T0202975

Lecture Notes in Computer Science 14371

Founding Editors

Gerhard Goos
Juris Hartmanis

Editorial Board Members

The series Lecture Notes in Computer Science (LNCS), including its subseries Lecture Notes in Artificial Intelligence (LNAI) and Lecture Notes in Bioinformatics (LNBI), has established itself as a medium for the publication of new developments in computer science and information technology research, teaching, and education.

LNCS enjoys close cooperation with the computer science R & D community, the series counts many renowned academics among its volume editors and paper authors, and collaborates with prestigious societies. Its mission is to serve this international community by providing an invaluable service, mainly focused on the publication of conference and workshop proceedings and postproceedings. LNCS commenced publication in 1973.

Guy Rothblum · Hoeteck Wee
Editors

Theory
of Cryptography

21st International Conference, TCC 2023
Taipei, Taiwan, November 29 – December 2, 2023
Proceedings, Part III

 Springer

Editors
Guy Rothblum 🆔
Apple
Cupertino, CA, USA

Hoeteck Wee
NTT Research
Sunnyvale, CA, USA

ISSN 0302-9743   ISSN 1611-3349 (electronic)
Lecture Notes in Computer Science
ISBN 978-3-031-48620-3   ISBN 978-3-031-48621-0 (eBook)
https://doi.org/10.1007/978-3-031-48621-0

This Springer imprint is published by the registered company Springer Nature Switzerland AG
The registered company address is: Gewerbestrasse 11, 6330 Cham, Switzerland

Paper in this product is recyclable.

Preface

The 21st Theory of Cryptography Conference (TCC 2023) was held during November 29 – December 2, 2023, at Academia Sinica in Taipei, Taiwan. It was sponsored by the International Association for Cryptologic Research (IACR). The general chairs of the conference were Kai-Min Chung and Bo-Yin Yang.

The conference received 168 submissions, of which the Program Committee (PC) selected 68 for presentation giving an acceptance rate of 40%. Each submission was reviewed by at least three PC members in a single-blind process. The 39 PC members (including PC chairs), all top researchers in our field, were helped by 195 external reviewers, who were consulted when appropriate. These proceedings consist of the revised versions of the 68 accepted papers. The revisions were not reviewed, and the authors bear full responsibility for the content of their papers.

We are extremely grateful to Kevin McCurley for providing fast and reliable technical support for the HotCRP review software. We also thank Kay McKelly for her help with the conference website.

This was the ninth year that TCC presented the Test of Time Award to an outstanding paper that was published at TCC at least eight years ago, making a significant contribution to the theory of cryptography, preferably with influence also in other areas of cryptography, theory, and beyond. This year, the Test of Time Award Committee selected the following paper, published at TCC 2007: "Multi-authority Attribute Based Encryption" by Melissa Chase. The award committee recognized this paper for "the first attribute-based encryption scheme in which no small subset of authorities can compromise user privacy, inspiring further work in decentralized functional encryption." The author was invited to deliver a talk at TCC 2023.

This year, TCC awarded a Best Young Researcher Award for the best paper authored solely by young researchers. The award was given to the paper "Memory Checking for Parallel RAMs" by Surya Mathialagan.

We are greatly indebted to the many people who were involved in making TCC 2023 a success. First of all, a big thanks to the most important contributors: all the authors who submitted fantastic papers to the conference. Next, we would like to thank the PC members for their hard work, dedication, and diligence in reviewing and selecting the papers. We are also thankful to the external reviewers for their volunteered hard work and investment in reviewing papers and answering questions. For running the conference itself, we are very grateful to the general chairs, Kai-Min Chung and Bo-Yin Yang, as well as the staff at Academia Sinica (Institute of Information Science and Research Center of Information Technology Innovation). For help with these proceedings, we thank the team at Springer. We appreciate the sponsorship from IACR, Hackers in Taiwan, Quantum Safe Migration Center (QSMC), NTT Research and BTQ. Finally, we are thankful to

Tal Malkin and the TCC Steering Committee as well as the entire thriving and vibrant TCC community.

October 2023   Guy Rothblum
                                                               Hoeteck Wee

Organization

General Chairs

Kai-Min Chung   Academia Sinica, Taiwan
Bo-Yin Yang   Academia Sinica, Taiwan

Program Committee Chairs

Guy N. Rothblum   Apple, USA and Weizmann Institute, Israel
Hoeteck Wee   NTT Research, USA and ENS, France

Steering Committee

Jesper Buus Nielsen   Aarhus University, Denmark
Krzysztof Pietrzak   Institute of Science and Technology, Austria
Huijia (Rachel) Lin   University of Washington, USA
Yuval Ishai   Technion, Israel
Tal Malkin   Columbia University, USA
Manoj M. Prabhakaran   IIT Bombay, India
Salil Vadhan   Harvard University, USA

Program Committee

Prabhanjan Ananth   UCSB, USA
Christian Badertscher   Input Output, Switzerland
Chris Brzuska   Aalto University, Finland
Ran Canetti   Boston University, USA
Nico Döttling   CISPA, Germany
Rosario Gennaro   CUNY and Protocol Labs, USA
Aarushi Goel   NTT Research, USA
Siyao Guo   NYU Shanghai, China
Shai Halevi   AWS, USA
Pavel Hubáček   Czech Academy of Sciences and Charles University, Czech Republic
Yuval Ishai   Technion, Israel

Aayush Jain   CMU, USA
Zhengzhong Jin   MIT, USA
Yael Kalai   Microsoft Research and MIT, USA
Chethan Kamath   Tel Aviv University, Israel
Bhavana Kanukurthi   IISc, India
Jiahui Liu   MIT, USA
Mohammad Mahmoody   University of Virginia, USA
Giulio Malavolta   Bocconi University, Italy and Max Planck
                               Institute for Security and Privacy, Germany
Peihan Miao   Brown University, USA
Eran Omri   Ariel University, Israel
Claudio Orlandi   Aarhus, Denmark
João Ribeiro   NOVA LINCS and NOVA University Lisbon,
                               Portugal
Doreen Riepel   UC San Diego, USA
Carla Ràfols   Universitat Pompeu Fabra, Spain
Luisa Siniscalchi   Technical University of Denmark, Denmark
Naomi Sirkin   Drexel University, USA
Nicholas Spooner   University of Warwick, USA
Akshayaram Srinivasan   University of Toronto, Canada
Stefano Tessaro   University of Washington, USA
Eliad Tsfadia   Georgetown University, USA
Mingyuan Wang   UC Berkeley, USA
Shota Yamada   AIST, Japan
Takashi Yamakawa   NTT Social Informatics Laboratories, Japan
Kevin Yeo   Google and Columbia University, USA
Eylon Yogev   Bar-Ilan University, Israel
Mark Zhandry   NTT Research, USA

Additional Reviewers

Damiano Abram   Benedikt Auerbach
Hamza Abusalah   Renas Bacho
Abtin Afshar   Saikrishna Badrinarayanan
Siddharth Agarwal   Chen Bai
Divesh Aggarwal   Laasya Bangalore
Shweta Agrawal   Khashayar Barooti
Martin Albrecht   James Bartusek
Nicolas Alhaddad   Balthazar Bauer
Bar Alon   Shany Ben-David
Benny Applebaum   Fabrice Benhamouda
Gal Arnon   Jean-François Biasse

Alexander Bienstock
Olivier Blazy
Jeremiah Blocki
Andrej Bogdanov
Madalina Bolboceanu
Jonathan Bootle
Pedro Branco
Jesper Buus Nielsen
Alper Çakan
Matteo Campanelli
Shujiao Cao
Jeffrey Champion
Megan Chen
Arka Rai Choudhuri
Valerio Cini
Henry Corrigan-Gibbs
Geoffroy Couteau
Elizabeth Crites
Hongrui Cui
Marcel Dall'Agnol
Quang Dao
Pratish Datta
Koen de Boer
Leo Decastro
Giovanni Deligios
Lalita Devadas
Jack Doerner
Jelle Don
Leo Ducas
Jesko Dujmovic
Julien Duman
Antonio Faonio
Oriol Farràs
Danilo Francati
Cody Freitag
Phillip Gajland
Chaya Ganesh
Rachit Garg
Gayathri Garimella
Romain Gay
Peter Gaži
Ashrujit Ghoshal
Emanuele Giunta
Rishab Goyal
Yanqi Gu

Ziyi Guan
Jiaxin Guan
Aditya Gulati
Iftach Haitner
Mohammad Hajiabadi
Mathias Hall-Andersen
Shuai Han
Dominik Hartmann
Aditya Hegde
Alexandra Henzinger
Shuichi Hirahara
Taiga Hiroka
Charlotte Hoffmann
Alex Hoover
Yao-Ching Hsieh
Zihan Hu
James Hulett
Joseph Jaeger
Fatih Kaleoglu
Ari Karchmer
Shuichi Katsumata
Jonathan Katz
Fuyuki Kitagawa
Ohad Klein
Karen Klein
Michael Klooß
Dimitris Kolonelos
Ilan Komargodski
Yashvanth Kondi
Venkata Koppula
Alexis Korb
Sabrina Kunzweiler
Thijs Laarhoven
Jonas Lehmann
Baiyu Li
Xiao Liang
Yao-Ting Lin
Wei-Kai Lin
Yanyi Liu
Qipeng Liu
Tianren Liu
Zeyu Liu
Chen-Da Liu Zhang
Julian Loss
Paul Lou

Steve Lu
Ji Luo
Fermi Ma
Nir Magrafta
Monosij Maitra
Christian Majenz
Alexander May
Noam Mazor
Bart Mennink
Hart Montgomery
Tamer Mour
Alice Murphy
Anne Müller
Mikito Nanashima
Varun Narayanan
Hai Nguyen
Olga Nissenbaum
Sai Lakshmi Bhavana Obbattu
Maciej Obremski
Kazuma Ohara
Aurel Page
Mahak Pancholi
Guillermo Pascual Perez
Anat Paskin-Cherniavsky
Shravani Patil
Sikhar Patranabis
Chris Peikert
Zach Pepin
Krzysztof Pietrzak
Guru Vamsi Policharla
Alexander Poremba
Alex Poremba
Ludo Pulles
Wei Qi
Luowen Qian
Willy Quach
Divya Ravi
Nicolas Resch
Leah Namisa Rosenbloom
Lior Rotem
Ron Rothblum
Lance Roy

Yusuke Sakai
Pratik Sarkar
Sruthi Sekar
Joon Young Seo
Akash Shah
Devika Sharma
Laura Shea
Sina Shiehian
Kazumasa Shinagawa
Omri Shmueli
Jad Silbak
Pratik Soni
Sriram Sridhar
Akira Takahashi
Ben Terner
Junichi Tomida
Max Tromanhauser
Rotem Tsabary
Yiannis Tselekounis
Nikhil Vanjani
Prashant Vasudevan
Marloes Venema
Muthuramakrishnan Venkitasubramaniam
Hendrik Waldner
Michael Walter
Zhedong Wang
Gaven Watson
Weiqiang Wen
Daniel Wichs
David Wu
Ke Wu
Zhiye Xie
Tiancheng Xie
Anshu Yadav
Michelle Yeo
Runzhi Zeng
Jiaheng Zhang
Rachel Zhang
Cong Zhang
Chenzhi Zhu
Jincheng Zhuang
Vassilis Zikas

Contents – Part III

IOPs and Succinctness

Anonymity, Surveillance and Tampering

Lower Bounds on Anonymous Whistleblowing

Willy Quach[1]($^{(\boxtimes)}$), LaKyah Tyner[2], and Daniel Wichs[2,3]

[1] Weizmann Institute of Science, Rehovot, Israel
quach.w@northeastern.edu
[2] Northeastern University, Boston, MA, USA
tyner.l@northeastern.edu, wichs@ccs.neu.edu
[3] NTT Research, Sunnyvale, CA, USA

Abstract. Anonymous transfer, recently introduced by Agrikola, Couteau and Maier [3] (TCC '22), allows a sender to leak a message anonymously by participating in a public non-anonymous discussion in which everyone knows who said what. This opens up the intriguing possibility of using cryptography to ensure strong anonymity guarantees in a seemingly non-anonymous environment.

The work of [3] presented a lower bound on anonymous transfer, ruling out constructions with strong anonymity guarantees (where the adversary's advantage in identifying the sender is negligible) against arbitrary polynomial-time adversaries. They also provided a (heuristic) upper bound, giving a scheme with weak anonymity guarantees (the adversary's advantage in identifying the sender is inverse in the number of rounds) against *fine-grained* adversaries whose run-time is bounded by some fixed polynomial that exceeds the run-time of the honest users. This leaves a large gap between the lower bound and the upper bound, raising the intriguing possibility that one may be able to achieve weak anonymity against arbitrary polynomial time adversaries, or strong anonymity against fine grained adversaries.

In this work, we present improved lower bounds on anonymous transfer, that rule out both of the above possibilities:
- We rule out the existence of anonymous transfer with any non-trivial anonymity guarantees against general polynomial time adversaries.
- Even if we restrict ourselves to fine-grained adversaries whose runtime is essentially equivalent to that of the honest parties, we cannot achieve strong anonymity, or even quantitatively improve over the inverse polynomial anonymity guarantees (heuristically) achieved by [3].

Consequently, constructions of anonymous transfer can only provide security against fine-grained adversaries, and even in that case they achieve at most weak quantitative forms of anonymity.

1 Introduction

Consider the following question:

Can a sender leak a message anonymously, by exclusively participating in a public non-anonymous discussion where everyone sees who said what?

© International Association for Cryptologic Research 2023
G. Rothblum and H. Wee (Eds.): TCC 2023, LNCS 14371, pp. 3–32, 2023.
https://doi.org/10.1007/978-3-031-48621-0_1

In particular, we consider a setting where the participants are having a seemingly innocuous discussion (e.g., about favorite cat videos). The discussion is public and non-anonymous, meaning that the participants are using their real identities and everyone knows who said what.[1] The non-sender participants are having a real conversation about this topic. On the other hand, the sender is carefully choosing what to say in a way that looks like she is participating in the conversation, but her real goal is to leak a secret document (e.g., NSA's polynomial-time factoring algorithm). At the end of the discussion, anyone should be able to look at the transcript of the conversation and reconstruct the secret document, without learning anything about which of the participants was the actual sender responsible for leaking it. Despite its conceptual importance and simplicity, this question has not been studied until recently, perhaps because it may appear "obviously impossible".

A formal study of the question was recently initiated by Agrikola, Couteau and Maier in [3], who, perhaps surprisingly, raise the intriguing possibility of answering it positively using cryptography. They do so by introducing a new cryptographic primitive, dubbed anonymous transfer (henceforth AT), to capture the setting above. An anonymous transfer involves a sender with a secret document, along with unaware dummy participants who send uniformly random messages.[2] The parties run for some number of rounds, where in each round the sender and each participant sends a message. At the end of the protocol anyone can reconstruct the secret document with high probability given the transcript. However, the transcript cannot be used to identify who the sender is among the participants.

Crucially, anonymous transfer does not rely on the availability of any (weak) anonymous channels, nor on the availability of trusted third parties during the execution. Instead, all protocol messages are assumed to be traceable to their respective senders, and all other dummy participants only passively send random messages. The simplicity of the setting makes it both a natural question to explore, and raises very intriguing possibility of "creating" anonymity in a seemingly non-anonymous environment.

Anonymous Transfer and Whistleblowing. One central motivation for studying anonymous transfer is its relation to whistleblowing, where whistleblowers wish to leak confidential and oftentimes sensitive information, while operating in a potentially untrusted environment. The whistleblowers themselves usually risk being subjected to both harsh social, financial, and even legal consequences if caught [1,4,13]. One natural mitigation for those risks is the use appropriate

---

[1] For concreteness, the public discussion could occur over Facebook or Twitter, and users need to be logged in with their true identity.

[2] This departs from our informal setting, where a real discussion occurred, while we now assume that "real discussions" are uniformly random. Various works, including [12,15,16] show how to embed uniform randomness into real discussions. Concretely, it suffices to (randomly) encode uniformly random messages to the distribution representing the (non-necessarily uniform) communication pattern, in a way that the random messages can be decoded.

tools, typically cryptographic ones, to ensure anonymity of the leak. And indeed, a large body of work is devoted to build such tools.

One crucial aspect of these tools is the assumptions made on resources available to the whistleblower, which we would ideally like to minimize. From a practical perspective, it seems unreasonable to assume the general availability of, say, anonymous channels or online trusted parties to whistleblowers. In fact, even given the availability of such anonymous channels, their use alone could potentially be incriminating. From a more theoretical perspective, cryptographic solutions leveraging such assumptions could be seen as bootstrapping weaker forms of anonymity. Unfortunately, as far as we are aware, except the work of [3], all prior work on whistleblowing assume the availability of an online form of trust, and thus do not seem to answer the initial question we consider. In contrast, [3] asks the intriguing question of whether cryptography can *create* forms of anonymity in a more fundamental sense.

Prior Work on Anonymous Transfer. Along with introducing anonymous transfer, [3] gives both lower bounds, and, perhaps surprisingly, plausibility results on its feasibility. Let us introduce some notation. The *correctness error* $\varepsilon = \varepsilon(\lambda)$ of an anonymous transfer is the probability secret documents fail to be reconstructed, and the *anonymity* $\delta = \delta(\lambda)$ of an AT is the advantage a transcript of the AT provides towards identifying the sender.[3] An AT is in general interactive, and consists of $c = c(\lambda)$ rounds of interaction.

On the negative side, [3] shows that no protocol can satisfy close to ideal forms of correctness and security, namely $\varepsilon, \delta = \mathrm{negl}(\lambda)$, against all polynomial time adversaries. They supplement this lower bound with a plausibility result, by giving heuristic constructions of anonymous transfer with *fine-grained* security. This heuristic construction provides negligible correctness error, but weaker anonymity guarantees (namely $\delta \approx 1/c$, where c is the number of rounds), and only against a restricted class of *fine-grained* adversaries, who are allowed restricted to be at most $O(c)$ times more powerful than honest users, which are argued secure by relying on ideal obfuscation.

Still, the work of [3] leaves open the possibility of building anonymous transfer with non-optimal correctness and security guarantees (e.g., $\delta \leq 1/c$) secure against arbitrary polynomial-time attacks.

Our Results. In this work, we give improved lower bounds for anonymous transfer, largely ruling out potential improvements over the heuristic upper bound from [3]. Throughout this exposition, we will consider the case of 2 participants, one sender and a non-sender; [3] shows that lower bounds in that setting translates to lower bounds for any larger number of parties. Our main theorem shows that anonymous transfer with any non-trivial anonymity against general polynomial-time attackers is impossible, solving a conjecture explicitly stated in [3].

---

[3] In this work, we use the convention that an AT is *stronger* as ε, δ tend to 0; this is the opposite convention of [3] where this held whenever ε, δ tend to 1.

Theorem 1 (Informal). *For any 2-party anonymous transfer protocol for* $\omega(\log \lambda)$-*bit messages with correctness error* ε, *for all polynomial* $\alpha = \alpha(\lambda)$, *there exists a polynomial-time adversary that identifies the sender with probability at least* $1 - \varepsilon - 1/\alpha$.

Note that, the probability of identifying the sender is essentially optimal, as, with probability ε, the sender might act as a dummy party, and therefore this rules out any non-trivial constructions.

Our attack runs in polynomial-time, but where the polynomial is fairly large. This unfortunately does not match the run-time of allowed adversaries in the heuristic construction of [3].

As a secondary result, we show that even in the setting of fine-grained adversaries whose run-time is essentially equivalent to that of the honest parties, we can identify senders with probability $1/c$ whenever the secret document can be reconstructed. This shows that, even in the fine-grained setting, one cannot improve on the quantitative anonymity guarantees achieved by the heuristic construction of [3].

Theorem 2 (Informal). *For any 2-party anonymous transfer protocol for* $\omega(\log \lambda)$-*bit messages, with correctness error* ε, *and having c-round of interaction, there exists a fine-grained adversary whose run-time matches that of the reconstruction procedure up to additive constant factors, that identifies the sender with probability at least* $(1 - \varepsilon - \mathrm{negl}(\lambda))/c$.

Theorem 2 in particular rules out all fine-grained protocols with a polynomial number of rounds, if both δ and ε are negligible. For comparison, the lower bound of [3] rules out very similar parameters, but where the run-time of the adversary is $m(\lambda) = \lambda \cdot c^g$ times larger than the one of the reconstruction procedure, for some arbitrary constant $g > 0$.

Related Work on Whistleblowing. Current solutions for anonymous messaging and anonymous whistleblowing include systems based on onion routing [10], mixnets [7], and Dining Cryptographer networks or DC-nets [2,6,9,11,14]. Additionally, there have been other applications developed that utilize new techniques inspired by the models mentioned previously [5,8,9]. Each of these solutions, however, intrinsically assumes that there exists non-colluding honest servers that participate to ensure anonymity. [3] is the first to introduce a model which does not rely on this assumption. Impossibility results could be interpreted as evidence that such an assumption *is* in fact necessary.

Open Problems. The main open question left by [3] and this work is the construction of fine-grained anonymous transfer matching their heuristic construction, but under standard assumptions.

Additionally, our attack in Theorem 1 runs in fairly large polynomial time, which does not tightly match the fine-grained security proved in the heuristic construction of [3]. We leave for future work the possibility of improving the run-time of an attack matching the properties of Theorem 1.

2 Technical Overview

Anonymous Transfer. Let us first recall some basic syntax and notations for anonymous transfer (henceforth AT), introduced in [3]. In this overview, we will focus on 2-party anonymous transfer, which features a *sender*, a *dummy party* and an external *receiver*.[4,5] The sender takes as input a message μ to transfer. The sender and the dummy party exchange messages in synchronous rounds, with the restriction that the dummy party only sends random bits. An execution of the transfer spans over c rounds of interaction, where both parties send a message at each round. Given a full transcript, the external receiver can (attempt to) reconstruct the original message. We say that an AT has ε correctness error if the reconstruction procedure fails to recover μ with probability at most ε; and that it is δ-anonymous if no adversary has advantage greater than δ in identifying the sender amongst the two participating parties over a random guess, where the adversary can choose the message to be sent.[6] We refer to Sect. 3.1 for formal definitions.

In that setting, [3] showed the following lower bound on AT.

Theorem 3 ([3], paraphrased). *Every (two-party, silent receiver) AT with ε-correctness and δ-anonymity against all polynomial-time adversary, and consisting of c rounds, satisfies $\delta \cdot c \geq \frac{1-\varepsilon}{2} - 1/m(\lambda)$ for all polynomial $m(\lambda)$.*

In particular, no AT can satisfy $\delta, \varepsilon = \mathrm{negl}(\lambda)$ (assuming $c = \mathrm{poly}(\lambda)$, which holds if participants are polynomial-time). More precisely, [3] show, for all polynomial $m(\lambda)$, an attack with runtime $m(\lambda) \cdot \mathrm{poly}(\lambda)$ with advantage at least $\frac{1}{c} \cdot (\frac{1-\varepsilon}{2} - 1/m(\lambda))$.

The main limitation of Theorem 3 is that it does not rule out the existence of AT protocols with anonymity δ scaling inverse-polynomially with the number of rounds c, e.g. $\delta = 1/c$. In other words, the trade-off between correctness and security could potentially be improved by relying on a large amount of interaction. And indeed, [3] does provide a plausibility result, where, assuming ideal obfuscation, there exists a *fine-grained* AT with $\delta \approx 1/c$, $\varepsilon = \mathrm{negl}(\lambda)$, so that anonymity does improve with the number of rounds. A secondary limitation is that, because the attack corresponding to Theorem 3 needs to call the honest algorithms a polynomial number of times (even though the polynomial can arbitrarily small), this potentially leaves room for "very fine-grained" protocols, where security would only hold against adversaries running in mild super-linear time compared to honest users.

---

[4] Anonymous transfer can also be defined with more than a single "dummy" party. We focus for simplicity on the 2-party case for this overview, and will show how to extend the attacks to the N-party case subsequently.

[5] We consider here "silent" receivers who do not send any messages—this is similarly known to be sufficient for lower bounds [3].

[6] We remind the reader that [3] takes different conventions than ours for ε and δ. With our notation, an AT satisfies stronger properties as ε and δ get smaller and closer to 0, and are ideally negligible in the security parameter.

Our main results are stronger generic attacks on anonymous transfer proto-cols.

A General Blueprint for Our Attacks. The core idea behind all our attacks is a simple notion of *progress* associated to any (potentially partial) transcript of an AT. We do so by associating a real *value* $p \in [0,1]_{\mathbb{R}}$ to partial transcripts of an AT, as follows. We can complete any partial transcripts, replacing all missing messages by uniformly random ones, and attempt to recover the input message $\mu \leftarrow \{0,1\}^{\ell}$ from the sender. For a partial transcript, we define $p \in [0,1]_{\mathbb{R}}$ to be the probability that a random completion of the transcript allows to recover μ.

The next step is to attribute partial evolutions of p, as the transcript gets longer, to parties in the protocol. Namely if, after party A sends the ith message in the transcript, the value of the protocol evolves from p_{i-1} to p_i, and we attribute to A some progress dependent on p_{i-1} and p_i. We then make the following observations: the empty transcript has value $p_0 = 1/2^{\ell}$ close to 0 (if μ is chosen uniformly at random), and full transcripts have (on expectation) value $p_{2c} = 1 - \varepsilon$ close to 1 by correctness. Our main leverage is that messages sent by the unaware, dummy participant in an AT do not significantly change the value of a partial transcript: this is because, in our random completion of transcripts, messages from the dummy party follow their real distribution. Furthermore, as long as the final value p_{2c} is significantly larger than the initial value p_0, then a significant amount of total progress has to be made *at some point*. Therefore the messages from the sender have to significantly bias the values of partial transcripts towards 1.

This results in the following blueprint for identifying the sender of the AT. We first estimate the contribution of each party towards total progress, namely, the evolution of the values p associated to partial transcripts where the last message was sent from that party.[7] Then, we argue that (1) the contribution of the dummy party is likely to be small overall and (2) the total contribution of both parties is fairly large (on expectation), from which we conclude that the party whose messages contributed the most to increasing the value p is likely to be the AT sender.

Covert Cheating Games. We abstract out this recipe as a natural game, that we call a covert cheating game. A covert cheating game played by two players A and B, who take $2c$ alternate turns moving a point, or current *state of the game*, on the real interval $[0,1]$. One player is designed to be a *bias inducer*, and the other a *neutral party*. The initial state is p_0, and the final state is p_{2c} is either 0 or 1. We say that a strategy has *success rate* $p_f > p_0$ if $\mathbb{E}[p_{2c}] \geq p_f$, regardless of the identity of the bias inducer. The neutral party is restricted to exclusively making randomized moves that do not affect the current state on expectation. The goal of a third player, the *observer* C, is to determine, given access to the states of the game, which player is the bias inducer. Our main technical contribution is

---

[7] In an AT, rounds are by default synchronous; for the sake of this general blueprint, any arbitrary sequentialization of the messages would be meaningful.

to show generic observer strategies for this game. We refer to Definition 3 for a more detailed definition.

We use this abstraction to capture the fact that our attacks use the AT in a specific black-box sense, namely, only to measure out values $p \in [0,1]_{\mathbb{R}}$, and using all the AT algorithms in a black-box manner. Overall, our abstraction of attacks on ATs as strategies in a game captures a natural family of black-box distinguishing algorithms, which we believe capture most reasonable attacks on AT.[8] Indeed, it is not clear how to leverage any non-black-box use of honest user algorithms, as they could potentially be obfuscated (and indeed, the plausibility result of [3] does rely on obfuscated programs to be run by honest users). We believe this game to be natural enough to see other applications in the future.

In the rest of the technical overview, we focus on describing generic attacks in the language of covert cheating games.

A Generic "Free-Lunch" Attack. We describe our first attack on the game introduced above, which corresponds to a proof sketch of Theorem 2. Our attack is very simple, and only leverages the fact that, on expectation over a random move, moves done by the bias inducer bias the outcome by an additive term $(p_f - p_0)/c$, while moves from the neutral party do not add any bias. Suppose the game consists of c rounds (each consisting of one move from each party A, B), and that party A makes the first move, so that A makes the odd moves $2k+1$, and B makes the even moves $2k$. Our strategy is to pick a random move $k \leftarrow [c]$ from A, whose kth move makes the game evolve from state p_{2k} to p_{2k+1}. We simply output "A is the bias inducer" with probability p_{2k+1} (and B with probability $1 - p_{2k+1}$).

The main idea is that if A is the neutral party, then on expectation $p_{2k+1} = p_{2k}$, and thus our strategy outputs A with probability p_k. On the other hand, if A is the bias inducer, our strategy outputs A with probability p_{2k+1}.[9] Because B is then a neutral party, B's total expected contribution is 0, namely $\mathbb{E}_k[p_{2k+2} - p_{2k+1}] = 0$, so that the advantage of our algorithm towards determining A is:

$$\mathbb{E}_k[p_{2k+1} - p_{2k}] = \mathbb{E}_k[p_{2k+1} - p_{2k} + \underbrace{(p_{2k+2} - p_{2k+1})}_{0}] = (p_f - p_0)/c.$$

The cost of our attack is the cost of obtaining a single sample with probability p_{2k+1}. Going back to AT, this corresponds to the cost of running the honest users' algorithms *once* (namely, attempting to reconstruct the message of a random completion of a randomly chosen partial transcript with last message from A). We conclude no AT can provide security with parameters from Theorem 2, in

---

[8] More precisely, strategies are black-box in the AT algorithms, but need to consider full transcripts in a slightly non-black-box way (namely, by separating messages and considering random continuations).

[9] Technically, the quantities p_k when A is the neutral party and p_k when A is the bias inducer are not necessarily related. But without loss of generality, the strategies used by the bias inducer and the neutral party are independent of their identity as A or B, in which case the quantities p_{2k} *are* equal.

any fine-grained setting (as long as adversaries are allowed to be in the same complexity class as honest users).

A Generic Attack with Large Advantage. We now describe a slightly more involved attack that achieves stronger advantage, at the cost of running in larger polynomial time. The main inspiration behind this new attack comes from taking a closer look on the restriction that the neutral party's moves do not change the game state on expectation. We observe that this is a more stringent restriction if the current game state p is close to 0. For concreteness, if the current state of the game is $p = 1/2$, then the neutral party could potentially move the state to $p' = 0$ or $p' = 1$ with probability $1/2$ each, inducing a large change of the value of p. However, starting at $p \gtrsim 0$, Markov's inequality ensures that p' cannot be too large.

This motivates us to consider a different quantification of progress where *additive* progress close to 0 is weighed more significantly than *additive* progress at large constants (e.g. $1/2$). We do so by considering a *multiplicative* form of progress associated to moves and players. Namely, if the ith move of the game transforms the game state from p_{i-1} to p_i, then we define the multiplicative progress associated with the move as[10]

$$r_i = \frac{p_i}{p_{i-1}}.$$

The total progress associated with a player would then be the product of the progress associated with its moves.

Our blueprint still applies in this context. The total progress of all the moves combined is[11]

$$\prod_{i\in[2c]} r_i = \prod_{i\in[2c]} \frac{p_i}{p_{i-1}} = \frac{p_f}{p_0},$$

and so one of the players (on expectation) needs to have progress at least $\sqrt{p_f/p_0}$. Furthermore, one can show that the restriction on neutral party's moves implies that the product of the r_i associated to the neutral party is 1 on expectation. Namely, denoting N the set of indices corresponding to moves made by the neutral party: $\mathbb{E}\left[\prod_N r_i\right] = 1$. Markov's inequality then gives:

$$\Pr\left[\prod_N r_i \geq \sqrt{\frac{p_f}{p_0}}\right] \leq \sqrt{\frac{p_0}{p_f}}.$$

---

[10] One technically needs to be careful handling cases where $p_i = 0$ for some i. We largely ignore this technicality in this overview. For concreteness, it will be enough to output a random guess if this happens, and observe that, for games resulting from an AT, this happens with probability at most $1 - p_f$, and therefore does not affect our advantage too much. We refer to Sect. 4.3 for more details.

[11] Actually, the total progress is only guaranteed to be p_f/p_0 *on expectation*, which induces several technical issues. We will assume the progress is always equal to p_f/p_0 for the sake of this overview, and we refer to Sect. 4.2 for more details on the issues and a solution.

Overall, this shows that with good probability $1 - \sqrt{p_0/p_f}$, the sender has a large total contribution, and the dummy party has a small contribution, so that an attacker can identify them with at least such a probability.

We are unfortunately not done yet, because observers do not have direct access to the real values $p \in [0,1]$: they are only given the ability to sample coins with probability p (going back to AT, recall that this is done by sampling a random completion of a transcript and testing whether the reconstructed message matched the sender's message). This is problematic: from the perspective of a polynomial-time observer, the values $p = \text{negl}(\lambda)$ and $p = 0$ are indistinguishable, given only sampling access. How can we then ensure that the ratios $r_i = p_i/p_{i-1}$ are even well-defined (that is, that $p_{i-1} \neq 0$)?

We solve this issue by conditioning our product to be over moves $i \geq i^*$, such that for all $i > i^*, p_i \geq \tau$ for some small accuracy threshold $p_0 < \tau < p_f$ (think $\tau = 1/\text{poly}(\lambda)$), and where we set the convention $p_{i^*} = \tau$. Now the ratios are well-defined, and the total contribution is now p_f/τ. It remains to argue that the product corresponding to the neutral party is small. While we might have biased the distribution of the neutral party by conditioning on the product starting at i^*, we argue by a union bound that, with sufficiently high probability $1 - c\sqrt{\tau/p_f}$, all "suffix-products" from the dummy party are small (namely, smaller than $\sqrt{p_f/\tau}$)

Summing up, our final observer strategy estimates all the p_i up to some sufficiently good precision (using Chernoff) so that the product of the $r_i = p_i/p_{i-1}$ is ensured to be accurate, as long as all the terms p_i that appear in the product are large enough compared to our threshold τ. We refer to Sect. 4.4 for more formal details.

Taking a step back, the major strength of Theorem 1 is that the advantage of the associated attack is independent of the number of rounds: only its running time scales with the number of rounds (in order to ensure sufficient precision with Chernoff bounds). This is in our eyes a quantitative justification that multiplicative progress is better suited to identify bias in a covert cheating game.

Extending the Lower Bound to N Parties. Last, we sketch how to extend our attack from Theorem 1 to the N-party setting, which consists of a sender interacting with $N - 1$ dummy parties. Our first step is to observe that our attacks described above directly translate to *targeted-predicting attacks*, which correctly identify the sender given the promise that the sender is either party $i \in [N]$ or $j \in [N]$ where $i \neq j$ are arbitrary but fixed for the targeted predictor. This follows from [3], which builds a 2-party AT from any N-party AT, while preserving targeted-predicting security.[12] In other words, given the promise that the sender is either party i or party j, we can correctly identify the sender with the same guarantees as in Theorem 1 (or even Theorem 2).

However, we ideally wish to obtain general predicting attacks that do not rely on any additional information to correctly output the identity of the sender.

---

[12] This is done by considering all the messages sent by parties $k \neq i,j$ as part of the CRS of the new 2-party protocol.

We generically upgrade any targeted-predicting attack to a standard predicting attack, while preserving the advantage δ, as follows. The attack simply runs the targeted-predicting attack on all pairs of distinct indices $\{(i,j) \mid i,j \in [N], i \neq j\}$, and outputs as the sender the party i^* that got designated as the sender in all the runs (i^*, j), $j \neq i^*$.[13] Now, if i^* is the sender of the N-party AT, an union bound implies that the probability that all the internal runs $(i^*, j), j \neq i^*$ of the targeted-predicting attack correctly point out to i^* as the sender is at least $\delta' \geq 1 - N(1 - \delta)$. Starting with the attack from Theorem 1 with $\alpha' = N \cdot \alpha$,[14] we obtain the same lower bound as Theorem 1 in the N-party setting, at the cost of a poly(N) overhead in the runtime of our attack.[15]

3 Preliminaries and Definitions

Notations. When X is a distribution, or a random variable following this distribution, we let $x \leftarrow X$ denote the process of sampling x according to the distribution X. If X is a set, we let $x \leftarrow X$ denote sampling x uniformly at random from X; if Alg is a randomized algorithm, we denote by $x \leftarrow$ Alg the process of sampling an output of Alg using uniformly random coins. We use the notation $[k]$ to denote the set $\{1, \ldots, k\}$ where $k \in \mathbb{N}$, and $[0,1]_{\mathbb{R}}$ to denote the real interval $\{x \in \mathbb{R} \mid 0 \leq x \leq 1\}$. We denote by negl$(\lambda)$ functions f such that $f(\lambda) = 1/\lambda^{\omega(1)}$.

Chernoff Bound. We will use the following (multiplicative) form of Chernoff-Hoeffding inequality.

Lemma 1 (Multiplicative Chernoff). *Suppose $X_1, \cdots, X_n$ are independent Bernouilli variables with common mean p. Then, for all $t > 0$, we have:*

$$\Pr\left[\sum_{i=1}^{n} X_i \notin [(1-t) \cdot np, (1+t) \cdot np)]\right] \leq 2e^{-2t^2 p^2 n}.$$

3.1 Anonymous Transfer

We recall here the notion anonymous transfer, introduced in [3]. Throughout most of this work, we focus the two-party setting, involving a sender, a dummy non-sender and a (silent) receiver.[16]

---

[13] Note that there is at most one such index. If no such index exist, our attack, say, outputs party 1.

[14] This corresponds to setting $\delta = 1 - 1/\alpha'$, conditioned on executions where the message can be correctly reconstructed. We refer to Sect. 5.3 for more details.

[15] The overhead arises from both the $O(N^2)$ calls to the internal distinguisher, and the runtime of the internal distinguisher itself which is poly$(\alpha') =$ poly$(N) \cdot \alpha$.

[16] The work of [3] more generally considers a setting with N parties, namely a sender and $N - 1$ dummy parties. Our work focuses on the two-party case, but our main result extend to the N-party case: see Remark 4 and Sect. 5.3 for more details.

Definition 1. ((Two-Party, Silent-Receiver) Anonymous Transfer); **adapted from [3]).** *A two-party anonymous transfer (AT)* Π_{AT}^{ℓ}, *with correctness error* $\varepsilon \in [0,1]_{\mathbb{R}}$, *anonymity* $\delta \in [0,1]_{\mathbb{R}}$, *consisting of* $c \in \mathbb{N}$ *rounds and message length* $\ell \in \mathbb{N}$ *(all possibly functions of* λ*), is a tuple of PPT algorithms* (Setup, Transfer, Reconstruct) *with the following specifications:*

- Setup(1^{λ}) *takes as input a unary encoding of the security parameter* λ *and outputs a common reference string* crs.
- Transfer(crs, b, μ) *takes as input a common reference string* crs, *the index of the sender* $b \in \{0,1\}$, *the message to be transferred* $\mu \in \{0,1\}^{\ell}$, *and outputs a transcript* π. *Transcripts* π *consists of* c *rounds of interaction between the sender and the dummy party, where the dummy party (with index* $1 - b$*) sends uniform and independent messages at each round, and the each message from the sender depends on the partial transcript so far, with a next message function implicitly defined by* Transfer(crs, b, μ). *By default, we assume that the receiver does not send any messages (namely, the receiver is silent).*[17]
- Reconstruct(crs, π) *takes as input a common reference string* crs, *a transcript* π *and outputs a message* $\mu' \in \{0,1\}^{\ell}$. *By default, we assume that* Reconstruct *is deterministic.*[18]

We require that the following properties are satisfied.

ε-*Correctness.* *An anonymous transfer* Π_{AT}^{ℓ} *has correctness error* ε *if, for all large enough security parameter* λ, *index* $b \in \{0,1\}$, *message length* $\ell \in \text{poly}(\lambda)$, *and all message* $\mu \in \{0,1\}^{\ell}$, *we have:*

$$\Pr \begin{bmatrix} \text{crs} \leftarrow \text{Setup}(1^{\lambda}) \\ \pi \leftarrow \text{Transfer}(\text{crs}, b, \mu) \quad : \mu' \neq \mu \\ \mu' \leftarrow \text{Reconstruct}(\text{crs}, \pi) \end{bmatrix} \leq \varepsilon.$$

δ-*Anonymity.* *An anonymous transfer* Π_{AT}^{ℓ} *is* δ-*anonymous if, for all PPT algorithm* D, *all large enough security parameter* λ, *message length* $\ell \in \text{poly}(\lambda)$, *and all message* $\mu \in \{0,1\}^{\ell}$,

$$\left| \begin{array}{l} \Pr[\pi^{(0)} \leftarrow \text{Transfer}(\text{crs}, 0, m) : D(\pi^{(0)}) = 1] \\ - \Pr[\pi^{(1)} \leftarrow \text{Transfer}(\text{crs}, 1, m) : D(\pi^{(1)}) = 1] \end{array} \right| \leq \delta, \tag{1}$$

where the probability is over the randomness of Setup, Transfer, *and the internal randomness of* D.

    We alternatively say that Π_{AT}^{ℓ} *is* δ-*anonymous with respect to a class of adversaries* $\mathcal{C}$, *if Eq. (1) holds instead for all distinguishers* $D \in \mathcal{C}$.

Definition 2. *We say that an anonymous transfer is* symmetric *if the next message function of the sender, implicitly defined by* Transfer(crs, b, μ) *where* b *is the sender, does not depend on* b, *and if* Reconstruct *does not depend on the identities of the participants.*

---

[17] This is without loss of generality; see Remark 2.
[18] This is without loss of generality; see Remark 3.

Remark 1. (Comparison with [3]*).* Our notation and definitions are slightly different but equivalent from the ones from [3]. With our conventions, ε denotes a correctness error, and δ denotes a (bound on a) distinguishing advantage, and therefore an AT has stronger correctness (resp. stronger anonymity) guarantees as ε, δ decrease. This is the opposite of [3], where guarantees gets better as their parameters ε, δ tend to 1.

Our definition of correctness error is over the random choice of crs $\leftarrow$ Setup, while it is worst case over crs in [3]. Because this defines a larger class of protocols, ruling out the definition above makes our lower bounds stronger.

Our definition of δ-anonymity is formulated specifically for the two-party case, and is worded differently from theirs, which states, up to the mapping $\delta \mapsto 1 - \delta$ discussed above:

$$\left| \Pr_{b \leftarrow \{0,1\}} \left[\pi^{(b)} \leftarrow \mathsf{Transfer}(\mathsf{crs}, b, m) : D(\pi^{(b)}) = b \right] - \frac{1}{2} \right| \le \frac{\delta}{2}. \tag{2}$$

However one can easily show that both definitions correspond to the same value δ .

Remark 2 (Silent Receivers). As noted in [3], without loss of generality, the receiver in an anonymous transfer can be made silent, namely, does not send any messages in the protocol execution. This is because its random tape can be hard-coded in the CRS.

Remark 3 (Deterministic reconstruction). We observe that Reconstruct can be assumed to be deterministic without loss of generality; this is because random coins for Reconstruct can be sampled and included in the common reference string crs.

Remark 4 (AT with larger number of parties). [3] more generally defines anonymous transfer with a larger number of participants $N \in \mathbb{N}$. We refer to [3, Definition 3] for a formal definition.[19] The main difference (in the silent receiver case), is that δ is defined as an advantage over random guessing among the N participants. Namely, Eq. (2) becomes:

$$\left| \Pr_{k \leftarrow [N]} \left[\pi^{(k)} \leftarrow \mathsf{Transfer}(\mathsf{crs}, k, m) : D(\pi^{(k)}) = k \right] - \frac{1}{N} \right| \le \delta \cdot \frac{N-1}{N}.$$

In particular, while the indistinguishability-based definition in Eq. (1) and the predicting-based definition in Eq. (2) are equivalent in the two-party setting, it is not immediately clear that this holds in the N-party setting. Looking ahead, in order to extend our results from the 2-party to the N-party setting, our main observation is to show that this equivalence in fact holds, up to some mild loss in the parameters. We refer to Sect. 5.3 for more details.

---

[19] We remind the reader that the quantity δ in [3] corresponds to $1 - \delta$ for us. Additionally, in this version of the definition, we do not include the receiver in the count for the number of parties.

4 Identifying Covert Cheaters

In this section, we introduce our abstraction of the *covert cheating games*, and then show generic strategies for the game.

4.1 Covert Cheating Game

We define a covert cheating game as follows.

Definition 3 (Covert Cheating Game). *Let $c \in \mathbb{N}$, $p_0 \in]0,1[_{\mathbb{R}}$ be parameters.*

- **Setup, players and roles.** *A* covert cheating game *is played by two (randomized) players A and B, who can agree on a strategy in advance. They play against an* observer *C. During setup, one party is (randomly) designated as the* bias inducer *while the other is designated as the* neutral party.
- **Execution and states of a game.** *An execution of the game consists of players A and B take alternate moves making moves in the game, with the convention that player A makes the first move. The game consists of c rounds (that is, $2c$ total moves, c moves from A and c moves from B), where $c \in \mathbb{N}$ is a parameter of the game. At any point during the game, the current* state *of a game is represented by a real number $p \in [0,1]_{\mathbb{R}}$. The final state of the game is a bit $p_{2c} \in \{0,1\}$ (where one can consider 1 as a winning outcome for the players A, B, and 0 as a losing outcome).*
  For $k \in [c]$, if A is the bias inducer, we will use either of the notations $X_{2k-1} = X_{2k-1}^{(A)}$ (resp. $X_{2k} = X_{2k}^{(B)}$), to denote the random variable associated to the state resulting from A (resp. B) making its kth move. In other words, the superscript in $X_{2k-1}^{(A)}$ (resp. $X_{2k}^{(B)}$) is a redundant notation to make remind the reader that A (resp. B) made the $(2k-1)$st (resp. $(2k)$th) move of the game.
  Similarly, for $k \in [c]$, if B is the bias inducer, we will use either of the notations $Y_{2k-1} = Y_{2k-1}^{(A)}$ (resp. $Y_{2k} = Y_{2k}^{(B)}$), to denote the random variable associated to the state resulting from A (resp. B) making its kth move. Again, the redundant superscript is used to make the player associated to the move explicit.
  The initial state of the game is defined as $p_0 \in]0,1[_{\mathbb{R}}$, where p_0 is a parameter of the game. In other words, $X_0 = Y_0 = p_0$.
  We say that a strategy for A and B has success rate *p_f if $\mathbb{E}[X_{2c}] \geq p_f$ and $\mathbb{E}[Y_{2c}] \geq p_f$.*
- **Rules on moves.** *The neutral party is restricted to making moves that do not change the state of the game on expectation, namely, the moves behave as martingales with respect to the current game state. More formally, with our*

notation, for all $k \in [c]$, we have:[20]

$$\mathbb{E}[X_{2k}^{(B)}|X_{2k-1}, \cdots, X_0] = X_{2k-1}. \tag{3}$$

$$E[Y_{2k-1}^{(A)}|Y_{2k}, \cdots, Y_0] = Y_{2k-2}. \tag{4}$$

where the first equation (resp. second equation) corresponds to A (resp. B) being the bias inducer.

- **Objective of the game.** *The goal of the game is, for the bias inducer, to be covert with respect to the observer C, while maintaining a high success rate p_f (namely, a high probability of ending up at 1 in the final state). The observer C has access to intermediate states of the execution $p_i \leftarrow X_i$ (if A is the bias inducer, or $p_i \leftarrow Y_i$ otherwise) via a (distribution of) oracles $\mathcal{O}$. In each oracle $\mathcal{O}$ is hard-coded a sequence of $2c$ states of the game $p_i, i \leq 2c$ induced by an execution of the game. We will respectively denote by $\mathcal{O}^{(A)}$ (resp. $\mathcal{O}^{(B)}$) (the distribution of) oracles corresponding to when A (resp. B) is designated as the bias inducer. We consider the following variants of the oracles $\mathcal{O} \in \{\mathcal{O}^{(A)}, \mathcal{O}^{(B)}\}$.*

  - *Sampling access. We say that the observer C gets sampling access to game states $p_i \in [0,1]_\mathbb{R}$, if oracles $\mathcal{O}$ are probabilistic oracles such that, for all $i \in [2c]$, $\mathcal{O}(i) = 1$ with probability p_i, and $\mathcal{O}(i) = 0$ with probability $1 - p_i$, where the randomness is uniformly and independently sampled at each oracle call. This is our default notion of access.*

  - *Direct access. We say that an observer gets direct access to game states $p_i \in [0,1]_\mathbb{R}$, if oracles $\mathcal{O}$ are defined as $\mathcal{O}_{\text{direct}}(i) = p_i \in [0,1]_\mathbb{R}$ for all $i \in [2c]$.*

  We say that the bias inducer successfully δ-fools a class $\mathcal{C}$ of observers with respect to sampling access if for every algorithm $C \in \mathcal{C}$, we have:

$$\left| \Pr\left[C^{\mathcal{O}^{(A)}} = 1 \right] - \Pr\left[C^{\mathcal{O}^{(B)}} = 1 \right] \right| \leq \delta,$$

  where $C^{\mathcal{O}^{(\mathcal{X})}}$, where $\mathcal{X} \in \{A, B\}$, denotes the experiment of sampling $\mathcal{O} \leftarrow \mathcal{O}^{(\mathcal{X})}$ (which is defined as sampling a random execution of the game when $\mathcal{X}$ is the bias inducer, yielding states $p_i, i \leq 2c$, and defining $\mathcal{O}$ with respect to $\{p_i\}$), and giving C oracle access to $\mathcal{O}$.

  We say that the bias inducer successfully δ-fools a class $\mathcal{C}$ of observers with respect to direct access if the observer C gets oracle access to $\mathcal{O}_{\text{direct}}$ instead.

- **(Optional Property): Symmetricity.** *We say that a strategy for players A and B is symmetric if:*

$$\forall k \in [c], \mathbb{E}\left[X_{2k}\right] = \mathbb{E}\left[Y_{2k}\right], \tag{5}$$

that is, the state of the game is (on expectation) independent of the identity of the bias inducer, whenever the bias inducer and the neutral party made an identical number of moves (which happens after an even number of total moves).

---

[20] We technically are also conditioning the expectations X, Y on all the prior moves instead, but are omitting them for ease of notation. See Remark 5.

– *(Optional Property): Absorption.* We say that a strategy is absorbent (*implicitly, with respect to states* 0 *and* 1) *if, for all* $i \in [2c]$ *and bit* $b \in \{0,1\}$:

$$\{X_i = b\} \implies \{\forall j \geq i, X_j = b\}. \tag{6}$$

Remark 5 (Implicit Conditioning on Prior Moves.). We allow the strategies from A and B to be adaptive, namely, to depend on prior moves. As a result, all the expectations on random variables X_i, Y_i are technically always considered conditioned on all the prior moves. For ease of notation, we will not make this conditioning explicit, and will always implicitly consider the conditional version of expectations for these variables (and resulting variables defined as a function of X_i, Y_i).

4.2   Attack 1: Free-Lunch Attack with Weak Distinguishing Guarantees

We show here that there exists a very efficient generic observer strategy given sampling access to game states with small but non-negligible distinguishing advantage. Namely:

Theorem 4 (Free-Lunch Distinguisher). *For any covert cheating game , consisting of $2c$ total moves, with starting state p_0 and satisfying symmetricity (see Definition 3, Eq. (5)), and any strategy for that game with success rate $p_f > p_0$, there exists an observer strategy C^* that determines the identity of the bias inducer with advantage $\delta = \frac{p_f - p_0}{c}$, by making a* single *call to the sampling oracle $\mathcal{O}$.*

In other words, the strategy does not δ-fool the class of observers making a single sampling oracle call.

Proof. We build our observer strategy as follows:

Observer C^*:

– Pick a random $k \leftarrow [c]$. Output $\mathcal{O}(2k - 1) \in \{0,1\}$.

In other words, C^* picks a random move from A, and outputs 1 with probability the state of the game after A's kth move. Let us analyze the advantage of C^*.

Suppose A is the bias inducer. Then:

$$\mathbb{E}_{k \leftarrow [c]} \left[\mathcal{O}^{(A)}(2k - 1) \right] = \mathbb{E}\left[X_{2k-1}\right],$$

and we furthermore have by Eq. (3) that for all $k \in [c]$[21]:

$$\mathbb{E}\left[X_{2k}^{(B)} - X_{2k-1}^{(A)}\right] = 0, \tag{7}$$

---

[21] Recall that each expectation is implicitly conditioned on prior moves (Remark 5).

namely, B's moves do not change X on expectation.

Suppose now that B is the bias inducer. Then, Eq. (4) gives that for all $k \in [c]$:

$$\mathbb{E}\left[Y_{2k-1}^{(A)} - Y_{2k-2}^{(B)}\right] = 0, \tag{8}$$

namely, A's moves do not change Y on expectation. This gives:

$$\mathbb{E}_{k \leftarrow [c]}\left[\mathcal{O}^{(B)}(2k-1)\right] = \mathbb{E}\left[Y_{2k-1}\right]$$
$$= \mathbb{E}\left[Y_{2k-2}\right]$$
$$= \mathbb{E}\left[X_{2k-2}\right],$$

where the second equality comes from Eq. (8), and the last equality follows by symmetry if $k > 1$ (Eq. (5)), or as $X_0 = Y_0 = p_0$ if $k = 1$.

Overall, we obtain that the advantage of C^* is, by telescoping:

$$\left|\Pr\left[C^{\mathcal{O}^{(A)}} = 1\right] - \Pr\left[C^{\mathcal{O}^{(B)}} = 1\right]\right|$$
$$\geq \Pr\left[C^{\mathcal{O}^{(A)}} = 1\right] - \Pr\left[C^{\mathcal{O}^{(B)}} = 1\right]$$
$$= \mathbb{E}_{k \xleftarrow{\$} [c]}\left[X_{2k-1}^{(A)} - Y_{2k-1}^{(A)}\right]$$
$$= \mathbb{E}_{k \xleftarrow{\$} [c]}\left[X_{2k-1}^{(A)} - X_{2k-2}^{(B)}\right]$$
$$= \sum_{k \in [c]} \frac{\mathbb{E}\left[X_{2k-1}^{(A)} - X_{2k-2}^{(B)}\right]}{c} + \underbrace{\frac{\mathbb{E}\left[X_{2k}^{(B)} - X_{2k-1}^{(A)}\right]}{c}}_{=0 \text{ (Eq.(7))}}$$
$$= \frac{\mathbb{E}\left[X_{2c} - X_0\right]}{c}$$
$$= \frac{p_f - p_0}{c}$$

which concludes the proof.

Remark 6 (Correct predictions). Our attack provides a slightly better guarantee than stated in Theorem 4: it correctly outputs the identity of the bias inducer (say by associating output 1 to A being the bias inducer), as opposed to simply distinguishing them. In other words, we have:

$$\Pr\left[C^{\mathcal{O}^{(A)}} = 1\right] - \Pr\left[C^{\mathcal{O}^{(B)}} = 1\right] = \frac{p_f - p_0}{c}.$$

4.3   Attack 2.1: A Strong Attack Given Direct Access to States

Next, we describe a generic attack with large advantage, given direct access to game states. We refer to the technical overview (Sect. 2) for an intuition of the attack. Compared to the exposition in the technical overview, the main difference is that we have to deal with games where the end state is not consistently p_f, but rather 0 or 1 with expectation p_f. This does lead to technical complications. Indeed, one crucial argument in our proof is that the (multiplicative) contribution of the neutral party is 1 on expectation, which allows us to call Markov's inequality. However, switching to the expectation statement, conditioning on the end state being 1 might skew the contribution of the neutral party, which might prevent us from concluding. Instead, we carefully define several useful events, which allows us to compute the advantage of our strategy without ever conditioning on successful runs. More precisely, we now prove the slightly stronger statement that for all winning executions (that is, such that $p_{2c} = 1$), we only fail to identify the sender with small probability $\sqrt{p_0}$.[22]

Last, there is a minor technicality in how to handle denominators being equal to 0 (again, where we do not wish to condition on denominators not being equal to 0), which we solve by requiring a stronger, but natural "absorption" property of the covert cheating game (Definition 3, Eq. (6)).

Theorem 5 (Strong Distinguisher given Direct Access). *For any covert cheating game satisfying absorption (Definition 3, Eq. (6)), consisting of $2c$ total moves, with starting state $p_0 > 0$, and any strategy for that game with success rate $p_f > 2\sqrt{p_0}$, there exists an observer strategy C^* that determines the identity of the bias inducer with advantage at least $p_f - 2\sqrt{p_0}$ given $2c$ oracle calls to the direct access oracle $\mathcal{O}_{\text{direct}}$ (Definition 3).*

Proof. We describe the observer strategy.

    Observer C^*:

– Compute for all $i \in [2c]$: $p_i = \mathcal{O}_{\text{direct}}(i)$. If $p_{2c} = 0$, output a random bit $\beta \leftarrow \{0, 1\}$.
  Otherwise, compute:

$$t^{(A)} = \prod_{k=1}^{c} \frac{p_{2k-1}}{p_{2k-2}},$$

$$t^{(B)} = \prod_{k=1}^{c} \frac{p_{2k}}{p_{2k-1}},$$

  with the convention that $t^{(A)} = 1$ (resp. $t^{(B)} = 1$) if $p_{2k-2} = 0$ for some $k \in [c]$ (resp. if $p_{2k-1} = 0$ for some $k \in [c]$).
– Output 1 (that we associate to outputting "A") if $t^{(A)} \geq \sqrt{\frac{1}{p_0}}$. Otherwise, if $t^{(B)} \geq \sqrt{\frac{1}{p_0}}$, output 0 (that we associate to outputting "B"). Otherwise, output $\bot$.[23]

---

[22] This is a stronger statement in the sense that observers can test whether an execution is winning, and therefore can output an arbitrary bit $p_{2c} \neq 1$.

[23] Technically, $\bot$ can be replaced by any arbitrary output, e.g. 0; but considering this output separately is in our eyes conceptually cleaner.

Let us analyze the advantage of C^*.

Case 1: A is the bias inducer. Suppose A is the bias inducer. We define the following events:

$$\mathsf{CORRECT}_A := \{X_{2c} = 1\};$$

$$\mathsf{LARGE}_A^{(A)} := \left\{t^{(A)} \geq \sqrt{\frac{1}{p_0}}\right\};$$

$$\mathsf{SMALL}_A^{(B)} := \left\{t^{(B)} < \sqrt{\frac{1}{p_0}}\right\};$$

$$\mathsf{GOOD}_A := \mathsf{CORRECT}_A \wedge \mathsf{LARGE}_A^{(A)} \wedge \mathsf{SMALL}_A^{(B)}.$$

Note that if GOOD_A occurs, our algorithm is correct when A is the bias inducer. We argue that GOOD_A occurs with high probability. We start by analyzing the contribution $t^{(B)}$ of B.

Lemma 2. *We have:*
$$\Pr[\mathsf{SMALL}_A^{(B)}] \geq 1 - \sqrt{p_0}.$$

Proof. For $k \in [c]$, let us define the partial product of ratios associated to B:

$$P_k^{(B)} = \prod_{j=1}^{k} \frac{X_{2j}^{(B)}}{X_{2j-1}^{(A)}},$$

with the convention that $P_k^{(B)} = 1$ if $p_{2j-1} = 0$ for some $j \in [k]$, and observe that:

$$t^{(B)} \leftarrow P_c^{(B)}.$$

First, observe that

$$\mathbb{E}[P_1^{(B)}] = \frac{\mathbb{E}[X_1^{(B)}]}{p_0} = 1,$$

by Eq. (4).

Let $k \in \{2, \cdots, c\}$; suppose that $\mathbb{E}[P_{k-1}^{(B)}] = 1$. We have:

$$\mathbb{E}[P_k^{(B)}] = \mathbb{E}_{Y_0, \cdots Y_{2k-1}} \left[\mathbb{E}[P_k^{(B)} | Y_0, \cdots, Y_{2k-1}]\right]$$

$$= \mathbb{E}_{p_0, \cdots p_{2k-1}} \left[\mathbb{E}\left[P_{k-1}^{(B)} \cdot \frac{X_{2k}^{(B)}}{X_{2k-1}^{(A)}} \middle| Y_0 = p_0, \cdots, Y_{2k-1} = p_{2k-1}\right]\right]$$

$$= \mathbb{E}_{p_0, \cdots p_{2k-1}} \left[\mathbb{E}\left[P_{k-1}^{(B)} \cdot \frac{X_{2k}^{(B)}}{p_{2k-1}} \middle| Y_0 = p_0, \cdots, Y_{2k-1} = p_{2k-1}\right]\right]$$

$$= \mathbb{E}_{p_0, \cdots p_{2k-1}} \left[t_{k-1}^{(B)} \cdot \frac{\mathbb{E}\left[X_{2k}^{(B)}\right]}{p_{2k-1}} \middle| Y_0 = p_0, \cdots, Y_{2k-1} = p_{2k-1}\right]$$

$$= \mathbb{E}_{p_0, \cdots p_{2k-1}} \left[t_{k-1}^{(B)} \middle| Y_0 = p_0, \cdots, Y_{2k-1} = p_{2k-1}\right]$$

$$= P_{k-1}^{(B)},$$

where we define $t_{k-1}^{(B)} = t_{k-1}^{(B)}(p_0, \cdots, p_{2k})$ as: $t_{k-1}^{(B)} = \prod_{j=1}^{k-1} \frac{p_{2j}}{p_{2j-1}}$, and where the second to last equality follows by Eq. (4), and with the convention that a fraction with denominator 0 is equal to 1. Therefore, for all $k \in [c]$ (and in particular $k = c - 1$), we have:

$$\mathbb{E}[P_k^{(B)}] = 1. \tag{9}$$

Markov's inequality thus gives:

$$\Pr[\neg\mathsf{SMALL}_A^{(B)}] = \Pr\left[P_k^{(B)} \geq \sqrt{\frac{1}{p_0}}\right] \leq \sqrt{p_0},$$

which concludes the proof of Lemma 2.

Next, by definition of success rate and p_f, we have $\Pr[\mathsf{CORRECT}_A] \geq p_f$. Thus:

$$\Pr\left[\mathsf{CORRECT}_A \wedge \mathsf{SMALL}_A^{(B)}\right] \geq \Pr\left[\mathsf{CORRECT}_A\right] - \Pr\left[\neg\mathsf{SMALL}_A^{(B)}\right] \geq p_f - \sqrt{p_0}.$$

Last, we observe that $\mathsf{CORRECT}_A \wedge \mathsf{SMALL}_A^{(B)}$ implies $\mathsf{CORRECT}_A \wedge \mathsf{LARGE}_A^{(A)} \wedge \mathsf{SMALL}_A^{(B)}$. Indeed, suppose $\mathsf{CORRECT}_A$ occurs. By absorption of the game Eq. (6), none of the terms used in a denominator equal 0 (otherwise the final state would be 0). Furthermore, whenever $\mathsf{CORRECT}_A$ occurs, we have by a telescoping product:

$$t^{(A)} \cdot t^{(B)} = 1,$$

and therefore, $t^{(B)} < \sqrt{1/p_0}$ (given by $\mathsf{SMALL}_A^{(B)}$) implies that $t^{(A)} \geq \sqrt{1/p_0}$, namely that $\mathsf{LARGE}_A^{(A)}$ occurs.

Overall, this ensures:

$$\Pr[\mathsf{GOOD}_A] \geq \Pr[\mathsf{CORRECT}_A \wedge \mathsf{SMALL}_A^{(B)}] \geq p_f - \sqrt{p_0},$$

and therefore C^* will be correct with probability at least $p_f - \sqrt{p_0}$ when A is the bias inducer when $\mathsf{CORRECT}_A$ occurs, and correct with probability $1/2$ when $\neg\mathsf{CORRECT}_A$ occurs (which occurs with probability $1 - p_f$ by definition of p_f). In other words, when A is the bias inducer, C^* outputs 1 with probability at least $p_f - \sqrt{p_0} + (1 - p_f)/2$.

Case 2: B is the bias inducer. Suppose now B is the bias inducer. We can similarly define:

$$\mathsf{CORRECT}_B := \{Y_{2c} = 1\};$$

$$\mathsf{LARGE}_B^{(B)} := \left\{t^{(B)} \geq \sqrt{\frac{1}{p_0}}\right\};$$

$$\mathsf{SMALL}_B^{(A)} := \left\{t^{(A)} < \sqrt{\frac{1}{p_0}}\right\};$$

$$\mathsf{GOOD}_B := \mathsf{LARGE}_A^{(A)} \wedge \mathsf{SMALL}_A^{(B)}.$$

An almost identical analysis (using random variables X instead of Y, and shifting the indices appropriately) shows that

$$\Pr[\mathsf{GOOD}_B] \geq p_f - \sqrt{p_0},$$

and therefore C^* will be correct with probability at least $p_f - \sqrt{p_0} + (1 - p_f)/2$ when B is the bias inducer.

Wrapping Up. Overall, the advantage of C^* is

$$\left| \Pr\left[C^{\mathcal{O}^{(A)}} = 1 \right] - \Pr\left[C^{\mathcal{O}^{(B)}} = 1 \right] \right| \geq \Pr\left[C^{\mathcal{O}^{(A)}} = 1 \right] - \Pr\left[C^{\mathcal{O}^{(B)}} = 1 \right]$$
$$\geq 2(p_f - \sqrt{p_0}) - 1 + (1 - p_f) = p_f - 2\sqrt{p_0},$$

which concludes the proof.

4.4   Attack 2.2: A Strong Attack Given Sampling Access to States

Next, we port our attack from Sect. 4.3 to the much weaker sampling setting. Overall, this new attack

- works in the much weaker sampling setting, and does not require the game to satisfy absorption (Eq. (6)),
- but has slightly weaker advantage $\approx p_f - 1/\mathrm{poly}(\lambda)$ while requiring p_0 to be fairly small (the advantage holding for any $\mathrm{poly}(\lambda)$ of our choice, as long as p_0 is small enough), and has a quite larger polynomial sample complexity $q \approx c^6 \cdot \mathrm{poly}(\lambda)$ with respect to the sampling oracle.[24]

Our new analysis is more involved, as to carefully estimate the multiplicative progress of the players despite having imperfect access to the game states p_i. The main problem arises when the state of the game becomes (say, exponentially close or even equal to) 0. Indeed, such states are indistinguishable from the state being actually 0 from the view of a polynomial-time observer with only sampling access to the state. However, they cannot be treated using an absorption argument (Eq. (6)), like in Theorem 5: this is because Eq. (6) only holds for the two states 0 and 1. We solve this by thresholdizing the (partial) products, and only considering "suffix-products" (that is, over indices $i \geq i^*$ for some index i^*) when all the probabilities handled are large enough (say $\gtrsim 1/c^2$). We refer to Sect. 2 for an intuition for the attack.

One difference with the overview in Sect. 2 is, again, that the strategy from the players A, B do not necessarily finish at state $p_{2c} \geq p_f$; this guarantee only holds on expectation. We solve this issue similarly to Theorem 5, by defining several useful events, and argue that products associated to the neutral party are small with high probability without (significantly) conditioning. And similarly to Theorem 5, we prove a slightly stronger result: for all winning executions of

---

[24] Looking ahead, this large sample complexity is a result of the techniques we use in our analysis which require us compute precise estimations for each game state.

the game (that is, such that $p_{2c} = 1$), we only fail to identify the sender with probability $\approx 1/\text{poly}(\lambda)$.

Overall, we present an attack with guarantees comparable with the ones from Theorem 5. Even if the analysis is quite tedious and notation-heavy, it is still very similar in spirit to the one of Theorem 5.

Theorem 6 (Strong Distinguisher given Sampling Access). *Let $\alpha(\lambda) \geq 1$ be a polynomial. For all covert cheating game satisfying $p_0 \leq O\left(\frac{1}{c^2\alpha^2}\right)$, and any strategy with success rate $p_f \geq 1/\alpha(\lambda)$, there exists an observer C^* that determines the identity of the bias inducer with advantage at least $p_f - 1/\alpha -$ negl(λ).*

Furthermore, the observer makes $c^6\alpha^4\omega(\log^2 \lambda)$ calls to the sampling oracle $\mathcal{O}$.

In particular, if $p_0 = \text{negl}(\lambda)$, there is, for all polynomial α, an observer strategy with advantage at least $p_f - 1/\alpha - \text{negl}(\lambda)$, with a query complexity of $c^6\alpha^4\omega(\log^2 \lambda)$.

Proof. Suppose the covert cheating game satisfies the constraints on p_0 and p_f; observe that in particular $p_0 \leq p_f$.

We describe our attack, which uses the following parameters:

- $\tau = \tau(\lambda, c) \in [0, 1]_{\mathbb{R}}$, a threshold precision for our estimation procedure. We will use $\tau = 1/(64c^2 \cdot \alpha^2(\lambda))$ where α is specified in Theorem 6.
- $t = t(\lambda, c) \in [0, 1]_{\mathbb{R}}$, a multiplicative approximation factor for our estimation. We will use $t = 1/2c$.
- $s = \text{poly}(\lambda, c, \tau, t)$, a number of repetitions for our estimation. We will set $s = c^6 \cdot \text{poly}(\lambda)$, so that $s = \frac{\log c \cdot \omega(\log \lambda)}{\tau^2 t^2}$.

<u>Observer C^*:</u>

1. (<u>Estimation of p_i's</u>):
   - Set $\widetilde{p_0} = p_0$.
   - For $i = 1$ to $2c$:
     - For $j = 1$ to s, sample $b_j \leftarrow \mathcal{O}(i)$.
     - Compute $\widetilde{p_i} = \frac{1}{s}\sum_{j=1}^{s} b_j$.
   - If $\widetilde{p_{2c}} \leq 1 - \tau$, output a random bit $\beta \leftarrow \{0, 1\}$.[25]
   - Otherwise, let i^* be the largest index in $[0, 2c]$ such that $\widetilde{p_i} \leq \tau$ (which exists as we set $p_0 = \widetilde{p_0} \leq \tau$).
2. (<u>Estimation of partial numerator and denominator</u>): Compute

$$\widetilde{t^{(A)}}_{\text{num}} = \prod_{k \,|\, 2k-2 \geq i^*}^{c} \widetilde{p_{2k-1}} \cdot \qquad \widetilde{t^{(B)}}_{\text{num}} = \frac{1}{\widetilde{p_{2c}}} \prod_{k \,|\, 2k-1 \geq i^*}^{c} \widetilde{p_{2k}}$$

$$\widetilde{t^{(A)}}_{\text{denom}} = K^{(A)} \cdot \prod_{k \,|\, 2k-1 \geq i^*}^{c} \widetilde{p_{2k-2}}, \qquad \widetilde{t^{(B)}}_{\text{denom}} = K^{(B)} \cdot \prod_{k \,|\, 2k \geq i^*}^{c} \widetilde{p_{2k-1}},$$

---

[25] The choice of the specific output doesn't matter for the sake of the analysis, as long as is the same distribution whenever A or B is the bias inducer.

where $K^{(A)} = \begin{cases} 1 \text{ if } i^* \text{ is odd} \\ \tau \text{ if } i^* \text{ is even,} \end{cases}$ and $K^{(B)} = \begin{cases} \tau \text{ if } i^* \text{ is odd} \\ 1 \text{ if } i^* \text{ is even.} \end{cases}$

In other words, this computes partial products starting at i^* with the convention $\widetilde{p_{i^*}} = \tau$ (which only appears in one denominator, according to the parity of i^*), and $\widetilde{p_{2c}} = 1$.

3. <u>Output:</u> Output 1 (that we associate to outputting "A") if

$$\widetilde{t^{(A)}} := \frac{\widetilde{t_{num}^{(A)}}}{\widetilde{t_{denom}^{(A)}}} \geq \sqrt{\frac{1}{\tau}}.$$

Otherwise, output 0 (that we associate to outputting "B") if

$$\widetilde{t^{(B)}} := \frac{\widetilde{t_{num}^{(B)}}}{\widetilde{t_{denom}^{(B)}}} \geq \sqrt{\frac{1}{\tau}}.$$

Otherwise, output $\perp$.[26]

Let us analyze the advantage of C^*.

Case 1. A is the bias inducer. We define the following events, similar to the proof of Theorem 5, adapted to the approximate setting:

$$\mathsf{CORRECT}_A := \{\widetilde{p_{2c}} \geq 1 - t\};$$

$$\mathsf{LARGE}_A^{(A)} := \left\{\widetilde{t^{(A)}} \geq \sqrt{\frac{1}{\tau}}\right\};$$

$$\mathsf{SMALL}_A^{(B)} := \left\{\widetilde{t^{(B)}} < \sqrt{\frac{1}{\tau}}\right\};$$

$$\mathsf{GOOD}_A := \mathsf{CORRECT}_A \wedge \mathsf{LARGE}_A^{(A)} \wedge \mathsf{SMALL}_A^{(B)}.$$

We furthermore define the following auxiliary events related to the accuracy of the estimation procedure:

$$\mathsf{BAD}_0 := \{\forall i \text{ s.t. } p_i \geq \tau, \widetilde{p}_i \notin [(1-t)\,p_i, (1+t)\,p_i]\};$$
$$\mathsf{BAD}_1 := \{p_{i^*} \leq 2\tau\}.$$

We first argue that these auxiliary events only hold with negligible probability.

Lemma 3. *We have:* $\Pr[\neg\mathsf{BAD}_0 \wedge \neg\mathsf{BAD}_1] = \mathsf{negl}(\lambda)$.

Proof. This follows from routine Chernoff bounds. Define:

$$\mathsf{BAD}_2 := \{\exists i > i^*, p_i \leq \tau/2\}.$$

---

[26] Again, $\perp$ can be replaced by any arbitrary output, e.g. 0; but considering this output separately is in our eyes conceptually cleaner.

Combining Chernoff (Lemma 1 with $t = 1$) with an union bound over the at most $2c$ indices i gives $\Pr[\mathsf{BAD}_2] \leq 2c \cdot e^{-8s\tau^2}$. Whenever BAD_2 does not occur, we have $\Pr[\mathsf{BAD}_0 \wedge \neg\mathsf{BAD}_2] \leq 4c \cdot e^{-2\tau^2 t^2 s}$ by another combination of Chernoff and an union bound, which overall yields:

$$\Pr[\mathsf{BAD}_0] \leq 6c \cdot e^{-8\tau^2 t^2 s} \leq \mathsf{negl}(\lambda),$$

as long as $\tau^2 t^2 s \geq \log(c)\omega(\log \lambda)$, which holds by our setting of s.

Similarly, a Chernoff bound with $t = 2$ gives $\Pr[\mathsf{BAD}_1] \leq e^{-8\tau^2 s}$, which is negligible as long as $\tau^2 s \geq \omega(\log \lambda)$.

We want to prove two main claims, namely:

(1) Whenever GOOD_A occurs, C^* correctly outputs 1.
(2) GOOD_A occurs with sufficiently high probability (Sect. 4.4).

Claim (1) follows, similarly to the case in the proof of Theorem 5, from the claim that $\mathsf{CORRECT}_A \wedge \mathsf{SMALL}_A^{(B)}$ holding implies $\mathsf{CORRECT}_A \wedge \mathsf{LARGE}_A^{(A)} \wedge \mathsf{SMALL}_A^{(B)}$ holds except with negligible probability. Indeed, whenever $\mathsf{CORRECT}_A$ and BAD_0 occur, we have

$$\widetilde{t^{(A)}} \cdot \widetilde{t^{(B)}} = 1,$$

and therefore $\widetilde{t^{(B)}} < \frac{1}{2} \cdot \sqrt{1/\tau}$ (given by $\mathsf{SMALL}_A^{(B)}$) implies that $t^{(A)} \geq 2\sqrt{1/\tau}$, namely that $\mathsf{LARGE}_A^{(A)}$ occurs, and Lemma 3 concludes the claim.

It therefore suffices to prove (2).

Claim. We have:

$$\Pr[\mathsf{GOOD}_A] \geq p_f - 4c \cdot \sqrt{\tau} - \mathsf{negl}(\lambda).$$

We first show a few intermediate lemmas.

Proof (Proof of Sect. 4.4). We proceed similarly as in Sect. 4.3. We start by showing that:

$$\Pr[\mathsf{SMALL}_A^{(B)}] \geq \Pr[\mathsf{SMALL}_A^{(B)} \wedge \neg\mathsf{BAD}_0 \wedge \neg\mathsf{BAD}_1] \geq 1 - c \cdot \sqrt{\tau} - \mathsf{negl}(\lambda). \quad (10)$$

By a similar analysis to Sect. 4.3, using Eq. (4), we have that for any fixed $i \in [2c]$:

$$\Pr\left[\prod_{k|2k-1 \geq i}^{c} \frac{p_{2k}^{(B)}}{p_{2k-1}^{(A)}} \geq \frac{1}{4} \cdot \sqrt{\frac{1}{\tau}} \right] \leq 4\sqrt{\tau}.$$

A union bound over $i = 2k - 1 \in [2c]$, (there are c different such products), then gives:

$$\Pr\left[\exists i \in [2c], \prod_{k|2k-1 \geq i}^{c} \frac{p_{2k}^{(B)}}{p_{2k-1}^{(a)}} \geq \frac{1}{4} \cdot \sqrt{\frac{1}{\tau}} \right] \leq 4c \cdot \sqrt{\tau}.$$

Furthermore, whenever $\neg \mathsf{BAD}_1$ occurs, we have $p_i^* \leq 2\tau$, that is $1/p_i^* \geq 2/\tau$, so that, using Lemma 3:

$$\Pr\left[\frac{1}{2} \cdot \prod_{k\,|\,2k-1 \geq i^*} \frac{p_{2k}^{\prime(B)}}{p_{2k-1}^{\prime(A)}} \geq \frac{1}{4} \cdot \sqrt{\frac{1}{\tau}}\right] \leq 4c \cdot \sqrt{\tau} + \mathrm{negl}(\lambda),$$

where p' are defined as $p_{i^*}' = \tau$, and $p_i' = p_i$ for all $i \neq i^*$.

Last, whenever $\neg \mathsf{BAD}_0$ additionally occurs, we have:

$$\frac{\widetilde{t_{\mathrm{num}}^{(B)}}}{t_{\mathrm{denom}}^{(B)}} = \frac{1}{K^{(B)}} \cdot \frac{1}{\widetilde{p_{2c}}} \cdot \frac{\prod_{k\,|\,2k-1 \geq i^*}^c \widetilde{p_{2k}}}{\prod_{k\,|\,2k \geq i^*}^c \widetilde{p_{2k-1}}}$$

$$\leq \left(\frac{1+t}{1-t}\right)^c \prod_{k\,|\,2k-1 \geq i^*}^c \frac{p_{2k}^{\prime(B)}}{p_{2k-1}^{\prime(A)}}$$

$$\leq 2 \cdot \prod_{k\,|\,2k-1 \geq i^*}^c \frac{p_{2k}^{\prime(B)}}{p_{2k-1}^{\prime(A)}},$$

whenever $t \leq 1/2c$. Therefore:

$$\Pr[\neg \mathsf{SMALL}_A^{(B)}] = \Pr\left[\frac{\widetilde{t_{\mathrm{num}}^{(B)}}}{t_{\mathrm{denom}}^{(B)}} \geq \sqrt{\frac{1}{\tau}}\right] \leq 4c \cdot \sqrt{\tau} + \mathrm{negl}(\lambda).$$

Next, we have that if $\neg \mathsf{BAD}_0$ holds, then $\Pr[\mathsf{CORRECT}_A] \geq p_f$ (by definition of p_f), and therefore $\Pr[\mathsf{CORRECT}_A] \geq p_f - \mathrm{negl}(\lambda)$, and thus

$$\Pr\left[\mathsf{CORRECT}_A \wedge \mathsf{SMALL}_A^{(B)} \wedge \mathsf{LARGE}_A^{(B)}\right]$$

$$\geq \Pr\left[\mathsf{CORRECT}_A \wedge \mathsf{SMALL}_A^{(B)}\right] - \mathrm{negl}(\lambda)$$

$$\geq \Pr[\mathsf{CORRECT}_A] - \Pr\left[\neg \mathsf{SMALL}_A^{(B)}\right] - \mathrm{negl}(\lambda)$$

$$\geq p_f - 4c\sqrt{\tau} - \mathrm{negl}(\lambda),$$

which concludes the proof of Sect. 4.4.

Overall, if A is the bias inducer, given C^* outputs 1 with probability $1/2$ whenever $\neg \mathsf{CORRECT}_A$ occurs, we have:

$$\Pr\left[C^{\mathcal{O}^{(A)}} = 1\right] \geq p_f - 4c\sqrt{\tau} + \frac{1 - p_f}{2} - \mathrm{negl}(\lambda).$$

Case 2. B is the bias inducer. Similarly to Sect. 4.3, we define and analyze the analogues of the events when B is the bias inducer, and conclude that in this case, C^* outputs 0 with probability at least $p_f - 4c\sqrt{\tau} + \frac{1-p_f}{2} - \mathrm{negl}(\lambda)$.

Wrapping Up. Overall, the advantage of C^* is

$$\left| \Pr\left[C^{\mathcal{O}^{(A)}} = 1 \right] - \Pr\left[C^{\mathcal{O}^{(B)}} = 1 \right] \right|$$

$$\geq \Pr\left[C^{\mathcal{O}^{(A)}} = 1 \right] - \Pr\left[C^{\mathcal{O}^{(B)}} = 1 \right]$$

$$\geq p_f - 4c\sqrt{\tau} + \frac{1 - p_f}{2} - 1 + (p_f - 4c\sqrt{\tau} + \frac{1 - p_f}{2}) - \text{negl}(\lambda)$$

$$= p_f - 8c\sqrt{\tau} - \text{negl}(\lambda), \tag{11}$$

and plugging in the parameters in the beginning of the proof gives $8c\sqrt{\tau} = 1/\alpha$, which concludes the proof.

Remark 7 (Correct predictions). Again, our attack provides a slightly better guarantee than stated in Theorem 6: it correctly outputs the identity of the bias inducer (say by associating output 1 to A being the bias inducer), as opposed to simply distinguishing them. In other words, we have:

$$\Pr\left[C^{\mathcal{O}^{(A)}} = 1 \right] - \Pr\left[C^{\mathcal{O}^{(B)}} = 1 \right] = p_f - 8c\sqrt{\tau} - \text{negl}(\lambda).$$

Looking ahead, we will crucially use this fact to extend our result to the many-party case.

Remark 8 (Cost of the Attack, and Fine-grained Guarantees). The sampling complexity of our strategy C^* is a large, but fixed polynomial $c^6 \cdot \alpha^4 \cdot \omega(\log^2 \lambda)$. Concretely, in the setting where $p_f \geq K$ for a constant K, and $p_0 = \text{negl}(\lambda)$, we obtain attack with *constant advantage* (or even advantage $1 - 1/\text{poly}$ if $p_f = 1 - 1/\text{poly}$) which has a fixed overhead sampling cost as a function of c.

In other words, our attack rules out combinations of games and strategies that δ-fool *fine-grained observers* with sample complexity $m(c)$, if m is allowed to be a large enough polynomial.[27]

5   Lower Bounds on Anonymous Transfer

In this section, we tie the attacks on covert cheating games in Sect. 4 to impossibility results for anonymous transfer, thus obtaining Theorem 8 and Theorem 9. Last, we show how to extend Theorem 8 to the N-party setting in Sect. 5.3.

5.1   Reducing Anonymous Transfer to Covert Cheating Games

Theorem 7. *Let Π_{AT}^ℓ be a two-party anonymous transfer protocol, with correctness error $\varepsilon \in [0,1]_{\mathbb{R}}$, anonymity $\delta \in [0,1]_{\mathbb{R}}$ with respect to a class $\mathcal{C}$ of*

---

[27] Here, we implicitly take the convention that, because players make c moves, they have complexity at least c. This is informal, and there is a mismatch: we are comparing sample complexity of C^* against standard complexity of A and B. The translation to AT lower bounds will make this statement more precise.

adversaries, consisting of $c \in \mathbb{N}$ rounds and message length $\ell \in \mathbb{N}$ (all possibly functions of λ) and satisfying deterministic reconstruction (which is without loss of generality, see Remark 3).

Then there exists a covert cheating game, along with player strategy, where the game consists of c rounds, the initial state of the game is $2^{-\ell}$, the expected final state is $p_f = 1 - \varepsilon$ and the player strategy δ-fools observers in $\mathcal{C}$.

Moreover, the covert cheating game satisfies absorption (Definition 3, Eq. (6)), and is symmetric if Π_{AT}^{ℓ} is symmetric (Definition 2).

Proof. Let $\Pi_{AT}^{\ell} = (\mathsf{Setup}, \mathsf{Transfer}, \mathsf{Reconstruct})$ be an AT with the notation of Theorem 7. We define our game as follows.

- **Players and roles.** The players of the game are the participants of the AT. The bias inducer is the sender of the AT using a uniformly random message $\mu \leftarrow \{0,1\}^{\ell}$, the neutral party is the dummy party of the AT, and observers are distinguishers.

- **Execution and states.** Moves in the covert cheating game are messages sent in the AT. In other words, a full execution of the game is a full AT transcript. Because moves in the covert cheating game are sequential, we sequentialize the messages of the AT by consider player A to move first within the round. This induces an order of messages, indexed by $i \in [2c]$.
  Let us fix an execution of the game, that is a full AT transcript $\pi \leftarrow \mathsf{Transfer}(\mathsf{crs}, b, \mu)$, where $\mathsf{crs} \leftarrow \mathsf{Setup}(1^{\lambda})$ and $\mu \leftarrow \{0,1\}^{\ell}$. The associated states of the game p_i, where $i \in [2c]$, are defined as follows. Let $\pi[i]$ denote the partial transcript consisting of the first i messages of the protocol $\mathsf{Transfer}$ (with the sequential order from above). Let $\overline{\pi[i]}$ denote the distribution of *randomly completed* partial transcripts, where $\pi[i]$ is completed with $2c - i$ uniformly sampled random message to obtain a full transcript. We then define:

$$p_i = p(\mathsf{crs}, \pi[i]) := \Pr\left[\mu' \leftarrow \mathsf{Reconstruct}(\mathsf{crs}, \overline{\pi[i]}) : \mu' = \mu\right],$$

  where $\mu \leftarrow \{0,1\}^{\ell}$ is the input to the AT sender. The probability is over the randomness of the random completion (recall that $\mathsf{Reconstruct}$ is deterministic).
  The initial state of the game is $p_0 = 1/2^{\ell}$, over the sole randomness of $\mu \leftarrow \{0,1\}^{\ell}$.
  Π_{AT}^{ℓ} having correctness error ε implies that the resulting covert cheating strategies have success rate $p_f = 1 - \varepsilon$. Furthermore, the final state satisfies $p_{2c} \in \{0,1\}$ by determinism of $\mathsf{Reconstruct}$ and definition of p_{2c} (as there is no randomness in $\mathsf{Reconstruct}(\mathsf{crs}, \overline{\pi})$).

- **Restriction on the neutral party.** We argue that Eqs. (3) and (4) hold. This is because in an AT, dummy messages are sampled uniformly at random, and are therefore identically distributed as its counterpart obtained from random completion. More formally, supposing A is the bias inducer/sender, we have for all $k \in [c]$ that the completions $\overline{(\pi[2k-1]\|\mathsf{msg})}$ where msg is a random AT protocol message, and $\overline{\pi[2k-1]}$ are identically distributed by definition of completion, so that

$$\mathbb{E}[X_{2k}^{(B)}|X_{2k-1},\cdots,X_0]$$

$$= \mathbb{E}_{\mathsf{msg}}\left[\Pr\left[\mu' \leftarrow \mathsf{Reconstruct}(\mathsf{crs}, \overline{(\pi[2k-1]\|\mathsf{msg})}) : \mu' = \mu\right]\right]$$

$$= \Pr\left[\mu' \leftarrow \mathsf{Reconstruct}(\mathsf{crs}, \overline{\pi[2k-1]}) : \mu' = \mu\right]$$

$$= X_{2k-1},$$

and similarly when B is the bias inducer/sender.

- **Observers and security.** Given an AT transcript, we implement a sampling oracle as follows. On input i, sample $\overline{\pi[i]}$ and compute $\mu' \leftarrow$ Reconstruct$(\mathsf{crs}, \overline{\pi[i]})$ Output 1 if $\mu' = \mu$, and 0 otherwise. By definition, this procedure tosses a coin with probability p_i.

  Overall, if an observer strategy distinguishes $\mathcal{O}^{(A)}$ from $\mathcal{O}^{(B)}$ in time t, with q sampling oracle queries and advantage δ, then there exists a distinguisher for the *AT* running in time $t + q \cdot (n + \rho(c))$ with advantage δ, where n is the complexity of computing Reconstruct and $\rho(c)$ is the complexity of sampling c uniformly random protocol messages.

- **Absorption.** Because completions are sampled uniformly random from the whole message space of the protocol, by definition of p_i, $p_i = 1$ implies that all completions of $\pi[i]$ recover μ, which implies that all possible continuations of $\pi[i]$ satisfy $p = 1$. Similarly, $p_i = 0$ implies that all completions of $\pi[i]$ fail to recover μ, so that all continuations of $\pi[i]$ satisfy $p = 0$.

- **Symmetricity.** Suppose the AT is symmetric (Definition 2), and let $k \in [c]$. Then (1) by symmetry of Reconstruct, Reconstruct$(\mathsf{crs}, \overline{\pi[2k]})$ is identically distributed as Reconstruct$(\mathsf{crs}, \overline{\mathsf{Mirror}(\pi[2k])})$, where Mirror flips the identities of the participants in the transcript and (2) by symmetry of Transfer, the unordered set $(\mathsf{dummy}^{(A)}, \mathsf{msg}^{(B)})$ is identically distributed as $(\mathsf{dummy}^{(B)}, \mathsf{msg}^{(A)})$. We can therefore replace all the consecutive pairs of messages $(2j-1, 2j)$ from $\{\mathsf{dummy}_{2j-1}^{(A)}, \mathsf{msg}_{2j}^{(B)}\}$ to $\{\mathsf{msg}_{2j-1}^{(A)}, \mathsf{dummy}_{2j}^{(B)}\}$, for all $j \leq k$, without changing the distribution of the outcome of Reconstruct. Doing so $2k$ times gives:

$$\mathbb{E}[X_{2k}] = \mathbb{E}[Y_{2k}].$$

5.2 Lower Bounds on Anonymous Transfer

We first rule out the existence of AT with non-trivial correctness error ε and anonymity δ, that are secure against arbitrary polynomial-time adversaries. We do so by combining Theorem 6 with Theorem 7, which gives the following:

Theorem 8. *Suppose Π_{AT}^{ℓ} is a (two-party, silent receiver) anonymous transfer satisfying deterministic reconstruction, and with $\ell \geq \omega(\log \lambda)$-bit messages, with correctness error ε, and δ-anonymous against all polynomial-time adversaries. Then, for all polynomial $\alpha = \alpha(\lambda)$:*

$$\delta \geq 1 - \varepsilon - 1/\alpha(\lambda).$$

We observe that the relation between δ and ε is almost tight (up to $1/\text{poly}(\lambda)$ factors), namely matches a trivial construction, (See full version).

Remark 9 (Ruling out other versions of AT). Thanks to the transformations in Sect. 3, Theorem 8 also rules out other versions of AT, including (all combinations of) the following: AT with non-silent receiver, AT with randomized reconstruction, AT with a large number N of parties (by considering $\delta' = (N-1) \cdot \delta$).

Remark 10 (Ruling out strong fine-grained results). In fact, denoting $n = n(\lambda)$ the running time of Reconstruct, the attack obtained by combining Theorem 6 with Theorem 7 runs in time $m(\lambda) = n \cdot c^6 \cdot \omega(\log^2(\lambda))$, and therefore Theorem 8 further rules out schemes that are secure against adversaries running in fixed polynomial overhead over honest users $m \leq n^7$. In other words, fine-grained results for non-trivial parameters will at most provide security against adversaries running in time m.

Next, we rule out the existence of fine-grained AT, but for a smaller set of parameters. We do so by combining Theorem 4 with Theorem 7. Note that Theorem 4 requires the AT to be symmetric; this is without loss of generality (See full version). This overall gives the following:

Theorem 9. *There are no fine-grained AT with ℓ-bit messages, correctness error ε, and anonymity δ, such that:*

$$\delta \cdot c \geq 1 - \varepsilon - 1/2^\ell.$$

More precisely, denoting $n = n(\lambda)$ the maximum runtime of Transfer, Reconstruct, and $\rho(c)$ is the cost of sampling c uniformly random protocol messages, combining Theorem 4 with Theorem 7 gives an attack with complexity $n(\lambda) + \rho(c) \leq 2n(\lambda)$.

5.3   Extension to Anonymous Transfer with Many Parties

In this section, we show that Theorem 8 extends to rule out anonymous transfer with any polynomial number N of parties.[28] More precisely, we prove the following result.

Theorem 10. *Let $N = N(\lambda)$ be any polynomial. Suppose Π_{AT}^ℓ is an N-party (silent receiver) anonymous transfer satisfying deterministic reconstruction, with $\ell \geq \omega(\log \lambda)$-bit messages, with correctness error ε, and δ-anonymous against all polynomial-time adversaries. Then, for all polynomial $\alpha = \alpha(\lambda)$:*

$$\delta \geq 1 - \varepsilon - 1/\alpha(\lambda).$$

---

[28] Looking ahead, doing so comes at a mild loss in the resulting anonymity δ. While this loss is mild starting from Theorem 8 yielding the main result of the section, it is quite significant when starting from Theorem 9, in which case the anonymity guarantees we obtain are similar to the ones of [3]. We therefore focus on Theorem 8 in this section.

We refer to the technical overview for a sketch, and the full version for a full proof.

Acknowledgements. Daniel Wichs was supported in part by the National Science Foundation under NSF CNS-1750795, CNS-2055510, and the JP Morgan faculty research award.

References

1. Navalny, A.: Russia's jailed vociferous putin critic. British Broadcasting Corporation (2022). https://www.bbc.com/news/world-europe-16057045
2. Abraham, I., Pinkas, B., Yanai, A.: Blinder - scalable, robust anonymous committed broadcast. In: Ligatti, J., Ou, X., Katz, J., Vigna, G. (eds.) ACM CCS 2020, pp. 1233–1252. ACM Press, November 2020. https://doi.org/10.1145/3372297.3417261
3. Agrikola, T., Couteau, G., Maier, S.: Anonymous whistleblowing over authenticated channels. In: Kiltz, E., Vaikuntanathan, V. (eds.) TCC 2022, Part II. LNCS, vol. 13748, pp. 685–714. Springer, Heidelberg (2022). https://doi.org/10.1007/978-3-031-22365-5_24
4. Andrews, S., Burrough, B., Ellison, S.: The Snowden saga. Vanity Fair (2014). https://archive.vanityfair.com/article/2014/5/the-snowden-saga
5. Berret, C. (2016). https://www.cjr.org/tow_center_reports/guide_to_securedrop.php
6. Chaum, D.: The dining cryptographers problem: unconditional sender and recipient untraceability. J. Cryptol. **1**(1), 65–75 (1988). https://doi.org/10.1007/BF00206326
7. Chaum, D.: Untraceable electronic mail, return addresses and digital pseudonyms. In: Gritzalis, D.A. (ed.) Secure Electronic Voting. Advances in Information Security, vol. 7, pp. 211–219. Springer, Boston (2003). https://doi.org/10.1007/978-1-4615-0239-5_14
8. Cohn-Gordon, K., Cremers, C., Dowling, B., Garratt, L., Stebila, D.: A formal security analysis of the signal messaging protocol. J. Cryptol. **33**(4), 1914–1983 (2020). https://doi.org/10.1007/s00145-020-09360-1
9. Corrigan-Gibbs, H., Boneh, D., Mazières, D.: Riposte: an anonymous messaging system handling millions of users. In: 2015 IEEE Symposium on Security and Privacy, pp. 321–338 (2015). https://doi.org/10.1109/SP.2015.27
10. Dingledine, R., Mathewson, N., Syverson, P.F.: Tor: The second-generation onion router. In: Blaze, M. (ed.) USENIX Security 2004, pp. 303–320. USENIX Association, August 2004
11. Eskandarian, S., Corrigan-Gibbs, H., Zaharia, M., Boneh, D.: Express: lowering the cost of metadata-hiding communication with cryptographic privacy. In: Bailey, M., Greenstadt, R. (eds.) USENIX Security 2021, pp. 1775–1792. USENIX Association, August 2021
12. Hopper, N.J., Langford, J., von Ahn, L.: Provably secure steganography. In: Yung, M. (ed.) CRYPTO 2002. LNCS, vol. 2442, pp. 77–92. Springer, Heidelberg (2002). https://doi.org/10.1007/3-540-45708-9_6
13. Inzaurralde, B.: The cybersecurity 202: leak charges against treasury official show encrypted apps only as secure as you make them. The Washinton Post (2018)
14. Newman, Z., Servan-Schreiber, S., Devadas, S.: Spectrum: high-bandwidth anonymous broadcast with malicious security. Cryptology ePrint Archive, Report 2021/325 (2021). https://eprint.iacr.org/2021/325

15. von Ahn, L., Hopper, N.J.: Public-key steganography. In: Cachin, C., Camenisch, J.L. (eds.) EUROCRYPT 2004. LNCS, vol. 3027, pp. 323–341. Springer, Heidelberg (2004). https://doi.org/10.1007/978-3-540-24676-3_20
16. von Ahn, L., Hopper, N.J., Langford, J.: Covert two-party computation. In: Gabow, H.N., Fagin, R. (eds.) 37th ACM STOC, pp. 513–522. ACM Press (2005). https://doi.org/10.1145/1060590.1060668

Anonymous Permutation Routing

Paul Bunn[1]([✉]), Eyal Kushilevitz[2], and Rafail Ostrovsky[3]

[1] Stealth Software Technologies, Inc., Los Angeles, USA
paul@stealthsoftwareinc.com
[2] Computer Science Department, Technion, Haifa, Israel
eyalk@cs.technion.ac.il
[3] Departments of Computer Science, Mathematics, UCLA, Los Angeles, USA
rafail@cs.ucla.edu

Abstract. The Non-Interactive Anonymous Router (NIAR) model was introduced by Shi and Wu [SW21] as an alternative to conventional solutions to the anonymous routing problem, in which a set of senders wish to send messages to a set of receivers. In contrast to most known approaches to support anonymous routing (e.g. mix-nets, DC-nets, etc.), which rely on a network of routers communicating with users via interactive protocols, the NIAR model assumes a *single* router and is inherently *non-interactive* (after an initial setup phase). In addition to being non-interactive, the NIAR model is compelling due to the security it provides: instead of relying on the honesty of some subset of the routers, the NIAR model requires anonymity even if the router (as well as an arbitrary subset of senders/receivers) is corrupted by an honest-but-curious adversary.

In this paper, we present a protocol for the NIAR model that improves upon the results from [SW21] in two ways:

- Improved computational efficiency (quadratic to near linear): Our protocol matches the communication complexity of [SW21] for each sender/receiver, while reducing the computational overhead for the router to polylog overhead instead of linear overhead.
- Relaxation of assumptions: Security of the protocol in [SW21] relies on the Decisional Linear assumption in bilinear groups; while security for our protocol follows from the existence of any rate-1 oblivious transfer (OT) protocol (instantiations of which are known to exist under the DDH, QR and LWE assumptions [DGI+19, GHO20]).

Keywords: Anonymous Routing · Private-Information Retrieval · Permutation Routing · Non-Interactive Protocols

1 Introduction

As the collection and access of digital information in our daily lives becomes ever-more ubiquitous (internet, local networks, mobile networks, IoT), so too does the need for the development of technologies to protect access and transmission of this data. While protecting the integrity and access to sensitive data

© International Association for Cryptologic Research 2023
G. Rothblum and H. Wee (Eds.): TCC 2023, LNCS 14371, pp. 33–61, 2023.
https://doi.org/10.1007/978-3-031-48621-0_2

remain important tasks, there has been a growing need for *anonymity* in protecting data access and communications between users. Throughout this paper, anonymity will refer to the inability to associate which nodes in a network are communicating with each other; i.e. the unlinkability between one or more senders and the associated receiver(s). The conventional approach to providing such protection (onion routing, mix-nets, and others) relies on a network of routers relaying messages, where anonymity is only guaranteed if there are sufficiently many uncorrupted routers. A markedly different approach to this problem was recently introduced by Shi and Wu [SW21], who proposed using cryptographic techniques to hide connectivity patterns. Namely, they introduce the Non-Interactive Anonymous Router (NIAR) model, in which a set of N receiving nodes wish to receive information from a set of N sending nodes, with all information passing through a central router. Anonymity in their model is defined to be the inability to link any sender to the corresponding receiver, even if the router and (up to $N - 2$) various (sender, receiver) pairs are susceptible to attack by an (honest-but-curious[1]) adversary.

There are a number of real-world scenarios in which the NIAR model as described above is relevant. The important characteristics of any such application is that a number of (sender, receiver) pairs wish to anonymously communicate with each other through a central server, where the messages to be transmitted are large and/or the communication channels are non-ephemeral/indefinite. These conditions are exhibited, for example, in the following scenarios:

ANONYMOUS PEER-TO-PEER COMMUNICATION. Relevant in settings where a large set of users wish to communicate anonymously through a central server, e.g. for a Messaging app, where every communication link is established as a separate pair of (anonymous) virtual users.

PUB/SUB WITH PRIVACY. Because our solution is quasi-linear in message size, the additional overhead of storing all messages is minimal. We can therefore view the central router of the NIAR model as delivering each stream of messages it receives from the N senders into N storage units, rather than delivering them directly to receivers. In this way, the set of receivers can (privately) subscribe to an information service/source, and periodically receive updates. Furthermore, our protocol allows receivers to (privately) subscribe to *multiple* services at the same time, without revealing which services they are subscribed to.

MULTI-CLIENT PIR/PIW. In a similar spirit as the previous point, viewing the receivers as storage units, the messages being streamed from the senders can accumulate (or update previous messages), thus implementing a form of Private Information Writing (PIW). Depending on the application (in terms

---

[1] Our limitation to HBC adversaries is only needed to ensure Correctness of our protocol - that receivers get the correct messages. We note that requiring HBC for correctness is unavoidable, as a malicious router can, for example, not forward any message (like in PIR and other related primitives). In terms of Security (privacy of the senders-receivers permutation): so long as the one-time Setup is performed properly, then security of our protocol will hold in the Malicious adversary setting.

of which users will ultimately access/read the PIW server), hiding the linkage between which location each sender writes to versus which location each receiver reads from may require stronger security requirements, e.g. for our protocol, any receiver colluding with the central router will learn which sender it is reading from.

OBLIVIOUS SHUFFLE. A common scenario encountered in MPC protocols is when two or more parties are secret sharing a list of values, and need to obliviously permute the list, so that no party knows the permutation. Our protocol can be used to implement this oblivious shuffle, by viewing one party as acting as all N senders (for its list of N secret shared values), and sending the permuted shares via the "central router" (also being simulated by the sending party) to the other party (who is acting as all N receivers). This process is then reversed, with the other party sending its shares to the first party, via the same permutation. There are subtleties that need to be specified, such as ensuring that the permutation remains unknown to each party (which can be handled as part of the Setup procedure), and how to amortize the process to ensure efficiency (so the Setup does not dominate overall cost), but in general a solution in the NIAR model can be viewed as an instantiation of oblivious shuffle.

PERMUTATION ROUTING WITH ANONYMITY. There has been substantial work in researching permutation routing (e.g. [AKS83, Lei84, Upf89, MS92]), which was inspired due to its relevance to parallel computing (for timing the connections between processors and memory) and fault tolerant routing. Since the NIAR model is essentially permutation routing with anonymity, any applications of permutation routing that stand to benefit from hiding the permutation are relevant to our work.

1.1 Technical Challenges

Notice that (assuming PKI) an immediate solution to anonymity in the NIAR model is to have each sender encrypt their message (under the desired receiver's public key or using a shared secret key with the recipient), send the encrypted message to the center router, and then simply have the router flood all N (encrypted) messages to each of the N receivers. While this naïve approach satisfies anonymity (as well as privacy, in that receivers only receive messages intended for them), it has the pitfall of excessive communication: $O(N)$ for each receiver, and $O(N^2)$ for the router. Shi and Wu [SW21] present a protocol which, under the Decisional Linear assumption (on certain bilinear groups), achieves anonymity with minimal *communication* overhead.

Having re-framed the goal of anonymity to the NIAR model and with the toolbox of cryptographic techniques at hand, a natural observation is that Private Information Retrieval (PIR) can be used as a potential solution. In a (single server) PIR protocol [KO97], a server stores a database DB of N elements, and a client issues a query to the server to retrieve the ith element $DB[i]$, for i of its choice. Security in the PIR model means that the server does not learn any information about the index i being queried. Thus, if N senders encrypt their messages and send them to the router, we can let the router act as a PIR server with the N concatenated (encrypted) messages forming the contents of the PIR database. Each receiver can then issue a PIR query to fetch the appropriate message, and anonymity follows from the security of PIR. As with the protocol of [SW21], this solution enjoys both the requisite security features, as well as having minimal communication overhead (e.g. $\log N$ overhead, depending on the PIR protocol; see survey of PIR results in [OS07]).

An important metric in determining the feasibility of a protocol in the NIAR model is the end-to-end message transmission time, which depends on the computational burden on each user, and especially that of the central router.

A significant drawback of both the protocol of [SW21][2] and the naïve PIR solution described above is that they require *quadratic* (in terms of the number of users) computation at the router. As this computation cost is likely prohibitive (or at least extremely inefficient) when there are a large number of users, we set out to explore the possibility of a NIAR protocol that maintained the minimal communication burden of the naïve PIR and [SW21] solutions, but reduced computation overhead (at the router) from $O(N^2)$ closer to the optimal $O(N)$.

Our first observation is that the NIAR model is similar to so-called "permutation routing" (see Sect. 2.1), but with an additional anonymity requirement. Namely, permutation routing seeks to connect N senders to N receivers through a network, which (from a communication standpoint) is what is required in the NIAR model. Our main idea was to leverage the efficient routing (and therefore minimal overhead) of a permutation-routing network, but then to administer PIR at each node to keep each routing decision hidden, thereby allowing for the anonymity required by the NIAR model. In particular, we envisioned a solution in which the central router simulates a virtual permutation-routing network by itself, where the actual path the messages take (from each of the N senders on one end of the network to the N receivers at the other end) is hidden (from the central router) by using PIR along each edge. Namely, at each node of the (virtual) network, a PIR query is applied to each of the node's outgoing edges, where the PIR query (privately) selects a message from one of the node's incoming edges.

While the above idea captures the spirit of our solution (and indeed, the idea of layering PIR on top of various routing networks/protocols may have other interesting applications for anonymizing communication), there are several complications that required additional consideration:

1. (Virtual) Network Size. Since each outgoing edge in the routing network is assigned a PIR query, and this PIR query is applied to a (virtual) database whose size is the number of incoming edges of the node in question, the computation cost of simulating routing in a virtual network is roughly $O(E \cdot I)$, where E is the number of edges and I is the number of incoming edges per

---

[2] Router computation is not explicitly measured in the protocol of [SW21], our analysis of their protocol yields $O(N^2)$ computation load on the router: their Multi-Client Functional Encryption (MCFE) protocol is invoked N times by the router, with each invocation processing N ciphertexts.

node. Since E is necessarily at least $\Omega(N)$, having a NIAR protocol with only polylog computation overhead requires that E is at most $O(N \cdot polylog\ N)$ and I is $O(polylog\ N)$.

2. **Standard PIR Won't Work.** Even if network size is small $(O(N \cdot polylog(N)))$, if the depth (number of nodes a message passes through from sender to receiver) is not constant, then standard PIR schemes will not work, since each invocation of PIR typically has $O(polylog(N))$ bits in the PIR server's response, and hence the message size will incur an exponential blow-up with network depth. For example, even log-depth networks will have messages of size $O(2^{\log N}) = O(N)$ by the time they reach the last layer of the network, which is no better than the naïve PIR approach mentioned above.

3. **Correctness Requires Edge-Disjoint Paths.** Since PIR is being used to hide routing decisions made at each node/routing gate in the network, this requires that each outgoing edge forwards the message on (at most) one of the node's incoming edges. In particular, if any two paths connecting two different sender-receiver pairs in the permutation network contain a common edge, then correctness is compromised. Since a *random* path selection algorithm will be crucial to proving anonymity, the given (virtual) permutation network must have the property that, with high probability, a random sample of paths connecting the sender-receiver pairs are edge-disjoint.

4. **Edge-Disjoint Property is Insufficient for Anonymity.** While having edge-disjoint paths is necessary for correctness, it is not sufficient to ensure anonymity. For example, if the central router is colluding with $(N\text{-}2)$ sender-receiver pairs (and therefore only needs to determine the linkage amongst the remaining two senders and two receivers), then knowledge that all paths are edge-disjoint can give the router an advantage in identifying the linkage between the remaining two senders and two receivers. Namely, the router knows (via collusion) N-2 paths, and thus can eliminate available options for the remaining two paths. For example, this attack is viable in the Beneš network (which is commonly used in permutation routing literature; see Sect. 3.1) making it unsuitable when anonymity is required, and justifying our usage of a more complex network. Indeed, since permutation-routing networks have been studied outside of the context of anonymity, to our knowledge there has not been any research into understanding how network properties and path selection protocols impact anonymity.

1.2 Overview of Our Results

Our solution to the NIAR problem, which blends techniques from permutation routing with techniques for hiding routing decisions made at each node of the (virtual) permutation network, overcomes the challenges outlined in the previous section as follows. By using familiar permutation-routing networks, which are inherently small $(O(N \cdot polylog(N)))$, we ensure the network size is suitably small, thus addressing the first potential issue. Furthermore, a common (and well-studied) feature of many permutation-routing networks is the edge-disjoint property, which inspired our choice to use an (extended) Beneš permutation Network, thus addressing the third issue. We observe that there is an inherent tension between network topology (number of nodes, edges, and depth) in terms of achieving correctness and anonymity versus low router computation. Our solution includes carefully selecting appropriate network parameters to balance these trade-offs. Meanwhile, recent works [DGI+19, GHO20, CGH+21] present so-called *rate-1 PIR* protocols, which can address the second issue of exponential growth of message size per network layer.

Addressing the fourth issue is one of our key technical achievements. In spirit, the edge-disjoint property is related to anonymity, but as mentioned above, it is in general insufficient. Identifying a property that *is* sufficient (and simultaneously not over-cumbersome in terms of network size), and then using such a property to formally argue anonymity, requires some thought and careful analysis. Informally, this property states that not only are N randomly chosen permutation paths through the network edge-disjoint (w.h.p), but even if the permutation swaps the output nodes of any two input nodes and two new paths are created to join these, then the collection of the old edges plus the two new sets of edges are still edge disjoint (w.h.p); see Definition 4.

Assuming rate-1 PIR, we present in Fig. 3 a routing protocol for the NIAR model that achieves $O(\log N)$ per-party communication and $O(N \cdot polylog(N))$ router computation. At a high level, our protocol dictates that the central router emulates routing in a permutation network, whereby each routing gate is (virtually) obliviously evaluated using a rate-1 PIR query/response for each outgoing edge. Our protocol consists of a setup phase in which the PIR queries that correspond to all outgoing edges of every routing gate are prepared, and then an online routing phase where a stream of (encrypted) messages are injected by the senders and routed to the receivers (re-using the setup).

A succinct comparison of our results to other relevant works is in Sect. 2.3.

2   Previous Work

2.1   Permutation Routing

In permutation routing [AKS83, Lei84, Upf89, MS92], messages from a set of N "input" nodes are routed through a network G to a set of N distinct "output" nodes. Such works attempt to identify networks G with various desired properties, and protocols within these networks that can efficiently route these messages, for any possible permutation σ that dictates which input node is connected to which output node. While our work is partially inspired by the routing networks considered in this line of work, the NIAR model is quite different than the permutation routing model, both because of the number of routers (one versus $\Theta(N \log N)$) and due to the required privacy of the permutation σ. In other words, we do not route the messages over a physical routing network (which is an iterative process that depends on the "depth" of the network), but rather we design our non-interactive routing protocol using a *virtual* sorting network.

2.2   PIR

There has been an extensive amount of work done on the original PIR problem [CGKS95, KO97] and its variants. Here, we discuss only a few of these works that are most relevant to us.

Multi-Client PIR. As discussed in the introduction, the NIAR problem can be solved using multi-client PIR. Indeed, a solution to generic multi-client PIR in which the PIR server's work does not scale with the number of users would imply an efficient solution for NIAR. While no such result is known, we discuss a few relevant works and why they are insufficient for the NIAR model.

In [IP07], it is demonstrated how a single user can efficiently issue multiple queries to a PIR server. However, their results rely on a single decoding algorithm, whereas the NIAR model would require distinct decoding keys for each of the N receivers. [HOWW19] present a related notion of private anonymous data access; we note that the results in their model do not scale to the full corruption threshold $(N - 2)$ required in the NIAR security model. Finally, results in the related areas of Batch Codes [IKOS04] and Public-Key Encryption with amortized updates [COS10] address a different model, and consequently do not seem to be directly applicable to the NIAR model.

Rate-1 PIR. A recent line of work [DGI+19, GHO20, CGH+21] has demonstrated the viability of rate-1 PIR, in which the server response is comparable in size to the database entry being fetched. Formally, for a database of N elements each of size B, rate-1 PIR means that the ratio of B to the server response size approaches 1 as $N \rightarrow \infty$. Stated differently, a rate-1 PIR scheme has an additive constant-stretch term δ_{PIR}, such that the server's response has size $B + \delta_{PIR}$. Rate-1 PIR is known to exist under the DDH, QR and LWE assumptions [DGI+19, GHO20].

Doubly Efficient PIR (DEPIR). In a recent result of Lin et al. [LMW22], they demonstrate a PIR protocol that, after a pre-processing phase that costs $O(N^{1+\epsilon})$ in server computation, enjoys polylog N communication and computation for each PIR query. If this DEPIR protocol were to be used to solve the NIAR problem (as per the straightforward application described in Sect. 1.1), the resulting protocol would have $O(N^{1+\epsilon})$ computation at the router for each new message packet/bit of the senders (since each database update would trigger a new "pre-processing" phase of the PIR server).

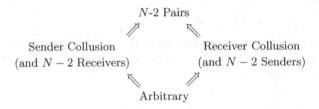

Fig. 1. *Various security requirements/settings relevant to the NIAR model. All four scenarios include collusion with router C, plus: - Top Setting (N-2 Pairs): Corruption of up to N-2 (sender, receiver) pairs; - Left Setting (Sender Collusion): Corruption of all senders (and N-2 receivers); - Right Setting (Receiver Collusion): Corruption of all receivers (and N-2 senders); - Bottom Setting (Arbitrary): Corruption of any $2N-2$ senders/receivers. The implication arrows indicate that a protocol that is secure in one setting is automatically secure in the other.*

2.3   Comparison with Other Results in NIAR Model

The NIAR model was introduced in [SW21], which included several variants of the security requirement, and offered solutions for these variants. As mentioned, our results improve upon those of [SW21] in three main ways: (i) Reduced router overhead ($O(N \cdot polylogN)$ versus $O(N^2)$); (ii) Seemingly simpler protocol based on weaker/more standard cryptographic assumptions; (iii) Improved practical/observed efficiency (not empirically verified). On the other hand, the protocol of [SW21] provides protection in different scenarios of security requirements. Namely, in terms of Fig. 1, our protocol focuses on the top and left settings, while [SW21] covers the top, right, and bottom settings. However, for all of the motivating examples discussed in the Introduction, security in the top and left settings (which our protocol provides) is sufficient.

A recent work of Fernando et al. [FSSV22] improves upon the work of [SW21], by reducing router computation to $O(N \cdot polylogN)$, which (asymptotically) matches our result. However, the other comparisons between our work and that of [SW21] are still valid; namely, our protocol benefits from simpler assumptions and protocol complexity (e.g. we do not require obfuscation) as well as practical efficiency, but ours does not offer protection against full receiver collusion.

A summary of the comparison of our results to other relevant results can be found in the table below, where $\widetilde{N} = O(N \cdot polylogN)$ denotes quasi-linear:

3   Preliminaries

3.1   Beneš Network

(The networks mentioned here are common in the permutation routing literature, see for example [AKS83, Lei84, Upf89, MS92]. Figures depicting each of the networks described below can be found in the extended version of this paper). In a butterfly network, N input nodes are connected to N output nodes via a leveled network of $(1 + \log N)$ levels, each with N nodes. A Beneš network appends a

Protocol	Anonymity Level[a]	Crypto Assumptions	Comm.	Router Comp.
Permutation Routing	None	N/A	$\tilde{N}$	$\tilde{N}$
Naïve PIR	Sender Collusion	PIR	$\tilde{N}$	N^2
DEPIR [LMW22][b]	Sender Collusion	Ring LWE	$\tilde{N}$	$N^{1+\epsilon}$
Original NIAR[SW21]	Receiver Collusion	DLIN	$\tilde{N}$	N^2
	Arbitrary	Obfuscation	N	N^2
Improved NIAR [FSSV22]	Arbitrary	Obfuscation	$\tilde{N}$	$\tilde{N}$
Our Results	Sender Collusion	DDH or QR or LWE	N	$\tilde{N}$

[a] Anonymity terminology as defined in Fig. 1. Namely, "Sender Collusion" refers to potential corruption of the central router, all senders, and up to $N-2$ receivers; and "Arbitrary" refers to potential corruption of the central router and any set of up to $2N-2$ senders/receivers.

[b] Analysis of [LMW22] in the context of the NIAR model is not done by Lin et al., and the stated characteristics of their protocol in the NIAR setting are ours.

second (inverted) butterfly network to the first; and more generally an extended Beneš network appends many "blocks" of butterfly networks together. We continue expanding on this model by replicating each node and edge c times, which can be conceptualized as coloring them with c distinct colors. Finally, our protocol will assume wide edges, which means that each edge can simultaneously route w messages (requiring specification of which of the w "slots" each message occupies).

3.2   Non-Interactive Anonymous Routing (NIAR)

We adopt the NIAR model of [SW21], in which N senders each has a series of m (e.g. single-bit) messages they wish to send to a distinct receiver *anonymously*. The anonymity guarantee refers to the unlinkability of each sender-receiver pair, and crucially it must be preserved even if the central router colludes with a subset of the senders/receivers. Depending on the application, there are various collusion patterns that may be of interest, see e.g. Fig. 1.

In this paper, we demonstrate our protocol is secure against the top and left settings (in Fig. 1). We do not consider the right and bottom settings (Receiver Collusion and Arbitrary) in this paper for two reasons: First, in the main application areas for the NIAR model (see Introduction above), the receivers already know the senders they wish to connect to, so anonymity of the senders (in the case that all receivers are colluding) is irrelevant. The second reason is because providing protection in settings when all Receivers collude with the router requires additional techniques than those considered in this paper. For example in [SW21] and [FSSV22], the protocol description, performance, and cryptographic hardness assumptions are all more complex in the Arbitrary collusion setting.

Formally, the (reformulated) NIAR model of [SW21] is as follows:

(Trusted) Setup. Upon input security parameters $(1^{\lambda_c}, 1^{\lambda_s})$, number of senders/receivers N, and permutation $\sigma : [N] \rightarrow [N]$, the Setup algorithm outputs sender keys $\{pk_i\}_{i \in [N]}$, receiver keys[3] $\{(sk_i, \kappa_i)\}_{i \in [N]}$, and token q for router C: $(\{pk_i\}_{i \in [N]}, \{(sk_i, \kappa_i)\}_{i \in [N]}, q) \leftarrow \textbf{Setup}(1^{\lambda_c}, 1^{\lambda_s}, N, \sigma)$.

Once Setup has been run, the Senders $\{S_i\}$ can communicate arbitrary messages $\{m_i\} = \{m_{i,\alpha}\}$ with the Receivers $\{R_i\}$ through router C.

Send Message. Using key pk_i, each Sender S_i encodes message $m_i = m_{i,\alpha}$ (where α denotes the αth bit of message m_i), and sends the result to router C: $c_{i,\alpha} \leftarrow \textbf{Enc}_{pk_i}(m_{i,\alpha})$.

Route Message. Upon inputs $\{c_i\}_{i \in [N]}$ from each Sender S_i, and using key q, router C prepares messages $\{z_i\}_{i \in [N]}$, and sends these to each Receiver R_i: $(z_1, z_2, \ldots, z_N) \leftarrow \textbf{Route}(q, c_1, c_2, \ldots, c_N)$.

Decode Message. Using keys (sk_i, κ_i), each Receiver R_i decodes the message $z_i = z_{i,\alpha}$ received from router C, and outputs $\tilde{m}_i = \tilde{m}_{i,\alpha}$: $\tilde{m}_{i,\alpha} \leftarrow \textbf{Dec}_{sk_i}(\kappa_i, z_{i,\alpha})$.

Correctness. An oblivious permutation routing protocol has:

<u>Perfect Correctness</u>: If each receiver R_i outputs message $\tilde{m}_i = m_i$ with probability 1.

<u>λ_c–Statistical Correctness</u>: If each receiver R_i outputs message $\tilde{m}_i = m_i$ with probability at least $\left(1 - \frac{1}{2^{\lambda_c}}\right)$, for security parameter λ_c.

Security. Informally, anonymity means that if a subset of parties collude (including router C), the permutation σ (namely, its restriction to non-colluding parties) should remain unknown. Formally, let $\mathcal{A}$ denote a (computationally bounded, honest-but-curious) adversary. Consider the following challenge game:

1. On input security parameter λ, Adversary $\mathcal{A}$ chooses N, two distinct permutations σ_0, σ_1 on $[N]$, a set of sender indices $S_\mathcal{A} \subseteq [N]$ to corrupt, and a set of receiver indices $R_\mathcal{A} \subseteq [N]$ to corrupt, subject to the following constraints:
   (a) $|R_\mathcal{A}| \leq N - 2$;
   (b) σ_0 and σ_1 match for all receivers in $R_\mathcal{A}$: $\forall i \in R_\mathcal{A} : \sigma_0^{-1}(i) = \sigma_1^{-1}(i)$.
2. Adversary $\mathcal{A}$ sends $\{\sigma_0, \sigma_1\}$ to Challenger $\mathcal{C}$.
3. Challenger $\mathcal{C}$ chooses $\sigma_b \in \{\sigma_0, \sigma_1\}$ for $b \leftarrow \{0, 1\}$ (e.g. by flipping a coin).
4. Challenger $\mathcal{C}$ chooses router token q, encryption keys $\{pk_i\}_{i \in [N]}$, and decryption keys $\{sk_i\}_{i \in [N]}$. $\mathcal{C}$ sends q, $\{pk_i\}_{i \in S_\mathcal{A}}$, and $\{sk_i\}_{i \in R_\mathcal{A}}$ to $\mathcal{A}$.
5. For each round α:
   (a) Based on knowledge of all prior ciphertexts $\{c_{i,\alpha'}\}_{\alpha' < \alpha}$ (see next step), Adversary $\mathcal{A}$ chooses messages $\{m_{i,\alpha}^{(0)}\}_{i \in [N]}$ and $\{m_{i,\alpha}^{(1)}\}_{i \in [N]}$, subject to the constraint that all messages bound for a corrupt receiver match: $\forall i$ s.t. $i = \sigma_0^{-1}(j)$ for some $j \in R_\mathcal{A}$: $m_{i,\alpha}^{(0)} = m_{i,\alpha}^{(1)}$. $\mathcal{A}$ sends $\{m_{i,\alpha}^{(0)}\}, \{m_{i,\alpha}^{(1)}\}$ to $\mathcal{C}$.

---

[3] The sender keys $\{pk_i\}$ are associated with the receiver keys $\{sk_i\}$ via the permutation σ; namely, secret key $sk_{\sigma(i)}$ can decrypt messages encrypted under pk_i.

(b) Challenger $\mathcal{C}$ outputs to $\mathcal{A}$ ciphertexts $\{c_{i,\alpha}\}_{i\in[N]}$, where each ciphertext is computed as (with b as chosen in Step 3): $c_{i,\alpha} = Enc_{\mathsf{pk}_i}(m_{i,\alpha}^{(b)})$.

6. Adversary $\mathcal{A}$ outputs a guess $b' \in \{0,1\}$ of which permutation $\{\sigma_0, \sigma_1\}$ Challenger $\mathcal{C}$ chose.

A NIAR protocol is λ_s-secure if the probability that any computationally bounded adversary $\mathcal{A}$ guesses b correctly is bounded by:

$$Pr[b' = b] \leq \frac{1}{2} + \frac{1}{2^{\lambda_s}} \tag{1}$$

3.3   Emulating Oblivious Routing in a Virtual Routing Network

In this section, we present the main ideas that connect the NIAR model to the permutation routing problem. At a high level, the idea is to have the NIAR router emulate message transmission through a (virtual) routing network that supports permutation routing between N senders and receivers. In particular, we view the N senders as *input* nodes in the routing network, and the N receivers as the *output* nodes, and then choose paths through the routing network connecting each sender to its receiver. The NIAR router then passes messages from each sender to the designate receiver by routing messages along this path. Note that this entire network, except the input nodes (corresponding to the senders) and output nodes (corresponding to the receivers), together with message routing within it, is entirely simulated by the NIAR router.

In order to preserve anonymity in terms of linkage between each (sender, receiver) pair, the paths that each message takes through this (virtual) routing network must remain hidden to the NIAR router. The key primitive that we utilize to achieve this is called an oblivious routing gate., informally defined as:

Definition 1 *(Informal). An oblivious routing gate describes a process in which the messages on w incoming wires of a gate are routed to its w outgoing wires, in such a way that the process that is performing the routing is unaware of the linkage between (incoming wire, outgoing wire) of each message.*

Notice that PIR can be used to instantiate an oblivious routing gate, by using PIR queries to secretly select the incoming edge to read from, and then having the PIR server (that is doing the actual routing) write its corresponding PIR response along that outgoing edge; see Fig. 2.

Routing in the NIAR model can be achieved by combining the oblivious routing gate paradigm with ordinary routing through a permutation network, as follows:

Definition 2 *(Informal). Denote NIAR parameters: N, permutation $\sigma : [N] \rightarrow [N]$, "central router" party C, "sender" parties $\{S_i\}_{i\in[N]}$ with messages $\{m_{i,\alpha}\}$, "receiver" parties $\{R_i\}_{i\in[N]}$, and let G denote a given routing network. An emulated permutation routing protocol Π_{EPR} performs NIAR routing by having C route the αth message of each sender $\{m_i\}$ through the (emulated) network G, in which messages are routing from the incoming edge of a network node to an outgoing edge via the oblivious routing gate paradigm.*

Due to space limitations, the formal definitions of *oblivious routing gate* and *emulated permutation routing*, as well as example instantiations via PIR, appear in the extended version.

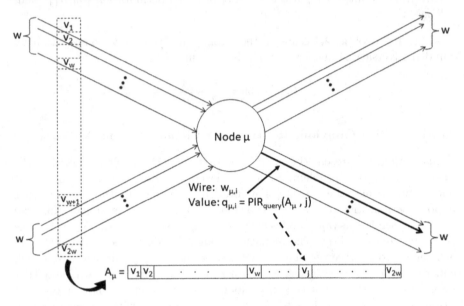

Fig. 2. Oblivious routing gate (Π_{ORG}) realization via PIR at node μ with $2w$ incoming and outgoing edges.

4   Our Protocol

4.1   Overview of Our Solution

Given N pairs of (sender, receiver) nodes and central router C, our protocol routes messages from the senders to the corresponding receivers via a virtual routing network G that C emulates where, for each node in the network, the router C obliviously executes a routing gate by simulating the functionality of a (rate-1) PIR query. Namely, (as part of trusted setup) each outgoing edge of a routing gate will have an assigned PIR query, and each incoming edge will have a value (which represents an encrypted message from one of the senders). Then the router C obliviously produces a message on each outgoing edge of the routing gate by running the associated PIR query on this wire against the (virtual) PIR database of messages (from the incoming wires). The determination of *which* incoming edge that a given PIR query (on a routing gate's outgoing edge) should specify is established offline during a setup phase, and specifically it is determined by choosing a random path $\mathcal{P}_i$, for each (sender$_i$, receiver$_i$) pair, through the (virtual) routing network G. Notice that once PIR queries are assigned (during an offline setup phase) as per all chosen paths $\{\mathcal{P}_i\}$, they may be reused indefinitely during the online routing phase to continuously route new messages for each (sender, receiver) pair. The main features of our solution are as follows:

- CORRECTNESS. Ensuring each receiver gets every message reduces to showing that the paths $\{\mathcal{P}_i\}$ connecting each (sender$_i$, receiver$_i$) pair are *edge-disjoint*.
- PRIVACY. Since each sender encrypts their messages under the intended receiver's public key, receivers can only decipher messages intended for them.
- ANONYMITY. This property is obtained so long as the paths $\{\mathcal{P}_i\}$ chosen are "sufficiently edge-disjoint" (for details see Definition 23).
- COMMUNICATION. To limit the expansion of message size through each (virtual) routing gate, we employ **rate-1** PIR, which ensures the final message size is proportional to the length of the chosen path $\mathcal{P}$ through the (virtual) routing network G; and that any such path is short (i.e. of *polylogN* length).
- END-TO-END TIME. Computation of central router C (which, together with communication, determines end-to-end transmission time) will depend on the size of the virtual graph $G = (V, E)$. Thus, in order to minimize computational overhead, $|E|$ should be close to N (e.g. $N \cdot polylogN$). Notice that there is inherent tension in minimizing end-to-end time versus satisfying the Correctness and Anonymity properties: the former requires small $|V|$ and $|E|$, while the latter two are readily achieved for larger $|V|$ and $|E|$. Our protocol finds appropriate (minimal) parameters to achieve correctness and anonymity, while introducing minimal end-to-end overhead.

We stress that some relaxed approaches to the NIAR problem actually fail to provide anonymity. Specifically, the approach of deploying an *arbitrary* permutation-routing network (without the extra features that we require), and the approach of just replacing each gate in the routing network (even a properly selected network) with PIR, do not seem sufficient, which we argue as follows.

While PIR is the main tool that hides (from central router C and any other parties it colludes with) the linkage between uncorrupted (sender, receiver) pairs, applying it naïvely will not provide the desired protection. Namely, if any two of the paths $\{\mathcal{P}_i\}$ through the virtual routing network have an edge in common, then a PIR query cannot be assigned to that edge, as there will be conflicting input edge indices (and conflicting messages on those edges) to select. Since, in proving anonymity, path selection must be a randomized process (in particular, edge conflicts cannot be deliberately avoided), our protocol will handle edge conflicts by producing garbage PIR queries for such edges. While this approach introduces failures in terms of delivering messages along the conflicting paths that were chosen for any such (sender, receiver) pairs, the threat to correctness is overcome by ensuring enough redundancy in the system to account for (the low probability event of) edge conflicts. However, edge conflicts (and the *lack* of edge conflicts), also threatens anonymity: for example, the router C could observe many messages from (sender, receiver) pairs it has corrupted all pass through a common node, and the router may also know that the message from an *uncorrupted* sender has some probability of passing through this same node. Thus, the presence or absence of an edge conflict on the set of outgoing edges of this node may give the router an advantage in determining if the uncorrupted sender's path goes through this node, and if so, some probabilistic advantage in knowing which outgoing edge the path used; and these advantages then threaten anonymity since the router may be able to have an advantage in guessing the ultimate destination (i.e. receiving node) of this path. Demonstrating that this approach cannot be used to give the router a non-negligible advantage in linking uncorrupted (sender, receiver) pairs will require: (i) Identifying what property a network should have to avoid this attack; (ii) Generating such a routing network that also supports the desired complexity and correctness requirements; (iii) An appropriate analysis that this property indeed proves anonymity. For example, the natural candidate property of exhibiting (with high probability on randomly chosen paths) the edge-disjoint property is insufficient, as it is susceptible to the above attack.

Figure 3 below gives pseudocode of our Π_{APR} protocol (due to space constraints, the full protocol can be found in the extended version).

4.2   Analysis of Our Protocol

Theorem 3. *Assuming the existence of rate-1 PIR, following trusted setup,[4] the protocol presented in Fig. 3 is λ_s-secure with λ_c-statistical correctness, $O(\log N)$ per-party communication, and $O(N \, polylog \, N)$ router computation.*

Remark. Instead of trusted setup, under appropriate cryptographic hardness assumptions the ideal functionality $\Pi_{ORG}(G, \widehat{c}, r, l, \Pi_{1-PIR})$ could instead be realized via generic secure multiparty computation (MPC) techniques. This would contribute $O(N^2 \, polylog \, N)$ to the asymptotic cost of the protocol (to deal the $O(N \, polylog \, N)$ rate-1 queries and $O(N^2 \, polylog \, N)$ reconstruction keys), but because $\Pi_{ORG}(G, \widehat{c}, r, l, \Pi_{1-PIR})$ is utilized only in the Setup Phase, this would be incurred as a one-time cost and would not impact cost of the Routing Phase.

Proof (Theorem 3, Sketch). Let $\lambda := \max(\lambda_c/(2-\log 3),\ 2\log N + \max(\lambda_s, 2 + \log\log N)$. Then the specific permutation network $G = B(\widehat{N}, b, c, w)$ used in Π_{APR} is a wide-edged, extended and colored Beneš network (see Sect. 3.1) with parameters $\widehat{N} = N$, $b = \lambda - 1$, $c = 4 \cdot a_\lambda$, and $w = 1.2 \cdot \lambda \cdot \log N \cdot (1 + \log N)$ (for $a_\lambda := \max(2, \lambda^{1/(\log N - 1)})$).

---

[4] Trusted setup is required for establishing public/secret key pairs for encryption and for instantiating ideal functionality $\Pi_{ORG}(G, \widehat{c}, r, l, \Pi_{1-PIR})$.

Anonymous Permutation Routing (APR) Protocol Π_{APR}

Input. APR parameters: N, permutation $\sigma:[N]\to[N]$, "central router" party C, "sender" parties $\{S_i\}_{i\in[N]}$ with messages $\{m_{i,\alpha}\}$, "receiver" parties $\{R_i\}_{i\in[N]}$.

Output. For each party index $1\le i\le N$, receiver $R_{\sigma(i)}$ outputs messages $\{\widetilde{m}_{i,\alpha}\}$.

Setup Phase.

1. Let $G = B(N, b, c, w)$ denote a wide-edged, extended and colored Beneš network (see proof details for appropriate choice of parameters b, c, and w).
2. For each $i\in[N]$: let (pk_i, sk_i) denote a public-key/secret-key pair.
   Output: $S_i \leftarrow pk_i$ and $R_{\sigma(i)} \leftarrow sk_i$.
3. Let $\lambda := \max(\lambda_c/(2\text{-}\log 3),\ 2\log N + \max(\lambda_s, 2 + \log\log N)$, where λ_c and λ_s denote the desired correctness and security parameters. Repeat λ times:
   (a) Choose N random paths $\{\mathcal{P}_i\}$ through G (respecting permutation σ).
   (b) Assign rate-1 PIR queries and reconstruction keys to each edge of G, as per $\{\mathcal{P}_i\}$. Namely, for a given node $\mu\in G$, if some path $\mathcal{P}_i$ passes through node μ along incoming edge $\mathcal{I}_{\mu,j}$ and outgoing edge $\mathcal{O}_{\mu,k}$, then write on edge $\mathcal{O}_{\mu,k}$ a rate-1 PIR query that selects the message on incoming edge $\mathcal{I}_{\mu,j}$, and give the reconstruction key for this PIR query to Receiver $R_{\sigma(i)}$.

Routing Phase. Repeat the following procedure for each message $\{m_{i,\alpha}\}$:

Senders $\{S_i\}$.

1. Sender S_i encrypts $m_i = m_{i,\alpha}$ under pk_i and sends $Enc_{pk_i}(m_i)$ to router C.

Central Router C. Repeat λ times:

1. C runs an *emulated permutation routing* protocol (Definition 2) with inputs $\{Enc_{pk_i}(m_i)\}$ (from each sender S_i's Routing Phase Step 1) and rate-1 PIR queries as per Step (3b) of Setup Phase; and sends the outputs to each Receiver.

Receivers $\{R_{\sigma(i)}\}$. Repeat λ times:

1. Use the reconstruction keys (received in Step (3b) of Setup Phase) to traverse $\mathcal{P}_i$ *backwards*, starting with the final value that it received from C. When $R_{\sigma(i)}$ has traversed backwards to level 0, it will have reconstructed value $Enc_{pk_i}(m_i)$.

Fig. 3. Anonymous Permutation Routing protocol Π_{APR}.

Cost. Per-party computation and communication costs for the routing phase are:

Party	Computation	Communication
S_i	$Cost(\Pi_{Enc})$	c_{Enc}
R_i	$Cost(\Pi_{Dec})+(1+b)\cdot(1+\log N)\cdot Cost(\Pi_{PIR\text{-}Rec})$	N/A
C	$M\cdot|E|\cdot Cost(\Pi_{PIR\text{-}Query})$	$N\cdot(2\cdot c_{Enc}+(1+b)\cdot\delta_{PIR})$

where:

- $|E| = (2 \log N + c) \cdot (c \cdot w \cdot N \cdot (1+b))$ is the number of edges in network $B(N, b, c, w)$.
- $Cost(\Pi_{Enc})$ is the (computation) cost of encrypting a message m.
- $Cost(\Pi_{Dec})$ is the (computation) cost of decrypting a ciphertext $Enc_{pk_i}(m)$.
- c_{Enc} is the size of a ciphertext $Enc_{pk_i}(m)$.
- δ_{PIR} is the constant stretch of the underlying rate-1 PIR protocol Π_{1-PIR}.
- $Cost(\Pi_{PIR-Query})$ is the PIR server cost of $\Pi_{1-PIR}(c \cdot w, c_{Enc} + (1+b) \cdot \delta_{PIR})$.
- $Cost(\Pi_{PIR-Rec})$ is the cost of running the reconstruction algorithm (on a PIR response) for $\Pi_{1-PIR}(c \cdot w, c_{Enc} + (1+b) \cdot \delta_{PIR})$.

Correctness. The intuition for the proof is as follows: Independent of adversarial presence, we first demonstrate bounds of certain properties of routing in the Beneš network, as per the protocols described in Fig. 3. Namely, we demonstrate in Corollary 19 that, with overwhelming probability, for any row index $i \in [N]$ there will exist (at least) one experiment $m \in [M]$ for which the path $\mathcal{P}_{m,i}$ is edge-disjoint from all other paths $\{\mathcal{P}_{m,j}\}_{j \neq i}$. Then as per protocol Π_{APR} specification (Step 2b of the Output Parties portion of the Routing Phase; see Fig. 3), the existence of an edge-disjoint path $\mathcal{P}_i$ means that $R_{\sigma(i)}$ will update $\widetilde{w}_i \leftarrow \widetilde{w}_{m,i}$. By the correctness property of the ideal functionality of Π_{ORG}, this value will be *correct* (i.e. it will equal p_i).

Formally, with $\lambda = \max(\frac{\lambda_c}{2 - \log 3}, 2 \log N + \max(\lambda_s, 2 + \log \log N)) \geq \frac{\lambda_c}{2 - \log 3}$, Lemma 19 states that the probability that there exists some row index $i \in [N]$ for which $\mathcal{P}_{m,i}$ is *not* edge-disjoint for *every* experiment $m \in [M]$ is bounded by:

$$\Pr[X = 0] < \left(\frac{3}{4}\right)^\lambda \leq \left(\left(\frac{3}{4}\right)^{\frac{1}{2 - \log 3}}\right)^{\lambda_c} = \frac{1}{2^{\lambda_c}}.$$

Security. As with the Correctness proof, we first demonstrate (probability bounds for) a version of the *edge-disjoint* property in the Beneš graph G (Sect. 3.1) used in Fig. 3. Namely, we demonstrate in Corollary 27 that, using the parameters as per Π_{APR} (Fig. 3), with overwhelming probability (in λ_s), for any pair of row indices $i, i' \in [N]$ and for every experiment $m \in [M]$, there will exist a block in which the chosen paths $\mathcal{P}_{m,i}$ and $\mathcal{P}_{m,i'}$ *as well as* their alternate paths $\mathcal{P}'_{m,i}$ and $\mathcal{P}'_{m,i'}$ are each edge-disjoint from all other paths in this block. Effectively, this means that for any two *uncorrupted* receiver nodes $i, i' \notin R_\mathcal{A}$, that for each experiment there exists some block in which the Adversary will necessarily lose all ability to distinguish between $\mathcal{P}_{m,i}$ and $\mathcal{P}_{m,i'}$ by the time these paths cross through this block. We then use a hybrid argument to show that the existence of an adversary that can distinguish between two arbitrary permutations (as per (1)) implies the existence of an adversary who can distinguish (with a smaller probability) between two permutations that differ only on two points; and then this contradicts the existence of a block in which any two paths become indistinguishable after that block.

Formally, the proof reduces the NIAR security game (with Challenger invoking the protocol Π_{APR} of Fig. 3) to Challenge Game 2, and then uses the indistinguishability of Challenge Game 2 (Lemma 29). To match notation of Π_{APR} with the communication sent to adversary $\mathcal{A}$ in the NIAR security game:

For Step 4 of the NIAR security game:
- Encryption keys $\{\mathsf{pk}_i\}$: The $\{pk_i\}$ from Step 1 of the Setup Phase (Fig. 3).
- Decryption keys $\{\mathsf{sk}_i\}$: The $\{sk_i\}$ from Step 1 of the Setup Phase, together with the reconstruction keys $\{\kappa_i\} = \{(\mu, j, \kappa_{\mu,j})\}$ from Step 2b of the Setup.
- Router token q: The rate-1 PIR queries $\{q_{\mu,j}\}$ from Step 2b of the Setup.

For Step 5b of the NIAR security game:
- Ciphertexts $\{c_{i,\alpha}\}$: The encrypted messages $\{Enc_{pk_i}(m_{i,\alpha})\}$ from Sender's Step 1 of the Routing Phase (Fig. 3).

First observe that indistinguishability of the distribution of ciphertexts $\{c_{i,\alpha}\} = \{Enc_{pk_i}(m_{i,\alpha})\}$ under $b = 0$ versus $b = 1$ follows from the security of the encryption scheme, together with the constraint that all messages bound for a corrupt receiver must match for $b = 0$ and $b = 1$ (see the specified constraint in Step 5a of the NIAR security game). Thus, for any ciphertext $c_{i,\alpha}$ for which Adversary $\mathcal{A}$ does not hold the decryption key, the security of the encryption scheme ensures indistinguishability of this as a ciphertext of $m_{i,\alpha}^{(0)}$ versus $m_{i,\alpha}^{(1)}$; and for any ciphertext $c_{i,\alpha}$ for which Adversary $\mathcal{A}$ does hold the decryption key, the constraint in Step 5a of the NIAR security game dictates that this ciphertext encodes a common message $m_{i,\alpha}^{(0)} = m_{i,\alpha}^{(1)}$.

Next we argue indistinguishability of the encryption keys $\{pk_i\}_{i \in S_\mathcal{A}}$ and the decryption keys $\{sk_i\}_{i \in R_\mathcal{A}}$. Notice first that due to the constraint in Step 1b of the NIAR security game, the distribution of decryption keys $\{sk_i\}_{i \in R_\mathcal{A}}$ looks the same for $b = 0$ and $b = 1$, since σ_0 and σ_1 necessarily agree here (i.e. they each map some index $j \in [N]$ to i. Meanwhile, for the distribution of encryption keys, we focus on indices $i \in [N]$ for which $\sigma_0(i) \neq \sigma_1(i)$. Fix any such i, and define $j = \sigma_0(i)$ and $j' = \sigma_1(i)$, so $j \neq j'$. Again due to the constraint in Step 1b of the NIAR security game, we have that neither j nor j' is in $R_\mathcal{A}$. This means that Adversary $\mathcal{A}$ does not hold the corresponding decryption key for pk_i regardless of whether $b = 0$ or $b = 1$, and thus by the security of the encryption scheme, the distribution of pk_i for $b = 0$ appears identical as the distribution when $b = 1$.

For indistinguishability of the router token q $= \{q_{\mu,j}\}$: for a given $q_{\mu,j}$ for which Adversary $\mathcal{A}$ does not hold the corresponding reconstruction key $\kappa_{\mu,j}$, indistinguishability follows from the security of the underlying rate-1 PIR scheme. Conversely, for a given $q_{\mu,j}$ for which Adversary $\mathcal{A}$ does hold the corresponding reconstruction key $\kappa_{\mu,j}$, $\mathcal{A}$ learns the input wire index that $q_{\mu,j}$ is selecting. However, the paths chosen through G (see Step (3a) of Setup Phase) are random and independent of each other and depend only on the given (sender, receiver) indices. Also, $\mathcal{A}$ knows reconstruction key $\kappa_{\mu,j}$ if and only if outgoing edge (μ, j) is on the path leading to a corrupt receiver $i \in R_\mathcal{A}$. Therefore, we again rely on the constraint in Step 1b of the NIAR security game to argue that σ_0 and σ_1 must agree on the (sender, receiver) indices for this path, so the input wire index that $q_{\mu,j}$ is selecting is the same.

It remains to argue indistinguishability of the reconstruction keys $\{\kappa_i\}_{i \in R_A} = \{(\mu, j, \kappa_{\mu,j})\}$. If for a given tuple $(\mu, j, \kappa_{\mu,j})$ the last component is a *valid* reconstruction key (i.e. $\kappa_{\mu,j} \neq \perp$), then indistinguishability follows the same argument as above for the router token. On the other hand, if $\kappa_{\mu,j} \neq \perp$, then as per the Correctness property of any Π_{ORG} protocol, Adversary $\mathcal{A}$ learns that at least two distinct paths chose outgoing edge (μ, j). Since this is the exact scenario as Challenge Game 2, the proof now follows from Lemma 29.

5   Correctness and Security

In this section, we present a series of definitions and lemmas that allow us to argue our main protocol (Fig. 3) satisfies the correctness and security properties of the NIAR model (Sect. 3.2). The main technical work lies in proving Security; this requires first defining a key property that networks can exhibit (Definition 23), then demonstrating that the Beneš Network we use satisfies this property (Corollary 27), and finally demonstrating how this property ensures security (see Challenge Games 1 and 2 in Sect. 5.3). As there are a number of lemmas and definitions to go through, to preserve the flow and focus on the main ideas, all proofs appear at the end of the paper.

5.1   Probabilities in a Beneš Network

The main goal of this section is to define a property of graphs that will allow us to formally argue that anonymity is achieved. As mentioned in the Introduction, this property is a stronger variant of edge-disjointness, which we call "local reversal edge-disjoint." Informally:

Definition 4 *(Informal). Given any permutation on N sets of (sender, receiver) pairs, a pairwise$_{i,j}$ reversal refers to swapping the receivers of senders i and j. When viewing a "block" of a permutation network (which also has N input nodes and N output nodes), a local pairwise$_{i,j}$ reversal refers to swapping the output nodes of two input nodes. A set of $N + 2$ paths through a block, which include one path for each (sender, receiver) pair plus two extra paths connecting sender i to receiver j (and sender j to receiver i) is said to be local pairwise$_{i,j}$ reversal edge-disjoint if these $N + 2$ paths are edge-disjoint. A permutation network is said to enjoy the local reversal edge-disjoint property if, for any pair of indices (i, j), w.h.p. there exists a block that is local pairwise$_{i,j}$ reversal edge-disjoint for $N + 2$ randomly chosen paths.*

Formally, Definitions 23 and 26 define the "*local reversal edge-disjoint*" property, and it is used to prove security via Corollary 27 and in the analysis of (12)).

Lemma 5. *Suppose that for each input node $\{\nu_i\}_{i=1}^{N}$ of a butterfly network, a random path $\mathcal{P}_i$ of $\log N$ steps is performed. For any node μ_l (at level $l \in [0, \log N]$), let X_{μ_l} denote the random variable that indicates how many of the paths $\{\mathcal{P}_i\}$ pass through node μ_l. Then for any integer $k \geq 1$:*

$$\Pr[X_{\mu_l} \geq k] \leq \frac{2^l}{k!} \tag{2}$$

Lemma 6. *Suppose that for each input node[5] $\{\nu_i\}_{i=1}^N$ of a **colored** butterfly network (with replication factor c), a random path $\mathcal{P}_i$ of $(1 + \log N)$ steps is performed (the first step chooses the color $\hat{c} \in [c]$). For any node $\mu_l = \mu_{\hat{c}, r, l}$ (at level $l \in [0, \log N]$, row $r \in [N]$, and color $\hat{c} \in [c]$), let X_{μ_l} denote the random variable that indicates how many of the paths $\{\mathcal{P}_i\}$ pass through node μ_l. Then for any integer $k \geq 1$:*

$$\Pr[X_{\mu_l} \geq k] \;\leq\; \frac{2^l}{k! \cdot c^k} \tag{3}$$

Lemma 7. *Suppose that for each input node $\{\nu_i\}_{i=1}^N$ of a **colored** butterfly network (with replication factor c), a random path $\mathcal{P}_i$ of $(1 + \log N)$ steps is performed (the first step chooses the color $\hat{c} \in [c]$). For any integer $k \geq 1$, let X_k denote an indicator variable on whether there exists **any** node μ (in the entire colored butterfly network) that has more than k (of the N total) random paths $\{\mathcal{P}_i\}$ pass through it. Then:*

$$\Pr[X_k = 1] \;\leq\; \frac{2c \cdot N^2}{k! \cdot c^k} \tag{4}$$

We now extend a (colored) butterfly network by concatenating several "blocks," each block consisting of $\log N$ levels, and then finishing with one final level that is the mirror reflection of a butterfly network:

Definition 8. *An **extended (colored) Beneš network** with b blocks consists of b butterfly networks concatenated together, followed by a single (reflected) butterfly network. Additionally, where each pair of blocks are connected, there is a single level inserted which consists of edges connecting all colors of each node (at each "row") to each other. A **block** j, for $j \in [1, (1+b)]$, refers to the $(1 + \log N)$ levels (and edges) between levels $(j - 1) \cdot (1 + \log N)$ and $j \cdot (1 + \log N)$. That is, a block corresponds to a contiguous set of $(1 + \log N)$ levels, whose first $\log N$ levels are a butterfly network, and the last level is the "connecting" level that consists of all edges connecting the different colors of all nodes on the same "row."[6] The **input level** of a block $j \in [1, 1 + b]$ is level $(j - 1) \cdot (1 + \log N)$, and the **output level** is $j \cdot (1 + \log N)$ (notice the input level of block b is the same as the output level of block $b - 1$).*

The following is analogous to Lemma 7, but bounds the probability with respect to each *block* of an extended, colored Beneš network:

---

[5] A colored butterfly network can be viewed as c disjoint butterfly networks overlaid on top of one another. Alternatively, we can view a colored butterfly network as a single (connected) graph by adding an extra input level (with level index -1) on the far left, consisting of N input nodes. Then there are c edges emanating from each input node, connecting it to each of the c colored nodes in level 0 of the corresponding row.

[6] In the special case of the $(1+b)^{th}$ block, the first $\log N$ levels of this block are a *reflected* butterfly network, and the last level of the block is the final "output" level of the entire network.

Lemma 9. *Let $\sigma : [N] \mapsto [N]$ be an arbitrary permutation on N items. Suppose that for each input node $\{\nu_i\}_{i=1}^N$ of an extended, colored Beneš network with replication factor c and b blocks, a random path $\mathcal{P}_i$ of $(1 + b \cdot (1 + \log N))$ steps is performed, and then each such path is extended (from level $(b \cdot (1 + \log N))$ to level $(1 + b) \cdot (1 + \log N))$ by traversing the unique path from the current node (on level $(b \cdot (1 + \log N)))$ to $\sigma(i)$. For any $j \in [1, (b + 1)]$ and for any integer $k \geq 1$, let $X_{j,k}$ denote an indicator variable on whether there exists **any** node μ_j within block j (i.e. between levels $[(j - 1) \cdot (1 + \log N), j \cdot (1 + \log N) - 1]$ that has more than k (of the N total) random paths $\{\mathcal{P}_i\}$ pass through it. Then:*

$$Pr[X_{1,k} = 1] = Pr[X_{1+b,k} = 1] \leq \frac{2c \cdot N^2}{k! \cdot c^k}$$

$$\forall j \in [2, b] : \quad Pr[X_{j,k} = 1] \leq \frac{c \cdot N^2 \cdot (1 + \log N)}{k! \cdot c^k} \tag{5}$$

5.2   Permutation Routing Problem

We begin with the definitions that are needed to describe the Permutation Routing Problem and the desired properties that a successful solution must exhibit.

Definition 10. *Given a graph $G = (V, E)$ and a collection of paths $\{\mathcal{P}_i\}$ within the graph, we say that any given path $\mathcal{P}_i$ is **edge-disjoint** from the others if no edge in $\mathcal{P}_i$ is contained/traversed by any other path. We say the entire collection of paths $\{\mathcal{P}_i\}$ is **edge-disjoint** if each individual edge is edge-disjoint.*

Definition 11. *A **Permutation Routing Problem**(N, σ, G) is defined as follows: For input integer $N \in \mathbb{N}$, permutation $\sigma : [N] \rightarrow [N]$, and graph G that has N designated "input" nodes $\{I_1, I_2, \ldots, I_N\}$ and N designated "output" nodes $\{O_1, O_2, \ldots, O_N\}$, construct N **edge-disjoint** paths through G that connect each input-output pair $(I_i, O_{\sigma(i)})$.*

We extend the notion of the extended, colored Beneš network to a *wide-edged* variant, in which each edge has been replicated w times (which can equivalently be viewed as each edge having capacity w):

Definition 12. *A **wide-edged, extended, colored Beneš** network $B(N, b, c, w)$ is an extended and colored Beneš network in which, for each level $l \in [1, (b + (1 + b) \cdot \log N)]$, each edge connecting levels $(l-1, l)$ is replicated w times.*

Notice that the added *color* and *edge-width* features serve a similar purpose: they each reduce the probability of an edge conflict (i.e. increase the probability of being edge-disjoint, as per Definition 10); but they do so in slightly different ways: the *color* feature not only introduces new edges, but also additional nodes, so that once a path chooses a color for a particular block (which happens only at the start of each block, when there is a transition between levels in which each edge connects the various "colors" corresponding to the nodes on a common "row;" it will not conflict (on the present block) with paths that chose another color. In contrast, the *edge-width* feature reduces the chances that two paths conflict across a given edge; but those same paths may still end up in the same node at the far end of this edge, and thus may conflict in a later edge.

We now describe a naïve protocol for randomly choosing paths through a Beneš network:

Definition 13. *Given permutation $\sigma : [N] \to [N]$ and a wide-edged, extended, colored Beneš network $G = B(N, b, c, w)$, the **Naïve Random Path** algorithm defines N paths $\{\mathcal{P}_i\}$ through G, connecting each input node to each output node as per σ, as follows: Path $\mathcal{P}_i$, which starts at input node I_i, chooses random edges for each level through the first b blocks of $G = B(N, b, c, w)$. Then from its current node on level $(b \cdot (1 + \log N))$, it follows the unique path to destination node $O_{\sigma(i)}$ (by choosing one of the w replicates of each edge along this path).*

Definition 14. *Given a wide-edged, extended, colored Beneš network $B(N, b, c, w)$, and given a routing algorithm $\Pi = \Pi_{N,\sigma,B(N,b,c,w)}$ that attempts to solve the Permutation Routing Problem (Definition 11), for each $i \in [N]$ and for each block $1 \leq j \leq (1+b)$, let $\mathsf{X}_\Pi(i,j)$ denote the boolean random variable that indicates whether Π constructs an edge-disjoint path **on the jth block** for the pair $(I_i, O_{\sigma(i)})$. That is, $X_\Pi(i,j) = 1$ if the path connecting I_i and $O_{\sigma(i)}$ within the jth block (as specified by Π) is edge-disjoint from all other paths specified by Π.*

We now demonstrate several properties that the Naïve Random Path algorithm (Definition 13) satisfies:

Lemma 15. *Let $\Pi = \Pi_{\sigma_N}$ denote the Naïve Random Path algorithm (Definition 13) on a wide-edged, extended, and colored Beneš network $B(N, b, c \geq 2, w)$. Then for any $i \in [0, N]$, for any $1 \leq j \leq (1 + b)$, and for any $1 \leq k \leq N$, the probability that $X_\Pi(i,j) = 0$ (as per Definition 14) is bounded by:*

$$Pr[X_\Pi(i,j) = 0] \leq (1 + \log N) \cdot \left(\frac{c \cdot N^2(1 + \log N)}{k! \cdot c^k} + \frac{k}{2w} \right) \qquad (6)$$

We now extend Definition 14 (and in particular the indicator random variable $X_\Pi(i,j) = 0$) to a statement about a path $\mathcal{P}_i$ being edge-disjoint across the entire network G:

Definition 16. *Given a routing algorithm $\Pi = \Pi_{N,\sigma,G}$ that attempts to solve the Permutation Routing Problem (Definition 11), for each $i \in [N]$, let $\mathsf{X}_\Pi(i)$ denote the boolean random variable that indicates whether Π constructs an edge-disjoint path for the pair $(I_i, O_{\sigma(i)})$. That is, $X_\Pi(i) = 1$ if the path connecting I_i and $O_{\sigma(i)}$ (as specified by Π) is edge-disjoint from all other paths specified by Π.*

Lemma 17. *Let $\Pi = \Pi_{\sigma_N}$ denote the Naïve Random Path algorithm (Definition 13) on a wide-edged, extended, and colored Beneš network $B(N, b, c \geq 2, w)$. Then for any $i \in [N]$ and for any $1 \leq k \leq N$, the probability that $X_\Pi(i) = 0$ (as per Definition 16) is bounded by:*

$$Pr[X_\Pi(i) = 0] \leq (1 + b) \cdot (1 + \log N) \cdot \left(\frac{c \cdot N^2 \cdot (1 + \log N)}{k! \cdot c^k} + \frac{k}{2w} \right) \qquad (7)$$

Proof. This follows immediately from Lemma 15 by applying a union bound on the $(1 + b)$ blocks of the Beneš network $B(N, b, c, w)$.

We are now ready to present the final definition and corresponding statement that will be required for the correctness property of the protocol in Fig. 3.

Definition 18. *Given an (independent) collection $\{\Pi_m\}$ of M routing algorithms that attempt to solve the Permutation Routing Problem (see Definition 11) in a wide-edged, extended and colored Beneš network $B(N, b, c, w)$, let* X *denote the boolean random variable that indicates if, for every $i \in [N]$, there exists (at least) one experiment $m \in [M]$ in which $X_{\Pi_m}(i) = 1$ (where $X_{\Pi_m}(i)$ is the random variable in Definition 16).*

Corollary 19. *For any security parameter λ and for any input parameters $2^n = N \geq 64$, $b = \lambda - 1$, $c = 4 \cdot a_\lambda$, and $w = 1.2 \cdot \lambda \cdot \log N \cdot (1 + \log N)$ (for[7] $a_\lambda := \max(2, \lambda^{1/(\log N - 1)}))$, if the Naïve Random Path algorithm (Definition 13) is repeated $M := \lambda$ times, then the probability that $X = 0$ (Definition 18) is bounded by:*

$$Pr[X = 0] < \left(\frac{3}{4}\right)^\lambda \tag{8}$$

Ultimately, Corollary 19 will demonstrate *correctness* of our routing protocol (3). However, for the *security* property, we will need to consider two sets of (input, output) node pairs. The following definition (which extends Definition 14, but for two sets of (input, output) pairs of nodes) will be used to capture the requisite probabilities for our security proof.

Definition 20. *Given a wide-edged, extended, colored Beneš network $B(N, b, c, w)$ and two routing algorithms $\Pi = \Pi_{N,\sigma,G=B(N,b,c,w)}$ and $\Pi' = \Pi'_{N,\sigma,G=B(N,b,c,w)}$ that attempt to solve the Permutation Routing Problem (Definition 11), for any pair of row indices $(i, i') \in [N]$ and for any block $1 \leq j \leq (1 + b)$, let $Y_{\Pi,\Pi'}(i, i', j)$ denote the boolean random variable that indicates whether each of the four paths $\{\mathcal{P}_i, \mathcal{P}_{i'}, \mathcal{P}'_i, \mathcal{P}'_{i'}\}$ are edge-disjoint from all other paths on block j.*

Aside. Notice that Definition 20 is only concerned about what happens on a single block of a wide-edged, extended, and colored Beneš network $B(N, b, c, w)$. In particular, we do not actually require two routing algorithms Π, Π' to be defined on the full network $B(N, b, c, w)$ in order to evaluate whether $Y_{\Pi,\Pi'}(i, i', j)$ equals zero or one on a given block $j \in [1, 1 + b]$ (as per Definition 20); rather, we only need to know what each algorithm does on block j. Also notice that there is no requirement that the four paths be edge-disjoint *from each other*.

Definition 21. *Given a wide-edged, extended, and colored Beneš network $G = B(N, b, c, w)$, and a routing algorithm $\Pi = \Pi_{N,\sigma,G}$ that attempts to solve the Permutation Routing Problem (Definition 11), and given any pair of row indices $i, i' \in [N]$ and any block index $j \in [1, (1 + b)]$, define the block j alternate routing algorithm $\Pi'_{i,i',j}$ as follows:*

---

[7] Notice $a_\lambda = 2$ if $\lambda \leq N/2$.

- $\Pi'_{i,i',j}$ is identical to Π on the first $(j-1)$ blocks.
- On the jth block:
  - For all $\widehat{i} \notin \{i,i'\}$: $\Pi'_{i,i',j}$ is identical to Π.
  - Let μ_i (respectively $\mu_{i'}$) denote the node on the output level (which has level index $j \cdot (1 + \log N)$) of block j that $\mathcal{P}_i$ (respectively $\mathcal{P}_{i'}$) passes through. Then $\Pi'_{i,i',j}$ is identical to Π except that the choice of μ_i versus $\mu_{i'}$ is swapped in Step 2a for i and i'.[8]
- For all blocks beyond the jth block:
  - For all $\widehat{i} \notin \{i,i'\}$: $\Pi'_{i,i',j}$ is identical to Π.
  - For i, i': $\Pi'_{i,i',j}$ is identical to Π, except that it has swapped paths $\mathcal{P}_i$ and $\mathcal{P}_{i'}$.[9]

With these definitions in hand, we provide an analogous probability bound for $Y_{\Pi,\Pi'}(i,i',j)$ as Lemma 15 provided for $X_\Pi(i,j)$.

Lemma 22. *Let $\Pi = \Pi_{\sigma_N}$ denote the Naïve Random Path algorithm (Definition 13) on a wide-edged, extended, and colored Beneš network $B(N,b,c \geq 2,w)$. Fix any pair of row indices $i, i' \in [N]$ and any block index $j \in [1,(1+b)]$, and let $\Pi' = \Pi'_{i,i',j}$ denote the "block j alternate routing protocol" (Definition 21). Then for any $1 \leq k \leq N$, the probability that $Y_{\Pi,\Pi'}(i,i',j) = 0$ (as per Definition 20) is bounded by:*

$$Pr[Y_{\Pi,\Pi'}(i,i',j) = 0] \leq 4 \cdot (1 + \log N) \cdot \left(\frac{c \cdot N^2 \cdot (1 + \log N)}{k! \cdot c^k} + \frac{k}{2w} \right) \quad (9)$$

Just as $X_\Pi(i,j)$ (Definition 14) and the corresponding bound for it (Lemma 15) were extended from variables/statements about *blocks* to variables/statements about the *entire network* (in the corresponding Definition 16 and Lemma 17), we likewise extend $Y_{\Pi,\Pi'}(i,i',j)$ (Definition 20) and the corresponding Lemma 22 to variables/statements about the entire network. However, these extensions differ slightly from before, as ultimately we only need the *existence* of a block that satisfies the key property, as opposed to requiring that *all blocks* satisfy some property.

Definition 23. *Given a wide-edged, extended, and colored Beneš network $G = B(N,b,c,w)$, and given two routing algorithms $\Pi = \Pi_{N,\sigma,G}$ and $\Pi' = \Pi'_{N,\sigma,G}$ that attempt to solve the Permutation Routing Problem (Definition 11), for any pair of row indices $(i,i') \in [N]$, let $Y_{\Pi,\Pi'}(i,i')$ denote the boolean random variable that indicates whether there exists some block $j \in [1,(1+b)]$ in which the four paths $\{\mathcal{P}_i, \mathcal{P}_{i'}, \mathcal{P}'_i, \mathcal{P}'_{i'}\}$ are each edge-disjoint from all other paths on block j.*

---

[8] Notice that if $\mu_i = \mu_{i'}$, then $\Pi'_{i,i',j}$ is identical to Π (for *all* paths $\{\mathcal{P}_i\}$) on all blocks through j (including block j).

[9] Swapping paths is only necessary for the sake of making sure the paths link up/connect between blocks (since output node μ_i and $\mu_{i'}$ were swapped in block j). However, as was noted in the Aside note following Definition 20, the details of what $\Pi'_{i,i',j}$ does beyond block j will be irrelevant for the context of Lemmas 22 and 25.

Definition 24. *Given a wide-edged, extended, and colored Beneš network* $G = B(N, b, c, w)$, *and a routing algorithm* $\Pi = \Pi_{N,\sigma,G}$ *that attempts to solve the Permutation Routing Problem (Definition 11), and given any pair of row indices* $i, i' \in [N]$, *define the* alternate routing algorithm $\Pi'_{i,i'}$ *as follows:*

1. $\forall j \in [1, (1+b)]$, *let* $\Pi'_j = \Pi'_{i,i',j}$ *denote the block* j *alternate routing algorithm (Definition 21).*
2. *Construct* $\Pi'_{i,i'}$ *from the family of alternate routing algorithms* $\{\Pi_j\}$ *as follows:*
   a. *If there exists an index* $j \in [1, (1+b)]$ *such that* $Y_{\Pi,\Pi'_j}(i, i', j) = 1$ *(as per Definition 14), then let* $\Pi'_{i,i'} = \Pi'_j$ *(for the minimal* j *satisfying* $Y_{\Pi,\Pi'_j}(i, i', j) = 1$).
   b. *Otherwise, define* $\Pi'_{i,i'} = \Pi$.

Lemma 25. *Let* $\Pi = \Pi_{\sigma_N}$ *denote the Naïve Random Path algorithm (Definition 13) on a wide-edged, extended, and colored Beneš network* $B(N, b, c \geq 2, w)$, *let* $i, i' \in [N]$ *be any two row indices, and let* $\Pi' = \Pi'_{i,i'}$ *be the alternate routing algorithm (as per Definition 24). Then for any* $1 \leq k \leq N$, *the probability that* $Y_{\Pi,\Pi'}(i, i') = 0$ *(as per Definition 23) is bounded by:*

$$Pr[Y_{\Pi,\Pi'}(i, i') = 0] \leq \left(4 \cdot (1 + \log N) \cdot \left(\frac{c \cdot N^2 (1 + \log N)}{k! \cdot c^k} + \frac{k}{2w} \right) \right)^{(1+b)}$$

(10)

We are now ready to present the final definition and corresponding statement that will be required for the security proof of the protocol in Fig. 3.

Definition 26. *Given an (independent) collection* $\{\Pi_m\}$ *of* M *routing algorithms that attempt to solve the Permutation Routing Problem (Definition 11) in a wide-edged, extended and colored Beneš network* $B(N, b, c, w)$, *let* Y *denote the boolean random variable that indicates if, for every* Π_m *and every pair of row indices* $i, i' \in [N]$, *that* $Y_{\Pi_m,\Pi'_m}(i, i') = 1$ *(where* $\Pi'_m = \Pi'_{m,i,i'}$ *is the alternate routing algorithm (Definition 24) and* $Y_{\Pi_m,\Pi'_m}(i, i')$ *is the corresponding random variable (Definition 23)).*

Corollary 27. *For[10] any security parameter* $\lambda \geq 8$ *and any input parameters* $2^n = N \geq 64$, $b = \lambda - 1$, $c = 4 \cdot a_\lambda$, *and* $w = 1.2 \cdot \lambda \cdot \log N \cdot (1 + \log N)$ *(for* $a_\lambda := \max(2, \lambda^{1/(\log N - 1)}))$, *if the Naïve Random Path algorithm (Definition 13) is repeated* $M := \lambda$ *times, then the probability that* $Y = 0$ *(Definition 26) is bounded by:*

$$Pr[Y = 0] < \frac{\lambda \cdot N^2}{4^\lambda}$$

(11)

---

[10] Notice that these parameter values all match those in the hypothesis of Corollary 19.

5.3   Security

Succinctly, security (anonymity) will follow for the routing protocol of Fig. 3 from:

Corollary 27 $\Rightarrow$ (!$\exists\mathcal{A}$ with non-negligible advantage in Challenge Game 1)
$\Rightarrow$ (!$\exists\mathcal{A}$ with non-negligible advantage in Challenge Game 2)
$\Rightarrow$ (Routing Protocol of Fig. 3 is secure (per Definition 11))   (12)

In this section, we define Challenge Games 1 and 2, and then demonstrate the first two implications in (12) (the third implication was already presented in the proof of Theorem 3).

Challenge Game 1

Input Parameters:

- Number of input/output nodes $2^n = N \geq 64$.
- Security parameter $\lambda \geq 8$.
- A wide-edged, extended and colored Beneš network $G = B(N, b, c, w)$, with parameters as per Corollaries 19 and 27: $b = \lambda - 1$, $c = 4 \cdot a_\lambda$, and $w = 1.2 \cdot \lambda \cdot \log N \cdot (1 + \log N)$ (for $a_\lambda := \max(2, \lambda^{1/(\log N - 1)})$).
- There are N "global input nodes" on level -1 of the Beneš network $G = B(N, b, c, w)$, which are denoted: $\mathcal{I} = \{I_1, I_2, \ldots, I_N\}$, and N global output nodes $\mathcal{O} = \{O_1, O_2, \ldots, O_N\}$.
- Set the experiment replication amount $M = \lambda$.

Challenge Game:

1. Challenger $\mathcal{C}$ chooses a permutation σ on N elements $\sigma : [N] \to [N]$.
2. For each experiment $m \in [M]$: Challenger $\mathcal{C}$ performs the Naïve Random Path algorithm (Definition 13) $\Pi_m = \Pi_{m,N,\sigma_b,G}$ (for $G = B(N, b, c, w)$). For each $i \in [N]$, let $\mathcal{P}_{m,i}$ denote the path chosen (by Π_m) that connects nodes $(I_i, \sigma_b(I_i))$.
3. Let Y be the boolean random variable from Definition 26. If $Y = 0$, Challenger $\mathcal{C}$ aborts (Adversary $\mathcal{A}$ wins).
4. Challenger $\mathcal{C}$ chooses any two distinct indices $i, i' \in [N]$, and gives[11] $\sigma|_{[N]\setminus\{i,i'\}}$ to Adversary $\mathcal{A}$, which is the mapping of σ on all indices *except* i and i'. Notice that since σ is a permutation, Adversary $\mathcal{A}$ now has complete knowledge of σ, *except* for what σ does to i and i'. In particular, there are two range indices $\sigma(i), \sigma(i') \in [N]$ that are *not* mapped to (based on what $\mathcal{C}$ gives to $\mathcal{A}$). Let τ denote the permutation that is identical to σ, except that it swaps where i and i' are mapped to (so $\tau(i) = \sigma(i')$ and $\tau(i') = \sigma(i)$). Notice that after this step, Adversary $\mathcal{A}$ knows that the permutation chosen by Challenger $\mathcal{C}$ is either σ or τ.

---

[11] This information is also available indirectly from what $\mathcal{C}$ gives to $\mathcal{A}$ in Step 5 a below.

5. (If this step is reached) Since $Y = 1$, for each run $1 \leq m \leq M$ of the experiment, we have that alternate routing algorithm $\Pi'_{m,i,i'}$ must have been constructed as per Step 2a of Definition 24 (as opposed to Step 2b). Therefore, let $j_m \in [1, (1+b)]$ denote the block index for which $\Pi'_{m,i,i'}$ is defined as in Step 2a; i.e. j_m (is the minimal index that) satisfies $Y_{\Pi_m, \Pi'_m, j_m}(i, i', j_m) = 1$. Then, for each experiment $m \in [M]$:

   (a) [Block Index]: Challenger $\mathcal{C}$ gives Adversary $\mathcal{A}$ the block index j_m (recall this is the first block for which $Y_{\Pi_m, \Pi'_m, j_m}(i, i', j_m) = 1$).

   (b) [All Non-Interesting Paths]: Challenger $\mathcal{C}$ gives Adversary $\mathcal{A}$ all paths $\{\mathcal{P}_{m,\hat{\imath}}\}_{\hat{\imath} \notin \{i,i'\}}$.

   (c) [Interesting Paths *Before* Block j_m]: Challenger $\mathcal{C}$ gives Adversary $\mathcal{A}$, *through the first (j_m-1) blocks only*, paths $\mathcal{P}_{m,i}$ and $\mathcal{P}_{m,i'}$.

   (d) [Interesting Paths + Alternate Paths for Block j_m]: Denote the two sub-paths of $\mathcal{P}_{m,i}$ and $\mathcal{P}_{m,i'}$ that are restricted to block j_m (i.e. just the edges of these paths within block j_m) and their two alternate sub-paths (as specified by alternate routing protocol $\Pi'_{i,i'}$ (Definition 24)) as: $\{\mathcal{P}_{m,i,j_m}, \mathcal{P}_{m,i',j_m}, \mathcal{P}'_{m,i,j_m}, \mathcal{P}'_{m,i',j_m}\}$. Then Challenger $\mathcal{C}$ gives Adversary $\mathcal{A}$ the *unordered* set $\{\mathcal{P}_{m,i,j_m}, \mathcal{P}_{m,i',j_m}, \mathcal{P}'_{m,i,j_m}, \mathcal{P}'_{m,i',j_m}\}$.

   (e) [(Unordered) Interesting Paths *Beyond* Block j_m]: For each level with index $j_m \cdot (1 + \log N) \leq l \leq (1+b) \cdot (1 + \log N)$ in $G = B(N, b, c, w)$ that lies *after* block j_m, Challenger $\mathcal{C}$ gives Adversary $\mathcal{A}$ the *unordered* set of edges $\{\mathcal{P}_{m,i,l}, \mathcal{P}_{m,i',l}\}_l$, where $\mathcal{P}_{m,i,l}$ (resp. $\mathcal{P}_{m,i',l}$) denotes the lth edge on the path $\mathcal{P}_{m,i}$ (resp. on the path $\mathcal{P}_{m,i'}$). In other words, $\mathcal{A}$ learns the edges (beyond block j_m) traversed by paths $\mathcal{P}_{m,i}$ and $\mathcal{P}_{m,i'}$, but $\mathcal{A}$ is *not* explicitly told which edges belong to which path ($\mathcal{P}_{m,i}$ versus $\mathcal{P}_{m,i'}$).

6. Adversary $\mathcal{A}$ outputs a guess whether Challenger's permutation was σ or τ.

The Adversary $\mathcal{A}$ wins Challenge Game 1 either if Challenger $\mathcal{C}$ aborts in Step 3, or if $\mathcal{A}$'s output guess in Step 6 is correct.

The main result for Challenge Game 1 (which is the first implication in (12)) is:

Lemma 28. *The probability that an (unbounded) Adversary $\mathcal{A}$ wins Challenge Game 1 is bounded by:*

$$Pr[\mathcal{A} \text{ wins Challenge Game 1}] \leq \frac{1}{2} + \frac{\lambda \cdot N^2}{4^\lambda} \tag{13}$$

Challenge Game 2

Input Parameters:

- Number of input/output nodes $2^n = N \geq 64$.
- Security parameter λ_s. Let $\lambda := 2 \log N + \max(\lambda_s, 2 + \log \log N)$.
- A wide-edged, extended and colored Beneš network $G = B(N, b, c, w)$, with parameters as per Corollaries 19 and 27: $b = \lambda - 1$, $c = 4 \cdot a_\lambda$, and $w = 1.2 \cdot \lambda \cdot \log N \cdot (1 + \log N)$ (for $a_\lambda := \max(2, \lambda^{1/(\log N - 1)})$).

- There are N "global input nodes" on level -1 of the Beneš network $G = B(N, b, c, w)$, which are denoted: $\mathcal{I} = \{I_1, I_2, \ldots, I_N\}$, and N global output nodes $\mathcal{O} = \{O_1, O_2, \ldots, O_N\}$.
- Set the experiment replication amount $M = \lambda$.

Challenge Game:

1. On input security parameter λ, Adversary $\mathcal{A}$ chooses N, two distinct permutations σ_0, σ_1 on $[N]$, a set of sender indices $S_\mathcal{A} \subseteq [N]$ to corrupt, and a set of receiver indices $R_\mathcal{A} \subseteq [N]$ to corrupt; subject to constraints:
   (a) $|R_\mathcal{A}| \leq N - 2$;
   (b) σ_0 and σ_1 match for all receivers in $R_\mathcal{A}$: $\forall\, i \in R_\mathcal{A} : \sigma_0^{-1}(i) = \sigma_1^{-1}(i)$.
2. Adversary $\mathcal{A}$ sends $\{\sigma_0, \sigma_1\}$ to a Challenger $\mathcal{C}$.
3. Challenger $\mathcal{C}$ chooses $b \in \{0, 1\}$ and selects $\sigma_b \in \{\sigma_0, \sigma_1\}$.
4. For each experiment $m \in [M]$:
   (a) Challenger $\mathcal{C}$ performs the Naïve Random Path algorithm (Definition 13) $\Pi_m = \Pi_{m,N,\sigma_b,G}$ (for $G = B(N, b, c, w)$). For each $i \in [N]$, let $\mathcal{P}_{m,i}$ denote the path chosen (by Π_m) that connects nodes $(I_i, O_{\sigma_b(i)})$.
   (b) Adversary $\mathcal{A}$ is given the following information:
      - For each $i \in R_\mathcal{A}$: all edges $e \in \mathcal{P}_{m,i}$ that are edge-disjoint from all other paths $\mathcal{P}_{m,j}$ (for $j \neq i$).
      - The list of edges $\{e\} \in G$ that have at least two distinct paths $\mathcal{P}_{m,i}, \mathcal{P}_{m,i'}$ pass through them, with $i' \neq i$ and $i \in R_\mathcal{A}$. Notice that $\mathcal{A}$ is given only the identity of the set of edges $\{e\}$; in particular, $\mathcal{A}$ *is not* given the information of *which* (nor even *how many*) indices in $[N] \setminus R_\mathcal{A}$ traverse each such edge.
5. Let Y be the boolean random variable from Definition 26. If $Y = 0$, Challenger $\mathcal{C}$ aborts (Adversary $\mathcal{A}$ wins).
6. Adversary $\mathcal{A}$ outputs a guess $b' \in \{0, 1\}$ of which permutation $\{\sigma_0, \sigma_1\}$ Challenger $\mathcal{C}$ chose.

We say that the Adversary wins the above challenge if its output is correct.

The main result for Challenge Game 2 (which is the second implication in (12)) is:

Lemma 29. *The probability that an (unbounded) Adversary $\mathcal{A}$ wins Challenge Game 2 is bounded by:* $Pr[\mathcal{A} \text{ wins Challenge Game 2}] \leq \frac{1}{2} + \frac{1}{2^{\lambda_s}}$.

Acknowledgements. This material is based upon work supported by the United States Air Force and DARPA – Distribution Statement "A" (Approved for Public Release, Distribution Unlimited) – under Contract No. FA8750-19-C-0031, DARPA under Cooperative Agreement HR0011-20-2-0025, the Algorand Centers of Excellence program managed by Algorand Foundation, NSF grants CNS-224635, CCF-2220450, CNS-2001096, US-Israel BSF grant 2018393, ISF grant 2774/20, Amazon Faculty Award, Cisco Research Award and Sunday Group. Any views, opinions, findings, conclusions or recommendations contained herein are those of the author(s) and should not be interpreted as necessarily representing the official policies, either expressed or implied, of DARPA, the Department of Defense, the United States Air Force, the Algorand Foundation, or the U.S. Government. The U.S. Government is authorized to reproduce and distribute reprints for governmental purposes not withstanding any copyright annotation therein.

References

[AKS83]   Ajtai, M., Komlós, J., Szemerédi, E.: An o(n log n) sorting network. In: Proceedings of the 15th Annual ACM Symposium on Theory of Computing, 25–27 April 1983, pp. 1–9. ACM (1983)

[CGH+21] Chase, M., Garg, S., Hajiabadi, M., Li, J., Miao, P.: Amortizing rate-1 OT and applications to PIR and PSI. In: Nissim, K., Waters, B. (eds.) TCC 2021. LNCS, vol. 13044, pp. 126–156. Springer, Cham (2021). https://doi.org/10.1007/978-3-030-90456-2_5

[CGKS95] Chor, B., Kushilevitz, E., Goldreich, O., Sudan, M.: Private information retrieval. In: 36th Annual Symposium on Foundations of Computer Science, Milwaukee, Wisconsin, USA, 23–25 October 1995, pp. 41–50. IEEE Computer Society (1995)

[COS10]   Chandran, N., Ostrovsky, R., Skeith, W.E.: Public-key encryption with efficient amortized updates. In: Garay, J.A., De Prisco, R. (eds.) SCN 2010. LNCS, vol. 6280, pp. 17–35. Springer, Heidelberg (2010). https://doi.org/10.1007/978-3-642-15317-4_2

[DGI+19] Döttling, N., Garg, S., Ishai, Y., Malavolta, G., Mour, T., Ostrovsky, R.: Trapdoor hash functions and their applications. In: Boldyreva, A., Micciancio, D. (eds.) CRYPTO 2019. LNCS, vol. 11694, pp. 3–32. Springer, Cham (2019). https://doi.org/10.1007/978-3-030-26954-8_1

[FSSV22] Fernando, R., Shi, E., Soni, P., Vanjani, N.: Non-interactive anonymous router with quasi-linear router computation. IACR Cryptology ePrint Archive, Paper 1395 (2022)

[GHO20]   Garg, S., Hajiabadi, M., Ostrovsky, R.: Efficient range-trapdoor functions and applications: rate-1 OT and more. In: Pass, R., Pietrzak, K. (eds.) TCC 2020. LNCS, vol. 12550, pp. 88–116. Springer, Cham (2020). https://doi.org/10.1007/978-3-030-64375-1_4

[HOWW19] Hamlin, A., Ostrovsky, R., Weiss, M., Wichs, D.: Private anonymous data access. In: Ishai, Y., Rijmen, V. (eds.) EUROCRYPT 2019. LNCS, vol. 11477, pp. 244–273. Springer, Cham (2019). https://doi.org/10.1007/978-3-030-17656-3_9

[IKOS04] Ishai, Y., Kushilevitz, E., Ostrovsky, R., Sahai, A.: Batch codes and their applications. In: Proceedings of the 36th Annual ACM Symposium on Theory of Computing, pp. 262–271. ACM (2004)

[IP07]   Ishai, Y., Paskin, A.: Evaluating branching programs on encrypted data. In: Vadhan, S.P. (ed.) TCC 2007. LNCS, vol. 4392, pp. 575–594. Springer, Heidelberg (2007). https://doi.org/10.1007/978-3-540-70936-7_31

[KO97]   Kushilevitz, E., Ostrovsky, R.: Replication is NOT needed: SINGLE database, computationally-private information retrieval. In: 38th Annual Symposium on Foundations of Computer Science, FOCS 1997, 19–22 October 1997, pp. 364–373. IEEE Computer Society (1997)

[Lei84]   Leighton, F.T.: Tight bounds on the complexity of parallel sorting. In: Proceedings of the 16th Annual ACM Symposium on Theory of Computing, pp. 71–80. ACM (1984)

[LMW22]   Lin, W.-K., Mook, E., Wichs, D.: Doubly efficient private information retrieval and fully homomorphic RAM computation from ring LWE. IACR Cryptology ePrint Archive, Paper 1703 (2022)

[MS92]   Maggs, B.M., Sitaraman, R.K.: Simple algorithms for routing on butterfly networks with bounded queues (ext. abstract). In: 24th Annual ACM Symposium on Theory of Computing, pp. 150–161. ACM (1992)

[OS07] Ostrovsky, R., Skeith, W.E.: A survey of single-database private information retrieval: techniques and applications. In: Okamoto, T., Wang, X. (eds.) PKC 2007. LNCS, vol. 4450, pp. 393–411. Springer, Heidelberg (2007). https://doi.org/10.1007/978-3-540-71677-8_26

[SW21] Shi, E., Wu, K.: Non-interactive anonymous router. In: Canteaut, A., Standaert, F.-X. (eds.) EUROCRYPT 2021. LNCS, vol. 12698, pp. 489–520. Springer, Cham (2021). https://doi.org/10.1007/978-3-030-77883-5_17

[Upf89] Upfal, E.: An o(log N) deterministic packet routing scheme (preliminary version). In: Proceedings of the 21st Annual ACM Symposium on Theory of Computing, pp. 241–250. ACM (1989)

Non-Interactive Anonymous Router
with Quasi-Linear Router Computation

Rex Fernando[1(✉)], Elaine Shi[1], Pratik Soni[2], Nikhil Vanjani[1],
and Brent Waters[3,4]

[1] Carnegie Mellon University, Pittsburgh, USA
rex1fernando@gmail.com, nvanjani@cmu.edu
[2] University of Utah, Salt Lake City, USA
[3] University of Texas at Austin, Austin, USA
[4] NTT Research, Sunnyvale, USA

Abstract. Anonymous routing is an important cryptographic primitive that allows users to communicate privately on the Internet, without revealing their message contents or their contacts. Until the very recent work of Shi and Wu (Eurocrypt'21), all classical anonymous routing schemes are *interactive* protocols, and their security rely on a *threshold* number of the routers being honest. The recent work of Shi and Wu suggested a new abstraction called Non-Interactive Anonymous Router (NIAR), and showed how to achieve anonymous routing *non-interactively* for the first time. In particular, a *single untrusted router* receives a token which allows it to obliviously apply a permutation to a set of encrypted messages from the senders. Shi and Wu's construction suffers from two drawbacks: 1) the router takes time *quadratic* in the number of senders to obliviously route their messages; and 2) the scheme is proven secure only in the presence of static corruptions.

In this work, we show how to construct a non-interactive anonymous router scheme with *sub-quadratic* router computation, and achieving security in the presence of *adaptive corruptions*. To get this result, we assume the existence of indistinguishability obfuscation and one-way functions. Our final result is obtained through a sequence of stepping stones. First, we show how to achieve the desired efficiency, but with security under static corruption and in a selective, single-challenge setting. Then, we go through a sequence of upgrades which eventually get us the final result. We devise various new techniques along the way which lead to some additional results. In particular, our techniques for reasoning about a *network of obfuscated programs* may be of independent interest.

1 Introduction

Anonymous communication systems allow users to communicate without revealing their identities and messages. The earliest design of an anonymous communication system goes back to Chaum [22] who proposed the design of an encrypted

P. Soni—Work was done partially when the author was visiting Carnegie Mellon University.

G. Rothblum and H. Wee (Eds.): TCC 2023, LNCS 14371, pp. 62–92, 2023.
https://doi.org/10.1007/978-3-031-48621-0_3

email service that additionally hides the identities of the sender and the receiver. Since then, numerous approaches have been proposed to build anonymous routing schemes $[1,10,22,23,27,28,30,38,51,55,56,58]$ – a key component of anonymous communication systems. These include mix-nets $[1,10,22]$, the Dining Cryptographers' nets $[3,23,28]$, onion routing $[19,29,30,38]$, multi-party-computation-based approaches $[4,42,54]$, multi-server PIR-write $[27,35,49]$, as well as variants $[55,56,58]$.

However, all of these routing schemes are *interactive*, where many servers or routers engage in an interactive protocol to achieve routing. The security relies on *threshold* type assumptions, e.g., majority or at least one of the routers must be honest. This is unsatisfactory since the threshold-based trust model increases the barrier of adoption, the interactivity leads to higher network latency, and finally, the schemes provide no guarantees when *all* routers may be malicious, or worse yet, colluding with a subset of the receivers and senders.

The recent work of Shi and Wu [53] was the first to study the feasibility of *non-interactive* anonymous routing (NIAR) with a *single, untrusted* router which can additionally collude with a subset of senders and receivers. The setting is as follows: there are n senders and n receivers, and each sender u wants to talk to a unique receiver $v = \pi(u)$ given by the routing permutation π. The NIAR scheme has a trusted setup that given a routing permutation π outputs encryption keys for senders, decryption keys for receivers, and a routing token for the router that secretly encrypts the routing permutation. In each time step, each sender uses its encryption key to encrypt a message. The router upon collecting all the n ciphertexts applies the routing token to permute them and convert them into n transformed ciphertexts, and delivers each receiver a single transformed ciphertext. Each receiver learns their message by decrypting the received ciphertext with their key. The computation of the permuted ciphertexts can be viewed as the router *obliviously* applying the routing permutation π, without learning π.

NIAR was shown to have numerous applications in [53] including realizing a non-interactive anonymous shuffle (NIAS) where n senders send encryptions of their private messages to an entity called *shuffler* who, upon decryption, learns a permutation of the senders' messages, without learning the mapping between each message and the corresponding sender. A NIAS scheme can be used to instantiate the *shuffle model* adopted in a line of work on distributed, differentially private mechanisms $[7,8,13,24,32,36]$. We can realize such a NIAS construction from NIAR by having the shuffler act on behalf of the NIAR router and all n receivers, as long as the underlying NIAR scheme provides meaningful security even when all the receivers collude with the router – termed as *receiver-insider* security by Shi and Wu [53].

Shi and Wu [53] give a NIAR scheme that satisfies receiver-insider security assuming the hardness of the decisional linear problem. Their scheme not only supports an *unbounded* number of time steps, but also has good efficiency features: each sender only needs to send $O_\lambda(1)$ bits per time step to encrypt a bit,[1]

---

[1] Throughout the paper, we use $O_\lambda(\cdot)$ to hide $\mathsf{poly}(\lambda)$ multiplicative factors where λ denotes the security parameter.

moreover, the sender and receiver keys are $O_\lambda(1)$ and the public parameters are $O_\lambda(n)$ in size. However, Shi and Wu's scheme suffers from two main drawbacks.

- First, their token size and router computation per time step are both *quadratic* in the number of users n, that is, $O_\lambda(n^2)$. We also stress that the quadratic router computation drawback pertains not only to the work of Shi and Wu [53]. As Gordon et al. [39] pointed out, even in classical, *interactive* anonymous routing constructions [22,23,42,54], the total router computation is typically $\Omega(nm)$ where n and m denote the number of clients and routers, respectively—therefore, in a peer-to-peer environment where the clients also act as routers, the total computation would be quadratic in n.
- Shi and Wu's construction is proven secure only under *static corruption*, i.e., the adversary must specify all corrupt senders and receivers upfront. This leaves open an interesting question whether we can construct a NIAR scheme that is secure against adaptive corruptions, i.e., when the adversary can dynamically decide which players to corrupt.

The status quo gives rise to the following natural questions:

1. *Can we have a NIAR scheme with* subquadratic *router computation?*
2. *Can we have a NIAR scheme secure against* adaptive *corruptions?*

1.1 Main Result

In this paper, we construct a new NIAR scheme that simultaneously answers both of the above questions affirmatively. In particular, our new NIAR construction achieves $\widetilde{O}_\lambda(n)$ router computation per time step where $\widetilde{O}_\lambda(\cdot)$ hides both $\mathrm{poly}(\lambda, \log n)$ factors; moreover, it achieves security in the presence of adaptive corruptions. In terms of assumptions, we need the existence of indistinguishability obfuscator (iO) [16,33,34,44,57] and one-way functions.

Theorem 1.1 (Informal: NIAR with subquadratic router computation). *Let λ be a security parameter. Let $n = n(\lambda)$ be the number of senders/receivers. Then, assuming the existence of indistinguishability obfuscator and one-way functions, there exists a NIAR scheme (in the receiver insider protection setting) that satisfies security under adaptive corruptions. Further, the asymptotical performance bounds are as follows:*

1. *the token size and router computation per time step is $\widetilde{O}_\lambda(n)$;*
2. *the per-sender communication and encryption time per bit of the message is $\widetilde{O}_\lambda(1)$;*
3. *each sender key is of length $\widetilde{O}_\lambda(1)$, each receiver key is of length $O_\lambda(1)$.*

Technical Highlights. The above result is obtained through a sequence of stepping stones.

- *Techniques for reasoning about a network of obfuscated programs.* First, we show how to achieve the desired efficiency, but under a relaxed notion of security, that is, assuming static corruptions and a selective, single-challenge setting. To achieve this, we use a gate-by-gate obfuscation approach. Specifically, we break up one big circuit into a network of smaller circuits to obfuscate, through the use of a quasilinear-sized routing network. In this network, each smaller circuit is of size polylogarithmic in the number of senders, thus helping us meet our efficiency goals even after obfuscating each of the smaller circuits. We also devise new techniques for reasoning about a network of obfuscated programs. Specifically, we propose a new notion of a Somewhere Statistically Unforgeable (SSU) signature which may be of independent interest, and we show how to construct SSU signatures from either iO + one-way functions, or from fully homomorphic encryption.

- *New techniques for upgrading from selective and static security to fully adaptive security.* Next, we want to remove the static corruption and selective-single-challenge restrictions. What is interesting is that the *standard complexity leveraging techniques completely fail* in our context due to our efficiency requirements. Therefore, we devise various new techniques for upgrading the security of the scheme, which eventually gets us the final result. An important consequence of our techniques is that we only incur a *polynomial security loss* when performing the upgrades. A key insight in our upgrade is to consider the following single-inversion restriction on the adversary: it must submit two permutations seperated by a single inversion in the two worlds, i.e., the two permutations are almost identical except for swapping the destinations of a pair of senders. We prove that security w.r.t. a single inversion is in fact equivalent to security w.r.t two arbitrary permutations.

Along the way, we also explore the relationship of different definitions of NIAR security, and get several additional results (see Sect. 1.2) which may be of independent interest.

1.2 Additional Results

Impossibility of Simulation Security for Adaptive Corruptions. Shi and Wu [53] showed that assuming static corruption, indistinguishability-based security is equivalent to simulation-based security for NIAR. We revisit the two definitional approaches in the context of adaptive corruption. Somewhat surprisingly, we show that indistinguishability-based security and simulation-based security are not equivalent in the context of adaptive corruption. In our paper, we focus on achieving indistinguishability-based security under adaptive corruptions, since we prove that the simulation-based notion is impossible for adaptive corruptions. However, our construction does satisfy simulation-based security under static corruptions due to the equivalence of the two notions under static corruptions.

Theorem 1.2 (Informal: Impossibility of simulation security for adaptive corruptions). *There does not exist a NIAR scheme (in the receiver insider protection setting) that achieves simulation-based security under adaptive corruptions (even with subexponential security assumptions).*

Adaptively Secure NIAR with $O(n^2)$ Router Computation from Standard Assumptions. Our techniques for upgrading from selective/static to adaptive security can be of independent interest. For example, we can apply the same upgrade techniques to the previous NIAR scheme by Shi and Wu [53], which gives an adaptively secure NIAR scheme with $O_\lambda(n^2)$ router computation from standard assumptions.

Corollary 1.3 (Informal: quadratic computation NIAR scheme assuming bilinear maps). *Assume standard bilinear map assumptions. There exists a NIAR scheme (in the receiver insider protection setting) that satisfies security under adaptive corruptions, and the asymptotical performance bounds are as follows:*

1. *the token size and router computation per time step is $O_\lambda(n^2)$;*
2. *the per-sender communication and encryption time per bit of the message is $\widetilde{O}_\lambda(1)$;*
3. *each sender key is of length $\widetilde{O}_\lambda(1)$, each receiver key is of length $O_\lambda(1)$.*

Static-to-Adaptive-Corruption Compiler for Other Settings. In Appendices H and I, we show that our static-to-adaptive-corruption compiler also works for non-interactive differentially anonymous router schemes as introduced by Bünz et al. [18], and NIAR schemes with sender insider protection as introduced by Bunn et al. [17].

1.3   Related Work and Open Questions

Techniques for Reasoning About a Network of Obfuscated Programs. To the best of our knowledge, the only other works that used the gate-by-gate obfuscation technique are the Jain and Jin [43] and Canetti et al. [21]. However, our techniques are fundamentally different in nature from the previous works. With Jain and Jin's techniques, the evaluator will need to spend $\mathsf{poly}(n)$ time to evaluate each obfuscated gate whereas for our construction, each obfuscated gate takes only $\mathsf{poly}(\lambda, \log n)$ time to evaluate, which is important for our efficiency claims. Our network of iOs idea also differs fundamentally from Canetti et al. [21], which builds leveled fully-homomorphic encryption scheme from iO. In our setting, there are *multiple* encrypters some of whom may be *corrupt*, whereas in the setting of Canetti et al. [21], there is a *single* encrypter who is assumed to be *honest*—so their setting is a lot easier.

Another line of works [5,12,20,43,46] constructs indistinguishability obfuscation for Turing machines and RAM programs. A natural question is whether obfuscating the routing network modelled as a Turing machine or RAM program can result in the required sub-quadratic routing efficiency. Unfortunately, prior approaches [5,12,20,43,46] suffer from evaluation time that is polynomial in the input length—in the case of the routing network, it would result in $\mathsf{poly}(n)$ runtime. Therefore, we cannot directly use existing iO for Turing machines or RAMs as a blackbox to achieve the desired efficiency. This is also another way to see why our results are non-trivial.

Additional Related Work. The recent work of Bünz, Hu, Matsuo and Shi [18] made an attempt at answering the question. They could not fully achieve the above goal, but did suggest a scheme with $O(\lambda^{\frac{1}{\gamma}} \cdot n^{1+\gamma})$ router computation for any $\gamma \in (0,1)$. Their scheme has two significant drawbacks. First, their subquadratic router computation comes at the price of relaxing the security definition to (ϵ, δ)-*differential privacy* [31]. In other words, their scheme ensures that the adversary's views are indistinguishable only for two *neighboring* routing permutations (whereas full security requires indistinguishability for any two routing permutations). Not only is differential privacy a significantly weaker security notion, it can also leads to additional complications in terms of managing the privacy budget. Second, their poly(λ) dependency is not a fixed one—to improve the dependence on the parameter n, we want to choose an arbitrarily small γ, however, this would significantly blow up the polynomial dependence on the security parameter λ.

Comparison with Concurrent Work. We stress that in this paper, we focus on constructing a NIAR scheme whose security is sufficient for instantiating a non-interactive anonymous shuffler. As mentioned earlier, the shuffler application is important in the context of distributed differentially private mechanisms in the so-called "shuffle model". For this application to work, we need the NIAR scheme to satisfy a notion of security called *receiver-insider protection*, that is, corrupt receivers (possibly colluding with the router and some corrupt senders) should not learn which honest senders have sent the message.

In comparison, the elegant concurrent work by Bunn, Kushilevitz, and Ostrovsky [17] solves the *dual* problem as ours. Their syntax is the same as ours, but their security guarantees are for the *sender insider protection* setting, and are not sufficient for instantiating the shuffler application. In particular, in the sender insider protection setting, corrupt senders (possibly colluding with the router and some corrupt receivers) should not learn which honest receivers are receiving their messages.

From a technical standpoint, *sender insider protection* is akin to Private Information Retrieval (PIR) [25,26]. In fact, if we allow quadratic router computation, a NIAR scheme with a sender insider protection is implied by PIR which is known from standard, polynomial-strength assumptions. By contrast, PIR does not directly lead to NIAR with *receiver*-insider security (even if router computation efficiency is a non-concern). In fact, NIAR with receiver insider protection is technically akin to *multi-client functional encryption (MCFE) with function-hiding security*. Technically, a NIAR scheme with receiver-insider protection implies a function-hiding MCFE for the selection functionality with the bounded, upfront key queries[2]. So far, the only known way to achieve receiver-insider security (i.e., the work by Shi and Wu [53]) also uses function-hiding,

---

[2] In this sense, our adaptive corruption result is also interesting in the context of function-hiding MCFE since how to get function-hiding MCFE under adaptive corruption was not known earlier. The recent work of Shi and Vanjani [52] showed a function-hiding MCFE scheme for inner-product computation under static corruption, relying on standard bilinear group assumptions.

multi-client functional encryption as a building block. For this reason, receiver insider protection is technically more challenging based on the existing knowledge and techniques.

Bunn et al. [17] did not discuss the issue of adaptive corruption in the context of their primitive. Interestingly, our work's static-to-adaptive compiler can also be applied to their sender insider protection setting.

Finally, from a technical perspective, Bunn et al.'s main idea is to use a rate-1 PIR scheme where they reuse the clients' PIR queries at the router over multiple sessions. To cut the router computation to quasi-linear, they also rely an oblivious routing network. In their paper, they construct and analyze a new oblivious routing network for this purpose. Alternatively, they can also directly use the same oblivious routing network that we use in our paper, which is directly borrowed from the earlier algorithms literature [6, 50].

Open Questions. Our feasibility results naturally raise several open questions for future work. Can we achieve subquadratic router computation from standard assumptions without using indistinguishability obfuscation? Can we construct a scheme with good concrete performance? Can we strengthen the security of the scheme to get full insider protection (as defined by [53]) from standard assumptions?

2   Technical Roadmap

To get the above result, we had to go through multiple intermediate steps, where we first construct schemes with relaxed security notions and then gradually lift them to full security. In this process, we develop several interesting new techniques and building blocks that may be of independent interest. At a very high level, our blueprint and techniques are summarized below:

2.1   Single Selective Challenge and Static Corruptions

Our first step is to construct a NIAR scheme with quasilinear router computation, but we relax the definitions and only require security when the adversary has to upfront commit to 1) all corrupt senders and receivers and 2) a single challenge time step along with the corresponding challenge plaintext vectors. In this step, we encounter multiple challenges.

Definitional Challenge for Single, Selective Security. First, it turns out that even defining a meaningful selective notion of security (in the static corruption setting) is non-trivial, because it is unclear how the non-challenge rounds should behave. This definition should satisfy two goals: first, the non-challenge rounds should contain no information about the permutation. This is because our techniques below crucially rely on this. Second, the definition should generalize naturally to full security. We discuss these issues in more detail in Appendix D.

Gate-by-Gate Obfuscation for Efficiency. Next, we consider how to get a NIAR scheme with quasilinear router computation under the relaxed security. To start with, it is helpful to imagine an inefficient scheme where the router's token is an obfuscated circuit that encodes the entire permutation π as well as encryption and decryption keys. Now, upon receiving the n incoming ciphertexts, the obfuscated circuit decrypts the incoming ciphertexts, applies the permutation π, and reencrypts the outcomes using each receiver's respective key. The intuition if we treat the obfuscation as a black box which completely hides its internals, then it should hide everything about π and the honest parties' plaintexts beyond what the corrupted parties are allowed to decrypt.

There are two problems with this approach. First, the seminal work of [9] showed that it is impossible to achieve an "virtual black-box" (VBB) obfuscation scheme that perfectly hides its internals. Second, even forgetting about the security analysis, all known obfuscation schemes have large polynomial blowup in the input size; there is no obfuscation scheme that even comes close to a quadratic blowup, let alone subquadratic. This clearly does not meet our efficiency requirement.

Our idea to solve this efficiency problem is to break up one big circuit into a network of smaller circuits to obfuscate, through the use of a quasilinear-sized routing network. In this routing network, each gate has only polylogarithmically sized inputs and outputs, and there are $O(n)$ such gates. Now, if we obfuscate each gate separately and create a network of obfuscated gates, then the total size of all obfuscated gates would be quasilinear.

It turns out that this idea would only work if the underlying routing network has a special "obliviousness" property, that is, a corrupt sender cannot infer from its own route the destinations of honest senders (see Definition B.1). Fortunately, we were able to get such a routing network using known techniques from the oblivious sorting literature (although the notion of "obliviousness" there is of a different nature).

New Techniques for Reasoning About a Network of Obfuscated Programs. We now turn to the challenges involved in reasoning about the security of "networked obfuscated programs". To solve these challenges, we develop techniques which we believe have potential to be useful in future applications. In particular, when the output of one obfuscated gate is fed into another, we want to ensure that the adversary does not tamper with the output in between. To achieve this, we would like to have each obfuscated gate authenticate its own outputs, and have the next obfuscated gate verify the authentication information before proceeding to the computation.

As mentioned before, it is well-known that VBB obfuscation is impossible, and it is only possible to achieve a much more restrictive notion called indistinguishability obfuscation (iO). iO achieves a much weaker notion of security: it only guarantees that obfuscations of two *functionally equivalent* programs are indistinguishable. As is evident from prior works, computationally secure primitives are generally incompatible with the functional equivalence requirements of iO. Therefore, we need to develop new iO-compatible techniques for authentication.

A New Notion of Somewhere-Statistically-Unforgeable Signatures. To this end, one of our contributions is to introduce a new building block called a *Somewhere Statistically Unforgeable (SSU)* signature scheme. Informally, in an SSU signature scheme, there are three modes to sample the signing and verification keys: *normal mode, punctured mode*, and the *binding mode*.

- Normal mode: the signing and verification keys behave same as in standard digital signatures.
- Punctured mode: the signing key is *punctured* w.r.t. a set of points X but the verification key is normal. Intuitively, this means that *no* valid signature can be computed using the signing algorithm for points outside of the set X when using the *punctured* signing key.
- Binding mode: here, both the signing and verification keys are *binding* w.r.t. a sets of points X. Intuitively, this means that, with overwhelming probability, *no* valid signatures exist for points outside of the set X w.r.t. a randomly sampled *binding* verification key. In other words, this means that statistical unforgeability holds *somewhere* (points outside the set X) in the binding mode.

SSU signatures can be used to sign/verify tuples of the form (t, m), where t denotes a round and m denotes a message. For a fixed round t^* and message m^*, we specifically focus on a set X_{t^*,m^*} which contains pairs (t, m) as follows:

- For all $t \neq t^*$, $(t, m) \in X_{t^*,m^*}$ for all $m \in \{0,1\}^{\mathsf{len}}$.
- For $t = t^*$, there is a single pair $(t^*, m^*) \in X_{t^*,m^*}$, and for all $m' \neq m^*$, $(t^*, m') \notin X_{t^*,m^*}$.

Intuitively, we can use this restriction to restrict the behavior of the network of circuits during the challenge round t^*. Note that both the round t^* and the message m^* must be fixed when generating the keys of the signature scheme, hence (among other reasons) why the techniques here achieve a selective notion of security for the NIAR scheme.

For our network of iO proof to go through, we need the following important property from the SSU signature. We require that the distributions to be computationally indistinguishable:

$$\begin{pmatrix} punctured\ signing\ key, \\ normal\ verification\ key \end{pmatrix} \equiv_c \begin{pmatrix} binding\ signing\ key, \\ binding\ verification\ key \end{pmatrix}$$

This property is critical when we perform a layer-by-layer hybrid argument in our proofs.

We stress that for technical reasons explained below, this property is important for our "networked obfuscated programs" techniques to work. This property also differentiates our SSU signature scheme from previous known puncturable signature schemes [11,40,41]. The main difference from previous puncturable signature schemes is that we need the two verification keys to be indistinguishable even in the presence of some signing key, whereas the previous schemes required that the two verification keys be indistinguishable in absence of any signing key.

We show how to construct such a SSU signature scheme from puncturable PRFs, single-point binding (SPB) signatures, and single-point binding (SPB) hash functions[3]. In Sect. 2.4, we provide some intuition of how we constuct such SSU signatures. We know how to construct puncturable PRFs from one-way functions [14,15,37,45], SPB signatures from one-way functions [40], and SPB hash function from indistinguishability obfuscation or leveled fully homomorphic encryption [40]. Plugging in these instantiations, we obtain the following theorem which may be of independent interest:

Theorem 2.1 (Informal: SSU signatures). *Assuming the existence of one-way functions and indistinguishability obfuscation, or assuming leveled fully homomorphic encryption, there exists a somewhere statistically unforgeable signature scheme for the family of sets X_{t^*,m^*} defined above.*

Network of iOs: Proof Highlight. We sketch our proof outline, focusing on the part that makes use of the aforementioned property of our SSU signature. In our construction, a ciphertext encrypts the message as well as the route it should be sent along. Imprecisely speaking then, each gate does the following: decrypts the incoming ciphertexts and verifies the input message signature (to authenticate the message) and route signature (to authenticate the route); and if valid, it performs the routing, encrypts the output messages (along with the routing information), and uses an output signing key to sign them. Our proof goes through a sequence of hybrids sketched below[4].

- First, starting from the real-world experiment, through a sequence of hybrids, we hard-wire the route signatures on corrupt wires (which are shared across all time steps)—we defer the details of these hybrids to the subsequent technical sections so we can focus on the part of proof that uses aforementioned property of our SSU signatures.
- Next, through a layer-by-layer hybrid sequence, we want to switch to a world in which for challenge time step t^*, honest and filler wires' ciphertexts and signatures (for both messages and routes) are hard-wired in the obfuscated gate and the obfuscated gate only accepts an incoming ciphertext that matches the hiredwired one. Except for the honest-to-corrupt wires in the last layers

---

[3] Informally speaking, SPB signatures have a special single-point binding property which states that it is possible to generate a special verification key w.r.t. a message m^* s.t. it only accepts a single signature for m^*. Similarly, SPB hash functions have a special single-point binding property which states that it is possible to generate a special hash key w.r.t. a message m^* s.t. no hash collisions exist on m^*.

[4] Our formal proof in the technical sections actually first proves single, selective-challenge, static security only for an adversary subject to the following restrictions: it must corrupt all receivers, and submit two permutations that differ by a single inversion. We prove that even this weaker version is sufficient for our upgrade all the way to full security under adaptive corruption.

which are hard-wired encryptions of the actual messages to be received by the corrupt receiver, for all other honest/filler wires, the hired-wired ciphertexts are encryptions of fillers. In this new world, the challenge ciphertexts for honest senders are also random encryptions of fillers; therefore, for the challenge time step t^*, the adversary's view contains no information about honest-to-honest and honest-to-corrupt routes, as well as honest-to-honest messages.

As described below, this layer-by-layer hybrid is where we critically need the aforementioned security property from the SSU signatures.

- Assuming that layer i's input verification key is already switched to binding, we can then switch layer i's output signing key to a punctured signing key by using iO security (since the binding verification key already ensure that the punctured messages will never pass through);

- Next, we make the following replacement by relying on the security of the SSU signature scheme:

  (punctured signing key: layer i, normal verification key: layer $i + 1$)
  $\implies$ (binding signing key: layer i,   binding verification key: layer $i + 1$)

- At this moment, by relying on iO security, we can hard-wire the ciphertexts and signatures for t^* on honest/filler wires, such that the obfuscated gate only accepts the input on the wire if it matches the hard-wired value.

2.2 Removing the Selective Challenge Restriction

Recall that the techniques above are able to achieve a limited notion of security, which we call "selective single-challenge" security. The selective notion requires that the adversary submit not just two permutations $\pi^{(0)}$ and $\pi^{(1)}$ upfront, but additionally commit to both a challenge round t^* and the set $\{x_{u,t^*}^{(0)}, x_{u,t^*}^{(1)}\}_{u \in \mathcal{H}_S}$ of challenge plaintexts to be used during round t^* for the honest senders $\mathcal{H}_S$, two for each honest sender. Recall that we use the SSU signature scheme above, and we puncture the signing and verification keys at round t^* and at the target plaintexts, which we hardcode in the obfuscated gates during the inner hybrids. This is essentially why we need this data upfront.

Standard Complexity Leveraging Fails. The standard tool to achieve such a transformation is complexity leveraging. Namely, to run the adaptive-query single-challenge with the selective scheme, we guess the values t^* and $\{x_{u,t^*}^{(0)}, x_{u,t^*}^{(1)}\}_{u \in \mathcal{H}_S}$ at the beginning of the experiment. This incurs a security loss proportional to 2^α, where α is the number of bits needed to represent t^* and $\{x_{u,t^*}^{(0)}, x_{u,t^*}^{(1)}\}_{u \in \mathcal{H}_S}$. We stress that due to our efficiency requirements, complexity leveraging fails completely even if we are willing to accept the (sub-)exponential loss in the security reduction. More specifically, α can be as large as $O(n)$, which means that the selective-secure NIAR scheme would have to be $2^{O(n)}$-secure for the reduction to be meaningful. Thus we must adopt a security parameter greater than n in all the underlying primitives, including the iO scheme, resulting in poly(n) cost and thus defeating our efficiency goals. This problem seems inherent with our techniques, because as explained above, we hardcode information about each $x_{u,t^*}^{(b)}$ for all honest u in the obfuscated gates.

Removing the Selective Challenge Restriction Through Equivalence to Single-Inversion Security. For removing the selective challenge restriction, our key insight is to define a single-inversion notion of NIAR security, and using single-inversion security as a stepping stone. In normal NIAR security (under static corruption), we want security to hold for two arbitrary admissible permutations. In single-inversion security, we consider two admissible permutations where only a pair of honest senders' destinations are swapped.

If we can prove equivalence to single-inversion security, then we can do the selective-query to adaptive-query upgrade for single-inversion security. In this case, a standard complexity leveraging argument has only polynomial security loss as explained below. Specifically, with single-inversion security, the reduction only needs to guess the challenge time step t^* and the challenge plaintexts of the two swapped honest users in the two worlds—without loss of generality, we can assume that each sender's plaintext is a single bit, since we can always get a multi-bit scheme by parallel composition of multiple single-bit schemes. Further, we assume that the reduction is given an upper bound on the p.p.t. adversary's running time. Therefore, the space of the guesses is polynomially bounded.

The remaining technicality is proving equivalence to single-inversion security. At first sight, it might be tempting to conclude that this is obvious, since given $\pi_{(0)}$ and $\pi_{(1)}$, we can always swap a pair of honest senders at a time to eventually transform $\pi_{(0)}$ to $\pi_{(1)}$. However, correctly implementing this idea is subtle. Specifically, we need any pair of adjacent hybrids to be not trivially distinguishable by the adversary, where the adversary is subject to the admissibility rules of the beginning and the end hybrids. We prove that given any beginning and end hybrids, we can indeed construct a sequence of intermediate hybrids, each time swapping a pair of honest senders' destinations and their messages, such that each pair of adjacent hybrids satisfy the aforementioned constraint.

2.3   Achieving Security for Adaptive Corruptions

So far, we have constructed a NIAR scheme that achieves security under static corruptions but adaptive queries. The last question remaining is how to upgrade the scheme to get security even under adaptive corruptions.

A first idea that comes to mind is to again attempt complexity leveraging. Again, unfortunately, due to our efficiency requirements, complexity leveraging completely does not work even if we are willing to suffer from (sub-)exponential losses in the reduction. Suppose that the reduction guesses which set of players the adversary will corrupt. Since there are 2^n possible guesses, for the parameters to work in the complexity leveraging, we must adopt a security parameter that is greater than n in the underlying iO scheme, which results in at least poly(n) blowup.

A New Compiler for Upgrading to Adaptive Corruptions. Instead of complexity leveraging, we construct a new compiler that compiles a NIAR scheme secure under static corruption to a NIAR scheme secure under adaptive corruption, with only polynomial loss in the security reduction.

The compiler is very simple: each sender will first encrypt their plaintext using a PRF that is secure against selective opening (which is implied by standard PRF security as shown by Abraham et al. [2]), before encrypting it using the NIAR scheme that is secure under static corruption. For proving that this construction secure against adaptive corruptions, we will go through the following key steps:

- First, suppose we want to prove single-inversion security when all the receivers are corrupt. Now, when the reduction receives the two permutations $\pi_{(0)}$ and $\pi_{(1)}$, it may assume that only the inverted pair of senders are honest. Therefore, in this case, security under adaptive corruption is the same as security under static corruption.
- Next, still assuming that all receivers are corrupt, we want to prove security under adaptive corruption for any two arbitrary permutations. For this step, we need to prove the equivalence of security under two arbitrary permutations and single-inversion security, but now for the scenario when the senders can be adaptively corrupted. The technicalities in this proof are similar to the counterpart for the static corruption case; however, the argument becomes somewhat more involved now that the senders can be adaptively corrupt.
- Finally, we show how to remove the assumption where the receivers must be all corrupted upfront, and allow the adversary to adaptively corrupt the receivers. This step will rely on the selective-opening security of the PRF which is implied by standard PRF security [2].

2.4   SSU Signature Construction

In this section, we give an informal overview of our SSU signature construction. Our scheme is inspired by the well-known Merkle signature scheme [48] which can upgrade a one-time signature scheme such as Lamport signatures [47] to a multi-use signature. Recall that the Merkle signature construction works as follows:

- There is a signing key and verification key pair (for a one-time signature scheme) at every node u in the tree denoted $(\mathsf{sk}_u, \mathsf{vk}_u)$, and the pair $(\mathsf{sk}_u, \mathsf{vk}_u)$ are sampled using $\mathsf{PRF}_k(u)$. The final verification key is $\mathsf{vk}_{\mathrm{root}}$, and the secret signing key is $(k, \mathsf{sk}_{\mathrm{root}})$.
- To sign a new message m, pick the next unused leaf, and consider the path from the root to the leaf. Let $\{\mathsf{vk}_0 = \mathsf{vk}_{\mathrm{root}}, \mathsf{vk}_1, \mathsf{vk}_2, \ldots, \mathsf{vk}_d\}$ be the verification keys corresponding to nodes on the path from the root to the selected leaf, and let $\{\mathsf{vk}_1', \ldots, \mathsf{vk}_d'\}$ denote the verification keys for the siblings of these nodes. The signer uses sk_0 to sign $H(\mathsf{vk}_1, \mathsf{vk}_1')$, uses sk_1 to sign $H(\mathsf{vk}_2, \mathsf{vk}_2')$, and so on where we use $H(\cdot)$ to denote a hash function. Finally, use sk_d to sign hash of the actual message $H(m)$. The resulting signature contains all $d+1$ signatures as well as $\{\mathsf{vk}_1, \mathsf{vk}_1', \ldots, \mathsf{vk}_d, \mathsf{vk}_d'\}$.

- Verification is done in the most natural manner.

Recall that we want to construct an SSU signature scheme for the set X_{t^*, m^*}, such that in the binding mode, the only message that can be signed for the time step t^* is m^*. We will modify the Merkle signature scheme as follows:

- Imagine that each leaf of the tree corresponds to some time step t. To sign a message x under the time step t, the signer will use the leaf node corresponding to t.
- We use a punctured PRF instead of a standard PRF to generate the $(\mathsf{vk}_u, \mathsf{sk}_u)$ pair for every tree node u.
- Instead of an arbitrary one-time signature scheme, we want to use a one-time signature scheme with a single-point binding (SPB) property, that is, there is a binding setup which takes a message m^* as input, and generates a verification key vk^* such that the only message that can pass verification is m^*; and moreover, a computationally bounded adversary cannot tell that vk^* is generated using the binding mode.
- Instead of using a normal hash function $H(\cdot)$, we will use a single-point binding (SPB) hash function. We will create one SPB hash instance per level of the tree, and include the hash keys in both the signing and verification keys. An SPB hash function has a binding setup mode that takes m^* as input and generates a binding hash key hk^* such that m^* does not have any collision; moreover, a computationally bounded adversary cannot tell that hk^* is a binding key.

Punctured Key. To puncture the signing key such that one can sign only x^* at t^*, puncture the PRF key such that one is unable to compute the signing and verification key pairs on the path from the root to the leaf t^*. Additionally, we can use the unpunctured key to pre-sign the message m^* and t^* and include this signature in the punctured signing key.

Binding Key. For the binding-mode setup, we want to generate a binding signing key and a binding verification key such that for t^*, only the message x^* has a unique valid signature. The binding mode also punctures the PRF key in the same way as the punctured mode. However, for the path from the root to the leaf at t^*, we no longer generate the $(\mathsf{sk}_u, \mathsf{vk}_u)$ honestly by using the unpunctured PRF key. Instead, we will call the binding setup of the SPB signatures and SPB hashes. Specifically, on the path from the root to the leaf t^*, we will run the binding setup algorithms of the SPB signature scheme such that at the leaf t^*, we can only sign hash of $t^* \| x^*$; and at any non-leaf node on the path, we can only sign a unique hash (of the two children's verification keys). Further, we run the binding setup algorithms of the SPB hash functions, such that at level i of the tree, the pair $(\mathsf{vk}_i, \mathsf{vk}_i')$ to be hashed has no collisions, where $(\mathsf{vk}_i, \mathsf{vk}_i')$ are verification keys corresponding to the level-i node on the path to leaf t^* (recall that vk_i is generated using the binding mode of the SPB signature), and its sibling. After we generate all these keys, we again pre-sign (t^*, x^*) using these keys.

As a result, the binding verification key is $\mathsf{vk_{root}}$ and the hash keys which are generated using the binding mode of the SPB signature and hash schemes; and the binding signing key is the punctured PRF key, as well as the pre-signed signature for (t^*, m^*), and the binding hash keys.

Formal Description and Proofs. We defer the formal description of the SSU signature and its proofs to Sect. 5 and Appendix C.

Organization of Rest of the Paper. In Sect. 3, we define NIAR, and in Sect. 4 and Appendix B, we present preliminaries. In Sect. 5, we define SSU signatures and in Appendix C, we present a construction along with proofs of correctness and security. In Sect. 6, we construct a NIAR scheme secure against a static and all-receiver-corrupting adversary and present the security proof in Appendices D and E. In Appendix F, we present a compiler that transforms the above NIAR scheme to one with full security, i.e., removing the static and all-receiver-corrupting restrictions on the adversary. In Appendices H and I, we show that this compiler also works for differentially anonymous and sender insider protection settings. In Appendix G, we present the impossibility of NIAR simulation security for adaptive corruptions. All appendices are available in the online full version: https://eprint.iacr.org/2022/1395.

3   Definitions for NIAR

In this section, we define the syntax and security for NIAR, focusing on the strongest definition of full security against adaptive corruptions.

3.1   Syntax

We begin with the syntax. A Non-Interactive Anonymous Router (NIAR) is a cryptographic scheme consisting of the following, possibly randomized algorithms:

- $(\{\mathsf{ek}_u\}_{u\in[n]}, \{\mathsf{rk}_u\}_{u\in[n]}, \mathsf{tk}) \leftarrow \mathbf{Setup}(1^\lambda, \mathsf{len}, n, \pi)$: the trusted **Setup** algorithm takes the security parameter 1^λ, the length of the messages len, the number of senders/receivers n, and a permuation π. The algorithm outputs a sender key for each sender denoted $\{\mathsf{ek}_u\}_{u\in[n]}$, a receiver key for each receiver denoted $\{\mathsf{rk}_u\}_{u\in[n]}$, and a token for the router denoted tk.
- $\mathsf{ct}_{u,t} \leftarrow \mathbf{Enc}(\mathsf{ek}_u, x_{u,t}, t)$: sender u uses its sender key ek_u to encrypt the message $x_{u,t} \in \{0,1\}^{\mathsf{len}}$ where t denotes the current time step. The **Enc** algorithm produces a ciphertext $\mathsf{ct}_{u,t}$.
- $(\mathsf{ct}'_{1,t}, \mathsf{ct}'_{2,t}, \dots, \mathsf{ct}'_{n,t}) \leftarrow \mathbf{Rte}(\mathsf{tk}, \mathsf{ct}_{1,t}, \mathsf{ct}_{2,t}, \dots, \mathsf{ct}_{n,t})$: the routing algorithm **Rte** takes pk and its token tk (which encodes some permutation π), and n ciphertexts received from the n senders denoted $\mathsf{ct}_{1,t}, \mathsf{ct}_{2,t}, \dots, \mathsf{ct}_{n,t}$, and produces *transformed ciphertexts* $\mathsf{ct}'_{1,t}, \mathsf{ct}'_{2,t}, \dots, \mathsf{ct}'_{n,t}$ where $\mathsf{ct}'_{u,t}$ is destined for the receiver $u \in [n]$.

- $x \leftarrow \mathbf{Dec}(\mathsf{rk}_u, \mathsf{ct}'_{u,t}, t)$: the decryption algorithm $\mathbf{Dec}$ takes a receiver key rk_u, a transformed ciphertext $\mathsf{ct}'_{u,t}$, a time step t, and outputs a message x.

Correctness of NIAR. Correctness requires that with probability 1, the following holds for any $\lambda, \mathsf{len} \in \mathbb{N}$, any $(x_1, x_2, \ldots, x_n) \in \{0,1\}^{\mathsf{len} \cdot n}$, and any t: let $(\{\mathsf{ek}_u\}_{u \in [n]}, \{\mathsf{rk}_u\}_{u \in [n]}, \mathsf{tk}) \leftarrow \mathbf{Setup}(1^\lambda, \mathsf{len}, n, \pi)$, let $\mathsf{ct}_{u,t} \leftarrow \mathbf{Enc}(\mathsf{ek}_u, x_u, t)$ for $u \in [n]$, let $(\mathsf{ct}'_{1,t}, \mathsf{ct}'_{2,t}, \ldots, \mathsf{ct}'_{n,t}) \leftarrow \mathbf{Rte}(\mathsf{tk}, \mathsf{ct}_{1,t}, \mathsf{ct}_{2,t}, \ldots, \mathsf{ct}_{n,t})$, and let $x'_u \leftarrow \mathbf{Dec}(\mathsf{rk}_u, \mathsf{ct}'_{u,t}, t)$ for $u \in [n]$; it must be that $x'_{\pi(u)} = x_u$ for every $u \in [n]$.

3.2 NIAR Full Security

In this section, we present a security notion for NIAR against a very strong adversary. In particular, we allow such an adversary to (a) adaptively corrupt the set of senders and receivers, and (b) adaptively ask for encryptions of chosen plaintext under the senders' keys that are not yet corrupted. Our security definition is a strict generalization of the "receiver-insider corruption" notion introduced by Shi and Wu [53] which captured only static corruptions of users.

We formalize our definition via the experiment $\mathsf{NIARFull}^{b,\mathcal{A}}$ which is parametrized by some challenge bit b and a **stateful** non-uniform p.p.t. adversary $\mathcal{A}$. At the beginning of the experiment, adversary $\mathcal{A}$ submits two challenge permutations $\pi^{(0)}$ and $\pi^{(1)}$ over $[n]$ for its choice of n. At any time in the experiment, the adversary can choose to corrupt a sender or receiver, and it will receive the secret key for the newly corrupted player. The adversary receives tk, and then in each time step, it can submit two plaintext vectors $\{x_{u,t}^{(0)}, x_{u,t}^{(1)}\}_{u \in \mathcal{H}_S}$ for the set of currently honest senders $\mathcal{H}_S$. The challenger will encrypt the plaintexts indexed by $b \in \{0,1\}$, and at the end of the experiment, the adversary's job is to distinguish which world b the challenger is in. The adversary must be subject to a set of admissibility rules such that it cannot trivially distinguish which world it is in.

More formally, our full NIAR security game is defined as follows, where $\mathsf{Cor}(\cdot)$ is the following oracle: upon receiving a sender or receiver identity,

- return its corresponding secret key;
- in case the newly corrupted player is a sender, additionally return all the historical random coins consumed by the $\mathbf{Enc}$ algorithm during the previous time steps;
- update the honest sender set $\mathcal{H}_S$ and honest receiver set $\mathcal{H}_R$ accordingly.

NIAR Full Security Experiment $\mathsf{NIARFull}^{b,\mathcal{A}}(1^\lambda)$.

1. $(n, \mathsf{len}, \pi^{(0)}, \pi^{(1)}) \leftarrow \mathcal{A}(1^\lambda)$.
2. $\mathcal{H}_S = [n]$, $\mathcal{H}_R = [n]$.
3. $(\{\mathsf{ek}_u\}_{u \in [n]}, \{\mathsf{rk}_u\}_{u \in [n]}, \mathsf{tk}) \leftarrow \mathbf{Setup}(1^\lambda, \mathsf{len}, n, \pi^{(b)})$.
4. For $t = 1, 2, \ldots$:
   - if $t = 1$: $\{x_{u,t}^{(0)}, x_{u,t}^{(1)}\}_{u \in \mathcal{H}_S} \leftarrow \mathcal{A}^{\mathsf{Cor}(\cdot)}(\mathsf{tk})$;
     else $\{x_{u,t}^{(0)}, x_{u,t}^{(1)}\}_{u \in \mathcal{H}_S} \leftarrow \mathcal{A}^{\mathsf{Cor}(\cdot)}(\{CT_{u,t-1}\}_{u \in \mathcal{H}_S})$.

- for all $u \in \mathcal{H}_S$, $\mathsf{CT}_{u,t} \leftarrow \mathbf{Enc}(\mathsf{ek}_u, x_{u,t}^{(b)}, t)$.
5. At any time, $\mathcal{A}$ may halt and output an arbitrary function of its view. The experiment then also halts and returns the output of $\mathcal{A}$.

In the above definition, if the adversary wants to specify an initially corrupt set, it can simply make calls to the corruption oracle $\mathsf{Cor}(\cdot)$ at the beginning of $t = 1$. Therefore, without loss of generality, we may assume that the initially corrupt set before the challenger calls **Setup** is empty.

Admissibility. We state some admissibility rules on the adversary to make sure that the adversary cannot trivially distinguish whether it is in world $b = 0$ or $b = 1$. Our admissibility rule corresponds to the "receiver-insider protection" version of Shi and Wu [53], which is sufficient for building a non-interactive anonymous shuffler. Basically, we assume that senders know their receivers but receivers do not know their senders. Therefore, if the adversary corrupts some senders, the adversary will know the corrupt senders' receivers. We remark that Shi and Wu [53] additionally described a "full insider protection" notion where it is assumed that neither senders nor receivers know who they are paired with. Their "full insider protection" construction requires polynomial in n evaluation time and uses indistinguishable obfuscation and bilinear group assumptions [53]. It remains an open question how to reduce the evaluation time for the "full insider protection" version.

Henceforth, if a player remains honest at the end of the execution, we say that it is *eventually honest*; otherwise we say that it is *eventually corrupt*. We say that $\mathcal{A}$ is *admissible* iff with probability 1, the following holds where $\mathcal{H}_S$ and $\mathcal{H}_R$ refer to the eventually honest sender and receiver set, and define $\mathcal{K}_R = [n] \setminus \mathcal{H}_R, \mathcal{K}_S = [n] \setminus \mathcal{H}_S$ to be the eventually corrupt sender and receiver sets:

1. For all eventually corrupt senders $u \in \mathcal{K}_S$, $\pi^{(0)}(u) = \pi^{(1)}(u)$.
2. For any eventually corrupt sender $u \in \mathcal{K}_S$, for any t in which u was not corrupt yet, $x_{u,t}^{(0)} = x_{u,t}^{(1)}$. In other words, here we require that in the two alternate worlds $b = 0$ or $b = 1$, every eventually corrupt sender should be sending the same message in all rounds before it was corrupted.
3. For all rounds t, and for any $v \in \mathcal{K}_R \cap \pi^{(0)}(\mathcal{H}_S) = \mathcal{K}_R \cap \pi^{(1)}(\mathcal{H}_S)$, $x_{u_0,t}^{(0)} = x_{u_1,t}^{(1)}$ where for $b \in \{0,1\}$, $u_b := (\pi^{(b)})^{-1}(v)$. In other words, here we require that in the two alternate worlds $b = 0$ or 1, every eventually corrupt receiver receiving from an eventually honest sender must receive the same message in all rounds.

Definition 3.1 (NIAR full security). We say that a NIAR scheme is fully secure iff for any non-uniform p.p.t. *admissible* $\mathcal{A}$, its views in the two experiments $\mathsf{NIARFull}^{0,\mathcal{A}}(1^\lambda)$ and $\mathsf{NIARFull}^{1,\mathcal{A}}(1^\lambda)$ are computationally indistinguishable.

4   Preliminaries

Whenever we refer to an adversary in the paper henceforth, we implicitly mean it to be a *non-uniform* adversary. We discuss the notations next and defer the additional preliminaries to Appendix B.

4.1   Notations

We say that a function $\mathsf{negl} : \mathbb{N} \to \mathbb{R}$ is negligible, if for every constant $c > 0$ and for all sufficiently large $\lambda \in \mathbb{N}$ we have $\mathsf{negl}(\lambda) < \lambda^{-c}$. Two distribution ensembles $\{X_0^\lambda\}_\lambda$ and $\{X_1^\lambda\}_\lambda$ are computationally indistinguishable if for every p.p.t. adversary $\mathcal{A}$, there exists a negligible function $\mathsf{negl}(\cdot)$ such that for all $\lambda \in \mathbb{N}$, $|\Pr[x \leftarrow X_0^\lambda : \mathcal{A}(x) = 0] - \Pr[x \leftarrow X_1^\lambda : \mathcal{A}(x) = 0]| \leq \mathsf{negl}(\lambda)$. We use '$\_$' to denote that a value is irrelevant. For instance, in $(a, \_, c)$ the second value is irrelevant and can be anything. Often times, we use a short hand $\{y_i : i \in [n]\}$ to denote an ordered sequence $(y_1, \ldots, y_n)$. For instance, $\{y_i : i \in [n]\} \leftarrow f(t, \{x_i : i \in [n]\})$ means $(y_1, \ldots, y_n) \leftarrow f(t, x_1, \ldots, x_n)$.

5   Somewhere Statistically Unforgeable (SSU) Signatures

In this section, we define SSU signatures and provide an informal construction.

5.1   Definition

We consider an SSU signature scheme where the signing and verification algorithms both take a counter t (i.e., time step) in addition to the message x to be signed. We refer to t as the *round*. Specifically, an SSU signature scheme contains the following algorithms:

- $(\mathsf{sk}, \mathsf{vk}, \mathsf{pp}) \leftarrow \mathbf{Setup}(1^\lambda, \mathsf{tlen}, \mathsf{len})$: takes as input the security parameter 1^λ, the length of the round $\mathsf{tlen} \geq 0$, the length of the messages to be signed $\mathsf{len} > 0$, and outputs a signing key sk, a verification key vk, and a public parameter pp.
- $\sigma \leftarrow \mathbf{Sign}(\mathsf{pp}, \mathsf{sk}, t, x)$: a *deterministic* algorithm that takes as input a public parameter pp, a singing key sk, along with a round $t \in \{0, 1\}^{\mathsf{tlen}}$ ($t = \bot$ in case $\mathsf{tlen} = 0$) and a message $x \in \{0, 1\}^{\mathsf{len}}$ and outputs a signature σ for x w.r.t. t.
- $(0 \text{ or } 1) \leftarrow \mathbf{Vf}(\mathsf{pp}, \mathsf{vk}, t, x, \sigma)$: takes as input a public paramter pp, a verification key vk, a round t, a message x, and a signature σ, and outputs either 1 for accept or 0 for reject.
- $(\mathsf{sk}, \tilde{\mathsf{sk}}, \mathsf{vk}, \mathsf{pp}) \leftarrow \mathbf{PuncturedSetup}(1^\lambda, \mathsf{tlen}, \mathsf{len}, t^*, x^*)$: takes as input the security parameter 1^λ, the length of the round tlen, the length of the messages to be signed len, a round $t^* \in \{0, 1\}^{\mathsf{tlen}}$ ($t^* = \bot$ in case $\mathsf{tlen} = 0$) and a message $x^* \in \{0, 1\}^{\mathsf{len}}$, and outputs a signing key sk, a punctured signing key $\tilde{\mathsf{sk}}$, a verification key vk, and a public paramter pp.

- $(\mathsf{sk}^*, \mathsf{vk}^*, \mathsf{pp}^*) \leftarrow \mathbf{BindingSetup}(1^\lambda, \mathsf{tlen}, \mathsf{len}, t^*, x^*)$: takes as input the security parameter 1^λ, the length of the round tlen, the length of the messages to be signed len, a round $t^* \in \{0,1\}^{\mathsf{tlen}}$ ($t^* = \bot$ in case $\mathsf{tlen} = 0$) and message $x^* \in \{0,1\}^{\mathsf{len}}$, and outputs a binding signing key sk^*, a binding verification key vk^*, and a binding public paramter pp^*.
- $\sigma \leftarrow \mathbf{PSign}(\mathsf{pp}, \widetilde{\mathsf{sk}}, t, x)$: a *deterministic* algorithm that takes as input a public paramter pp, a punctured signing key $\widetilde{\mathsf{sk}}$ generated by $\mathbf{PuncturedSetup}$, a round t and a message x, and outputs a signature σ for x w.r.t. t.

Correctness of SSU signature. An SSU signature is said to be correct iff the following holds,

- For all $\lambda, \mathsf{len}, \mathsf{tlen} \in \mathbb{N}$, $t \in \{0,1\}^{\mathsf{tlen}}$, $x \in \{0,1\}^{\mathsf{len}}$,

$$\Pr\left[\begin{array}{c}(\mathsf{sk}, \mathsf{vk}, \mathsf{pp}) \leftarrow \mathbf{Setup}(1^\lambda, \mathsf{tlen}, \mathsf{len}) \\ \sigma \leftarrow \mathbf{Sign}(\mathsf{pp}, \mathsf{sk}, t, x)\end{array} : \mathbf{Vf}(\mathsf{pp}, \mathsf{vk}, t, x, \sigma) = 1\right] = 1.$$

- For all $\lambda, \mathsf{len}, \mathsf{tlen} \in \mathbb{N}$, $t^*, t \in \{0,1\}^{\mathsf{tlen}}$, $x^*, x \in \{0,1\}^{\mathsf{len}}$ such that it is *not* the case that $t = t^*$ and $x \neq x^*$,

$$\Pr\left[\begin{array}{c}(\mathsf{sk}, \widetilde{\mathsf{sk}}, \mathsf{vk}, \mathsf{pp}) \leftarrow \mathbf{PuncturedSetup}(1^\lambda, \mathsf{tlen}, \mathsf{len}, t^*, x^*): \\ \mathbf{Sign}(\mathsf{pp}, \mathsf{sk}, t, x) = \mathbf{PSign}(\mathsf{pp}, \widetilde{\mathsf{sk}}, t, x)\end{array}\right] = 1.$$

Definition 5.1 (Security for SSU Signatures). An SSU signature is said to be secure if it has the following properties:

- **Identical distribution of normal keys output by Setup and PuncturedSetup.** For any λ, $\mathsf{len}, \mathsf{tlen} \in \mathbb{N}$, any $t^* \in \{0,1\}^{\mathsf{tlen}}$, any $x^* \in \{0,1\}^{\mathsf{len}}$, we have the following where $\equiv$ denotes identical distribution:

$$\{(\mathsf{sk}, \mathsf{vk}, \mathsf{pp}) \leftarrow \mathbf{Setup}(1^\lambda, \mathsf{tlen}, \mathsf{len}) : \text{output } (\mathsf{sk}, \mathsf{vk}, \mathsf{pp})\}$$
$$\equiv \{(\mathsf{sk}, \widetilde{\mathsf{sk}}, \mathsf{vk}, \mathsf{pp}) \leftarrow \mathbf{PuncturedSetup}(1^\lambda, \mathsf{tlen}, \mathsf{len}, t^*, x^*) : \text{output } (\mathsf{sk}, \mathsf{vk}, \mathsf{pp})\}$$

- **Indistinguishability of punctured and binding setups.** For any len and tlen that are polynomially bounded by λ, any $t^* \in \{0,1\}^{\mathsf{tlen}}$, any $x^* \in \{0,1\}^{\mathsf{len}}$, we have the following where $\approx$ denotes computational indistinguishability:

$$\{(\mathsf{sk}, \widetilde{\mathsf{sk}}, \mathsf{vk}, \mathsf{pp}) \leftarrow \mathbf{PuncturedSetup}(1^\lambda, \mathsf{tlen}, \mathsf{len}, t^*, x^*) : \text{output } (\widetilde{\mathsf{sk}}, \mathsf{vk}, \mathsf{pp})\}$$
$$\approx \{(\mathsf{sk}^*, \mathsf{vk}^*, \mathsf{pp}^*) \leftarrow \mathbf{BindingSetup}(1^\lambda, \mathsf{tlen}, \mathsf{len}, t^*, x^*) : \text{output } (\mathsf{sk}^*, \mathsf{vk}^*, \mathsf{pp}^*)\}$$

- **Statistical unforgeability at (t^*, x^*).** For any $\mathsf{len}, \mathsf{tlen}$ that are polynomially bounded in λ, there exists a negligible function $\mathsf{negl}(\cdot)$, such that for any $t^* \in \{0,1\}^{\mathsf{tlen}}$, $x^* \in \{0,1\}^{\mathsf{len}}$, for any λ,

$$\Pr\left[\begin{array}{c}(\mathsf{sk}^*, \mathsf{vk}^*, \mathsf{pp}^*) \leftarrow \mathbf{BindingSetup}(1^\lambda, \mathsf{tlen}, \mathsf{len}, t^*, x^*): \\ \exists\, (\sigma, x) \text{ s.t. } x \neq x^* \wedge \mathbf{Vf}(\mathsf{pp}^*, \mathsf{vk}^*, t^*, x, \sigma) = 1\end{array}\right] \leq \mathsf{negl}(\lambda),$$

$$\Pr\left[\begin{array}{c}(\mathsf{sk}^*, \mathsf{vk}^*, \mathsf{pp}^*) \leftarrow \mathbf{BindingSetup}(1^\lambda, \mathsf{tlen}, \mathsf{len}, t^*, x^*): \\ \exists\, \sigma \neq \mathbf{PSign}(\mathsf{pp}^*, \mathsf{sk}^*, t^*, x^*) \text{ s.t. } \mathbf{Vf}(\mathsf{pp}^*, \mathsf{vk}^*, t^*, x^*, \sigma) = 1\end{array}\right] \leq \mathsf{negl}(\lambda).$$

5.2 SSU Signatures: Informal Construction

Let $\Sigma = (\Sigma.\mathbf{Gen}, \Sigma.\mathbf{Sign}, \Sigma.\mathbf{Vf}, \Sigma.\mathbf{GenBind})$ be a single-point binding (SPB) signature scheme. Let $\mathsf{H} = (\mathsf{H}.\mathbf{Gen}, \mathsf{H}.\mathbf{Hash}, \mathsf{H}.\mathbf{GenBind})$ be a single-point binding (SPB) hash function. Let PPRF be a puncturable PRF. The SSU signature scheme is based on a binary tree of SPB signatures intuitively described in Figs. 1a and 1b. We present the formal construction in Appendix C.

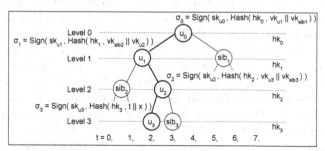

(a) Sign and PuncturedSetup. For each node u_i, $(\mathsf{sk}_{u_i}, \mathsf{vk}_{u_i})$ is generated using $\Sigma.\mathbf{Gen}$ with $\mathsf{PPRF}.\mathsf{Eval}(K, u_i)$ as the randomness seed. A signature σ on message x for $t = 2$ consists of $\sigma := ((\sigma_0, \mathsf{vk}_{u_1}, \mathsf{vk}_{\mathsf{sib}_1}), (\sigma_1, vk_{u_2}, \mathsf{vk}_{\mathsf{sib}_2}), (\sigma_2, \mathsf{vk}_{u_3}, \mathsf{vk}_{\mathsf{sib}_3}), \sigma_3)$.
PuncturedSetup at the point (t, x) outputs a punctured key $\tilde{\mathsf{sk}}$ that consists of the PPRF key punctured at the set $\{u_0, u_1, u_2, u_3\}$ and σ.

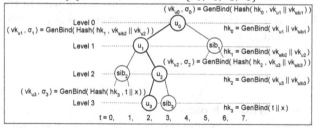

(b) BindingSetup. For nodes $u_i \in \{u_0, u_1, u_2, u_3\}$, $(\mathsf{vk}_{u_i}, \sigma_u)$ is generated using $\Sigma.\mathbf{GenBind}$ with $\mathsf{PPRF}.\mathsf{Eval}(K, u_i)$ as the randomness seed. **BindingSetup** at the point (t, x) outputs a binding key sk^* that consists of the PPRF key punctured at the set $\{u_0, u_1, u_2, u_3\}$ and a signature σ on message x for $t = 2$, where
$$\sigma := ((\sigma_0, \mathsf{vk}_{u_1}, \mathsf{vk}_{\mathsf{sib}_1}), (\sigma_1, vk_{u_2}, \mathsf{vk}_{\mathsf{sib}_2}), (\sigma_2, \mathsf{vk}_{u_3}, \mathsf{vk}_{\mathsf{sib}_3}), \sigma_3).$$

Fig. 1. SSU Signatures informal construction

6 NIAR for a Static and All-Receiver-Corrupting Adversary

In this section, we first introduce a basic NIAR scheme which we prove secure under an adversary who is restricted to make all corruption queries upfront, and moreover, it must always corrupt all receivers—we call such an adversary a static, all-receiver-corrupting adversary. This is same as the adversary in the full security game in Definition 3.1 except with the aforementioned restrictions. For sake of completeness, we define this version of security in Definition A.1.

Later in Appendix F, we give a compiler that transforms the scheme in this section to one with full security, i.e., removing the static and all-receiver-corrupting restrictions on the adversary.

Notation. To describe our construction more formally, it will be helpful to introduce some notation for the routing network. Recall that a routing network for n senders and n receivers is a layered directed acyclic graph that has $O(\log n)$ layers numbered from $0, 1, \ldots, L$. Each sender $u \in [n]$ is assigned to the $(2u-1)$-th wire in the input layer (i.e., layer-0), and each receiver $v \in [n]$ is assigned to the $(2v-1)$-th wire in the output layer (i.e., layer-L). Let G be the number of gates contained in each of the $L-1$ intermediate layers. There are $(L-1) \cdot G$ gates overall, and we refer to the g-th gate in the ℓ-th layer by the tuple $(\ell, g) \in [L-1] \times [G]$. Let $W = O(\log^2 \lambda)$ be the number of incoming and outgoing wires in each gate. Overall, there are $L \times [2n]$ wires where we index the i-th wire in the ℓ-th layer by the tuple $(\ell, i) \in [L] \times [2n]$.[5] We refer to the W incoming wires of every gate (ℓ, g) by the set $\mathsf{Input}_{(\ell, g)} \subseteq [2n]$ and the W outgoing wires by the set $\mathsf{Output}_{(\ell, g)} \subseteq [2n]$. In other words, the wires coming into gate (ℓ, g) are the set $\{(\ell, w)\}_{w \in \mathsf{Input}_{(\ell, g)}}$, and the wires outgoing from gate (ℓ, g) are the set $\{(\ell+1, w)\}_{w \in \mathsf{Output}_{(\ell, g)}}$. Finally, recall that a route rte_u from sender u to receiver v is a sequence of wires $(j_1, \ldots, j_L)$ where j_ℓ is a wire in the ℓ-th layer for all $\ell \in [L]$. Based on the description of routing network, also recall that $j_1 = 2u - 1 \in [2n]$ and $j_L = 2v - 1 \in [2n]$.

6.1   Construction

Simplifying assumption. Throughout this section, we shall assume that the message length $\mathsf{len} = 1$. This assumption is without loss of generality, since we can always parallel-compose multiple NIAR schemes where $\mathsf{len} = 1$ to get a NIAR scheme for $\mathsf{len} > 1$.

We now describe our basic NIAR scheme in detail.

Keys associated with wires. In our construction, each wire (ℓ, i) in the routing network will have the following associated with it:

- A PRF key $k_{(\ell, i)}$, which will be used to encrypt and decrypt the (signed) message along with its routing information on the wire;
- A message signing key tuple $(\mathsf{mpp}_{(\ell, i)}, \mathsf{msk}_{(\ell, i)}, \mathsf{mvk}_{(\ell, i)})$, which will later be used by the corresponding sender or obfuscated gate to sign the message to be sent to the wire;

---

[5] To be more precise there are $c \cdot n$ wires in each layer for constant $c \geq 2$, but for simplicity we assume $c = 2$ as this is achieved by our proposed instantiation.

– A route signing key tuple $(\mathsf{rpp}_{(\ell,i)}, \mathsf{rsk}_{(\ell,i)}, \mathsf{rvk}_{(\ell,i)})$, which will be used by the **Setup** algorithm to sign the routes and by the obfuscated gates to verify the routes before performing the routing.

Hardcoded values. $\mathsf{Gate}_{(\ell,g)}$ has hardcoded the following values:

– For each wire $i \in \mathsf{Input}_{(\ell,g)}$ in layer ℓ: $k_{(\ell,i)}, \mathsf{mpp}_{(\ell,i)}, \mathsf{mvk}_{(\ell,i)}, \mathsf{rpp}_{(\ell,i)}, \mathsf{rvk}_{(\ell,i)}$.

– For each wire $i \in \mathsf{Output}_{(\ell,g)}$ in layer $\ell+1$: $k_{(\ell+1,i)}, \mathsf{mpp}_{(\ell+1,i)}, \mathsf{msk}_{(\ell+1,i)}$.

Procedure. $\mathsf{Gate}_{(\ell,g)}$ takes as input a round t and a set of ciphertexts $\{\mathsf{CT}_{(\ell,i)} : i \in \mathsf{Input}_{(\ell,g)}\}$ corresponding to the input wires. It computes as follows.

1. For each input wire $i \in \mathsf{Input}_{(\ell,g)}$:
   (a) If $\ell = 1$ and i is even, continue to next i. // Filler, ignored.

   (b) **Decrypt and authenticate the message/route:**
      i. Compute $y = \mathsf{CT}_{(\ell,i)} \oplus \mathsf{PRF}(k_{(\ell,i)}, t)$ and parse y as $(x, \overline{\mathsf{rte}}, \mathsf{msig})$.

      ii. Abort if $\mathsf{Sig.Vf}(\mathsf{mpp}_{(\ell,i)}, \mathsf{mvk}_{(\ell,i)}, t, (x, \overline{\mathsf{rte}}), \mathsf{msig}) = 0$.

      iii. If $x = \perp_{\mathsf{filler}}$ and $\overline{\mathsf{rte}} = \perp_{\mathsf{filler}}$, continue to the next i. // Filler, ignored.

      iv. Parse $\overline{\mathsf{rte}}$ as $(\mathsf{rte}, \mathsf{rsig})$, rte as $(j_1, \ldots, j_L)$, and rsig as $(\mathsf{rsig}_1, \ldots, \mathsf{rsig}_L)$. Abort if $j_\ell \neq i$ or the next hop $j_{\ell+1} \notin \mathsf{Output}_{(\ell,g)}$ or $\mathsf{Sig.Vf}(\mathsf{rpp}_{(\ell,i)}, \mathsf{rvk}_{(\ell,i)}, 1, \mathsf{rte}, \mathsf{rsig}_\ell) = 0$.

   (c) **Prepare the output ciphertext $\mathsf{CT}_{(\ell+1,j_{\ell+1})}$:**
      i. For convenience, set $j = j_{\ell+1}$.

      ii. If $\mathsf{CT}_{(\ell+1,j)}$ has already been computed, then abort.

      iii. Else if $\ell + 1 < L$ (intermediate layer), first compute a new message signature $\mathsf{msig}' = \mathsf{Sig.Sign}(\mathsf{mpp}_{(\ell+1,j)}, \mathsf{msk}_{(\ell+1,j)}, t, (x, \overline{\mathsf{rte}}))$. Then, compute the ciphertext $\mathsf{CT}_{(\ell+1,j)} = (x, \overline{\mathsf{rte}}, \mathsf{msig}') \oplus \mathsf{PRF}(k_{(\ell+1,j)}, t)$.

      iv. Else if $\ell + 1 = L$ (output layer), compute the ciphertext $\mathsf{CT}_{(L,j)} = x \oplus \mathsf{PRF}(k_{(L,j)}, t)$.

2. For each $j \in \mathsf{Output}_{(\ell,g)}$ such that $\mathsf{CT}_{(\ell+1,j)}$ has not been computed yet, compute filler ciphertexts:
   (a) Set $x = \perp_{\mathsf{filler}}$ and $\overline{\mathsf{rte}} = \perp_{\mathsf{filler}}$.

   (b) Compute $\mathsf{msig}' = \mathsf{Sig.Sign}(\mathsf{mpp}_{(\ell+1,j)}, \mathsf{msk}_{(\ell+1,j)}, t, (x, \overline{\mathsf{rte}}))$.

   (c) Compute $\mathsf{CT}_{(\ell+1,j)} = (x, \overline{\mathsf{rte}}, \mathsf{msig}') \oplus \mathsf{PRF}(k_{(\ell+1,j)}, t)$.

3. Output $\{\mathsf{CT}_{(\ell+1,i)} : i \in \mathsf{Output}_{(\ell,g)}\}$.

Fig. 2. The circuit $\mathsf{Gate}_{(\ell,g)}$.

Circuit for Each Gate. We first describe the circuit for each gate to be obfuscated later in our construction. The circuit $\mathsf{Gate}_{(\ell,g)}$ denotes the g-th gate in the ℓ-th layer. It receives a ciphertext on each input wire and decrypts it using a PRF key to obtain a tuple $(x, \overline{\mathsf{rte}}, \mathsf{msig})$, where x is a message, $\overline{\mathsf{rte}}$ is the authenticated route, and msig is a message signature. It verifies the message signature msig on the tuple $(x, \overline{\mathsf{rte}})$. Next, it performs route authentication and prepares the output ciphertext which varies depending on whether the wire is filler or not. A wire is filler if $x = \perp_{\mathsf{filler}}$ and $\overline{\mathsf{rte}} = \perp_{\mathsf{filler}}$. For a filler input wire, no route authentication is performed as there is no route associated with it. Computing output ciphertext for filler output wires is deferred to later as the circuit does not know which are filler output wires at the moment. For a non-filler input wire i, the circuit parses $\overline{\mathsf{rte}} = (\mathsf{rte}, \mathsf{rsig})$ and verifies that the route rte is valid using rsig. Then, it parses $\mathsf{rte} = (j_1, \ldots, j_L)$. If $j_\ell = i$, then it finds the corresponding non-filler output wire $j_{\ell+1}$ from the rte and computes a new message signature msig' and then a new ciphertext for the output wire in the natural manner. At the end, all output wires which do not have any ciphertext assigned to them are interpreted as filler wires and the circuit computes message signature and ciphertext similarly by setting $x = \perp_{\mathsf{filler}}$ and $\overline{\mathsf{rte}} = \perp_{\mathsf{filler}}$. In Fig. 2 we describe the circuit formally and in more detail, where Sig is a SSU signature scheme constructed in Sect. 5 and PRF is a puncturable PRF.

We next describe the **Setup** algorithm.

Setup Algorithm. Given a routing permutation π, the **Setup** algorithm first sets $\mathsf{tlen} = \log^2(\lambda)$. Then, it runs the $\mathsf{AssignRoutes}$ algorithm to sample a set of edge-disjoint routes $\{\mathsf{rte}_u\}_{u \in [n]}$ between each sender/receiver pair. Then, for every wire $(\ell, i) \in [L] \times [2n]$ in the routing network we sample (a) PRF key $k_{(\ell,i)}$ for encryption, (b) a signature key pair $(\mathsf{rsk}_{(\ell,i)}, \mathsf{rvk}_{(\ell,i)}, \mathsf{rpp}_{(\ell,i)})$ for signing routes, and (c) a signature key pair $(\mathsf{msk}_{(\ell,i)}, \mathsf{mvk}_{(\ell,i)}, \mathsf{mpp}_{(\ell,i)})$ for signing messages. Looking ahead, when proving security, the route signature keys for wires assigned to corrupt senders' routes, and the message signature keys for all other wires will be punctured to ensure "uniqueness of routes and plaintexts".

Given the above set of keys, consider a sender/receiver pair (u, v) with route $\mathsf{rte}_u = (j_1, \ldots, j_L)$. Then sender u's sender key ek_u and receiver v's decryption key rk_v are defined as follows, where rsig_ℓ is the signature on rte_u computed using the route public param $\mathsf{rpp}_{(\ell,j_\ell)}$ and route signing key $\mathsf{rsk}_{(\ell,j_\ell)}$.

$$\mathsf{ek}_u = \left(k_{(1,j_1)}, \mathsf{mpp}_{(1,j_1)}, \mathsf{msk}_{(1,j_1)}, \overline{\mathsf{rte}}_u = (\mathsf{rte}_u, \mathsf{rsig}_u = (\mathsf{rsig}_1, \ldots, \mathsf{rsig}_L))\right), \mathsf{rk}_v = k_{(L,j_L)} .$$

Lastly, the routing token tk is then defined as follows, where the circuit $\mathsf{Gate}_{(\ell,g)}$ is as described in Fig. 2.

$$\mathsf{tk} = \{\mathsf{iO}(\mathsf{Gate}_{(\ell,g)}) : (\ell,g) \times [L-1] \times [G]\}.$$

More formally, the **Setup** algorithm is as in Fig. 3.

Setup$(1^\lambda, \mathsf{len} = 1, n, \pi)$: on inputs the security parameter 1^λ, the individual message length $\mathsf{len} = 1$, the number of parties n, and the permutation π, **Setup** does the following:

1. Set $\mathsf{tlen} = \log^2(\lambda)$.

2. **Sampling Routes**: Run the AssignRoutes procedure (Appendix B.1) on inputs $(1^\lambda, n, \pi)$. Abort if it outputs $\bot$. Else parse the output as a set of edge-disjoint routes $\{\mathsf{rte}_u\}_{u \in [n]}$ between each sender/receiver pair. Let $0, \ldots, L$ be the layers in the resulting network. Let G be the number of gates contained in each of the $L - 1$ intermediate layers. Let W be the number of incoming and outgoing wires in each gate. Then, for all $u \in [n]$, the size of the string rte_u is $\mathsf{len}_{\mathsf{rte}} = L \cdot \log(2n)$.

3. **Sampling Wire Keys**: For each wire (ℓ, i) in $[L] \times [2n]$:
   (a) Sample PRF key $k_{(\ell,i)} \leftarrow \mathsf{PRF.Gen}(1^\lambda)$ as the encryption key for this wire.

   (b) To sign and verify routes of length $\mathsf{len}_{\mathsf{rte}}$, sample route signature keys

   $$(\mathsf{rsk}_{(\ell,i)}, \mathsf{rvk}_{(\ell,i)}, \mathsf{rpp}_{(\ell,i)}) \leftarrow \mathsf{Sig.Setup}(1^\lambda, 0, \mathsf{len}_{\mathsf{rte}}) \ .$$

   Suppose that the resulting route signatures will be of size $\mathsf{poly}_{\mathsf{rsig}}(\lambda)$ for some polynomials $\mathsf{poly}_{\mathsf{rsig}}$. Then, the messages signed will be of length $\mathsf{len}_m = \mathsf{tlen} + 1 + L \cdot \log(2n) + L \cdot \mathsf{poly}_{\mathsf{rsig}}(\lambda)$. To sign and verify messages of length len_m, sample message signature keys

   $$(\mathsf{msk}_{(\ell,i)}, \mathsf{mvk}_{(\ell,i)}, \mathsf{mpp}_{(\ell,i)}) \leftarrow \mathsf{Sig.Setup}(1^\lambda, \mathsf{tlen}, \mathsf{len}_m) \ .$$

4. **Signing Routes**: For each sender $u \in [n]$ do the following:
   (a) Parse $\mathsf{rte}_u = (j_1, \ldots, j_L)$. Sign rte_u using route signing keys for each wire along rte_u, that is, for $\ell \in [L]$ compute $\mathsf{rsig}_\ell = \mathsf{Sig.Sign}(\mathsf{rpp}_{(\ell,j_\ell)}, \mathsf{rsk}_{(\ell,j_\ell)}, 1, \mathsf{rte})$.

   (b) Set $\overline{\mathsf{rte}}_u = (\mathsf{rte}_u, \mathsf{rsig}_u = (\mathsf{rsig}_1, \ldots, \mathsf{rsig}_L))$.

5. **Setting Routing Token**:
   (a) For each merge-split gate (ℓ, g) in $[L-1] \times [G]$, compute an indistinguishability obfuscation $\overline{\mathsf{Gate}}_{(\ell,g)} \leftarrow \mathsf{iO}(1^\lambda, \mathsf{Gate}_{(\ell,g)})$ of the circuit $\mathsf{Gate}_{(\ell,g)}$ described in Figure 2.

   (b) Set $\mathsf{tk} = \{\overline{\mathsf{Gate}}_{(\ell,g)} : \ell \in [L-1], g \in [G]\}$.

6. **Setting Sender Keys**: For each $u \in [n]$, set $\mathsf{ek}_u = (k_{(1,j_1)}, \mathsf{mpp}_{(1,j_1)}, \mathsf{msk}_{(1,j_1)}, \overline{\mathsf{rte}}_u)$.

7. **Setting Receiver Keys**: For each $v \in [n]$, set $\mathsf{rk}_v = k_{(L,2v-1)}$.

8. Output $(\{\mathsf{ek}_u\}_{u \in [n]}, \{\mathsf{rk}_u\}_{u \in [n]}, \mathsf{tk})$.

Fig. 3. The **Setup** algorithm

Next, we describe how encryption, routing and decryption work.

Encryption Algorithm. For a sender u to send a message x to its receiver for time step t, the sender first computes a message signature msig for the tuple $(x, \overline{\text{rte}}_u)$ for round t, and encrypts the tuple $(x, \overline{\text{rte}}_u, \text{msig})$ using its PRF key.

$\text{Enc}(\text{ek}_u, x_u, t)$ on input user u's encryption key ek_u and plaintext x_u and the round t, does the following:
1. Parse ek_u as $(k, \text{mpp}, \text{msk}, \overline{\text{rte}}_u)$.
2. Compute the message signature $\text{msig} = \text{Sig.Sign}(\text{mpp}, \text{msk}, t, (x_u, \overline{\text{rte}}_u))$.
3. Compute the ciphertext $\text{CT}_u = (x_u, \overline{\text{rte}}_u, \text{msig}) \oplus \text{PRF}(k, t)$.
4. Output CT_u.

Routing Algorithm. The router receives a routing token tk from the **Setup** algorithm. It consists of obfuscation of each gate in the routing network as described in Fig. 2. During each round t, the router receives n ciphertexts $\text{CT}_1, \ldots, \text{CT}_n$ from the n senders. Before processing the ciphertexts through the routing network, the router sets the $2n$ ciphertexts $\text{CT}_{(1,1)}, \ldots, \text{CT}_{(1,2n)}$ for the first layer as follows. For all $i \in [n]$, it sets $\text{CT}_{(1,2i-1)} = \text{CT}_i$ as the real ciphertexts and $\text{CT}_{(1,2i)} = \perp_{\text{filler}}$ as the *filler* ciphertexts, where $\perp_{\text{filler}}$ is a special string. Next, the router uses the token tk to route the $2n$ ciphertexts in the first layer through the routing network to obtain the $2n$ ciphertexts in the last layer L: $\text{CT}_{(L,1)}, \ldots, \text{CT}_{(L,2n)}$. Finally, to all receivers $i \in [n]$, the router sends the ciphertexts $\text{CT}'_i = \text{CT}_{(L,2i-1)}$. More formally,

---

$\text{Rte}(\text{tk}, t, \text{CT}_1, \text{CT}_2, \ldots, \text{CT}_n)$ on input the router token tk along with the round number t, and ciphertexts $\text{CT}_1, \ldots, \text{CT}_n$, does the following:
1. Parse $\text{tk} = \{\overline{\text{Gate}}_{(\ell,g)} : \ell \in [L-1], g \in [G]\}$.
2. Compute ciphertexts for the input layer:
   (a) For all $k \in [n]$, set $\text{CT}_{(1,2k-1)} = \text{CT}_k$. // *Real ciphertexts*
   (b) For all $k \in [n]$, set $\text{CT}_{(1,2k)} = \perp_{\text{filler}}$. // *Filler ciphertexts*
3. Compute network of iO obfuscated gates layer-by-layer, that is, for layer $\ell = 1, \ldots, L-1$, evaluate all the obfuscated gates at this layer as follows. For each $g \in [G]$, let $\text{Input}_{(\ell,g)}$ and $\text{Output}_{(\ell,g)}$ be the set of input and output wires of gate $\text{Gate}_{(\ell,g)}$. Then, evaluate the circuit

$$\{\text{CT}_{(\ell+1,i)} : i \in \text{Output}_{(\ell,g)}\} = \overline{\text{Gate}}_{(\ell,g)}(t, \{\text{CT}_{(\ell,i)} : i \in \text{Input}_{(\ell,g)}\}).$$

4. Output $(\text{CT}'_1 = \text{CT}_{(L,1)}, \text{CT}'_2 = \text{CT}_{(L,3)}, \ldots, \text{CT}'_n = \text{CT}_{(L,2n-1)})$.

Decryption Algorithm. A receiver u learns its intended message by just decrypting the received ciphertext using its PRF key. More formally,

---

$\mathbf{Dec}(\mathsf{rk}_u, \mathsf{CT}'_u, t)$ on input user u's receiver key rk_u, output ciphertext CT'_u, and a time step t, does the following: Output $y = \mathsf{CT}'_u \oplus \mathsf{PRF}(\mathsf{rk}_u, t)$.

6.2   Efficiency Analysis

Recall that we assume $\mathsf{len} = 1$ since for multi-bit messages, since we can always parallel-compose multiple NIAR schemes where $\mathsf{len} = 1$ to get a NIAR scheme for $\mathsf{len} > 1$. In the analysis below, we argue that the router computation per time is bounded by $\widetilde{O}_\lambda(n)$ where $\widetilde{O}_\lambda$ hides $\mathsf{poly}(\lambda, \log n)$ factors for some fixed $\mathsf{poly}(\cdot)$.

Recall that the routing network consists of layers $0, \ldots, L$, where $L = O(\log n)$. In each of the $L - 1$ intermediate layers, there are $G = 2n/W$ number of gates, where $W = O(\log^2 \lambda)$ is the number of incoming and outgoing wires in each gate.

Size of Hardcoded Values in Each Gate. Each incoming wire has the following hardcoded: PRF key of size $\mathsf{poly}(\lambda)$, route public parameters of size $\mathsf{poly}(\lambda)$ and route verification key of size $\mathsf{poly}(\lambda)$, message public parameters of size $\mathsf{poly}(\lambda)$ and message verification key of size $\mathsf{poly}(\lambda)$. Each outgoing wire has the following hardcoded: PRF key of size $\mathsf{poly}(\lambda)$, message public parameters of size $\mathsf{poly}(\lambda)$ and message signing key of size $\mathsf{poly}(\lambda, \mathsf{tlen}) = \mathsf{poly}(\lambda)$ as $\mathsf{tlen} = \log^2(\lambda)$.

Size of Ciphertexts. Each route signature is of size $\mathsf{poly}_{\mathsf{rsig}}(\lambda)$. and each message signature is of size $\mathsf{poly}_{\mathsf{msig}}(\lambda)$. Therefore, the ciphertexts are of size $\mathsf{tlen} + 1 + L \cdot \log(2n) + L \cdot \mathsf{poly}_{\mathsf{rsig}}(\lambda) + \mathsf{poly}_{\mathsf{msig}}(\lambda) = \mathsf{poly}(\lambda, \log n)$.

Size and Running Time of Each Gate. Each gate has W incoming and outgoing wires and each gate processes W ciphertexts, where $W = O(\log^2 \lambda)$. Therefore, each gate has $\mathsf{poly}(\lambda)$ amount of hardcoded information and processes $\mathsf{poly}(\lambda, \log n)$ amount of inputs. Based on the operations inside each gate, we can then conclude that each gate is of size $\mathsf{poly}(\lambda, \log n)$. Then, accounting for the polynomial blowup of the iO obfuscator, we can conclude that the size of each obfuscated gate is still $\mathsf{poly}(\lambda, \log n)$ and the router can run each obfuscated circuit in time $\mathsf{poly}(\lambda, \log n)$.

Router Computation per Time Step. Observe that for each time step, the router computes each of the obfuscated circuits at most once. Since there are at most $\widetilde{O}(n)$ gates, we can conclude that the router computation per time step is bounded by $\widetilde{O}_\lambda(n)$ where $\widetilde{O}_\lambda$ hides $\mathsf{poly}(\lambda, \log n)$ factors for some fixed $\mathsf{poly}(\cdot)$.

Sender and Receiver Key Sizes, Computation and Communication per Time Step. Sender key size is bounded by the size of the route which is $\tilde{O}_\lambda(1)$. For every sender, computation and communication per time step is $\tilde{O}_\lambda(1)$. Each receiver's key contains a PRF key which is $O_\lambda(1)$ in size. For every receiver, computation and communication per time step is $O_\lambda(1)$.

6.3   Static Security Theorem

In Appendices D and E, we prove the following theorem, which shows that the above construction satisfies static security as long as the adversary always corrupts all receivers. In Appendix F, we give a compiler that further compiles the scheme to one that satisfies full security under adaptive corruptions, and without any restrictions on the adversary.

Theorem 6.1. *Suppose* PRF *is a secure puncturable PRF,* Sig *is a secure deterministic SSU signature scheme, and* iO *is a secure indistinguishability obfuscation scheme. Then, our NIAR construction in Sect. 6.1 satisfies full static corruption security (Definition A.1) subject to an all-receiver-corrupting adversary.*

We give a proof roadmap of Theorem 6.1 below.

Proof Roadmap. We prove Theorem 6.1 through a sequence of steps.

- In Definition D.1, we define indistinguishability w.r.t. inversions against an adversary that additionally satisfies the selective single-challenge restriction. Then, we present an Upgrade Theorem stated in Theorem D.2 which shows how to remove the selective single-challenge and inversion restrictions.
- Next, to complete the proof of Theorem 6.1, it suffices to prove security under the selective single-challenge and single inversion restrictions. We show this in Theorem E.1.

Acknowledgements. Elaine Shi was supported by a DARPA SIEVE grant, a Packard Fellowship, a grant from Algorand Foundation, NSF awards under the grant numbers 2128519 and 2044679, and a grant from ONR under the award number N000142212064. Brent Waters was supported by NSF CNS-1908611, CNS-2318701 and Simons Investigator award.

References

1. Abe, M.: Mix-networks on permutation networks. In: Lam, K.-Y., Okamoto, E., Xing, C. (eds.) ASIACRYPT 1999. LNCS, vol. 1716, pp. 258–273. Springer, Heidelberg (1999). https://doi.org/10.1007/978-3-540-48000-6_21
2. Abraham, I., et al.: Communication complexity of byzantine agreement, revisited. In: PODC (2019)
3. Abraham, I., Pinkas, B., Yanai, A.: Blinder: MPC based scalable and robust anonymous committed broadcast. In: ACM CCS (2020)
4. Alexopoulos, N., Kiayias, A., Talviste, R., Zacharias, T.: MCMix: anonymous messaging via secure multiparty computation. In: Usenix Security (2017)

5. Ananth, P., Jain, A., Sahai, A.: Indistinguishability obfuscation for turing machines: constant overhead and amortization. In: Katz, J., Shacham, H. (eds.) CRYPTO 2017. LNCS, vol. 10402, pp. 252–279. Springer, Cham (2017). https://doi.org/10.1007/978-3-319-63715-0_9

6. Asharov, G., Chan, T.H., Nayak, K., Pass, R., Ren, L., Shi, E.: Bucket oblivious sort: an extremely simple oblivious sort. In: SOSA (2020)

7. Balle, B., Bell, J., Gascón, A., Nissim, K.: Differentially private summation with multi-message shuffling. CoRR, abs/1906.09116 (2019)

8. Balle, B., Bell, J., Gascón, A., Nissim, K.: The privacy blanket of the shuffle model. In: Boldyreva, A., Micciancio, D. (eds.) CRYPTO 2019. LNCS, vol. 11693, pp. 638–667. Springer, Cham (2019). https://doi.org/10.1007/978-3-030-26951-7_22

9. Barak, B., Goldreich, O., Impagliazzo, R., Rudich, S., Sahai, A., Vadhan, S., Yang, K.: On the (im)possibility of obfuscating programs. In: Kilian, J. (ed.) CRYPTO 2001. LNCS, vol. 2139, pp. 1–18. Springer, Heidelberg (2001). https://doi.org/10.1007/3-540-44647-8_1

10. Bayer, S., Groth, J.: Efficient zero-knowledge argument for correctness of a shuffle. In: Pointcheval, D., Johansson, T. (eds.) EUROCRYPT 2012. LNCS, vol. 7237, pp. 263–280. Springer, Heidelberg (2012). https://doi.org/10.1007/978-3-642-29011-4_17

11. Bellare, M., Stepanovs, I., Waters, B.: New negative results on differing-inputs obfuscation. In: Fischlin, M., Coron, J.-S. (eds.) EUROCRYPT 2016. LNCS, vol. 9666, pp. 792–821. Springer, Heidelberg (2016). https://doi.org/10.1007/978-3-662-49896-5_28

12. Bitansky, N., Garg, S., Lin, H., Pass, R., Telang, S.: Succinct randomized encodings and their applications. In: Proceedings of the Forty-Seventh Annual ACM Symposium on Theory of Computing, pp. 439–448 (2015)

13. Bittau, A., et al.: Prochlo: strong privacy for analytics in the crowd. CoRR, abs/1710.00901 (2017)

14. Boneh, D., Waters, B.: Constrained pseudorandom functions and their applications. In: Sako, K., Sarkar, P. (eds.) ASIACRYPT 2013. LNCS, vol. 8270, pp. 280–300. Springer, Heidelberg (2013). https://doi.org/10.1007/978-3-642-42045-0_15

15. Boyle, E., Goldwasser, S., Ivan, I.: Functional signatures and pseudorandom functions. In: Krawczyk, H. (ed.) PKC 2014. LNCS, vol. 8383, pp. 501–519. Springer, Heidelberg (2014). https://doi.org/10.1007/978-3-642-54631-0_29

16. Brakerski, Z., Dottling, N., Garg, S., Malavolta, G.: Factoring and pairings are not necessary for IO: circular-secure LWE suffices. Cryptology ePrint Archive, Report 2020/1024 (2020)

17. Bunn, P., Kushilevitz, E., Ostrovsky, R.: Anonymous permutation routing. Cryptology ePrint Archive, Paper 2022/1353 (2022). https://eprint.iacr.org/2022/1353

18. Bünz, B., Hu, Y., Matsuo, S., Shi, E.: Non-interactive differentially anonymous router. Cryptology ePrint Archive, Paper 2021/1242 (2021). https://eprint.iacr.org/2021/1242

19. Camenisch, J., Lysyanskaya, A.: A formal treatment of onion routing. In: Shoup, V. (ed.) CRYPTO 2005. LNCS, vol. 3621, pp. 169–187. Springer, Heidelberg (2005). https://doi.org/10.1007/11535218_11

20. Canetti, R., Holmgren, J., Jain, A., Vaikuntanathan, V.: Indistinguishability obfuscation of iterated circuits and ram programs. Cryptology ePrint Archive (2014)
21. Canetti, R., Lin, H., Tessaro, S., Vaikuntanathan, V.: Obfuscation of probabilistic circuits and applications. In: Dodis, Y., Nielsen, J.B. (eds.) TCC 2015. LNCS, vol. 9015, pp. 468–497. Springer, Heidelberg (2015). https://doi.org/10.1007/978-3-662-46497-7_19
22. Chaum, D.L.: Untraceable electronic mail, return addresses, and digital pseudonyms. Commun. ACM **24**(2), 84–90 (1981)
23. Chaum, D.L.: The dining cryptographers problem: unconditional sender and recipient untraceability. J. Cryptol. **1**(1), 65–75 (1988)
24. Cheu, A., Smith, A., Ullman, J., Zeber, D., Zhilyaev, M.: Distributed differential privacy via shuffling. In: Ishai, Y., Rijmen, V. (eds.) EUROCRYPT 2019. LNCS, vol. 11476, pp. 375–403. Springer, Cham (2019). https://doi.org/10.1007/978-3-030-17653-2_13
25. Chor, B., Gilboa, N.: Computationally private information retrieval (extended abstract). In: Proceedings of the Twenty-Ninth Annual ACM Symposium on Theory of Computing, STOC 1997, New York, NY, USA, pp. 304–313. ACM (1997)
26. Chor, B., Goldreich, O., Kushilevitz, E., Sudan, M.: Private information retrieval. In: IEEE Symposium on Foundations of Computer Science (FOCS), pp. 41–50 (1995)
27. Corrigan-Gibbs, H., Boneh, D., Mazières, D.: Riposte: an anonymous messaging system handling millions of users. In: S & P (2015)
28. Corrigan-Gibbs, H., Ford, B.: Dissent: accountable anonymous group messaging. In: CCS, pp. 340–350 (2010)
29. Degabriele, J.P., Stam, M.: Untagging tor: a formal treatment of onion encryption. In: Nielsen, J.B., Rijmen, V. (eds.) EUROCRYPT 2018. LNCS, vol. 10822, pp. 259–293. Springer, Cham (2018). https://doi.org/10.1007/978-3-319-78372-7_9
30. Dingledine, R., Mathewson, N., Syverson, P.: Tor: the second-generation onion router. In: USENIX Security Symposium (2004)
31. Dwork, C., McSherry, F., Nissim, K., Smith, A.: Calibrating noise to sensitivity in private data analysis. In: Halevi, S., Rabin, T. (eds.) TCC 2006. LNCS, vol. 3876, pp. 265–284. Springer, Heidelberg (2006). https://doi.org/10.1007/11681878_14
32. Erlingsson, Ú., Feldman, V., Mironov, I., Raghunathan, A., Talwar, K., Thakurta, A.: Amplification by shuffling: from local to central differential privacy via anonymity. In: SODA (2019)
33. Garg, S., Gentry, C., Halevi, S., Raykova, M. Sahai, A., Waters, B.: Candidate indistinguishability obfuscation and functional encryption for all circuits. In: IEEE Symposium on Foundations of Computer Science (FOCS) (2013)
34. Gay, R., Pass, R.: Indistinguishability obfuscation from circular security. Cryptology ePrint Archive, Report 2020/1010 (2020)
35. Gertner, Y., Ishai, Y., Kushilevitz, E., Malkin, T.: Protecting data privacy in private information retrieval schemes. J. Comput. Syst. Sci. **60**(3) (2000)
36. Ghazi, B., Pagh, R., Velingker, A.: Scalable and differentially private distributed aggregation in the shuffled model. CoRR, abs/1906.08320 (2019)
37. Goldreich, O., Goldwasser, S., Micali, S.: How to construct random functions. J. ACM (JACM) **33**(4), 792–807 (1986)

38. Goldschlag, D., Reed, M., Syverson, P.: Onion routing for anonymous and private internet connections. Commun. ACM **42**, 39–41 (1999)

39. Gordon, S.D., Katz, J., Liang, M., Xu, J.: Spreading the privacy blanket: differentially oblivious shuffling for differential privacy. In: Ateniese, G., Venturi, D. (eds.) ACNS 2022. LNCS, vol. 13269, pp. 501–520. Springer, Cham (2022). https://doi.org/10.1007/978-3-031-09234-3_25

40. Guan, J., Wichs, D., Zhandry, M.: Incompressible cryptography. In: Dunkelman, O., Dziembowski, S. (eds.) EUROCRYPT 2022, Part I. LNCS, vol. 13275, pp. 700–730. Springer, Cham (2022). https://doi.org/10.1007/978-3-031-06944-4_24

41. Halevi, S., Ishai, Y., Jain, A., Komargodski, I., Sahai, A., Yogev, E.: Non-interactive multiparty computation without correlated randomness. In: Takagi, T., Peyrin, T. (eds.) ASIACRYPT 2017. LNCS, vol. 10626, pp. 181–211. Springer, Cham (2017). https://doi.org/10.1007/978-3-319-70700-6_7

42. Huang, Y., Evans, D., Katz, J.: Private set intersection: are garbled circuits better than custom protocols? In NDSS (2012)

43. Jain, A., Jin, Z.: Indistinguishability obfuscation via mathematical proofs of equivalence. In: 63rd IEEE Annual Symposium on Foundations of Computer Science, FOCS 2022, Denver, CO, USA, 31 October–3 November 2022, pp. 1023–1034. IEEE (2022)

44. Jain, A., Lin, H., Sahai, A.: Indistinguishability obfuscation from well-founded assumptions. In: Proceedings of the 53rd Annual ACM SIGACT Symposium on Theory of Computing, pp. 60–73 (2021)

45. Kiayias, A., Papadopoulos, S., Triandopoulos, N., Zacharias, T.: Delegatable pseudorandom functions and applications. In: Proceedings of the 2013 ACM SIGSAC conference on Computer & communications security, pp. 669–684 (2013)

46. Koppula, V., Lewko, A.B., Waters, B.: Indistinguishability obfuscation for turing machines with unbounded memory. In: Proceedings of the Forty-Seventh Annual ACM Symposium on Theory of Computing, pp. 419–428 (2015)

47. Lamport, L.: Constructing digital signatures from a one way function (1979)

48. Merkle, R.C.: Secrecy, authentication, and public key systems. Stanford University (1979)

49. Ostrovsky, R., Shoup, V.: Private information storage (extended abstract). In: STOC, pp. 294–303 (1997)

50. Ramachandran, V., Shi, E.: Data oblivious algorithms for multicores. In: Agrawal, K., Azar, Y. (eds.) SPAA 2021: 33rd ACM Symposium on Parallelism in Algorithms and Architectures, Virtual Event, USA, 6–8 July 2021, pp. 373–384. ACM (2021)

51. Sherwood, R., Bhattacharjee, B., Srinivasan, A.: P5: a protocol for scalable anonymous communication. In: IEEE Symposium on Security and Privacy (2002)

52. Shi, E., Vanjani, N.: Multi-client inner product encryption: function-hiding instantiations without random oracles. In: Boldyreva, A., Kolesnikov, V. (eds.) PKC 2023. LNCS, vol. 13940, pp. 622–651. Springer, Cham (2023). https://doi.org/10.1007/978-3-031-31368-4_22

53. Shi, E., Wu, K.: Non-interactive anonymous router. In: Canteaut, A., Standaert, F.-X. (eds.) EUROCRYPT 2021. LNCS, vol. 12698, pp. 489–520. Springer, Cham (2021). https://doi.org/10.1007/978-3-030-77883-5_17

54. Smart, N.P., Talibi Alaoui, Y.: Distributing any elliptic curve based protocol. In: Albrecht, M. (ed.) IMACC 2019. LNCS, vol. 11929, pp. 342–366. Springer, Cham (2019). https://doi.org/10.1007/978-3-030-35199-1_17

55. Tyagi, N., Gilad, Y., Leung, D., Zaharia, M., Zeldovich, N.: Stadium: a distributed metadata-private messaging system. In: SOSP (2017)

56. van den Hooff, J., Lazar, D., Zaharia, M., Zeldovich, N.: Vuvuzela: scalable private messaging resistant to traffic analysis. In: SOSP (2015)
57. Wee, H., Wichs, D.: Candidate obfuscation via oblivious LWE sampling. Cryptology ePrint Archive, Report 2020/1042 (2020)
58. Zhuang, L., Zhou, F., Zhao, B.Y., Rowstron, A.: Cashmere: resilient anonymous routing. In: NSDI (2005)

Multi-instance Randomness Extraction and Security Against Bounded-Storage Mass Surveillance

Jiaxin Guan[1] , Daniel Wichs[2,3] , and Mark Zhandry[3(✉)]

[1] Princeton University, Princeton, NJ 08544, USA
[2] Northeastern University, Boston, MA 02115, USA
[3] NTT Research, Inc., Sunnyvale, CA 94085, USA
mzhandry@gmail.com

Abstract. Consider a state-level adversary who observes and stores large amounts of encrypted data from all users on the Internet, but does not have the capacity to store it all. Later, it may target certain "persons of interest" in order to obtain their decryption keys. We would like to guarantee that, if the adversary's storage capacity is only (say) 1% of the total encrypted data size, then even if it can later obtain the decryption keys of arbitrary users, it can only learn something about the contents of (roughly) 1% of the ciphertexts, while the rest will maintain full security. This can be seen as an extension of *incompressible cryptography* (Dziembowski CRYPTO'06, Guan, Wichs and Zhandry EUROCRYPT'22) to the *multi-user* setting. We provide solutions in both the symmetric key and public key setting with various trade-offs in terms of computational assumptions and efficiency.

As the core technical tool, we study an information-theoretic problem which we refer to as "multi-instance randomness extraction". Suppose $X_1, \ldots, X_t$ are correlated random variables whose total joint min-entropy rate is α, but we know nothing else about their individual entropies. We choose t random and independent seeds $S_1, \ldots, S_t$ and attempt to individually extract some small amount of randomness $Y_i = \mathsf{Ext}(X_i; S_i)$ from each X_i. We'd like to say that roughly an α-fraction of the extracted outputs Y_i should be indistinguishable from uniform even given all the remaining extracted outputs and all the seeds. We show that this indeed holds for specific extractors based on Hadamard and Reed-Muller codes.

1 Introduction

Bounded-Storage Mass Surveillance. We consider a scenario where a powerful (e.g., state-level) adversary wants to perform mass surveillance of the population. Even if the population uses encryption to secure all communication, the adversary can collect large amounts of encrypted data from the users (e.g., by monitoring encrypted traffic on the Internet). The data is encrypted and hence

---

Supplementary Information The online version contains supplementary material available at https://doi.org/10.1007/978-3-031-48621-0_4.

G. Rothblum and H. Wee (Eds.): TCC 2023, LNCS 14371, pp. 93–122, 2023.
https://doi.org/10.1007/978-3-031-48621-0_4

the adversary does not learn anything about its contents when it is collected. However, the adversary may store this data for the future. Later, it may identify various "persons of interest" and perform expensive targeted attacks to get their secret keys (e.g., by remote hacking or by physically compromising their devices). We will assume the adversary is capable of eventually getting any secret key of any user of its choosing. Can we still achieve any meaningful notion of security against such mass-surveillance?

One option is to rely on cryptosystems having *forward secrecy* [19], which exactly addresses the problem of maintaining security even if the secret key is later compromised. Unfortunately, forward-secure encryption schemes inherently require either multi-round interaction between the sender and receiver or for the receiver to perform key updates, both of which can be impractical or impossible in many natural scenarios. Without these, it may seem that no reasonable security is possible – if the adversary collects all the ciphertexts and later can get any secret key, clearly it can also get any plaintext!

In this work, we restrict the adversary to have *bounded storage*, which is much smaller than the total of size of all the encrypted data it can observe. This is a reasonable assumption since the total communication of an entire population is likely huge.[1] As a running example throughout the introduction, we will assume that the adversary's storage capacity is 1% of the total encrypted data size. We allow the adversary to observe all the encrypted data simultaneously and then compress it in some arbitrary way to fit within its storage budget. Later, the adversary can get any secret key of any user of its choosing, and eventually it may even get all the keys of all the users. What kind of security guarantees can we provide in this setting?

Clearly, the adversary can simply store 1% of the ciphertexts and discard the remaining 99%, which will allow it to later compromise the security of 1% of the users by getting their secret keys. While one may pessimistically see this as a significant privacy violation already, we optimistically regard this as a potentially reasonable privacy outcome that's vastly preferable to the adversary being able to compromise all the users. For example, if the adversary later chooses a random user and wants to learn something about their data, it will only be able to do so with 1% probability, even if it can get their secret key. But can we argue that this is the best that the adversary can do? In particular, we'd like to say that, no mater what compression strategy the adversary employs, it will be unable to learn anything about the contents of 99% of the ciphertexts, even if it later gets all the secret keys. Unfortunately, this is not generically true. For example, the adversary could store the first 1% of the bits of every ciphertext. If the encryption scheme is (e.g.,) the one-time pad, then an adversary who later learns the secret keys would later be able to learn the first 1% of every encrypted message of every user, which may provide a pretty good idea of the overall message contents. In fact, it can get even worse than this. If the encryption scheme is fully homomorphic, the adversary can individually compress each ciphertext

---

[1] Global annual Internet traffic has long surpassed 1 zettabyte (10^{21} bytes) [4], while *total* world-wide datacenter storage is only a couple zettabytes in 2022 [11].

into a small evaluated ciphertext encrypting some arbitrary predicate of the data (e.g., was the message insulting of the supreme leader), and therefore learn the outcome of this predicate about the encrypted data of every user. Even worse, if the encryption scheme is multi-key fully homomorphic, the adversary can derive a compressed ciphertext that encrypts the output of a joint computation over all the data of all the users, as long as the output is sufficiently small. Thus, in general, an adversary whose storage capacity is only 1%, may still be able to learn some partial information about the encrypted messages of a 100% of the users. The question is then, whether or not it is indeed possible to guarantee only 1% of users are compromised, and if so to actually design such a scheme.

Connection to Incompressible Cryptography. Encryption schemes that offer protection against bounded-storage mass surveillance can be seen as a generalization of *incompressible encryption* [6,15,17] to the setting of multiple ciphertexts. To clarify the distinction, we refer to the earlier notion of incompressible encryption as *individually incompressible* and our new notion as *multi-incompressible*.

In an *individually incompressible encryption* scheme, we can make the size of a ciphertext flexibly large, and potentially huge (e.g., many gigabytes). An adversary observes a single ciphertext, but cannot store it in its entirety and can instead only store some compressed version of it. Security dictates that even if the adversary later gets the user's secret key, it cannot learn anything about the encrypted message. The work of [15] gave a construction of one-time symmetric-key encryption with information-theoretic security in this setting, and the work of [17] showed how to achieve public-key encryption in this setting, under the minimal assumption that standard public-key encryption exists. The works of [6,17] also constructed such public-key encryption schemes having rate 1, meaning that the size of the message can be almost as large as the ciphertext size, and the latter work even showed how to do so under specific but standard public-key assumptions.

In our new notion of *multi-incompressible encryption*, we also have the flexibility to make the ciphertext size arbitrarily large. But now the adversary observes a large number of ciphertexts from many users and compresses them down to something that's roughly an α-fraction of the size of all the original ciphertexts, for some α. In particular, the adversary's storage may be much larger than a single ciphertext. Later the adversary gets all the secret keys, and we want to say that the adversary can only learn something about a (roughly) α-fraction of the messages, but cannot learn anything about the rest.

Our new notion of multi-incompressibility implies individual incompressibility. In particular, in the case of a single ciphertext, unless the adversary stores essentially all of it (i.e., $\alpha \approx 1$), it cannot learn anything about the encrypted message ($= 100\%$ of the messages). But our notion is significantly more general. For example, individual incompressibility does not even offer any guarantees if an adversary can take even 2 ciphertexts and compress them down to the size of 1, while multi-incompressibility ensures that one of the messages stays secure.

Formalizing multi-incompressibility is tricky: the natural indistinguishability-based approach would be to insist that the encryptions of two lists of messages are indistinguishable. But unlike individually incompressible encryption, in our setting the adversary can always learn *something*, namely the messages contained in ciphertexts it chose to store. We therefore need a fine-grained notion which captures that some messages to be learned, but other messages remain completely hidden. We give details on our solution below.

Extracting Randomness Against Correlated Sources. Before getting to our results, we discuss randomness extraction, which is a central tool in all existing constructions of incompressible encryption. A randomness extractor Ext takes as input a source of imperfect randomness X and uses it to distill out some (nearly) uniformly random string Y. Here, we consider seeded extractors, which use a public uniformly random seed S as a catalyst to extract $Y = \mathsf{Ext}(X; S)$, such that Y should be (nearly) uniform even conditioned on the seed S.

While randomness extraction is very well studied, it is most often in the *single-use* case, where a single string $Y = \mathsf{Ext}(X; S)$ is extracted from a single source X having sufficient entropy. Here we ask: what if many strings $Y_i = \mathsf{Ext}(X_i; S_i)$ are extracted from multiple sources X_i respectively (using independent random seeds S_i), but where the sources X_i may be arbitrarily correlated? What guarantees can be made? We consider the case where we only know that the total joint entropy of all the sources is high, but we know nothing else about their individual entropies; indeed some of the sources may have no entropy at all! In this case, clearly not all of the extracted values Y_i can be uniform, and some may even be entirely deterministic. One may nevertheless hope that *some* of the extracted values remain uniform, where the fraction of uniform values roughly correlates to combined total entropy rate of all the sources. To the best of our knowledge, randomness extraction in this setting has not been studied before.

1.1 Our Results

Formalizing Multi-user Incompressible Encryption. We first provide definitions for multi-user incompressible encryption. We depart from the indistinguishability-based definitions of the prior work on incompressible cryptography [6,15,17], and instead give a *simulation*-based definition. Essentially, it says that anything that an adversary can learn by taking many ciphertexts of different users, compressing them down sufficiently, and later getting all the secret keys, can be simulated by a simulator that can only ask to see some small fraction of the plaintexts but learns nothing about the remaining ones. In the single-instance case, this definition implies indistinguishability-based security, but appears stronger. Nevertheless, existing constructions and proofs are readily adapted to satisfy simulation security. The distinction becomes more important in the multi-user setting, however, where simulation security allows us to naturally define what it means for some messages to be revealed and some to remain hidden.

Multi-instance Randomness Extractors. As our main technical tool, we explore a new kind of extractor that we call a multi-instance randomness extractor, which aims to solve the extraction problem outlined above. Syntactically, this is a standard extractor $Y = \mathsf{Ext}(X; S)$ that takes as input a source X and a seed S and outputs some short randomness Y. However, we now imagine that the extractor is applied separately to t correlated sources X_i, with each invocation using an independent seed S_i, to derive extracted values $Y_i = \mathsf{Ext}(X_i; S_i)$. The only guarantee on the sources is that the total joint min-entropy of $X = (X_1, \ldots, X_t)$ is sufficiently high. Any individual source X_i, however, may actually be deterministic (have 0 entropy), in which case the corresponding extracted value Y_i is of course not random. However, provided the total min-enropy rate of X is high, it is guaranteed that *many* of the t extracted values are statistically-close uniform. Ideally, if the joint min-entropy rate of X is α, we would hope that roughly αt of the extracted values are uniform.

Formalizing the above requires some care. For example, it may be the case that X is chosen by selecting a random index $i^* \leftarrow [t]$, setting X_{i^*} to be all 0's, and choosing the remaining block X_j for $j \neq i^*$ uniformly at random. In that case X has a very high entropy rate, but for any fixed index i, the min-entropy of X_i is small (at most $\log t$ since with polynomial probability $1/t$ the value of X_i is all 0's), and not enough to extract even 1 bit with negligible bias. Therefore, we cannot argue that $Y_i = \mathsf{Ext}(X_i; S_i)$ is close to uniform for any particular index i! Instead, we allow the set of indices i, for which Y_i is close to uniform, itself be a random variable correlated with X. (See Definition 3.)

We show constructions of multi-instance randomness extractors nearing the optimal number of uniform extracted values. In particular, we show that if the joint min-entropy rate of $X = (X_1, \ldots, X_t)$ is α then there exists some random variable I_X denoting a subset of $\approx \alpha \cdot t$ indices in $[t]$ such that nobody can distinguish between seeing all the extracted values $Y_i = \mathsf{Ext}(X_i; S_i)$ versus replacing all the Y_i for $i \in I_X$ by uniform, even given all the seeds S_i. (See Corollary 1.) Our constructions are based on Hadamard codes (long seed) and Reed-Muller codes (short seed). While the constructions themselves are standard, our analysis is novel, leveraging the list-decodability of the codes, plus a property we identify called *hinting*. Hinting roughly means that the values of $\{\mathsf{Ext}(x; S_i)\}_i$ on some particular exponentially large set of pairwise independent seeds S_i can be compressed into a single small hint, of size much smaller than x. This hinting property is a crucial feature in the *local* list-decoding algorithms for these codes, but appears not to have been separately formalized/utilized as a design goal for an extractor.[2]

Applications. We then show that multi-instance randomness extraction can be used essentially as a drop-in replacement for standard randomness extractors in prior constructions of individual incompressible encryption, lifting them to multi-incompressible encryption. As concrete applications, we obtain multi-incompressible encryption in a variety of settings:

---

[2] The work of [1] studied a notion of extractors for "Somewhere Honest Entropic Look Ahead" (SHELA) sources. The notions are largely different and unrelated. In particular: (i) in our work X is an arbitrary source of sufficient entropy while [1] places additional restrictions, (ii) we use a seeded extractor while [1] wants a deterministic extractor, (iii) we apply the seeded extractor separately on each X_i while [1] applies it jointly on the entire X, (iv) we guarantee that a large fraction of extracted outputs is uniform even if the adversary sees the rest, while in [1] the adversary cannot see the rest.

- A symmetric key scheme with information-theoretic security, by replacing the extractor in [15].
- A "rate-1" symmetric key scheme, meaning the ciphertext is only slightly larger than the message. Here, we assume either decisional composite residuosity (DCR) or learning with errors (LWE), matching [6][3].
- A public key scheme, assuming any ordinary public key encryption scheme, matching [17].
- A rate-1 public key scheme, under the same assumptions as [6][4]. The scheme has large public keys.
- A rate-1 public key scheme that additionally has succinct public keys, assuming general functional encryption, matching [17].

In all cases, we guarantee that if the adversary's storage is an α fraction of the total size of all the ciphertexts, then it can only learn something about a $\beta \approx \alpha$ fraction of the encrypted messages. We can make $\beta = \alpha - 1/p(\lambda)$ for any polynomial p in the security parameter λ, by choosing a sufficiently large ciphertext size.

Multiple Ciphertexts Per User. Prior work, in addition to only considering a single user, also only considers a single ciphertext per user. Perhaps surprisingly, security does not compose, and indeed for any fixed secret key size, we explain that simulation security for unbounded messages is impossible.

We therefore develop schemes for achieving a bounded number of ciphertexts per user. We show how to modify each of the constructions above to achieve multi-ciphertext security under the same assumptions.

The Random Oracle Model. In the full version [18] of the paper, we also show how to construct symmetric key multi-user incompressible encryption with an unbounded number of ciphertexts per user and also essentially optimal secret key and ciphertext sizes, from random oracles. This shows that public key tools are potentially not inherent to rate-1 symmetric incompressible encryption.

1.2 Concurrent Work

A concurrent and independent work of Dinur et al. [12] (Sect. 6.2) considers an extraction problem that turns out to be equivalent to our notion of *Multi-Instance Randomness Extractor*. They study this problem in a completely different context of differential-privacy lower bounds. They show that (in our language) universal hash functions are "multi-instance randomness extractors" with good parameters, similar to the ones in our work. While conceptually similar, the results are technically incomparable since we show our result for hinting

---

[3] One subtlety is that, for all of our rate-1 constructions, we need a PRG secure against *non-uniform* adversaries, whereas the prior work could have used a PRG against uniform adversaries.

[4] [6] explores CCA security, but in this work for simplicity we focus only on CPA security.

extractors while they show it for universal hash functions. One advantage of our result is that we show how to construct hinting extractors with short seeds, while universal hash functions inherently require a long seed. Their proof is completely different from the one in our paper.

The fact that multi-instance randomness extractors have applications in different contexts, as demonstrated in our work and Dinur et al. [12], further justifies them as a fundamental primitive of independent interest. We believe that having two completely different techniques/approaches to this problem is both interesting and valuable.

1.3   Our Techniques: Multi-instance Randomness Extraction

We discuss how to construct a multi-instance randomness extractor Ext. Recall, we want to show that, if the joint min-entropy rate of $X = (X_1, \ldots, X_t)$ is α then there exists some random variable I_X denoting a subset of $\approx \alpha \cdot t$ indices in $[t]$ such that the distribution $(S_i, Y_i = \mathsf{Ext}(X_i; S_i))_{i \in [t]}$ is statistically indistinguishable from $(S_i, Z_i)_{i \in [t]}$ where Z_i is uniformly random for $i \in I_X$ and $Z_i = Y_i$ otherwise.

A Failed Approach. A natural approach would be to try to show that every standard seeded extractor is also a "multi-instance randomness extractor". As a first step, we would show that there is some random variable I_X denoting a large subset of $[t]$ such that the values X_i for $i \in I_X$ have large min-entropy conditioned on $i \in I_X$. Indeed, such results are known; see for example the "block-entropy lemma" of [13] (also [9,16]). In fact, one can even show a slightly stronger statement that the random variables X_i for $i \in I_X$ have high min-entropy even conditioned on all past blocks $X_1, \ldots, X_{i-1}$. However, it cannot be true that X_i has high min-entropy conditioned on *all* other blocks past and future (for example, think of X being uniform subject to $\bigoplus_{i=1}^t X_i = 0$). Unfortunately, this prevents us for using the block-entropy lemma to analyze multi-instance extraction, where the adversary sees some extracted outputs from all the blocks.[5] It remains as a fascinating open problem whether every standard seeded extractor is also a multi-instance randomness extractor or if there is some counterexample.[6]

Our Approach. We are able to show that particular seeded extractors Ext based on Hadamard or Reed-Muller codes are good multi-instance randomness

---

[5] This strategy would allow us to only prove a very weak version of multi-instance extraction when the number of blocks t is sufficiently small. In this case we can afford to lose the t extracted output bits from the entropy of *each* block. However, in our setting, we think of the number of blocks t as huge, much larger than the size/entropy of each individual block.

[6] We were initially convinced that the general result does hold and invested much effort trying to prove it via some variant of the above approach without success. We also mentioned the problem to several experts in the field who had a similar initial reaction, but were not able to come up with a proof.

extractors. For concreteness, let us consider the Hadamard extractor $\mathsf{Ext}(x; s) = \langle x, s \rangle$.[7] Our proof proceeds in 3 steps:

Step 1: Switch quantifiers. We need to show that there *exists* some random variable I_X such that *every* statistical distinguisher fails to distinguish between the two distributions $(S_i, Y_i)_{i \in [t]}$ and $(S_i, Z_i)_{i \in [t]}$. We can use von Neumann's minimax theorem to switch the order quantifiers.[8] Therefore, it suffices to show that for every (randomized) statistical distinguisher D there is some random variable I_X such that D fails to distinguish the above distributions.

Step 2: Define I_X. For any fixed $x = (x_1, \ldots, x_t)$ we define the set I_x to consist of indices $i \in [t]$ such that D fails to distinguish between the hybrid distributions $(\{S_j\}_{j \in [t]}, Z_1, \ldots, Z_{i-1}, Y_i, \ldots, Y_t)$ versus $(\{S_j\}_{j \in [t]}, Z_1, \ldots, Z_i, Y_{i+1}, \ldots, Y_t)$, where in both distributions we condition on $X = x$. In other words, these are the indices where we can replace the next extracted output by random and fool the distinguisher. We then define the random variable I_X that chooses the correct set I_x according to X. It is easy to show via a simple hybrid argument that with this definition of I_X it is indeed true that D fails to distinguish $(S_i, Y_i)_{i \in [t]}$ and $(S_i, Z_i)_{i \in [t]}$.

Step 3: Argue that I_X is large. We still need to show that I_X is a large set, containing $\approx \alpha \cdot t$ indices. To do so, we show that if I_X were small (with non negligible probability) then we could "guess" X with sufficiently high probability that would contradict X having high min-entropy. In particular, we provide a guessing strategy such that for any x for which I_x is small, our strategy has a sufficiently high chance of guessing x. First, we guess the small set $I_x \subseteq [t]$ as well as all of the blocks x_i for $i \in I_x$ uniformly at random. For the rest of the blocks $i \notin I_x$, we come up with a guessing strategy that does significantly better than guessing randomly. We rely on the fact that distinguishing implies predicting, to convert the distinguisher D into a predictor P such that for all $i \notin I_x$ we have: $P(S_i, \{S_j, \mathsf{Ext}(x_j; S_j)\}_{j \in [t] \setminus \{i\}}) = \mathsf{Ext}(x_i; S_i)$ with probability significantly better than $1/2$. Now we would like to use the fact that the Hadamard code $(\mathsf{Ext}(x; s) = \langle x, s \rangle)_s$ is list-decodable to argue that we can use such predictor P to derive a small list of possibilities for x. Unfortunately, there is a problem with this argument. To call the predictor, the predictor requires an auxiliary input, namely $\mathsf{aux}_i = \{S_j, \mathsf{Ext}(x_j; S_j)\}_{j \in [t] \setminus \{i\}}$. Supplying the aux_i in turn requires knowing at least t bits about x. We could hope to guess a good choice of aux_i, but there may be a different good choice for each $i \in [t]$, and therefore we would need to guess a fresh t bits of information about x just to recover each block x_i, which when $|x_i| < t$ is worse than the trivial approach of guessing x_i directly! Instead, we use a trick inspired by the proof of the Goldreich-Levin theorem. For each

---

[7] For the sake of exposition, here we only show the case where the extractor output is a single bit. In Sect. 3, we construct extractors with multiple-bit outputs.

[8] Think of the above as a 2 player game where one player chooses I_X, the other chooses the distinguisher and the payout is the distinguishing advantage; the minimax theorem says that the value of the game is the same no matter which order the players go in.

block $j \in [t]$, we guess the values of $b^{(k)} := \langle x_j, S_j^{(k)} \rangle$ for a very small "base set" of h random seeds $S_j^{(1)}, \ldots, S_j^{(h)}$. We can then expand this small "base set" of seeds into an exponentially larger "expanded set" of $Q = 2^h - 1$ seeds $S_j^{(K)} := \sum_{k \in K} S_j^{(k)}$ for $K \subseteq [h] \setminus \emptyset$, and derive guesses for $b^{(K)} := \langle x_j, S_j^{(K)} \rangle$ by setting $b^{(K)} = \sum_{k \in K} b^{(k)}$. By linearity, the expanded set of guesses is correct if the base set is correct, and moreover the expanded sets of seeds $(S_j^{(K)})_K$ are pairwise independent for different sets K. Therefore, for each set K, we can derive the corresponding $\mathsf{aux}_i^{(K)}$. We can now apply Chebyshev's bound to argue that if for each i we take the majority value for $P(S_i, \mathsf{aux}_i^{(K)})$ across all Q sets K, it is likely equal to $\mathsf{Ext}(x_i; S_i)$ with probability significantly better than $1/2$. Notice that we got our saving by only guessing ht bits about $x = (x_1, \ldots, x_t)$ for some small value h (roughly $\log(1/\varepsilon)$ if we want indistinguishability ε) and were able to use these guesses to recover all the blocks x_i for $i \notin I_x$.

Generalizing. We generalize the above analysis for the Hadamard extractor to any extractor that is list-decodable and has a "hinting" property as discussed above. In particular, this also allows us to use a Reed-Muller based extractor construction with a much smaller seed and longer output length.

1.4   Our Techniques: Multi-incompressible Encryption

We then move to considering incompressible encryption in the multi-user setting.

Definition. We propose a simulation-based security definition for multi-instance incompressible encryption. Roughly, the simulator first needs to simulate all the ciphertexts for all the instances *without* seeing any of the message queries, corresponding to the fact that at this point the adversary can't learn anything about any of the messages. To model the adversary then learning the secret keys, we add a second phase where the simulator can query for a *subset* of the messages, and then must simulate *all* the private keys. We require that no *space-bounded* distinguisher can distinguish between the receiving real encryptions/real private keys vs receiving simulated encryptions/keys. The number of messages the simulator can query will be related to the storage bound of the distinguisher.

Upgrading to Multi-incompressible Encryption Using Multi-instance Randomness Extraction. All prior standard-model constructions of individual incompressible encryption [6,15,17] utilize a randomness extractor. For example, Dziembowski [15] gives the following simple construction of a symmetric key incompressible encryption scheme:

- The secret key k is parsed as (s, k') where s is a seed for a randomness extractor, and k' is another random key.
- To encrypt a message m, choose a large random string R, and output $c = (R, d = \mathsf{Ext}(R; s) \oplus k' \oplus m)$.

The intuition for (individual) incompressible security is that an adversary that cannot store essentially all of c can in particular not store all of R, meaning

R has min-entropy conditioned on the adversary's state. The extraction guarantee then shows that $\mathsf{Ext}(R; s)$ can be replaced with a random string, thus masking the message m.

We demonstrate that our multi-instance randomness extractors can be used as a drop-in replacement for ordinary random extractors in all prior constructions of individual incompressible encryption, upgrading them to multi-incompressible encryption. In the case of [15], this is almost an immediate consequence of our multi-instance randomness extractor definition. Our simulator works by first choosing random s for each user, and sets the ciphertexts of each user to be random strings. Then it obtains from the multi-instance randomness extractor guarantee the set of indices i where Y_i is close to uniform. For these indices, it sets k' to be a uniform random string. This correctly simulates the secret keys for these i.

For i where Y_i is not uniform, the simulator then queries for messages for these i. It programs k' as $k' = d \oplus \mathsf{Ext}(R; s) \oplus m$; decryption under such k' will correctly yield m. Thus, we correctly simulate the view of the adversary, demonstrating multi-incompressible security.   .

Remark 1. The set of indices where Y_i is uniform will in general not be efficiently computable, and multi-instance randomness extraction only implies that the set of indices exist. Since our simulator must know these indices, our simulator is therefore inefficient. In general, an inefficient simulator seems inherent in the standard model, since the adversary's state could be scrambled in a way that hides which ciphertexts it is storing.

We proceed to show that various constructions from [6,17] are also secure in the multi-user setting, when plugging in multi-instance randomness extractors. In all cases, the proof is essentially identical to the original single-user counterpart, except that the crucial step involving extraction is replaced with the multi-instance randomness extraction guarantee. We thus obtain a variety of parameter size/security assumption trade-offs, essentially matching what is known for the single-user setting.

One small issue that comes up is that, once we have invoked the multi-instance randomness extractor, the simulation is inefficient. This presents a problem in some of the security proofs, specifically in the "rate-1" setting where messages can be almost as large as ciphertexts. In the existing proofs in this setting, there is a computational hybrid step that comes *after* applying the extractor. Naively, this hybrid step would seem to be invalid since the reduction now has to be inefficient. We show, however, that the reduction can be made efficient as long as it is *non-uniform*, essentially having the choice of indices (and maybe some other quantities) provided as non-uniform advice. As long as the underlying primitive for these post-extraction hybrids has non-uniform security, the security proof follows.

Multiple Ciphertexts Per User. We also consider the setting where there may be multiple ciphertexts per user, which has not been considered previously.

It is not hard to see that having an *unbounded* number of ciphertexts per user is impossible in the standard model. This is because the simulator has to simulate everything but the secret key without knowing the message. Then, for the ciphertexts stored by the adversary, the simulator queries for the underlying messages and must generate the secret key so that those ciphertexts decrypt to the given messages. By incompressiblity, this means the secret key length must be at least as large as the number of messages.

We instead consider the case of bounded ciphertexts per user. For a stateful encryption scheme, it is trivial to upgrade a scheme supporting one ciphertext per user into one supporting many: simply have the secret key be a list of one-time secret keys. In the symmetric key setting, this can be made stateless by utilizing k-wise independent hash functions.

In the public key setting, achieving a stateless construction requires more work, and we do not believe there is a simple generic construction. We show instead how to modify all the existing constructions to achieve multiple cipher-texts per user. Along the way, we show an interesting combinatorial approach to generically lifting non-committing encryption to the many-time setting without sacrificing ciphertext rate.

2   Preliminaries

Notation-wise, for $n \in \mathbb{N}$, we let $[n]$ denote the ordered set $\{1, 2, \ldots, n\}$. We use capital bold letters to denote a matrix $\mathbf{M}$. Lowercase bold letters denote vectors $\mathbf{v}$. Let $\mathbf{M}_{i,j}$ denote the element on the i-th row, and j-th column of $\mathbf{M}$, and $\mathbf{v}_i$ denote the i-th element of $\mathbf{v}$.

Lemma 1 (Johnson Bound, Theorem 3.1 of [20]). *Let $\mathcal{C} \subseteq \Sigma^n$ with $|\Sigma| = q$ be any q-ary error-correcting code with relative distance $p_0 = 1 - (1 + \rho)\frac{1}{q}$ for $\rho > 0$, meaning that for any two distinct values $x, y \in \mathcal{C}$, the Hamming distance between x, y is at least $p_0 \cdot n$. Then for any $\delta > \sqrt{\rho(q-1)}$ there exists some $L \leq \frac{(q-1)^2}{\delta^2 - \rho(q-1)}$ such that the code is $(p_1 = (1 - (1 + \delta)\frac{1}{q}), L)$-list decodable, meaning that for any $y \in \Sigma_q^n$ there exist at most L codewords $x \in \mathcal{C}$ that are within Hamming distance $p_1 n$ of y.*

Lemma 2 (Distinguishing implies Predicting). *For any randomized function $D : \{0,1\}^n \times \{0,1\}^m \rightarrow \{0,1\}$ there exists some randomized function $P : \{0,1\}^n \rightarrow \{0,1\}^m$ such that for any jointly distributed random variables (A, B) over $\{0,1\}^n \times \{0,1\}^m$:*
if $\Pr[D(A, B) = 1] - \Pr[D(A, U_m) = 1] \geq \varepsilon$ then $\Pr[P(A) = B] \geq \frac{1}{2^m}(1 + \varepsilon)$.

Proof. Define $P(a)$ as follows. Sample a random $b_0 \leftarrow \{0,1\}^m$, if $D(a, b_0) = 1$ output b_0 else sample a fresh $b_1 \leftarrow \{0,1\}^m$ and output b_1.

Define $p = \Pr[D(A, U_m) = 1]$. Let B_0, B_1 be independent random variables that are uniform over $\{0,1\}^m$ corresponding to the strings b_0, b_1 . Then we have

$$\Pr[P(A) = B] = \Pr[D(A, B_0) = 1 \wedge B_0 = B] + \Pr[D(A, B_0) = 0 \wedge B_1 = B]$$
$$= \Pr[B_0 = B] \Pr[D(A, B) = 1] + \Pr[D(A, B_0) = 0] \Pr[B_1 = B]$$
$$= \frac{1}{2^m}(\varepsilon + p) + (1 - p)\frac{1}{2^m} = \frac{1}{2^m}(1 + \varepsilon).$$

□

Min-Entropy Extractor. Recall the definition for average min-entropy:

Definition 1 (Average Min-Entropy). *For two jointly distributed random variables* (X, Y), *the average min-entropy of* X *conditioned on* Y *is defined as*

$$H_\infty(X|Y) = -\log \mathbf{E}_{y \xleftarrow{\$} Y}[\max_x \Pr[X = x|Y = y]].$$

Lemma 3 ([14]). *For random variables* X, Y *where* Y *is supported over a set of size* T, *we have* $H_\infty(X|Y) \geq H_\infty(X, Y) - \log T \geq H_\infty(X) - \log T$.

Definition 2 (Extractor [23]). *A function* Extract : $\{0,1\}^n \times \{0,1\}^d \to \{0,1\}^m$ *is a* (k, ϵ) *strong average min-entropy extractor if, for all jointly distributed random variables* (X, Y) *where* X *takes values in* $\{0,1\}^n$ *and* $H_\infty(X|Y) \geq k$, *we have that* $(U_d, \mathsf{Extract}(X; U_d), Y)$ *is* ϵ-*close to* (s, U_m, Y), *where* U_d *and* U_m *are uniformly random strings of length* d *and* m *respectively.*

Remark 2. Any strong randomness extractor is also a strong *average* min-entropy extractor, with a constant loss in ϵ.

Definitions of incompressible encryption and functional encryption can be found in the full version [18] of the paper.

3   Multi-instance Randomness Extraction

3.1   Defining Multi-instance Extraction

Definition 3 (Multi-instance Randomness Extraction). *A function* Ext : $\{0,1\}^n \times \{0,1\}^d \to \{0,1\}^m$ *is* $(t, \alpha, \beta, \varepsilon)$-*multi-instance extracting if the following holds. Let* $X = (X_1, \ldots, X_t)$ *be any random variable consisting of blocks* $X_i \in \{0,1\}^n$ *such that* $H_\infty(X) \geq \alpha \cdot tn$. *Then, there exists some random variable* I_X *jointly distributed with* X, *such that* I_X *is supported over sets* $\mathcal{I} \subseteq [t]$ *of size* $|\mathcal{I}| \geq \beta \cdot t$ *and:*

$$(S_1, \ldots, S_t, \mathsf{Ext}(X_1; S_1), \ldots, \mathsf{Ext}(X_t; S_t)) \approx_\varepsilon (S_1, \ldots, S_t, Z_1, \ldots, Z_t)$$

where $S_i \in \{0,1\}^d$ *are uniformly random and independent seeds, and* $Z_i \in \{0,1\}^m$ *is sampled independently and uniformly random for* $i \in I_X$ *while* $Z_i = \mathsf{Ext}(X_i; S_i)$ *for* $i \notin I_X$.

In other words, the above definition says that if we use a "multi-instance extracting" extractor with independent seeds to individually extract from t correlated blocks that have a joint entropy-rate of α, then seeing all the extracted outputs is indistinguishable from replacing some carefully chosen β-fraction by uniform.

3.2   Hinting Extractors

Definition 4 (Hinting Extractor). *A function* $\mathsf{Ext} : \{0,1\}^n \times \{0,1\}^d \to \{0,1\}^m$ *is a* (δ, L, h, Q)-*hinting extractor if it satisfies the following:*

- *List Decodable: If we think of* $\mathsf{ECC}(x) = (\mathsf{Ext}(x;s))_{s \in \{0,1\}^d}$ *as a* $(2^d, n)_{\Sigma = \{0,1\}^m}$ *error-correcting code over the alphabet* $\Sigma = \{0,1\}^m$, *then the code is* $(p = 1 - (1+\delta)2^{-m}, L)$-*list decodable, meaning that for any* $y \in \Sigma^{2^d}$, *the number of codewords that are within Hamming distance* $p \cdot 2^d$ *of* y *is at most* L.
- *Pairwise-Independent Hint: There exist some functions* $\mathsf{hint} : \{0,1\}^n \times \{0,1\}^\tau \to \{0,1\}^h$, *along with* rec_0 *and* rec_1 *such that:*
  - *For all* $x \in \{0,1\}^n, r \in \{0,1\}^\tau$, *if we define* $\sigma = \mathsf{hint}(x;r)$, $\{s_1, \ldots, s_Q\} = \mathsf{rec}_0(r)$, *and* $\{y_1, \ldots, y_Q\} = \mathsf{rec}_1(\sigma, r)$, *then* $\mathsf{Ext}(x;s_i) = y_i$ *for all* $i \in [Q]$.
  - *Over a uniformly random* $r \leftarrow \{0,1\}^\tau$, *the* Q *seeds* $\{s_1, \ldots, s_Q\} = \mathsf{rec}_0(r)$, *are individually uniform over* $\{0,1\}^d$ *and pairwise independent.*

Intuitively, the pairwise-independent hint property says that there is a small (size h) hint about x that allows us to compute $\mathsf{Ext}(x;s_i)$ for a large (size Q) set of pairwise independent seeds s_i. We generally want Q to be exponential in h.

The list-decoding property, on the other hand, is closely related to the standard definition of strong randomness extractors. Namely, if Ext is a (k, ε)-extractor then it is also $(p = 1 - (1+\delta)2^{-m}, 2^k)$-list decodable for $\delta = \varepsilon \cdot 2^m$, and conversely, if it is $(p = 1 - (1+\delta)2^{-m}, 2^k)$-list deocdable then it is a $(k + m + \log(1/\delta), \delta)$-extractor (see Proposition 6.25 in [26]).

Construction 1: Hadamard. Define $\mathsf{Ext} : \{0,1\}^n \times \{0,1\}^n \to \{0,1\}^m$ via $\mathsf{Ext}(x;s) = \langle x, s \rangle$, where we interpret x, s as elements of $\mathbb{F}_{2^m}^{\hat{n}}$ for $\hat{n} := n/m$ and all the operations are over $\mathbb{F}_{2^m}$. The seed length is $d = n$ bits and the output length is m bits.

Lemma 4. *The above* $\mathsf{Ext} : \{0,1\}^n \times \{0,1\}^n \to \{0,1\}^m$ *is a* (δ, L, h, Q)-*hinting extractor for any* $h, \delta > 0$ *with* $Q \geq 2^{h-m}$ *and* $L \leq 2^{2m}/\delta^2$.

Proof. The list-decoding bounds on δ, L come from the Johnson bound (Lemma 1) with $q = 2^m$, $\rho = 0$. For pairwise-independent hints, let $\hat{h} = h/m$ and define $\mathsf{hint}(x; R)$ to parse $R \in \mathbb{F}_{2^m}^{\hat{h} \times \hat{n}}$ and output $\sigma = R \cdot x^\top$, which has bit-size h. Let $\mathcal{V} \subseteq \mathbb{F}_{2^m}^{\hat{h}}$ be a set of vectors such that any two distinct vectors $v_1 \neq v_2 \in \mathcal{V}$ are linearly independent. Such a set $\mathcal{V}$ exists of size $Q = (2^m)^{\hat{h}-1} + (2^m)^{\hat{h}-2} + \cdots + 2^m + 1 \geq 2^{h-m}$, e.g., by letting $\mathcal{V}$ be the set of all non-zero vectors whose left-most non-zero entry is a 1. Define $\mathsf{rec}_0(R)$ so that it outputs $\{s_v = v \cdot R\}_{v \in \mathcal{V}}$. Correspondingly, $\mathsf{rec}_1(\sigma, R)$ outputs $\{y_v = \langle v, \sigma \rangle\}_{v \in \mathcal{V}}$. It's easy to see that the seeds s_v are individually uniform and pairwise independent, since for any linearly-independent $v_1 \neq v_2 \in \mathcal{V}$ and the value $s_{v_1} = v_1 R$ and $s_{v_2} = v_2 R$ are random and independent over a random choice of the matrix R. Moreover for all seeds s_v we have

$$\mathsf{Ext}(x, s_v) = \langle s_v, x \rangle = v \cdot R \cdot x^\top = \langle v, \sigma \rangle = y_v.$$

$\square$

Construction 2: Hadamard ∘ Reed-Muller. Define $\mathsf{Ext}(f; s = (s_1, s_2)) = \langle f(s_1),$
$s_2 \rangle$, where $f \in \mathbb{F}_{2^w}^{\binom{\ell+g}{g}}$ is interpreted as a ℓ-variate polynomial of total degree
g over some field of size $2^w > g$, and $s_1 \in \mathbb{F}_{2^w}^{\ell}$ is interpreted as an input to
the polynomial (this is Reed-Muller).[9] Then $y = f(s_1)$ and s_2 are interpreted
as a values in $\mathbb{F}_{2^m}^{w/m}$ and the inner-product $\langle y, s_2 \rangle$ is computed over $\mathbb{F}_{2^m}$ (this is
Hadamard). So overall, in bits, the input length is $n = w \cdot \binom{\ell+g}{g}$, the seed length
is $d = w(\ell + 1)$ and the output length is m. This code has relative distance
$1 - (\frac{1}{2^m} + \frac{g}{2^w}) = 1 - \frac{1}{2^m}(1 + \frac{g}{2^{w-m}})$.

Lemma 5. *For any w, ℓ, g, m, δ such that $2^w > g$ and m divides w, if we set*
$n = w \cdot \binom{\ell+g}{g}$, $d = w(\ell+1)$ *then the above* $\mathsf{Ext} : \{0,1\}^n \times \{0,1\}^d \to \{0,1\}^m$
is an (δ, L, h, Q)-hinting extractor with $\delta = \sqrt{g2^{2m}/2^w}$, $L = \frac{2^{2m}}{\delta^2 - g2^{2m}/2^w}$, $h = $
$w \cdot (g + 1)$, $Q = 2^w$.
In particular, for any n, m, w such that m divides w, we can set $\ell = g = \log n$
to get an (δ, L, h, Q)-hinting extractor $\mathsf{Ext} : \{0,1\}^n \times \{0,1\}^d \to \{0,1\}^m$ *with*
$d = O(w \log n)$, $\delta = 2^{m+\log\log n - w/2}$, $h = O(w \log n)$ *and $Q = 2^w$.*

Proof. The list-decoding bounds on δ, L come from the Johnson bound (Lemma
1) with $q = 2^m$, $\rho = \frac{g}{2^{w-m}}$. On the other hand, for pairwise-independent hints,
we can define $\mathsf{hint}(f; r)$ as follows. Parse $r = (r^0, r^1, s_1^1, \ldots, s_1^Q)$ with $r^0, r^1 \in \mathbb{F}_{2^w}^{\ell}$
and $s_1^i \in \mathbb{F}_{2^m}^{w/m}$. Let $\hat{f}(i) = f(r^0 + i \cdot r^1)$ be a univariate polynomial of degree g
and define the hint $\sigma = \hat{f}$ to be the description of this polynomial. Define $\{s_i =$
$(s_0^i, s_1^i))\} = \mathsf{rec}_0(r)$ for $i \in \mathbb{F}_{2^w}$ by setting $s_0^i = r^0 + i \cdot r^1$. Define $\{y_i\} = \mathsf{rec}_1(\sigma, r)$
via $y_i = \langle \hat{f}(i), s_1^i \rangle$. It is easy to check correctness and pairwise independence
follows from the fact that the values $s_0^i = r^0 + i \cdot r^1$ are pairwise independent
over the randomness r^0, r^1.   □

3.3   Hinting-Extractors Are Multi-instance-Extracting

Lemma 6 (Multi-instance-Extraction Lemma). *Let* $\mathsf{Ext} : \{0,1\}^n \times \{0,1\}^d$
$\to \{0,1\}^m$ *be a (δ, L, h, Q)-hinting extractor. Then, for any $t, \alpha > 0$ such that*
$Q \geq 2t\frac{2^{2m}}{\delta^2}$, *it is also $(t, \alpha, \beta, \varepsilon)$-multi-instance extracting with $\varepsilon = 6t\delta$ and $\beta = $*
$\alpha - \frac{\log L + h + \log t + \log(1/\varepsilon) + 3}{n}$.

Proof. Our proof follows a sequence of steps.

Step 0: Relax the Size Requirement. We modify the statement of the lemma as
follows. Instead of requiring that $|I_X| \geq \beta \cdot t$ holds with probability 1, we relax
this to requiring that $\Pr[|I_X| < \beta \cdot t] \leq \varepsilon/4$. On the other hand, we strengthen
the requirement on statistical indisitnguishability from ε to $\varepsilon/2$:

$$(S_1, \ldots, S_t, \mathsf{Ext}(X_1; S_1), \ldots, \mathsf{Ext}(X_1; S_t)) \approx_{\varepsilon/2} (S_1, \ldots, S_t, Z_1, \ldots, Z_t).$$

This modified variant of the lemma implies the original.

---

[9] Since the the input to the extractor is interpreted as a polynomial, we will denote
it by f rather than the usual x to simplify notation.

To see this, notice that we can replace the set I_X that satisfies the modified variant with I'_X which is defined as $I'_X := I_X$ when $|I_X| \geq \beta t$ and $I'_X := \{1, \ldots, \beta t\}$ else. The set I'_X then satisfies the original variant. In particular, we can prove the indisintinguishability guarantee of the original lemma via a hybrid argument: replace I'_X by I_X ($\varepsilon/4$ statistical distance), switch from the left distribution to right distribution ($\varepsilon/2$ statistical distance), replace I_X back by I'_X ($\varepsilon/4$ statistical distance) for a total distance of ε.

Step 1: Change quantifiers. We need to prove that: *for all X with $H_\infty(X) \geq \alpha \cdot tn$, there **exists** some random variable $I_X \subseteq [t]$ with $\Pr[|I_X| < \beta t] \leq \varepsilon/4$ such that **for all** (inefficient) distinguishers D:*

$$|\Pr[D(S_1, \ldots, S_t, Y_1, \ldots, Y_t) = 1] - \Pr[D(S_1, \ldots, S_t, Z_1, \ldots, Z_t) = 1]| \leq \varepsilon/2 \tag{1}$$

where we define $Y_i = \mathsf{Ext}(X_i; S_i)$, and the random variables Z_i are defined as in the Lemma. By the min-max theorem, we can switch the order of the last two quantifiers. In particular, it suffices to prove that: *for all X with $H_\infty(X) \geq \alpha \cdot tn$ and **for all** (inefficient, randomized) distinguishers D there **exists** some random variable $I_X \subseteq [t]$ with $\Pr[|I_X| < \beta t] \leq \varepsilon/4$ such that Eq. (1) holds.*

We can apply min-max because a distribution over inefficient distinguishers D is the same as a single randomized inefficient distinguisher D and a distribution over random variables I_X is the same as a single random variable I_X.

Step 2: Define I_X. Fix a (inefficient/randomized) distinguisher D.

For any fixed value $x \in \{0,1\}^{n \cdot t}$, we define a set $I_x \subseteq [t]$ iteratively as follows. Start with $I_x := \emptyset$. For $i = 1, \ldots, t$ add i to I_x if

$$\left(\begin{array}{c} \Pr[D(S_1, \ldots, S_t, Z_1^x \ldots, Z_{i-1}^x, Y_i^x, Y_{i+1}^x, \ldots, Y_t^x) = 1] \\ - \Pr[D(S_1, \ldots, S_t, Z_1^x, \ldots, Z_{i-1}^x, U_m, Y_{1+1}^x, \ldots, Y_t^x) = 1] \end{array} \right) \leq 3\delta \tag{2}$$

where S_i is uniform over $\{0,1\}^d$, $Y_j^x = \mathsf{Ext}(x_j; S_j)$ and for $j < i$ we define Z_j^x to be uniformly random over $\{0,1\}^m$ for $j \in I_x$, while $Z_j^x = Y_j^x$ for $j \notin I_x$. Note that $Y_i^x = (Y_i | X = x)$ and $Z_i^x = (Z_i | X = x)$.

Define I_X to be the random variable over the above sets I_x where x is chosen according to X. With the above definition, Eq. 1 holds since:

$$\Pr[D(S_1, \ldots, S_t, Y_1, \ldots, Y_t) = 1] - \Pr[D(S_1, \ldots, S_t, Z_1, \ldots, Z_t) = 1]$$
$$= \mathbb{E}_{x \leftarrow X} \Pr[D(S_1, \ldots, S_t, Y_1, \ldots, Y_t) = 1 | X = x]$$
$$\quad - \Pr[[D(S_1, \ldots, S_t, Z_1, \ldots, Z_t) = 1 | X = x]$$
$$= \mathbb{E}_{x \leftarrow X} \Pr[D(S_1, \ldots, S_t, Y_1^x, \ldots, Y_t^x) = 1] - \Pr[D(S_1, \ldots, S_t, Z_1^x, \ldots, Z_t^x) = 1]$$
$$= \mathbb{E}_{x \leftarrow X} \sum_{i \in [t]} \underbrace{\left(\begin{array}{c} \Pr[D(S_1, \ldots, S_t, Z_1^x, \ldots, Z_{i-1}^x, Y_i^x, Y_{i+1}^x, \ldots, Y_t^x) = 1] \\ - \Pr[D(S_1, \ldots, S_t, Z_1^x, \ldots, Z_{i-1}^x, Z_i^x, Y_{i+1}^x, \ldots, Y_t^x) = 1] \end{array} \right)}_{(*)}$$
$$\leq 3t\delta = \varepsilon/2$$

The last line follows since, for any x and any $i \in [t]$, if $i \notin I_x$ then $Y_i^x = Z_i^x$ and therefore $(*) = 0$, and if $i \in I_x$ then $(*) \leq 3\delta$ by the way we defined I_x in Eq. (2).

Step 3: Argue I_X is large. We are left to show that

$$\Pr[|I_X| < \beta \cdot t] \leq \varepsilon/4. \tag{3}$$

We do this via a proof by contradiction. Assume otherwise that (3) does not hold. Then we show that we can guess X with high probability, which contradicts the fact that X has high min-entropy. In particular, we define a randomized function guess() such that, for any x for which $|I_x| < \beta \cdot t$, we have:

$$\Pr_{\hat{x} \leftarrow \text{guess}()} [\hat{x} = x] \geq \frac{1}{4} \left(t^{\beta t + 1} 2^{ht} L^t 2^{\beta tn} \right)^{-1}. \tag{4}$$

Then, assuming (3) does not hold, we have

$$\Pr_{\hat{x} \leftarrow \text{guess}(), x \leftarrow X} [\hat{x} = x] \geq \Pr_{x \leftarrow X} [|I_x| < \beta t] \Pr_{\hat{x} \leftarrow \text{guess}(), x \leftarrow X} [\hat{x} = x \mid |I_x| < \beta t]$$

$$\geq \frac{\varepsilon}{16} \left(t^{\beta t + 1} 2^{ht} L^t 2^{\beta tn} \right)^{-1}.$$

which contradicts $H_\infty(X) \geq \alpha tn$.

Before defining the function guess(), we note that by the definition of I_x in Eq. (2) and the "distinguishing implies predicting" lemma (Lemma 2), there exist some predictors P_i (depending only on D), such that, for all $x \in \{0,1\}^n$ and $i \notin I_x$, we have:

$$\Pr[P_i(S_1, \ldots, S_t, Z_1^x, \ldots, Z_{i-1}^x, Y_{i+1}^x, \ldots, Y_t^x) = Y_i^x] \geq \frac{1}{2^m}(1 + 3\delta) \tag{5}$$

The guessing strategy. We define guess() using these predictors P_i as follows:

1. Sample values $r_1, \ldots, r_t$ with $r_i \leftarrow \{0,1\}^\tau$.
2. Sample a set $\hat{I}_x \subseteq [t]$ of size $|\hat{I}_x| \leq \beta t$ uniformly at random.
3. Sample values $\hat{\sigma}_i \leftarrow \{0,1\}^h$ for $i \notin \hat{I}_x$ uniformly at random.
4. Sample values $\hat{x}_i \leftarrow \{0,1\}^n$ for $i \in \hat{I}_x$ uniformly at random.
5. Let $\{s_i^1, \ldots, s_i^Q\} = \text{rec}_0(r_i)$, and $\{y_i^1, \ldots, y_i^Q\} = \text{rec}_1(\hat{\sigma}_i, r_i)$.
6. Use all of the above values to define, for each $i \notin \hat{I}_x$, a randomized function $\hat{P}_i(s)$ which chooses a random $j^* \leftarrow [Q]$ and outputs:

$$\hat{P}_i(s) = P_i(s_1^{j^*}, \ldots, s_{i-1}^{j^*}, s, s_{i+1}^{j^*}, \ldots, s_t^{j^*}, z_1^{j^*}, \ldots, z_{i-1}^{j^*}, y_{i+1}^{j^*}, \ldots, y_t^{j^*})$$

where $z_i^{j^*} := y_i^{j^*}$ if $i \notin \hat{I}_x$ and $z_i^{j^*} \leftarrow \{0,1\}^m$ if $i \in \hat{I}_x$.

7. For each $i \notin \hat{I}_x$, define $\text{cw}_i \in \Sigma^{2^d}$ by setting $\text{cw}_i[s] \leftarrow \hat{P}_i(s)$, where $\Sigma = \{0,1\}^m$. Let $\mathcal{X}_i$ be the list of at most L values $\tilde{x}_i$ such that the Hamming distance between $\text{ECC}(\tilde{x}_i)$ and cw_i is at most $(1 + \delta)2^d$, as in Definition 4.

8. For each $i \notin \hat{I}_x$, sample $\hat{x}_i \leftarrow \mathcal{X}_i$.
9. Output $\hat{x} = (\hat{x}_1, \ldots, \hat{x}_t)$.

Fix any x such that $|I_x| < \beta t$ and let us analyze $\Pr_{\hat{x} \leftarrow \mathsf{guess}()}[\hat{x} = x]$.

Event E_0. Let E_0 be the event that $\hat{I}_x = I_x$ and, for all $i \in I_x$: $\hat{x}_i = x_i$ and $\hat{\sigma}_i = \mathsf{hint}(x_i, r_i)$. Then $\Pr[E_0] \geq (t^{\beta t + 1} 2^{ht} 2^{\beta tn})^{-1}$. Let us condition on E_0 occurring for the rest of the analysis. In this case, we can replace all the "hatted" values $\hat{I}_x, \hat{\sigma}_i, \hat{x}_i$ with their "unhatted" counterparts $I_x, \sigma_i = \mathsf{hint}(x_i, r_i), x_i$ and we have $y_i^j = \mathsf{Ext}(x_i; s_i^j)$. Furthermore, since the "hatted" values were chosen uniformly at random, E_0 is independent of the choice of $r_1, \ldots, r_t$ and of all the "unhatted" values above; therefore conditioning on E_0 does not change their distribution.

Event E_1. Now, for any fixed choice of $r_1, \ldots, r_t$, define the corresponding procedure $\hat{P}_i$ to be "good" if

$$\Pr_{s \leftarrow \{0,1\}^d}[\hat{P}_i(s) = \mathsf{Ext}(x_i; s)] \geq (1 + 2\delta)\frac{1}{2^m},$$

where the probability is over the choice of $s \leftarrow \{0,1\}^d$ and the internal randomness of $\hat{P}_i$ (i.e., the choice of the index $j^* \leftarrow [Q]$ and the values $z_i^{j^*} \leftarrow \{0,1\}^m$ for $i \in I_x$). Let E_1 be the event that for all $i \notin I_x$ we have $\hat{P}_i$ is good, where the event is over the choice of $r_1, \ldots, r_t$. Define random variables V_i^j over the choice of $r_1, \ldots, r_t$ where

$$V_i^j = \Pr_{s \leftarrow \{0,1\}^d}[\hat{P}_i(s) = \mathsf{Ext}(x_i; s) \mid j^* = j]$$

$$= \Pr_{s \leftarrow \{0,1\}^d}[P_i(s_1^j, \ldots, s_{i-1}^j, s, s_{i+1}^j, \ldots, s_t^j, z_1^j, \ldots, z_{i-1}^j, y_{i+1}^j, \ldots, y_t^j) = \mathsf{Ext}(x_i; s)].$$

and $V_i := \sum_{j \in Q} V_i^j$. Then $\hat{P}_i$ is good iff $V_i \geq Q(1 + 2\delta)\frac{1}{2^m}$. By Eq. (5), we have $E[V_i] = \sum_j E[V_i^j] \geq Q(1 + 3\delta)\frac{1}{2^m}$. Furthermore, for any fixed i, the variables V_i^j are pairwise independent by Definition 4 and the fact that V_i^j only depends on s_i^j. Therefore $Var[V_i] = \sum_j Var[V_i^j] \leq Q$. We can apply the Chebyshev inequality to get:

$$\Pr[E_1 | E_0] \geq 1 - \Pr\left[\exists i \notin I_x : V_i < Q(1 + 2\delta)\frac{1}{2^m}\right]$$

$$\geq 1 - \sum_{i \notin I_x} \Pr\left[V_i < Q(1 + 2\delta)\frac{1}{2^m}\right]$$

$$\geq 1 - \sum_{i \notin I_x} \Pr\left[|V_i - E[V_i]| > Q\delta\frac{1}{2^m}\right] \geq 1 - t\frac{2^{2m}}{\delta^2 Q} \geq \frac{1}{2}$$

Event E_2. Now fix any choice of the values in steps (1)–(6) such that E_0, E_1 hold. Let cw_i be the values sampled in step 7. Define the event E_2 to hold if for all $i \notin I_x$ the value cw_i agrees with $\mathsf{ECC}(x_i)$ in at least $(1+\delta)2^{d-m}$ coordinates, where the probability is only over the internal randomness used to sample the components $\mathsf{cw}_i(s) \leftarrow \hat{P}_i(s)$. We can define random variables W_i^s which are 1 if $\mathsf{cw}_i(s) = \mathsf{Ext}(x_i; s)$ and 0 otherwise. These variables are mutually independent (since each invocation of $\hat{P}_i$ uses fresh internal randomness) and $E[\sum_s W_i^s] = 2^d \Pr_s[\hat{P}_i(s) = \mathsf{Ext}(x_i; s)] \geq (1+2\delta)2^{d-m}$. Therefore, by the Chernoff bound:

$$\Pr[E_2|E_1 \wedge E_0] = 1 - \Pr[\exists i \notin I_x \; : \; \sum_s W_i^s \leq (1+\delta)2^{d-m}]$$

$$\geq 1 - \sum_{i \notin I_x} \Pr[\sum_s W_i^s \leq (1+\delta)2^{d-m}]$$

$$\geq 1 - t \cdot e^{-\delta^2 2^{d-m}/8} \geq \frac{1}{2}$$

Event E_3. Finally, fix any choice of the values in steps (1)–(7) such that E_0, E_1, E_2 hold. Let E_3 be the event that for each $i \notin \hat{I}_x$ if $\hat{x}_i \leftarrow X_i$ is the value sampled in step (8) then $\hat{x}_i = x_i$. Then $\Pr[E_3|E_2 \wedge E_1 \wedge E_0] \geq \left(\frac{1}{L}\right)^t$. Therefore, our guess is correct if E_0, E_1, E_2, E_3 all occur, which gives us the bound in Eq. (4). □

Corollary 1. *For any $n, m, t, \varepsilon > 0, \alpha > 0$, there exist extractors $\mathsf{Ext} : \{0,1\}^n \times \{0,1\}^d \to \{0,1\}^m$ that are $(t, \alpha, \beta, \varepsilon)$-multi-instance extracting with either:*

1. *seed length $d = n$ and $\beta = \alpha - \frac{O(m + \log t + \log(1/\varepsilon))}{n}$, or*
2. *seed length $d = O((\log n)(m + \log \log n + \log t + \log(1/\varepsilon)))$ and $\beta = \alpha - \frac{O(d)}{n}$.*

In particular, letting λ denote the security parameter, for any input length $n = \omega(\lambda \log \lambda)$ with $n < 2^\lambda$, for number of blocks $t < 2^\lambda$, any entropy rate $\alpha > 0$, there exists an extractor $\mathsf{Ext} : \{0,1\}^n \times \{0,1\}^d \to \{0,1\}^m$ with output length $m = \lambda$ and seed length $d = O(\lambda \log n)$, which is a $(t, \alpha, \beta, \epsilon = 2^{-\lambda})$-multi-instance randomness extractor with $\beta = \alpha - o(1)$. In other words, the fraction of extracted values that can be replaced by uniform is nearly α.

4   Multi-user Security for Incompressible Encryption

Utilizing multi-instance randomness extractors, we can now explore the multi-user setting for incompressible encryptions. But first, we need to formally define what it means for an incompressible PKE or SKE scheme to be multi-user secure.

We propose a simulation-based security definition. Roughly, the simulator first needs to simulate all the ciphertexts for all the instances *without* seeing any of the message queries. So far, this is akin to the standard semantic security notion for encryption. But we need to now model the fact that the adversary can store ciphertexts for later decryption, at which point it has all the private keys. We therefore add a second phase where the simulator can query for a *subset* of the messages, and then must simulate *all* the private keys. We require that no space-bounded distinguisher can distinguish between receiving real encryptions/real private keys vs receiving simulated encryptions/keys. The number of messages the simulator can query is related to the storage bound of the distinguisher.

Put formally, let $\Pi = (\mathsf{Gen}, \mathsf{Enc}, \mathsf{Dec})$ be a public key encryption scheme, to define simulation-based incompressible ciphertext security for the multiple-instance setting, consider the following two experiments:

- In the real mode experiment, the adversary $\mathcal{A} = (\mathcal{A}_1, \mathcal{A}_2)$ interacts with the challenger $\mathcal{C}$, who has knowledge of all the adversary's challenge messages.
  Real Mode $\mathsf{ExpReal}^{\Pi}_{\mathcal{C}, \mathcal{A}=(\mathcal{A}_1, \mathcal{A}_2)}(\lambda, \eta, \ell, S)$:
  1. For $i \in [\eta]$, the challenger $\mathcal{C}$ runs $\mathsf{Gen}(1^\lambda, 1^S)$ to sample $(\mathsf{pk}_i, \mathsf{sk}_i)$.
  2. The challenger $\mathcal{C}$ sends all the pk_i's to $\mathcal{A}_1$.
  3. For each $i \in [\eta]$, $\mathcal{A}_1$ can produce up to ℓ message queries $\{m_{i,j}\}_{j \in [\ell]}$. The adversary submits all of the message queries *in one single batch* $\{m_{i,j}\}_{i,j}$ and receives $\{\mathsf{ct}_{i,j}\}_{i,j}$ where $\mathsf{ct}_{i,j} \leftarrow \mathsf{Enc}(\mathsf{pk}_i, m_{i,j})$.
  4. $\mathcal{A}_1$ produces a state st of size at most S.
  5. On input of $\mathsf{st}, \{m_{i,j}\}_{i,j}, \{(\mathsf{pk}_i, \mathsf{sk}_i)\}_i$, $\mathcal{A}_2$ outputs a bit $1/0$.
- In the ideal mode experiment, the adversary $\mathcal{A} = (\mathcal{A}_1, \mathcal{A}_2)$ interacts with a simulator $\mathcal{S}$, which needs to simulate the view of the adversary with no/partial knowledge of the challenge messages.
  Ideal Mode $\mathsf{ExpIdeal}^{\Pi}_{\mathcal{S}, \mathcal{A}=(\mathcal{A}_1, \mathcal{A}_2)}(\lambda, \eta, \ell, q, S)$:
  1. For $i \in [\eta]$, the simulator $\mathcal{S}$ samples pk_i.
  2. The simulator $\mathcal{S}$ sends all the pk_i's to $\mathcal{A}_1$.
  3. For each $i \in [\eta]$, and $j \in [\ell]$, $\mathcal{A}_1$ produces $m_{i,j}$. All of the queries $\{m_{i,j}\}_{i,j}$ are submitted in one batch and the simulator $\mathcal{S}$ produces $\{\mathsf{ct}_{i,j}\}_{i,j}$ *without seeing* $\{m_{i,j}\}_{i,j}$.
  4. $\mathcal{A}_1$ produces a state st of size at most S.
  5. The simulator now submits up to q number of (i,j) index pairs, and receives the corresponding messages $m_{i,j}$'s. Then $\mathcal{S}$ simulates all the secret keys sk_i's.
  6. On input of $\mathsf{st}, \{m_{i,j}\}_{i,j}, \{(\mathsf{pk}_i, \mathsf{sk}_i)\}_i$, $\mathcal{A}_2$ outputs a bit $1/0$.

Notice that the simulator needs to simulate the ciphertexts first without knowing the corresponding messages, and then sample the secret keys so that the ciphertexts appear appropriate under the given messages.

Definition 5 (Multi-instance Simulation-Based CPA Security). *For security parameters $\lambda, \eta(\lambda), \ell(\lambda), q(\lambda)$ and $S(\lambda)$, a public key encryption scheme $\Pi = (\mathsf{Gen}, \mathsf{Enc}, \mathsf{Dec})$ is (η, ℓ, q, S)-MULT-SIM-CPA secure if for all PPT adversaries $\mathcal{A} = (\mathcal{A}_1, \mathcal{A}_2)$, there exists a simulator $\mathcal{S}$ such that:*

$$\left| \Pr\left[\mathsf{ExpReal}^{\Pi}_{\mathcal{C}, \mathcal{A}}(\lambda, \eta, \ell, S) = 1 \right] - \Pr\left[\mathsf{ExpIdeal}^{\Pi}_{\mathcal{S}, \mathcal{A}}(\lambda, \eta, \ell, q, S) = 1 \right] \right| \leq \mathsf{negl}(\lambda).$$

Remark 3. If $\ell = 1$, we say that the scheme has only single-ciphertext-per-user security. For $\ell > 1$, we say that the scheme has multi-ciphertext-per-user security.

Remark 4. Notice that by replacing the underlying PKE scheme with a Symmetric Key Encryption (SKE) scheme and modifying corresponding syntaxes (sample only sk's instead of $(\mathsf{pk}, \mathsf{sk})$ pairs, and remove step 2 of the experiments where the adversary receives the pk's), we can also get a MULT-SIM-CPA security definition for SKE schemes.

5 Symmetric Key Incompressible Encryption

In this section, we explore the multi-user security of incompressible SKEs, both in the low-rate setting and the rate-1 setting. We also present a generic lifting technique to obtain an SKE with multi-ciphertext-per-user security from an SKE with single-ciphertext-per-user security.

5.1 Low Rate Incompressible SKE

For low rate incompressible SKE, it follows almost immediately from multi-instance randomness extractors that the forward-secure storage by Dziembowski [15] is MULT-SIM-CPA secure (by using multi-instance randomness extractors as the "BSM function" and One Time Pad (OTP) as the underlying SKE primitive).

First, let us recall the construction by Dziembowski [15], with the multi-instance randomness extractors and OTP plugged in.

Construction 1 (Forward-Secure Storage [15]). Let λ and S be security parameters. Given $\mathsf{Ext} : \{0,1\}^n \times \{0,1\}^d \to \{0,1\}^w$ a $(t, \alpha, \beta, \epsilon)$-multi-instance randomness extractor as defined in Definition 3 where the seed length $d = \mathsf{poly}(\lambda)$, output length $w = \mathsf{poly}(\lambda)$ and $n = \frac{S}{(1-\alpha)t} + \mathsf{poly}(\lambda)$, the construction $\Pi = (\mathsf{Gen}, \mathsf{Enc}, \mathsf{Dec})$ for message space $\{0,1\}^w$ works as follows:

- $\mathsf{Gen}(1^\lambda, 1^S)$: Sample a seed $s \leftarrow \{0,1\}^d$ for the randomness extractor, and a key $k' \leftarrow \{0,1\}^w$. Output $k = (s, k')$.
- $\mathsf{Enc}(k, m)$: To encrypt a message m, first parse $k = (s, k')$ and sample a long randomness $R \leftarrow \{0,1\}^n$. Compute the ciphertext as $\mathsf{ct} = (R, \mathsf{ct}' = \mathsf{Ext}(R; s) \oplus k' \oplus m)$.
- $\mathsf{Dec}(k, \mathsf{ct})$: First, parse $\mathsf{ct} = (R, \mathsf{ct}')$ and $k = (s, k')$. Then compute $m = \mathsf{Ext}(R; s) \oplus k' \oplus \mathsf{ct}'$.

Correctness is straightforward. Construction 1 is also MULT-SIM-CPA secure. Essentially, the simulator simply sends ct_i's as uniformly random strings. Then when the simulator sends the keys, it would use the simulator for the multi-instance randomness extractor to get the index subset $I \subset [\eta]$, and for $i \in I$, send k_i as a uniformly random string. For $i \notin I$, it samples the extractor seed s_i and then compute $k'_i = m_i \oplus \mathsf{Ext}(R_i; s_i) \oplus \mathsf{ct}'_i$. Notice that for $i \notin I$, $\mathsf{ct}'_i = m_i \oplus \mathsf{Ext}(R_i; s_i) \oplus k'_i$, and for $i \in I$, $\mathsf{ct}'_i = m_i \oplus u_i \oplus k'_i$ where u_i is a w-bit uniform string. This is now just the definition of multi-instance randomness extractors.

Theorem 1. *Let λ, S be security parameters. If $\mathsf{Ext} : \{0,1\}^n \times \{0,1\}^d \to \{0,1\}^w$ is a $(t, \alpha, \beta, \epsilon)$-multi-instance randomness extractor with $d, w = \mathsf{poly}(\lambda)$ and $n = \frac{S}{(1-\alpha)t} + \mathsf{poly}(\lambda)$, then Construction 1 is $(t, 1, (1-\beta)t, S)$-MULT-SIM-CPA secure.*

For a formal hybrid proof of Theorem 1, see the full version [18].

Remark 5. While MULT-SIM-CPA security only requires that no *PPT* adversaries can distinguish between the real mode and the ideal mode experiments, what we have proved for construction 1 here is that it is actually MULT-SIM-CPA secure against *all (potentially computationally unbounded)* adversaries, and hence is information theoretically MULT-SIM-CPA secure.

5.2 Rate-1 Incompressible SKE

Branco, Döttling and Dujmovic [6] construct rate-1 incompressible SKE from HILL-Entropic Encodings [22], extractors and PRGs. We show that by replacing the extractors with multi-instance randomness extractors and slightly modifying the scheme, we get MULT-SIM-CPA security.

First, we recall the definitions and security requirements of a HILL-Entropic Encoding scheme [22].

Definition 6 (HILL-Entropic Encoding [22]). *Let λ be the security parameter. An (α, β)-HILL-Entropic Encoding in the common random string setting is a pair of PPT algorithms* Code $=$ (Enc, Dec) *that works as follows:*

- $\mathsf{Enc}_{\mathsf{crs}}(1^\lambda, m) \rightarrow c$: *On input the common random string* crs, *the security parameter, and a message, outputs a codeword c.*
- $\mathsf{Dec}_{\mathsf{crs}}(c) \rightarrow m$: *On input the common random string and a codeword, outputs the decoded message m.*

It satisfies the following properties.

Correctness. *For all $\lambda \in \mathbb{N}$ and $m \in \{0,1\}^*$, $\Pr[\mathsf{Dec}_{\mathsf{crs}}(\mathsf{Enc}_{\mathsf{crs}}(1^\lambda, m)) = m] \geq 1 - \mathsf{negl}(\lambda)$.*

α-Expansion. *For all $\lambda, k \in \mathbb{N}$ and for all $m \in \{0,1\}^k$, $|\mathsf{Enc}_{\mathsf{crs}}(1^\lambda, m)| \leq \alpha(\lambda, k)$.*

β-HILL-Entropy. *There exists a simulator algorithm* SimEnc *such that for all polynomial $k = k(\lambda)$ and any ensemble of messages $m = \{m_\lambda\}$ of length $k(\lambda)$, consider the following real mode experiment:*

- crs $\leftarrow \{0,1\}^{t(\lambda, k)}$
- $c \leftarrow \mathsf{Enc}_{\mathsf{crs}}(1^\lambda, m_\lambda)$

and let CRS, C *denote the random variables for the corresponding values in the real mode experiment. Also consider the following simulated experiment:*

- $(\mathsf{crs}', c') \leftarrow \mathsf{SimEnc}(1^\lambda, m_\lambda)$

and let CRS$'$, C' *be the corresponding random variables in the simulated experiment. We require that* (CRS, C) $\approx_c$ (CRS$'$, C') *and that $H_\infty(C'|\mathsf{CRS}') \geq \beta(\lambda, k)$.*

Moran and Wichs [22] show that we can construct HILL-Entropic Encodings in the CRS model from either the Decisional Composite Residuosity (DCR) assumption [10,24] or the Learning with Errors (LWE) problem [25]. Their construction achieves $\alpha(\lambda, k) = k(1 + o(1)) + \mathsf{poly}(\lambda)$ and $\beta(\lambda, k) = k(1 - o(1)) - \mathsf{poly}(\lambda)$, which we call a "good" HILL-entropic encoding.

Now we reproduce the construction from [6] with the multi-instance randomness extractors and some other minor changes (highlighted below).

Construction 2 ([6]). Let λ and S be security parameters. Given $\mathsf{Ext} : \{0,1\}^n \times \{0,1\}^d \to \{0,1\}^w$ a $(t, \alpha, \beta, \epsilon)$-multi-instance randomness extractor where the seed length $d = \mathsf{poly}(\lambda)$, $w = \mathsf{poly}(\lambda)$ and $n = \frac{S}{(1-\alpha)t} + \mathsf{poly}(\lambda)$, $\mathsf{Code} = (\mathsf{Enc}, \mathsf{Dec})$ a "good" (α', β')-HILL-Entropic Encoding scheme, and $\mathsf{PRG} : \{0,1\}^w \to \{0,1\}^n$ a pseudorandom generator secure against non-uniform adversaries, the construction $\Pi = (\mathsf{Gen}, \mathsf{Enc}, \mathsf{Dec})$ for message space $\{0,1\}^n$ works as follows:

- $\mathsf{Gen}(1^\lambda, 1^S)$: Sample a seed $s \leftarrow \{0,1\}^d$ for the randomness extractor, a common random string $\mathsf{crs} \in \{0,1\}^{\mathsf{poly}(\lambda,n)}$ for the HILL-Entropic Encoding, and a random pad $r \leftarrow \{0,1\}^n$. Output $k = (s, r, \mathsf{crs})$.
- $\mathsf{Enc}(k, m)$: To encrypt a message m, first parse $k = (s, r, \mathsf{crs})$ and sample a random PRG seed $s' \leftarrow \{0,1\}^w$. Compute $c_1 = \mathsf{Code}.\mathsf{Enc}_{\mathsf{crs}}(1^\lambda, \mathsf{PRG}(s') \oplus r \oplus m)$ and $c_2 = s' \oplus \mathsf{Ext}(c_1, s)$. The final ciphertext is $\mathsf{ct} = (c_1, c_2)$.
- $\mathsf{Dec}(k, \mathsf{ct})$: First, parse $\mathsf{ct} = (c_1, c_2)$ and $k = (s, r, \mathsf{crs})$. Then compute $s' = \mathsf{Ext}(c_1; s) \oplus c_2$ and obtain $m = \mathsf{Code}.\mathsf{Dec}_{\mathsf{crs}}(c_1) \oplus \mathsf{PRG}(s') \oplus r$.

Correctness follows from the original construction and should be easy to verify. Notice that by the α'-expansion of the "good" HILL-entropic encoding, the ciphertexts have length $(1 + o(1))n + w + \mathsf{poly}(\lambda) = (1 + o(1))n + \mathsf{poly}(\lambda)$ (the $\mathsf{poly}(\lambda)$ part is independent of n), while the messages have length n. Hence the scheme achieves an optimal rate of 1 $((1 - o(1))$ to be exact). The keys are bit longer though, having size $d + n + \mathsf{poly}(\lambda, n) = n + \mathsf{poly}(\lambda, n)$. Furthermore, Moran and Wichs [22] show that the CRS needs to be at least as long as the message being encoded. Thus the key has length at least $2n + \mathsf{poly}(\lambda)$.

Theorem 2. *If* $\mathsf{Ext} : \{0,1\}^n \times \{0,1\}^d \to \{0,1\}^w$ *is a* $(t, \alpha, \beta, \epsilon)$-*multi-instance randomness extractor with* $n = \frac{S}{(1-\alpha)t} + \mathsf{poly}(\lambda)$, $\mathsf{Code} = (\mathsf{Enc}, \mathsf{Dec})$ *is a "good" HILL-entropic encoding with* β'-*HILL-entropy, and* PRG *is a pseudorandom generator secure against non-uniform adversaries, then Construction 2 is* $(t, 1, (1 - \beta)t, S)$-*MULT-SIM-CPA secure.*

The hybrid proof essentially follows the same structure from [6], except for a different extractor step, the inclusion of the random pad r and the requirement of PRG to be secure against non-uniform attackers. For the detailed hybrid proof of Theorem 2, see the full version [18].

5.3 Dealing with Multiple Messages per User

Above we have showed MULT-SIM-CPA security for SKE schemes where the number of messages per user ℓ is equal to 1. Here, we show how we can generically lift a SKE scheme with single-message-per-user MULT-SIM-CPA security to multiple-messages-per-user MULT-SIM-CPA security.

Construction 3. Let λ, S be security parameters. Given $\mathsf{SKE} = (\mathsf{Gen}, \mathsf{Enc}, \mathsf{Dec})$ a $(\eta, 1, q, S)$-MULT-SIM-CPA secure SKE with key space $\{0,1\}^{n}$ [10] and $\mathcal{F}$ a

---

[10] Here we assume SKE's keys are uniformly random n-bit strings. This is without loss of generality since we can always take the key to be the random coins for Gen.

class of ℓ-wise independent functions with range $\{0,1\}^n$, we construct $\Pi = (\mathsf{Gen}, \mathsf{Enc}, \mathsf{Dec})$ as follows.

- $\mathsf{Gen}(1^\lambda, 1^S)$: Sample a random function $f \leftarrow \mathcal{F}$. Output $k = f$.
- $\mathsf{Enc}(k = f, m)$: Sample a short random string r with $|r| = \mathsf{polylog}(\ell)$, compute $k' = f(r)$, and get $c \leftarrow \mathsf{SKE.Enc}(k', m)$. Output $\mathsf{ct} = (r, c)$.
- $\mathsf{Dec}(k = f, \mathsf{ct} = (r, c))$: Compute $k' = f(r)$, and output $m \leftarrow \mathsf{SKE.Dec}(k', c)$.

Correctness should be easy to verify given the correctness of the underlying SKE scheme and the deterministic property of the ℓ-wise independent functions.

Lemma 7. *If* SKE *is a* $(\eta, 1, q, S)$-MULT-SIM-CPA *secure SKE with key space* $\{0,1\}^n$ *and* $\mathcal{F}$ *is a class of* ℓ-wise independent functions with range $\{0,1\}^n$, then Construction 3 is $(\eta/\ell, \ell, q, S - \eta \cdot \mathsf{polylog}(\ell))$-MULT-SIM-CPA *secure.*

Proof. We prove this through a reduction. We show that if there is an adversary $\mathcal{A} = (\mathcal{A}_1, \mathcal{A}_2)$ that breaks the $(\eta/\ell, \ell, q, S - \eta \cdot \mathsf{polylog}(\ell))$-MULT-SIM-CPA security of Π, then we can construct an adversary $\mathcal{A}' = (\mathcal{A}'_1, \mathcal{A}'_2)$ that breaks the $(\eta, 1, q, S)$-MULT-SIM-CPA security of SKE. $\mathcal{A}' = (\mathcal{A}'_1, \mathcal{A}'_2)$ works as follows:

- $\mathcal{A}'_1$: First, run $\mathcal{A}_1$ to get a list of message queries $\{m_{i,j}\}_{i \in [\eta/\ell], j \in [\ell]}$. Let $m'_i = m_{(i/\ell)+1,((i-1) \bmod \ell)+1}$ for $i \in [\eta]$. Notice that here we are essentially flattening the list of messages. Submit the list $\{m'_i\}_{i \in [\eta]}$ and receive $\{\mathsf{ct}'_i\}_{i \in [\eta]}$. Reconstruct $\mathsf{ct}_{i,j} = (r_{i,j}, \mathsf{ct}'_{(i-1)\cdot\ell+j})$ for $i \in [\eta/\ell]$ and $j \in [\ell]$, where $r_{i,j}$ is a uniformly random string sampled from $\{0,1\}^{\mathsf{polylog}(\ell)}$. Notice that the $r_{i,j}$'s have no collisions under the same i with overwhelming probability. Send the list of ciphertexts $\{\mathsf{ct}_{i,j}\}_{i,j}$ back to $\mathcal{A}_1$ and receive a state st. Output the state $\mathsf{st}' = (\mathsf{st}, \{r_{i,j}\}_{i,j})$. The size of the state is $|\mathsf{st}| + \eta \cdot \mathsf{polylog}(\ell) \leq S - \eta \cdot \mathsf{polylog}(\ell) + \eta \cdot \mathsf{polylog}(\ell) = S$.
- $\mathcal{A}'_2$: First receive $\mathsf{st}' = (\mathsf{st}, \{r_{i,j}\}_{i,j}), \{m'_i\}_{i \in [\eta]}, \{k'_i\}_{i \in [\eta]}$ from the challenger / simulator. Reorganize $m_{i,j} = m'_{(i-1)\cdot\ell+j}$ for $i \in [\eta/\ell]$ and $j \in [\ell]$. Construct k_i as an ℓ-wise independent function f_i s.t. for all $i \in [\eta/\ell]$ and $j \in [\ell]$, $f_i(r_{i,j}) = k'_{(i-1)\cdot\ell+j}$. Send $\mathsf{st}, \{m_{i,j}\}_{i \in [\eta/\ell], j \in [\ell]}, \{k_i = f_i\}_{i \in [\eta/\ell]}$ to $\mathcal{A}_2$ and receive a bit b. Output b.

Notice that $\mathcal{A}'$ perfectly simulates the view for $\mathcal{A}$. If $\mathcal{A}$ says it is in the real mode, this means the ciphertexts are faithful encryptions of the message queries, and hence $\mathcal{A}'$ should be in the real mode as well, and vice versa. Therefore, construction 3 is $(\eta/\ell, \ell, q, S - \eta \cdot \mathsf{polylog}(\ell))$-MULT-SIM-CPA secure. □

6   Public Key Incompressible Encryption

Here we explore multi-user security of incompressible Public Key Encryptions (PKEs), considering constructions from [6,17]. Unlike the SKE setting, where we can generically lift single-ciphertext-per-user security to multi-ciphertext-per-user security, here we show how to obtain multi-ciphertext security by modifying each construction specifically.

6.1   Low Rate Incompressible PKE

For low rate incompressible PKE, we show that the construction from [17] is MULT-SIM-CPA secure by plugging in the multi-instance randomness extractor. Then, we upgrade the construction to have multi-ciphertext-per-user security by upgrading the functionality of the underlying functional encryption scheme.

Construction 4 ([17] with Multi-Instance Randomness Extractor). Given FE = (Setup, KeyGen, Enc, Dec) a single-key selectively secure functional encryption scheme and a $(t, \alpha, \beta, \epsilon)$-multi-instance randomness extractor Ext : $\{0,1\}^n \times \{0,1\}^d \to \{0,1\}^w$, with $d = \mathsf{poly}(\lambda)$, $w = \mathsf{poly}(\lambda)$ and $n = \frac{S}{(1-\alpha)t} + \mathsf{poly}(\lambda)$, the construction $\Pi = (\mathsf{Gen}, \mathsf{Enc}, \mathsf{Dec})$ with message space $\{0,1\}^w$ works as follows:

- $\mathsf{Gen}(1^\lambda, 1^S)$: First, obtain (FE.mpk, FE.msk) $\leftarrow$ FE.Setup(1^λ). Then, generate the secret key for the following function f_v with a hardcoded $v \in \{0,1\}^{d+w}$:

$$f_v(s' = (s, \mathsf{pad}), \mathsf{flag}) = \begin{cases} s' & \text{if flag} = 0 \\ s' \oplus v & \text{if flag} = 1 \end{cases}.$$

  Output pk = FE.mpk and sk = FE.sk$_{f_v}$ $\leftarrow$ FE.KeyGen(FE.msk, f_v).
- $\mathsf{Enc}(\mathsf{pk}, m)$: Sample a random tuple $s' = (s, \mathsf{pad})$ where $s \in \{0,1\}^d$ is used as a seed for the extractor and pad $\in \{0,1\}^w$ is used as a one-time pad. The ciphertext consists of three parts: FE.ct $\leftarrow$ FE.Enc(FE.mpk, $(s', 0)$), a long randomness $R \in \{0,1\}^n$, and $z = \mathsf{Ext}(R; s) \oplus \mathsf{pad} \oplus m$.
- $\mathsf{Dec}(\mathsf{sk}, \mathsf{ct} = (\mathsf{FE.ct}, R, z))$: First, obtain $s' \leftarrow$ FE.Dec(FE.sk$_{f_v}$, FE.ct), and then use the seed s to compute $\mathsf{Ext}(R; s) \oplus z \oplus \mathsf{pad}$ to recover m.

The correctness follows from the original construction.

Theorem 3. *If FE is a single-key selectively secure functional encryption scheme and Ext : $\{0,1\}^n \times \{0,1\}^d \to \{0,1\}^w$ is a $(t, \alpha, \beta, \epsilon)$-multi-instance randomness extractor with $d, w = \mathsf{poly}(\lambda)$ and $n = \frac{S}{(1-\alpha)t} + \mathsf{poly}(\lambda)$, then Construction 4 is $(t, 1, (1-\beta)t, S)$-MULT-SIM-CPA secure.*

For the sequence of hybrids, see the full version [18]. The proofs of the hybrid arguments are identical to those from [17], except for the extractor step, which is analogous to the proof of Lemma 5.2 in the full version [18].

Upgrading to Multiple Ciphertexts per User. Additionally, We show that the constructions from [17] can be upgraded to have multi-ciphertext-per-user security. Essentially, all we need is to upgrade the functionality of the underlying functional encryption scheme to work for a slightly more generalized class of functions. We will need functions $f_{\{v_i\}_i}(s, \mathsf{flag}) = s \oplus v_{\mathsf{flag}}$ for hard coded values $v_1, \ldots, v_\ell$ and a special v_0 being the all 0 string. Notice that the original GWZ construction [17] can be viewed as using functions that are a special case where $\ell = 1$. We show how to construct FE schemes for such $f_{\{v_i\}_i}$ functions from plain PKE in the full version [18]. With this new class of functions, we can achieve $(t, \ell, (1 - \beta)\ell t, S)$-MULT-SIM-CPA security. In the hybrid proof where we replace FE.Enc(FE.mpk, $(s', 0)$) with FE.Enc(FE.mpk, $(s' \oplus v, 1)$), now for the j-th message query for the i-th user where $i \in [t]$ and $j \in [\ell]$, we replace FE.Enc(FE.mpk$_i$, $(s'_{i,j}, 0)$) with FE.Enc(FE.mpk$_i$, $(s'_{i,j} \oplus v_{i,j}, j)$). The rest of the hybrid proof follows analogously.

6.2   Rate-1 Incompressible PKE

For rate-1 incompressible PKE, we first show that we can easily plug in the multi-instance randomness extractor to the construction by Guan, Wichs and Zhandry [17]. We also provide a generalization on the construction by Branco, Döttling and Dujmovic [6] using a Key Encapsulation Mechanism (KEM) with a special *non-committing* property. For both constructions, we show how to adapt them to allow for multi-ciphertext-per-user security.

Construction by [17]. We first reproduce the rate-1 PKE construction from [17], with the multi-instance randomness extractors plugged in.

Construction 5 ([17]). Given FE = (Setup, KeyGen, Enc, Dec) a rate-1 functional encryption scheme satisfying single-key semi-adaptive security, Ext : $\{0,1\}^n \times \{0,1\}^d \to \{0,1\}^w$ a $(t, \alpha, \beta, \epsilon)$-multi-instance randomness extractor with $d, w = \mathsf{poly}(\lambda)$, $n = \frac{S}{(1-\alpha)t} + \mathsf{poly}(\lambda)$ and PRG : $\{0,1\}^w \to \{0,1\}^n$ a secure PRG against non-uniform adversaries, the construction $\Pi = $ (Gen, Enc, Dec) for message space $\{0,1\}^n$ works as follows:

- Gen($1^\lambda, 1^S$): First, obtain (FE.mpk, FE.msk) $\leftarrow$ FE.Setup(1^λ). Then, generate the secret key for the following function $f_{v,s}$ with a hardcoded large random pad $v \in \{0,1\}^n$ and a small extractor seed $s \in \{0,1\}^d$:

$$f_{v,s}(x, \mathsf{flag}) = \begin{cases} x & \text{if flag} = 0 \\ \mathsf{PRG}(\mathsf{Extract}(x; s)) \oplus v & \text{if flag} = 1 \end{cases}.$$

  Output pk = FE.mpk and sk = FE.sk$_{f_{v,s}} \leftarrow$ FE.KeyGen(FE.msk, $f_{v,s}$).
- Enc(pk, m): The ciphertext is simply an encryption of $(m, 0)$ using the underlying FE scheme, i.e. FE.ct $\leftarrow$ FE.Enc(FE.mpk, $(m, 0)$).
- Dec(sk, ct): Decryption also corresponds to FE decryption. The output is simply FE.Dec(FE.sk$_{f_{v,s}}$, ct) = $f_{v,s}(m, 0) = m$ as desired.

Correctness easily follows from the original construction. The rate of the construction is the rate of the underlying FE multiplied by $\frac{n}{n+1}$. If the FE has rate $(1 - o(1))$, the construction has rate $(1 - o(1))$ as desired.

Theorem 4. *If* FE = (Setup, KeyGen, Enc, Dec) *is a single-key semi-adaptively secure FE scheme,* Ext : $\{0,1\}^n \times \{0,1\}^d \to \{0,1\}^w$ *is a* $(t, \alpha, \beta, \epsilon)$-*multi-instance randomness extractor, with* $d, w = \mathsf{poly}(\lambda)$ *and* $n = \frac{S}{(1-\alpha)t} + \mathsf{poly}(\lambda)$, *and* PRG : $\{0,1\}^w \to \{0,1\}^n$ *is a PRG secure against non-uniform adversaries, then Construction 5 is* $(t, 1, (1 - \beta)t, S)$-MULT-SIM-CPA *secure.*

For the sequence of hybrids to prove Theorem 4, see the full version [18]. For the proofs of each hybrid argument, see the original [17] paper, since they are identical except for the extractor step (analogous to Lemma 5.2 in the full version [18]) and the PRG against non-uniform attackers step (analogous to Lemma 5.8 in the full version [18]).

Upgrading to Multiple Ciphertexts per User. Upgrading Construction 5 to multi-ciphertext-per-user security is rather straightforward. Since the construction already requires a full functionality FE scheme, we just modify the class of functions that the underlying FE scheme uses, without introducing any new assumptions. Specifically, we now use $f_{\{v_j\}_j, \{s_j\}_j}$ with hard-coded values $v_j \in \{0,1\}^n$ and $s_j \in \{0,1\}^d$ for $j \in [\ell]$ that behaves as follows:

$$f_{\{v_j\}_j, \{s_j\}_j}(x, \mathsf{flag}) = \begin{cases} x & \text{if flag} = 0 \\ \mathsf{PRG}(\mathsf{Extract}(x; s_{\mathsf{flag}})) \oplus v_{\mathsf{flag}} & \text{if flag} \in [\ell] \end{cases}.$$

This gives us $(t, \ell, (1 - \alpha)\ell t, S)$-MULT-SIM-CPA security. Notice that this modification does slightly harm the rate of the scheme, since the flag is now $\log(\ell)$ bits instead of one bit, but asymptotically the rate is still $(1 - o(1))$.

The hybrid proof works analogously to that of Theorem 4, except that in the hybrid proof where we swap the FE encryption of $(m, 0)$ to $(R, 1)$, we now swap from $(m_{i,j}, 0)$ to $(R_{i,j}, j)$ for the j-th ciphertext from the i-th user.

Generalization of Construction by [6]. [6] show how to lift a rate-1 incompressible SKE scheme to a rate-1 incompressible PKE scheme using a Key Encapsulation Mechanism [8] from programmable Hash Proof Systems (HPS) [7,21]. Their construction satisfies CCA2 security. We show that if we are to relax the security notion to only CPA security, all we need for the lifting is a Key Encapsulation Mechanism with a *non-committing* property, defined below.

Definition 7 (Key Encapsulation Mechanism [8]). *Let λ be the security parameters, a Key Encapsulation Mechanism (KEM) is a tuple of algorithms $\Pi = (\mathsf{KeyGen}, \mathsf{Encap}, \mathsf{Decap})$ that works as follows:*

- $\mathsf{KeyGen}(1^\lambda, 1^{\mathcal{L}_k}) \to (\mathsf{pk}, \mathsf{sk})$: *The key generation algorithm takes as input the security parameter and the desired symmetric key length $\mathcal{L}_k$, outputs a pair of public key and private key $(\mathsf{pk}, \mathsf{sk})$.*
- $\mathsf{Encap}(\mathsf{pk}) \to (k, c)$: *The encapsulation algorithm takes the public key pk, produces a symmetric key $k \in \{0,1\}^{\mathcal{L}_k}$, and a header c that encapsulates k.*
- $\mathsf{Decap}(\mathsf{sk}, c) \to k$: *The decapsulation algorithm takes as input the private key sk and a header c, and decapsulates the header to get the symmetric key k.*

Definition 8 (Correctness of KEM). *A key encapsulation mechanism $\mathsf{KEM} = (\mathsf{KeyGen}, \mathsf{Encap}, \mathsf{Decap})$ is said to be correct if:*

$$\Pr\left[k' = k : \begin{array}{c} (\mathsf{pk}, \mathsf{sk}) \leftarrow \mathsf{KeyGen}(1^\lambda, 1^{\mathcal{L}_k}) \\ (k, c) \leftarrow \mathsf{Encap}(\mathsf{pk}) \\ k' \leftarrow \mathsf{Decap}(\mathsf{sk}, c) \end{array} \right] \geq 1 - \mathsf{negl}(\lambda).$$

Definition 9 (Non-Committing). *A key encapsulation mechanism* KEM = (KeyGen, Encap, Decap) *is said to be* non-committing *if there exists a pair of simulator algorithm* $(\mathsf{Sim}_1, \mathsf{Sim}_2)$ *such that* $\mathsf{Sim}_1(1^\lambda, 1^{\mathcal{L}_k})$ *outputs a simulated public key* pk′, *a header* c′ *and a state* st *with* $|\mathsf{st}| = \mathsf{poly}(\lambda, \mathcal{L}_k)$, *and for any given target key* $k' \in \{0,1\}^{\mathcal{L}_k}$, $\mathsf{Sim}_2(\mathsf{st}, k')$ *outputs the random coins* r^{KeyGen} *and* r^{Encap}. *We require that if we run the key generation and encapsulation algorithm using these random coins, we will get the desired* pk′, c′, *and* k′, .:

$$\Pr \left[\begin{array}{l} \mathsf{pk}' = \mathsf{pk} \\ k' = k \\ c' = c \end{array} : \begin{array}{l} (\mathsf{pk}, \mathsf{sk}) \leftarrow \mathsf{KeyGen}(1^\lambda, 1^{\mathcal{L}_k}; r^{\mathsf{KeyGen}}) \\ (k, c) \leftarrow \mathsf{Encap}(\mathsf{pk}; r^{\mathsf{Encap}}) \end{array} \right] \geq 1 - \mathsf{negl}(\lambda).$$

Kindly notice that by the correctness property, $\mathsf{Decap}(\mathsf{sk}, c') \to k'$.

This *non-committing* property allows us to commit to a public key and header first, but then later able to reveal it as an encapsulation of an arbitrary symmetric key in the key space. And it will be impossible to distinguish the simulated public key and header from the ones we get from faithfully running KeyGen and Encap.

Using this non-committing KEM, we are able to construct rate-1 incompressible PKE from rate-1 incompressible SKE, with multi-user security in mind. This is a generalization of the construction by [6].

Construction 6 (Generalization of [6]). For security parameters λ, S, given KEM = (KeyGen, Encap, Decap) a non-commiting KEM and SKE = (Gen, Enc, Dec) a rate-1 incompressible SKE for message space $\{0,1\}^n$, we construct rate-1 incompressible PKE Π = (Gen, Enc, Dec) for message space $\{0,1\}^n$ as follows:

- Gen($1^\lambda, 1^S$): First, run SKE.Gen($1^\lambda, 1^S$) to determine the required symmetric key length $\mathcal{L}_k$ under security parameters λ, S. Then run (pk, sk) ← KEM.KeyGen($1^\lambda, 1^{\mathcal{L}_k}$) and output (pk, sk).
- Enc(pk, m): First, run (k, c_0) ← KEM.Encap(pk) to sample a symmetric key k, and encapsulate it into a header c_0. Then compute c_1 ← SKE.Enc(k, m). The ciphertext is the tuple (c_0, c_1).
- Dec(sk, ct = (c_0, c_1)): Decapsulate c_0 with sk to obtain k ← KEM.Decap(sk, c_0), and then use k to decrypt c_1 and get m ← SKE.Dec(k, c_1).

Correctness follows from the correctness of the underlying incompressible SKE and the KEM scheme. In terms of the rate, to achieve a rate-1 incompressible PKE, we would require the KEM to produce "short" headers, i.e. $|c_0| = \mathsf{poly}(\lambda)$ independent of $\mathcal{L}_k$ (notice that $\mathcal{L}_k = \mathsf{poly}(\lambda, n)$ and needs to be at least as large as n). We can build such KEMs using various efficient encapsulation techniques [2,3,5]. With the short header and an incompressible SKE with rate $(1 - o(1))$, the ciphertext length is $n/(1 - o(1)) + \mathsf{poly}(\lambda)$, yielding an ideal rate of $(1 - o(1))$ for the construction. However, these KEMs require long public keys, as opposed to the short public keys in Construction 5.

For security, we prove that if the underlying SKE has MULT-SIM-CPA security, then Construction 6 has MULT-SIM-CPA security as well.

Theorem 5. *If* KEM *is a non-commiting KEM, and* SKE *is a* $(\eta, 1, q, S)$-MULT-SIM-CPA *secure SKE with message space* $\{0,1\}^n$, *then Construction 6 is* $(\eta, 1, q, S - \eta \cdot \mathsf{poly}(\lambda, n))$-MULT-SIM-CPA *secure.*

Proof. We prove this through a reduction. We show that if there is an adversary $\mathcal{A} = (\mathcal{A}_1, \mathcal{A}_2)$ that breaks the $(\eta, 1, q, S - \eta \cdot \mathsf{poly}(\lambda, n))$-MULT-SIM-CPA security of Π, then we can construct an adversary $\mathcal{A}' = (\mathcal{A}'_1, \mathcal{A}'_2)$ that breaks the $(\eta, 1, q, S)$-MULT-SIM-CPA security of SKE. $\mathcal{A}' = (\mathcal{A}'_1, \mathcal{A}'_2)$ works as follows:

- $\mathcal{A}'_1$: Use the security parameters λ, S to determine the key length $\mathcal{L}_k$ for the underlying SKE[11]. For each $i \in [\eta]$, obtain $(\mathsf{pk}_i, c_{0,i}, \mathsf{KEM.st}_i) \leftarrow \mathsf{KEM.Sim}_1(1^\lambda, 1^{\mathcal{L}_k})$. Send $\{\mathsf{pk}_i\}_i$ to $\mathcal{A}_1$ to get a list of message queries $\{m_i\}_i$. Then, forward the list $\{m_i\}_i$ to the challenger/simulator and receive a list of ciphertexts $\{\mathsf{ct}'_i\}_i$. Construct $\mathsf{ct}_i = (c_{0,i}, \mathsf{ct}'_i)$, and send all $\{\mathsf{ct}_i\}_i$ to $\mathcal{A}_1$ to receive a state st. Output the state $\mathsf{st}' = (\mathsf{st}, \{\mathsf{KEM.st}_i\}_i)$. The size of the state is $|\mathsf{st}| + \eta \cdot \mathsf{poly}(\lambda, \mathcal{L}_k) \leq S - \eta \cdot \mathsf{poly}(\lambda, n) + \eta \cdot \mathsf{poly}(\lambda, n) = S$.
- $\mathcal{A}'_2$: First receive $\mathsf{st}' = (\mathsf{st}, \{\mathsf{KEM.st}_i\}_i), \{m_i\}_i, \{k_i\}_i$ from the challenger/simulator. For each $i \in [\eta]$, run $(r_i^{\mathsf{KeyGen}}, r_i^{\mathsf{Encap}}) \leftarrow \mathsf{KEM.Sim}_2(\mathsf{KEM.st}_i, k_i)$, and $(\mathsf{pk}_i, \mathsf{sk}_i) \leftarrow \mathsf{KEM.KeyGen}(1^\lambda, 1^{\mathcal{L}_k}; r_i^{\mathsf{KeyGen}})$. Notice that pk_i matches the pk_i produced previously by $\mathcal{A}'_1$ due to the non-committing property of the KEM. Send $\mathsf{st}, \{m_i\}_i, \{(\mathsf{pk}_i, \mathsf{sk}_i)\}_i$ to $\mathcal{A}_2$ and receive a bit b. Output b.

Notice that $\mathcal{A}'$ perfectly simulates the view for $\mathcal{A}$. If $\mathcal{A}$ says it is in the real mode interacting with the challenger, this means the ciphertexts ct_i's are faithful encryptions of the message queries m_i's for all $i \in [\eta]$. Then we have $\mathsf{SKE.Dec}(k_i, \mathsf{ct}'_i) = m_i$, and hence $\mathcal{A}'$ is also in the real mode. The converse also holds true. Therefore, construction 6 is $(\eta, 1, q, S - \eta \cdot \mathsf{poly}(\lambda, n))$-MULT-SIM-CPA secure. $\square$

Upgrading to Multiple Ciphertexts per User. Next we show how to upgrade Construction 6 to have multi-ciphertext-per-user security. All we need is to upgrade the KEM to be ℓ-*strongly non-committing*, defined as below.

Definition 10 (ℓ-Strongly Non-Committing). *A key encapsulation mechanism* KEM = (KeyGen, Encap, Decap) *is said to be* ℓ-*strongly non-committing if there exists a pair of simulator algorithm* $(\mathsf{Sim}_1, \mathsf{Sim}_2)$ *such that* $\mathsf{Sim}_1(1^\lambda, 1^{\mathcal{L}_k})$ *outputs a simulated public key* pk', *a set of simulated headers* $\mathcal{C}' = \{c'_1, c'_2, \ldots, c'_\ell\}$ *and a state* st *with* $|\mathsf{st}| = \mathsf{poly}(\lambda, \mathcal{L}_k, \ell)$, *and for any given set of target keys* $\mathcal{K}' = \{k'_1, k'_2, \ldots, k'_\ell\}$ *where* $k'_i \in \{0,1\}^{\mathcal{L}_k}$ *for all* $i \in [\ell]$, $\mathsf{Sim}_2(\mathsf{st}, \mathcal{K}')$ *outputs a set of random coin pairs* $\{(r_i^{\mathsf{KeyGen}}, r_i^{\mathsf{Encap}})\}_{i \in [\ell]}$. *We require that if we run the key generation and encapsulation algorithm using the* i-*th pair of these random coins, we will get the desired* pk', c'_i, *and* k'_i, *i.e. for all* $i \in [\ell]$:

$$\Pr \left[\begin{array}{cc} \mathsf{pk}' = \mathsf{pk} \\ k'_i = k & : & (\mathsf{pk}, \mathsf{sk}) \leftarrow \mathsf{KeyGen}(1^\lambda, 1^{\mathcal{L}_k}; r_i^{\mathsf{KeyGen}}) \\ c'_i = c & (k, c) \leftarrow \mathsf{Encap}(\mathsf{pk}; r_i^{\mathsf{Encap}}) \end{array} \right] \geq 1 - \mathsf{negl}(\lambda).$$

Kindly notice that by the correctness property, $\mathsf{Decap}(\mathsf{sk}, c'_i) \to k'_i$.

---

[11] For the ease of syntax, we imagine the security parameters to be part of the public parameters always accessible to the adversary.

We show how to construct ℓ-strongly non-committing KEMs by composing plain non-committing KEMs in the full version [18].

To get multi-ciphertext security, we simply plug in the ℓ-strongly non-committing KEM in place of the plain non-committing KEM in construction 6. The resulting construction has $(\eta/\ell, \ell, q, S - \eta \cdot \mathsf{poly}(\lambda, n, \ell))$-MULT-SIM-CPA security. The security proof follows analogous from that of Theorem 5.

References

1. Aggarwal, D., Obremski, M., Ribeiro, J., Siniscalchi, L., Visconti, I.: How to extract useful randomness from unreliable sources. In: Canteaut, A., Ishai, Y. (eds.) EUROCRYPT 2020. LNCS, vol. 12105, pp. 343–372. Springer, Cham (2020). https://doi.org/10.1007/978-3-030-45721-1_13
2. Albrecht, M., Cid, C., Paterson, K.G., Tjhai, C.J., Tomlinson, M.: Nts-kem. NIST Submissions **2**, 4–13 (2019)
3. Bardet, M., et al.: Big quake binary goppa quasi-cyclic key encapsulation. NIST Submissions (2017)
4. Barnett Jr., T.: The zettabyte era officially begins (how much is that?). https://blogs.cisco.com/sp/the-zettabyte-era-officially-begins-how-much-is-that
5. Bernstein, D.J., et al.: Classic mceliece: conservative code-based cryptography. NIST Submissions (2017)
6. Branco, P., Döttling, N., Dujmovic, J.: Rate-1 incompressible encryption from standard assumptions. In: Kiltz, E., Vaikuntanathan, V. (eds.) TCC 2022, Part II. LNCS, vol. 13748, pp. 33–69. Springer, Heidelberg (2022). https://doi.org/10.1007/978-3-031-22365-5_2
7. Cramer, R., Shoup, V.: Universal hash proofs and a paradigm for adaptive chosen ciphertext secure public-key encryption. In: Knudsen, L.R. (ed.) EUROCRYPT 2002. LNCS, vol. 2332, pp. 45–64. Springer, Heidelberg (2002). https://doi.org/10.1007/3-540-46035-7_4
8. Cramer, R., Shoup, V.: Design and analysis of practical public-key encryption schemes secure against adaptive chosen ciphertext attack. SIAM J. Comput. **33**(1), 167–226 (2003)
9. Damgård, I.B., Fehr, S., Renner, R., Salvail, L., Schaffner, C.: A tight high-order entropic quantum uncertainty relation with applications. In: Menezes, A. (ed.) CRYPTO 2007. LNCS, vol. 4622, pp. 360–378. Springer, Heidelberg (2007). https://doi.org/10.1007/978-3-540-74143-5_20
10. Damgård, I., Jurik, M.: A generalisation, a simplification and some applications of Paillier's probabilistic public-key system. In: Kim, K. (ed.) PKC 2001. LNCS, vol. 1992, pp. 119–136. Springer, Heidelberg (2001). https://doi.org/10.1007/3-540-44586-2_9
11. Department, S.R.: Data center storage capacity worldwide from 2016 to 2021, by segment. https://www.statista.com/statistics/638593/worldwide-data-center-storage-capacity-cloud-vs-traditional/
12. Dinur, I., Stemmer, U., Woodruff, D.P., Zhou, S.: On differential privacy and adaptive data analysis with bounded space. Cryptology ePrint Archive, Report 2023/171 (2023). https://eprint.iacr.org/2023/171
13. Dodis, Y., Quach, W., Wichs, D.: Authentication in the bounded storage model. In: Dunkelman, O., Dziembowski, S. (eds.) EUROCRYPT 2022, Part III. LNCS, vol. 13277, pp. 737–766. Springer, Heidelberg (2022). https://doi.org/10.1007/978-3-031-07082-2_26

14. Dodis, Y., Reyzin, L., Smith, A.: Fuzzy extractors: how to generate strong keys from biometrics and other noisy data. In: Cachin, C., Camenisch, J.L. (eds.) EUROCRYPT 2004. LNCS, vol. 3027, pp. 523–540. Springer, Heidelberg (2004). https://doi.org/10.1007/978-3-540-24676-3_31

15. Dziembowski, S.: On forward-secure storage. In: Dwork, C. (ed.) CRYPTO 2006. LNCS, vol. 4117, pp. 251–270. Springer, Heidelberg (2006). https://doi.org/10.1007/11818175_15

16. Dziembowski, S., Kazana, T., Zdanowicz, M.: Quasi chain rule for min-entropy. Inf. Process. Lett. **134**, 62–66 (2018). https://doi.org/10.1016/j.ipl.2018.02.007. https://www.sciencedirect.com/science/article/pii/S002001901830036X

17. Guan, J., Wichs, D., Zhandry, M.: Incompressible cryptography. In: Dunkelman, O., Dziembowski, S. (eds.) EUROCRYPT 2022, Part I. LNCS, vol. 13275, pp. 700–730. Springer, Heidelberg (2022). https://doi.org/10.1007/978-3-031-06944-4_24

18. Guan, J., Wichs, D., Zhandry, M.: Multi-instance randomness extraction and security against bounded-storage mass surveillance. Cryptology ePrint Archive (2023)

19. Günther, C.G.: An identity-based key-exchange protocol. In: Quisquater, J.-J., Vandewalle, J. (eds.) EUROCRYPT 1989. LNCS, vol. 434, pp. 29–37. Springer, Heidelberg (1990). https://doi.org/10.1007/3-540-46885-4_5

20. Guruswami, V.: List Decoding of Error-Correcting Codes. LNCS, vol. 3282. Springer, Heidelberg (2005). https://doi.org/10.1007/b104335

21. Kalai, Y.T.: Smooth projective hashing and two-message oblivious transfer. In: Cramer, R. (ed.) EUROCRYPT 2005. LNCS, vol. 3494, pp. 78–95. Springer, Heidelberg (2005). https://doi.org/10.1007/11426639_5

22. Moran, T., Wichs, D.: Incompressible encodings. In: Micciancio, D., Ristenpart, T. (eds.) CRYPTO 2020. LNCS, vol. 12170, pp. 494–523. Springer, Cham (2020). https://doi.org/10.1007/978-3-030-56784-2_17

23. Nisan, N.: Psuedorandom generators for space-bounded computation. In: 22nd ACM STOC, pp. 204–212. ACM Press (1990). https://doi.org/10.1145/100216.100242

24. Paillier, P.: Public-key cryptosystems based on composite degree residuosity classes. In: Stern, J. (ed.) EUROCRYPT 1999. LNCS, vol. 1592, pp. 223–238. Springer, Heidelberg (1999). https://doi.org/10.1007/3-540-48910-X_16

25. Regev, O.: On lattices, learning with errors, random linear codes, and cryptography. In: Gabow, H.N., Fagin, R. (eds.) 37th ACM STOC, pp. 84–93. ACM Press (2005). https://doi.org/10.1145/1060590.1060603

26. Vadhan, S.P., et al.: Pseudorandomness. Found. Trends® Theor. Comput. Sci. **7**(1–3), 1–336 (2012)

Efficiently Testable Circuits Without Conductivity

Mirza Ahad Baig[1]([⊠])(ID), Suvradip Chakraborty[2](ID), Stefan Dziembowski[3,4](ID), Małgorzata Gałązka[3], Tomasz Lizurej[3,4](ID), and Krzysztof Pietrzak[1]

[1] ISTA, Zurich, Switzerland
mirzaahad.baig@ist.ac.at
[2] Visa Research, Santa Clara, USA
[3] University of Warsaw, Warsaw, Poland
[4] IDEAS NCBR, Warsaw, Poland

Abstract. The notion of "efficiently testable circuits" (ETC) was recently put forward by Baig et al. (ITCS'23). Informally, an ETC compiler takes as input any Boolean circuit C and outputs a circuit/inputs tuple $(C', \mathbb{T})$ where (completeness) C' is functionally equivalent to C and (security) if C' is tampered in some restricted way, then this can be detected as C' will err on at least one input in the small test set $\mathbb{T}$. The compiler of Baig et al. detects tampering even if the adversary can tamper with *all* wires in the compiled circuit. Unfortunately, the model requires a strong "conductivity" restriction: the compiled circuit has gates with fan-out up to 3, but wires can only be tampered in one way even if they have fan-out greater than one. In this paper, we solve the main open question from their work and construct an ETC compiler without this conductivity restriction. While Baig et al. use gadgets computing the AND and OR of particular subsets of the wires, our compiler computes inner products with random vectors. We slightly relax their security notion and only require that tampering is detected with high probability over the choice of the randomness. Our compiler increases the size of the circuit by only a small constant factor. For a parameter λ (think $\lambda \leq 5$), the number of additional input and output wires is $|C|^{1/\lambda}$, while the number of test queries to detect an error with constant probability is around $2^{2\lambda}$.

1 Introduction

Circuit Testing. Detecting errors in circuits is of interest in various areas of engineering and computer science. In circuit manufacturing, the focus is on efficiently detecting errors that randomly occur during production [10]. Querying circuits on a few carefully chosen inputs and checking the output for correctness will typically detect a large fraction of the faulty ones.

Private Circuits (PC). The cryptographic community has long focused on errors that are intentionally introduced by an adversary, as such "tampering" or "fault

© International Association for Cryptologic Research 2023
G. Rothblum and H. Wee (Eds.): TCC 2023, LNCS 14371, pp. 123–152, 2023.
https://doi.org/10.1007/978-3-031-48621-0_5

attacks" can be used to extract cryptographic secrets [7,8]. Compared to testing in manufacturing, protecting circuits against fault attacks is more difficult for at least two reasons (1) the errors are not just random but can be targeted on specific wires or gates in the circuit (2) the errors introduced by tampering must not just be detected, but the circuit must be prevented to leak any information.

For this challenging setting of *private circuits* (PC), Ishai, Prabhakaran, Sahai, and Wagner [24] construct a *circuit compiler* that given (the description of) any circuit C and some parameter k outputs (the description of) a functionally equivalent circuit C_k (i.e., $C(X) = C_k(X)$ for all X) which is secure against fault attacks that can tamper with up to k wires with each query (the faults can be persistent, so ultimately the entire circuit can be tampered with), while blowing up the circuit size by a factor of k^2. The efficacy of the compiler can be somewhat improved by allowing some small information leakage [22].

Efficiently Testable Circuits (ETC). Efficiently testable circuits (ETC), recently introduced in [3], considers a setting that "lies in between" testing for benign errors and private circuits. An ETC compiler takes any Boolean circuit C : $\mathbb{Z}_2^s \to \mathbb{Z}_2^t$ and maps it to a tuple $(C_{\text{test}} : \mathbb{Z}_2^{s+s'} \to \mathbb{Z}_2^{t+t'}, \mathbb{T}_{\text{test}} \subset \mathbb{Z}_2^{s+s'})$ where C_{test} is functionally equivalent to C and $\mathbb{T}_{\text{test}}$ is a test set that will catch any (nontrivial) tampering on C_{test}. A bit more formally, by saying C_{test} is functionally equivalent to C we mean $\forall X \in \mathbb{Z}_2^s : C_{\text{test}}(X\|0^{s'})_{|t} = C(X)$ ($S_{|t}$ denotes the t bit prefix of S, $\|$ is concatenation and 0^s is the string of s zeros).

The security property states that if for a wire tampering τ on C_{test} the tampered circuit C_{test}^τ errs on at least one of the (exponentially many) inputs $X\|0^{s'}$ (i.e., the t bit prefix of the output is not $C(X)$), then C_{test}^τ will err on at least one input in the (small) test set

$$\forall \tau : \exists X \in \mathbb{Z}_2^s \ s.t. \ C_{\text{test}}^\tau(X\|0^s)_{|t} \neq \overbrace{C_{\text{test}}(X\|0^{s'})_{|t}}^{=C(X)} \Rightarrow$$
$$\exists T \in \mathbb{T}_{\text{test}} \ s.t. \ C_{\text{test}}^\tau(T) \neq C_{\text{test}}(T) \tag{1}$$

ETC aims at detecting *adversarial* errors like PC, but unlike PC, this detection only happens during a dedicated testing phase, not implicitly with every query. Thus ETC cannot be used to replace PCs which aim to protect secrets on a device that is under adversarial control and can be tampered with. Instead, they ensure that a circuit correctly evaluates on all inputs, even if it was under adversarial control in the past.

Using ETC can also be useful to detect benign errors, particularly in settings where one doesn't want to accept a non-trivial probability of missing a fault, which is the case for the heuristic techniques currently deployed in circuit manufacturing. One such setting is in space exploration where faults can be catastrophic, and to make matters worse, the high radiation in outer space is likely to cause additional faults. Here the ability to run a cheap test repeatedly in a black-box way is useful.

While ETCs provide a weaker security guarantee than PC in terms of how tampering is detected, the construction of the ETC from [3] achieves security under a much stronger tampering model than what is known for PC. Furthermore, ETCs are much more efficient and rely on weaker assumptions: the ETC compiler from [3] blows the circuit up by a small constant factor while allowing for tampering *with all wires*. On the other hand, in *Private Circuits II* [24], to detect tampering with k wires already requires a blow up of k^2.

Conductivity. A major restriction of both, the PC compiler [24] and the ETC compiler from [3], is the fact that wire tamperings are assumed to be *conductive*: while a wire can be tampered (set to constant 0 or 1, or toggling) arbitrarily, if this wire has fan-out greater than 1, i.e., leads to more than one destination which can be an input to another gate or an output wire, all must carry the same value and cannot be tampered individually.[1] This is an arguably unrealistic assumption and not does not capture real tampering attacks: Why should, say, cutting the wire at the input of one gate affect the value at another gate to which this wire is connected? While any circuit can easily be turned into a functionally equivalent one where all wires have fan-out 1 by using copy gates $\mathsf{COPY}(b) = (b, b)$, applying this to the circuit produced by the compiler from [3] will completely break its security as we will sketch below.

Our Contribution. In this work we solve the main open problem left in [3] and construct an ETC compiler that maps a circuit C to an ETC $(C_{\text{test}}, \mathbb{T}_{\text{test}})$ where $|\mathbb{T}_{\text{test}}| \leq 6$ and C_{test} has fan-out 1, which means it doesn't rely on the conductivity assumption as there's nothing to conduct.[2]

To get a practical construction with few extra output wires, we need to generalize the notion of ETCs and make it probabilistic. Whether efficient *deterministic* ETCs without the conductivity assumption exist is an interesting open question (our construction can be "derandomized", but this would lead to an impractically large test set of size $|C|^2$). Concretely, the inputs in our test set $\mathbb{T}_{\text{test}}$ are shorter than C_{test}'s input, and during testing the remaining inputs must be chosen at random. The soundness guarantee $\exists T \in \mathbb{T}_{\text{test}}$ $s.t.$ $C_{\text{test}}^\tau(T) \neq C_{\text{test}}(T)$ from Eq. (1) is adapted to a probabilistic guarantee

$$\exists T \in \mathbb{T}_{\text{test}} \; s.t. \; \Pr_R[C_{\text{test}}^\tau(T \| R) \neq C_{\text{test}}(T \| R)] \geq 1/2^{2\lambda} \tag{2}$$

where $\lambda \in \mathbb{N}_0$ is a parameter specifying the number of layers in the testing subcircuit. A larger λ will decrease the extra input/output wires but will increase the required number of test queries, a reasonable range for λ is 1 to 4.

---

[1] The conductivity assumption for the PC compiler from [24] is slightly stronger than ours, as they additionally assume that "faults on the output side of a NOT gate propagate to the input side".

[2] Ensuring non-conductivity by making sure the fan-out is 1 is done for clarity of exposition. To get a fan-out 1 circuit our complied circuit requires numerous COPY gates. In an actual physical circuit any of those COPY gates can be simply removed by increasing the fan-out of the input wire to that gate by one.

Size, Query and Randomness Efficiency. The number of extra input/output wires is roughly (cf. Table 1 for the exact numbers) $\lambda \cdot |C|^{1/(\lambda+1)}$, e.g. for a circuit with 2^{32} ($\approx$ four billion) gates and $\lambda = 3$ we need roughly $3 \cdot 2^8 = 768$ extra input and output wires. By repeating the testing κ times with fresh randomness, the probability that we fail to detect a non-trivial tampering is at most $(1 - 1/2^{2\lambda})^\kappa$, which for our example is < 0.5 for $\lambda = 3, \kappa = 45$. The number of test queries required for this testing is $|\mathbb{T}_{\text{test}}| \cdot \kappa = 6 \cdot 45 = 270$ (as we don't know which of the $T \in \mathbb{T}_{\text{test}}$ satisfies Eq. (2) we have to query with all of them). The number of random bits required for this testing is $\kappa \cdot \lambda \cdot |C|^{1/(\lambda+1)} = 45 \cdot 768 = 34560$ (each test query $T \in \mathbb{T}_{\text{test}}$ must be concatenated with $\lambda \cdot |C|^{1/(\lambda+1)}$ random bits, we can use the same randomness for each $T \in \mathbb{T}_{\text{test}}$, but assume fresh randomness for each of the κ runs of the test). We can get the probability of missing a fault down to any $2^{-\alpha}$ by repeating the above test α times. This is already quite practical despite the fact that in this work we focused on a clean exposition rather than improving concrete parameters.

2   ETC Compilers and Their Security

2.1   The Construction from [3] Using Conductivity

Before we describe our construction, let us first give a short summary of the ETC compiler from [3]. The basic construction using a toy circuit $C(x_1, x_2, x_3, x_4) = (x_1 \wedge x_2) \vee (x_3 \vee x_4)$ as input is illustrated in Fig. 1.

Wire Covering. In a first step, they compile the basic circuit C into a tuple $(C_{\text{wire}}, \mathbb{T}_{\text{wire}})$ where C_{wire} is functionally equivalent to C and $\mathbb{T}_{\text{wire}}$ is a wire covering for C_{wire}, which means for every wire w in C and $b \in \{0, 1\}$ there is some $X \in \mathbb{T}_{\text{wire}}$ such that w carries the value b if C is evaluated on X. For the toy circuit C we can use $(C_{\text{wire}} = C, \mathbb{T}_{\text{wire}} = \{0000, 1111\})$ (here $C_{\text{wire}} = C$, but in general we need up to 3 extra input wires and some extra XOR gates to compile C to C_{wire}).

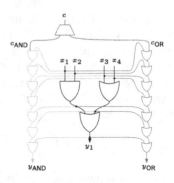

Fig. 1. The compiler from [3] illustrated on a toy circuit.

A Naive Construction with Conductivity. From $(C_{\text{wire}}, \mathbb{T}_{\text{wire}})$ [3] then further construct their ETC $(C_{\text{test}}, \mathbb{T}_{\text{test}})$. A naive construction is to let the test set be the wire covering set, i.e., $\mathbb{T}_{\text{test}} = \mathbb{T}_{\text{wire}}$, and derive C_{test} from C_{wire} by increasing the fan-out of every internal wire by one, and use the extra wire as an output. This way any tampering of a wire will be observable on one of the outputs.

Of course, having $|C_{\text{wire}}|$ many output wires is completely impractical so they must be compressed, and we'll sketch how this is done below, but let us first emphasize here that *conductivity* is absolutely crucial even for this naive construction, a concrete example is given in [3]. Looking ahead, a key observation we make in this work is that by using a more general "gate covering" set, this naive construction will detect tampering even without conductivity.

Compressing the Output. The work of [3] reduce the number of additional output wires by connecting every wire w in C_{wire} to one "OR gadget" and one "AND gadget" in a careful way (so they get fan-out 3, in the figure those gadgets are the purple and cyan subcircuits). These gadgets have just a one bit output (for our toy example we just need one OR and one AND gadget). There's also an extra input bit c (for control) and for every $X \in \mathbb{T}_{\mathsf{wire}}$ in the wire covering, the test set $\mathbb{T}_{\mathsf{test}}$ contains two inputs, $X\|0$ and $X\|1$, i.e., one where the control is 0 and one where it's 1. The wires are connected to the gadgets such that whenever there's some tampering on the internal circuit, some gadget will compute the wrong value on some $X \in \mathbb{T}_{\mathsf{test}}$. The extra control bit is necessary so this holds even if the adversary can also tamper with the gadgets themselves. Understanding the details of their construction and proof are not necessary for the current paper, so we refer to their paper for more details.

2.2   Our Construction Without Conductivity

Overcoming Conductivity. Without conductivity, the design principle outlined above, i.e., routing internal wires to some gadgets that try to catch errors, is not sufficient as errors on the internal wires can potentially be "tampered back" to the correct value on the external wires. Our construction makes this approach work even when we cannot rely on conductivity. Instead of trying to catch any tampering error, our gadgets (which compute inner products) are only guaranteed to catch tamperings on a test set if some wire "loses information", which means the wire carries different values on two inputs from the test set, but after tampering the values are identical. A key observation is that one can't undo information loss by tampering a wire. Fortunately, this already will be enough; we prove a dichotomy showing that every tampering either loses information on a "gate covering" set of inputs, or the tampering is additive. The latter case can easily be detected by checking the correctness of the regular (as opposed to the gadget) output on an arbitrary input. We will now illustrate our compiler using the toy circuit C shown in Fig. 2.(A).

Gate Covering. Like in [3], in a first step we compile our circuit C into a wire covering. That is, a tuple $(C_{\mathsf{wire}}, \mathbb{T}_{\mathsf{wire}})$ where C_{wire} is functionally equivalent to C and for every wire in C_{wire} and every $b \in \{0, 1\}$ there's an $X \in C_{\mathsf{wire}}$ s.t. w takes value b on evaluation $C_{\mathsf{wire}}(X)$. For our toy example, we use $(C_{\mathsf{wire}} = C, \mathbb{T}_{\mathsf{wire}} = \{0000, 1010, 1101\})$ as shown in Fig. 2.(A).

We then compile $(C_{\mathsf{wire}}, \mathbb{T}_{\mathsf{wire}})$ into a gate covering $(C_{\mathsf{gate}}, \mathbb{T}_{\mathsf{gate}})$. By this we mean a tuple where C_{gate} is functionally equivalent to C_{wire} when padding the (at most two) new inputs to 0, i.e., $C_{\mathsf{wire}}(X) = C_{\mathsf{gate}}(X\|0^2)$. A gate covering is a wire covering, but additionally, we require that for every gate g, and for every

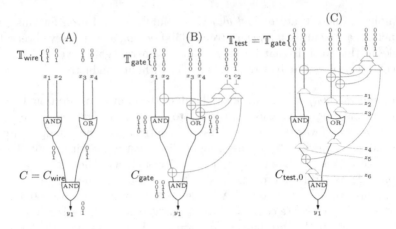

Fig. 2. Illustration of our toy circuit C (A) with a wire covering set $\mathbb{T}_{\text{wire}} = \{0000, 1010, 1101\}$ (B) after adding two extra control inputs c_1, c_2 and XORing them into the circuit to get a gate covering set $\mathbb{T}_{\text{gate}} = \{X\|00 : X \in \mathbb{T}_{\text{wire}}\} \cup 000010$ (in our toy example the 2nd control c_2 and the 2nd input 000001 is not required). (C) We get our 0th layer ETC ($C_{\text{test},0}, \mathbb{T}_{\text{test}}$) setting $\mathbb{T}_{\text{test}} = \mathbb{T}_{\text{gate}}$ and adding copy gates to route the output of every AND,OR and XOR to a new output z_i.

possible input to that gate, there's a $X \in \mathbb{T}_{\text{gate}}$ such that g is queried on those inputs. There's one relaxation, for XOR gates we just require that three out of the four inputs $\{00, 01, 10, 11\}$ are covered. In Fig. 2.(B) we illustrate how to compile the wire covering into a gate covering. This requires adding two extra control bits c_1, c_2 as inputs, some copy gates to create enough copies of those controls, and some XOR gates which add those controls to some carefully chosen wires. The gate cover set $\mathbb{T}_{\text{gate}}$ contains $X\|00$ for every $X \in \mathbb{T}_{\text{wire}}$, and additional two inputs which are all 0 except on c_1 and c_2, respectively. For our toy example we actually just need one control c_1.

Our "0th layer" ETC ($C_{\text{test},0}, \mathbb{T}_{\text{test}}$), as illustrated in Fig. 2.(C), is derived from ($C_{\text{gate}}, \mathbb{T}_{\text{gate}}$) by setting $\mathbb{T}_{\text{test}} = \mathbb{T}_{\text{gate}}$, and $C_{\text{test},0}$ is derived from C_{gate} by adding a copy gate to the output of every AND,OR and XOR gate (except if that wire is an output already) to create fresh outputs $z_1, z_2, \ldots, z_6$. Note that by adding copy gates $\mathbb{T}_{\text{test}}$ remains a gate covering for $C_{\text{test},0}$. We will need this fact below.

Of course, the ETC is not practical as there are way too many output wires. Before describing how to compress those outputs we discuss why ($C_{\text{test},0}, \mathbb{T}_{\text{test}}$) is an ETC, i.e., why any non-trivial tampering on the circuit will already cause an error on the outputs for some input in $\mathbb{T}_{\text{test}}$.

Information Loss. As we want a non-conductive circuit, we must use copy gates to route the internal wire values to the outputs and can't just use gates with higher fan-out as in [3]. But now the adversary can tamper with the wires leading to the z_i's individually and thus potentially undo any error in the circuit (Fig. 3).

We show that for any circuit with a gate covering – we'll use ($C_{\text{test},0}, \mathbb{T}_{\text{test}}$) from Fig. 2 as running example – every tampering τ is either additive in the sense

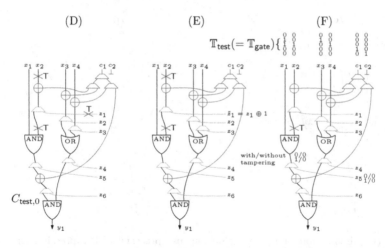

Fig. 3. Illustration of the types on tamperings τ on circuits with gate coverings using the toy example $(C, \mathbb{T}_{gate})$ from Fig. 2. Toggling three wires as indicated in (D) has no effect, i.e., $C^\tau(X) = C(X)$ for all inputs X. Toggling two wires as in (E) creates an additive tampering where $C^\tau(X) = C(X) \oplus B$ (here $B = 100000$), and thus is easily detected with just one query on any input. Tamperings that are not additive create "information loss" at the output of some internal gate, i.e., for two inputs $T_0, T_1 \in \mathbb{T}_{test}$, some wire will have different values without tampering, but the same value with tampering as illustrated in (F). As we copy all output wires and use them as outputs (and tampering a wire cannot "undo" information loss), we'll observe information loss also on one of the z_i values (illustrated is the loss on z_5 for inputs 000000 and 110100).

that for some fixed B we have $\forall X : C_0^\tau(X) = C_0(X) \oplus B$ or there's *information loss* on some wire w that is the output of a AND, OR or XOR gate, which means there are two inputs $X_0, X_1 \in \mathbb{T}_{test}$ such that the wire w carries different values in the evaluations $C_0(X_0)$ and $C_0(X_1)$, but the same value in the evaluations $C_0^\tau(X_0)$ and $C_0^\tau(X_1)$ of the tampered circuit.

By construction, in our C_0 circuit every such wire w is copied $(w', w'') \leftarrow \mathsf{COPY}(w)$ and w'' is then routed to the output. Here we crucially rely on the fact that we don't merely have arbitrary errors like in [3] but information loss, which cannot be undone even by tampering w'' independently from w, w'.

Let us shortly sketch why $(C_0, \mathbb{T}_{test})$ is an ETC. Consider any tampering τ. As argued above, the tampering is either (1) additive or (2) we have information loss on the outputs. In case (1) for some B we have $C_0^\tau(X) = C_0(X) \oplus B$. Recall that C_0's outputs contain the actual outputs y_i and the z_i's used for the testing. If B doesn't flip any of the y_i's, then this tampering does not affect correctness and we don't have to bother. If B flips (i.e., XORs a 1 to 0) at least one y_i, we'll observe the mistake by querying C_0 on an arbitrary input. In case (2) there is at least one output *out* (could be a y_i or z_i value) and two inputs $T_0, T_1 \in \mathbb{T}_{test}$ s.t. *out* has the same value in evaluations $C_0^\tau(T_0), C_0^\tau(T_1)$, but it should be different, thus it will be wrong in one of the two evaluations.

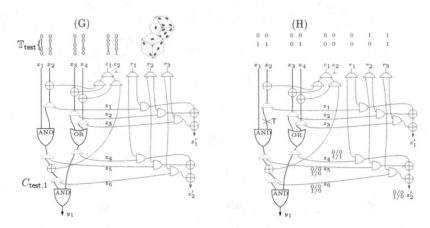

Fig. 4. (G) Illustration of the "information loss preserving" compression circuit (in purple) attached to 0th layer ETC $C_{test,0}$ from Fig. 2.(C) to get a 1st layer ETC C_1. (H) For the two inputs $T_0 = 000000, T_1 = 110100$ to $C_{test,0}$ we have information loss on the z_5 and also z_6 output. For randomness $R = 011, Q = 001$ we then also observe information loss at the z_2' output of $C_{test,1}$ on inputs $T_0\|R, T_1\|Q$.

Compressing the Output. The 0th layer ETC $(C_0, \mathbb{T}_{test})$ is not practical as the number of output wires required for testing is linear in the size of the circuit.

To compress the output we construct a gadget circuit $G : \{0,1\}^{n_{in}+r} \rightarrow \{0,1\}^{n_{in}/r}$ that takes an n_{in} bit string and r random bits as input and outputs an $n_{out} = n_{in}/r$ bits. This compressing circuit on input $X\|R$ chops X into n_{out} strings $X_1, \ldots, X_{n_{out}}$, it then computes and outputs the inner products $\langle X_i, R \rangle$ of each X_i with R. For $n_{in} = 6, r = 3$ this gadget is illustrated by the purple subcircuit in Fig. 4.G.

We will prove that even if the compressing circuit is tampered with, it will "preserve information loss" with good probability over the randomness. More formally, we consider any four inputs X_0, X_1, X_0', X_1' where at least in one position i the X_0, X_1 values are distinct, but the X_0', X_1' values are not, i.e., $\exists i : X_0[i] \neq X_1[i]$ and $X_0'[i] = X_1'[i]$. Now for any tampering τ and random R, Q consider the values

$$(Y_0, Y_1, Y_2, Y_3) = (G(X_0\|R), G(X_1\|R), G(X_0\|Q), G(X_1\|Q))$$
$$(Y_0', Y_1', Y_2', Y_3') = (G^\tau(X_0'\|R), G^\tau(X_1'\|R), G^\tau(X_0'\|Q), G^\tau(X_1'\|Q))$$

Then $\Pr_{R,Q}\left[\exists i, k < j : Y_k[i] \neq Y_j[i] \text{ and } Y_k'[i] = Y_j'[i]\right] \geq 1/2$.

Setting $r \approx \sqrt{n_{in}}$ we get $n_{out} = n_{in}/r \approx \sqrt{n_{in}}$ and thus can replace n_{in} output wires with $\sqrt{n_{in}}$ input and output wires (in our toy example we had $n_{in} = 6$ and $r = \lceil\sqrt{6}\rceil = 3, n_{out} = \lfloor\sqrt{6}\rfloor = 2$).

If we apply the compression gadget just once, it is sufficient to prove that with good probability some of the outputs are wrong, i.e., that for some $j : Y_j \neq Y_j'$. We prove a more general property of information loss at the output of the gadget so we can cascade them. To balance the number of additional input and output wires, for λ layers we compress the number of wires at each layer by a factor $\lambda+\sqrt[1]{n}$ which results in just $\lambda+\sqrt[1]{n}$ additional output and $\lambda \cdot {}^{\lambda+1}\sqrt{n}$ input wires.

The main disadvantage of choosing a larger λ is the fact that the probability of detecting a tampering decreases, and one thus must make more test queries. Concretely, we must make $|\mathbb{T}_{test}|2^\lambda \leq 6 \cdot 2^\lambda$ queries to be guaranteed to catch a tampering with probability $2^{-\lambda}$. By repeating this κ times we can amplify the success probability to $1 - (1 - 2^{-\lambda})^\kappa$ at the cost of making $\kappa \cdot 6 \cdot 2^\lambda$ queries.

In practice, a very small λ will be sufficient, for example with $\lambda = 4$ we get a total of around 64 output and 256 input wires for a circuit with 2^{32} (around 4 billion) gates, and setting $\kappa = 11$ requires $11 \cdot 6 \cdot 2^4 = 1056$ queries to get a > 0.5 detection probability (that's what's guaranteed in the worst case by our security proof, as we did not optimize for constant, the practical security is certainly much better). Table 1 summarizes the efficiency of our ETC compiler.

Table 1. Summary of the efficiency of our ETC compiler which first compiles the input circuit C into a (functionally equivalent) C_{wire} with a wire covering set $\mathbb{T}_{wire}$. This is then compiled into a circuit C_{gate} with a gate covering set $\mathbb{T}_{gate}$, which is then compiled into the 0th later ETC $C_{test,0}$ with the test set $\mathbb{T}_{test}$. We then compress the additional output wires from $4n$ (i.e., linear in $|C| = n$) to the $\lambda + 1$th root of that by applying $\lambda \geq 1$ layers of our compression gadget. The testing is now probabilistic but can be repeated with fresh randomness until one gets the desired.

	C	C_{wire}	C_{gate}	$C_{test,0}$	$C_{test,\lambda}, \lambda \in \mathbb{N}^+$
Number of gates	n	$\leq (3 + o(1))|C|$ $\leq 3n + o(n)$	$\leq (7 + o(1))|C|$ $\leq 7n + o(n)$	$\leq |C_{gate}| + 2 \cdot 4n$ $\leq 15n + o(n)$	$\leq |C_{test,0}| + 2 \cdot 4n$ $\leq 23n + o(n)$
Input size	s	$\leq s + 3$	$\leq s + 5$	$\leq s + 5$	$\leq s + 5 + \lambda \cdot {}^{\lambda+1}\sqrt{4n}$
Output size	t	t	t	$\leq t + 4n$	$\leq t + {}^{\lambda+1}\sqrt{4n}$
Cover/Test size		$|\mathbb{T}_{wire}| \leq 4$	$|\mathbb{T}_{gate}| \leq 6$	$|\mathbb{T}_{test}| \leq 6$	$|\mathbb{T}_{test}| \leq 6$
Success Probability		N/A	N/A	1	$2^{-2\lambda}$
Randomness (bits)		0	0	0	$\lambda \cdot {}^{\lambda+1}\sqrt{4n}$

2.3 More Related Work

Testing circuits is a major topic in hardware manufacturing, the books [6,10] discuss heuristics for testing and practical issues of the problem. Circuit-compilers (as used in this work) which harden a circuit against some "physical attacks" in a provably secure way were first introduced for leakage attacks (concretely, leaking values of a small number of wires) by Ishai et al. in [25]. Based on this compiler they later also gave a compiler to protect against tampering [24]. This line of research was continued in a sequence of papers on tampering wires [13,14,21,23] or gates [19,26,28]. As discussed in the introduction, these compilers aim at protecting secrets in the circuit, while efficiently testable circuits [3] only aim at detecting tampering in a special test phase.

Apart from compilers, a line of research was pioneered by Micali and Reyzin in [30] on reductions or composition of cryptographic building blocks to prevent "general" leakage. The first cryptographic primitive achieving security against a general notion of leakage (bounded leakage) from standard cryptographic building blocks is the leakage-resilient cipher from [17], by now we have leakage-resilient variants of most basic cryptographic primitives including signatures [9,20] or MACS [5], an excellent overview on the area is [27]. Unfortunately for tampering no construction secure against general tampering – or even a notion of what "general tampering" means – exists. Although Non-malleable codes [18] can protect data in memory (rather than during computation) from very general classes of tampering attacks [1,4,12,15,29].

The most powerful physical attack model is Trojans, where an attacker can not just tamper the circuit, but completely replace it. Some limited provable-security results against this class of attacks are [11,16]. There are few attempts to use general verifiable computation to certify the output of circuits [2,31].

3   Preliminaries

We use notations and a tampering model similar to [3].

3.1   Notation for Circuits

Circuits can be modeled as directed acyclic graphs (DAGs), and we will extensively use standard graph theory notation. Concretely, a circuit is modeled as a DAG $C_\gamma = (V, E)$ where vertices refer to gates and the directed edges refer to wires. The circuit definition C_γ comes with a labeling function $\gamma : V \to \mathfrak{G}$ which assigns specific gates to the vertices, where $\mathfrak{G}$ is the set of gates allowed. We will often omit the parameter γ since it is chosen when specifying the circuit and cannot be changed. Each wire carries a bit from $\mathbb{Z}_2$, and each gate is taken from the set of allowed gates $\mathfrak{G}$ (including $\{\mathsf{AND}, \mathsf{OR}, \mathsf{XOR}, \mathsf{COPY}, \mathsf{NOT}\}$ and two special $\{\mathbf{in}, \mathbf{out}\}$ gates).

For $v \in V$, let $E^-(v) = \{(u, v) \in E\}$ and $E^+(v) = \{(v, u) \in E\}$ be the sets of v's incoming and outgoing edges, respectively. For $e = (u, v) \in E$ we define $V^-(e) = u$ and $V^+(e) = v$. We split the vertices into three sets $V = \mathcal{I} \cup \mathcal{G} \cup \mathcal{O}$, where $\mathcal{I} = \{I_1, I_2, ..., I_s\}$ are vertices which are assigned to $\mathbf{in}$, and $\mathcal{O} = \{O_1, O_2, ..., O_t\}$ are these assigned to $\mathbf{out}$. Given $C_\gamma = (V, E)$ and an input $X = (x_1, \ldots, x_s) \in \mathbb{Z}_2^s$ we define a valuation function

$$\mathrm{val}_{C_\gamma, X} : V \cup E \to \mathbb{Z}_2 \tag{3}$$

which assigns each gate the value it outputs and each wire the value it holds when the circuit is evaluated on X. More formally the valuation function for vertices $v \in V$ and edges $e \in E$ is defined as

$$\text{val}_{C_\gamma, X=(x_1, x_2, \dots, x_s)}(v) = \begin{cases} x_i, & \text{if } v = I_i. \\ \gamma(v)(\text{val}_{C_\gamma, X}(E^-(v))), & \text{otherwise.} \end{cases}$$

$$\text{val}_{C_\gamma, X}(e) = \text{val}_{C_\gamma, X}(V^-(e)).$$

We will sometimes just write val_X if the circuit considered is clear from the context. The behaviour of the circuit C can be associated with the function that it evaluates, i.e. $C : \mathbb{Z}_2^s \to \mathbb{Z}_2^t$. We can define this function as follows: $C(X) = (\text{val}_{C,X}(O_1), \text{val}_{C,X}(O_2), \dots, \text{val}_{C,X}(O_t))$.

3.2 Tampering Model

We consider an adversary who can arbitrarily tamper with every wire of the circuit, i.e. flip its value, set it to 0, set it to 1, or leave it untampered. Unlike [3] or [24], we *do not* take advantage of the *conductivity* assumption. This means, we operate on circuits with conductivity 1, where all nodes $n \in V$ of a circuit C have fan-in and fan-out equal to an inherent fan in, fan-out of $\gamma(n)$, and all output wires of all nodes can be tampered independently. We assume that the input circuit is not conductive. In [3], the authors assumed k-conductivity, i.e. a value of some wire in the circuit could be copied to at most k distinct destinations with a restriction that all of them must be tampered equally. Without loss of generality, every k-conductive circuit can be transformed into a 1-conductive circuit, as by using COPY gates, every k-conductive circuit can be turned into a non-conductive one while at most doubling the circuit size and increasing the depth by a factor $\lceil \log(k) \rceil$.

The tampering of a wire is described by a function $\mathbb{Z}_2 \to \mathbb{Z}_2$ from the set of possible bit tamper functions $\mathcal{T} = \{\text{id}, \text{neg}, \text{one}, \text{zero}\}$. The tampering of an entire circuit $C = (V, E)$ is defined by a function $\tau : E \to \mathcal{T}$ mapping each wire to a tampering function. For convenience, we sometimes write τ_e to denote $\tau(e)$.

Now we can extend our notion of the valuation to also take tampering into account in order to define the valuation of a tampered circuit

$$\text{val}_X^\tau : V \cup E \to \mathbb{Z}_2.$$

The only difference to the (non-tampered) valuation function from Eq. (3) is that we apply the tampering to each value of an edge after it is being computed, formally:

$$\text{val}_{C_\gamma, X=(x_1, 2, \dots, x_s)}^\tau(v) = \begin{cases} x_i, & \text{if } v = I_i. \\ \gamma(v)(\text{val}_{C_\gamma, X}^\tau(E^-(v))), & \text{otherwise.} \end{cases}$$

$$\text{val}_{C_\gamma, X}^\tau(e) = \tau_e(\text{val}_{C_\gamma, X}^\tau(V^-(e))).$$

By C^τ we can again understand a function that describes the input-output behavior of the *tampered* circuit: $C^\tau(X) = (\text{val}_{C,X}^\tau(O_1), \text{val}_{C,X}^\tau(O_2), \dots, \text{val}_{C,X}^\tau(O_t))$ (Fig. 5).

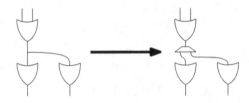

Fig. 5. Examples of $2 - conductive$ (left circuit) and $1 - conductive$ (right circuit) circuits. A single wire on the left circuit is copied to two destinations. The adversary can apply only a single tampering to this wire. On the right circuit, this wire is divided into three parts with a COPY gate. The adversary can apply separate tampering to each of these parts.

4   Gate Covering Sets

The authors of [3] developed a notion of *wire covering set* $\mathbb{T}_{\text{wire}}$. It is a set of inputs to a specific circuit, such that every wire is evaluated to both 0 and 1, given some inputs from the test set $\mathbb{T}_{\text{wire}}$ (see Definition 1 below). Moreover, the paper states that every circuit can be efficiently compiled into its wire-covered version (Theorem 10 from [3]). We denote the compilation procedure (Algorithm 10 from [3]) as Algorithm A. It compiles a circuit C into a functionally equivalent C_{wire}, along with its wire covering set $\mathbb{T}_{\text{wire}}$.

Definition 1 (Definition 4 from [3]). *The set* $\mathbb{T}_{\text{wire}}$ *is a wire covering set for a circuit* C *if* $\forall\, e \in E(C)$, $b \in \{0,1\}\ \exists\, X \in \mathbb{T}_{\text{wire}}\ :\ \text{val}_{C,X}(e) = b$.

In this paper, we develop a stronger notion called *gate covering set*. Here, we not only require covering all wires of the circuit, but also pairs of wires that form an input to multi-input gates (in our model the **and, or, xor** gates).

Before we proceed, we expand our notation by the sequences of the input values to the gate *i.e.*, by $(\text{val}_{C,X}(e))_{e\in E^{-}(v)}$ we understand the sequence of the values given to v, when the circuit is evaluated on the input X. E.g. for a gate v in a circuit C that is evaluated on 0 and 1 given input X to C, we write $(\text{val}_{C,X}(e))_{e\in E^{-}(v)} = 01$. Now, we give the definition of the gate covering set.

Definition 2. $\mathbb{T}_{\text{gate}}$ *is a gate covering set for a circuit* C *with gate assignment* γ *if it satisfies:*

- $\forall_{v\in V(C)}\,:\,\gamma(v)\in\{\text{COPY,NOT,OUTPUT}\}\,:\,|\{(\text{val}_{C,X}(e))_{e\in E^{-}(v)} : X \in \mathbb{T}_{\text{gate}}\}| \geq 2,$
- $\forall_{v\in V(C)}\,:\,\gamma(v)\in\{\text{AND,OR}\}\,:\,|\{(\text{val}_{C,X}(e))_{e\in E^{-}(v)} : X \in \mathbb{T}_{\text{gate}}\}| = 4,$
- $\forall_{v\in V(C)}\,:\,\gamma(v)\in\{\text{XOR}\}\,:\,|\{(\text{val}_{C,X}(e))_{e\in E^{-}(v)} : X \in \mathbb{T}_{\text{gate}}\}| \geq 3.$

We call a circuit with a gate-covering set a gate-covered circuit. Any node in a circuit that has enough evaluation sequences as in the Definition 2, given any test set, we call gate-covered.

To construct a gate covering of a circuit we first use the recalled Algorithm A to obtain a wire covering of the circuit and then we go through the multi-input gates of the intermediary circuit topologically to ensure that they are evaluated on a sufficient number of their inputs combinations. In the algorithm, it is sufficient to add XOR gates to the input wires of the topologically traversed gates of the circuit to gate-cover them. The Algorithm 1 describes a procedure that takes as input a circuit C and outputs a functionally-equivalent circuit C_{gate} along with a gate-covering set $\mathbb{T}_{\text{gate}}$ for C_{gate}.

Algorithm 1: Algorithm for constructing a gate covering set for C

Input: $C : \mathbb{Z}_2^s \to \mathbb{Z}_2^t$
Output: $C_{\text{gate}}, \mathbb{T}_{\text{gate}}$

1   $(C_{\text{wire}} : \mathbb{Z}_2^{s+s_w} \to \mathbb{Z}_2^t, \mathbb{T}_{\text{wire}}) = Algorithm\ A(C)$ /* Wire-covered intermediary circuit */

2   Initialize $C_{\text{gate}} = C_{\text{wire}}$

3   Initialize $\mathbb{T}_{\text{gate}} = \mathbb{T}_{\text{wire}}$

4   Append 00 to every $X \in \mathbb{T}_{\text{gate}}$

5   $X_0 = 0^{s+s_w}10$

6   $X_1 = 0^{s+s_w}01$

7   **for** $v \in V(C_{\text{gate}}) : \gamma(v) \in \{\text{OR}, \text{AND}, \text{XOR}\}$ (processed in a *topological* order) **do**

8      $S = \{(\text{val}_{C,X}(e))_{e \in E^-(v)} : X \in \mathbb{T}_{\text{gate}}\}$ /* Assert $|S| \geq 2$ */

9   **for** $e_i \in \{00, 01, 10, 11\} \setminus S$ **do**

10        $p_i = (\text{val}_{C,X_i}(e))_{e \in E^-(v)}$ /* Get current valuation of the v's input wires on the input X_i */

11   **for** $j \in \{0, 1\}$ **do**

12   **if** $e_i[j] \neq p_i[j]$ **then**

            /* Given the input X_i, the $s + s_w + i$'th input wire of the circuit has value 1 */

13   Update C_{gate} by adding a XOR gate that has one of the inputs connected $s + s_w + i$'th input wire of the circuit and its second input is the j'th input wire of v. The output of the XOR gate will be a new j'th input of v /* When the control bits X_0, X_1 are used at least twice, one needs to use linear number of COPY gates in the construction to assure that C_{gate} remains non-conductive */

14   **return** $C_{\text{gate}}, \mathbb{T}_{\text{gate}} \cup \{X_0, X_1\}$

Proposition 1. *The Algorithm 1 transforms a circuit C into a functionally equivalent circuit C_{gate} along with gate-covering set $\mathbb{T}_{\text{gate}}$.*

Proof. It is easy to see that the circuit C_{gate} is functionally equivalent to C, since it does not add any new output bits to the circuit, and all the new gates are XOR gates connected via a sequence of COPY gates to the new control bits. Whenever these bits are set to 0, the new XOR gates do not affect the behaviour of the circuit. Note that after adding the new XOR gates, all of the wires connected directly to the old gates of the circuit remain wire-covered by the old test set adjusted by adding 00 to its every input. What is more, the new control bits wire-cover every new wire added to the circuit. This implies that every gate from the set $\{\mathsf{COPY}, \mathsf{NOT}, \mathsf{OUTPUT}\}$ in the updated circuit is trivially gate-covered (evaluated to both $0, 1$ given some inputs from the test set).

When we topologically go through the gates from the set $\{\mathsf{OR}, \mathsf{AND}, \mathsf{XOR}\}$ of the intermediary circuit, we can see that since the input wires to the circuit are wire-covered by the adjusted old test set, then these gates are partially covered before and after adding new XOR gates to their input wires (i.e. $\{(\mathrm{val}_{C,X}(e))_{e \in E^-(v)} : X \in \mathbb{T}_{\mathsf{gate}}\} \geq 2$). In the step 9 of the Algorithm, we add XOR gates connected to the new control bits to cover at most two missing evaluation sequences. The XOR gates added during the topological procedure are evaluated on two distinct input sequences, given inputs from the adjusted old wire-covering set. The third distinct input comes from setting their respective control bit to 1   □

Proposition 2. *For any circuit C with max fan-in 2, number of gates n, the Algorithm 1 creates a circuit with additional 5 input bits, test set of size 6, additional $6n$ gates.*

Proof. The Algorithm A from [3] compiles into a circuit with additional 3 input bits, test set of size 4 and adds at most n XOR gates and n COPY gates. Now, adding 2 input bits and 2 test inputs to the test set in the second part of Algorithm 1, and adding at most $2n$ XOR gates and $2n$ COPY gates during the iteration concludes the result   □

5   Information Loss in Gate-Covered Circuits

In this section, we define information loss and show that it is easily trackable in any C_{gate} that has a gate-covering set $\mathbb{T}_{\mathsf{gate}}$. For any such circuit, we show the following property: for any tampering applied to the wires of the C_{gate}, either we observe an information loss on one of the output wires of the multi-input gates $\mathsf{AND}, \mathsf{OR}, \mathsf{XOR}$ (given only the inputs from the gate-covering set $\mathbb{T}_{\mathsf{gate}}$), or the output wires of the circuit are always set to a constant value or always toggled or always correctly evaluated.

Theorem 1. *For any circuit $C_{\mathsf{gate}} : \mathbb{Z}_2^s \rightarrow \mathbb{Z}_2^t$ with gate-covering set $\mathbb{T}_{\mathsf{gate}}$, for any tampering function τ applied to the circuit then at least one of the following holds:*

- *Information loss on multi-input gates*

$$\exists_{X_0, X_1 \in \mathbb{T}_{\mathsf{gate}}, \; n \in V(C_{\mathsf{gate}})} : \gamma(n) \in \{\mathsf{AND}, \mathsf{OR}, \mathsf{XOR}\} :$$

$$\left(\mathrm{val}_{X_0, C_{\mathsf{gate}}}(n) = 0 \wedge \mathrm{val}_{X_1, C_{\mathsf{gate}}}(n) = 1 \right) \wedge \left(\mathrm{val}_{X_0, C_{\mathsf{gate}}}^\tau(n) = \mathrm{val}_{X_1, C_{\mathsf{gate}}}^\tau(n) \right)$$

- *Constant output*

$$\exists_{i \in [t], c \in \{0,1\}} \forall X \in \mathbb{Z}_2^s : C_{\mathsf{gate}}^\tau(X)[i] = c$$

- *At most toggled output*

$$\exists_{T \in \{0,1\}^t} \forall X \in \mathbb{Z}_2^s : \ C_{\text{gate}}^\tau(X) = C_{\text{gate}}(X) + T$$

Proof. The proof follows a modular argument. For this, we need a definition of Topological Layers of Computation on any circuit C_γ. In the definition below, we say that a wire e is connected to a gate g in a circuit C_γ described with a DAG (denoted by predicate $connected_{C_\gamma}(g, e)$ holds) if and only if there exists a direct connection or connection going through a path of COPY or NOT gates between g and the predecessor of e in the circuit.

Definition 3 (Topological Layers of Computation). *For any circuit C, we recursively define its Topological Layers of Computation:*

- 0th-*layer of Computation* $\mathcal{L}_0 = \mathcal{I}(C)$
- i^{th}-*layer of Computation* $\mathcal{L}_i = \{g \in V(C_\gamma) : \forall_{e \in E^-(g)} : connected_{C_\gamma}(g', e)$ *for some* $g' \in \mathcal{L}_0 \cup \ldots \cup \mathcal{L}_{i-1}$ *and* $\gamma(g) \in \{\text{XOR, AND, OR}\}\}$.

By $G_i(C)$ we denote a subgraph induced by the layers $\mathcal{L}_0, \ldots, \mathcal{L}_i$ of the circuit.

Below we consider $C = C_{\text{gate}}$. We run an experiment that evaluates layer by layer the tampered C (assuming C has $L + 1$ layers). In the i'th layer either there is an information loss and we stop the experiment or the output of the layer is at most toggled [see event $\mathcal{E}_2$ below] and the experiment proceeds to the next layer. We define the following predicates for a gate g in layer i:

- $\mathcal{E}_1(g, i)$ holds if $g \in \mathcal{L}_i \ \wedge \ \exists_{X_0, X_1 \in \mathbb{T}'} \text{val}_{X_0, C}(g) = 0 \ \wedge \ \text{val}_{X_1, C}(g) = 1 \ \wedge$ $\text{val}_{X_0, C}^\tau(g) = \text{val}_{X_1, C}^\tau(g)$,
- $\mathcal{E}_2(g, i)$ holds if $g \in \mathcal{L}_i \ \wedge \ \forall_{X \in \mathbb{Z}_2^s} : \text{val}_{X, C}^\tau(g) = \text{val}_{X, C}(g) + f\Big[\tau(e) : e \in E(G_i(C))\Big]$.

In the 0th-layer of the circuit, by definition of the tampering function, for any node $g \in \mathcal{L}_0(C): X \in \mathbb{Z}_2^s : \text{val}_{X, C}^\tau(g) = \text{val}_{X, C}(g)$. This implies event $\mathcal{E}_2(g, 0)$ on any gate from this layer. We prove the following for the tampered circuit C:

$$\forall_{\tau(C), i \in \{1, \ldots, L\}} : \forall_{j \in \{0, \ldots, i-1\}, g' \in \mathcal{L}_j} : \mathcal{E}_2(g', j) \implies \forall_{g \in \mathcal{L}_i(C)} : \mathcal{E}_1(g, i) \vee \mathcal{E}_2(g, i)$$

We first study the gates of the first layer:

- The AND gate in the 1st-layer is connected to the input gates only via a sequence of COPY and NOT gates. The computation on this gate can be described as $P_g(a, b) = a \cdot b$. The tampered output of the gate is $\tilde{P}_g(a, b) = \tilde{a} \cdot \tilde{b}$, where $\tilde{a} \in \{a, a + 1, 0, 1\}$, $\tilde{b} \in \{b, b + 1, 0, 1\}$. The tampering of a wire a is set to 1 or 0 whenever there is a constant tampering on its path from the 0th layer, $a + 1$ or $b + 1$ whenever on the path there is an odd number of toggle tamperings, and a or b whenever there is an even number of toggle tamperings on the path. Whenever $\tilde{a} = 0 \lor \tilde{b} = 0$, then $\tilde{P}_g(a, 1) = 0$ and $P(a, 1) = a$, we get an information loss. Now, since by the construction of the Algorithm 2, the wire P is connected via a COPY to the output, the event $\mathcal{E}_1(g, 1)$ occurs. In other cases:

- if $\tilde{a} = 1$ (or $\tilde{b} = 1$), $P(a, 1) = a$ and $\tilde{P}(a, 1) = const.$ (resp. $P(b, 1) = b$ and $\tilde{P}(b, 1) = const.$) $[\mathcal{E}_1(g, 1)$ occurs],
- when $\tilde{a} = a + 1$ (or $\tilde{b} = b + 1$), then $P(1, b) = b$ and $\tilde{P}(1, b) = 0$ (resp. $P(1, a) = 1$ and $\tilde{P}(a, 1) = 0$) $[\mathcal{E}_1(g, 1)$ occurs],
- otherwise $\tilde{P}(a, b) = ab$ $[\mathcal{E}_2(g, 1)$ occurs].

- Similar argument as above applies for the OR gate,
- The input wires of the XOR gate are also connected only via a sequence of COPY and NOT gates to the input. We observe that $P_g(a, b) = a + b$, and the tampered output $\tilde{P}_g(a, b) = \tilde{a} + \tilde{b}$, where $\tilde{a} \in \{a, a+1, 0, 1\}$, $\tilde{b} \in \{b, b+1, 0, 1\}$.

  - if $\tilde{a} = const.$ (or $\tilde{b} = const.$), $P(a, 0) = a$ and $\tilde{P}(a, 0) = const.$ (resp. $P(0, b) = b$ and $\tilde{P}(0, b) = const.$) $[\mathcal{E}_1(g, 1)$ occurs],
  - when $\tilde{a} = a + c_a, \tilde{b} = b + c_b$, then $P(a, b) = a + b$, $\tilde{P}(a, b) = a + b + c_a + c_b$ $[\mathcal{E}_2(g, 1)$ occurs].

In the i'th layer, the inputs to all of the gates are, again, connected to the gates of the previous layers only via a sequence of COPY, NOT gates. Now, once the induction assumption holds in the layers $\{1, \dots, i-1\}$, the event $\mathcal{E}_2$ on all gates assures that the case analysis from the first layer may be repeated, but the tampered wires $\tilde{a}, \tilde{b}$ will now get a constant tampering 0 or 1, or a toggle bit depending on the tamperings chosen on the edges of the graph induced by layers from the set $\{0, \dots, i\}$.

This implies that on multi-input gates of the circuit, we either get event $\mathcal{E}_1$ or $\mathcal{E}_2$. Whenever the event $\mathcal{E}_1$ occurs, the information loss on one of the multi-input gates of the circuit occurs. Otherwise only the event $\mathcal{E}_2$ on these gates may occur. The OUTPUT gates of the circuit are connected via a sequence of COPY and NOT gates to the gates of the topological layers of computation of the circuit. If on their paths one finds a constant tampering, then some output bit is set constant; if only toggles are found there, the output bits are at most toggled □

5.1   Routing the Information Loss in Gate-Covered Circuits

In this section, we show that any gate-covered circuit can be converted to another gate-covered circuit for which any information loss that appears on its multi-input gates is routed to the output of the circuit. We present Algorithm 2 that adds a COPY gate to the output wires of the multi-input gates in the gate-covered circuit. The added COPY gates forward one copy of the original wires to their previous destinations and another copy directly to the output (Fig 6).

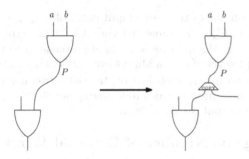

Fig. 6. Adding a COPY gate to the wire P in the Algorithm 2. This creates two wires; the left one is connected to the previous successor of the wire P, and the right one is sent to the output of the circuit. Algorithm 2 takes into account only the wires P which originate at AND, OR, XOR gates in the original circuit.

Algorithm 2: Algorithm for Routing the Information Loss in a Gate-Covered C

Input: $C_{\text{gate}} : \mathbb{Z}_2^s \to \mathbb{Z}_2^t, \mathbb{T}_{\text{gate}}$
Output: $C_{\text{test},0}, \mathbb{T}_0$

1 Initialize $C_{\text{test},0} = C_{\text{gate}}, \mathbb{T}_0 = \mathbb{T}_{\text{gate}}$
2 **for** $g \in V(C_{\text{gate}})$ **do**
3   **if** $g \in \{\text{AND}, \text{OR}, \text{XOR}\} \wedge E^+(g)$ *is not an output wire of* $C_{\text{test},0}$ **then**
4   Insert to $C_{\text{test},0}$ a COPY gate between g and $V^+(w)$.
5   One of the output wires of the new gate should go to $V^+(w)$, the other one should be left as an additional output wire of the modified circuit.
6 **return** $C_{\text{test},0}, \mathbb{T}_0$

Proposition 3 *The Algorithm 2 transforms a gate-covered circuit $C_{\text{gate}} : \mathbb{Z}_2^s \to \mathbb{Z}_2^t$ with gate-covering set $\mathbb{T}_{\text{gate}}$ into another gate-covered circuit $C_{\text{test},0} : \mathbb{Z}_2^s \to \mathbb{Z}_2^{t+t_0}$ with additional output bits and the same gate-covering set, $\mathbb{T}_0 = \mathbb{T}_{\text{gate}}$, where one observes for any tampering τ of the circuit $C_{\text{test},0}$ at least one of the following holds:*

- **Information loss on output:** $\exists b \in \{0,1\}, X_0, X_1 \in \mathbb{T}_0, i \in \{1, \ldots, t + t_0\}$ *such that*

$$\text{val}_{X_0}(C_{\text{test},0})[i] = 0, \text{val}_{X_1}(C_{\text{test},0})[i] = 1, \text{val}_{X_0}^\tau(C_{\text{test},0})[i] = \text{val}_{X_1}^\tau(C_{\text{test},0})[i] = b$$

- **At most toggled output**

$$\exists_{B \in \{0,1\}^t} \forall X \in \mathbb{Z}_2^s \; \exists Y \in \mathbb{Z}_2^{t_0} : \; C_{\text{test},0}^\tau(X) = C_{\text{gate}}(X) \| Y + B \| 0^{t_0}$$

Proof. It is easy to see that the same test set $\mathbb{T}_0 = \mathbb{T}_{\text{gate}}$ is a gate covering set for the transformed $C_{\text{test},0}$. Now, according to Theorem 1 on the transformed circuit the following cases may follow:

1. Information-loss on one of the multi-input gates of $C_{test,0}$: in this case, one of the output wires of $C_{test,0}$ is connected via a COPY gate to the output of the multi-input gate and the information loss is propagated to this wire.
2. One of the output wires of $C_{test,0}$ always evaluates to a constant value: in this case, we observe an information loss on this wire because it is wire-covered according to the definition of the gate-covering set $\mathbb{T}_0$.
3. At most, toggled output on the circuit.

6   Minimizing the Number of External Wires

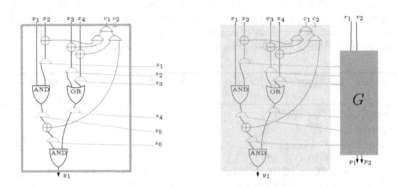

Fig. 7. To reduce the number of external wires, we add a compressing gadget $G_{n,\lambda,d}$.

In the previous Section, we introduced the notion of information loss and showed that without limitations on the number of *additional* input/output wires, the tamper-resilience can be achieved for 1-conductive circuits. For practical reasons, the number of the external wires, $n_{external}$, is more limited compared to the number of internal wires, $n_{internal}$. Typically, the external wires are on the border of a square which contains internal wires [6,10], thus a convincing relation between these numbers can be given by $n_{external}^2 \leq c \cdot n_{internal}$, where c is some constant. Unfortunately, in the construction given in the previous Section, the number of external wires in the compiled circuit is *linear* in the number of the internal wires in the original ones, which is not practical to implement in a real-life circuit. Thus, in this section, we focus on minimizing the number of external wires in our precompiled circuit.

We will define a *compressing gadget* $G_{n,\lambda,d}$. The gadget will compress an input of length n. It will be composed of λ layers of smaller sub-gadgets each of which will need d additional wires with uniformly random bits as input. The gadget $G_{n,\lambda,d}$ will take $\lambda \cdot d$ additional input wires and will have a limited number of output wires (much lower than the number of its input wires - see Fig. 7). We will show that even if the adversary tampers with the compressing gadget $G_{n,\lambda,d}$, the information loss on any of its input wires will survive through it and can be detected on the output of the gadget with sufficiently high probability. In practice, we will be able to keep λ at most 5.

6.1   Construction of One Layer Compression

The $G_{n,\lambda,d}$ gadget consists of λ layers that we define as subgadgets $S_{m,d}$ (with varying parameter m). The single-layer compression gadget $S_{m,d}$ compresses m bit input into $\lceil \frac{m}{d} \rceil$ bit output (using d additional input wires which will be uniformly random bits during the testing procedure). For ease of analysis, we can consider m to be a multiple of d (otherwise we can add $m - \lfloor \frac{m}{d} \rfloor$ spare input wires set to 0 to the $S_{m,d}$ single-layer gadget). Sometimes we refer to $S_{m,d}$ as simply S_d when m is clear from the context.

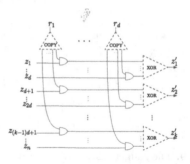

Fig. 8. Construction of - $S_{m,d}$. The dotted red triangle represents the copying tree, $\triangle_k$. The dotted green triangle represents the xoring tree, $\rhd_d$.

$S_{m,d}$ takes $m + d$ wires as input, where d are additional inputs composed of uniformly random bits, and outputs $\frac{m}{d}$ wires. First, $S_{m,d}$ divides the input sequence that it receives (say $z_1, z_2, \ldots, z_m$) into $\frac{m}{d}$ blocks of length d

$$\left((z_1, \ldots, z_d), (z_{d+1}, \ldots, z_{2d}), \ldots, (z_{(\frac{m}{d}-1)d+1}, \ldots z_{(\frac{m}{d}-1)d+d}) \right).$$

Then using the additional sequence of d input bits $r_1, \ldots, r_d$ it outputs the value of the inner product of each length d block of $z's$ and the additional sequence. More formally, for $S_{m,d}$ given input wires $(z_1, \ldots, z_m)$ and additional input wires $(r_1, \ldots, r_d)$, $S_{m,d}$ outputs $\frac{m}{d}$ bits:

$$S_{m,d} \left((z_i)_{i=1,\ldots,m}, (r_i)_{i=1,\ldots,d} \right) = \left(\sum_{j=1,\ldots,d} z_{id+j} \cdot r_j \right)_{i=0,\ldots,\frac{m}{d}-1}.$$

The construction of $S_{m,d}$ is shown in Fig. 8. An instantiation with $m = 8, d = 4$ is shown in Fig. 10. Construction of $S_{m,d}$ needs as building blocks 2 types of gadgets: copying tree (with fan-in 1, but high fan-out) consisting of COPY gates and xoring tree (with high fan-in, but fan-out 1) consisting of XOR gates. They are realized by tree-like gadgets that we denote with the following symbols - $\triangle_{m'}, \rhd_d$ (see Fig. 9).

The *copying tree*, $\triangle_{m'}$, takes a single wire as input and outputs m' wires which, as the name suggests, are copies of the input in untampered computation. This is achieved by a complete binary tree with m' leaves where the root is the input, the leaves are the output and all internal nodes are COPY gates. The direction of computation is from the root to the leaves.

The *xoring tree*, $\rhd_d$ takes d wires as input and outputs 1 wire which in the untampered circuit is the **xor** of all the inputs. It achieves this by a complete binary tree with d leaves, where leaves are the input, the root is the output and all nodes are XOR gates. The direction of computation is from the leaves to the root. From the construction above, we obtain the following properties of $S_{m,d}$.

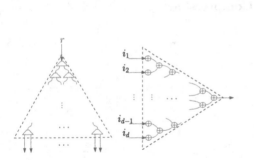
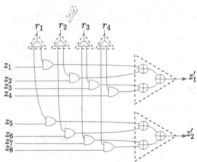

Fig. 9. The gadgets $\triangle, \triangleright$ are realized by complete binary trees with COPY, XOR in nodes, respectively.

Fig. 10. A single layer of compression - $S_{m,d}$ (in this case $m = 8, d = 4$). Trapeziums represent copy gates. The dotted red triangle represents the copying tree, $\triangle_2$. The dotted green triangle represents the xoring tree, $\triangleright_4$.

Lemma 1. *For the $S_{m,d}$ gadget with m input wires and additional d input wires for randomness (Fig. 8), the following holds: (1) The number of output wires is $\frac{m}{d}$, (2) The depth is less than $\log \frac{m}{d} + \log d + 1 = \log m + 1$, (3) The total number of gates is less than $d \cdot \frac{m}{d} + n + \frac{m}{d} \cdot d = 3m$ (number of gates in the copying trees, plus the number of multiplication gates plus number of gates in the xoring trees).*

6.2 Composing the Layers

Now we are ready to present the full construction of $G_{n,\lambda,d}$. This is achieved by simply adding λ layers of $S_{m,d}$ gadgets, with varying parameter m depending on the layer (see Fig. 11). The first layer of S takes as input the input wires to the gadget G; the next layer takes as input the output of the previous layer, and so on. We change the parameter m of inputs to $S_{m,d}$ in each layer accordingly. The output of the last layer is the output of the G. Every layer reduces the number of output wires by a factor of d. Every layer is given d extra input wires which would be uniformly random bits.

Intuition: In Proposition 3, it was shown, that any non-trivial tampering implies an error on the standard output wires or an information loss on the auxiliary output wires (which are input wires to the compressing gadget G). Here we focus on the second case. We can conclude, that if there is any error on the input wire corresponding to the value z_i (what is implied by the information loss), we may hope it to survive through λ of the S_d layers - sometimes the value on this particular wire will be changing the value of the respective inner product, and sometimes not, independent of everything else except the value of some r_j.

From the construction above, we obtain the following.

Lemma 2. *Let* $G_{n,\lambda,d}$ *receive a sequence of length* $n = m \cdot d^\lambda$ *as an input to be compressed. Then the following statements are true:*
(1) $G_{n,\lambda,d}$ *outputs* m *bits. (2) It needs* $\lambda \cdot d$ *auxiliary random bits. (3) The depth of* $G_{n,\lambda,d}$ *is bounded by* $\lambda \cdot (\log n + 1)$. *(4) The total number of its gates is not greater than* $\sum_{i=0}^{\lambda-1}\left(3\frac{n}{d^i}\right) = 3n\frac{d-d^{1-\lambda}}{d-1}$.

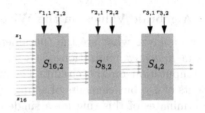

Fig. 11. The compressing gadget $G_{n,\lambda,d}$ consists of λ layers of the compression subgadgets $S_{m,d}$, where the number of input wires m decreases layer by layer. Example parameters are $n = 16, \lambda = 3, d = 2$.

6.3 Information Losing Tuples

Recall that in Proposition 3, we show that any meaningful error of computation will result in an information loss on one of the output wires of the precompiled circuit. In the following Sections, we will describe that the $G_{n,\lambda,d}$ gadget propagates the information loss on some of its input wires to one of its output wires with good probability. The reason that we focus on the propagation of the information loss, not a single error on computation is that the values of the input the $G_{n,\lambda,d}$ gadget and the tamperings may be adversarially chosen in a way that the error vanishes. E.g. imagine a wire in $G_{n,\lambda,d}$ that is (almost) always evaluated to 0 on the test inputs in an untampered evaluation, and the adversarial tampering flips the value of this wire to 1, given some specific inputs. Then the adversary may undo the wrong evaluation on this wire with another constant tampering. In general, it is easy for an adversary to undo the (almost) always correct or (almost) always incorrect evaluations. We will thus make use of the information loss - a pair of evaluations on a single wire that ensures that this wire evaluates to both 0 and 1, and an error occurs on one of these evaluations.

We introduce the notion of information-losing tuples which separates the idea of information loss from the process of evaluation of the whole circuit. In the definition below the n-ary vectors over $\mathbb{Z}_2$ denoted with X_i denote honest evaluations of n wires and the vectors denoted with Y_i denote tampered evaluations of the same wires of some circuit C.

Definition 4. *We say that* $(X_1, ..., X_m; Y_1, ..., Y_m)$ - *a tuple of* n-ary vectors over $\mathbb{Z}_2$ - *is an information-losing tuple if* $\exists_{i,j,k}((X_i[k] \neq X_j[k]) \wedge (Y_i[k] = Y_j[k]))$. *The triple* (i, j, k) *is called an information-losing witness for* $(X_1, ..., X_m; Y_1, ..., Y_m)$

Recall Proposition 3. Let $(X_i), (Y_i)$ denote the values on the output wires of $C_{\text{gate}}, C_{\text{gate}}^\tau$ for the gate covering set $\mathbb{T}_{\text{gate}} = (T_i)$. Then *information loss on the output* means, that $((X_i), (Y_i))$ forms an information-losing tuple if the information loss occurs on the output of the circuit.

6.4   Algebraic Values on the Wires

Now we analyze what are the (parameterized by the input) possible values on wires in *tampered* realization of $G_{n,\lambda,d}$. We will use an algebraic notation for the computation on the circuit. The wires of the circuit carry not only the elements of $\mathbb{Z}_2$, but elements of a ring of multivariate polynomials over $\mathbb{Z}_2$. The indeterminates of this ring for a single circuit will be associated with its input wires and will be denoted with lowercase letters; sometimes we will be using auxiliary indeterminates. To compute the results of the val function, we simply extrapolate the functions from $\mathfrak{G}$ to the ring. From now on, whenever we refer to *value* on the wire, we allow the value to be an element of the ring.

In this setting, how does the tampering of the wire affect its value? It works the same way as before - toggling is simply adding 1 to the polynomial, and setting $0/1$ is setting the polynomial to be equal to $0/1$, without indeterminates. Therefore we can make some observations on the gadgets $\triangleright, \triangle$ (from Fig. 9), and the output of the multiplication gates in S_d.

Proposition 4 (Output of the Copying Trees). *Let $\triangle^\tau$ be given r as input, and r' be any of its output. Then $r' \in \{0, 1, r, r+1\}$.*

Every output of a copying tree is either constant, toggled or the original value of its single input wire, depending on the number of toggling or constant tamperings on the path from the root of the copying tree to the output wire.

Proposition 5 (Output of the Xoring Trees). *Let $a_1, ..., a_d$ be the input values to $\triangleright^\tau$ and p be its output. Then $p = \beta + \sum_{i=1,...,d} \alpha_i a_i$, where $\alpha_i, \beta \in \{0, 1\}$.*

The single output of the xoring tree is a linear combination of its input. If there is a constant tampering on a path from some input wire to the output wire, the coefficient α_i of the input value a_i is set to 0, the coefficient β depends on the number of toggling tamperings and values of the constant tamperings.

Proposition 6 (Output of the Multiplication Gates). *Let (z_i, r_i) be a pair of input wires to some multiplication gate in S^τ and let $mult_i$ denote the output value of this multiplication gate. Then $mult_i = \alpha_i(z_i)r_i + \beta_i(z_i)$, where α_i, β_i are linear functions over $\mathbb{Z}_2$ for all i's.*

Given that for any fixed τ on S^τ, $tamp(z_i) \in \{0, 1, z_i, z_i + 1\}$, $tamp(r_i) \in \{0, 1, r_i, r_i + 1\}$, we can set $mult_i = tamp(z_i) \cdot tamp(r_i)$. The above Proposition states that for the fixed tampering τ, the output value of the multiplication gate m_i can be described as a linear function of r_i.

Proposition 7 (Output of the One Layer Compression Gagdet). *Let p_m be the output value of the gadget $\triangleright^\tau$ from the construction of S_d^τ which takes as input values $z_{md+1}, z_{md+2}, ..., z_{md+d}, r_1, r_2, ..., r_d$. Then $p_m = \beta(z_{md+1}, ..., z_{md+d}) + \sum_{i=1,...,d} \alpha_i(z_{md+i})r_i$, where α_i and β_i are linear (multilinear) functions over $\mathbb{Z}_2$.*

Given the Propositions 4, 5, 6, in Proposition 7 we can conclude on the output values of $S_{m'd,d}$ given values $z_1, ..., z_{m'd}; r_1, ..., r_d$ as input in the above statement.

6.5   Information Loss Survival for S_d

Now, we will prove that information loss survives a single-layer computation S_d with probability at least $\frac{1}{2}$. Since the full compression gadget $G_{n,\lambda,d}$ is built using λ layers of S_d gadgets, this result will lead us to the final conclusion, that $G_{n,\lambda,d}$ compresses the size of the output and propagates the information loss to the output with a probability at least $1/2^\lambda$.

We are given an information-losing tuple $(X_1, ..., X_z; X_1^\tau, ..., X_z^\tau)$ which represents z different (untampered and tampered) evaluation vectors of input wires to the single layer compressing gadget S_d. Given z uniformly random pairs of randomness vectors R_i, Q_i each of the evaluation vectors X_i will be used twice as the input to the gadget S_d. This will suffice to propagate the information loss to the output of the gadget with good probability.

Theorem 2 (Information Loss Through One Layer). *Let* $(X_1, ..., X_z; X_1^\tau,$ $..., X_z^\tau)$ *be an information-losing tuple. Let* R_i, Q_i *for* $i = 1, ..., z$ *be vectors in* $\mathbb{Z}_2^d$ *chosen independently and uniformly at random. Let*

$$Y_i = S_d(X_i|R_i),\ Y_{i+z} = S_d(X_i|Q_i),\ Y_i^\tau = S_d^\tau(X_i^\tau|R_i),\ Y_{i+z}^\tau = S_d^\tau(X_i^\tau|Q_i),$$

for $i = 1, ..., z$. *Then* $(Y_1, ..., Y_{2z}; Y_1^\tau, ..., Y_{2z}^\tau)$ *is an information-losing tuple with probability at least* $\frac{1}{2}$.

Proof. Let (i, j, k) be a information-loss witness for $(X_1, ..., X_z; X_1^\tau, ..., X_z^\tau)$. Then

$$(X_i[k] \neq X_j[k]) \wedge (X_i^\tau[k] = X_j^\tau[k]). \tag{4}$$

Denote the input to S_d by $U = (x_1, ..., x_d, r_1, ..., r_d)$. Let O_s be the s'th output wire of S which is possibly affected by the value of x_k. Obviously $s = \lceil \frac{k}{d} \rceil$, and $k = sd + k'$ where $k' \in [d]$. Then the value of the selected output wire in the untampered S_d is:

$$\mathrm{val}_U(O_s) = \sum_{t=1,...,d} x_{sd+t} r_t = \sum_{t=1,...,d} \gamma_t(x_{sd+t}) r_t, \tag{5}$$

where γ_t is the identity function. From Proposition 7 we know, that the tampered value of the selected output wire can be described with the following expression:

$$\mathrm{val}_U^\tau(O_s) = \sum_{t=1,...,d} \alpha_t (x_{sd+t}) r_t + \beta_t (x_{sd+t}), \tag{6}$$

where α_i and β_i are linear (multilinear) functions over $\mathbb{Z}_2$.

Now we can instantiate $(x_1, ..., x_z)$ four times, with $X_i, X_j, X_i'X_j'$. In every such case $\alpha_t(\cdot), \beta_t(\cdot), \gamma_t(\cdot)$ are evaluated to some elements of $\mathbb{Z}_2$. Let us denote these elements with $\beta_t^{X_i'} = \beta_t(X_i'[sd + t])$. Since (i, j, k) is the witness of information loss we know, that $\gamma_{k'}^{X_i} \neq \gamma_{k'}^{X_j}$, $\alpha_{k'}^{X_i'} = \alpha_{k'}^{X_j'}$. WLOG let $\gamma_{k'}^{X_i} \neq \alpha_{k'}^{X_i}$.

Moreover, the evaluations 5, 6 are simply linear/affine combinations of $r_1, ... r_d$ over $\mathbb{Z}_2$, respectively. Consider,

$$\mathrm{DIFF}_i(r_1, ..., r_t) := \mathrm{val}_{X_i|r_1,...,r_d}(O_s) - \mathrm{val}^{\tau}_{X'_i|r_1,...,r_d}(O_s) = r_{k'} + \sum_{t=1,...,d; t \neq t'} \delta_t r_t + \epsilon_i, \quad (7)$$

for some $\epsilon_i, \delta_t \in \mathbb{Z}_2$.

Now let instantiate $(r_1, ..., r_d)$ with uniform random variable R over $\mathbb{Z}_2^d$. Firstly, observe that $\Pr[\mathrm{DIFF}_i(R) = 1] = \frac{1}{2}$ which means, that for the pair X_i, X'_i for exactly half of the choices of R there will occur an error on the O_s - i.e. the expected and actual values will differ. Since $\mathrm{DIFF}_j(r_1, ..., r_t) = \mathrm{val}_{X_j|r_1,...,r_d}(O_s) - \mathrm{val}^{\tau}_{X'_j|r_1,...,r_d}(O_s) = \sum_{t=1,...,d} \kappa_t r_t + \epsilon_j$, for some $\epsilon_j, \kappa_t \in \mathbb{Z}_2$, we know that $\Pr[\mathrm{DIFF}_j(R) = 1] \in \{0, \frac{1}{2}, 1\}$. Thus for the pair X_j, X'_j there is an error never or always or for half of the choices of R. Finally,

$$\left\{ \frac{1}{2} \right\} \subseteq \{ \Pr[\mathrm{val}_{X_i|R}(O_s) = 0], \Pr[\mathrm{val}_{X_j|R}(O_s) = 0] \} \subseteq \left\{ 0, \frac{1}{2} \right\}. \quad (8)$$

The first inclusion is true since $1 \in \{\gamma_{k'}^{X_i}, \gamma_{k'}^{X_j}\}$. The second inclusion is true, since $\mathrm{val}_{X_i|R}(O_s), \mathrm{val}_{X_j|R}(O_s)$ are linear combinations of r_t's.

Let us denote $x_1(R) = S(X_i|R)[k']$, $x_2(R) = S(X_j|R)[k']$, $y_1(R) = S^{\tau}(X_i^{\tau}|R)[k']$, $y_2(R) = S^{\tau}(X_j^{\tau}|R)[k']$. Informally speaking, for independent and uniformly random R_i, R_j, Q_i, Q_j the tuple $\mathcal{V}$ below
$\mathcal{V} = (x_1(R_i), x_1(Q_i), x_2(R_j), x_2(Q_j); y_1(R_i), y_1(Q_i), y_2(R_j), y_2(Q_j))$ contains a tampered evaluation y_1 that has an error with probability $1/2$ with respect to its correct evaluation x_1 and at least one evaluation x_1 or x_2 that is correctly evaluated to 1. Now, we can use Lemma 3 below to prove the above informal statement and say that given uniformly random R_i, R_j, Q_i, Q_j, the tuple $\mathcal{V}$ is an information-losing tuple with a probability of at least $1/2$.

Thus we conclude that $(Y_1, ..., Y_{2z}; Y_1^{\tau}, ..., Y_{2z}^{\tau})$ is an information-losing tuple with at least one of $(i, j, k'), (i, j+z, k'), (i+z, j, k'), (i+z, j+z, k')$ as a witness with probability at least $1/2$. □

Finally, we formulate the Lemma which lets us conclude that the information loss survives a single layer of compression S_d with probability at least $1/2$.

Lemma 3. Let x_1, x_2, y_1, y_2 be functions from $\mathbb{Z}_2^d$ to $\mathbb{Z}_2$, and let R be a random variable over $\mathbb{Z}_2^d$, such that:

$$\Pr[x_1(R) = y_1(R)] = \frac{1}{2}, \quad (9)$$

$$\Pr[x_2(R) = y_2(R)] \in \left\{ 0, \frac{1}{2}, 1 \right\}, \quad (10)$$

$$\left\{ \frac{1}{2} \right\} \subseteq \{ \Pr[x_1(R) = 0], \Pr[x_2(R) = 0] \} \subseteq \left\{ \frac{1}{2}, 1 \right\}, \quad (11)$$

Then for independent and uniformly random R_1, R_2, Q_1, Q_2 the tuple

$$(x_1(R_1), x_1(Q_1), x_2(R_2), x_2(Q_2); y_1(R_1), y_1(Q_1), y_2(R_2), y_2(Q_2))$$

is information losing with probability $\geq \frac{1}{2}$.

Proof. We want to show that for any constraints with probability $\geq \frac{1}{2}$ the tuple $(x_1(R_1), x_1(Q_1), x_2(R_2), x_2(Q_2); y_1(R_1), y_1(Q_1), y_2(R_2), y_2(Q_2))$ has some two $x's$ different and corresponding $y's$ being equal. Consider any four tuples $(a, a'), (b, b'), (c, c')$ and (d, d') where $a, b, c, d, a', b', c', d' \in \{0, 1\}$. First, we claim that $(a, b, c, d; a', b', c', d')$ forms an information-losing tuple if and only if none of the following is true: (1) $a = b = c = d$, (2) $(a = a') \wedge (b = b') \wedge (c = c') \wedge (d = d')$, (3) $(a = 1 - a') \wedge (b = 1 - b') \wedge (c = 1 - c') \wedge (d = 1 - d')$.

Clearly, if any of the above conditions is true then $(a, b, c, d; a', b', c', d')$ is not information-losing. For the reverse, assume none of the conditions is true. WLOG let $a = 1, b = 0$. WLOG we have two cases $c = 1, d = 1$ or $c = 1, d = 0$. In the first case, if $b' = 0$, then at least one of a', c', d' must be 0, otherwise, condition 2 above would hold. WLOG let $a' = 0$. Thus $a \neq b$ but $a' = b'$ and we get information loss. Similarly, if $b' = 1$ using condition 3, we will find information loss. In the second case of $a = 1, b = 0, c = 1, d = 0$, if $a' \neq c'$, then $b' = a'$ or c' hence information loss. If $a' = c'$, then we get information loss if either b' or d' is equal to a'. The only way for neither b' nor d' to be equal to a' is for one of conditions 2 or 3 to hold true, but this would be a contradiction.

Thus we define three events corresponding to the three conditions above:

E_1: $x_1(R_1) = x_1(Q_1) = x_2(R_2) = x_2(Q_2)$

E_2: $(x_1(R_1) = y_1(R_1)) \wedge (x_1(Q_1) = y_1(Q_1)) \wedge (x_2(R_2) = y_2(R_2)) \wedge (x_2(Q_2) = y_2(Q_2))$

E_3: $(x_1(R_1) = 1 - y_1(R_1)) \wedge (x_1(Q_1) = 1 - y_1(Q_1)) \wedge (x_2(R_2) = 1 - y_2(R_2)) \wedge (x_2(Q_2) = 1 - y_2(Q_2))$

Thus given a tuple of evaluations

$$\mathcal{V} = (x_1(R_1), x_1(Q_1), x_2(R_2), x_2(Q_2); y_1(R_1), y_1(Q_1), y_2(R_2), y_2(Q_2)),$$

we get that $\Pr[\mathcal{V}$ is information losing$] = 1 - \Pr[E_1 \vee E_2 \vee E_3]$.

We will bound $\Pr[E_1 \vee E_2 \vee E_3] \leq \frac{1}{2}$, thus proving the desired result. For this we first use union bound to get $\Pr[E_1 \vee E_2 \vee E_3] \leq \Pr[E_1] + \Pr[E_2 \vee E_3]$. Now for $\Pr[E_1]$, we have that at either $\Pr[x_1 = 0] = \frac{1}{2}$ or $\Pr[x_2 = 0] = \frac{1}{2}$ (eq. 11). Thus $\Pr[x_1(R_1) = x_1(Q_1) = x_2(R_2) = x_2(Q_2)] \leq \frac{1}{4}$.

For $\Pr[E_2 \vee E_3] \leq \Pr[E_2] + \Pr[E_3]$. We have three cases by eq. 10:

1. $\Pr[x_2(R) = y_2(R)] = 0$: In this case $\Pr[E_2] = 0$. Additionally using eq. 9 we get that $\Pr[E_3] = \frac{1}{4}$. Hence, $\Pr[E_2 \vee E_3] = \frac{1}{4}$
2. $\Pr[x_2(R) = y_2(R)] = 1$: In this case $\Pr[E_3] = 0$. Additionally using eq. 9 we get that $\Pr[E_2] = \frac{1}{4}$. Hence, $\Pr[E_2 \vee E_3] = \frac{1}{4}$
3. $\Pr[x_2(R) = y_2(R)] = \frac{1}{2}$: Additionally using eq. 9 we get $\Pr[E_2] = \Pr[E_3] = \frac{1}{16}$. Hence, $\Pr[E_2 \vee E_3] \leq \frac{1}{8}$

We get $\Pr[E_1 \vee E_2 \vee E_3] \leq \frac{1}{2}$, and the probability of inf. loss at least $\frac{1}{2}$. ∎

7   The Compiler

Finally, building upon results from the previous sections, we define a compiler that compiles any circuit $C : \mathbb{Z}_2^s \to \mathbb{Z}_2^t$ into another functionally equivalent circuit $C_{\text{test},\lambda} : \mathbb{Z}_2^{s+s'} \to \mathbb{Z}_2^{t+t'}$ such that for any non-trivial tampering of the circuit $C_{\text{test},\lambda}$, running the testing procedure on the tampered $C_{\text{test},\lambda}$, one always detects an error with high probability.

Algorithm 3: The Compiler

Input: $C : \mathbb{Z}_2^s \to \mathbb{Z}_2^t, \lambda$
Output: $C_{\text{test},\lambda}$

1 Compile circuit C into a gate-covered $C_{\text{gate}} : \mathbb{Z}_2^{s+s_g} \to \mathbb{Z}_2^t, \mathbb{T}_{\text{gate}}$, by running Algorithm 1 on it

2 Add the COPY gates that route the information loss in the gate-covered circuit to the testing gadget, by running Algorithm 2 on the pair $C_{\text{gate}}, \mathbb{T}_{\text{gate}}$. This procedure gives a circuit with additional t_0 output bits - $C_{\text{test},0} : \mathbb{Z}_2^{s+s_g} \to \mathbb{Z}_2^{t+t_0}$ along with a test set $\mathbb{T}_0$

3 Append the $G_{n,\lambda,d}$ gadget to the t_0 wires added in the previous step, where $d = \lceil t_0^{\frac{1}{\lambda+1}} \rceil$. This step adds s_λ wires to the input of the circuit, but replaces the t_0 output bits created in the previous step with λ new output bits, producing a circuit $C_{\text{test},\lambda} : \mathbb{Z}_2^{s+s_g+s_\lambda} \to \mathbb{Z}_2^{t+t_\lambda}$

4 **return** $C_{\text{test},\lambda}$

Theorem 3 (Testing Probability of Final Circuit). *On input circuit* $C : \mathbb{Z}_2^s \to \mathbb{Z}_2^t$ *along with parameter* λ, *Algorithm 3 outputs a circuit* $C_{\text{test},\lambda} : \mathbb{Z}_2^{s+s_g+s_\lambda} \to \mathbb{Z}_2^{t+t_\lambda}$ *such that for any tampering* τ *of* $C_{\text{test},\lambda}$ *if*

$$\exists X \in \mathbb{Z}_2^s : C_{\text{test},\lambda}^\tau(X||0^{s_g+s_\lambda}) \neq C_{\text{test},\lambda}(X||0^{s_g+s_\lambda})$$

then when observing behaviour of the circuit $C_{\text{test},\lambda}$ *on its test set* $\mathbb{T}_{\text{test}}$,

- *Either the output is wrong:*

$$\exists X \in \mathbb{T}_{\text{test}} : C_{\text{test},\lambda}^\tau(X||0^{s_\lambda}) \neq C_{\text{test},\lambda}(X||0^{s_\lambda}),$$

- *or the testing gadget detects an inconsistency:*

$$\exists X \in \mathbb{T}_{\text{test}} : \Pr_{R \leftarrow \mathbb{Z}_2^{s_\lambda}} \left[C_{\text{test},\lambda}^\tau(X||R) \neq C_{\text{test},\lambda}(X||R) \right] \geq \frac{1}{2^{2\lambda}}.$$

Proof. By the Proposition 3 we know that either we observe an information loss on the first t bits of the intermediary circuit $C_{\text{test},0}$ or its output is toggled, or we observe information loss on t_0 wires added during Step 2 of the Algorithm 3, or the output is always correct. Any error on the first t bits of the circuit will be detected on at least of query from ($\mathbb{T}_0 \subseteq \mathbb{T}_{\text{test}}$ is the gate-covering set of the $C_{\text{test},0}$ (Propositions 1 and 3)). Next, when we append the gadget $G_{n,\lambda,d}$ to the remaining t_0 wires of the construction. By Theorem 2 we know that the information loss on these wires survives with probability $1/2$ in each layer when queried with fresh randomness twice. Hence the information loss would survive with probability $1/2^\lambda$ if we query with two fresh randomness vectors in each layer. Thus if we query with only one random string the probability of information loss surviving and hence the error showing up on the output is $\frac{1}{2^\lambda}/2^\lambda = 1/2^{2\lambda}$. ∎

Testing Procedure. Given any circuit $C^\tau_{\text{test},\lambda}$ with any tampering τ on its wires we test it by querying it on all the test inputs in $\mathbb{T}_{\text{test}}$ along with uniform random $R \in \mathbb{Z}_2^{s_\lambda}$. We can repeat the testing procedure κ times with fresh randomness to get the probability of catching an error $1 - (1 - 1/2^{2\lambda})^\kappa$

Circuit Parameters. For any circuit $C : \mathbb{Z}_2^s \to \mathbb{Z}_2^t$ with n gates, using the Algorithm 3 with parameter λ. The first step of the Algorithm produces a gate-covered circuit C_{gate} with 5 new input bits and a test set of size 6 and creates a circuit of size $\approx 7n$ gates (see Proposition 2). The second step of the algorithm adds XOR and COPY gate to every nonlinear gate of the circuit, adding $\approx 2 \cdot 4n$ gates and roughly $\approx 4n$ output wires (in the previous estimation at least $3n$ out of $7n$ gates are the COPY gates). The third step of the algorithm replaces the $4n$ intermediary wires with $\approx L \cdot {}^{\lambda+1}\!\sqrt{4n}$ input bits and $\approx {}^{\lambda+1}\!\sqrt{4n}$ output bits.

8 Conclusions and Open Problems

In this work, we construct an efficiently testable circuit compiler that detects tampering on all wires and does not assume conductivity, solving one of the two open problems put forward in [3] (the other being a construction that can handle tampering of all *gates*). Unlike in [3], our testing procedure is randomized, and it's an interesting open question whether this is inherent. We can "derandomize" our construction by using $\lambda = \log(n)$ layers and then making test queries for all $2^{2\lambda} = n^2$ possible choices of the randomness. The number of test queries will be quadratic in the size of the circuit, which is not practical.

We hope that more applications, besides testing and security against tampering, will be found in the future as was the case for non-malleable codes [18] (like ETC, non-malleable codes originally also aimed at preventing tampering, but only on static memory). E.g., an arithmetic version of our ETC could have applications to multiparty computation (as it would strengthen the additive tampering notion used in [23]), or to the construction of succinct proofs systems, where starting from an ETC rather than a general (arithmetic) circuit could give some security benefits, like avoiding a trusted setup, and instead just checking whether the setup works on all the values in the testset.

References

1. Aggarwal, D., Dodis, Y., Lovett, S.: Non-malleable codes from additive combinatorics. In: Shmoys, D.B. (ed.), Symposium on Theory of Computing, STOC 2014,

New York, NY, USA, May 31–June 03, 2014, pp. 774–783. ACM (2014). https://doi.org/10.1145/2591796.2591804

2. Ateniese, G., Kiayias, A., Magri, B., Tselekounis, Y., Venturi, D.: Secure outsourcing of cryptographic circuits manufacturing. In: Baek, J., Susilo, W., Kim, J. (eds.) ProvSec 2018. LNCS, vol. 11192, pp. 75–93. Springer, Cham (2018). https://doi.org/10.1007/978-3-030-01446-9_5

3. Baig, M.A., Chakraborty, S., Dziembowski, S., Gałczka, M., Lizurej, T., Pietrzak, K.: Efficiently testable circuits. In: ITCS - Innovations in Theoretical Computer Science (2023)

4. Marshall Ball, Dana Dachman-Soled, Siyao Guo, Tal Malkin, and Li-Yang Tan. Non-malleable codes for small-depth circuits. In Mikkel Thorup, editor, 59th IEEE Annual Symposium on Foundations of Computer Science, FOCS 2018, Paris, France, October 7–9, 2018, pages 826–837. IEEE Computer Society, 2018. https://doi.org/10.1109/FOCS.2018.00083

5. Berti, F., Guo, C., Peters, T., Standaert, F.-X.: Efficient leakage-resilient MACs without idealized assumptions. In: Tibouchi, M., Wang, H. (eds.) ASIACRYPT 2021. LNCS, vol. 13091, pp. 95–123. Springer, Cham (2021). https://doi.org/10.1007/978-3-030-92075-3_4

6. Bhunia, S., Tehranipoor, M.: The Hardware Trojan War. Springer, Cham (2018). https://doi.org/10.1007/978-3-319-68511-3

7. Biham, E., Shamir, A.: Differential fault analysis of secret key cryptosystems. In: Kaliski, B.S. (ed.) CRYPTO 1997. LNCS, vol. 1294, pp. 513–525. Springer, Heidelberg (1997). https://doi.org/10.1007/BFb0052259

8. Boneh, D., DeMillo, R.A., Lipton, R.J.: On the importance of eliminating errors in cryptographic computations. J. Cryptol. $14(2)$, 101–119 (2001)

9. Boyle, E., Segev, G., Wichs, D.: Fully Leakage-Resilient Signatures. J. Cryptol. $26(3)$, 513–558 (2012). https://doi.org/10.1007/s00145-012-9136-3

10. Bushnell, M., Agrawal, V.: Essentials of Electronic Testing for Digital, Memory and Mixed-signal VLSI Circuits, vol. 17. Springer Science & Business Media, Cham (2004). https://doi.org/10.1007/b117406

11. Chakraborty, S., Dziembowski, S., Gałązka, M., Lizurej, T., Pietrzak, K., Yeo, M.: Trojan-resilience without cryptography. In: Nissim, K., Waters, B. (eds.) TCC 2021. LNCS, vol. 13043, pp. 397–428. Springer, Cham (2021). https://doi.org/10.1007/978-3-030-90453-1_14

12. Chattopadhyay, E., Li, X.: Non-malleable codes and extractors for small-depth circuits, and affine functions. In: Hatami, H., McKenzie, P., King, V., (eds.), Proceedings of the 49th Annual ACM SIGACT Symposium on Theory of Computing, STOC 2017, Montreal, QC, Canada, June 19–23, 2017, pp. 1171–1184. ACM (2017). https://doi.org/10.1145/3055399.3055483

13. Dachman-Soled, D., Kalai, Y.T.: Securing circuits against constant-rate tampering. In: Safavi-Naini, R., Canetti, R. (eds.) CRYPTO 2012. LNCS, vol. 7417, pp. 533–551. Springer, Heidelberg (2012). https://doi.org/10.1007/978-3-642-32009-5_31

14. Dachman-Soled, D., Kalai, Y.T.: Securing circuits and protocols against $1/\mathrm{poly}(k)$ tampering rate. In: Lindell, Y. (ed.) TCC 2014. LNCS, vol. 8349, pp. 540–565. Springer, Heidelberg (2014). https://doi.org/10.1007/978-3-642-54242-8_23

15. Dachman-Soled, D., Liu, F.-H., Shi, E., Zhou, H.-S.: Locally decodable and updatable non-malleable codes and their applications. J. Cryptol. $33(1)$, 319–355 (2018). https://doi.org/10.1007/s00145-018-9306-z

16. Dziembowski, S., Faust, S., Standaert, F.-X.: Private circuits III: hardware trojan-resilience via testing amplification. In: Weippl, E.R., Katzenbeisser, S., Kruegel,

C., Myers, A.C., Halevi, S., (eds.), ACM CCS, pp. 142–153. ACM (2016). https:// doi.org/10.1145/2976749.2978419

17. Dziembowski, S., Pietrzak, K.: Leakage-resilient cryptography. In: 49th Annual IEEE Symposium on Foundations of Computer Science, FOCS 2008, October 25–28, 2008, Philadelphia, PA, USA, pp. 293–302. IEEE Computer Society (2008). https://doi.org/10.1109/FOCS.2008.56

18. Dziembowski, S., Pietrzak, K., Wichs, D.: Non-malleable codes. J. ACM **65**(4), 20:1-20:32 (2018). https://doi.org/10.1145/3178432

19. Efremenko, K., et al.: Circuits resilient to short-circuit errors. In: Proceedings of the 54th Annual ACM SIGACT Symposium on Theory of Computing, STOC 2022, pp. 582–594. Association for Computing Machinery, New York, NY, USA (2022). ISBN 9781450392648. https://doi.org/10.1145/3519935.3520007

20. Faust, S., Kiltz, E., Pietrzak, K., Rothblum, G.N.: Leakage-resilient signatures. In: Micciancio, D. (ed.) TCC 2010. LNCS, vol. 5978, pp. 343–360. Springer, Heidelberg (2010). https://doi.org/10.1007/978-3-642-11799-2_21

21. Faust, S., Mukherjee, P., Nielsen, J.B., Venturi, D.: A tamper and leakage resilient von Neumann architecture. In: Katz, J. (ed.) PKC 2015. LNCS, vol. 9020, pp. 579–603. Springer, Heidelberg (2015). https://doi.org/10.1007/978-3-662-46447-2_26

22. Faust, S., Pietrzak, K., Venturi, D.: Tamper-proof circuits: how to trade leakage for tamper-resilience, pp. 391–402 (2011). https://doi.org/10.1007/978-3-642-22006-7_33

23. Genkin, D., Ishai, Y., Prabhakaran, M.M., Sahai, A., Tromer, E.: Circuits resilient to additive attacks with applications to secure computation. In: Proceedings of the Forty-Sixth Annual ACM Symposium on Theory of Computing, STOC 2014, pp. 495–504. Association for Computing Machinery, New York, NY, USA (2014). ISBN 9781450327107. https://doi.org/10.1145/2591796.2591861

24. Ishai, Y., Prabhakaran, M., Sahai, A., Wagner, D.: Private circuits II: keeping secrets in tamperable circuits. In: Vaudenay, S. (ed.) EUROCRYPT 2006. LNCS, vol. 4004, pp. 308–327. Springer, Heidelberg (2006). https://doi.org/10.1007/11761679_19

25. Ishai, Y., Sahai, A., Wagner, D.: Private circuits: securing hardware against probing attacks. In: Boneh, D. (ed.) CRYPTO 2003. LNCS, vol. 2729, pp. 463–481. Springer, Heidelberg (2003). https://doi.org/10.1007/978-3-540-45146-4_27

26. Kalai, Y.T., Lewko, A.B., Rao, A.: Formulas resilient to short-circuit errors. In: 53rd Annual IEEE Symposium on Foundations of Computer Science, FOCS 2012, New Brunswick, NJ, USA, October 20–23, 2012, pp. 490–499. IEEE Computer Society (2012). https://doi.org/10.1109/FOCS.2012.69

27. Kalai, Y.T., Reyzin, L.: A survey of leakage-resilient cryptography. In: Goldreich, O., (ed.) Providing Sound Foundations for Cryptography: On the Work of Shafi Goldwasser and Silvio Micali, pp. 727–794. ACM (2019). https://doi.org/10.1145/3335741.3335768

28. Kiayias, A., Tselekounis, Y.: Tamper resilient circuits: the adversary at the gates. In: Sako, K., Sarkar, P. (eds.) ASIACRYPT 2013. LNCS, vol. 8270, pp. 161–180. Springer, Heidelberg (2013). https://doi.org/10.1007/978-3-642-42045-0_9

29. Li, X.: Improved non-malleable extractors, non-malleable codes and independent source extractors. In: Hatami, H., McKenzie, P., King, V. (eds.), Proceedings of the 49th Annual ACM SIGACT Symposium on Theory of Computing, STOC 2017, Montreal, QC, Canada, June 19–23, 2017, pp. 1144–1156. ACM (2017). https:// doi.org/10.1145/3055399.3055486

30. Micali, S., Reyzin, L.: Physically observable cryptography. In: Naor, M. (ed.) TCC
    2004. LNCS, vol. 2951, pp. 278–296. Springer, Heidelberg (2004). https://doi.org/
    10.1007/978-3-540-24638-1_16
31. Wahby, R.S. Howald, M., Garg, S., Shelat, A., Walfish, M., Verifiable Asics. In:
    IEEE SP, pp. 759–778. IEEE Computer Society (2016). https://doi.org/10.1109/
    SP.2016.51

Immunizing Backdoored PRGs

Marshall Ball[✉] , Yevgeniy Dodis , and Eli Goldin

New York University, New York, USA
{marshall,dodis}@cs.nyu.edu, eli.goldin@nyu.edu

Abstract. A backdoored Pseudorandom Generator (PRG) is a PRG which looks pseudorandom to the outside world, but a saboteur can break PRG security by planting a backdoor into a seemingly honest choice of *public parameters*, *pk*, for the system. Backdoored PRGs became increasingly important due to revelations about NIST's backdoored Dual EC PRG, and later results about its practical exploitability.

Motivated by this, at Eurocrypt'15 Dodis et al. [22] initiated the question of *immunizing* backdoored PRGs. A k-immunization scheme repeatedly applies a post-processing function to the output of k backdoored PRGs, to render any (unknown) backdoors provably useless. For $k = 1$, [22] showed that no deterministic immunization is possible, but then constructed "seeded" 1-immunizer either in the random oracle model, or under strong non-falsifiable assumptions. As our first result, we show that no seeded 1-immunization scheme can be black-box reduced to any efficiently falsifiable assumption.

This motivates studying k-immunizers for $k \geq 2$, which have an additional advantage of being deterministic (i.e., "seedless"). Indeed, prior work at CCS'17 [37] and CRYPTO'18 [8] gave supporting evidence that simple k-immunizers might exist, albeit in slightly different settings. Unfortunately, we show that simple standard model proposals of [8,37] (including the XOR function [8]) provably do not work in our setting. On a positive, we confirm the intuition of [37] that a (seedless) random oracle is a provably secure 2-immunizer. On a negative, no (seedless) 2-immunization scheme can be black-box reduced to any efficiently falsifiable assumption, at least for a large class of natural 2-immunizers which includes all "cryptographic hash functions."

In summary, our results show that k-immunizers occupy a peculiar place in the cryptographic world. While they likely exist, and can be made practical and efficient, it is unlikely one can reduce their security to a "clean" standard-model assumption.

1 Introduction

Pseudorandom number generators (PRGs) expand a short, uniform bit string s (the "seed") to a larger sequence of pseudorandom bits X. Beyond their status

M. Ball—Supported in part by the Simons Foundation.

Y. Dodis—Research Supported by NSF grant CNS-2055578, and gifts from JP Morgan, Protocol Labs and Algorand Foundation.

E. Goldin—Partially supported by a National Science Foundation Graduate Research Fellowship.

G. Rothblum and H. Wee (Eds.): TCC 2023, LNCS 14371, pp. 153–182, 2023.
https://doi.org/10.1007/978-3-031-48621-0_6

as a fundamental primitive in cryptography, they are used widely in practical random number generators, including those in all major operating systems. Unsurprisingly, PRGs have been target of many attacks over the years. In this work we focus on a specific, yet prominent, type of PRG attack which arises by planting a *backdoor* inside the PRG. This type of attack goes far back to 1983, when Vazirani and Vazirani [42,43] introduced the notion of "trapdoored PRGs" and showed the Blum-Blum-Shub PRG is one such example [13]. Their purpose was not for sabotaging systems, however, but instead they used the property constructively in a higher level protocol.

NIST DUAL EC PRG. Perhaps the most infamous demonstration of the potential for sabotage is the backdoored NIST Dual EC PRG [1]. Oversimplifying this example for the sake of presentation (see [17,22,39] for the "real-world" description), the attack works as follows. The (simplified) PRG is parameterized by two elliptic curve points; call them P and Q. These points are supposed to be selected at random and independent from each other, forming the PRG public parameter $pk = (P, Q)$ which can be reused by multiple PRG instances. Each new PRG instance then selects a random initial seed s, and can expand into random-looking elliptic curve points $X = sP$ and $Y = sQ$. Ignoring the details of mapping elliptic curve points into bit-strings,[1] as well as subsequent iterations of this process, one can conclude that the points (X, Y) are pseudorandom conditioned on $pk = (P, Q)$. In fact, this is *provably so* under to widely believed Decisional Diffie-Hellman (DDH) assumption.

Yet, imagine that the entity selecting points P and Q chooses the second point Q as $Q = dP$ for a random multiple ("discrete log") d, and secretly keeps this multiple as its backdoor $sk = d$. Notice, the resulting public parameter distribution $pk = (P, Q)$ is *identical* to the supposed "honest" distribution, when Q was selected independently from P. Thus, the outside world cannot detect any cheating in this step, and could be swayed to use the PRG due to its provable security under the DDH assumption. Yet, the knowledge of d can easily allow the attacker to distinguish the output (X, Y) from random; or, worse, predict Y from X, by noticing that

$$Y = sQ = s(dP) = d(sP) = dX$$

While we considerably simplified various low level details of the Dual EC PRG, the works of [17,39] showed that the above attack idea can be extended to attacking the actual NIST PRG. Moreover, the famous "Juniper Dual EC incident" (see [16] and references therein) showed that this vulnerability was likely used for years in a real setting of Juniper Networks VPN system!

BACKDOORED PRGs. Motivated by these real-world considerations, the work of Dodis et al. [22] initiated a systematic study of so called *backdoored PRGs*, abstracting and generalizing the Dual EC PRG example from above. A backdoored PRG (K, G) is specified by a (unknown to the public) key generation algorithm K which outputs public parameters pk, and a hidden backdoor sk.

---

[1] And instead thinking of PRG as outputting pseudorandom elliptic curve points.

The "actual PRG" G takes pk and a current PRG state s as input, and generates the next block of output bits R and the updated (internal) state s. The initial seed/state $s = s_0$ is assumed to be chosen at random and not controlled/sabotaged by the attacker. We call this modeling *honest initialization*, emphasizing that the Dual EC PRG attack was possible even under such assumption. The PRG can then be iterated any number of times q, producing successive outputs (R_i) and corresponding internal states (s_i). The basic constraint on the saboteur is that the joint output $X = (R_1, \ldots, R_q)$ should be indistinguishable from uniform given only the public parameters pk (but not the secret backdoor sk). We call this constraint *public security*.

Unfortunately, the dual EC PRG example shows that public security—even when accompanied by a "security proof"—does not make the backdoor PRG secure against the *saboteur, who also knows sk*. In fact, [22] showed that the necessary and sufficient assumption for building effective backdoor PRGs (secure to public but broken using sk) is the existence of any public-key encryption scheme with pseudorandom ciphertexts.

1.1   Our Questions: Immunization Countermeasures

While the question of designing backdoored PRGs is fascinating, in this work we are interested in various countermeasures against backdoor PRGs, a topic of interest given the reduced trust in PRGs engendered by the possibility of backdooring. Obviously, the best countermeasure would be to use only trusted PRGs, if this is feasible. Alternatively, one could still agree to use a given backdoor PRG, but attempt to overwrite its public parameters pk. For example, this latter approach is advocated (and formally proven secure) in [5,35]. Unfortunately, these techniques cannot be applied in many situations. For example, existing proprietary software or hardware modules may not be easily changed, or PRG choices may be mandated by standards, as in the case of FIPS. Additionally, the user might not have not have direct control over the implementation itself (for example, if it is implemented in hardware or the kernel), or might not have capability or expertise to properly overwrite (potentially hidden or hardwired) value of pk. Fortunately, there is another approach which is much less intrusive, and seems to be applicable to virtually any setting: to efficiently *post-process the output* of a PRG in an online manner in order to prevent exploitation of the backdoor. We call such a post-processing strategy an *immunizer*.[2]

The question of building such immunizers was formally introduced and studied by Dodis et al. [22]. For example, the most natural such immunizer would simply apply a cryptographic hash function C, such as SHA-256 (or SHA-3), to the current output R_i of the PRG, only providing the saboteur with value

---

[2] Note that the immunizer only processes pseudorandom outputs and does not have access to the internal state (which is not necessarily available to a user). Indeed, if one has access to a random initial state, there is a trivial "immunizer" that ignores the given backdoor PRG, and instead uses the random state to bootstrap a different (non-backdoored) PRG.

$Z_i = C(R_i)$ instead of R_i itself. The hope being that hashing the output of a PRG will provide security even against the suspected backdoor sk.[3] Unfortunately, [22] showed that this natural immunizer does not work in general, even if C is modeled as a Random Oracle (RO)! Moreover, this result easily extends to any deterministic immunizer C (e.g., bit truncation, etc.).

Instead, the solution proposed by [22] considers a weaker model of probabilistic/seeded immunizers, where it is assumed that some additional, random-but-public parameter can be chosen after the attacker finalized design of the backdoor PRG (K, G), and published the public parameters pk. While [22] provide some positive results for such *seeded immunizers*, these results were either in the random oracle model, or based on the existence of so called universal computational extractors (UCEs) [9]. Thus, we ask the question:

Question 1. Can one built a seeded backdoor PRG immunizer in the standard model, under an efficiently falsifiable[4] assumption?

It turns out that we can use the elegant black-box separation technique of Wichs [44] to give a negative answer to this question (proof included in the full version [6]).

Theorem 1. *If there is a black-box reduction showing security of a seeded immunizer C from the security of some cryptographic game $\mathcal{G}$, then $\mathcal{G}$ is not secure.*

Moreover, the availability and trust issues in generating and agreeing on the public seed required for the immunization make this solution undesirable or inapplicable for many settings. Thus, we ask the question if *deterministic* immunizers could exist in another meaningful model, despite the impossibility result of [22] mentioned above. And, as a secondary question, if they can be based on efficiently falsifiable assumptions.

2-IMMUNIZERS TO RESCUE? We notice that the impossibility result of [22] implicitly (but *critically*) assumes that only a *single* honestly-initialized backdoor PRG is being immunized. Namely, the immunizer C is applied to the output(s) R_i of a single backdoor PRG (K, G). Instead, we notice that many PRGs allow to explicitly initialize *multiple independent copies*. For example, a natural idea would be to initialize two (random and independent) initial states s and s' of the PRG, run these PRGs in parallel, but instead of directly outputting these outputs R_i and R_i', respectively, the ("seedless") immunizer C will output the value $Z_i = C(R_i, R_i')$ to the attacker.[5] We call such post-processing procedures *2-immunizers*.[6] More generally, one can consider k-immunizers for $k \geq 2$, but

---

[3] This assumption presumes that such C itself is not backdoored.

[4] Recall that, loosely speaking, an assumption is efficiently falsifiable if the falseness of the assumption can be verified (efficiently), given an appropriate witness.

[5] Note that again if the post-processing is not sufficiently "simple" (here this means statelessly processing outputs in an online manner), one can trivially bootstrap "honest" public parameters from many fresh PRG invocations.

[6] Drawing inspiration from 2-source extractors [18] to similarly overcome the impossibility of deterministic extraction from a single weak source of randomness.

setting $k = 2$ is obviously the most preferable in practice. As before, our hope would be that the final outputs $(Z_1, \ldots, Z_q)$ will be pseudorandom even conditioned on the (unknown) backdoor sk, and even if the key generation algorithm K could depend on the choice of our 2-immunizer C. This is the main question we study in this work:

Question 2. (Main Question). Can one construct a provably secure 2-immunizer C against all efficient backdoored PRGs (K, G)?

We note that several natural candidates for such 2-immunizers include XOR, inner product, or a cryptographic hash function C.

A NOTE ON IMMUNIZERS FROM COMPUTATIONAL ASSUMPTIONS. One may wonder whether it is worth considering immunizers whose security depends on a computational assumption. After all, if the computational assumption is sufficiently strong to imply that pseudorandom generators exist (as most assumptions are), then why would we not just use the corresponding PRG? However, we think that building a immunizer in this setting is still interesting for two reasons. First, if we can show that a immunizer exists in this regime, then this gives evidence that an information-theoretic style immunizer also exists. Second, there are some scenarios where one has access to PRG outputs but no access to true randomness (for example if the kernel does not give direct access to its random number generator). In this setting, we can use a computational immunizer to recover full security.

1.2 Related Immunization Settings

Before describing our results, it might be helpful to look at the two conceptually similar settings considered by Bauer at al. [8,21] and Russell et al. [37].

DETOUR 1: BACKDOORED RANDOM ORACLES. In this model [8], one assumes the existence of a truly random oracle G. However, the fact that G might have been "backdoored" is modeled by providing the attacker with the following *leakage oracle* any polynomial number of times: given any (potentially inefficient) function g, the attacker can learn the output of g applied to the entire truthtable of G. For example, one can trivially break the PRG security of a length-expanding random oracle $R = G(s)$, by simply asking the leakage oracle $g_R(G)$ whether there is a shorter-than-R seed s s.t. $G(s) = R$.

With this modeling, [8] asked (among other things) whether one can build 2-immunizers for two independent BROs F and G. For example, in case of pseudorandomness, they explicitly asked if $H(s) = F(s) \oplus G(s)$ is pseudo-random (for random seed s), even if the distinguisher can have polynomial number of leakage oracle calls to F and G separately (but not jointly). Somewhat surprisingly, they reduce this question to a plausible conjecture regarding communication complexity of the classical set-intersection problem (see [15] for a survey of this problem). Thus, despite not settling this question unconditionally, the results of [8] suggest that XOR might actually work for the case of PRGs.

In addition, [38] studies the question of k-immunizers in the related setting of "subverted" random oracles (where the subverted oracle differs from the true one on a small number of inputs). There, a simple yet slightly more complicated "xor-then-hash" framework is shown to provide a good immunizer.

DETOUR 2: KLEPTOGRAPHIC SETTING. While the study of kleptography goes back to the seminal works of Young and Yung [45–47] (and many others), let us consider a more recent variant of [37]. This model is quite general, attempting to formalize the ability of the public to test if a given black-box implementation is done according to some ideal specification. As a special case, this could in particular cover the problem of public parameter subversion of PRGs, where the PRG designer kept some secret information sk, instead of simply choosing pk at random.

We will comment on the subtleties "kleptographic PRGs" vs "backdoored PRGs" a bit later, but remark that [37] claimed very simple k-immunizers in their setting. Specifically they showed that for one-shot PRGs (where there is no internal state for deriving arbitrarily many pseudorandom bits) in the kleptographic setting, random oracle C is a good 2-immunizer, while for $k \gg 2$, one can even have very simple k-immunizers in the standard model. For example, have each of k PRGs shrink its output to a single bit, and then concatenate these bits together. Again this suggests that something might work for the more general case of (stateful) PRGs.

1.3   Our Results for 2-Immunizers

As we see, in both of these related settings it turns out that simple k-immunizers exist, including XOR and random oracle for $k = 2$. Can these positive results be extended to the backdoored PRG setting?

XOR IS INSECURE. First we start with the simple XOR 2-immunizer $C(x, y) = x \oplus y$, which is probably the simplest and most natural scheme to consider. Moreover, as we mentioned, the PRG results of [8] for BROs give some supporting evidence that this 2-immunizer might be secure in the setting of backdoor PRGs. Unfortunately, we show that this is not the case.[7] Intuitively, the BRO modeling assumes that both generators F and G are modeled as true random oracles with bounded leakage, which means that both of them have a lot of entropy hidden from the attacker. In contrast, the backdoor PRG model of [22] (and this work) allows the attacker to build F and G which are extremely far from having any non-trivial amount of entropy to the attacker who knows the backdoor sk.

Indeed, our counter-example for the XOR immunizer comes from a more general observation, which rules out all 2-immunizers C for which one can build a public key encryption scheme (Enc, Dec) which has pseudorandom ciphertexts, and is what we call C-homomorphic. Oversimplifying for the sake of presentation (see Definition 13), we need an encryption scheme where the message

---

[7] Under a widely believed cryptographic assumption mentioned shortly.

m—independently encrypted twice under the same public key pk with corresponding ciphertexts x and y—can still be recovered using the secrete key sk and "C-combined" ciphertext $z = C(x, y)$. If such a scheme exists, the backdoor PRG can simply output independent encryptions of a fixed message (say, 0) as its pseudorandom bits. The C-homomorphic property then ensures that the attacker can still figure that 0 was encrypted after seeing the combined ciphertext $z = C(x, y)$, where x and y are now (individually pseudorandom, and hence secure to public) encryptions of 0. Moreover, we build a simple "XOR-homomorphic" public key encryption under a variant of the LPN assumption due to Alekhnovich [3]. Thus, under this assumption we conclude that XOR is not a secure 2-immunizer.

Theorem 2. *Assuming the Alekhnovich assumption (listed in Proposition 1) holds, XOR is not a secure 2-immunizer.*

INADEQUACY OF KLEPTOGRAPHIC SETTING FOR PRGS. Our second observation is that the kleptographic setting considered by [37]—which extremely elegant and useful for many other cryptographic primitives (and additionally considers the dimension of corrupted implementations, which we do not consider) – does not adequately model the practical problem of backdoored PRGs. In essence, the subverted PRG modeling of [36, 37] yields meaningful results in the stateless (one-time output production) setting, but does not extend to the practically relevant stateful setting. It is worth noting that while [37] informally claim (see Remark 3.2 in [36]) a trivial composition theorem to move from stateless to the (practically relevant) stateful setting, that result happens to be vacuous.[8] In particular, the "ideal specification" of stateful PRGs (implicitly assumed by the authors in their proofs) requires that stateful PRG would produce fresh and unrelated outputs, even after rewinding the PRG state to some prior state. However, PRGs are deterministic after the initial seed is chosen. As such, even the most secure and "stego-free" implementation will never pass such rewinding test, as future outputs are predetermined once and for all. Stated differently, the "ideal specification" of stateful PRG implicitly assumed by [36, 37] in Remark 3.2 is too strong, and no construction can meet it.[9]

To see this modeling inadequacy directly, recall that one of the standard model k-immunizers from [36, 37] simply concatenates the first bit of each PRG's output. For a stateless (one-time) PRG case, this is secure for trivial (and practically useless) reasons: each PRG bit should be statistically random, or the "public" (called the "watchdog" by the authors) will easily catch it. But now

---

[8] In general, we conjecture no such composition result is true under proper modeling of backdoor PRGs, such as the one in this work. For example, 2-immunization for stateless PRGs can be effectively instantiated with a sufficiently strong 2-source extractor. In contrast, our negative result (mentioned later in the Introduction) rules out such extractors as sufficient for stateful PRGs.

[9] Note however, that their modeling does capture *pseudorandom number generators (PRNGs)* which accumulate entropy albeit in a setting where one has rewinding access and the entropy sources are not too adversarial.

let us look at the stateful extension,—which could be potentially useful if it was secure,—and apply it to the the following Dual-EC variant. On a given initial state s, in round i the variant will output the ith bit of Dual-EC initialized with s. Syntactically, this is the same (very dangerous) backdoor PRG we would like to defend against, although made artificially less efficient. Yet, when the "concatenation" k-immunizer above is applied to this (stateful) variant, the attacker still learns full outputs of each of the k PRG copies, and can just do the standard attack on Dual-EC separately on each copy. This means that this k-immunizer is blatantly insecure in our setting, for any value of k.

RANDOM ORACLE IS SECURE. Despite the inability to generically import the positive results of [36,37] to our setting, we can still ask if the random oracle 2-immunizer result claimed by [36,37] is actually true for backdoored PRGs. Fortunately, we show that this is indeed the case, by giving a direct security proof.[10] In fact, it works even is the so called *auxiliary-input ROM* (AI-ROM) defined by Unruh [41] and recently studied by [19,23]. In this model we allow the saboteur to prepare the backdoor sk and public parameters pk after *unbounded preprocessing* of the Random Oracle C. The only constraint of the resulting backdoored PRG G is that it has to be secure to the public in the standard ROM (since the public might not have enough resources to run the expensive preprocessing stage). Still, when being fed with outputs $z_i = C(x_i, y_i)$, the saboteur cannot distinguish them from random even given its polynomial-sized backdoor sk (which also models whatever auxiliary information about RO C the attacker computed), and additional polynomial number of queries to C.

Despite appearing rather expected, the proof of this result is quite subtle. It uses the fact that each independently initialized PRG instances F and G are unlikely to ever query the random oracle on any of the outputs produced by the other instance (i.e., F on $C(\cdot, y_i)$ and G on $C(x_i, \cdot)$), because we show that this will contradict the assumed PRG security of F and G from the public.

Theorem 3. $C(X, Y) = RO(X\|Y)$ *is a secure 2-immunizer in the AI-ROM.*

BACK-BOX SEPARATION FROM EFFICIENTLY FALSIFIABLE ASSUMPTIONS. Finally, we consider the question of building a secure 2-immunizer in the standard model. In this setting, we again use the black-box separation technique of Wichs [44] to show the following negative result. No function $C(x, y)$, which is *highly dependent on both inputs x ad y*, can be proven as a secure 2-immunizer for backdoor PRGs, via a black-box reduction to any efficiently falsifiable assumption.

The formal definition of "highly dependent" is given in Definition 18, but intuitively states that there are few "influential" inputs x^* (resp., y^*) which

---

[10] In particular, the key piece of our proof that was missing in [36,37], is contained in Lemma 8 of our paper. The important observation (adapted from the seeded 1-immunizers proof in [22]) is that the random oracle outputs reveal negligible information about its inputs, and so every PRG round can inductively be treated as the first round.

fix the output of C to a constant, irrespective of the other input. We notice that most natural functions are clearly highly dependent on both inputs. *This includes XOR, the inner product function, and any cryptographic hash function heuristically replacing a random oracle, such as SHA-256 or SHA-3.*

The latter category is unfortunate, though. While our main positive result gave plausible evidence that cryptographic hash functions are likely secure as 2-immunizers, our negative result shows that there is no efficiently falsifiable assumption in the standard model under which we can formally show security of any such 2-immunizer C.

Theorem 4. *Let C be a 2-immunizer which is highly dependent on both inputs. If there is a black-box reduction showing that C is secure from the security of some cryptographic game $\mathcal{G}$, then $\mathcal{G}$ is not secure.*

WEAK 2-IMMUNIZERS. Given our main positive result is proven in the random oracle model, we also consider another meaningful type of immunizer which we call *weak 2-immunizer*, in hope that it might be easier to instantiate in the standard model. (For contrast, we will call the stronger immunizer concept considered so far as *strong 2-immunizer.*) Recall, in the strong setting the immunizer C was applied to two independently initialized copies of the *same* backdoor PRG (K, G). In particular, both copies shared the same public parameters pk. In contrast, in the weak setting,—in addition to independent seed initialization above,—we assume the backdoor PRGs were designed by two *independent key generation processes K and K'*, producing independent key pairs (pk, sk) and (pk', sk'). For example, this could model the fact that competing PRGs were designed by two different standards bodies (say, US and China). Of course, at the end we will allow the two saboteurs to "join forces" and try to use both sk and sk' when breaking the combined outputs $Z_i = C(R_i, R_i')$. Curiously, it is not immediately obvious that a strong 2-immunizer is also a weak one, but we show that this is indeed the case, modulo a small security loss. In particular, this implies that our positive result in the random oracle model also gives a weak 2-immunizer.

Of course, the interesting question is whether the relaxation to the weak setting makes it easier to have standard model instantiations. Unfortunately, *we show that this does not appear to be the case*, by extending most of our impossibility/separation results to the weak setting (as can be seen in their formal statements). The only exception is the explicit counter-example to the insecurity of XOR as a weak 2-immunizer, which we leave open (but conjecture to be true). As partial evidence, we show that the pairing operation (which looks similar to XOR) is not a weak 2-immunizer under a widely believed SXDH assumption in pairing based groups [4,7].

Theorem 5. *Assuming the SXDH assumption (listed in Conjecture 1) holds for groups G_X, G_Y, G_T, a bilinear map $e : G_X \times G_Y \to G_T$ is not a secure weak 2-immunizer.*

OPEN QUESTION. Summarizing, our results largely settle the feasibility of designing secure 2-immunizers for backdoor PRGs, but leave the following fascinating question open: *Is there a 2-immunizer C in the standard model whose security can be black-box reduced to an efficiently falsifiable assumption?*

While we know such C cannot be "highly dependent on both inputs", which rules out most natural choices one would consider (including cryptographic hash function), we do not know if other "unnatural" functions C might actually work.

In the absence of such a function/reduction, there are two alternatives:

First, it may be possible to give a *non-black-box* reduction from a non-highly input-dependent function (such as a very good two-source extractor).

Or alternatively, one might try to base the security of C on a *non-falsifiable* assumption likely satisfied by a real-world cryptographic hash function. For example, [22] built seeded 1-immunizers based on the existence of so called universal computational extractors (UCEs) [9]. Unfortunately, the UCE definition seems to be inherently fitted for 1-immunizers, and it is unclear (and perhaps unlikely) that something similar can be done in the 2-immunizer setting, at least with a security definition that is noticeably simpler than that of 2-immunizers.

1.4   Further Related Work

We briefly mention several related works not mentioned so far.

EXTRACTORS. Randomness Extractors convert a weak random source into an output which is statistically close to uniform. Similar to our setting, while deterministic extraction is impossible in this generality [18], these results can either be overcome using seeded extractors [31], or two-source extractors [18].

A special class of seeded extractors consider consider sources which could partially depend on the prior outputs of the extractor (and, hence, indirectly on the random seed). Such sources are called *extractor-dependent* [25,33], and generalize the corresponding notion of oracle-dependent extractors considered by [20] in the ROM. Conceptually similar to our results, [25] showed a black-box separation for constructing such extractors from cryptographic hash functions in the standard model, despite the fact that cryptographic hash functions provably worked in the ROM [20].

KLEPTOGRAPHY. Young and Yung studied what they called kleptography: subversion of cryptosystems by modifying encryption algorithms in order to leak information subliminally [45–47]. Juels and Guajardo [29] propose an immunization scheme for kleptographic key-generation protocols that involves publicly-verifiable injection of private randomness by a trusted entity. More recent work by Bellare, Paterson, and Rogaway [10] treats a special case of Young and Yung's setting for symmetric encryption.

As described in detail above, the works [36,37] consider the idea of using a random oracle as a 2-immunizer, however their results do not extend to the stateful setting considered here.

The works [5,34] also consider immunizing corrupted PRGs, however these results success by modifying the public parameters, as opposed to operating on the PRG output. In other words, the immunizers are not simple and stateless, and thus not relevant in a situations where a user cannot control the implementation itself (e.g. if it is implemented in hardware or the kernel).

STEGANOGRAPHY AND RELATED NOTIONS. Steganography (see [27,40]) is the problem of sending a hidden message in communications over a public channel so that an adversary eavesdropping on the channel cannot even detect the presence of the hidden message. In this sense backdoor PRG could be viewed as a steganographic channel where the PRG is trying to communicate information back to the malicious PRG designer, without the "public" being able to detect such communication (thinking instead that a random stream is transmitted).

More recently, the works of [28,32] looked at certain types of encryption schemes which can always be turned into stegonagraphic channels, even if the dictator demands the users to reveal their purported secret keys.

Finally, the works of [24,30] looked at constructing so called *reverse firewalls*, which probably remove steganographic communication by carefully re-randomizing messages supposedly exchanged by the parties for some other cryptographic task.

BACKDOORED RANDOM ORACLES. The work of [8] and [12] consider the task of immunizing random oracles with XOR. However, these consider information theoretic models of PRG security. An intriguing observation about the findings of our work is that information theoretic models (such as the backdoored random oracle model) do not capture the computational advantage that backdoors can achieve, as is shown by our counterexamples in Sect. 3.

2   Definitions

Definition 1. *Two distributions X and Y are called (t, ϵ)-indistinguishable (denoted by $\boldsymbol{CD}_t(X, Y) \leq \epsilon$) if for any algorithm D running in time t,*

$$|\Pr[D(X) = 1] - \Pr[D(Y) = 1]| \leq \epsilon.$$

Definition 2. *Let X_λ and Y_λ be two families of distributions indexed by λ. If for all polynomial $t(\lambda)$ and some negligible $\epsilon(\lambda)$, X_λ and Y_λ are $(t(\lambda), \epsilon(\lambda))$-indistinguishable, then we say X and Y are computationally indistinguishable (denoted by $\boldsymbol{CD}(X, Y) \leq negl(\lambda)$).*

2.1   Pseudorandom Generators

A pseudorandom generator is a pair of algorithms (K, G). Traditionally, K takes in randomness and outputs a public parameter. We additionally allow K to output a secret key to be used for defining trapdoors. To go with our notation of secret keys, we will denote the public parameter as the public key. For non-trapdoored PRGs, the secret key is set to null. G is a function that takes in a public key and a state, and outputs an n-bit output as well as a new state. More formally, we give the following definitions, adapted from [22]:

Definition 3. *Let* $\mathcal{PK}, \mathcal{SK}$ *be sets of public and secret keys respectively. Let* $\mathcal{S}$ *be a set we call the state space. A* <u>*pseudorandom generator (PRG)*</u> *is a pair of algorithms* (K, G) *where*

- $K : \{0,1\}^\ell \to \mathcal{PK} \times \mathcal{SK}$ *takes in randomness and outputs a public key* pk *and secret key* sk. *We will denote running* K *on uniform input as* $(pk, sk) \xleftarrow{\$} K$.
- $G : \mathcal{PK} \times \mathcal{S} \to \{0,1\}^n \times \mathcal{S}$ *takes in the public key and a state and outputs* n *bits as well as the new state.*

For ease of notation, we may write G instead of G_{pk} when the public key is clear from context.

Definition 4. *Let* (K, G) *be a PRG,* $pk \in \mathcal{PK}, s \in \mathcal{S}$. *Let* $s_0 = s$ *and let* $(r_i, s_i) \leftarrow G_{pk}(s_i)$ *for* $i \geq 1$. *We call the sequence* $(r_1, \ldots, r_q)$ *the* <u>*output of*</u> <u>(K, G)</u>, *and denote it by* $\boldsymbol{out}^q(G_{pk}, s)$ *(or* $\boldsymbol{out}^q(G, s)$).

For n an integer we will denote by $\mathcal{U}_n$ the uniform distribution over $\{0,1\}^n$.

Definition 5. *A PRG* (K, G) *is a* <u>(t, q, δ) *publicly secure PRG*</u> *if* K, G *both run in time* t *and*

$$pk \xleftarrow{\$} K$$

$$\boldsymbol{CD}_t((pk, \boldsymbol{out}^q(G_{pk}, \mathcal{S})), (pk, \mathcal{U}_{qn})) \leq \delta.$$

Note that here there is some implied initial distribution over $\mathcal{S}$. This will depend on the construction, but when unstated we will assume that this distribution is uniform.

Definition 6. *A PRG* (K, G) *is a* <u>(t, q, δ) *backdoor secure PRG*</u> *if* K, G *both run in time* t *and*

$$(pk, sk) \xleftarrow{\$} K$$

$$\boldsymbol{CD}_t((pk, sk, \boldsymbol{out}^q(G_{pk}, \mathcal{U}_{\mathcal{S}})), (pk, sk, \mathcal{U}_{qn})) \leq \delta.$$

Note that there are PRGs that are (t, q, δ) publicly secure, but not (t', q, δ') backdoor secure even for some $t' << t$ and $\delta' >> \delta$ [22]. The goal of an immunizer is to take in as input some (K, G) which is publicly secure but not backdoor secure, and transform it generically into a new PRG which is backdoor secure.

2.2   2-Immunizers

Our definition of 2-immunizers will also be based on the definition of immunizers given in [22]. Note in particular that while the [22] definition of immunizers takes in the output of one PRG and a random seed, we define 2-immunizers to be deterministic functions of the output of two PRGs.

We first define notation to express what it means to apply an immunizer to two PRGs.

Definition 7. *Let* $(K^X, G^X), (K^Y, G^Y)$ *be two PRGs and let* $C : \{0,1\}^n \times \{0,1\}^n \to \{0,1\}^m$ *be a function on the output spaces of the PRGs. We define a new PRG as follows:*

-The key generation algorithm (denoted (K^X, K^Y)*) will be the concatenation of the original two key generation algorithms. More formally, it will run* $K^X \to pk^X, sk^X$, $K^Y \to pk^Y, sk^Y$ *and will return* $pk = (pk^X, pk^Y)$ *and* $sk = (sk^X, sk^Y)$.

-The pseudorandom generation algorithm, denoted $C(G^X, G^Y)$ *will run both PRGs independently and apply* C *to the output. Formally, let us denote* $s = (s^X, s^Y)$. *If* $G^X(s^X) = (r^X, s'^X)$ *and* $G^Y(s^Y) = (r^Y, s'^Y)$, *then*

$$C(G^X, G^Y)(s) := (C(r^X, r^Y), (s'^X, s'^Y)).$$

Note that the output of the PRG will be C applied to the outputs of the original PRGs. Formally, if $\mathbf{out}^q(G^X, s^X) = x_1, \ldots, x_q$ and $\mathbf{out}^q(G^Y, s^Y) = y_1, \ldots, y_q$, then

$$\mathbf{out}^q(C(G^X, G^Y), (s^X, s^Y)) = C(x_1, y_1), \ldots, C(x_q, y_q).$$

Definition 8. *A two-input function* C *is a* (t, q, δ, δ')-*secure weak 2-immunizer, if for any* (t, q, δ) *publicly secure PRGs* $(K^X, G^X), (K^Y, G^Y)$, *the PRG* $((K^X, K^Y), C(G^X, G^Y))$ *is a* (t, q, δ') *backdoor secure PRG.*

A weak 2-immunizer is effective at immunizing two PRGs as long as the public parameters are independently sampled. We can also consider the case where the designers of the two PRGs collude and share public parameters. Identically, we can consider the case where we run one backdoored PRG on multiple honest initializations. If a 2-immunizer effectively immunizes in this setting, we call it a strong 2-immunizer.

Let us first define the syntax

Definition 9. *Let* (K, G) *be a PRG and let* $C : \{0,1\}^n \times \{0,1\}^n \to \{0,1\}^m$ *be a function on the output space of* G. *We define a new PRG (denoted* $(K, C(G, G))$*) as follows:*

-The key generation algorithm will be K

-The pseudorandom generation algorithm, denoted $C(G_{pk}, G_{pk})$ *will run* G *twice (with the same public key) on two initial seeds, and apply* C *to the output. Formally, let us denote* $s = (s^X, s^Y)$. *If* $G_{pk}(s^X) = (r^X, s'^X)$ *and* $G_{pk}(s^Y) = (r^Y, s'^Y)$, *then*

$$C(G, G)(s) := (C(r^X, r^Y), (s'^X, s'^Y))$$

If $x_1, \ldots, x_q = \mathbf{out}^q(G_{pk}, s^X)$ *and* $y_1, \ldots, y_q = \mathbf{out}^q(G_{pk}, s^Y)$ *are two outputs of* G *on the same public key and freshly sampled initial states, then*

$$\mathbf{out}^q(C(G, G), (s^X, s^Y)) = C(x_1, y_1), \ldots, C(x_q, y_q).$$

Definition 10. *A two-input function* C *is called a* (t, q, δ, δ')-*secure strong 2-immunizer, if for any* (t, q, δ) *publicly secure PRG* (K, G), *the PRG* $(K, C(G, G))$ *is a* (t, q, δ') *backdoor secure PRG.*

Lemma 1. *If C is a (t, q, δ, δ')-secure strong 2-immunizer, then C is a $(t, q, \delta, 4\delta')$-secure weak 2-immunizer.*

For a proof of this lemma, see a full version of this paper [6].

Remark 1. Some traditional definitions of PRGs [11] consider the notion of forward-secrecy. That is, even PRG security for the first q outputs should still be maintained even if the $q + 1$st output is leaked. However, it is impossible for a 2-immunizer in our model to preserve public forward secrecy. Informally, given any PRG satisfying forward-secrecy, we can append an encryption of the initial state to the $q + 1$st state. This would result in a PRG satisfying public forward-secrecy but not backdoor forward-secrecy. Since we do not allow the 2-immunizer to view or modify the internal state of the corresponding PRGs in any way, it is impossible for any 2-immunizer to remove this vulnerability.

3   Counterexamples for Simple 2-Immunizers

In this section we will outline a framework for arguing that simple functions (for example XOR) do not work as 2-immunizers. To argue that some C is not a strong 2-immunizer, we will construct a public key encryption scheme suitably homomorphic under C. We will then note that the PRG which simply encrypts 0 using the randomness of its honest initialization will have a backdoor after immunization, where the backdoor will be given by the homomorphic property of the underlying encryption scheme.

To argue that C is not a weak 2-immunizer, we will need to instead construct two public key encryption schemes which are in jointly homomorphic in a suitable manner. In this case, the PRGs defined by encrypting 0 under the two public key encryption schemes defined will allow us to perform an analogous attack on C.

In particular, we will generically define what it means for public key encryption schemes to be suitably homomorphic under C, and argue that this property is enough to show that C is not a 2-immunizer. Note that the definition of suitably homomorphic will depend on whether we are attacking the weak or strong security of C.

We will then instantiate our generic result with specific public key encryption schemes, leading to the following theorems.

Theorem 6 (Theorem 2 restated). *Assuming the Alekhnovich assumption (listed in Proposition 1) holds, XOR is not a $(poly(\lambda), 1, negl(\lambda), negl(\lambda))$-secure strong 2-immunizer.*

Note that there is no simple way to adapt the public key encryption scheme used to prove this theorem to be sufficiently homomorphic to prove that XOR is not a weak 2-immunizer. We leave the question as to whether XOR is a weak 2-immunizer as an open question.

Definition 11. *Let G_X, G_Y, G_T be groups of prime order exponential in λ with generators g_X, g_Y, g_T. A bilinear map $e : G_X \times G_Y \to G_T$ is a function satisfying*

$$e(g_X^a, g_Y^b) = e(g_X, g_Y)^{ab} = g_T^{ab}$$

Note that requiring $e(g_X, g_Y) = g_T$ is a non-standard requirement for bilinear maps, but will always occur when we restrict the codomain of the bilinear group to the subgroup defined by its image.

Theorem 7 (Theorem 5 restated). *Assuming the SXDH assumption (listed in Conjecture 1) holds for groups G_X, G_Y, G_T, a bilinear map $e : G_X \times G_Y \to G_T$ is not a $(poly(\lambda), 2, negl(\lambda),$
$negl(\lambda))$-secure weak 2-immunizer.*

Note that although [8] does not directly argue that a bilinear map is a 2-immunizer in their model, it is clear that the argument for XOR can be generalized to apply for bilinear maps.

3.1 Public Key Encryption

A public key encryption scheme (PKE) is a triple (Gen, Enc, Dec) where

- Gen outputs a public key, secret key pair (pk, sk),
- Enc takes in the public key pk and a message m, and outputs a ciphertext c,
- Dec takes in the secret key sk and a ciphertext c, and outputs the original message m.

For security, as we are working with pseudorandom generators, it is useful for us to require that the encryption schemes themselves be pseudorandom. More formally,

Definition 12. *We say that a public key encryption scheme (Gen, Enc, Dec) is pseudorandom if for all m,*

$$pk \xleftarrow{\$} \text{Gen}$$
$$CD_{poly(\lambda)}((pk, \text{Enc}(m)), (pk, \mathcal{U})) \le negl(\lambda)$$

Note that for our purposes we will require all public key encryption schemes to be pseudorandom. We remark that this assumption is strictly stronger than traditional PKE security.

3.2 Strong 2-Immunizers

Definition 13. *Let $C^e : \{0, 1\}^n \times \{0, 1\}^n \to \{0, 1\}^m$ be some operation. We say that a public key encryption scheme (Gen, Enc, Dec) is $\underline{C^e\text{-homomorphic}}$ if there exists some function $\text{Dec}_{sk}^{C^e}$ such that for all m,*

$$\Pr_{\substack{(pk, sk) \xleftarrow{\$} \text{Gen} \\ \alpha, \alpha' \xleftarrow{\$} \mathcal{U}}} [\text{Dec}_{sk}^{C^e}(C^e(\text{Enc}_{pk}(m; \alpha), \text{Enc}_{pk}(m; \alpha'))) = m] \ge \frac{2}{3}.$$

Theorem 8. *Let* (Gen, Enc, Dec) *be a public key encryption scheme and let* C^e *be some operation. Then, if* (Gen, Enc, Dec) *is pseudorandom and* C^e-*homomorphic (with homomorphic decryption algorithm* Dec^{C^e} *), then* C^e *is not a* $(poly(\lambda), 1, negl(\lambda), negl(\lambda))$-*secure strong 2-immunizer.*

Proof. We will first construct a PRG (K, G) using (Gen, Enc, Dec), and then we will show that $C^e(G, G)$ has a backdoor.

Let us first observe that $\Pr[\mathrm{Dec}^{C^e}(\mathcal{U}) \to 0] + \Pr[\mathrm{Dec}^{C^e}(\mathcal{U}) \to 1] \leq 1$, and so one of these probabilities will be less than $\frac{1}{2}$. Without loss of generality, assume $\Pr[\mathrm{Dec}^{C^e}(\mathcal{U}) \to 0] \leq \frac{1}{2}$.

Define (K, G) by $K := \mathrm{Gen}$, $G_{pk}(s) := \mathrm{Enc}_{pk}(0; s)$. It is clear to see that (K, G) is a $(poly(\lambda), 1, negl(\lambda))$ publicly secure PRG by the definition of a pseudorandom PKE. Thus, it remains to show an adversary D that can distinguish

$$(pk, sk, C^e(\mathrm{Enc}_{pk}(0; \mathcal{U}), \mathrm{Enc}_{pk}(0; \mathcal{U})))$$

from

$$(pk, sk, \mathcal{U})$$

with probability $\geq \frac{1}{poly(\lambda)}$.

On input (pk, sk, r), D will run $\mathrm{Dec}^{C^e}_{sk}(r) \to m$ and output 1 if and only if $m = 0$. It is clear that

$$\Pr[D(pk, sk, C^e(\mathrm{Enc}_{pk}(0; \mathcal{U}), \mathrm{Enc}_{pk}(0; \mathcal{U}))) \to 1] \geq \frac{2}{3}$$

by the definition of Dec^{C^e}. But note that we assumed $\Pr[\mathrm{Dec}^{C^e}(\mathcal{U}) \to 0] \leq \frac{1}{2}$, and so

$$\Pr[D(pk, sk, \mathcal{U}) \to 1] \leq \frac{1}{2}$$

Thus, the advantage of D is $\geq \frac{2}{3} - \frac{1}{2} = \frac{1}{6} \geq \frac{1}{poly(\lambda)}$.

We remark that while this theorem is stated for $q = 1$, it is fairly easy to extend this to arbitrary q by simply appending the corrupted PRGs with a genuine one.

[3] gives a construction of a public key encryption scheme based off of a variant of the learning parity with noise problem (which we will call the Alekhnovich assumption, it is Conjecture 4.7 in his paper). Instead of presenting his underlying assumption directly, we will refer to the following proposition:

Proposition 1 [3]: *Suppose that the Alekhnovich assumption holds, then for every* $m = O(n), k = \Theta(\sqrt{n}), \ell, t \leq poly(n)$ *then*

$$A_i \xleftarrow{\$} \mathcal{U}_{m \times n}, x_i \xleftarrow{\$} \mathcal{U}_n, e_i \xleftarrow{\$} \binom{\{0, 1\}^m}{k}$$

$$CD_t((A_i, A_i x_i + e_i)_{i=1}^{\ell}, (A_i, \mathcal{U}_m)_{i=1}^{\ell}) \leq negl(n)$$

That is, given a uniformly random $m \times n$ binary matrix A, a vector which differs from an element in the image of the matrix in exactly k places is computationally indistinguishable from random.

Let us proceed now to the proof of Theorem 6.

We will prove this by showing a pseudorandom $\oplus$-homomorphic public key encryption scheme based off of the Alekhnovich assumption.

We claim that if the Alekhnovich assumption holds, the public key encryption scheme presented in [2] (along with a minor variation) is both pseudorandom and $\oplus$-homomorphic. Therefore, by Theorem 8, XOR is not a strong 2-immunizer.

First, we present Alekhnovich's public key encryption scheme in Fig. 1. We make one minor change to the original scheme, namely we change the value of the parameter k from $\sqrt{\frac{n}{2}}$ to $\sqrt{\frac{n}{4}}$. Note that since the underlying proposition only requires that $k = \Theta(\sqrt{n})$, this does not affect the proof of security

---

Notation:

$k = \sqrt{\dfrac{n}{4}}$, $m = 2n$.

$\{0,1\}^\ell$ are vectors in $\mathbb{Z}_2^\ell$.

$\dbinom{\{0,1\}^m}{k} :=$ vectors in $\{0,1\}^m$ with exactly k 1s.

Gen-A:

$A \xleftarrow{\$} \mathcal{U}_{m \times n}$.

$x \xleftarrow{\$} \mathcal{U}_n$

$e \xleftarrow{\$} \dbinom{\{0,1\}^m}{k}$

$b \leftarrow Ax + e$, $M = (b|A)$.

$B \xleftarrow{\$} \mathcal{U}_{m \times (m-n-1)}$ conditioned on $M^T B = 0_n$.

Output $pk = B$, $sk = (B, e)$.

Enc-A(1):

$c \xleftarrow{\$} \mathcal{U}_m$.

Output c.

Enc-A(0):

$x' \xleftarrow{\$} \mathcal{U}_{n-1}$,

$e' \xleftarrow{\$} \dbinom{\{0,1\}^m}{k}$.

Output $c = Bx' + e'$.

Dec-A$((B, e), c)$:

Output 0 if $e^T c = 0$.

Otherwise, output 1.

Fig. 1. Alekhnovich's PKE scheme (From Sect. 4.4.3).

Proposition 2 [3]: *Assuming the Alekhnovich assumption holds,*

$$CD((pk, \text{Enc-A}(0)), (pk, \text{Enc-A}(1))) \le negl(\lambda)$$

Corollary 1. *Assuming the Alekhnovich assumption holds,* (Gen-A, Enc-A, Dec-A) *is pseudorandom.*

Proposition 3. *Assuming the Alekhnovich assumption holds, (Gen-A, Enc-A, Dec-A) as presented above is $\oplus$-homomorphic.*

The proof of Proposition 3 is in the full version of this paper [6].

3.3   Weak 2-Immunizers

Definition 14. *Let $C^e : \{0,1\}^n \times \{0,1\}^n \to \{0,1\}^m$ be some operation. We say a pair of public key encryption schemes (Gen, Enc, Dec) and (Gen', Enc', Dec') are jointly C^e-homomorphic if there exists some function $\mathrm{Dec}^{C^e}_{sk,sk'}$ such that for all m,*

$$\Pr_{\substack{(pk,sk) \xleftarrow{\$} \mathrm{Gen} \\ (pk',sk') \xleftarrow{\$} \mathrm{Gen}' \\ \alpha, \alpha' \xleftarrow{\$} \mathcal{U}}} [\mathrm{Dec}^{C^e}_{sk,sk'}(C^e(\mathrm{Enc}_{pk}(m;\alpha), \mathrm{Enc}'_{pk'}(m;\alpha'))) = m] \geq \frac{2}{3}.$$

Theorem 9. *Let (Gen, Enc, Dec), (Gen', Enc', Dec') be two public key encryption schemes and let C^e be some operation. Then, if (Gen, Enc, Dec), (Gen', Enc', Dec') are pseudorandom and jointly C^e-homomorphic (with homomorphic decryption algorithm Dec^{C^e}), then C^e is not a $(poly(\lambda), 1, negl(\lambda), negl(\lambda))$-secure weak 2-immunizer.*

Proof. This proof is analogous to the proof of Theorem 8. The corresponding PRGs are $(K^X, G^X) = (\mathrm{Gen}, \mathrm{Enc}(0;s))$ and $(K^Y, G^Y) = (\mathrm{Gen}', \mathrm{Enc}'(0;s))$. The distinguisher again runs $\mathrm{Dec}^{C^e} \to 0$ and returns 1 if and only if $m = 0$.

Corollary 2. *If there exists (Gen, Enc, Dec), (Gen', Enc', Dec') pseudorandom and jointly $\oplus$-homomorphic, then $\oplus$ is not a $(poly(\lambda), 1, negl(\lambda), negl(\lambda))$-secure weak 2-immunizer.*

We remark that the Alekhnovich PKE is not jointly $\oplus$-homomorphic with itself. We leave it as an open question as to whether such a pair of encryption schemes exist for XOR, but we suspect that its existence is likely.

Instead, we show that another simple 2-immunizer (namely a bilinear pairing) is not secure assuming a suitable computational assumption. In particular, we will rely on the SXDH assumption, defined in [4,7].

Conjecture 1. *The Symmetric External Diffie Hellman Assumption (SXDH) states that there exist groups G_X, G_Y, G_T with generators g_X, g_Y, g_T such that -there exists an efficiently computable bilinear map $e : G_X \times G_Y \to G_T$, -for uniformly random $a, b, c \xleftarrow{\$} \mathbb{Z}_{|G_X|}$ $\mathbf{CD}((g_X^a, g_X^b, g_X^{ab}), (g_X^a, g_X^b, g_X^c)) \leq negl(\lambda)$ (the Diffie Hellman assumption holds for G_X), -for uniformly random $a, b, c \xleftarrow{\$} \mathbb{Z}_{|G_Y|}$ $\mathbf{CD}((g_Y^a, g_Y^b, g_Y^{ab}), (g_Y^a, g_Y^b, g_Y^c)) \leq negl(\lambda)$ (the Diffie Hellman assumption holds for G_Y).*

Note that, as stated in Definition 11 we will require that $e(g_X, g_Y) = g_T$ and that G_X, G_Y, G_T are of prime order exponential in λ.

Note that instead of constructing jointly homomorphic public key encryption schemes under e, we will instead create public key encryption schemes jointly homomorphic under a related operation. We will then use the fact that this related operation is not a weak 2-immunizer to show that e is not a weak 2-immmunizer.

Let G_X, G_Y, G_T be cyclic groups of size exponential in λ with an efficiently computable bilinear map $e : G_X \times G_Y \to G_T$. Define the 2-immunizer $C^e :$ $(G_X \times G_X) \times (G_Y \times G_Y) \to G_T$ by

$$C^e((a_X, b_X), (a_Y, b_Y)) = (e(a_X, b_X), e(a_Y, b_Y)).$$

Lemma 2. *Assuming the SXDH assumption holds, C^e is not a $(poly(\lambda), 1, negl(\lambda), negl(\lambda))$-secure weak 2-immunizer.*

We defer the proof of this lemma and the proof of Theorem 7 using Lemma 2 to the full version [6].

4 Positive Result in Random Oracle Model

Although it seems that simple functions will not function well as a 2-immunizer, we show that a random oracle is a strong 2-immunizer. Heuristically, this means that a good hash function can be used in practice as a 2-immunizer. Furthermore, it gives some hope that 2-immunizers may exist in the standard model.

In fact, a random oracle is a strong 2-immunizer even if we allow the adversary to perform arbitrary preprocessing on the random oracle. This model, introduced in [41], is known as the Auxiliary Input Random Oracle Model (AI-ROM).

Theorem 10. *Let $RO : \{0,1\}^{2n} \to \{0,1\}^m$ be a random oracle. For t sufficiently large to allow for simple computations, $f(X, Y) = RO(X||Y)$ is a (t, q, δ, δ')-secure strong 2-immunizer with*

$$\delta' = \left(\delta + \frac{q^2}{2^n}\right) + 2(t + t^2)q\sqrt{\delta + \frac{q}{2^n}}.$$

Corollary 3. *$f(X, Y) = RO(X||Y)$ is a $(poly(\lambda), poly(\lambda), negl(\lambda), negl(\lambda))$-secure strong 2-immunizer in the ROM.*

Theorem 11 (Theorem 3 restated). *$f(X, Y) = RO(X||Y)$ is a $(poly(\lambda), poly(\lambda), negl(\lambda), negl(\lambda))$-secure strong 2-immunizer in the AI-ROM.*

The intuition behind Theorem 10 is as follows. Even given the secret and public keys for a PRG, public security guarantees that the output of each PRG is unpredicable. Let $x_1, \ldots, x_q$ and $y_1, \ldots, y_q$ be two outputs of a PRG, and let us consider the perspective of the compromised PRG generating x. Since this algorithm does not know the seed generating y, each y_i is unpredictable to it.

Thus, it has no way of seeing any of the outputs of the functions $RO(\cdot\|y_i)$. But as long as neither call to the PRG queries the random oracle on $x_i\|y_i$, there will be no detectable relationship between the x_i's and $RO(x_i\|y_i)$, and so the immunizer output will seem truly random.

The extension to the AI-ROM in Theorem 11 comes from standard presampling techniques [23,41], with a full proof included in the full version [6].

4.1 Random Oracle Model Definitions

In the random oracle model (ROM), we treat some function RO as a function chosen uniformly at random. This provides a good heuristic for security when the random oracle is instantiated with some suitable hash function. To argue that some cryptographic primitive is secure in the random oracle model, the randomness of the random oracle must be baked into the underlying game.

Definition 15. *We will denote the random oracle by $\mathcal{O} : A \to B$. Two distributions X and Y are (q, t, ϵ)-indistinguishable in the random oracle model if for any oracle algorithm $D^{\mathcal{O}}$ running in time t making at most q random oracle calls,*

$$\left| \Pr_{\mathcal{O} \xleftarrow{\$} \{f : A \to B\}} [D^{\mathcal{O}}(X) = 1] - \Pr_{\mathcal{O} \xleftarrow{\$} \{f : A \to B\}} [D^{\mathcal{O}}(Y) = 1] \right| \le \epsilon$$

For simplicity, we will typically set $q = t$. We will define PRG security in the random oracle model to be identical to typical PRG security, but with the computational indistinguishability to be also set in the random oracle model.

Definition 16. *Two distributions X and Y are (s, t, ϵ)-indistinguishable in the AI-ROM if for any oracle function $z^{\mathcal{O}}$ into strings of length s and for any oracle algorithm $D^{\mathcal{O}}$ running in time t,*

$$\left| \Pr_{\mathcal{O} \xleftarrow{\$} \{f : A \to B\}} [D^{\mathcal{O}}(z^{\mathcal{O}}, X) = 1] - \Pr_{\mathcal{O} \xleftarrow{\$} \{f : A \to B\}} [D^{\mathcal{O}}(z^{\mathcal{O}}, Y) = 1] \right| \le \epsilon$$

We similarly define PRG security in the AI-ROM.

Definition 17. *A two-input function C is a $\underline{(t, q, \delta, \delta')\text{-secure strong 2-immu-}}$* $\underline{\textit{nizer in the ROM (respectively AI-ROM), if for any PRG } (K, G) \textit{ which is } (t, q, \delta)}$ $\underline{\textit{publicly secure in the ROM, the PRG } (K, C(G, G)) \textit{ is a } (t, q, \delta') \textit{ backdoor secure}}$ $\underline{\textit{PRG in the ROM (respectively AI-ROM)}}.$

The definition of a (t, q, δ, δ')-secure weak 2-immunizer in the ROM/AI-ROM will be analogous.

Note that in particular our definition for 2-immunizer security in the AI-ROM only requires that the underlying PRG be secure in the ROM. This is a stronger definition, and we do this to model the situation where the auxiliary input represents a backdoor for the underlying PRGs.

4.2   Random Oracle is a 2-Immunizer

To show that a random oracle is a strong 2-immunizer, we adapt the proof structure from [22]. That is, we prove a key information theoretic property about publicly secure PRGs, and then use this property to bound the probability that some adversary queries the random oracle on key values.

In particular, let G^X, G^Y be two PRGs with outputs $x_1, \ldots, x_q$ and $y_1, \ldots, y_q$, and let RO be a random oracle. We will argue that the only part of the PRG game for $RO(G^X, G^Y)$ which queries $RO(x_i, y_i)$ is when the 2-immunizer is directly called by the game. This is because all parts of the game will only have access to at most one of x_i or y_i, and so therefore as the other is information theoretically unpredictable, they will be unable to query x_i and y_i to the oracle at the same time.

Afterwards, we will show that RO is still a strong 2-immunizer even in the presence of auxiliary input. We will show this by using the presampling lemma (Theorem ??). The trick we will use is that since our key property is information theoretic, we can set p for the presampling lemma to be exponential in λ, and so the security loss we suffer will be negligible.

We begin by stating the following information theoretic lemma. The proof is in the full version of this paper [6].

Lemma 3. *(KEY LEMMA) Let* $K : \{0,1\}^\ell \to \mathcal{PK} \times \mathcal{SK}$, $G : \mathcal{PK} \times \mathcal{S} \to \{0,1\}^n \times \mathcal{S}$ *be a* (t, q, δ) *publicly secure PRG. Let* $r \in \{0,1\}^\ell$ *be some initial randomness. For* $p \in (0,1)$, *we say that* r *is* p-*weak if for* $(pk, sk) \leftarrow K(r)$,

$$\max_{\widetilde{x} \in \{0,1\}^n} \Pr_{x_1, \ldots, x_q \xleftarrow{\$} out^q(G_{pk}, \mathcal{U}_S)} [x_i = \widetilde{x} \text{ for some } i \in [q]] \geq p.$$

Denote

$$p' := \Pr_{r \in \{0,1\}^\ell} [r \text{ is } p\text{-weak}]$$

Then,

$$p' \cdot p^2 \leq q^2 \left(\delta + \frac{q}{2^n} \right).$$

Intuitively, we call a public key pk (described using its initial randomness r) weak if the output of G_{pk} is predictable. The above lemma gives an upper bound on the probability of a public key being weak. That is, we show (through an averaging argument) that every publicly secure PRG has unpredictable output for most choices of its public parameters.

We now proceed to the proof of Theorem 10.

Proof. Let $K : \{0,1\}^\ell \to \mathcal{PK} \times \mathcal{SK}$, $G : \mathcal{PK} \times \mathcal{S} \to \{0,1\}^n \times \mathcal{S}$ be a (t, q, δ)-secure PRG. Let D be a distinguisher against $f(G, G)$ running in time t. Let $HONEST$ be the distribution

$$(sk, pk) \xleftarrow{\$} K, s_X, s_Y \xleftarrow{\$} \mathcal{S}$$

$$(pk, sk, \mathbf{out}^q(C(G_{pk}, G_{pk}), (s^X, s^Y)))$$

and let $RANDOM$ be the distribution

$$(sk, pk) \xleftarrow{\$} K, (r_1, \ldots, r_q) \xleftarrow{\$} \mathcal{U}_{qm}$$

$$(pk, sk, r_1, \ldots, r_q)$$

We want to bound

$$\delta' = |\Pr[D(HONEST) = 1] - \Pr[D(RANDOM) = 1]|$$

Let q_K, q_G, q_D be bounds on the number of times K, G, D query the random oracle respectively. Note that these are all bounded by t.

Let us consider the case where the distinguisher is given the output of the honest 2-immunizer. We will denote $\mathbf{out}^q(G, s^X) = x_1, \ldots, x_q$ and $\mathbf{out}^q(G, s^Y) = y_1, \ldots, y_q$. Let BAD be the event that there is some i such that (x_i, y_i) is queried to the random oracle more than once. Note that conditioned on $\overline{BAD}$, the two distributions in the distinguishing game are identical. Thus, $\delta' \leq \Pr[BAD]$.

We will break BAD up into five cases, and bound each case separately.

- We define BAD_1 to be the event where there exists i, j such that $x_i = x_j$ and $y_i = y_j$. This corresponds to (x_i, y_i) be queried to the random oracle more than once by the game itself.
- We define BAD_2 to be the event that K queries x_i, y_i for some i.
- We define BAD_3 to be the event that G queries x_i, y_i in the process of calculating $\mathbf{out}^q(G_{pk}, s^X)$.
- We define BAD_4 to be the event that G queries x_i, y_i in the process of calculating $\mathbf{out}^q(G_{pk}, s^Y)$.
- We define BAD_5 to be the event that D queries x_i, y_i.

Lemma 4. $\Pr[BAD_1] \leq \delta + \frac{q^2}{2^n}$

First, we will bound $\Pr[BAD_1]$. Let $\mathcal{A}$ be an attacker for the underlying PRG game on (K, G) which on input $r_1, \ldots, r_q$ outputs 1 if $r_i = r_j$ for some $i \neq j$. It is clear that $\Pr[\mathcal{A}(pk, \mathbf{out}^q(G_{pk}, \mathcal{U}_S)) \to 1] \geq \Pr[BAD_1]$, and $\Pr[\mathcal{A}(pk, \mathcal{U}_{qn}) \to 1] \leq \frac{q^2}{2^n}$. But by public security of the PRG, $\Pr[\mathcal{A}(pk, \mathbf{out}^q(G_{pk}, \mathcal{U}_S)) \to 1] - \Pr[\mathcal{A}(pk, \mathcal{U}_{qn}) \to 1] \leq \delta$ Thus, we have

$$\Pr[BAD_1] \leq \delta + \frac{q^2}{2^n}$$

Lemma 5. $\Pr[BAD_2] \leq qq_K \sqrt{\delta + \frac{q}{2^n}}$

We will bound $\Pr[BAD_2]$ using the key lemma. We claim that

$$\Pr_{r \xleftarrow{\$} \mathcal{U}_\ell} [r \text{ is } p\text{-weak}] \geq \sqrt{\Pr[BAD_2]}$$

for some suitable value of p. We will then use the key lemma to get an upper bound on $\Pr[BAD_2]$.

Let r be such that

$$\Pr[BAD_2|(pk, sk) \leftarrow K(r)] \geq \sqrt{\Pr[BAD_2]}$$

We claim then that r is p-weak for some p to be specified later. Let F_r be the set of random oracle queries made by $K(r)$. We can more precisely state

$$\Pr[BAD_2|(pk, sk) \leftarrow K(r)] = \Pr[(x_i, y_i) \in F_r \text{ for some index } i|(pk, sk) \leftarrow K(r)]$$

In particular, we can ignore one output and see that this means

$$\Pr_{x_1,\ldots,x_q \xleftarrow{\$} \mathbf{out}^q(G_{pk}, \mathcal{U}_S)} [x_i \in F_r \text{ for some index } i] \geq \sqrt{\Pr[BAD_2]}$$

But since $|F_r| \leq q_K$, this means there must be some element $\tilde{x} \in F_r$ such that

$$\Pr_{x_1,\ldots,x_q \xleftarrow{\$} \mathbf{out}^q(G_{pk}, \mathcal{U}_S)} [x_i = \tilde{x} \text{ for some index } i] \geq \frac{\sqrt{\Pr[BAD_2]}}{q_K}.$$

But this precisely means that r is p-weak, for $p = \frac{\sqrt{\Pr[BAD_2]}}{q_K}$. Thus,

$$\sqrt{\Pr[BAD_2]}\,\Pr[BAD_2] \leq q_K^2 q^2 \left(\delta + \frac{q}{2^n}\right)$$

and so as

$$\Pr[BAD_2]^2 \leq \sqrt{\Pr[BAD_2]}\,\Pr[BAD_2],$$

we have

$$\Pr[BAD_2] \leq q q_K \sqrt{\delta + \frac{q}{2^n}}.$$

Lemma 6. $\Pr[BAD_3] \leq q^2 q_G \sqrt{\delta + \frac{q}{2^n}}$

To bound $\Pr[BAD_3]$, we will again use the key lemma and show that

$$\Pr_{r \xleftarrow{\$} \mathcal{U}_\ell} [r \text{ is } p\text{-weak}] \geq \sqrt{\Pr[BAD_3]}$$

for some suitable value of p.

Let r be such that

$$\Pr[BAD_3|(pk, sk) \leftarrow K(r)] \geq \sqrt{\Pr[BAD_3]}.$$

We claim then that r is p-weak for some p to be specified later. Note that since this probability is the average over s of $\Pr[BAD_3|(pk, sk) \leftarrow K(r), s^X = s]$, there must be some $\tilde{s}$ such that

$$\Pr[BAD_3|(pk, sk) \leftarrow K(r), s^X = \tilde{s}] \geq \sqrt{\Pr[BAD_3]}.$$

Let $F_{r,\widetilde{s}}$ be the queries made by G when calculating $\mathbf{out}^q(G_{pk}, \widetilde{s})$. Using a similar argument as in the previous paragraph, we see that there must be some pair $(\widetilde{x}, \widetilde{y}) \in F_{r,\widetilde{s}}$ such that

$$\Pr_{y_1,\ldots,y_q \overset{\$}{\leftarrow} \mathbf{out}^q(G_{pk}, \mathcal{U}_S)} [y_i = \widetilde{y} \text{ for some index } i] \geq \frac{\sqrt{\Pr[BAD_3]}}{|F_{r,\widetilde{s}}|}.$$

But note that $|F_{r,\widetilde{s}}| \leq q \cdot q_G$ as it is generated by running G q times. Thus, r is p-weak for $p = \frac{\sqrt{\Pr[BAD_3]}}{q \cdot q_G}$. The same algebra as the previous lemma gives us

$$\Pr[BAD_3] \leq q^2 q_G \sqrt{\delta + \frac{q}{2^n}}$$

Lemma 7. $\Pr[BAD_4] \leq q^2 q_G \sqrt{\delta + \frac{q}{2^n}}$

The proof of this lemma is analogous to the proof for $\Pr[BAD_3]$.

Lemma 8. $\Pr[BAD_5] \leq q q_D \sqrt{\delta + \frac{q}{2^n}}$

To bound $\Pr[BAD_5]$, we first notice that at the point when D first queries x_i, y_i, the only information available to D is the secret key and the output of $i-1$ random oracle calls. As at this point D has never queried any of its inputs, the probability that D succeeds at querying any input is the same as if D were given only the secret key.

Let us fix any initial randomness $r \in \{0,1\}^\ell$ such that

$$\Pr[BAD_5|(pk, sk) \leftarrow K(r)] \geq \sqrt{\Pr[BAD_5]}.$$

We can clearly see that

$$\Pr[BAD_5|(pk, sk) \leftarrow K(r)]$$

$$\leq \max_{\substack{F \subseteq \{0,1\}^n \\ |F| \leq q_D}} \Pr[(x_i, y_i) \in F \text{ for some index } i|(pk, sk) \leftarrow K(r)]$$

But by union bound we then have

$$\Pr[BAD_5|(pk, sk) \leftarrow K(r)] \leq q_D \max_{\widetilde{x} \in \{0,1\}^n} \Pr[x_i = \widetilde{x} \text{ for some } i \in [q]].$$

The same reasoning as the previous arguments shows us that r is p-weak for $p = \frac{\sqrt{\Pr[BAD_5]}}{q_D}$. Applying the key lemma gives us

$$\Pr[BAD_5] \leq q q_D \sqrt{\delta + \frac{q}{2^n}}$$

Putting all the lemmas together, we have

$$\delta' \leq \Pr[BAD] \leq \left(\delta + \frac{q^2}{2^n}\right) + (qq_K + 2q^2q_G + qq_D)\sqrt{\delta + \frac{q}{2^n}}$$

Noting that $q_K, q_G, q_D \leq t$ gives us our theorem.

5 Black Box Separation (with Limitations)

Definition 18. *Let* $C : \{0,1\}^n \times \{0,1\}^n \rightarrow \{0,1\}^m$ *be a function. We call an input* $x \in \{0,1\}^n$ *"left-bad" if* $\max_{z \in \{0,1\}^m} \Pr_{y \in \{0,1\}^n}[C(x,y) = z] > \frac{1}{2}$. *We define what it means for an input to be "right-bad" analogously.*

We say that C *is* highly dependent on both inputs *if*

$$\Pr_{(x,y) \xleftarrow{\$} \{0,1\}^{2n}} [x \text{ is "left-bad" OR } y \text{ is "right-bad"}] \leq negl(\lambda).$$

Informally, a two-input function C is highly dependent on both inputs if it ignores one of its inputs at most a negligible proportion of the time. This is a rather broad category of functions. In particular, XOR, pairings, inner product, and random oracles are all highly dependent on both inputs. Furthermore, any collision resistant hash function must also be highly dependent on both inputs, otherwise it would be trivial to find a collision.

We show that it is hard to prove security (either weak or strong) for any 2-immunizer C which is highly dependent on both inputs. Note that one of the most common and useful techniques for proving security of cryptographic primitives is to create a black box reduction to some cryptographic assumption. Informally, a black box reduction transforms an attacker for some cryptographic primitive into an attacker for a cryptographic assumption. Thus, if the cryptographic assumption is immune to attack, the cryptographic primitive will be secure.

We show that if a 2-immunizer is highly dependent on both inputs, then there cannot be any black-box reduction of its security to any falsifiable cryptographic assumption.

Theorem 12 (Theorem 4 restated). *Let* C *be a weak 2-immunizer which is highly dependent on both inputs. If there is a black-box reduction showing that* C *is* $(poly(\lambda), \lambda, negl(\lambda), negl(\lambda))$*-secure from the security of some cryptographic game* $\mathcal{G}$*, then* $\mathcal{G}$ *is not secure.*

As a random oracle is highly dependent on both inputs, any reasonable hash function should also be highly dependent on both inputs. This implies that despite the fact that a random oracle is a strong 2-immunizer, it may be hard to argue security for any particular instantiation of the random oracle. We sketch the proof of this theorem in the next subsection. For the full argument, see the full version [6].

5.1   Proof Sketch for Theorem 12

THE SIMULATABLE ATTACKER PARADIGM. The simulatable attacker paradigm, first introduced by [14] and formalized by [44], is a method for transforming a black-box reduction into an attack against the underlying assumption. This paradigm was first used to prove black-box separations from all falsifiable assumptions in [26].

In particular, let C be a cryptographic protocol with a black-box reduction to a cryptographic assumption $\mathcal{G}$. Formally, we will describe the black-box reduction as an oracle algorithm $\mathcal{B}^{\cdot}$ which breaks the security of $\mathcal{G}$ whenever its oracle is a (possibly inefficient) adversary breaking the security of C.

A *simulatable attack* against C is an (inefficient) attack $\mathcal{A}$ which breaks the security game of C, but which can be simulated by an efficient algorithm **Sim**. In particular, oracle access to $\mathcal{A}$ and **Sim** should be indistinguishable to the black-box reduction $\mathcal{B}^{\cdot}$. If this occurs, then since $\mathcal{B}^{\mathbf{Sim}}$ is indistinguishable from $\mathcal{B}^{\mathcal{A}}$, $\mathcal{B}^{\mathbf{Sim}}$ is an efficient attack breaking the security game of $\mathcal{G}$.

Note that in order for this paradigm to make sense, it needs to be the case that the simulator has more capabilities than the inefficient adversary, otherwise the simulator itself would be an attack for C. In practice, this is done by either restricting the oracle queries made by the black-box separation $\mathcal{B}^{\cdot}$ or by restricting the power of the attacker $\mathcal{A}$.

BLACK-BOX SEPARATIONS FOR 2-STAGE GAMES. In 2013, Wichs showed a a general framework for proving that two-stage games cannot be reduced to any falsifiable assumption [44]. In a two-stage security game the adversary consists of two algorithms which each have individual state, but are not allowed to communicate. Thus, a simulatable attack consists of the inefficient attack as well as two simulators where the simulators *do* have shared state. This means that it is conceivable to have a simulator **Sim** for which oracle access is *indistinguishable* from $\mathcal{A}$.

Note that if we have a simulatable attack of this form, then this simulator will fool every (efficient) black-box reduction. Thus, if we can prove that for every construction there exists an simulatable attack, this gives a black-box separation of the security definition from any falsifiable assumption.

OUR SIMULATABLE ATTACK. Note that an adversary against a 2-immunizer consists of both a set of PRGs and a distinguisher. Here, the PRGs and the distinguisher are not allowed to share state, and so we can hope to construct a simulatable attack in the style of [44].

Given C any candidate 2-immunizer, let G^X, G^Y be random functions and let $D(y)$ be the algorithm which outputs 1 if there exists an (s^X, s^Y) such that $y = \mathbf{out}^q(C(G^X, G^Y), (s^X, s^Y))$. It is clear that G^X, G^Y, D is an inefficient attack breaking the security of C.

To simulate this, we simply replace G^X, G^Y with a lazy sampling oracle. That is, the first time G^X sees s, it will respond with a random value, and it will use the same response for future queries of s. To simulate D, the simulator will check if there exists *an already queried* (s^X, s^Y) such that

$y = \mathbf{out}^q(C(G^X, G^Y), (s^X, s^Y))$. Since the adversary is polynomially bounded, there will only be a polynomial number of already queried points, and so this simulator is efficient.

It turns out that the only way to distinguish this simulator from the inefficient adversary is to find some y such that $y = \mathbf{out}^q(C(G^X, G^Y), (s^X, s^Y))$ for either s^X or s^Y unqueried. If neither s^X or s^Y has been queried before, then by a counting argument it is impossible to guess such a y. But if s^X has been queried before, if C ignores s^Y then it is possible to guess $\mathbf{out}^q(C(G^X, G^Y), (s^X, s^Y))$ without querying s^Y. To avoid this problem, we simply assume that the output of C is dependent on both of its inputs, as in Definition 18.

References

1. Recommendation for random number generation using deterministic random bit generators. National Institute of Standards and Technology: Special Publication (2012). https://csrc.nist.gov/publications/PubsSPs.html#800-90A
2. Alekhnovich, M.: More on average case vs approximation complexity. In: 44th FOCS, pp. 298–307. IEEE Computer Society Press (2003)
3. Alekhnovich, M.: More on average case vs approximation complexity. Comput. Complex. **20**(4), 755–786 (2011)
4. Ateniese, G., Camenisch, J., Hohenberger, S., de Medeiros, B.: Practical group signatures without random oracles. Cryptology ePrint Archive, Report 2005/385 (2005). https://eprint.iacr.org/2005/385
5. Ateniese, G., Francati, D., Magri, B., Venturi, D.: Immunization against complete subversion without random oracles. Theor. Comput. Sci. **859**, 1–36 (2021)
6. Ball, M., Dodis, Y., Goldin, E.: Immunizing backdoored prgs. eprint (2023). https://eprint.iacr.org
7. Ballard, L., Green, M., de Medeiros, B., Monrose, F.: Correlation-resistant storage via keyword-searchable encryption. Cryptology ePrint Archive, Report 2005/417 (2005). https://eprint.iacr.org/2005/417
8. Bauer, B., Farshim, P., Mazaheri, S.: Combiners for backdoored random oracles. In: Shacham, H., Boldyreva, A. (eds.) CRYPTO 2018. LNCS, vol. 10992, pp. 272–302. Springer, Cham (2018). https://doi.org/10.1007/978-3-319-96881-0_10
9. Bellare, M., Hoang, V.T., Keelveedhi, S.: Instantiating random oracles via UCEs. In: Canetti, R., Garay, J.A. (eds.) CRYPTO 2013. LNCS, vol. 8043, pp. 398–415. Springer, Heidelberg (2013). https://doi.org/10.1007/978-3-642-40084-1_23
10. Bellare, M., Paterson, K.G., Rogaway, P.: Security of symmetric encryption against mass surveillance. In: Garay, J.A., Gennaro, R. (eds.) CRYPTO 2014. LNCS, vol. 8616, pp. 1–19. Springer, Heidelberg (2014). https://doi.org/10.1007/978-3-662-44371-2_1
11. Bellare, M., Yee, B.: Forward-security in private-key cryptography. In: Joye, M. (ed.) CT-RSA 2003. LNCS, vol. 2612, pp. 1–18. Springer, Heidelberg (2003). https://doi.org/10.1007/3-540-36563-X_1
12. Bhattacharyya, R., Nandi, M., Raychaudhuri, A.: Crooked indifferentiability of enveloped XOR revisited. In: Adhikari, A., Küsters, R., Preneel, B. (eds.) INDOCRYPT 2021. LNCS, vol. 13143, pp. 73–92. Springer, Cham (2021). https://doi.org/10.1007/978-3-030-92518-5_4
13. Blum, L., Blum, M., Shub, M.: A simple unpredictable pseudo-random number generator. SIAM J. Comput. **15**(2), 364–383 (1986)

14. Boneh, D., Venkatesan, R.: Breaking RSA may not be equivalent to factoring. In: Nyberg, K. (ed.) EUROCRYPT 1998. LNCS, vol. 1403, pp. 59–71. Springer, Heidelberg (1998). https://doi.org/10.1007/BFb0054117
15. Chattopadhyay, A., Pitassi, T.: The story of set disjointness. SIGACT News **41**(3), 59–85 (2010)
16. Checkoway, S., et al.: A systematic analysis of the juniper dual ec incident. In: Proceedings of the 2016 ACM SIGSAC Conference on Computer and Communications Security, CCS 2016, pp. 468–479. Association for Computing Machinery, New York (2016)
17. Checkoway, S., et al.: On the practical exploitability of dual EC in TLS implementations. In: Fu, K., Jung, J. (eds.) USENIX Security 2014, pp. 319–335. USENIX Association (2014)
18. Chor, B., Goldreich, O.: Unbiased bits from sources of weak randomness and probabilistic communication complexity (extended abstract). In: 26th FOCS, pp. 429–442. IEEE Computer Society Press (1985)
19. Coretti, S., Dodis, Y., Guo, S., Steinberger, J.: Random oracles and non-uniformity. In: Nielsen, J.B., Rijmen, V. (eds.) EUROCRYPT 2018. LNCS, vol. 10820, pp. 227–258. Springer, Cham (2018). https://doi.org/10.1007/978-3-319-78381-9_9
20. Coretti, S., Dodis, Y., Karthikeyan, H., Tessaro, S.: Seedless fruit is the sweetest: random number generation, revisited. In: Boldyreva, A., Micciancio, D. (eds.) CRYPTO 2019. LNCS, vol. 11692, pp. 205–234. Springer, Cham (2019). https://doi.org/10.1007/978-3-030-26948-7_8
21. Dodis, Y., Farshim, P., Mazaheri, S., Tessaro, S.: Towards defeating backdoored random oracles: indifferentiability with bounded adaptivity. In: Pass, R., Pietrzak, K. (eds.) TCC 2020. LNCS, vol. 12552, pp. 241–273. Springer, Cham (2020). https://doi.org/10.1007/978-3-030-64381-2_9
22. Dodis, Y., Ganesh, C., Golovnev, A., Juels, A., Ristenpart, T.: A formal treatment of backdoored pseudorandom generators. In: Oswald, E., Fischlin, M. (eds.) EUROCRYPT 2015. LNCS, vol. 9056, pp. 101–126. Springer, Heidelberg (2015). https://doi.org/10.1007/978-3-662-46800-5_5
23. Dodis, Y., Guo, S., Katz, J.: Fixing cracks in the concrete: random oracles with auxiliary input, revisited. In: Coron, J.-S., Nielsen, J.B. (eds.) EUROCRYPT 2017. LNCS, vol. 10211, pp. 473–495. Springer, Cham (2017). https://doi.org/10.1007/978-3-319-56614-6_16
24. Dodis, Y., Mironov, I., Stephens-Davidowitz, N.: Message transmission with reverse firewalls—secure communication on corrupted machines. In: Robshaw, M., Katz, J. (eds.) CRYPTO 2016. LNCS, vol. 9814, pp. 341–372. Springer, Heidelberg (2016). https://doi.org/10.1007/978-3-662-53018-4_13
25. Dodis, Y., Vaikuntanathan, V., Wichs, D.: Extracting randomness from extractor-dependent sources. In: Canteaut, A., Ishai, Y. (eds.) EUROCRYPT 2020. LNCS, vol. 12105, pp. 313–342. Springer, Cham (2020). https://doi.org/10.1007/978-3-030-45721-1_12
26. Gentry, C., Wichs, D.: Separating succinct non-interactive arguments from all falsifiable assumptions. In: Fortnow, L., Vadhan, S.P. (eds.) 43rd ACM STOC, pp. 99–108. ACM Press (2011)
27. Hopper, N.J., Langford, J., von Ahn, L.: Provably secure steganography. In: Yung, M. (ed.) CRYPTO 2002. LNCS, vol. 2442, pp. 77–92. Springer, Heidelberg (2002). https://doi.org/10.1007/3-540-45708-9_6
28. Horel, T., Park, S., Richelson, S., Vaikuntanathan, V.: How to subvert backdoored encryption: Security against adversaries that decrypt all ciphertexts. In: Blum, A. (ed.) ITCS 2019, vol. 124, pp. 42:1–42:20. LIPIcs (2019)

29. Juels, A., Guajardo, J.: RSA key generation with verifiable randomness. In: Naccache, D., Paillier, P. (eds.) PKC 2002. LNCS, vol. 2274, pp. 357–374. Springer, Heidelberg (2002). https://doi.org/10.1007/3-540-45664-3_26

30. Mironov, I., Stephens-Davidowitz, N.: Cryptographic Reverse Firewalls. In: Oswald, E., Fischlin, M. (eds.) EUROCRYPT 2015. LNCS, vol. 9057, pp. 657–686. Springer, Heidelberg (2015). https://doi.org/10.1007/978-3-662-46803-6_22

31. Nisan, N., Zuckerman, D.: Randomness is linear in space. J. Comput. Syst. Sci. **52**(1), 43–52 (1996)

32. Persiano, G., Phan, D.H., Yung, M.: Anamorphic encryption: private communication against a dictator. In: Dunkelman, O., Dziembowski, S. (eds.) EUROCRYPT 2022. LNCS, vol. 13276, pp. 34–63. Springer, Heidelberg (2022). https://doi.org/10.1007/978-3-031-07085-3_2

33. Quach, W., Waters, B., Wichs, D.: Targeted lossy functions and applications. In: Malkin, T., Peikert, C. (eds.) CRYPTO 2021. LNCS, vol. 12828, pp. 424–453. Springer, Cham (2021). https://doi.org/10.1007/978-3-030-84259-8_15

34. Russell, A., Tang, Q., Yung, M., Zhou, H.S.: Cliptography: clipping the power of kleptographic attacks. Cryptology ePrint Archive, Report 2015/695 (2015). https://eprint.iacr.org/2015/695

35. Russell, A., Tang, Q., Yung, M., Zhou, H.-S.: Cliptography: clipping the power of kleptographic attacks. In: Cheon, J.H., Takagi, T. (eds.) ASIACRYPT 2016. LNCS, vol. 10032, pp. 34–64. Springer, Heidelberg (2016). https://doi.org/10.1007/978-3-662-53890-6_2

36. Russell, A., Tang, Q., Yung, M., Zhou, H.S.: Generic semantic security against a kleptographic adversary. Cryptology ePrint Archive, Paper 2016/530 (2016). https://eprint.iacr.org/2016/530

37. Russell, A., Tang, Q., Yung, M., Zhou, H.S.: Generic semantic security against a kleptographic adversary. In: Thuraisingham, B.M., Evans, D., Malkin, T., Xu, D. (eds.) ACM CCS 2017, pp. 907–922. ACM Press (2017)

38. Russell, A., Tang, Q., Yung, M., Zhou, H.-S.: Correcting subverted random oracles. In: Shacham, H., Boldyreva, A. (eds.) CRYPTO 2018. LNCS, vol. 10992, pp. 241–271. Springer, Cham (2018). https://doi.org/10.1007/978-3-319-96881-0_9

39. Shumow, D., Ferguson, N.: On the possibility of a back door in the nist sp800-90 dual ec prng. In: Proceedings of Crypto 2007 (2007). https://rump2007.cr.yp.to/15-shumow.pdf

40. Simmons, G.J.: The prisoners' problem and the subliminal channel. In: Chaum, D. (ed.) CRYPTO 1983, Plenum Press, New York, USA, pp. 51–67 (1983)

41. Unruh, D.: Random oracles and auxiliary input. In: Menezes, A. (ed.) CRYPTO 2007. LNCS, vol. 4622, pp. 205–223. Springer, Heidelberg (2007). https://doi.org/10.1007/978-3-540-74143-5_12

42. Vazirani, U.V., Vazirani, V.V.: Trapdoor pseudo-random number generators, with applications to protocol design. In: 24th FOCS, pp. 23–30. IEEE Computer Society Press (1983)

43. Vazirani, U.V., Vazirani, V.V.: Efficient and secure pseudo-random number generation (extended abstract). In: Blakley, G.R., Chaum, D. (eds.) CRYPTO 1984. LNCS, vol. 196, pp. 193–202. Springer, Heidelberg (1985). https://doi.org/10.1007/3-540-39568-7_17

44. Wichs, D.: Barriers in cryptography with weak, correlated and leaky sources. In: Kleinberg, R.D. (ed.) ITCS 2013, pp. 111–126. ACM (2013)

45. Young, A., Yung, M.: The dark side of "Black-Box" cryptography or: should we trust capstone? In: Koblitz, N. (ed.) CRYPTO 1996. LNCS, vol. 1109, pp. 89–103. Springer, Heidelberg (1996). https://doi.org/10.1007/3-540-68697-5_8

46. Young, A., Yung, M.: Kleptography: using cryptography against cryptography. In: Fumy, W. (ed.) EUROCRYPT 1997. LNCS, vol. 1233, pp. 62–74. Springer, Heidelberg (1997). https://doi.org/10.1007/3-540-69053-0_6
47. Young, A., Yung, M.: Kleptography from standard assumptions and applications. In: Garay, J.A., De Prisco, R. (eds.) SCN 2010. LNCS, vol. 6280, pp. 271–290. Springer, Heidelberg (2010). https://doi.org/10.1007/978-3-642-15317-4_18

Lower Bounds

Communication Lower Bounds
of Key-Agreement Protocols via Density
Increment Arguments

Mi-Ying Huang$^{(\boxtimes)}$, Xinyu Mao, Guangxu Yang, and Jiapeng Zhang

Thomas Lord Department of Computer Science, University of Southern California,
Los Angeles, CA 90007, USA
{miying.huang,xinyumao,guangxuy,jiapengz}@usc.edu

Abstract. Constructing key-agreement protocols in the random oracle model (ROM) is a viable method to assess the feasibility of developing public-key cryptography within Minicrypt. Unfortunately, as shown by Impagliazzo and Rudich (STOC 1989) and Barak and Mahmoody (Crypto 2009), such protocols can only guarantee limited security: any ℓ-query protocol can be attacked by an $O(\ell^2)$-query adversary. This quadratic gap matches the key-agreement protocol proposed by Merkle (CACM 78), known as Merkle's Puzzles.

Besides query complexity, the communication complexity of key-agreement protocols in the ROM is also an interesting question in the realm of find-grained cryptography, even though only limited security is achievable. Haitner et al. (ITCS 2019) first observed that in Merkle's Puzzles, to obtain secrecy against an eavesdropper with $O(\ell^2)$ queries, the honest parties must exchange $\Omega(\ell)$ bits. Therefore, they conjectured that high communication complexity is unavoidable, any ℓ-query protocols with c bits of communication could be attacked by an $O(c \cdot \ell)$-query adversary. This, if true, will suggest that Merkle's Puzzle is also optimal regarding communication complexity. Building upon techniques from communication complexity, Haitner et al. (ITCS 2019) confirmed this conjecture for two types of key agreement protocols with certain natural properties.

This work affirms the above conjecture for all non-adaptive protocols with perfect completeness. Our proof uses a novel idea called *density increment argument*. This method could be of independent interest as it differs from previous communication lower bounds techniques (and bypasses some technical barriers).

Keywords: Key-Agreement · Communication Complexity · Random Oracle

1 Introduction

Key-agreement protocols [DH76] allow two parties, Alice and Bob, to agree on a shared private key by communicating over an insecure public channel. Its

Supported by NSF CAREER award 2141536.

G. Rothblum and H. Wee (Eds.): TCC 2023, LNCS 14371, pp. 185–206, 2023.
https://doi.org/10.1007/978-3-031-48621-0_7

security requires that any (efficient) eavesdropper cannot learn the key from the transcript. In an early work, Merkle [Mer78] first proposed an ingenious key-agreement protocol, known as *Merkle's Puzzles*, as follows.

Protocol 1 (Merkle's Puzzles). *Let $f : [N] \rightarrow [M]$ be a cryptographic hash function and let ℓ be a parameter measuring the query complexity of this protocol. Alice and Bob first agree on a set $W \subseteq [N]$ of size ℓ^2. Then, at the beginning of the protocol, Alice makes ℓ random queries in W, i.e., $f(w_1), \ldots, f(w_\ell)$. Similarly, Bob makes another ℓ random queries $f(w'_1), \ldots, f(w'_\ell)$. By the birthday paradox, there is a good chance that $\{w_1, \ldots, w_\ell\} \cap \{w'_1, \ldots, w'_\ell\} \neq \emptyset$. Alice then sends $z_1 = f(w_1), \ldots, z_\ell = f(w_\ell)$ to Bob, and Bob checks if there is a w'_j in his query such that $f(w'_j) = z_i$ for some $i \in [\ell]$. If such a pair (w'_j, z_i) exists, then Bob sends z_i back to Alice and sets w'_j as his key; otherwise, Bob aborts. Finally, according to z_i, Alice chooses w_i as her key.*

As long as the function f is collision-free on W, Alice and Bob will agree on the same key with high probability. In terms of security, if f is modeled as a random function, we can show that any eavesdropper that breaks this protocol with constant probability has to query a constant fraction of inputs in W; consequently, the query complexity of any eavesdropper must be $\Omega(\ell^2)$.

On the other hand, Impagliazzo and Rudich [IR89], followed by Barak and Mahmoody [BMG09], showed that key-agreement protocol is essentially a public-key primitive and is unlikely to be based only on hardness assumptions for symmetric cryptography—any key-agreement protocol only guarantees limited security as long as the symmetric hardness is used in a black-box way. Specifically, they studied key-agreement protocols in the *random oracle model* (ROM). In the ROM, all parties, including the eavesdropper, have oracle access to a random function $f : [N] \rightarrow [M]$, which is an idealization of symmetric primitives like collision-resistant hash function. The efficiency of parties is measured by the number of queries they make to the oracle (in the worst case). [IR89] proved that any key-agreement protocols in the ROM with ℓ queries can be attacked by an eavesdropper with $O(\ell^6)$ queries. [BMG09] further improved the efficiency of the eavesdropper to $O(\ell^2)$ queries. This result indicates that Merkle's puzzle is optimal in terms of the number of oracle queries since it reaches quadratic security. Despite its limited security, the complexity of key-agreement protocols in the ROM is still an interesting question of fine-grained cryptography. A long line of research has been conducted on the limitation and possibility of key-agreement protocols in the ROM, in both classical setting [DH76, Mer78, IR89, BMG09, HMO+19, ACMS23], distributed setting [DH21] and quantum setting [ACC+22].

Besides oracle queries, another important cost in key-agreement protocols is the communication cost between Alice and Bob. The communication complexity of (multi-party) protocols, such as key-agreement, optimally-fair coin tossing, statistically hiding commitment schemes, and multi-party computation, has garnered considerable attention recently [DSLMM11, HHRS15, HMO+19, Cou19, AHMS20, CN22].

In this paper, we focus on the communication complexity of key-agreement protocols: a problem initiated by Haitner et al. [HMO+19]. Concretely, they observed that the communication complexity of Merkle's Puzzle is also $\widetilde{\Omega}(\ell)^1$, and they conjectured that high communication cost is unavoidable.

Conjecture 1 ([HMO+19]*, informal).* Let $\Pi = (\mathsf{A}, \mathsf{B})$ be a key-agreement protocol such that:

1. A and B agree on the same key with high probability;
2. A and B each make at most ℓ queries to the random function (oracle);
3. Π is secure against any adversary with q queries to the random oracle.

Then A and B must communicate $\Omega(q/\ell)$ bits.

As we discussed, Merkle's puzzle matches the lower bound in this conjecture for $q = \Theta(\ell^2)$. For $q = o(\ell^2)$, an asymmetric version of Merkle's puzzle also matches this lower bound.

Protocol 2 (Asymmetric version of Merkle's Puzzles). *Alice and Bob first fix a domain W of size q. Then Alice makes $c := q/\ell$ random queries in W and sends them to Bob. Bob also makes ℓ random queries (in W) and checks if there is a common query in accordance with the original Merkle's Puzzles.*

[HMO+19] partly tackled this conjecture for two types of key-agreement protocols. We say a protocol is *non-adaptive* if both parties choose all their queries at the beginning of the protocol (before querying the oracle and communicating); that is, their queries are determined by their internal randomness. Haitner el al. [HMO+19] proved that for any protocol $\Pi = (\mathsf{A}, \mathsf{B})$ that satisfies the conditions in Conjecture 1:

- If Π is non-adaptive and has only two rounds, A and B must exchange $\Omega(q/\ell)$ bits.
- If the queries are uniformly sampled, then A and B must communicate $\Omega(q^2/\ell^3)$ bits.

Note that protocols with uniform queries are also special non-adaptive protocols.

In this paper, we affirm Conjecture 1 for non-adaptive protocols with *perfect completeness*, i.e., Alice and Bob agree on the same key with probability 1. Specifically, we prove the following theorem.

Theorem 3 (Informal). *Let $\Pi = (\mathsf{A}, \mathsf{B})$ be a non-adaptive key-agreement protocol such that:*

1. *A and B agree on the same key with probability 1;*
2. *A and B each make at most ℓ queries to the random oracle;*
3. *Π is secure against any adversary with q queries to the random oracle.*

Then A and B must communicate $\Omega(q/\ell)$ bits.

---

[1] We drop low order terms such as $\log N$ and $\log M$ here.

Our proof is built on the density increment argument introduced by Yang and Zhang [YZ22, YZ23], which they used to prove communication lower bounds for the *unique disjointness problem*. Looking at our main theorem carefully, we acknowledge two non-trivial requirements in our statement: non-adaptivity and perfect completeness. However, these limitations are not inherent in this method. Therefore, we are optimistic that our method has a good chance to overcome these two limitations; more details will be discussed in Sect. 1.2.

It is worth noting that Mazor [Maz23] recently devised a non-adaptive protocol with perfect completeness and quadratic security guarantee. We observed that this protocol, with minor adjustments, allows a trade-off between communication and security in a similar fashion to Protocol 2. Our result shows that Mazor's construction is optimal among non-adaptive protocols with perfect completeness.

1.1   Proof Overview

Now we give a high-level overview of our proof. Since the execution of key-agreement protocols and the attacking process involve many random variables, we first explain our notations.

- We use bold and uppercase letters for random variables and corresponding regular letters for samples and values, such as $f, r_A, r_B, Q_A, Q_B, \tau, Q_E$ and f_E (uppercase for sets and lowercase for elements and functions).
- Let $\boldsymbol{F}$ be the RO that the parties have access to, which is a random function from $[N]$ to $[M]$. Moreover, let $\boldsymbol{R}_A, \boldsymbol{R}_B$ be Alice's and Bob's internal randomness. $(\boldsymbol{R}_A, \boldsymbol{R}_B, \boldsymbol{F})$ determines the entire execution of key-agreement protocols.
- Let $\boldsymbol{Q}_A, \boldsymbol{Q}_B \subseteq [N]$ be the queries made by Alice and Bob in the execution, respectively. Notice that $\boldsymbol{Q}_A, \boldsymbol{Q}_B$ is fully determined by $\boldsymbol{R}_A, \boldsymbol{R}_B$ for non-adaptive protocols. $\boldsymbol{Q}_A$ and $\boldsymbol{Q}_B$ are usually ordered sets since Alice and Bob make oracle queries one at a time. For the sake of notation convenience, we sometimes regard $\boldsymbol{Q}_A$ and $\boldsymbol{Q}_B$ as unordered sets.
- Let $\boldsymbol{T}$ be the communication transcript between Alice and Bob. Notice that $\boldsymbol{T}$ is observed by the attacker Eve.
- Let $\boldsymbol{Q}_E \subseteq [N]$ be Eve's queries. Let $\boldsymbol{F}_E = \boldsymbol{F}(\boldsymbol{Q}_E)$ be Eve's observations of the random oracle $\boldsymbol{F}$. We interpret $\boldsymbol{F}_E$ as a partial function: for every $x \in \boldsymbol{Q}_E$, $\boldsymbol{F}_E(x) = \boldsymbol{F}(x)$; for all other x, $\boldsymbol{F}_E(x) = \perp$.

To study the security of key-agreement protocols, Impagliazzo and Rudich [IR89] observed that the advantage of Alice and Bob over Eve mainly comes from their intersection queries which have not been queried by Eve, i.e., the knowledge from $(\boldsymbol{Q}_A \cap \boldsymbol{Q}_B) \backslash \boldsymbol{Q}_E$ and $\boldsymbol{F}((\boldsymbol{Q}_A \cap \boldsymbol{Q}_B) \backslash \boldsymbol{Q}_E)$. Based on this insight, they devised an attacker that aims to guess (and query) the set $(\boldsymbol{Q}_A \cap \boldsymbol{Q}_B)$. In order to learn intersection queries more efficiently, [BMG09] introduced the notion of *heavy query*. Given Eve's current observation, which consists of a transcript τ and a partial function f_E, an input $w \in [N] \setminus Q_E$ is said to be ε-*heavy* with respect to (τ, f_E) if

$$\mathbf{Pr}[w \in (Q_A \cap Q_B) \mid \tau, f_E] \geq \varepsilon.$$

Now we give an informal description of Eve's strategy[2]:

- **Stage I.** Eve checks if there exists a heavy query conditioned on transcript τ and her observations of the random oracle f_E. If yes, then query them, update f_E, and repeat until there are no heavy queries.
- **Stage II.** Eve simulates Alice and Bob based on observed information and outputs Alice's key in her simulation. In other words, Eve simply outputs a sample from the distribution of Alice's key conditioned on observed information.

Suppose that Alice and Bob each make at most ℓ queries and set $\varepsilon = \Theta(1/\ell)$. A standard technique can prove that Stage I stops within $O(\ell/\varepsilon) = O(\ell^2)$ queries. We can also show that in order to clean up all heavy queries (Stage I), $\Omega(\ell^2)$ queries are inevitable. This querying process does not explore strong connections to communication complexity.

Our Approach. Our main observation is that if Alice and Bob communicate too little, they cannot utilize their common queries and thus have no advantage over Eve! Hence, we focus on queries correlated with the transcript τ instead of all intersection queries. With this in mind, we introduce *correlated query* as a refined notion of heavy query.

Definition 1 (ε-correlated set, informal; see Definition 3). *Eve's view consists of a transcript τ and a partial function f_E. We say a set $S = \{w_1, \ldots, w_r\} \subseteq [N]$ is ε-**correlated** with respect to (τ, f_E) if*

$$\mathbf{H}\left(F(w_1), \ldots, F(w_r) \mid R_A, R_B, f_E\right) - \mathbf{H}\left(F(w_1), \ldots, F(w_r) \mid R_A, R_B, f_E, \tau\right) \geq \varepsilon,$$

where $\mathbf{H}(\cdot)$ denotes the Shannon entropy.

We use $F(S)$ to denote $(F(w_1), \ldots, F(w_r))$ in the future, and $F(S)$ can also be viewed as a partial function with domain S. A main difference between our attacker and [BMG09] is that: instead of making ε-heavy queries, we clean up all ε-correlated sets of size at most 2ℓ. Another difference is that we choose $\varepsilon = \Theta(1)$ and [BMG09] set $\varepsilon = \Theta(1/\ell)$. Intuitively, this is because a correlated set of size ℓ is as effective as ℓ single heavy queries. Along these lines, we then have to prove two things:

- **Success.** Eve can guess the key of Alice/Bob if there is no ε-correlated set of size at most 2ℓ.
- **Efficiency.** Eve can remove all ε-correlated sets (of size at most 2ℓ) after querying $O(c)$ correlated sets, where c is the number of communication bits between Alice and Bob. Thus, the query complexity of Eve is $O(c \cdot \ell)$.

---

[2] This is not exactly the same as [BMG09] due to some technical challenges in [BMG09].

Eve Can Guess the Key if There are No Small ε-Correlated Sets. Assume that the protocol Π is non-adaptive, i.e., Q_A (or Q_B) is determined by r_A (resp., r_B). To study the success probability of Eve, we consider a rectangle $\mathcal{X} \times \mathcal{Y}$ as follows. Every $x \in \mathcal{X}$ has the form $x = (r_A, f_A)$ (Alice's view) and every $y \in \mathcal{Y}$ has the form $y = (r_B, f_B)$ (Bob's view), where f_A, f_B have domain Q_A, Q_B respectively. Note that we enumerate x and y independently in the rectangle. Consequently, some pairs (x, y) in this rectangle may be *inconsistent*. Concretely, we say that a pair $x = (r_A, f_A)$ and $y = (r_B, f_B)$ is inconsistent if there exists an input $w \in Q_A \cap Q_B$ such that $f_A(w) \neq f_B(w)$. Define an output table as follows:

$$\mathcal{M}(x,y) \stackrel{\text{def}}{=} \begin{cases} \text{Alice's key output by } \Pi(r_A, r_B, f_A \cup f_B), & \text{if } f_A \text{ and } f_B \text{ are consistent;} \\ *, & \text{otherwise.} \end{cases}$$

This table indeed captures all possible executions of the protocol Π. This table is a partial function because many entries are undefined (the $*$ entries).

During the attack, Eve observes the transcript τ and makes queries to f. Whenever Eve has observed (τ, f_E), we update the table $\mathcal{M}$ by removing the entries that are inconsistent with Eve's observation, i.e., we update the table to

$$\mathcal{M}_{\tau, f_E}(x, y) \stackrel{\text{def}}{=} \begin{cases} \mathcal{M}(x, y), & \text{if } (x, y) \text{ are consistent with } (\tau, f_E); \\ *, & \text{otherwise.} \end{cases}$$

Given this observation (τ, f_E), the defined entries of $\mathcal{M}_{\tau, f_E}$ capture all possible views of Alice and Bob. Now we say $\mathcal{M}_{\tau, f_E}$ is almost monochromatic if almost all defined entries of $\mathcal{M}_{\tau, f_E}$ are equal to the same output $b \in \{0, 1\}$. [3] A key step in our proof is to show $\mathcal{M}_{\tau, f_E}$ is almost monochromatic provided that the following conditions are met:

1. Π has perfect completeness;
2. there is no small ε-correlated set respect to (τ, f_E).

Once Eve realizes $\mathcal{M}_{\tau, f_E}$ is almost monochromatic, she knows that Alice's key is b with high probability.

Upper Bound the Number of Eve's Queries via Density Increment Argument. This part of our proof is based on the density increment argument in [YZ22, YZ23]. We first define a density function to capture the amount of hidden information in the transcript τ about the random function $\boldsymbol{F}$, which is not known by Eve. For every τ and f_E, its density function $\Phi(\tau, f_E)$ is defined as

$$\Phi(\tau, f_E) \stackrel{\text{def}}{=} \mathbf{H}(\boldsymbol{F} \mid \boldsymbol{R}_A, \boldsymbol{R}_B, f_E) - \mathbf{H}(\boldsymbol{F} \mid \boldsymbol{R}_A, \boldsymbol{R}_B, f_E, \tau).$$

If we replace τ and f_E with corresponding random variables, $\boldsymbol{T}$ and $\boldsymbol{F}_E$, then $\Phi(\boldsymbol{T}, \boldsymbol{F}_E)$ equals to $\mathrm{I}(\boldsymbol{F}; \boldsymbol{T} \mid \boldsymbol{R}_A, \boldsymbol{R}_B, \boldsymbol{F}_E)$, the mutual information of $\boldsymbol{F}$ and $\boldsymbol{T}$ conditioned on $\boldsymbol{R}_A, \boldsymbol{R}_B, \boldsymbol{F}_E$. This quantity is strongly related to the *information*

---

[3] More precisely, 'almost all' means if we sample an entry (x, y) according to the probability that it appears in real execution (conditioned on τ, f_E), we have $\mathcal{M}(x, y) = b$ with high probability.

complexity (IC), a powerful tool for proving lower bounds in communication complexity [CSWY01, BBCR10]. IC usually refers to the mutual information of Alice's input and Bob's input conditioned on the transcript, so the IC for key-agreement should look like $I(R_A, R_B; T)$. However, in the ROM, the random function F is another random resource involved in the computation. Therefore, we cannot use IC *as a black box* to study such key-agreement protocols. Instead, we use the density increment argument proposed by [YZ23], which reinterprets IC in a white-box manner.

Let us turn back to our proof. The key idea is that whenever Eve *queries an ε-correlated set*, the density function *decreases by at least ε* in expectation. To make things clearer, we first explain our sampling procedure. There are several random variables involved in the analysis, including $(R_A, R_B, F, T, S_1, S_2, \dots)$. Here S_i is the query set made by Eve in the i-th round. In our analysis, we *do not* sample (R_A, R_B, F) all at once. Instead, we consider these random variables to be sampled in the following order.

---

1. We first sample the transcript $\tau \leftarrow T$ and send it to the attacker.
2. In the i-th round of the attack,
   - Eve samples her next query set S_i conditioned on $(\tau, S_1, f(S_1), \dots, S_{i-1}, f(S_{i-1}))$.
   - We sample $f(S_i)$ conditional on $(\tau, S_1, f(S_1), \dots, S_{i-1}, f(S_{i-1}), S_i)$, and Eve receives $f(S_i)$.

Suppose that at some point, Eve has already observed f_E, e.g., $f_E = f(S_1 \cup \cdots \cup S_{i-1})$ and decided to query S_i next. By definition, Eve only queries correlated sets, i.e., S_i is ε-correlated w.r.t. (τ, f_E). And we prove that for any ε-correlated set S_i,

$$\mathop{\mathbf{E}}_{f(S_i) \leftarrow F(S_i)|_{\tau, f_E}} [\Phi(T, f_E \cup f(S_i))] \leq \Phi(T, f_E) - \varepsilon, \tag{1}$$

where $f_E \cup f(S_i)$ is Eve's updated observation after making oracle queries on S_i. We then finish our argument by observing the following two properties of Φ:

- In the beginning, $\Phi(T, f_\emptyset) \leq c$. Here $f_\emptyset$ denotes the all-empty function since Eve has no information about the oracle before making any queries.
- Φ is non-negative: $\Phi(\tau, f_E) \geq 0$ for all τ, f_E.

Equation (1) says that each time Eve queries an ε-correlated set, Φ decreases by ε (in expectation), so Eve can query at most $O(c/\varepsilon) = O(c)$ sets (in expectation), as we set $\varepsilon = \Theta(1)$. Since each set queried by Eve is of size at most 2ℓ, we conclude that the total number of Eve's queries is $O(c\ell)$.

Comparison with [HMO+19]. The paper by Haitner et al. uses mostly direct calculations to derive an upper bound of the mutual information characterizing the advantage of Alice and Bob over Eve. An important ingredient in their proof is that conditioning on Eve's view does not introduce significant dependency between Alice and Bob; this is true for two-round protocols but fails for multi-round protocols. Even with perfect completeness, their approach encounters similar barriers. In contrast, our proof mainly depends on the investigation of the structure of the table $\mathcal{M}_{\tau, f_E}$, and hence the number of rounds is no longer a restriction.

1.2   Discussions and Open Problems

In this section, we discuss some open problems and future directions. An immediate question is how to remove the restrictions in our main theorem. We briefly discuss some potential ways to solve them below.

Protocols with Imperfect Completeness. In our proof, the property of perfect completeness is used in Lemma 3. The perfect completeness restriction is an analog of proving *deterministic* communication complexity, while key-agreement protocols with imperfect completeness can be likened to *randomized* communication protocols. The density increment argument used in this paper was originally inspired by the proofs of *query-to-communication lifting theorems* in communication complexity [RM97, GPW15, GPW17, YZ22]. In communication complexity, past experience suggests that the density increment argument is robust in the sense that it usually extends to proving randomized communication lower bounds. For example, the deterministic query-to-communication lifting theorem was formalized by [GPW15], then [GPW17] proved the extension to the randomized query-to-communication lifting theorem, even though it took several years.

Protocols with Adaptive Queries. The density increment argument has a good chance of proving communication lower bounds for adaptive protocols. Particularly, our efficiency proof directly applies to adaptive protocols. Our proof only utilized the non-adaptivity in Lemma 3. The round-by-round analysis introduced by Barak and Mahmoody [BMG09] might be helpful to circumvent this obstacle. Admittedly, the analysis might be slightly more complicated, but we do not see a fundamental barrier here.

Further Potential Applications. The heavy query technique used in the proof of [BMG09] has found applications in the context of black-box separations and black-box security in the random oracle model (see, e.g., [DSLMM11, KSY11, BKSY11, MP12, HOZ16]). Likewise, it will be interesting to check if our approach offers fresh perspectives and potential solutions to some open problems. The following is a list of potential questions.

1. Devise an $O(\ell)$-round and $O(\ell^2)$-query attack for key-argeement protocols in the ROM [BMG09, MMV11].
2. Consider an M-party protocol where all pairs among M players agree on secret keys. Given an attack that recovers a constant fraction of the $\binom{M}{2}$ keys with $O(M \cdot \ell^2)$ oracle queries [DH21].

3. In the quantum setting, Alice and Bob are capable of conducting quantum computation and classical communication, and the random oracle allows quantum queries. [ACC+22] introduced the Polynomial Compatibility Conjecture and gave an attack (only for protocols with perfect completeness) assuming this conjecture holds. Devise an attack that has better efficiency or fewer restrictions.

2   Preliminary

2.1   Notations

For a random variable X, denote x is sampled from (the distribution of) X as $x \leftarrow X$; the support of X is defined as $\mathrm{supp}(X) \overset{\text{def}}{=} \{x : \mathbf{Pr}\left[X = x\right] > 0\}$.

Partial Functions. There are many ways to view a partial function $f : [N] \to [M] \cup \{\bot\}$ with domain $Q \overset{\text{def}}{=} \{w \in [N] : f(w) \neq \bot\}$: It can be viewed as a function $f_Q : Q \to [M]$, or a list $((w_i, f(w_i))_{i \in [Q]}$. We say two partial functions are *consistent* if they agree on the intersection of their domains. For consistent partial functions f_1 and f_2, we use $f_1 \cup f_2$ to denote the partial function with domain $Q_1 \cup Q_2$ and is consistent with f_1 and f_2.

2.2   Key-Agreement Protocols

Let $\Pi = (\mathsf{A}, \mathsf{B})$ be a two-party protocol consisting of a pair of probabilistic interactive Turing machines, where the two parties A and B are often referred to as Alice and Bob. A protocol is called ℓ-*oracle-aided* if Alice and Bob have access to an oracle $f : [N] \to [M]$ and each party makes at most ℓ queries to f. An oracle-aided protocol is called *non-adaptive* when both parties choose their queries before querying the oracle and communicating. Π produces a *transcript* τ which is the communication bits between players. The *communication complexity* of Π, denoted by $\mathrm{CC}(\Pi)$, is the length of the transcript of Π in the worst case.

We focus on oracle-aided key-agreement protocols in the random oracle model, where the oracle f is uniformly sampled from the collection of all functions from $[N]$ to $[M]$. Note that the execution of the key-agreement protocol is completely determined by r_A, r_B and f, where r_A (resp., r_B) is Alice's (resp., Bob's) internal randomness. We call the tuple (r_A, r_B, f) an *extended view*. Let $EV = (R_A, R_B, F)$ denote the distribution of the extended view in a random execution. For every extended view $v = (r_A, r_B, f)$, let $\mathsf{tran}(v), \mathsf{out}_\mathsf{A}(v), \mathsf{out}_\mathsf{B}(v)$ be the communication transcript, A's output, and B's output respectively, given the extended view v.

Definition 2 (Key-agreement protocols). *Let* $\alpha, \gamma \in [0, 1], q \in \mathbb{N}$. *A protocol* $\Pi = (\mathsf{A}, \mathsf{B})$ *is a* (α, q, γ)-*key-agreement if the following conditions hold:*

1. $(1 - \alpha)$-*completeness.* $\mathbf{Pr}_{v \leftarrow EV}\left[\mathsf{out}_\mathsf{A}(v) = \mathsf{out}_\mathsf{B}(v)\right] \geq 1 - \alpha$.

2. (q, γ)-**security**. *For any q-oracle-aided adversary* E,

$$\Pr_{v=(r_A, r_B, f) \leftarrow EV} \left[E^f(\operatorname{tran}(v)) = \operatorname{out}_A(v) \right] \leq \gamma.$$

Since we aim to prove lower bounds, we assume each party outputs one bit, as per [HMO+19]. Moreover, [HMO+19] proved that studying the following normalized key-agreement protocols suffices.

Normalized Key-Agreement Protocols. Following [HMO+19], to simplify the proof of the lower bound, we can transform the key-agreement protocol Π into a normalized protocol called Π', such that the secret key output by Bob in Π' is the first bit of his last query. Formally,

Proposition 1. *Let Π be a non-adaptive, ℓ-oracle-aided (α, q, γ)-key-agreement protocol with communication complexity c. Then there is a non-adaptive $(\ell+1)$-oracle-aided (α, q, γ)-key-agreement protocol Π' with communication complexity $c + 1$, in which Bob's output is the first bit of his last query.*

2.3   Basic Information Theory

The Shannon entropy of a random variable X is defined as

$$\mathbf{H}(X) \stackrel{\text{def}}{=} \sum_{x \in \operatorname{supp}(X)} \mathbf{Pr}\left[X = x\right] \log\left(\frac{1}{\mathbf{Pr}\left[X = x\right]}\right).$$

The conditional entropy of a random variable X given Y is defined as

$$\mathbf{H}\left(X \mid Y\right) \stackrel{\text{def}}{=} \mathop{\mathbf{E}}_{y \leftarrow Y} \left[\mathbf{H}\left(X \mid Y = y\right)\right].$$

We often use (conditional) entropy conditioned on some event E, which is defined by the same formula where the probability measure $\mathbf{Pr}\left[\cdot\right]$ is replace by $\mathbf{Pr}'[\cdot] \stackrel{\text{def}}{=} \mathbf{Pr}\left[\cdot | E\right]$. Entropy conditioned on event E is denoted as $\mathbf{H}(X|E), \mathbf{H}(X|Y, E)$.

Let X and Y be two (possibly correlated) random variables. The mutual information of X and Y is defined by

$$\mathbf{I}\left(X; Y\right) \stackrel{\text{def}}{=} \mathbf{H}(X) - \mathbf{H}\left(X \mid Y\right) = \mathbf{H}(Y) - \mathbf{H}\left(Y \mid X\right).$$

The conditional mutual information is

$$\mathbf{I}\left(X_i; Y \mid X_1, \ldots, X_{i-1}\right) \stackrel{\text{def}}{=} \mathbf{H}\left(X_i \mid X_1, \ldots, X_{i-1}\right) - \mathbf{H}\left(X_i \mid Y, X_1, \ldots, X_{i-1}\right).$$

Proposition 2 (Entropy chain rule). *For random variables $X_1, X_2, \ldots, X_n$, it holds that*

$$\mathbf{H}(X_1, X_2, \ldots, X_n) = \sum_{i=1}^{n} \mathbf{H}\left(X_i \mid X_1, X_2, \ldots, X_{i-1}\right).$$

Proposition 3. *(Chain rule for mutual information) For* $X_1, X_2, \ldots, X_n$ *are* n *random variables and* Y *is another random variable,*

$$\mathrm{I}(X_1, X_2, \ldots, X_n; Y) = \sum_{i=1}^{n} \mathrm{I}(X_i; Y \mid X_1, X_2, \ldots, X_{i-1}).$$

Proposition 4. *(Data processing inequality) For two random variables* X, Y *and a function* f,

$$\mathbf{H}(f(X)) \le \mathbf{H}(X) \ and \ \mathrm{I}(f(X); Y) \le \mathrm{I}(X; Y)$$

3   Communication Complexity of Key-Agreement Protocols

This section proves the main theorem:

Theorem 4 (Formal version of Theorem 3). *Let* $\Pi = (\mathsf{A}, \mathsf{B})$ *be an* ℓ-*query-aided, non-adaptive* $(0, q, \gamma)$-*key-agreement (i.e.,* Π *enjoys perfect completeness), then*

$$\mathrm{CC}(\Pi) \ge \frac{q}{2(\ell + 1)} \cdot \frac{(1 - \gamma)^3}{27} - 1 = \Omega\left(\frac{q}{\ell}\right).$$

By Proposition 1, it suffices to show that

$$\mathrm{CC}(\Pi) \ge \frac{q}{2\ell} \cdot \frac{(1 - \gamma)^3}{27}, \tag{2}$$

for all normalized protocol Π that satisfies the conditions in Theorem 4.

Correlated sets play a central role in our proof; here we give the formal definition.

Definition 3 (ε-correlated). *Let* τ *be a transcript and* f_E *be a partial function with domain* Q_E. *We say a set* $S \subseteq [N]$ *is* ε-**correlated** *with respect to* (τ, f_E) *if*

$$\mathbf{H}(F(S) \mid R_A, R_B, F(Q_E) = f_E) - \mathbf{H}(F(S) \mid R_A, R_B, F(Q_E) = f_E \wedge T = \tau) \ge \varepsilon,$$

where (R_A, R_B, F) *is a random extended view and* $T \stackrel{\mathrm{def}}{=} \mathrm{tran}(R_A, R_B, F)$.

3.1   Description of the Attacker

The attacker is described in Algorithm 1. In the algorithm, $f_E^{(i)}$ stands for the observations of Eve till the end of the i-th iteration. Moreover, we use $EV(\tau, f_E^{(i)})$

to denote the distribution of the extended view $\boldsymbol{EV}$ conditioned on the following two events: (1) the random oracle is consistent with $f_E^{(i)}$; (2) the transcript is τ.

Algorithm 1: The attacker E

Input: transcript τ
Oracle : $f : [N] \to [M]$
Output: $b \in \{0, 1, \bot\}$
Set $\varepsilon := (1 - \gamma)^2/9$
Initialize $i := 0$ and $f_E^{(0)}$ as the empty function
while $\exists\, S \subseteq [N]$ *s.t.* $|S| \le 2\ell$ *and is ε-correlated w.r.t.* $(\tau, f_E^{(i)})$ **do**
    Let S_{i+1} be any ε-correlated set of size at most 2ℓ
    Query f on S_{i+1} and receive $f(S_{i+1})$
    Set $f_E^{(i+1)} := f_E^{(i)} \cup f(S_{i+1})$.
    $i := i + 1$
if $\exists\, b \in \{0, 1\}$ *s.t.* $\mathbf{Pr}_{v \leftarrow EV(\tau, f_E^{(i)})}[\mathsf{out}_\mathsf{A}(v) = b] \ge 1 - \sqrt{2\varepsilon}$ **then**
    Output b
else
    Output $\bot$

3.2   Success Probability of the Attacker

This subsection analyzes the attacker's success probability for perfect completeness. We will first introduce the language of the combinatorial rectangle and then use it to analyze the attacker's success probability.

Through the Lens of Rectangles. *Combinatorial rectangle* is a standard tool in communication complexity. We thus develop this language for key-agreement protocols in the following.

Let Π be a non-adaptive key-agreement protocol, meaning that queries of Alice is a function $\mathcal{Q}_\mathsf{A}(r_A)$ of her internal randomness r_A. If f_A is a partial function with domain $\mathcal{Q}_\mathsf{A}(r_A)$, we call the pair (r_A, f_A) a **profile** of Alice. The profile space of Alice, denoted by $\mathcal{X}$, consists of all possible profiles of Alice, namely,

$$\mathcal{X} \overset{\text{def}}{=} \{(r_A, f_A) : f_A \text{ is a partial function with domain } \mathcal{Q}_\mathsf{A}(r_A)\}.$$

For Bob, we analogously define $\mathcal{Q}_\mathsf{B}$ and

$$\mathcal{Y} \overset{\text{def}}{=} \{(r_B, f_B) : f_B \text{ is a partial function with domain } \mathcal{Q}_\mathsf{B}(r_B)\}.$$

Given a profile pair $(x = (r_A, f_A), y = (r_B, f_B)) \in \mathcal{X} \times \mathcal{Y}$, Alice and Bob can run the protocol by using f_A and f_B respectively as oracle answers: when Alice needs to issue an oracle query w, she takes $f_A(w)$ as oracle answer; similarly, Bob takes $f_B(w)$ as oracle answer when querying w. Hence, we can still define the transcript $\mathtt{tran}(x, y)$ and output $\mathsf{out}_\mathsf{A}(x, y)$, $\mathsf{out}_\mathsf{B}(x, y)$.

Note that some profile pairs are imaginary in the sense that the oracle answers of Alice and Bob are inconsistent. We say $x = (r_A, f_A) \in \mathcal{X}$ and $y = (r_B, f_B) \in \mathcal{Y}$ are **consistent** if f_A and f_B are consistent. Define the output table $\mathcal{M}_\Pi \in \{0, 1, *\}^{\mathcal{X} \times \mathcal{Y}}$ via

$$\mathcal{M}_\Pi(x, y) \overset{\text{def}}{=} \begin{cases} \mathsf{out}_A(x, y), & \text{if } x, y \text{ are consistent;} \\ *, & \text{otherwise.} \end{cases}$$

Let $D \overset{\text{def}}{=} \{(x, y) \in \mathcal{X} \times \mathcal{Y} : \mathcal{M}_\Pi(x, y) \neq *\}$ be the set of all consistent profile pairs; such profile pairs can be witnessed in real execution.

A set $R \subseteq \mathcal{X} \times \mathcal{Y}$ is called a **rectangle** if $R = \mathcal{X}_R \times \mathcal{Y}_R$ for some $\mathcal{X}_R \subseteq \mathcal{X}$ and $\mathcal{Y}_R \subseteq \mathcal{Y}$. Let τ be a transcript and f_E be a partial function with domain Q_E. We care about the profiles that are consistent with f_E and produce transcript τ; formally, we consider the rectangle $\mathcal{X}_{\tau, f_E} \times \mathcal{Y}_{\tau, f_E}$ where

$$\mathcal{X}_{\tau, f_E} \overset{\text{def}}{=} \left\{ x = (r_A, f_A) \in \mathcal{X} : \exists y = (r_B, f_B) \in \mathcal{Y} \text{ s.t. } \begin{matrix} f_A, f_B, f_E \text{ are consistent and} \\ \mathsf{tran}(x, y) = \tau \end{matrix} \right\},$$

and

$$\mathcal{Y}_{\tau, f_E} \overset{\text{def}}{=} \left\{ y = (r_B, f_B) \in \mathcal{Y} : \exists x = (r_A, f_A) \in \mathcal{X} \text{ s.t. } \begin{matrix} f_A, f_B, f_E \text{ are consistent and} \\ \mathsf{tran}(x, y) = \tau \end{matrix} \right\}.$$

If Π has perfect completeness, the rectangle $\mathcal{X}_{\tau, f_E} \times \mathcal{Y}_{\tau, f_E}$ has the following simple but useful property.

Lemma 1. *Assume that Π has perfect completeness. Let $(x, y), (x', y') \in \mathcal{X}_{\tau, f_E} \times \mathcal{Y}_{\tau, f_E}$ for some τ and f_E. If $\mathcal{M}_\Pi(x, y) = 0$ and $\mathcal{M}_\Pi(x', y') = 1$, then $\mathcal{M}_\Pi(x, y') = \mathcal{M}_\Pi(x', y) = *$.*

Proof. Assume $\mathcal{M}_\Pi(x, y') \neq *$. Since (x, y') appears in some execution of Π, by perfect completeness, we have $\mathsf{out}_A(x, y') = \mathsf{out}_B(x, y')$. However, $\mathsf{out}_A(x, y') = \mathsf{out}_A(x, y') = 0$ while $\mathsf{out}_B(x, y') = \mathsf{out}_B(x', y') = 1$, a contradiction. The argument for (x', y) is similar.

Let $QV(\tau, f_E)$ denote the query set of Alice and Bob conditioned on (τ, f_E), namely, $QV(\tau, f_E) \overset{\text{def}}{=} (\mathcal{Q}_A(R_A), \mathcal{Q}_B(R_B))$, where $(R_A, R_B, \cdot) = EV(\tau, f_E)$. Given $(Q_A, Q_B) \in \mathsf{supp}QV(\tau, f_E)$, we obtain a subrectangle of $\mathcal{X}_{\tau, f_E} \times \mathcal{Y}_{\tau, f_E}$ by adding the restriction that Alice's (resp., Bob's) queries is Q_A (resp., Q_B). That is, we consider $\mathcal{X}_{\tau, f_E}(Q_A) \times \mathcal{Y}_{\tau, f_E}(Q_B)$ where

$$\mathcal{X}_{\tau, f_E}(Q_A) \overset{\text{def}}{=} \{x = (r_A, f_A) \in \mathcal{X}_{\tau, f_E} : \mathcal{Q}_A(r_A) = Q_A\},$$

$$\mathcal{Y}_{\tau, f_E}(Q_B) \overset{\text{def}}{=} \{y = (r_B, f_B) \in \mathcal{Y}_{\tau, f_E} : \mathcal{Q}_B(r_B) = Q_B\}.$$

Definition 4 (Monochromatic Rectangle). *A rectangle $R \subseteq \mathcal{X} \times \mathcal{Y}$ is called b-monochromatic if $R \cap D \neq \emptyset$ and for every $(x, y) \in R \cap D$, $\mathcal{M}_\Pi(x, y) = b$; R is said to be monochromatic if it is b-monochromatic for some $b \in \{0, 1\}$.*

The following lemma shows that if the protocol is normalized and has perfect completeness, the rectangle $\mathcal{X}_{\tau,f_E} \times \mathcal{Y}_{\tau,f_E}$ has a special structure: It can be partitioned into monochromatic rectangles according to the queries.

Lemma 2. *Suppose Π is normalized and has perfect completeness. Let τ be a transcript and f_E be a partial function. For all $(Q_A, Q_B) \in \mathrm{supp}\boldsymbol{QV}(\tau, f_E)$, the rectangle $\mathcal{X}_{\tau,f_E}(Q_A) \times \mathcal{Y}_{\tau,f_E}(Q_B)$ is monochromatic.*

Proof. Since Π is normalized, for any $(x, y) \in \mathcal{X}_{\tau,f_E}(Q_A) \times \mathcal{Y}_{\tau,f_E}(Q_B)$, $\mathrm{out_B}(x, y)$ is determined by Q_B. Moreover, because of perfect completeness, $\mathrm{out_A}(x, y) = \mathrm{out_B}(x, y)$ for all $(x, y) \in \mathcal{X}_{\tau,f_E}(Q_A) \times \mathcal{Y}_{\tau,f_E}(Q_B)$. Thus, $\mathcal{X}_{\tau,f_E}(Q_A) \times \mathcal{Y}_{\tau,f_E}(Q_B)$ is monochromatic.

Analyzing the Attacker's Success Probability. Next, we show that Algorithm 1 breaks the security of normalized protocols. The following lemma characterizes what happens after all small ε-correlated sets are cleaned up; it roughly says that if there exists no small ε-correlated set, the key is almost determined conditioned on Eve's information.

Lemma 3. *Let τ be a transcript and f_E be a partial function with domain Q_E. If there exists no ε-correlated set of size at most 2ℓ w.r.t. (τ, f_E), then $\exists b \in \{0, 1\}$ s.t.*

$$\Pr_{v \leftarrow \boldsymbol{EV}(\tau,f_E)} [\mathrm{out_A}(v) = b] \geq 1 - \sqrt{2\varepsilon}.$$

Proof. Write $\delta \stackrel{\mathrm{def}}{=} \sqrt{2\varepsilon}$. Assume towards contradiction that

$$\Pr_{v \leftarrow \boldsymbol{EV}(\tau,f_E)} [\mathrm{out_A}(v) = b] > \delta, \forall b \in \{0, 1\}.$$

For $b \in \{0, 1\}$, define

$$\mathcal{G}_b \stackrel{\mathrm{def}}{=} \{(Q_A, Q_B) \in \mathrm{supp}\boldsymbol{QV}(\tau, f_E) : \mathcal{X}_{\tau,f_E}(Q_A) \times \mathcal{Y}_{\tau,f_E}(Q_B) \text{ is } b\text{-monochromatic}\}.$$

By Lemma 2, $\forall b \in \{0, 1\}$,

$$\Pr_{v \leftarrow \boldsymbol{EV}(\tau,f_E)} [(\mathcal{Q}_{\mathsf{A}}(v), \mathcal{Q}_{\mathsf{B}}(v)) \in \mathcal{G}_b] = \Pr_{v \leftarrow \boldsymbol{EV}(\tau,f_E)} [\mathrm{out_A}(v) = b] > \delta. \quad (3)$$

For $Q = (Q_A, Q_B), Q' = (Q'_A, Q'_B)$, define

$$h(Q, Q') \stackrel{\mathrm{def}}{=} \boldsymbol{H}(\boldsymbol{F}(Q_A \cup Q_B) \mid \boldsymbol{F}(Q_E) = f_E)$$
$$- \boldsymbol{H}(\boldsymbol{F}(Q_A \cup Q_B) \mid \mathcal{Q}_{\mathsf{A}}(\boldsymbol{R}_A) = Q'_A \wedge \mathcal{Q}_{\mathsf{B}}(\boldsymbol{R}_B) = Q'_B \wedge \boldsymbol{F}(Q_E) = f_E \wedge \boldsymbol{T} = \tau),$$

where $(\boldsymbol{R}_A, \boldsymbol{R}_B, \boldsymbol{F})$ is a random extended view and $\boldsymbol{T} = \mathrm{tran}(\boldsymbol{R}_A, \boldsymbol{R}_B, \boldsymbol{F})$ as usual. Then, we have

Claim. For all $Q_0 = (Q^0_A, Q^0_B) \in \mathcal{G}_0$ and $Q_1 = (Q^1_A, Q^1_B) \in \mathcal{G}_1$, we have $h(Q_b, Q_{1-b}) \geq 1$ for some $b \in \{0, 1\}$.

The above claim suggests some kind of correlation with the transcript exists; next, we prove such correlation gives rise to an ε-correlated set.

Consider the following complete bipartite graph, denoted by G:

1. The left vertex set is V_0 and each vertex $v \in V_0$ is associated with some $Q(v) \in \mathcal{G}_0$.
2. The right vertex set is V_1 and each vertex $v \in V_1$ is associated with some $Q(v) \in \mathcal{G}_1$.
3. For each $Q \in \mathcal{G}_0 \cup \mathcal{G}_1$, the number of vertices associated with Q is proportional to $\mathbf{Pr}_{QV(\tau, f_E)}[Q]$.

We assign an orientation to G as follows: for all $v_0 \in V_0, v_1 \in V_1$, if $h(Q(v_0), Q(v_1)) \geq 1$, then the edge $\{v_0, v_1\}$ is directed towards v_1; otherwise, $\{v_0, v_1\}$ is directed towards v_0. Let $E(G)$ denote the set of all directed edges. By the above claim, each directed edge $v \to v'$ satisfies $h(Q(v), Q(v')) \geq 1$. Let $\Gamma(v) \overset{\text{def}}{=} \{v' : (v \to v') \in E(G)\}$ denote the set of out-neighbors of v. WLOG, assume that $|V_0| \leq |V_1|$. By average argument, there exists some $v^* \in V_0 \cup V_1$ such that $|\Gamma(v^*)| \geq \frac{|V_0| \cdot |V_1|}{|V_0| + |V_1|} \geq |V_0|/2$.
Say $v^* \in V_{b^*}$, then we have

$$
\begin{aligned}
\Pr_{v \leftarrow V_{1-b^*}} [(v^* \to v) \in E(G)] = \frac{|\Gamma(v^*)|}{|V_{1-b^*}|} &\geq \frac{|V_0|}{2|V_{1-b^*}|} \\
&= \frac{1}{2} \cdot \frac{\mathbf{Pr}_{v \leftarrow EV(\tau, f_E)}[(\mathcal{Q}_A(v), \mathcal{Q}_B(v)) \in \mathcal{G}_0]}{\mathbf{Pr}_{v \leftarrow EV(\tau, f_E)}[(\mathcal{Q}_A(v), \mathcal{Q}_B(v)) \in \mathcal{G}_{1-b^*}]} \\
&> \frac{\delta}{2}.
\end{aligned}
$$

Let $Q^* \overset{\text{def}}{=} Q(v^*)$. Then we have

$$
\begin{aligned}
\mathop{\mathbf{E}}_{Q \leftarrow QV(\tau, f_E)} & [h(Q^*, Q)] \\
&\geq \mathop{\mathbf{E}}_{Q \leftarrow QV(\tau, f_E)} [h(Q^*, Q) \mid Q \in \mathcal{G}_{1-b^*}] \mathop{\mathbf{Pr}}_{Q \leftarrow QV(\tau, f_E)} [Q \in \mathcal{G}_{1-b^*}] \\
&\geq \mathop{\mathbf{E}}_{v \leftarrow V_{1-b^*}} [h(Q(v^*), Q(v))] \cdot \delta \\
&\geq \mathop{\mathbf{Pr}}_{v \leftarrow V_{1-b^*}} [(v^* \to v) \in E(G)] \cdot \delta \\
&= \frac{\delta^2}{2} = \varepsilon,
\end{aligned}
$$

(4)

where the second inequality follows from Eq. (3) and the construction of G, and the third inequality holds because $h(Q(v^*), Q(v)) \geq \mathbb{1}[(v^* \to v) \in E(G)]$.

Note that $\mathbf{E}_{Q \leftarrow QV(\tau, f_E)}[h(Q^*, Q)] \geq \varepsilon$ means that

$$
\begin{aligned}
&\mathbf{H}\left(F(Q_A^* \cup Q_B^*) \mid F(Q_E) = f_E\right) \\
&- \mathbf{H}\left(F(Q_A^* \cup Q_B^*) \mid \mathcal{Q}_A(R_A), \mathcal{Q}_B(R_B), F(Q_E) = f_E \wedge T = \tau\right) \geq \varepsilon,
\end{aligned}
$$

where $Q^* = (Q_A^*, Q_B^*)$. Thus, letting $\widehat{Q} = Q_A^* \cup Q_B^*$, we have

$$\mathbf{H}\left(\mathbf{F}(\widehat{Q}) \mid \mathbf{R}_A, \mathbf{R}_B, \mathbf{F}(Q_E) = f_E\right) - \mathbf{H}\left(\mathbf{F}(\widehat{Q}) \mid \mathbf{R}_A, \mathbf{R}_B, \mathbf{F}(Q_E) = f_E \wedge \mathbf{T} = \tau\right)$$

$$\geq \mathbf{H}\left(\mathbf{F}(\widehat{Q}) \mid \mathbf{R}_A, \mathbf{R}_B, \mathbf{F}(Q_E) = f_E\right)$$

$$- \mathbf{H}\left(\mathbf{F}(\widehat{Q}) \mid \mathcal{Q}_A(\mathbf{R}_A), \mathcal{Q}_B(\mathbf{R}_B), \mathbf{F}(Q_E) = f_E \wedge \mathbf{T} = \tau\right)$$

$$= \mathbf{H}\left(\mathbf{F}(\widehat{Q}) \mid \mathbf{F}(Q_E) = f_E\right) - \mathbf{H}\left(\mathbf{F}(\widehat{Q}) \mid \mathcal{Q}_A(\mathbf{R}_A), \mathcal{Q}_B(\mathbf{R}_B), \mathbf{F}(Q_E) = f_E \wedge \mathbf{T} = \tau\right)$$

$$\geq \varepsilon,$$

where the first inequality is by data processing inequality and the second step holds as $\mathbf{F}(\widehat{Q}), \mathbf{R}_A, \mathbf{R}_B$ are independent. That is, $\widehat{Q}$ is ε-correlated w.r.t. (τ, f_E), a contradiction.

It remains to prove the claim involved in the above proof.

Proof (of Claim). Define

$$R_b \stackrel{\text{def}}{=} \mathcal{X}_{\tau, f_E}(Q_A^b) \times \mathcal{Y}_{\tau, f_E}(Q_B^b) \text{ where } b \in \{0, 1\}.$$

For all $(x, y) \in R_0, (x', y') \in R_1$, we have $\mathcal{M}_\Pi(x, y) = 0$ and $\mathcal{M}_\Pi(x', y') = 1$, and hence $\mathcal{M}_\Pi(x, y') = *$ according to Lemma 1. This means that oracle answers in profile x and profile y' are inconsistent. Note that all inconsistent queries are in $S \stackrel{\text{def}}{=} Q_A^0 \cap Q_B^1$. Therefore,

$$\text{supp}\left(\mathbf{F}(S)|_{\mathcal{Q}_A(\mathbf{R}_A) = Q_A^0 \wedge \mathcal{Q}_A(\mathbf{R}_B) = Q_B^0 \wedge \mathbf{T} = \tau \wedge \mathbf{F}(Q_E) = f_E}\right)$$

$$\cap \text{supp}\left(\mathbf{F}(S)|_{\mathcal{Q}_A(\mathbf{R}_A) = Q_A^1 \wedge \mathcal{Q}_A(\mathbf{R}_B) = Q_B^1 \wedge \mathbf{T} = \tau \wedge \mathbf{F}(Q_E) = f_E}\right) = \emptyset.$$

A simple average argument shows that for some $b^* \in \{0, 1\}$,

$$\left|\text{supp}\left(\mathbf{F}(S)|_{\mathcal{Q}_A(\mathbf{R}_A) = Q_A^{b^*} \wedge \mathcal{Q}_A(\mathbf{R}_B) = Q_B^{b^*} \wedge \mathbf{T} = \tau \wedge \mathbf{F}(Q_E) = f_E}\right)\right|$$

$$\leq \frac{\left|\text{supp}\left(\mathbf{F}(S)|_{\mathbf{F}(Q_E) = f_E}\right)\right|}{2}. \tag{5}$$

Consequently,

$$\Delta \stackrel{\text{def}}{=} \mathbf{H}\left(\mathbf{F}(S) \mid \mathbf{F}(Q_E) = f_E\right)$$

$$- \mathbf{H}\left(\mathbf{F}(S) \mid \mathcal{Q}_A(\mathbf{R}_A) = Q_A^{b^*} \wedge \mathcal{Q}_B(\mathbf{R}_B) = Q_B^{b^*} \wedge \mathbf{F}(Q_E) = f_E \wedge \mathbf{T} = \tau\right)$$

$$\geq \mathbf{H}\left(\mathbf{F}(S) \mid \mathbf{F}(Q_E) = f_E\right)$$

$$- \log\left|\text{supp}\left(\mathbf{F}(S)|_{\mathcal{Q}_A(\mathbf{R}_A) = Q_A^{b^*} \wedge \mathcal{Q}_A(\mathbf{R}_B) = Q_B^{b^*} \wedge \mathbf{T} = \tau \wedge \mathbf{F}(Q_E) = f_E}\right)\right|$$

$$\geq \log\left|\text{supp}\left(\mathbf{F}(S)|_{\mathbf{F}|_{Q_E} = f_E}\right)\right| - \log \frac{\left|\text{supp}\left(\mathbf{F}(S)|_{\mathbf{F}(Q_E) = f_E}\right)\right|}{2}$$

$$= 1,$$

where the second inequality follows from Eq. 5 and the fact that $F(S)|_{F(Q_E)=f_E}$ is uniform distribution.

Now that $\Delta \geq 1$, it suffice to show $h(Q_{1-b^*}, Q_{b^*}) \geq \Delta$. Since $S \subseteq Q_A^{1-b^*} \cup Q_B^{1-b^*}$, this follows from chain rule:

$$h(Q_{1-b^*}, Q_{b^*}) - \Delta$$
$$= \mathbf{H}\left(F(\overline{S}) \mid F(Q_E) = f_E\right)$$
$$- \mathbf{H}\left(F(\overline{S}) \mid F(S), \mathcal{Q}_A(R_A) = Q_A^{b^*} \wedge \mathcal{Q}_B(R_B) = Q_B^{b^*} \wedge F(Q_E) = f_E \wedge T = \tau\right)$$
$$\geq 0,$$

where $\overline{S} \stackrel{\text{def}}{=} (Q_A^{1-b^*} \cup Q_B^{1-b^*}) \setminus S$ and the inequality holds since $F(\overline{S})|_{F(Q_E)=f_E}$ is uniform distribution (and uniform distribution has maximum entropy).

Corollary 1 (Accuracy of E). *Let Π be an ℓ-oracle-aided, non-adaptive $(1, q, \gamma)-$key-agreement. Assume the Π is normalized, then Algorithm 1 guesses the key correctly with probability at least $1 - \sqrt{2\varepsilon}$, i.e.,*

$$\Pr_{v=(r_A, r_B, f) \leftarrow EV} \left[E^f(\mathrm{tran}(v)) = \mathrm{out}_A(v)\right] > 1 - \sqrt{2\varepsilon}.$$

Proof. By Lemma 3, E outputs $\mathrm{out}_A(v)$ except with probability less than $\sqrt{2\varepsilon}$.

3.3   Efficiency of the Attacker

In this subsection, we analyze the efficiency of the attacker Eve (Algorithm 1) via the density increment argument [YZ22, YZ23]. We first introduce the density function. Intuitively, the density function $\Phi(\tau, f_E)$ captures the amount of hidden information contained in the transcript τ about the random function F given Eve's observation of oracle f_E. As Eve makes effective queries, she learns (a constant amount of) information in each iteration, so the density function decreases by a constant.

Definition 5 (Density function). *Let τ be a transcript and f_E be a partial function with domain Q_E. Define density function Φ via*

$$\Phi(\tau, f_E) \stackrel{\text{def}}{=} \mathbf{H}(F \mid R_A, R_B, F(Q_E) = f_E) - \mathbf{H}(F \mid R_A, R_B, F(Q_E) = f_E \wedge T = \tau),$$

where (R_A, R_B, F) is a random extended view and $T \stackrel{\text{def}}{=} \mathrm{tran}(R_A, R_B, F)$.

Lemma 4. *The density function Φ satisfies the following properties:*

1. Φ is non-negative.
2. $\mathbf{E}_{\tau \leftarrow T}[\Phi(\tau, f_\emptyset)] \leq \mathrm{CC}(\Pi)$, where $f_\emptyset$ denotes the empty function.
3. If S if ε-correlated w.r.t. (τ, f_E), then

$$\mathop{\mathbf{E}}_{f_S \leftarrow F(S)|_{T=\tau, F(Q_E)=f_E}} [\Phi(\tau, f_E \cup f_S)] \leq \Phi(\tau, f_E) - \varepsilon.$$

Proof. We prove these statements as follows.

1. F is uniform distribution conditioned on R_A, R_B and the event $F(Q_E) = f_E$. Hence Φ is non-negative.

2. By definition, we have that

$$\mathop{\mathbf{E}}_{\tau \leftarrow T} [\Phi(\tau, f_\emptyset)] = \mathop{\mathbf{E}}_{\tau \leftarrow T} [\mathbf{H}(F \mid R_A, R_B) - \mathbf{H}(F \mid R_A, R_B, T = \tau)]$$
$$= \mathbf{H}(F \mid R_A, R_B) - \mathbf{H}(F \mid R_A, R_B, T)$$
$$= \mathbf{I}(F; T \mid R_A, R_B)$$
$$\leq \mathbf{H}(T)$$
$$\leq \mathrm{CC}(\Pi).$$

3. Write $Q'_E \overset{\text{def}}{=} Q_E \cup S$. We decompose

$$\Phi(\tau, f_E) - \mathop{\mathbf{E}}_{f_S \leftarrow F(S)|_{T = \tau, F(Q_E) = f_E}} [\Phi(\tau, f_E \cup f_S)] = \phi_1 - \phi_2,$$

where

$$\phi_1 \overset{\text{def}}{=} \mathbf{H}(F \mid R_A, R_B, F(Q_E) = f_E)$$
$$- \mathop{\mathbf{E}}_{f_S \leftarrow F(S)|_{T = \tau, F(Q_E) = f_E}} [\mathbf{H}(F \mid R_A, R_B, F(Q'_E) = (f_E \cup f_S))],$$

and

$$\phi_2 \overset{\text{def}}{=} \mathbf{H}(F \mid R_A, R_B, F(Q_E) = f_E \wedge T = \tau)$$
$$- \mathop{\mathbf{E}}_{f_S \leftarrow F(S)|_{\tau, f_E}} [\mathbf{H}(F \mid R_A, R_B, F(Q'_E) = (f_E \cup f_S) \wedge T = \tau)].$$

Since R_A, R_B, F are independent, we have (by chain rule)

$$\phi_1 = \mathbf{H}(F(S) \mid R_A, R_B, F(Q_E) = f_E).$$

Observe that by the definition of conditional entropy,

$$\mathop{\mathbf{E}}_{f_S \leftarrow F(S)|_{\tau, f_E}} [\mathbf{H}(F \mid R_A, R_B, F(Q'_E) = (f_E \cup f_S) \wedge T = \tau)]$$
$$= \mathbf{H}(F \mid R_A, R_B, F(S), F(Q_E) = f_E \wedge T = \tau).$$

By the chain rule,

$$\phi_2 = \mathbf{H}(F \mid R_A, R_B, F(Q_E) = f_E \wedge T = \tau)$$
$$- \mathbf{H}(F \mid R_A, R_B, F(S), F(Q_E) = f_E \wedge T = \tau) \qquad (6)$$
$$= \mathbf{H}(F(S) \mid R_A, R_B, F(Q_E) = f_E \wedge T = \tau).$$

Since S is ε-correlated, we have

$$\mathbf{H}(F(S) \mid R_A, R_B, F(Q_E) = f_E) - \mathbf{H}(F(S) \mid R_A, R_B, F(Q_E) = f_E \wedge T = \tau) \geq \varepsilon,$$

and hence

$$\Phi(\tau, f_E) - \mathop{\mathbf{E}}_{f_S \leftarrow F(S)|_{T = \tau, F(Q_E) = f_E}} [\Phi(\tau, f_E \cup f_S] = \phi_1 - \phi_2 \geq \varepsilon.$$

Following Lemma 4, we can deduce that our attacker E (Algorithm 1) makes at most $CC(\Pi)/\varepsilon$ iterations in expectation.

Lemma 5 (Efficiency of E). $\mathbf{E}[\#$ *of iterations in the running of* E$] \leq \frac{CC(\Pi)}{\varepsilon}$.

Proof. Recall the sampling procedure in Sect. 1.1. Then, we define some random variables in a random execution for analysis. Let $\boldsymbol{F}_E^{(i)} = \boldsymbol{F}_E^{(i-1)} \cup \boldsymbol{F}(S_i)$ be the observations of Eve until the end of the i-th iteration, where $\boldsymbol{F}_E^{(0)}$ is the empty function. If E does not enter the i-th iteration, we define $\boldsymbol{F}_E^{(i)} = \boldsymbol{F}_E^{(i-1)}$. Define a counter variable to record the number of iterations as follows: $C_0 \overset{\text{def}}{=} 0$ and for $i \geq 0$

$$C_{i+1} \overset{\text{def}}{=} \begin{cases} C_i + 1, & \text{if E enters the } i\text{-th iteration;} \\ C_i, & \text{otherwise.} \end{cases}$$

We claim that for every τ and f_E,

$$\mathbf{E}\left[\Phi(\boldsymbol{T}, \boldsymbol{F}_E^{(i)}) - \Phi(\boldsymbol{T}, \boldsymbol{F}_E^{(i+1)}) - \varepsilon(C_{i+1} - C_i) \mid \boldsymbol{T} = \tau \wedge \boldsymbol{F}_E^{(i)} = f_E\right] \geq 0. \quad (7)$$

To see this, consider the event $\mathsf{Enter}_i \overset{\text{def}}{=}$ 'E enters the i-th iteration'. Conditioned on Enter_i, $C_{i+1} - C_i = 1$ and by the third item of Lemma 4, the underlined part is non-negative; conditioned on $\neg\mathsf{Enter}_i$, the underlined part equals zero by definition.

Since Eq. (7) holds for all (τ, f_E), we get

$$\mathbf{E}\left[\Phi(\boldsymbol{T}, \boldsymbol{F}_E^{(i)}) - \Phi(\boldsymbol{T}, \boldsymbol{F}_E^{(i+1)}) - \varepsilon(C_{i+1} - C_i)\right] \geq 0.$$

Summing over $i = 0, \cdots, N-1$, we obtain

$$\mathbf{E}[\Phi(\boldsymbol{T}, \boldsymbol{F}_E^{(0)})] - \mathbf{E}[\Phi(\boldsymbol{T}, \boldsymbol{F}_E^{(N)})] - \varepsilon\,\mathbf{E}[C_N - C_0] \geq 0.$$

By the first and second items of Lemma 4, we have $\mathbf{E}[\Phi(\boldsymbol{T}, \boldsymbol{F}_E^{(N)})] \geq 0$ and $\mathbf{E}[\Phi(\boldsymbol{T}, \boldsymbol{F}_E^{(0)})] \leq CC(\Pi)$. Note that $C_0 = 0$ and C_N equals the total number of iterations because there can never be more than N iterations. Therefore, we get

$$\mathbf{E}[\# \text{ of iterations in the running of E}] = \mathbf{E}[C_N] \leq \frac{CC(\Pi)}{\varepsilon}.$$

So far, we have bounded the expected number of iterations of Algorithm 1 from above; however, Algorithm 1 could make too many queries in the worst case. To prove our main theorem, we need an attacker who makes a bounded number of queries in the worst case. We construct such an attacker by running E for a limited number of iterations.

Theorem 5. *Let* E′ *be an attacker who runs* E *but aborts when the number of iterations exceeds* $\frac{CC(\Pi)}{\varepsilon^{3/2}}$. *Then the following statements hold:*

1. *Efficiency:* E′ *makes at most* $q_{E′} = 2\ell \cdot CC(\Pi)/\varepsilon^{3/2}$ *oracle queries.*
2. *Accuracy: The success probability of* E′ *is at least* γ.

Proof. Efficiency holds because E′ queries at most $CC(\Pi)/\varepsilon^{3/2}$ sets and each set has size at most 2ℓ. As for accuracy, let β, β' be the success probability of E, E′ respectively. By the definition of E′, we have

$$|\beta' - \beta| \leq \mathbf{Pr}\left[E′ \text{ aborts}\right]$$

$$= \mathbf{Pr}\left[\# \text{ of iterations in the running of E is more than } CC(\Pi)/\varepsilon^{3/2}\right].$$

Lemma 5 together with Markov's inequality shows that this quantity is at most $\sqrt{\varepsilon}$. Therefore, we have $\beta' \geq \beta - \sqrt{\varepsilon}$. By the accuracy of E (Corollary 1) and our choice of ε (i.e., $\varepsilon = (1 - \gamma)^2/9$), we obtain $\beta' \geq 1 - \sqrt{2\varepsilon} - \sqrt{\varepsilon} > 1 - 3\sqrt{\varepsilon} = \gamma$.

Proving the Main Theorem. Theorem 4 immediately follows from the above lemma.

Proof (of Theorem 4). Let Π be a protocol that satisfies the conditions of Theorem 4. It suffices to prove $CC(\Pi) \geq \frac{q}{2\ell} \cdot \frac{(1-\gamma)^3}{27}$ (Eq. 2), provided that Π is normalized. Since E′ in theorem 5 succeeds with probability γ and Π is a (q, γ)-secure by assumption, we must have $q_{E′} > q$, which implies

$$CC(\Pi) > \frac{q}{2\ell} \cdot \varepsilon^{3/2} = \frac{q}{2\ell} \cdot \frac{(1 - \gamma)^3}{27}.$$

Acknowledgements. We thank Noam Mazor for presenting us with this intriguing question and for giving the ingenious construction of a key-agreement protocol with perfect completeness. We are grateful to the anonymous reviewers for their insightful comments and suggestions, which have significantly enhanced the presentation of this work.

References

[ACC+22] Young, A., Yung, M.: Kleptography from standard assumptions and applications. In: Garay, J.A., De Prisco, R. (eds.) SCN 2010. LNCS, vol. 6280, pp. 271–290. Springer, Heidelberg (2010). https://doi.org/10.1007/978-3-642-15317-4_18

[ACMS23] Afshar, A., Couteau, G., Mahmoody, M., Sadeghi, E.: Fine-grained non-interactive key-exchange: constructions and lower bounds. In: Hazay, C., Stam, M. (eds.) EUROCRYPT 2023. LNCS, vol. 14004, pp. 55–85. Springer, Heidelberg (2023). https://doi.org/10.1007/978-3-031-30545-0_3

[AHMS20] Applebaum, B., Holenstein, T., Mishra, M., Shayevitz, O.: The communication complexity of private simultaneous messages, revisited. J. Cryptol. **33**(3), 917–953 (2020)

[BBCR10] Barak, B., Braverman, M., Chen, X., Rao, A.: How to compress interactive communication. In: Proceedings of the Forty-Second ACM Symposium on Theory of Computing, pp. 67–76 (2010)

[BKSY11] Brakerski, Z., Katz, J., Segev, G., Yerukhimovich, A.: Limits on the power of zero-knowledge proofs in cryptographic constructions. In: Ishai, Y. (ed.) TCC 2011. LNCS, vol. 6597, pp. 559–578. Springer, Heidelberg (2011). https://doi.org/10.1007/978-3-642-19571-6_34

[BMG09] Barak, B., Mahmoody-Ghidary, M.: Merkle puzzles are optimal–an $O(n^2)$-query attack on any key exchange from a random oracle. In: Halevi, S. (ed.) CRYPTO 2009. LNCS, vol. 5677, pp. 374–390. Springer, Heidelberg (2009). https://doi.org/10.1007/978-3-642-03356-8_22

[CN22] Cohen, S.P., Naor, M.: Low communication complexity protocols, collision resistant hash functions and secret key-agreement protocols. Cryptology ePrint Archive (2022)

[Cou19] Couteau, G.: A note on the communication complexity of multiparty computation in the correlated randomness model. In: Ishai, Y., Rijmen, V. (eds.) EUROCRYPT 2019. LNCS, vol. 11477, pp. 473–503. Springer, Cham (2019). https://doi.org/10.1007/978-3-030-17656-3_17

[CSWY01] Chakrabarti, A., Shi, Y., Wirth, A., Yao, A.: Informational complexity and the direct sum problem for simultaneous message complexity. In: Proceedings 42nd IEEE Symposium on Foundations of Computer Science, pp. 270–278. IEEE (2001)

[DH76] Diffie, W., Hellman, M.: New directions in cryptography. IEEE Trans. Inf. Theory 22(6), 644–654 (1976)

[DH21] Dinur, I., Hasson, B.: Distributed Merkle's puzzles. In: Nissim, K., Waters, B. (eds.) TCC 2021. LNCS, vol. 13043, pp. 310–332. Springer, Cham (2021). https://doi.org/10.1007/978-3-030-90453-1_11

[DSLMM11] Dachman-Soled, D., Lindell, Y., Mahmoody, M., Malkin, T.: On the black-box complexity of optimally-fair coin tossing. In: Ishai, Y. (ed.) TCC 2011. LNCS, vol. 6597, pp. 450–467. Springer, Heidelberg (2011). https://doi.org/10.1007/978-3-642-19571-6_27

[GPW15] Göös, M., Pitassi, T., Watson, T.: Deterministic communication vs. partition number. In: 2015 IEEE 56th Annual Symposium on Foundations of Computer Science, pp. 1077–1088. IEEE (2015)

[GPW17] Göös, M., Pitassi, T., Watson, T.: Query-to-communication lifting for bpp. In: 2017 IEEE 58th Annual Symposium on Foundations of Computer Science (FOCS), pp. 132–143. IEEE (2017)

[HHRS15] Haitner, I., Hoch, J.J., Reingold, O., Segev, G.: Finding collisions in interactive protocols-tight lower bounds on the round and communication complexities of statistically hiding commitments. SIAM J. Comput. 44(1), 193–242 (2015)

[HMO+19] Haitner, I., Mazor, N., Oshman, R., Reingold, O., Yehudayoff, A.: On the communication complexity of key-agreement protocols. In: 10th Innovations in Theoretical Computer Science, vol. 124 of LIPIcs. Leibniz Int. Proc. Inform., Art. No. 40, p. 16. Schloss Dagstuhl. Leibniz-Zent. Inform., Wadern (2019)

[HOZ16] Haitner, I., Omri, E., Zarosim, H.: Limits on the usefulness of random oracles. J. Cryptol. 29(2), 283–335 (2016)

[IR89] Impagliazzo, R., Rudich, S.: Limits on the provable consequences of one-way permutations. In: Proceedings of the Twenty-First Annual ACM Symposium on Theory of Computing, pp. 44–61 (1989)

[KSY11] Katz, J., Schröder, D., Yerukhimovich, A.: Impossibility of blind signatures from one-way permutations. In: Ishai, Y. (ed.) TCC 2011. LNCS, vol. 6597, pp. 615–629. Springer, Heidelberg (2011). https://doi.org/10.1007/978-3-642-19571-6_37

[Maz23] Mazor, N.: Key-agreement with perfect completeness from random oracles. Cryptology ePrint Archive (2023)

[Mer78] Merkle, R.C.: Secure communications over insecure channels. Commun. ACM **21**(4), 294–299 (1978)

[MMV11] Mahmoody, M., Moran, T., Vadhan, S.: Time-lock puzzles in the random oracle model. In: Rogaway, P. (ed.) CRYPTO 2011. LNCS, vol. 6841, pp. 39–50. Springer, Heidelberg (2011). https://doi.org/10.1007/978-3-642-22792-9_3

[MP12] Mahmoody, M., Pass, R.: The curious case of non-interactive commitments – on the power of black-box vs. non-black-box use of primitives. In: Safavi-Naini, R., Canetti, R. (eds.) CRYPTO 2012. LNCS, vol. 7417, pp. 701–718. Springer, Heidelberg (2012). https://doi.org/10.1007/978-3-642-32009-5_41

[RM97] Raz, R., McKenzie, P.: Separation of the monotone NC hierarchy. In: Proceedings 38th Annual Symposium on Foundations of Computer Science, pp. 234–243. IEEE (1997)

[YZ22] Yang, G., Zhang, J.: Simulation methods in communication complexity, revisited. In: Electron. Colloquium Comput. Complex., TR22-019 (2022)

[YZ23] Yang, G., Zhang, J.: Lifting theorems meet information complexity: known and new lower bounds of set-disjointness (2023)

Searching for ELFs in the Cryptographic Forest

Marc Fischlin[✉][iD] and Felix Rohrbach[iD]

Cryptoplexity, Technische Universität Darmstadt, Darmstadt, Germany
{marc.fischlin,felix.rohrbach}@cryptoplexity.de
http://www.cryptoplexity.de

Abstract. Extremely Lossy Functions (ELFs) are families of functions that, depending on the choice during key generation, either operate in injective mode or instead have only a polynomial image size. The choice of the mode is indistinguishable to an outsider. ELFs were introduced by Zhandry (Crypto 2016) and have been shown to be very useful in replacing random oracles in a number of applications.

One open question is to determine the minimal assumption needed to instantiate ELFs. While all constructions of ELFs depend on some form of exponentially-secure public-key primitive, it was conjectured that exponentially-secure secret-key primitives, such as one-way functions, hash functions or one-way product functions, might be sufficient to build ELFs. In this work we answer this conjecture mostly negative: We show that no primitive, which can be derived from a random oracle (which includes all secret-key primitives mentioned above), is enough to construct even moderately lossy functions in a black-box manner. However, we also show that (extremely) lossy functions themselves do not imply public-key cryptography, leaving open the option to build ELFs from some intermediate primitive between the classical categories of secret-key and public-key cryptography. (The full version can be found at https://eprint.iacr.org/2023/1403.)

1 Introduction

Extremely lossy functions, or short ELFs, are collections of functions that support two modes: the injective mode, in which each image has exactly one preimage, and the lossy mode, in which the function merely has a polynomial image size. The mode is defined by a seed or public key pk which parameterizes the function. The key pk itself should not reveal whether it describes the injective mode or the lossy mode. In case the lossy mode does not result in a polynomially-sized image, but the function compresses by at least a factor of 2, we will speak of a (moderately) lossy function (LF).

Extremely lossy functions were introduced by Zhandry [31,32] to replace the use of the random oracle model in some cases. The random oracle model (ROM) [4] introduces a truly random function to which all parties have access to. This random function turned out to be useful in modeling hash functions for security proofs of real-world protocols. However, such a truly random function

© International Association for Cryptologic Research 2023
G. Rothblum and H. Wee (Eds.): TCC 2023, LNCS 14371, pp. 207–236, 2023.
https://doi.org/10.1007/978-3-031-48621-0_8

clearly does not exist in reality and it has been shown that no hash function can replace such an oracle without some protocols becoming insecure [11]. Therefore, a long line of research aims to replace the random oracle by different modeling of hash functions, e.g., by the notion of correlation intractability [11] or by Universal Computational Extractors (UCEs) [3]. However, all these attempts seem to have their own problems: Current constructions of correlation intractability require extremely strong assumptions [10], while for UCEs, it is not quite clear which versions are instantiable [5,9]. Extremely lossy functions, in turn, can be built from relatively standard assumptions.

Indeed, it turns out that extremely lossy functions are useful in removing the need for a random oracle in many applications: Zhandry shows it can be used to generically boost selective security to adaptive security in signatures and identity-based encryption, construct a hash function which is output intractable, point obfuscation in the presence of auxiliary information and many more [31,32]. Agrikola, Couteau and Hofheinz [1] show that ELFs can be used to construct probabilistic indistinguishability obfuscation from only polynomially-secure indistinguishability obfuscation. In 2022, Murphy, O'Neill and Zaheri [23] used ELFs to give full instantiations of the OAEP and Fujisaki-Okamoto transforms. Recently, Brzuska et al. [8] improve on the instantiation of the Fujisaki-Okamoto transform and instantiate the hash-then-evaluate paradigm for pseudorandom functions using ELFs.

While maybe not as popular as their extreme counterpart, moderately lossy functions have their own applications as well: Braverman, Hassidim and Kalai [7] build leakage-resistant pseudo-entropy functions from lossy functions, and Dodis, Vaikuntanathan and Wichs [12] use lossy functions to construct extractor-dependent extractors with auxiliary information.

1.1   Our Contributions

One important open question for extremely lossy functions, as well as for moderately lossy functions, is the minimal assumption to build them. The constructions presented by Zhandry are based on the exponential security of the decisional Diffie-Hellman problem, but he conjectures that public-key cryptography should not be necessary and suggests for future work to try to construct ELFs from exponentially-secure symmetric primitives (As Zhandry shows as well in his work, polynomial security assumptions are unlikely to be enough for ELFs[1]). Holmgren and Lombardi [17] wondered whether their definition of one-way product functions might suffice to construct ELFs.

For moderately lossy functions, the picture is quite similar: While all current constructions require (polynomially-secure) public-key cryptography, it is gen-

---

[1] ELFs can be distinguished efficiently using a super-logarithmic amount of non-determinism. It is consistent with our knowledge, however, that NP with an super-logarithmic amount of non-determinism is solvable in polynomial time while polynomially-secure cryptographic primitives exist. Any construction of ELFs from polynomially-secure cryptographic primitives would therefore change our understanding of NP-hardness.

erally assumed that public-key cryptography should not be necessary for them and that private-key assumptions should suffice (see, e.g., [28]).

In this work, we answer the questions about building (extremely) lossy functions from symmetric-key primitive mostly negative: There exists no fully-black box construction of extremely lossy functions, or even moderately lossy functions, from a large number of primitives, including exponentially-secure one-way functions, exponentially-secure collision resistant hash functions or one-way product functions. Indeed, any primitive that exists unconditionally relative to a random oracle is not enough. We will call this family of primitives *Oraclecrypt*, in reference to the famous naming convention by Impagliazzo [19], in which Minicrypt refers to the family of primitives that can be built from one-way functions in a black-box way.

Note that most of the previous reductions and impossibility results, such as the renowned result about the impossibility of building key exchange protocols from black-box one-wayness [20], are in fact already cast in the Oraclecrypt world. We only use this term to emphasize that we also rule out primitives that are usually not included in Minicrypt, like collision resistant hash functions [30].

On the other hand, we show that public-key primitives might not strictly be needed to construct ELFs or moderately lossy functions. Specifically, we show that no fully black-box construction of key agreement is possible from (moderately) lossy functions, and extend this result to prevent any fully black-box construction even from extremely lossy functions (for a slightly weaker setting, though). This puts the primitives lossy functions and extremely lossy functions into the intermediate area between the two classes Oraclecrypt and Public-Key Cryptography.

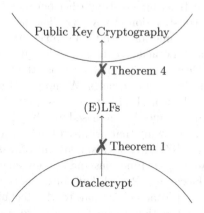

Fig. 1. We show both an oracle separation between Oraclecrypt and (E)LFs as well as (E)LFs and key agreement.

Finally, we discuss the relationship of lossy functions to hard-on-average problems in SZK, the class of problems that have a statistical zero-knowledge proof. We see hard-on-average SZK as a promising minimal assumption to build lossy functions from – indeed, it is already known that hard-on-average SZK problems follow from lossy functions with sufficient lossiness. While we leave open the question of building such a construction for future work, we give a lower bound for hard-on-average SZK problems that might be of independent interest, showing that hard-on-average SZK problems cannot be built from any Oraclecrypt primitive in a fully black-box way. While this is already known for some primitives in Oraclecrypt [6], these results do not generalize to all Oraclecrypt primitives as our proof does.

Note that all our impossibility results only rule out black-box constructions, leaving the possibility of future non-black-box constructions. However, while there is a growing number of non-black-box constructions in the area of cryptography, the overwhelming majority of constructions are still black-box constructions. Further, as all mentioned primitives like exponentially-secure one-way functions, extremely lossy functions or key agreement might exist unconditionally, ruling out black-box constructions is the best we can hope for to show that a construction probably does not exist.

1.2   Our Techniques

Our separation of Oraclecrypt primitives and extremely/moderately lossy functions is based on the famous oracle separation by Impagliazzo and Rudich [20]: We first introduce a strong oracle that makes sure no complexity-based cryptography exists unconditionally, and then add an independent random oracle that allows for specific cryptographic primitives (specifically, all Oraclecrypt primitives) to exist again. We then show that relative to these oracles, (extremely) lossy functions do not exist by constructing a distinguisher between the injective and lossy mode for any candidate construction. A key ingredient here is that we can identify the *heavy queries* in a lossy function with high probability with just polynomially many queries to the random oracle, a common technique used for example in the work by Bitansky and Degwekar [6]. Finally, we use the two-oracle technique by Hsiao and Reyzin [18] to fix a set of oracles. We note that our proof technique is similar to a technique in the work by Pietrzak, Rosen and Segev to show that the lossiness of lossy functions cannot be increased well in a black-box way [27]. Our separation result for SZK, showing that primitives in Oraclecrypt may not suffice to derive hard problems in SZK, follows a similar line of reasoning.

Our separation between lossy functions and key agreement is once more based on the work by Impagliazzo and Rudich [20], but this time using their specific result for key agreement protocols. Similar to the techniques in [14], we try to compile out the lossy function to be then able to apply the Impagliazzo-Rudich adversary: We first show that one can build (extremely) lossy function oracles relative to a random oracle (where the lossy function itself is efficiently computable via oracle calls, but internally makes an exponentially number of random oracle evaluations). The heart of our separation is then a simulation lemma showing that any efficient game relative to our (extremely) lossy function oracle can be simulated efficiently and sufficiently close given only access to a random oracle. Here, sufficiently close means an inverse polynomial gap between the two cases but where the polynomial can be set arbitrarily. Given this we can apply the key agreement separation result of Impagliazzo and Rudich [20], with a careful argument that the simulation gap does not infringe with their separation.

1.3 Related Work

Lossy Trapdoor Functions. Lossy trapdoor functions were defined by Peikert and Waters in [25,26] who exclusively considered such functions to have a trapdoor in injective mode. Whenever we talk about lossy functions in this work, we refer to the moderate version of extremely lossy functions which does not necessarily have a trapdoor. The term extremely lossy function (ELFs) is used as before to capture strongly compressing lossy functions, once more without requiring a trapdoor for the injective case.

Targeted Lossy Functions. Targeted lossy functions were introduced by Quach, Waters and Wichs [28] and are a relaxed version of lossy functions in which the lossiness only applies to a small set of specified inputs. The motivation of the authors is the lack of progress in creating lossy functions from other assumptions than public-key cryptography. Targeted lossy functions, however, can be built from Minicrypt assumptions, and, as the authors show, already suffices for many applications, such as construct extractor-dependent extractors with auxiliary information and pseudo-entropy functions. Our work very much supports this line of research, as it shows that any further progress in creating lossy functions from Minicrypt/Oraclecrypt assumptions is unlikely (barring some construction using non-black-box techniques) and underlines the need of such a relaxation for lossy functions, if one wants to build them from Minicrypt assumptions.

Amplification of Lossy Functions. Pietrzak, Rosen and Segev [27] show that it is impossible to improve the relative lossiness of a lossy function in a black-box way by more than a logarithmic amount. This translates into another obstacle in building ELFs, even when having access to a moderately lossy function. Note that this result strengthens our result, as we show that even moderately lossy functions cannot be built from anything in Oraclecrypt.

2   Preliminaries

This is a shortened version of the preliminaries, omitting some standard definitions. The full version [13] of the paper contains the complete preliminaries.

2.1   Lossy Functions

A lossy function can be either injective or compressing, depending on the mode the public key pk has been generated with. The desired mode (inj or loss) is passed as argument to a (randomized) key generating algorithm Gen, together with the security parameter 1^λ. We sometimes write $\mathsf{pk}_{\mathsf{inj}}$ or $\mathsf{pk}_{\mathsf{loss}}$ to emphasize that the public key has been generated in either mode, and also $\mathsf{Gen}_{\mathsf{inj}}(\cdot) = \mathsf{Gen}(\cdot, \mathsf{inj})$ as well as $\mathsf{Gen}_{\mathsf{loss}}(\cdot) = \mathsf{Gen}(\cdot, \mathsf{loss})$ to explicitly refer to key generation in injective and lossy mode, respectively. The type of key is indistinguishable to outsiders. This holds even though the adversary can evaluate the function via deterministic algorithm Eval under this key, taking 1^λ, a key pk and a value x of input length $\mathsf{in}(\lambda)$ as input, and returning an image $f_{\mathsf{pk}}(x)$ of an implicitly defined function f. We usually assume that 1^λ is included in pk and thus omit 1^λ for Eval's input.

In the literature, one can find two slightly different definitions of lossy function. One, which we call the strict variant, requires that for any key generated in injective or lossy mode, the corresponding function is perfectly injective or lossy. In the non-strict variant this only has to hold with overwhelming probability over the choice of the key pk. We define both variants together:

Definition 1 (Lossy Functions). *An ω-lossy function consists of two efficient algorithms* (Gen, Eval) *of which Gen is probabilistic and Eval is deterministic and it holds that:*

(a) *For* $\mathsf{pk}_{\mathsf{inj}} \leftarrow\!\!{\$}\ \mathsf{Gen}(1^\lambda, \mathsf{inj})$ *the function* $\mathsf{Eval}(\mathsf{pk}_{\mathsf{inj}}, \cdot) : \{0,1\}^{\mathsf{in}(\lambda)} \to \{0,1\}^*$ *is injective with overwhelming probability over the choice of* $\mathsf{pk}_{\mathsf{inj}}$.

(b) *For* $\mathsf{pk}_{\mathsf{loss}} \leftarrow\!\!{\$}\ \mathsf{Gen}(1^\lambda, \mathsf{loss})$, *the function* $\mathsf{Eval}(\mathsf{pk}_{\mathsf{loss}}, \cdot) : \{0,1\}^{\mathsf{in}(\lambda)} \to \{0,1\}^*$ *is ω-compressing i.e.,* $\left|\{\mathsf{Eval}(\mathsf{pk}_{\mathsf{loss}}, \{0,1\}^{\mathsf{in}(\lambda)})\}\right| \le 2^{\mathsf{in}(\lambda)-\omega}$, *with overwhelming probability over the choice of* $\mathsf{pk}_{\mathsf{loss}}$.

(c) *The random variables* $\mathsf{Gen}_{\mathsf{inj}}$ *and* $\mathsf{Gen}_{\mathsf{loss}}$ *are computationally indistinguishable.*

We call the function strict *if properties (a) and (b) hold with probability 1.*

Extremely lossy functions need a more fine-grained approach where the key generation algorithm takes an integer r between 1 and $2^{\mathsf{in}(\lambda)}$ instead of inj or loss. This integer determines the image size, with $r = 2^{\mathsf{in}(\lambda)}$ asking for an injective function. As we want to have functions with a sufficiently high lossiness that the image size is polynomial, say, $p(\lambda)$, we cannot allow for any polynomial adversary. This is so because an adversary making $p(\lambda) + 1$ many random (but distinct) queries to the evaluating function will find a collision in case that pk was lossy, while no collision will be found for an injective key. Instead, we define the minimal r such that $\mathsf{Gen}(1^\lambda, 2^\lambda)$ and $\mathsf{Gen}(1^\lambda, r)$ are indistinguishable based on the runtime and desired advantage of the adversary:

Definition 2 (Extremely Lossy Function). *An extremely lossy function consists of two efficient algorithms* (Gen, Eval) *of which Gen is probabilistic and Eval is deterministic and it holds that:*

(a) *For* $r = 2^{in(\lambda)}$ *and* $\mathsf{pk} \leftarrow\!\!{\$}\ \mathsf{Gen}(1^\lambda, r)$ *the function* $\mathsf{Eval}(\mathsf{pk}, \cdot) : \{0,1\}^{in(\lambda)} \to \{0,1\}^*$ *is injective with overwhelming probability.*

(b) *For* $r < 2^{in(\lambda)}$ *and* $\mathsf{pk} \leftarrow\!\!{\$}\ \mathsf{Gen}(1^\lambda, r)$ *the function* $\mathsf{Eval}(\mathsf{pk}, \cdot) : \{0,1\}^{in(\lambda)} \to \{0,1\}^*$ *has an image size of at most r with overwhelming probability.*

(c) *For any polynomials p and d there exists a polynomial q such that for any adversary $\mathcal{A}$ with a runtime bounded by $p(\lambda)$ and any $r \in [q(\lambda), 2^{in(\lambda)}]$, algorithm $\mathcal{A}$ distinguishes $\mathsf{Gen}(1^\lambda, 2^{in(\lambda)})$ from $\mathsf{Gen}(1^\lambda, r)$ with advantage at most $\frac{1}{d(\lambda)}$.*

Note that extremely lossy functions do indeed imply the definition of (moderately) lossy functions (as long as the lossiness-parameter ω still leaves an exponential-sized image size in the lossy mode):

Lemma 1. *Let* (Gen, Eval) *be an extremely lossy function. Then* (Gen, Eval) *is also a (moderately) lossy function with lossiness parameter $\omega = 0.9\lambda$.*

The proof for this lemma can be found in the full version [13].

2.2   Oraclecrypt

In his seminal work [19], Impagliazzo introduced five possible worlds we might be living in, including two in which computational cryptography exists: Minicrypt, in which one-way functions exist, but public-key cryptography does not, and Cryptomania, in which public-key cryptography exists as well. In reference to this classification, cryptographic primitives that can be built from one-way functions in a black-box way are often called Minicrypt primitives.

In this work, we are interested in the set of all primitives that exist relative to a truly random function. This of course includes all Minicrypt primitives, as one-way functions exist relative to a truly random function (with high probability), but it also includes a number of other primitives, like collision-resistant hash functions and exponentially-secure one-way functions, for which we don't know that they exist relative to a one-way function, or even have a black-box impossibility result. In reference to the set of Minicrypt primitives, we will call all primitives existing relative to a truly random function *Oraclecrypt* primitives.

Definition 3 (Oraclecrypt). *We say that a cryptographic primitive is an Oraclecrypt primitive, if there exists an implementation relative to truly random function oracle (except for a measure zero of random oracles).*

We will now show that by this definition, indeed, many symmetric primitives are Oraclecrypt primitives:

Lemma 2. *The following primitives are Oraclecrypt primitives:*

– *Exponentially-secure one-way functions,*
– *Exponentially-secure collision resistant hash functions,*
– *One-way product functions.*

We moved the proof for this lemma to the full version [13].

3   On the Impossibility of Building (E)LFs in Oraclecrypt

In this chapter, we will show that we cannot build lossy functions from a number of symmetric primitives, including (exponentially-secure) one-way functions, collision-resistant hash functions and one-way product functions, in a black-box way. Indeed, we will show that any primitive in Oraclecrypt is not enough to build lossy functions. As extremely lossy functions imply (moderately) lossy functions, this result applies to them as well.

Note that for exponentially-secure one-way functions, this was already known for lossy functions that are sufficiently lossy: Lossy functions with sufficient lossiness imply collision-resistant hash functions, and Simon's result [30] separates these from (exponentially-secure) one-way functions. However, this does not apply for lossy functions with e.g. only a constant number of bits of lossiness.

Theorem 1. *There exists no fully black-box construction of lossy functions from any Oraclecrypt primitive, including exponentially-secure one-way functions, collision resistant hash functions, and one-way product functions.*

Our proof for this Theorem follows a proof idea by Pietrzak, Rosen and Segev [27], which they used to show that lossy functions cannot be amplified well, i.e., one cannot build a lossy function which is very compressing in the lossy mode from a lossy function that is only slightly compressing in the lossy mode. Conceptually, we show an oracle separation between lossy functions and Oraclecrypt: For this, we will start by introducing two oracles, a random oracle and a modified PSPACE oracle. We will then, for a candidate construction of a lossy function based on the random oracle and a public key pk, approximate the heavy queries asked by $\mathsf{Eval}(\mathsf{pk}, \cdot)$ to the random oracle. Next, we show that this approximation of the set of heavy queries is actually enough for us approximating the image size of $\mathsf{Eval}(\mathsf{pk}, \cdot)$ (using our modified PSPACE oracle) and therefore gives an efficient way to distinguish lossy keys from injective keys. Finally, we have to fix a set of oracles (instead of arguing with a distribution of oracles) and then use the two-oracle technique [18] to show the theorem. Due to the use of the two-oracle techique, we only get an impossibility result for *fully* black-box constructions (see [18] and [2] for a discussion of different types of black-box constructions).

3.1   Introducing the Oracles

A common oracle to use in an oracle separation in cryptography is the PSPACE oracle, as relative to this oracle, all non-information theoretic cryptography is broken. As we do not know which (or whether any) cryptographic primitives exist unconditionally, this is a good way to level the playing field. However, in our case, PSPACE is not quite enough. In our proof, we want to calculate the image size of a function relative to a (newly chosen) random oracle. It is not possible to simulate this oracle by lazy-sampling, though, as to calculate the image size of a function, we might have to save an exponentially large set of queries, which is not possible in PSPACE. Therefore, we give the PSPACE oracle access to its own random oracle $\mathcal{O}' : \{0,1\}^\lambda \to \{0,1\}^\lambda$ and will give every adversary access to PSPACE$^{\mathcal{O}'}$.

The second oracle is a random oracle $\mathcal{O} : \{0,1\}^\lambda \to \{0,1\}^\lambda$. Now, we know that a number of primitives exist relative to a random function, including exponentially-secure one-way functions, collision-resistant hash functions and even more complicated primitives like one-way product functions. Further, they still exist if we give the adversary access to PSPACE$^{\mathcal{O}'}$, too, as $\mathcal{O}'$ is independent from $\mathcal{O}$ and PSPACE$^{\mathcal{O}'}$ does not have direct access to $\mathcal{O}$.

We will now show that every candidate construction of a lossy function with access to $\mathcal{O}$ can be broken by an adversary $\mathcal{A}^{\mathcal{O},\text{PSPACE}^{\mathcal{O}'}}$. Note that we do not give the construction access to PSPACE$^{\mathcal{O}'}$—this is necessary, as $\mathcal{O}'$ should look like a randomly sampled oracle to the construction. However, giving the construction access to PSPACE$^{\mathcal{O}'}$ would enable the construction to behave differently for this specific oracle $\mathcal{O}'$. Not giving the construction access to the oracle is fine, however, as we are using the two-oracle technique.

Our proof for Theorem 1 will now work in two steps. First, we will show that with overwhelming probability over independently sampled $\mathcal{O}$ and $\mathcal{O}'$, no lossy functions exist relative to $\mathcal{O}$ and PSPACE$^{\mathcal{O}'}$. However, for an oracle separation, we need one fixed oracle. Therefore, as a second step (Sect. 3.4), we will use standard techniques to select one set of oracles relative to which any of our Oraclecrypt primitives exist, but lossy functions do not.

For the first step, we will now define how our definition of lossy functions with access to both oracles looks like:

Definition 4 (Lossy functions with Oracle Access). *A family of functions* $\mathsf{Eval}^{\mathcal{O}}(\mathsf{pk}, \cdot) : \{0,1\}^{in(\lambda)} \to \{0,1\}^*$ *with public key* pk *and access to the oracles* $\mathcal{O}$ *is called ω-lossy if there exist two PPT algorithms* Gen_{inj} *and* Gen_{loss} *such that for all* $\lambda \in \mathbb{N}$,

(a) *For all* pk *in* $[\mathsf{Gen}_{inj}^{\mathcal{O}}(1^\lambda)] \cup [\mathsf{Gen}_{loss}^{\mathcal{O}}(1^\lambda)]$, $\mathsf{Eval}^{\mathcal{O}}(\mathsf{pk}, \cdot)$ *is computable in polynomial time in* λ,
(b) *For* $\mathsf{pk} \leftarrow\!\!\$\, \mathsf{Gen}_{inj}^{\mathcal{O}}(1^\lambda)$, $\mathsf{Eval}^{\mathcal{O}}(\mathsf{pk}, \cdot)$ *is injective with overwhelming probability (over the choice of* pk *as well as the random oracle* $\mathcal{O}$*),*
(c) *For* $\mathsf{pk} \leftarrow\!\!\$\, \mathsf{Gen}_{loss}^{\mathcal{O}}(1^\lambda)$, $\mathsf{Eval}^{\mathcal{O}}(\mathsf{pk}, \cdot)$ *is ω-compressing with overwhelming probability (over the choice of* pk *as well as the random oracle* $\mathcal{O}$*)*
(d) *The random variables* $\mathsf{Gen}_{inj}^{\mathcal{O}}$ *and* $\mathsf{Gen}_{loss}^{\mathcal{O}}$ *are computationally indistinguishable for any polynomial-time adversary* $\mathcal{A}^{\mathcal{O},\text{PSPACE}^{\mathcal{O}'}}$ *with access to both* $\mathcal{O}$ *and* PSPACE$^{\mathcal{O}'}$.

3.2 Approximating the Set of Heavy Queries

In the next two subsections, we will construct an adversary $\mathcal{A}^{\mathcal{O},\text{PSPACE}^{\mathcal{O}'}}$ against lossy functions with access to the random oracle $\mathcal{O}$ as described in Definition 4.

Let $(\mathsf{Gen}^{\mathcal{O}}, \mathsf{Eval}^{\mathcal{O}})$ be some candidate implementation of a lossy function relative to the oracle $\mathcal{O}$. Further, let $\mathsf{pk} \leftarrow \mathsf{Gen}_?^{\mathcal{O}}$ be some public key generated by either $\mathsf{Gen}_{\mathsf{inj}}$ or $\mathsf{Gen}_{\mathsf{loss}}$. Looking at the queries asked by the lossy function to $\mathcal{O}$, we can divide them into two parts: The queries asked during the generation of the key pk, and the queries asked during the execution of $\mathsf{Eval}^{\mathcal{O}}(\mathsf{pk}, \cdot)$. We will denote the queries asked during the generation of pk by the set Q_G. As the generation algorithm has to be efficient, Q_G has polynomial size. Let k_G be the maximal number of queries asked by any of the two generators. Further, denote by k_f the maximum number of queries of $\mathsf{Eval}^{\mathcal{O}}(\mathsf{pk}, x)$ for any pk and x—again, k_f is polynomial. Finally, let $k = \max\{k_G, k_f\}$.

The set of all queries done by $\mathsf{Eval}(\mathsf{pk},)$ for a fixed key pk might be of exponential size, as the function might ask different queries for each input x. However, we are able to shrink the size of the relevant subset significantly, if we concentrate on *heavy* queries—queries that appear for a significant fraction of all inputs x:

Definition 5 (Heavy Queries). *Let k be the maximum number of $\mathcal{O}$-queries made by the generator $\mathsf{Gen}_?^{\mathcal{O}}$, or the maximum number of queries of $\mathsf{Eval}(\mathsf{pk}, \cdot)$ over all inputs $x \in \{0,1\}^{in(\lambda)}$, whichever is higher. Fix some key pk and a random oracle $\mathcal{O}$. We call a query q to $\mathcal{O}$ heavy if, for at least a $\frac{1}{10k}$-fraction of $x \in \{0,1\}^{in(\lambda)}$, the evaluation $\mathsf{Eval}(\mathsf{pk}, x)$ queries $\mathcal{O}$ about q at some point. We denote by Q_H the set of all heavy queries (for $\mathsf{pk}, \mathcal{O}$).*

The set of heavy queries is polynomial, as $\mathsf{Eval}^{\mathcal{O}}(\mathsf{pk}, \cdot)$ only queries the oracle a polynomial number of times and each heavy query has to appear in a polynomial fraction of all x. Further, we will show that the adversary $\mathcal{A}^{\mathcal{O}, \mathrm{PSPACE}^{\mathcal{O}'}}$ is able to approximate the set of heavy queries, and that this approximation is actually enough to decide whether pk was generated in injective or in lossy mode. We will start with a few key observations that help us prove this statement.

The first one is that the generator, as it is an efficiently-computable function, will only query $\mathcal{O}$ at polynomially-many positions, and these polynomially-many queries already define whether the function is injective or lossy:

Observation 1. *Let Q_G denote the queries by the generator. For a random $\mathsf{pk} \leftarrow \mathsf{Gen}_{\mathsf{inj}}^{\mathcal{O}}$ generated in injective mode and a random $\mathcal{O}'$ that is consistent with Q_G, the image size of $\mathsf{Eval}^{\mathcal{O}'}(\mathsf{pk}, \cdot)$ is 2^{λ} (except with a negligible probability over the choice of pk and $\mathcal{O}'$). Similarly, for a random $\mathsf{pk} \leftarrow \mathsf{Gen}_{\mathsf{loss}}^{\mathcal{O}}$ generated in lossy mode and a random $\mathcal{O}'$ that is consistent with Q_G, the image size of $\mathsf{Eval}^{\mathcal{O}'}(\mathsf{pk}, \cdot)$ is at most $2^{\lambda-1}$ (except with a negligible probability over the choice of pk and $\mathcal{O}'$).*

This follows directly from the definition: As $\mathsf{Gen}_?^{\mathcal{O}}$ has no information about $\mathcal{O}$ except the queries Q_G, properties (2) and (3) of Definition 1 have to hold for every random oracle that is consistent with $\mathcal{O}$ on Q_G. We will use this multiple times in the proof to argue that queries to $\mathcal{O}$ that are not in Q_G are, essentially, useless randomness for the construction, as the construction has to work with almost any possible answer returned by these queries.

An adversary is probably very much interested in learning the queries Q_G. There is no way to capture them in general, though. Here, we need our second key observation. Lossiness is very much a global property: to switch a function from lossy to injective, at least half of all inputs x to $\mathsf{Eval}^{\mathcal{O}}(\mathsf{pk}, x)$ must produce a different result, and vice versa. However, as we learned from the first observation, whether $\mathsf{Eval}^{\mathcal{O}}(\mathsf{pk}, \cdot)$ is lossy or injective, depends just on Q_G. Therefore, some queries in Q_G must be used over and over again for different inputs x—and will therefore appear in the heavy set Q_H. Further, due to the heaviness of these queries, the adversary is indeed able to learn them!

Our proof works alongside these two observations: First, we show in Lemma 3 that for any candidate lossy function, an adversary is able to compute a set $\hat{Q}_H$ of the interesting heavy queries. Afterwards, we show in Lemma 5 that we can use $\hat{Q}_H$ to decide whether $\mathsf{Eval}^{\mathcal{O}}(\mathsf{pk}, \cdot)$ is lossy or injective, breaking the indistinguishability property of the lossy function.

Lemma 3. *Let* $\mathsf{Eval}^{\mathcal{O}}(\mathsf{pk}, \cdot)$ *be a (non-strict) lossy function and* $\mathsf{pk} \leftarrow \mathsf{Gen}^{\mathcal{O}}_?(1^{\lambda})$ *for oracle* $\mathcal{O}$. *Then we can compute in probabilistic polynomial-time (in* λ) *a set* $\hat{Q}_H$ *which contains all heavy queries of* $\mathsf{Eval}^{\mathcal{O}}(\mathsf{pk}, \cdot)$ *for* $\mathsf{pk}, \mathcal{O}$ *with overwhelming probability.*

Proof. To find the heavy queries we will execute $\mathsf{Eval}^{\mathcal{O}}(\mathsf{pk}, x)$ for t random inputs x and record all queries to $\mathcal{O}$ in $\hat{Q}_H$. We will now argue that, with high probability, $\hat{Q}_H$ contains all heavy queries.

First, recall that a query is heavy if it appears for at least an ε-fraction of inputs to $\mathsf{Eval}^{\mathcal{O}}(\mathsf{pk}, \cdot)$ for $\varepsilon = \frac{1}{10k}$. Therefore, the probability for any specific heavy query q_{heavy} to not appear in $\hat{Q}_H$ after the t evaluations can be bounded by

$$\Pr\left[q_{\mathsf{heavy}} \notin \hat{Q}_H\right] = (1 - \varepsilon)^t \le 2^{-\varepsilon t}.$$

Furthermore, there exist at most $\frac{k}{\varepsilon}$ heavy queries, because each heavy query accounts for at least $\varepsilon \cdot 2^{\mathrm{in}(\lambda)}$ of the at most $k \cdot 2^{\mathrm{in}(\lambda)}$ possible queries of $\mathsf{Eval}^{\mathcal{O}}(\mathsf{pk}, x)$ when iterating over all x. Therefore, the probability that any heavy query q_{heavy} is not included in $\hat{Q}_H$ is given by

$$\Pr\left[\exists q_{\mathsf{heavy}} \notin \hat{Q}_H\right] \le \frac{k}{\varepsilon} \cdot 2^{-\varepsilon t}$$

Choosing $t = 10k\lambda$ we get

$$\Pr\left[\exists q_{\mathsf{heavy}} \notin \hat{Q}_H\right] \le 10k^2 \cdot 2^{-\lambda}$$

which is negligible. Therefore, with all but negligible probability, all heavy queries are included in $\hat{Q}_H$. □

3.3   Distinguishing Lossiness from Injectivity

We next make the transition from oracle $\mathcal{O}$ to our PSPACE-augmenting oracle $\mathcal{O}'$. According to the previous subsection, we can compute (a superset $\hat{Q}_H$

of) the heavy queries efficiently. Then we can fix the answers of oracle $\mathcal{O}$ on such frequently asked queries in $\hat{Q}_H$, but otherwise use the independent oracle $\mathcal{O}'$ instead. Denote this partly-set oracle by $\mathcal{O}'_{|\hat{Q}_H}$. Then the distinguisher for injective and lossy keys, given some pk, can approximate the image size of $\#im(\text{Eval}^{\mathcal{O}'_{|\hat{Q}_H}}(\text{pk},\cdot))$ with the help of its PSPACE$^{\mathcal{O}'}$ oracle and thus also derives a good approximimation for the actual oracle $\mathcal{O}$. This will be done in Lemma 5.

We still have to show that the non-heavy queries do not violate the above approach. According to the proof of Lemma 4 it suffices to look at the case that the image sizes of oracles $\mathcal{R} := \mathcal{O}'_{|\hat{Q}_H}$ and for oracle $\mathcal{R}' := \mathcal{O}'_{|\hat{Q}_H \cup Q_G}$, where we als fix on the key generator's non-heavy queries to values from $\mathcal{O}$, cannot differ significantly. Put differently, missing out the generator's non-heavy queries Q_G in $\hat{Q}_H$ only slightly affects the image size of $\text{Eval}^{\mathcal{O}'_{|\hat{Q}_H}}(\text{pk},\cdot)$, and we can proceed with our approach to consider only heavy queries.

Lemma 4. *Let* pk $\leftarrow$ Gen$_?^{\mathcal{R}}(1^\lambda)$ *and* $Q_G^{nonh} = \{q_1,\ldots,q_{k'}\}$ *be the k' generator's queries to $\mathcal{R}$ in Q_G when computing* pk *that are not heavy for* pk, $\mathcal{R}$. *Then, for any oracle $\mathcal{R}'$ that is identical to $\mathcal{R}$ everywhere except for the queries in Q_G^{nonh}, i.e., $\mathcal{R}(q) = \mathcal{R}'(q)$ for any $q \notin Q_G^{nonh}$, the image sizes of* Eval$^{\mathcal{R}}(\text{pk},\cdot)$ *and* Eval$^{\mathcal{R}'}(\text{pk},\cdot)$ *differ by at most $\frac{2^{in(\lambda)}}{10}$.*

Proof. As the queries in Q_G^{nonh} are non-heavy, every $q_i \in Q_G^{nonh}$ is queried for at most $\frac{2^{in(\lambda)}}{10k}$ inputs x to Eval$^{\mathcal{R}}(\text{pk},\cdot)$ when evaluating the function. Therefore, any change in the oracle $\mathcal{R}$ at $q_i \in Q_G^{nonh}$ affects the output of Eval$^{\mathcal{R}}(\text{pk},\cdot)$ for at most $\frac{2^{in(\lambda)}}{10k}$ inputs. Hence, when considering the oracle $\mathcal{R}'$, which differs from $\mathcal{R}$ only on the k' queries from Q_G^{nonh}, moving from $\mathcal{R}$ to $\mathcal{R}'$ for evaluating Eval$^{\mathcal{R}}(\text{pk},\cdot)$ changes the output for at most $\frac{k'2^{in(\lambda)}}{10k}$ inputs x. In other words, letting Δ_f denote the set of all x such that Eval$^{\mathcal{R}}(\text{pk},x)$ queries some $q \in Q_G^{nonh}$ during the evaluation, we know that

$$|\Delta_f| \le \frac{k'2^{in(\lambda)}}{10k}$$

and

$$\text{Eval}^{\mathcal{R}}(\text{pk},x) = \text{Eval}^{\mathcal{R}'}(\text{pk},x) \text{ for all } x \notin \Delta_f.$$

We are interested in the difference of the two image sizes of Eval$^{\mathcal{R}}(\text{pk},\cdot)$ and Eval$^{\mathcal{R}'}(\text{pk},\cdot)$. Each $x \in \Delta_f$ may add or subtract an image in the difference, depending on whether the modified output Eval$^{\mathcal{R}'}(\text{pk},x)$ introduces a new image or redirects the only image Eval$^{\mathcal{R}}(\text{pk},x)$ to an already existing one. Therefore, the difference between the image sizes is at most

$$\left| \#im(\text{Eval}^{\mathcal{R}}(\text{pk},\cdot)) - \#im(\text{Eval}^{\mathcal{R}'}(\text{pk},\cdot)) \right| \le \frac{k'2^{in(\lambda)}}{10k} \le \frac{2^{in(\lambda)}}{10},$$

where the last inequality is due to $k' \le k$.   □

Lemma 5. *Given $\hat{Q}_H \supseteq Q_H$, we can decide correctly whether $\mathsf{Eval}^{\mathcal{O}}(\mathsf{pk}, \cdot)$ is lossy or injective with overwhelming probability.*

Proof. As described in Sect. 3.1, we give the adversary, who has to distinguish a lossy key from a injective key, access to $\mathrm{PSPACE}^{\mathcal{O}'}$, where $\mathcal{O}'$ is another random oracle sampled independently of $\mathcal{O}$. This is necessary for the adversary, as we want to calculate the image size of $\mathsf{Eval}^{\mathcal{O}'}(\mathsf{pk}, \cdot)$ relative to a random oracle $\mathcal{O}'$, and we cannot do this in PSPACE with lazy sampling.

We will consider the following adversary $\mathcal{A}$: It defines an oracle $\mathcal{O}'_{|\hat{Q}_H}$ that is identical to $\mathcal{O}'$ for all queries $q \notin \hat{Q}_H$ and identical to $\mathcal{O}$ for all queries $q \in \hat{Q}_H$. Then, it calculates the image size

$$\#im(\mathsf{Eval}^{\mathcal{O}'_{|\hat{Q}_H}}(\mathsf{pk}, \cdot)) = \left| \{ \mathsf{Eval}^{\mathcal{O}'_{|\hat{Q}_H}}(\mathsf{pk}, \{0,1\}^{\mathrm{in}(\lambda)}) \} \right| .$$

Note that this can be done efficiently using $\mathrm{PSPACE}^{\mathcal{O}'}$ as well as polynomially many queries to $\mathcal{O}$. If $\#im(\mathsf{Eval}^{\mathcal{O}'_{|\hat{Q}_H}}(\mathsf{pk}, \cdot))$ is bigger than $\frac{3}{4} 2^{\mathrm{in}(\lambda)}$, $\mathcal{A}$ will guess that $\mathsf{Eval}^{\mathcal{O}}(\mathsf{pk}, \cdot)$ is injective, and lossy otherwise. For simplicity reasons, we will assume from now on that pk was generated by $\mathsf{Gen}_{\mathsf{inj}}$—the case where pk was generated by $\mathsf{Gen}_{\mathsf{loss}}$ follows by a symmetric argument.

First, assume that all queries Q_G of the generator are included in $\hat{Q}_H$. In this case, any $\mathcal{O}'$ that is consistent with Q_H is also consistent with all the information $\mathsf{Gen}_{\mathsf{inj}}$ have about $\mathcal{O}$. However, this means that by definition, $\mathsf{Eval}^{\mathcal{O}}(\mathsf{pk}, \cdot)$ has to be injective with overwhelming probability, and therefore, an adversary can easily check whether pk was created by $\mathsf{Gen}_{\mathsf{inj}}$.

Otherwise, let $q_1, \ldots, q_{k'}$ be a set of queries in Q_G which are not included in $\hat{Q}_H$. With overwhelming probability, this means that $q_1, \ldots, q_{k'}$ are all non-heavy. We now apply Lemma 4 for oracles $\mathcal{R} := \mathcal{O}'_{|\hat{Q}_H}$ and $\mathcal{R}' := \mathcal{O}'_{|\hat{Q}_H \cup Q_G}$. These two oracles may only differ on the non-heavy queries in Q_G, where $\mathcal{R}$ coincides with $\mathcal{O}'$ and $\mathcal{R}'$ coincides with $\mathcal{O}$; otherwise the oracles are identical. Lemma 4 tells us that this will change the image size by at most $\frac{2^{\mathrm{in}(\lambda)}}{10}$. Therefore, with overwhelming probability, the image size calculated by the distinguisher is bounded from below by

$$\#im(\mathsf{Eval}^{\mathcal{O}'_{|\hat{Q}_H}}(\mathsf{pk}, \cdot)) \geq 2^{\mathrm{in}(\lambda)} - \frac{2^{\mathrm{in}(\lambda)}}{10} \geq \frac{3}{4} 2^{\mathrm{in}(\lambda)}$$

and the distinguisher will therefore correctly decide that $\mathsf{Eval}^{\mathcal{O}}(\mathsf{pk}, \cdot)$ is in injective mode. $\square$

Theorem 2. *Let $\mathcal{O}$ and $\mathcal{O}'$ be two independent random oracles. Then, with overwhelming probability over the choice of the two random oracles, lossy functions do not exist relative the oracles $\mathcal{O}$ and $\mathrm{PSPACE}^{\mathcal{O}'}$.*

Proof. Given the key pk, our distinguisher (with oracle access to random oracle $\mathcal{O}$) against the injective and lossy mode first runs the algorithm of Lemma 3 to efficiently construct a super set $\hat{Q}_H$ of the heavy queries Q_H for $\mathsf{pk}, \mathcal{O}$. This succeeds with overwhelming probability, and from now on we assume that indeed $Q_H \subseteq \hat{Q}_H$. Then our algorithm continues by running the decision procedure of Lemma 5 to distinguish the cases. Using the $\mathrm{PSPACE}^{\mathcal{O}'}$ oracle, the latter can also be carried out efficiently. □

3.4   Fixing an Oracle

We have shown now (in Theorem 2) that no lossy function exists relative to a random oracle with overwhelming probability. However, to prove our main theorem, we have to show that there exists one fixed oracle relative to which one-way functions (or collision-resistant hash functions, or one-way product functions) exist, but lossy functions do not.

In Lemma 2, we have already shown that (exponentially-secure) one-way functions, collision-resistant hash functions and one-way product functions exist relative to a random oracle with high probability. In the next lemma, we will show that there exists a fixed oracle relative to which exponentially-secure one-way functions exist, but lossy functions do not. The proofs for existence of oracles relative to which exponentially-secure collision-resistant hash functions or one-way product functions, but no lossy functions exist follow similarly.

Lemma 6. *There exists a fixed set of oracles $\mathcal{O}$, $\mathrm{PSPACE}^{\mathcal{O}'}$ such that relative to these oracles, one-way functions using $\mathcal{O}$ exist, but no construction of lossy functions from $\mathcal{O}$ exists.*

Now, our main theorem of this section directly follows from this lemma (and its variants for the other primitives):

Theorem 1 (restated). *There exists no fully black-box construction of lossy functions from any Oraclecrypt primitive, including exponentially-secure one-way functions, collision resistant hash functions, and one-way product functions.*

The proof of Lemma 6 and Theorem 1 follow from standard techniques for fixing oracles and can be found in the full version [13].

4   On the Impossibility of Building Key Agreement Protocols from (Extremely) Lossy Functions

In the previous section we showed that lossy functions cannot be built from many symmetric primitives in a black-box way. This raises the question if lossy functions and extremely lossy functions might be inherent asymmetric primitives. In this section we provide evidence to the contrary, showing that key agreement cannot be built from lossy functions in a black-box way. For this, we adapt the proof by Impagliazzo and Rudich [20] showing that key agreement cannot be built from one-way functions to our setting. We extend this result to also hold for extremely lossy functions, but in a slightly weaker setting.

4.1   Lossy Function Oracle

We specify our lossy function oracle relative to a (random) permutation oracle Π, and further sample (independently of Π) a second random permutation Γ as integral part of our lossy function oracle. The core idea of the oracle is to evaluate $\mathsf{Eval}^{\Gamma,\Pi}(\mathsf{pk}_{\mathsf{inj}}, x) = \Pi(\mathsf{pk}_{\mathsf{inj}}\|ax + b)$ for the injective mode, but set $\mathsf{Eval}^{\Gamma,\Pi}(\mathsf{pk}_{\mathsf{loss}}, x) = \Pi(\mathsf{pk}_{\mathsf{loss}}\|\mathsf{setlsb}(ax+b))$ for the lossy mode, where a, b describe a pairwise independent hash permutation $ax + b$ over the field $GF(2^\mu)$ with $a \neq 0$ and setlsb sets the least significant bit to 0. Then the lossy function is clearly two to one. The values a, b will be chosen during key generation and placed into the public key, but we need to hide them from the adversary in order to make the keys of the two modes indistinguishable. Else a distinguisher, given pk, could check if $\mathsf{Eval}^{\Gamma,\Pi}(\mathsf{pk}, x) = \mathsf{Eval}^{\Gamma,\Pi}(\mathsf{pk}, x')$ for appropriately computed $x \neq x'$ with $\mathsf{setlsb}(ax + b) = \mathsf{setlsb}(ax' + b)$. Therefore, we will use the secret permutation Γ to hide the values in the public key. We will denote the preimage of pk under Γ as pre-key.

Another feature of our construction is to ensure that the adversary cannot generate a lossy key $\mathsf{pk}_{\mathsf{loss}}$ without calling $\mathsf{Gen}^{\Gamma,\Pi}$ in lossy mode, while allowing it to generate keys in injective mode. We accomplish this by having a value k in our public pre-key that is zero for lossy keys and may take any non-zero value for an injective public key. Therefore, with overwhelming probability, any key generated by the adversary without a call to the $\mathsf{Gen}^{\Gamma,\Pi}$ oracle will be an injective key.

We finally put both ideas together. For key generation we hide a, b and also the string k by creating pk as a commitment to the values, $\mathsf{pk} \leftarrow \Gamma(k\|a\|b\|z)$ for random z. To unify calls to Γ in regard of the security parameter λ, we will choose all entries in the range of $\lambda/5$.[2] When receiving pk the evaluation algorithm $\mathsf{Eval}^{\Gamma,\Pi}$ first recovers the preimage $k\|a\|b\|z$ under Π, then checks if k signals injective or lossy mode, and then computes $\Pi(a\|b\|ax + b)$ resp. $\Pi(a\|b\|\mathsf{setlsb}(ax + b))$ as the output.

Definition 6 (Lossy Function Oracle). *Let* Π, Γ *be permutation oracles with* $\Pi, \Gamma : \{0,1\}^\lambda \to \{0,1\}^\lambda$ *for all* λ. *Let* $\mu = \mu(\lambda) = \lfloor (\lambda - 2)/5 \rfloor$ *and* $\mathsf{pad} = \mathsf{pad}(\lambda) = \lambda - 2 - 5\mu$ *define the length that the rounding-off loses to* $\lambda - 2$ *in total (such that* $\mathsf{pad} \in \{0, 1, 2, 3, 4\}$). *Define the lossy function* $(\mathsf{Gen}^{\Gamma,\Pi}, \mathsf{Eval}^{\Gamma,\Pi})$ *with input length* $in(\lambda) = \mu(\lambda)$ *relative to* Π *and* Γ *now as follows:*

Key Generation: *Oracle* $\mathsf{Gen}^{\Gamma,\Pi}$ *on input* 1^λ *and either mode* inj *or* loss *picks random* $b \leftarrow_\$ \{0,1\}^\mu$, $z \leftarrow_\$ \{0,1\}^{2\mu+\mathsf{pad}}$ *and random* $a, k \leftarrow_\$ \{0,1\}^\mu \setminus \{0^\mu\}$. *For mode* inj *the algorithm returns* $\Gamma(k\|a\|b\|z)$. *For mode* loss *the algorithm returns* $\Gamma(0^\mu\|a\|b\|z)$ *instead.*

Evaluation: *On input* $\mathsf{pk} \in \{0,1\}^\lambda$ *and* $x \in \{0,1\}^\mu$ *algorithm* $\mathsf{Eval}^{\Gamma,\Pi}$ *first recovers (via exhaustive search) the preimage* $k\|a\|b\|z$ *of* pk *under* Γ *for* $k, a, b \in \{0,1\}^\mu$, $z \in \{0,1\}^{2\mu+\mathsf{pad}}$. *Check that* $a \neq 0$ *in the field* $GF(2^\mu)$. *If any check fails then return* $\bot$. *Else, next check if* $k = 0^\mu$. *If so, return* $\Pi(a\|b\|\mathsf{setlsb}(ax + b))$, *else return* $\Pi(a\|b\|ax + b)$.

---

[2] For moderately lossy function we could actually use $\lambda/4$ but for compatibility to the extremely lossy case it is convenient to use $\lambda/5$ already here.

We now show that there exist permutations Π and Γ such that relative to Π and the lossy function oracle $(\mathsf{Gen}^{\Gamma,\Pi}, \mathsf{Eval}^{\Gamma,\Pi})$, lossy functions exist, but key agreement does not. We will rely on the seminal result by Impagliazzo and Rudich [20] showing that no key agreement exists relative to a random permutation. Note that we do not give direct access to Γ—it will only be accessed by the lossy functions oracle and is considered an integral part of it.

The following lemma is the technical core of our results. It says that the partly exponential steps of the lossy-function oracles $\mathsf{Gen}^{\Gamma,\Pi}$ and $\mathsf{Eval}^{\Gamma,\Pi}$ in our construction can be simulated sufficiently close and efficiently through a stateful algorithm Wrap, given only oracle access to Π, even if we filter out the mode for key generation calls. For this we define security experiments as efficient algorithms Game with oracle access to an adversary $\mathcal{A}$ and lossy function oracles $\mathsf{Gen}^{\Gamma,\Pi}, \mathsf{Eval}^{\Gamma,\Pi}, \Pi$ and which produces some output, usually indicating if the adversary has won or not. We note that we can assume for simplicity that $\mathcal{A}$ makes oracle queries to the lossy function oracles and Π via the game only. Algorithm Wrap will be black-box with respect to $\mathcal{A}$ and Game but needs to know the total number $p(\lambda)$ of queries the adversary and the game make to the primitive and the quality level $\alpha(\lambda)$ of the simulation upfront.

Lemma 7 (Simulation Lemma). *Let* Filter *be a deterministic algorithm which for calls* $(1^\lambda, \mathsf{mode})$ *to* $\mathsf{Gen}^{\Gamma,\Pi}$ *only outputs* 1^λ *and leaves any input to calls to* $\mathsf{Eval}^{\Gamma,\Pi}$ *and to* Π *unchanged. For any polynomial* $p(\lambda)$ *and any inverse polynomial* $\alpha(\lambda)$ *there exists an efficient algorithm* Wrap *such that for any efficient algorithm* $\mathcal{A}$, *any efficient experiment* Game *making at most* $p(\lambda)$ *calls to the oracle, the statistical distance between* $\mathsf{Game}^{\mathcal{A},(\mathsf{Gen}^{\Gamma,\Pi},\mathsf{Eval}^{\Gamma,\Pi},\Pi)}(1^\lambda)$ *and* $\mathsf{Game}^{\mathcal{A},\mathsf{Wrap}^{\mathsf{Gen}^{\Gamma,\Pi},\Pi} \circ \mathsf{Filter}}$ *is at most* $\alpha(\lambda)$. *Furthermore* Wrap *initially makes a polynomial number of oracle calls to* $\mathsf{Gen}^{\Gamma,\Pi}$, *but then makes at most two calls to* Π *for each query.*

In fact, since $\mathsf{Gen}^{\Gamma,\Pi}$ is efficient relative to Γ, and Wrap only makes calls to $\mathsf{Gen}^{\Gamma,\Pi}$ for all values up to a logarithmic length L_0, we can also write $\mathsf{Wrap}^{\Gamma_{|L_0},\Pi}$ to denote the limited access to the Γ-oracle. We also note that the (local) state of Wrap only consists of such small preimage-image pairs of Γ and Π for such small values (but Wrap later calls Π also about longer inputs).

Proof. The proof strategy is to process queries of Game and $\mathcal{A}$ efficiently given only access to Π, making changes to the oracle gradually, depending on the type of query. The changes will be actually implemented by our stateful algorithm Wrap, and eventually we will add Filter at the end. To do so, we will perform a series of games hops where we change the behavior of the key generation and evaluation oracles. For each game $\mathsf{Game}_1, \mathsf{Game}_2, \ldots$ let $\mathsf{Game}_i(\lambda)$ be the randomized output of the game with access to $\mathcal{A}$. Let $p(\lambda)$ denote the total number of oracle queries the game itself and $\mathcal{A}$ make through the game, and let $\mathsf{Game}_0(\lambda)$ be the original attack of $\mathcal{A}$ with the defined oracles. The final game will then immediately give our algorithm Wrap with the upstream Filter. We give an overview over all the game hops in Fig. 2.

Game	$\mathsf{Gen}_{\mathsf{loss}}$	$\mathsf{Gen}_{\mathsf{inj}}$	$\mathsf{Eval}(\mathsf{pk}, x)$	$\Pi(x)$
Game_0	$\mathsf{pk} \leftarrow \mathsf{Gen}_{\mathsf{loss}}^{\ulcorner\Gamma,\Pi\urcorner}(1^\lambda)$ **return** pk	$\mathsf{pk} \leftarrow \mathsf{Gen}_{\mathsf{inj}}^{\ulcorner\Gamma,\Pi\urcorner}(1^\lambda)$ **return** pk	$y \leftarrow \mathsf{Eval}^{\ulcorner\Gamma,\Pi\urcorner}(\mathsf{pk}, x)$ **return** y	$\Pi(x)$
Game_2	$(\mathsf{pk}, b) \leftarrow\!\!\$\ \{0,1\}^{6\mu}$ $a \leftarrow\!\!\$\ \{0,1\}^\mu_{\neq 0^\mu}$ $k \leftarrow\!\!\$\ \{0,1\}^\mu_{\neq 0^\mu}$ $\mathsf{st}_{\mathsf{pk}} \leftarrow (k,a,b)$ **return** pk	$(\mathsf{pk}, b) \leftarrow\!\!\$\ \{0,1\}^{6\mu}$ $a \leftarrow\!\!\$\ \{0,1\}^\mu_{\neq 0^\mu}$ $\mathsf{st}_{\mathsf{pk}} \leftarrow (0^\mu, a, b)$ **return** pk	**if** $\mathsf{st}_{\mathsf{pk}} = \bot$ $\quad k,b \leftarrow\!\!\$\ \{0,1\}^{2\mu}$ $\quad a \leftarrow\!\!\$\ \{0,1\}^\mu_{\neq 0^\mu}$ $\quad \mathsf{st}_{\mathsf{pk}} \leftarrow (k,a,b)$ $(k,a,b) \leftarrow \mathsf{st}_{\mathsf{pk}}$ **if** $k = 0^\mu$ $\quad$ **return** $\Pi(\mathsf{pk}\|\mathsf{setlsb}(ax+b))$ **else** $\quad$ **return** $\Pi(\mathsf{pk}\|ax+b)$	$\Pi(x)$
Game_3	$[\dots]$ $\mathsf{st}_{\mathsf{pk}} \leftarrow (\mathsf{loss}, a, b)$ $[\dots]$	$[\dots]$ $\mathsf{st}_{\mathsf{pk}} \leftarrow (\mathsf{inj}, a, b)$ $[\dots]$	**if** $\mathsf{st}_{\mathsf{pk}} = \emptyset$ $\quad b \leftarrow\!\!\$\ \{0,1\}^\mu$ $\quad a \leftarrow\!\!\$\ \{0,1\}^\mu_{\neq 0^\mu}$ $\quad \mathsf{st}_{\mathsf{pk}} \leftarrow (\mathsf{inj}, a, b)$ $(\mathsf{mode}, a, b) \leftarrow \mathsf{st}_{\mathsf{pk}}$ **if** $\mathsf{mode} = \mathsf{loss}$ $\quad$ **return** $\Pi(\mathsf{pk}\|\mathsf{setlsb}(ax+b))$ **else** $\quad$ **return** $\Pi(\mathsf{pk}\|ax+b)$	$\Pi(x)$
Game_4	$[\dots]$ $\mathsf{st}_{\mathsf{pk}} \leftarrow (a, b)$ $[\dots]$	$[\dots]$ $\mathsf{st}_{\mathsf{pk}} \leftarrow (a, b)$ $[\dots]$	$[\dots]$ $\quad \mathsf{st}_{\mathsf{pk}} \leftarrow (a, b)$ $a, b \leftarrow \mathsf{st}_{\mathsf{pk}}$ **return** $\Pi(\mathsf{pk}\|ax+b)$	$\Pi(x)$
Game_5	$[\dots]$	$[\dots]$	$[\dots]$ **return** $\Pi_1(\mathsf{pk}\|ax+b)$	$\Pi_1(x)$
Game_6	$\mathsf{pk} \leftarrow\!\!\$\ \{0,1\}^{5\mu}$ **return** pk	$\mathsf{pk} \leftarrow\!\!\$\ \{0,1\}^{5\mu}$ **return** pk	$a\|b\|\cdots \leftarrow \Pi_0(\mathsf{pk})$ **return** $\Pi_1(\mathsf{pk}\|ax+b)$	$\Pi_1(x)$
Game_7	$[\dots]$	$[\dots]$	**return** $\Pi_0(\mathsf{pk}\|x)$	$\Pi_1(x)$

Fig. 2. An overview of all the game hops. Note that for simplicity we ignored the modifications related to inputs of length L_0 here, in particular the game hop to Game_1.

Game_1. In the first game hops we let Wrap collect all information about very short queries (of length related to L_0) in a list and use this list to answer subsequent queries. Change the oracles as follows. Let

$$L_0 := L_0(\lambda) := \lceil \log_2(80\alpha^{-1}(\lambda) \cdot p(\lambda)^2 + p(\lambda)) \rceil.$$

Then our current version of algorithm Wrap, upon initialization, queries Π about all inputs of size at most $2L_0$ and stores the list of queries and answers. The reason for using $2L_0$ is that the evaluation algorithm takes as input a key of security parameter λ and some input of size $\mu \approx \lambda/5$, such that we safely cover all evaluations for keys of security size $\lambda \leq L_0$.

Further, for any security parameter less than $2L_0$, our algorithm queries $\mathsf{Gen}^{\Gamma,\Pi}$ for $\lambda 2^{2L_0}$ times; recall that we do not assume that parties have direct access to Γ but only via $\mathsf{Gen}^{\Gamma,\Pi}$. This way, for any valid key, we know that it was created at some point except with probability $(1 - 2^{-2L_0})^{\lambda 2^{2L_0}} \leq 2^{-\lambda}$ and therefore the probability that any key was not generated is at most $2^{L_0} 2^{-\lambda}$, which is negligible. Further, for every public key, it evaluates $\mathsf{Eval}^{\Gamma,\Pi}$ at $x = 0$ and uses the precomputed list for Π to invert, revealing the corresponding a and b. Note that all of this can be done in polynomial time.

Any subsequent query to $\mathsf{Gen}^{\Gamma,\Pi}$ for security parameter at most L_0, as well as to $\mathsf{Eval}^{\Gamma,\Pi}$ for a public keys of size at most L_0 (which corresponds to a key for security parameter at most L_0), as well as to Π for inputs of size at most $2L_0$, are answered by looking up all necessary data in the list. If any data is missing, we will return $\perp$. Note that as long as we do not return $\perp$, this is only a syntactical change. As returning $\perp$ happens at most with negligible probability over the randomness of Wrap,

$$\mathsf{SD}\,(\mathsf{Game}_0, \mathsf{Game}_1) \leq 2^{2L_0} 2^{-\lambda}.$$

From now one we will implicitly assume that queries of short security length up to L_0 are answered genuinely with the help of tables and do not mention this explicitly anymore.

Game_2. In this game, we will stop using the lossy function oracles altogether, and instead introduce a global state for the Wrap algorithm. Note that this state will be shared between all parties having access to the oracles (via Wrap). Now, for every call to $\mathsf{Gen}^{\Gamma,\Pi}$, we do the following: If the key is created in injective mode, Wrap will sample $b \leftarrow_\$ \{0,1\}^\mu$ and $a, k \leftarrow_\$ \{0,1\}^\mu \setminus \{0^\mu\}$, if the key is created in lossy mode, it sets $k = 0^\mu$. Further, it samples a public key $\mathsf{pk} \leftarrow_\$ \{0,1\}^{5\mu + \mathsf{pad}}$, and sets the state $\mathsf{st}_{\mathsf{pk}} \leftarrow (k, a, b)$. Finally it returns pk. Any call to $\mathsf{Eval}^{\Gamma,\Pi}(\mathsf{pk}, x)$ will be handled as follows: First, Wrap checks whether a state for pk exists. If this is not the case, we generate $k, a, b \leftarrow_\$ \{0,1\}^\mu$ (with checking that $a \neq 0$) and save $\mathsf{st}_{\mathsf{pk}} \leftarrow (k, a, b)$. Then, we read $(k, a, b) \leftarrow \mathsf{st}_{\mathsf{pk}}$ from the (possibly just initialized) state and return $\Pi(a\|b\|ax + b)$.

What algorithm Wrap does here can be seen as emulating Γ. However, there are two differences: We do not sample z, and we allow for collisions. The collisions can be of either of two types: Either we sample the same (random) public key $\mathsf{pk} = \mathsf{pk}'$ but for different state values $(k, a, b) \neq (k', a', b')$, or we sample the same values $(k, a, b) = (k', a', b')$ but end up with different public keys $\mathsf{pk} \neq \mathsf{pk}'$. In this case, an algorithm that finds such a collision of size at least μ for $\mu \geq L_0/5$ —smaller values are precomputed and still answered as before— could be able to distinguish the two games. Still, the two games are statistically close since such collisions happen with probability at most $2^{-2L_0/5+1}$ for each pair of generated keys:

$$\mathsf{SD}\,(\mathsf{Game}_2, \mathsf{Game}_1) \leq 2p(\lambda)^2 \cdot 2^{-2L_0/5+1} \leq \frac{\alpha(\lambda)}{8}$$

Game$_3$. Next, instead of generating and saving a value k depending on the lossy or injective mode, we just save a label inj or loss for the mode the key was created for. Further, whenever $\mathsf{Eval}^{\Gamma,\Pi}(\mathsf{pk}, x)$ is called on a public key without saved state, i.e., if it has not been created via key generation, then we always label this key as injective.

The only way the adversary is able to recognize the game hop change is because a self-chosen public key, not determined by key generation, will now never be lossy (or will be invalid because $a = 0$). However, any adversarially chosen string of size at least $5\mu \geq L_0$ would only describe a lossy key with probability at most $\frac{1}{2^\mu - p(\lambda)}$ and yield an invalid $a = 0$ with the same probability. Hence, taking into account that the adversary learns at most $p(\lambda)$ values about Γ though genuinely generated keys, and the adversary makes at most $p(\lambda)$ queries, the statistical difference between the two games is small:

$$\mathsf{SD}\left(\mathsf{Game}_2, \mathsf{Game}_3\right) \leq 2p(\lambda) \cdot \frac{1}{2^{-L_0/5+1} - p(\lambda)} \leq \frac{\alpha(\lambda)}{8}.$$

Game$_4$. Now, we remove the label inj or loss again. Wrap will now, for any call to Eval, calculate everything in injective mode.

There are two ways an adversary can distinguish between the two games: Either by inverting Π, e.g., noting that the last bit in the preimage is not as expected, or by finding a pair $x \neq x'$ for a lossy key $\mathsf{pk}_{\mathsf{loss}}$ such that $\mathsf{Eval}(\mathsf{pk}_{\mathsf{loss}}, x) = \mathsf{Eval}(\mathsf{pk}_{\mathsf{loss}}, x')$ in Game$_3$. Inverting Π (or guessing a and b) only succeeds with probability $\frac{2(p(\lambda)+1)}{2^\mu}$. For the probability of finding a collision, note that viewing the random permutation Π as being lazy sampled shows that the answers are chosen independently of the input (except for repeating previous answers), and especially of a, b for any lossy public key of the type considered here. Hence, we can imagine to choose a, b for any possible pairs of inputs only after x, x' have been determined. But then the probability of creating a collision among the $p(\lambda)^2$ many pairs for the same key is at most $\frac{2p(\lambda)^2}{2^\mu}$ for $\mu > L_0/5$. Therefore, the distance between these two games is bounded by

$$\mathsf{SD}\left(\mathsf{Game}_3, \mathsf{Game}_4\right) \leq 3(p(\lambda) + p(\lambda)^2) \cdot 2^{-L_0/5+1} \leq \frac{\alpha(\lambda)}{8}.$$

Game$_5$. We split the random permutation Π to have two oracles. For $\beta \in \{0,1\}$ and $x \in \{0,1\}^{5\mu}$, we now define $\Pi_\beta(x) = \Pi(\beta\|x)_{1\ldots5\mu-1}$, i.e., we add a prefix β and drop the last bit. We now replace any use of Π in Wrap, including direct queries to Π, by Π_1.

Would Π_1 be a permutation, this would be a perfect simulation. However, Π_1 is not even injective anymore, but finding a collision is still very unlikely (as random functions are collision resistant). In particular, using once more that we only look at sufficiently large values, the statistical distance of the games is still small:

$$\mathsf{SD}\left(\mathsf{Game}_4, \mathsf{Game}_5\right) \leq \frac{2p(\lambda)^2}{2^{5\mu}} \leq \frac{\alpha(\lambda)}{8}.$$

Game$_6$. Next, we stop using the global state st for information about the values related to a public key (except for keys of security parameter at most L_0). The wrapper for Gen now only generates a uniformly random pk and returns it. For Eval calls, Wrap instead calculates $a\|b \leftarrow \Pi_0(\text{pk})$ on the fly. Note that there is a small probability of $2^{-L_0/5+1}$ of $a = 0$, yielding an invalid key. Except for this, since the adversary does not have access to Π_0, this game otherwise looks completely identical to the adversary:

$$\mathsf{SD}\left(\mathsf{Game}_5, \mathsf{Game}_6\right) \leq p(\lambda) \cdot 2^{-L_0/5+1} \leq \frac{\alpha(\lambda)}{8}.$$

Game$_7$. For our final game, we use Π_0 to evaluate the lossy function:

$$\mathsf{Eval}^\Pi(\text{pk}, x) = \Pi_0(\text{pk}\|x).$$

Note that, as $\mathcal{A}$ has no access to Π_0, calls to Eval in Game$_7$ are random for $\mathcal{A}$. For Game$_6$, calls to Eval looks random as long as $\mathcal{A}$ does not invert Π_1, which happens at most with probability $\frac{2(p(\lambda)+1)}{2^\mu}$. Therefore, the statistical distance between the two games is bound by

$$\mathsf{SD}\left(\mathsf{Game}_6, \mathsf{Game}_7\right) \leq 3p(\lambda) \cdot 2^{-2L_0/5+1} \leq \frac{\alpha(\lambda)}{8}.$$

In the final game the algorithm Wrap now does not need to save any state related to large public keys, and it behaves identically for the lossy and injective generators. We can therefore safely add our algorithm Filter, stripping off the mode before passing key generation requests to Wrap. Summing up the statistical distances we obtain a maximal statistical of $\frac{7}{8}\alpha(\lambda) \leq \alpha(\lambda)$ between the original game and the one with our algorithms Wrap and Filter.   □

We next argue that the simulation lemma allows us to conclude immediately that the function oracle in Definition 6 is indeed a lossy function:

Theorem 3. *The function in Definition 6 is a lossy function for lossiness parameter 2.*

The proof can be found in the full version [13].

4.2   Key Exchange

We next argue that given our oracle-based lossy function in the previous section one cannot build a secure key agreement protocol based only this lossy function (and having also access to Π). The line of reasoning follows the one in the renowned work by Impagliazzo and Rudich [20]. They show that one cannot build a secure key agreement protocol between Alice and Bob, given only a random permutation oracle Π. To this end they argue that, if we can find NP-witnesses efficiently, say, if we have access to a PSPACE oracle, then the adversary with oracle access to Π can efficiently compute Alice's key given only a transcript of a protocol run between Alice and Bob (both having access to Π).

We use the same argument as in [20] here, noting that according to our Simulation Lemma 7 we could replace the lossy function oracle relative to Π by our algorithm Wrap^{Π}. This, however, requires some care, especially as Wrap does not provide access to the original Π.

We first define (weakly) secure key exchange protocols relative to some oracle (or a set of oracles) $\mathcal{O}$. We assume that we have an interactive protocol $\langle \mathrm{Alice}^{\mathcal{O}}, \mathrm{Bob}^{\mathcal{O}} \rangle$ between two efficient parties, both having access to the oracle $\mathcal{O}$. The interactive protocol execution for security parameter 1^{λ} runs the interactive protocol between $\mathrm{Alice}^{\mathcal{O}}(1^{\lambda}; z_A)$ for randomness z_A and $\mathrm{Bob}^{\mathcal{O}}(1^{\lambda}, z_B)$ with randomness z_B, and we define the output to be a triple $(k_A, T, k_B) \leftarrow \langle \mathrm{Alice}^{\mathcal{O}}(1^{\lambda}; z_A), \mathrm{Bob}^{\mathcal{O}}(1^{\lambda}; z_B) \rangle$, where k_A is the local key output by Alice, T is the transcript of communication between the two parties, and k_B is the local key output by Bob. When talking about probabilities over this output we refer to the random choice of randomness z_A and z_B.

Note that we define completeness in a slightly non-standard way by allowing the protocol to create non-matching keys with a polynomial (but non-constant) probability, compared to the negligible probability the standard definition would allow. The main motivation for this definition is that it makes our proof easier, but as we will prove a negative result, this relaxed definition makes our result even stronger.

Definition 7. *A key agreement protocol $\langle Alice, Bob \rangle$ relative to an oracle $\mathcal{O}$ is*

complete *if there exists an at least linear polynomial $p(\lambda)$ such that for all large enough security parameters λ:*

$$\Pr\left[k_A \neq k_B : (k_A, T, k_B) \leftarrow_\$ \left\langle Alice^{\Pi}(1^{\lambda}), Bob^{\mathcal{O}}(1^{\lambda}) \right\rangle \right] \leq \frac{1}{p(\lambda)}.$$

secure *if for any efficient adversary $\mathcal{A}$ the probability that*

$$\Pr\left[k^* = k_A : (k_A, T, k_B) \leftarrow_\$ \left\langle Alice^{\mathcal{O}}(1^{\lambda}), Bob^{\mathcal{O}}(1^{\lambda}) \right\rangle, k^* \leftarrow_\$ \mathcal{A}^{\mathcal{O}}(1^{\lambda}, T) \right]$$

is negligible.

Theorem 4. *There exist random oracles Π and Γ such that relative to $\mathsf{Gen}^{\Gamma, \Pi}$, $\mathsf{Eval}^{\Gamma, \Pi}$, Π and PSPACE, the function oracle $(\mathsf{Gen}^{\Gamma, \Pi}, \mathsf{Eval}^{\Gamma, \Pi})$ from Definition 6 is a lossy function, but no construction of secure key agreement from $\mathsf{Gen}^{\Gamma, \Pi}$, $\mathsf{Eval}^{\Gamma, \Pi}$ and Π exists.*

From this theorem and using the two-oracle technique, the following corollary follows directly:

Corollary 1. *There exists no fully black-box construction of a secure key agreement protocol from lossy functions.*

Proof (Theorem 4). Assume, to the contrary, that a secure key agreement exists relative to these oracles. We first note that it suffices to consider adversaries in the Wrap-based scenario. That is, $\mathcal{A}$ obtains a transcript T generated by the execution of $\text{Alice}^{\text{Wrap}^{\Gamma,\Pi}\circ\text{Filter}}(1^\lambda; z_A)$ with $\text{Bob}^{\text{Wrap}^{\Gamma,\Pi}\circ\text{Filter}}(1^\lambda; z_A)$ where Wrap is initialized with randomness z_W and itself interacts with Π. Note that $\text{Wrap}^\Pi \circ$ Filter is efficiently computable and only requires local state (holding the oracle tables for small values), so we can interpret the wrapper as part of Alice and Bob without needing any additional communication between the two parties— see Fig. 3.

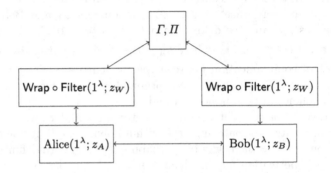

Fig. 3. The two parties Alice and Bob get access to the Wrap ∘ Filter algorithm with internal access to the permutations Γ and Π, instead of having access to the lossy function oracles as well as direct access to Π.

We now prove the following two statements about the key agreement protocol in the wrapped mode:

1. For non-constant $\alpha(\lambda)$, the protocol $\langle \text{Alice}^{\text{Wrap}^{\Gamma,\Pi}\circ\text{Filter}}, \text{Bob}^{\text{Wrap}^{\Gamma,\Pi}\circ\text{Filter}} \rangle$ still fulfills the completeness property of the key agreement, i.e., at most with polynomial probability, the keys generated by Alice and Bob differ; and
2. there exists a successful adversary $\mathcal{E}^{\text{Wrap}^{\Gamma,\Pi}\circ\text{Filter},\text{PSPACE}}$ with additional PSPACE access, that, with at least polynomial probability, recovers the key from the transcript of Alice and Bob.

If we show these two properties, we have derived a contradiction: If there exists a successful adversary against the wrapped version of the protocol, then this adversary must also be successful against the protocol with the original oracles with at most a negligible difference in the success probability – otherwise, this adversary could be used as a distinguisher between the original and the wrapped oracles, contradicting the Simulation Lemma 7.

Completeness. The first property holds by the Simulation Lemma: Assume there exists a protocol between Alice and Bob such that in the original game, the keys generated differ for at most a polynomial probability $\frac{1}{p(\lambda)}$, while in the case where we replace the access to the oracles by $\mathsf{Wrap}^{\Gamma,\Pi} \circ \mathsf{Filter}$ for some $\alpha(\lambda)$, the keys differ with constant probability $\frac{1}{c_\alpha}$. In such a case, we could—in a thought experiment— modify Alice and Bob to end their protocol by revealing their keys. A distinguisher could now tell from the transcripts whether the keys of the parties differ or match. Such a distinguisher would however now be able to distinguish between the oracles and the wrapper with probability $\frac{1}{c_\alpha} - \frac{1}{p(\lambda)}$, which is larger than $\alpha(\lambda)$ for large enough security parameters, which is a contradiction to the Simulation Lemma.

Attack. For the second property, we will argue that the adversary by Impagliazzo and Rudich from their seminal work on key agreement from one-way functions [20] works in our case as well. For this, first note that the adversary has access to both Π_1 (by Π-calls to Wrap) and Π_0 (by Eval-calls to Wrap) and Wrap also makes the initial calls to Γ. Combining Γ, Π_0 and Π_1 into a single function we can apply the Impagliazzo-Rudich adversary. Specifically, [20, Theorem 6.4] relates the agreement error, denoted ϵ here, to the success probability approximately $1 - 2\epsilon$ of breaking the key agreement protocol. Hence, let $\epsilon(\lambda)$ be the at most polynomial error rate of the original key exchange protocol. We choose now $\alpha(\lambda)$ sufficiently small such that $\epsilon(\lambda) + \alpha(\lambda)$ is an acceptable error rate for a key exchange, i.e., at most $1/4$. Then this key exchange using the wrapped oracles is a valid key exchange using only our combined random oracle, and therefore, we can use the Impagliazzo-Rudich adversary to recover the key with non-negligible probability.

Fixing the Oracles. Finally, we have to fix the random permutations Π and Γ such that the Simulation Lemma holds and the Impagliazzo-Rudich attack works. This happens again using standard techniques – see the full version [13] for a proof. □

4.3 ELFs

We will show next that our result can also be extended to show that no fully black-box construction of key agreement from *extremely* lossy functions is possible. However, we are only able to show a slightly weaker result: In our separation, we only consider constructions that access the extremely lossy function on the same security parameter as used in the key agreement protocol. We call such constructions *security-level-preserving*. This leaves the theoretic possibility of building key agreement from extremely lossy functions of (significantly) smaller security parameters. At the same time it simplifies the proof of the Simulation Lemma for this case significantly since we can omit the step where Wrap samples Γ for all small inputs, and we can immediately work with the common negligible terms.

We start by defining an ELF oracle. In general, the oracle is quite similar to our lossy function oracle. Especially, we still distinguish between an injective and a lossy mode, and make sure that any key sampled without a call to the $\mathsf{Gen}_{\mathsf{ELF}}^{\Gamma,\Pi}$ oracle will be injective with overwhelming probability. For the lossy mode, we now of course have to save the parameter r in the public key. Instead of using setlsb to lose one bit of information, we take the result of $ax + b$ (calculated in $GF(2^\mu)$) modulo r (calculated on the integers) to allow for the more fine-grained lossiness that is required by ELFs.

Definition 8 (Extremely Lossy Function Oracle). *Let Π, Γ be permutation oracles with $\Pi, \Gamma : \{0,1\}^\lambda \to \{0,1\}^\lambda$ for all λ. Let $\mu = \mu(\lambda) = \lfloor (\lambda - 2)/5 \rfloor$ and $\mathsf{pad} = \mathsf{pad}(\lambda) = \lambda - 2 - 5\mu$ defines the length that the rounding-off loses to $\lambda - 2$ in total (such that $\mathsf{pad} \in \{0,1,2,3,4\}$). Define the extremely lossy function $(\mathsf{Gen}_{\mathsf{ELF}}^{\Gamma,\Pi}, \mathsf{Eval}_{\mathsf{ELF}}^{\Gamma,\Pi})$ with input length $\mathsf{in}(\lambda) = \mu(\lambda)$ relative to Γ and Π now as follows:*

Key Generation: *The oracle $\mathsf{Gen}_{\mathsf{ELF}}^{\Gamma,\Pi}$, on input 1^λ and mode r, picks random $b \leftarrow_\$ \{0,1\}^\mu$, $z \leftarrow_\$ \{0,1\}^{\mu+\mathsf{pad}}$ and random $a, k \leftarrow_\$ \{0,1\}^\mu \setminus \{0^\mu\}$. For mode $r = 2^{\mathsf{in}(\lambda)}$ the algorithm returns $\Gamma(k\|a\|b\|r\|z)$. For mode $r < 2^{\mathsf{in}(\lambda)}$ the algorithm returns $\Gamma(0^\mu\|a\|b\|r\|z)$ instead.*

Evaluation: *On input $\mathsf{pk} \in \{0,1\}^\lambda$ and $x \in \{0,1\}^\mu$ algorithm $\mathsf{Eval}_{\mathsf{ELF}}^{\Gamma,\Pi}$ first recovers (via exhaustive search) the preimage $k\|a\|b\|r\|z$ of pk under Γ for $k, a, b, r \in \{0,1\}^\mu$, $z \in \{0,1\}^{\mu+\mathsf{pad}}$. Check that $a \neq 0$ in the field $GF(2^\mu)$. If any check fails then return $\bot$. Else, next check if $k = 0^m$. If so, return $\Pi(a\|b\|(ax + b \bmod r))$, else return $\Pi(a\|b\|ax + b)$.*

We can now formulate versions of Theorem 4 and Corollary 1 for the extremely lossy case.

Theorem 5. *There exist random oracles Π and Γ such that relative to $\mathsf{Gen}_{\mathsf{ELF}}^{\Gamma,\Pi}$, $\mathsf{Eval}_{\mathsf{ELF}}^{\Gamma,\Pi}$, Π and PSPACE, the extremely lossy function oracle $(\mathsf{Gen}_{\mathsf{ELF}}^{\Gamma,\Pi}, \mathsf{Eval}_{\mathsf{ELF}}^{\Gamma,\Pi})$ from Definition 8 is indeed an ELF, but no security-level-preserving construction of secure key agreement from $\mathsf{Gen}_{\mathsf{ELF}}^{\Gamma,\Pi}, \mathsf{Eval}_{\mathsf{ELF}}^{\Gamma,\Pi}$ and Π exists.*

Corollary 2. *There exists no fully black-box security-level-preserving construction of a secure key agreement protocol from extremely lossy functions.*

Proving Theorem 5 only needs minor modifications of the proof of Theorem 4 to go through. Indeed, the only real difference lies in a modified Simulation Lemma for ELFs, which we will formulate next, together with a proof sketch that explains where differences arrive in the proof compared to the original Simulation Lemma. To stay as close to the previous proof as possible, we will continue to distinguish between an injective generator $\mathsf{Gen}_{\mathsf{inj}}(1^\lambda)$ and a lossy generator $\mathsf{Gen}_{\mathsf{loss}}(1^\lambda, r)$, where the latter also receives the parameter r.

Lemma 8 (Simulation Lemma (ELFs)). *Let Filter be a·deterministic algorithm which for calls $(1^\lambda, \mathsf{mode})$ to $\mathsf{Gen}_{\mathsf{ELF}}^{\Gamma,\Pi}$ only outputs 1^λ and leaves any input to calls to $\mathsf{Eval}_{\mathsf{ELF}}^{\Gamma,\Pi}$ and to Π unchanged. There exists an efficient algorithm Wrap such that for any polynomials p and d' there exists a polynomial q such that for any adversary $\mathcal{A}$ which makes at most $p(\lambda)$ queries to the oracles, any efficient* *experiment* Game *making calls to the* $\text{Gen}_{\text{ELF}}^{r,\Pi}$ *oracle with* $r > q(\lambda)$ *the distinguishing advantage between* $\text{Game}^{\mathcal{A},(\text{Gen}_{\text{ELF}}^{r,\Pi},\text{Eval}_{\text{ELF}}^{r,\Pi},\Pi)}(1^\lambda)$ *and* $\text{Game}^{\mathcal{A},\text{Wrap}^\Pi\circ\text{Filter}}$ *is at most* $\frac{1}{d'(\lambda)}$ *for sufficiently large* λ. *Furthermore* Wrap *makes at most two calls to* Π *for each query.*

Proof (Sketch). We will now describe how the game hops differ from the proof of Lemma 7, and how these changes affect the advantage of the distinguisher. Note that allowing only access to the ELF oracle at the current security parameter allows us to argue that differences between game hops are negligible, instead of having to give a concrete bound.

Game_1. stays identical to Game_0 – as we only allow access to the ELF oracle at the current security level, precomputing all values smaller than some L_0 is not necessary here.

Game_2. introduces changes similar to Game_2 in Lemma 7 – however, we now of course also have to save the parameter r in the state. Again, the only notable difference to the distinguisher is that we sample pk independently of the public key parameters and therefore, collisions might happen more often. However, the probability for this is clearly negligible:

$$\text{SD}\,(\text{Game}_1, \text{Game}_2) \leq \text{negl}(\lambda)$$

Game_3. replaces k with a label inj or loss. Again, the only noticeable difference is that keys sampled without calling Gen_{inj} or Gen_{loss} will now always be injective, while they are lossy with probability $2^{-\mu}$ in Game_2, yielding only a negligible difference between the two games however.

$$\text{SD}\,(\text{Game}_2, \text{Game}_3) \leq \text{negl}(\lambda)$$

Game_4. is the game where we start to always evaluate in injective mode. There are two options a distinguisher might distinguish between the two games: Either by inverting Π, or by finding a collision for a lossy key. Inverting Π only happens with probability $\frac{2(p(\lambda)+1)}{2^\mu}$, while finding a collision happens with probability $\frac{2p(\lambda)^2}{r}$. Let $d(\lambda) = \frac{d'(\lambda)}{2}$ be the advantage we want to allow for the distinguisher in this game hop. Choosing $q(\lambda) = 4p(\lambda)^2 d(\lambda)$ for the bound on r of the ELF, we get

$$\text{Adv}_{\mathcal{A}}^{\text{Game}_3,\text{Game}_4} \leq \frac{1}{d(\lambda)}$$

Game_4 is now identical to Game_4 in the proof of Lemma 7 (except for the different handling of calls to security parameters smaller than L_0). Therefore, all game hops up to Game_7 are identical to the ones in the proof of Lemma 7, with the statistical difference being negligible for all of them. Therefore, the overall advantage of an distinguisher is bounded by $\frac{1}{d(\lambda)} + \text{negl}(\lambda) \leq \frac{1}{d'(\lambda)}$ for large enough security parameters λ.

$\square$

Let $\langle \text{Alice}^{\text{Gen}_{\text{ELF}}^{\Gamma,\Pi},\text{Eval}_{\text{ELF}}^{\Gamma,\Pi},\Pi}, \text{Bob}^{\text{Gen}_{\text{ELF}}^{\Gamma,\Pi},\text{Eval}_{\text{ELF}}^{\Gamma,\Pi},\Pi} \rangle$ be some candidate key agreement protocol with completeness error $\frac{1}{\epsilon(\lambda)} < \frac{1}{8}$ that makes at most $p(\lambda)$ queries in sum, and let $\frac{1}{d'(\lambda)} < \frac{1}{8}$ be the advantage bound for any adversary against the key agreement we are trying to reach.

To determine the correct parameters for the ELF oracle, we need to know how many queries the Impagliazzo-Rudich adversary makes against the transcript of the wrapped version of the protocol $\langle \text{Alice}^{\text{Wrap}^\Pi \circ \text{Filter}}, \text{Bob}^{\text{Wrap}^\Pi \circ \text{Filter}} \rangle$, which depends on the number of queries of the protocol. Note that we know that Wrap^Π makes at most two queries to Π for each internal query of Alice or Bob, so we know that the wrapped version makes at most $2p(\lambda)$ queries to Π. Let $p'(\lambda)$ be the number of queries needed by the Impagliazzo-Rudich protocol.

First, we have to show that completeness still holds for the wrapped version of the protocol. The wrapped protocol has an error rate of at most $\frac{1}{\epsilon'} < \frac{1}{\epsilon} + \frac{1}{d'} \leq \frac{1}{4}$, as otherwise, we would have a successful distinguisher for the Simulation Lemma. Further, as the error rate $\frac{1}{\epsilon'}$ is smaller than $\frac{1}{4}$, we know that Impagliazzo-Rudich will have a success probability of at least $\frac{1}{2}$.

Further, we know from the Simulation Lemma that we need $d(\lambda) = \frac{d'(\lambda)}{2}$ for it to hold. Therefore, we set the bound for r in the ELF oracle to $q(\lambda) = 4p'(\lambda)^2 d(\lambda)$. Now, the Impagliazzo-Rudich attack has to be successful for the original protocol with polynomial probability $\frac{1}{d''}$, as otherwise, there would be an distinguisher for the Simulation Lemma with advantage $\frac{1}{2} - \text{negl}(\lambda) > \frac{1}{d'(\lambda)}$.

Fixing oracles Π, Γ such that $(\text{Gen}_{\text{ELF}}^{\Gamma,\Pi}, \text{Eval}_{\text{ELF}}^{\Gamma,\Pi})$ is an ELF, while the Impagliazzo-Rudich attack is successful yields the Theorem.

5 Relationship of Lossy Functions to Statistical Zero-Knowledge

The complexity class (average-case) SZK, introduced by Goldwasser, Micali and Rackoff [16], contains all languages that can be proven by a statistical zero-knowledge proof, and is often characterized by its complete promise problem (average-case) Statistical Distance [29]. Hardness of Statistical Zero-Knowledge follows from a number of algebraic assumptions like Discrete Logarithm [15] and lattice problems [22] and the existence of some Minicrypt primitives like one-way functions [24] and distributional collision resistant hash functions [21] follow from hard problems in SZK – it is not known to follow from any Minicrypt assumptions, however, and for some, e.g., collision-resistant hash functions, there exist black-box separations [6].

Therefore, average-case hard problems in SZK seem to be a natural candidate for a non-public key assumption to build lossy functions from. Intuitively, one can see similarities between lossy functions and statistical distance: Both are, in a sense, promise problems, if one looks at the image size of a lossy function with a large gap between the injective mode and the lossy mode. Further, it is known that hard problems in SZK follow from lossy functions (this seems to be folklore knowledge – we give a proof for this fact in the full version.

Note that a construction of lossy functions would also be interesting from a different perspective: As collision-resistant hash functions can be build from sufficiently lossy functions, a construction of (sufficiently) lossy functions from average-case SZK hardness would mean that collision resistance follows from average-case SZK hardness. However, right now, this is only known for *distributional* collision resistance, a weaker primitive [21].

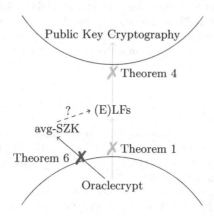

Fig. 4. We show an oracle separation between Oraclecrypt and average-case SZK as well. The question whether lossy functions can be build from average-case SZK is still open.

Alas, we are unable to either give a construction of a lossy function from a hard-on-average statistical zero-knowledge problem or to prove an black-box impossibility result between the two, leaving this as an interesting open question for future work. Instead, we give a lower bound on the needed assumptions for hard-on-average problems in SZK by showing that no Oraclecrypt primitive can be used in a black-box way to construct a hard-on-average problem in SZK – this serves as hint that indeed SZK is an interesting class of problems to look at for building lossy functions, but the result might also be interesting independently.

Note some Oraclecrypt primitives, such a separation already exists: For example, Bitansky and Degwekar give an oracle separation between collision-resistant hash functions and (even worst-case) hard problems in SZK. However, this result uses a Simon-style oracle separation (using a *break*-oracle that depends on the random oracle), which means that the result is specific to the primitive and does not easily generalize to all Oraclecrypt primitives.

Theorem 6. *There exists no black-box construction of an hard-on-average problem in SZK from any Oraclecrypt primitive.*

Our proof techniques is quite similar to Chap. 3: First, we will reuse the oracles $\mathcal{O}$ and $\mathrm{PSPACE}^{\mathcal{O}'}$. We assume there exists an hard-on-average statistical distance problem relative to these random oracles. We will then calculate the heavy queries of the circuits produced by the statistical distance problem and show that the heavy queries are sufficient to decide whether the circuits are statistically far from each other or not, yielding a contradiction to the assumed hardness-on-average of statistical distance. The complete proof can be found in the full version.

Acknowledgments. We thank the anonymous reviewers for valuable comments.

Funded by the Deutsche Forschungsgemeinschaft (DFG, German Research Foundation) - SFB 1119 - 236615297 and by the German Federal Ministry of Education and Research and the Hessian Ministry of Higher Education, Research, Science and the Arts within their joint support of the National Research Center for Applied Cybersecurity ATHENE.

References

1. Agrikola, T., Couteau, G., Hofheinz, D.: The usefulness of sparsifiable inputs: how to avoid Subexponential iO. In: Kiayias, A., Kohlweiss, M., Wallden, P., Zikas, V. (eds.) PKC 2020. LNCS, vol. 12110, pp. 187–219. Springer, Cham (2020). https://doi.org/10.1007/978-3-030-45374-9_7

2. Jutla, C.S., Roy, A.: Shorter quasi-adaptive NIZK proofs for linear subspaces. In: Sako, K., Sarkar, P. (eds.) ASIACRYPT 2013. LNCS, vol. 8269, pp. 1–20. Springer, Heidelberg (2013). https://doi.org/10.1007/978-3-642-42033-7_1

3. Bellare, M., Hoang, V.T., Keelveedhi, S.: Instantiating random oracles via UCEs. In: Canetti, R., Garay, J.A. (eds.) CRYPTO 2013. LNCS, vol. 8043, pp. 398–415. Springer, Heidelberg (2013). https://doi.org/10.1007/978-3-642-40084-1_23

4. Bellare, M., Rogaway, P.: Random oracles are practical: a paradigm for designing efficient protocols. In: Denning, D.E., Pyle, R., Ganesan, R., Sandhu, R.S., Ashby, V. (eds.) ACM CCS 1993, pp. 62–73. ACM Press (1993). https://doi.org/10.1145/168588.168596

5. Bellare, M., Stepanovs, I., Tessaro, S.: Contention in cryptoland: obfuscation, leakage and UCE. In: Kushilevitz, E., Malkin, T. (eds.) TCC 2016, Part II. LNCS, vol. 9563, pp. 542–564. Springer, Heidelberg (2016). https://doi.org/10.1007/978-3-662-49099-0_20

6. Bitansky, N., Degwekar, A.: On the complexity of collision resistant hash functions: new and old black-box separations. In: Hofheinz, D., Rosen, A. (eds.) Theory of Cryptography. LNCS, vol. 11891, pp. 422–450. Springer, Cham (2019). https://doi.org/10.1007/978-3-030-36030-6_17

7. Braverman, M., Hassidim, A., Kalai, Y.T.: Leaky pseudo-entropy functions. In: Chazelle, B. (ed.) Innovations in Computer Science - ICS 2011, Tsinghua University, Beijing, China, January 7–9, 2011. Proceedings, pp. 353–366. Tsinghua University Press (2011). http://conference.iiis.tsinghua.edu.cn/ICS2011/content/papers/17.html

8. Brzuska, C., Couteau, G., Egger, C., Karanko, P., Meyer, P.: New random oracle instantiations from extremely lossy functions. Cryptology ePrint Archive, Report 2023/1145 (2023). https://eprint.iacr.org/2023/1145

9. Brzuska, C., Farshim, P., Mittelbach, A.: Indistinguishability obfuscation and UCEs: the case of computationally unpredictable sources. In: Garay, J.A., Gennaro, R. (eds.) CRYPTO 2014. LNCS, vol. 8616, pp. 188–205. Springer, Heidelberg (2014). https://doi.org/10.1007/978-3-662-44371-2_11

10. Canetti, R., Chen, Y., Reyzin, L.: On the correlation intractability of obfuscated pseudorandom functions. In: Kushilevitz, E., Malkin, T. (eds.) TCC 2016, Part I. LNCS, vol. 9562, pp. 389–415. Springer, Heidelberg (2016). https://doi.org/10.1007/978-3-662-49096-9_17
11. Canetti, R., Goldreich, O., Halevi, S.: The random oracle methodology, revisited (preliminary version). In: 30th ACM STOC, pp. 209–218. ACM Press (1998). https://doi.org/10.1145/276698.276741
12. Dodis, Y., Vaikuntanathan, V., Wichs, D.: Extracting Randomness from Extractor-Dependent Sources. In: Canteaut, A., Ishai, Y. (eds.) EUROCRYPT 2020, Part I. LNCS, vol. 12105, pp. 313–342. Springer, Cham (2020). https://doi.org/10.1007/978-3-030-45721-1_12
13. Fischlin, M., Rohrbach, F.: Searching for ELFs in the cryptographic forest. Cryptology ePrint Archive, Report 2023/1403. https://eprint.iacr.org/2023/1403
14. Garg, S., Hajiabadi, M., Mahmoody, M., Mohammed, A.: Limits on the power of garbling techniques for public-key encryption. In: Shacham, H., Boldyreva, A. (eds.) CRYPTO 2018, Part III. LNCS, vol. 10993, pp. 335–364. Springer, Cham (2018). https://doi.org/10.1007/978-3-319-96878-0_12
15. Goldreich, O., Kushilevitz, E.: A perfect zero-knowledge proof system for a problem equivalent to the discrete logarithm. J. Cryptol. 6(2), 97–116 (1993). https://doi.org/10.1007/BF02620137
16. Goldwasser, S., Micali, S., Rackoff, C.: The knowledge complexity of interactive proof-systems (extended abstract). In: 17th ACM STOC, pp. 291–304. ACM Press (1985). https://doi.org/10.1145/22145.22178
17. Holmgren, J., Lombardi, A.: Cryptographic hashing from strong one-way functions (or: One-way product functions and their applications). In: Thorup, M. (ed.) 59th FOCS, pp. 850–858. IEEE Computer Society Press (2018). https://doi.org/10.1109/FOCS.2018.00085
18. Hsiao, C.-Y., Reyzin, L.: Finding collisions on a public road, or do secure hash functions need secret coins? In: Franklin, M. (ed.) CRYPTO 2004. LNCS, vol. 3152, pp. 92–105. Springer, Heidelberg (2004). https://doi.org/10.1007/978-3-540-28628-8_6
19. Impagliazzo, R.: A personal view of average-case complexity. In: Proceedings of the Tenth Annual Structure in Complexity Theory Conference, Minneapolis, Minnesota, USA, June 19–22, 1995, pp. 134–147. IEEE Computer Society (1995). https://doi.org/10.1109/SCT.1995.514853
20. Impagliazzo, R., Rudich, S.: Limits on the provable consequences of one-way permutations. In: 21st ACM STOC, pp. 44–61. ACM Press (1989). https://doi.org/10.1145/73007.73012
21. Komargodski, I., Yogev, E.: On distributional collision resistant hashing. In: Shacham, H., Boldyreva, A. (eds.) CRYPTO 2018, Part II. LNCS, vol. 10992, pp. 303–327. Springer, Cham (2018). https://doi.org/10.1007/978-3-319-96881-0_11
22. Micciancio, D., Vadhan, S.P.: Statistical zero-knowledge proofs with efficient provers: lattice problems and more. In: Boneh, D. (ed.) CRYPTO 2003. LNCS, vol. 2729, pp. 282–298. Springer, Heidelberg (2003). https://doi.org/10.1007/978-3-540-45146-4_17
23. Murphy, A., O'Neill, A., Zaheri, M.: Instantiability of classical random-oracle-model encryption transforms. In: Agrawal, S., Lin, D. (eds.) ASIACRYPT 2022, Part IV. LNCS, vol. 13794, pp. 323–352. Springer, Heidelberg (2022). https://doi.org/10.1007/978-3-031-22972-5_12

24. Ostrovsky, R.: One-way functions, hard on average problems, and statistical zero-knowledge proofs. In: Proceedings of the Sixth Annual Structure in Complexity Theory Conference, Chicago, Illinois, USA, June 30 - July 3, 1991, pp. 133–138. IEEE Computer Society (1991). https://doi.org/10.1109/SCT.1991.160253

25. Peikert, C., Waters, B.: Lossy trapdoor functions and their applications. In: Ladner, R.E., Dwork, C. (eds.) 40th ACM STOC, pp. 187–196. ACM Press (2008). https://doi.org/10.1145/1374376.1374406

26. Peikert, C., Waters, B.: Lossy trapdoor functions and their applications. SIAM J. Comput. 40(6), 1803–1844 (2011)

27. Pietrzak, K., Rosen, A., Segev, G.: Lossy functions do not amplify well. In: Cramer, R. (ed.) TCC 2012. LNCS, vol. 7194, pp. 458–475. Springer, Heidelberg (2012). https://doi.org/10.1007/978-3-642-28914-9_26

28. Quach, W., Waters, B., Wichs, D.: Targeted lossy functions and applications. In: Malkin, T., Peikert, C. (eds.) CRYPTO 2021, Part IV. LNCS, vol. 12828, pp. 424–453. Springer, Cham (2021). https://doi.org/10.1007/978-3-030-84259-8_15

29. Sahai, A., Vadhan, S.P.: A complete problem for statistical zero knowledge. J. ACM 50(2), 196–249 (2003). https://doi.org/10.1145/636865.636868

30. Simon, D.R.: Finding collisions on a one-way street: can secure hash functions be based on general assumptions? In: Nyberg, K. (ed.) EUROCRYPT 1998, Part I. LNCS, vol. 1403, pp. 334–345. Springer, Heidelberg (1998). https://doi.org/10.1007/BFb0054137

31. Zhandry, M.: The magic of ELFs. In: Robshaw, M., Katz, J. (eds.) CRYPTO 2016, Part I. LNCS, vol. 9814, pp. 479–508. Springer, Heidelberg (2016). https://doi.org/10.1007/978-3-662-53018-4_18

32. Zhandry, M.: The Magic of ELFs. J. Cryptol. 32(3), 825–866 (2018). https://doi.org/10.1007/s00145-018-9289-9

On Time-Space Lower Bounds for Finding Short Collisions in Sponge Hash Functions

Akshima[1]([✉]), Xiaoqi Duan[2], Siyao Guo[1]([✉]), and Qipeng Liu[3]

[1] Shanghai Frontiers Science Center of Artificial Intelligence and Deep Learning, NYU Shanghai, Shanghai, China
{akshima,siyao.guo}@nyu.edu
[2] ETH Zürich, Zürich, Switzerland
dogther66@gmail.com
[3] UC San Diego, San Diego, USA
qipengliu0@gmail.com

Abstract. Sponge paradigm, used in the design of SHA-3, is an alternative hashing technique to the popular Merkle-Damgård paradigm. We revisit the problem of finding B-block-long collisions in sponge hash functions in the auxiliary-input random permutation model, in which an attacker gets a piece of S-bit advice about the random permutation and makes T (forward or inverse) oracle queries to the random permutation.

Recently, significant progress has been made in the Merkle-Damgård setting and optimal bounds are known for a large range of parameters, including all constant values of B. However, the sponge setting is widely open: there exist significant gaps between known attacks and security bounds even for $B = 1$.

Freitag, Ghoshal and Komargodski (CRYPTO 2022) showed a novel attack for $B = 1$ that takes advantage of the inverse queries and achieves advantage $\widetilde{\Omega}(\min(S^2T^2/2^{2c}, (S^2T/2^{2c})^{2/3}) + T^2/2^r)$, where r is bit-rate and c is the capacity of the random permutation. However, they only showed an $\widetilde{O}(ST/2^c + T^2/2^r)$ security bound, leaving open an intriguing quadratic gap. For $B = 2$, they beat the general security bound by Coretti, Dodis, Guo (CRYPTO 2018) for arbitrary values of B. However, their highly non-trivial argument is quite laborious, and no better (than the general) bounds are known for $B \geq 3$.

In this work, we study the possibility of proving better security bounds in the sponge setting. To this end,

- For $B = 1$, we prove an improved $\widetilde{O}(S^2T^2/2^{2c} + S/2^c + T/2^c + T^2/2^r)$ bound. Our bound strictly improves the bound by Freitag et al., and is optimal for $ST^2 \leq 2^c$.
- For $B = 2$, we give a considerably simpler and more modular proof, recovering the bound obtained by Freitag et al.
- We obtain our bounds by adapting the recent multi-instance technique of Akshima, Guo and Liu (CRYPTO 2022) which bypasses the limitations of prior techniques in the Merkle-Damgård setting. To complement our results, we provably show that the recent multi-instance technique cannot further improve our bounds for $B = 1, 2$, and the general bound by Correti et al., for $B \geq 3$.

© International Association for Cryptologic Research 2023
G. Rothblum and H. Wee (Eds.): TCC 2023, LNCS 14371, pp. 237–270, 2023.
https://doi.org/10.1007/978-3-031-48621-0_9

Overall, our results yield state-of-the-art security bounds for finding short collisions and fully characterize the power of the multi-instance technique in the sponge setting.

Keywords: Collision · hash functions · Sponge · multi-instance · pre-computation · auxiliary input

1 Introduction

Sponge paradigm [BDPA07, BDPA08] is a novel domain extension technique for handling arbitrary long inputs based on a permutation $F : [R] \times [C] \to [R] \times [C]$ (where $C := 2^c$, $R := 2^r$ for bit-rate r and capacity c) with fixed input length. Specifically, a B-block message $\mathbf{m} = (m_1, \cdots, m_B)$ with $m_i \in [R]$ is hashed into $\mathsf{SP}_F(a, \mathbf{m})$ as follows: initialize $(x_0, y_0) = (0, a)$, and compute

$$(x_i, y_i) = F(x_{i-1} \oplus m_i, y_{i-1}) \text{ for } 1 \leq i \leq B; \text{ finally output } x_B$$

where $a \in [C]$ is the initialization salt[1]. We say $\mathbf{m} \neq \mathbf{m}'$ is a pair of B-block collision with respect to a salt a if they both have at most B blocks and $\mathsf{SP}_F(a, \mathbf{m}) = \mathsf{SP}_F(a, \mathbf{m}')$.

Sponge paradigm is an important alternative hashing technique to the popular Merkle-Damgård (MD) paradigm [Mer89, Dam89]. Notably, it has been used in the most recent hashing standard SHA-3. In this work, we are interested in the collision resistance property of sponge hash functions against preprocessing attackers, which can have an arbitrary (but bounded) precomputed advice about F to help.

Recently, several works have rigorously studied the algorithms for collision finding using preprocessing for Merkle-Damgård hash functions [DGK17, CDGS18, ACDW20, GK22, AGL22, FGK23], and significant progress has been made towards fully determining the optimal security bounds for all values of B [GK22, AGL22]. However, unlike the MD setting, the sponge setting draws much less attention [CDG18, FGK22], and our understanding is quite unsatisfactory. Significant gaps exist between known attacks and security bounds even for $B = 1$.

All of them [CDG18, FGK22] studied this question in the auxiliary-input random permutation model (AI-RPM) proposed by Coretti, Dodis and Guo [CDG18]. In this model, F is treated as a random permutation, and an adversary $\mathcal{A}$ consists of a pair of algorithms $(\mathcal{A}_1, \mathcal{A}_2)$. In the offline stage, (computationally unbounded) $\mathcal{A}_1$ precomputes S bits of advice about F. In the online

---

[1] In some practical sponge applications like SHA-3, this salt is usually set to 0. However, when we study the collision resistance of sponge hash functions in the *auxiliary input* model, such a fixed salt will make finding collisions trivial. [CDG18] identified this need for salting the hash functions for collision resistance in the *auxiliary input* model and so we are interested in the security bounds against a random initialization salt (just like what prior works [CDG18, ACDW20, AGL22, FGK22] did). See more details on the definition of the *auxiliary input* model below in Sect. 2.4.

stage, $\mathcal{A}_2$ takes this advice, and receive a random challenge salt a as the initialization salt of F. Next, it makes T oracle queries to F or F^{-1} during the attack, and finally output two messages that form the collision. We remark that inverse queries are not allowed in the MD setting, since the hash functions used by MD are usually one-way functions, while in sponge F is a invertible permutation.

Freitag, Ghoshal and Komargodski [FGK22] showed a novel attack for $B = 1$ that takes advantage of the inverse queries and applies the function inversion algorithms by Hellman [Hel80]. This attack achieves advantage $\Omega(\min(S^2T^2/C^2, (S^2T/C^2)^{2/3}) + T^2/R)$. This is particularly interesting because it suggests that for some range of parameters (e.g., $ST^2 \geq C$), 1-block sponge hashing is less secure than 1-block MD hashing (for which the trivial attack by storing S collisions is known to be optimal [DGK17]). For $B \geq 2$, Freitag et al., based on an analogous attack for MD hashing given by Akshima, Cash, Drucker and Wee [ACDW20], showed an attack with advantage $\widetilde{\Omega}(STB/C + T^2/\min(C, R))$ (the notations $\widetilde{\Omega}, \widetilde{O}$ hides poly-log factors).

In terms of security upper bounds, Coretti, Dodis and Guo [CDG18] proved an $\widetilde{O}(ST^2/C + T^2/R)$ bound for any B, showing the optimality of the attack for finding $B \approx T$-length collisions. For other choices of B, only sub-optimal bounds are known for $B \leq 2$, and no better bound than $\widetilde{O}(ST^2/C + T^2/R)$ is known for any $B \geq 3$. Specifically, Freitag et al. showed an $\widetilde{O}(ST/C + T^2/R)$ bound for $B = 1$ and $\widetilde{O}(ST/C + S^2T^4/C^2 + T^2/\min(C, R))$ bound for $B = 2$. Therefore, there is still a quadratic gap between the attack and security upper bound even for $B = 1$. On the contrast, optimal bounds are known for all constant values of B in the MD setting [DGK17, ACDW20, GK22, AGL22].

That motivates us to study the following question in this paper:

What is the optimal bound for B=1?
Is there a better attack or security upper bound?

From the technical level, we are particularly interested in the multi-instance technique used to prove nearly optimal bounds for MD hashing [AGL22]. Specifically, it has recently been observed that the sequential random multi-instance technique by [AGL22] (referred to as multi-instance games technique in [AGL22]) subsumes the popular presampling technique [CDGS18, CDG18] and sequential distinct multi-instance technique [ACDW20] (referred to as multi-instance problem technique in [AGL22]). In the MD setting, it bypasses provable limitations of presampling technique [CDG18] and gives more modular proofs than sequential distinct multi-instance technique [ACDW20]. Moreover, the sequential random multi-instance technique successfully gave optimal bounds for various primitives even in the quantum setting [CGLQ20]. Therefore, we set out to understand the following question,

Can we prove better bounds or provide simpler proofs using multi-instance games?

In this work, we answer both questions.

1.1 Our Results

Our first contribution is an improved bound for $B = 1$.

Theorem 1 (Informal). *The advantage of the best adversary with S-bit advice and T queries for finding 1-block collisions in sponge hash functions in the auxiliary-input random permutation model, is*

$$\tilde{O}\left(\frac{S^2T^2}{C^2} + \frac{S}{C} + \frac{T}{C} + \frac{T^2}{R}\right).$$

Our bound strictly improves the $\tilde{O}(ST/C + T^2/R)$ bound, and matches the best known attacks for most ranges of parameters. Note that $S/C, T/C, T^2/R$ terms match trivial or standard attacks, and the S^2T^2/C^2 term matches the attack $\min(S^2T^2/C^2, (S^2T/C^2)^{2/3})$ by [FGK22] as long as $ST^2 \leq C$. Notably, our bound is optimal for $ST^2 \leq C$.

We believe that further bridging the gap between the attack by [FGK22] and our bound is challenging. This is because their attack is obtained via connections with the function inversion problem for which an analogues gap exists. Bridging the gap for function inversion problem is a long standing open problem, and better security bounds would imply new classical circuit lower bounds, as shown by Corrigan-Gibbs and Kogan [CGK19].

Our second contribution is a considerably simpler proof for $B = 2$, recovering one of the main results of [FGK22]. The original proof classified the collision structure into over 20 types, while we only need 8 types. This is possible because we do a careful analysis using the MI-games technique from [AGL22].

Theorem 2 (Informal). *The advantage of the best adversary with S-bit advice and T queries for finding 2-block collisions in sponge hash functions in the auxiliary-input random permutation model, is*

$$\tilde{O}\left(\frac{ST}{C} + \frac{S^2T^4}{C^2} + \frac{T^2}{\min(C,R)}\right).$$

We note that the term $ST/C + T^2/\min(C, R)$ matches the best known attack by [FGK22]. Therefore the above bound is optimal when the S^2T^4/C^2 term doesn't dominate the sum, i.e., $ST^3 \leq C$. However, this leaves an intriguing possibility of obtaining a better attack than ST/C for $ST^3 > C$, which will further confirm that sponge hashing is less secure than the MD hashing against preprocessing attackers (this message has been conveyed for $B = 1$ by [FGK22]).

We prove our results using the sequential distinct multi-instance technique (referred to as multi-instance problem technique in [AGL22]), and the sequential random multi-instance technique (referred to as the multi-instance game techniques in [AGL22]). It illustrates the power of the multi-instance technique over prior techniques in the sponge setting. The sequential distinct MI technique bypasses the limitation of the presampling technique (for $B = 1$) and sequential random MI technique gives more modular proofs (for $B = 2$). A comparison of our results with the prior works is summarized in Table 1.

The difference between sequential distinct MI technique and sequential random MI technique is in how the challenge games are defined. As the name suggests, in sequential distinct MI technique the game picks a random set of distinct challenge problems, the adversary is presented with one instance of the challenge problem at a time and has to solve all the instances of the distinct challenge problems to win. Whereas in the sequential random MI technique, the game picks a new randomly chosen instance of challenge problem each time, and the adversary gets that challenge only after solving all the previous challenges. Picking a random instance of the challenge problem allows the sequence of challenges to be independent of each other.

Roughly speaking, the sequential MI technique reduces proving ε security in the auxiliary input model against (S,T)-algorithms to proving $(\varepsilon/2)^S$ security in the (S,T)-multi-instance game. There are S stages in this game, and the adversary need to win all the S stages to win the whole game. In the ith stage, the adversary will first receive a challenge salt a_i, then make T queries to F (or F^{-1} for sponge), and finally output a pair of messages m_A, m_B such that $SP_F(a_i, m_A) = SP_F(a_i, m_B)$. The adversary is allowed to use the queries from previous stages, but is no longer allowed to store advice bits. (See Sect. 2.4 for relevant definitions.)

Given that the sequential MI technique is used successfully to prove optimal bounds for various problems, such as finding 2-block collision in MD hash functions [AGL22], we wonder why we cannot prove better bounds for $B = 2$ in the sponge setting: is it an issue of our proofs or the technique. Therefore, we set out to understand the limitation of this technique.

Our third contribution is the following theorem, which implies that it is impossible to prove better bounds for any B using the sequential multi-instance technique in the sponge setting.

Theorem 3 (Informal). *Suppose $S, T, R \geq 16$. There are adversaries for finding 1-block collisions with advantage $(\widetilde{\Omega}(S^2T^2/C^2))^S$, and adversaries for finding 2-block collisions with advantage $(\widetilde{\Omega}(S^2T^4/C))^S$, and adversaries for finding 3-block collisions with advantage $(\widetilde{\Omega}(ST^2/C))^S$ when $T^2 < R$, in the (S,T)-multi-instance games of sponge hash functions.*

These lower bounds give limitations on the bound one can prove with multi-instance techniques. In particular, it implies that (using the multi-instance technique) the S^2T^2/C^2 term obtained in Theorem 1 cannot be improved. It also explains why Theorem 2 (also [FGK22]) cannot prove better than S^2T^4/C^2, and why no non-trivial bounds (i.e., better than ST^2/C) can be proved for $B \geq 3$. Together with our new security upper bounds and the general known bound[2] for the multi-instance games (summarized in Table 2), we fully characterize the power of the multi-instance technique in the sponge setting. As the bounds in Theorem 1, Theorem 2 and the general $O(ST^2/C + T^2/R)$ bound are the best

---

[2] [CDG18] proved an $\widetilde{O}(\frac{ST^2}{C} + \frac{T^2}{R})$ bound using presampling which implies an $(\widetilde{O}(\frac{ST^2}{C} + \frac{T^2}{R}))^S$ multi-instance security.

one can prove using the multi-instance technique, other novel techniques are required to obtain optimal bounds for collision resistance of sponge in the AI setting. In Sect. 1.3, we point out potential techniques for future directions.

Table 1. Asymptotic security bounds on the security of finding B-block-long collisions in sponge hash functions constructed from a random permutation $F : [R] \times [C] \mapsto [R] \times [C]$ against (S,T)-algorithms. For simplicity, logarithmic terms and constant factors are omitted and $S, T \geq 1$.

	Best known attacks	Previous Security bounds	Our Security bounds
$B = 1$	$\min(\frac{S^2T^2}{C^2}, (\frac{S^2T}{C^2})^{2/3}) +$ $\frac{T^2}{R} + \frac{S}{C} + \frac{T}{C}$	$\frac{ST}{C} + \frac{T^2}{R}$ [FGK22]	$\frac{S^2T^2}{C^2} + \frac{S}{C} + \frac{T}{C} + \frac{T^2}{R}$ [Theorem 1]
$B = 2$	$\frac{ST}{C} + \frac{T^2}{\min(C,R)}$	$\frac{ST}{C} + \frac{S^2T^4}{C^2} + \frac{T^2}{\min(C,R)}$ [FGK22]	$\frac{ST}{C} + \frac{S^2T^4}{C^2} + \frac{T^2}{\min(C,R)}$ [Theorem 2]
$3 \leq B \leq T$	$\frac{STB}{C} + \frac{T^2}{\min(R,C)}$	$\frac{ST^2}{C} + \frac{T^2}{R}$ [CDG18]	–

Table 2. Asymptotic bounds on the security finding B-block-long collisions in sponge hash functions constructed from a random permutation $F : [R] \times [C] \mapsto [R] \times [C]$ in the (S,T)-multi-instance games. We note that naive attacks can achieve $(\widetilde{\Omega}(S/C))^S$, $(\widetilde{\Omega}(T/C))^S$ and $(\widetilde{\Omega}(T^2/R))^S$ advantage in (S,T)-MI games model.

	Our attacks	Security bounds
$B = 1$	$\left(\widetilde{\Omega}\left(\frac{S^2T^2}{C^2}\right)\right)^S$ [Theorem 10]	$\left(\widetilde{O}\left(\frac{S^2T^2}{C^2} + \frac{S}{C} + \frac{T}{C} + \frac{T^2}{R}\right)\right)^S$ [Theorem 8]
$B = 2$	$\left(\widetilde{\Omega}\left(\frac{S^2T^4}{C^2}\right)\right)^S$ [Theorem 11]	$\left(\widetilde{O}\left(\frac{ST}{C} + \frac{S^2T^4}{C^2} + \frac{T}{\min(C,R)}\right)\right)^S$ [Lemma 2]
$3 \leq B \leq T$	$\left(\widetilde{\Omega}\left(\frac{ST^2}{C}\right)\right)^S$ [Theorem 12]	$\left(\widetilde{O}\left(\frac{ST^2}{C} + \frac{T^2}{R}\right)\right)^S$

1.2 Technical Overview

In this section, we present an overview of our proofs using reduction to the the multi-instance game model to analyze security bounds of B-block collision finding for $B = 1$ and $B = 2$, followed by our attacks for $B = 1$, $B = 2$ and $B \geq 3$ in the multi-instance game model.

The high level idea is: the multi-instance approach [AGL22, CGLQ20, IK10, ACDW20, GK22, FGK22] reduces proving the security of a problem with S-bit advice to proving the security of S random instances of the problem. If the instances are given at once, then we call it "parallel" multiple instance problem, and if the instances are presented one at a time, we call it "sequential" multi-instance game. [AGL22] showed that if any adversary (with no advice) can solve S random instances of the problem "sequentially" with success probability at most δ^S, then any adversary with S-bit advice can solve one instance of the problem with success probability at most 2δ. We note that security bounds for "parallel" multiple instance problem implies security bounds for corresponding "sequential" multiple instance games. Henceforth, we always mean sequential multi-instance games when we refer to multi-instance games in this paper.

Our Proof for B = 1. We use the compression technique from [DTT10] to analyze our multi-instance games. The compression technique (refer to Theorem 5 for the precise statement) states that for a pair of encoding and decoding algorithms that can compress a random function by at least $\log 1/\varepsilon$ bits, succeeds with probability at most ε. Here, we will design a pair of encoding and decoding algorithm, such that whenever an adversary $\mathcal{A}$ wins the multi-instance game, the encoder can use this adversary $\mathcal{A}$ to compress F. The challenge is to show that the encoder can compress 'enough' bits using this $\mathcal{A}$ to obtain the desired (upper) bound on the success probability of the adversary $\mathcal{A}$.

To get an idea, we first look at the simplest case. Say there is only 1 stage in the game (i.e., $S = 1$), and the adversary makes two **forward** queries that collide for the challenge salt a. In other words the adversary queries $F(m_1, a)$ and $F(m_2, a)$ such that their outputs are in $(m, *)$. This means the first part of the outputs for both the queries is the same (which is m in this case). Here we can use 2 pointers, each $\log T$ bits long, to store the positions of the two colliding forward queries among the adversary's forward queries, and remove m from F's mapping table corresponding to the second query (Since we know it equals to the first part of output of the first query). This saves $\log R$ bits. Therefore, we can get an $O(T^2/R)$ upper bound as per Theorem 5.

However, for $S > 1$, pointing to the forward colliding queries trivially requires $\log(ST)$-sized pointers (as the adversary makes a total of ST queries). This gives the bound $\varepsilon \leq S^2T^2/C$ which is not good enough. We can do better by storing the colliding queries for all the challenge salts together in an unordered set. The same idea works when the first occurring of the colliding queries is an inverse query and second one is a forward query. Refer to Sect. 3.1.2 for more details about compressing in these cases.

Another possibility is that the adversary always outputs two **inverse** queries, say $F^{-1}(m_i, a_{i_1}) = (m_{i_1}, a_i)$ and $F^{-1}(m_i, a_{i_2}) = (m_{i_2}, a_i)$, as the collision. Then we can compress using that the second part of the output for all these queries will be in $a_1, \ldots, a_S$.

The trickiest case is when the adversary first makes a forward query, say $F(m_{i_1}, a_i) = (m_i, a_{i_1})$, then an inverse query, say $F^{-1}(m_i, a_{i_2}) = (m_{i_2}, a_i)$ as the collision. The trivial thing to do is to compress only the inverse query as above. However, it will only achieve an $O(ST/C)^S$ bound, which is not enough for our results. We use the idea that the output salt of the inverse query is not just in $a_1, \ldots, a_S$ but in fact it is one of the salts that is input to a forward query with output of the form $(m_i, *)$. The issue is the number of salts in $a_1, \ldots, a_S$ meeting this requirement could still be 'large'. When that happens we have to compress the output of the forward queries as well to get enough compression. Refer to Sect. 3.1.2 for more details about this case and how to deal with an adversary that finds different types of collisions for different challenge salts.

Our Proof for B = 2. For $B = 2$, we will use the proof strategy of Akshima et al. [AGL22] for dealing with $B = 2$ in the MD setting. The main difference is that we have to additionally deal with inverse queries in our analysis. We provide a high level overview of their proof, and describe where our proof differs due to inverse queries.

Recall that, to prove the sequential multi-instance security, it is sufficient to bound the advantage of any adversary that finds a 2-block collision for a fresh salt a, conditioned on it finds 2-block collisions for all the previous random challenge salts $a_1, \cdots, a_S$.

Following the terminology of Akshima et al. [AGL22], we call these ST queries made during the first S rounds as offline queries, and among the T queries made for a, we call the queries that were not made during the first S rounds as online queries. Moreover, we focus on the case that the new salt a has never been queried among the offline queries (because the other case happens with probability at most ST/N). As a result, all queries starting with the challenge salt a have to be online queries.

Akshima et al. [AGL22] studied how can the previous ST queries be helpful for this round of game? The main observation of Akshima et al. [AGL22] is that although the adversary learns about the function from the offline queries, and in the worst case, the offline queries could be very helpful. However, the helpful worst offline queries are not typical and can be tolerated by refining the technique. To do this, they define a bunch of helpful "high knowledge gaining" events among previous ST queries including, 1) there are more than S distinct salts with 1-block collision, 2) there are more than S^2 pairs of queries forming collisions, 3) there are more than S distinct salts with self-loops. They show that these events happen with sufficiently small probability, and conditioned on none of them happens, no online algorithms can find 2-block collisions with advantage better than the desired bound.

Now the question is what changes when inverse queries are allowed? The high knowledge gaining events are essentially the same, however some of these events can easily happen when inverse queries are allowed. In particular, for event 2), it was hard to form collisions (under the first part of output) among ST forward queries $F(x_1, y_1), \ldots, F(x_{ST}, y_{ST})$. However, if we make ST inverse queries with form $F^{-1}(0, y_1), \ldots, F^{-1}(0, y_{ST})$, then we have $\Omega((ST)^2)$ pairs of input pairs such that their evaluations in the forward direction form collision (under the first part of output). Given such a set of offline queries, one can find 2-block collisions for a new salt with probability at least $\Omega(S^2 T^4/C^2)$. Fortunately, this is the worst we can get, and we can prove the advantage is at most $\mathcal{O}(S^2 T^4/C^2)$ with adjusted high knowledge gaining events.

Our Attacks for $B = 1, 2, 3$ in the MI Model. We present three simple attacks for finding collisions in the multi-instance model and show their analysis. The main high level idea for all of these attacks is to accumulate relevant high knowledge events in each round to help with the next round.

We briefly illustrate the core idea of our attacks, starting with the attack for $B = 1$. In the ith round, the adversary makes T queries $F^{-1}(0, iT + j)$ for $j = 0, \ldots, T-1$. The intuition is that via these inverse queries, the expected number of salts for which a collision is found (i.e. For a salt a, there exist two inverse queries $F^{-1}(0, x) = (m_1, a)$ and $F^{-1}(0, y) = (m_2, a)$) is $\Omega((iT)^2/C^2)$ in previous i-rounds. Therefore, once the random challenge salt in the i_{th} round is one of these 'solved' salt, then we are already done. Overall, the probability of finding collisions in each of the S rounds in this manner is at least $(\Omega(S^2 T^2/C^2))^S$. We note that this is just the intuition, and we have to carefully deal with the correlations between winning in previous rounds and the expected events happening in previous rounds.

For $B = 2$, the most helpful event is to accumulate a lot of pairs of queries whose first part of output forms a collision. The best way of doing so is to spend an half of the queries in each round to make inverse queries of queries of form $F^{-1}(0, *)$, and spend the other half of the queries trying to hit two of these queries from the current challenge salt a_i. With high probability there will be $\Omega(i^2 T^2 / C^2)$ such pairs, and one can win the i_{th} stage with probability at least $\Omega(i^2 T^4 / C^2)$.

For $B = 3$, the most helpful event is to have at least $\Omega(iT)$ salts such that there are 2-block collisions starting from these salts. Specifically, we first try to find 1-block collision collisions starting from a salt y, and then make queries of form $F^{-1}(*, y)$ to generate these $\Omega(iT)$ salts. Then, with $\Omega(iT^2 / C)$ probability one can hit one of these salts from the challenge salt and form a 3-block collision. We refer to Fig. 7 and Sect. 5 for the details and analysis of these attacks.

1.3 Discussions and Open Problems

Is STB-Conjecture True for Sponge Hashing? Akshima et al. [ACDW20] conjectured that the best attack with time T and space S for finding collisions of length $B \geq 2$ in salted MD hash functions built using compression functions with n-bit output achieves advantage $\Theta((STB + T^2)/2^n)$. It is natural to consider a similar STB-conjecture for sponge hash functions, conjecturing the $\Theta(STB/C + T^2/\min(R, C))$ attack by Freitag et al. [FGK22] is optimal for $B \geq 2$. However, this conjecture is only proved for very large $B \approx T$ [CDG18], and sponge hash is provably less secure than MD hash [FGK22] for $B = 1$. It will be extremely interesting to either prove or refute the sponge STB-conjecture. To start with, is the STB-conjecture true for $B = 2$ in sponge?

Better Attacks for $B = 2$? The current security upper bound for $B = 2$ suggests that there may exist an attack with advantage $\Omega(S^2 T^4 / C^2)$ in the auxiliary-input random permutation model. And we show an attack in the multi-instance model with advantage $(\Omega(S^2 T^4 / C^2))^S$. Can we utilize similar ideas to show a corresponding attack in the auxiliary-input random permutation model?

Better Bounds via Stateless Multi-instance Games? Our results characterize the power of the multi-instance technique in the sponge setting by presenting attacks in the model of Akshima et al. [AGL22]. We observe that, a variant of the reduction of Akshima et al. [AGL22] allows one to consider more restricted multiple-instance games, where the adversary is stateless and doesn't remember information from previous rounds. Because our attacks require knowing queries from previous rounds, our attacks don't apply to stateless multi-instance games. We remark that analyzing stateless adversary for multi-instance games is non-trivial because, although the challenges are independent, the same random permutation is reused in multiple rounds. We hope that the study of stateless multi-instance games will shed light on how to obtain optimal bounds for finding collisions in sponge and potentially close the gap for MD other major open problem (such as function inversion) in this area.

Other Related Works. In a recent work [GGPS23], Golovnev et al. presented an algorithm for function inversion which works for any S, T such that $TS^2 \cdot \max\{S, T\} = \widetilde{\Theta}(C^3)$ (where C is the size of the range of function) and improves over the Fiat and Noar algorithm when $S < T$. We mention that the time-space tradeoffs of many other cryptographic primitives, such as one-way functions, pseudorandom random generators, discrete discrete logarithm have been studied in various idealized models [DTT10, CHM20, CGK18, CGK19, GGKL21, DGK17, CDG18, CDGS18]. Recently, Ghoshal and Tessaro studied the pre-image resistance and collision-resistance security of preprocessing attacks with bounded offline and online queries for Merkle-Damgård construction in [GT23].

2   Preliminaries

2.1   Notations

For any positive integer N, we write $[N]$ to denote the set $\{1, \ldots, N\}$. For any non-negative integers N, k, $\binom{[N]}{k}$ is used to denote the collection of all k-sized subsets of $[N]$. For any finite set X, $\mathbf{x} \leftarrow_\$ X$ indicates $\mathbf{x}$ is a uniform random variable in X. We write X^+ to indicate a tuple of one or more elements from X.

2.2   Random Permutation Model

Random Permutation model is an idealized model where a function is modelled as a random permutation sampled uniformly from all possible permutations.

Lazy Sampling. One useful property of modelling a function, say F, as a random permutation is that sampling F uniformly at random is equivalent to initializing F with $\perp$ for every input and sampling the responses uniformly at random without replacement as and when the input is queried.

2.3   Sponge Hash Functions

A cryptographic hash function is a function that takes input of arbitrary length and outputs a fixed length string. They are widely used in security applications such as digital signatures, message authentication codes and password hashing. In practice, several hash functions, including SHA-3, are based on the popular Sponge Construction.

A sponge based hash function internally uses a permutation function of fixed length domain. We will treat this permutation as a random permutation for the purpose of analyzing it's security.

We will parameterize our sponge function SP as a function in $[R]^+ \times [C] \to [R]$ such that it uses a random permutation, denoted by F, on $[R] \times [C]$ where $[R]$ corresponds to the set of messages and $[C]$ corresponds to the set of salts. Note that as F is a permutation, its inverse, denoted F^{-1}, is an efficiently computable function. Hence, any entity that can query F can also query F^{-1}.

Say $F(m,a) = (m',a')$ for some $m, m' \in [R]$ and $a, a' \in [C]$, then will use $F(m,a)[1], F(m,a)[2]$ to denote the first and second element from the output tuple. In other words, $F(m,a)[1] = m'$ and $F(m,a)[2] = a'$.

A message m is called a B-block message if it can be written as $m = m_1\|\ldots\|m_B$ where each $m_i \in [R]$. Then for a B-block message $m = m_1\|m_2\|\ldots\|m_B$ and some $a \in [C]$, we define the function $\mathsf{SP}_F(m,a)$ as follows:

1. Initialize $(x_0, y_0) = (0, a)$.
2. For the ith block, compute $(x_i, y_i) = F(x_{i-1} \oplus m_i, y_{i-1})$.
3. Return x_B.

Collisions. For a given $a \in [C]$, two distinct messages $m, m' \in [R]^+$ are said to form a **collision**, if

$$\mathsf{SP}_F(m,a) = \mathsf{SP}_F(m',a)$$

2.4   Definitions

We establish some definitions in this subsection which will be used throughtout the paper.

Definition 1. *We refer to two queries (m_1, a_1) and (m_2, a_2) as **same** or not distinct if one of the following holds true:*

1. *when both queries are made to F (or F^{-1}), $a_1 = a_2$ and $m_1 = m_2$*
2. *(m_1, a_1) is made to F (or F^{-1}), (m_2, a_2) is made to F^{-1} (or F) and $F(m_1, a_1) = (m_2, a_2)$ (or $F^{-1}(m_1, a_1) = (m_2, a_2)$)*

*If two queries are not same, then they are referred to as **distinct**.*

Next, we define an AI-adversary against collision resistance in Sponge functions.

Definition 2. *A pair of algorithms $\mathcal{A} = (\mathcal{A}_1, \mathcal{A}_2)$ is an (S,T)-AI adversary for SP_F if*

- *$\mathcal{A}_1$ has unbounded access to F (and F^{-1}), and outputs S bits of advice, denoted σ*
- *$\mathcal{A}_2$ takes σ and a challenge salt $a \in [C]$ as input, makes T queries to F or F^{-1}, and outputs m, m'.*

Next, we define the security game for B-block collision-resistance against the (S,T)-AI adversary.

Definition 3. *For any fixed random permutation $F : [R] \times [C] \to [R] \times [C]$, a salt $a \in [C]$ and B which is a function of R, C, we define the game B-AICR in Fig. 1.*

Game B-AICR$_{F,a}(\mathcal{A})$

$\sigma \leftarrow \mathcal{A}_1^F$

$m, m' \leftarrow \mathcal{A}_2^{F/F^{-1}}(\sigma, a)$

If m or m' consists of more than B blocks

   Then Return 0

If $m \neq m'$ and $\mathsf{SP}_F(m, a) = \mathsf{SP}_F(m', a)$

   Then Return 1

Else Return 0

Fig. 1. Security game B-AICR$_{F,a}(\mathcal{A})$

For any (S, T)-AI adversary $\mathcal{A}$, its advantage is denoted by $\mathsf{Adv}_{B\text{-}SP}^{AICR}(\mathcal{A})$ and defined as the probability that for a uniformly random permutation F and a random salt $a \in [C]$, the game B-AICR$_{F,a}(\mathcal{A})$ returns 1. For any functions S, T, B, we define (S, T, B)-auxiliary input collision resistance of Sponge functions, denoted by $\mathsf{Adv}_{B\text{-}SP}^{AICR}(S, T)$, as the maximum advantage taken over all (S, T)-AI adversaries.

It is known from several prior works that security in the AI model is closely related to the security in the multi-instance model. In this work, we will analyze the security in the MI model and use this relation to obtain security bounds in the AI model. To this end, we formally define the multi-instance (MI) adversary and two versions of the security game for collision resistance against the MI adversary next.

Definition 4. *A stateful algorithm $\mathcal{A}$ is an (S, T)-MI adversary against collision resistance in SP_F if for every $i \in [S]$:*

- *$\mathcal{A}$ takes a salt $a_i \in [C]$ as input*
- *$\mathcal{A}$ makes T queries to F or F^{-1}*
- *$\mathcal{A}$ outputs m_i, m_i'.*

We define the security games next.

Definition 5. *For any fixed random permutation $F : [R] \times [C] \to [R] \times [C]$, fixed B and S that are functions of R, C, we define the game B-MICR^S in Fig. 2.*

Game B-MICR$_F^S(\mathcal{A})$

   For $i \in [S]$:

      Sample $a_i \leftarrow [C]$ at uniformly random without replacement

      $m_i, m_i' \leftarrow \mathcal{A}^{F/F^{-1}}(a_i)$

      If m_i or m_i' consists of more than B blocks

         Then Return 0

      If $m_i = m_i'$ or $\mathsf{SP}_F(m_i, a_i) \neq \mathsf{SP}_F(m_i', a_i)$

         Then Return 0

   Return 1

Fig. 2. Security game B-MICR$_F^S(\mathcal{A})$

For any (S, T)-MI adversary $\mathcal{A}$, its advantage is denoted by $\mathsf{Adv}^{\mathsf{MICR}}_{\mathsf{B\text{-}SP}}(\mathcal{A})$ and defined as the probability that for a uniformly random permutation F, the game $\mathsf{B\text{-}MICR}^S_F(\mathcal{A})$ returns 1. For any functions S, T, B, we define (S, T, B)-multi-instance collision resistance of Sponge functions, denoted by $\mathsf{Adv}^{\mathsf{MICR}}_{\mathsf{B\text{-}SP}}(S, T)$, as the maximum advantage taken over all (S, T)-MI adversaries.

Next, we define another game for the MI adversary and it is differs from the one above only in the way it samples salts uniformly at random with replacement.

Definition 6. *For any fixed random permutation $F : [R] \times [C] \to [R] \times [C]$, fixed B and S that are functions of R, C, we define the game $\mathsf{B\text{-}rand\text{-}MICR}^S$ in Fig. 3.*

Game $\mathsf{B\text{-}rand\text{-}MICR}^S_F(\mathcal{A})$

    For $i \in [S]$:

        Sample $a_i \leftarrow_\$ [C]$

        $m_i, m'_i \leftarrow \mathcal{A}^{F/F^{-1}}(a_i)$

        If m_i or m'_i consists of more than B blocks

            Then Return 0

        If $m_i = m'_i$ or $\mathsf{SP}_F(m_i, a_i) \neq \mathsf{SP}_F(m'_i, a_i)$

            Then Return 0

    Return 1

Fig. 3. Security game $\mathsf{B\text{-}rand\text{-}MICR}^S_F(\mathcal{A})$

$\mathsf{Adv}^{\mathsf{rand\text{-}MICR}}_{\mathsf{B\text{-}SP}}(\mathcal{A})$ and $\mathsf{Adv}^{\mathsf{rand\text{-}MICR}}_{\mathsf{B\text{-}SP}}(S, T)$ are analogously defined for (S, T)-MI adversaries as in Definition 5.

2.5 Relevant Results

We will use the following theorems in our proofs:

Theorem 4 (Chernoff bounds). *Suppose $\mathbf{x}_1, \ldots, \mathbf{x}_t$ are independent random variables. Let $\mathbf{x} = \sum_{i=1}^t \mathbf{x}_i$ and $\mu = \mathbb{E}[\mathbf{x}]$. For any $\delta \geq 0$, it holds that*

$$\Pr[\mathbf{x} \geq (1 + \delta)\mu] \leq \exp\left(\frac{-\delta^2 \mu}{2 + \delta}\right).$$

Theorem 5 ([DTT10]). *For any pair of encoding and decoding algorithms (Enc, Dec), where $Enc : \{0, 1\}^x \to \{0, 1\}^y$ and $Dec : \{0, 1\}^y \to \{0, 1\}^x$, such that $Dec(Enc(z)) = z$ with probability at least ϵ where $z \leftarrow \{0, 1\}^x$, then $y \geq x - \log \frac{1}{\epsilon}$.*

This is the compression theorem we mentioned earlier, and we will use it frequently in our proofs.

Theorem 6. *For any S, T, B and $\delta \in [0, 1]$, if $\mathsf{Adv}^{\mathsf{rand\text{-}MICR}}_{\mathsf{B\text{-}SP}}(S, T) \leq \delta^S$, then $\mathsf{Adv}^{\mathsf{AICR}}_{\mathsf{B\text{-}SP}} \leq 2\delta$.*

Such a theorem relating AI-security to MI-security has been used in several prior works. Refer to theorem 3 in [AGL22] for more details and proof.

Theorem 7. *For any S, T, B, C, if $\mathsf{Adv}^{\mathsf{MICR}}_{\mathsf{B\text{-}SP}}(u, T) \leq \delta^u$ for all $u \in [S]$, then $\mathsf{Adv}^{\mathsf{rand\text{-}MICR}}_{\mathsf{B\text{-}SP}}(S, T) \leq (\delta + \frac{S}{C})^S$.*

Proof. Fix an arbitrary (S, T)-MI adversary $\mathcal{A}$. Let X_i be an indicator that $\mathcal{A}$ wins on the ith instance, i.e., finds B-block collision on a_i (i^{th} challenge salt). Then

$$\mathsf{Adv}^{\mathsf{rand\text{-}MICR}}_{\mathsf{B\text{-}SP}}(\mathcal{A}) = \Pr[X_1 \wedge \cdots \wedge X_S] = \prod_{i=1}^{S} \Pr[X_i | X_{<i}]$$

$$\leq \prod_{i=1}^{S} \left(\Pr[a_i = a_j \text{ for some } j < i] + \Pr[X_i | X_{<i} \wedge a_i \neq a_j \text{ for all } j < i] \right)$$

$$= \prod_{i=1}^{S} \left(\frac{i-1}{C} + \delta \right) \leq \left(\frac{S}{C} + \delta \right)^S$$

where the third equality follows from the fact that $\mathsf{Adv}^{\mathsf{MICR}}_{\mathsf{B\text{-}SP}}(u, T) \leq \delta^u$ for every $u \in [S]$. □

This theorem relates the advantage of an MI-adversary that receives random challenge salts (which can possibly repeat) to an MI-adversary that always receives distinct challenge salts.

3 Improved Bound for $B = 1$ (Optimal When $ST^2 \leq C$)

Theorem 8. *For any S, T, R, C such that $S \geq 2^{12}, \max\{\frac{ST}{C}, \frac{T^2}{R}\} < \frac{1}{8e^9}$, then*

$$\mathsf{Adv}^{\mathsf{AICR}}_{\mathsf{1\text{-}SP}}(S, T) = \tilde{O}\left(\frac{T^2}{R} + \frac{S}{C} + \frac{T}{C} + \left(\frac{ST}{C}\right)^2 \right)$$

To prove this theorem, we first reduce AI-security to MI-security via Theorem 6 and Theorem 7. Now we only need to look at the advantage bound for any MI-adversary $\mathcal{A}$ in game B-MICR$^S_F(\mathcal{A})$. In this game, all the challenge salts $a_1, \ldots, a_S$ are different, and unlike the AI model, here the adversary doesn't have any advice (except the information from previous stages).

In fact, we have the following lemma, which we will prove in the next section:

Lemma 1. *For any S, T, R, C such that $S \geq 2^{12}, \max\{\frac{ST}{C}, \frac{T^2}{R}\} < \frac{1}{8e^9}$, then*

$$\mathsf{Adv}^{\mathsf{MICR}}_{\mathsf{1\text{-}SP}} = \left(\tilde{O}\left(\frac{T^2}{R} + \frac{T}{C} + \left(\frac{ST}{C}\right)^2 \right) \right)^S$$

Now we can prove the main theorem.

Proof. (Proof of Theorem 8). The Theorem is immediate from Theorem 6, Theorem 7 and Lemma 1.

3.1   Proof of Lemma 1

We will prove the lemma via compression. In Sect. 3.1.1 and 3.1.2, we will design a set of encoding and decoding algorithms, such that given any MI-adversary $\mathcal{A}$, if $\mathcal{A}$ wins on 'too many' S-sized subsets of $[C]$, we can use fewer bits to describe the function F (i.e. compress it). However, this contradicts with Theorem 5 and thus bounds the number of S-sized subsets of $[C]$ any adversary can succeed on. In Sect. 3.1.3, we will first analyze the number of bits our algorithm can save, and then finally prove Lemma 1 via compression argument. To this end, we first identify the types of 1-block collisions.

3.1.1   Type of Collisions

Due to the existence of F^{-1}, there are 3 possible types of collisions when $B = 1$. A pair of collision (m_1, m_2) on salt a, such that $F(m_1, a) = (m, a_1)$ and $F(m_2, a) = (m, a_2)$, can be classified into cases according to the type and relative position of the corresponding "fresh" queries as made by the adversary.

Here a query $F(m_1, a) = (m, a_1)$ is "fresh" means that neither $F(m_1, a)$ nor $F^{-1}(m, a_1)$ has been queried previously. A query to F is referred to as a forward query and a query to F^{-1} is referred to as an inverse query.

WLOG we assume $F(m_1, a)$ or $F^{-1}(m, a_1)$ is queried for the first time before $F(m_2, a)$ or $F^{-1}(m, a_2)$ is queried for the first time. Then the 3 types of collisions are as follows:

- Type 1: The second fresh query is of the form $F(m_2, a)$, i.e. the first fresh query from the collision can be either a forward query or an inverse query but the second one is a forward query.
- Type 2: The fresh queries are of the form $F^{-1}(m, a_1)$ and $F^{-1}(m, a_2)$, i.e. both fresh queries are inverse queries (that queries F^{-1}).
- Type 3: The fresh queries are of the form $F(m_1, a)$ and $F^{-1}(m, a_2)$ (i.e. the first fresh query is a forward query, and the second fresh query is an inverse query).

See Fig. 4 for details.

3.1.2   Encoding and Decoding Algorithms

Now we state our encoding and decoding algorithms for the random permutation function $F : [R] \times [C] \to [R] \times [C]$. Let $\mathcal{A}$ be an (S, T)-MI adversary that wins the game, i.e. succeeds on S different challenge salts $a_1, \ldots, a_S$. Generally, in the encoding algorithm, we will store a partial mapping table of F that contains answers to all the queries made by $\mathcal{A}$ in order, except the entries (corresponding to the mappings) we delete from the table, followed by the remaining of the function table (not queried by $\mathcal{A}$) in the lexicographic order. Note that we will store some extra bits apart from the function table that will help recover the deleted entries from the table. In the decoding algorithm, we will restore the removed entries using these extra bits, and thus restore the entire function table.

The encoding algorithm is as follows:

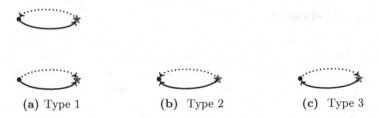

Fig. 4. All 3 types of collisions. Line directed $\rightarrow$ represents query to F and line directed $\leftarrow$ represents query to F^{-1}. $\bullet$ represents that (output/input of) the two queries share the salt. $\star$ represents that (output/input of) the two queries share the message. The dotted line means this query occurs first, and the solid line means this query occurs later than the dotted line query.

1. Simulate $\mathcal{A}$ on F and $a_1, \ldots, a_S$, and maintain a table that contains the response to each query made by $\mathcal{A}$ in order (e.g. If the first query made by the adversary is $F(m', a') = (m, a)$, then the first entry will be (m, a)).
2. As $\mathcal{A}$ succeeds on $a_1, \ldots, a_S$, it is guaranteed to output S pairs of messages that form collision with each of $a_1, \ldots, a_S$ under SP_F in the simulation. According to the collision types in Sect. 3.1.1, divide the salts into 3 sets $\mathbb{S}_1, \mathbb{S}_2, \mathbb{S}_3$, respectively. Denote $S_i = |\mathbb{S}_i|$ for $i = 1, 2, 3$, i.e. S_i is the size for set $\mathbb{S}_i$.
3. For salts in set $\mathbb{S}_1$:
   (a) Use $\log S$ bits to store S_1 (i.e. the number of salts in $\mathbb{S}_1$).
   (b) Use $2 \log \binom{ST}{S_1}$ bits to store in an unordered fashion the set containing indices of **fresh** queries that form collisions for each salt in $\mathbb{S}_1$. (Since for each salt there are exactly 2 queries that form the collision, and there are ST possible locations for each such query, we need $2 \log \binom{ST}{S_1}$ to store this set.)
   (c) For each pair of collision $F(m_{i_1}, a_i) = (m_i, a')$ (or $F^{-1}(m_i, a') = (m_{i_1}, a_i)$) and $F(m_{i_2}, a_i) = (m_i, a'')$ in the order of occurrence, remove m_i in the output of the second query (i.e. the first part of output), but keep the second part. Namely, we remove the the response to $F(m_{i_2}, a_i)$ in the function table, but use extra $\log C$ bits to store the second part, i.e. a''. So after this step, we remove S_1 entries from the function table, and stored the size of $\mathbb{S}_1$ in $\log S$ bits, the set in $2 \log \binom{ST}{S_1}$ bits and second part of the S_1 entries in $S_1 \log C$ bits.
4. For salts in set $\mathbb{S}_2$:
   (a) Use $\log S$ bits to store S_2.
   (b) Use $2 \log \binom{ST}{S_2}$ bits to store the set of indices of **fresh** queries that form collision for each salt in $\mathbb{S}_2$.
   (c) For each stored query $F^{-1}(m, a') = (m', a_i)$, use $\log S$ bits to store the salt index i (since a_i is among $a_1, \ldots, a_S$), and remove a_i from the response of the query. (Still, it means that we remove the corresponding entry in the function table, and use $\log R$ extra bits to store m'.)

5. For salts in set $\mathbb{S}_3$, depending on the parameters S, T, R, there are two corresponding strategies of compression:
   (a) When $ST > R$:
      i. Use $\log S$ bits to store S_3.
      ii. Use $2 \log \binom{ST}{S_3}$ bits to store the positions of fresh queries which form the collision for each salt $a_i \in \mathbb{S}_3$. (There will be S_3 inverse queries and S_3 forward queries.)
      iii. For each stored inverse query $F^{-1}(m_i, a') = (m_{i_2}, a_i)$, count the number of **stored** forward query $F(m_{j_1}, a_j) = (m_j, a'')$ in previous step, such that $j < i$ and $m_j = m_i$. Denote this number by q_{m_i}. Then we use extra $\log q_{m_i}$ bits to indicate which forward query is exactly the matching query for the current inverse query (Since the matching query must be within these q_{m_i} stored queries). Finally, remove the second part of output of these S_3 inverse queries (i.e. remove a_i).
      iv. For $m \in [R]$, let $Q(m)$ be the set of **stored** forward queries $F(m_{i_1}, a_i) = (m_i, a')$ in step 5(a)ii where $m_i = m$. Denote $Q_m = |Q(m)|$, i.e. the size of $Q(m)$. Notice all the values q_m defined in step 5(a)iii also satisfy $q_m \le Q_m$ (since q_m only counts the previous queries).

      Now, if there exists m such that $Q_m > \log STR$, we will use extra bits to save information about these forward queries (since their first part of output are all m):
         (a) Use $\log S$ bits to indicate the number of m such that $Q_m > \log STR$.
         (b) For each such m:
            – Use $\log R$ bits to store m.
            – Use $\log S_3$ bits to store Q_m. (Since all the elements in $Q(m)$ are from stored forward queries, the size is at most S_3.)
            – Use $\log \binom{S_3}{Q_m}$ bits to store the positions of queries in $Q(m)$ (among stored forward queries in step 5(a)ii), i.e. the queries with first part of output being m.
            – Remove the first part of output of all these Q_m queries (i.e. remove m in the output).
         For convenience, we denote $Q_{tot} = \sum_{m \in [R]: Q_m > \log STR} Q_m$.
   (b) When $ST \le R$:
      i. Use $\log S$ bits to store S_3.
      ii. Use $\log \binom{ST}{S_3}$ bits to store the positions of fresh **inverse** queries which find the collision for each salt $a_i \in \mathbb{S}_3$. (There will be S_3 inverse queries.) Notice we no longer store forward queries.
      iii. For each stored inverse query $F^{-1}(m_i, a') = (m_{i_2}, a_i)$, count the number of **all** forward queries $F(m_{j_1}, a_j) = (m_j, a'')$ such that $j < i$ and $m_j = m_i$. Denote this number be q_{m_i}. Then we use extra $\log q_{m_i}$ bits to indicate which forward query is exactly the matching query for the current inverse query. (Notice q_{m_i} can be as large as ST.) Finally, remove the second part of output of these S_3 inverse queries (i.e. remove a_i).

iv. For $m \in [R]$, denote $Q(m)$ be the set of **all** queries $F(m_{i_1}, a_i) = (m_i, a')$ (or $F^{-1}(m_i, a') = (m_{i_1}, a_i)$) such that $m_i = m$, and Q_m be the size of $Q(m)$. Further, denote K_m be the number of **stored** inverse queries $F^{-1}(m_i, a'') = (m_{i_2}, a_i)$ in step 5(b)ii such that $m_i = m$. Obviously $K_m \leq Q_m$. Further, all the values q_m occurred in step 5(b)iii also satisfy $q_m \leq Q_m$ (since q_m only counts the previous queries).

Now, if there exists m such that $Q_m > \log STR$ and $K_m \geq 1$, we will use extra bits to save information about these forward queries (since their first part of output are all m):

A. Use $\log S$ bits to indicate the number of m such that $Q_m > \log STR$.

B. For each such m:
   - Use $\log R$ bits to store m.
   - Use $\log ST$ bits to store Q_m. (Notice now Q_m can be as large as ST.)
   - Use $\log \binom{ST}{Q_m}$ bits to store the indices of the queries whose first part of response is m. (Notice since we don't store the forward queries in step 5(b)ii, here we need $\log \binom{ST}{Q_m}$ instead of $\log \binom{S_3}{Q_m}$.)
   - Remove the first part of the response to all these Q_m queries (i.e. remove m in the output).

   For convenience, we denote $Q_{tot} = \sum_{m \in [R]: Q_m > \log STR, K_m \geq 1} Q_m$, and $K_{tot} = \sum_{m \in [R]: Q_m > \log STR, K_m \geq 1} K_m$. Since $K_m \leq Q_m$ for any m, we have $K_{tot} \leq Q_{tot}$.

6. The final output of the encoding algorithm will be the extra bits generated in steps 3-5 (except step 5(a)iii and 5(b)iii), followed by the function table (with some entries deleted) that contains responses of the queries, followed by the remaining function table of F that remains unqueried by the adversary, followed by the extra bits in step 5(a)iii and 5(b)iii in the order that the corresponding query is made by the adversary.

Next, we state our decoding algorithm which can fully recover the random permutation function F (for a succeeding adversary).

1. Read out the first part of generated extra bits according to encoding step 3-5. For example, for step 3, we first read S_1, then according to S_1 we know the value of $2 \log \binom{ST}{S_1}$, so we can continue reading out the indices of the stored queries, etc. After this step we will know the total number of removed queries in the table, and thus we know the starting point of the second part of extra bits.

2. Now simulate the adversary $\mathcal{A}$ on the given salts $a_1, \ldots, a_S$. During the process, $\mathcal{A}$ will make several oracle queries to either F or F^{-1}, and we know from the extra bits whether we have removed the corresponding entry in the (partial) function table or not.
   - If the query is not removed from the function table, we simply read the next entry from the table and answer it directly.

- Otherwise, it must have been deleted in one of the encoding steps 3–5. Formally, we must have stored information about this query in either step 3b, 4b, 5(a)ii, 5(a)ivB, 5(b)ii or 5(b)ivB.
  - It is stored in encoding step 3b. Thus it must be a forward query with form $F(m_0, a) = (?, a')$ (we know a' since we have stored it when encoding, but we don't know the first part). Then we look at the whole stored query set in step 3b. Since all challenge salts are different, we can uniquely determine its corresponding first occurring query $F(m_1, a) = (m, a')$ or $F^{-1}(m, a') = (m_1, a)$ according to a . Hence, we know $F(m_0, a) = (m, a')$.
  - It is stored in encoding step 4b. Thus it must be an inverse query of the form $F^{-1}(m, a) = (m', ?)$. From the stored index i we immediately know $F^{-1}(m, a) = (m', a_i)$.
  - It is stored in encoding step 5(a)ii or 5(b)iii. Thus it must be an inverse query of the form $F^{-1}(m, a_0) = (m', ?)$. Further, we also know a $\log q_m$ pointer to its corresponding forward query $F(m_1, a) = (m, a_1)$ or $F^{-1}(m, a_1) = (m_1, a)$. (Since we already know all the previous queries, we can easily recover the set $Q(m)$ and know the value q_m, and then we can read the next $\log q_m$ bits from the second part of extra bits, and determine the specific query.) Then we know $F^{-1}(m, a_0) = (m', a)$.
  - It is stored in encoding step 5(a)ivB or 5(b)ivB. Then it must be a forward query of the form $F(m', a') = (?, a'')$. Since we have stored the corresponding m for this query, we know $F(m', a') = (m, a'')$.
3. Continue reading out the function table of F that are not queried by the adversary.

Therefore, as long as the adversary $\mathcal{A}$ can successfully find all the S collisions, we can correctly restore the the function F.

3.1.3   Number of Bits Saved

In this section, we will analyze the number of bits we can compress using our encoding algorithm, and then prove Lemma 1.

In our algorithm, the compression comes from deleting several entries of the function table of F and storing some extra (lesser number of) bits for learning those deleted entries. The following claim shows the compression from removing these entries:

Claim 1. *Suppose in the encoding algorithm we removed y entries from the function table, and stored x extra bits for information. Then we can save at least $y(\log RC - 1) - x$ bits via the compression.*

Proof. In order to count the saving, we first need to know how many bits are needed to store these rows originally. Note that the adversary $\mathcal{A}$ only queries at most ST values of F, and touches at most $2ST$ (message,salt) pairs (either in the input of the query, or from output of the query), so there will be at least

$RC - 2ST \geq \frac{RC}{2}$ untouched pairs. Therefore, for each query, there are at least $\frac{RC}{2}$ different possible outputs (since the output can be any of the untouched pairs), and we need at least $\log RC - 1$ bits to store these entries. Since it's true for any query, we originally need at least $y(\log RC - 1)$ to store all these removed entries, so we can save at least $y(\log RC - 1) - x$ bits. $\qquad \square$

Next, we analyze the savings according to the types of collisions:

- In step 3, we stored $\log S + 2 \log \binom{ST}{S_1} + S_1 \log C$ extra bits. Besides, we deleted S_1 entries from the function table. Therefore, according to the above claim, we can save at least

$$L_1 := S_1(\log RC - 1) - \log S - 2 \log \binom{ST}{S_1} - S_1 \log C$$
$$= S_1(\log R - 1) - \log S - 2 \log \binom{ST}{S_1}$$

bits.

- In step 4, we stored $\log S + 2 \log \binom{ST}{S_2} + 2S_2 \log S + 2S_2 \log R$ bits, and deleted $2S_2$ entries from the function table. Then we can save at least

$$L_2 := 2S_2(\log C - 1) - \log S - 2S_2 \log S - 2 \log \binom{ST}{S_2}$$

bits.

- In step 5:
  - When $ST > R$, we first stored $\log S + 2 \log \binom{ST}{S_3} + \log S$ bits, and for each query we stored an $\log q_{m_i}$ bit pointer. Further, for each large Q_i, we stored $\log R + \log S_3 + \log \binom{S_3}{Q_i}$ bits. What we saved is the second part of output of S_3 inverse queries, which is at least $S_3(\log C - 1)$ bits, and the first part of the response to the queries in Q_i, which is at least $Q_i(\log R - 1)$ bits. Therefore, we can save at least

$$L_3 := S_3(\log C - 1) + \sum_{i:Q_i > \log STR} Q_i(\log R - 1) - 2 \log S$$
$$- 2 \log \binom{ST}{S_3} - \sum_{i:Q_i > \log STR} \left(\log S_3 + \log \binom{S_3}{Q_i} + \log R \right) - \sum_i Q_i \log Q_i$$

bits.
  - When $ST \leq R$, similarly we can save at least

$$L_3 := S_3(\log C - 1) + \sum_{i:Q_i > \log STR, K_i \geq 1} Q_i(\log R - 1) - 2 \log S$$
$$log\binom{ST}{S_3} - \sum_{i:Q_i > \log STR, K_i \geq 1} \left(\log ST + \log \binom{ST}{Q_i} + \log R \right) - \sum_i K_i \log Q_i$$

bits.

Based on the above analysis, we have the following claims:

Claim 2. *Suppose* $S \geq 2^{12}, \max\{\frac{ST}{C}, \frac{T^2}{R}\} < \frac{1}{8e^9}$. *When* $ST > R$:

$$2^{L_1+L_2+L_3} = \left(\tilde{O}\left(\frac{T^2}{R} + \left(\frac{ST}{C}\right)^2\right)\right)^S$$

Claim 3. *Suppose* $S \geq 2^{12}, \max\{\frac{ST}{C}, \frac{T^2}{R}\} < \frac{1}{8e^9}$. *When* $ST \leq R$:

$$2^{L_1+L_2+L_3} = \left(\tilde{O}\left(\frac{T^2}{R} + \left(\frac{ST}{C}\right)^2 + \frac{T}{C}\right)\right)^S$$

The proof for these claims can be found in the full version of the paper on ePrint Archive.

Proof. (Proof of Lemma 1). For any adversary $\mathcal{A}$, denote $\epsilon = \mathsf{Adv}_{1\text{-SP}}^{\mathsf{MICR}}(\mathcal{A})$. According to Theorem 5, Claim 2 and Claim 3:

$$\log \epsilon \leq L_1 + L_2 + L_3$$
$$\epsilon \leq 2^{L_1+L_2+L_3}$$
$$\leq \left(\tilde{O}\left(\frac{T^2}{R} + \left(\frac{ST}{C}\right)^2 + \frac{T}{C}\right)\right)^S$$

Since it holds for any $\mathcal{A}$, according to definition of $\mathsf{Adv}_{1\text{-SP}}^{\mathsf{MICR}}$, this completes the proof. □

4 A Simpler Proof for $B = 2$

In this section we analyze the lower bound for 2-block collisions in Sponge hash functions in the AI model via reduction to MI model. Our bound in the MI model matches the attack in the MI model (refer to Sect. 5.2).

Theorem 9. *For any* S, T, C *and* R,

$$\mathsf{Adv}_{2\text{-SP}}^{\mathsf{AICR}}(S, T) = \tilde{O}\left(\left(\frac{ST^2}{C}\right)^2 + \frac{ST}{C} + \frac{T^2}{C} + \frac{T^2}{R}\right).$$

From Theorem 6 , we know it suffices to prove the following lemma in order to prove Theorem 9.

Lemma 2. *For any* S, T, C *and* R,

$$\mathsf{Adv}_{2\text{-SP}}^{\mathsf{rand\text{-}MICR}}(S, T) = \left(\tilde{O}\left(\left(\frac{ST^2}{C}\right)^2 + \frac{ST}{C} + \frac{T^2}{C} + \frac{T^2}{R}\right)\right)^S.$$

Next, we present the proof for Lemma 2 with several details omitted to save space. For full details please refer to the full version of the paper on Cryptology ePrint Archive.

(Proof of Lemma 2). We assume F is a random permutation from $[R] \times [C] \rightarrow [R] \times [C]$ which is lazily sampled. Fix an arbitrary (S, T)-MI adversary $\mathcal{A}$.

Let X_i be the indicator that $\mathcal{A}$ wins on the ith instance, i.e., finds 2-block collision on a_i. Then we make the following claim:

Claim 4.

$$\Pr[X_1 \wedge \cdots \wedge X_S] \leq \prod_{i=1}^{S} \left(\Pr[X_i | X_{<i} \wedge \overline{E^i}] + \frac{\Pr[E^i]}{\Pr[X_{<i}]} \right)$$

for any event E^i.

The proof of Claim 4 can be found in the full version of the paper.

Say we want to bound $\Pr[X_1 \wedge \cdots \wedge X_S]$ by δ^S, then it is sufficient to bound $\Pr[X_i | X_{<i}]$ by δ for an arbitrary $i \in [S]$. As in [AGL22], when analyzing $\Pr[X_i | X_{<i}]$, we will refer to the stage before receiving the ith challenge salt a_i as the offline stage and the stage after receiving a_i as online stage.

Definition 7. *Database is defined as the set of sampled distinct queries on F/F^{-1} and their responses.*
*The set of distinct queries made in the offline stage (i.e., before receiving the challenge salt as input) are referred to as **offline queries**. The set of distinct queries made in the online stage (i.e., after receiving the challenge salt as input) that had not been made in the offline phase are referred to as the **online queries**.*

Following the Claim 4, our high-level strategy would be to define the 'good' events and then bound the two terms separately to obtain our results. It is worth noting that we can assume $\Pr[X_{<i}] \geq \delta^i$. Otherwise $\Pr[X_{<i+1}] \leq \delta^i$ holds trivially.

To this end we first define the 'good' events. For $j \in [4]$, let's define E_j^i to be the event that there exists at least $10i \log R$ of Type j structures (shown in Fig. 5) from distinct a in the offline queries of ith instance. Let's define the event $E^i := E_1^i \vee E_2^i \vee E_3^i \vee E_4^i$.

Next, we analyze the probability of the events E_j^i for all $j \in [4]$.

Claim 5. *For any $i \in [S]$ and $T^2 \leq R/2$, $\Pr[E_j^i] \leq R^{-10i}$ for $j \in \{1, 2\}$.*

Claim 6. *For any $i \in [S]$ and $ST^2 \leq C/2$, $\Pr[E_j^i] \leq R^{-10i}$ for $j \in \{3, 4\}$.*

We omit the proofs of Claim 5 and 6 here and those proofs can be found in the full version of the paper.

Claims 5 and 6 are sufficient to show that $\frac{\Pr[E^i]}{\Pr[X_{<i}]} \leq \sum_{j=1}^{4} \frac{\Pr[E_j^i]}{\Pr[X_{<i}]}$ is small enough. Now we need to bound the term $\Pr[X_i | X_{<i} \wedge \overline{E^i}]$. To this end, we will have to analyze all the types of two block collisions that can be found in Sponge hash functions. First, we give some definitions and then identify all the types of 2-block collisions in the next claim.

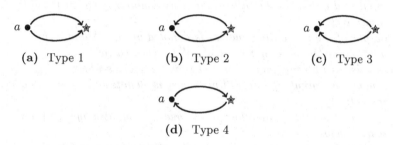

(a) Type 1   **(b)** Type 2   **(c)** Type 3

(d) Type 4

Fig. 5. The top line represents the query that occurs first, and the bottom line represents the query that occurs later. $\rightarrow$ represents a query to F and $\leftarrow$ represents a query to F^{-1}. ● represents that (output/input of) the two queries share the salt. ☆ represents that (output/input of) the two queries share the message.

Claim 7. *To find a 2-block collision on a_i for any $i \in [S]$, the queries in the database should satisfy at least one of the following conditions:*

1. *There exists an offline query that takes $(*, a_i)$ as input or outputs $(*, a_i)$.*
2. *There exists an online query such that it's output is $(*, a_i)$.*
3. *There exist two online queries with corresponding outputs (m', a') and (m'', a'') such that either $m' = m''$ or $a' = a''$.*
4. *There exist an online query, say it's output is denoted by (m, a), and an offline query, say it's input is denoted by (m', a') and output is denoted by (m'', a''), such that $a \in \{a', a''\}$ and $m \in \{m', m''\}$.*
5. *There exist two offline queries and one online query where:*
   - *input and output of the first (occurring) offline query is denoted by (m', a') and (m'', a'') respectively*
   - *the second offline query is to F and it's input and output is denoted by (ℓ', b') and (ℓ'', b'') respectively*
   - *the output of the online query is denoted by (m, a)*
   Then either $a = b' = a'$ and $\ell'' = m''$ or $a = b' = a''$ and $\ell'' = m'$. In other words, the offline queries form either Type 1 or Type 2 structure and the output salt of the online is the same as the input salt of the second offline query.
6. *There exist two offline queries and one online query where:*
   - *input and output of the first (occurring) offline query is denoted by (m', a') and (m'', a'') respectively*
   - *the second offline query is to F^{-1} and it's input and output is denoted by (ℓ', b') and (ℓ'', b'') respectively*
   - *the output of the online query is denoted by (m, a)*
   Then either $a = b'' = a'$ and $\ell' = m''$ or $a = b'' = a''$ and $\ell' = m'$. In other words, the offline queries form either Type 3 or Type 4 structure and the output salt of the online is the same as the output salt of the second offline query.
7. *There exist an offline query and two online queries where:*

– *input and output of the offline query us denoted by* (m', a') *and* (m'', a'')
respectively
– *output of the two online queries is denoted by* (m, a) *and* (ℓ, b)
Then $a \in \{a', a''\}$ *and either* $\ell \in \{m', m''\}$ *or* $b \in \{a', a''\}$.
8. *There exist two offline queries and two online queries where:*
– *input and output of one offline query is denoted by* $(*, a')$ *and* $(*, a'')$
respectively
– *input and output of the other offline query is denoted by* $(*, b')$ *and* $(*, b'')$
respectively
– *output of the two online queries is denoted by* $(*, a)$ *and* $(*, b)$
Then $a \in \{a', a''\}$ *and* $b \in \{b', b''\}$.

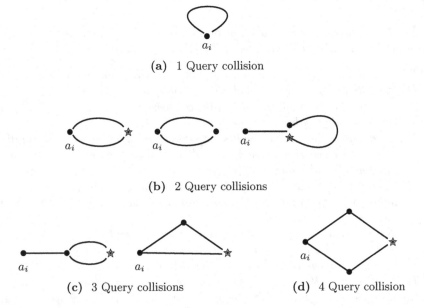

(a) 1 Query collision

(b) 2 Query collisions

(c) 3 Query collisions   **(d)** 4 Query collision

Fig. 6. Line represents query to F/F^{-1}. Each line could be directed $\rightarrow$ for query to F or $\leftarrow$ for query to F^{-1}. ● represents that (output/input of) the two queries share the salt. ★ represents that (output/input of) the two queries share the message.

Proof. First, we identify all the types of 2-block collisions for Sponge hash functions in Fig. 6. Note that each line shown in the figure could be depicting an offline/online query and a query to F/F^{-1}. We next show that all the possible types of collisions satisfy at least one of the cases in the claim.

First let's consider when none of the colliding queries (i.e., queries involved in collision) is an offline query. Then for the type of collision depicted in Fig. 6a will satisfy case 2 in the claim. And all the other types of collisions (depicted in

Fig. 6b, 6c, 6d) will satisfy case 3 in the claim when all the colliding queries are online queries.

Next, let's consider when exactly one of the colliding queries is an offline query. For the collision types depicted in Fig. 6a and the first two in Fig. 6b, this one offline query will necessary have the node a_i at one end (in other words, the offline query will have input/output of the form $(*, a_i)$) and will satisfy case 1 in the claim. Similarly for the remaining collision types, if the offline query is the one with node a_i at one end, the colliding queries will satisfy case 1 in the claim. For the third collision type in Fig. 6b, when the offline query is the one depicted by the curved line, it will satisfy case 4 in the claim. All the remaining collision types will satisfy case 7 in the claim when the one offline query is depicted by a line that does not have the node a_i at one of its ends.

Next, we consider when two or more of the colliding queries are offline queries. Again if even one of these offline queries is depicted by a line that has the node a_i at one end, they will satisfy case 1 in the claim. Otherwise, the first collision type depicted in Fig. 6c will satisfy one of case 5 or 6 in the claim. The collision type depicted in Fig. 6d will satisfy case 8 in the claim.   □

Finally, we analyze each case in Claim 7 and show that it's advantage is bounded by $\widetilde{O}((ST^2/C)^2 + ST/C + T^2/C + T^2/R)$ for any $i \in [S]$ when $X_{<i} \wedge \overline{E^i}$.

Case 1: As F/F^{-1} are lazily sampled and there are at most iT offline queries, the probability is bounded by $2iT/C$.

Case 2: For each of the T online queries, the probability it's output is $(*, a)$ is $1/C$. Therefore, the probability is bounded by T/C.

Case 3: By birthday bound, T online queries implies the probability of finding collision is bounded by $T^2/C + T^2/R$.

Case 4: Fix an offline query and the probability that output of at least one of the T online queries can be completely determined by the input and output of the fixed offline query is $4/RC$. Thus, the probability is bounded by $4ST^2/RC$.

Case 5: Conditioned on $\overline{E_1^i} \wedge \overline{E_2^i}$, there exists at most $10i \log R$ pair of offline queries each that form Type 1 and Type 2 structure. Thus, the probability that the output salt of each of the T online queries hitting either Type 1 or Type 2 structure is $20i \log R/C$. Thus, the probability is bounded by $20iT \log R/C$.

Case 6: Conditioned on $\overline{E_3^i} \wedge \overline{E_4^i}$, there exists at most $10i \log R$ pair of offline queries each that form Type 3 and Type 4 structure. Thus, the probability that the output salt of each of the T online queries hitting either Type 3 or Type 4 structure is $20i \log R/C$. Thus, the probability is bounded by $20iT \log R/C$.

Case 7: Fix an offline query. Then the probability that output salt of one online query is input/output salt of the fixed offline query and output salt or message of one online query is input/output salt or message respectively of the fixed offline query is $2/C \cdot (2/R + 2/C)$. Thus, the probability is bounded by $4ST \cdot T^2/C \cdot (1/R + 1/C)$.

Case 8: Fix two offline queries. Then the probability that output of two online queries is input/output salt of one fixed offline query each is $2/C \cdot 2/C$. Then the probability is bounded by $4ST^2/C \cdot ST^2/C$.

$\square$

5   Limitations for the Multi-instance Model

In this section, we will show that finding collisions is easy in the multi-instance model. For sponge, we will present 3 different attacks, one for each of parameter range $B = 1, B = 2$ and $B \geq 3$. It's worth noticing that the advantage of our attack matches the security bound given by Theorem 8 and [FGK22] in all cases. Therefore, we can not hope to prove better bounds unless we find a better model.

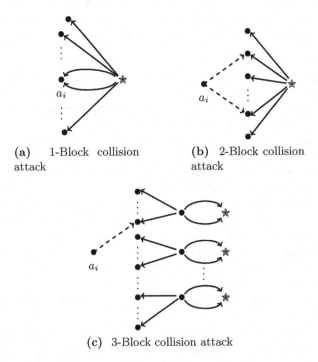

(a)   1-Block collision attack

(b)   2-Block collision attack

(c)   3-Block collision attack

Fig. 7. Attacks for sponge in multi-instance model. Dashed line represent online query. Solid line represents offline/online query. Line directed $\rightarrow$ represents query to F and line directed $\leftarrow$ represents query to F^{-1}. $\bullet$ represents that (output/input of) the two queries share the salt. $\bigstar$ represents that (output/input of) the two queries share the message.

5.1 Attacks for Sponge in Multi-instance Model When $B = 1$

Theorem 10. *Suppose $S, T \geq 8$ and $\frac{ST}{C} \leq \frac{1}{2}$. There exists an (S,T)-MI adversary $\mathcal{A}$ such that:*

$$\mathsf{Adv}^{\mathsf{MICR}}_{\text{1-SP}}(\mathcal{A}) = \left(\widetilde{\Omega} \left(\frac{S^2 T^2}{C^2} \right) \right)^S.$$

$\square$

Proof. For the ith stage of an MI game, let the challenge salt be denoted by a_i. In this stage, we will use the following strategy:

- We make T queries $F^{-1}(0, (i-1) \cdot T + j)$ where $j \in [T]$.
- Among all the (online and offline) queries, if there are two different queries $F^{-1}(0, j_1) = (m_1, a_{j_1})$ and $F^{-1}(0, j_2) = (m_2, a_{j_2})$, such that

$$a_{j_1} = a_{j_2} = a_i$$

Then we output the message pair $(m_1), (m_2)$ as the collision.

See Fig. 7a for reference. The correctness of the attack is immediate.

Next we analyze the lower bound on the success probability of the attack stated above. Define event E_i: There are **exactly** 2 queries (among the iT queries in the first i stages) hitting a_i. If E_i happens, then we will definitely win the ith stage. Consider the event $E_1 \wedge E_2 \wedge \ldots \wedge E_S$:

$$
\begin{aligned}
\Pr[E_1 \wedge E_2 \wedge \ldots \wedge E_S] &= \left(\prod_{i=1}^{S} \binom{iT - 2(i-1)}{2} \frac{1}{C^2} \right) \left(1 - \frac{S}{C} \right)^{ST - 2S} \\
&\geq \prod_{i=1}^{S} \left(\frac{iT}{2} \cdot \frac{iT}{4} \cdot \frac{1}{2C^2} \left(1 - \frac{S}{C} \right)^{T-2} \right) \\
&\geq \prod_{i=1}^{S} \left(\frac{i^2 T^2}{16 C^2} \left(1 - \frac{S(T-2)}{C} \right) \right) \\
&\geq \left(\frac{T^2}{16 C^2} \cdot \frac{1}{2} \right)^S \prod_{i=1}^{S} i^2 \geq \left(\frac{S^2 T^2}{16 \, C^2 \log^2 S} \right)^S
\end{aligned}
$$

where the first inequality holds using $i(T-2) \geq \frac{iT}{2}$ (as $T \geq 8$), second to last inequality holds using $\frac{ST}{C} \leq \frac{1}{2}$, and the last inequality is due to the fact $S! \geq \left(\frac{S}{e} \right)^S$ and $e < \log S$.

This event gives a lower bound of success probability of our attack, which is already $\left(\widetilde{\Omega} \left(\frac{S^2 T^2}{C^2} \right) \right)^S$.

5.2 Attacks for Sponge in Multi-instance Model When $B = 2$

Theorem 11. *Suppose $S, T \geq 8$ and $\frac{ST^2}{C} \leq \frac{1}{2}$. There exists an (S,T)-MI adversary $\mathcal{A}$ such that:*

$$\mathsf{Adv}^{\mathsf{MICR}}_{2\text{-SP}}(\mathcal{A}) = \left(\widetilde{\Omega} \left(\frac{S^2 T^4}{C^2} \right) \right)^S.$$

Proof. Again we denote the challenge salt for the ith stage of the MI game by a_i. We maintain a counter x (initially set to 0) through the whole game. The strategy in the ith stage of the game for any $i \in [S]$ will be as follows:

---

1. First, we make $\frac{T}{2}$ queries in the following way:
   (a) If the query $F^{-1}(0, x)$ is **fresh**, we make this query. (Recall that a query $F^{-1}(m, a) = (m', a')$ is fresh if neither $F^{-1}(m, a)$ nor $F(m', a')$ is queried before.)
   (b) Set $x \leftarrow x + 1$.
   We will repeat until $\frac{T}{2}$ fresh queries have been made in step (a).
2. Next, we make $\frac{T}{2}$ queries $F(j, a_i)$ where $j \in [\frac{T}{2}]$.
3. If there are at least 2 queries in step 2 that are **not** fresh, they must have the form $F(m_1, a_i) = (0, j_1)$ and $F(m_2, a_i) = (0, j_2)$ (Since all the challenge salts a_i are different, their first occurrence must be in step 1 of some previous stages, which must have form $F^{-1}(0, *) = (*, a_i)$). Then we output the message pair $(m_1), (m_2)$ as the collision.
4. Otherwise, if there exist two different online queries $F(j_1, a_i) = (m_1, a_{i_1}), F(j_2, a_i) = (m_2, a_{i_2})$ from step 2, and two different (online or offline) queries $F^{-1}(0, j_3) = (m_3, a_{i_3}), F^{-1}(0, j_4) = (m_4, a_{i_4})$ from step 1 such that

   $$a_{i_1} = a_{i_3}$$
   $$a_{i_2} = a_{i_4}$$

   Then we output the message pair $(j_1, m_1 \oplus m_3), (j_2, m_2 \oplus m_4)$ as the collision.

See Fig. 7b for reference. One may wonder that the adversary may not find enough queries in step 1(a). However, if it happens, since all the C queries $F^{-1}(0, i)$ (where $i \in [0, C)$) are different, it means at least $C - \frac{iT}{2} > 3ST$ queries are not fresh (since $ST < \frac{C}{2}$), which is impossible since there are at most iT different queries till now. Hence, as long as we can find such queries in step 3 or 4, we will succeed in this stage.

Next, we analyze the success probability of this attack. Suppose we are in stage i. Let Q_i be the indicator variable whether the adversary can find such queries in step 3 or 4. Similarly, let $Q_{<i}$ be the indicator variable that the adversary succeeds in finding such queries in each of the stages $1, \ldots, i - 1$.

We define another indicator variable E_i for the event: number of new salts a' appeared in the output of queries $F(j', a_i) = (j'', a')$ in step 1 for stage i is no less than $\frac{T}{4}$ (here "new salt" means that this salt has not been the output of any queries in step 1, including the previous stages). Analogous to $Q_{<i}$, we define $E_{<i}$ to be the indicator variable that $E_j = 1$ for all $j < i$. We will show that despite the extra requirement of these events happening, our attack still achieves the desired advantage.

To solve the problem, we analyze the conditional probability $\Pr[Q_i = 1 \wedge E_i = 1 | Q_{<i} = 1 \wedge E_{<i} = 1]$ for each stage i. To begin with, given that $E_{<i} = 1 \wedge Q_{<i} = 1$, we know that at least $\frac{(i-1)T}{4}$ distinct salts appeared in step 1 from previous stages. Therefore, for $E_i = 0$ to happen $\frac{T}{2}$ queries in step 1 will generate less than $\frac{T}{4}$ new salts (i.e. more than $\frac{T}{4}$ queries generate old salts). However, there are at most $\frac{iT}{2}$ salts visited in step 1 so far. Hence, we have

$$\Pr[E_i = 0 | Q_{<i} = 1 \wedge E_{<i} = 1] \leq \binom{\frac{T}{2}}{\frac{T}{4}} \left(\frac{iT}{2C}\right)^{\frac{T}{4}} \leq (2e)^{\frac{T}{4}} \left(\frac{iT}{2C}\right)^{\frac{T}{4}} = \left(\frac{eiT}{C}\right)^{\frac{T}{4}}$$

Therefore,

$$\Pr[E_i = 1 | Q_{<i} = 1 \wedge E_{<i} = 1] \geq 1 - \left(\frac{eiT}{C}\right)^{\frac{T}{4}} \geq 1 - \left(\frac{eiT^2}{4C}\right) \geq \frac{1}{2}$$

Since $\frac{ST^2}{C} < \frac{1}{2}$.

Next, given $E_i = 1$, we compute a lower bound of the probability for $Q_i = 1$. Since $E_i = 1$ and $E_{<i} = 1$, we know there are at least $\frac{iT}{4}$ salts visited in step 1. Besides, if the adversary fails in step 3, then there are at least $\frac{T}{2} - 1 \geq \frac{T}{4}$ fresh queries in step 2. Now we only consider a special case that the adversary can succeed (which gives a lower bound on probability of event $Q_i = 1$): The adversary fails in step 3, and among the **first** $\frac{T}{4}$ fresh online queries in step 2, **exactly** 2 of them hits two of the **first** $\frac{iT}{4}$ new salts in step 1:

$$\Pr[Q_i = 1 | E_i = 1 \wedge Q_{<i} = 1 \wedge E_{<i} = 1] \geq \binom{\frac{T}{4}}{2} \left(\frac{iT}{4C}\right)^2 \left(1 - \frac{iT}{4C}\right)^{\frac{T}{4} - 2}$$

$$\geq \frac{T^2}{64} \left(\frac{iT}{4C}\right)^2 \left(1 - \frac{iT^2}{16C}\right) \geq \frac{i^2 T^4}{2^{11}C}$$

Since $\frac{ST^2}{C} \leq \frac{1}{2}$.

Hence,

$$\Pr[Q_i = 1 \wedge E_i = 1 | Q_{<i} = 1 \wedge E_{<i} = 1]$$
$$= \Pr[E_i = 1 | Q_{<i} = 1 \wedge E_{<i} = 1] \cdot \Pr[Q_i = 1 | E_i = 1 \wedge Q_{<i} = 1 \wedge E_{<i} = 1]$$
$$\geq \frac{1}{2} \cdot \frac{i^2 T^4}{2^{11}C} = \frac{i^2 T^4}{2^{12}C^2}$$

Finally, the advantage of our attack is at least:

$$\Pr[Q_1 = 1 \wedge Q_2 = 1 \ldots \wedge Q_S = 1]$$
$$\geq \Pr[Q_1 = 1 \wedge Q_2 = 1 \ldots \wedge Q_S = 1 \wedge E_1 = 1 \wedge E_2 = 1 \ldots \wedge E_S = 1]$$
$$= \prod_{i=1}^{S} \Pr[Q_i = 1 \wedge E_i = 1 | Q_{<i} = 1 \wedge E_{<i} = 1]$$
$$\geq \prod_{i=1}^{S} \left(\frac{i^2 T^4}{2^{12} C^2} \right) \geq \left(\frac{S^2 T^4}{2^{12} C^2 \log^2 S} \right)^S$$

which proves the theorem. $\square$

5.3   Attacks for Sponge in Multi-instance Model When $B \geq 3$

Theorem 12. *Suppose $R, S, T \geq 16$, $\frac{ST^2}{C} \leq \frac{1}{2}$ and $\frac{T^2}{R} \leq 1$. For any $B \geq 3$, there exists an (S,T)-MI adversary $\mathcal{A}$ such that:*

$$\mathsf{Adv}_{\text{B-SP}}^{\text{MICR}}(\mathcal{A}) = \left(\widetilde{\Omega} \left(\frac{ST^2}{C} \right) \right)^S.$$

The assumption $\frac{T^2}{R} \leq 1$ is required, otherwise the trivial birthday attack will already have $\Omega(1)$ advantage even in the Auxiliary-Input setting.

Proof. We will propose an attack that only uses 3-block messages, which is valid for any $B \geq 3$. Our attack is as follows:

- Initially set $x \leftarrow 0, y \leftarrow 0$.
- For stage i of the MI game (let the challenge salt in this stage be a_i):
    1. First, we make $\frac{T}{2}$ queries in the following fashion:
        (a) If $F^{-1}(x, y)$ is **fresh**, we make this query.
        (b) Set $x \leftarrow x + 1$.
        (c) If $x \geq R$, we set $y \leftarrow y + 1$ and $x \leftarrow 0$.
        We repeat until $T/2$ new fresh queries are made in (a).
    2. Next, we make $T/2 - 2$ queries of the form $F(j, a_i)$ where $j \in [\frac{T}{2}]$.
    3. If any query in step 2 is **not** fresh, it must have form $F(m_1, a_i) = (j_1, y')$ where $0 \leq y' \leq y$ (Similarly, this is since that the first occurrence of this query must be in step 1(a), which has form $F^{-1}(*, y') = (*, a_i)$). Then we make two extra queries $F(0, y')$ and $F(1, y')$. If $F(0, y')[1] = F(1, y')[1]$, we output the message pair $(m_1, j_1), (m_1, j_1 \oplus 1)$ as the collision.
    4. Otherwise, if there exists one online query $F(j_1, a_i) = (m_1, a_{i_1})$ and one (online or offline) query $F^{-1}(j_2, y') = (m_2, a_{i_2})$ such that $a_{i_1} = a_{i_2}$, then we make two extra queries $F(0, y')$ and $F(1, y')$. If $F(0, y')[1] = F(1, y')[1]$, we output the message pair $(j_1, m_1 \oplus m_2, j_2), (j_1, m_1 \oplus m_2, j_2 \oplus 1)$ as the collision.

See Fig. 7c for reference. Recall that $F(0, y')[1]$ means the first part of output (i.e. message) of query $F(0, y')$. Our attack will need to form $y + 1$ of the structures shown in the figure. Notice that since we introduced y, the adversary may eventually check all possible $F^{-1}(x, y)$, and thus will always find enough queries in step 1(a) (since $\frac{ST}{RC} < \frac{1}{2}$).

First, we claim that $y \leq \frac{ST}{R}$ after all S stages of execution. This is because if any query in step 1(a) is not fresh, then it has occurred before in step 2–4 (of a previous stage). However, there are at most $\frac{ST}{2}$ such queries in total. Therefore, the number of queries that are fresh in step 1(a) is at least $yR - \frac{ST}{2}$ (There can be more fresh queries if any of $F^{-1}(i, y)$ is fresh for some $0 \leq i < x$). Further, we know that there are exactly $\frac{ST}{2}$ fresh queries in step 1(a) after S stages, so we have $yR - \frac{ST}{2} \leq \frac{ST}{2}$, which means $y \leq \frac{ST}{R}$.

Let us define an indicator variable W_i as whether $F(0, i)[1] = F(1, i)[1]$, and variable $W = W_0 \wedge W_1 \wedge \ldots \wedge W_y$. If $W = 1$ and that we find such queries in step 3 or 4, it's not hard to check that our output forms a valid collision and we win this stage.

First, we claim that the event $W = 1$ will happen with large enough probability via lazy-sampling. For $i \in [y]$, $F(0, i)$ and $F(1, i)$ are sampled in order without replacement. For any $i \in [y]$ and for some m, the probability $F(1, i)[1] = m$ depends on the number of previous samples that had output $(m, *)$. Note that there can be at most $2i + 1$ such samples. Therefore,

$$\Pr[W = 1] = \prod_{i=0}^{y} \Pr[W_i = 1 | W_{<i} = 1] = \prod_{i=0}^{y} \Pr[F(1, i)[1] = F(0, i)[1] | W_{<i} = 1]$$

$$\geq \prod_{i=0}^{y} \frac{C - (2i + 1)}{RC - (2i + 1)} \geq \left(\frac{C - (2y + 1)}{RC} \right)^{y+1} \geq \left(\frac{C/2}{RC} \right)^{y+1} = \left(\frac{1}{2R} \right)^{y+1}$$

where the last inequality uses that $2y + 1 \leq 4ST/R \leq C/2$.

Next, we focus on the probability of finding such queries. We define $Q_i, Q_{<i}, E_i, E_{<i}$ the same way as in Sect. 5.2. With the same analysis, we have

$$\Pr[E_i = 1 | Q_{<i} = 1 \wedge E_{<i} = 1] \geq \frac{1}{2}$$

Now, given $E_i = 1$, we need to lower bound the probability for $Q_i = 1$ again. Here, we consider the case that the adversary fails in step 3, and that there is **exactly** 1 online query (Since the adversary fails in step 3, this query must be fresh) that hits the **first** $\frac{iT}{4}$ new salts (from step 1):

$$\Pr[Q_i = 1 | E_i = 1 \wedge Q_{<i} = 1 \wedge E_{<i} = 1] \geq \left(\frac{T}{2} - 2 \right) \cdot \frac{iT}{4C} \left(1 - \frac{iT}{4C} \right)^{\frac{T}{2} - 3}$$

$$\geq \frac{iT^2}{16C} \left(1 - \frac{iT^2}{8C} \right) \geq \frac{iT^2}{32C}$$

Hence

$$\Pr[Q_i = 1 \wedge E_i = 1 | Q_{<i} = 1 \wedge E_{<i} = 1]$$
$$= \Pr[E_i = 1 | Q_{<i} = 1 \wedge E_{<i} = 1] \cdot \Pr[Q_i = 1 | E_i = 1 \wedge Q_{<i} = 1 \wedge E_{<i} = 1]$$
$$\geq \frac{iT^2}{64\,C}$$

Finally, the success probability of our attack will be at least

$$\Pr[W = 1 \wedge Q_1 = 1 \wedge Q_2 = 1 \ldots \wedge Q_S = 1]$$
$$\geq \Pr[W \wedge Q_1 = 1 \wedge Q_2 = 1 \ldots \wedge Q_S = 1 \wedge E_1 = 1 \wedge E_2 = 1 \ldots \wedge E_S = 1]$$
$$= \Pr[W = 1] \cdot \prod_{i=1}^{S} \Pr[Q_i = 1 \wedge E_i = 1 | Q_{<i} = 1 \wedge E_{<i} = 1]$$
$$\geq \left(\frac{1}{R}\right)^{y+1} \prod_{i=1}^{S} \left(\frac{iT^2}{64\,C}\right) \geq \left(\frac{T^2}{64C} \left(\frac{1}{R}\right)^{\frac{2T}{R}}\right)^{S} \prod_{i=1}^{S} i$$
$$\geq \left(\frac{T^2}{64C} \left(\frac{1}{2}\right)^{\frac{2\,T\log R}{R}}\right)^{S} \left(\frac{S}{\log S}\right)^{S} \geq \left(\frac{ST^2}{256\,C\log S}\right)^{S}$$

where third to last inequality holds as $y + 1 \leq \frac{2ST}{R}$ (as explained above), while the last inequality holds since $\frac{T}{\sqrt{R}} \leq 1$ and $\frac{\log R}{\sqrt{R}} \leq 1$ $\square$.

Acknowledgements. We thank TCC reviewers for their constructive comments. Siyao Guo and Akshima are supported by National Natural Science Foundation of China Grant No.62102260, Shanghai Municipal Education Commission (SMEC) Grant No. 0920000169, NYTP Grant No. 20121201 and NYU Shanghai Boost Fund. The work was done while Xiaoqi Duan was a research assistant at Shanghai Qi Zhi Institute and supported by the Shanghai Qi Zhi Institute. Most of the work was done while Qipeng Liu was a Postdoctoral researcher in Simons Institute, supported in part by the Simons Institute for Theory of Computing, through a Quantum Postdoctoral Fellowship and by the DARPA SIEVE-VESPA grant No. HR00112020023. Any opinions, findings and conclusions or recommendations expressed in this material are those of the author(s) and do not necessarily reflect the views of the supporting institutions.

References

[ACDW20] Akshima, C.D., Drucker, A., Wee, H.: Time-space tradeoffs and short collisions in merkle-damgård hash functions. In: Micciancio, D., Ristenpart, T. (eds.) CRYPTO 2020. LNCS, vol. 12170, pp. 157–186. Springer, Heidelberg (2020). https://doi.org/10.1007/978-3-030-56784-2_6

[AGL22] Akshima, G.S., Liu, Q.: Time-space lower bounds for finding collisions in merkle-damgård hash functions. In: Dodis, Y., Shrimpton, T. (eds.) CRYPTO 2022. LNCS, vol. 13509, pp. 192–221. Springer, Heidelberg (2022). https://doi.org/10.1007/978-3-031-15982-4_7

[BDPA07] Bertoni, G., Daemen, J., Peeters, M., Van Assche, G.: On the indifferentia-bility of the sponge construction. In: ECRYPT Hash Workshop, vol. 2007. Citeseer (2007)

[BDPA08] Bertoni, G., Daemen, J., Peeters, M., Van Assche, G.: On the indifferentia-bility of the sponge construction. In: Smart, N. (ed.) EUROCRYPT 2008. LNCS, vol. 4965, pp. 181–197. Springer, Heidelberg (2008). https://doi.org/10.1007/978-3-540-78967-3_11

[CDG18] Coretti, S., Dodis, Y., Guo, S.: Non-uniform bounds in the random-permutation, ideal-cipher, and generic-group models. In: Shacham, H., Boldyreva, A. (eds.) CRYPTO 2018. LNCS, vol. 10991, pp. 693–721. Springer, Cham (2018). https://doi.org/10.1007/978-3-319-96884-1_23

[CDGS18] Coretti, S., Dodis, Y., Guo, S., Steinberger, J.: Random oracles and non-uniformity. In: Nielsen, J.B., Rijmen, V. (eds.) EUROCRYPT 2018. LNCS, vol. 10820, pp. 227–258. Springer, Cham (2018). https://doi.org/10.1007/978-3-319-78381-9_9

[CGK18] Corrigan-Gibbs, H., Kogan, D.: The discrete-logarithm problem with pre-processing. In: Nielsen, J.B., Rijmen, V. (eds.) EUROCRYPT 2018. LNCS, vol. 10821, pp. 415–447. Springer, Cham (2018). https://doi.org/10.1007/978-3-319-78375-8_14

[CGK19] Corrigan-Gibbs, H., Kogan, D.: The function-inversion problem: barriers and opportunities. In: Hofheinz, D., Rosen, A. (eds.) TCC 2019. LNCS, vol. 11891, pp. 393–421. Springer, Cham (2019). https://doi.org/10.1007/978-3-030-36030-6_16

[CGLQ20] Chung, K.M., Guo, S., Liu, Q., Qian, L.: Tight quantum time-space trade-offs for function inversion. In: Irani, S. (ed.) 61st IEEE Annual Symposium on Foundations of Computer Science, FOCS 2020, Durham, NC, USA, 16–19 November 2020, pp. 673–684. IEEE (2020)

[CHM20] Chawin, D., Haitner, I., Mazor, N.: Lower bounds on the time/memory tradeoff of function inversion. In: Theory of Cryptography - 18th Interna-tional Conference, TCC 2020, Durham, NC, USA, 16–19 November 2020, Proceedings, Part III, pp. 305–334 (2020)

[Dam89] Damgård, I.B.: A design principle for hash functions. In: Brassard, G. (ed.) CRYPTO 1989. LNCS, vol. 435, pp. 416–427. Springer, New York (1990). https://doi.org/10.1007/0-387-34805-0_39

[DGK17] Dodis, Y., Guo, S., Katz, J.: Fixing cracks in the concrete: random oracles with auxiliary input, revisited. In: Coron, J.-S., Nielsen, J.B. (eds.) EURO-CRYPT 2017. LNCS, vol. 10211, pp. 473–495. Springer, Cham (2017). https://doi.org/10.1007/978-3-319-56614-6_16

[DTT10] De, A., Trevisan, L., Tulsiani, M.: Time space tradeoffs for attacks against one-way functions and PRGs. In: Rabin, T. (ed.) CRYPTO 2010. LNCS, vol. 6223, pp. 649–665. Springer, Heidelberg (2010). https://doi.org/10.1007/978-3-642-14623-7_35

[FGK22] Freitag, C., Ghoshal, A., Komargodski, I.: Time-space tradeoffs for sponge hashing: attacks and limitations for short collisions. In: Dodis, Y., Shrimp-ton, T. (eds.) CRYPTO 2022. LNCS, vol. 13509, pp. 131–160. Springer, Heidelberg (2022). https://doi.org/10.1007/978-3-031-15982-4_5

[FGK23] Freitag, C., Ghoshal, A., Komargodski, I.: Optimal security for keyed hash functions: avoiding time-space tradeoffs for finding collisions. In: Hazay, C., Stam, M. (eds.) EUROCRYPT 2023. LNCS, vol. 14007, pp. 440–469. Springer, Heidelberg (2023). https://doi.org/10.1007/978-3-031-30634-1_15

[GGKL21] Gravin, N., Guo, S., Kwok, T.C., Lu, P.: Concentration bounds for almost k-wise independence with applications to non-uniform security. In: Proceedings of the 2021 ACM-SIAM Symposium on Discrete Algorithms, SODA 2021, Virtual Conference, 10–13 January 2021, pp. 2404–2423 (2021)

[GGPS23] Golovnev, A., Guo, S., Peters, S., Stephens-Davidowitz, N.: Revisiting time-space tradeoffs for function inversion. In: Handschuh, H., Lysyanskaya, A. (eds.) CRYPTO 2023. LNCS, vol. 14082, pp. 453–481. Springer, Heidelberg (2023). https://doi.org/10.1007/978-3-031-38545-2_15

[GK22] Ghoshal, A., Komargodski, I.: On time-space tradeoffs for bounded-length collisions in merkle-damgård hashing. In: Dodis, Y., Shrimpton, T. (eds.) CRYPTO 202. LNCS, vol. 13509, pp. 161–191. Springer, Heidelberg (2022)

[GT23] Ghoshal, A., Tessaro, S.: The Query-Complexity of Preprocessing Attacks. In: Handschuh, H., Lysyanskaya, A. (eds.) CRYPTO 2023. LNCS, vol. 14082, pp. 482–513. Springer, Heidelberg (2023). https://doi.org/10.1007/978-3-031-38545-2_16

[Hel80] Hellman, M.: A cryptanalytic time-memory trade-off. IEEE Trans. Inf. Theory **26**(4), 401–406 (1980)

[IK10] Impagliazzo, R., Kabanets, V.: Constructive proofs of concentration bounds. In: Serna, M., Shaltiel, R., Jansen, K., Rolim, J. (eds.) APPROX/RANDOM -2010. LNCS, vol. 6302, pp. 617–631. Springer, Heidelberg (2010). https://doi.org/10.1007/978-3-642-15369-3_46

[Mer89] Merkle, R.C.: A certified digital signature. In: Brassard, G. (ed.) CRYPTO 1989. LNCS, vol. 435, pp. 218–238. Springer, New York (1990). https://doi.org/10.1007/0-387-34805-0_21

On the Cost of Post-compromise Security in Concurrent Continuous Group-Key Agreement

Benedikt Auerbach[(✉)] , Miguel Cueto Noval , Guillermo Pascual-Perez ,
and Krzysztof Pietrzak

ISTA, Klosterneuburg, Austria
{bauerbac,mcuetono,gpascual,pietrzak}@ista.ac.at

Abstract. Continuous Group-Key Agreement (CGKA) allows a group
of users to maintain a shared key. It is the fundamental cryptographic
primitive underlying group messaging schemes and related protocols,
most notably TreeKEM, the underlying key agreement protocol of the
Messaging Layer Security (MLS) protocol, a standard for group messaging by the IETF. CKGA works in an asynchronous setting where parties
only occasionally must come online, and their messages are relayed by
an untrusted server. The most expensive operation provided by CKGA
is that which allows for a user to refresh their key material in order to
achieve forward secrecy (old messages are secure when a user is compromised) and post-compromise security (users can heal from compromise).
One caveat of early CGKA protocols is that these update operations had
to be performed sequentially, with any user wanting to update their key
material having had to receive and process all previous updates. Late
versions of TreeKEM do allow for concurrent updates at the cost of a
communication overhead per update message that is linear in the number of updating parties. This was shown to be indeed necessary when
achieving PCS in just two rounds of communication by [Bienstock et
al. TCC'20].

The recently proposed protocol CoCoA [Alwen et al. Eurocrypt'22],
however, shows that this overhead can be reduced if PCS requirements
are relaxed, and only a logarithmic number of rounds is required. The
natural question, thus, is whether CoCoA is optimal in this setting.

In this work we answer this question, providing a lower bound on the
cost (concretely, the amount of data to be uploaded to the server) for
CGKA protocols that heal in an arbitrary k number of rounds, that shows
that CoCoA is very close to optimal. Additionally, we extend CoCoA to
heal in an arbitrary number of rounds, and propose a modification of it,
with a reduced communication cost for certain k.

We prove our bound in a combinatorial setting where the state of the
protocol progresses in rounds, and the state of the protocol in each round
is captured by a set system, each set specifying a set of users who share a
secret key. We show this combinatorial model is equivalent to a symbolic
model capturing building blocks including PRFs and public-key encryption, related to the one used by Bienstock et al.

© International Association for Cryptologic Research 2023
G. Rothblum and H. Wee (Eds.): TCC 2023, LNCS 14371, pp. 271–300, 2023.
https://doi.org/10.1007/978-3-031-48621-0_10

Our lower bound is of order $k \cdot n^{1+1/(k-1)}/\log(k)$, where $2 \leq k \leq \log(n)$ is the number of updates per user the protocol requires to heal. This generalizes the n^2 bound for $k = 2$ from Bienstock *et al.*. This bound almost matches the $k \cdot n^{1+2/(k-1)}$ or $k^2 \cdot n^{1+1/(k-1)}$ efficiency we get for the variants of the CoCoA protocol also introduced in this paper.

1 Introduction

A fundamental task underlying various cryptographic protocols is to agree upon, and maintain, a secret key amongst a group of users. A prominent example is *continuous group-key agreement* (CGKA) [3], which underlies group messaging applications. Here, a group of users wants to maintain a shared secret key, that then can be used for private communication amongst the group members.

CGKA is defined in an asynchronous setting, where parties are online only occasionally, and the exchanged messages are relayed through an untrusted server (only trusted to provide liveness and thus correctness). CGKA allows for users to be added or removed from the group. Moreover users can update their keys, which allows the group to achieve forward secrecy (FS) and post-compromise security (PCS). FS guarantees that, should a user's secrets be compromised, messages sent in the past remain secure. PCS, in turn, allows the group to "heal", i.e. to recover privacy after a compromise occurs.

The most efficient existing protocols for CGKA are TreeKEM [10] and variants thereof [2,3,7,22,23], which are inspired by logical key hierarchies (LKH) [25], a popular protocol for multicast encryption (ME) [14]. The study of these protocols has received a great deal of attention recently, motivated by the IETF working group on *Message Layer Security* (MLS) [9], which aims to output standard for instant group messaging. Said standard employs TreeKEM as the underlying CGKA. These schemes all arrange keys from a public-key encryption scheme in trees, known as *ratchet trees*, where each node is associated with a key, each user is associated with a leaf, and users should know exactly the (secret) keys on the path from their leaf to the root (also known as the *tree invariant*).

A simple ratchet tree with four users is illustrated in Fig. 1. The advantage of using such a hierarchical tree structure is that replacing a user's keys in a group of size n just requires the creation of $\lceil \log(n) \rceil$ ciphertexts, while e.g. maintaining pairwise keys between the users would require $n - 1$.

Concurrent Updates. Updating keys in a ratchet tree as illustrated in Fig. 1 only works if updates are sequential. That is, if two users want to update, then they need to do it in order, with the second processing the first user's update before creating their own. TreeKEM supports concurrent updates through the "propose and commit" (P&C) paradigm, but handling concurrency in this way degrades the nice tree structure and thus efficiency of the protocol. Indeed, after several users update concurrently, all of their paths to the root but one will lose their keys, a.k.a. become *blank*, increasing the in-degrees of nodes in the tree and thus the cost of that and subsequent operations. This incurs an overhead that is linear in the number of updating parties, something which was shown to be

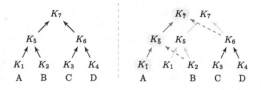

Fig. 1. Left: Illustration of a ratchet tree with $n = 4$ users $\{A, B, C, D\}$ where each key $K_i = (pk_i, sk_i)$ is a public/secret key tuple. Right: To update and achieve PCS Alice rotates keys $\{K_1, K_5, K_7\}$ by sampling new keys $\{K_{\bar{1}}, K_{\bar{5}}, K_{\bar{7}}\}$ (blue, shaded background) and encrypting each secret key under the public key of their parent (blue, dashed arrows), e.g. $K_2 \to K_{\bar{5}}$ corresponds to a ciphertext $\mathsf{Enc}_{pk_2}(sk_{\bar{5}})$. Given those ciphertexts, all users can learn the new keys on their path to the root. For example Bob must decrypt the ciphertexts $\mathsf{Enc}_{pk_2}(sk_{\bar{5}})$ and $\mathsf{Enc}_{pk_{\bar{5}}}(sk_{\bar{7}})$. This requires $2\lceil \log(n) \rceil = 4$ ciphertexts. However, by deriving the keys $\{K_{\bar{1}}, K_{\bar{5}}, K_{\bar{7}}\}$ deterministically from a single seed using a PRG as suggested in [14], we can save the ciphertexts for the solid blue arrows and only need $\lceil \log(n) \rceil = 2$ ciphertexts. (Color figure online)

optimal by Bienstock, Dodis and Rösler [12], whenever PCS is to be achieved as soon as all corrupted users update once.

CoCoA [2] takes a different approach, and simply choses a "winner" whenever there is a conflict, i.e., when two users want to concurrently replace the same key, as illustrated in Fig. 2. As opposed to the previous scenario, this does not immediately "heal" the state of the concurrently updating parties (in the Figure, key $K_{\bar{7}}$ is not secure if Dave's key K_6 was compromised). However, in [2] it is shown that the group heals (i.e., achieves PCS) after all corrupted users participate in $\log(n)$ (possibly concurrent) update rounds. This is a middle ground between the immediate concurrent healing of P&C TreeKEM, and the n sequential rounds needed for non-concurrent versions of TreeKEM.

In this work we prove a lower bound on the communication cost of CGKA protocols that heal in any number of (up to logarithmic in the group size) rounds.

A Combinatorial Model. Conceptually, our lower bound proof proceed in two steps. We first derive the lower bounds in a clean and simple combinatorial model which proceeds in rounds. The state of the protocol for n users in round t is captured by a set system $\mathcal{S}_t \subseteq 2^{[n]}$, where $S \in \mathcal{S}_t$ means that after round t there is a shared secret amongst the users S *not* known to the adversary.

In particular, $[n] \in \mathcal{S}_t$ means the group $[n] = \{1, \ldots, n\}$ shares a secret, which has to be satisfied in all rounds with a secure group key.

For example, in the ratchet tree example from Fig. 1 (where users are denoted $\{A, B, C, D\}$ not $\{1, 2, 3, 4\}$), the sets corresponding to the keys $K_1, .., K_7$ are

$$\mathcal{S}_t = \{\{1\}, \{2\}, \{3\}, \{4\}, \{1, 2\}, \{3, 4\}, \{1, 2, 3, 4\}\}.$$

If a user u gets compromised, all secrets corresponding to sets containing u become known to the adversary and thus the sets must be removed, e.g., if we compromise user 1, the set system becomes

$$\mathcal{S}_{t+1} = \{\{2\}, \{3\}, \{4\}, \{3, 4\}\}.$$

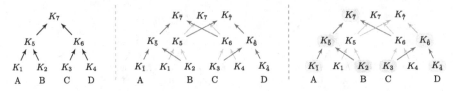

Fig. 2. Illustration of CoCoA where Alice and Dave concurrently rotate their keys. Left: state of the ratchet tree before the updates. Middle: Keys $\{K_{\bar{1}}, K_{\bar{5}}, K_{\bar{7}}\}$ and $\{K_{\bar{4}}, K_{\bar{6}}, K_{\bar{7}}\}$ generated by Alice and Dave's updates respectively. There's a collision at the (root) key K_7, and the server chooses a "winner" (any rule for choosing winners will do), in this case Alice. Right: New state of the ratchet tree (Keys in the tree depicted with shaded background). The new root key is $K_{\bar{7}}$ while Dave's $K_{\hat{7}}$ is ignored. As $K_{\bar{7}}$ was encrypted to K_6 we do not achieve PCS if Dave's state $\{K_4, K_6, K_7\}$ prior to the update was compromised. But latest once all corrupted parties updated $\log(n)$ times PCS will be achieved (in particular, if Dave updates once more PCS is achieved).

A user u can update and create new sets (keys) as follows. They can always locally sample a key, creating the singleton $\{u\}$. For two sets $S, S' \in \mathcal{S}$, where $u \in S$ (or $u \in S'$), they can create a new set $S \cup S'$, by deterministically deriving a secret from that of S using a PRF, and encrypting it under the public key of S'. This would get added to $\mathcal{S}$ in the next round. Note that indeed all users in $S \cup S'$ are able to derive the secret either deterministically from the secret associated to S or by decrypting the ciphertext. In the simplest version of TreeKEM, user 1 performs an update by creating $\{1\}$, then $\{1, 2\} = \{1\} \cup \{2\}$, then $\{1, 2, 3, 4\} = \{1, 2\} \cup \{3, 4\}$ (i.e., the keys $K_{1'}, K_{5'}, K_{7'}$ in Fig. 1). Of course, u is not restricted to create new sets as the union of only two sets, but could also encrypt the secret using the keys of sets $S_1, \dots, S_k$ to form the set $S \cup \bigcup_{i=1}^{k} S_i$. The communication cost of this operation, i.e., the number of ciphertexts that have to be uploaded to the server to communicate the new secret to all members of the corresponding set, would in this example be k. In Sect. 3.1 we extend this idea into a self-contained combinatorial model consisting of set system $\mathcal{S}_t$ and an accompanying cost function Cost required to satisfy properties matching the intuition given above. In Sect. 3.2 we use it to prove our lower bounds.

The Symbolic Model. While the combinatorial model offers a clean model for proving lower bounds, it is not obvious how it captures real-world protocols. We show that any lower bound in the combinatorial model implies a lower bound in a symbolic model capturing pseudorandom functions and public-key encryption. Most existing CGKA protocols can be captured in this symbolic model and the fact that lower bounds in the combinatorial model carry over to the symbolic model justifies the interest of the combinatorial model we propose. Symbolic models were introduced by Dolev and Yao [18] in public key encryption, used in multicast encryption by Micciancio and Panjwani [24] and in CGKA by Bienstock, Dodis, and Rösler [12] and Alwen et al. [1]. In the symbolic model pseudorandom functions and public-key encryption are treated in an idealized way by seeing their inputs and outputs as variables with a data type, which, in turn, follow some grammar rules, and ignoring other considerations that an actual construction may have. The functionality and security of these primitives are captured by the grammar rules and entailment relations in Sect. 4.1.

1.1 Our Bounds

In this work we prove lower bounds on the communication cost of CGKA protocols achieving PCS. Moreover, in Sect. 5 we introduce a new protocol, a modification and generalization of CoCoA. It introduces the necessary number of rounds to heal as a parameter and, in some cases, improves over the natural generalization of CoCoA in this setting.

We measure the cost of a protocol in terms of the number of ciphertexts that users in a group must create (and upload to a server for the other users to download) to achieve post-compromise security.[1] Sometimes, we additionally put a bound on the number of rounds required for parties to heal. We do not require forward-secrecy and will also consider groups of a fixed size, i.e., without removals or additions of users, just updates. Note that both of these make the lower bounds stronger, as an adversary could always choose to not use add/removes. Additionally, FS is relatively well understood [3].

We consider the setting where the users do not know who is compromised or who else will update in any given communication round, and the adversary schedules who does updates in each round. This is similar to that of [12].

When a user is corrupted, we assume its entire secret state is leaked to the adversary, who can also observe all its local randomness. We call this the "randomness corruption" model (RC for short), but we also consider a weaker "no-randomness corruption" ($\neg$RC) model, where only the secret state is leaked. In this model, a corrupted user can still create encrypted secrets for other users. Most protocols are proven secure in the stronger RC model, whereas lower bounds are naturally stronger in the $\neg$RC model. Our lower bounds require some additional restrictions on the CGKAs discussed at the end of the introduction.

Lower Bound. The number k of updates a user is required to make before their state is guaranteed to heal plays a crucial role. Our security game is parameterized by the number of users n and k. The adversary schedules who updates in each round, and we require that, at any point, the group key is secure provided every party who was corrupted in the past was asked to update at least k times (since their last corruption). Table 1 states our lower bound and upper bound, as well as existing ones. Our lower bound is roughly $n^{1+1/k} \cdot k/\log(k)$.

The main message here is that we need to allow for logarithmically many rounds for healing (as in CoCoA) if we want a small logarithmic sender communication cost per user. In particular, if we insist on a constant number of rounds, the average cost per user will be of order $n^{1/k}$.

---

[1] It is possible, as in [2,5], to reduce recipient communication by introducing additional reliance on the server. We focus on sender communication.

Table 1. Upper-bounds (top) and lower-bounds (bottom) in the no-information setting for $\Omega(n)$ corrupted users. Communication is measured as total number of ciphertexts sent to recover from corruption, column "Rounds" indicates the number of update rounds after which schemes are required to recover from corruption, column "Rand. corr.", whether the security model allows the adversary to learn internal randomness of algorithms. The protocol [12] improves over TreeKEM in that concurrent operations do not degrade future performance, which is not captured in the table. Our lower-bounds require CGKA to not allow distributed work (NDW) and not use nested encryption (NNE). Our bound holds without the extra assumption requiring the protocols to have publicly-computable update cost (PCU). However, additional properties of it hold when this assumption is present. We refer the reader to the discussion in Sect. 1.3 below for more details. Here, $\alpha_\varepsilon \approx \varepsilon$ is some constant depending on ε.

Upper bounds				
Scheme	Communication	Rounds	Rand. corr	See
TreeKEM and related	n^2	2	RC	[10]
Bienstock, Dodis, Rösler	n^2	2	¬RC	[12]
CoCoA on $^{k-}\sqrt[k]{n}$-ary trees	$n\,k^2\,^{k-}\sqrt[k]{n}$	k	RC	Sect. 5
CoCoA on 2-ary trees	$n\log(n)^2$	$\log(n)$	RC	[2]
CoCoALight on $^{(k-1)/2}\sqrt[2]{n}$-ary trees	$n\,k\,^{(k-1)/2}\sqrt[2]{n}$	k	RC	Sect. 5
Lower bounds				
Restrictions	Communication	Rounds	Rand. corr	See
None	n^2	2	¬RC	[12]
NDW, NNE, PCU*	$n\log(n)/\log(\log(n))$	$\log(n)$	¬RC	Cor. 5
NDW, NNE, PCU*	$\varepsilon \cdot n \cdot {}^{(1+\varepsilon)k-}\sqrt[\varepsilon]{\alpha_\varepsilon n} \cdot k/\log(k)$	k	¬RC	Cor. 5

Upper Bound. We introduce in Sect. 5 the protocol CoCoALight, a modification of CoCoA that achieves PCS in $k \in [4, 2\lceil\log(n)\rceil + 1]$ rounds. This protocol has a cost $k \cdot n^{1+2/(k-1)}$, which matches the lower bound up to a factor $\log(k)/n^{1/(k-1)}$. In particular, our protocol is only a factor of $\log(\log(n))$ from optimal for k in the order of $\log(n)$. In turn, CoCoA (or rather, a straightforward generalization of it we propose for $k \in [2, \lceil\log(n)\rceil + 1]$, as opposed to $k = \lceil\log(n)\rceil + 1$ in the original protocol) has better efficiency for low values of k. The key insight in our protocol is that users do not need to update all the keys in their path to heal. In fact, it suffices for them to update keys one by one, as long as every key in the path is updated twice. We formalize and discuss this further in Sect. 5 of this paper's full version [8].

1.2 Our Proofs

The details of the proofs are omitted in this version of the paper and can be found in the full version [8]. Below we give an intuition.

Proof of the Lower Bound. To prove the lower bound we first show that, if the protocol can heal from c corruptions in k rounds, then there is some user whose cost is $c^{1/k}$. In particular, if $c = \Theta(n)$, we get a cost of $\Theta(n^{1/k})$. The intuition for this is quite simple, let us give it for $c = n$. Initially everyone is corrupted, so our set system is simply $\{1\}, \ldots, \{n\}$, after the kth round $[n] = \{1, \ldots, n\}$ is in our set system. If we denote with s_i the size of the largest set in round i, we have $s_1 = 1, s_k = n$, which means there must be a round i where $s_{i+1}/s_i \geq n^{1/(k-1)}$. Therefore, in this round, the user creating the new set of size s_i has cost $\geq n^{1/(k-1)}$. A slightly more careful argument shows that the maximum cost of a user in each round adds up to $k \cdot c^{1/(k-1)}$.

To prove our bound we will show that for $c = \Theta(n)$ corruptions, we can adversarially schedule the updates so that a $1/\log(k)$ fraction of users (and not just a single one) can be forced to pay close to the maximum cost in each round, which then adds up to $n^{1+1/(k-1)} \cdot k/\log(k)$.

This adversarial scheduling goes as follows: before each round, the adversary investigates each user's cost, should they be asked to update in the next round. Then, it simply picks a $1/\log(k)$ fraction of users, all having either very small cost or, if such a set does not exist, a set of users with roughly the same cost (we show that such a set of users always exists).

Proof of the Upper Bound. We prove our protocol secure by following the framework set by [22], which reduces the adaptive security of a CGKA protocol to that of a game played on graphs. One first defines a so-called *safe predicate*, which captures the settings in which security should be guaranteed (i.e. every corrupted user performed k updates since their last corruption, in our case). This is implicit in our security game. Then, in order to apply previous results, one needs to essentially show that key satisfying the safe predicate trivially leaked as a result of a user corruption during the execution. We do this by associating to each group key in the execution a *recovery graph*, made up of those keys that trivially allow recovery of the group key. Then, through a combinatorial argument, we show that if the safe predicate holds all keys ever leaked through a corruption cannot belong to the recovery graph of the challenge key. Security of the protocol thus follows using the aforementioned framework, in a fashion similar to that of previous works, such as [2].

1.3   Overcoming Lower Bounds

Proving lower bounds for important protocols serves several purposes. On the one hand, it can tell us when constructions *falling into the model of the lower-bound* cannot be further improved. As we identify a protocol that almost match our lower bound, this question is basically answered.

However, lower bound proofs can also hint as to where one should look for constructions overcoming them. One such possibility is to consider building blocks not captured by the bounds, or seemingly technical assumptions, which seem crucial for the lower-bound proofs to go through.

More Powerful Building Blocks. The symbolic model we consider (and which is captured by our combinatorial model) allows the basic primitives of PRFs or public-key encryption, and thus does not rule out protocols overcoming our lower bounds if they use more sophisticated tools.

The "big hammer" in this context is multiparty non-interactive key-agreement (mNIKE). With this primitive, each user could simply create a single message to be broadcast, after which any subset of users can locally compute a shared secret. While this overcomes our lower-bounds, it is just of theoretical interest, as currently no practical instantiations of mNIKE exist.

There already do exist CGKA protocols using primitives not captured by our model, in particular rTreeKEM [3] and DeCAF [7]. The variant rTreeKEM uses secretly-updatable public-key encryption [21] (skUPKE), but this primitive is used to improve the forward secrecy of the protocol, with no difference to the (asymptotic) communication cost of the protocol. The CGKA DeCAF also uses skUPKE, but in order to improve the round complexity for healing: instead of $\log(n)$ rounds as in CoCoA, DeCAF only needs $\log(c)$ rounds, with c being the number of users corrupted.

Note that our lower bound is independent of the number of corrupted users, but the proof argues based on an adversary which corrupts $c = \Theta(n)$ parties. In this setting DeCAF's cost matches that of CoCoA and thus adheres to our lower bound. However, under the promise that few, say constant, users are actually corrupted, DeCAF heals in a constant number of rounds with cost $\mathcal{O}(n \log(n))$.

Finally, two recent works [5,19], explore the use of multi-recipient multi-message PKE (mmPKE), which allows for much more efficient updates. However, the improvements save a constant factor in the ciphertext size, and do not have an influence in the asymptotic cost of the protocols.

Distributing Work. Our bound is restricted to schemes that do not "distribute the workload of communicating a secret on several users", in the following sense. We require that, if in any round a user gets access to a secret they did not previously possess, then they must have recovered it from a single update message, or sampled it themselves. All CGKA schemes we are aware of satisfy this property.

Nested Encryption. Finally, we require that users do not create layered ciphertexts, i.e., those of the form $\mathsf{Enc}(pk_1, \mathsf{Enc}(pk_2, m))$. Again, this is a property that is satisfied by all CGKA protocols we are aware of. This condition has a similar flavor as the one of distributing work, with the difference being that, instead of splitting the communication cost between several users, would enable a user to spread out communication cost over several rounds.

Publicly-Computable Update Cost. We show that there exists a sequence of updates such that the lower bound holds. However, this does not mean that the sequence can be found using only public information. We introduce this assumption to guarantee that the adversary can tell what cost a user will incur if asked to update in round t using only public information available at the end of round $t - 1$ and this suffices to find the update sequence used in the proof of the lower bound. We also introduce a stronger version of this property, which we call offline publicly-computable update cost, that makes it possible to use public information available at the end of the initialization phase and the sequence of users who have performed updates in the previous rounds. While the strong property is satisfied by all protocols we are aware of, it is conceivable that protocols exist that overcome our bound, by having a user toss a coin when asked to update, with the outcome determining whether a "cheap" or "expensive" update is made.

1.4 Related Work

Protocols. The primitive of CGKA was introduced by Alwen *et al.* [3], but constructions existed earlier, notably ART [15] and TreeKEM [10]. These two were the starting point for the Message Layer Security (MLS) working group by the IETF. A variety of protocols have since been published, aiming to improve TreeKEM across different axes.

First, in the non-concurrent setting, [3] propose the use of UPKE in order to improve on FS; Klein *et al.* [22] propose an alternative way to handle dynamic operations with a lower communication cost in certain scenarios; Devigne, Duguey and Fouque [17] propose to use zero-knowledge proof to enhance the protocol robustness; Alwen *et al.* [1] initiates the study of efficiency of CGKAs in the multi-group setting; Hashimoto, Katsumata and Prest [20] provide a wrapper upgrading non-metadata-hiding CGKAs into metadata-hiding ones.

Concurrency was already mentioned in the initial TreeKEM versions, and indeed, as mentioned, its new versions allow for a certain degree of it. The first protocol to explore the idea was Weidner's Causal TreeKEM [23] with the idea of updates by re-randomizing (and combining) key material, instead of overwriting it. The work of Weidner *et al.* [26] puts forth the notion of decentralized CGKA. Alwen *et al.*'s CoCoA [2] analyzes a variant allowing for concurrent healing in $\log(n)$ rounds. A follow-up of this work by Alwen *et al.* [7] picked up the idea of [23] and extended it and formally analyzed it, showing that it allows for PCS in a logarithmic number of rounds in the number of corrupted parties.

Lowerbounds. The main approach is to make use of the symbolic security model, first introduced by Dolev and Yao [18] and later used by Micciancio and Panjwani [24] to prove worst case bounds on the update cost of multicast encryption schemes for a single group.

Regarding CGKAs, in the non-concurrent setting, Alwen *et al.* [1] provide lower bounds for the average update cost of an update in any CGKA protocol in the symbolic model, following and generalizing the approach of [24]. This shows TreeKEM or other related protocols are indeed optimal in this setting. In the concurrent setting, i.e. that where we consider the case of healing c corruptions in less than c rounds, the study of lower bounds was initiated by Bienstock, Dodis and Rösler [12], who establish lower bounds for protocols achieving PCS in exactly 2 rounds.[2] Last, Bienstock *et al.* [11] establish a lower bound on the cost of certain sequences of adds and removes. In particular, they show that any CGKA has a worst-case communication cost linear in the number of users.

---

[2] Here, we have a tradeoff between the time needed to achieve PCS, and the communication needed to do so. The picture is slightly more complicated, as in protocols like TreeKEM, or the protocol proposed in [12], the bigger tradeoff is in the increased cost of subsequent updates.

Security. Finally, security of CGKAs has been studied by multiple papers. Security against adaptive adversaries with a sub-exponential loss was first proved by Klein *et al.* [22]. Active security has been studied by Alwen *et al.* [4,6] in the UC model. PCS in the multi-group setting has been studied by Cremers, Hale and Kohbrok [16], who show shortcomings of a certain version of MLS compared to the (inefficient) pairwise-channels construction. Brzuska, Cornelissen and Kohbrok [13] apply the State Separating Proofs methodology to analyze the security of a certain version MLS.

2   Preliminaries

2.1   Definitions and Results from Combinatorics

Definition 1 (Minimal set cover). *Let $n \in \mathbb{N}$ and $\mathcal{S} \subseteq 2^{[n]}$. Then for $X \subseteq [n]$ we define the min cover of X with respect to $\mathcal{S}$. A minimal set cover (min cover) $\mathrm{minCover}_{\supseteq}(X, \mathcal{S})$ of X with respect to $\mathcal{S}$ is a set $\mathcal{T} \subseteq \mathcal{S}$ of minimal cardinality such that $X \subseteq \bigcup_{T \in \mathcal{T}} T$, i.e., a minimal subset of $\mathcal{S}$ that covers X. Note that we only require $\mathcal{S}$ be contained in the union but no equality.*

Proposition 1 (Inequality of arithmetic and geometric means). *For $k \in \mathbb{N}$ let $x_1, \ldots, x_k \in \mathbb{R}$ be non-negative such that $\sum_{i=1}^{k} x_i = x$. Then*

$$\prod_{i=1}^{k} x_i \leq \left(\frac{x}{k}\right)^k .$$

2.2   Continuous Group-Key Agreement

We now establish syntax for *continuous group-key agreement* (CGKA) schemes. A CGKA scheme allows a group G of users to agree on a group key that is to be used to secure communication within the group. In order to be able to recover from corruption users can also, possibly concurrently, send update messages, which rotate their key material. On top of this, CGKA schemes normally allow for group membership to evolve throughout the execution, by adding or removing users. However, while schemes allowing for theses additional operations are desirable in practice, the main goal of this work is to establish lower bounds on the communication complexity of recovering from corruption by concurrent updates. Thus, we restrict our view to static groups, i.e., we do not require the functionality of adding users to or removing users from the group. Not considering adds and removes allows for less technical notation, and we point out that lower bounds only profit from this restriction, as they hold even for schemes restricted to static groups. In doing so, our syntax essentially follows that of [12], with a couple of small differences mentioned below.

A continuous group-key agreement scheme CGKA specifies algorithms Setup, Init, Update, Process, and GetKey. Algorithms Setup and Init can be used to initialize the a group G, that since we restrict our view to static groups, throughout this work we simply identify with $G = [n]$ for some $n \in \mathbb{N}$. Here, Setup is used to generate every user's initial internal state and can be thought of as the users generating a key pair and registering it with a PKI. Init, on the other hand, is called by one of the users to initialize the group. It generates a control message that, when processed by the other users, establishes the initial group-key K_G^0. Afterwards, the scheme proceeds in rounds t, in each of which a subset of users in G concurrently generate update messages using algorithm Update. The update messages are in turn processed by the group members resulting in a new group key K_G^t that can be recovered from a user's internal state using algorithm GetKey.

More formally,

- Setup$(n; r)$ on input the group size n and random coins r belonging to randomness space Rnd outputs public information pub, as well as an initial state st_u for every user $u \in G = [n]$.
- Init$(st_u, pub; r)$ receives as input a user's (initial) state, the public information pub, and random coins r. Its output (st_u', MI_u) consists of the initializing user's updated state and a control message MI_u.
- Update$(st_u, pub; r)$ in round t takes as input a user's current state, the public information pub, and random coins r. It returns updated state st_u' and a update message MU_u^t.
- Deterministic algorithm Process(st_u, pub, M) gets as input a user u's state, the public information pub, and a set M of control messages that either consists of a single group initialization message MI_v, or a family of update messages $(MU_v)_v$. Its output is the processing user's updated state st_u'.
- Deterministic algorithm GetKey(st_u) on input a user's state returns u's view of current group key K_G belonging to key space CGKA.KS.

When comparing to the syntax of [12], one can find two differences. On the one hand, we chose not to merge algorithms Setup and Init, as in [12], although this would be possible since we consider the simple setting where a single static group is created. On the other hand, we include the algorithm GetKey, present in the original CGKA definition from [3]. This makes it easier to argue the

---

```
Game CORRECT^CGKA(n, u_0, (U_t)_{t=1}^{t_max})        Oracle ROUND(U_t)
00  t ← 0                                             13  MU ← ∅
01  INIT(n, u_0)                                       14  for u ∈ U_t:
02  while t ≤ t_max:                                   15     (st_u, MU_u^t) ← Update(st_u, pub)
03     t ← t + 1                                       16     MU ←_∪ MU_u^t
04     ROUND(U_t)                                      17  for u ∈ [n]:
05  return 0                                           18     st_u ← Process(st_u, pub, MU)
                                                       19     K_G^u ← GetKey(st_u)
Oracle INIT(n, u_0)                                    20  if ∃u, v ∈ [n] : K_G^u ≠ K_G^v:      \\disagreement on group key
06  (pub, (st_u)_{u∈[n]}) ← Setup(n)                   21     return 1
07  (st_{u_0}, MI_{u_0}^0) ← Init(st_{u_0}, pub, n; r)
08  for u ∈ [n]:
09     st_u ← Process(st_u, pub, MI_{u_0}^0)
10     K_G^u ← GetKey(st_u)
11  if ∃u, v ∈ [n] : K_G^u ≠ K_G^v:
12     return 1
```

Fig. 3. Correctness game for continuous group-key agreement scheme CGKA.

connection between the combinatorial and symbolic models. The two main properties that we require from a CGKA scheme are correctness and security.

Correctness. For correctness we require that, for every valid sequence of operations, in every round t, all users agree on the current group key K_G^t where $G = [n]$ is a static group of size $n \in \mathbb{N}$. We formalize the notion of correctness in the game of Fig. 3. The game gets as input n, the user $u_0 \in G$ initializing the group, and a sequence $(U_t)_t$ of updates to be applied in every round where $U_t \subseteq G$. The game returns the value 0 if the execution was correct and 1 otherwise. Accordingly, we say that a scheme CGKA is *perfectly correct* if, for every input $(n, u_0, (U_t)_{t=1}^{t_{\max}})$ and all choices of random coins, we have that $0 = \text{CORRECT}^{\text{CGKA}}(n, u_0, (U_t)_{t=1}^{t_{\max}})$. For a perfectly correct scheme, we denote the current group key by K_G, instead of K_G^u since all users agree on it.

Security. For security, we require that the group key of a CGKA scheme recovers from corruption assuming that every party did at least k updates since their last corruption. More formally, we consider the security notions of indistinguishability of the group key from random (IND-k-PCS$_{\text{mode}}$), and one-wayness (OW-k-PCS$_{\text{mode}}$). Here, mode $\in \{\neg\text{RC}, \text{RC}\}$ indicates whether the corruption of a user reveals only their private state in the current round, or also additionally the random coins they sampled in the round. Thus, we end up with 4 different

---

Game IND-k-PCS$_{\text{mode}}^{\text{CGKA}}$(A)
00 $b^* \leftarrow_\$ \{0,1\}$
01 $b \leftarrow A^{\text{INIT,ROUND,CORR,CHALL}}$
02 **return** $[b = b^*] \wedge \text{safe}_{k\text{-PCS}}$

Game OW-k-PCS$_{\text{mode}}^{\text{CGKA}}$(A)
03 $K \leftarrow A^{\text{INIT,ROUND,CORR,CHALL}}$
04 **return** $[K^* = K] \wedge \text{safe}_{k\text{-PCS}}$

Oracle INIT(n, u_0)   \\one call; called first
05 $t \leftarrow 0$
06 $\text{Cor}[u] \leftarrow \emptyset$, $\text{Upd}[u] \leftarrow \emptyset$ for all $u \in [n]$
07 $\text{Coins}[u,t] \leftarrow \emptyset$ for all $u \in [n]$, $\forall t$
08 $r_{\text{setup}} \leftarrow_\$ \text{Rnd}$
09 $(pub, (st_u)_{u \in [n]}) \leftarrow \text{Setup}(n; r_{\text{setup}})$
10 $r \leftarrow_\$ \text{Rnd}$; $\text{Coins}[u_0, t] \leftarrow_\cup \{r\}$
11 $(st_{u_0}, MI_{u_0}^0) \leftarrow \text{Init}(st_{u_0}, pub, n; r)$
12 **for** $u \in [n]$:
13 $\quad st_u \leftarrow \text{Process}(st_u, pub, MI_{u_0}^0)$
14 $\quad K_G \leftarrow \text{GetKey}(st_u)$
15 **return** $pub, MI_{u_0}^0$

Oracle CHALL   \\one call, Game IND-k-PCS$_{\text{mode}}^{\text{CGKA}}$(A)
16 $t^* \leftarrow t$
17 $K_0 \leftarrow_\$ \text{CGKA.KS}$; $K_1 \leftarrow K_G$
18 **return** K_{b^*}

Oracle CHALL   \\one call, Game OW-k-PCS$_{\text{mode}}^{\text{CGKA}}$(A)
19 $t^* \leftarrow t$
20 $K^* \leftarrow K_G$

Oracle ROUND(U_t)
21 $t \leftarrow t + 1$
22 $MU \leftarrow \emptyset$
23 **for** $u \in U_t$:
24 $\quad$ **require** $u \in [n]$
25 $\quad \text{Upd}[u] \leftarrow_\cup \{t\}$
26 $\quad r \leftarrow_\$ \text{Rnd}$; $\text{Coins}[u, t] \leftarrow_\cup \{r\}$
27 $\quad (st_u, MU_u^t) \leftarrow \text{Update}(st_u, pub; r)$
28 $\quad MU \leftarrow_\cup MU_u^t$
29 **for** $u \in [n]$:
30 $\quad st_u \leftarrow \text{Process}(st_u, pub, MU)$
31 $\quad K_G \leftarrow \text{GetKey}(st_u)$
32 **return** MU

Predicate safe$_{k\text{-PCS}}$
33 **for** $u \in [n]$:
34 $\quad$ **if** $\text{Cor}[u] \neq \emptyset$
35 $\quad\quad$ **if** $\exists t \in \text{Cor}[u] : t \geq t^*$:   \\corruption after challenge
36 $\quad\quad\quad$ **return** 0
37 $\quad\quad t_u^c \leftarrow \max\{t \in \text{Cor}[u]\}$
38 $\quad\quad$ **if** $|\{t \in \text{Upd}[u] : t_u^c < t \leq t^*\}| < k$:   \\too few updates
39 $\quad\quad\quad$ **return** 0
40 **return** 1

Oracle CORR(u)
41 $\text{Cor}[u] \leftarrow_\cup \{t\}$
42 **return** $(st_u, \text{Coins}[u, t])$ \\if mode = RC
43 **return** st_u \\if mode = $\neg$RC

Fig. 4. Security games IND-k-PCS$_{\text{mode}}$ for indistinguishability and OW-k-PCS$_{\text{mode}}$ for one-wayness of group keys with respect to mode $\in \{\text{RC}, \neg\text{RC}\}$. The game is defined with respect to a scheme CGKA and an adversary A. We require that the adversary's first call is to oracle INIT, which can only be queried once.

security notions. The weakest, OW-k-PCS$_{\neg RC}$, is used for our lower bounds in Sect. 3.2 and the strongest, IND-k-PCS$_{RC}$, for our upper bound of Sect. 5.

The security games are formally defined in Fig. 4. They provide the adversary A with an initialization oracle INIT that allows for a single query, that has to be made before using any of the other oracles. It enables A to set up a universe of users and initialize a group. Using oracle ROUND, the adversary can specify sets of users to concurrently perform updates. All operations are then processed by the members of the group, and the round counter t is increased. Further, A can, at any point in time, use the corruption oracle CORR(u) to reveal user u's current internal state st_u, and, in the case that mode = RC, additionally the random coins u sampled in the current round while updating. Finally, A, at an arbitrary point in time t^*, can make a single query to the challenge oracle CHALL, which in Game IND-k-PCS$^{CGKA}_{mode}$(A), depending on challenge bit b^*, returns either the current group key or a uniformly random key. The adversary wins if it is able to correctly guess b^* and safety predicate safe-k-PCS holds. In Game OW-k-PCS$^{CGKA}_{mode}$(A), the oracle instead stores the current group key as challenge key K^*. This has to be computed by A in order to win, again with the restriction that safe-k-PCS holds. The predicate safe-k-PCS verifies that, for every user that at time t^* is a member of the group, (a) they were never corrupted after t^* and (b) since their last corruption before t^* they performed at least k updates.

Definition 2 (k-PCS security).   *Let* CGKA *be a continuous group-key agreement scheme, $k \in \mathbb{N}$, and* mode $\in \{RC, \neg RC\}$. *Then* CGKA *is* IND-k-PCS$_{mode}$ *secure, if for every PPT adversary the advantage function* $|\Pr[\text{IND-}k\text{-PCS}^{CGKA}_{mode}(A) \Rightarrow 1 \mid b^* = 1] - \Pr[\text{IND-}k\text{-PCS}^{CGKA}_{mode}(A) \Rightarrow 1 \mid b^* = 0]|$ *is negligible.*

Further, CGKA *is* OW-k-PCS$_{mode}$ *secure, if for every PPT adversary the advantage function* $\Pr[\text{OW-}k\text{-PCS}^{CGKA}_{mode}(A) \Rightarrow 1]$ *is negligible.*

Remark 1. We make the following observation about the security model.

(i) In this work we are interested in the communication cost of achieving post-compromise security, and thus ignore attacks breaching forward secrecy, i.e., learning group keys from previous rounds by corrupting users. This is encoded in lines 35 and 36 of the safe predicate, which disallow corrupting users after the challenged round t^*.

(ii) Our security model is quite weak. In particular, all initialization and update operations are honestly generated and immediately processed by all users in synchronous rounds. We point out that this only strengthens our lower bounds, as they hold even for a security notion far weaker than what one would aim for in practice. While this leaves open the possibility of improving on our bounds by switching to a stronger security notion, we point out that they are closely matched by the upper bound of Sect. 5, which we expect to be easily made secure in asynchronous settings with a semi-honest server using standard techniques to ensure consistency (e.g. signatures, a key schedule, transcript and parent hashes, etc. [2,6,10]).

Restrictions. Our lower bounds apply to CGKA schemes CGKA satisfying the following two restrictions.

- CGKA does not use nested encryption (NNE). This means that users do not create layered ciphertexts of the form $\mathsf{Enc}(pk_1, \mathsf{Enc}(pk_2, m))$.
- CGKA does not distribute work (NDW). This means that, if in any round a user get access to a secret they did not previously possess, then they must have either sampled it by themselves or recovered it from the update message of a single user.

The properties are not directly exploited in our proofs in the combinatorial model. Instead, we use them to show that bounds in the combinatorial model also hold in the symbolic model. We defer the restrictions' formal definitions to Sect. 4 (Definition 5 and Definition 7), where we will also formally justify their impact on the combinatorial model. We point out that all CGKA schemes that we are aware of satisfy both properties.

We also consider an additional property. We say that CGKA has publicly-computable update cost (PCU) if it is always possible to determine the size $|MU_u|$ of an update that a user u would produce if asked to update given access only to public information, i.e., *pub*, as well as the sets of update messages sent so far. With this additional property we can show that not only there exists a sequence of updates for which the total communication cost is at least roughly $n^{1+1/k} \cdot k/\log(k)$, but it is also possible to find the sequence using only public information. Formally, CGKA schemes with publicly-computable update cost are defined as follows.

Definition 3 (Publicly-computable update cost). *Let CGKA be a CGKA scheme. Consider an execution of game* IND-k-PCS$_{\mathrm{mode}}$ *(or* OW-k-PCS$_{\mathrm{mode}}$*). We say that CGKA has* publicly-computable update cost *if, for every round t and for every user $u \in G_t$ with internal state st_u^t and public information pub, it is possible to efficiently compute $|MU|$, where $(st', MU) \leftarrow \mathsf{Update}(st_u^t, pub; r)$ would be the output of calling the update procedure, from public information at the end of round $t-1$ (i.e., all messages $MI_{u_0}^0$ and $MU_u^{t'}$ sent in any round $t' \leq t-1$, the sequence $(U_{t'})_{t' \leq t-1}$, n, k, pub and u_0). Note that, in particular, the size of MU must be independent of the random coins r used to generate the update message. We say that CGKA has* offline publicly-computable update cost *if the same property holds using only the initialization messages $MI_{u_0}^0$, the sequence $(U_{t'})_{t' \leq t-1}$, n, k, pub and u_0.*

All CGKA schemes that we are aware of have offline publicly-computable update cost. For example, for schemes based on ratchet trees, as for example TreeKEM or CoCoA, the size of every user's next update is fully determined by the position of blank and non-blank nodes in the ratchet tree, which can be determined given just the sequence of update/propose-commit operations.

3   Lower Bounds in the Combinatorial Model

In this section we define a self-contained combinatorial model capturing CGKA schemes recovering from corruption in k rounds of updates and then prove a lower bound on the communication complexity of such schemes. The model is given in Sect. 3.1, the bound in Sect. 3.2.

3.1 The Combinatorial Model

We now present a purely combinatorial model capturing an adversary interacting with a correct and secure CGKA scheme built from public-key encryption and pseudorandom functions. The interaction proceeds in rounds, during which users schedule update operations and at the end of which a set of users is corrupted.

High-Level Structure. An instance of the combinatorial model is characterized by a tuple (n, k, t_{max}, C_0) and a sequence $(U_t, C_t)_{t=1}^{t_{max}}$, where $n, k, t_{max} \in \mathbb{N}$, $C_0 \subseteq [n]$, and $U_t, C_t \subseteq [n]$ for all t. This corresponds to setting up the group $G = [n]$ and in round 0 corrupting the set of users C_0. The sequence $(U_t, C_t)_{t=1}^{t_{max}}$ determines the operations performed in the following t_{max} rounds, where

- U_t is the set of users performing an update in round t, and
- C_t is the set of users corrupted at the end of round t.

Integer k determines the safety requirement imposed on the CGKA scheme. More precisely, we aim to capture CGKA schemes that recover from corruption after k updates, meaning that if every user did at least k updates since the last round in which they were corrupted, then the group must agree on a secure key. Formally, consider an instantiation of the combinatorial model with respect to (n, k, t_{max}, C_0) and $(U_t, C_t)_t$ as described above. We say that a round $t \in \{0, \ldots, t_{max}\}$ is *safe*, if for every user $u \in G$ such that $u \in C_{t'}$ for some t' there exist rounds $t_1, \ldots, t_k$ such that

$$u \in U_{t_i} \text{ for all } i \in \{1, \ldots, k\} \tag{1}$$

and

$$\max\{t_c \in \{0, \ldots, t_{max}\} : u \in C_{t_c}\} < t_1 < \cdots < t_k \leq t \ . \tag{2}$$

Recall that since we want to only argue about post-compromise security but not forward-secrecy the condition also excludes the corruption of users *after* round t.

Set System and Cost Function. The main intuition behind the combinatorial model is to associate the secure PKE and PRF keys present in the CGKA scheme in round t to the set of users in G that have access to them at this point in time, i.e., can recover them from their current internal state. Here 'secure key' refers to keys that were established by update operations and cannot be trivially recovered from the adversary. The adversary is able to get access to keys directly by corrupting users' states, or by recovering them from protocol messages. The latter is possible if the message contains an encryption of the key under a key the adversary has access to, or if it contains the key in plain. In every round the sets $S(sk)$ of users having access to secure keys sk form a subset of 2^G. Intuitively, security and correctness of a CGKA scheme imply that the system

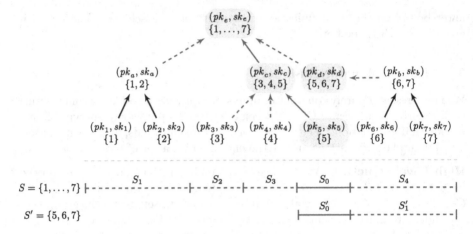

Fig. 5. Top: Illustration of a ratchet tree and its associated set system $\mathcal{S}_t$. Vertices contain key-pairs (above) and the associated set (below). Keys already present in the system at time $t-1$ are depicted in black and keys added by user 5 in round t in blue with shaded background. Edges indicate that knowledge secret key of the source implies knowledge of the one of the sink. Dashed, blue edges correspond to ciphertexts $\mathsf{Enc}_{pk_{\text{source}}}(sk_{\text{sink}})$ sent by user 5 in round t, solid edges either to keys derived using a PRF in round t (depicted in blue) or to keys communicated in a previous round (depicted in black). Accordingly, user 5 generated key-pairs (pk_5, sk_5) and (pk_d, sk_d) using fresh randomness, and (pk_c, sk_c) and (pk_e, sk_e) using a PRF. Bottom: Depiction of the sets required to exist by property (iii) using the examples $S = \{1, \ldots, 7\} = \bigcup_{i=0}^{k} S_i$ and $S' = \{5, 6, 7\} = \bigcup_{i=0}^{k'} S_i'$ with $k = 4$ and $k' = 1$ corresponding to the secret keys sk_e and sk_d respectively. We have $S_0 = \{5\} = S_0'$, $S_1 = \{1, 2\}$, $S_2 = \{3\}$, $S_3 = \{4\}$, and $S_4 = \{6, 7\} = S_1'$. Note that the number of ciphertexts sent to communicate the secret keys corresponding to S and S' to their members are $5 > k$ and $1 = k'$ respectively, thus satisfying the inequality on the user's cost function required by property (iii). (Color figure online)

of associated sets should satisfy certain properties, and that adding sets to it by scheduling updates comes at the cost of sending ciphertexts. These properties are stated below and, looking ahead, will serve as the main tools to derive our lower bound. For an illustration of the set system corresponding to a ratchet tree as described in the introduction see Fig. 5 (Top).

Formally, consider an instantiation of the combinatorial model with respect to $(n, k, t_{\max}, C_0)$ and $(U_t, C_t)_t$. We require the existence of a cost function Cost and a sequence $(\mathcal{S}_t)_{0 \le t \le t_{\max}}$ of set systems $\mathcal{S}_t \subseteq 2^G$. The cost function and sequences are required to satisfy three properties to be given further below. The cost function takes as input

- the user $u \in G$ performing the update operation,
- the round t with $1 \le t \le t_{\max}$, and
- the history $M_t = (n, k, (U_{t'})_{1 \le t' < t})$ of sets of users performing updates in the previous rounds.

Its output is an integer $\text{Cost}(u, t, M_t)$. For better legibility, we will simply write $\text{Cost}(u, t)$ whenever the third input is clear from context.

Note that while the cost of a user's update in a given round depends on the operations performed in previous rounds, it does not depend on the sets $C_{t'}$ of users corrupted in previous rounds. The latter is justified, since, looking ahead, in the security game in the symbolic model, users are not aware whether they are corrupted or not. However, if asked to update by the adversary, they may decide to create particular ciphertexts depending on the history of operations performed so far, as these may have impacted their internal state.

Requirements on Set System and Cost Function. We now give three properties to be satisfied by the cost function and the set system.

(i) Correctness of the CGKA scheme implies that group members share a common key. Further, by security, whenever a round is safe, the corresponding shared key must not be known to the adversary at this point in time.
Formally, if round t is safe we require that $G = [n] \in \mathcal{S}_t$.

(ii) If a user is corrupted in some round, all keys they currently have access to can also be recovered by the adversary and therefore should be considered insecure. This is represented by $\mathcal{S}_t$ not containing any sets that include a party corrupted in round t.
Formally, for all $t \in \{0, \ldots, t_{\max}\}$ and all $u \in C_t$ we have that $S \in \mathcal{S}_t$ implies that $u \notin S$.

(iii) The third property captures how users agree on new keys when using basic cryptographic primitives (PRFs and PKE) and which cost in terms of ciphertexts sent is incurred by communicating these keys to other users. A user $u \in G$ can always sample a new key locally. Further, from such a key or one already present in the system they can derive a chain of new keys using PRF evaluations. To communicate the key sk to other users they can encrypt it under a public key pk' that must have either been present in the system at the end of round $t-1$ or been previously generated by u in round t. From the resulting ciphertext, every user with access to the corresponding sk' is able to derive sk as well as all keys derived from sk using PRF evaluations. Note that if sk' is insecure, then the adversary can recover sk.
In terms of sets this essentially means that the set $S \in \mathcal{S}_t$ of users able to recover sk can be covered by a union of sets in $\mathcal{S}_{t-1}$ (and potentially a singleton $\{u\}$ in case user u generated the starting point of the PRF evaluation chain from fresh randomness) and that the cost of the user communicating sk to the other members of S should be at least the number of sets forming the union (where sometimes one ciphertext can be saved, as the key serving as a starting point of a chain of PRF evaluations needs not be communicated).
Formally, for every $t \geq 1$ and every $S \in \mathcal{S}_t$ we require that there exist $h \in \mathbb{N}_{\geq 0}$ and $S_0, \ldots, S_h$, such that either

$$S_0 = \{u\} \text{ for some } u \in U_t \quad \text{or} \quad S_0 \in \mathcal{S}_{t-1}\ , \tag{3}$$

and if $h \geq 1$ then $S_i \in \mathcal{S}_{t-1}$ for all $i \in \{1, \ldots, h\}$. Further, we require that

$$S \cap C_{\leq t} \subseteq \bigcup_{i=0}^{h} S_i \qquad (4)$$

where $C_{\leq t} = \bigcup_{0 \leq t' \leq t} C_{t'}$ are the users that have been corrupted at least once in or before round t. And, regarding the cost function, we require that

$$\exists u \in S_0 \cap U_t \text{ such that } \mathrm{Cost}(u, t) \geq h \ . \qquad (5)$$

Note that if in Eq. 3 we have $S_0 = \{u\}$ then the user in Eq. 5 must be u. Finally, we can connect the cost of adding a set to the set system $\mathcal{S}_t$ to its MinCover with respect to $\mathcal{S}_{t-1}$. Indeed, for $S \in \mathcal{S}_t$, if u is the user required to exist by Eq. 5, then by Eqs. 3, 4, and 5

$$\mathrm{Cost}(u, t) \geq |\mathrm{minCover}_{\supseteq}(S \cap C_{\leq t}, \mathcal{S}_{t-1} \cup \{u\})| - 1 \ . \qquad (6)$$

The precise connection between the combinatorial model and the symbolic model is established in Sect. 4. There, we essentially show that an adversary playing the OW security game in the symbolic model with respect to a correct and secure CGKA scheme that satisfies the restrictions described in Sect. 2.2 implies the existence of a set system $\mathcal{S}_t$ satisfying Properties (i)–(iii) if one uses the number of ciphertexts sent by a user u in round t as cost function $\mathrm{Cost}(u, t)$.

3.2   Lower Bound in the Combinatorial Model

We now give a lower bound on the communication cost required to recover from compromise within k rounds in the combinatorial model. Conceptually, our proof proceeds in two steps. First, we lower bound the sum of the maximal per-user update cost over all rounds. This bound is a best-case bound, i.e., it holds with respect to every sequence $(U_t)_t$ of updating users. In a second step we then prove our main result, a bound on the total cost required to recover from corruption. This bound is worst case, i.e., it holds with respect to an adversarially chosen sequence of updating users. Concretely, we will exploit that the cost of a user $u \in U_t$ updating in round t does not depend on the cost of other members of U_t updating concurrently. This enables us to find a sequence $(U_t)_t$ for which all members of U_t have roughly the same update cost, which yields the desired bound as the bound on the maximal per-user update cost implies that the cost of the users in U_t in sufficiently many rounds t must be quite large.

Lower Bound on the Maximal Per-user Update Cost. We first consider the scenario that after an arbitrary setup phase of t_c rounds a set of c users in $G = [n]$ is corrupted and that after m subsequent rounds of updates we have $G \in \mathcal{S}_t$ (intuitively corresponding to the existence of a secure group key). Below, we bound the sum of the maximal per-user update cost over the m rounds. Note that this bound holds irrespective of how the sets U_t of updating users are chosen. The proposition's proof is in the full version of this paper [8].

Proposition 2. *Let* $n, k, t_c, m \in \mathbb{N}$, $C \subseteq [n]$, *and* $c = |C|$ *such that* $\ln(c) \geq m - 1$. *Let* $t_{\max} = t_c + m$ *and consider an instantiation of the combinatorial model with respect to* $(n, k, t_{\max}, C_0)$, $(U_t, C_t)_t$, *where* $C_{t_c} = C$, $C_t = \emptyset$ *for* $t \neq t_c$, *and* $(U_t)_t$ *is an arbitrary sequence.*

If $G = [n]$ *is contained in the set-system* $\mathcal{S}_{t_{\max}}$ *at the end of round* $t_{\max} = t_c + m$, *then we have*

$$\sum_{t=1}^{m} \max_{u \in U_{t_c+t}} \text{Cost}(u, t_c + t) \geq (m-1) \left(\sqrt[m-1]{c} - 1 \right).$$

From Maximal Per-user Cost to Total-Communication Cost. We now show that for an adversarially chosen sequence $(U_t)_t$ of sets of updating users actually almost all users have to adhere to the bound derived in the previous paragraph. Intuitively, after an arbitrary warm up phase of t_c rounds and corrupting a linear fraction of users in round t_c, we construct $(U_t)_t$ such that either all updating users have roughly the same update cost, or all users have a very small update cost. This procedure will then be repeated for sufficiently many rounds to force that a linear fraction of all users in the group has updated at least k times. In this case the final round $t_{\max}$ must be secure enforcing that $G \in \mathcal{S}_{t_{\max}}$. This allows us to use the bound derived in the previous paragraph to show that the communication cost of rounds corresponding to the former case must be substantial. We obtain the following theorem, its proof, as well as the one of the following corollary, being in the full version of this paper [8].

Theorem 3. *Let* $k, n, t_c \in \mathbb{N}$ *and* $0 < \varepsilon < 2/5$ *be a constant such that* $(1+\varepsilon)k \in \mathbb{N}$. *Set* $\alpha_\varepsilon = \frac{\varepsilon - 5/2\varepsilon^2 + \varepsilon^3}{8(1+\varepsilon)} > 0$ *and* $t_{\max} = t_c + (1+\varepsilon)k$. *If* $3 \leq k \leq \ln(\alpha_\varepsilon n)$, *then for every sequence* $(U_t)_{t=1}^{t_c}$ *there exists a set* $C \subseteq [n]$ *of size* $\lceil \alpha_\varepsilon n \rceil$ *and a sequence* $(U_t)_{t=t_c+1}^{t_{\max}}$ *such that the instantiation of the combinatorial model with respect to* $(n, k, t_{\max}, \emptyset)$ *and* $(U_t, C_t)_{t=1}^{t_{\max}}$, *where* $C_{t_c} = C$ *and* $C_t = \emptyset$ *if* $t \neq t_c$, *satisfies*

$$\sum_{t=1}^{(1+\varepsilon)k} \text{Cost}(U_{t_c+t}) \geq \frac{(k-1)}{4} \cdot \left\lfloor \frac{2\varepsilon n}{5(1+\varepsilon)\lceil \log(k) \rceil} \right\rfloor \left((\alpha_\varepsilon n)^{\frac{1}{(1+\varepsilon)k-1}} - 1 \right).$$

While we phrased Theorem 3 as a single-stage experiment, i.e., only consider the communication required to recover from corruptions made in a single round, it easily carries over to a repeated experiment consisting of repeatedly corrupting a linear fraction of the users from which the group has to recover within $(1+\varepsilon)k$ rounds of updates. Note, that the setting of Theorem 3 allows for an arbitrary setup phase $(U_t)_{t \leq t_c}$ of t_c rounds. Thus, by simply applying the arguments in the proof iteratively to each recovery phase, we obtain that the derived bound holds even in an amortized sense, i.e., even in this setting the recovery from each corruption requires communication of order $nk^{(1+\varepsilon)k}\sqrt{n}/\log(k)$.

Corollary 4. *Let* k, n, t_c, ε, *and* α_ε *be as in Theorem 3. Let* $z_{\max} \in \mathbb{N}$ *and for* $0 \leq z < z_{\max}$ *set* $t_{c,z} = t_c + z \cdot (t_c + (1+\varepsilon)k)$ *and* $t_{\max} = z_{\max} \cdot (t_c + (1+\varepsilon)k)$. *For all* collections of sequences $(U_t)_{t=t_{c,z}-t_c+1}^{t_{c,z}}$ with $0 \leq z < z_{\max}$, there exist sets $C_z \subseteq$ $[n]$ each of size $\lceil \alpha_\varepsilon n \rceil$ and collections of updates $(U_t)_{t=t_{c,z}+1}^{t_{c,z}+(1+\varepsilon)k}$ such that for every instantiation of the combinatorial model with respect to $(n, k, t_{\max}, \emptyset)$ and $(U_t, C_t)_{t=1}^{t_{\max}}$, where $C_{t_{c,z}} = C_z$ and $C_t = \emptyset$ if $t \notin \{t_{c,z} \mid 0 \leq z < z_{\max}\}$, we have

$$\sum_{t=t_{c,z}+1}^{t_{c,z}+(1+\varepsilon)k} \mathrm{Cost}(U_{t_{c,z}+t}) \geq \frac{(k-1)}{4} \cdot \left\lfloor \frac{2\varepsilon n}{5(1+\varepsilon)\lceil \log(k)\rceil} \right\rfloor \left((\alpha_\varepsilon n)^{\frac{1}{(1+\varepsilon)k-1}} - 1 \right)$$

for very $0 \leq z < z_{\max}$.

4   Lower Bounds in the Symbolic Model

In this section define CGKA in a symbolic model, an approach introduced for public key encryption by Dolev and Yao [18], following the work on multicast encryption by Micciancio and Panjwani [24], and generalized to CGKA by Bienstock, Dodis, and Rösler [12], who considered concurrent updates for schemes recovering in two rounds. A similar model was also used to lower bound the communication incurred by users in CGKA schemes in order to achieve PCS, in a setting of multiple groups [1]. We show how the questions we are interested in can be translated from the symbolic to the combinatorial model of Sect. 3, which allows us to conclude that the bounds derived in the combinatorial model also hold with respect to the symbolic model.

4.1   The Symbolic Model

We consider schemes constructed from pseudorandom functions and public-key encryption, both modeled as idealized primitives that take as input symbolic variables, and output symbolic variables. To more easily distinguish these from non-symbolic variables we use typewriter font. We use the following syntax.

(i) *Pseudorandom function:* Algorithm PRF takes as input a key K and a message m and returns a key $K' = \mathsf{PRF}(K, m)$.

(ii) *Public-key Encryption:* A PKE scheme consists of algorithms (PKE.Gen, PKE.Enc, PKE.Dec), where PKE.Gen on input of secret key sk returns the corresponding public key pk. PKE.Enc takes as input a public key pk and a message m, and outputs a ciphertext c ← PKE.Enc(pk, m) with message data type. PKE.Dec takes as input a secret key sk and a ciphertext c, and outputs a message m = PKE.Dec(sk, c). We assume perfect correctness: PKE.Dec(sk, PKE.Enc(pk, m)) = m for all sk, pk = PKE.Gen(sk), and messages m.

As data types, we consider messages, public keys, secret keys, symmetric keys, and random coins, the latter being a terminal type. Which variables can be recovered from a set of messages M, is captured by the *entailment relation* ⊢.

Data type		Grammar rules
Message m	$\leftarrow$	$\mathsf{sk}, \mathsf{pk}, \mathsf{PKE.Enc}(\mathsf{pk}, \mathsf{m})$
Public key pk	$\leftarrow$	$\mathsf{PKE.Gen}(\mathsf{sk})$
Secret key sk	$\leftarrow$	K
Key K	$\leftarrow$	$\mathsf{r}, \mathsf{PRF}(\mathsf{K}, \mathsf{m})$
Random coin r		terminal type

Entailment relation

$\mathsf{m} \in \mathsf{M}$	$\Rightarrow$	$\mathsf{M} \vdash \mathsf{m}$
$\mathsf{M} \vdash \mathsf{m}, \mathsf{pk}$	$\Rightarrow$	$\mathsf{M} \vdash \mathsf{PKE.Enc}(\mathsf{pk}, \mathsf{m})$
$\mathsf{M} \vdash \mathsf{K}$	$\Rightarrow$	$\mathsf{M} \vdash \mathsf{PRF}(\mathsf{K}, \mathsf{m})$ for all m
$\mathsf{M} \vdash \mathsf{PKE.Enc}(\mathsf{pk}, \mathsf{m}), \mathsf{sk} : \mathsf{pk} = \mathsf{PKE.Gen}(\mathsf{sk})$	$\Rightarrow$	$\mathsf{M} \vdash \mathsf{m}$

Note that the entailment relation captures (ideal) correctness and (ideal) security of PRF and PKE, as recovering a PRF output or an encrypted message from a ciphertext requires knowledge of the secret key. Security is effectively captured by the of a sequence of entailment relations that recover the appropriate message. Examples and further comments (in the setting of multicast encryption) can be found in [24, Sect. 3.2]. The set of messages which can be recovered from M using relation $\vdash$ is denoted by $\mathsf{Der}(\mathsf{M}) := \{\mathsf{m} : \mathsf{M} \vdash \mathsf{m}\}$.

We point out that the model of [12] covers more primitives, concretely, dual PRFs, updatable PKE, and broadcast encryption. It is an interesting open question to consider whether a translation to our combinatorial model is also possible if one takes these additional primitives into account. For a brief discussion on challenges to overcome if one would allow dual PRFs see Remark 3.

Continuous Group-Key Agreement in the Symbolic Model. A CGKA scheme CGKA in the symbolic model follows the syntax of Sect. 2.2. Additionally, we require some of the inputs to CGKA's algorithms to be symbolic variables. Concretely, we require that the group keys K, public and internal states pub and st, random coins r as well as the control messages MI and MU are symbolic. They can also have a non-symbolic counterpart which we omit as the properties we study and the security game we consider in the symbolic model do not depend on the non-symbolic variables. However, we often distinguish between symbolic random coins r and non-symbolic randomness r as this is used in some of the proofs. Intuitively, symbolic randomness represents the new secrets being sampled, while non-symbolic randomness allows to capture the fact that the algorithms may flip a coin in order to determine their actions (e.g., the update algorithm might flip random coins to decide whether to generate certain ciphertexts or not). Further, we assume that the context symbolic variables, e.g., which key corresponds to a certain ciphertext, or which keys correspond to a particular set of users, are implicitly known to the algorithms.

We use the game of Fig. 3 to define correctness of CGKA, where we additionally require that, for every algorithm, each of its symbolic outputs can be derived from its symbolic inputs using the entailment relation $\vdash$. E.g., if user u computes $(\mathsf{st}'_u, \mathsf{MU}_u) \leftarrow \mathsf{Update}(\mathsf{st}_u, \mathsf{pub}; \mathbf{r}, r)$, then we require that $\mathsf{st}'_u, \mathsf{MU}_u \in \mathsf{Der}(\{\mathsf{st}_u, \mathsf{pub}, \mathbf{r}\})$, and similarly if $\mathsf{st}'_u \leftarrow \mathsf{Process}(\mathsf{st}_u, \mathsf{pub}, \mathsf{M})$ then it must hold that $\mathsf{st}'_u \in \mathsf{Der}(\{\mathsf{st}_u, \mathsf{pub}, \mathsf{M}\})$.

Regarding security, we target the notion of OW-k-PCS$_{\neg \mathrm{RC}}$ of Definition 2. As our goal is to prove lower bounds, using one-wayness as the targeted security notion only makes our results stronger compared to using indistinguishability.

We structure the game in rounds, that correspond to the oracle calls that occur between two subsequent calls to oracle ROUND. We say a query to some oracle was made in round 0 if it was made before the first query to ROUND, and in round t for $t \in \{1, \ldots, t_{\max}\}$, if it was either the tth query to ROUND, or, for calls to CHALL or CORR, if it was made after the tth and before the $(t+1)$st query to ROUND. This allows us to fully characterize adversaries A by the sequence of inputs to the oracles made in each round. For round 0, these are the input (n, G_0, u_0) to INIT and the set C_0 of corrupted users; for round t, the set U_t of updating users queried to ROUND, as well as the set C_t of users corrupted during the round; and finally, t^* indicating in which round the single call to CHALL is made. An explicit description of the OW-k-PCS$_{\neg \mathrm{RC}}$ security game in the symbolic model can be found in Fig. 7.

Definition 4 (Symbolic k-PCS security). *Let* CGKA *be a continuous group-key agreement scheme, $k \in \mathbb{N}$. Then* CGKA *is* OW-k-PCS$_{\neg \mathrm{RC}}$ *secure, if for all* $(n, u_0, C_0, (U_t, C_t)_{t=1}^{t_{\max}}, t^*)$ *it holds that*

$$\Pr[\text{OW-}k\text{-PCS}_{\neg \mathrm{RC}}^{\mathsf{CGKA}}(n, u_0, C_0, (U_t, C_t)_{t=1}^{t_{\max}}, t^*) \Rightarrow 1] = 0$$

where the probability is taken over the non-symbolic randomness.

This notion of security, in which for any sequence $(n, u_0, C_0, (U_t, C_t)_{t=1}^{t_{\max}}, t^*)$ the game is lost, is standard in the literature of symbolic security and used, for instance, in [24] and [12]. The requirement that the probability be zero, implies that the game is not won for every possible choice of non-symbolic randomness. The reason for this choice rather than requiring that it be a negligible function in $\log|R|$, where R denotes the set of non-symbolic randomness, is that it may very well be the case that $|R|$ is small since this is not the randomness used to sample new keys (when it would be reasonable to work with $\log|R|$ as a security parameter). For instance, one could just flip a coin (i.e., $R = \{0, 1\}$).

In the game we require that all symbolic random coins used by users are generated disjointly. More precisely, if $\mathbf{r}_u^t$ denotes the set of random coins used by user u in round t in the init/update procedures, then we require that $\mathbf{r} \in \mathbf{r}_u^t$ implies $\mathbf{r} \notin \mathbf{r}_{u'}^{t'}$ for all $(u, t) \neq (u', t')$.

We now define a property of CGKA schemes that we will require for our bounds. It essentially forbids schemes to generate layered ciphertexts of the form PKE.Enc(pk_2, PKE.Enc(pk_2, m)). For some intuition on how it factors into our translation to the combinatorial model see Remark 3.

Definition 5 (No nested encryption). *We say a scheme* CGKA *does not use* nested encryption *if, for all ciphertexts* c $\leftarrow$ PKE.Enc(pk, m), *the encrypted message is either a secret key or a random coin, i.e., of type* sk, K, *or* r.

Our goal for the remainder of this section is to show that the task of deriving lower bounds on the communication complexity of correct and secure CGKA schemes translates to the analogue in the combinatorial model. To this end, we define *useful secrets*, i.e., secret symbolic variables that the adversary is not able to derive, and associate them to the set of users with knowledge of them. We prove that these sets satisfy the properties described in Sect. 3.1 for a cost function that counts the number of messages sent in a given round by a user.

Useful Secrets and Associated Sets. First, we establish some notation. Consider an adversary playing OW-k-PCS$_{\neg RC}$. We denote the set of public messages sent up to and including round t by M_t, i.e., for $t = 0$ we set $M_0 = \{\text{pub}, \text{MI}^0_{u_0}\}$ to be the output of oracle Init; and for every round $t \geq 1$ we extend the set by the output of oracle ROUND: $M_t \leftarrow M_{t-1} \cup MU$, where $MU = \text{ROUND}(U_t)$. Further, for $t \geq 0$ we track all variables the adversary learned up to and including round t, via the corruption oracle, in a set COR_t. I.e., at the beginning of round t, the set COR_t is initialized to COR_{t-1} and, if user u is corrupted in round t, then their current state st_u (meaning the one after all oracle calls of the round) is added to the set. Note that COR_t matches the set COR_t, defined in game OW-k-PCS$_{\neg RC}$, that tracks the values known to the adversary via corruption. This allows us to define the notion of useful secrets s, i.e., variables of type r, K, and sk that cannot be derived by the adversary, and associate to them the set of users that in round t have access to s.

Definition 6 (Useful secrets and associated sets). *Consider adversary A playing game* OW-k-PCS$_{\neg RC}$ *in the symbolic model and let* $t \in \mathbb{N}$*, and* s *be a variable of type* r*,* K*, or* sk *generated during the game, before or in round t. We say that s is* useful *in round t if* $s \notin \text{Der}(\{M_t, \text{COR}_t\})$*. Let* s *be useful in round t. We define the* associated set *of* s *in round t as*

$$S(s,t) := \{u \in [n] \mid s \in \text{Der}(\text{st}_u^{t_{c,u}}, (r_u^{t'})_{t_{c,u}+1 \leq t' \leq t}, M_t)\} \subseteq [n]$$

where $t_{c,u} := \max\{\tilde{t} \mid u \in C_{\tilde{t}}$ *and* $\tilde{t} \leq t\}$ *($t_{c,u} = -1$ if u has never been corrupted). We define the* associated set *of* s *after the setup as*

$$S(s,-1) := \{u \in [n] \mid s \in \text{Der}(\text{st}_u^{-1}, \text{pub})\} \subseteq [n] \ .$$

We define the set system *in round t as*

$$\mathcal{S}_t := \{S(s,t) \mid s \text{ is useful in round } t\} \subseteq 2^{[n]} \ .$$

The intuition behind the definition of $S(s,t)$ is that any user who can derive the secret s in a round t' such that $t_{c,u}+1 \leq t' \leq t$ (i.e., $s \in \text{Der}(\text{st}_u^{t'}, M_{t'})$) should belong to the set $S(s,t)$. This is indeed the case since $\text{st}_u^{t'} \subseteq \text{Der}(\text{st}_u^{t'-1}, r_u^{t'}, M_{t'})$ because symbolic outputs of algorithms can always be derived symbolically from their symbolic inputs. The notation st_u^{-1} refers to the state that u is assigned by the Setup algorithm.

We now define what it means for a scheme to not allow users to distribute work. Intuitively, this requirement says that whenever a secret (be it already existing or newly generated) is communicated to a set of users, who did not yet have access to it, then this communication must have been done by a *single* user. For example, this notion excludes schemes in which two users u_1, u_2, already sharing a common key, communicate this key to users u_3 and u_4 by having u_1 encrypt it to u_3, and u_2 encrypt it to u_4.

See Fig. 6 for an illustration of a scheme that *does* make use of distributed work at hand of a ratchet tree.

Definition 7 (No distributed work). *Consider a scheme* CGKA *and an execution of game* OW-k-PCS$_{\neg \mathrm{RC}}$ *with respect to* CGKA *in the symbolic model. For user u and round t let* st_u^t *denote the user's state in round t and* $\mathbf{r}_u^t$ *the random coins generated in round t. We say that* CGKA *does not allow users to distribute work if, for all t and every secret symbolic variable* s*, we have that there exists a user u' such that for every $u \in S(\mathsf{s}, t) \setminus (S(\mathsf{s}, t-1) \cup \{u'\})$ it holds that* $\mathsf{s} \in \mathsf{Der}(\mathsf{st}_u^{t-1}, \mathsf{M}_{t-1}, \mathsf{MU}_{u'}^t)$ *and* $\mathsf{s} \in \mathsf{Der}(\mathsf{st}_{u'}^{t-1}, \mathbf{r}_{u'}^t, \mathsf{M}_{t-1})$.

Connection to Combinatorial Model. In the following we show that the three properties required in the combinatorial model are satisfied by the symbolic model's associated set system. The first two are quite natural observations, the last essentially corresponds to a generalization of a statement that is shown in the proof of [12, Theorem 2] and can be seen as quantifying the cost of adding new sets to the set system $\mathcal{S}_t$ by updating. We measure the cost in terms of the number of symbolic variables sent by a user u in round t and denote this quantity $|\mathsf{MU}_u^t|$. When interested in the cost of a round t, we take the sum over all users $u \in U_t$.

Intuitively, Property (i) is enforced by correctness and security, as on one hand every member of G_t must be able to derive the current group key from their state, and the safety predicate being satisfied implies that the group key at time t^* must be useful, i.e., $G_{t^*} \in \mathcal{S}_{t^*}$. Property (ii) corresponds to the simple fact that no secret derivable from st_u can be useful in a round in which the user gets corrupted, as in this case it can be derived by the adversary as well. Equivalently, a set $S \in \mathcal{S}_t$ cannot contain any users in C_t. Finally, Property (iii) corresponds to the intuition, that the secret s belonging to a new set $S = S(\mathsf{s}, t)$ needs to be communicated to (at least) every member u of S. If s cannot be derived using PRF evaluations from a secret already known to u, then either it, or a secret which can be derived from using PRF, must be communicated to u by encrypting it to a useful key that was known to the party in the previous round, i.e., in round $t-1$. In other words, this determines a covering of the set S with sets in $\mathcal{S}_{t-1}$ and possibly a singleton $\{u\}$ for some updating user $u \in U_t$ with the property that the number of symbolic variables contained in the messages exchanged in round t is at least the number of sets in the said cover minus one. When we consider schemes in which users do not distribute work, we obtain a simpler statement for property (iii) and it matches Eq. 5 from the combinatorial model.

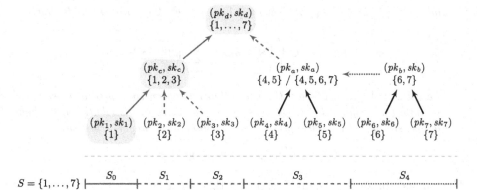

Fig. 6. Top: Example of a ratchet tree and its associated set system $\mathcal{S}_t$ making use of distributed work. Vertices contain key-pairs (above) and the associated set (below). Edges indicate that knowledge of the secret key of the source implies knowledge of the one of the sink. Dashed edges correspond to ciphertexts $\mathsf{Enc}_{pk_{\mathrm{source}}}(sk_{\mathrm{sink}})$ sent by user 1 in round t, solid edges either to keys derived using a PRF in round t or to keys communicated in a previous round. Keys already present in the system at time $t-1$ are depicted in black and keys added by user 1 in round t in blue with shaded background. The dotted edge corresponds to a ciphertext sent by user 5 in round t. Note that the associated set of (pk_a, sk_a) changes in round t as an effect of this ciphertext, and that users 6 and 7 need to decrypt ciphertexts sent by two different users, namely users 1 and 5, in order to recover sk_d, implying that the scheme does indeed use distributed work. Bottom: Depiction of the sets proven to exist in Lemma 1 using the example $S = \{1, \dots, 7\} = \bigcup_{i=0}^{k} S_i$ in the set system depicted above. Note that $k = 4$ matches the number of ciphertexts sent in round t to establish S, which, however, stem from more than a single user (compare Lemma 1; (iii)). (Color figure online)

Lemma 1. *Let* CGKA *be a perfectly correct continuous group-key agreement scheme that is* OW-k-PCS$_{\neg\mathrm{RC}}$-*secure and does not use nested encryption. Consider an adversary playing game* OW-k-PCS$_{\neg\mathrm{RC}}$ *of Fig. 7 in the symbolic model.*

(i) *If* K_{G_t} *is the group key in round* t, *then* $S(\mathsf{K}_{G_t}, t) = G_t$. *In particular, if oracle* CHALL *is queried in round* t^* *and the safety predicate is satisfied then we have* $G_{t^*} \in \mathcal{S}_{t^*}$.

(ii) *If user* u *was corrupted by the adversary in round* t, *then for every* $S \in \mathcal{S}_t$ *it holds that* $u \notin S$.

(iii) *Let* $t \geq 1$. *Recall, that* $U_t \subseteq [n]$ *indicate the users that updated and for user* u *the sets* MU_u^t *correspond to the control messages generated by performing the corresponding update operation. Then for every set* $S \in \mathcal{S}_t$ *there exist* $k \in \mathbb{N}_{\geq 0}$ *and sets* $\{S_i\}_{i=0}^{k}$ *such that either*

$$(a)\ S_0 = \{u\}\ \text{for some } u \in U_t,\quad \text{or } (b)\ S_0 \in \mathcal{S}_{t-1}$$

and, if $k \geq 1$, $S_i \in \mathcal{S}_{t-1}$ for every $i = 1, \ldots, k$. Furthermore, it holds that

$$S \cap C_{\leq t} \subseteq \bigcup_{i=0}^{k} S_i \quad and \quad \sum_{u \in U_t} |\mathsf{MU}_u^t| \geq k .$$

where $C_{\leq t} = \bigcup_{0 < t' \leq t} C_{t'}$ are the users that have been corrupted at least once in round t or before. If CGKA does not allow users to distribute work, then the last statement can be replaced by the following stronger expression:

$$\exists u \in S_0 \cap U_t \ such \ that \ |\mathsf{MU}_u^t| \geq k .$$

The lemma's proof is in the full version of this paper [8].

Remark 2. Looking ahead, we observe the following. Consider an execution of game OW-k-PCS$_{\neg \mathrm{RC}}$ in the symbolic model, where CGKA is a perfectly correct, OW-k-PCS$_{\neg \mathrm{RC}}$-secure CGKA scheme which does not use nested encryption and does not allow users to distribute work, and set $\mathrm{Cost}(u, t) = |\mathsf{MU}_u^t|$ to be the number of symbolic variables sent by u in round t. Then, by Lemma 1 the associated set system $\mathcal{S}_t$ (Definition 6) and Cost satisfy all properties of the combinatorial model described in Sect. 3.1. As a consequence, to prove lower bounds on the communication cost of CGKA, i.e., the number of ciphertexts sent during the execution of the game, it is sufficient to lower bound the cost function for a scheme satisfying the combinatorial model.

Remark 3. Lemma 1 requires that CGKA not use nested encryption, i.e., not generate encryptions of ciphertexts. On a technical level, this restriction guarantees that for the graph constructed in the lemma's proof for every edge $(\mathsf{s}_1, \mathsf{s}_2)$ we have that knowledge of secret s_1 implies knowledge of s_2. On a more intuitive level, allowing ciphertexts of the form $\mathsf{c} = \mathsf{Enc}(\mathsf{pk}_2, \mathsf{Enc}(\mathsf{pk}_1, \mathsf{m}))$ would enable users to send ciphertext c in one round but release message m in a later round by at this point in time sending sk_2 in the plain, at cost of no additional ciphertexts. While this does not seem to help with the total communication cost, it could in principle enable users to distribute their workload over several rounds. An analogous statement holds, if one allows the use of dual PRFs (as in [12]).

Following the idea outlined in Remark 2 it can be shown that the worst-case lower bound on the communication cost of CGKA schemes in the combinatorial model carries over to the symbolic model for OW-k-PCS$_{\neg \mathrm{RC}}$-secure schemes.

Corollary 5. *Let k, n, t_c, ε, and α_ε be as in Corollary 5 and let CGKA be a correct and OW-k-PCS$_{\neg \mathrm{RC}}$-secure CGKA scheme that does not use nested encryption, and does not allow users to distribute work. Let $z_{\max} \in \mathbb{N}$ and for every integer $0 \leq z < z_{\max}$ set $t_{c,z} = t_c + z \cdot (t_c + (1 + \varepsilon)k)$ and $t_{\max} = z_{\max} \cdot (t_c + (1 + \varepsilon)k)$.*
If $3 \leq k \leq \ln(\alpha_\varepsilon n)$, then for an arbitrary setup phase of the group $G_0 = G_t = [n]$ and $z_{\max}$ arbitrary phases of t_c rounds of updates $(U_t)_{t=t_{c,z}-t_c+1}^{t_{c,z}}$ with $0 \leq z < z_{\max}$ and any choice of non-symbolic randomness in the security game

```
Game OW-k-PCS_¬RC^CGKA (n, u₀, C₀, (Uₜ, Cₜ)ₜ₌₁^tmax, t*)   Oracle ROUND(Uₜ)
00 INIT(n, u₀)                                             21 MU ← ∅
01 for u ∈ C₀: call CORR(u)                                22 for u ∈ Uₜ:
02 for t = 1, ..., tmax:                                   23    Upd[u] ←∪ {t}
03   ROUND(Uₜ)                                             24    r ←ₛ Rnd; Coins[u, t] ←∪ {r}
04   CORₜ ← CORₜ₋₁                                         25    (stᵤ, MUᵤᵗ) ← Update(stᵤ, pub; r)
05   for u ∈ Cₜ: call CORR(u)                              26    MU ←∪ {MUᵤᵗ}
06   if t = t*: call CHALL                                 27 for u ∈ [n]:
07 return [K* ∈ Der(CORₜmₐₓ, M) ∧ safe_k-PCS]             28    stᵤ ← Process(stᵤ, pub, MU)
                                                           29    K_G ← GetKey(stᵤ)
Oracle INIT(n, u₀)              \\ one call; called first  30 M ←∪ MU
08 t ← 0
09 M ← ∅, COR₀ ← ∅                                         Predicate safe_k-PCS
10 Cor[u] ← ∅, Upd[u] ← ∅ for all u ∈ [n]                 31 for u ∈ [n]:
11 Coins[u, t] ← ∅ for all u ∈ [n], ∀t                    32    if Cor[u] ≠ ∅
12 r_setup ←ₛ Rnd                                          33       if ∃t ∈ Cor[u] : t ≥ t*:     \\ corruption after challenge
13 (pub, (stᵤ)ᵤ∈[n]) ← Setup(n; r_setup)                 34          return 0
14 r ←ₛ Rnd; Coins[u₀, t] ←∪ {r}                         35       tᵤᶜ ← max{t ∈ Cor[u]}
15 (stᵤ₀, MIᵤ₀⁰) ← Init(stᵤ₀, pub, n; r)                 36       if |{t ∈ Upd[u] : tᵤᶜ < t ≤ t*}| < k:   \\ too few updates
16 for u ∈ [n]:                                            37          return 0
17    stᵤ ← Process(stᵤ, pub, MIᵤ₀⁰)                     38 return 1
18    K_G ← GetKey(stᵤ)
19 M ←∪ {pub, MIᵤ₀⁰}                                      Oracle CORR(u)
                                                           39 Cor[u] ←∪ {t}
Oracle CHALL                         \\ one call          40 CORₜ ←∪ {stᵤ}
20 K* ← K_G
```

Fig. 7. Security game OW-k-PCS$_{\neg RC}$ in the symbolic model with respect to the sequence $(n, u_0, C_0, (U_t, C_t)_{t=1}^{t_{\max}}, t^*)$ of inputs to the oracles.

OW-k-PCS$_{\neg RC}$, there exist sequences of updates $(U_t)_{t=t_{c,z}+1}^{t_{c,z}+(1+\varepsilon)k}$ and sets of corrupted users $C_z \subseteq [n]$ each of cardinality $\lceil \alpha_\varepsilon n \rceil$ such that the total communication cost satisfies

$$\sum_{t=t_{c,z}+1}^{t_{c,z}+(1+\varepsilon)k} \text{Cost}(U_{t_{c,z}+t}) \geq \frac{(k-1)}{4} \cdot \left\lfloor \frac{2\varepsilon n}{5(1+\varepsilon)\lceil \log(k) \rceil} \right\rfloor \left((\alpha_\varepsilon n)^{\frac{1}{(1+\varepsilon)k-1}} - 1 \right)$$

for every $0 \leq z < z_{\max}$.

If CGKA has publicly-computable update cost (Definition 3), the sequences of sets $(U_t)_{t=t_{c,z}+1}^{t_{c,z}+(1+\varepsilon)k}$ can be computed online, i.e., $U_{t_{c,z}+t}$ can be computed using public information from the previous rounds. Furthermore, if CGKA has offline publicly-computable update cost, the sequence of updates $(U_t)_{t=t_{c,z}+1}^{t_{c,z}+(1+\varepsilon)k}$ can be computed after round $t_{c,z}$ and is independent of the non-symbolic randomness.

The corollary's proof is in the full version of this paper [8].

5   Upper Bound on the Update Cost

In this section we briefly outline a simple CGKA protocol, inspired by CoCoA [2], but both more general and, for certain values of k, with a lower total upload communication cost. Accordingly, we termed it CoCoALight.

This short section assumes knowledge of CoCoA and only aims to give an intuitive understanding of the ideas behind the proposed protocol. For space reasons we defer a more thorough discussion on CoCoA and our protocol, as well as the formal description and security proof to the full version of this work [8].

The key feature of the protocol is that, as opposed to in CoCoA, users will not rotate the keys for all nodes in their path in each update, but instead just rotate the key of a single node. Users keep track, by means of a counter, of which node they last refreshed, and will, in the following update, sample a new key for its child, increasing the counter by 1. In the case that two users send ciphertexts corresponding to the same node in the same round, the server will decide a winner, as in CoCoA, and thus whose key will be the next one associated to said node, according to any agreed-upon (potentially deterministic) rule. In the case of such a collision, the user losing will still "make progress" and increase their counter, and so, in the following update will attempt to rotate the key at the next node in their path.

A consequence of rotating a single key per update is that knowledge of parts of the old state might allow the recovery of this new key. In particular, the knowledge of the secret key of the parent key of v, when v's key is being refreshed, allows the recovery of the latter (as its seed will be encrypted under the former). Thus, informally, what ensures healing is the progressive rotation of all the path's keys after corruption, and *starting* from the leaf. Thus, in order to guarantee healing in k rounds, CoCoALight uses trees of depth $\approx k/2$, to ensure a rotation of all keys in the path *starting at the leaf* happens within that period.

In particular, it can recover from an arbitrary number of corruptions in k rounds and with a total communication cost in the order of $nk \sqrt[k/2]{n}$ ciphertexts, without any user coordination. While CoCoA's communication complexity is lower for low values of k, CoCoALight's improves for values of k closer to $\log(n)$. This improvement comes at the drawback of non-immediate forward secrecy, which requires at least $k/2$ updates from each user prior to their corruption. Likewise, we not prove it secure against any type of active adversary and, indeed, only describe a simple protocol satisfying IND-k-PCS$_{RC}$ security. Nevertheless, it shows that the lower bound on PCS from the previous section is only $\log(k)/\sqrt[k/2]{n}$ from being tight, for $k \in [4, 2\lceil\log(n)\rceil + 1]$. Concretely, for the case $k = \log(n)$, the gap is of order just $\log(\log(n))$.

References

1. Alwen, J., et al.: Grafting key trees: efficient key management for overlapping groups. In: Nissim, K., Waters, B. (eds.) TCC 2021, Part III. LNCS, vol. 13044, pp. 222–253. Springer, Heidelberg (2021). https://doi.org/10.1007/978-3-030-90456-2_8

2. Alwen, J., et al.: CoCoA: concurrent continuous group key agreement. In: Dunkelman, O., Dziembowski, S. (eds.) EUROCRYPT 2022, Part II. LNCS, vol. 13276, pp. 815–844. Springer, Heidelberg (2022). https://doi.org/10.1007/978-3-031-07085-3_28

3. Alwen, J., Coretti, S., Dodis, Y., Tselekounis, Y.: Security analysis and improvements for the IETF MLS standard for group messaging. In: Micciancio, D., Ristenpart, T. (eds.) CRYPTO 2020, Part I. LNCS, vol. 12170, pp. 248–277. Springer, Heidelberg (2020). https://doi.org/10.1007/978-3-030-56784-2_9

4. Alwen, J., Coretti, S., Jost, D., Mularczyk, M.: Continuous group key agreement with active security. In: Pass, R., Pietrzak, K. (eds.) TCC 2020, Part II. LNCS, vol. 12551, pp. 261–290. Springer, Heidelberg (2020). https://doi.org/10.1007/978-3-030-64378-2_10

5. Alwen, J., Hartmann, D., Kiltz, E., Mularczyk, M.: Server-aided continuous group key agreement. In: Yin, H., Stavrou, A., Cremers, C., Shi, E. (eds.) ACM CCS 2022, pp. 69–82. ACM Press, November 2022

6. Alwen, J., Jost, D., Mularczyk, M.: On the insider security of MLS. In: Dodis, Y., Shrimpton, T. (eds.) CRYPTO 2022, Part II. LNCS, vol. 13508, pp. 34–68. Springer, Heidelberg (2022). https://doi.org/10.1007/978-3-031-15979-4_2

7. Alwen, J., Auerbach, B., Noval, M.C., Klein, K., Pascual-Perez, G., Pietrzak, K.: DeCAF: decentralizable continuous group key agreement with fast healing. Cryptology ePrint Archive, Paper 2022/559 (2022). https://eprint.iacr.org/2022/559

8. Auerbach, B., Noval, M.C., Pascual-Perez, G., Pietrzak, K.: On the cost of post-compromise security in concurrent continuous group-key agreement. Cryptology ePrint Archive, Paper 2023/1123 (2023). https://eprint.iacr.org/2023/1123

9. Barnes, R., Beurdouche, B., Robert, R., Millican, J., Omara, E., Cohn-Gordon, K.: The Messaging Layer Security (MLS) Protocol. RFC 9420, July 2023. https://www.rfc-editor.org/info/rfc9420

10. Bhargavan, K., Barnes, R., Rescorla, E.: TreeKEM: Asynchronous Decentralized Key Management for Large Dynamic Groups, May 2018. https://mailarchive.ietf.org/arch/attach/mls/pdf1XUH6o.pdf

11. Bienstock, A., Dodis, Y., Garg, S., Grogan, G., Hajiabadi, M., Rösler, P.: On the worst-case inefficiency of CGKA. In: Kiltz, E., Vaikuntanathan, V. (eds.) TCC 2022, Part II. LNCS, vol. 13748, pp. 213–243. Springer, Heidelberg (2022). https://doi.org/10.1007/978-3-031-22365-5_8

12. Bienstock, A., Dodis, Y., Rösler, P.: On the price of concurrency in group ratcheting protocols. In: Pass, R., Pietrzak, K. (eds.) TCC 2020, Part II. LNCS, vol. 12551, pp. 198–228. Springer, Heidelberg (2020). https://doi.org/10.1007/978-3-030-64378-2_8

13. Brzuska, C., Cornelissen, E., Kohbrok, K.: Cryptographic security of the MLS RFC, draft 11. Cryptology ePrint Archive, Report 2021/137 (2021). https://eprint.iacr.org/2021/137

14. Canetti, R., Garay, J.A., Itkis, G., Micciancio, D., Naor, M., Pinkas, B.: Multicast security: a taxonomy and some efficient constructions. In: IEEE INFOCOM 1999, pp. 708–716, New York, NY, USA, 21–25 March 1999

15. Cohn-Gordon, K., Cremers, C., Garratt, L., Millican, J., Milner, K.: On ends-to-ends encryption: asynchronous group messaging with strong security guarantees. In: Lie, D., Mannan, M., Backes, M., Wang, X. (eds.) ACM CCS 2018, pp. 1802–1819. ACM Press, October 2018

16. Cremers, C., Hale, B., Kohbrok, K.: The complexities of healing in secure group messaging: Why cross-group effects matter. In: Bailey, M., Greenstadt, R. (eds.) USENIX Security 2021, pp. 1847–1864. USENIX Association, August 2021

17. Devigne, J., Duguey, C., Fouque, P.A.: MLS group messaging: how zero-knowledge can secure updates. In: Bertino, E., Shulman, H., Waidner, M. (eds.) ESORICS 2021, Part II. LNCS, vol. 12973, pp. 587–607. Springer, Heidelberg (2021). https://doi.org/10.1007/978-3-030-88428-4_29

18. Dolev, D., Yao, A.: On the security of public key protocols. IEEE Trans. Inf. Theory **29**(2), 198–208 (1983)

19. Hashimoto, K., Katsumata, S., Postlethwaite, E., Prest, T., Westerbaan, B.: A concrete treatment of efficient continuous group key agreement via multi-recipient PKEs. In: Vigna, G., Shi, E. (eds.) ACM CCS 2021, pp. 1441–1462. ACM Press, November 2021

20. Hashimoto, K., Katsumata, S., Prest, T.: How to hide MetaData in MLS-like secure group messaging: simple, modular, and post-quantum. In: Yin, H., Stavrou, A., Cremers, C., Shi, E. (eds.) ACM CCS 2022, pp. 1399–1412. ACM Press, November 2022

21. Jost, D., Maurer, U., Mularczyk, M.: A unified and composable take on ratcheting. In: Hofheinz, D., Rosen, A. (eds.) TCC 2019, Part II. LNCS, vol. 11892, pp. 180–210. Springer, Heidelberg (2019). https://doi.org/10.1007/978-3-030-36033-7_7

22. Klein, K., et al.: Keep the dirt: tainted TreeKEM, adaptively and actively secure continuous group key agreement. In: 2021 IEEE Symposium on Security and Privacy, pp. 268–284. IEEE Computer Society Press, May 2021

23. Weidner, M.A.: Group messaging for secure asynchronous collaboration. Master's thesis, University of Cambridge, June 2019

24. Micciancio, D., Panjwani, S.: Optimal communication complexity of generic multicast key distribution. In: Cachin, C., Camenisch, J. (eds.) EUROCRYPT 2004. LNCS, vol. 3027, pp. 153–170. Springer, Heidelberg (2004). https://doi.org/10.1007/978-3-540-24676-3_10

25. Wallner, D., Harder, E., Agee, R.: Key management for multicast: issues and architectures. Request for Comments: 2627, Internet Engineering Task Force (1999)

26. Weidner, M., Kleppmann, M., Hugenroth, D., Beresford, A.R.: Key agreement for decentralized secure group messaging with strong security guarantees. In: Vigna, G., Shi, E. (eds.) ACM CCS 2021, pp. 2024–2045. ACM Press, November 2021

Generic-Group Lower Bounds via Reductions Between Geometric-Search Problems: With and Without Preprocessing

Benedikt Auerbach[✉][iD], Charlotte Hoffmann[iD],
and Guillermo Pascual-Perez[iD]

ISTA, Klosterneuburg, Austria
{bauerbac,choffman,gpascual}@ista.ac.at

Abstract. The generic-group model (GGM) aims to capture algorithms working over groups of prime order that only rely on the group operation, but do not exploit any additional structure given by the concrete implementation of the group. In it, it is possible to prove information-theoretic lower bounds on the hardness of problems like the discrete logarithm (DL) or computational Diffie-Hellman (CDH). Thus, since its introduction, it has served as a valuable tool to assess the concrete security provided by cryptographic schemes based on such problems. A work on the related algebraic-group model (AGM) introduced a method, used by many subsequent works, to adapt GGM lower bounds for one problem to another, by means of conceptually simple reductions.

In this work, we propose an alternative approach to extend GGM bounds from one problem to another. Following an idea by Yun [EC15], we show that, in the GGM, the security of a large class of problems can be reduced to that of geometric search-problems. By reducing the security of the resulting geometric-search problems to variants of the search-by-hypersurface problem, for which information theoretic lower bounds exist, we give alternative proofs of several results that used the AGM approach.

The main advantage of our approach is that our reduction from geometric search-problems works, as well, for the GGM with preprocessing (more precisely the bit-fixing GGM introduced by Coretti, Dodis and Guo [Crypto18]). As a consequence, this opens up the possibility of transferring preprocessing GGM bounds from one problem to another, also by means of simple reductions. Concretely, we prove novel preprocessing bounds on the hardness of the d-strong discrete logarithm, the d-strong Diffie-Hellman inversion, and multi-instance CDH problems, as well as a large class of Uber assumptions. Additionally, our approach applies to Shoup's GGM without additional restrictions on the query behavior of the adversary, while the recent works of Zhang, Zhou, and Katz [AC22] and Zhandry [Crypto22] highlight that this is not the case for the AGM approach.

© International Association for Cryptologic Research 2023
G. Rothblum and H. Wee (Eds.): TCC 2023, LNCS 14371, pp. 301–330, 2023.
https://doi.org/10.1007/978-3-031-48621-0_11

1   Introduction

The Generic Group Model. The concrete security provided by a cryptographic scheme is typically assessed following the reductionist approach: one first shows that its security is implied by the hardness of a problem, and then analyzes the best running times of algorithms solving said problem. Regarding the second step, for schemes defined over a group $\mathbb{G} = \langle g \rangle$ of prime order p, the generic-group model (GGM) has proven itself a valuable tool. It is an idealized model that, on the one hand, is assumed to be meaningful for elliptic-curve groups, which are heavily relied on in practice. On the other hand, it allows to derive information-theoretic lower bounds on the number of group operations required to solve problems, like the discrete logarithm and Diffie-Hellman problems (as well as many of their variants).

The model aims to capture algorithms that are generic in the sense of being applicable to any group $\mathbb{G}$ of prime order p. Algorithms of this type only make use of the group operation, but do not exploit any additional structure given by the concrete implementation of the group. There have been several efforts of formalize this requirement. In Shoup's definition [28] of the model, the adversary gets access to group elements via abstract labels, i.e., uniformly random bitstrings, and to the group operation via an oracle. The variant by Maurer [21], on the other hand, gives access to group elements using abstract handles. All problems that are definable in Maurer's GGM are also definable in Shoup's, but the other direction does not hold. In fact, Zhandry [32] recently showed that Maurer's GGM (and the more commonly used extension thereof, which Zhandry calls type-safe model) fails to capture many textbook techniques that are captured by Shoup's GGM. An additional difference is that Maurer's model does not capture preprocessing algorithms. For more details on the differences between the models we refer to [32].

In this work we focus on Shoup's model, which we will simply refer to as the *generic-group model*, or GGM, from here on. In it, group elements g^x are represented by labels $\sigma \in \{0, 1\}^\ell$. A generic algorithm receives as input some labels and, typically, either has to compute a discrete logarithm or the label of a certain group element. To do so, it has access to a group operation oracle GrpOp. This takes as input two labels and returns the label of the product of the corresponding group elements.

As an example of how one typically argues hardness of problems in the GGM, we briefly sketch the bound on the discrete logarithm (DL) problem, as proven in [28]. Here, a secret exponent $x \leftarrow_{\$} \mathbb{Z}_p$ is sampled and the adversary receives as input labels σ_g, σ_{g^x} corresponding to g and g^x. In the proof, each label σ is associated to a linear function $F_\sigma \in \mathbb{Z}_p[X]$ as follows. The adversary's inputs σ_g, σ_{g^x} are associated to 1 and X, and whenever the group-operation oracle is queried on labels σ, σ', their product $\mathrm{GrpOp}(\sigma, \sigma')$ is associated to the function $F_{\sigma''} = F_\sigma + F_{\sigma'}$. Then, one checks whether $F_{\sigma''}$ equals any of the functions defined previously. If so, the corresponding label is used; if not, a fresh label σ'' is sampled. The idea being that, in this way, group elements which are equal can be identified, as every label σ corresponds to a group element of the form

$g^{F_\sigma(x)}$. However, this simulation of the GGM works only as long as there exists no $F_\sigma \neq F_{\sigma'}$ with $F_\sigma(x) = F_{\sigma'}(x)$, in which case the adversary would receive two different labels for the same group element. Accordingly, the proof bounds the probability of this event happening, and, in case that it does not, the probability of the adversary winning.

In [31], Yun considers a natural generalization of the discrete-logarithm problem, namely the task to solve several DL instances. In the proof of his bound, he shows that one can *perfectly* simulate the GGM group-operation oracle in a reduction from the so-called search-by-hyperplane problem (SHP). In this problem, the adversary has to find a hidden value $\vec{x} \in \mathbb{Z}_p^m$ (here m is the number of discrete logarithm instances that have to be solved) by using hyperplane queries that, on input an affine function F, return whether $F(\vec{x}) = 0$ or not; exactly what is needed in the GGM to check whether a group operation query should be answered with an already defined label. By proving an information-theoretic lower bound on the hardness of SHP, one then is able to obtain bounds on the hardness of the original problem in the GGM. This approach was later generalized by Auerbach, Giacon, and Kiltz [2] to allow the function F to be a multivariate polynomial of bounded degree. This is needed, for example, if one wants to argue about problems involving decisional Diffie-Hellman oracles, or "higher-degree" problems like the d-strong discrete-logarithm problem.

The GGM and Preprocessing. In practice most cryptosystems rely only on a few standardized groups, which makes preprocessing attacks particularly viable. The power of those attacks was demonstrated by Mihalcik [22]; Lee, Cheon, and Hong [20]; and Bernstein and Lange [6], who construct generic algorithms with preprocessing that solve the DL problem in a group of order p in time $p^{1/3}$. The authors thereby circumvented the lower bound in the GGM of $p^{1/2}$ without preprocessing established by Shoup [28].

Two recent works extend the GGM to adversaries allowed to perform unbounded preprocessing before the problem instance is sampled. Both derive lower bounds on the hardness of variants of the discrete logarithm and Diffie-Hellman problems. Corrigan-Gibbs and Kogan [15] leverage compression arguments, Coretti, Dodis and Guo [14] a pre-sampling technique by Unruh [29]. The latter work defines two variants of the GGM allowing for preprocessing: the auxiliary input (AI-GGM) and bit-fixing (BF-GGM) generic-group models. In the AI-GGM, the adversary is able to perform unbounded preprocessing on the whole labeling function to generate an advice string of bounded size before receiving the problem instance. In the preprocessing phase of the BF-GGM, on the other hand, it is able to choose labels of a bounded number of group elements, but does not have access to the remainder of the labeling function. The authors show that, under certain conditions, bounds in the BF-GGM, which is typically easier to work with, also hold in the AI-GGM. To derive a preprocessing bound on the hardness of computing multiple discrete logarithms, the latter work also uses a reduction from SHP.

Generic Group Lower Bounds via Algebraic Reductions. A related restricted class of algorithms working over $\mathbb{G}$ consists of so called *algebraic* algorithms, first considered by Boneh and Venkatesan [12], and later further formalized by Pallier and Vergnaud [25]. Fuchsbauer, Kiltz, and Loss [16] abstract such algorithms in their *algebraic-group model* (AGM) as follows. While an algorithm with input $g_0, \ldots, g_k \in \mathbb{G}$ in the AGM gets explicit access to the group $\mathbb{G}$, it has to provide an algebraic justification for every element $h \in \mathbb{G}$ that it outputs. More precisely, together with h, it has to produce $a_0, \ldots, a_k \in \mathbb{Z}_p$ such that $h = \prod_{i=0}^{k} g_i^{a_i}$.

In the paper, the authors introduce an approach that, assuming existing generic-group lower bounds for problem P_1, allows to extend the bound to a different problem P_2 by means of a conceptually simple reduction, which they describe as follows.

(i) If adversary A against P_2 is generic, we may assume w.l.o.g. that it is algebraic.

(ii) Construct a generic reduction from P_1 to P_2 that exploits the algebraic justifications that A has to provide for all group elements it computes.

(iii) Now, since the existence of generic solver for P_2 implies a generic solver for P_1, and since P_1 is hard, P_2 must be as well.

As this approach is conceptually simpler than establishing GGM bounds for P_2 from scratch, and typically leads to cleaner proofs, the idea of analyzing problems and schemes in the algebraic group model was picked up by many subsequent works [1,2,5,17–19,23].

As it is relevant to our discussion on preprocessing below, we provide some intuition on point (i). Here, the idea is that a generic reduction interacting with generic adversary A is able to compute the required algebraic justification by itself, as long as A queries the group-operation oracle only on labels it previously received as input. Indeed, in this case the justification can be computed inductively as follows. If σ_1 and σ_2 are the labels, and the reduction already recorded their algebraic justifications $\vec{a_1}$ and $\vec{a_2}$ in a previous step, then a justification of the product of the two group elements is given by $\vec{a_1} + \vec{a_2}$.

The AGM and Preprocessing. Despite the fact that both the work on the algebraic-group model [16] and the one on the GGM with preprocessing [14] have been taken up in many subsequent works, the approach of transferring preprocessing bounds from one problem to ones for another with simple reductions has stayed elusive so far. One presumed reason for this is that, in this setting, one cannot argue that the reduction is able to compute an algebraic justification from the generic adversary's queries. Indeed, the argument outlined above crucially relies on the adversary only querying labels of group elements it previously received as input. However, in the preprocessing setting, the adversary receives as input an advice string, computed during an unbounded precomputation phase. And, as the advice might contain labels not accessible to the reduction, e.g. encryptions of labels under a key hard coded into the adversary's code, this poses an obstacle to the reduction's ability to compute algebraic justifications for group elements computed by the adversary. Maurer's GGM does not allow for preprocessing (see e.g. [32]).

The AGM and Shoup's GGM. A recent work by Zhang, Zhou, and Katz [33] showed that the AGM approach of transferring lower bounds in Shoups's GGM outlined above requires caution. Concretely, they construct a problem, the so called bit-encoding problem, that is at least as hard as the discrete logarithm problem in the AGM, but can be trivially solved in the GGM. This shows that point (i) in the approach outlined above does not hold in general. As discussed above, one would like to argue that the reduction is able to compute the required justification of group elements produced by the adversary A by itself, which is possible if A never queries for group operations on labels it did not previously receive as input. However, this cannot be guaranteed in general, a fact that is exploited in the bit-encoding problem of [33], which can be won by returning such a label.

Note that the bit-encoding problem is definable in Shoup's GGM but not in Maurer's GGM. In fact, Zhandry [32] formally proved that the AGM approach is valid for all problems that are definable in Maurer's GGM, so the AGM approach is valid for most "natural" problems. However, we point out that several results in prior work [1,2,16–19] argue about the generic-group model in the presence of a random oracle, as is often the case when analyzing cryptographic schemes, instead of problems purely defined over groups. Opposed to Shoup's model, random oracles have to be explicitly modeled in Maurer's model. However, it is unclear, as far as we know, whether one may assume generic algorithms to be algebraic given this additional oracle.

1.1   Our Contributions

In this work we present a new proof technique to derive lower bounds in the GGM that improves over the AGM approach in the following ways:

– It also applies to the bit-fixing generic-group model of [14]. Since bounds in the BF-GGM can be carried over to the AI-GGM, this opens up the possibility of extending preprocessing bounds from one problem to another by means of a reduction between the problems;
– It applies to Shoup's GGM in its full generality.

Generalizing the idea introduced in [31], we show that, in the GGM, the security of a large class of computational problems can be reduced to that of analogous geometric search-problems. We then propose to construct reductions between the obtained geometric search-problems. Interestingly, several reductions from prior work using the AGM approach turn out to have a geometric equivalent. Further, the geometric analogue of several discrete-logarithm type problems are special cases of the search-by-hypersurface problem [2], for which information theoretic bounds exist. As a consequence, we obtain alternative proofs of several GGM bounds from prior work that relied on AGM reductions with the additional benefit, that for all considered problems that can also be expressed in the AI-GGM we obtain the corresponding preprocessing lower bounds essentially for free.

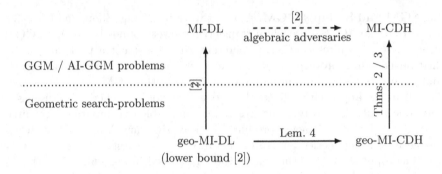

Fig. 1. Our proposed way of deriving GGM and AI-GGM lower bounds at the example of the multi-instance CDH problem, compared to the approach taken in [2]. Arrows indicate reductions from source to sink. The dashed arrow indicates that the reduction holds with respect to algebraic adversaries, and thus is restricted to (Maurer's) GGM, but does not apply to the AI-GGM.

For a visualization, through a concrete example, of our proposed approach compared to the one using the AGM, see Fig. 1. We now describe our results in more detail.

From Generic-Group Problems to Geometry. In Sect. 3 we show that, in the GGM, the security of a large class of computational problems can be reduced to the security of a corresponding geometric search-problem. We try to capture as many problems of interest as possible to prevent that this technical step has to be redone in future work. Thus, we phrase our result in terms of a family of Uber problems MI-Uber, in the style of [10,27]. In this type of problems, a vector of secret exponents $\vec{x} = (x_1, \ldots, x_t)$ is sampled from $\mathbb{Z}_p^t$, and the adversary receives as input group elements of the form $g^{F(\vec{x})}$, where $F \in \mathbb{Z}_p[X_1, \ldots, X_t]$. Then, it has to compute group elements of the form $g^{F^*(\vec{x})}$, for some $F^* \in \mathbb{Z}_p(\vec{X})$. Note that our definition of MI-Uber *extends* the definitions of Uber problems in [10,27]. It captures many Diffie-Hellman-type problems including e.g. the d-strong Diffie-Hellman-inversion [8] problem, as we allow the target function to be rational. Further, we cover m-out-of-n multi-instance problems, in which the adversary has to produce at least m out of n target group elements, and allow access to decisional oracles, such as, for example, a decisional Diffie-Hellman (DDH) oracle.

The corresponding geometric search-problem geo-MI-Uber roughly looks as follows. A secret vector $\vec{x} = (x_1, \ldots x_t)$ is sampled uniformly at random from $\mathbb{Z}_p^t$ and the adversary has access to an evaluation oracle Eval that, on input a polynomial $\hat{F}$, returns whether the point $\vec{x}$ satisfies $\hat{F}(\vec{x}) = 0$ or not.[1] As in prior work, queries of this form are sufficient to (almost) perfectly simulate the

---

[1] We refer to these problems as geometric search-problems, since queries of this type can be seen as testing whether the hypersurface in $\mathbb{Z}_p^t$ defined by $\hat{F}$ contains $\vec{x}$ or not.

group-operation oracle in the GGM. The problems considered in previous works were connected to variants of the discrete logarithm problem, and so the adversary's goal was to compute $\vec{x}$. In geo-MI-Uber, on the other hand, the adversary has to compute a polynomial $\hat{F}$ such that $(F^* - \hat{F})(\vec{x}) = 0$ for the challenge polynomial F^*. To prevent ending up with a trivial problem, e.g., by having the adversary simply output F^*, we have to restrict the space of admissible $\hat{F}$. Our main observation regarding this is that all solutions our reduction will obtain from a generic adversary interacting with MI-Uber will be an affine combinations of the input polynomials $\vec{F}$. Restricting the solutions in geo-MI-Uber to this form turns out to be sufficient to not end up with trivial problems. Essentially, we show the following.

For every adversary A against MI-Uber making at most q queries, there exists an adversary B making at most $\mathcal{O}(q^2)$ queries such that

$$\mathrm{Adv}^{\mathrm{MI\text{-}Uber}}(\mathsf{B}) \geq \mathrm{Adv}^{\mathrm{geo\text{-}MI\text{-}Uber}}(\mathsf{A}) - \frac{\mathcal{O}(d_{\max}q^2)}{p} \ ,$$

where $d_{\max}$ is the highest degree of the polynomials $\vec{F}$.

The loss in our reduction stems from carefully accounting for the possibility of the adversary querying its group-operation oracle on labels it did not previously receive. We point out that our formal result allows for more flexibility regarding this error term, and shows that it can reduced exponentially, albeit at the cost of increasing the reductions query count (see Theorem 2). When reducing from a geometric search-problem, queries of this type turn out to not be an issue, in contrast to a generic reduction interacting with a generic algorithm. The main difference is that, here, the reduction simulates the labeling function. Thus, undefined labels simply correspond to uniformly random, unused group elements, that can be sampled by the reduction itself. However, additional Eval queries are required to ensure consistency with the previous simulation and, in unlikely events, the reduction might get unlucky and not find an appropriate group element. We point out that, so far, queries of this type were either assumed to not occur [2,31] or not accounted for in the advantage [14].

We extend our result in two ways. First, we show that an analogous result holds in the bit-fixing generic-group model (BF-GGM) of [14]. As the paper uses a reduction from SHP to argue about the hardness of solving multiple discrete logarithms in the preprocessing setting, it is not surprising that our reduction from geo-MI-Uber to MI-Uber carries over to the BF-GGM. However, it requires additional queries to account for the labels chosen by the adversary.

Finally, we show an analogous result for the generic-group model for bilinear groups. We cover groups of types 1, 2, and 3. The main additional challenge in this setting is to carefully restrict the range of admissible queries to the evaluation oracle according to the bilinear group's type.

As we work in Shoup's model, our approach is compatible with nonprogrammable random oracles, which in this setting either take as input or have as output labels in $\{0, 1\}^{\ell}$. As an example of a reduction to a geometric search-problem in the programmable ROM, we revisit the treatment of BLS signatures from [16], establishing the same GGM bound of q^2/p.

Reductions Between Geometric Search-Problems and Application to Concrete Problems. In Sect. 4 we derive generic group lower bounds on the hardness of several problems in the GGM, the AI-GGM, and the bilinear GGM. To do so, we construct simple reductions between the geometric analogue geo-P of the problem P and variants of the search-by-hypersurface (SHS) problem of [2]. In the easiest case, both problems are defined with respect to the same oracle Eval, and the reduction can simply forward all queries and find the solution to SHS among the roots of polynomials related to the one output by the geo-P solver as a solution. In other cases, where SHS is defined with respect to secrets $(z_1, \ldots, z_s)$, and P expects input $(x_1, \ldots, x_t)$ with $s \leq t$, our reductions will implicitly set $x_i = a_0 + \sum_{i=0}^{s} a_i z_i$ with known $a_i \in \mathbb{Z}_p$. This enables them to answer $\mathrm{Eval}_{\text{geo-P}}(F)$ queries by the adversary, for $F \in \mathbb{Z}_p[X_1, \ldots, X_t]$, with the response to $\mathrm{Eval}_{\text{SHS}}(F(X_1'(\vec{Z}), \ldots, X_t'(\vec{Z})))$, where $X_i' = a_0 + \sum_{i=0}^{s} a_i Z_i$. Again, the reduction will solve its SHS challenge by returning a root of a polynomial related to the one output as a solution by the geo-P solver.

We point out that our reductions are very close in concept to typical reductions in the AGM. In those, the reduction also translates an algebraic justification into a polynomial, and solves its DL challenge by finding its roots. Similarly, the processing of Eval challenges corresponds to an AGM reduction re-randomizing and expanding its challenge. An example of this would be the generation of a CDH challenge $(X = Z^{a_x} g^{b_x}, Y = Z^{a_y} g^{b_y})$ from a discrete-logarithm challenge $Z \in \mathbb{G}$ using known exponents $a_x, a_y, b_x, b_y \in \mathbb{Z}_p$.

As a consequence, some of our reductions can be seen as easy, direct translations of reductions from prior work to the geometric setting. We see this as an attractive feature of our approach. Concretely, we are able to formally justify the bounds using the AGM + RO approach for the multi-instance gap-CDH problem [2] (targeted at Hashed-ElGamal key-encapsulation) and BLS signatures [16]. Further, we derive new preprocessing bounds for the d-strong discrete logarithm, d-strong Diffie-Hellman inversion, and multi-instance CDH problems, as well as a large class of Uber assumptions. Regarding the latter, a recent work by Bauer, Farshim, Harasser, and O'Neill [4] proves a lower bound in the AI-GGM for a decisional Uber problem. In turn their bound holds also for the easier, corresponding computational Uber problem. However, the bound obtained with our approach substantially improves on it. For an overview on our bounds see Table 1.

Table 1. Our GGM and AI-GGM bounds on the advantage of adversaries in groups of size p. Integer q denotes the number of queries, s the size of the advice string, the expressions are to be understood as $\tilde{\mathcal{O}}$. For problem (m,n)MI-CDH, n denotes the number of challenges, m the number of required solutions, and the bounds hold for arbitrary r (see Remark 1 for a comparison to prior work). For problems Uber and Uber$_\phi$ we denote by d the largest degree of the input polynomials. For BLS signatures, we denote by q_{RO} the number of random oracle queries made by the adversary. Bounds without references are new and for the other ones we give alternative proofs. References marked with * proved the respective bounds using AGM + RO.

Model	Problem	Bound	See
GGM			
	(m,n)MI-gap-DL, (m,n)MI-gap-CDH	$\left(\frac{rq^2}{mp}\right)^m + q\left(\frac{q}{p}\right)^r$	[2]*, Corollary 9
AI-GGM			
	d-strong-DL, d-strong-DHI	$\frac{d(sq^2+q^2)}{p}$	Corollary 5
	(m,n)MI-DL, (m,n)MI-CDH	$\left(\frac{q^2s+rq^2}{mp}\right)^m + q\left(\frac{q}{p}\right)^r$	Corollary 10
	Uber	$\frac{dq^2}{p} + \sqrt{\frac{sq^2}{p}}$	[4]
	Uber	$\frac{d(sq^2+q^2)}{p}$	Corollary 8
Bil GGM			
	Uber$_\phi$	$\frac{dq^2}{p}$	[10,27], Corollary 12
	BLS signatures	$\frac{q^2+q_{RO}^2}{p}$	[16]*, Corollary 14

Open Questions and Future Work. Our results are limited to computational problems. So, a natural question is whether decisional problems like DDH also have a geometric equivalent; and, if so, whether reductions to SHS variants are possible, e.g., following an analogous approach to the one taken by Rotem and Segev [26], who extend the definition of the AGM to capture decisional problems. A second interesting direction would be to extend the equivalence results of BF-GGM and AI-GGM from [14] to allow for decisional oracles, as this would open up the possibility of proving preprocessing bounds in the bilinear GGM via simple reductions.

Further Related Work. The gap-CDH problem was first introduced by Okamoto and Pointcheval [24]. Ying and Kunihiro [30] prove GGM lower bounds on the hardness of (m,n)MI-DL. Bauer, Fuchsbauer, and Plouviez [17] on the hardness of the one-more-discrete logarithm problem. The latter uses techniques reminiscent of [31]. Blocki and Lee [7] prove preprocessing GGM bounds on the hardness of $(1,n)$MI-DL.

2 Preliminaries

2.1 Notation

We use the following conventions. We denote the set of natural numbers up to n by $[n] := \{1,\dots,n\}$ and the set including 0 by $[n]_0 := \{0,\dots,n\}$. Typically we use lower case letters to refer to elements of $\mathbb{Z}$ or $\mathbb{R}$, and upper case letters for indeterminants or functions. For prime p and vector of indeterminants $\vec{X}$ we often work over the multivariate ring of polynomials $\mathbb{Z}_p[\vec{X}]$, which we will sometimes see as a vector space over $\mathbb{Z}_p$. For a set of polynomials $\mathcal{F} = \{F_1, \ldots, F_k\}$, we denote by $\text{Span}(\mathcal{F}) := \{F \in \mathbb{Z}_p[\vec{X}] \mid \exists a_i \in \mathbb{Z}_p : F = \sum_{i=1}^{k} a_i F_i\}$ its linear span. The ring of rational functions is denoted by $\mathbb{Z}_p(\vec{X}) := \{F_1/F_2 \mid F_1, F_2 \in \mathbb{Z}_p[\vec{X}], F_2 \neq 0\}$.

Algorithms A are typically depicted using sans-serif font. Throughout this work we assume that $p \in \mathbb{N}$ is a fixed prime, known to all adversaries and reductions. We denote the truth value of a statement E by $[E]$.

2.2 Generic-Group Model

We recall Shoup's generic group model (GGM). We consider 4 variants of it: the original one as introduced in [28], its extension to bilinear groups [9], and the auxiliar-input (i.e., preprocessing) and bit-fixing variants introduced in [14].

Generic-Group Model. We consider groups $\mathbb{G} = \langle g \rangle$ of prime order p generated by g. While we use this notation for ease of exposition when giving intuitive descriptions of problems over $\mathbb{G}$, if we explicitly work in the generic group model, we identify $(\mathbb{G}, \cdot)$ with $(\mathbb{Z}_p, +)$ via the isomorphism $x \mapsto g^x$. In the GGM, adversaries get access to group elements via abstract labels, and to the group operation via an oracle. More precisely, let $\ell \geq \lceil \log(p) \rceil$ and let $\mathcal{L} : \mathbb{Z}_p \hookrightarrow \{0,1\}^\ell$ be an injection sampled uniformly at random from the set of all injections into $\{0,1\}^\ell$. We denote the range of $\mathcal{L}$ by $\mathcal{R} := \mathcal{L}(\mathbb{Z}_p) \subseteq \{0,1\}^\ell$. An adversary A in the generic group model receives as input labels $\sigma_0, \ldots, \sigma_t$, with $\sigma_i = \mathcal{L}(h_i)$ for some group elements $h_i \in \mathbb{Z}_p$. Typically, it has to compute either the label of some group element or some discrete logarithm. It has access to the group operation via the oracle $\text{GrpOp}(\sigma_1, \sigma_2)$, which first checks whether both input labels σ_1 and σ_2 are in $\mathcal{R}$, returning $\perp$ if not, and then returns the label $\sigma = \mathcal{L}(\mathcal{L}^{-1}(\sigma_1) + \mathcal{L}^{-1}(\sigma_2))$ corresponding to the group operation applied to the two group elements. In some problems, A additionally will have access to decisional oracles such as, for example, a decisional Diffie-Hellman oracle. These take as input one or more labels and return 0 or 1 depending on whether a certain relation of the corresponding group elements holds. We measure the running time of A as the (worst-case) number of oracle queries made and typically denote this value by q. As this work only considers computational problems P, the advantage of adversary A in this model and any of its variants is given by $\text{Adv}^P(A) := \Pr[A \text{ solves } P]$.

Preprocessing and Bit-Fixing Generic-Group Models. We now recall the auxiliary-input (AI-GGM) and bit-fixing (BF-GGM) generic group models. Again, both models consider a group isomorphic to $(\mathbb{Z}_p, +)$. Adversaries A = (A_1, A_2) proceed in two stages, and are parameterized by both advice size s and the number of oracle queries q made by A_2. We refer to such adversaries as (s, q)-adversaries. BF-GGM is additionally parameterized by $M \leq p$, the number of values of the labeling function that can be chosen by A_1.

For problems P defined in the AI-GGM, the unbounded preprocessing phase A_1 receives as input the full description of the labeling function $\mathcal{L} : \mathbb{Z}_p \to \{0,1\}^\ell$, that is a uniformly random sampled injection, and returns a state Γ of bit-size at most s. A_2 receives as input Γ and the problem instance. It has access to the group-operation oracle $\mathrm{GrpOp}(\sigma_1, \sigma_2) = \mathcal{L}(\mathcal{L}^{-1}(\sigma_1) + \mathcal{L}^{-1}(\sigma_2))$, that it can query up to q times. As before, A's advantage is defined as $\mathrm{Adv}^{\mathrm{P}}(A) := \Pr[\text{A solves P}]$.

For problems P defined in the BF-GGM, the range $\mathcal{R}$ of the labeling function is first sampled uniformly at random from all size p subsets of $\{0,1\}^\ell$. Unbounded algorithm A_1 receives $\mathcal{R}$ as input and returns a state Γ of bit size at most s, as well as a list $(\sigma_i, a_i)_i$ of at most M elements, with $\sigma_i \in \mathcal{R}$ and $a_i \in \mathbb{Z}_p$, such that all σ_i and all a_i are distinct. Then, the labeling function $\mathcal{L}$ is chosen uniformly at random from all bijections between $\mathbb{Z}_p$ and $\mathcal{R}$ that satisfy $\mathcal{L}(a_i) = \sigma_i$ for all i, and A_2 is invoked on Γ and the problem instance. It has access to group-operation oracle $\mathrm{GrpOp}(\sigma_1, \sigma_2) = \mathcal{L}(\mathcal{L}^{-1}(\sigma_1) + \mathcal{L}^{-1}(\sigma_2))$, that it can query up to q times.

We recall the following theorem, which establishes that hardness in the BF-GGM implies hardness in the AI-GGM.

Theorem 1 ([14] Thm. 1). *Let P be a single-stage computational problem defined over generic groups, and $\gamma > 0$. Assume that for $M \geq 6(q + \log(\gamma^{-1})) \cdot q_{\mathrm{comb}}$ the advantage of every (s,q)-adversary solving P in the BF-GGM is bounded by ε', where q_{comb} is the combined query count of A and the problem environment P. Then, in the AI-GGM every (s,q)-adversary has advantage bounded by*

$$\varepsilon \leq 2\varepsilon' + \gamma ,$$

Generic Group Model for Bilinear Groups. In the setting of bilinear groups one considers groups $\mathbb{G}_1, \mathbb{G}_2, \mathbb{G}_T$, all of prime order p, equipped with a bilinear map $e : \mathbb{G}_1 \times \mathbb{G}_2 \to \mathbb{G}_T$. Accordingly, the extension of the GGM to bilinear groups is obtained by considering three different i.i.d. random injections $\mathcal{L}_j : \mathbb{Z}_p \hookrightarrow \{0,1\}^\ell$ for $j \in \{1, 2, T\}$, with images $\mathcal{R}_j$ respectively. The group-operation oracle $\mathrm{GrpOp}(j, \sigma_1, \sigma_2)$ can now be queried with respect to any of the label functions, and thus takes an extra input. The bilinear-map oracle $\mathrm{Bil}(\sigma_1, \sigma_2)$ takes as input two labels $\sigma_1 \in \mathcal{R}_1$ and $\sigma_2 \in \mathcal{R}_2$, and outputs the label $\sigma = \mathcal{L}_T(\mathcal{L}_1^{-1}(\sigma_1) \cdot \mathcal{L}_2^{-1}(\sigma_2)) \in \mathcal{R}_T$.

Different types of bilinear group used in practice differ by the (non)-existence of efficiently computable isomorphisms between $\mathbb{G}_1$ and $\mathbb{G}_2$. Thus, depending on type $\phi \in \{1, 2, 3\}$, algorithms might additionally have access to oracles $\mathrm{Iso} : \mathbb{G}_2 \to \mathbb{G}_1$ mapping $\sigma \mapsto \mathcal{L}_1(\mathcal{L}_2^{-1}(\sigma))$; and $\mathrm{Iso}^{-1} : \mathbb{G}_1 \to \mathbb{G}_2$ mapping $\sigma \mapsto \mathcal{L}_2(\mathcal{L}_1^{-1}(\sigma))$. If $\phi = 1$ algorithms have access to both Iso and Iso^{-1}, if $\phi = 2$ only to Iso, and if $\phi = 3$ to none of the two.

Problem SHS(n, d)	Oracle Eval(F)
00 $\vec{a} \leftarrow_\$ \mathbb{Z}_p^n$	03 if $\deg(F) > d$
01 $\vec{b} \leftarrow \mathsf{A}^{\mathrm{Eval}}$	04 return $\perp$
02 return $[\vec{a} = \vec{b}]$	05 return $[F(\vec{a}) = 0]$

Fig. 2. Search-by-Hypersurface problem parameterized dimension n and degree d.

2.3 Search-by-Hypersurface Problem

We recall the *Search-by-Hypersurface problem* (SHS(n, d)) [2] for dimension n and degree d, that can be seen as a generalization of Yun's *Search-by-Hyperplane problem* [31] to degrees larger than 1. In the problem, a vector $\vec{a} = (a_1, \ldots, a_n)$ sampled uniformly at random from $\mathbb{Z}_p^n$ has to be recovered by an adversary A. To do so, A receives no input, but has access to oracle Eval that, on input a hypersurface in $\mathbb{Z}_p^n$ of degree at most d, tells whether $\vec{a}$ lies on the hypersurface or not. More precisely, Eval takes as input polynomials $F \in \mathbb{Z}[X_1, \ldots, X_n]$ of degree at most d and returns 1 if $F(\vec{a}) = 0$ and 0 else. For a formal definition see Fig. 2. We now recall an information theoretic lower bound on the hardness of SHS.

Lemma 1 ([2], Lemma 6). *Let $n, d, q \in \mathbb{N}$. Then, every adversary A that makes at most q queries in game SHS(n, d) has an advantage bounded by*

$$\mathrm{Adv}^{\mathrm{SHS}(n,d)}(\mathsf{A}) \le \left(\frac{d}{p}\right)^n \cdot \sum_{i=0}^{n} \binom{q}{i} \le \frac{1}{2} \cdot \left(\frac{e\, d q}{p n}\right)^n ,$$

where e is Euler's number.

3 From Generic Group Problems to Geometric Search-Problems

In this section we show that the hardness of a large class of problems in the generic group model(s) can be reduced to the hardness of a corresponding geometric search-problem. In prior work (plain GGM [2,31], bit-fixing GGM [14]) this approach was taken to prove bounds on the hardness of specific discrete-logarithm type problems. We show that it can be generalized as follows.

We introduce the first geometric search-problems corresponding to problems that require the adversary to compute group elements instead of hidden exponents. For these problems the solution is going to be a polynomial/hypersurface (similar to the ones the adversary is allowed to query for) from a restricted range of admittable solutions. The latter is necessary to not end up with a trivial problem. We define such problems both for the plain GGM and the bit-fixing GGM and then extend our approach to the setting of bilinear groups. We phrase our results in terms of Uber-assumptions in the style of [10,27], where we in particular allow multi-instance problems and access to decisional oracles. The latter, as well as the bilinear map e in the case of bilinear groups, require us to carefully restrict the geometric-search problem's range of admittable evaluation-oracle inputs in a way that enables us to carry over AGM reductions to reductions between the corresponding geometric search-problems to in Sect. 4. This restriction is in contrast to prior work, where the only restriction was the degree of the queried polynomial.

Section 3.1 covers the plain GGM, Sect. 3.2 the bit-fixing GGM, and Sect. 3.3 the bilinear GGM.

3.1 From GGM to Geometric Search-Problems

Considered Problems. Our goal is to capture as many problems in the generic group model as possible, so we state our transformation to geometric search-problems for Uber problem

$$\text{MI-Uber}(t, (m, n), F_1, \ldots, F_k, F_1^*, \ldots, F_n^*, W_1, \ldots, W_s)$$

where $t, m, n \in \mathbb{N}$ with $m \leq n$, $F_i \in \mathbb{Z}_p[X_1, \ldots, X_t]$, $F_i^* \in \mathbb{Z}_p(X_1, \ldots, X_t)$, and $W_i \in \mathbb{Z}_p[Z_1, \ldots, Z_{s_i}]$ for some s_i. The parameters have the following role.

Parameter	Role	Example: gap-CDH
t	# secrets $x_1, \ldots, x_t$ in $\mathbb{Z}_p$	$t = 2$, secrets x, y
n	# target group elements	1
m	required solutions	1
$F_1, \ldots, F_k$	input group elements	$F_1 = X \sim g^x$, $F_2 = Y \sim g^y$
$F_1^*, \ldots, F_n^*$	target group elements	$F_1^* = XY \sim g^{xy}$
$W_1, \ldots, W_s$	decisional oracles	DDH-oracle: $W_1 = X'Y' - Z'$

A MI-Uber adversary A for vector of secrets $\vec{x} = (x_1, \ldots, x_t)$ receives as input $(g, g^{F_1(\vec{x})}, \ldots, g^{F_k(\vec{x})})$ and has to output an index set $I \subseteq [n]$ of size at least m as well as group elements h_i such that $h_i = g^{F_i^*(\vec{x})}$ for all $i \in I$. It has access to the group operation, as well as decisional oracles W_i which, on input s_i many group elements $h_j = g^{y_j}$, returns 1 if $g^{W_i(\vec{y_j})} = 1$ (or equivalently $W_i(\vec{y_j}) = 0$) and 0 if not. For a formal definition of MI-Uber in the generic-group model see Fig. 3. We point out that the binary encoding game of [33] used to separate the GGM and AGM does not fall under the umbrella of MI-Uber because the adversary of the binary encoding game does not get a description of the target group element via a polynomial.

Associated Geometric Search-Problem. We now define the geometric search problem associated to MI-Uber$(t, (m, n), \vec{F}, \vec{F^*}, \vec{W})$, called geo-MI-Uber $(t, (m, n), \vec{F}, \vec{F^*}, \vec{W})$. It is parameterized by a set of integers and variables with the same restrictions as MI-Uber, some of which take different roles, as follows. A vector $\vec{x} = (x_1, \ldots, x_t) \leftarrow_s \mathbb{Z}_p^t$ is sampled uniformly at random. The goal of adversary A is to return index set $I \subseteq [n]$ of size m, and polynomials $\hat{F}_i \in \mathbb{Z}_p[X_1, \ldots, X_t]$ such that $\hat{F}_i(\vec{x}) - F_i^*(\vec{x}) = 0$ for all $i \in I$. To do so, A receives no input, but has access to oracle Eval, which on input a polynomial $F' \in \mathbb{Z}_p[X_1, \ldots, X_t]$ returns 1 if $F'(\vec{x}) = 0$ and 0 else. Note that this corresponds to the query, whether the hypersurface in $\mathbb{Z}_p^t$ defined by F' contains $\vec{x}$ or not. We make the additional requirement that all output solutions $\hat{F}_i$ lie in the linear span $\mathrm{Span}(1, F_1, \ldots, F_k)$ of the input polynomials and impose the same requirement on inputs to Eval.[2] The restriction on solutions ensures that geo-MI-Uber is non-trivial as long as MI-Uber is; If MI-Uber cannot be trivially solved, we must have that (sufficiently many) $F_i^* \notin \mathrm{Span}(\vec{F})$ as else one could compute a valid solution with a small number of group-operation queries. Accordingly, in this case geo-MI-Uber does not admit the trivial solution of simply outputting m of the F_i^*. The restriction on the inputs to Eval, on the other hand, turns out to be useful when construction reductions between geometric search-problems. Finally, each $W_i \in \mathbb{Z}_p[Z_1, \ldots, Z_{s_i}]$ corresponds to oracle Dec_{W_i}, which on input of $F_1', \ldots, F_{s_i}' \in \mathrm{Span}(1, F_1, \ldots, F_k)$ returns 1 if $(W_i(F_1', \ldots, F_{s_i}'))(\vec{x}) = W_i(F_1'(\vec{x}), \ldots, F_{s_i}'(\vec{x})) = 0$, and 0 if not.[3] For a formal definition of the problem see Fig. 3.

In the following we give the reduction from geo-MI-Uber to MI-Uber. The key observation is that, by using the oracle Eval, the reduction can simulate the view of the MI-Uber adversary A without knowledge of the secret $\vec{x}$.

Theorem 2. *Let $t, m, n, k, s \in \mathbb{N}$ with $m \leq n$, and consider vectors $\vec{F} = (F_1, \ldots, F_k)$, $\vec{F}^* = (F_1^*, \ldots, F_n^*)$ of polynomials and rational functions with $F_i \in \mathbb{Z}_p[X_1, \ldots, X_t]$, $F_i^* \in \mathbb{Z}_p(X_1, \ldots, X_t)$ for all i, and $\vec{W} = (W_1, \ldots, W_s)$ with $W_i \in \mathbb{Z}_p[Z_1, \ldots, Z_{s_i}]$ for some $s_i \in \mathbb{N}$.*

Let $r \in \mathbb{N}$ and A a MI-Uber$(t, (m, n), \vec{F}, \vec{F}^*, \vec{W})$-solver in the GGM, which makes at most q oracle queries. Then, there exists a geo-MI-Uber $(t, (m, n), \vec{F}, \vec{F}^*, \vec{W})$ solver B that for $d_{\max} := \max_i(\deg(F_i))$ and $s_{\max} := \max(\max_i(s_i), 2)$ makes at most

$$q^2 \cdot s_{\max} r + q \cdot \big((k s_{\max} + m)(r - 1) + k + 1\big) + k\big(k + 1 + m(r - 1)\big) \approx q^2 s_{\max} r$$

---

[2] Alternatively, one could also make this requirement explicit by changing the inputs to Eval to be a vector $(a_0, \ldots, a_k) \in \mathbb{Z}_p^k$ and return whether $\vec{x}$ lies on the hypersurface defined by $a_0 + \sum_{i=1}^k a_i F_i$. The requirement for solutions $\hat{F}_i$ could be adapted accordingly.

[3] As is the case for Eval, oracle Dec corresponds to evaluating containment in a hypersurface, albeit, one of degree possibly higher than the ones in the linear span of the input polynomials. Thus, one could incorporate Dec_{W_i} into Eval by expanding the range of admissible polynomials for the latter from $\mathrm{Span}(1, F_1, \ldots, F_k)$ to also include polynomials of the form $W_i(F_1', \ldots, F_{s_i}') \in \mathbb{Z}_p[X_1, \ldots, X_t]$ for $F_j' \in \mathrm{Span}(1, F_1, \ldots, F_k)$. However, we decided to keep the oracles separated in order to have a clearer conceptual distinction between the group-operation oracle and decisional oracles.

Problem MI-Uber$(t, (m,n), \vec{F}, \vec{F^*}, \vec{W})$	Oracle GrpOp(σ, σ')
00 $\mathcal{L} \leftarrow_{\$} \mathrm{Inj}(\mathbb{Z}_p, \{0,1\}^\ell)$	08 **require** $\sigma, \sigma' \in \mathcal{L}(\mathbb{Z}_p)$
01 $\vec{x} \leftarrow_{\$} \mathbb{Z}_p^t$	09 **return** $\mathcal{L}(\mathcal{L}^{-1}(\sigma) + \mathcal{L}^{-1}(\sigma'))$
02 $\sigma_0 \leftarrow \mathcal{L}(1)$	
03 **for** $i = 1, \ldots, k$	Oracle Dec$_{W_i}(\sigma'_1, \ldots, \sigma'_{s_i})$
04 $\quad \sigma_i \leftarrow \mathcal{L}(F_i(\vec{x}))$	10 **require** $\sigma'_j \in \mathcal{L}(\mathbb{Z}_p)$ for $j \in [s_i]$
05 $(I, (\hat{\sigma}_i)_{i \in I}) \leftarrow \mathsf{A}^{\mathrm{GrpOp}, (\mathrm{Dec}_{W_i})_i}(\sigma_0, \ldots, \sigma_k)$	11 **return** $[W_i(\mathcal{L}^{-1}(\tilde{\sigma}_1), \ldots, \mathcal{L}^{-1}(\tilde{\sigma}_{s_i})) = 0]$
06 **require** $I \subseteq [n] \wedge |I| \geq m$	
07 **return** $[\forall i \in [I] : \hat{\sigma}_i = \mathcal{L}(F_i^*(\vec{x}))]$	

Problem geo-MI-Uber$(t, (m,n), \vec{F}, \vec{F^*}, \vec{W})$	Oracle Eval(F')
12 $\vec{x} \leftarrow_{\$} \mathbb{Z}_p^t$	17 **require** $F' \in \mathrm{Span}(1, \vec{F})$
13 $(I, (\hat{F}_i)_{i \in I}) \leftarrow \mathsf{A}^{\mathrm{Eval}, (\mathrm{Dec}_{W_i})_i}$	18 **return** $[F'(\vec{x}) = 0]$
14 **require** $\hat{F}_i \in \mathrm{Span}(1, \vec{F})$ for all $i \in I$	
15 **require** $I \subseteq [n] \wedge |I| \geq m$	Oracle Dec$_{W_i}(F'_1, \ldots, F'_{s_i})$
16 **return** $[\forall i \in I : (F_i^* - \hat{F}_i)(\vec{x}) = 0]$	19 **require** $F'_j \in \mathrm{Span}(1, \vec{F})$ for all $j \in [s_i]$
	20 **return** $[W_i(F'_1(\vec{x}), \ldots, F'_{s_i}(\vec{x})) = 0]$

Fig. 3. Problems MI-Uber (in the GGM) and the corresponding geometric search problem geo-MI-Uber parameterized by $t, m, n \in \mathbb{N}$, and polynomials $\vec{F} = (F_1, \ldots, F_k)$, $\vec{F^*} = (F_1^*, \ldots, F_n^*)$ with $F_i \in \mathbb{Z}_p[X_1, \ldots, X_t]$, $F_i^* \in \mathbb{Z}_p(X_1, \ldots, X_t)$ for all i, in the presence of decisional oracles defined by polynomials $\vec{W} = (W_1, \ldots, W_s)$ with $W_i \in \mathbb{Z}_p[Z_1, \ldots, Z_{s_i}]$ for some $s_i \in \mathbb{N}$. $\mathrm{Inj}(\mathbb{Z}_p, \{0,1\}^\ell)$ denotes the set of injections from $\mathbb{Z}_p$ to label space $\{0,1\}^\ell$.

queries and satisfies

$$\mathrm{Adv}^{\text{geo-MI-Uber}(t, (m,n), \vec{F}, \vec{F^*}, \vec{W})}(\mathsf{B})$$

$$\geq \mathrm{Adv}^{\text{MI-Uber}(t, (m,n), \vec{F}, \vec{F^*}, \vec{W})}(\mathsf{A}) - (q s_{\max} + m) \cdot \left(\frac{(q+k) \cdot d_{\max}}{p} \right)^r .$$

Proof. The geo-MI-Uber solver B receives as input the number of indeterminates t and the polynomials $\vec{F}$ rational functions $\vec{F^*}$ and has access to oracles Eval, $(\mathrm{Dec}_{W_i})_i$. To simulate the view of the MI-Uber solver A, B needs to construct input $(\sigma_0, \ldots, \sigma_k)$ and reply to oracle queries made by A. To do this in a consistent manner, B samples labels on the fly and maintains a table T that stores all previously recorded labels σ, each together with a corresponding polynomial $P(\vec{X}) \in \mathrm{Span}(1, \vec{F})$ in the indeterminates $X_1, \ldots, X_t$. The labels σ will correspond to a perfect simulation of MI-Uber such that we have $\mathcal{L}^{-1}(\sigma) = P(\vec{x})$ for every entry (P, σ) in T. To make sure that the simulation is consistent, B needs to check that no two polynomials P, P' such that $P(\vec{x}) = P'(\vec{x})$ get paired with different labels. This would be equivalent to a group element receiving two different labels. Hence, before sampling a new label for a polynomial P, B needs to check that there is no previously recorded polynomial P' in T such that $(P - P')(\vec{x}) = 0$ using the oracle Eval. Note that, if $P, P' \in \mathrm{Span}(1, \vec{F})$ then so is $P - P'$, and thus the oracle will not return $\perp$. In more detail, B does the following.

- It samples the range $\mathcal{R} \subseteq \{0,1\}^\ell$ uniformly at random from all subsets of $\{0,1\}^\ell$ of size p.[4]
- To create the input $(\sigma_0, \sigma_1, \ldots, \sigma_k)$ for A, B does the following: first, it samples $\sigma_0 \leftarrow_{\$} \mathcal{R}$, stores $(0, \sigma_0)$ in T, and then iteratively defines σ_i as follows. To create σ_i for $i \in [k]$, it queries Eval on $F_i - P'$ for all previously recorded polynomials P' in T. If the answer is 1 for some P', it sets σ_i to the corresponding label of P'. Otherwise, it chooses a random unused value from $\mathcal{R}$ and stores (F_i, σ_i). Note that all polynomials stored so far in T trivially lie in $\mathrm{Span}(1, F_1, \ldots, F_k)$, and entries (P, σ) defined so far are consistent with the property $\mathcal{L}^{-1}(\sigma) = P(\vec{x})$.
- Then B runs $\mathsf{A}(\sigma_0, \sigma_1, \ldots, \sigma_k)$. When A makes a query (σ, σ') to GrpOp, B does the following:
  - First, it checks if σ and σ' have been recorded in T. If σ has not been recorded, checks if $\sigma \in \mathcal{R}$ and answers $\bot$ if not. Otherwise, B makes r attempts at assigning σ a constant unused element in $\mathbb{Z}_p$ that is consistent with the simulation so far. In particular, B will repeat the following steps up to r times. It starts by sampling a random unused element $a \leftarrow_{\$} \mathbb{Z}_p$. If this is the $\tilde{r}$th attempt, with $\tilde{r} < r$, it queries Eval on $a - P$ for all previously recorded (non-constant) polynomials P in T. If Eval outputs 1 for some P, adversary B tries again with a new random unrecorded $a \leftarrow_{\$} \mathbb{Z}_p$. If Eval does not output 1 for any of the queries or if it is the rth time of sampling a, it stores the pair (a, σ) in T, where a is to be interpreted as a constant polynomial. It then does the same if σ' has not been recorded.
  - Let P, P' be the polynomials corresponding to labels σ, σ'. For all previously recorded polynomials P'' in T, B queries $P + P' - P''$ to oracle Eval. If Eval outputs 1 for any of the P'', it looks up the corresponding label σ'' in T and sends σ'' to A. Otherwise, B samples a random σ'' from the unused values in $\mathcal{R}$ and sends it to A. Then it stores $(P + P', \sigma'')$ in T.
  - Note that, again, all newly stored polynomials are elements of $\mathrm{Span}(1, \vec{F})$ and that, if for all $(\hat{P}, \hat{\sigma}) \in T$ we had that $\mathcal{L}^{-1}(\hat{\sigma}) = \hat{P}(\vec{x})$, then the same holds for all elements added to the table during either of these steps.
- When A makes a query $(\sigma'_1, \ldots, \sigma'_{s_i})$ to one of the decisional oracles Dec_{W_i}, B does the following:
  - It first checks if for all $j \in [s_i]$, σ'_j has been recorded in T. If not, it proceeds as in the analogous case of group operation queries described above, assigning a random constant to it.
  - Then, it queries Dec_{W_i} on $(F'_1, \ldots, F'_{s_i})$, where $F'_1, \ldots, F'_r$ are the polynomials corresponding to $\sigma'_1 \ldots, \sigma'_{s_i}$ respectively. Sends the answer of Dec_{W_i} to A.

---

[4] We measure the running time of generic algorithms by their query count. So, both sampling from $\mathcal{R}$ and checking whether $\sigma \in \mathcal{R}$ need not be efficiently computable. We use this approach for ease of exposition, but point out that these operations can easily be adapted to be done efficiently by sampling $\mathcal{R}$ on the fly.

– Note that for all j it holds that $\mathcal{L}^{-1}(\sigma'_j) = F'_j(\vec{x})$, and so the query is answered correctly, since we have that

$$W_i(\mathcal{L}^{-1}(\sigma'_1), \ldots, \mathcal{L}^{-1}(\sigma'_{s_i})) = W_i(F'_1(\vec{x}), \ldots, F'_{s_i}\vec{x}) \ .$$

– When A outputs $(I, (\hat{\sigma}_i)_{i \in I})$, B checks for every $i \in I$ whether $\hat{\sigma}_i$ has previously been recorded in T with corresponding polynomial $\hat{F}_i$. If not, it is treated as in the analogous case of group operation queries described above. Then B outputs $(I, (\hat{F}_i)_{i \in I})$ as its solution. Note that the check of line 14 will succeed, as $\hat{F}_i \in \mathrm{Span}(1, \vec{F})$ for all i.

We now count the number of queries made by B. First, note that to set up A's input, B adds 1 constant and k arbitrary entries to T and makes at most $k(k+1)$ queries to Eval. During the execution of A, every query to GrpOp or Dec_{W_i} adds up to $s_{\max}$ constant and one arbitrary polynomial to T. Thus, at the q'th query, T contains at most $k + 1 + (s_{\max} + 1)q'$ entries, of which at most $k + q'$ are not constant. As the check against previously unrecorded labels needs to be done only with respect to non-constant polynomials, the q'th query requires at most $(r-1)s_{\max}(k+q') + (k + 1 + (s_{\max}+1)q')$ queries to Eval. Finally, to handle A's output, B makes up to $(r-1)m$ additional checks against the at most $(k+q)$ non-constant entries in T. Summing up we can bound the number of queries made by B by $q^2 \cdot s_{\max}r + q \cdot ((ks_{\max} + m)(r - 1) + k + 1) + k(k + 1 + m(r - 1))$. To show that

$$\mathrm{Adv}^{\text{geo-MI-Uber}(t,(m,n),\vec{F},\vec{F}^*,\vec{W})}(\mathsf{B})$$

$$\geq \mathrm{Adv}^{\text{MI-Uber}(t,(m,n),\vec{F},\vec{F}^*,\vec{W})}(\mathsf{A}) - (qs_{\max} + m) \cdot \left(\frac{(q+k) \cdot d_{\max}}{p}\right)^r,$$

we define the event $\mathtt{bad} = \{\exists (a, \sigma_a), (P, \sigma_P) \in T \mid a \text{ constant}, P \text{ not constant} : P(\vec{x}) - a = 0\}$, which corresponds to B assigning a label σ it did not previously receive to a constant in a way not consistent with the simulation. Observe that in the case that $\mathtt{bad}$ does not occur, we have $\mathcal{L}^{-1}(\sigma) = P(\vec{x})$ for all (P, σ) stored in T, and the view of A is a perfect simulation of the MI-Uber game with hidden value $\vec{x}$. Thus, in this case we have that $(\hat{F}_i - F_i^*)(\vec{x}) = 0 \Leftrightarrow \mathcal{L}^{-1}(\hat{\sigma}_i) = \hat{F}_i(\vec{x}) = F_i^*(\vec{x})$ for all $i \in I$, and B wins exactly if A wins.

Finally, when assigning a constant to a previously unseen σ the probability that B does so inconsistently is at most $((q+k)d_{\max}/p)^r$. Indeed, by the Schwartz-Zippel Lemma, the probability the sampled constant is in the set of roots of any polynomial P is at most $d_{\max}/p$ and, for each of the r attempts at finding a constant, at most $(q + k)$ polynomials have to be checked. As the reduction has to sample at most $(qs_{\max} + m)$ constants, the bound follows. □

Before turning to the setting of BF-GGM we make a couple observations.

Remark 1. (i) As opposed to prior work, our reduction does not fully preserve the advantage of A, but introduces an error term of order $\sim q\left(\frac{qd_{\max}}{p}\right)^r$. The term, as well as some of the additional queries that B has to make, stems from handling group-operation queries on labels, that the adversary did not previously receive. The reduction B handles such queries by assigning them a random, unused discrete logarithm. The number r corresponds to the number of attempts made for each such query to find a constant that is consistent with the simulation so far.

Looking ahead, the loss in advantage will not cause issues when deriving lower bounds, as the bounds we obtain on the advantage of B will, for most problems, be of order $q^2 d_{\max}/p$. Hence, in this case we can simply choose $r = 1$. The only exception are multi-instance (gap) CDH problems, for which the advantage of B decays exponentially in the number of instances that have to be solved. For these we end up with worse bounds than the ones from literature (However, if one only considers the number of queries required to achieve *constant* success probability the bound stays the same). We point out that in the reductions of [2,31] it is assumed that A never queries on labels it did not previously receive. In light of the work by Zhang, Zhou, and Katz [33] this seems hard to formally justify unless the range of labels is very sparse in $\{0,1\}^\ell$, as is assumed in [31]. In [14], such queries are handled in the same way that we do. However, neither the probability of failing to sample an adequate discrete logarithm, nor the additional Eval queries to verify its consistency with the simulation, were factored in the advantage and query count, respectively, of their reduction.

(ii) One can easily adapt Theorem 2 to discrete-logarithm variants of MI-Uber, in which A receives the same input and has access to the same oracles, but instead of computing target group elements has to compute at least m of the $x_1, \ldots, x_t$. The corresponding geometric search-problem would have access to the same oracles as in geo-MI-Uber, and also have to compute at least m of the x_i.

(iii) Theorem 2 also holds if in both problems the adversaries have oracle access to a random oracle, i.e., a uniformly random function $\mathsf{RO}\colon \mathcal{R} \to \{0,1\}^{\ell'}$ for some ℓ'. In this case, the reduction can simply forward all RO queries. Thus, the computed GGM bounds also apply to cryptographic schemes making use of such oracles, as for example in [2,7,17,18]. In the case of a random oracle into the group, i.e., $\mathsf{RO}; \{0,1\}^* \to \{0,1\}^\ell$, the reduction can simulate the random oracle, and associate previously unseen labels to a constant polynomial as discussed in point (i). For an example of this type of reduction, see our result for BLS signatures in Sect. 4.2 and [1,19].

3.2 Extension to the Bit-Fixing Generic-Group Model

In this section we show that the translation of problems to geometric search-problems also works in the BF-GGM. In combination with Theorem 1 and a reduction between the corresponding geometric problems, like the ones presented in Sect. 4, this enables us to carry over preprocessing lower-bounds from one problem to another.

We again consider Uber problems MI-Uber and geo-MI-Uber of Fig. 3. However, in this section we will restrict to problems without decision oracles, i.e., we assume that $\vec{W} = \epsilon$ is the empty vector. We stress that the reason for this is that the preprocessing GGM and bit-fixing GGM, as well as the translation between the two in Theorem 1, are defined without decisional oracles. If one was able to extend both models to allow for such oracles (or to the setting of bilinear groups) and establish their equivalence, we do not see any obstacles for our translation to geometric search-problems to carry over as well.

We show that the security of MI-Uber in the bit-fixing GGM reduces to the security of geo-MI-Uber (which does not have a preprocessing phase). The proof follows the one of Theorem 2, the main difference being that, since in the preprocessing phase A_1 fixes the labels of a number of group elements, the reduction is required to add a corresponding amount of constant polynomials to its table T. This leads to a larger amount of queries to oracle Eval.

Recall that the BF-GGM is parameterized by $M \in \mathbb{N}$, the number of labels chosen by A_1 in the preprocessing phase. A_2 receives as input both the advice $\Gamma \leftarrow A_1(\mathcal{R})$ and the problem instance as defined in Fig. 3. We obtain the following result. Its proof is in the full version of this paper [3].

Theorem 3. *Let* $t, m, n, k \in \mathbb{N}$ *with* $m \leq n$, *and consider vectors* $\vec{F} = (F_1, \ldots, F_k)$, $\vec{F}^* = (F_1^*, \ldots, F_n^*)$ *of polynomials and rational functions with* $F_i \in \mathbb{Z}_p[X_1, \ldots, X_t]$, $F_i^* \in \mathbb{Z}_p(X_1, \ldots, X_t)$ *for all* i. *Further, let* $d_{\max} := \max_i(\deg(F_i))$. *Let* $r \in \mathbb{N}$ *and let* $A = (A_1, A_2)$ *be a* MI-Uber$(t, (m, n), \vec{F}, \vec{F}^*)$ *solver in the BF-GGM which makes at most* q *queries. Using* A, *we can construct a* geo-MI-Uber *solver* B *that makes at most*

$$q\big(M + (2r+1)q\big) + kM + q\big(rk + 1 + m(r-1)\big) + k\big(k + 1 + m(r-1)\big) \approx q(M + (2r+1)q)$$

queries and satisfies

$$\mathrm{Adv}^{\mathrm{geo\text{-}MI\text{-}Uber}(t,(m,n),\vec{F},\vec{F}^*)}(B)$$
$$\geq \mathrm{Adv}^{\mathrm{MI\text{-}Uber}(t,(m,n),\vec{F},\vec{F}^*)}(A) - (2q + m)\left(\frac{(q+k) \cdot d_{\max}}{p}\right)^r .$$

3.3   Extension to the GGM for Bilinear Groups

In this section we generalize the result of Sect. 3.1 to the setting of bilinear groups. In Fig. 4 we define the

$$\mathrm{MI\text{-}Uber}_\phi(t, (m, n_1, n_2, n_T), \vec{F}_1, \vec{F}_2, \vec{F}_T, \vec{F}_1^*, \vec{F}_2^* \vec{F}_T^*, W_1, \ldots, W_s)$$

problem for bilinear groups of type ϕ and the corresponding geometric problem

$$\mathrm{geo\text{-}MI\text{-}Uber}_\phi(t, (m, n_1, n_2, n_T), \vec{F}_1, \vec{F}_2, \vec{F}_T, \vec{F}_1^*, \vec{F}_2^* \vec{F}_T^*, W_1, \ldots, W_s) .$$

Again, $t \in \mathbb{N}$ is the number of secrets in $\mathbb{Z}_p$ and $m \in \mathbb{N}$ is the number of solutions the adversary A is required to output. The input and target polynomials are now divided into three vectors $\vec{F}_1, \vec{F}_2, \vec{F}_T$ and $\vec{F}_1^*, \vec{F}_2^*, \vec{F}_T^*$ respectively, that correspond to the three groups $\mathbb{G}_1, \mathbb{G}_2, \mathbb{G}_T$, where we have $\dim(\vec{F}_J^*) = n_J$ for $J \in \{1, 2, T\}$. The polynomials W_i define decisional oracles which, on input s_i many group elements defined by exponents $y_{1,1}, \ldots y_{1,r_1}, y_{2,1}, \ldots y_{2,r_2}, y_{T,1}, \ldots y_{T,r_T}$ for generators g_1, g_2, g_T, return 1 if $W_i(y_{1,1}, \ldots y_{1,r_1}, y_{2,1}, \ldots y_{2,r_2}, y_{T,1}, \ldots y_{T,r_T}) = 0$ and 0 if not. In MI-Uber$_\phi$, the adversary A receives as input

$$\left(g_1, g_2, g_T, g_1^{\vec{F}_{1,1}(\vec{x})}, \ldots, g_1^{F_{1,k_1}(\vec{x})}, g_2^{F_{2,1}(\vec{x})}, \ldots, g_2^{F_{2,k_2}(\vec{x})}, g_T^{F_{T,1}(\vec{x})}, \ldots, g_T^{F_{T,k_T}(\vec{x})}\right)$$

and has to output three index sets $I_1 \subseteq [n_1]$, $I_2 \subseteq [n_2]$, $I_T \subseteq [n_T]$ such that $|I_1| + |I_2| + |I_T| \geq m$, as well as group elements $h_{J,i} = g_J^{F_{J,i}^*(\vec{x})}$ for all $J \in \{1, 2, T\}$ and all $i \in I_J$.

In geo-MI-Uber$_\phi$, a vector $\vec{x} = (x_1, \ldots, x_t) \leftarrow \mathbb{Z}_p^t$ is sampled uniformly at random and A has to output three sets $I_1 \subseteq [n_1]$, $I_2 \subseteq [n_2]$, $I_T \subseteq [n_T]$ such that $|I_1| + |I_2| + |I_T| \geq m$, as well as polynomials $P_{J,i}$ such that $P_{J,i}(\vec{x}) = F_{J,i}^*(\vec{x})$ for all $J \in \{1, 2, T\}$ and all $i \in I_J$. The adversary A does not receive any input but has access to the oracle Eval, that takes queries of the form (J, P) and returns 1 if $P(\vec{x}) = 0$ and 0 else. Here, $P \in \mathbb{Z}_p[X_1, \ldots, X_t]$ is a polynomial that satisfies certain restrictions depending on the type ϕ of the bilinear group, which we explain in more detail below. Before we give the reduction from geo-MI-Uber$_\phi$ to MI-Uber$_\phi$ in Theorem 4, we define some useful notation.

Notation. Let $\vec{R}, \vec{S}, \vec{F}$ be vectors of polynomials. In this section we will use the following notation:

$$\text{Span}(\vec{R}, \vec{S}) := \text{Span}(R_1, \ldots, R_{\dim(\vec{R})}, S_1, \ldots, S_{\dim(\vec{S})})$$

denotes the linear span of the polynomials in the entries of the vectors $\vec{R}$ and $\vec{S}$. We further define three different types of spans:

$$\text{Span}_1(\vec{R}, \vec{S}, \vec{F}, \phi) := \begin{cases} \text{Span}(\vec{R}, \vec{S}) & \text{if } \phi \in \{1, 2\}, \\ \text{Span}(\vec{R}) & \text{if } \phi = 3; \end{cases}$$

$$\text{Span}_2(\vec{R}, \vec{S}, \vec{F}, \phi) := \begin{cases} \text{Span}(\vec{R}, \vec{S}) & \text{if } \phi = 1, \\ \text{Span}(\vec{S}) & \text{if } \phi \in \{2, 3\}; \end{cases}$$

$$\text{Span}_T(\vec{R}, \vec{S}, \vec{F}, \phi) := \text{Span}(\vec{F}, \text{Span}_1(\vec{R}, \vec{S}, \vec{F}, \phi) \cdot \text{Span}_2(\vec{R}, \vec{S}, \vec{F}, \phi)).$$

If $\vec{R}$ defines elements in $\mathbb{G}_1$, $\vec{S}$ defines elements in $\mathbb{G}_2$ and $\vec{F}$ defines elements in $\mathbb{G}_T$, we have that the elements in $\text{Span}_J(\vec{R}, \vec{S}, \vec{F}, \phi)$ correspond to exactly those elements in group $\mathbb{G}_J$ that can be obtained from the input elements by performing group operations, evaluating the bilinear map and applying the isomorphism between groups $\mathbb{G}_1$ and $\mathbb{G}_2$.

We obtain the following result. Its proof is in the full version of this paper [3].

Theorem 4. *Let* $t, m, n_1, n_2, n_T, k_1, k_2, k_T \in \mathbb{N}$ *with* $m \leq n_1 + n_2 + n_T$, *and consider vectors* $\vec{F}_1 = (F_{1,1}, \ldots, F_{1,k_1})$, $\vec{F}_2 = (F_{2,1}, \ldots, F_{2,k_2})$, $\vec{F}_T = (F_{T,1}, \ldots, F_{T,k_T})$, $\vec{F}_1^* = (F_{1,1}^*, \ldots, F_{1,n_1}^*)$, $\vec{F}_2^* = (F_{2,1}^*, \ldots, F_{2,n_2}^*)$, $\vec{F}_T^* = (F_{T,1}^*, \ldots, F_{T,n_T}^*)$*

```
Problem MI-Uber_φ(t, (m, n_1, n_2, n_T), F⃗_1, F⃗_2, F⃗_T, F⃗*_1, F⃗*_2, F⃗*_T, W_1, ..., W_s)
00  x⃗ ←_$ Z_p^t
01  σ_{1,0} ← L_1(1)
02  σ_{2,0} ← L_2(1)
03  σ_{T,0} ← L_T(1)
04  for J ∈ {1, 2, T}
05    for i = 1, ..., k_J
06      σ_{J,i} ← L_J(F_{J,i}(x⃗))
07  (I_1, I_2, I_T, (σ̂_{1,i})_{i∈I_1}, (σ̂_{2,i})_{i∈I_2}, (σ̂_{T,i})_{i∈I_T}) ← A^{Iso,Iso^{-1},GrpOp,Bil,(Dec_{W_i})_{i∈[s]}}((σ_{1,i})_{i∈[k_1]_0}, (σ_{2,i})_{i∈[k_2]_0}, (σ_{T,i})_{i∈[k_T]_0})
08  require I_1 ⊆ [n_1] ∧ I_2 ⊆ [n_2] ∧ I_T ⊆ [n_T] ∧ |I_1| + |I_2| + |I_T| ≥ m
09  return [∀J ∈ {1, 2, T} ∀i ∈ [I_J] : σ̂_{J,i} = L_J(F*_{J,i}(x⃗))]

Oracle Iso(σ)                                    Oracle GrpOp(J, σ, σ̂)
10  require φ ∈ {1, 2} ∧ σ ∈ L_2(Z_p)            14  require J ∈ {1, 2, T} ∧ σ, σ̂ ∈ L_J(Z_p)
11  return L_1(L_2^{-1}(σ))                       15  return L_J(L_J^{-1}(σ) + L_J^{-1}(σ̂))

Oracle Iso^{-1}(σ)                               Oracle Bil(σ, σ̂)
12  require φ = 1 ∧ σ ∈ L_1(Z_p)                  16  require σ ∈ L_1(Z_p) ∧ σ̂ ∈ L_2(Z_p)
13  return L_2(L_1^{-1}(σ))                        17  return L_T(L_1^{-1}(σ) · L_2^{-1}(σ̂))

Oracle Dec_{W_i}(σ̂_{1,1}, ..., σ̂_{1,s_1}, σ̂_{2,1}, ..., σ̂_{2,s_2}, σ̂_{T,1}, ..., σ̂_{T,s_T})
18  require σ̂_{J,j} ∈ L_J(Z_p) for all J ∈ {1, 2, T} and j ∈ [s_J]
19  return [W_i((L_1^{-1}(σ̂_{1,j}))_{j∈[s_1]}, (L_2^{-1}(σ̂_{2,j}))_{j∈[s_2]}, (L_T^{-1}(σ̂_{T,j}))_{j∈[s_T]}) = 0]
```

```
Problem geo-MI-Uber_φ(t, (m, n_1, n_2, n_T), F⃗_1, F⃗_2, F⃗_T, F⃗*_1, F⃗*_2, F⃗*_T, W_1, ..., W_s)
00  x⃗ ←_$ Z_p^t
01  (I_1, I_2, I_T, (P̂_{1,i})_{i∈I_1}, (P̂_{2,i})_{i∈I_2}, (P̂_{T,i})_{i∈I_T}) ← A^{Iso,Eval,Bil,(Dec_{W_i})_{i∈[s]}}
02  require I_1 ⊆ [n_1], I_2 ⊆ [n_2], I_T ⊆ [n_T] ∧ |I_1| + |I_2| + |I_T| ≥ m
03  require ∀J ∈ {1, 2, T} ∀i ∈ I_J : P̂_{J,i} ∈ Span_J(F⃗_1, F⃗_2, F⃗_T, φ)
04  return [∀J ∈ {1, 2, T} ∀i ∈ I_J : (P̂_i - F*_{J,i})(x⃗) = 0]

Oracle Iso(P_1, P_2)
05  require P_J ∈ Span_J(F⃗_1, F⃗_2, F⃗_T, φ) for all J ∈ {1, 2}
06  return [(P_1 - P_2)(x⃗) = 0]
Oracle Eval(J, P)
07  require J ∈ {1, 2, T} and P ∈ Span_J(F⃗_1, F⃗_2, F⃗_T, φ)
08  return [P(x⃗) = 0]
Oracle Bil(P_1, P_2, P_3)
09  require P_J ∈ Span_J(F⃗_1, F⃗_2, F⃗_T, φ) for all J ∈ {1, 2, T}
10  return [(P_1 · P_2 - P_3)(x⃗) = 0]
Oracle Dec_{W_i}(P̂_{1,1}, ..., P̂_{1,s_1}, P̂_{2,1}, ..., P̂_{2,s_2}, P̂_{T,1}, ..., P̂_{T,s_T})
11  require P̂_{J,j} ∈ Span_J(F⃗_1, F⃗_2, F⃗_T, φ) for all J ∈ {1, 2, T} and all j ∈ [s_J]
12  return [W_i(P̂_{1,1}, ..., P̂_{1,s_1}, P̂_{2,1}, ..., P̂_{2,s_2}, P̂_{T,1}, ..., P̂_{T,s_T})(x⃗) = 0]
```

Fig. 4. The problems MI-Uber$_φ$ (in the bilinear GGM) and geo-MI-Uber$_φ$ for bilinear groups of type $φ ∈ \{1, 2, 3\}$ parameterized by t, m, n_1, n_2, n_T, and vectors of polynomials $F⃗_1, F⃗_2, F⃗_T, F⃗*_1, F⃗*_2 F⃗*_T$ of different dimensions with entries in $\mathbb{Z}_p[X_1, ..., X_t]$ and in $\mathbb{Z}_p(X_1, ..., X_t)$ respectively, where $\dim(F⃗_J) = n_J$ for $J ∈ \{1, 2, T\}$. The polynomials $W_1, ..., W_s$ define decisional oracles Dec_{W_i}.

of polynomials with $F_{J,i} ∈ \mathbb{Z}_p[X_1, ..., X_t]$, $F^*_{J,i} ∈ \mathbb{Z}_p(X_1, ..., X_t)$ for all $J ∈ \{1, 2, T\}$ and all i and $\vec{W} = (W_1, ..., W_s)$ with $W_i ∈ \mathbb{Z}_p[Z_1, ..., Z_{s_i}]$ for some $s_i ∈ \mathbb{N}$. Let $k = k_1 + k_2 + k_T$.

Let $r ∈ \mathbb{N}$ and A be a MI-Uber-*solver in the GGM, which makes at most q oracle queries. Then, there exists a geo-MI-Uber solver B that, for

$$d_{\max} := \max\left(\max_i(\deg(F_{T,i})), 2\max_i(\deg(F_{1,i})), 2\max_i(\deg(F_{2,i}))\right)$$

and $s_{\max} := \max(\max_i(s_i), 2)$, makes at most $k(k + 3) + q((r - 1)s_{\max}(k + q) + k + 3 + (s_{\max} + 1)q) + (r - 1)m(k + q) ≈ s_{\max}q^2r$ queries and satisfies

$$\text{Adv}^{\text{geo-MI-Uber}(t,(m,n_1,n_2,n_3),F⃗_1,F⃗_2,F⃗_T,F⃗*_1,F⃗*_2 F⃗*_T,W_1,...,W_s)}(\text{B})$$

$$≥ \text{Adv}^{\text{MI-Uber}(t,(m,n_1,n_2,n_3),F⃗_1,F⃗_2,F⃗_T,F⃗*_1,F⃗*_2 F⃗*_T,W_1,...,W_s)}(\text{A})$$

$$- (qs_{\max} + m)\left(\frac{(q + k) · d_{\max}}{p}\right)^r.$$

4 Reductions Between Geometric Search-Problems

In this section we derive bounds in the GGM and AI-GGM (in Sect. 4.1) and bilinear GGM (in Sect. 4.2) for several problems. Building on the results from Sect. 3, which show a reduction to the considered problem from its geometric version, we show that there is a reduction from a variant of the search-by-hyperplane problem to the geometric problem. Using the lower bounds on the hardness of SHS then gives us the desired GGM bounds. Interestingly, several of our reductions closely mirror generic reductions in the AGM following the approach introduced in [16]. While the bounds in the GGM and bilinear GGM are not new and either have been proven directly in the GGM or by following the AGM approach, we think they serve as nice examples on how reductions between geometric-search problems can serve as a replacement of the AGM approach. The bounds in the AI-GGM, on the other hand, are novel. In particular, we point out that preprocessing bounds for the multi-instance CDH problem seem hard to obtain with a direct reduction from $SHS(m, 2)$ (compare Fig. 1).

As a further result, in Sect. 4.2 we revisit the tight AGM+RO reduction of [16] between the security of BLS signatures [11] and the discrete logarithm problem. We give a reduction from $SHS(1, 2)$ to BLS security in the bilinear GGM + RO and thus obtain a GGM lower bound of order q^2/p, matching that of [16].

4.1 Reductions Between Geometric Search-Problems in the GGM and AI-GGM

Preprocessing Bounds for d-strong-DL and d-strong-DHI in the GGM. As a warm-up, in this section we give a simple reduction between the geometric search variants of the d-strong discrete logarithm (d-strong-DL) and d-strong Diffie-Hellman inversion [8] (d-strong-DHI) problems. Since we identify the former with the special case $SHS(1, d)$ of the search-by-hypersurface problem, for which bounds of its hardness exist, we obtain new bounds on the hardness of the two problems in the AI-GGM. While the problems are arguably more interesting in the bilinear GGM, which is unfortunately not covered in the translation between BF-GGM and AI-GGM, we think this example nicely illustrates the simplicity of our approach compared to directly proving the corresponding bounds in the BF-GGM.

Recall that in both problems the adversary receives as input group elements $(g, g^x, \ldots, g^{x^d})$ for $x \leftarrow_{\$} \mathbb{Z}_p$ and has access to no decisional oracles. In d-strong-DL the goal is to compute x, in d-strong-DHI the group element $g^{1/x}$ (assuming $x \neq 0$). We define geo-d-strong-DL = $SHS(1, d)$, i.e., adversary A has access to oracle Eval accepting all univariate polynomials of degree at most d, and has to return x. Note that the d-strong Diffie-Hellman inversion problem is the special case MI-Uber$(1, (1, 1), (X, \ldots, X^d), (1/X))$ of the Uber problem. We obtain the following.

Lemma 2. *Let $d \in \mathbb{N}$. Then, for every adversary* A *against* geo-d-strong-DHI *making at most q queries, there exist adversary* B *against* geo-d-strong-DL *making at most $q + d + 1$ queries such that*

$$\mathrm{Adv}^{\text{geo-}d\text{-strong-DL}}(\mathsf{B}) \geq \mathrm{Adv}^{\text{geo-}d\text{-strong-DHI}}(\mathsf{A}) \ .$$

Proof. Note that the case $x = 0$ can be efficiently recognized by B. Thus assume $x \neq 0$. Further, note that the two games only differ by the expected solution and winning condition. Indeed in both games oracle Eval is defined with respect to indeterminate x and answers queries for polynomials in $\mathrm{Span}(1, X, \ldots, X^d)$, i.e., all polynomials of degree at most d. Thus, adversary B can provide A with a perfect simulation of d-strong-DHI by simply forwarding all Eval queries. Let $\hat{F} \leftarrow \mathsf{A}^{\text{Eval}}$. If A wins, then we have $\sum_{i=0}^{d} a_i X_i = \hat{F} \in \mathrm{Span}(1, \vec{X})$, and $1/x = \sum_{i=0}^{d} a_i x^i = \hat{F}(x)$. As $x \neq 0$ there exists $a_i \neq 0$. Thus the polynomial $F = X \cdot \hat{F}(X) - 1$ is nontrivial, of degree at most $d + 1$, and x must be one of its at most $d + 1$ roots. B computes all roots y_j of F, uses at most $d + 1$ queries of the form $X - y_j$ to Eval to determine x, and returns it as its solution. $\qquad\square$

As a consequence we obtain the following preprocessing bounds.

Corollary 5. *Let* A, B *be (s, q)-adversaries with $q \geq d$ in the AI-GGM against d-strong-DL and d-strong-DHI, respectively. Then we have* $\mathrm{Adv}^{d\text{-strong-DL}}(\mathsf{A}) \in \tilde{\mathcal{O}}\left(\frac{d(sq^2 + q^2)}{p}\right)$ *and* $\mathrm{Adv}^{d\text{-strong-DHI}}(\mathsf{B}) \in \tilde{\mathcal{O}}\left(\frac{d(sq^2 + q^2)}{p}\right)$.

Proof. By Lemma 1, every adversary against geo-d-strong-DL $=$ SHS$(1, d)$ making at most q' queries has advantage bounded by $e\,dq'/p$. Thus, if we set $q' = q(M + 3q) + Mq + q(k + 1) + k(k + 1) \in \mathcal{O}(q^2 + qM)$ and $r = 1$, by Theorem 3, every (s, q)-adversary against d-strong-DL in BF-GGM has advantage bounded by

$$\frac{edq'}{p} + \frac{2dq^2 + 2d^2q + dq + d^2}{p} \in \mathcal{O}\left(\frac{dq^2 + dqM}{p}\right)$$

as a larger advantage would contradict the bound for geo-d-strong-DL. Now the statement follows from Theorem 1 by observing that $q_{\mathrm{comb}} = q + d\lceil\log(p)\rceil$, and setting $\gamma = 1/p$ and $M = 6(s + \log(p))(q + d\lceil\log(p)\rceil)$.

Regarding the bound for d-strong-DHI, by Lemma 2 we can bound the advantage of every q'-adversary against geo-d-strong-DHI by $e\,d(q' + d + 1)/p$. Then, the second part of the statement follows analogously to the above. $\qquad\square$

From geo-d-strong-DL to geo-Uber. We now consider $\mathrm{Uber}(t, F_1, \ldots, F_k, F^*) := \mathrm{MI\text{-}Uber}(t, (1, 1), \vec{F}, F^*)$, the subclass of single instance Uber problems without decisional oracles. As before, to make the problem nontrivial, we require that $F^* \notin \mathrm{Span}(\vec{F})$. Note that this class contains several problems considered in the AGM setting in prior work as, for example, the CDH, square Diffie-Hellman, and strong Diffie-Hellman assumptions [16], as well as the CDH variants in cyclic groups and bilinear groups of [23].

We give a reduction from geo-d-strong-DL = SHS$(1, d)$ to geo-Uber by translating the AGM reduction from d-strong-DL to Uber in [5] to the geometric setting. A key idea of the reduction in [5] is to rerandomize the element g^x obtained from the d-strong-DL game by raising it to random powers y_i and multiplying the result by g^{z_i} for random z_i. This implicitly sets the secrets for the Uber adversary to $x_i = y_i x + z_i$. We adapt this idea to our setting by letting the reduction explicitly set the secrets for the geo-Uber solver to $P_i = y_i X + z_i$ for random values y_i, z_i, where X is an indeterminate. Then, when the geo-Uber outputs a multivariate polynomial, the reduction substitutes in the P_i for the corresponding variables and solves the resulting univariate polynomial for X. In the proof of Theorem 6 we make use of the following fact.

Lemma 3 ([5, **Lemma 2.1**]). *Let* $F(X_1, \ldots, X_t) \in \mathbb{Z}_p[X_1, \ldots, X_t]$ *be a multivariate polynomial of degree* d. *Then* $F(y_1 X + z_1, y_2 X + z_2, \ldots, y_t X + z_t)$ *is a polynomial in* $\mathbb{Z}_p([y_1, \ldots, y_t, z_1, \ldots, z_t])[X]$ *and its coefficient of maximal degree is a polynomial in* $\mathbb{Z}_p[y_1, \ldots, y_t]$ *of degree* d.

Theorem 6. *Let* A *be a* geo-Uber$(t, F_1, ..., F_k, F^*)$ *solver which makes at most* q *queries, where* $F^*, F_1, \ldots, F_k$ *are polynomials in* t *indeterminates of degree at most* d, *such that* $F^* \notin \mathrm{Span}(1, F_1, \ldots, F_k)$. *Using* A, *we can construct a* geo-d-strong-DL *solver* B *that makes* $q + d$ *queries and satisfies*

$$\mathrm{Adv}^{\text{geo-}d\text{-strong-DL}}(\mathsf{B}) = \mathrm{Adv}^{\text{geo-Uber}(t, F_1, \ldots, F_k, F^*)}(\mathsf{A}) - \frac{d}{p} \ .$$

Proof. The geo-d-strong-DL solver B needs to find one hidden value $x \in \mathbb{Z}_p$, but construct t independent hidden values $\vec{x} = (x_1, \ldots, x_t) \in \mathbb{Z}_p^t$ for the geo-Uber solver A. To this end, B sets up polynomials $P_i = y_i X + z_i$ for all $i \in [t]$, where X is an indeterminate, and y_i, z_i are i.i.d. uniform values from $\mathbb{Z}_p$. It then provides A with a perfect simulation of geo-Uber for the choice of secrets $x_i = P_i(x) = y_i x + z_i$ as described below. Note that, indeed, $\vec{x}$ is uniformly random in $\mathbb{Z}_p^t$.

B has access to the geo-d-strong-DL oracle Eval, that takes as input univariate polynomials of degree at most d. In order to run A, it needs to answer evaluation queries made by the latter, which consist of n-dimensional polynomials spanned by $1, F_1, \ldots, F_k$. When A makes a hypersurface query P, B first checks whether P is a polynomial in t variables $X_1, \ldots, X_t$ in the span of $1, F_1, \ldots, F_k$, and outputs $\perp$ if not. Otherwise, B sets $X_i = P_i$ for all $i \in [t]$ and then queries the resulting univariate polynomial $P(P_1(X), ..., P_k(X))$ to the geo-d-strong-DL oracle Eval. Note that, since P is in the span of $1, F_1, \ldots, F_k$, which have total degree at most d, the degree of the resulting univariate polynomial is at most d, by Lemma 3. So, Eval answers the query with 0 or 1. By choice of the x_i, we have that $P(x_1, \ldots, x_t) = 0 \Leftrightarrow P(P_1(x), \ldots, P_t(x)) = 0$, so B can simply forward this answer to A.

Finally, A outputs a t-dimensional polynomial $\hat{F}(X_1, \ldots, X_t)$. Consider the polynomial $F(X_1, \ldots, X_t) = F^* - \hat{F}$. B checks whether F has at least one (non-constant) non-zero coefficient and aborts if not. Observe that, since $F^* \notin$

$\text{Span}(1, F_1, \ldots, F_k)$, if we also have $\hat{F} \in \text{Span}(1, F_1, \ldots, F_k)$ (which is a condition for A to succeed), we obtain that F will indeed have at least one (non-constant) non-zero coefficient.

Now, B sets $X_i = P_i(X)$ in $F(X_1, \ldots, X_t)$ to obtain a univariate polynomial of degree at most d. By Lemma 3, this polynomial is non-zero with probability $1-d/p$, since the highest degree coefficient depends on the y_i, which are uniformly random. B computes the roots $r_1, \ldots, r_d$ of this polynomial and then queries $X - r_i$ to Eval for all $i \in [d]$. If Eval outputs 1 for one of the roots, B outputs that root. To show that

$$\text{Adv}^{\text{geo-}d\text{-strong-DL}}(\mathsf{B}) = \text{Adv}^{\text{geo-Uber}(n, F_1, \ldots, F_k, F^*)}(\mathsf{A}) - \frac{d}{p} \ ,$$

we note that the view of A is a perfect simulation of the geo-Uber game. Further, by the definition of geo-Uber, if A succeeds, then $\vec{x}$ must be a root of F. □

We obtain the following bounds in the GGM and AI-GGM.

Corollary 7. *In the GGM, every adversary* A *against problem* $\text{Uber}(t, \vec{F}, F^*)$ *making at most q queries, has advantage*

$$\text{Adv}^{\text{Uber}(t, \vec{F}, F^*)}(\mathsf{A}) \in \tilde{\mathcal{O}}\left(\frac{dq^2}{p}\right) \ ,$$

where d is the maximum among the total degrees of $\vec{F}$ and F^*.

Corollary 8. *Every (s, q)-adversary* A *against problem* $\text{Uber}(t, \vec{F}, F^*)$ *in the AI-GGM, has advantage*

$$\text{Adv}^{\text{Uber}(t, \vec{F}, F^*)}(\mathsf{A}) \in \tilde{\mathcal{O}}\left(\frac{d(sq^2 + q^2)}{p}\right) \ .$$

The proofs of the corollaries are in the full version of this paper [3].

From (m, m)geo-MI-gap-DL to (m, n)geo-MI-gap-CDH. In this section we revisit the GGM lower bounds for the multi-instance gap-CDH problem from [2]. We (re)establish the claimed bound in the GGM and additionally obtain new preprocessing bounds for the (m, n)MI-CDH problem. To do so, we show that, for $m, n \in \mathbb{N}$ with $m \leq n$, the algebraic reduction from (m, m)MI-gap-DL to (m, n)MI-gap-CDH in [2, Thm. 5] can easily be translated to one for the corresponding geometric search problems.

Recall that the (m, m)MI-gap-DL problem requires A, on input $(g, g^{x_1} \ldots, g^{x_m})$, to return all discrete logarithms $x_1, \ldots, x_m$. In the (m, n)MI-gap-CDH problem, on the other hand, the adversary gets as input $(g, g^{x_1}, \ldots, g^{x_n}, g^{y_1}, \ldots, g^{y_n})$, and has to return an index set $I \subseteq [n]$ of size at least m, as well as the group elements $g^{x_i y_i}$ for all $i \in I$. In both problems the term "gap" refers to the fact that the adversary has access to a DDH oracle that, on input group elements $(g^{x'}, g^{y'}, g^{z'})$, returns 1 if $g^{x'y'} = g^{z'}$ and 0 else. Thus, (m, n)MI-gap-CDH corresponds to the special case of MI-Uber, where $2n$ indeterminates $x_1, \ldots, x_n$,

$y_1, \ldots, y_n$ are sampled, the input polynomials are $X_1, \ldots, X_n, Y_1, \ldots, Y_n$, the target polynomials $X_1 Y_1, \ldots, X_n Y_n$, and there is one decisional oracle defined by the polynomial $Z_1 Z_2 - Z_3$.

The corresponding geometric search problem (m, n)geo-MI-gap-CDH thus samples $\vec{x}, \vec{y} \leftarrow_\$ \mathbb{Z}_p^n$, and requires adversary A to return an index set $I \subseteq [n]$ of size at least m, as well as polynomials $\hat{F}_i \in \mathrm{Span}(1, \vec{X}, \vec{Y})$, such that for all $i \in I$ we have $\hat{F}_i(\vec{x}, \vec{y}) - x_i y_i = 0$. To do so, A has access to oracles Eval, that on input $F \in \mathrm{Span}(1, \vec{X}, \vec{Y})$ returns $[F(\vec{x}, \vec{y}) = 0]$, and Dec, that on input $F_1, F_2, F_3 \in \mathrm{Span}(1, \vec{X}, \vec{Y})$ returns $[(F_1 \cdot F_2 - F_3)(\vec{x}, \vec{y}) = 0]$.

Problem (m, m)geo-MI-gap-DL samples $\vec{z} \leftarrow_\$ \mathbb{Z}_p^m$, and requires adversary A to return all of $\vec{z}$. A has access to oracles Eval, that on input of $F \in \mathrm{Span}(1, \vec{Z})$ returns $[F(\vec{Z}) = 0]$, and Dec, that on input of $F_1, F_2, F_3 \in \mathrm{Span}(1, \vec{Z})$ returns $[(F_1 \cdot F_2 - F_3)(\vec{z}) = 0]$.

Regarding our reduction between the geometric search-problems we obtain the following result. It allows to formally reestablish the lower bounds from [2] on the hardness of (m, n)MI-gap-CDH in the generic group model. Afterwards, we derive new preprocessing bounds for (m, n)MI-CDH. The proofs are in the full version of this paper [3].

Lemma 4. *Let* $m \leq n \in \mathbb{N}$ *and let* A *be an adversary against* (m, n)geo-MI-gap-CDH *that makes at most* q *queries to oracles* Eval *and* Dec. *Then, there exists an adversary* B *against* (m, m)geo-MI-gap-DL *making the same number of oracles queries such that*

$$\mathrm{Adv}^{(m,m)\text{geo-MI-gap-DL}}(\mathsf{B}) \geq 2^{-m} \mathrm{Adv}^{(m,n)\text{geo-MI-gap-CDH}}(\mathsf{A}) .$$

Corollary 9. *Let* $m \leq n \leq p$. *For every* $r \in \mathbb{N}$, *in the generic group model every adversary* A *against problem* (m, n)MI-gap-CDH *that makes at most* q *oracle queries has advantage bounded by*

$$\mathrm{Adv}^{(m,m)\text{MI-gap-CDH}}(\mathsf{A}) \in \tilde{\mathcal{O}}\left(\left(\frac{rq^2}{mp} \right)^m + q \left(\frac{q}{p} \right)^r \right)$$

In particular, to achieve constant success probability it is necessary that $q \in \Omega(\sqrt{mp})$. *The same bound holds with respect to* (m, n)MI-gap-DL.

Regarding preprocessing we obtain the following new lower bound.

Corollary 10. *Let* $m \leq n \leq p$. *For every* $r \in \mathbb{N}$, *in the generic group model with preprocessing every adversary* A *against problem* (m, n)MI-CDH *that receives advice bounded by* s *and makes at most* q *oracle queries has advantage bounded by*

$$\mathrm{Adv}^{(m,m)\text{MI-CDH}}(\mathsf{A}) \in \tilde{\mathcal{O}}\left(\left(\frac{q^2 s + rq^2}{mp} \right)^m + q \left(\frac{q}{p} \right)^r \right) .$$

In particular, to achieve constant success probability it is necessary that $q^2 s \in \tilde{\Omega}(mp)$. *The same bound holds for* (m, n)MI-DL.

4.2 Reductions Between Geometric Search-Problems Corresponding to the Bilinear GGM

From geo-2d-strong-DL to geo-MI-Uber$_\phi$ in bilinear groups. In this section we revisit the lower bound for the

$$\text{Uber}_\phi := \text{MI-Uber}_\phi(t, (1,0,0,1), \vec{F}_1, \vec{F}_2, \vec{F}_T, F_1^*, F_2^*, F_T^*)$$

problem in the bilinear GGM from [10,13]. While the bound in Theorem 11 is of the same order as in [10,13], it demonstrates how to apply our techniques in bilinear groups. Their proofs are similar to the ones for Uber in the GGM and AI-GGM. The proof of Theorem 11 closely follows the proof of [5, Theorem 3.5] and can be found in the full version of his paper [3].

Theorem 11. *Let* A *be a* geo-MI-Uber$_\phi(t, (1,0,0,1), \vec{F}_1, \vec{F}_2, \vec{F}_T, F_1^*, F_2^*, F_T^*)$ *solver which makes at most* q *queries, where* $F_J^*, F_{J,i}$ *for* $J \in \{1,2,T\}$ *and* $i \in [k_J]$ *are polynomials in* t *indeterminates of total degree at most* d; *and such that there is* $\tilde{J} \in \{1,2,T\}$ *such that* $F_{\tilde{J}}^* \notin \text{Span}_{\tilde{J}}(\vec{F}_1, \vec{F}_2, \vec{F}_T, \phi)$. *Using* A, *we can construct a* geo-2d-strong-DL *solver* B *in* $\mathbb{G}_{\tilde{J}}$ *that makes* $q + 2d$ *queries and satisfies*

$$\text{Adv}^{\text{geo-2}d\text{-strong-DL}}(\text{B}) = \text{Adv}^{\text{geo-MI-Uber}(t,(1,0,0,1),\vec{F}_1,\vec{F}_2,\vec{F}_T,F_T^*)}(\text{A}) - \frac{2d}{p} .$$

Corollary 12. *Let* A *be an adversary against* Uber$_\phi$ *in the bilinear GGM that makes at most* q *oracle queries. Then* $\text{Adv}^{\text{Uber}_\phi}(\text{A}) \in \tilde{\mathcal{O}}\left(\frac{q^2 d + dqk + d^2 + dk^2}{p}\right)$.

The corollary's proof can be found in the full version of this paper [3].

Security of BLS Signatures in the Bilinear GGM. In this section we give a tight reduction from geo-2-strong-DL = SHS(1, 2) to the unforgeability of BLS signatures under chosen-message attacks defined in Fig. 5. We closely follow the proof in [16, Section 6]. Recall that we work in the generic group model for bilinear groups that we presented in Sect. 2.2. The bilinear groups are of type 1 so, to not explicitly have to work with the isomorphism oracle, we can simply set $\mathbb{G} := \mathbb{G}_1 = \mathbb{G}_2$.

Theorem 13. *Let* A *be an* UF-CMA$_{\text{BLS}}(p, \mathbb{G}, \mathbb{G}_T, g, e)$ *solver in the random-oracle model which makes at most* q *group-operation, bilinear map, and signing queries and at most* q_{RO} *random-oracle queries. Using* A, *we can construct a* geo-2-strong-DL *solver* B *that makes* $\mathcal{O}(q^2)$ *queries and satisfies*

$$\text{Adv}^{\text{geo-2-strong-DL}}(\text{B})$$
$$\geq \frac{1}{2}\text{Adv}^{\text{UF-CMA}_{\text{BLS}}(p,\mathbb{G},\mathbb{G}_T,g,e)}(\text{A}) - \frac{4q(3q + 2)}{p} - \frac{q_{\text{RO}}(q_{\text{RO}} + q)}{p} .$$

BLSGen($p, \mathbb{G}, \mathbb{G}_T, g, e$)	BLSSig(m, sk)	BLSVer(m, s)
00 $sk = x \leftarrow \mathbb{Z}_p$	03 $s := H(m)^{sk}$	05 return $[e(H(m), pk) = e(s, g)]$
01 $pk := g^x$	04 return s	
02 return (pk, sk)		

Problem UF-CMA$_{\text{BLS}}(p, \mathbb{G}, \mathbb{G}_T, g, e)$	**Oracle** Sign(σ_m)	**Oracle** GrpOp($\sigma, \hat{\sigma}$)
06 $sk = x \leftarrow \mathbb{Z}_p$	14 $m := \mathcal{L}_1^{-1}(\sigma_m)$	23 **require** $\sigma, \hat{\sigma} \in \mathcal{L}_1(\mathbb{Z}_p)$
07 $pk := g^x$	15 $Q := Q \cup \{m\}$	24 **return** $\mathcal{L}_1(\mathcal{L}_1^{-1}(\sigma) + \mathcal{L}_1^{-1}(\hat{\sigma}))$
08 $Q := \emptyset$	16 $s \leftarrow \text{RO}(m)^{sk}$	
09 $\sigma_0 \leftarrow \mathcal{L}_1(g)$	17 $\sigma_s \leftarrow \mathcal{L}_1(s)$	**Oracle** Bil($\sigma, \hat{\sigma}$)
10 $\sigma_{pk} \leftarrow \mathcal{L}_1(pk)$	18 **return** σ_s	25 **require** $\sigma, \hat{\sigma} \in \mathcal{L}_1(\mathbb{Z}_p)$
11 $(m^*, \sigma_{s^*}) \leftarrow \mathsf{A}^{\text{Sign,RO,GrpOp,Bil}}(\sigma_0, \sigma_{pk})$	**Oracle** RO(m)	26 **return** $\mathcal{L}_T(\mathcal{L}_1^{-1}(\sigma) + \mathcal{L}_1^{-1}(\hat{\sigma}))$
12 $s^* := \mathcal{L}_1^{-1}(\sigma_{s^*})$	19 **if** $\nexists(m, \sigma_m) \in T_{\text{RO}}$	
13 **return** $[m^* \notin Q \wedge \text{BLSVer}(m^*, s^*)]$	20 $\sigma_m \leftarrow_\$ \{0,1\}^\ell$	
	21 $T_{\text{RO}} \leftarrow_\cup (m, \sigma_m)$	
	22 **return** σ_m	

Fig. 5. Top: BLS signature scheme. Bottom: Unforgeability-under-chosen-message-attack problem for with respect to BLS signatures in the bilinear GGM + ROM, where the random oracle returns group elements of $\mathbb{G}_1$.

Corollary 14. *In the bilinear* GGM *for groups of type 1 and programmable random-oracle model every adversary* A *that make at most q group-operation, bilinear map, and signing queries and at most* q_{RO} *random-oracle queries has advantage of order* $\mathcal{O}((q^2 + q_{\text{RO}}^2)/p)$.

The theorem's and corollary's proofs can be found in the full version of this paper [3].

References

1. Abdalla, M., Barbosa, M., Bradley, T., Jarecki, S., Katz, J., Xu, J.: Universally composable relaxed password authenticated key exchange. In: Micciancio, D., Ristenpart, T. (eds.) CRYPTO 2020, Part I. LNCS, vol. 12170, pp. 278–307. Springer, Cham (2020). https://doi.org/10.1007/978-3-030-56784-2_10

2. Auerbach, B., Giacon, F., Kiltz, E.: Everybody's a target: scalability in public-key encryption. In: Canteaut, A., Ishai, Y. (eds.) EUROCRYPT 2020, Part III. LNCS, vol. 12107, pp. 475–506. Springer, Cham (2020). https://doi.org/10.1007/978-3-030-45727-3_16

3. Auerbach, B., Hoffmann, C., Pascual-Perez, G.: Generic-group lower bounds via reductions between geometric-search problems: With and without preprocessing. Cryptology ePrint Archive, Paper 2023/808 (2023). https://eprint.iacr.org/2023/808

4. Bauer, B., Farshim, P., Harasser, P., O'Neill, A.: Beyond Uber: instantiating generic groups via PGGs. In: Kiltz, E., Vaikuntanathan, V. (eds.) TCC 2022, Part III. LNCS, vol. 13749, pp. 212–242. Springer, Heidelberg (Nov 2022). https://doi.org/10.1007/978-3-031-22368-6_8

5. Bauer, B., Fuchsbauer, G., Loss, J.: A classification of computational assumptions in the algebraic group model. In: Micciancio, D., Ristenpart, T. (eds.) CRYPTO 2020, Part III. LNCS, vol. 12171, pp. 121–151. Springer, Cham (2020). https://doi.org/10.1007/978-3-030-56880-1_5

6. Bernstein, D.J., Lange, T.: Non-uniform cracks in the concrete: the power of free precomputation. In: Sako, K., Sarkar, P. (eds.) ASIACRYPT 2013, Part II. LNCS, vol. 8270, pp. 321–340. Springer, Heidelberg (Dec (2013)

7. Blocki, J., Lee, S.: On the multi-user security of short Schnorr signatures with preprocessing. In: Dunkelman, O., Dziembowski, S. (eds.) EUROCRYPT 2022, Part II. LNCS, vol. 13276, pp. 614–643. Springer, Heidelberg (May / Jun (2022). https://doi.org/10.1007/978-3-031-07085-3_21

8. Boneh, D., Boyen, X.: Efficient selective-ID secure identity based encryption without random oracles. In: Cachin, C., Camenisch, J. (eds.) EUROCRYPT 2004. LNCS, vol. 3027, pp. 223–238. Springer, Heidelberg (May (2004). https://doi.org/10.1007/978-3-540-24676-3_14

9. Boneh, D., Boyen, X.: Short signatures without random oracles. In: Cachin, C., Camenisch, J. (eds.) EUROCRYPT 2004. LNCS, vol. 3027, pp. 56–73. Springer, Heidelberg (May (2004). https://doi.org/10.1007/978-3-540-24676-3_4

10. Boneh, D., Boyen, X., Goh, E.-J.: Hierarchical identity based encryption with constant size ciphertext. In: Cramer, R. (ed.) EUROCRYPT 2005. LNCS, vol. 3494, pp. 440–456. Springer, Heidelberg (2005). https://doi.org/10.1007/11426639_26

11. Boneh, D., Lynn, B., Shacham, H.: Short signatures from the Weil pairing. J. Cryptol. **17**(4), 297–319 (2004)

12. Boneh, D., Venkatesan, R.: Breaking RSA may not be equivalent to factoring. In: Nyberg, K. (ed.) EUROCRYPT 1998. LNCS, vol. 1403, pp. 59–71. Springer, Heidelberg (1998). https://doi.org/10.1007/BFb0054117

13. Boyen, X.: The uber-assumption family (invited talk). In: Galbraith, S.D., Paterson, K.G. (eds.) PAIRING 2008. LNCS, vol. 5209, pp. 39–56. Springer, Heidelberg (Sep (2008). https://doi.org/10.1007/978-3-540-85538-5_3

14. Coretti, S., Dodis, Y., Guo, S.: Non-uniform bounds in the random-permutation, ideal-cipher, and generic-group models. In: Shacham, H., Boldyreva, A. (eds.) CRYPTO 2018, Part I. LNCS, vol. 10991, pp. 693–721. Springer, Heidelberg (Aug (2018). https://doi.org/10.1007/978-3-319-96884-1_23

15. Corrigan-Gibbs, H., Kogan, D.: The discrete-logarithm problem with preprocessing. In: Nielsen, J.B., Rijmen, V. (eds.) EUROCRYPT 2018, Part II. LNCS, vol. 10821, pp. 415–447. Springer, Cham (2018). https://doi.org/10.1007/978-3-319-78375-8_14

16. Fuchsbauer, G., Kiltz, E., Loss, J.: The algebraic group model and its applications. In: Shacham, H., Boldyreva, A. (eds.) CRYPTO 2018, Part II. LNCS, vol. 10992, pp. 33–62. Springer, Cham (2018). https://doi.org/10.1007/978-3-319-96881-0_2

17. Fuchsbauer, G., Plouviez, A., Seurin, Y.: Blind Schnorr signatures and signed ElGamal encryption in the algebraic group model. In: Canteaut, A., Ishai, Y. (eds.) EUROCRYPT 2020, Part II. LNCS, vol. 12106, pp. 63–95. Springer, Cham (2020). https://doi.org/10.1007/978-3-030-45724-2_3

18. Ghoshal, A., Tessaro, S.: State-restoration soundness in the algebraic group model. In: Malkin, T., Peikert, C. (eds.) CRYPTO 2021, Part III. LNCS, vol. 12827, pp. 64–93. Springer, Cham (2021). https://doi.org/10.1007/978-3-030-84252-9_3

19. Kastner, J., Loss, J., Xu, J.: On pairing-free blind signature schemes in the algebraic group model. In: Hanaoka, G., Shikata, J., Watanabe, Y. (eds.) PKC 2022, Part II. LNCS, vol. 13178, pp. 468–497. Springer, Heidelberg (Mar (2022). https://doi.org/10.1007/978-3-030-97131-1_16

20. Lee, H.T., Cheon, J.H., Hong, J.: Accelerating ID-based encryption based on trapdoor DL using pre-computation. Cryptology ePrint Archive, Paper 2011/187 (2011). https://eprint.iacr.org/2011/187

21. Maurer, U.M.: Abstract models of computation in cryptography (invited paper). In: Smart, N.P. (ed.) Cryptography and Coding 2005. LNCS, vol. 3796, pp. 1–12. Springer, Heidelberg (Dec (2005). https://doi.org/10.1007/11586821_1

22. Mihalcik, J.P.: An analysis of algorithms for solving discrete logarithms in fixed groups. Master's thesis, Naval Postgraduate School (2010). https://calhoun.nps. edu/bitstream/handle/10945/5395/10Mar_Mihalcik.pdf

23. Mizuide, T., Takayasu, A., Takagi, T.: Tight reductions for Diffie-Hellman variants in the algebraic group model. In: Matsui, M. (ed.) CT-RSA 2019. LNCS, vol. 11405, pp. 169–188. Springer, Cham (2019). https://doi.org/10.1007/978-3-030-12612-4_9

24. Okamoto, T., Pointcheval, D.: The gap-problems: a new class of problems for the security of cryptographic schemes. In: Kim, K. (ed.) PKC 2001. LNCS, vol. 1992, pp. 104–118. Springer, Heidelberg (2001). https://doi.org/10.1007/3-540-44586-2_8

25. Paillier, P., Vergnaud, D.: Discrete-log-based signatures may not be equivalent to discrete log. In: Roy, B. (ed.) ASIACRYPT 2005. LNCS, vol. 3788, pp. 1–20. Springer, Heidelberg (2005). https://doi.org/10.1007/11593447_1

26. Rotem, L., Segev, G.: Algebraic distinguishers: from discrete logarithms to decisional uber assumptions. In: Pass, R., Pietrzak, K. (eds.) TCC 2020, Part III. LNCS, vol. 12552, pp. 366–389. Springer, Cham (2020). https://doi.org/10.1007/978-3-030-64381-2_13

27. Rupp, A., Leander, G., Bangerter, E., Dent, A.W., Sadeghi, A.-R.: Sufficient conditions for intractability over black-box groups: generic lower bounds for generalized DL and DH problems. In: Pieprzyk, J. (ed.) ASIACRYPT 2008. LNCS, vol. 5350, pp. 489–505. Springer, Heidelberg (2008). https://doi.org/10.1007/978-3-540-89255-7_30

28. Shoup, V.: Lower bounds for discrete logarithms and related problems. In: Fumy, W. (ed.) EUROCRYPT 1997. LNCS, vol. 1233, pp. 256–266. Springer, Heidelberg (1997). https://doi.org/10.1007/3-540-69053-0_18

29. Unruh, D.: Random oracles and auxiliary input. In: Menezes, A. (ed.) CRYPTO 2007. LNCS, vol. 4622, pp. 205–223. Springer, Heidelberg (2007). https://doi.org/10.1007/978-3-540-74143-5_12

30. Ying, J.H.M., Kunihiro, N.: Bounds in various generalized settings of the discrete logarithm problem. In: Gollmann, D., Miyaji, A., Kikuchi, H. (eds.) ACNS 2017. LNCS, vol. 10355, pp. 498–517. Springer, Cham (2017). https://doi.org/10.1007/978-3-319-61204-1_25

31. Yun, A.: Generic hardness of the multiple discrete logarithm problem. In: Oswald, E., Fischlin, M. (eds.) EUROCRYPT 2015, Part II. LNCS, vol. 9057, pp. 817–836. Springer, Heidelberg (2015). https://doi.org/10.1007/978-3-662-46803-6_27

32. Zhandry, M.: To label, or not to label (in generic groups). In: Dodis, Y., Shrimpton, T. (eds.) CRYPTO 2022, Part III. LNCS, vol. 13509, pp. 66–96. Springer, Heidelberg (Aug (2022). https://doi.org/10.1007/978-3-031-15982-4_3

33. Zhang, C., Zhou, H.S., Katz, J.: An analysis of the algebraic group model. In: Agrawal, S., Lin, D. (eds.) ASIACRYPT 2022, Part IV. LNCS, vol. 13794, pp. 310–322. Springer, Heidelberg (Dec (2022). https://doi.org/10.1007/978-3-031-22972-5_11

IOPs and Succinctness

Holographic SNARGs for P
and Batch-NP from (Polynomially Hard)
Learning with Errors

Susumu Kiyoshima[✉]

NTT Social Informatics Laboratories, Tokyo, Japan
susumu.kiyoshima@ntt.com

Abstract. A succinct non-interactive argument (SNARG) is called *holographic* if the verifier runs in time sub-linear in the input length when given oracle access to an encoding of the input. We present holographic SNARGs for P and Batch-NP under the learning with errors (LWE) assumption. Our holographic SNARG for P has a verifier that runs in time $\mathsf{poly}(\lambda, \log T, \log n)$ for T-time computations and n-bit inputs (λ is the security parameter), while our holographic SNARG for Batch-NP has a verifier that runs in time $\mathsf{poly}(\lambda, T, \log k)$ for k instances of T-time computations. Before this work, constructions with the same asymptotic efficiency were known in the designated-verifier setting or under the subexponential hardness of the LWE assumption. We obtain our holographic SNARGs (in the public-verification setting under the polynomial hardness of the LWE assumption) by constructing holographic SNARGs for certain hash computations and then applying known/trivial transformations.

As an application, we use our holographic SNARGs to weaken the assumption needed for a recent public-coin 3-round zero-knowledge (ZK) argument [Kiyoshima, CRYPTO 2022]. Specifically, we use our holographic SNARGs to show that a public-coin 3-round ZK argument exists under the same assumptions as the state-of-the-art private-coin 3-round ZK argument [Bitansky et al., STOC 2018].

1 Introduction

SNARGs. Informally speaking, a *succinct argument* [29] (or *delegation scheme* [14]) is an argument system with small communication complexity and fast verification time. In a typical setting, the statement to be proven contains a description of a computation and an input to the computation; the prover's task is to convince the verifier that the output of the computation is 1. A typical efficiency requirement is that the communication complexity and the verification time are polylogarithmic in the complexity of the computation.

When succinct arguments are non-interactive in the common random/reference string (CRS) model, they are commonly referred to as *succinct non-interactive arguments (SNARGs)*. Initially, the study of SNARGs

---

This work was done while the author was a member of NTT Research.

G. Rothblum and H. Wee (Eds.): TCC 2023, LNCS 14371, pp. 333–362, 2023.
https://doi.org/10.1007/978-3-031-48621-0_12

was focused on constructing SNARGs for all NP computations (i.e., the goal was to design SNARGs that can prove the correctness of any NP computations). However, for such a large class of computations, positive results were only obtained in the idealized model (e.g., the random oracle model) or under non-standard cryptographic assumptions (e.g., extractability assumptions). Recently, a growing number of works showed that SNARGs for useful subclasses of NP computations, such as deterministic computations and Batch-NP computations,[1] can be obtained in the standard model under standard cryptographic assumptions. Specifically, Kalai, Raz, and Rothblum [26] and subsequent works (e.g., [2,4,18,24]) constructed *designated-verifier SNARGs* for such subclasses under the learning with errors (LWE) assumption. (Designated-verifier SNARGs are weaker than standard SNARGs in that they are not publicly verifiable, i.e., only the owner of a secret verification key can verify the correctness of proofs.) More recently, Choudhuri, Jain, and Jin [11] and other works (e.g., [9,13,21,22,28,31,33]) constructed (publicly verifiable) SNARGs for such subclasses under various standard cryptographic assumptions (e.g., the LWE assumption).

Holographic SNARGs. SNARGs are called *holographic* if the verifier runs in time sub-linear in the length of the input when given oracle access to an encoding of the input.[2] In many cases, the holographic property is naturally satisfied when SNARGs are constructed based on code-theoretic techniques, and it often comes with additional useful properties such as (i) input encoding having a simple algebraic structure (e.g., a low-degree polynomial) and (ii) verification that only makes non-adaptive queries to the encoding of the input.

The holographic property of existing SNARGs has been used crucially in some applications. For example, in the application to 2-message arguments of proximity [27], the holographic property of the underlying SNARG [26] was used to reduce the task of proving the correctness of an arbitrary deterministic computation to a much simpler task of proving that the encoding of the computation input has certain values at certain positions. Other examples include applications to succinct probabilistically checkable arguments [5] and 3-round zero-knowledge argument [3,30], where the holographic property of the underlying SNARGs was used to have succinct verification in the setting where the entire input is not available to the verifier.

Existing holographic SNARGs are, however, less powerful than state-of-the-art non-holographic SNARGs. Concretely, compared with the non-holographic SNARGs of Choudhuri et al. [11] and subsequent works [13,28,31,33] (which are publicly verifiable, can be used for deterministic polynomial-time computations

---

[1] In SNARGs for Batch-NP computations, a statement consists of multiple instances of an NP language, and the prover tries to convince the verifier that all the instances belong to the language. The communication complexity and the verification time are required to be smaller than the naive check.

[2] The holographic property has also been considered for *interactive oracle proofs* (IOPs) [7,8] and interactive proofs/arguments [5,15]. The term "holography" was initially used in the context of *probabilistically checkable proofs* (PCPs) [1].

and Batch-NP computations, and are based on standard polynomial hardness assumptions), existing holographic SNARGs are either (i) not publicly verifiable [4,26] or (ii) based on sub-exponential hardness assumptions [22,30].

Because of this gap, some applications of holographic SNARGs only obtained sub-optimal results. For example, in the application to 3-round zero-knowledge arguments [3,30], the existing constructions are either (i) private-coin (as the underlying holographic SNARG [26] is not publicly verifiable) or (ii) based on a sub-exponential hardness assumption (as the underlying holographic SNARG [22] is based on a sub-exponential hardness assumption).

1.1 Our Results

We give holographic SNARGs for deterministic polynomial-time computations and Batch-NP computations under the polynomial hardness of the LWE assumption. The holographic verifier of our SNARGs makes non-adaptive queries to the *low-degree extension* (LDE) of the computation input.[3]

Theorem (informal, see Theorem 5 and Corollary 2). *Under the LWE assumption, there exist holographic SNARGs for deterministic polynomial-time computations and Batch-NP computations.*

- *For security parameter λ and any deterministic T-time computation with input length n, the CRS generator runs in time $\mathsf{poly}(\lambda, \log T, \log n)$, the prover runs in time $\mathsf{poly}(\lambda, T, n)$, and the verifier runs in time $\mathsf{poly}(\lambda, \log T, \log n)$ given oracle access to the LDE of the computation input.*
- *For security parameter λ and any Batch-NP computation that consists of k instances of a T-time non-deterministic computation, the CRS generator runs in time $\mathsf{poly}(\lambda, T, \log k)$, the prover runs in time $\mathsf{poly}(\lambda, T, k)$, and the verifier runs in time $\mathsf{poly}(\lambda, T, \log k)$ given oracle access to the LDE of the concatenation of the k instances.*

Given the LDE of a long input, our SNARG verifiers run in time sub-linear in the input length.

At a high level, our result can be seen as a holographic version of the result of Choudhuri, Jain, and Jin [11] (where SNARGs for deterministic computations and Batch-NP computations are given under the LWE assumption). However, in the adaptive-statement setting, our holographic soundness notion is weaker than the non-holographic counterparts since the input to be encoded is required to be fixed non-adaptively before the CRS is sampled (see, e.g., Definition 13 for the soundness notion that our holographic SNARG for Batch-NP satisfies).

As an application of the above result, we give the following result.

Theorem (informal, see Theorem 6). *Assume the existence of (polynomially compressing) keyless hash functions that are multi-collision resistant against slightly super-polynomial-time adversaries, and additionally assume slightly super-polynomial hardness of the LWE assumption. Then, there exists a public-coin 3-round zero-knowledge argument for NP.*

---

[3] For the definition of low-degree extensions, see, e.g., [14].

We obtain this result by relying on a known transformation [3,30]. The assumptions in this result are the same as those that are needed for the state-of-the-art private-coin 3-round zero-knowledge argument [3], and they are weaker than those that are needed for the state-of-the-art public-coin 3-round zero-knowledge argument [30] (concretely, sub-exponential hardness is not necessary for the LWE assumption). In short, this result closes the gap between the assumptions needed for private-coin 3-round zero-knowledge arguments and those needed for public-coin ones.

1.2 Related Work

The following is a brief review of existing SNARGs that have verification time sub-linear in the input length. (We focus on those that are publicly verifiable and based on well-studied falsifiable assumptions.) For deterministic computations, the aforementioned work by Choudhuri et al. [11] constructed a *SNARG for RAM computations* [12,24], where the verifier runs in time sub-linear in the length of the initial memory when given a short digest of the initial memory. (The digest can be computed by the verifier in a one-time expensive pre-processing phase.) For Batch-NP computations, some of the existing constructions (e.g., [11,33]) have the verifier that first runs in an expensive offline phase and subsequently checks the proof in time sub-linear in the number of the instances. As a special case of SNARGs for Batch-NP, the work by Choudhuri et al. [11] defined and constructed a *batch argument (BARG) for the index language*, where the statement to be proven is restricted to the form $\forall i \in [k] \exists w_i \in \{0,1\}^*$ s.t. $C(i, w_i) = 1$ for a Boolean circuit C, and the verifier runs in time sub-linear in k if C is of size sub-linear in k. (A similar notion was also considered by Kalai, Vaikuntanathan, and Zhang [28].) As a related notion, Devadas, Goyal, Kalai, and Vaikuntanathan [13] considered *hashed BARGs*, where the verifier runs in sub-linear time when given a (*somewhere extractable* [11,20]) hash of the instances.

2   Technical Overviews

2.1   Holographic SNARG for P

Overall Approach. Our starting point is the work by Choudhuri, Jain, and Jin (CJJ) [11], which gives a (non-holographic) SNARG for deterministic polynomial-time computation under the LWE assumption. In the CJJ SNARG, the computation to be proven is modeled as a RAM computation, and the input to the computation is viewed as the initial memory. Importantly, the verifier only uses the input to obtain the digest of the initial memory, and the digest is simply the Merkle tree-hash of the input. Thus, the CJJ SANRG is non-holographic only because the verifier needs to compute the Merkle tree-hash of the input.[4]

---

[4] Most of the existing schemes (e.g., [21,28,31,33]) are also (implicitly) designed for RAM computations and are non-holographic for the same reason.

Recently, it was shown that the CJJ SNARG can be made holographic under the sub-exponential hardness of the LWE assumption [30]. The main idea was to delegate the computation of the Merkle tree-hash to the prover. That is, the prover was modified to additionally create the Merkle tree-hash of the input along with a holographic proof about the correctness of the Merkle tree-hash. The key point was that the correctness of Merkle tree-hash computations can be proved in a holographic way using the SNARG by Jawale, Kalai, Khurana, and Zhang (JKKZ) [22] (which is holographic and can be used for any log-uniform bounded-depth deterministic computations). This approach requires the sub-exponential hardness of the LWE assumption since the JKKZ SNARG is based on the sub-exponential hardness of the LWE assumption.

We make the CJJ SNARG holographic under the polynomial hardness of the LWE assumption. Our approach is to design a holographic SNARG that is tailored to Merkle tree-hash computations, expecting that such a restricted SNARG is easier to construct under the polynomial hardness assumption. Concretely, our target is a SNARG such that (i) for a statement of the form (x, h, rt), the prover can prove that $\mathsf{rt} \in \{0,1\}^\lambda$ is the Merkle tree-hash of $x \in \{0,1\}^*$ under the hash function $h : \{0,1\}^{2\lambda} \to \{0,1\}^\lambda$, (ii) the soundness holds even against cheating provers that adaptively choose rt, and (iii) the verifier runs in time sub-linear in $|x|$ when it is given oracle access to an encoding of x.

We achieve our goal in two steps. First, we obtain a holographic SNARG for tree-hash computations under the LWE assumption while assuming the existence of a holographic SNARG for another specific computation with a weak soundness guarantee. Next, we construct the required holographic SNARG under the LWE assumption. Below, we use the following tools in both steps.

1. **Somewhere extractable (SE) hash functions** [11,20]: Like the Merkle tree-hash scheme, an SE hash function SEH.Hash with a random public key h can create a hash value $\mathsf{rt} = \mathsf{SEH.Hash}(h, x)$ and short certificates $\{\mathsf{cert}_i\}_{i \in [N]}$ for a long message $x = (x_1, \ldots, x_N)$. Moreover, for any $i^* \in [N]$, we can sample h with trapdoor information td so that the following hold.
   - *Somewhere extractability.* With overwhelming probability over the sampling of h, any hash value rt uniquely determines its pre-image in position i^*. Furthermore, a PPT extractor SEH.Ext can extract the unique i^*-th position value v given $(\mathsf{td}, \mathsf{rt})$.
   - *Index hiding.* The public key h hides the binding index i^*.
   An SE hash function can be obtained under the LWE assumption [20]. It can be generalized to support multiple binding indices naturally, and its complexity (such as the description size of the hash function) scales linearly in the number of binding indices.
2. **Batch arguments (BARGs) for the index language** [11]: BARGs for the index language are a special case of SNARGs for Batch-NP computations: for a Boolean circuit C and an integer $k \in \mathbb{N}$, the statement to be proven is that $\forall i \in [k] \exists w_i \in \{0,1\}^*$ s.t. $C(i, w_i) = 1$. (Unlike the general case, BARGs for the index language can have verification time sub-linear in k since the verifier no longer needs to take k instances explicitly.) A BARG for the index

language can be obtained under the LWE assumption [11]. Its CRS generation and verifier run in time polylogarithmic in k, and it satisfies a stronger notion of soundness, *semi-adaptive somewhere soundness*, guaranteeing that for any $i^* \in [k]$, the CRS can be sampled so that giving an accepting proof for an adaptively chosen circuit C is infeasible as long as $\nexists w$ s.t. $C(i^*, w) = 1$.

Step 1. Holographic SNARG for Tree-Hashing from Somewhere-Sound Holographic SNARG for SE-Hashing. We construct a holographic SNARG for tree-hashing computations by using what we call a *somewhere-sound holographic SNARG for SE-hash computations*.

We start by giving an insecure candidate construction as a motivating example. Recall that in SNARGs for tree-hash computations, for a statement (x, h, rt), the prover proves that $\mathsf{rt} \in \{0,1\}^\lambda$ is the Merkle tree-hash of $x \in \{0,1\}^*$ under the hash function $h : \{0,1\}^{2\lambda} \to \{0,1\}^\lambda$, where the verifier is given oracle access to an encoding of x. At a high level, we consider a construction that follows the commit-and-prove paradigm, where the prover (i) hashes all the nodes of the tree-hash of x in the layer-by-layer basis and (ii) uses a BARG for the index language to prove that the hashed nodes constitute a Merkle tree; the verifier verifies all the BARG proofs and checks whether the hash of the top layer is the hash of rt. See Fig. 1 for a detailed description. Clearly, the construction in Fig. 1 is not sound since nothing is proved about the consistency between x and the hash values. More concretely, the problem is that the verifier does not check whether rt_ℓ is the hash value of x w.r.t. the hash function h_ℓ^{SEH}. Since we want the verifier to be holographic, we cannot let the verifier check $\mathsf{SEH.Hash}(h_\ell^{\mathsf{SEH}}, x) \overset{?}{=} \mathsf{rt}_\ell$ directly. We thus augment the candidate construction with a holographic SNARG that proves the consistency between rt_ℓ and x.

To see in more detail what type of SNARGs is needed to make the candidate construction secure, assume that a cheating prover P^* breaks the soundness of the candidate construction. That is, given (x, h), the cheating prover P^* adaptively chooses rt and makes V output 1 despite $\mathsf{TreeHash}_h(x) \neq \mathsf{rt}$, where $\mathsf{TreeHash}_h(x)$ denotes the tree-hash of x under the hash function h. (For simplicity, we assume that P^* succeeds with probability 1.) Let $\{\mathsf{node}_{i,\sigma}\}_{i \in \{0,\dots,\ell\}, \sigma \in \{0,\dots,2^i-1\}}$ denote the correct nodes of $\mathsf{TreeHash}_h(x)$. Then, we consider the following claim.

Claim (Informal). $\forall i \in \{0, \dots, \ell\}, \exists \sigma \in \{0, \dots, 2^i - 1\}$ s.t. if h_i^{SEH} is sampled in the CRS generation in a way that it is binding in position σ, the hash value rt_i that P^* provides as a part of an accepting proof π satisfies $\mathsf{SEH.Ext}(\mathsf{td}_i^{\mathsf{SEH}}, \mathsf{rt}_i) \neq \mathsf{node}_{i,\sigma},$[5] where $\mathsf{td}_i^{\mathsf{SEH}}$ is the trapdoor corresponding to h_i^{SEH}.

In words, this claim says that from each of the hash values $\{\mathsf{rt}_i\}_{i \in \{0,\dots,\ell\}}$ that P^* provides as the layer-by-layer hashes of the nodes of $\mathsf{TreeHash}_h(x)$, we can extract

---

[5] In this overview, we view rt_i as a hash of a vector that consists of 2^i blocks, where each block is a λ-bit string. Thus, $\mathsf{SEH.Ext}$ extracts a λ-bit string as the σ-th position of the pre-image. .

Building blocks: (i) SEH.Hash—an SE hash function. (ii) $\mathsf{BARG_{idx}}$—a BARG for the index language.

- -

CRS generation: The CRS generation algorithm samples λ public keys $h_0^{\mathsf{SEH}}, \ldots, h_{\lambda-1}^{\mathsf{SEH}}$ of SEH.Hash and a CRS of $\mathsf{BARG_{idx}}$.

Prover P: The prover P is given a binary string $x \in \{0,1\}^*$, a hash function $h : \{0,1\}^{2\lambda} \to \{0,1\}^\lambda$, and a hash value $\mathsf{rt} \in \{0,1\}^\lambda$.

1. Compute the nodes $\{\mathsf{node}_{i,\sigma}\}_{i \in \{0,\ldots,\ell\}, \sigma \in \{0,\ldots,2^i-1\}}$ of the tree-hash of x using h. That is, do the following.
   (a) Partition x into 2^ℓ blocks $\mathsf{blk}_0, \ldots, \mathsf{blk}_{2^\ell-1}$ such that $|\mathsf{blk}_0| = \cdots = |\mathsf{blk}_{2^\ell-1}| = \lambda$. (We assume for simplicity that $|x| = 2^\ell \lambda$ for $\ell \in \mathbb{N}$.)
   (b) Let $\mathsf{node}_{\ell,\sigma} := \mathsf{blk}_\sigma$ for $\forall \sigma \in \{0,\ldots,2^\ell-1\}$, and let $\mathsf{node}_{i,\sigma} := h(\mathsf{node}_{i+1,2\sigma} \| \mathsf{node}_{i+1,2\sigma+1})$ for $\forall i \in \{\ell-1,\ldots,0\}, \sigma \in \{0,\ldots,2^i-1\}$.
2. Compute $\mathsf{rt}_i := \mathsf{SEH.Hash}(h_i^{\mathsf{SEH}}, x_i)$ for $\forall i \in \{0,\ldots,\ell\}$, where $x_i := \mathsf{node}_{i,0} \| \cdots \| \mathsf{node}_{i,2^i-1}$ is the concatenation of the nodes at the i-th level.
3. For $\forall i \in \{0,\ldots,\ell-1\}$, use $\mathsf{BARG_{idx}}$ to compute a proof π_i about the consistency between rt_i and rt_{i+1}, i.e., prove that for $\forall \sigma \in \{0,\ldots,2^i-1\}$, there exists a pair of triples $(\mathsf{node}^{(P)}, \mathsf{node}^{(L)}, \mathsf{node}^{(R)})$, $(\mathsf{cert}^{(P)}, \mathsf{cert}^{(L)}, \mathsf{cert}^{(R)})$ s.t. (i) $\mathsf{cert}^{(P)}$ certifies that the σ-th position of the pre-image of rt_i is $\mathsf{node}^{(P)}$, (ii) $(\mathsf{cert}^{(L)}, \mathsf{cert}^{(R)})$ certifies that the 2σ-th and $2\sigma+1$-st positions of the pre-image of rt_{i+1} are $(\mathsf{node}^{(L)}, \mathsf{node}^{(R)})$, and (iii) $h(\mathsf{node}^{(L)} \| \mathsf{node}^{(R)}) = \mathsf{node}^{(P)}$.
4. Output $\pi := (\{\mathsf{rt}_i\}_{i \in \{0,\ldots,\ell\}}, \{\pi_i\}_{i \in \{0,\ldots,\ell-1\}})$ as a proof.

Verifier V: The verifier V is given (h, rt) and $\pi = (\{\mathsf{rt}_i\}_{i \in \{0,\ldots,\ell\}}, \{\pi_i\}_{i \in \{0,\ldots,\ell-1\}})$ along with oracle access to an encoding of x. Then, V outputs 1 iff (i) each π_i is an accepting w.r.t. $(\mathsf{rt}_i, \mathsf{rt}_{i+1})$ and (ii) $\mathsf{SEH.Hash}(h_0^{\mathsf{SEH}}, \mathsf{rt}) = \mathsf{rt}_0$.

Fig. 1. A candidate construction of holographic tree-hash SNARGs

a node that disagrees with the correct nodes $\{\mathsf{node}_{i,\sigma}\}_{i \in \{0,\ldots,\ell\}, \sigma \in \{0,\ldots,2^i-1\}}$ in a certain position σ. We prove this claim by induction on i.

Base case. When $i = 0$ and $\sigma = 0$, the claim holds trivially because of our assumption that P^* breaks the soundness of the candidate construction.

Inductive step. Assume that the claim holds for $i-1$ and σ_{i-1}. The index hiding property of h_i^{SEH} guarantees that the claim remains to hold even when h_i^{SEH} is statistically binding in positions $2\sigma_{i-1}$ and $2\sigma_{i-1}+1$. Then, the semi-adaptive somewhere soundness of π_i guarantees that when we extract the statistically fixed values $\widetilde{\mathsf{node}}_{i-1,\sigma_{i-1}} := \mathsf{SEH.Ext}(\mathsf{td}_{i-1}^{\mathsf{SEH}}, \mathsf{rt}_{i-1})$ and $(\widetilde{\mathsf{node}}_{i,2\sigma_{i-1}}, \widetilde{\mathsf{node}}_{i,2\sigma_{i-1}+1}) := \mathsf{SEH.Ext}(\mathsf{td}_i^{\mathsf{SEH}}, \mathsf{rt}_i)$, they satisfy $h(\widetilde{\mathsf{node}}_{i,2\sigma_{i-1}} \| \widetilde{\mathsf{node}}_{i,2\sigma_{i-1}+1}) = \widetilde{\mathsf{node}}_{i-1,\sigma_{i-1}}$. Since we assumed $\widetilde{\mathsf{node}}_{i-1,\sigma_{i-1}} \neq \mathsf{node}_{i-1,\sigma_{i-1}}$, we conclude that $\exists \sigma_i \in \{2\sigma_{i-1}, 2\sigma_{i-1}+1\} \subseteq \{0,\ldots,2^i-1\}$ s.t. $\widetilde{\mathsf{node}}_{i,\sigma_i} \neq \mathsf{node}_{i,\sigma_i}$ as desired.

For $i = \ell$, the above claim implies that a cheating prover can break the soundness of the candidate scheme only when $\exists \sigma \in \{0, \ldots, 2^\ell - 1\}$ s.t. the hash value rt_ℓ that the prover provides satisfies $\mathsf{Ext}(\mathsf{td}_\ell^{\mathsf{SEH}}, \mathsf{rt}_\ell) \neq \mathsf{blk}_\sigma$, i.e., the extractor extracts a node that disagrees with the σ-th block of x. Thus, we need a holographic SNARG that prevents this type of inconsistency.

In conclusion, to make the candidate construction secure, we need a holographic SNARG that satisfies the following.

Holographic completeness. The prover can convince the verifier when given a statement (x, h, rt) s.t. $\mathsf{SEH.Hash}(h, x) = \mathsf{rt}$. The verifier is given (h, rt) as explicit inputs and is given oracle access to an encoding of x. The verifier runs in time sub-linear in $|x|$ (ideally, polylogarithmic in $|x|$).

Somewhere soundness. For any x and $\sigma \in \{0, \ldots, |x| - 1\}$, and for an honest CRS and a random SE hash function key h that is statistically binding in position σ, no PPT prover can provide a hash value rt and an accepting proof satisfying $\mathsf{SEH.Ext}(\mathsf{td}^{\mathsf{SEH}}, \mathsf{rt}) \neq x_\sigma$, where $\mathsf{td}^{\mathsf{SEH}}$ is the trapdoor corresponding to h.

Note that the somewhere soundness does not guarantee $\mathsf{SEH.Hash}(h, x) = \mathsf{rt}$. It only guarantees that for any σ, if we extract the σ-th position value from rt, the extracted value agrees with x. This guarantee is sufficient since the above claim guarantees that any successful cheating prover breaks this type of consistency in a randomly chosen σ with non-negligible probability.

Step 2. Somewhere Sound Holographic SNARG for SE-Hashing from LWE. Similarly to recent SNARGs (e.g., [11,21,22,28]), our construction is obtained by using a *correlation-intractable (CI) hash function* [6]. Roughly speaking, a hash function family $\{\mathcal{H}_\lambda = \{h : X_\lambda \to Y_\lambda\}\}_{\lambda \in \mathbb{N}}$ is correlation intractable for a relation ensemble $\mathbf{R} = \{\mathbf{R}_\lambda \subseteq X_\lambda \times Y_\lambda\}_{\lambda \in \mathbb{N}}$ if no PPT adversary can find $x \in X_\lambda$ s.t. $(x, h(x)) \in \mathbf{R}_\lambda$ for a random $h \in \mathcal{H}_\lambda$. It is known that a CI hash function family exists for *efficiently product verifiable relation ensembles* under the LWE assumption [17], where a relation $\mathbf{R}_\lambda \subseteq X_\lambda \times Y_\lambda^t$ is efficiently product verifiable if we have $(x, (y_1, \ldots, y_t)) \in \mathbf{R}_\lambda$ iff each y_i is included in a small efficiently verifiable set. More concretely, we use the following result [17].

Theorem (Informal. See Sect. 3.2). *Fix any (arbitrarily small) constant* $\delta, \rho \in [0, 1]$ *and any function* $t(\lambda) = \Omega(\lambda^\delta)$. *Then, under the LWE assumption, there exists a hash function family that is correlation intractable for any relation ensemble* $\mathbf{R} = \{\mathbf{R}_\lambda \subseteq X_\lambda \times Y_\lambda^{t(\lambda)}\}_{\lambda \in \mathbb{N}}$ *that satisfies the following: for every* λ *and* $x \in X_\lambda$, *(i) the set* $\mathbf{R}_x := \{(y_1, \ldots, y_t) \mid (x, (y_1, \ldots, y_t)) \in \mathbf{R}_\lambda\} \subseteq Y_\lambda^{t(\lambda)}$ *has a decomposition* $\mathbf{R}_x = S_1 \times S_2 \times \cdots \times S_{t(\lambda)}$, *(ii) each* S_i *satisfies* $|S_i| \leq \rho|Y_\lambda|$, *and (iii) each* S_i *is efficiently verifiable, i.e., there exists a polynomial-size circuit* C *such that* $C(x, y, i) = 1$ *iff* $y \in S_i$. *Furthermore, each hash function in the family can be evaluated in time* $\mathsf{poly}(\log|X_\lambda|, |Y_\lambda|, t_\lambda, |C|)$.

In our SNARG construction, we use the following encoding scheme for holographic verification. For a finite field $\mathbb{F}$ and a subset $\mathbb{H} \subseteq \mathbb{F}$, the *low-degree extension (LDE)* $\widehat{x}$ of $x \in \{0,1\}^n$ is defined by first viewing x as a function $x : \mathbb{H}^m \to \{0,1\}$ for $m := \lceil \log_{|\mathbb{H}|} n \rceil$ and next defining $\widehat{x} : \mathbb{F}^m \to \mathbb{F}$ as the unique m-variate polynomial that satisfies $\widehat{x}|_{\mathbb{H}^m} \equiv x$ with individual degree at most $|\mathbb{H}| - 1$. (In this paper, $\mathbb{F}$ and $\mathbb{H}$ are chosen so that $|\mathbb{H}| = O(\log n)$ and $|\mathbb{F}| = \text{poly}(|\mathbb{H}|)$.) What is crucial for us is that LDEs are *linear tensor codes*. In particular, the LDE $\widehat{x}$ of x satisfies the following for any $m' \in \{1, \ldots, m-1\}$.

Property 1. View $\widehat{x} : \mathbb{F}^m \to \mathbb{F}$ as a $|\mathbb{F}|^{m'} \times |\mathbb{F}|^{m-m'}$ matrix s.t. the i-th row is the truth table of $\widehat{x}(i, \cdot) : \mathbb{F}^{m-m'} \to \mathbb{F}$, where $i \in \{1, \ldots, |\mathbb{F}|^{m'}\}$ is mapped to an element of $\mathbb{F}^{m'}$ by a canonical bijection. Then, each row is a valid LDE of length $\mathbb{F}^{m-m'}$. In particular, the i-th row $\widehat{x}(i, \cdot)$ is the LDE of $\widehat{x}(i, \cdot)|_{\mathbb{H}^{m-m'}}$, where $\widehat{x}(i, \cdot)|_{\mathbb{H}^{m-m'}}$ is the restriction of $\widehat{x}(i, \cdot)$ to the domain $\mathbb{H}^{m-m'}$. Similarly, the j-th column $\widehat{x}(\cdot, j)$ is the LDE of $\widehat{x}(\cdot, j)|_{\mathbb{H}^{m'}}$ for $\forall j \in \{1, \ldots, |\mathbb{F}|^{m-m'}\}$.

Jumping ahead, we use the above property to obtain our SNARG in a recursive way. The prover creates a proof for x by recursively creating a proof for $\widehat{x}(i, \cdot)|_{\mathbb{H}^{m-m'}}$ for certain i. To verify the recursive proof, the verifier makes queries to $\widehat{x}(i, \cdot)$, which is indeed the LDE of $\widehat{x}(i, \cdot)|_{\mathbb{H}^{m-m'}}$ because of the above property. (The above property was used previously in a similar context by [32].)

Now, let us describe our construction. Recall that in holographic SNARGs for SE-hash computations, a statement consists of an input x, an SE hash function key h, and a hash value rt, which are supposed to satisfy $\mathsf{SEH.Hash}(h, x) = \mathsf{rt}$. For simplicity, we view x as a function $x : \mathbb{H}^m \to \mathbb{F}$, where $\mathbb{F}$ and $\mathbb{H}$ are those to be used to compute the LDE for the verifier. Also, we assume for simplicity that the security parameter λ is a power of $|\mathbb{H}|$. Let $m_\lambda := \log_{|\mathbb{H}|} \lambda$, $\delta := 1/(\lfloor m/m_\lambda \rfloor + 1)$, and $\alpha := \lfloor \lambda^\delta \rfloor$. Then, our construction is obtained recursively based on the input length m. When $m < m_\lambda$, the CRS generation and the prover do nothing, and the verifier directly checks $\mathsf{SEH.Hash}(h, x) \overset{?}{=} \mathsf{rt}$, where the verifier obtains x by using its oracle access to the LDE of x. When $m \geq m_\lambda$, our construction proceeds as described in Fig. 2. At a high level, the prover first views the LDE $\widehat{x}$ as a $|\mathbb{F}|^{m_\lambda} \times |\mathbb{F}|^{m-m_\lambda}$ matrix and obtains an SE hash value for each row (restricted to $\mathbb{H}^{m-m_\lambda}$ as suggested above). Then, the prover selects α rows based on the indices that are obtained by applying a CI hash function to the SE hash values, and recursively creates proofs about these rows. (The prover also creates batch proofs about the correctness of the SE hash values.)

Completeness can be verified by inspection. In particular, the verifier accepts the batch proof π^{idx} and the recursive proofs $\{\pi_{\mathbf{c}_i}\}_{\mathbf{c}_i \in S_{\mathbf{c}}}$ because of the above-described property of LDEs. Also, intuitively the efficiency requirement holds since the number of recursive executions is at most $\alpha^{\lfloor m/m_\lambda \rfloor + 1} \leq \lambda$.

To see somewhere soundness, we start with a toy case. For a statement (x, h, rt), consider a prover that behaves honestly for an incorrect statement (x', h, rt') s.t. $x' \neq x$ and $\mathsf{SEH.Hash}(h, x') = \mathsf{rt}'$. Since $x' \neq x$, their LDEs $\widehat{x}, \widehat{x}'$ (viewed as matrices) disagree in a certain column, say, the $\mathbf{v}^*$-th one. Since the $\mathbf{v}^*$-th columns of $\widehat{x}, \widehat{x}'$ are valid LDEs of length $|\mathbb{F}|^{m_\lambda}$ (i.e., they are m_λ-variate polynomials of individual degree at most $|\mathbb{H}| - 1$), it follows that they agree in at most a $\rho := m_\lambda(|\mathbb{H}| - 1)/|\mathbb{F}|$ fraction of the positions. Thus, if we set $|\mathbb{F}|$ large

Building blocks: (i) SEH.Hash—an SE hash function. (ii) $\mathsf{BARG}_{\mathrm{idx}}$—a BARG for the index language. (iii) $\mathcal{H} = \{\mathcal{H}_\lambda\}_{\lambda \in \mathbb{N}}$—a hash function family that is correlation intractable for efficiently product verifiable relation ensembles.

- -

CRS generation: Sample an SE hash function key h', a CI hash function $h^{\mathrm{CIH}} \in \mathcal{H}_\lambda$, and a CRS of $\mathsf{BARG}_{\mathrm{idx}}$. Also, recursively sample a CRS of itself for input length $m - m_\lambda$.

Prover P: Given (x, h, rt) and the CRS, compute a proof π as follows.

1. Compute the LDE $\widehat{x} : \mathbb{F}^m \to \mathbb{F}$ of x and view $\widehat{x}$ as a $|\mathbb{F}|^{m_\lambda} \times |\mathbb{F}|^{m-m_\lambda}$ matrix. For each $\mathbf{u} \in \mathbb{F}^{m_\lambda}$, let $\widehat{x}_{(\mathbf{u},*)}$ denote the $\mathbf{u}$-th row of the matrix.
   (a) Compute $\mathsf{rt}_\mathbf{u} := \mathsf{SEH.Hash}(h', x_{(\mathbf{u},*)})$ for $\forall \mathbf{u} \in \mathbb{F}^{m_\lambda}$, where $x_{(\mathbf{u},*)} := \widehat{x}_{(\mathbf{u},*)}|_{\mathbb{H}^{m-m_\lambda}}$.
   (b) For $\forall \mathbf{u} \in \mathbb{H}^{m_\lambda}$, use $\mathsf{BARG}_{\mathrm{idx}}$ to compute a proof $\pi_\mathbf{u}^{\mathrm{idx}}$ for the consistency between rt and $\mathsf{rt}_\mathbf{u}$ (i.e., prove that $\forall \mathbf{v} \in \mathbb{H}^{m-m_\lambda} \exists x'_{\mathbf{u},\mathbf{v}} \in \mathbb{F}$ s.t. both rt and $\mathsf{rt}_\mathbf{u}$ have $x'_{\mathbf{u},\mathbf{v}}$ in the appropriate positions of their pre-images).
   (c) Use $\mathsf{BARG}_{\mathrm{idx}}$ to compute a proof π^{idx} proving that each column that is hashed to $\{\mathsf{rt}_\mathbf{u}\}_{\mathbf{u} \in \mathbb{F}^{m_\lambda}}$ is a valid LDE (i.e., prove that $\forall \mathbf{v} \in \mathbb{H}^{m-m_\lambda} \exists x'_{(*,\mathbf{v})} : \mathbb{H}^{m_\lambda} \to \mathbb{F}$ s.t. the values in the $\mathbf{v}$-th position of the pre-images of $\{\mathsf{rt}_\mathbf{u}\}_{\mathbf{u} \in \mathbb{F}^{m_\lambda}}$ constitute the LDE of $x'_{(*,\mathbf{v})}$).
2. Apply h^{CIH} to $\{\mathsf{rt}_\mathbf{u}\}_{\mathbf{u} \in \mathbb{H}^{m_\lambda}}$ to obtain $S_\mathbf{c} := (\mathbf{c}_1, \ldots, \mathbf{c}_\alpha) \in \mathbb{F}^{m_\lambda} \times \cdots \times \mathbb{F}^{m_\lambda}$.
3. For $\forall \mathbf{c}_i \in S_\mathbf{c}$, recursively invoke the prover P for the statement $(x_{(\mathbf{c}_i,*)}, h', \mathsf{rt}_{\mathbf{c}_i})$ to obtain a proof $\pi_{\mathbf{c}_i}$.
4. Output $\pi := (\{\mathsf{rt}_\mathbf{u}\}_{\mathbf{u} \in \mathbb{F}^{m_\lambda}}, \{\pi_\mathbf{u}^{\mathrm{idx}}\}_{\mathbf{u} \in \mathbb{H}^{m_\lambda}}, \pi^{\mathrm{idx}}, \{\pi_{\mathbf{c}_i}\}_{\mathbf{c}_i \in S_\mathbf{c}})$.

Verifier V: Given (h, rt, π), the CRS, and oracle access to the LDE $\widehat{x}$:

1. Parse π as $(\{\mathsf{rt}_\mathbf{u}\}_{\mathbf{u} \in \mathbb{F}^{m_\lambda}}, \{\pi_\mathbf{u}^{\mathrm{idx}}\}_{\mathbf{u} \in \mathbb{H}^{m_\lambda}}, \pi^{\mathrm{idx}}, \{\pi_{\mathbf{c}_i}\}_{\mathbf{c}_i \in S_\mathbf{c}})$.
2. Apply h^{CIH} to $\{\mathsf{rt}_\mathbf{u}\}_{\mathbf{u} \in \mathbb{H}^{m_\lambda}}$ to obtain $S_\mathbf{c} := (\mathbf{c}_1, \ldots, \mathbf{c}_\alpha) \in \mathbb{F}^{m_\lambda} \times \cdots \times \mathbb{F}^{m_\lambda}$.
3. Output 1 iff all of the proofs $\{\pi_\mathbf{u}^{\mathrm{idx}}\}_{\mathbf{u} \in \mathbb{H}^{m_\lambda}}, \pi^{\mathrm{idx}}, \{\pi_{\mathbf{c}_i}\}_{\mathbf{c}_i \in S_\mathbf{c}}$ are accepting, where each recursive proof $\pi_{\mathbf{c}_i}$ is verified for the statement $(x_{(\mathbf{c}_i,*)}, h', \mathsf{rt}_{\mathbf{c}_i})$ by recursively invoking the verifier V with oracle $\widehat{x}(\mathbf{c}_i, \cdot)$.

Fig. 2. Overview of our holographic SNARG for SE-hashing (when $m \geq m_\lambda$).

enough, $\widehat{x}$ and $\widehat{x}'$ disagree in a constant fraction of the rows. By temporarily thinking as if h^{CIH} is a truly random function, we conclude that with high probability, one of the recursive proofs is created for a row in which $\widehat{x}$ and $\widehat{x}'$ disagree. Thus, after the recursions, the verifier rejects the proof in the base case.

Let us observe somewhere soundness in more detail. Naturally, we show the somewhere soundness by relying on the somewhere soundness of the recursive executions. Assume for contradiction that a PPT cheating prover P^* breaks the somewhere soundness, i.e., $\exists x : \mathbb{H}^m \to \mathbb{F}$ and $\sigma = (\mathbf{u}^*, \mathbf{v}^*) \in \mathbb{H}^{m_\lambda} \times \mathbb{H}^{m-m_\lambda} = \mathbb{H}^m$ s.t. for a random SE hash function key h that is statistically binding in position $(\mathbf{u}^*, \mathbf{v}^*)$, the cheating prover P^* produces an accepting proof π along with a hash value rt s.t. $\mathsf{SEH.Ext}(\mathsf{td}, \mathsf{rt}) \neq x(\mathbf{u}^*, \mathbf{v}^*)$, where td is the trapdoor corresponding to h. Note that, due to the index hiding property of the underlying SE hash function, P^* breaks the somewhere soundness even when the CRS generation algorithm samples the SE hash function key h' in a way that h' is statistically binding in position $\mathbf{v}^*$. Let $\{\widetilde{x}_{(\mathbf{u},\mathbf{v}^*)}\}_{\mathbf{u}\in\mathbb{F}^{m\lambda}}$ denote the column that we can extract by using SEH.Ext for the hash values $\{\mathsf{rt}_\mathbf{u}\}_{\mathbf{u}\in\mathbb{F}^{m\lambda}}$ that P^* provides as the hashes of the rows. To use P^* to break the soundness of a recursive proof, we show that $\exists i \in [\alpha]$ s.t. the i-th recursive statement $(x_{(\mathbf{c}_i,*)}, h', \mathsf{rt}_{\mathbf{c}_i})$ is false, i.e., the $\mathbf{c}_i$-th row of the extracted column $\{\widetilde{x}_{(\mathbf{u},\mathbf{v}^*)}\}_{\mathbf{u}\in\mathbb{F}^{m\lambda}}$ disagrees with the correct value $\widehat{x}(\mathbf{c}_i, \mathbf{v}^*)$. Put differently, we show that the output $(\mathbf{c}_1, \ldots, \mathbf{c}_\alpha)$ of the CI hash function is not included in the set $S_1 \times \cdots \times S_\alpha$ s.t. $S_i := \{\mathbf{c} \in \mathbb{F}^{m\lambda} \mid \widetilde{x}_{(\mathbf{c},\mathbf{v}^*)} = \widehat{x}(\mathbf{c}, \mathbf{v}^*)\}$. Toward this goal, we can use the correlation intractability of h^{CIH} straightforwardly since we have $|S_i| \leq \rho|\mathbb{F}|^{m\lambda}$ for a constant ρ as shown below.[6]

Let $\widetilde{x}_{(*,\mathbf{v}^*)} : \mathbb{F}^{m\lambda} \to \mathbb{F}$ be the function representing the extracted column, i.e., $\widetilde{x}_{(*,\mathbf{v}^*)} : \mathbf{u} \mapsto \widetilde{x}_{(\mathbf{u},\mathbf{v}^*)}$. The somewhere soundness of $\mathsf{BARG}_{\mathrm{idx}}$ guarantees that $\widetilde{x}_{(*,\mathbf{v}^*)}$ is a valid LDE s.t. $\widetilde{x}_{(*,\mathbf{v}^*)}(\mathbf{u}^*) = \mathsf{SEH.Ext}(\mathsf{td}, \mathsf{rt})$. Since we assumed $\mathsf{SEH.Ext}(\mathsf{td}, \mathsf{rt}) \neq x(\mathbf{u}^*, \mathbf{v}^*)$ for contradiction, it follows that $\widetilde{x}_{(*,\mathbf{v}^*)}$ and $\widehat{x}(\cdot, \mathbf{v}^*)$ are valid LDEs that disagree in position $\mathbf{u}^*$. Thus, by appropriately setting the parameter of the LDE, we can guarantee that $\widetilde{x}_{(*,\mathbf{v}^*)}$ and $\widehat{x}(\cdot, \mathbf{v}^*)$ disagree in a constant fraction of positions.

Thus, the correlation intractability of h^{CIH} guarantees that $\exists i \in [\alpha]$ s.t. $\widetilde{x}_{(\mathbf{c}_i,\mathbf{v}^*)} \neq \widehat{x}(\mathbf{c}_i, \mathbf{v}^*)$, i.e., the recursive statement $(x_{(\mathbf{c}_i,*)}, h', \mathsf{rt}_{\mathbf{c}_i})$ is false. Thus, we can break the soundness of a recursive execution and reach a contradiction.

2.2   Holographic SNARG for Batch-NP

Our starting point is the non-holographic SNARG for Batch-NP by Choudhuri, Jain, and Jin (CJJ) [11], which is non-holographic only in that the verifier computes an SE hash of the instances. Concretely, the CJJ SNARG works as follows. For k instances $x_1, \ldots, x_k$ of an NP language $\mathbf{L}$, the prover computes a hash rt of the instances using an SE hash function and then uses a BARG for the index language to prove the following for each $i \in [k]$: (i) the i-th position of the preimage of the hash rt can be opened to an instance $\widetilde{x}_i$ and (ii) $\widetilde{x}_i \in \mathbf{L}$. The verifier computes the SE hash of the instances and verifies the BARG proof.

We make the CJJ SNARG holographic by letting the prover send the hash of the instances along with a holographic proof about the correctness of the hash. For the analysis of the CJJ SNARG to go through, the proof about the SE hash needs to have the following weak form of soundness: if the i-th instance is extracted from the hash, the extracted instance is equal to x_i. This form of soundness is precisely what our somewhere-sound holographic SNARG for SE-hashing guarantees. Thus, combining it with the CJJ SNARG suffices.

---

[6] S_i is efficiently verifiable by a circuit that has $\{\mathsf{td}_\mathbf{u}\}_{\mathbf{u}\in\mathbb{F}^{m\lambda}}$ and $\{\widehat{x}(\mathbf{u}, \mathbf{v}^*)\}_{\mathbf{u}\in\mathbb{F}^{m\lambda}}$ as hardwired inputs.

3   Preliminaries

We use λ to denote the security parameter. For any finite field $\mathbb{F}$, a subset $\mathbb{H} \subseteq \mathbb{F}$, and an integer $m \in \mathbb{N}$, the *low-degree extension (LDE)* of a function $x : \mathbb{H}^m \to \mathbb{F}$ (or its truth table) is denoted by $\mathsf{LDE}_{\mathbb{F},\mathbb{H},m}(x)$. More details about LDEs and other standard notations are explained in the full version of this paper.

3.1   Hash Functions

A *hash function family* for a domain-codomain ensemble $\{(X_\lambda, Y_\lambda)\}_{\lambda \in \mathbb{N}}$ can be modeled by two algorithms $\mathcal{H} = (\mathsf{Gen}, \mathsf{Hash})$, where $\mathsf{Gen}(1^\lambda)$ outputs a key h and $\mathsf{Hash}(h, x)$ outputs the hash value $y \in Y_\lambda$ of $x \in X_\lambda$. A hash function family is called *public-coin* [19] if $\mathsf{Gen}(1^\lambda)$ outputs a uniformly random string. We use $\mathcal{H}_\lambda$ to denote the range of $\mathsf{Gen}(1^\lambda)$, use $h \leftarrow \mathcal{H}_\lambda$ as a shorthand of $h \leftarrow \mathsf{Gen}(1^\lambda)$, and use $h(x)$ as a shorthand of $\mathsf{Hash}(h, x)$.

For any $h : \{0,1\}^{2\lambda} \to \{0,1\}^\lambda$ and $\ell \in \mathbb{N}$, the *tree-hash* of a string $x \in \{0,1\}^{2^\ell \lambda}$ is defined as follows: (i) partition x into 2^ℓ blocks $\mathsf{blk}_0, \ldots, \mathsf{blk}_{2^\ell - 1}$ of length λ; (ii) let $\mathsf{node}_{\ell,\sigma} := \mathsf{blk}_\sigma$ for $\forall \sigma \in \{0, \ldots, 2^\ell - 1\}$ and $\mathsf{node}_{i,\sigma} := h(\mathsf{node}_{i+1,2\sigma} \,\|\, \mathsf{node}_{i+1,2\sigma+1})$ for $\forall i \in \{\ell - 1, \ldots, 0\}, \sigma \in \{0, \ldots, 2^i - 1\}$, and (iii) define the tree-hash, denoted as $\mathsf{TreeHash}_h(x)$, to be $\mathsf{node}_{0,0}$.

3.2   Correlation-Intractable Hash Functions

We recall the definition of *correlation-intractable hash functions* [6].

Definition 1. *Let* $\mathcal{H} = (\mathsf{Gen}, \mathsf{Hash})$ *be a hash function family and* $\{(X_\lambda, Y_\lambda)\}_{\lambda \in \mathbb{N}}$ *be its domain-codomain ensemble. Then,* $\mathcal{H}$ *is* **correlation intractable** *for a relation ensemble* $\boldsymbol{R} = \{\boldsymbol{R}_\lambda \subseteq X_\lambda \times Y_\lambda\}_{\lambda \in \mathbb{N}}$ *if for every* PPT *algorithm* $\mathcal{A}$, *there exists a negligible function* negl *such that for every* $\lambda \in \mathbb{N}$ *and* $z \in \{0,1\}^*$,

$$\Pr\left[(x,y) \in \boldsymbol{R}_\lambda \mid h \leftarrow \mathsf{Gen}(1^\lambda);\ x \leftarrow \mathcal{A}(h,z);\ y := \mathsf{Hash}(h,x)\right] \leq \mathsf{negl}(\lambda) \ .$$

Next, we recall a result by Holmgren, Lombardi, and Rothblum [17] about correlation intractability for *efficiently verifiable product relations*.

Definition 2. ([16, Definition 3.1]). *A relation* $\boldsymbol{R} \subseteq X \times Y^t$ *is said to be a* **product relation** *if for every* $x \in X$, *the set* $\boldsymbol{R}_x := \{(y_1, \ldots, y_t) \mid (x, (y_1, \ldots, y_t)) \in \boldsymbol{R}\} \subseteq Y^t$ *has a decomposition* $\boldsymbol{R}_x = S_1 \times S_2 \times \cdots \times S_t$, *where* $S_1, \ldots, S_t \subseteq Y$ *may depend on* x.

Definition 3. ([16, Definition 3.3], slightly generalized). *For any* $T \in \mathbb{N}$, *a product relation* $\boldsymbol{R} \subseteq X \times Y^t$ *is called* T**-time product verifiable** *if there exists a size-T circuit* C *such that for every input* $x \in X$ *with the corresponding sets* $S_1, \ldots, S_t$ *as in Definition 2, it holds that* $C(x, y, i) = 1$ *iff* $y \in S_i$.[7]

---

[7] The definition is slightly modified in that the size of C is required to be bounded by T rather than an arbitrary polynomial.

Definition 4. ([16, Definition 3.4]). *For any $\rho \in [0,1]$, a product relation $\boldsymbol{R} \subseteq X \times Y^t$ is said to have **product sparsity** ρ if for every input $x \in X$, the sets $S_1, \ldots, S_t$ as in Definition 2 have size at most $\rho|Y|$.*

Theorem 1 ([16, Theorem 5.1]). *Let $T : \mathbb{N} \to \mathbb{N}$ and $\rho : \mathbb{N} \to [0,1]$ be functions and $\boldsymbol{R} = \{\boldsymbol{R}_\lambda \subseteq X_\lambda \times Y_\lambda^{t_\lambda}\}_{\lambda \in \mathbb{N}}$ be an ensemble of product relations such that (i) each $\boldsymbol{R}_\lambda$ is $T(\lambda)$-time product verifiable with product sparsity $\rho(\lambda)$, (ii) $|Y_\lambda|$, $\log|X_\lambda|$, $T(\lambda)$, and t_λ are all upper bounded by $\lambda^{O(1)}$, and (iii) $t_\lambda \geq \lambda/\log(1/\rho(\lambda))$. Let $X := \{X_\lambda\}_{\lambda \in \mathbb{N}}$, $Y := \{Y_\lambda\}_{\lambda \in \mathbb{N}}$ and $t := \{t_\lambda\}_{\lambda \in \mathbb{N}}$. Then, for the domain-codomain ensemble $\{X_\lambda, Y_\lambda^{t_\lambda}\}_{\lambda \in \mathbb{N}}$, there exists a hash function family $\mathcal{H}$ that is correlation intractable for $\boldsymbol{R}$ under the LWE assumption. Moreover, $\mathcal{H}$ depends only on (X, Y, ρ, t, T) (and is otherwise independent of $\boldsymbol{R}$) and can be evaluated in time $\mathsf{poly}(\log|X_\lambda|, |Y_\lambda|, t_\lambda, T(\lambda))$.*

Several remarks about Theorem 1 are given below. First, the correlation-intractable hash function family $\mathcal{H}$ of Theorem 1 can be made public-coin. Also, $\mathcal{H}$ can be efficiently determined given (X, Y, ρ, t, T), and its correlation intractability holds for a negligible function that depends only on (X, Y, ρ, t, T) (and is otherwise independent of $\boldsymbol{R}$). Additionally, as mentioned in [16, Section 5.1], the condition $t_\lambda \geq \lambda/\log(1/\rho(\lambda))$ in Theorem 1 can be weakened to $t_\lambda \geq \lambda^\delta/\log(1/\rho(\lambda))$ for an arbitrarily small constant $\delta > 0$. Similarly, if the LWE assumption holds against slightly super-polynomial-time adversaries, the condition can be weakened to $t_\lambda \geq \lambda^{1/\tau(\lambda)}/\log(1/\rho(\lambda))$ for a super-constant function $\tau(\lambda) = \omega(1)$. (For details, see the full version of this paper.)

3.3 Somewhere Extractable Hash Functions

We recall the definition of *somewhere extractable hash functions* [9,11,20]. The following definition is adapted from [10, Section 3.5]. For the differences from the original definition, see the full version of this paper.

Definition 5. *A **somewhere extractable hash function family** consists of a tuple of algorithms $(\mathsf{Gen}, \mathsf{TGen}, \mathsf{Hash}, \mathsf{Open}, \mathsf{Ver}, \mathsf{Ext})$ satisfying the following.*

- *Syntax. Gen and TGen are probabilistic and the others are deterministic.*
- *Opening correctness. For every $\lambda \in \mathbb{N}$, $N \in [2^\lambda]$, $M_I \in [N]$, $i \in [N]$, and $m = (m_1, \ldots, m_N) \in \{0,1\}^N$,*

$$\Pr\left[\mathsf{Ver}(h, \mathsf{rt}, m_i, i, \mathsf{cert}_i) = 1 \,\middle|\, \begin{array}{l} h \leftarrow \mathsf{Gen}(1^\lambda, N, 1^{M_I}); \ \mathsf{rt} := \mathsf{Hash}(h, m) \\ \mathsf{cert}_i := \mathsf{Open}(h, m, i) \end{array}\right] = 1 \ .$$

- *Key indistinguishability. For every PPT algorithms $(\mathcal{A}_1, \mathcal{A}_2)$ and polynomial poly_N, there exists a negligible function negl such that for every $\lambda \in \mathbb{N}$, $N \leq \mathsf{poly}_N(\lambda)$, and $z \in \{0,1\}^*$,*

$$\left| \Pr\left[\mathcal{A}_2(\mathsf{st}, h) = 1 \,\middle|\, \begin{array}{l} (\mathsf{st}, I) \leftarrow \mathcal{A}_1(1^\lambda, N, z) \\ h \leftarrow \mathsf{Gen}(1^\lambda, N, 1^{|I|}) \end{array}\right] - \Pr\left[\mathcal{A}_2(\mathsf{st}, h) = 1 \,\middle|\, \begin{array}{l} (\mathsf{st}, I) \leftarrow \mathcal{A}_1(1^\lambda, N, z) \\ (h, \mathsf{td}) \leftarrow \mathsf{TGen}(1^\lambda, N, I) \end{array}\right] \right| \leq \mathsf{negl}(\lambda) \ .$$

- **Somewhere (statistical) extractability.** For any polynomial poly_I, there exists a negligible function negl such that for every $\lambda \in \mathbb{N}$, $N \in [2^\lambda]$, and $I \subseteq [N]$ such that $|I| \le \mathsf{poly}_I(\lambda)$,

$$\Pr\left[\begin{array}{l} \exists \; \mathsf{rt}, m_{i^*}, i^*, \mathsf{cert}_{i^*} \; s.t. \\ i^* \in I \wedge \mathsf{Ver}(h, \mathsf{rt}, m_{i^*}, i^*, \mathsf{cert}_{i^*}) = 1 \wedge \widetilde{m}_{i^*} \ne m_{i^*} \end{array}\right] \le \mathsf{negl}(\lambda) \; ,$$

where (i) the probability is taken over $(h, \mathsf{td}) \leftarrow \mathsf{TGen}(1^\lambda, N, I)$ and (ii) $\widetilde{m}_{i^*}$ is defined by $\{\widetilde{m}_i\}_{i \in I} := \mathsf{Ext}(\mathsf{td}, \mathsf{rt})$.

- **Efficiency.** In the above opening correctness experiment, the following hold.
  - The key generation Gen runs in time $\mathsf{poly}(\lambda, \log N, M_I)$.
  - The hashing algorithm Hash runs in time $\mathsf{poly}(\lambda, N)$ and outputs a hash value rt of length $\mathsf{poly}(\lambda, \log N, M_I)$.
  - The opening algorithm Open runs in time $\mathsf{poly}(\lambda, N)$ and outputs a certificate cert_i of length $\mathsf{poly}(\lambda, \log N, M_I)$.
  - The verifier Ver runs in time $\mathsf{poly}(\lambda, \log N, M_I)$.

Also, in the above extractability experiment, the following hold.
  - The trapdoor key generation TGen runs in time $\mathsf{poly}(\lambda, \log N, M_I)$.
  - The extractor Ext runs in time $\mathsf{poly}(\lambda, \log N, M_I)$.

As observed in [11], the LWE-based (public-coin) hash functions family by Hubacek and Wichs [20] is somewhere extractable.

Theorem 2. *Under the LWE assumption, there exists a (public-coin) somewhere extractable hash function family.*

Somewhere Extractable Hash for Non-binary Alphabets. In this paper, somewhere extractable hash functions are also used for strings over a finite field $\mathbb{F}$, where Definition 5 is straightforwardly generalized for non-binary alphabets. Concretely, $\mathbf{v} = (v_1, \ldots, v_N) \in \mathbb{F}^N$ is hashed by hashing $(v_{1,j}, \ldots, v_{N,j})$ for every $j \in [\log|\mathbb{F}|]$, where $v_{i,j}$ is the j-th bit of v_i. The running time of Gen remains the same since the same key can be used for all the hashes, while the complexities related to the other algorithms increase by a multiplicative factor $\log|\mathbb{F}|$.

3.4 SNARGs for P (a.k.a. Non-Interactive TM Delegations)

We recall the definition of SNARGs for P, a.k.a. *publicly verifiable non-interactive Turing-machine delegation schemes*. The following definitions are adapted from those given in [23, Section 3.1]. A major difference from the original definitions is that we consider schemes for two-input Turing machines and define soundness in the *partially adaptive setting* [5], where the first input is non-adaptively determined while the second one is adaptively chosen by the prover. For other differences, see the full version of this paper.

Definition 6. *For a (deterministic) Turing machine M, let*

$$L_M := \{(\chi, T) \mid M \text{ accepts } \chi \text{ within } T \text{ steps}\} \; .$$

Definition 7. *For a (deterministic) two-input Turing machine M and pair of functions $T_{\mathsf{Gen}} : \mathbb{N} \times \mathbb{N} \to \mathbb{N}$, $L_\pi : \mathbb{N} \times \mathbb{N} \to \mathbb{N}$, a triple of algorithms $(\mathsf{Gen}, \mathsf{P}, \mathsf{V})$ is called a **partially adaptive publicly verifiable non-interactive delegation scheme for M with setup time T_{Gen} and proof length L_π** if it satisfies the following.*

- *Syntax. Gen is probabilistic and the others are deterministic.*
- *Completeness. For every $\lambda, T, n_1, n_2 \in \mathbb{N}$ and $\chi = (\chi_1, \chi_2) \in \{0,1\}^{n_1} \times \{0,1\}^{n_2}$ such that $n := n_1 + n_2 \leq T \leq 2^\lambda$ and $(\chi, T) \in \boldsymbol{L}_M$,*

$$\Pr\left[\mathsf{V}(\mathsf{crs}, \chi, \pi) = 1 \mid \mathsf{crs} \leftarrow \mathsf{Gen}(1^\lambda, T, n_1, n_2); \; \pi := \mathsf{P}(\mathsf{crs}, \chi)\right] = 1 \;.$$

- *Partially adaptive soundness. For every PPT algorithm P^* and triple of polynomials poly_T, poly_{n_1}, poly_{n_2}, there exists a negligible function negl such that for every $\lambda \in \mathbb{N}$, $T \leq \mathsf{poly}_T(\lambda)$, $n_1 \leq \mathsf{poly}_{n_1}(\lambda)$, $n_2 \leq \mathsf{poly}_{n_2}(\lambda)$, $\chi_1 \in \{0,1\}^{n_1}$, and $z \in \{0,1\}^*$,*

$$\Pr\left[\begin{array}{l}\mathsf{V}(\mathsf{crs}, \chi, \pi) = 1 \\ \wedge \; (\chi, T) \notin \boldsymbol{L}_M \end{array} \middle| \begin{array}{l}\mathsf{crs} \leftarrow \mathsf{Gen}(1^\lambda, T, n_1, n_2) \\ (\chi_2, \pi) \leftarrow \mathsf{P}^*(\mathsf{crs}, \chi_1, z); \; \chi := (\chi_1, \chi_2)\end{array}\right] \leq \mathsf{negl}(\lambda) \;.$$

- *Efficiency. In the above completeness experiment, the following hold.*
  - *The setup algorithm Gen runs in time $T_{\mathsf{Gen}}(\lambda, T, n_1, n_2)$.*
  - *The prover P runs in time $\mathsf{poly}(\lambda, T)$ and outputs a proof π of length $L_\pi(\lambda, T, n_1, n_2)$.*
  - *The verifier V runs in time $O(L_\pi) + \mathsf{poly}(\lambda, n)$.[8]*

*A publicly verifiable non-interactive delegation scheme is called **public-coin** if the setup algorithm Gen is public-coin, i.e., it just outputs a string that is sampled uniformly randomly (possibly along with various parameters that are determined deterministically based on the input of Gen).*

Definition 8. *For a super-polynomial function γ, a partially adaptive publicly verifiable non-interactive delegation scheme is called γ-secure if the partial adaptive soundness holds even when (i) the adversary P^* runs in time $\mathsf{poly}(\gamma(\lambda))$ and (ii) the polynomials poly_T, poly_{n_1}, poly_{n_2} are all replaced with γ.*

3.5 SNARGs for Batch-NP (a.k.a Non-Interactive BARGs)

We recall the definition of SNARGs for Batch-NP, a.k.a. *publicly verifiable non-interactive batch arguments (BARGs)*. The following definitions are adapted from those given in [10, Section 4.1]. For the differences from the original definitions, see the full version of this paper.

Definition 9. *Let $\boldsymbol{R}_{\mathbf{CSAT}}$ be the relation defined as $\boldsymbol{R}_{\mathbf{CSAT}} := \{((C, x), w) \mid C$ is a Boolean circuit s.t. $C(x, w) = 1\}$. Then, $\mathbf{CSAT}$ is the language defined as $\mathbf{CSAT} := \{(C, x) \mid \exists w \; s.t. \; ((C, x), w) \in \boldsymbol{R}_{\mathbf{CSAT}}\}$.*

---

[8] For convenience, we use a slightly weaker bound than prior works [25], where the bound is $O(L_\pi) + n \cdot \mathsf{poly}(\lambda)$.

Definition 10. *For any $k \in \mathbb{N}$, let*

$$R_{\mathrm{CSAT}}^{\otimes k} := \left\{ ((C, \mathbf{x}), \mathbf{w}) \;\middle|\; \begin{array}{l} \mathbf{x} = (x_1, \ldots, x_k) \text{ and } \mathbf{w} = (w_1, \ldots, w_k) \text{ satisfy} \\ ((C, x_i), w_i) \in R_{\mathrm{CSAT}} \text{ for } \forall i \in [k] \end{array} \right\} .$$

Then, for any $k \in \mathbb{N}$, $\mathbf{CSAT}^{\otimes k}$ is the language defined as $\mathbf{CSAT}^{\otimes k} := \{(C, \mathbf{x}) \mid \exists \mathbf{w} \; s.t. \; ((C, \mathbf{x}), \mathbf{w}) \in R_{\mathrm{CSAT}}^{\otimes k}\}$.

Definition 11. *A triple of algorithms $(\mathsf{Gen}, \mathsf{P}, \mathsf{V})$ is called a **(non-adaptive) publicly verifiable non-interactive batch argument for CSAT** if it satisfies the following.*

- **Syntax.** Gen *is probabilistic and the others are deterministic.*
- **Completeness.** *For every $\lambda, k, n \in \mathbb{N}$ and $((C, \mathbf{x}), \mathbf{w}) \in R_{\mathrm{CSAT}}^{\otimes k}$ such that $\mathbf{x} \in (\{0,1\}^n)^k$,*

$$\Pr\left[\mathsf{V}(\mathsf{crs}, C, \mathbf{x}, \pi) = 1 \;\middle|\; \mathsf{crs} \leftarrow \mathsf{Gen}(1^\lambda, 1^n, 1^{|C|}, k); \; \pi := \mathsf{P}(\mathsf{crs}, C, \mathbf{x}, \mathbf{w}) \right] = 1 .$$

- **(Non-adaptive) Soundness.** *For every PPT algorithm P^* and pair of polynomials $\mathsf{poly}_k, \mathsf{poly}_C$, there exists a negligible function negl such that for every $\lambda \in \mathbb{N}$, $k \leq \mathsf{poly}_k(\lambda)$, $M_C \leq \mathsf{poly}_C(\lambda)$, $n \leq M_C$, $(C, \mathbf{x}) \notin \mathbf{CSAT}^{\otimes k}$, and $z \in \{0,1\}^*$ such that $|C| \leq M_C$ and $\mathbf{x} \in (\{0,1\}^n)^k$,*

$$\Pr\left[\mathsf{V}(\mathsf{crs}, C, \mathbf{x}, \pi) = 1 \;\middle|\; \begin{array}{l} \mathsf{crs} \leftarrow \mathsf{Gen}(1^\lambda, 1^n, 1^{M_C}, k) \\ \pi \leftarrow \mathsf{P}^*(\mathsf{crs}, C, \mathbf{x}, z) \end{array} \right] \leq \mathsf{negl}(\lambda) .$$

- **Efficiency.** *In the above completeness experiment, the following hold.*
  - *The setup algorithm Gen runs in time $\mathsf{poly}(\lambda, |C|, \log k)$.*
  - *The prover P runs in time $\mathsf{poly}(\lambda, |C|, k)$ and outputs a proof π of length $\mathsf{poly}(\lambda, |C|, \log k)$.*
  - *The verifier V runs in time $\mathsf{poly}(\lambda, n, k) + \mathsf{poly}(\lambda, M_C, \log k)$.*

*A publicly verifiable non-interactive batch argument is called **public-coin** if the setup algorithm Gen is public-coin, i.e., it just outputs a string that is sampled uniformly randomly (possibly along with various parameters that are determined deterministically based on the input of Gen).*

Definition 12. *A publicly verifiable non-interactive batch argument $(\mathsf{Gen}, \mathsf{P}, \mathsf{V})$ for CSAT is called **semi-adaptive somewhere sound** if there exists a PPT algorithm TGen that satisfies the following.*

- **CRS indistinguishability.** *For every PPT algorithms $(\mathcal{A}_1, \mathcal{A}_2)$ and pair of polynomials $\mathsf{poly}_k, \mathsf{poly}_C$, there exists a negligible function negl such that for every $\lambda \in \mathbb{N}$, $k \leq \mathsf{poly}_k(\lambda)$, $M_C \leq \mathsf{poly}_C(\lambda)$, $n \leq M_C$, and $z \in \{0,1\}^*$,*

$$\left| \begin{array}{l} \Pr\left[\mathcal{A}_2(\mathsf{st}, \mathsf{crs}) = 1 \;\middle|\; \begin{array}{l} (\mathsf{st}, i^*) \leftarrow \mathcal{A}_1(1^\lambda, 1^n, 1^{M_C}, k, z) \\ \mathsf{crs} \leftarrow \mathsf{Gen}(1^\lambda, 1^n, 1^{M_C}, k) \end{array} \right] \\ - \Pr\left[\mathcal{A}_2(\mathsf{st}, \mathsf{crs}) = 1 \;\middle|\; \begin{array}{l} (\mathsf{st}, i^*) \leftarrow \mathcal{A}_1(1^\lambda, 1^n, 1^{M_C}, k, z) \\ (\mathsf{crs}, \mathsf{td}) \leftarrow \mathsf{TGen}(1^\lambda, 1^n, 1^{M_C}, k, i^*) \end{array} \right] \end{array} \right| \leq \mathsf{negl}(\lambda) .$$

- **Semi-adaptive somewhere soundness.** *For every* PPT *algorithm* P^* *and pair of polynomials* poly_k, poly_C, *there exists a negligible function* negl *such that for every* $\lambda \in \mathbb{N}$, $k \leq \text{poly}_k(\lambda)$, $M_C \leq \text{poly}_C(\lambda)$, $n \leq M_C$, *and* $z \in \{0,1\}^*$,

$$\Pr\left[\begin{array}{l} V(\text{crs}, C, \mathbf{x}, \pi) = 1 \\ \wedge\, i^* \in [k] \\ \wedge\, (C, x_{i^*}) \notin \mathbf{CSAT} \end{array} \middle| \begin{array}{l} (\text{st}, i^*) \leftarrow P_1^*(1^\lambda, 1^n, 1^{M_C}, k, z) \\ \text{crs} \leftarrow \text{TGen}(1^\lambda, 1^n, 1^{M_C}, k, i^*) \\ (C, \mathbf{x}, \pi) \leftarrow P_2^*(\text{st}, \text{crs}), \\ \text{where } \mathbf{x} = (x_1, \ldots, x_k) \in (\{0,1\}^n)^k \end{array}\right] \leq \text{negl}(\lambda)\ .$$

Weakly Semi-adaptive Somewhere Soundness. We define a new soundness notion that lies between non-adaptive soundness and semi-adaptive somewhere soundness. The difference from semi-adaptive somewhere soundness is that the instances $\mathbf{x}$ are fixed non-adaptively (the circuit C is still chosen adaptively).

Definition 13. *A publicly verifiable non-interactive batch argument* (Gen, P, V) *for* **CSAT** *is called **weakly semi-adaptive somewhere sound** if there exists a* PPT *algorithm* TGen *that satisfies the following.*

- **CRS indistinguishability.** *Identical with the one in Definition 12.*
- **Weakly semi-adaptive somewhere soundness.** *For every* PPT *algorithm* P^* *and pair of polynomials* poly_k, poly_C, *there exists a negligible function* negl *such that for every* $\lambda \in \mathbb{N}$, $k \leq \text{poly}_k(\lambda)$, $M_C \leq \text{poly}_C(\lambda)$, $n \leq M_C$, *and* $z \in \{0,1\}^*$,

$$\Pr\left[\begin{array}{l} V(\text{crs}, C, \mathbf{x}, \pi) = 1 \\ \wedge\, i^* \in [k] \\ \wedge\, (C, x_{i^*}) \notin \mathbf{CSAT} \end{array} \middle| \begin{array}{l} (\text{st}, i^*, \mathbf{x}) \leftarrow P_1^*(1^\lambda, 1^n, 1^{M_C}, k, z), \\ \text{where } \mathbf{x} = (x_1, \ldots, x_k) \in (\{0,1\}^n)^k \\ \text{crs} \leftarrow \text{TGen}(1^\lambda, 1^n, 1^{M_C}, k, i^*) \\ (C, \pi) \leftarrow P_2^*(\text{st}, \text{crs}) \end{array}\right] \leq \text{negl}(\lambda)\ .$$

Non-interactive BARGs for the Index Language. We recall the definition and a known result of *publicly verifiable non-interactive BARGs for the index language* [11].

Definition 14. *Publicly verifiable non-interactive batch arguments for the indexed language are a special case of publicly verifiable non-interactive batch arguments for* **CSAT** *(Definition 11), with the following differences.*

- **Syntax.** *The instances* $\mathbf{x} = (x_1, \ldots, x_k)$ *are fixed to be the indices* $\mathbf{x} = (1, \ldots, k)$, *and they are not given to the prover* P *and the verifier* V. *Also, the instance length* n *is not given to the setup algorithm* Gen. *(It is assumed that* P *and* V *can learn* k *from the common reference string* crs.*)*
- **Efficiency.** *The requirement about the running time of the verifier* V *is strengthened to* $\text{poly}(\lambda, M_C, \log k)$.

Theorem 3 ([11]). *Under the LWE assumption, there exists a public-coin non-interactive batch argument for the index language. Furthermore, it satisfies semi-adaptive somewhere soundness.*

3.6   Holographic SNARGs for P and Batch-NP

We define holographic SNARGs for P and Batch-NP by naturally combining the definitions of non-interactive Turing-machine delegations and BARGs with the definitions of holographic interactive proofs/arguments [5,15].

Definition 15. *Let M be a two-input Turing machine. A publicly verifiable non-interactive delegation scheme $(\mathsf{Gen}, \mathsf{P}, \mathsf{V})$ for M is called **holographic** if there exists a deterministic polynomial-time algorithm Encode such that the execution of the verifier on input $(\mathsf{crs}, (\chi_1, \chi_2), \pi)$ can be written as $\mathsf{V}^{\widehat{\chi}_1}(\mathsf{crs}, (|\chi_1|, \chi_2), \pi)$ for $\widehat{\chi}_1 := \mathsf{Encode}(\lambda, \chi_1)$, where the verifier works in two steps as follows.*

1. *Without making queries to $\widehat{\chi}_1$, the verifier either immediately outputs 0 (i.e., rejects the proof) or computes a set $I \subseteq [\widehat{n}]$ of queries along with a set $Z \subseteq \Sigma^{\widehat{n}}$ of expected responses. (Σ is the alphabet of $\widehat{\chi}_1$ and $\widehat{n}$ is the block length.) This step takes time at most $O(L_\pi) + \mathsf{poly}(\lambda, \log|\chi_1|, |\chi_2|)$, where L_π is the length of the proof π.*
2. *The verifier makes the queries to $\widehat{\chi}_1$, and it outputs 1 iff $\widehat{\chi}_1|_I = Z$.*

Definition 16. *A publicly verifiable non-interactive batch argument $(\mathsf{Gen}, \mathsf{P}, \mathsf{V})$ is called **holographic** if there exists a deterministic polynomial-time algorithm Encode such that the execution of the verifier on input $(\mathsf{crs}, C, \mathbf{x}, \pi)$ can be written as $\mathsf{V}^{\widehat{\mathbf{x}}}(\mathsf{crs}, C, k, \pi)$ for $\widehat{\mathbf{x}} := \mathsf{Encode}(\lambda, \mathbf{x})$, where the verifier proceeds in two steps as follows.*

1. *Without making queries to $\widehat{\mathbf{x}}$, the verifier either immediately outputs 0 (i.e., rejects the proof) or computes a set $I \subseteq [\widehat{n}]$ of queries along with a set $Z \subseteq \Sigma^{\widehat{n}}$ of expected responses. (Σ is the alphabet of $\widehat{\mathbf{x}}$ and $\widehat{n}$ is the block length.) This step takes time at most $\mathsf{poly}(\lambda, |C|, \log k)$.*
2. *The verifier makes the queries to $\widehat{\mathbf{x}}$, and it outputs 1 iff $\widehat{\mathbf{x}}|_I = Z$.*

The following is a special case of the above definitions.

Definition 17. *A publicly verifiable non-interactive delegation scheme (resp., a publicly verifiable non-interactive batch argument) is called **LDE-holographic** if it is holographic w.r.t. the encoding algorithm Encode that outputs the low-degree extension $\mathsf{LDE}_{\mathbb{F}, \mathbb{H}, m}(\chi)$ of the input χ for the parameter $(\mathbb{F}, \mathbb{H}, m)$ that is determined based on $(\lambda, |\chi|)$ (resp., the low-degree extension $\mathsf{LDE}_{\mathbb{F}, \mathbb{H}, m}(\mathbf{x})$ of the instances $\mathbf{x} = (x_1, \ldots, x_k)$ for the parameter $(\mathbb{F}, \mathbb{H}, m)$ that is determined based on $(\lambda, |x_1| + \cdots + |x_k|)$, where $\mathbf{x}$ is viewed as a binary string $x_1 \| \cdots \| x_k$).*

4   Somewhere-Sound Holographic SNARG for SE Hash

In this section, we construct a specific type of holographic SNARGs that we use as a tool in the subsequent sections. The target of this section is defined as follows based on the definition of holographic publicly verifiable non-interactive Turing-machine delegations schemes (Definition 7, Definition 15).

Definition 18. *Let* $\mathsf{SEH} = (\mathsf{SEH.Gen}, \mathsf{SEH.TGen}, \mathsf{SEH.Hash}, \mathsf{SEH.Open}, \mathsf{SEH.Ver},$ $\mathsf{SEH.Ext})$ *be a somewhere extractable hash function family. A **partially adaptive somewhere-sound holographic non-interactive delegation scheme** for* SEH *consists of four algorithms* $(\mathsf{Gen}, \mathsf{P}, \mathsf{V}, \mathsf{Encode})$ *satisfying the following.*

- **Holographic completeness.** *For every* $\lambda \in \mathbb{N}$, $N \in [2^\lambda]$, $x \in \{0,1\}^N$, *and* $M_I \in [N]$,

$$\Pr \left[\mathsf{V}^{\widehat{x}}(\mathsf{crs}, (h, \mathsf{rt}), \pi) = 1 \; \middle| \; \begin{array}{l} \mathsf{crs} \leftarrow \mathsf{Gen}(1^\lambda, N, 1^{M_I}) \\ h \leftarrow \mathsf{SEH.Gen}(1^\lambda, N, 1^{M_I}) \\ \mathsf{rt} := \mathsf{SEH.Hash}(h, x) \\ \pi := \mathsf{P}(\mathsf{crs}, (x, (h, \mathsf{rt}))) \\ \widehat{x} := \mathsf{Encode}(\lambda, x) \end{array} \right] = 1 \; .$$

Furthermore, the execution of $\mathsf{V}^{\widehat{x}}(\mathsf{crs}, (h, \mathsf{rt}), \pi)$ *proceeds in two steps as specified in the definition of holographic delegations (Definition 15).*
- **Partially adaptive somewhere soundness.** *For every* PPT *algorithm* P^* *and pair of polynomials* poly_N, poly_I, *there exists a negligible function* negl *such that for every* $\lambda \in \mathbb{N}$, $N \in [2^\lambda]$, $x = (x_1, \ldots, x_N) \in \{0,1\}^N$, $I \subseteq [N]$, *and* $z \in \{0,1\}^*$ *such that* $N \leq \mathsf{poly}_N(\lambda)$ *and* $|I| \leq \mathsf{poly}_I(\lambda)$,

$$\Pr \left[\begin{array}{l} \mathsf{V}^{\widehat{x}}(\mathsf{crs}, (h, \mathsf{rt}), \pi) = 1 \\ \wedge \; \exists i \in I \; s.t. \; x_i \neq \widetilde{x}_i \end{array} \; \middle| \; \begin{array}{l} \mathsf{crs} \leftarrow \mathsf{Gen}(1^\lambda, N, 1^{|I|}) \\ (h, \mathsf{td}) \leftarrow \mathsf{SEH.TGen}(1^\lambda, N, I) \\ (\mathsf{rt}, \pi) \leftarrow \mathsf{P}^*(\mathsf{crs}, (x, h), z) \\ \widehat{x} := \mathsf{Encode}(\lambda, x) \\ \{\widetilde{x}_i\}_{i \in I} := \mathsf{SEH.Ext}(\mathsf{td}, \mathsf{rt}) \end{array} \right] \leq \mathsf{negl}(\lambda) \; .$$

- **Efficiency.** *In the above completeness experiment, the following hold.*
  - *The setup algorithm* Gen *runs in time* $\mathsf{poly}(\lambda, \log N, M_I)$.
  - *The prover* P *runs in time* $\mathsf{poly}(\lambda, N)$ *and outputs a proof* π *of length* $\mathsf{poly}(\lambda, \log N, M_I)$.
  - *The verifier* V *runs in time* $\mathsf{poly}(\lambda, \log N, M_I)$.

A holographic delegation scheme for SEH *is called **public-coin** if the setup algorithm* Gen *is public-coin, i.e., it just outputs a string that is sampled uniformly randomly (possibly along with various parameters that are determined deterministically based on the input of* Gen*). A holographic delegation scheme for* SEH *is called **LDE-holographic** if the encoding algorithm* Encode *outputs the low-degree extension* $\mathsf{LDE}_{\mathbb{F},\mathbb{H},m}(x)$ *of the input* x *for the parameter* $(\mathbb{F}, \mathbb{H}, m)$ *that is determined based on* $(\lambda, |x|)$.

The goal of this section is to prove the following lemma.

Lemma 1. *Under the LWE assumption, there exists a partially adaptive somewhere-sound holographic non-interactive delegation scheme for any somewhere extractable hash function family. The scheme is public-coin and LDE-holographic, where for the security parameter* λ *and an input* x *of length* N, *the encoding algorithm* Encode *outputs the LDE of* x *w.r.t. an arbitrary LDE parameter* $(\mathbb{F}, \mathbb{H}, m)$ *such that* $|\mathbb{F}| \leq \mathsf{poly}(|\mathbb{H}|) \leq \mathsf{poly}(\log N)$, $|\mathbb{H}|^m \leq \mathsf{poly}(N)$, *and* $m|\mathbb{H}|/|\mathbb{F}| \leq O(1)$.

Proof. Fix any somewhere extractable hash function family SEH = (SEH.Gen, SEH.TGen, SEH.Hash, SEH.Open, SEH.Ver, SEH.Ext). Our goal is to give a partially adaptive somewhere-sound holographic non-interactive delegation scheme for SEH. For simplicity, we assume SEH is public-coin.[9]

First, we introduce notations. Let $\mathsf{param}_{\mathsf{LDE}}$ be any efficiently computable mapping that maps each $(\lambda, N) \in \mathbb{N} \times \mathbb{N}$ to an LDE parameter $(\mathbb{F}, \mathbb{H}, m)$ such that $|\mathbb{F}| \leq \mathsf{poly}(|\mathbb{H}|) \leq \mathsf{poly}(\log N)$, $|\mathbb{H}|^m \leq \mathsf{poly}(N)$, and $m|\mathbb{H}|/|\mathbb{F}| \leq O(1)$.[10] For a security parameter $\lambda \in \mathbb{N}$ and an LDE parameter $(\mathbb{F}, \mathbb{H}, m) := \mathsf{param}_{\mathsf{LDE}}(\lambda, N)$, define m_λ as $m_\lambda := \lceil \log_{|\mathbb{H}|} \lambda \rceil$ so that $\lambda \leq |\mathbb{H}|^{m_\lambda} < \lambda|\mathbb{H}|$. We identify $\mathbb{H}^m$ with $\{1, \ldots, |\mathbb{H}|^m\}$ by the lexicographical order.

Next, we introduce the building blocks that we use in our scheme.

- Let $\mathsf{BARG}_{\mathsf{idx}} = (\mathsf{BARG.Gen}_{\mathsf{idx}}, \mathsf{BARG.P}_{\mathsf{idx}}, \mathsf{BARG.V}_{\mathsf{idx}})$ be a semi-adaptive somewhere-sound public-coin non-interactive BARG for the index language.
- For each (arbitrarily small) constant $\delta > 0$ and $\alpha := \lfloor \lambda^\delta \rfloor$, let CIH_α be a public-coin correlation-intractable hash function family that satisfies the following. For sufficiently large polynomials $\mathsf{poly}_X, \mathsf{poly}_Y, \mathsf{poly}_T$ and a constant $\rho \in [0, 1]$,[11] (i) the domain-codomain ensemble of CIH_α is $\{(X_\lambda, Y_\lambda^\alpha)\}_{\lambda \in \mathbb{N}}$ for $X_\lambda := \{0, 1\}^{\mathsf{poly}_X(\lambda)}$ and $Y_\lambda := \{1, \ldots, \mathsf{poly}_Y(\lambda)\}$, (ii) the correlation intractability of CIH_α holds for any product relation ensemble that is poly_T-time product verifiable with product sparsity ρ, and (iii) CIH_α can be evaluated in time $\mathsf{poly}(\log|X_\lambda|, |Y_\lambda|, \alpha, \mathsf{poly}_T(\lambda)) = \mathsf{poly}(\lambda, \alpha)$.

Both of the above exist under the LWE assumption (cf. Theorem 3 and Sect. 3.2).

Now, we describe our scheme $\mathsf{SEH\text{-}Del} = (\mathsf{Gen}, \mathsf{P}, \mathsf{V}, \mathsf{Encode})$ using a subroutine scheme $\mathsf{SEH\text{-}Del}_{\mathsf{sub}} = (\mathsf{Gen}_{\mathsf{sub}}, \mathsf{P}_{\mathsf{sub}}, \mathsf{V}_{\mathsf{sub}})$. Intuitively, $\mathsf{SEH\text{-}Del}_{\mathsf{sub}}$ is a holographic SNARG for SEH w.r.t. strings over finite fields (rather than binary strings), and $\mathsf{SEH\text{-}Del}$ is a wrapper scheme that enables us to use $\mathsf{SEH\text{-}Del}_{\mathsf{sub}}$ w.r.t. strings over binary strings. That is, given a binary string x and its SE hash value rt, $\mathsf{SEH\text{-}Del}$ converts x into an equivalent string x' over a finite field, computes the SE hash value rt' of x', and invokes $\mathsf{SEH\text{-}Del}_{\mathsf{sub}}$ for x' and rt' while using $\mathsf{BARG}_{\mathsf{idx}}$ to prove the consistency between rt and rt'. The formal description of $\mathsf{SEH\text{-}Del}$ is given in Fig. 3. The subroutine scheme $\mathsf{SEH\text{-}Del}_{\mathsf{sub}}$ is defined recursively in Fig. 4 (a high-level idea is explained in Sect. 2.1).[12] [13]

Since the correctness and efficiency can be verified by inspection, we focus on the proof of soundness below. (See the full version of this paper about the correctness and efficiency.) We prove the partially adaptive somewhere soundness of $\mathsf{SEH\text{-}Del}$ by proving a related soundness notion for $\mathsf{SEH\text{-}Del}_{\mathsf{sub}}$. Concretely, we consider the following two claims about $\mathsf{SEH\text{-}Del}_{\mathsf{sub}}$.

---

[9] If not, it suffices to additionally use any LWE-based somewhere extractable hash function family (cf. Theorem 2) as a building block in our scheme.

[10] E.g, $|\mathbb{H}| = \lceil \log N \rceil$, $|\mathbb{F}| = \mathsf{poly}(|\mathbb{H}|)$, and $m = \lceil \log_{|\mathbb{H}|} N \rceil$.

[11] The concrete requirements about poly_X, poly_Y, poly_T, and ρ are determined based on SEH and $\mathsf{param}_{\mathsf{LDE}}$ (cf. the proof of Claim 2).

[12] In $\mathsf{SEH\text{-}Del}$ and $\mathsf{SEH\text{-}Del}_{\mathsf{sub}}$, SEH is used for strings over a finite field (cf. Sect. 3.3).

[13] The recursive structure of $\mathsf{SEH\text{-}Del}_{\mathsf{sub}}$ is the reason why we define it w.r.t. strings over finite fields.

Claim 1 (Base case). *For every* PPT *algorithm* P^* *and polynomial* poly_N, *there exists a negligible function* negl *such that for every* $\lambda \in \mathbb{N}$, $N \leq \text{poly}_N(\lambda)$, $(\mathbb{F}, \mathbb{H}, m_N) := \text{param}_{\text{LDE}}(\lambda, N)$, $m := m_N - \lfloor m_N/m_\lambda \rfloor \cdot m_\lambda$, $x : \mathbb{H}^m \to \mathbb{F}$, $i^* \in [|\mathbb{H}|^m]$, $\alpha := \lfloor \lambda^{1/(\lfloor m_N/m_\lambda \rfloor + 1)} \rfloor$, *and* $z \in \{0,1\}^*$,

$$\Pr\left[\begin{array}{l} V_{\text{sub}}^{\widehat{x}}(\text{crs}, (h, \text{rt}), \pi) = 1 \\ \wedge\ x(i^*) \neq \widetilde{x}_{i^*} \end{array} \middle|\ \begin{array}{l} \text{crs} \leftarrow \text{Gen}_{\text{sub}}(1^\lambda, (\mathbb{F}, \mathbb{H}, m), \alpha) \\ (h, \text{td}) \leftarrow \text{SEH.TGen}(1^\lambda, |\mathbb{H}|^m, \{i^*\}) \\ (\text{rt}, \pi) \leftarrow P^*(\text{crs}, (x, h), z) \\ \widehat{x} := \text{LDE}_{\mathbb{F}, \mathbb{H}, m}(x) \\ \widetilde{x}_{i^*} := \text{SEH.Ext}(\text{td}, \text{rt}) \end{array} \right] \leq \text{negl}(\lambda)\ .$$

$$(1)$$

$\underline{\text{crs} \leftarrow \text{Gen}(1^\lambda, N, 1^{M_I})}:$

1. Let $(\mathbb{F}, \mathbb{H}, m_N) := \text{param}_{\text{LDE}}(\lambda, N)$.
2. Sample $h' \leftarrow \text{SEH.Gen}(1^\lambda, |\mathbb{H}|^{m_N}, 1^{M_I'})$, where $M_I' := 1$.
3. Sample $\text{crs}^{\text{idx}} \leftarrow \text{BARG.Gen}_{\text{idx}}(1^\lambda, 1^{M_C}, N)$, where $M_C = \text{poly}(\lambda, \log N, M_I)$ is the size of the circuit C that is defined in the prover P below.
4. Sample $\text{crs}' \leftarrow \text{Gen}_{\text{sub}}(1^\lambda, (\mathbb{F}, \mathbb{H}, m_N), \alpha)$, where $\alpha := \lfloor \lambda^{1/(\lfloor m_N/m_\lambda \rfloor + 1)} \rfloor$.
5. Output $\text{crs} \leftarrow (1^\lambda, N, h', \text{crs}^{\text{idx}}, \text{crs}')$.

$\underline{\pi := P(\text{crs}, (x, (h, \text{rt})))}:$

1. Parse crs as $(1^\lambda, N, h', \text{crs}^{\text{idx}}, \text{crs}')$. Let $(\mathbb{F}, \mathbb{H}, m_N) := \text{param}_{\text{LDE}}(\lambda, N)$.
2. Let $x' : \mathbb{H}^{m_N} \to \mathbb{F}$ be the function that is obtained from $x = (x_1, \ldots, x_N) \in \{0,1\}^N$ by letting $x'(i) := x_i$ for $1 \leq i \leq N$ and $x'(i) := 0$ for $N < i \leq |\mathbb{H}|^{m_N}$, where $\mathbb{H}^{m_N}$ is identified with $\{1, \ldots, |\mathbb{H}|^{m_N}\}$ by the lexicographical order.
3. Compute $\text{rt}' := \text{SEH.Hash}(h', x')$. Also, compute $\text{cert}_i := \text{SEH.Open}(h, x, i)$ and $\text{cert}_i' := \text{SEH.Open}(h', x', i)$ for $\forall i \in [N]$.
4. Compute $\pi^{\text{idx}} := \text{BARG.P}_{\text{idx}}(\text{crs}^{\text{idx}}, C, \mathbf{w})$, where $\mathbf{w} := \{w_i\}_{i \in [N]}$, $w_i := (x_i, \text{cert}_i, \text{cert}_i')$, and C is the following circuit.
   - C has $(h, \text{rt}, h', \text{rt}')$ as hardwired inputs, takes an index $i \in [N]$ and a witness $w_i = (x_i, \text{cert}_i, \text{cert}_i')$ as inputs, and outputs 1 iff $\text{SEH.Ver}(h, \text{rt}, x_i, i, \text{cert}_i) = 1$ and $\text{SEH.Ver}(h', \text{rt}', x_i, i, \text{cert}_i') = 1$.
5. Compute $\pi' \leftarrow P_{\text{sub}}(\text{crs}', (x', (h', \text{rt}')))$.
6. Output $\pi := (\text{rt}', \pi^{\text{idx}}, \pi')$.

$\underline{b := V^{\widehat{x}}(\text{crs}, (h, \text{rt}), \pi)}:$

1. Parse crs as $(1^\lambda, N, h', \text{crs}^{\text{idx}}, \text{crs}')$ and π as $(\text{rt}', \pi^{\text{idx}}, \pi')$.
2. Output 1 iff $\text{BARG.V}_{\text{idx}}(\text{crs}^{\text{idx}}, C, \pi^{\text{idx}}) = 1$ and $V_{\text{sub}}^{\widehat{x}}(\text{crs}', (h', \text{rt}'), \pi') = 1$.

$\underline{\widehat{x} := \text{Encode}(\lambda, x)}:$

1. Output $\widehat{x} := \text{LDE}_{\mathbb{F}, \mathbb{H}, m_N}(x)$, where $(\mathbb{F}, \mathbb{H}, m_N) := \text{param}_{\text{LDE}}(\lambda, N)$, $N := |x|$.

Fig. 3. SEH-Del $= (\text{Gen}, P, V, \text{Encode})$.

$\mathsf{crs} \leftarrow \mathsf{Gen_{sub}}(1^\lambda, (\mathbb{F}, \mathbb{H}, m), \alpha)$:

1. If $m < m_\lambda$, output $\mathsf{crs} := (1^\lambda, (\mathbb{F}, \mathbb{H}, m), \bot, \bot, \bot, \bot)$. If $m \geq m_\lambda$, do the following.
2. Sample $h^+ \leftarrow \mathsf{SEH.Gen}(1^\lambda, |\mathbb{H}|^{m-m_\lambda}, 1^{M_I})$, where $M_I := 1$.
3. Sample $\mathsf{crs^{idx}} \leftarrow \mathsf{BARG.Gen_{idx}}(1^\lambda, 1^{M_C}, |\mathbb{H}|^{m-m_\lambda})$, where $M_C := \max(|C_\mathbf{u}|, |C|)$ for the circuits $C_\mathbf{u}, C$ that are defined in the prover $\mathsf{P_{sub}}$.
4. Sample $h^{\mathrm{CIH}} \leftarrow \mathsf{CIH.Gen}_\alpha(1^\lambda)$.
5. Sample $\mathsf{crs^+} \leftarrow \mathsf{Gen_{sub}}(1^\lambda, (\mathbb{F}, \mathbb{H}, m - m_\lambda), \alpha)$.
6. Output $\mathsf{crs} := (1^\lambda, (\mathbb{F}, \mathbb{H}, m), \alpha, h^+, \mathsf{crs^{idx}}, h^{\mathrm{CIH}}, \mathsf{crs^+})$.

$\pi \leftarrow \mathsf{P_{sub}}(\mathsf{crs}, (x, (h, \mathsf{rt})))$:

1. Parse crs as $(1^\lambda, (\mathbb{F}, \mathbb{H}, m), \alpha, h^+, \mathsf{crs^{idx}}, h^{\mathrm{CIH}}, \mathsf{crs^+})$, where $(\mathbb{F}, \mathbb{H}, m)$ is expected to be an LDE parameter such that $x : \mathbb{H}^m \to \mathbb{F}$. If $m < m_\lambda$, output $\pi := x$. If $m \geq m_\lambda$, compute $\widehat{x} := \mathsf{LDE}_{\mathbb{F}, \mathbb{H}, m}(x)$ and do the following.
2. Compute $\mathsf{rt}_\mathbf{u}^+ := \mathsf{SEH.Hash}(h^+, x_{(\mathbf{u},*)})$ for $\forall \mathbf{u} \in \mathbb{F}^{m_\lambda}$, where $x_{(\mathbf{u},*)} : \mathbb{H}^{m-m_\lambda} \to \mathbb{F}$ is defined as $x_{(\mathbf{u},*)} : \mathbf{v} \mapsto \widehat{x}(\mathbf{u}, \mathbf{v})$. Also, compute $\mathsf{cert}_{(\mathbf{u},\mathbf{v})} := \mathsf{SEH.Open}(h, x, (\mathbf{u}, \mathbf{v}))$ for $\forall (\mathbf{u}, \mathbf{v}) \in \mathbb{H}^{m_\lambda} \times \mathbb{H}^{m-m_\lambda}$ and $\mathsf{cert}_{(\mathbf{u},\mathbf{v})}^+ := \mathsf{SEH.Open}(h^+, x_{(\mathbf{u},*)}, \mathbf{v})$ for $\forall (\mathbf{u}, \mathbf{v}) \in \mathbb{F}^{m_\lambda} \times \mathbb{H}^{m-m_\lambda}$.
3. Compute $\pi_\mathbf{u}^{\mathrm{idx}} := \mathsf{BARG.P_{idx}}(\mathsf{crs^{idx}}, C_\mathbf{u}, \mathbf{w})$ for $\forall \mathbf{u} \in \mathbb{H}^{m_\lambda}$, where $\mathbf{w} := \{w_\mathbf{v}\}_{\mathbf{v} \in \mathbb{H}^{m-m_\lambda}}$, $w_\mathbf{v} := (x(\mathbf{u}, \mathbf{v}), \mathsf{cert}_{(\mathbf{u},\mathbf{v})}, \mathsf{cert}_{(\mathbf{u},\mathbf{v})}^+)$, and $C_\mathbf{u}$ is as follows.
   - $C_\mathbf{u}$ has $(h, \mathsf{rt}, h^+, \mathsf{rt}_\mathbf{u}^+)$ as hardwired inputs, takes an index $\mathbf{v}$ and a witness $w = (y, \mathsf{cert}, \mathsf{cert}^+)$ as inputs, and outputs 1 iff $\mathsf{SEH.Ver}(h, \mathsf{rt}, y, (\mathbf{u}, \mathbf{v}), \mathsf{cert}) = 1$ and $\mathsf{SEH.Ver}(h^+, \mathsf{rt}_\mathbf{u}^+, y, \mathbf{v}, \mathsf{cert}') = 1$.
4. Compute $\pi^{\mathrm{idx}} := \mathsf{BARG.P_{idx}}(\mathsf{crs^{idx}}, C, \mathbf{w})$, where $\mathbf{w} := \{w_\mathbf{v}\}_{\mathbf{v} \in \mathbb{H}^{m-m_\lambda}}$, $w_\mathbf{v} = \{\widehat{x}(\mathbf{u}, \mathbf{v}), \mathsf{cert}_{(\mathbf{u},\mathbf{v})}^+\}_{\mathbf{u} \in \mathbb{F}^{m_\lambda}}$, and C is the following circuit.
   - C has $(h^+, \{\mathsf{rt}_\mathbf{u}^+\}_{\mathbf{u} \in \mathbb{F}^{m_\lambda}})$ as hardwired inputs, takes an index $\mathbf{v} \in \mathbb{H}^{m-m_\lambda}$ and a witness $w = \{y_{(\mathbf{u},\mathbf{v})}, \mathsf{cert}_{(\mathbf{u},\mathbf{v})}\}_{\mathbf{u} \in \mathbb{F}^{m_\lambda}}$ as inputs, and outputs 1 iff (i) $\mathsf{SEH.Ver}(h^+, \mathsf{rt}_\mathbf{u}^+, y_{(\mathbf{u},\mathbf{v})}, \mathbf{v}, \mathsf{cert}_{(\mathbf{u},\mathbf{v})}) = 1$ for $\forall \mathbf{u} \in \mathbb{F}^{m_\lambda}$ and (ii) the function $\widehat{y}_{(*,\mathbf{v})} : \mathbb{F}^{m_\lambda} \to \mathbb{F}$ defined as $\widehat{y}_{(*,\mathbf{v})} : \mathbf{u} \mapsto y_{(\mathbf{u},\mathbf{v})}$ is the LDE of $y_{(*,\mathbf{v})} := \widehat{y}_{(*,\mathbf{v})}|_{\mathbb{H}^{m_\lambda}}$ w.r.t. $(\mathbb{F}, \mathbb{H}, m_\lambda)$.
5. Compute $(\mathbf{c}_1, \ldots, \mathbf{c}_\alpha) := \mathsf{CIH.Hash}_\alpha(h^{\mathrm{CIH}}, \{\mathsf{rt}_\mathbf{u}^+\}_{\mathbf{u} \in \mathbb{H}^{m_\lambda}})$, where each $\mathbf{c}_i$ is viewed as an element of $\mathbb{F}^{m_\lambda}$. Let $S_\mathbf{c} := \{\mathbf{c}_1, \ldots, \mathbf{c}_\alpha\}$.
6. Compute $\pi_{\mathbf{c}_i}^+ \leftarrow \mathsf{P_{sub}}(\mathsf{crs^+}, (x_{(\mathbf{c}_i,*)}, (h^+, \mathsf{rt}_{\mathbf{c}_i}^+)))$ for $\forall \mathbf{c}_i \in S_\mathbf{c}$.
7. Output $\pi := (\{\mathsf{rt}_\mathbf{u}^+\}_{\mathbf{u} \in \mathbb{F}^{m_\lambda}}, \{\pi_\mathbf{u}^{\mathrm{idx}}\}_{\mathbf{u} \in \mathbb{H}^{m_\lambda}}, \pi^{\mathrm{idx}}, \{\pi_{\mathbf{c}_i}^+\}_{\mathbf{c}_i \in S_\mathbf{c}})$.

$b := \mathsf{V_{sub}^{\widehat{x}}}(\mathsf{crs}, (h, \mathsf{rt}), \pi)$:

1. Parse crs as $(1^\lambda, (\mathbb{F}, \mathbb{H}, m), \alpha, h^+, \mathsf{crs^{idx}}, h^{\mathrm{CIH}}, \mathsf{crs^+})$. If $m < m_\lambda$, output 1 iff $\mathsf{SEH.Hash}(h, \pi) = \mathsf{rt}$ and $\pi = \widehat{x}|_{\mathbb{H}^m}$. If $m \geq m_\lambda$, do the following.
2. Parse π as $(\{\mathsf{rt}_\mathbf{u}^+\}_{\mathbf{u} \in \mathbb{F}^{m_\lambda}}, \{\pi_\mathbf{u}^{\mathrm{idx}}\}_{\mathbf{u} \in \mathbb{H}^{m_\lambda}}, \pi^{\mathrm{idx}}, \{\pi_{\mathbf{c}_i}^+\}_{\mathbf{c}_i \in S_\mathbf{c}})$.
3. Compute $(\mathbf{c}_1, \ldots, \mathbf{c}_\alpha) := \mathsf{CIH.Hash}_\alpha(h^{\mathrm{CIH}}, \{\mathsf{rt}_\mathbf{u}^+\}_{\mathbf{u} \in \mathbb{H}^{m_\lambda}})$, where each $\mathbf{c}_i$ is viewed as an element in $\mathbb{F}^{m_\lambda}$. Let $S_\mathbf{c} := \{\mathbf{c}_1, \ldots, \mathbf{c}_\alpha\}$.
4. Output 1 iff (i) $\mathsf{BARG.V_{idx}}(\mathsf{crs^{idx}}, C_\mathbf{u}, \pi_\mathbf{u}^{\mathrm{idx}}) = 1$ for $\forall \mathbf{u} \in \mathbb{H}^{m_\lambda}$, (ii) $\mathsf{BARG.V_{idx}}(\mathsf{crs^{idx}}, C, \pi^{\mathrm{idx}}) = 1$, and (iii) $\mathsf{V_{sub}^{\widehat{x}(\mathbf{c}_i,\cdot)}}(\mathsf{crs^+}, (h^+, \mathsf{rt}_{\mathbf{c}_i}^+), \pi_{\mathbf{c}_i}^+) = 1$ for $\forall \mathbf{c}_i \in S_\mathbf{c}$.

Fig. 4. $\mathsf{SEH\text{-}Del_{sub}} = (\mathsf{Gen_{sub}}, \mathsf{P_{sub}}, \mathsf{V_{sub}})$.

Claim 2 (Inductive step). *For every* PPT *algorithm* P* *and polynomial* poly_N, *there exists a* PPT *algorithm* P+ *and a negligible function* negl *such that the following holds. Assume there exists a polynomial* poly_{P*} *such that for infinitely many* $\lambda \in \mathbb{N}$, *there exist* $N \leq \mathsf{poly}_N(\lambda)$, $(\mathbb{F}, \mathbb{H}, m_N) := \mathsf{param}_{\mathrm{LDE}}(\lambda, N)$, $m \in \{m_N, m_N - m_\lambda, \ldots, m_N - (\lfloor m_N/m_\lambda \rfloor - 1) \cdot m_\lambda\}$, $x : \mathbb{H}^m \rightarrow \mathbb{F}$, $i^* \in [|\mathbb{H}|^m]$, $\alpha := \lfloor \lambda^{1/(\lfloor m_N/m_\lambda \rfloor + 1)} \rfloor$, *and* $z \in \{0,1\}^*$ *such that*

$$
\Pr \left[
\begin{array}{l|l}
\mathsf{V}^{\hat{x}}_{\mathrm{sub}}(\mathsf{crs}, (h, \mathsf{rt}), \pi) = 1 \\
\wedge\ x(i^*) \neq \widetilde{x}_{i^*}
\end{array}
\right.
\left|
\begin{array}{l}
\mathsf{crs} \leftarrow \mathsf{Gen}_{\mathrm{sub}}(1^\lambda, (\mathbb{F}, \mathbb{H}, m), \alpha) \\
(h, \mathsf{td}) \leftarrow \mathsf{SEH.TGen}(1^\lambda, |\mathbb{H}|^m, \{i^*\}) \\
(\mathsf{rt}, \pi) \leftarrow \mathsf{P}^*(\mathsf{crs}, (x, h), z) \\
\hat{x} := \mathsf{LDE}_{\mathbb{F}, \mathbb{H}, m}(x) \\
\widetilde{x}_{i^*} := \mathsf{SEH.Ext}(\mathsf{td}, \mathsf{rt})
\end{array}
\right]
\geq \frac{1}{\mathsf{poly}_{P*}(\lambda)}.
$$

$$(2)$$

Then, for such a polynomial poly_{P*} *and for infinitely many such* λ, N, $(\mathbb{F}, \mathbb{H}, m_N)$, m, *and* α, *there exist* $x^+ : \mathbb{H}^{m-m_\lambda} \rightarrow \mathbb{F}$, $i^+ \in [|\mathbb{H}|^{m-m_\lambda}]$, *and* $z^+ \in \{0,1\}^*$ *such that*

$$
\Pr \left[
\begin{array}{l|l}
\mathsf{V}^{\hat{x}^+}_{\mathrm{sub}}(\mathsf{crs}, (h, \mathsf{rt}), \pi) = 1 \\
\wedge\ x^+(i^*) \neq \widetilde{x}_{i^+}
\end{array}
\right.
\left|
\begin{array}{l}
\mathsf{crs} \leftarrow \mathsf{Gen}_{\mathrm{sub}}(1^\lambda, (\mathbb{F}, \mathbb{H}, m - m_\lambda), \alpha) \\
(h, \mathsf{td}) \leftarrow \mathsf{SEH.TGen}(1^\lambda, |\mathbb{H}|^{m-m_\lambda}, \{i^+\}) \\
(\mathsf{rt}, \pi) \leftarrow \mathsf{P}^+(\mathsf{crs}, (x^+, h), z^+) \\
\hat{x}^+ := \mathsf{LDE}_{\mathbb{F}, \mathbb{H}, m}(x^+) \\
\widetilde{x}_{i^+} := \mathsf{SEH.Ext}(\mathsf{td}, \mathsf{rt})
\end{array}
\right]
$$

$$
\geq \frac{1}{|\mathbb{F}|^{m_\lambda}} \left(\frac{1}{\mathsf{poly}_{P*}(\lambda)} - \mathsf{negl}(\lambda) \right). \quad (3)
$$

Furthermore, the running time of P+ *is upper bounded by* $T_{P*}(\lambda) + \mathsf{poly}(\lambda)$, *where* T_{P*} *is the running time of* P* *and* poly *is independent of* T_{P*}.

First, we observe that the soundness of SEH-Del follows from Claim 1 and Claim 2. Assume for contradiction that SEH-Del is not partially adaptive somewhere sound, i.e., a cheating prover P* provides an accepting proof π and a hash value rt from which the extractor fails to extract the correct values. Then, the semi-adaptive somewhere soundness of $\mathsf{BARG}_{\mathrm{idx}}$ (together with the key indistinguishability of SEH and the CRS indistinguishability of $\mathsf{BARG}_{\mathrm{idx}}$) guarantees that the extractor fails to extract the correct values even from the hash value rt' that is included in π as the statement of the subroutine scheme. Thus, we can use P* to obtain a successful cheating prover against the subroutine scheme, and after repeated applications of Claim 2, we can derive a contradiction using Claim 1. (For details, see the full version of this paper.)

It remains to prove Claim 1 and Claim 2. Claim 1 holds trivially since $m = m_N - \lfloor m_N/m_\lambda \rfloor \cdot m_\lambda < m_\lambda$. Regarding Claim 2, we prove it following the idea given in the technical overview (Sect. 2.1). That is, using the security of SEH and $\mathsf{BARG}_{\mathrm{idx}}$ as above and also relying on the correlation intractability of CIH_α, we show that any successful cheating prover P* against SEH-Del$_{\mathrm{sub}}$ can be used to obtain a successful cheating prover P+ against one of the recursive proofs. A subtlety is that the correlation intractability of CIH_α is non-adaptive in the sense that the relation ensemble in the security experiment needs to be fixed in advance (cf. Definition 1). Since P* chooses the indices $\{c_i\}_{i\in[\alpha]} \in \mathbb{F}^{m\lambda}$ of the recursive proofs adaptively, we can rely on the correlation intractability of CIH_α only when we correctly guess the index on which the prover cheats. Consequently, we can only show that P^+ succeeds with probability that decreases by a multiplicative factor $1/|\mathbb{F}|^{m\lambda}$. For the formal proofs, see the full version of this paper.   □

5 Holographic SNARG for Tree-Hash

In this section, we construct a holographic SNARG for the correctness of Merkle tree-hash computations. The target of this section is defined as follows.

Definition 19. *Publicly verifiable non-interactive delegation schemes for tree-hash computations (or publicly verifiable non-interactive tree-hash delegation schemes in short) are a special case of publicly verifiable non-interactive delegation schemes for Turing machines (Definition 7), where the following restrictions are imposed.*

- *The instance χ is restricted to the form $\chi = (x, (h, \mathsf{rt}))$, where $x \in \{0,1\}^{2^\ell\lambda}$ ($\ell \in \mathbb{N}$) is a binary string, $h : \{0,1\}^{2\lambda} \to \{0,1\}^\lambda$ is a hash function (represented as a circuit), and $\mathsf{rt} \in \{0,1\}^\lambda$ is a binary string.*
- *The Turing machine M is fixed to be the two-input Turing machine $M_{\text{tree-hash}}$ that takes an input of the form $\chi = (x, (h, \mathsf{rt}))$ and outputs 1 iff $\mathsf{TreeHash}_h(x) = \mathsf{rt}$. Also, the time bound T (given to Gen along with the input length bounds n_1, n_2) is fixed to be $T_{\text{tree-hash}}(n_1, n_2)$, where $T_{\text{tree-hash}}$ is a polynomial upper bound of the running time of $M_{\text{tree-hash}}$.*

The goal of this section is to prove the following lemma.

Lemma 2. *Assume the existence of (i) a somewhere extractable hash function family SEH, (ii) a semi-adaptive somewhere-sound publicly verifiable non-interactive BARG for the index language, and (iii) a partially adaptive somewhere-sound holographic delegation scheme SEH-Del for SEH. Then, there exists a partially adaptive publicly verifiable non-interactive tree-hash delegation scheme that satisfies the following.*

- *The scheme is holographic w.r.t. the same encoding algorithm as SEH-Del.*
- *The setup time $T_{\mathsf{Gen}}(\lambda, T, n_1, n_2)$ and the proof length $L_\pi(\lambda, T, n_1, n_2)$ are both at most $\mathsf{poly}(\lambda, \log n_1, n_2)$.*
- *The scheme is public-coin if the above-listed primitives are public-coin.*

Since the primitives listed in Lemma 2 exist under the LWE assumption (Theorem 2, Theorem 3, Lemma 1), we can obtain the following corollary.

Corollary 1. *Under the LWE assumption, there exists a partially adaptive public-coin non-interactive tree-hash delegation scheme.*

– *The scheme is LDE-holographic, where for the security parameter λ and an input x of length N, the encoding algorithm* Encode *outputs the LDE of x w.r.t. an arbitrary LDE parameter $(\mathbb{F}, \mathbb{H}, m)$ such that $|\mathbb{F}| \leq$ poly$(|\mathbb{H}|) \leq$ poly$(\log N)$, $|\mathbb{H}|^m \leq$ poly(N), and $m|\mathbb{H}|/|\mathbb{F}| \leq O(1)$.*
– *The setup time $T_{\mathsf{Gen}}(\lambda, T, n_1, n_2)$ and the proof length $L_\pi(\lambda, T, n_1, n_2)$ are both at most* poly$(\lambda, \log n_1, n_2)$.

Proof (of Lemma 2). Let SEH = (SEH.Gen, SEH.TGen, SEH.Hash, SEH.Open, SEH.Ver, SEH.Ext) be a somewhere extractable hash function family, BARG$_{\mathsf{idx}}$ = (BARG.Gen$_{\mathsf{idx}}$, BARG.P$_{\mathsf{idx}}$, BARG.V$_{\mathsf{idx}}$) be a semi-adaptive somewhere-sound publicly verifiable non-interactive BARG for the index language, and SEH-Del = (SEH-Del.Gen, SEH-Del.P, SEH-Del.V, SEH-Del.Encode) be a partially adaptive somewhere-sound holographic delegation scheme for SEH. For simplicity, we adjust the definition of somewhere extractable hash functions (Definition 5) so that the set of the indices is $\{0, \ldots, N - 1\}$ rather than $\{1, \ldots, N\}$. The same adjustment is also made to the definition of BARGs (Definition 11).

Our scheme TH-Del = (Gen, P, V) is given in Fig. 5. We prove the security of TH-Del following the idea given in the technical overview (Sect. 2.1). For the formal proof, see the full version of this paper.

□

6   Holographic SNARG for Batch-NP

In this section, we construct a holographic SNARG for batch NP.

Theorem 4. *Assume the existence of a somewhere extractable hash function family* SEH, *a semi-adaptive somewhere-sound publicly verifiable non-interactive BARG for the index language, and a partially adaptive somewhere-sound holographic delegation scheme* SEH-Del *for* SEH. *Then, there exists a publicly verifiable non-interactive BARG for* **CSAT** *that is (i) weakly semi-adaptive somewhere sound and (ii) holographic w.r.t. the same encoding algorithm as* SEH-Del. *The scheme is public-coin if the above-listed primitives are public-coin.*

Since all the primitives listed in Theorem 4 exist under the LWE assumption (Theorem 2, Theorem 3, Lemma 1), we obtain the following corollary.

Corollary 2. *Under the LWE assumption, there exists a public-coin non-interactive BARG for* **CSAT** *that is (i) weakly semi-adaptive somewhere sound and (ii) LDE-holographic, where for the security parameter λ and an input x of length N, the encoding algorithm* Encode *outputs the LDE of x w.r.t. an arbitrary LDE parameter $(\mathbb{F}, \mathbb{H}, m)$ such that $|\mathbb{F}| \leq$ poly$(|\mathbb{H}|) \leq$ poly$(\log N)$, $|\mathbb{H}|^m \leq$ poly(N), and $m|\mathbb{H}|/|\mathbb{F}| \leq O(1)$.*

As sketched in Sect. 2.2, we prove Theorem 4 by considering a scheme that works roughly as follows. For instances $\mathbf{x} = (x_1, \ldots, x_k)$ and a circuit C, the prover first computes a hash value of $\mathbf{x}$ using a somewhere extractable hash function. Next, the prover uses SEH-Del to compute a holographic proof about

---

$\mathsf{crs} \leftarrow \mathsf{Gen}(1^\lambda, T, n_1, n_2)$:

1. Let $\ell := \log(n_1/\lambda)$.
2. Sample $h_0^{\mathsf{SEH}} \leftarrow \mathsf{SEH.Gen}(1^\lambda, \lambda, 1^\lambda)$ and $h_i^{\mathsf{SEH}} \leftarrow \mathsf{SEH.Gen}(1^\lambda, 2^i\lambda, 1^{2\lambda})$ for $\forall i \in \{1, \ldots, \ell\}$.
3. Sample $\mathsf{crs}_i^{\mathsf{idx}} \leftarrow \mathsf{BARG.Gen}_{\mathsf{idx}}(1^\lambda, 1^{|C_i|}, 2^i)$ for $\forall i \in \{0, \ldots, \ell-1\}$, where the circuit C_i is defined in the prover P below.
4. Sample $\mathsf{crs}^{\mathsf{SEH\text{-}Del}} \leftarrow \mathsf{SEH\text{-}Del.Gen}(1^\lambda, 2^\lambda\lambda, 1^{2\lambda})$.
5. Output $\mathsf{crs} := (1^\lambda, \{h_i^{\mathsf{SEH}}\}_{i \in \{0,\ldots,\ell\}}, \{\mathsf{crs}_i^{\mathsf{idx}}\}_{i \in \{0,\ldots,\ell-1\}}, \mathsf{crs}^{\mathsf{SEH\text{-}Del}})$.

$\pi := \mathsf{P}(\mathsf{crs}, (x, (h, \mathsf{rt})))$:

1. Parse crs as $(1^\lambda, \{h_i^{\mathsf{SEH}}\}_{i \in \{0,\ldots,\ell\}}, \{\mathsf{crs}_i^{\mathsf{idx}}\}_{i \in \{0,\ldots,\ell-1\}}, \mathsf{crs}^{\mathsf{SEH\text{-}Del}})$.
2. Compute $\mathsf{TreeHash}_h(x)$ along with its nodes $\{\mathsf{node}_{i,\sigma}\}_{i \in \{0,\ldots,\ell\}, \sigma \in \{0,\ldots,2^i-1\}}$ (cf. Sect. 3.1).
3. Compute $\mathsf{rt}_i := \mathsf{SEH.Hash}(h_i^{\mathsf{SEH}}, x_i)$ for each $i \in \{0, \ldots, \ell\}$, where $x_i := \mathsf{node}_{i,0} \| \cdots \| \mathsf{node}_{i,2^i-1} \in \{0,1\}^{2^i\lambda}$. For each $i \in \{0, \ldots, \ell-1\}$ and $\sigma \in \{0, \ldots, 2^i-1\}$, let $\mathsf{cert}_{i,\sigma}$ be the certificates that open the appropriate positions of the pre-image of rt_i to $\mathsf{node}_{i,\sigma}$; i.e., $\mathsf{cert}_{i,\sigma} := (\mathsf{cert}_{i,\sigma,0}, \ldots, \mathsf{cert}_{i,\sigma,\lambda-1})$ and $\mathsf{cert}_{i,\sigma,j} := \mathsf{SEH.Open}(h_i^{\mathsf{SEH}}, b_{i,\sigma,j}, \lambda\sigma + j)$ for $\forall j \in \{0, \ldots, \lambda-1\}$, where $b_{i,\sigma,j}$ is the j-th bit of $\mathsf{node}_{i,\sigma} \in \{0,1\}^\lambda$.
4. For each $i \in \{0, \ldots, \ell-1\}$, compute $\pi_i := \mathsf{BARG.P}_{\mathsf{idx}}(\mathsf{crs}_i^{\mathsf{idx}}, C_i, \mathbf{w}_i)$, where $\mathbf{w}_i := \{w_{i,\sigma}\}_{\sigma \in \{0,\ldots,2^i-1\}}$, $w_{i,\sigma} := (\mathsf{node}_{i,\sigma}, \mathsf{cert}_{i,\sigma}, \mathsf{node}_{i+1,2\sigma}, \mathsf{cert}_{i+1,2\sigma}, \mathsf{node}_{i+1,2\sigma+1}, \mathsf{cert}_{i+1,2\sigma+1})$, and C_i is the following circuit.
   - C_i has $(h, h_i^{\mathsf{SEH}}, \mathsf{rt}_i, h_{i+1}^{\mathsf{SEH}}, \mathsf{rt}_{i+1})$ as hardwired inputs, and takes an index $\sigma \in \{0, \ldots, 2^i-1\}$ and a witness $w = (\mathsf{node}^{(0,0)}, \mathsf{cert}^{(0,0)}, \mathsf{node}^{(1,0)}, \mathsf{cert}^{(1,0)}, \mathsf{node}^{(1,1)}, \mathsf{cert}^{(1,1)})$ as inputs. First, C_i parses $\mathsf{node}^{(u,v)}$ as $(b_0^{(u,v)}, \ldots, b_{\lambda-1}^{(u,v)})$ and $\mathsf{cert}^{(u,v)}$ as $(\mathsf{cert}_0^{(u,v)}, \ldots, \mathsf{cert}_{\lambda-1}^{(u,v)})$ for each $(u,v) \in \{(0,0),(1,0),(1,1)\}$. Then, C_i outputs 1 iff (i) $\mathsf{SEH.Ver}(h_{i+u}^{\mathsf{SEH}}, \mathsf{rt}_{i+u}, b_j^{(u,v)}, \lambda(2^u\sigma + v) + j, \mathsf{cert}_j^{(u,v)}) = 1$ for $\forall (u,v) \in \{(0,0),(1,0),(1,1)\}$, $j \in \{0, \ldots \lambda-1\}$ and (ii) $h(\mathsf{node}^{(1,0)} \| \mathsf{node}^{(1,1)}) = \mathsf{node}^{(0,0)}$.
5. Compute $\pi_\ell := \mathsf{SEH\text{-}Del.P}(\mathsf{crs}^{\mathsf{SEH\text{-}Del}}, (x_\ell, (h_\ell^{\mathsf{SEH}}, \mathsf{rt}_\ell)))$.
6. Output $\pi := \{\mathsf{rt}_i, \pi_i\}_{i \in \{0,\ldots,\ell\}}$.

$b := \mathsf{V}(\mathsf{crs}, (x, (h, \mathsf{rt})), \pi)$:

1. Parse crs as $(1^\lambda, \{h_i^{\mathsf{SEH}}\}_{i \in \{0,\ldots,\ell\}}, \{\mathsf{crs}_i^{\mathsf{idx}}\}_{i \in \{0,\ldots,\ell-1\}}, \mathsf{crs}^{\mathsf{SEH\text{-}Del}})$ and π as $\{\mathsf{rt}_i, \pi_i\}_{i \in \{0,\ldots,\ell\}}$. Abort unless $|\mathsf{rt}| = \lambda$ and $h : \{0,1\}^{2\lambda} \to \{0,1\}^\lambda$.
2. Output 1 iff all of the following hold.
   - $\mathsf{SEH.Hash}(h_0^{\mathsf{SEH}}, \mathsf{rt}) = \mathsf{rt}_0$.
   - $\mathsf{BARG.V}_{\mathsf{idx}}(\mathsf{crs}_i^{\mathsf{idx}}, C_i, \pi_i) = 1$ for $\forall i \in \{0, \ldots, \ell-1\}$.
   - $\mathsf{SEH\text{-}Del.V}^{\widehat{x}}(\mathsf{crs}^{\mathsf{SEH\text{-}Del}}, (h_\ell^{\mathsf{SEH}}, \mathsf{rt}_\ell), \pi_\ell) = 1$, where $\widehat{x} := \mathsf{SEH\text{-}Del.Encode}(\lambda, x)$.

Fig. 5. A publicly verifiable non-interactive tree-hash delegation scheme TH-Del = (Gen, P, V).

the consistency between rt and **x**. Finally, the prover uses $\mathsf{BARG}_{\mathsf{idx}}$ to prove that for each $i \in [k]$, there exists an instance $\widetilde{x}_i$ such that (i) the i-th instance in the pre-image of rt can be opened to $\widetilde{x}_i$ and (ii) $(C, \widetilde{x}_i) \in \mathbf{CSAT}$. Intuitively speaking, the somewhere soundness follows from that of $\mathsf{BARG}_{\mathsf{idx}}$ since for each $i \in [k]$, the i-th instance in the pre-image of rt can be statistically fixed to x_i by the somewhere soundness of SEH-Del. The holographic property follows from that of SEH-Del. The formal proof is given in the full version of this paper.

7 Holographic SNARG for P

In this section, we observe that we can obtain a holographic SNARG for P by combining a holographic tree-hash SNARG with a known transformation.

Theorem 5. *Assume the hardness of the LWE assumption. Then, for every Turing machine, there exists a partially adaptive public-coin non-interactive delegation scheme that satisfies the following properties.*

- *The scheme is LDE-holographic, where for the security parameter λ and an input x of length N, the encoding algorithm Encode outputs the LDE of x w.r.t. an arbitrary LDE parameter $(\mathbb{F}, \mathbb{H}, m)$ such that $|\mathbb{F}| \leq \mathsf{poly}(|\mathbb{H}|) \leq \mathsf{poly}(\log N)$, $|\mathbb{H}|^m \leq \mathsf{poly}(N)$, and $m|\mathbb{H}|/|\mathbb{F}| \leq O(1)$.*
- *The setup time $T_{\mathsf{Gen}}(\lambda, T, n_1, n_2)$ and the proof length $L_\pi(\lambda, T, n_1, n_2)$ are both at most $\mathsf{poly}(\lambda, \log T, \log n_1, n_2)$.*

As mentioned in Sect. 2.1, the above theorem is obtained by combining our LWE-based holographic tree-hash SNARG (Corollary 1) with a known transformation [30], which uses the LWE-based *RAM delegation scheme* of Choudhuri, Jain, and Jin [11]. At a high level, the RAM delegation scheme of Choudhuri et al. is a public-coin non-interactive delegation scheme where (i) the prover can prove the correctness of an arbitrary polynomial-time computation and (ii) the verifier only needs to have the Merkle tree-hash of the computation input rather than the input itself. Naturally, their RAM delegation scheme can be converted to a holographic SNARG for P by augmenting it with a holographic tree-hash SNARG, i.e., by requiring the prover to send the tree-hash of the computation input along with a holographic proof about the correctness of the tree-hash. Thus, by using our LWE-based holographic tree-hash SNARG (Corollary 1), we can obtain a holographic SNARG for P as desired.

8 Application: Public-Coin Three-Round Zero-Knowledge

As an application of our holographic SNARGs, we give a public-coin 3-round zero-knowledge argument based on the slightly super-polynomial hardness of the LWE assumption and keyless multi-collision-resistant hash functions. (For the definition of keyless multi-collision-resistant hash functions, see, e.g., [3].)

Theorem 6. *For arbitrary super-polynomial functions $\gamma_{\mathsf{LWE}}, \gamma_{\mathsf{mCRH}}$ and an arbitrary polynomial K, assume the γ_{LWE}-hardness of the LWE assumption and the existence of a keyless weakly $(K, \gamma_{\mathsf{mCRH}})$-collision-resistant hash function. Then, there exists a public-coin 3-round zero-knowledge argument for NP.*

Proof. We use the transformation shown in [30], summarized as follows.

Lemma 3. *Assume the γ_{LWE}-hardness of the LWE assumption and the existence of a keyless weakly $(K, \gamma_{\mathsf{mCRH}})$-collision-resistant hash function as in Theorem 6. Also, assume the existence of a public-coin non-interactive tree-hash delegation scheme that satisfies the following properties.*

- *The scheme satisfies partial adaptive soundness and is γ_{Del}-secure for a super-polynomial function γ_{Del}.*
- *The scheme is LDE-holographic w.r.t. the encoding algorithm* Encode *such that, for the security parameter λ and an input x of length $N = 2^\ell \lambda$ ($\ell \leq \lfloor \log^2 \lambda \rfloor$), it outputs the LDE of x w.r.t. an LDE parameter $(\mathbb{F}, \mathbb{H}, m)$ such that $2m|\mathbb{H}| < |\mathbb{F}| = \mathsf{poly}(\log \lambda)$ and $N \leq |\mathbb{H}|^m \leq |\mathbb{F}|^m \leq \mathsf{poly}(N)$.*
- *The setup time $T_{\mathsf{Gen}}(\lambda, T, n_1, n_2)$ and the proof length $L_\pi(\lambda, T, n_1, n_2)$ are both at most $\mathsf{poly}(\lambda, \log n_1, n_2)$.*

Then, there exists a public-coin 3-round zero-knowledge argument for NP.

(For details about how we obtain Lemma 3 from [30], see the full version of this paper.) Given Lemma 3, we can prove Theorem 6 by observing that the desired tree-hash delegation scheme can be obtained by straightforwardly adjusting the proofs of Lemma 1 and Lemma 2 (namely, by using the super-polynomial hardness of the LWE assumption rather than the standard polynomial hardness). □

References

1. Babai, L., Fortnow, L., Levin, L.A., Szegedy, M.: Checking computations in polylogarithmic time. In: 23rd ACM STOC, pp. 21–31. ACM Press, May 1991. https://doi.org/10.1145/103418.103428
2. Badrinarayanan, S., Kalai, Y.T., Khurana, D., Sahai, A., Wichs, D.: Succinct delegation for low-space non-deterministic computation. In: Diakonikolas, I., Kempe, D., Henzinger, M. (eds.) 50th ACM STOC, pp. 709–721. ACM Press, June 2018. https://doi.org/10.1145/3188745.3188924
3. Bitansky, N., Kalai, Y.T., Paneth, O.: Multi-collision resistance: a paradigm for keyless hash functions. In: Diakonikolas, I., Kempe, D., Henzinger, M. (eds.) 50th ACM STOC, pp. 671–684. ACM Press, June 2018. https://doi.org/10.1145/3188745.3188870
4. Brakerski, Z., Holmgren, J., Kalai, Y.T.: Non-interactive delegation and batch NP verification from standard computational assumptions. In: Hatami, H., McKenzie, P., King, V. (eds.) 49th ACM STOC, pp. 474–482. ACM Press, June 2017. https://doi.org/10.1145/3055399.3055497

5. Bronfman, L., Rothblum, R.D.: PCPs and instance compression from a cryptographic lens. In: Braverman, M. (ed.) 13th Innovations in Theoretical Computer Science Conference (ITCS 2022). Leibniz International Proceedings in Informatics (LIPIcs), vol. 215, pp. 30:1–30:19. Schloss Dagstuhl - Leibniz-Zentrum für Informatik, Dagstuhl, Germany (2022). https://doi.org/10.4230/LIPIcs.ITCS.2022.30. https://drops.dagstuhl.de/opus/volltexte/2022/15626

6. Canetti, R., Goldreich, O., Halevi, S.: The random oracle methodology, revisited. J. ACM **51**(4), 557–594 (2004). https://doi.org/10.1145/1008731.1008734

7. Chiesa, A., Hu, Y., Maller, M., Mishra, P., Vesely, N., Ward, N.: Marlin: preprocessing zkSNARKs with universal and updatable SRS. In: Canteaut, A., Ishai, Y. (eds.) EUROCRYPT 2020. LNCS, vol. 12105, pp. 738–768. Springer, Cham (2020). https://doi.org/10.1007/978-3-030-45721-1_26

8. Chiesa, A., Ojha, D., Spooner, N.: FRACTAL: post-quantum and transparent recursive proofs from holography. In: Canteaut, A., Ishai, Y. (eds.) EUROCRYPT 2020. LNCS, vol. 12105, pp. 769–793. Springer, Cham (2020). https://doi.org/10.1007/978-3-030-45721-1_27

9. Choudhuri, A.R., Jain, A., Jin, Z.: Non-interactive batch arguments for NP from standard assumptions. In: Malkin, T., Peikert, C. (eds.) CRYPTO 2021. LNCS, vol. 12828, pp. 394–423. Springer, Cham (2021). https://doi.org/10.1007/978-3-030-84259-8_14

10. Choudhuri, A.R., Jain, A., Jin, Z.: SNARGs for $\mathcal{P}$ from LWE. Cryptology ePrint Archive, Report 2021/808, Version 20211108:181325 (2021). https://eprint.iacr.org/2021/808. An extended version of [11]

11. Choudhuri, A.R., Jain, A., Jin, Z.: SNARGs for $\mathcal{P}$ from LWE. In: 62nd FOCS, pp. 68–79. IEEE Computer Society Press, February 2022. https://doi.org/10.1109/FOCS52979.2021.00016

12. Chung, K.-M., Kalai, Y.T., Liu, F.-H., Raz, R.: Memory delegation. In: Rogaway, P. (ed.) CRYPTO 2011. LNCS, vol. 6841, pp. 151–168. Springer, Heidelberg (2011). https://doi.org/10.1007/978-3-642-22792-9_9

13. Devadas, L., Goyal, R., Kalai, Y., Vaikuntanathan, V.: Rate-1 non-interactive arguments for batch-NP and applications. In: 63rd FOCS, pp. 1057–1068. IEEE Computer Society Press, October/November 2022. https://doi.org/10.1109/FOCS54457.2022.00103

14. Goldwasser, S., Kalai, Y.T., Rothblum, G.N.: Delegating computation: interactive proofs for muggles. J. ACM **62**(4), 27:1–27:64 (2015)

15. Gur, T., Rothblum, R.D.: A hierarchy theorem for interactive proofs of proximity. In: Papadimitriou, C.H. (ed.) ITCS 2017, vol. 4266, pp. 39:1–39:43. LIPIcs, 67, January 2017. https://doi.org/10.4230/LIPIcs.ITCS.2017.39

16. Holmgren, J., Lombardi, A., Rothblum, R.D.: Fiat-Shamir via list-recoverable codes (or: Parallel repetition of GMW is not zero-knowledge). Cryptology ePrint Archive, Report 2021/286, Version 20210307:022349 (2021). https://eprint.iacr.org/2021/286. An extended version of [17]

17. Holmgren, J., Lombardi, A., Rothblum, R.D.: Fiat-Shamir via list-recoverable codes (or: parallel repetition of GMW is not zero-knowledge). In: Khuller, S., Williams, V.V. (eds.) 53rd ACM STOC, p. 750–760. ACM Press, June 2021. https://doi.org/10.1145/3406325.3451116

18. Holmgren, J., Rothblum, R.: Delegating computations with (almost) minimal time and space overhead. In: Thorup, M. (ed.) 59th FOCS, pp. 124–135. IEEE Computer Society Press, October 2018. https://doi.org/10.1109/FOCS.2018.00021

19. Hsiao, C.Y., Reyzin, L.: Finding collisions on a public road, or do secure hash functions need secret coins? In: Franklin, M. (ed.) CRYPTO 2004. LNCS, vol. 3152, pp. 92–105. Springer, Heidelberg (Aug 2004). https://doi.org/10.1007/978-3-540-28628-8_6

20. Hubacek, P., Wichs, D.: On the communication complexity of secure function evaluation with long output. In: Roughgarden, T. (ed.) ITCS 2015, pp. 163–172. ACM, January 2015. https://doi.org/10.1145/2688073.2688105

21. Hulett, J., Jawale, R., Khurana, D., Srinivasan, A.: SNARGs for P from subexponential DDH and QR. In: Dunkelman, O., Dziembowski, S. (eds.) EUROCRYPT 2022, Part II. LNCS, vol. 13276, pp. 520–549. Springer, Heidelberg (2022). https://doi.org/10.1007/978-3-031-07085-3_18

22. Jawale, R., Kalai, Y.T., Khurana, D., Zhang, R.Y.: SNARGs for bounded depth computations and PPAD hardness from sub-exponential LWE. In: Khuller, S., Williams, V.V. (eds.) 53rd ACM STOC, pp. 708–721. ACM Press, June 2021. https://doi.org/10.1145/3406325.3451055

23. Kalai, Y., Paneth, O., Yang, L.: How to delegate computations publicly. Cryptology ePrint Archive, Report 2019/603, Version 20190602:113205 (2019). https://eprint.iacr.org/2019/603. An extended version of [25]

24. Kalai, Y.T., Paneth, O.: Delegating RAM computations. In: Hirt, M., Smith, A.D. (eds.) TCC 2016-B, Part II. LNCS, vol. 9986, pp. 91–118. Springer, Heidelberg (2016). https://doi.org/10.1007/978-3-662-53644-5_4

25. Kalai, Y.T., Paneth, O., Yang, L.: How to delegate computations publicly. In: Charikar, M., Cohen, E. (eds.) 51st ACM STOC, pp. 1115–1124. ACM Press, June 2019. https://doi.org/10.1145/3313276.3316411

26. Kalai, Y.T., Raz, R., Rothblum, R.D.: How to delegate computations: the power of no-signaling proofs. J. ACM **69**(1), 1–82 (2022). https://doi.org/10.1145/3456867

27. Kalai, Y.T., Rothblum, R.D.: Arguments of proximity - [extended abstract]. In: Gennaro, R., Robshaw, M. (eds.) CRYPTO 2015. LNCS, vol. 9216, pp. 422–442. Springer, Heidelberg (2015). https://doi.org/10.1007/978-3-662-48000-7_21

28. Kalai, Y.T., Vaikuntanathan, V., Zhang, R.Y.: Somewhere statistical soundness, post-quantum security, and SNARGs. In: Nissim, K., Waters, B. (eds.) TCC 2021, Part I. LNCS, vol. 13042, pp. 330–368. Springer, Heidelberg (2021). https://doi.org/10.1007/978-3-030-90459-3_12

29. Kilian, J.: A note on efficient zero-knowledge proofs and arguments (extended abstract). In: 24th ACM STOC, pp. 723–732. ACM Press, May 1992. https://doi.org/10.1145/129712.129782

30. Kiyoshima, S.: Public-coin 3-round zero-knowledge from Learning with Errors and keyless multi-collision-resistant hash. In: Dodis, Y., Shrimpton, T. (eds.) CRYPTO 2022, Part I. LNCS, vol. 13507, pp. 444–473. Springer, Heidelberg (2022). https://doi.org/10.1007/978-3-031-15802-5_16

31. Paneth, O., Pass, R.: Incrementally verifiable computation via rate-1 batch arguments. In: 63rd FOCS, pp. 1045–1056. IEEE Computer Society Press, October/November 2022. https://doi.org/10.1109/FOCS54457.2022.00102

32. Rothblum, G.N., Vadhan, S.P., Wigderson, A.: Interactive proofs of proximity: delegating computation in sublinear time. In: Boneh, D., Roughgarden, T., Feigenbaum, J. (eds.) 45th ACM STOC, pp. 793–802. ACM Press, June 2013. https://doi.org/10.1145/2488608.2488709

33. Waters, B., Wu, D.J.: Batch arguments for NP and more from standard bilinear group assumptions. In: Dodis, Y., Shrimpton, T. (eds.) CRYPTO 2022, Part II. LNCS, vol. 13508, pp. 433–463. Springer, Heidelberg (2022). https://doi.org/10.1007/978-3-031-15979-4_15

Chainable Functional Commitments
for Unbounded-Depth Circuits

David Balbás[1,2](✉) (iD), Dario Catalano[3] (iD), Dario Fiore[1] (iD),
and Russell W. F. Lai[4] (iD)

[1] IMDEA Software Institute, Madrid, Spain
{david.balbas,dario.fiore}@imdea.org
[2] Universidad Politécnica de Madrid, Madrid, Spain
[3] University of Catania, Catania, Italy
catalano@dmi.unict.it
[4] Aalto University, Espoo, Finland
russell.lai@aalto.fi

Abstract. A functional commitment (FC) scheme allows one to commit to a vector x and later produce a short opening proof of $(f, f(x))$ for any admissible function f. Since their inception, FC schemes supporting ever more expressive classes of functions have been proposed.

In this work, we introduce a novel primitive that we call *chainable functional commitment* (CFC), which extends the functionality of FCs by allowing one to 1) open to functions of multiple inputs $f(x_1, \ldots, x_m)$ that are committed independently, 2) while preserving the output also in committed form. We show that CFCs for quadratic polynomial maps generically imply FCs for circuits. Then, we efficiently realize CFCs for quadratic polynomials over pairing groups and lattices, resulting in the *first FC schemes for circuits of unbounded depth* based on either pairing-based or lattice-based falsifiable assumptions. Our FCs require fixing a-priori only the maximal width of the circuit to be evaluated, and have opening proof size depending only on the circuit depth. Additionally, our FCs feature other nice properties such as being additively homomorphic and supporting sublinear-time verification after offline preprocessing.

Using a recent transformation that constructs homomorphic signatures (HS) from FCs, we obtain the first pairing- and lattice-based realisations of HS for bounded-width, but unbounded-depth, circuits. Prior to this work, the only HS for general circuits is lattice-based and requires bounding the circuit depth at setup time.

1 Introduction

Commitment schemes allow a sender to commit to a message x in such a way that the message remains secret until the moment she decides to open the commitment and reveal it (*hiding*), and they allow the receiver to get convinced that the opened message is the same x originally used at commitment time (*binding*).

© International Association for Cryptologic Research 2023
G. Rothblum and H. Wee (Eds.): TCC 2023, LNCS 14371, pp. 363–393, 2023.
https://doi.org/10.1007/978-3-031-48621-0_13

Today, commitments are a ubiquitous building block in cryptographic protocols, including digital signatures, zero-knowledge proofs and multiparty computation, to name a few. As applications become more and more sophisticated, the basic commitment functionality may fall short. One particular limitation is that the opening mechanism is *all-or-nothing*: either the sender opens in full the commitment and the receiver learns the whole message, or the receiver gets nothing. A more flexible and useful functionality would be to open the commitment to a *function of the committed message*, that is to reveal $f(x)$ for some function f.

This advanced commitment notion has been formalized by Libert, Ramanna and Yung who called this primitive *Functional Commitments* (FC) [24]. The property that makes functional commitments unique (and nontrivial to realize) is *succinctness*: assuming that the message is a large vector x, then both the commitment and the openings should be short, e.g., polylogarithmic or constant in the size of x. The main security requirement of functional commitments is *evaluation binding*: no polynomially bounded adversary should be able to, validly, open the commitment to two different values $y \neq y'$ for the same f. Additionally, FCs can also be hiding and zero-knowledge (a commitment and possibly several openings should not reveal additional information about x).

Functional commitments are essentially a class of (commit-and-prove) succinct non-interactive arguments (SNARGs) with a weaker security property, that is evaluation binding instead of soundness. The notion of evaluation binding is not necessarily a weakness but can also be a feature: it is a falsifiable security notion that makes FCs potentially realizable from falsifiable assumptions in the standard model (i.e., without random oracles), without contradicting the celebrated result of Gentry and Wichs about impossibility of SNARGs from falsifiable assumptions [14]. For this reason, functional commitments can be an attractive alternative to SNARGs for implementing succinct arguments in cryptographic protocols where evaluation binding is sufficient (notably, without carrying the need of non-falsifiable assumptions). Examples of this case include homomorphic signatures and verifiable databases as shown in [8], as well as the numerous applications that employ vector commitments [6,7,25] or polynomial commitments [21] (two primitives that are a special case of the FC notion). An additional motivation for studying evaluation binding FCs is that they can provide a different approach to construct SNARKs since any evaluation binding FC can be compiled into a SNARK by adding a simpler SNARK proof of "I know x that opens the commitment".

The state-of-the-art on realizations of FCs encompasses a limited set of functionalities that (besides the special cases of vector and polynomial commitments) include linear maps [23,24], semi-sparse polynomials [26] and constant-degree polynomials [1,8] (see Sect. 1.2 for a discussion on related and concurrent work).

We note that the full version of our work containing all results and proofs is available as [3].

1.1 Our Contribution

In this paper, we propose the first constructions of Functional Commitments that support the evaluation of arbitrary arithmetic circuits of unbounded depth[1] and are based on falsifiable assumptions. Our FC schemes are also *chainable*, meaning that it is possible to open to functions of multiple committed inputs while preserving the output to be in committed form. To capture such functionality, we introduce a novel primitive called *Chainable Functional Commitment* (CFC).

In our FC schemes only the maximal *width* of the circuits has to be fixed at setup time. The size of the commitments is succinct in the input size; the size of opening proofs grows with the multiplicative depth d_C of the evaluated circuit C, but is otherwise independent of the circuit's size or the input length. Notably, our FCs provide an exponential improvement compared to previous ones that could only support polynomials of degree $\delta = O(1)$ with an efficiency (prover time and parameter size) degrading exponentially in δ (as $O(n^\delta))^2$ [1,8].

We design our FCs for circuits in two steps: (1) a generic construction of an FC for unbounded-depth circuits based on CFCs for quadratic functions, and (2) two realizations of CFCs, one based on bilinear pairings and one based on lattices. The pairing-based CFC relies on a new falsifiable assumption that we justify in the bilinear generic group model, while the lattice-based CFC relies on a slight extension of the k-R-ISIS assumption recently introduced in [1]. Using either one of these two CFC constructions (and considering a few tradeoffs of our generic construction), we obtain a variety of FC schemes; we summarize in Table 1 the most representative ones.

Our FC schemes enjoy useful additional properties.

1. They are *additively homomorphic*, which as shown in [8] makes the FC updatable and allows for building homomorphic signatures (HS). Notably, our new FC for circuits yields new HS realizations that advance the state of the art (see slightly below for details).
2. They enjoy *amortized efficient verification*, which means that the verifier can precompute a verification key vk_C associated to a circuit C and use this key (an unbounded number of times) to verify openings for C in time (asymptotically) faster than evaluating C.
3. Our FC schemes can be trivially modified to have *perfectly hiding commitments* and efficiently compiled into FCs with *zero-knowledge openings*.

Both efficient verification and zero-knowledge openings are relevant in the construction of HS from FCs since, as showed in [8], they imply the analogous properties of efficient verification [9,18] and *context hiding* [4] in the resulting HS schemes.

---

[1] Looking ahead, our pairing-based instantiation supports arithmetic circuits over $\mathbb{Z}_q$, while our lattice-based instantiation supports arithmetic circuits over cyclotomic rings $\mathbb{Z}[\zeta]$ where wires carry values of bounded norm.

[2] Note, when used for a circuit of depth d these solutions may have efficiency doubly exponential in d since in general $\delta \approx 2^d$.

Table 1. Comparison of FCs for functions with n inputs and ℓ outputs. Constants are omitted, e.g., λn means $O(\lambda n)$ and $p(\cdot)$ represents some arbitrary polynomial function. For semi-sparse polynomials $\mu \geq n$ is a sparsity-dependent parameter (cf. [26]). For constant-degree polynomials δ_f is the degree of the polynomial f used in opening while δ is the maximum degree fixed at setup. AC means arithmetic circuits, $d_{\mathcal{C}}$ the depth of the circuit $\mathcal{C}$ used in opening, and note that $w \geq n, \ell$. AH means 'additively homomorphic'; schemes meeting this property can be turned into homomorphic signatures.

FC scheme	Functions	|pp|	|com|	|π|	**AH**
[24] (pair.)	linear maps	λn	λ	$\lambda \ell$	✓
[23] (pair.)	linear maps	$\lambda \ell n$	λ	λ	✓
[26] (pair.)	semi-sparse poly	$\lambda \mu$	$\lambda \ell$	λ	–
[1] (latt.)	const. deg. poly	$p(\lambda)(n^{2\delta}+\ell)$	$p(\lambda) \log n$	$p(\lambda) \log^2 \ell n$	✓
[8] (pair.)	const. deg. poly	$\lambda \ell n^{2\delta}$	$\lambda \delta_f$	$\lambda \delta_f$	✓
This work:					
Corol. 1.1 (pair.)	AC of width $\leq w$	λw^5	λ	$\lambda d_{\mathcal{C}}^2$	✓
Corol. 1.3 (pair.)	AC of size $\leq S$	λS^5	λ	$\lambda d_{\mathcal{C}}$	✓
Corol. 2.2 (latt.)	AC of width $\leq w$	$p(\lambda) w^5$	$p(\lambda) \log w$	$p(\lambda) d_{\mathcal{C}} \log^2 w$	✓

Application to Homomorphic Signatures. Homomorphic signatures (HS) [4,20] allow a signer to sign a large dataset x in such a way that anyone, holding a signature on x, can perform a computation f on this data and derive a signature $\sigma_{f,y}$ on the output $y = f(x)$. This signature vouches for the correctness of y as output of f on some legitimately signed data and is publicly verifiable given a verification key, a description of f, and the result y. The most expressive HS in the state of the art is the scheme of Gorbunov, Vaikuntanathan and Wichs [18] that is based on lattices and supports circuits with bounded number of inputs n and bounded (polynomial) depth d. In their scheme, the signature size grows polynomially with the depth of the evaluated circuit (precisely, as $d^3 \cdot \mathsf{poly}(\lambda)$).

By applying a recently proposed transformation [8], our new FCs for circuits yield new HS that support the same class of functions and succinctness as supported by the FC, advancing the state of the art. Notably, we obtain:

- *The first HS for circuits based on pairings.* Previously existing HS based on pairings can capture at most circuits in NC^1 [8,22] and need a bound on the circuit size. In contrast, our HS can evaluate circuits of any polynomial depth, achieving virtually the same capability of the lattice-based HS of [18] and with better succinctness. We believe this result is interesting as it shows for the first time that we can build HS for circuits without the need of algebraic structures, such as lattices, that are notoriously powerful.
- *The first HS that do not require an a-priori bound on the depth.* The work of Gorbunov, Vaikuntanathan and Wichs [18] left open the problem of constructing *fully-homomorphic* signatures, i.e., HS that can evaluate any computation in the class P without having to fix any bound at key generation time. In our

new HS we do not need to fix a bound on the depth but we rather need a bound on the width of the circuits at key generation time. Although this result does not fully solve the open problem of realizing fully-homomorphic signatures, we believe that our schemes make one step ahead in this direction. Our observation is that dealing with a bound on the circuit's depth is more difficult than dealing with a bound on the width. As evidence for this, we show a variant of our FC scheme (in the full version) for which one can fix a bound n and support circuits of larger width $O(n)$ with an $O(1)$ increase in proof size. Therefore, while our solution needs a bound on the width, this is not strict, as opposed to the depth bound in the HS of [18].

Like the scheme of [18], our HS constructions have efficient (offline/online) verification and are context-hiding. As a drawback, our HS allow only a limited form of multi-hop evaluation, that is the ability of computing on already evaluated signatures. In our case, we can compose computations sequentially (i.e., given a signature $\sigma_{f,y}$ for $y = f(x)$ we can generate one for $z = g(y) = g(f(x))$), while [18] supports arbitrary compositions (e.g., given signatures for $\{y_i = f_i(x)\}_i$, one can generate one for $z = g(f_1(x), \ldots, f_n(x))$). On the other hand, for circuits with multiple outputs, the size of our signatures is independent of the output size, whereas in [18] signatures grow linearly with the number of outputs.

Our Novel Tool: Chainable Functional Commitments. The key novelty that allows us to overcome the barrier in the state of the art and build the first FCs for circuits is the introduction and realization of chainable functional commitments (CFC) – a new primitive of potentially independent interest.

In brief, a CFC is a functional commitment where one can "open" to *committed outputs*. More concretely, while a (basic) FC allows proving statements of the form "$f(x) = y$" for committed x and publicly known y, a CFC allows generating a proof π_f that com_y is a commitment to $y = f(x_1, \ldots x_m)$ for vectors $x_1, \ldots x_m$, each independently committed in $\mathsf{com}_1, \ldots, \mathsf{com}_m$. In terms of security, CFCs must satisfy the analogue of evaluation binding, that is one cannot open the same input commitments $(\mathsf{com}_1, \ldots, \mathsf{com}_m)$ to two distinct output commitments $\mathsf{com}_y \neq \mathsf{com}'_y$ for the same f.

Keeping outputs committed is what makes CFCs "chainable", in the sense that committed outputs can serve as (committed) inputs for other openings. For instance, using the syntax above, one can compute an opening π_g proving that com_z is a commitment to $z = g(y)$. This way, the concatenation of $\mathsf{com}_y, \pi_f, \pi_g$ yields a proof that $z = g(f(x_1, \ldots x_m))$.

The introduction and realization of CFCs are in our opinion the main conceptual and technical contributions of this paper. From a conceptual point of view, the chaining functionality turns out to be a fundamental feature to tackle the challenge of supporting a computation as expressive as an arithmetic circuit. Indeed, we show that from a CFC for quadratic polynomial maps it is possible to construct a (C)FC for arithmetic circuits. From the technical point of view, we propose new techniques that depart from the ones of existing FCs for polynomials [1,8] in that the latter only work when the output vector is known to the verifier and there is a single input commitment. We refer to Sect. 2 for an informal explanation of our techniques.

1.2 Related and Concurrent Work

As noticed in previous work, it is possible to construct an FC for arbitrary computations from a universal SNARK and a succinct commitment scheme by generating a succinct commitment to the input x and a SNARK proof for the statement "$f(x) = y$ and x opens the commitment correctly". The drawback of this solution is that, by reducing to the knowledge-soundness of the SNARK, it would require non-falsifiable assumptions [14]. Alternatively, one could also reduce the security of this construction to the tautological (but falsifiable) assumption that the very same construction is secure. While such an argument is logically correct, it yields a non-standard assumption against the spirit of modern complexity-based cryptography. Hence, one of the goals in the FC literature is to construct schemes based on simple assumptions, which is the direction taken in this work.

The idea of a commitment scheme where one can open to functions of the committed data was implicitly suggested by Gorbunov, Vaikuntanathan and Wichs [18], though their construction is not succinct as the commitment size is linear in the length of the vector. Libert, Ramanna and Yung [24] were the first to formalize *succinct* functional commitments. They proposed a succinct FC for linear forms and showed applications of this primitive to polynomial commitments [21] and accumulators. Recent works have extended FCs to support more expressive functions, including linear maps [23], semi-sparse polynomials [26], and constant-degree polynomials [1,8]. Table 1 presents a comparison of these works with our results. Catalano, Fiore and Tucker [8] also proposed an FC for monotone span programs, which only achieves a weaker notion of evaluation binding where the adversary must reveal the committed vector. A weaker security model is also considered in [29], who introduced a lattice-based FC scheme where a trusted authority is assumed to generate, using a secret key, an opening key for each function for which the prover wants to release an opening.

Compared to these prior works, ours addresses the main question left open in the state of the art, which is to construct FCs for arbitrary computation from falsifiable assumptions.

Verifiable Computation. The functionality of functional commitments has similarities with verifiable computation (VC) schemes (also known as SNARGs for P). The main difference between VC and FC schemes is that in the latter, the input is committed as opposed to publicly known. Looking ahead, our generic construction of FC from CFCs presents a similar high-level approach as the SNARGs for P in [16,17]. In particular, both constructions proceed level-by-level in the circuit (an idea that dates back to the GKR protocol [15]). Then, the prover 1) computes a set of commitments to the wires at each level, and 2) proves that the committed vectors are consistent with respect to the circuit evaluation.

Beyond this similarity, our construction and [16,17] differ in techniques and the level of security that we achieve. Notably, even though the verifier in [16,17] may not need to see the opening of the commitment at each level, soundness only holds with respect to adversaries that reveal such opening. This translates into requiring the verifier to know the input (which is sufficient for VC but not for FC). Besides, [16,17] have a function-specific setup, as opposed to FCs in which public parameters should be universal and functions are to be chosen at opening time.

Concurrent Work. Concurrently to our work, de Castro and Peikert [5], and Wee and Wu [30], also propose lattice-based constructions of functional commitments for circuits (as well as polynomial and vector commitments). Their approaches differ significantly from ours, as they both rely on homomorphic evaluation techniques [13].

The work of [5] constructs a "dual" FC (where one commits to the function f and proves that $f(x) = y$ for a given x)[3] for bounded-depth boolean circuits. Their construction is selectively secure under the standard SIS assumption and admits a transparent setup (i.e., the public parameters are a uniformly random string). Their FC does not have succinct openings though, as the opening size is linear in either the input size or the size of f (in our setting where one commits to f and opens to x).

The FC in [30] supports circuits of bounded depth, needs a structured setup, and is secure under a new structured-BASIS assumption introduced in the same work. Their FC has succinct openings that are polylogarithmic in the input size and polynomial in the circuit depth.

In comparison to [5,30], our FC schemes support circuits of bounded width but *unbounded depth*, with succinct openings that grow only with the depth of the circuit but are independent of the input size. As [30], we require a trusted setup and achieve adaptive security based on new falsifiable assumptions on either pairings or lattices. For the lattice-based FC we rely on the Twin-k-R-ISIS assumption which is weaker than the BASIS assumption of [30] (see Sect. 7 for a comparison). Our FC schemes are the only ones that (i) have openings succinct also in the output size,[4] and (ii) achieve fast verification with pre-processing (i.e., after an input-independent preprocessing verification time is sub-linear in the size of $|f|$ and $|x|$).

2 A Technical Overview of Our Work

We construct our FCs for circuits in two main steps: (1) a generic construction of (C)FC for circuits from CFCs for quadratic polynomial maps (Sect. 5), and (2) the realization of these CFCs based on either pairings (Sect. 6) or lattices (Sect. 7). Below we give an informal overview of these constructions.

---

[3] One can recover the standard notion of committing to x and opening to f via universal evaluators.

[4] This means that our FCs satisfy compactness as defined in [23] for subvector and linear map commitments.

2.1   (C)FC for Circuits from CFCs for Quadratic Functions

Our first result is a transformation from CFCs for quadratic polynomials to FCs for circuits that is summarized in the following theorem.

Theorem 2 (Informal). *Let* CFC *be a Chainable functional commitment for quadratic polynomial maps* $f(x_1, \ldots, x_m) = y$ *for any number of inputs* m, *such that each committed input vector* x_i *and the committed output* y *have length* n. *Then, there exist a functional commitment* FC *for arithmetic circuits of bounded width* n *and unbounded depth* d, *such that:*

– FC*'s commitment size is the same as that of* CFC;
– *if* CFC *has opening proofs of size* $s(n, m)$, *then* FC *has openings of size at most* $d \cdot s(n, d)$. *Moreover, if* CFC *is additively homomorphic and/or efficiently verifiable, so is* FC.

Our transform starts from the observation that the gates of an arithmetic circuit[5] can be partitioned into "levels" according to their multiplicative depth, i.e., level h contains all the gates of multiplicative depth h and level 0 contains the inputs. All the outputs of level h, denoted by $x^{(h)}$, are computed by a quadratic polynomial map taking inputs from previous levels $< h$, and thus the evaluation of a circuit $\mathcal{C}$ of width $\leq n$ and depth d can be described as the sequential evaluation of quadratic polynomial maps $f^{(h)} : \mathcal{X}^{nh} \to \mathcal{X}^n$ for $h = 1$ to d.

The basic idea of our generic FC is that, starting with a commitment com_0 to the inputs $x^{(0)}$, we can open it to $y = \mathcal{C}(x^{(0)})$ in two steps. First, we commit to the outputs of every level. Second, we use the CFC opening functionality to prove that these values are computed correctly from values committed in previous levels. Slightly more in detail, at level h we create a commitment com_h to the outputs $x^{(h)} = f^{(h)}(x^{(0)}, \ldots, x^{(h-1)})$ and generate a CFC opening proof π_h to show consistency w.r.t. commitments $\mathsf{com}_0, \ldots, \mathsf{com}_h$. Eventually, this strategy reaches the commitment com_d of the last level that includes the outputs, which can be opened to y (or kept committed if one wants to build a CFC for circuits). The final proof π consists of all intermediate proofs and commitments, $\pi := (\pi_1, \ldots, \pi_d, \mathsf{com}_1, \ldots, \mathsf{com}_{d-1})$. Security reduces to the security of the CFC for quadratic functions.

2.2   A Framework for CFCs for Quadratic Functions

We next overview our general strategy of construction CFCs for quadratic functions, which admits pairing- and lattice-based instantiations. Our constructions rely on new cryptographic assumptions that we describe in later sections. For our pairing-based construction, we introduce the HiKer assumption, which can be seen as a "hinted" version of the KerMDH assumptions of [28]. For our lattice-based construction, we define the Twin-k-R-ISIS assumption which extends the k-R-ISIS assumption from [1].

---

[5] In our model we assume wlog arithmetic circuits where every gate is a quadratic polynomial of unbounded fan-in.

Theorems 4 and 5 (Informal). *Assuming the n-HiKer assumption (resp. the Twin-k-R-ISIS assumption), our pairing-based (resp. lattice-based) CFC construction is a succinct CFC scheme for quadratic functions over any m vectors of length $\leq n$ that admits efficient verification, is additively homomorphic, and whose openings can be made zero-knowledge. For arbitrary quadratic functions, the opening proofs have size $s(n,m) = \mathcal{O}(m^2)$ (resp. $s(n,m) = \mathcal{O}(m \cdot \text{polylog}(m \cdot n)))^6$.*

To build our CFCs we devise new commitment and opening techniques that capture a quadratic polynomial map $\boldsymbol{y} = f(\boldsymbol{x}_1, \ldots, \boldsymbol{x}_m)$ where each input is committed in com_i, and the output is committed too in $\text{com}_{\boldsymbol{y}}$. Our two constructions (pairing-based and lattice-based) of CFCs for quadratic functions have a similar high-level design that we introduce below.

For the pairing setting we adopt the implicit notation for bilinear groups $\mathbb{G}_1, \mathbb{G}_2, \mathbb{G}_T$ of prime order q by which $[\boldsymbol{x}]_s$ denotes the vector of group elements $(g_s^{x_1}, \ldots, g_s^{x_n}) \in \mathbb{G}_s^n$ for a fixed generator g_s. For the lattice setting, we let $\mathcal{R}$ be a cyclotomic ring and q be a large enough rational prime. In this overview, we adopt the bracket notation $[x]$ to express the representation of a given group or ring element without further distinction.

Abstract Functionality. To start, we define three (vectors of) commitment keys $[\boldsymbol{\alpha}]$, $[\boldsymbol{\beta}]$, and $[\boldsymbol{\gamma}]$, that live either in $\mathbb{G}_1^n$ in the pairing setting, or in $\mathcal{R}_q^n$ in the lattice setting. A commitment of type α to a vector $\boldsymbol{x} \in \mathbb{Z}_q^n$ is computed à la Pedersen, i.e., via an inner product, as $X^{(\alpha)} = [\langle \boldsymbol{x}, \boldsymbol{\alpha} \rangle]$. Commitments of type β and γ are defined analogously.

In our CFCs the commitments generated by the commit algorithm Com and used by the opening algorithm Open are only those of type α, whereas commitments of type β and γ are used as auxiliary values in the opening proofs. In order to create a CFC opening to a quadratic polynomial, our main tool is a technique realizing the following functionality:

- $[(\alpha, \beta) \to \gamma]$-Quadratic opening: given m commitments for each of the keys $\{X_i^{(\alpha)} = [\langle \boldsymbol{x}_i, \boldsymbol{\alpha} \rangle], X_i^{(\beta)} = [\langle \boldsymbol{x}_i, \boldsymbol{\beta} \rangle]\}_{i=1\ldots m}$ and a commitment $Y^{(\gamma)} = [\langle \boldsymbol{y}, \boldsymbol{\gamma} \rangle]$ generate a succinct opening proof $\pi_f^{(\gamma)}$ that $\boldsymbol{y} = f(\boldsymbol{x}_1, \ldots, \boldsymbol{x}_m)$.

Before seeing how we generate this opening, we observe that $\pi_f^{(\gamma)}$ does not yet achieve our goal since it assumes the availability of both type-α and type-β commitments on the inputs, and it only allows us to "move" to a type-γ commitment of the output, preventing us from achieving chainability.

We solve both issues by designing two special cases of the functionality above:

- $[\alpha \to \beta]$-Identity opening: given a type-α commitment $X^{(\alpha)} = [\langle \boldsymbol{x}, \boldsymbol{\alpha} \rangle]$ show that a type-β commitment $X^{(\beta)}$ commits to the same $\boldsymbol{x}$, i.e., $X^{(\beta)} = [\langle \boldsymbol{x}, \boldsymbol{\beta} \rangle]$;

---

^{6} Following Theorem 2, this gives a proof size of $\mathcal{O}(d^3)$ for our pairing-based FC and $\mathcal{O}(d^2 \cdot \text{polylog}(d \cdot w))$ for our lattice-based FC for circuits of depth d and width w. Nevertheless, the proof size can be reduced by a factor of d in both cases, as we show in Table 1. We refer to Sects. 6 and 7 for details.

- [$\gamma \to \alpha$]-Identity opening: given a type-γ commitment $Y^{(\gamma)} = [\langle \boldsymbol{y}, \boldsymbol{\gamma} \rangle]$ show that a type-α commitment $Y^{(\alpha)}$ commits to the same $\boldsymbol{y}$, i.e., $Y^{(\alpha)} = [\langle \boldsymbol{y}, \boldsymbol{\alpha} \rangle]$.

We use the identity opening mechanisms to "close the circle" in such a way to obtain a quadratic opening mechanism where all inputs and outputs are only type-α commitments. To summarize, our CFC Open algorithm consists of the following steps:

(i) compute a type-β commitment $X_i^{(\beta)}$ to each input along with an [$\alpha \to \beta$]-Identity opening proof that $X_i^{(\beta)}$ commits to the same $\boldsymbol{x}_i$ in $X_i^{(\alpha)}$;
(ii) compute a type-γ commitment $Y^{(\gamma)}$ to the result $\boldsymbol{y} = f(\boldsymbol{x}_1, \ldots, \boldsymbol{x}_m)$ and a [$(\alpha, \beta) \to \gamma$]-Quadratic opening proof attesting the validity of $\boldsymbol{y}$ w.r.t. the input commitment pairs $(X_i^{(\alpha)}, X_i^{(\beta)})$;
(iii) finally, use the [$\gamma \to \alpha$]-identity opening to ensure that $Y^{(\alpha)}$ is a commitment to the same $\boldsymbol{y}$ in the $Y^{(\gamma)}$ computed in (ii).

In the full version, we provide an overview of each of the opening methods in greater detail, as well as for each of our pairing- and lattice-based constructions.

3 Preliminaries

Notation. We denote by $\mathbb{N}$ the set of natural numbers > 0. We denote the security parameter by $\lambda \in \mathbb{N}$. We call a function ϵ *negligible*, denoted $\epsilon(\lambda) = \mathsf{negl}(\lambda)$, if $\epsilon(\lambda) = O(\lambda^{-c})$ for every constant $c > 0$, and call a function $p(\lambda)$ *polynomial*, denoted $p(\lambda) = \mathsf{poly}$, if $p(\lambda) = O(\lambda^c)$ for some constant $c > 0$. We say that an algorithm is *probabilistic polynomial time* (PPT) if it consumes randomness and its running time is bounded by some $p(\lambda) = \mathsf{poly}(\lambda)$. For a finite set S, $x \leftarrow_{\$} S$ denotes sampling x uniformly at random in S. For an algorithm A, we write $y \leftarrow A(x)$ for the output of A on input x. For a positive $n \in \mathbb{N}$, $[n]$ is the set $\{1, \ldots, n\}$. We denote vectors $\boldsymbol{x}$ and matrices $\mathbf{M}$ using bold fonts. For a ring $\mathcal{R}$, given two vectors $\boldsymbol{x}, \boldsymbol{y} \in \mathcal{R}^n$, $\boldsymbol{z} := (\boldsymbol{x} \otimes \boldsymbol{y}) \in \mathcal{R}^{n^2}$ denotes their Kronecker product (that is a vectorization of the outer product), i.e., $\forall i, j \in [n] : z_{i+(j-1)n} = x_i y_j$.

3.1 Functional Commitments

In this section we give the definition of functional commitments (FC) for generic classes of functions, by generalizing the one given in [24] for linear functions. For notational simplicity and without loss of generality, we give our definitions for functions that have n inputs and n outputs.

Definition 1 (Functional Commitments). *Let $\mathcal{X}$ be some domain and let $\mathcal{F} \subseteq \{f : \mathcal{X}^n \to \mathcal{X}^n\}$ be a family of functions over $\mathcal{X}$, with n inputs and n outputs. A functional commitment scheme for $\mathcal{F}$ is a tuple of algorithms $\mathsf{FC} = (\mathsf{Setup}, \mathsf{Com}, \mathsf{Open}, \mathsf{Ver})$ that work as follows and that satisfy correctness and succinctness defined below.*

Setup$(1^\lambda, 1^n) \to$ ck *on input the security parameter λ and the functions parameters n, outputs a commitment key* ck.

Com$(\text{ck}, \boldsymbol{x}; r) \to (\text{com}, \text{aux})$ *on input a vector $\boldsymbol{x} \in \mathcal{X}^n$ and (possibly) randomness r, outputs a commitment* com *and related auxiliary information* aux.[7]

Open$(\text{ck}, \text{aux}, f) \to \pi$ *on input an auxiliary information* aux *and a function $f \in \mathcal{F}$, outputs an opening proof π.*

Ver$(\text{ck}, \text{com}, f, \boldsymbol{y}, \pi) \to b \in \{0, 1\}$ *on input a commitment* com, *an opening proof π, a function $f \in \mathcal{F}$ and a value $\boldsymbol{y} \in \mathcal{X}^n$, accepts (b = 1) or rejects (b = 0).*

Correctness. FC *is correct if for any $n \in \mathbb{N}$, all* ck $\leftarrow_\$$ Setup$(1^\lambda, 1^n)$, *any $f : \mathcal{X}^n \to \mathcal{X}^n$ in the class $\mathcal{F}$, and any $\boldsymbol{x} \in \mathcal{X}^n$, if* (com, aux) $\leftarrow$ Com$(\text{ck}, \boldsymbol{x})$, *then*

$$\Pr[\text{Ver}(\text{ck}, \text{com}, f, f(\boldsymbol{x}), \text{Open}(\text{ck}, \text{aux}, f)) = 1] = 1.$$

Succinctness. *Let us assume that the admissible functions can be partitioned as $\mathcal{F} = \{\mathcal{F}_\kappa\}_{\kappa \in \mathcal{K}}$ for some set $\mathcal{K}$, and let $s : \mathbb{N} \times \mathcal{K} \to \mathbb{N}$ be a function. A functional commitment FC for $\mathcal{F}$ is said to be $s(n, \kappa)$-succinct if there exists a polynomial $p(\lambda) = \text{poly}(\lambda)$ such that for any $\kappa \in \mathcal{K}$, function $f : \mathcal{X}^n \to \mathcal{X}^n$ s.t. $f \in \mathcal{F}_\kappa$, honestly generated commitment key* ck $\leftarrow$ Setup$(1^\lambda, 1^n)$, *vector $\boldsymbol{x} \in \mathcal{X}^n$, commitment* (com, aux) $\leftarrow$ Com$(\text{ck}, \boldsymbol{x})$ *and opening $\pi \leftarrow$ Open$(\text{ck}, \text{aux}, f)$, it holds that $|\text{com}| \le p(\lambda)$ and $|\pi| \le p(\lambda) \cdot s(n, \kappa)$.*

In order to model and compare different constructions, the notion of succinctness that we introduce is parametric with respect to a function $s(n, \kappa)$ that depends on the input-output length n and some parameter κ of the evaluated function. In some cases we will express the function s using asymptotic notation. To give some examples, κ could be an integer expressing the depth/size of a circuit (and thus $\mathcal{F}_\kappa$ are all circuits of depth/size κ), the degree of a polynomial, or the running time of a Turing machine. Accordingly, $\mathcal{K}$ is a set that partitions the class of admissible functions, e.g., $\mathcal{K} = [D]$ if the admissible functions are all circuits of depth $\le D$, or $\mathcal{K} = \mathbb{N}$ if one wants to capture circuits of any depth. The security definition of FCs proposed in [24] is called evaluation binding and says that a PPT adversary cannot open a commitment to two distinct outputs for the same function.

Definition 2 (Evaluation Binding). *For any PPT adversary $\mathcal{A}$, the following probability is* negl(λ):

$$\mathbf{Adv}_{\mathcal{A}, \text{FC}}^{\text{EvBind}}(\lambda) = \Pr \left[\begin{array}{c} \text{Ver}(\text{ck}, \text{com}, f, \boldsymbol{y}, \pi) = 1 \\ \wedge \ \boldsymbol{y} \ne \boldsymbol{y}' \ \wedge \\ \text{Ver}(\text{ck}, \text{com}, f, \boldsymbol{y}', \pi') = 1 \end{array} : \begin{array}{c} \text{ck} \leftarrow \text{Setup}(1^\lambda, 1^n) \\ (\text{com}, f, \boldsymbol{y}, \pi, \boldsymbol{y}', \pi') \leftarrow \mathcal{A}(\text{ck}) \end{array} \right]$$

---

[7] In our constructions, we often omit r from the inputs; in such a case we assume either that r is randomly sampled or that the commitment algorithm is deterministic.

For simplicity of presentation, in all our security definitions, we omit checking the domains of the elements returned by the adversary, e.g., that $f \in \mathcal{F}$ and $y \in \mathcal{X}^n$ etc. In the full version we show that evaluation binding also implies the classical binding notion. There we also recall a stronger security definition called strong evaluation binding, introduced in [23], and a definition of extractability.

3.2   Additional Properties of FCs

We informally present three additional properties of functional commitments satisfied by our constructions (see the full version for the formal definitions).

Additive-Homomorphic FCs. These are functional commitments where, given two commitments com_1 and com_2 to vectors x_1 and x_2 respectively, one can compute a commitment to $x_1 + x_2$.

Efficient Amortized Verification. An FC with this property enables the verifier to precompute a verification key vk_f associated to the function f, with which they can check any opening for f in time asymptotically faster than running f.

Definition 3 (Amortized Efficient Verification). *A functional commitment scheme* FC *for* $\mathcal{F}$ *has* amortized efficient verification *if there exist two additional algorithms* $vk_f \leftarrow \mathsf{VerPrep}(ck, f)$ *and* $b \leftarrow \mathsf{EffVer}(vk_f, com, y, \pi)$ *such that for any* $n = \mathsf{poly}(\lambda)$, *function* $f : \mathcal{X}^n \rightarrow \mathcal{X}^n$ *s.t.* $f \in \mathcal{F}$, *any honestly generated commitment key* $ck \leftarrow \mathsf{Setup}(1^\lambda, 1^n)$, *vector* $x \in \mathcal{X}^n$, *commitment* $(com, aux) \leftarrow \mathsf{Com}(ck, x)$ *and opening* $\pi \leftarrow \mathsf{Open}(ck, aux, f)$, *it holds: (a)* $\mathsf{EffVer}(\mathsf{VerPrep}(ck, f), com, y, \pi) = \mathsf{Ver}(ck, com, f, y, \pi)$, *and (b) the running time of* EffVer *is* $o(T)$ *where* $T = T(\lambda)$ *is the running time of* $\mathsf{Ver}(ck, com, f, y, \pi)$.

Hiding and Zero Knowledge. Intuitively, an FC is hiding if the commitments produced through Com are hiding, in the classical sense. For zero-knowledge, the goal is that the openings produced by Open should not reveal more information about the committed vector beyond what can be deduced from the output, i.e., that x is such that $y = f(x)$.

We state a simple result showing that an FC with hiding commitments (but not necessarily zero-knowledge openings) can be converted, via the use of a NIZK scheme, into one that also achieves zero-knowledge openings. The proof is straightforward and appears in the full version.

Theorem 1. *Let* FC *be an FC scheme that satisfies com-hiding and let* Π *be a knowledge-sound NIZK for the NP relation* $R_{\mathsf{FC}} = \{((ck, com, f, y); \pi) : \mathsf{Ver}(ck, com, f, y, \pi) = 1\}$. *Then there exists an FC scheme* FC* *for the same class of functions supported by* FC *that has com-hiding and zero-knowledge openings. Furthermore, if* FC *is additive-homomorphic, so is* FC*; *if* FC *has efficient verification and* Π *supports* $R'_{\mathsf{FC}} = \{(vk_f, com, y; \pi) : \mathsf{EffVer}(vk_f, com, y, \pi) = 1\}$, *then* FC* *has also efficient verification.*

4   Chainable Functional Commitments

As described in the introduction, we introduce the notion of Chainable Functional Commitments (CFC), which is an extension of the FC primitive that allows one to "chain" multiple openings to different functions.

Definition 4 (Chainable Functional Commitments). *Let $\mathcal{X}$ be some domain, $n = \mathsf{poly}(\lambda)$ and let $\mathcal{F} \subseteq \{f : \mathcal{X}^{nm} \to \mathcal{X}^n\}$ be a family of functions over $\mathcal{X}$ for any integer $m = \mathsf{poly}(\lambda)$. A chainable functional commitment scheme for $\mathcal{F}$ is a tuple of algorithms $\mathsf{CFC} = (\mathsf{Setup}, \mathsf{Com}, \mathsf{Open}, \mathsf{Ver})$ that works as follows and that satisfies correctness and succinctness.*

$\mathsf{Setup}(1^\lambda, 1^n) \to \mathsf{ck}$ *on input the security parameter λ and the vector length n, outputs a commitment key ck.*

$\mathsf{Com}(\mathsf{ck}, x; r) \to (\mathsf{com}, \mathsf{aux})$ *on input a vector $x \in \mathcal{X}^n$ and (possibly) randomness r, outputs a commitment com and related auxiliary information aux.*

$\mathsf{Open}(\mathsf{ck}, (\mathsf{aux}_i)_{i \in [m]}, f) \to \pi$ *given auxiliary informations $(\mathsf{aux}_i)_{i \in [m]}$, one for every committed input, and a function $f \in \mathcal{F}$, returns an opening proof π.*

$\mathsf{Ver}(\mathsf{ck}, (\mathsf{com}_i)_{i \in [m]}, \mathsf{com}_y, f, \pi) \to b \in \{0, 1\}$ *on input commitments $(\mathsf{com}_i)_{i \in [m]}$ to the m inputs and com_y to the output, an opening proof π, and a function $f \in \mathcal{F}$, accepts ($b = 1$) or rejects ($b = 0$).*

Correctness. *CFC is correct if for any $n, m \in \mathbb{N}$, all $\mathsf{ck} \leftarrow_{\$} \mathsf{Setup}(1^\lambda, 1^n)$, any $f : \mathcal{X}^{nm} \to \mathcal{X}^n$ in the class $\mathcal{F}$, and any set of vectors $\{x_i\}_{i \in [m]}$ such that $x_i \in \mathcal{X}^n$, if $(\mathsf{com}_i, \mathsf{aux}_i) \leftarrow \mathsf{Com}(\mathsf{ck}, x_i)$ for every $i \in [m]$ and $(\mathsf{com}_y, \mathsf{aux}_y) \leftarrow \mathsf{Com}(\mathsf{ck}, f(x_1, \dots, x_m))$,*

$$\Pr\left[\mathsf{Ver}(\mathsf{ck}, (\mathsf{com}_i)_{i \in [m]}, \mathsf{com}_y, f, \mathsf{Open}(\mathsf{ck}, (\mathsf{aux}_i)_{i \in [m]}, f)) = 1\right] = 1.$$

Succinctness. *Let $\mathcal{F} = \{\mathcal{F}_\kappa\}_{\kappa \in \mathcal{K}}$ for some set $\mathcal{K}$ and let $s : \mathbb{N} \times \mathbb{N} \times \mathcal{K}$ be a function. A chainable functional commitment CFC is $s(n, m, \kappa)$-succinct if there exists a polynomial $p(\lambda) = \mathsf{poly}(\lambda)$ such that for any n, m and $\kappa \in \mathcal{K}$, function $f : \mathcal{X}^{mn} \to \mathcal{X}^n$, $f \in \mathcal{F}_\kappa$, honestly generated commitment key $\mathsf{ck} \leftarrow \mathsf{Setup}(1^\lambda, 1^n)$, vectors $x_i \in \mathcal{X}^n$ and commitments $(\mathsf{com}_i, \mathsf{aux}_i) \leftarrow \mathsf{Com}(\mathsf{ck}, x_i)$ for $i \in [m]$, $(\mathsf{com}_y, \mathsf{aux}_y) \leftarrow \mathsf{Com}(\mathsf{ck}, f(x_1, \dots, x_m))$, and opening $\pi \leftarrow \mathsf{Open}(\mathsf{ck}, (\mathsf{aux}_i)_{i \in [m]}, f)$, it holds that $|\mathsf{com}_i|, |\mathsf{com}_y| \leq p(\lambda)$ for every $i \in [m]$ and $|\pi| \leq p(\lambda) \cdot s(n, m, \kappa)$.*

As in the case of FCs (Definition 1) we define succinctness in a parametric way, and we are interested in CFC constructions supporting non-trivial functions $s(n, m, \kappa)$ that are sublinear or constant in n, m.

Additive Homomorphism and Efficient Verification. As for functional commitments, a CFC can also be additively homomorphic and have amortized efficient verification. These properties are analogous to these of FCs.

Definition 5 (Evaluation Binding). *For any PPT adversary $\mathcal{A}$, the following probability is $\mathsf{negl}(\lambda)$:*

$$\Pr\left[\begin{array}{l} \mathsf{Ver}(\mathsf{ck},(\mathsf{com}_i)_{i\in[m]},\mathsf{com}_y,f,\pi)=1 \\ \wedge\ \mathsf{com}_y\neq\mathsf{com}'_y\ \wedge \\ \mathsf{Ver}(\mathsf{ck},(\mathsf{com}_i)_{i\in[m]},\mathsf{com}'_y,f,\pi')=1 \end{array}\ :\ \begin{array}{c} \mathsf{ck}\leftarrow\mathsf{Setup}(1^\lambda,1^n) \\ \\ \left((\mathsf{com}_i)_{i\in[m]},f,\ \begin{array}{c}\mathsf{com}_y,\pi,\\ \mathsf{com}'_y,\pi'\end{array}\right)\leftarrow\mathcal{A}(\mathsf{ck}) \end{array}\right]$$

As one can notice, the above notion of evaluation binding can only hold in the case when the output commitments com_y are generated deterministically. This is still enough for using CFCs to construct FCs with hiding commitments to inputs and zero-knowledge openings (thanks to Theorem 1). We leave the definition of CFCs with hiding output commitments for future work.

5   FC for Circuits from CFC for Quadratic Polynomials

In this section we introduce a generic construction of a Functional Commitment scheme for arithmetic circuits of bounded width n, from any Chainable Functional Commitment for quadratic functions over inputs of length n.

Circuit Model and Notation. Let $\mathcal{R}$ be a commutative ring. We consider arithmetic circuits $\mathcal{C} : \mathcal{R}^n \to \mathcal{R}^n$ where every gate is a quadratic polynomial with bounded coefficients. It is not hard to see that such a model captures the more common model of arithmetic circuits consisting of fan-in-2 gates that compute either addition or multiplication.

More in detail, we model $\mathcal{C}$ as a directed acyclic graph (DAG) where every node is either an *input*, an *output* or a *gate*, and input (resp. output) nodes have in-degree (resp. out-degree) 0. We partition the nodes in the DAG defined by $\mathcal{C}$ in *levels* as follows. Level 0 contains all the input nodes. Let the *depth* of a gate g be the length of the longest path from any input to g, in the DAG defined by the circuit. Then, for $h \geq 1$, we define level h as the subset of gates of depth h. Note that any gate in level h has *at least* one input coming from a gate at level $h - 1$ (while other inputs may come from gates at any other previous level $0, \ldots, h-2$). The *depth* of the circuit $\mathcal{C}$, denoted $d_\mathcal{C}$ (or simply d when clear from the context), is the number of levels of $\mathcal{C}$. Finally, we assume that the last level $d_\mathcal{C}$ also contains output nodes.[8]

In this model, we define the *width* of $\mathcal{C}$, denoted by n, as the maximum number of nodes in any level $h = 0$ to $d_\mathcal{C}$. Note that the width upper bounds the input length. For simplicity, we assume without loss of generality circuits with maximal n inputs and n gates in every level.

When we evaluate $\mathcal{C}$ on an input $\boldsymbol{x}$, we denote the input values by $\boldsymbol{x}^{(0)}$, and the outputs of the gates in level h by the vector $\boldsymbol{x}^{(h)}$. We note that, for every $k \in [n]$, the output of the k-th gate in level h can be defined as $x_k^{(h)} = f_k^{(h)}(\boldsymbol{x}^{(0)}, \ldots, \boldsymbol{x}^{(h-1)})$ where $f_k^{(h)} : \mathcal{R}^{nh} \to \mathcal{R}$ is a quadratic polynomial. We

---

[8] This can be assumed without loss of generality. If we have an output $x_i^{(h)}$ at level $h < d$, we can introduce a linear gate at level d that takes $x_i^{(h)}$ and some arbitrary $x_j^{(d-1)}$ as input, and outputs $x_k^{(d)} = x_i^{(h)} + 0 \cdot x_j^{(d-1)}$.

group all these n polynomials $f_1^{(h)}, \ldots, f_n^{(h)}$ into the quadratic polynomial map $f^{(h)} : \mathcal{R}^{nh} \to \mathcal{R}^n$ such that $\boldsymbol{x}^{(h)} = f^{(h)}(\boldsymbol{x}^{(0)}, \ldots, \boldsymbol{x}^{(h-1)})$. We denote the operation that extracts these functions $\{f^{(h)}\}$ from $\mathcal{C}$ by $(f^{(1)}, \ldots, f^{(d)}) \leftarrow \mathsf{Parse}(\mathcal{C})$.

Quadratic Functions. As we mentioned above, a gate in our circuit model computes a quadratic polynomial. Thus all the gates at a given level form a vector of n quadratic polynomials that take up to $m = \mathsf{poly}(\lambda)$ vectors and output a single vector. We define this class of functions as

$$\mathcal{F}_{\mathsf{quad}} = \{f : \mathcal{R}^{nm} \to \mathcal{R}^n \ : f = (f_k)_{k \in [n]} \wedge \forall k \in [n] \, f_k \in \mathcal{R}[X_1^{(1)}, \ldots, X_n^{(m)}]^{\leq 2}\}.$$

A quadratic polynomial map $f \in \mathcal{F}_{\mathsf{quad}}$, $f : \mathcal{R}^{mn} \to \mathcal{R}^n$, such as those representing the computation done at a given level of a circuit, can be expressed in a compact form. For $f(\boldsymbol{x}^{(1)}, \ldots, \boldsymbol{x}^{(m)}) = \boldsymbol{y}$, we can define d matrices $\mathbf{F}^{(h)} \in \mathcal{R}^{n \times n}$, $d(d+1)/2$ matrices $\mathbf{G}^{(h,h')} \in \mathcal{R}^{n \times n^2}$, and a vector $\boldsymbol{e} \in \mathbb{F}^n$ such that

$$f(\boldsymbol{x}^{(1)}, \ldots, \boldsymbol{x}^{(m)}) = \boldsymbol{e} + \sum_{h \in \mathcal{S}_1(f)} \mathbf{F}^{(h)} \cdot \boldsymbol{x}^{(h)} + \sum_{(h,h') \in \mathcal{S}_2^{\otimes}(f)} \mathbf{G}^{(h,h')} \cdot (\boldsymbol{x}^{(h)} \otimes \boldsymbol{x}^{(h')}). \quad (1)$$

The sets $\mathcal{S}_1(f)$ and $\mathcal{S}_2^{\otimes}(f)$ are the *linear support* and the *quadratic support* of f that we define below; for now $\mathcal{S}_1 = [m]$, $\mathcal{S}_2^{\otimes} = \{(h, h') \in [m] \times [m] : h \leq h'\}$.[9]

We note that, in an arbitrary circuit, the function $f^{(h)}$ at each level may depend on values from *any* previous level, but not necessarily from all of them. To capture such connectivity precisely, we define the *linear support* of $f \in \mathcal{F}_{\mathsf{quad}}$, denoted $\mathcal{S}_1(f) \subseteq [m]$, as the set of indices h where the linear part of f is nonzero with respect to any term $X_i^{(h)}$. Formally, $\mathcal{S}_1(f) := \{h \in [m] : \mathbf{F}^{(h)} \neq \mathbf{0}\}$.

Analogously, we define the *quadratic support* of f, denoted $\mathcal{S}_2(f) \subseteq [m]$, as $\mathcal{S}_2(f) := \{h \in [m] : \exists h' \in [m] \mathbf{G}^{(h,h')} \neq \mathbf{0}\}$. We also express the quadratic support using pairs of indices, $\mathcal{S}_2^{\otimes}(f) := \{(h, h') \in [m] \times [m] : h \leq h' \wedge \mathbf{G}^{(h,h)} \neq \mathbf{0}\}$.

Finally, we define the *support* of f as the union of its linear and quadratic supports, namely $\mathcal{S}(f) = \mathcal{S}_1(f) \cup \mathcal{S}_2(f)$.

Consider a circuit $\mathcal{C}$ and let $(f^{(1)}, \ldots, f^{(d)}) \leftarrow \mathsf{Parse}(\mathcal{C})$. Then every function $f^{(h)}$ can be expressed and computed using only the inputs in $\mathcal{S}(f^{(h)})$, namely $f^{(h)}((\boldsymbol{x}^{(h')})_{h' \in \mathcal{S}(f^{(h)})}) = f^{(h)}(\boldsymbol{x}^{(0)}, \ldots, \boldsymbol{x}^{(h-1)})$.

We call the number of inputs in the support of $f^{(h)}$, namely $|\mathcal{S}(f^{(h)})|$, the *in-degree of level* h. We say that *a circuit $\mathcal{C}$ has in-degree $t_{\mathcal{C}}$* if $t_{\mathcal{C}} = \max_{h \in [d_{\mathcal{C}}]} |\mathcal{S}(f^{(h)})|$. We call $\mathcal{C}$ a *layered circuit* if it has in-degree 1. Notice that for a layered circuit it holds that $\boldsymbol{x}^{(d)} = \mathcal{C}(\boldsymbol{x}^{(0)})$ where $\boldsymbol{x}^{(h)} = f^{(h)}(\boldsymbol{x}^{(h-1)})$ for all $h = 1$ to d.

Classes of Circuits. To properly define the succinctness and the functions supported by our FC construction, we parametrize the circuits according to three parameters, the depth, the in-degree, and the width. Let $\mathcal{F}_{(d,t,w)} = \{\mathcal{C} :$

---

[9] This representation is not unique as $\boldsymbol{x}^{(h)} \otimes \boldsymbol{x}^{(h')}$ contains repeated entries, but this can be solved by agreeing on appropriately placing zero coefficients.

FC.Setup($1^\lambda, 1^n$)	FC.Com(ck, x)
1 : **return** CFC.Setup($1^\lambda, 1^n$)	1 : **return** CFC.Com(ck, x)

FC.Open(ck, aux, $\mathcal{C}$)	FC.Ver(ck, com, $\mathcal{C}, y, \pi$)
1 : $(f^{(1)}, \ldots, f^{(d)}) \leftarrow$ Parse($\mathcal{C}$)	1 : $(f^{(1)}, \ldots, f^{(d)}) \leftarrow$ Parse($\mathcal{C}$)
2 : $x^{(0)} \leftarrow$ Parse(aux)	2 : $\text{com}_0 \leftarrow$ com
3 : **for** $h \in [d]$:	3 : $(\pi_1, \ldots, \pi_d,$
// Evaluate and commit to each level	$\text{com}_1, \ldots, \text{com}_{d-1}) \leftarrow \pi$
4 : $x^{(h)} \leftarrow f^{(h)}(x^{(0)}, x^{(1)}, \ldots, x^{(h-1)})$	// Recompute commitment to output
5 : $(\text{com}_h, \text{aux}_h) \leftarrow$ CFC.Com(ck, $x^{(h)}$)	4 : $\text{com}_d \leftarrow$ CFC.Com(ck, y)
// Compute the opening for the level	5 : **for** $h \in [d]$:
6 : $\pi_h \leftarrow$ CFC.Open(ck,	// Verify all proofs
$(\text{aux}_{h'})_{h' \in \mathcal{S}_h}, f^{(h)})$	6 : $b_h \leftarrow$ CFC.Ver(ck,
7 : **return** $(\pi_1, \ldots, \pi_d, \text{com}_1, \ldots, \text{com}_{d-1})$	$(\text{com}_{h'})_{h' \in \mathcal{S}_h}, \text{com}_h, f^{(h)}, \pi_h)$
	7 : **return** $b_1 \wedge \cdots \wedge b_d$

Fig. 1. Construction of our FC for circuits from a CFC for the class $\mathcal{F}_{\text{quad}}$. For notational succinctness, we let $\mathcal{S}_h := \mathcal{S}(f^{(h)})$.

$\mathcal{R}^n \rightarrow \mathcal{R}^n : d_{\mathcal{C}} = d, t_{\mathcal{C}} = t, w_{\mathcal{C}} = w\}$, where $d_{\mathcal{C}} \in \mathbb{N}$, $t_{\mathcal{C}} \leq d$, $w_{\mathcal{C}} \leq w$ are the depth, in-degree, and width of $\mathcal{C}$, respectively. Then our FC scheme supports any arithmetic circuit of width at most n, in the model described above. We denote this class by $\mathcal{F}_n := \{\mathcal{F}_{(d,t,w)}\}_{d \in \mathbb{N}, t \leq d, w \leq n}$.

Construction. In Fig. 1 we present our FC construction for $\mathcal{F}_n$. We assume, without loss of generality, that the auxiliary input aux generated by CFC.Com contains the committed input x. In the protocol, we retrieve x from aux via a Parse function. Note that the same construction becomes a CFC for $\mathcal{F}_n$ if the verifier takes com_d as input and skips line 4 of Fig. 1.

Our goal in this section is to prove the following theorem.

Theorem 2. *Let* CFC = (Setup, Com, Open, Ver) *be a chainable functional commitment scheme for the class of functions* $\mathcal{F}_{\text{quad}}$. *Then, the scheme* FC *in Fig. 1 is an FC for the class* $\mathcal{F}_n$ *of arithmetic circuits* $\mathcal{C} : \mathcal{R}^n \rightarrow \mathcal{R}^n$ *of width* $\leq n$.

Let $\mathcal{K}$ *be a partitioning of* $\mathcal{F}_{\text{quad}}$ *such that* CFC *is* $s(n, m, \kappa)$-*succinct for* $\mathcal{F}_{\text{quad}} = \{\mathcal{F}_{\text{quad},\kappa}\}$. *Then* FC *is* $d \cdot (s_{\max}(n, t) + 1)$-*succinct for the class* $\mathcal{F}_n = \{\mathcal{F}_{(d,t,w)}\}_{d \in \mathbb{N}, t \leq d, w \leq n}$, *where* $s_{\max}(n, t) := \max_{\kappa \in \mathcal{K}} s(n, t, \kappa)$. *Moreover, given an additively homomorphic and/or efficiently verifiable* CFC, *so is* FC.

Proof. Correctness and additive homomorphism of FC follow immediately from the respective properties of CFC.

Succinctness. If CFC is $s(n, m, \kappa)$-succinct for the class of quadratic polynomials in $\mathcal{F}_{\text{quad}} = \{\mathcal{F}_{\text{quad},\kappa}\}$, then FC is $s'(n, (d, t))$-succinct for $\mathcal{F}_n = \{\mathcal{F}_{(d,t,n)}\}$

where $s'(n, (d, t)) = d \cdot (s_{\max}(n, t) + 1)$. Indeed, FC.Open produces $d - 1$ commitments com_h for $h \in [d - 1]$, each of them having size bounded by a fixed polynomial $p(\lambda) = \mathsf{poly}(\lambda)$. Besides, it generates d CFC evaluation proofs π_h, each of them involving $|\mathcal{S}(f^{(h)})| \leq t$ input commitments, and thus having size $\leq p(\lambda) \cdot s(n, |\mathcal{S}(f^{(h)})|, \kappa) \leq p(\lambda) \cdot s_{\max}(n, t)$. Hence, we can bound the size of an FC.Open proof by $|\pi| \leq p(\lambda) \cdot d \cdot (s_{\max}(n, t) + 1)$. A particularly relevant case is that for layered circuits we obtain $|\pi| \leq p(\lambda) \cdot d \cdot (s_{\max}(n, 1) + 1)$.

We obtain better succinctness by using a slightly different, yet general, circuit model. To keep the presentation of the main scheme simpler, we present this optimization in the full version only. The proof size reduction is specific to our CFC construction from pairings (see Sect. 6.3 for the resulting efficiency).

Efficient Verification. If CFC has amortized efficient verification (Definition 3), we can set FC.VerPrep(ck, f) to obtain $\mathsf{vk}_h \leftarrow$ CFC.VerPrep(ck, $f^{(h)}$) for $h \in [d]$ and output $\mathsf{vk}_f := (\mathsf{vk}_1, \ldots, \mathsf{vk}_d)$. Then, FC.EffVer simply recomputes the commitment to the output com_d and runs CFC.EffVer for each circuit level. It is not hard to see that FC has amortized efficient verification unless $d = \mathcal{O}(|\mathcal{C}|)$, a case in which the proof size also becomes very large. We remark that for both our pairing-based and lattice-based CFC instances, the running time of FC.EffVer is actually bounded by $p(\lambda)(|\boldsymbol{y}| + |\pi|)$ where $p(\lambda) = \mathsf{poly}(\lambda)$, which is optimal since the verifier at least needs to parse the proof and the output.

Security. In the full version, we prove that if CFC is evaluation binding, then so is FC. We also show an analogous result for knowledge extractability. $\square$

Various optimization strategies and efficiency trade-offs are described in the full version. These allow for reducing the proof size in many cases, and also for supporting circuits of larger width than initially specified at setup time.

6   Paring-Based CFC for Quadratic Functions

We present our construction of a chainable functional commitment for quadratic functions based on pairings. With our CFC, one can commit to a set of vectors $\boldsymbol{x}_1, \ldots \boldsymbol{x}_m$ of length n and then open the commitment to a quadratic function $f :$ $\mathbb{F}^{mn} \rightarrow \mathbb{F}^n$, for any $m = \mathsf{poly}(\lambda)$. The opening proofs of our scheme are quadratic in the number m of input vectors, but constant in the (possibly padded) length n of each input vector and of the output. Security is proven in the standard model based on a new falsifiable assumption that we justify in the generic bilinear group model. In Sect. 6.3 we discuss the FCs for circuits that we obtain by applying the generic transform of Sect. 5 to this pairing-based CFC.

We present our CFC with deterministic commitments and openings. We detail how to make our commitments perfectly com-hiding in the full version. We note that the FCs for circuits obtained from the com-hiding CFC are also com-hiding, and their openings can be made zero-knowledge by applying Theorem 1, which we can efficiently instantiate using, e.g., the Groth-Sahai [19] NIZK.

6.1   Preliminaries on Bilinear Groups and Assumption

A *bilinear group generator* $\mathcal{BG}(1^\lambda)$ is an algorithm that returns bgp := $(q, \mathbb{G}_1, \mathbb{G}_2, \mathbb{G}_T, e, g_1, g_2)$, where $\mathbb{G}_1$, $\mathbb{G}_2$, $\mathbb{G}_T$ are groups of prime order q, $g_1 \in \mathbb{G}_1$ and $g_2 \in \mathbb{G}_2$ are fixed generators, and $e : \mathbb{G}_1 \times \mathbb{G}_2 \to \mathbb{G}_T$ is an efficiently computable, non-degenerate, bilinear map. We use Type-3 groups where it is assumed that there is no efficiently computable isomorphism between $\mathbb{G}_1$ and $\mathbb{G}_2$. As in Sect. 2, we use the bracket notation of [10] for group elements: $[x]_s$ denotes $g_s^x \in \mathbb{G}_s$.

We prove that our construction satisfies evaluation binding under a new falsifiable assumption, called HintedKernel (HiKer), that we justify in the generic group model (see full version). The name of the assumption comes from its similarity with the KerMDH assumption of [28] which for matrices $[\mathbf{A}]_2$ from certain (random) distributions asks the adversary to find a nonzero vector $[\mathbf{z}]_1$ such that $\mathbf{Az} = \mathbf{0}$. In our case the adversary is challenged to find a nonzero $[u, v]_1$ such that $u\eta + v = 0$, when given $[1, \eta]_2$ but also other group elements, the "hints", that depend on η and other random variables.

Definition 6 (n-HiKer Assumption). *Let* bgp = $(q, \mathbb{G}_1, \mathbb{G}_2, \mathbb{G}_T, e, g_1, g_2)$ *be a bilinear group setting, let* $n \in \mathbb{N}$ *and let* $\mathcal{G}_1(\boldsymbol{S}, \boldsymbol{T}, H), \mathcal{G}_2(\boldsymbol{S}, \boldsymbol{T}, H)$ *be the following two sets of Laurent monomials in* $\mathbb{Z}_q[S_1, T_1, \ldots, S_n, T_n, H]$:

$$\mathcal{G}_1 := \{S_i, T_i\}_{i \in [n]} \cup \{S_i \cdot T_j\}_{i,j \in [n]} \cup \left\{ \frac{S_{i'}}{S_i} \cdot T_i \cdot H \right\}_{\substack{i,i' \in [n] \\ i \neq i'}} \cup \left\{ \frac{S_{i'} \cdot T_{j'}}{S_i \cdot T_j} \cdot H \right\}_{\substack{i,j,i',j' \in [n] \\ (i,j) \neq (i',j')}}$$

$$\mathcal{G}_2 := \{H\} \cup \{S_i\}_{i \in [n]} \cup \left\{ \frac{1}{S_i} \cdot T_i \cdot H, \frac{1}{S_i} \cdot H \right\}_{i \in [n]} \cup \left\{ \frac{1}{S_i} \frac{1}{T_j} \cdot H \right\}_{i,j \in [n]}$$

The n-HintedKernel (n-HiKer) assumption holds if for every $n = \mathsf{poly}(\lambda)$ *and any PPT $\mathcal{A}$, the following advantage is negligible*

$$\mathbf{Adv}_{\mathcal{A}}^{n\text{-}HiKer}(\lambda) = Pr\left[\begin{array}{c} (U,V) \neq (1,1)_{\mathbb{G}_1} \wedge \\ e(U, [\eta]_2) = e(V, [1]_2) \end{array} \middle| (U,V) \leftarrow \mathcal{A}\left(\mathsf{bgp}, \begin{array}{c} [\mathcal{G}_1(\sigma, \tau, \eta)]_1, \\ [\mathcal{G}_2(\sigma, \tau, \eta)]_2 \end{array} \right) \right]$$

where the probability is over the random choices of $\boldsymbol{\sigma}, \boldsymbol{\tau}, \eta$ *and $\mathcal{A}$'s random coins.*

6.2   Our CFC Construction

As defined in the previous section we express $f \in \mathcal{F}_{\mathsf{quad}}$ through a set of matrices $\mathbf{F}^{(h)} \in \mathbb{F}^{n \times n}$ and $\mathbf{G}^{(h,h')} \in \mathbb{F}^{n \times n^2}$, and a vector $\boldsymbol{e} \in \mathbb{F}^n$ such that

$$f(\boldsymbol{x}^{(1)}, \ldots, \boldsymbol{x}^{(m)}) = \boldsymbol{e} + \sum_{h \in \mathcal{S}_1(f)} \mathbf{F}^{(h)} \cdot \boldsymbol{x}^{(h)} + \sum_{(h,h') \in \mathcal{S}_2^{\otimes}(f)} \mathbf{G}^{(h,h')} \cdot (\boldsymbol{x}^{(h)} \otimes \boldsymbol{x}^{(h')}) \quad (2)$$

For the sake of defining the succinctness of our CFC we parametrize the class $\mathcal{F}_{\mathsf{quad}}$ by the size of the quadratic support of f. Formally, let $\mathcal{K} = \{0, 1, \ldots, m(m+1)/2\}$. Then we partition $\mathcal{F}_{\mathsf{quad}}$ as $\{\mathcal{F}_{\mathsf{quad},\kappa}\}_{\kappa \in \mathcal{K}}$ where each $\mathcal{F}_{\mathsf{quad},\kappa} = \{f \in \mathcal{F}_{\mathsf{quad}} : \mathcal{S}_2^{\otimes}(f) = \kappa\}$.

Setup($1^\lambda, 1^n$) Let $n \geq 1$ be an integer representing the width of each of the inputs of the functions to be computed at opening time. Generate a bilinear group description $\mathsf{bgp} := (q, \mathbb{G}_1, \mathbb{G}_2, \mathbb{G}_T, e, g_1, g_2) \leftarrow \mathcal{BG}(1^\lambda)$, and let $\mathbb{F} := \mathbb{Z}_q$. Next, sample random $\boldsymbol{\alpha}, \boldsymbol{\beta}, \boldsymbol{\gamma} \leftarrow_s \mathbb{F}^n$, $\eta_\alpha, \eta_\beta, \eta_\gamma \leftarrow_s \mathbb{F}$, and output

$$
\mathsf{ck} := \begin{pmatrix}
[\boldsymbol{\alpha}]_1, [\boldsymbol{\alpha}]_2, [\boldsymbol{\beta}]_1, [\boldsymbol{\gamma}]_1, [\boldsymbol{\alpha} \otimes \boldsymbol{\beta}]_1, [\eta_\alpha]_2, [\eta_\beta]_2, [\eta_\gamma]_2 \\
\left\{ \left[\alpha_i \frac{\gamma_{i'}}{\gamma_i} \eta_\alpha\right]_1, \left[\frac{\alpha_{i'}}{\alpha_i} \beta_i \eta_\beta\right]_1 \right\}_{\substack{i,i' \in [n] \\ i \neq i'}} \left\{ \left[\frac{\alpha_{i'} \beta_{j'}}{\alpha_i \beta_j} \gamma_k \eta_\gamma\right]_1 \right\}_{\substack{i,j,i',j',k \in [n] \\ (i,j) \neq (i',j')}} \\
\left\{ \left[\frac{\alpha_i \eta_\alpha}{\gamma_i}\right]_2, \left[\frac{\beta_i \eta_\beta}{\alpha_i}\right]_2 \right\}_{i \in [n]}, \left\{ \left[\frac{\gamma_k \eta_\gamma}{\alpha_i}\right]_2 \right\}_{i,k \in [n]} \left\{, \left[\frac{\gamma_k \eta_\gamma}{\alpha_i \beta_j}\right]_2 \right\}_{i,j,k \in [n]}
\end{pmatrix}.
$$

Com($\mathsf{ck}, \boldsymbol{x}$)] output $\mathsf{com} := [\langle \boldsymbol{x}, \boldsymbol{\alpha}\rangle]_1$ and $\mathsf{aux} = \boldsymbol{x}$.

Open($\mathsf{ck}, (\mathsf{aux}_i)_{i \in [m]}, f$) $\to \pi$ Let $\mathbf{F}^{(h)} \in \mathbb{F}^{n \times n}$ for $h \in \mathcal{S}_1(f)$, $\mathbf{G}^{(h,h')} \in \mathbb{F}^{n \times n^2}$ for $(h, h') \in \mathcal{S}_2^\otimes(f)$, and $\boldsymbol{e} \in \mathbb{F}^n$ be the matrices and vectors associated to $f : \mathbb{F}^{mn} \to \mathbb{F}^n$. The opening algorithm computes the output $\boldsymbol{y} = f(\boldsymbol{x}^{(1)}, \ldots, \boldsymbol{x}^{(m)})$ and proceeds as follows.

- For every $h \in \mathcal{S}_2(f)$: compute $X_h^{(2)} := [\langle \boldsymbol{x}^{(h)}, \boldsymbol{\alpha}\rangle]_2$, $X_h^{(\beta)} := [\langle \boldsymbol{x}^{(h)}, \boldsymbol{\beta}\rangle]_1$, which are commitments to $\boldsymbol{x}^{(h)}$ under $\boldsymbol{\alpha}$ in $\mathbb{G}_2$ and under $\boldsymbol{\beta}$ in $\mathbb{G}_1$, resp.
- For every $h \in \mathcal{S}_2(f)$: compute a linear map opening proof for the identity function, to show that X_h and $X_h^{(\beta)}$ open to the same value:

$$
\pi_h^{(\beta)} := \sum_{\substack{i,i' \in [n] \\ i \neq i'}} x_{i'}^{(h)} \cdot \left[\frac{\alpha_{i'}}{\alpha_i} \beta_i \eta_\beta\right]_1
$$

- For every pair of inputs $\boldsymbol{x}^{(h)}, \boldsymbol{x}^{(h')}$ such that $(h, h') \in \mathcal{S}_2^\otimes(f)$, compute a commitment to their tensor products as follows:

$$
Z_{h,h'} := \sum_{i,j \in [n]} x_i^{(h)} x_j^{(h')} \cdot [\alpha_i \beta_j]_1 = [\langle \boldsymbol{x}^{(h)} \otimes \boldsymbol{x}^{(h')}, \boldsymbol{\alpha} \otimes \boldsymbol{\beta}\rangle]_1.
$$

- Compute a linear map opening proof to show that the vector $\boldsymbol{y}$ satisfies Eq. (2), with respect to all the inputs $\boldsymbol{x}^{(h)}$ committed in X_h and the inputs $\boldsymbol{x}^{(h)} \otimes \boldsymbol{x}^{(h')}$ committed in $Z_{h,h'}$:

$$
\pi^{(\gamma)} := \sum_{h \in \mathcal{S}_1(f)} \sum_{\substack{i,i',k \in [n] \\ i \neq i'}} F_{k,i}^{(h)} \cdot x_{i'}^{(h)} \cdot \left[\frac{\alpha_{i'}}{\alpha_i} \gamma_k \eta_\gamma\right]_1
$$

$$
+ \sum_{(h,h') \in \mathcal{S}_2^\otimes(f)} \sum_{\substack{i,j,i',j',k \in [n] \\ (i,j) \neq (i',j')}} G_{k,(i,j)}^{(h,h')} \cdot x_{i'}^{(h)} x_{j'}^{(h')} \cdot \left[\frac{\alpha_{i'} \beta_{j'}}{\alpha_i \beta_j} \gamma_k \eta_\gamma\right]_1
$$

Note that $\pi^{(\gamma)}$ is in fact a proof for the vector $\boldsymbol{e} - \boldsymbol{t}$; the linear shift will be addressed by the verifier in Eq. (8).

- Commit to the output y under γ by computing $Y^{(\gamma)} := [\langle y, \gamma \rangle]_1$. Then, compute a linear map opening proof for the identity function, to show that $Y^{(\gamma)}$ and the commitment to the output $\mathsf{com}_y \leftarrow \mathsf{Com}(\mathsf{ck}, y)$ (which is under α) open to the same value:

$$\pi^{(\alpha)} := \sum_{\substack{i,i' \in [n] \\ i \neq i'}} y_{i'} \cdot \left[\alpha_i \frac{\gamma_{i'}}{\gamma_i} \eta_\alpha \right]_1$$

- Return $\pi \quad := \quad \left(\{ X_h^{(2)}, X_h^{(\beta)}, \pi_h^{(\beta)} \}_{h \in \mathcal{S}_2(f)}, \{ Z_{h,h'} \}_{(h,h') \in \mathcal{S}_2^\otimes(f)}, Y^{(\gamma)}, \pi^{(\alpha)}, \pi^{(\gamma)} \right)$.

$\mathsf{Ver}(\mathsf{ck}, (\mathsf{com}_i)_{i \in [m]}, \mathsf{com}_y, f, \pi) \to b \in \{0,1\}]$ Parse the proof π as above and set $X_h := \mathsf{com}_h$. Output 1 if all the following checks pass and 0 otherwise:
- Verify the consistency of all the commitments. Namely, verify that each X_h and $X_h^{(2)}$ are commitments to the same value in $\mathbb{G}_1$ and $\mathbb{G}_2$:

$$\forall h \in \mathcal{S}_2(f) : e\left(X_h, [1]_2 \right) \stackrel{?}{=} e\left([1]_1, X_h^{(2)} \right) \tag{3}$$

- Verify the linear map commitment proofs $\pi_h^{(\beta)}$ that both $X_h^{(\beta)}, X_h$ commit to the same value in different sets of parameters:

$$\forall h \in \mathcal{S}_2(f) : e\left(X_h, \sum_{i \in [n]} \left[\frac{\beta_i \eta_\beta}{\alpha_i} \right]_2 \right) \stackrel{?}{=} e\left(\pi_h^{(\beta)}, [1]_2 \right) e\left(X_h^{(\beta)}, [\eta_\beta]_2 \right) \tag{4}$$

- Verify the consistency of the commitments to the tensor products, i.e., verify that $Z_{h,h'}$ is a commitment to $x^{(h)} \otimes x^{(h')}$:

$$\forall (h, h') \in \mathcal{S}_2^\otimes(f) : e\left(Z_{h,h'}, [1]_2 \right) \stackrel{?}{=} e\left(X_{h'}^{(\beta)}, X_h^{(2)} \right) \tag{5}$$

- Verify the linear map commitment proof $\pi^{(\alpha)}$ that both $\mathsf{com}_y, Y^{(\gamma)}$ commit to the same value in different sets of parameters:

$$e\left(Y^{(\gamma)}, \sum_{i \in [n]} \left[\frac{\alpha_i \eta_\alpha}{\gamma_i} \right]_2 \right) \stackrel{?}{=} e\left(\pi^{(\alpha)}, [1]_2 \right) e\left(\mathsf{com}_y, [\eta_\alpha]_2 \right) \tag{6}$$

- Verify the linear map commitment proof to check that, intuitively, $Y^{(\gamma)}$ is a commitment under γ to the output of f, computed from the inputs committed in X_h and $Z_{h,h'}$. To this end, compute the encoding of the matrices $\mathbf{F}^{(h)}$ for $h \in \mathcal{S}_1(f)$, $\mathbf{G}^{(h,h')}$ for $(h, h') \in \mathcal{S}_2^\otimes(f)$ and the vector e as follows. Let $\Theta = [\langle e, \gamma \rangle]_1$ and

$$\Phi_h := \sum_{i,k \in [n]} F_{k,i}^{(h)} \cdot \left[\frac{\gamma_k \eta_\gamma}{\alpha_i} \right]_2, \quad \Gamma_{h,h'} := \sum_{i,j,k \in [n]} G_{k,(i,j)}^{(h,h')} \cdot \left[\frac{\gamma_k \eta_\gamma}{\alpha_i \beta_j} \right]_2 \tag{7}$$

and then verify that

$$\prod_{h \in \mathcal{S}_1(f)} e\left(X_h, \Phi_h\right) \cdot \prod_{(h,h') \in \mathcal{S}_2^{\otimes}(f)} e\left(Z_{h,h'}, \Gamma_{h,h'}\right) \stackrel{?}{=} e\left(\pi^{(\gamma)}, [1]_2\right) e\left(Y^{(\gamma)} \cdot \Theta^{-1}, [\eta_\gamma]_2\right).$$

(8)

Theorem 3. *Assume that the n-HiKer assumption holds for a bilinear group setting generated by $\mathcal{BG}$. Then the construction CFC described above is an evaluation binding CFC scheme for the class $\mathcal{F}_{\mathsf{quad}}$ of quadratic functions over any $m = \mathsf{poly}(\lambda)$ vectors of length $\leq n$, that has efficient verification and is additively homomorphic. Considering the partitioning of $\mathcal{F}_{\mathsf{quad}} = \{\mathcal{F}_{\mathsf{quad},\kappa}\}_{\kappa=0}^{m(m+1)/2}$, CFC is $s(n, m, \kappa)$-succinct for $s(n, m, \kappa) = (\kappa + 3m + 3)$. Furthermore, when executed on a more adequately chosen circuit parametrization (see the full version for details) then CFC is $(4\kappa + 3)$-succinct.*

Due to space constraints, we only include a sketch of the security proof. The full proof of the theorem is available in the full version.

6.3   Resulting Instantiations of FC for Circuits

We summarize the FC schemes that result from instantiating our generic construction of Sect. 5 with our pairing-based CFC. The results follow by combining Theorems 2 and 3 and from the circuit optimizations that we describe in our full version.

Corollary 1. *Assume that the n-HiKer assumption holds for $\mathcal{BG}$. Then the following statements hold:*

1. *There exists an FC scheme for the class $\mathcal{F}_n = \{\mathcal{F}_{(d,t,w)}\}$ of arithmetic circuits of width $w \leq n$ that is $O(d \cdot t)$-succinct. In particular, the FC is $O(d^2)$-succinct for an arbitrary arithmetic circuit of multiplicative depth d, and is $O(d)$-succinct for a layered arithmetic circuit of multiplicative depth d.*
2. *There exists an FC scheme for the class $\mathcal{F}_n = \{\mathcal{F}_{(d,t,w)}\}$ of arithmetic circuits of width $w \leq n$ that is $\mathcal{O}(d^2 \cdot w \cdot n^{-1})$-succinct.*
3. *There exists an FC scheme for the class of arithmetic circuits of size $\leq S$, that is $\mathcal{O}(d)$-succinct where d is the multiplicative depth of the circuit.*
4. *For any $w_0 \geq 2$, there exists an FC scheme for the class $\mathcal{F} = \{\mathcal{F}_{(d,t,w)}\}$ of circuits of arbitrary width $w > w_0$ that is $\mathcal{O}(d \cdot t \cdot (w/w_0)^2)$-succinct.*

6.4   Proof of Security

In this section, we present a detailed sketch of the proof that our CFC satisfies evaluation binding. The full proof can be found in the full version, where we also show knowledge extractability by relying on a non-falsifiable assumption.

Consider an adversary $\mathcal{A}$ who returns a tuple $((\mathsf{com}_h)_{h \in [m]}, \mathsf{com}_y, f, \pi,$ $\tilde{\mathsf{com}}_y, \tilde{\pi})$ that breaks evaluation binding, set $X_h := \mathsf{com}_h$, and parse the proofs as follows

$$\pi := \left(\{X_h^{(2)}, X_h^{(\beta)}, \pi_h^{(\beta)}\}_{h \in \mathcal{S}_2(f)}, \{Z_{h,h'}\}_{(h,h') \in \mathcal{S}_2^\otimes(f)}, Y^{(\gamma)}, \pi^{(\alpha)}, \pi^{(\gamma)} \right)$$

$$\tilde{\pi} := \left(\{\tilde{X}_h^{(2)}, \tilde{X}_h^{(2)}, \tilde{\pi}_h^{(\beta)}\}_{h \in \mathcal{S}_2(f)}, \{\tilde{Z}_{h,h'}\}_{(h,h') \in \mathcal{S}_2^\otimes(f)}, \tilde{Y}^{(\gamma)}, \tilde{\pi}^{(\alpha)}, \tilde{\pi}^{(\gamma)} \right)$$

By evaluation binding, both proofs must verify for the same function f, the same input commitments $\{X_h\}_{h \in [m]}$, and different output $\mathsf{com}_y \neq \tilde{\mathsf{com}}_y$ commitments.

We show how to turn $\mathcal{A}$ into an adversary $\mathcal{B}$ against the assumption. $\mathcal{A}$ can cheat in three possible ways, for which we define events E_1, E_2, E_3 as:

- E_1 is the event that $Y^{(\gamma)} = \tilde{Y}^{(\gamma)}$. As $\mathsf{com}_y \neq \tilde{\mathsf{com}}_y$, this implies an evaluation binding break in the linear map opening proof in Eq. (6).
- E_2 is the event that E_1 does not happen (i.e., $Y^{(\gamma)} \neq \tilde{Y}^{(\gamma)}$) and that $X_{h^*}^{(\beta)} \neq \tilde{X}_{h^*}^{(\beta)}$ for some $h^* \in \mathcal{S}_2(f)$. This means that the proofs $\pi_{h^*}^{(\beta)}, \tilde{\pi}_{h^*}^{(\beta)}$ open the commitment com_{h^*} to two different output commitments for the identity function, which breaks evaluation binding in Eq. (4).
- E_3 is the event that neither E_1 nor E_2 occur. In this case, we will show that evaluation binding breaks in Eq. (8).

For any of these events, we will use $\mathcal{A}$'s output to break the n-HiKer assumption if this is embedded into ck. For this embedding, $\mathcal{B}$ makes a secret guess $\hat{s} \in \{0, 1\}$ such that $\hat{s} = 0$ corresponds to a guess that event E_1 occurs while $\hat{s} = 1$ corresponds to E_2 or E_3.

Commitment Key Generation. We sketch how $\mathcal{B}$ can generate ck and embed into it the input of the n-HiKer assumption. For $\hat{s} = 0$, $\mathcal{B}$ samples $\boldsymbol{\alpha}, \boldsymbol{\beta} \leftarrow_{\!s} \mathbb{F}^n$, $\eta_\beta, \eta_\gamma \leftarrow_{\!s} \mathbb{F}$ and implicitly sets $\boldsymbol{\gamma} := \boldsymbol{\sigma}$ and $\eta_\alpha := \eta$ from the input of the assumption. It is easy to see that this implicit setting allows $\mathcal{B}$ to compute all the elements in the first row of ck, namely $[\boldsymbol{\alpha}, \boldsymbol{\beta}, \boldsymbol{\gamma}, \boldsymbol{\alpha} \otimes \boldsymbol{\beta}]_1$, $[\boldsymbol{\alpha}, \eta_\alpha, \eta_\beta, \eta_\gamma]_2$. Then, $\mathcal{B}$ can simulate the remaining elements analogously. For instance, for the first element in the second row, $\mathcal{B}$ sets $\left[\alpha_i \frac{\gamma_{i'}}{\gamma_i} \eta_\alpha\right]_1 := \alpha_i \left[\frac{\eta \sigma_{i'}}{\sigma_i}\right]_1$ for all $i, i' \in [n], i \neq i'$.

For $\hat{s} = 1$, $\mathcal{B}$ samples $\eta_\alpha, r_\beta, r_\gamma \leftarrow_{\!s} \mathbb{F}$, $\boldsymbol{\gamma} \leftarrow_{\!s} \mathbb{F}^n$ and implicitly sets $\boldsymbol{\alpha} := \boldsymbol{\sigma}, \boldsymbol{\beta} := \boldsymbol{\tau}, \eta_\beta := r_\beta \cdot \eta, \eta_\gamma := r_\gamma \cdot \eta$. Then, she proceeds as before. It is not hard to show that ck is perfectly distributed and that $\hat{s}$ is perfectly hidden to $\mathcal{A}$.

Execution of $\mathcal{A}$. Having generated ck, $\mathcal{B}$ runs $\mathcal{A}(\mathsf{ck})$, and parses the output as before. Then, $\mathcal{B}$ proceeds differently according to the events E_1, E_2, E_3 above.

If E_1 occurs, $\mathcal{B}$ first checks that $\hat{s} = 1$ (and aborts otherwise). If $\mathcal{B}$ proceeds, we have that as $Y^{(\gamma)} = \tilde{Y}^{(\gamma)}$, then $\pi^{(\alpha)}, \tilde{\pi}^{(\alpha)}$ open to different $\mathsf{com}_y, \tilde{\mathsf{com}}_y$. Therefore, by Eq. (6), we have

$$e\left(\pi^{(\alpha)}, [1]_2\right) e\left(\mathsf{com}_y, [\eta_\alpha]_2\right) = e\left(\tilde{\pi}^{(\alpha)}, [1]_2\right) e\left(\tilde{\mathsf{com}}_y, [\eta_\alpha]_2\right)$$

Then, $\mathcal{B}$ returns (U, V) such that $U := \tilde{\mathsf{com}}_y / \mathsf{com}_y$, $V := \pi^{(\alpha)} / \tilde{\pi}^{(\alpha)}$. If $\mathcal{B}$ did not abort, then $\hat{s} = 0$ and we have that $\eta_\alpha = \eta$ and $e(U, [\eta]_2) = e(V, [1]_2)$, which breaks the HiKer assumption.

We use a similar argument for events E_2 and E_3, for which $\mathcal{B}$ aborts if $\hat{s} = 0$. Since $\hat{s}$ is perfectly hidden $\mathcal{B}$ aborts with probability $1/2$. Hence, if $\mathcal{A}$ is successful with probability ϵ, then $\mathcal{B}$ breaks the assumption with probability $\epsilon/2$.

7 Lattice-Based CFC for Quadratic Functions

In this section, we present a lattice-based construction of a CFC for quadratic functions, that can be seen as a lattice analogue of our pairing-based CFC obtained via a slight generalisation of the translation technique in [1].

7.1 Lattice Preliminaries

Let $\mathcal{R} = \mathbb{Z}[\zeta]$, where ζ is a fixed primitive m-th root of unity, be the ring of integers of the m-th cyclotomic field of degree $d = \varphi(m)$, where elements are represented by their coefficient embedding $x = \sum_{i=0}^{d-1} x_i \cdot \zeta^i$. If m is a prime-power (resp. power of 2), we call $\mathcal{R}$ a prime-power (resp. power-of-two) cyclotomic ring. For the rest of this section we will assume that $m = \mathsf{poly}(\lambda)$.

For $x \in \mathcal{R}$, write $\|x\| := \max_{i=0}^{d-1} |x_i|$ for the infinity norm induced on $\mathcal{R}$ by $\mathbb{Z}$. The norm generalises naturally to vectors $\boldsymbol{u} = (u_1, \ldots, u_n) \in \mathcal{R}^n$, with $\|\boldsymbol{u}\| := \max_{i=1}^{n} \|u_i\|$. For $q \in \mathbb{N}$, write $\mathcal{R}_q := \mathcal{R}/q\mathcal{R}$. We always assume that q is a (rational) prime. By a slight abuse of notation, we identity $\mathcal{R}_q$ with its balanced representation, i.e. if $x = \sum_{i=0}^{d-1} x_i \cdot \zeta^i \in \mathcal{R}_q$ then $|x_i| \le q/2$ for all i. The set of units, i.e., invertible elements, in $\mathcal{R}_q$ is denoted by $\mathcal{R}_q^\times$.

The ring expansion factor $\gamma_\mathcal{R}$ of $\mathcal{R}$ is defined as $\gamma_\mathcal{R} := \max_{a,b \in \mathcal{R}} \frac{\|a \cdot b\|}{\|a\| \cdot \|b\|}$. It is known [2] that if $\mathcal{R}$ is a prime-power cyclotomic ring then $\gamma_\mathcal{R} \le 2 \cdot d$, and if $\mathcal{R}$ is a power-of-two cyclotomic ring then $\gamma_\mathcal{R} \le d$.

Lattice Trapdoors. We recall the following standard algorithms (e.g., [11, 12, 27]) associated to lattice trapdoors and their properties for sufficiently large "leftover hash lemma parameter" $\mathsf{lhl}(\mathcal{R}, \eta, q, \beta) = O(\eta \log_\beta q)$:

- $(\mathbf{A}, \mathsf{td}_\mathbf{A}) \leftarrow \mathsf{TrapGen}(\mathcal{R}, 1^\eta, 1^\ell, q, \beta)$: The trapdoor generation algorithm generates a matrix $\mathbf{A} \in \mathcal{R}_q^{\eta \times \ell}$ along with a trapdoor $\mathsf{td}_\mathbf{A}$. It is assumed that (η, ℓ, q, β) are implicitly specified by $\mathsf{td}_\mathbf{A}$. When $\ell \ge \mathsf{lhl}(\mathcal{R}, \eta, q, \beta)$, the distribution of $\mathbf{A}$ is within $\mathsf{negl}(\lambda)$ statistical distance of $U(\mathcal{R}_q^{\eta \times \ell})$.
- $\boldsymbol{u} \leftarrow \mathsf{SampD}(\mathcal{R}, 1^\eta, 1^\ell, q, \beta')$: The domain sampling algorithm samples a vector $\boldsymbol{u} \in \mathcal{R}^\ell$ with norm $\|\boldsymbol{u}\| \le \beta'$. When $\beta' \ge \beta$ and $\ell \ge \mathsf{lhl}(\mathcal{R}, \eta, q, \beta)$, then the distribution of $(\mathbf{A}, \mathbf{A} \cdot \boldsymbol{u} \bmod q)$ for a uniformly random $\mathbf{A} \leftarrow_{\$} \mathcal{R}_q^{\eta \times \ell}$ is within $\mathsf{negl}(\lambda)$ statistical distance of $U(\mathcal{R}_q^{\eta \times \ell} \times \mathcal{R}_q^\eta)$.

- $u \leftarrow \mathsf{SampPre}(\mathsf{td_A}, v, \beta')$: The preimage sampling algorithm inputs a vector $v \in \mathcal{R}_q^n$ and outputs a vector $u \in \mathcal{R}^\ell$. If the parameters (η, ℓ, q, β) of $\mathsf{td_A}$ satisfy $\beta' \geq \beta$ and $\ell \geq \mathsf{lhl}(\mathcal{R}, \eta, q, \beta)$, then u and v satisfy $\mathbf{A} \cdot u = v \bmod q$ and $\|u\| \leq \beta'$. Furthermore, u is within $\mathsf{negl}(\lambda)$ statistical distance to $u \leftarrow \mathsf{SampD}(\mathcal{R}, 1^n, 1^\ell, q, \beta')$ conditioned on $\mathbf{A} \cdot u = v \bmod q$.

7.2 Hardness Assumptions

The k-R-ISIS assumption family[10] was recently introduced in [1] as a natural extention of the standard short integer solution (SIS) assumption and a natural lattice-analogue of a certain class of pairing-based assumptions. The k-R-ISIS family was accompanied by a translation technique outlined in [1] for translating pairing-based schemes and assumptions to their lattice-analogues.

For instance, a certain k-R-ISIS assumption could be parametrised by a set $\mathcal{G}$ of monomials. It states that even when given short preimages u_g satisfying $\mathbf{A} \cdot u_g = t \cdot g(v) \bmod q$ for all $g \in \mathcal{G}$, it is hard to find a short non-zero preimage u^* satisfying $\mathbf{A} \cdot u^* = 0 \bmod q$.

Applying the translation technique in [1] to the pairing-based assumption (Definition 6) which underlies the security of the pairing-based CFC construction, we encounter an obstacle that there is no translation for the term $[\eta]_2$ in the challenge relation $e(U, [\eta]_2) = e(V, [1]_2)$.

To overcome the above obstacle, in the following, we introduce (a special case of) a generalisation of the k-R-ISIS assumption which we call the Twin-k-R-ISIS assumption. In a nutshell, instead of a single set $\mathcal{G}$ of monomials, we now have two (or in general more) sets $\mathcal{G}_A$ and $\mathcal{G}_B$ of non-overlapping monomials. The Twin-k-R-ISIS assumption states that even when given short preimages u_g satisfying $\mathbf{A} \cdot u_g = t \cdot g(v) \bmod q$ for all $g \in \mathcal{G}_A$ and short preimages w_g satisfying $\mathbf{B} \cdot u_g = t \cdot g(v) \bmod q$ for all $g \in \mathcal{G}_B$, it is hard to find a short non-zero preimage (u^*, w^*) satisfying $\mathbf{A} \cdot u^* + \mathbf{B} \cdot w^* = 0 \bmod q$. We stress that the non-overlapping requirement of $\mathcal{G}_A$ and $\mathcal{G}_B$ is crucial, for otherwise $(u_g, -w_g)$ would be a trivial solution for any $g \in \mathcal{G}_A \cap \mathcal{G}_B$. Other than this trivial attack (which is ruled out), it could be verified that the (failed) attack strategies discussed in [1] against the k-R-ISIS assumption also fail against the Twin-k-R-ISIS assumption. [11]

---

[10] We use k-R-ISIS to refer to both the ring and module version. In [1], the module version is given the name k-M-ISIS.

[11] We refer to the attack strategies discussed in [1, Section 4.1]. There, the authors discussed two (they gave three, but the third generalises the second) attacks: 1) Direct SIS attack: Finding a short vector in the kernel of $(\mathbf{A} | - t \cdot g^*(v))$. 2) Find a (not necessarily short) linear combination $(z_1, \ldots, z_k)$ so that $s^* \cdot g^*(v) = \sum_i z_i \cdot g_i(v)$ and $u_{g^*} = \sum_i z_i \cdot u_{g_i}$ is short. There seems to be no obvious way that either attack can take advantage of the two-slotted structure in the twin-kMISIS assumption.

Definition 7 (*Twin-k-R-ISIS* **Assumption**). *Let* $\ell, \eta \in \mathbb{N}$, q *be a rational prime,* $\beta, \beta^* \in \mathbb{R}^+$,

$$\mathcal{G}_A := \left\{ \frac{X_{i'}}{X_i} \cdot \bar{X}_k, \ \frac{X_{i'}}{X_i} \cdot \check{X}_k, \ \frac{\bar{X}_{i'}}{\bar{X}_i} \cdot X_k \right\}_{i,i',k \in [n], i \neq i'} \cup \left\{ \frac{X_{i'} \cdot \check{X}_{j'}}{X_i \cdot \check{X}_j} \cdot \bar{X}_k \right\}_{\substack{i,i',j,j',k \in [n] \\ i \neq i', j \neq j'}},$$

$\mathcal{G}_B := \left\{ X_k, \bar{X}_k, \check{X}_k \right\}_{k \in [n]}$, *and* $\mathcal{G} := \mathcal{G}_A \cup \mathcal{G}_B$. *Let* $\mathcal{D}$ *be a distribution over* $\mathcal{R}^\ell$. *Write* $\mathsf{pp} := (\mathcal{R}_q, \eta, \ell, n, \beta, \beta^*, \mathcal{G}_A, \mathcal{G}_B, \mathcal{D})$. *The k-R-ISIS$_{\mathsf{pp}}$ assumption states that for any PPT adversary* $\mathcal{A}$ *we have* $\mathsf{Adv}_{\mathsf{pp},\mathcal{A}}^{\mathsf{k\text{-}r\text{-}isis}}(\lambda) \leq \mathsf{negl}(\lambda)$, *where* $\mathsf{Adv}_{\mathsf{pp},\mathcal{A}}^{\mathsf{k\text{-}r\text{-}isis}}(\lambda)$ *is given by*

$$Pr\left[\begin{array}{c} \mathbf{A}\boldsymbol{u}^* + \mathbf{B}\boldsymbol{w}^* \equiv 0 \bmod q \\ \wedge \ 0 < \|(\boldsymbol{u}^*, \boldsymbol{w}^*)\| \leq \beta^* \end{array} \middle| \begin{array}{l} \mathbf{A} \leftarrow_\$ \mathcal{R}_q^{\eta \times \ell} \bmod q; \ \mathbf{B} \leftarrow_\$ \mathcal{R}_q^{\eta \times \ell} \bmod q \\ \boldsymbol{t} \leftarrow_\$ (\mathcal{R}_q^\times)^\eta; \ \boldsymbol{v}, \bar{\boldsymbol{v}}, \check{\boldsymbol{v}} \leftarrow_\$ (\mathcal{R}^\times)^n \\ \boldsymbol{u}_g \leftarrow_\$ \mathcal{D} : \mathbf{A}\boldsymbol{u}_g \equiv \boldsymbol{t}g(\boldsymbol{v}, \bar{\boldsymbol{v}}, \check{\boldsymbol{v}}) \bmod q, \ \forall g \in \mathcal{G}_A \\ \boldsymbol{w}_g \leftarrow_\$ \mathcal{D} : \mathbf{B}\boldsymbol{w}_g \equiv \boldsymbol{t}g(\boldsymbol{v}, \bar{\boldsymbol{v}}, \check{\boldsymbol{v}}) \bmod q, \ \forall g \in \mathcal{G}_B \\ (\boldsymbol{u}^*, \boldsymbol{v}^*) \leftarrow \mathcal{A}(\mathbf{A}, \mathbf{B}, \boldsymbol{t}, \boldsymbol{v}, \bar{\boldsymbol{v}}, \check{\boldsymbol{v}}, \{\boldsymbol{u}_{\mathcal{G}_A}, \boldsymbol{w}_{\mathcal{G}_B}\}) \end{array} \right].$$

In the full version, we discuss the relation between Twin-k-R-ISIS, the original k-R-ISIS [1], and the recent BASIS assumption [30].

7.3   Construction

In the following, we construct a lattice-based chainable functional commitment scheme. Our construction is parametrised by a ring $\mathcal{R}$, dimensions η, ℓ, modulus q, norm bound β, an input length n, and the number of inputs m. Before describing the construction, we first introduce the following shorthands and notation.

For a quadratic polynomial map $f : \mathcal{R}^{mn} \to \mathcal{R}^n$, we express $f(\boldsymbol{x}_1, \dots, \boldsymbol{x}_m)$

$$f(\boldsymbol{x}_1, \dots, \boldsymbol{x}_m) = \boldsymbol{e} + \sum_{h \in \mathcal{S}_1(f)} \mathbf{F}_h \cdot \boldsymbol{x}_h + \sum_{(h,h') \in \mathcal{S}_2^\otimes(f)} \mathbf{G}_{h,h'} \cdot (\boldsymbol{x}_h \otimes \boldsymbol{x}_{h'})$$

for some $\mathbf{G}_{h,h'} \in \mathcal{R}^{n \times n^2}$, $\mathbf{F}_h \in \mathcal{R}^{n \times n}$, and $\boldsymbol{e} \in \mathcal{R}^n$, similarly to previous sections. Our lattice-based construction is additionally parametrised by a norm bound $\alpha \in \mathbb{R}^+$. We assume that messages $\boldsymbol{x}$ and each coefficient of any quadratic polynomial map f to be opened have norm at most α, and f is such that for any $\boldsymbol{x}_1, \dots, \boldsymbol{x}_m$ of norm at most α, it holds that $\|f(\boldsymbol{x}_1, \dots, \boldsymbol{x}_m)\| \leq \alpha$.

For a vector $\boldsymbol{v} \in (\mathcal{R}_q^\times)^n$, denote its component-wise inverse by $\boldsymbol{v}^\dagger := (v_i^{-1})_{i=1}^n$. Define $\mathbf{Z}_{\boldsymbol{v}} := \boldsymbol{v}^\dagger \cdot \boldsymbol{v}^\mathsf{T} - \mathbf{I} = (z_{i,j})_{i,j}$ where $z_{i,j} = 0$ if $i = j$, and $z_{i,j} = v_i^{-1} \cdot v_j$ if $i \neq j$. We are now ready to describe the construction as follows.

$\underline{\mathsf{Setup}(1^\lambda, 1^n)}$

– Sample trapdoored matrices $(\mathbf{A}, \mathsf{td_A}), (\mathbf{B}, \mathsf{td_B}) \leftarrow \mathsf{TrapGen}(\mathcal{R}, 1^\eta, 1^\ell, q, \beta)$.

- Sample submodule generator $t \leftarrow_{\$} (\mathcal{R}_q^{\times})^{\eta}$.
- Sample commitment key vectors $v, \bar{v}, \check{v} \leftarrow_{\$} \mathcal{R}_q^n$.
- Sample a short preimage $u_g \leftarrow \mathsf{SampPre}(\mathsf{td_A}, t \cdot g(v, \bar{v}, \check{v}) \bmod q)$ for each $g \in \mathcal{G}_A$, where

$$\mathcal{G}_A := \left\{ \frac{X_{i'}}{X_i} \cdot \bar{X}_k, \ \frac{X_{i'}}{X_i} \cdot \check{X}_k, \ \frac{\bar{X}_{i'}}{\bar{X}_i} \cdot X_k \right\}_{i,i',k\in[n],i\neq i'} \cup \left\{ \frac{X_{i'} \cdot \check{X}_{j'}}{X_i \cdot \check{X}_j} \cdot \bar{X}_k \right\}_{\substack{i,i',j,j',k\in[n] \\ i\neq i',j\neq j'}}$$

- Sample a short preimage $w_g \leftarrow \mathsf{SampPre}(\mathsf{td_B}, t \cdot g(v, \bar{v}, \check{v}) \bmod q)$ for each $g \in \mathcal{G}_B$, where

$$\mathcal{G}_B := \left\{ X_k, \bar{X}_k, \check{X}_k \right\}_{k\in[n]}.$$

- Output $\mathsf{ck} := (\mathbf{A}, \mathbf{B}, t, v, \bar{v}, \check{v}, (u_g)_{g\in\mathcal{G}_A}, (w_g)_{g\in\mathcal{G}_B})$.

$\mathsf{Com}(\mathsf{ck}, x)$ Compute $c := \langle v, x \rangle \bmod q$ and output $, := c$, $\mathsf{aux} := x$.

$\overline{\mathsf{Open}(\mathsf{ck}, (\mathsf{aux}_h)_{h\in[m]}, f)}$

- Parse aux_h as x_h for all $h \in [m]$ and let $y := f(x_1, \ldots, x_m)$.
- Compute $v_1 := \mathsf{vec}(\mathbf{Z}_v) \otimes \bar{v}$ and $v_2 := \mathsf{vec}((\mathbf{I} + \mathbf{Z}_v) \otimes (\mathbf{I} + \mathbf{Z}_{\check{v}}) - \mathbf{I}) \otimes \bar{v}$.
- Pack the preimages vectors given in the public parameters as columns of the following matrices:
  - $\mathbf{U}_i$ such that $\mathbf{A} \cdot \mathbf{U}_i = t \cdot v_i^{\mathsf{T}} \bmod q$ for $i \in [2]$.
    For example, for $i = 1$, the first few columns of the R.H.S. of the equation are of the form

    $$t \cdot v_1^{\mathsf{T}} = t \cdot \left(0 \quad \frac{v_1}{v_2} \cdot \bar{v}_1 \quad \frac{v_1}{v_3} \cdot \bar{v}_1 \quad \ldots \right).$$

    Notice that each column is either $0 \in \mathcal{R}_q^{\eta}$, for which $0 \in \mathcal{R}^{\ell}$ is a trivial preimage, or of the form $t \cdot \frac{v_{i'}}{v_i} \cdot \bar{v}_k$ for some $i, i', k \in [n]$ with $i \neq i'$, for which a preimage is given in ck.
  - $\bar{\mathbf{U}}$ such that $\mathbf{A} \cdot \bar{\mathbf{U}} = t \cdot v^{\mathsf{T}} \cdot \mathbf{Z}_{\bar{v}} \bmod q$.
  - $\check{\mathbf{U}}$ such that $\mathbf{A} \cdot \check{\mathbf{U}} = t \cdot \check{v}^{\mathsf{T}} \cdot \mathbf{Z}_v \bmod q$.
  - $\mathbf{W}$ such that $\mathbf{B} \cdot \mathbf{W} = t \cdot v^{\mathsf{T}} \bmod q$.
  - $\bar{\mathbf{W}}$ such that $\mathbf{B} \cdot \bar{\mathbf{W}} = t \cdot \bar{v}^{\mathsf{T}} \bmod q$.
  - $\check{\mathbf{W}}$ such that $\mathbf{B} \cdot \check{\mathbf{W}} = t \cdot \check{v}^{\mathsf{T}} \bmod q$.
- Compute $u := \sum_{h\in\mathcal{S}_1(f)} \mathbf{U}_1 \cdot \mathsf{vec}(x_h^{\mathsf{T}} \otimes \mathbf{F}_h) + \sum_{(h,h')\in\mathcal{S}_2^{\otimes}(f)} \mathbf{U}_2 \cdot \mathsf{vec}((x_h^{\mathsf{T}} \otimes x_{h'}^{\mathsf{T}}) \otimes \mathbf{G}_{h,h'})$.
- Compute $w_0 := \mathbf{W} \cdot y$.
- Compute $\bar{u}_0 := \bar{\mathbf{U}} \cdot y$ and $\bar{w}_0 := \bar{\mathbf{W}} \cdot y$.
- Compute $\check{u}_h := \check{\mathbf{U}} \cdot x_h$ and $\check{w}_h := \check{\mathbf{W}} \cdot x_h$ for $h \in \mathcal{S}_2(f)$.
- Output $(u, w_0, \bar{u}_0, \bar{w}_0, (\check{u}_h, \check{w}_h)_{h\in\mathcal{S}_2(f)})$.

$\mathsf{Ver}(\mathsf{ck}, (\mathsf{com}_h)_{h\in[m]}, \mathsf{com}_0, f, \pi)$

- Define $\hat{f}(C_1, \ldots, C_m, \check{C}_1, \ldots, \check{C}_m)$

$$:= \bar{v}^{\mathsf{T}} \cdot \left(\sum_{(h,h')\in\mathcal{S}_2(f)} \mathbf{G}_{h,h'} \cdot (v^{\dagger} \otimes \check{v}^{\dagger}) \cdot C_h \cdot \check{C}_{h'} + \sum_{h\in\mathcal{S}_1(f)} \mathbf{F}_h \cdot v^{\dagger} \cdot C_h + e^{\mathsf{T}} \right).$$

- Check if $\|\boldsymbol{w}_0\| \leq \beta^*$ and $\|\bar{\boldsymbol{w}}_0\| \leq \beta^*$.
- For $h \in [m] \setminus \mathcal{S}_2(f)$, set $\check{c}_h = 0$ and check if $\|\check{\boldsymbol{w}}_h\| \leq \beta^*$.
- Check if $\mathbf{B} \cdot \boldsymbol{w}_0 = \boldsymbol{t} \cdot c_0 \bmod q$.
- Check if there exists (unique) $\bar{c}_0$ such that $\mathbf{B} \cdot \bar{\boldsymbol{w}}_0 = \boldsymbol{t} \cdot \bar{c}_0 \bmod q$.
- Check if there exists (unique) $\check{c}_h$ such that $\mathbf{B} \cdot \check{\boldsymbol{w}}_h = \boldsymbol{t} \cdot \check{c}_h \bmod q$ for $h \in \mathcal{S}_2(f)$.
- Check if $\mathbf{A} \cdot \boldsymbol{u} = \boldsymbol{t} \cdot (\hat{f}(c_1, \ldots, c_m, \check{c}_1, \ldots, \check{c}_m) - \bar{c}_0) \bmod q$ and $\|\boldsymbol{u}\| \leq \beta^*$.
- Check if $\mathbf{A} \cdot \bar{\boldsymbol{u}}_0 = \boldsymbol{t} \cdot (\boldsymbol{v}^\mathsf{T} \cdot \bar{\boldsymbol{v}}^\dagger \cdot \bar{c}_0 - c_0) \bmod q$ and $\|\bar{\boldsymbol{u}}_0\| \leq \beta^*$.
- Check if $\mathbf{A} \cdot \check{\boldsymbol{u}}_h = \boldsymbol{t} \cdot (\check{\boldsymbol{v}}^\mathsf{T} \cdot \boldsymbol{v}^\dagger \cdot c_h - \check{c}_h) \bmod q$ and $\|\check{\boldsymbol{u}}_h\| \leq \beta^*$ for $h \in \mathcal{S}_2(f)$.
- Accept, i.e. output 1, if all checks pass. Otherwise, output 0.

Theorem 4. *Let $\ell \geq \mathsf{lhl}(\mathcal{R}, \eta, q, \beta)$, $\beta^* \geq 2 \cdot n^4 \cdot \hat{m}^2 \cdot \alpha^3 \cdot \beta \cdot \gamma_\mathcal{R}^3$, and $\mathcal{D} = \mathsf{SampD}(\mathcal{R}, 1^n, 1^\ell, q, \beta)$, and assume that the twin-k-R-$\mathsf{ISIS}_{\mathcal{R}_q, \eta, \ell, n, \beta, \beta^*, \mathcal{G}_A, \mathcal{G}_B, \mathcal{D}}$ assumption holds. Then, the construction CFC described above is an evaluation binding CFC for the class $\mathcal{F}_{\mathsf{quad}}$ of quadratic functions over any $m \leq \hat{m}$ vectors of length $\leq n$, has efficient verification, and is (almost) additively homomorphic. For a function $f \in \mathcal{F}_{\mathsf{quad}}$, the proof size of CFC is $|\pi| = |\mathcal{S}_2(f)| \cdot \log^2(m \cdot n) \cdot \mathsf{poly}(\lambda)$, and for the class $\mathcal{F}_{\mathsf{level}} = \{\mathcal{F}_{\mathsf{level}, \kappa}\}$, our CFC is $s(n, m, \kappa)$-succinct where $s(n, m, \kappa) = \kappa \cdot \log^2(m \cdot n)$. Furthermore, by setting $\hat{m} = \lambda^{\omega(1)}$ the CFC supports quadratic functions over any $m = \mathsf{poly}(\lambda)$ vectors and is $\kappa \cdot \log^2(n)$-succinct.*

Due to space constraints, we only provide the proof of security. The remaining proofs are available in the full version.

7.4 Resulting Instantiations of FC for Circuits

As in the previous section, we summarize the FC schemes that result from instantiating our generic construction of Sect. 5 with our lattice-based CFC.

Corollary 2. *Assume that all the conditions of Theorem 4 are satisfied. Then the following statements hold:*

1. *There exists an FC scheme for the class $\mathcal{F}_n = \{\mathcal{F}_{(d,t,w)}\}$ of arithmetic circuits of width w bounded by $\leq n$ and in-degree bounded by $\leq t_{\max}$ that is $O(d \cdot \log^2(t_{\max} \cdot n))$-succinct.*
2. *Using adequate parameters, there exists an FC scheme for $\mathcal{F}_n = \{\mathcal{F}_{(d,t,w)}\}$ of width $w \leq n$ that is $\mathcal{O}(d)$-succinct.*
3. *For any $w_0 \geq 2$, there exists an FC scheme for the class $\mathcal{F} = \{\mathcal{F}_{(d,t,w)}\}$ of circuits of arbitrary width $w > w_0$ that is $\mathcal{O}(d \cdot (w/w_0)^2)$-succinct.*

We provide the proof in the full version. As opposed to our pairing-based construction, the linear dependency on the depth does not follow from a black-box application of our FC from CFC construction. In fact, Theorem 2 gives a proof size of $\mathcal{O}(d \cdot t \cdot \log^2(t_{\max} \cdot n))$. We can supress the t factor by noticing that, for each circuit layer h, the *same* vectors $(\check{\boldsymbol{u}}_h, \check{\boldsymbol{w}}_h)$ are included in the openings at every layer h' such that $h \in \mathcal{S}_2(f^{(h')})$.

7.5 Proof of Security

Suppose there exists a PPT adversary $\mathcal{A}$ against evaluation binding of the CFC construction, we construct a PPT algorithm $\mathcal{B}$ for the Twin-k-R-ISIS problem as follows. Given a Twin-k-R-ISIS instance ck, $\mathcal{B}$ passes ck to $\mathcal{A}$. The adversary $\mathcal{A}$ returns input commitments $(c_h)_{h \in [m]}$, a quadratic function f, two output commitments c_0 and c_0', and two opening proofs π and π', where $\pi = (\boldsymbol{u}, \boldsymbol{w}_0, \bar{\boldsymbol{u}}_0, \bar{\boldsymbol{w}}_0, (\check{\boldsymbol{u}}_h, \check{\boldsymbol{w}}_h)_{h \in \mathcal{S}(f)})$ and $\pi' = (\boldsymbol{u}', \boldsymbol{w}_0', \bar{\boldsymbol{u}}_0', \bar{\boldsymbol{w}}_0', (\check{\boldsymbol{u}}_h', \check{\boldsymbol{w}}_h')_{h \in \mathcal{S}_2(f)})$. By our assumption on $\mathcal{A}$, with non-negligible probability, π (and analogously π') satisfies

$$\mathbf{A} \cdot \boldsymbol{u} = \boldsymbol{t} \cdot (\hat{f}(c_1, \ldots, c_m, \check{c}_1, \ldots, \check{c}_m) - \bar{c}_0) \bmod q,$$

$$\mathbf{A} \cdot \bar{\boldsymbol{u}}_0 = \boldsymbol{t} \cdot (\boldsymbol{v}^{\mathsf{T}} \cdot \bar{\boldsymbol{v}}^\dagger \cdot \bar{c}_0 - c_0) \bmod q, \text{ and}$$

$$\mathbf{A} \cdot \check{\boldsymbol{u}}_h = \boldsymbol{t} \cdot (\check{\boldsymbol{v}}^{\mathsf{T}} \cdot \boldsymbol{v}^\dagger \cdot c_h - \check{c}_h) \bmod q \text{ for all } h \in \mathcal{S}_2(f),$$

where $\mathbf{B} \cdot \bar{\boldsymbol{w}}_0 = \boldsymbol{t} \cdot \bar{c}_0 \bmod q$ and $\mathbf{B} \cdot \check{\boldsymbol{w}}_h = \boldsymbol{t} \cdot \check{c}_h \bmod q$.

For any $h \in \mathcal{S}_2(f)$, suppose $\check{\boldsymbol{w}}_h \neq \check{\boldsymbol{w}}_h'$, then from the third equation $(\check{\boldsymbol{u}}_h - \check{\boldsymbol{u}}_h', \check{\boldsymbol{w}}_h - \check{\boldsymbol{w}}_h')$ would be a non-zero vector of norm at most $2\beta^*$ satisfying $\mathbf{A} \cdot (\check{\boldsymbol{u}}_h - \check{\boldsymbol{u}}_h') + \mathbf{B} \cdot (\check{\boldsymbol{w}}_h - \check{\boldsymbol{w}}_h') = \mathbf{0} \bmod q$, contradicting the twin-k-R-ISIS assumption. We therefore have $\check{\boldsymbol{w}}_h = \check{\boldsymbol{w}}_h'$ and hence $\check{c}_h = \check{c}_h'$ for all $h \in \mathcal{S}_2(f)$.

Next, suppose $\bar{\boldsymbol{w}}_0 \neq \bar{\boldsymbol{w}}_0'$, then from the first equation $(\boldsymbol{u} - \boldsymbol{u}', \bar{\boldsymbol{w}}_0 - \bar{\boldsymbol{w}}_0')$ would be a non-zero vector of norm at most $2\beta^*$ satisfying $\mathbf{A} \cdot (\boldsymbol{u} - \boldsymbol{u}') + \mathbf{B} \cdot (\bar{\boldsymbol{w}}_0 - \bar{\boldsymbol{w}}_0') = \mathbf{0} \bmod q$, contradicting the twin-k-R-ISIS assumption. We therefore have $\bar{\boldsymbol{w}}_0 = \bar{\boldsymbol{w}}_0'$ and hence $\bar{c}_0 = \bar{c}_0'$.

Finally, suppose $\boldsymbol{w}_0 \neq \boldsymbol{w}_0'$, then from the second equation $(\bar{\boldsymbol{u}}_0 - \bar{\boldsymbol{u}}_0', \boldsymbol{w}_0 - \boldsymbol{w}_0')$ would be a non-zero vector of norm at most $2\beta^*$ satisfying $\mathbf{A} \cdot (\bar{\boldsymbol{u}}_0 - \bar{\boldsymbol{u}}_0') + \mathbf{B} \cdot (\boldsymbol{w}_0 - \boldsymbol{w}_0') = \mathbf{0} \bmod q$, contradicting the twin-k-R-ISIS assumption. We therefore have $\boldsymbol{w}_0 = \boldsymbol{w}_0'$ and hence $c_0 = c_0'$, meaning that $\mathcal{A}$ cannot be a successful adversary against evaluation binding.

Acknowledgements. This work is supported by the PICOCRYPT project that has received funding from the European Research Council (ERC) under the European Union's Horizon 2020 research and innovation programme (Grant agreement No. 101001283), partially supported by projects PRODIGY (TED2021-132464B-I00) and ESPADA (PID2022-142290OB-I00) funded by MCIN/AEI/10.13039/501100011033/ and the European Union NextGenerationEU/PRTR, and partially funded by Ministerio de Universidades (FPU21/00600). This research has been supported in part by the Programma ricerca di ateneo UNICT 35 2020-22 linea 2 and by research gifts from Protocol Labs.

References

1. Albrecht, M.R., Cini, V., Lai, R.W.F., Malavolta, G., Thyagarajan, S.A.K.: Lattice-based SNARKs: Publicly verifiable, preprocessing, and recursively composable - (extended abstract). In: Dodis, Y., Shrimpton, T. (eds.) CRYPTO 2022, Part II. LNCS, vol. 13508, pp. 102–132. Springer, Heidelberg (Aug 2022). https://doi.org/10.1007/978-3-031-15979-4_4

2. Albrecht, M.R., Lai, R.W.F.: Subtractive sets over cyclotomic rings - limits of Schnorr-like arguments over lattices. In: Malkin, T., Peikert, C. (eds.) CRYPTO 2021, Part II. LNCS, vol. 12826, pp. 519–548. Springer, Heidelberg, Virtual Event (Aug 2021). https://doi.org/10.1007/978-3-030-84245-1_18

3. Balbás, D., Catalano, D., Fiore, D., Lai, R.W.F.: Chainable functional commitments for unbounded-depth circuits. Cryptology ePrint Archive, Paper 2022/1365 (2022). https://eprint.iacr.org/2022/1365,https://eprint.iacr.org/2022/1365

4. Boneh, D., Freeman, D.M.: Homomorphic signatures for polynomial functions. In: Paterson, K.G. (ed.) EUROCRYPT 2011. LNCS, vol. 6632, pp. 149–168. Springer, Heidelberg (May 2011). https://doi.org/10.1007/978-3-642-20465-4_10

5. de Castro, L., Peikert, C.: Functional commitments for all functions, with transparent setup and from SIS. In: Hazay, C., Stam, M. (eds.) Advances in Cryptology – EUROCRYPT 2023, Part III. LNCS, vol. 14006, pp. 287–320. Springer, Cham (2023). https://doi.org/10.1007/978-3-031-30620-4_10

6. Catalano, D., Fiore, D.: Vector commitments and their applications. In: Kurosawa, K., Hanaoka, G. (eds.) PKC 2013. LNCS, vol. 7778, pp. 55–72. Springer, Heidelberg (Feb/Mar 2013). https://doi.org/10.1007/978-3-642-36362-7_5

7. Catalano, D., Fiore, D., Messina, M.: Zero-knowledge sets with short proofs. In: Smart, N.P. (ed.) EUROCRYPT 2008. LNCS, vol. 4965, pp. 433–450. Springer, Heidelberg (Apr 2008). https://doi.org/10.1007/978-3-540-78967-3_25

8. Catalano, D., Fiore, D., Tucker, I.: Additive-homomorphic functional commitments and applications to homomorphic signatures. In: Agrawal, S., Lin, D. (eds.) Advances in Cryptology – ASIACRYPT 2022, Part IV. LNCS, vol. 13794, pp. 159–188. Springer, Cham (2022). https://doi.org/10.1007/978-3-031-22972-5_6

9. Catalano, D., Fiore, D., Warinschi, B.: Homomorphic signatures with efficient verification for polynomial functions. In: Garay, J.A., Gennaro, R. (eds.) CRYPTO 2014, Part I. LNCS, vol. 8616, pp. 371–389. Springer, Heidelberg (Aug 2014). https://doi.org/10.1007/978-3-662-44371-2_21

10. Escala, A., Herold, G., Kiltz, E., Ràfols, C., Villar, J.: An algebraic framework for Diffie-Hellman assumptions. In: Canetti, R., Garay, J.A. (eds.) CRYPTO 2013, Part II. LNCS, vol. 8043, pp. 129–147. Springer, Heidelberg (Aug 2013). https://doi.org/10.1007/978-3-642-40084-1_8

11. Genise, N., Micciancio, D.: Faster Gaussian sampling for trapdoor lattices with arbitrary modulus. In: Nielsen, J.B., Rijmen, V. (eds.) EUROCRYPT 2018, Part I. LNCS, vol. 10820, pp. 174–203. Springer, Heidelberg (Apr/May 2018). https://doi.org/10.1007/978-3-319-78381-9_7

12. Gentry, C., Peikert, C., Vaikuntanathan, V.: Trapdoors for hard lattices and new cryptographic constructions. In: Ladner, R.E., Dwork, C. (eds.) 40th ACM STOC, pp. 197–206. ACM Press (May 2008). https://doi.org/10.1145/1374376.1374407

13. Gentry, C., Sahai, A., Waters, B.: Homomorphic encryption from learning with errors: conceptually-simpler, asymptotically-faster, attribute-based. In: Canetti, R., Garay, J.A. (eds.) CRYPTO 2013, Part I. LNCS, vol. 8042, pp. 75–92. Springer, Heidelberg (Aug 2013). https://doi.org/10.1007/978-3-642-40041-4_5

14. Gentry, C., Wichs, D.: Separating succinct non-interactive arguments from all falsifiable assumptions. In: Fortnow, L., Vadhan, S.P. (eds.) 43rd ACM STOC, pp. 99–108. ACM Press (Jun 2011). https://doi.org/10.1145/1993636.1993651

15. Goldwasser, S., Kalai, Y.T., Rothblum, G.N.: Delegating computation: interactive proofs for muggles. In: Ladner, R.E., Dwork, C. (eds.) 40th ACM STOC, pp. 113–122. ACM Press (May 2008). https://doi.org/10.1145/1374376.1374396

16. González, A., Ràfols, C.: Shorter pairing-based arguments under standard assumptions. In: Galbraith, S.D., Moriai, S. (eds.) ASIACRYPT 2019, Part III. LNCS, vol. 11923, pp. 728–757. Springer, Heidelberg (Dec 2019). https://doi.org/10.1007/978-3-030-34618-8_25

17. González, A., Zacharakis, A.: Fully-succinct publicly verifiable delegation from constant-size assumptions. In: Nissim, K., Waters, B. (eds.) TCC 2021, Part I. LNCS, vol. 13042, pp. 529–557. Springer, Heidelberg (Nov 2021). https://doi.org/10.1007/978-3-030-90459-3_18

18. Gorbunov, S., Vaikuntanathan, V., Wichs, D.: Leveled fully homomorphic signatures from standard lattices. In: Servedio, R.A., Rubinfeld, R. (eds.) 47th ACM STOC, pp. 469–477. ACM Press (Jun 2015). https://doi.org/10.1145/2746539.2746576

19. Groth, J., Sahai, A.: Efficient non-interactive proof systems for bilinear groups. In: Smart, N.P. (ed.) EUROCRYPT 2008. LNCS, vol. 4965, pp. 415–432. Springer, Heidelberg (Apr 2008). https://doi.org/10.1007/978-3-540-78967-3_24

20. Johnson, R., Molnar, D., Song, D.X., Wagner, D.: Homomorphic signature schemes. In: Preneel, B. (ed.) CT-RSA 2002. LNCS, vol. 2271, pp. 244–262. Springer, Heidelberg (Feb 2002). https://doi.org/10.1007/3-540-45760-7_17

21. Kate, A., Zaverucha, G.M., Goldberg, I.: Constant-size commitments to polynomials and their applications. In: Abe, M. (ed.) ASIACRYPT 2010. LNCS, vol. 6477, pp. 177–194. Springer, Heidelberg (Dec 2010). https://doi.org/10.1007/978-3-642-17373-8_11

22. Katsumata, S., Nishimaki, R., Yamada, S., Yamakawa, T.: Designated verifier/prover and preprocessing NIZKs from Diffie-Hellman assumptions. In: Ishai, Y., Rijmen, V. (eds.) EUROCRYPT 2019, Part II. LNCS, vol. 11477, pp. 622–651. Springer, Heidelberg (May 2019). https://doi.org/10.1007/978-3-030-17656-3_22

23. Lai, R.W.F., Malavolta, G.: Subvector commitments with application to succinct arguments. In: Boldyreva, A., Micciancio, D. (eds.) CRYPTO 2019, Part I. LNCS, vol. 11692, pp. 530–560. Springer, Heidelberg (Aug 2019). https://doi.org/10.1007/978-3-030-26948-7_19

24. Libert, B., Ramanna, S.C., Yung, M.: Functional commitment schemes: from polynomial commitments to pairing-based accumulators from simple assumptions. In: Chatzigiannakis, I., Mitzenmacher, M., Rabani, Y., Sangiorgi, D. (eds.) ICALP 2016. LIPIcs, vol. 55, pp. 30:1–30:14. Schloss Dagstuhl (Jul 2016). https://doi.org/10.4230/LIPIcs.ICALP.2016.30

25. Libert, B., Yung, M.: Concise mercurial vector commitments and independent zero-knowledge sets with short proofs. In: Micciancio, D. (ed.) TCC 2010. LNCS, vol. 5978, pp. 499–517. Springer, Heidelberg (Feb 2010). https://doi.org/10.1007/978-3-642-11799-2_30

26. Lipmaa, H., Pavlyk, K.: Succinct functional commitment for a large class of arithmetic circuits. In: Moriai, S., Wang, H. (eds.) ASIACRYPT 2020, Part III. LNCS, vol. 12493, pp. 686–716. Springer, Heidelberg (Dec 2020). https://doi.org/10.1007/978-3-030-64840-4_23

27. Micciancio, D., Peikert, C.: Trapdoors for lattices: simpler, tighter, faster, smaller. In: Pointcheval, D., Johansson, T. (eds.) EUROCRYPT 2012. LNCS, vol. 7237, pp. 700–718. Springer, Heidelberg (Apr 2012). https://doi.org/10.1007/978-3-642-29011-4_41

28. Morillo, P., Ràfols, C., Villar, J.L.: The kernel matrix Diffie-Hellman assumption. In: Cheon, J.H., Takagi, T. (eds.) ASIACRYPT 2016, Part I. LNCS, vol. 10031, pp. 729–758. Springer, Heidelberg (Dec 2016). https://doi.org/10.1007/978-3-662-53887-6_27

29. Peikert, C., Pepin, Z., Sharp, C.: Vector and functional commitments from lattices. In: Nissim, K., Waters, B. (eds.) TCC 2021, Part III. LNCS, vol. 13044, pp. 480–511. Springer, Heidelberg (Nov 2021). https://doi.org/10.1007/978-3-030-90456-2_16

30. Wee, H., Wu, D.J.: Succinct vector, polynomial, and functional commitments from lattices. In: Hazay, C., Stam, M. (eds.) Advances in Cryptology – EUROCRYPT 2023, Part III. LNCS 14006, pp. 385–416. Springer, Cham (2023). https://doi.org/10.1007/978-3-031-30620-4_13

Multilinear Schwartz-Zippel Mod N and Lattice-Based Succinct Arguments

Benedikt Bünz[1(✉)] and Ben Fisch[2]

[1] New York University, New York, USA
bb@nyu.edu
[2] Yale University, New Haven, USA
ben.fisch@yale.edu

Abstract. We show that for $\mathbf{x} \xleftarrow{\$} [0, 2^\lambda)^\mu$ and any integer N the probability that $f(\mathbf{x}) \equiv 0 \bmod N$ for any non-zero multilinear polynomial $f \in \mathbb{Z}[X_1, \ldots, X_\mu]$, co-prime to N is inversely proportional to N. As a corollary we show that if $\log_2 N \geq \log_2(2\mu)\lambda + 8\mu^2$ then the probability is bounded by $\frac{\mu+1}{2^\lambda}$. We also give tighter numerically derived bounds, showing that if $\log_2 N \geq 418$, and $\mu \leq 20$ the probability is bounded by $\frac{\mu}{2^\lambda} + 2^{-120}$.

We then apply this Multilinear Composite Schwartz-Zippel Lemma (LCSZ) to resolve an open problem in the literature on succinct arguments: that the *Bulletproofs* protocol for linear relations over classical Pedersen commitments in prime-order groups remains knowledge sound when generalized to commitment schemes that are binding only over short integer vectors. In particular, this means that the Bulletproofs protocol can be instantiated with plausibly post-quantum commitments from lattice hardness assumptions (SIS/R-SIS/M-SIS). It can also be instantiated with commitments based on groups of unknown order (GUOs), in which case the verification time becomes logarithmic instead of linear time.[1]

Prior work on lattice-based Bulletproofs (Crypto 2020) and its extensions required modifying the protocol to sample challenges from special sets of polynomial size. This results in a non-negligible knowledge error, necessitating parallel repetition to amplify soundness, which impacts efficiency and poses issues for the Fiat-Shamir transform. Our analysis shows knowledge soundness for the original Bulletproofs protocol with the exponential-size integer challenge set $[0, 2^\lambda]$ and thus achieves a negligible soundness error without repetition, circumventing a previous impossibility result (Crypto 2021). Our analysis also closes a critical gap in the original security proof of DARK, a GUO-based polynomial commitment scheme (Eurocrypt 2020). Along the way to achieving our result we also define *Almost Special Soundness* (AMSS), a generalization of Special-Soundness. Our main result is divided into two parts: (1) that the Bulletproofs protocol over generalized commitments is AMSS, and (2) that AMSS implies knowledge soundness. This framework serves to simplify the application of our analytical techniques to protocols beyond Bulletproofs in the future([1]This paper incorporates content published in the updated EPRINT of DARK [18]. The full version of this paper containing proofs is available online [17].).

© International Association for Cryptologic Research 2023
G. Rothblum and H. Wee (Eds.): TCC 2023, LNCS 14371, pp. 394–423, 2023.
https://doi.org/10.1007/978-3-031-48621-0_14

1   Introduction

The famous DeMillo-Lipton-Schwartz-Zippel (DLSZ) lemma [22,35,39] states that for any field $\mathbb{F}$, non-empty finite subset $S \subseteq \mathbb{F}$, and non-zero μ-variate polynomial f over $\mathbb{F}$ of total degree d, the number of zeros of f contained in S^μ is bounded by $d \cdot |S|^{\mu-1}$ (or equivalently, the probability that $f(\mathbf{x}) = 0$ for $\mathbf{x}$ sampled uniformly from S^μ is bounded by $\frac{d}{|S|}$). For $\mu = 1$ this simply follows from the Fundamental Theorem of Algebra, but for multivariate polynomials, the number of zeros over the whole field could be unbounded. The computational significance of this lemma is that sampling an element from S only takes $n \cdot \log_2(|S|)$ random bits but the probability of randomly sampling a zero of f from S^μ is inversely proportional to $|S|$, which is exponential in the number of random bits. One of its original motivations was an efficient randomized algorithm for polynomial identity testing, but it has since found widespread application in computer science [27].

The classical lemma applies more broadly to integral domains, but not to more general commutative rings such as the ring $\mathbb{Z}_N$. As a simple counterexample, over the ring of integers modulo $N = 2p$ the polynomial $f(X) = pX \bmod N$ vanishes on half of the points in $[0, N)$. This counterexample exploits the fact that f is of the form $f(X) = u \cdot g(X)$ where u is a zero-divisor. There are also simple counterexamples for f co-prime to N: setting $N = 2^\lambda$ the polynomial $f(X) = X^\lambda \bmod N$ vanishes on half of the points in $[0, N)$. However, there are no such counterexamples when f is both multilinear and co-prime to N. In fact, we will show in this work the probability a random vector from $S^\mu = [0, m)^\mu$ is a zero of a μ-linear polynomial (multilinear with μ variables) co-prime to N is negligible in the minimum of $\log m$ and $\log N$. As we will show in our main result, this special case of f and N still has a surprisingly powerful application to cryptography that resolves multiple recent open questions in the area of succinct arguments.

The DLSZ lemma has previously been extended to commutative rings by restricting the set S to special subsets in which the difference of any two elements is not a zero divisor [8]. For example, in the case of $\mathbb{Z}_N$ this would require the difference of any two elements in S to be co-prime to N. All examples of such sets have $O(\log N)$ size. Our present work explores the setting where S is the contiguous interval $[0, m)$ and thus does not have this restriction.

As a warmup, it is easy to see that any univariate linear polynomial $f(X) = c \cdot X + b$ co-prime to N has at most one root modulo N. If there were two such roots $x_1 \neq x_2 \bmod N$ then $c(x_1 - x_2) \equiv 0 \bmod N$ implies c is a zero divisor (i.e., $gcd(c, N) \neq 1$). Furthermore, $c \cdot x_1 \equiv -b \bmod N$ implies $-b = c \cdot x_1 + q \cdot N$ for some $q \in \mathbb{Z}$, and thus, $gcd(c, N)$ also divides b. This would contradict the co-primality of f and N. So for x uniformly distributed in $S = [0, m)$ the probability of $f(x) \equiv 0 \bmod N$ in this case is indeed at most $\frac{1}{|S|}$. Unfortunately, this does not generalize nicely to polynomials of arbitrary degree as illustrated by the counterexample above. On the other hand, we are able to generalize the lemma in a meaningful way to multivariate *linear* polynomials (i.e., at most degree 1 in each variable). We bound the probability of sampling a zero from $S^\mu = [0, m)^\mu$

of a μ-linear polynomial co-prime to N by $\epsilon + \frac{\mu}{|S|}$, where ϵ is tightly bounded by a product of regularized beta functions.

We also formulate an inverse lemma showing that for all sufficiently large N, ϵ is negligibly small. In particular, for $\log N \geq 8\mu^2 + (1 + \log \mu)\lambda$, ϵ is at most $2^{-\lambda}$, showing that the probability decays exponentially. Our technique for deriving this threshold lower bound $t(\lambda, \mu)$ on N for a target λ formulates $t(\lambda, \mu)$ as the objective function of a knapsack problem. We derive an analytical solution by deriving bounds on the regularized beta function. We also apply a knapsack approximation algorithm to find tighter values of $t(\lambda, \mu)$ for specific values of μ and λ. We call our new lemma the *multilinear composite Schwartz-Zippel* (LCSZ) lemma.

1.1   Bulletproofs for Short Pre-images

Using the multi-linear composite Schwartz-Zippel lemma (LCSZ), we can prove that a generalization of the Bulletproofs Polynomial Commitment [11,16,36] is secure even with large challenge sets. The generalization allows for commitments to "short" (i.e., bounded norm) integer vectors. This includes groups of unknown order, such as the RSA group or class groups, as well as lattice-based commitments (i.e. Ajtai commitments based on the Integer SIS or Ring-SIS assumptions). The instantiation using commitments based on groups of unknown order is essentially a variation of DARK [19], and our analysis closes a vital gap in the security proof that was first discovered by [9].[1] Unlike the fix proposed by [9], our analysis covers the original DARK protocol and enables the use of a large challenge space instead of relying on binary challenges. Our analysis is also the first to show that lattice-based Bulletproofs [13] (i.e., Bulletproofs instantiated with Ajtai commitments) with a challenge space of exponential size (e.g., $[0, 2^\lambda)$) has a negligible knowledge error (without parallel repetition). All previous attempts [1,4,13] had analyzed small, specially constructed challenge sets, which result in a knowledge error $o(\frac{1}{\text{poly}(\lambda)})$, and thus these protocols used parallel repetition to amplify soundness. In fact, [1] give an impossibility result, showing that the approach of specially constructing such sets is limited and unlikely to result in a negligible soundness error. Furthermore, parallel-repetition is not always compatible with the Fiat-Shamir transform [5,38].

In a bit more detail, lattice-based Bulletproofs use commitments to an integer vector $\mathbf{x} \in \mathbb{Z}^n$ of the form $C = \mathbf{A}\mathbf{x} \bmod q$ where $\mathbf{A}$ is a matrix over a $\mathbb{Z}$-module $\mathcal{R}$ and q is a prime number. When $\mathcal{R} = \mathbb{Z}$, the commitment is binding to integer vectors of bounded L2 norm B under the *short-integer solution* (SIS) assumption for a matrix of appropriate dimensions and q sufficiently larger than B. A more general assumption called *module SIS* (M-SIS) allows for $\mathcal{R}$ to be an m-th cyclotomic ring $\mathcal{R} = \mathbb{Z}[X]/\Phi_m(X)$. The goal of the protocol is to argue, for a public input $\mathbf{z} \in \mathbb{Z}^n$ and prime p, that $\langle \mathbf{z}, \mathbf{x} \rangle = y \bmod p$. The protocol is knowledge sound if there is a knowledge extractor that can obtain an integer

---

[1] The analysis we provide in this paper also applies to DARK in its original form. We include this in an updated appendix of the original DARK paper.

vector $\tilde{\mathbf{x}} \in \mathbb{Z}^n$ of sufficiently small norm and a sufficiently small positive integer s such that $\mathbf{A}\tilde{\mathbf{x}} = s \cdot C$ and $\langle \mathbf{z}, \tilde{\mathbf{x}} \rangle = s \cdot y \bmod p$. The protocol has knowledge error δ if for any adversary succeeding with probability ϵ the extractor runs in time $\mathsf{poly}(n)/\epsilon$ and succeeds with probability at least $1 - \delta/\epsilon$. The pair $(\tilde{\mathbf{x}}, s)$ is also known as a "relaxed" opening of the commitment C, which can be interpreted as an opening to the rational $\tilde{\mathbf{x}}/s$. This is binding under M-SIS if $s \cdot \|\tilde{\mathbf{x}}\|_2 \leq B$. The recent work by Albrecht and Lai [1] called s the *slack* and the norm increase factor $t = \|\tilde{\mathbf{x}}\|_2/\|\mathbf{x}\|_2$ the *stretch*. It is important to keep $s \cdot t \cdot \|\mathbf{x}\|_2 \leq B$ for the protocol to be meaningfully sound as otherwise the commitment is no longer binding. While the size of q could always be increased to accommodate a larger B, this increases the communication complexity of the protocol. Thus, for the protocol to remain succinct it is important that $s \cdot t \in 2^{O(\mathsf{polylog}(n))}$. The impossibility result of [1] suggested that prior approaches to analyzing lattice-based Bulletproofs would not be able to demonstrate knowledge soundness with small slack using challenge sets of size greater than $\mathsf{poly}(\lambda)$, and thus would have knowledge soundness error $o(1/\mathsf{poly}(\lambda))$ without parallel repetition. Our work gets around this barrier with new analysis techniques, achieving exponentially small knowledge error $2^{-\lambda}$ with $s \cdot t \in 2^{O(\mathsf{polylog}(n))}$.

Prior analysis of DARK and lattice Bulletproofs considered the special-soundness of the protocol. Informally, a public-coin interactive argument for a given relation is special-sound if an extractor can obtain a witness from *any* tree of accepting transcripts with distinct challenges at any branch. By the "forking lemma", which shows how to generate such trees, special-soundness implies knowledge soundness. DARK and lattice Bulletproofs both have a similar structure, the main difference being the instantiation of the vector commitment, although in both cases the vector commitment is only binding to short vectors in $\mathbb{Z}^n$ of norm at most $B \in 2^{O(\mathsf{polylog}(n))}$. This restriction on the size of B is for succinctness in the case of lattice Bulletproofs and for quasilinear prover complexity in the case of DARK (the time complexity of creating a DARK commitment is $\Omega(n \log B)$ group operations). Special-soundness of these protocol thus requires that the extractor can obtain from any such transcript tree a relaxed opening to the integer vector commitment with slack s and stretch t such that $s \cdot t \in 2^{O(\mathsf{polylog}(n))}$. In a special-soundness analysis, the differences of challenges in a transcript tree are arbitrary. The strech and slack of the extracted opening grow multiplicatively with those differences, which makes it difficult to bind them tightly. In fact, with challenges chosen from the set $[0, 2^\lambda)$, the extractor might obtain an opening with slack $2^{o(\lambda n)}$, which is far too large for either DARK or lattice Bulletproofs. However, using the LCSZ, we are able to show that Bulletproofs with vector commitments binding to short vectors (which generalize both DARK and lattice Bulletproofs) satisfies a less stringent requirement we call *almost-special soundness* (AMSS), which we show also implies knowledge soundness.

Almost Special Soundness. We introduce almost-special soundness (AMSS) as a generalization of special-soundness. AMSS protocols are multi-round protocols where every round is associated with a commitment that is binding over openings to messages in a set $\mathcal{W}$. This does not have to be an explicit message sent to the verifier but roughly represents the prover's state at a round of the protocol. At a very high level, protocols are AMSS if there exists an algorithm that extracts from any forking transcript tree an opening to these commitments, and if the opening is not inside a subset $\mathcal{W}' \subset \mathcal{W}$ then re-running (or completing) the protocol starting from this extracted state on fresh challenges would fail (with overwhelmingly high probability) to result in a transcript accepted by the verifier. One additional key requirement, stated informally here, is that re-running the protocol on the *same* challenges would either result in the same transcript or a break of the commitment scheme. We leverage these combined properties to show that AMSS protocols are knowledge-sound. We then show that Bulletproofs with commitments to short pre-images are almost-special sound, which relies on the inverse LCSZ.

As a brief overview, we begin by viewing the relaxed openings of the commitment scheme as *rational openings*. For any commitment C the opening $(\mathbf{f}, N)$ such that $\mathsf{com}(\mathbf{f}) = N \cdot C$ is interpreted as an opening of C to the rational vector $\mathbf{f}/N$. In the terminology of [1], the slack is thus the size of the absolute value of the denominator $|N|$ and the stretch is the L2 norm of the numerator $\|\mathbf{f}\|_2$. The Bulletproofs verifier accepts the protocol transcript only if the final message is a "small" integer (of bounded absolute value). This suggests that if the prover were to run the honest protocol starting with $\mathbf{f}/N$ as its private state, then its success would imply $f(\mathbf{r}) \equiv 0 \bmod N$ where f is a multilinear polynomial with the coefficients defined by $\mathbf{f}$ and $\mathbf{r}$ are the verifier challenges. We can use the inverse LCSZ to show that if N is too "large" and $\mathbf{r}$ is sampled randomly then this probability is negligible. Making this analysis formal is non-trivial, and we present a summary of the ideas in the technical overview below.

Along the way to showing that AMSS implies knowledge soundness we also introduce a variant of the standard forking lemma, which we call the *path predicate forking lemma*. This lemma shows the existence of a PPT algorithm to generate a transcript tree satisfying additional properties for AMSS protocols that enable the efficient extraction of a witness.

Fiat-Shamir Transform. The Fiat-Shamir transform is a method for transforming an interactive protocol with a public coin verifier into a non-interactive publicly verifiable protocol by replacing the verifier public-coin challenges with hashes of the prover's messages. Recent work [3,38] has shown that the Fiat-Shamir transform is secure for multi-round special-sound protocols. However, the security proof does not translate immediately to almost special-sound (AMSS) protocols. We prove security of the Fiat-Shamir transform for AMSS protocols with *computationally unique commitments*, where it is infeasible to open two distinct commitments to the same message. The deterministic variants of DARK and Ajtai commitments have this property.

1.2   Related Work

Lattice-Based Bulletproofs. Most practical lattice-based succinct proof systems have focused on single-round protocols. These protocols [6,23,30,32] have $o(\sqrt(m))$ communication complexity. Bulletproofs [11,16] is a multiround argument of knowledge for the opening of Pedersen vector commitments, which are binding based on the discrete-logarithm assumption. The Bulletproofs protocol has a recursive structure involving $\log n$ rounds for commitments to vectors of length n, and is public-coin, where the verifier's challenges are integers uniformly sampled from $[0, 2^\lambda)$. The overall communication is only $2\log_2(n)$ λ-bit sized messages. Bootle et al. [13] adapted the protocol to the lattice setting by replacing the Pedersen commitments with vector commitments based on Ring SIS or Module SIS over a cyclotomic ring $\mathcal{R}$. They also replace the challenge set $[0, 2^\lambda)$ with a smaller subset of $\mathcal{R}$. The challenges are monomials with binary coefficients such that the differences of any two challenges divide 2 in the ring. This allows them to demonstrate special-soundness, i.e. an extractor that can obtain an opening to the lattice-based vector commitment from any ternary tree of valid transcripts with distinct challenges on each edge. However, the smaller challenge set results in a larger soundness error and thus necessitates parallel repetition. This combined with the slack of the extractor leads to total communication $O(\lambda^2 \log^2(n))$, compared with the $O(\lambda \log(n))$ complexity of the original Bulletproofs protocol for Pedersen commitments.

Bulletproofs with Subtractive Sets. [4] generalize the techniques of [13] to allow for commitments based on Module SIS (M-SIS) and also more general challenge sets: special sets where differences in challenges are invertible. [1] further generalize the protocol, allowing for more general challenge sets they call $(k, 3)$-subtractive over $\mathcal{R}$. A set S is $(k, 3)$-subtractive if for any triple of challenges $\{c_1, c_2, c_3\} \subseteq S$ and $i \in \{1, 2, 3\}$ the product $\prod_{j \neq i}(c_i - c_j)$ divides s. They show that the Bulletproofs protocol using M-SIS commitments and $(k, 3)$-subtractive challenge sets achieves slack $k^{\log n}$ and knowledge error $\log n/|S|$. They construct a $(2, 3)$-subtractive set of size $O(m)$ for an order m power-of-two cyclotomic ring $\mathcal{R}$ and show that it is nearly optimal: there is no $(2, 3)$-subtractive set in such a ring of size greater than $m + 1$. This means that the size of the challenge set is at most linear in the bit-length of the commitments (i.e., polynomial rather than exponential in the security parameter λ), necessitating $O(\lambda/\log m)$ parallel repetitions of the protocol to amplify soundness. Beyond increasing the communication complexity this also poses difficulties for the security of the Fiat-Shamir transform [5,38].

Their upper bounds on the size of (k, r)-subtractive sets relative to k extends to prime-power cyclotomic rings and even larger values of k, suggesting that using small challenge sets (and boosting soundness through parallel repetition) was fundamentally required for achieving a sufficiently small extraction slack, at least based on the prior analysis techniques. [1] state that "unless fundamentally new techniques are discovered" their impossibility result "represents a barrier to practically efficient lattice-based succinct arguments in the Bulletproof framework".

Comparison to Our Work. Our work overcomes this barrier, showing that lattice-based Bulletproofs can indeed be instantiated with the exponential-sized challenge set $[0, 2^\lambda)$ and still achieve sufficiently small slack and stretch. The analysis is based on our variant of the DLSZ lemma for multilinear polynomials mod composite N (i.e., our LCSZ lemma). This also demonstrates compatibility of lattice-based Bulletproofs with the Fiat-Shamir transform. Specifically, our analysis is able to achieve both slack and stretch of $2^{O(\lambda \log n)}$ and knowledge error $\lambda n \cdot 2^{-\Omega(\lambda)}$. Prior analysis of lattice-Bulletproofs [1,4,13] instantiated with smaller challenges sets required $O(\lambda / \log(m))$ parallel repetitions where m is the degree of the cyclotomic polynomial of the ring used for M-SIS commitments. On the other hand, they achieved a smaller slack of $2^{O(\log m \log n)}$, thus allowing for a smaller modulus q than what our analysis of lattice-based Bulletproofs over the challenge set $[0, 2^\lambda)$ requires. Specifically, with vectors of length n over $\mathbb{Z}_p$, the modulus q is $O(\log m \log n + \log p)$ bits in their case and $O(\lambda \log n + \log p)$ bits in ours. Overall, for a commitment matrix in $\mathcal{R}^{\kappa \times n}$, according to prior analysis the prover needs to send $O(\kappa m(\lambda \log^2 n + \log p \log n \cdot \lambda / \log m))$ bits whereas according to our analysis the prover needs to send $O(\kappa m(\lambda \log^2 n + \log p \log n))$ bits. The reduction in overall complexity is most significant when $\log p \gg \log m \log n$. In other words, this is practically relevant for succinct-arguments applied to statements with a large field size relative to arithmetic complexity (e.g., $\log p = 256$, $\log m = 10$, and $\log n = 15$). An interesting direction for future work is to look at ways to pack the coefficients of vectors over a smaller modulus $p' \ll p$ into vectors over the larger modulus and still make use of the linear form opening. Another direction is to use an exponential-size challenge set of smaller norm elements (i.e., over the polynomial ring rather than integers), but this would require further generalizations of the LCSZ lemma.

Comparison of Our Work to LaBRADOR [7]. Recently, LaBRADOR [7] presented a new argument system for dot product constraints that circumvented the prior limitations of slack and knowledge error in lattice-based arguments that have a recursive structure like Bulletproofs. In contrast to our work, which provides a tighter analysis of the original simple Bulletproofs protocol in the lattice setting without modification, LaBRADOR changes the way the protocol works, allowing the verifier to request additional random linear projections of the committed vectors at each level of recursion, which are folded into prover's original claim. The projection is a map $\Pi : \mathbb{Z}^n \to \mathbb{Z}^{256}$ with entries sampled randomly and independently from a distribution over $\{-1, 0, 1\}$ with probability $1/4$, $1/2$, and $1/4$ respectively. If the prover is committed to $\mathbf{x}$ then the verifier learns $y = \Pi \mathbf{x} \bmod q$ and checks that its L2 norm is appropriately bounded. Since Π is independent of the challenges used for extraction, the knowledge extractor is able to obtain $\tilde{\mathbf{x}}$, independent of Π, such that $\Pi \tilde{\mathbf{x}} \bmod q$ has bounded norm. Based on the modular Johnson-Lindenstrauss Lemma [24], for sufficiently large q this implies on bound on the L2 norm of the extracted vector. This allows for tightly bounding the slack at each level of extraction even when using challenges sampled from an exponential size set over $\mathcal{R}$.

This is closely related to how we are able to a tighter slack/stretch of the original Bulletproofs protocol without modification, leveraging the fact that final message sent in the protocol is a certain random linear projection of the original vector $\mathbf{x}$: it is an evaluation of a multilinear polynomial $f_{\mathbf{x}}$ with $\log n$ variables and coefficients $\mathbf{x}$ on the random challenges $c_1, ..., c_{\log n}$ sampled by the verifier from $[0, 2^\lambda)$ in each round. Unlike the analysis of LaBRADOR, our extractor does not operate modulo q. Instead, we allow for slack in the opening of a commitment C, extracting $\tilde{\mathbf{x}} \in \mathcal{R}^n$ and $s \in \mathbb{Z}$ such that $\mathbf{A}\tilde{\mathbf{x}} = s \cdot C \bmod q$ and the multilinear polynomial h with rational coefficient vector $\frac{1}{s} \cdot \tilde{\mathbf{x}}$ satisfies $h(c_1, ..., c_{\log n}) \in \mathbb{Z}$. Our analysis applies our new composite Schwartz-Zippel lemma in a similar way to how the modular Johnson-Lindenstrauss lemma functions in the analysis of LaBRADOR. It implies for large s and $\mathbf{c} = (c_1, ..., c_{\log n})$ uniformly distributed independent of h that $h(\mathbf{c}) \notin \mathbb{Z}$ with overwhelming probability, thus bounding the size of the slack s for the extracted opening. However, unlike LaBRADOR, the coefficients of g are derived by the extractor using the verifier's challenges and are thus not independent. This complicates the analysis. We get around this by using 4-ary transcript trees, where h can be extracted from a 3-ary subtree and the challenges $c_1, ..., c_{\log n}$ come from an independent path. We provide a more detailed overview in the next section.

DARK and Groups of Unknown Order. The DARK Polynomial Commitment [19] is a polynomial commitment with succinct verification using groups of unknown order. If instantiated with class groups (see [15]) the protocol does not require a trusted setup. The scheme is particularly interesting because of the short proof sizes. Unfortunately, the original scheme had a gap in the security proof that was first discovered by [9]. This paper provides a fix to this security proof and shows that a slight modification to the original protocol is secure. Our protocol is a generalization that applies to general linear-homomorphisms of which polynomial evaluations are a special case. It also uses a Bulletproofs-style folding which makes it easier to generalize. Concretely, however, the group-of-unknown order instantiation of our protocol has the same concrete efficiencies as the original DARK protocol when used as a polynomial commitment. We also applied the techniques (The CSZ and AMSS) developed in this paper to the original DARK protocol and added that to the appendix of the eprint [18]. [9] had originally provided a fix to DARK using binary challenges. This blows up the communication complexity. Concretely each round requires sending λ commitments, whereas we prove that a slight modification of the original DARK protocol is correct, which only requires sending 2 commitments per round. Both [9] and our scheme are secure under the hidden order assumption (Assumption 1). However, interestingly, when applying the Fiat-Shamir heuristic to AMSS protocols (see full version), we require that the commitment be *computationally unique*. For the DARK-style commitment in groups of unknown order, this requires the stronger subgroup hidden-order assumption.

2 Technical Overview

The regular DeMillo-Lipton-Schwartz-Zippel lemma is relatively simple to prove. Consider the special case of a multilinear polynomial over a field. As a base case, a univariate linear polynomial has at most one root over the field. For the induction step, express $f(X_1, ..., X_{\mu+1}) = g(X_1, ..., X_\mu) + X_{\mu+1}h(X_1, ..., X_\mu)$ for random variables $X_1, \ldots, X_{\mu+1}$. The probability that $h(x_1, ..., x_n) = 0$ over random x_i sampled from S is at most $\mu/|S|$ by the inductive hypothesis, and if $h(x_1, ..., x_\mu) = w \neq 0$ and $g(x_1, \ldots, x_\mu) = u$, then $u + X_{\mu+1}w$ has at most one root (base case). By the union bound, the overall probability is at most $\mu/|S| + 1/|S| = (\mu+1)/|S|$. This simple proof does not work for multilinear polynomials modulo a composite integer. The base case is the same for f coprime to N, which has at most one root. However, in the induction step, it isn't enough that $h(x_1, ..., x_\mu) \neq 0$ as it still may be a zero divisor, in which case the polynomial $u + X_{\mu+1}w$ is not necessarily coprime to N and the base case no longer applies. The number of roots depends on $\gcd(u + X_{\mu+1}w, N)$ and our new analysis takes into account its distribution. For each prime divisor p_i of N, the highest power of p_i that divides $u + X_{\mu+1}w$ follows a geometric distribution. Using a modified inductive argument, we are able to show that the probability $f(x_1, \ldots, x_\mu) \equiv 0 \bmod p^r$ is bounded by the probability that $\sum_{i=1}^{n} Z_i \geq r$ for i.i.d. geometric variables with success parameter $1 - \frac{1}{p}$. This probability is equal to a $I_{\frac{1}{p}}(r, \mu)$ where I is the regularized beta function. Furthermore, by CRT this probability is independent for each prime factor of N, and thus, the overall probability can be bounded by a product of regularized beta functions.

"Inverse" Multilinear Composite Schwartz-Zippel (LCSZ) Lemma. While our main theorem gives a tight bound on the probability for particular values of N, μ, and m, cryptographic applications require finding concrete parameters such that the probability is exponentially small in a security parameter λ. Concretely, we want to find a value N^* such that for all $N \geq N^*$ the probability that $f(X_1, \ldots, X_\mu) \equiv 0 \bmod N$ is bounded by $2^{-\lambda}$. To do this, we first derive simple and useful bounds for the regularized beta function:

- $I_{\frac{1}{p}}(r, \mu) \leq \left(\frac{n}{p}\right)^r$ for $p \geq 2\mu$
- $I_{\frac{1}{p}}(r, \mu) \leq \frac{r^n}{p^r}$ for $r \geq 2\mu$
- $\log(I_{1/p}(r - 1, \mu)) - \log(I_{1/p}(r, \mu))$ is non-increasing in r for any $p > \mu$ and for $r = 1$ in p.

We then formulate finding N^* as an optimization problem. N^* is the maximum value of N such that the probability of $f(\mathbf{x}) \equiv 0 \bmod N$ is greater than $2^{-\lambda}$. For any N let $S(N)$ denote the set of pairs (p, r) where p is a prime divisor of N with multiplicity r. Taking the logarithm of both the objective and the constraint yields a knapsack-like constraint maximization problem where the objective is $\log(N^*) = \sum_{(p_i, r_i) \in S(N^*)} r_i \cdot \log(p_i)$ and the constraint is $\sum_{(p_i, r_i) \in S(N^*)} - \log(I_{\frac{1}{p_i}}(r, \mu)) \leq \lambda$. Using the bounds on $I_{\frac{1}{p_i}}$ and several transformations of the problem we show that any optimal solution to this problem must be bounded by $t = 8\mu^2 + \log_2(2\mu)\lambda$, which in turn implies that $N^* \leq 2^t$.

Tighter Computational Solution. We further show that a simple greedy knapsack algorithm computes an upper bound to the knapsack problem. The algorithm uses the fact that $\frac{\log(p)}{\log(I_{1/p}(r-1,\mu))-\log(I_{1/p}(r,\mu))}$ the so-called marginal density of each item is non increasing over certain regions. Adding the densest items to the knapsack computes an upper bound to the objective. We run the algorithm on a large number of values for μ and λ and report the result.

2.1 Bulletproofs for Short Pre-Images and Almost Special Soundness

In the Bulletproofs Inner Product Argument a prover convinces a verifier that it knows the opening $\mathbf{f} \in \mathbb{F}_p^n$ to a homomorphic commitment $C = \mathsf{com}(\mathbf{f}) \in \mathbb{G}$ where $\mathbb{G}$ is a prime-order group. At a very high level, it does this by iteratively computing $\mathbf{f}' = \mathbf{f}_L + x \cdot \mathbf{f}_R \in \mathbb{F}^{n/2}$, where $\mathbf{f}_L, \mathbf{f}_R$ are the left and right half of $\mathbf{f}$ respectively and $x \in \mathbb{F}$ is a verifier generated challenge, and sending a commitment to the new $\mathbf{f}'$ to the verifier. After $\log_2(n)$ rounds, the prover sends a single field element as the final message. This naturally generalizes to homomorphic commitments that map vectors in $\mathbb{Z}^n$ to a group $\mathbb{G}$. The Bulletproofs protocol operates in exactly the same way over integer vectors but using more general instantiations of the commitment scheme. In particular, we consider schemes that may only be binding to *short* vectors in $\mathbb{Z}^n$, such as the DARK commitment using groups of unknown order or lattice-based (Ajtai) commitments. Additionally, the verifier checks that the final message is a "small" integer. Furthermore, we consider commitments that are binding under what we call *short rational openings* that open C to $\mathbf{h} = \mathbf{f}/s$ by showing $s \cdot C = \mathsf{com}(\mathbf{f})$, where the numerator and denominator of $\mathbf{h}$ have bounded norms in reduced form. We consider such rational openings due to "slack" in the knowledge extractor for Bulletproofs over rings like $\mathbb{Z}$ instead of fields, where the extractor obtains $\mathbf{f}$ and s satisfying $s \cdot C = \mathsf{com}(\mathbf{f})$, but cannot invert s to obtain a direct pre-image of C. In the soundness analysis, we leverage the fact that the final integer is small in order to bound the numerator/denominator (i.e., stretch and slack) of the extracted opening. This is where we invoke the new LCSZ lemma for multilinear polynomials. To gain some intuition in how we apply LCSZ, if the prover's private state at the start of protocol were a rational vector $\mathbf{f}/s$ such that $\mathsf{com}(\mathbf{f}) = s \cdot C$, then running protocol would result in an integer y that is the evaluation of a multilinear polynomial h with rational coefficients $\mathbf{f}/s$ at the $\log_2(n)$ challenges $\mathbf{c} = (c_1, ..., c_{\log n})$ sampled by the verifier, i.e. $y = h(\mathbf{c})$. Equivalently, $f(\mathbf{c}) \equiv 0 \bmod s$. If $\mathbf{c}$ were sampled uniformly and independent from f, then the LCSZ lemma states that as s grows too large this probability becomes vanishingly small.

For commitments binding over $\mathbb{Z}_p$, Bulletproofs satisfies special-soundness: there exists an efficient extractor that can extract a witness (i.e., an opening to the input commitment) from *any* forking tree of transcripts. Special-soundness implies knowledge-soundness by the classic *forking lemma*, which shows how to generate a transcript tree in polynomial time. Unfortunately, Bulletproofs with commitments that are only binding over small norm (rational) openings fails to satisfy special-soundness because the opening extracted from a forking tree of transcripts may have a very large norm (i.e., large slack or stretch). On the other hand, it turns out that we can leverage the intuition above in order to bound the size (slack and stretch) of extracted openings. Along the way, we introduce a new notion called almost-special soundness.

Almost Special Soundness. A k-ary transcript tree for a μ-round public-coin interactive proof labels each node of a k-ary μ-depth tree with a prover message and each edge with a verifier public-coin challenge so that the labels along any root-to-leaf path in the tree form a valid transcript between the prover and verifier that would cause the verifier to accept. An interactive proof for a relation $\mathcal{R}$ is $k^{(\mu)}$-special-sound if there exists an extractor that can efficiently extract a witness w from any k-ary tree of protocol transcripts for input x so that $(x, w) \in \mathcal{R}$. Bulletproofs for standard Pedersen vector commitments has this property for 3-ary trees, but not for vector commitments with bounded-norm openings because the extractor may obtain an opening that has a too large norm. On the other hand, if a prover running the protocol honestly were to start in its head with an opening of the commitment that has a too large norm there is a negligible probability over the random challenges that it would result in a valid transcript, whose last message is an integer of bounded norm. This applies to rational openings as well with a large norm numerator or denominator. This probability analysis relies on LCSZ, as explained in the paragraph above. We will say that rational openings have "large. norm" if they have either a large numerator (stretch), large denominator (slack), or both.

This observation suggests the following strawman extraction analysis: show that one of the valid transcripts in the tree corresponds to running the honest prover on the extracted opening, and conclude that if the extracted rational opening had large norm then it would have a negligible probability of resulting in a valid transcript. A fallacy in this argument is that the extracted witness is computed from the transcripts, and is thus dependent on the challenges appearing in the transcripts, whereas running the prover on a large norm opening only results in an invalid transcript with high probability over challenges sampled independently from this opening. To address this we could attempt the following: generate a 4-ary tree T via rejection sampling from polynomially many random simulations, extract an opening w* from its 3-ary left subtree T_L, show that some transcript tr in $T \setminus T_L$ is the result of running the prover on w*. The extracted witness is now independent of the challenges appearing in tr and was well-defined during the generation of T, after T_L was created and before tr was added. Given that T was generated via polynomially many random simulations we can argue this event had a negligible probability of occurring.

The remaining challenge, however, is to show that some transcript tr in $T \setminus T_L$ is consistent with running the honest prover on the extracted opening w*. It turns out that for protocols like Bulletproofs this is only true when the extracted opening of the input commitment is within the space over which the scheme is binding, which seems to bring us back to square one. For example, the transcript for a single round Bulletproofs protocol over an input commitment C to a vector in $\mathbb{Z}^2$ and commitment basis $\mathbf{g} = (g_L, g_R) \in \mathbb{G}^2$ consists of $(C, C_L, C_R, r, f') \in \mathbb{G}^3 \times \mathbb{Z}$ such that $f' \cdot (g_R + r g_L) = C_R + r^2 C_L + rC$. Given an opening $\mathbf{f} = (f_L, f_R)$ such that $\mathsf{com}(\mathbf{f}) = \langle \mathbf{f}, \mathbf{g} \rangle = C$ and $\langle (0, f_L), \mathbf{g} \rangle = C_L$ and $\langle (f_R, 0), \mathbf{g} \rangle = C_R$ then "re-running" the protocol on the openings with challenge r gives $f^* = f_L + r \cdot f_R$ such that $f^* \cdot (g_R + r g_L) = C_R + r^2 C_L + rC = C^*$. If f^* is sufficiently small then this implies $f^* = f'$, otherwise it is a break of the commitment scheme as it provides conflicting openings to C^*. However, f^* is only guaranteed to be small if the extracted opening $\mathbf{f}$ has low norm.

To get around this issue, we can increase the parameters of the commitment scheme so that it is binding over slightly larger openings, and we will argue level by level that the extracted openings remain small (using the independent path and the fact that re-generation of transcripts either returns the same commitments/messages or a break of the commitment scheme). In other words, while we want to show that every extracted value remains below some norm bound A, each extraction step produces a value that might be as large as some bound $B > A$, but for which the scheme is still binding, and thus re-running the protocol on this value will conflict with some path in the transcript tree with overwhelmingly high probability if too much larger than A. **This is precisely where we apply our new LCSZ lemma.** If the extracted opening with numerator $\mathbf{f}$ and denominator s has too large norm then re-running the protocol with this opening as the prover's private state and using the challenges $c_1, ..., c_\mu$ from the independent path would conflict with the transcript along the independent path (the final message will not be a small integer) except with negligible probability over the random challenges. The final message is equal to the evaluation $h(c_1, ..., c_\mu)$ where h is a multilinear polynomial with coefficient vector $\mathbf{f}/s$. This allows us to bound the norm growth at each level by some sufficiently small value $C \in (A, B)$. Crucially, while the growth from A to B is at least quadratic in A, the growth from A to C will be constant.

We generalize this to the notion of *Almost Special Sound*(AMSS) protocols and replace the bounds A and B with arbitrary predicates ϕ_a and ϕ_b. We prove that all protocols with this structure are knowledge sound, just like special-sound protocols, where the knowledge error is dependent on the probability that a random completion of a transcript starting from a message that fails predicate ϕ_a results in a valid transcript. Intuitively, this captures the fact that once the adversary has a private state that fails the desired extraction predicate, it will fail with overwhelming probability over fresh challenges to complete the proof transcript successfully.

Our proof that AMSS implies knowledge-soundness relies on a lemma that we call the *path predicate forking lemma*. The usual forking lemma shows how to generate forking transcript tree, which in special-sound protocols can be passed directly to the extractor. In our case, we need to generate transcript tree that satisfies additional predicates on each node. In the standard forking lemma [11], the predicate would simply be that challenges on each child of a node in the transcript tree are distinct from previous challenges. Our new lemma considers more general predicates, which may depend on partial transcripts that have already been generated in the course of the transcript generation algorithm. The analysis is similar and uses a union bound over all polynomial steps of the transcript tree generation process.

Fiat-Shamir Transform. The analysis showing that AMSS protocols are knowledge-sound critically relies on the fact that in the transcript tree generation process for an interactive protocol, the challenges on any given branch are sampled uniformly and independently. This is used to show that the transcript tree generated satisfies a certain property with overwhelming probability. The Fiat-Shamir transform converts an interactive public-coin protocol into a non-interactive protocol by replacing the verifier's messages with a transcript hash. The problem with applying the Fiat-Shamir transform to an AMSS protocol is that the adversary can now grind the challenges in each round when generating a transcript, breaking uniformity and independence of challenges. Using a union bound, we could still bound the probability that the transcript tree does not have the desired property, but this would result in a factor Q^μ loss where Q is the number of queries an adversary performs, and μ is the number of rounds in the protocol. However, we can instead focus on protocols where grinding challenges is impossible for the adversary. To do this, we introduce the notion of *computationally unique* commitments. In a computationally unique commitment scheme, it is infeasible to open two distinct commitments to the same message. We prove that this property is held by a large class of deterministic homomorphic commitment schemes, which include those from groups of unknown order and lattice assumptions. We prove security of the Fiat-Shamir transform for AMSS protocols in the random oracle model with computationally unique commitments. This analysis is in the full version.

3   Main Theorem Statement (LCSZ)

Theorem 1 (Multilinear Composite Schwartz-Zippel (LCSZ)). *Let $N = \prod_{i=1}^{\ell} p_i^{r_i}$ for distinct primes $p_1, ..., p_\ell$. Let f be any μ-linear integer polynomial co-prime to N. For any integer $m > 1$ and $\mathbf{x}$ sampled uniformly from $[0, m)^\mu$, then*

$$\mathbb{P}_{\mathbf{x} \leftarrow [0,m)^\mu}[f(\mathbf{x}) \equiv 0 \bmod N] \leq \frac{\mu}{m} + \prod_{i=1}^{\ell} I_{\frac{1}{p_i}}(r_i, \mu),$$

where $I_{\frac{1}{p}}(r, \mu) = (1 - \frac{1}{p})^\mu \sum_{j=r}^{\infty} \binom{\mu+r-1}{r} \left(\frac{1}{p}\right)^j$ is the regularized beta function.

Remark 1. The regularized beta function characterizes the tail distribution of the sum of independent geometric random variables. If $Y = \sum_{i=1}^{\mu} Z_i$ where each Z_i is an independent geometric random variable with parameter ϵ then $P[Y \geq r] = I_{1-\epsilon}(r, \mu)$. Y is a negative binomial variable with parameters ϵ, μ.

Remark 2. A close reading of the proof reveals that if $m = N$, then the theorem statement simplifies to $\mathbb{P}_{\mathbf{x}\leftarrow[0,N)^\mu}[f(\mathbf{x}) \equiv 0 \bmod N] \leq \prod_{i=1}^{\ell} I_{\frac{1}{p_i}}(r_i, \mu)$. This is because $\mathbf{x}$ is uniform mod N and thus uniform mod any $N^*|N$.

Remark 3. The theorem is nearly tight for all N. Setting $f(\mathbf{x}) = \prod_{i=1}^{\mu} x_i$ and $m = N$ gives $P_{\mathbf{x}\leftarrow[0,m)^\mu}[f(\mathbf{x}) \equiv 0 \bmod N] = \mathbb{P}_{\mathbf{x}\leftarrow[0,N)^\mu}[f(\mathbf{x}) \equiv 0 \bmod N] = \prod_{i=1}^{\ell} I_{\frac{1}{p_i}}(r_i, \mu)$.

Remark 4. $1 - e^{-\mu/p_i} \leq I_{\frac{1}{p_i}}(1, \mu) = 1 - (1 - \frac{1}{p_i})^\mu \leq \frac{\mu}{p_i}$. Hence, for square-free N the probability in Theorem 1 is upper bounded by $\frac{\mu}{m} + \frac{\mu^\ell}{N}$, but for $\ell > 1$ this is a loose upper bound unless $\mu \ll p_i$ for all $p_i|N$. For $\ell = 1$ (i.e., prime N), Theorem 1 coincides with the Schwartz-Zippel lemma.

Remark 5. $I_{\frac{1}{p_i}}(r_i, 1) = \left(\frac{1}{p_i}\right)^{r_i}$. Hence, for $\mu = 1$, the bound in Theorem 1 is $\frac{1}{N} + \frac{1}{m}$.

We defer all proofs including the proof of Theorem 1 to the full version.

4 Inverse LCSZ

Theorem 1 (LCSZ) bounds the probability $\mathbb{P}_{\mathbf{x}\leftarrow[0,m)^\mu}[f(\mathbf{x}) \equiv 0 \bmod N]$ for given values of μ, N, and m, which has the form $\frac{\mu}{m} + \delta_{N,\mu}$. In the case that N is prime, $\delta_{N,\mu} = \frac{\mu}{N}$, which agrees with the standard Schwartz-Zippel lemma applied to μ-linear polynomials. The term $\delta_{N,\mu}$ for composite N, which is dependent on both μ and the factorization of N, has a complicated closed form expression in terms of a product of regularized beta functions.

This section analyzes the inverse: for a given $\mu, \lambda \in \mathbb{N}$ what size threshold $t(\lambda, \mu) \in \mathbb{N}$ is sufficient such that $\delta_{N,\mu} \leq 2^{-\lambda}$ for all $N \geq t(\lambda, \mu)$? In other words:

$$t(\lambda, \mu) := \sup\{N \in \mathbb{N} : \prod_{(p,r)\in S(N)} I_{\frac{1}{p}}(r, \mu) \geq 2^{-\lambda}\}. \qquad (t(\lambda,\mu) \text{ def})$$

For $\mu = 1$, since $I_{1/p}(r, 1) = \frac{1}{p^r}$ and $\prod_{(p,r)\in S(N)} I_{\frac{1}{p}}(r, \mu) = \frac{1}{N}$, it is easy to see that $t(\lambda, \mu) = 2^\lambda$. For $\mu \geq 2$, the value of $t(\lambda, \mu)$ (or even an upper bound) is not nearly as easy to derive. For the rest of this section we will focus on this $\mu \geq 2$ case. We will analytically derive an upper bound to $t(\lambda, \mu)$, showing that $\log t(\lambda, \mu) \in O(\mu^{2+\epsilon} + \frac{\lambda}{\epsilon})$ for any $\epsilon \geq \log_\mu(2)$.

Theorem 2 (Inverse LCSZ). *For all $\mu \geq 2$, $\epsilon \geq \log_\mu(2)$, and all N such that*

$$\log N \geq 4\mu^{2+\epsilon} + (1 + \frac{1}{\epsilon}) \cdot \lambda.$$

we have that for any μ-linear polynomial f that is coprime with N

$$\mathbb{P}_{x\leftarrow[0,m)^\mu}[f(x) \equiv 0 \bmod N] \leq 2^{-\lambda} + \frac{\mu}{m}.$$

By setting $\epsilon = \log_\mu(2)$ we get:

Corollary 1. *For all N such that*

$$\log N \geq 8\mu^2 + \log_2(2\mu) \cdot \lambda.$$

we have that for any n-linear polynomial f that is coprime with N

$$P_{x \leftarrow [0,m)^\mu}[f(x) \equiv 0 \bmod N] \leq 2^{-\lambda} + \frac{\mu}{m}.$$

5   Definitions and Notations

5.1   Integer Polynomials

If f is a multivariate polynomial, then $||f||_\infty$ denotes the maximum over the absolute values of all coefficients of f.

Lemma 1 (Evaluation Bound). *For any μ-linear integer polynomial f and $m \geq 2$:*

$$\mathbb{P}_{\mathbf{x} \leftarrow [0,m)^\mu}[|f(\mathbf{x})| \leq \frac{1}{m^\mu} \cdot ||f||_\infty] \leq \frac{3\mu}{m}$$

Fact 1 *Let $q \in \mathbb{Z}$ be any positive integer. For any integer $E \in \mathbb{Z}$ such that $|E| \leq \frac{q^{d+2} - q}{2(q-1)}$ there exists a unique degree d integer polynomial $f \in \mathbb{Z}[X]$ with $||f||_\infty \leq q/2$ such that $f(q) = E$.*

Lemma 2 (Rational Encoding of multi-linear polynomials). *Let $q \in \mathbb{Z}$ be any positive integer. Let $\mathbf{q} = [q^{2^{i-1}}]_{i=1}^\mu \in \mathbb{Z}^\mu$. Consider any $\beta_d, \beta_n \in \mathbb{N}$ such that $\beta_d \cdot \beta_n \leq \frac{q}{2}$. Let $Z = \{z \in \mathbb{Z} : |z| \leq \beta_d\}$, let $\mathcal{F} = \{f \in \mathbb{Z}[X_1, \ldots, X_\mu] : ||f||_\infty \leq \beta_n\}$ be a μ-linear polynomial, and let $\mathcal{H} = \{f/z \in \mathbb{Q}[X_1, \ldots X_\mu] : f \in \mathcal{F} \wedge z \in Z\}$. Then for any $h_1, h_2 \in \mathcal{H}$, if $h_1(\mathbf{q}) = h_2(\mathbf{q})$ then $h_1 = h_2$.*

5.2   Groups of Unknown Order

A group of unknown order is a group where the order is computationally hard to compute. It is defined by an algorithm *GGen* that on input security parameter, samples a group $\mathbb{G}$, along with size bounds on the group that depend on the security parameter (we omit the size bounds for simplicity). We define three assumptions in these groups. The hidden order assumption which is the most basic, minimal assumption, saying that it is hard to compute the order of random group elements. The stronger sub-group hidden order assumption states that it is hard to compute any information about the order of a sampled subgroup, e.g., a subgroup generated by a commitment key. And finally, the famous RSA assumption which states that it is hard to compute roots of random elements in the group and implies the hidden order assumption.

Assumption 1 (Hidden Order Assumption). The hidden order assumption holds for a group sampling algorithm $GGen$ if for any probabilistic polynomial time adversary $\mathcal{A}$:

$$\Pr\left[a \cdot \mathsf{G} = 0 : \begin{array}{c} \mathbb{G} \leftarrow GGen(1^\lambda) \\ \mathsf{G} \xleftarrow{\$} \mathbb{G} \\ a \in \mathbb{Z} \leftarrow \mathcal{A}(\mathbb{G}, \mathsf{G}) \end{array}\right] \leq \mathsf{negl}(\lambda) \ .$$

Assumption 2 (Subgroup Hidden Order Assumption). The subgroup hidden order assumption is a generalization of the hidden order assumption. It says that it is difficult to compute a multiple of the order of any element in a subgroup sampled according to some distribution. It holds for a group sampling algorithm $GGen$ and subgroup sampling[2] algorithm $SGGen$ if for any probabilistic polynomial time adversary $\mathcal{A}$:

$$\Pr\left[\gcd(a, |\mathbb{H}|) \neq 1 : \begin{array}{c} \mathbb{G} \leftarrow GGen(1^\lambda) \\ \mathbb{H} \leftarrow SGGen(\mathbb{G}) \\ a \in \mathbb{Z} \leftarrow \mathcal{A}(\mathbb{G}, \mathbb{H}) \end{array}\right] \leq \mathsf{negl}(\lambda) \ .$$

Assumption 3 (RSA assumption, [21,34]). The RSA assumption holds for $GGen$ if for any probabilistic polynomial time adversary $\mathcal{A}$:

$$\Pr\left[\ell \cdot \mathsf{U} = \mathsf{G} : \begin{array}{c} \mathbb{G}, N \leftarrow GGen(1^\lambda) \\ \mathsf{G} \xleftarrow{\$} \mathbb{G}, \ell \xleftarrow{\$} [N] \\ \mathsf{U} \in \mathbb{G} \leftarrow \mathcal{A}(\mathbb{G}, \mathsf{G}) \end{array}\right] \leq \mathsf{negl}(\lambda) \ .$$

The RSA Assumption implies Assumption 1 [18].

5.3   Knowledge Soundness

An NP relation $\mathcal{R}$ is a subset of strings $x, w \in \{0, 1\}^*$ such that there is a decision algorithm to decide $(x, w) \in \mathcal{R}$ that runs in time polynomial in $|x|$ and $|w|$. The language of $\mathcal{R}$, denoted $\mathcal{L}_R$, is the set $\{x \in \{0, 1\}^* : \exists w \in \{0, 1\}^* \ s.t. \ (x, w) \in \mathcal{R}\}$. The string w is called the *witness* and x the *instance*. An **interactive proof of knowledge** for an NP relation $\mathcal{R}$ is a special kind of two-party interactive protocol between a prover denoted $\mathcal{P}$ and a verifier denoted $\mathcal{V}$, where $\mathcal{P}$ has a private input w and both parties have a common public input x such that $(x, w) \in \mathcal{R}$. Informally, the protocol is *complete* if $\mathcal{P}(x, w)$ always causes $\mathcal{V}(x)$ to output 1 for any $(x, w) \in \mathcal{R}$. The protocol is *knowledge sound* if there exists an extraction algorithm $\mathcal{E}$ called the *extractor* such that for every x and adversarial prover $\mathcal{A}$ that causes $\mathcal{V}(x)$ to output 1 with non-negligible probability, $\mathcal{E}$ outputs w such that $(x, w) \in \mathcal{R}$ with overwhelming probability given access[3] to $\mathcal{A}$.

---

[2] The subgroup sampling algorithm takes $\mathbb{G}$ as input, which is interpreted as a succinct description of $\mathbb{G}$, such as a list of generators, not necessarily the list of all elements in $\mathbb{G}$.

[3] The extractor can run $\mathcal{A}$ for any specified number of steps, inspect the internal state of $\mathcal{A}$, and even rewind $\mathcal{A}$ to a previous state.

Definition 1 (Interactive Proof of Knowledge).

An interactive protocol $\Pi = (\mathcal{P}, \mathcal{V})$ between a prover $\mathcal{P}$ and verifier $\mathcal{V}$ is a proof of knowledge for a relation $\mathcal{R}$ with knowledge error $\delta : \mathbb{N} \to [0,1]$ if the following properties hold, where on common input x and prover witness w the output of the verifier is denoted by the random variable $\langle \mathcal{P}(x,w), \mathcal{V}(x) \rangle$:

- *Perfect Completeness: for all $(x,w) \in \mathcal{R}$*

$$\Pr[\, \langle \mathcal{P}(x,w), \mathcal{V}(x) \rangle = 1] = 1$$

- *$\delta - KnowledgeSoundness$: There exists a polynomial $\mathsf{poly}(\cdot)$ and a probabilistic oracle machine $\mathcal{E}$ called the extractor such that given oracle access to any adversarial interactive prover algorithm $\mathcal{A}$ and any input $x \in \mathcal{L}_R$ the following holds: if*

$$\mathbb{P}[\langle \mathcal{A}(x), \mathcal{V}(x) \rangle = 1] = \epsilon(x)$$

then $\mathcal{E}^{\mathcal{A}}(x)$ with oracle access to $\mathcal{A}$ runs in time $\frac{\mathsf{poly}(|x|)}{\epsilon(x)}$ and outputs w such that $(x,w) \in R$ with probability at least $1 - \frac{\delta(|x|)}{\epsilon(x)}$.

An interactive proof is "knowledge sound", or simply a "proof of knowledge", if has negligible knowledge error δ.

6 Almost-Special-Soundness

We first define deterministic (non-hiding) commitment scheme over a message space $\mathcal{M}$ and opening space $\mathcal{W} \supseteq \mathcal{M}$. When $\mathcal{M} = \mathcal{W}$ it is identical to collision-resistant hash functions. More generally, the commitment function is a collision-resistant hash function $H : \mathcal{M} \to \{0,1\}^\lambda$, but the algorithm that verifies an opening of C to m is not restricted to checking $H(m) = C$ (e.g., this may not be possible when $m \notin \mathcal{M}$).

These schemes do not provide a way to commit to $\mathbf{x} \in \mathcal{W} \setminus \mathcal{M}$, but is nonetheless useful to define in the context of arguments of knowledge. Suppose a party commits to a message $m \in \mathcal{M}$ as $C = H(m)$ and is asked to prove knowledge of an opening of C using an argument system for which the knowledge extractor is only guaranteed to extract an opening to a message in the superset $\mathcal{W}$. There are applications where it doesn't matter whether the prover knows an actual input $m \in \mathcal{M}$ to H such that $H(m) = C$ as long as it is committed in a binding way to some message in $\mathcal{W}$ that it knows. In fact, commitment schemes where $\mathcal{M} = \mathbb{Z}^n$ and $\mathcal{W} \subseteq \mathbb{Q}^n$ together with arguments of knowledge that extract openings to $\mathcal{W}$ suffice to construct linear-map vector commitments over prime fields $\mathbb{F}_p$, with polynomial commitment schemes as a special case. These have very powerful applications including the construction of generic succinct non-interactive argument (SNARK) systems for all of NP.

Definition 2 (Deterministic Commitment Scheme). *A deterministic commitment scheme Γ is a tuple $\Gamma = (\mathsf{Setup}, \mathcal{G}, \mathsf{Commit}, \mathsf{Open})$ where:*

- $Setup(1^\lambda) \to pp$ *is a PPT algorithm that generates public parameters* pp, *which define a finite set of indices* $\mathcal{I}$, *a message space* $\mathcal{M}$, *and an opening space* $\mathcal{W} \supseteq \mathcal{M}$;
- $\mathcal{G}(pp, \iota) \to pp^*$ *is a PPT algorithm that generates parameters for the index* $\iota \in \mathcal{I}$;
- $Commit(pp^*, m) \to C$ *is a polynomial time computable function that takes a secret message* m *and returns a public commitment* C.
- $Open(pp^*, C, w, \sigma) \to b \in \{0, 1\}$ *is a PPT algorithm that verifies the opening of commitment* C *to the message* $w \in \mathcal{W}$ *provided with an opening hint* $\sigma \in \{0, 1\}^*$.

A commitment scheme Γ *is* **binding** *if for all PPT adversaries* $\mathcal{A}$:

$$\Pr \left[b_0 = b_1 = 1 \wedge m_0 \neq m_1 : \begin{array}{l} pp \leftarrow Setup(1^\lambda) \\ (\iota, C, m_0, m_1, \sigma_0, \sigma_1) \leftarrow \mathcal{A}(pp) \\ pp^* \leftarrow \mathcal{G}(pp, \iota) \\ b_0 \leftarrow Open(pp^*, C, m_0, \sigma_0) \\ b_1 \leftarrow Open(pp^*, C, m_1, \sigma_1) \end{array} \right] \leq \mathsf{negl}(\lambda).$$

We say that a tuple $(C, (m_0, \sigma_0), (m_1, \sigma_1))$ *is a* break *of the commitment scheme, if* $Open(pp^*, C, x_1, \sigma_1) = Open(pp^*, C, m_1, \sigma_1) = 1$ *and* $m_0 \neq m_1$.

Remark on $\mathcal{I}$**:** The standard definition of commitment schemes does not have an indexing set $\mathcal{I}$, or equivalently has $|\mathcal{I}| = 1$. The more general definition we presented is important for our applications, and it is important for the scheme to be binding even for an adversarially sampled index. As a simple example, Setup might determine a prime-order group $\mathcal{G}$ in which the discrete logarithm is hard and $\mathcal{I} \subset \mathcal{G}$ is the set of $p - 1$ generators. The commitment function at index $g \in \mathcal{I}$ computes $x \mapsto g^x$ for $x \in \mathbb{F}_p$.

Definition 3 (Almost-Special-Soundness (new)).
   Let χ *denote any set of size* 2^λ. *Let* $\Gamma = (Setup, \mathcal{G}, Commit, Open)$ *denote a deterministic commitment scheme with message space* $\mathcal{M}$, *opening space* $\mathcal{W}$, *and indexing set* $\mathcal{I}$. *Let* Π *be* μ-*round public-coin interactive proof with challenge space* χ *for a relation* $\mathcal{R}_{pp}$, *such that the commitment parameters* $pp \leftarrow Setup(1^\lambda)$ *are generated as part of the setup of* Π *and where the relation is possibly dependent on* pp. Π *is* $(k^{(\mu)}, \delta(\cdot), \Gamma, \phi)$-*almost-special-sound if there exists*

1. *A pair of predicates* $\phi = (\phi_a, \phi_b)$ *where* $\phi_a, \phi_b : [\mu] \times \mathcal{M} \to \{0, 1\}$ *and* $\phi_a(i, m_i) = 1 \implies \phi_b(i, m_i) = 1$.
2. *A negligible function* $\delta : \mathbb{N} \to \mathbb{R}$.
3. *There is a localized transcript tree labeling* F *that assigns to each node* ν *of a valid transcript tree for* Π *a commitment label* $C^{(\nu)}$ *for the scheme* Γ *at an index* $\iota_\nu \in \mathcal{I}$.[4] *Additionally, any leaf node* ν *of the transcript tree is labelled*

---

[4] Crucially, the definition does not require the ith position of all transcripts to use the same commitment index. The commitment index μ_i used in a particular transcript for the ith commitment $C^{(i)}$ might be a function of the transcript prefix preceding $C^{(i)}$.

with $C^{(\nu)}$ for some index $\iota_\nu \in \mathcal{I}$ together with an opening (m_ν, o_ν) such that $\mathsf{Open}(\mathsf{pp}_{\iota_\nu}, C^{(\nu)}, m_\nu, o_\nu) = 1$ *and* $\phi_a(\mu, m_\mu) = 1$.

Extract Witness: $\mathsf{ExtractWitness}(x, F, \mathsf{tree}, \mathsf{treeOpenings}) \to w$ *takes as input an instance x, the tree labeling function F, a k-ary transcript tree* tree *and purported openings* $\mathsf{treeOpenings} = [(m_1, \sigma_1), \ldots, (m_N, \sigma_N)]$, *to the commitments of each node in the tree, that are defined by F. If* $\mathsf{tree}, \mathsf{treeOpenings}$, *satisfy the following properties then* $(x, w) \in \mathbb{R}_{\mathsf{pp}}$

1. *The challenge labels for the children of each node are distinct.*
2. *For each $\nu \in \mathsf{tree}$,* $\mathsf{Open}(\mathsf{pp}_\nu, C^\nu, m_\nu, \sigma_\nu) = 1$
3. *For each $\nu \in \mathsf{tree}$,* $\phi_a(\sigma_\nu) = 1$.

.

Extract Internal: $\mathsf{ExtractInternal}(F, \nu, \mathsf{subtree} = [(\iota_1, m_1, \sigma_1), \ldots, (\iota_t, m_t, \sigma_t)])$ $\to (m, \sigma)$ *takes as input a node ν such that $C^\nu = F(\nu)$ is the commitment assigned to ν by F, as well as the transcript subtree of size t, spanned at ν, defined by the indices ι of the subtree along with purported openings to each commitment $F(\iota) = C^\iota$ in the subtree.*

Given that each nodes children in the subtree have distinct challenge labels, the algorithm either outputs a break of Γ (Definition 2) or satisfies the following property:

$$\forall i \in [t] \phi_a(\mathsf{level}(\iota_i), m_i) = 1 \wedge \mathsf{Open}(\mathsf{pp}_{\iota_i}, C^{(\iota_i)}, m_i, \sigma_i) = 1$$
$$\Downarrow$$
$$\mathsf{Open}(\mathsf{pp}_\nu, C^\nu, m, \sigma) = 1 \wedge \phi_b(\mathsf{level}(\nu), m) = 1$$

Here $\mathsf{level} : [k^\mu] \to [\mu]$ *maps from a node to its level in the tree.* **Extend algorithm** $\mathsf{Extend}(\iota, \mathsf{tr}) \to ((m'_{\ell_\iota = \mathsf{level}(\iota)+1}, \sigma'_{\ell_\iota}), \ldots, (m'_\mu, \sigma_\mu))$, *such that* $\mathsf{tr} = [C, (C_1, \alpha_1), \ldots, (C_\mu, \alpha_\mu)]$ *is an accepting transcript that includes the node ι, i.e.* $C_{\ell_\iota} = C^{(\iota)}$. *For any openings to $C_i, \ldots, C_\mu$, $(m_i, \sigma_i), \ldots, (m_\mu, \sigma_\mu)$, one of the following cases holds:*

1. $\exists j \in [i, \mu]$ *such that* $(C_j, (m_j, \sigma_j), (m'_j, \sigma'_j))$ *is a break of Γ*
2.

$$P_{\alpha_i, \ldots, \alpha_\mu \leftarrow \chi}\left[\phi_a(\mathsf{level}(\iota), m) = 0 \,\middle|\, \begin{array}{l} m_i = m'_i \forall i \in [\ell_\iota + 1, \mu] \\ \phi_a(m'_i) = 1 \forall i \in [\ell_\iota + 1, \mu] \\ \phi_b(m_{\ell_\iota}) = 1 \end{array}\right] \leq \delta(\lambda)$$

Short-hand notation: *An interactive proof is $(k^{(\mu)}, \delta)$-almost-special-sound if it is $(k^{(\mu)}, \delta, \mathsf{com}, \phi)$-almost-special-sound for some commitment scheme* com *and some predicate pair ϕ. We may omit δ and simply write $k^{(\mu)}$-almost-special-soundness if this holds for some negligible function $\delta : \mathbb{N} \to \mathbb{R}$.*

Remark 6. Any special sound protocol satisfies almost-special-soundness as 3) essentially captures the special soundness definition. More precisely a $k^{(\mu)}$-special sound satisfies $k^{(\mu)}$-almost-special-soundness by setting the commitment scheme to be trivial (i.e., identity function) and the ith round commitment $C^{(i)}$ to the prover's ith round message and setting the predicates $\phi_a = 1, \phi_b = 0$ to be trivial as well (i.e., always return 1 and 0 respectively). The algorithm Extend can output an arbitrary set of messages because the condition on the algorithm is vacuously true as $\phi_a(i, m) \neq 0$ for any (i, m). The algorithm Extract$(\nu, C^{(\nu)}, *)$ is trivial because $C^{(\nu)}$ is the message itself. The algorithm Break is also trivial as ϕ_b is always 0. The algorithm Extract$(x, \mathsf{openTree}) \to w$ exists by the definition of $k^{(\mu)}$-special soundness.

Theorem 3 (AMSS implies Knowledge Soundness). *If a μ-round inter-active proof for a relation $\mathcal{R}$ with λ-bit challenges, $\mu \in O(\log(\lambda + |x|))$, and verifier decision algorithm runtime $t_V \in \mathsf{poly}(|pp|, |x|, \lambda)$ on input $x \in \mathcal{L}_{\mathcal{R}}$ and parameters $pp \leftarrow \Gamma.\mathsf{Setup}(1^\lambda)$ is $(k^{(\mu)}, \delta, \Gamma, \phi)$-almost-special-sound then for $\delta'(\lambda) = 2\lambda(k+1)^\mu(\mu + t_V) \cdot \max(\delta(\lambda), k \cdot 2^{-\lambda}) + 2^{-\lambda}$ it is δ'-knowledge sound for the modified relation:*

$$\mathcal{R}'(pp) = \{(x, w) : \mathcal{R}(x, w) = 1 \ \lor\ w \in \mathcal{L}_{break}(pp)\}$$

where

$$\mathcal{L}_{break}(pp) = \{(\mathcal{C}, \sigma_1, \sigma_2, \iota) : \iota \in \mathcal{I} \ \land\ \sigma_1 \neq \sigma_2 \ \land\ \mathsf{Open}(pp_\iota, \mathcal{C}, \sigma_1) = \mathsf{Open}(pp_\iota, \mathcal{C}, \sigma_2) = 1\}$$

Remark 7. $\delta'(\lambda)$ is a negligible function if $\delta(\lambda)$ is negligible, assuming $k \in O(1)$, $\mu \in O(\log(\lambda + |x|))$, $t_V \in \mathsf{poly}(|x|, \lambda)$, and $|x| \in \mathsf{poly}(\lambda)$.

This theorem has the following corollary:

Corollary 2. *An interactive proof with λ-bit challenges that is $k^{(\mu)}$-almost-special-sound for a relation $\mathcal{R}$ and has at most $\mu \in O(\log(\lambda + |x|))$ rounds on any instance $x \in \mathcal{L}_{\mathcal{R}}$ has witness-extended emulation for $\mathcal{R}$.*

7 Argument of Knowledge of "short" Rational Opening

For any deterministic homomorphic commitment to vectors in $\mathbb{Z}_p^n$, where the commitment function is a homomorphism com $: \mathbb{Z}_p^n \to \mathbb{G}$, there is a generic succinct argument of knowledge of a commitment opening (i.e., a homomorphism preimage) with $O(\log n)$ communication complexity [2,10,12]. This same protocol can also be used to argue knowledge of any linear form of the committed vector. This is also known as a linear-map vector commitment (LMVC) [20,28], and captures polynomial commitments as a special case.

We generalize this result to work with deterministic homomorphic integer vector commitments that are only binding over *short* vectors in $\mathbb{Z}^n$, which includes vector commitment schemes based on lattices and groups of unknown order. Furthermore, the protocol can still be used to argue knowledge of any linear form $h : \mathbb{Z}^n \to \mathbb{G}$ of the committed vector, where $\mathbb{G}$ is a prime order group.

The protocol is essentially the same as the succinct homomorphism preimage protocol [2,10], but where the verifier additionally checks a bound on the prover's final message. This can also be viewed as a special case of the sumcheck argument with a bound check, as described in [12], but we provide a much tighter soundness analysis.

A bit more precisely, the protocol is not an argument of knowledge of a short integer vector pre-image per se, but rather a *short rational* opening of the commitment $C = \mathsf{com}(\mathbf{x})$, which is some $\mathbf{x}' \in \mathbb{Z}^n$ and $z \in \mathbb{Z}$ such that $\mathsf{com}(\mathbf{x}') = z \cdot C$ and $\mathbf{x}'/z \in \mathcal{M} \subseteq \mathbb{Q}^n$ where $\mathcal{M} = \{\mathbf{x}/z \in \mathbb{Q}^n : z \in \mathbb{Z}, gcd(\mathbf{x}, z) = 1, \|\mathbf{x}\| \leq \beta_n, |z| \leq \beta_d\}$ is a subset of rational vectors with bounded norm denominators and numerators in reduced form. We call this an opening of the commitment C to the rational vector $\mathbf{x}'/z \in \mathcal{M}$. If the commitment scheme is binding over such rational openings to vectors in $\mathcal{M}$ and $[0, p)^n \subseteq \mathcal{M}$, then it also functions as a binding commitment scheme for vectors in $\mathbb{Z}_p^n$ where an opening to $m \in \mathcal{M}$ is also an opening to $m \bmod p \in \mathbb{Z}_p^n$ and the protocol is thus an argument of knowledge of an opening to a unique vector in $\mathbb{Z}_p^n$. Finally, for any linear form $h : \mathbb{Z}_p^n \to \mathbb{G}$ the modified commitment $\mathsf{com}^*(\mathbf{x}) = (\mathsf{com}(\mathbf{x}), h(\mathbf{x}))$ preserves binding over $\mathcal{M}$ and running the same protocol for com^* becomes an argument of knowledge for an opening of the commitment (C, y) to a unique $\mathbf{x}^* \in \mathbb{Z}_p^n$ such that $h(\mathbf{x}^*) = y$.

Remark on Zero-Knowledge. Deterministic commitment schemes are non-hiding and our construction is focussed on producing a succinct argument of knowledge without concern for zero-knowledge. To obtain a zero-knowledge argument, the succinct argument can be composed with (i.e., applied as the pivot to) a sigma protocol for pre-images of ϕ. See [4] for further details.

Definition 4 (Z-linear commitment scheme). *Let* $\Gamma = (\mathsf{Setup}, \mathcal{G}, \mathsf{Commit}, \mathsf{Open})$ *be a deterministic commitment scheme such that for any* $\mathsf{pp} = (\mathcal{I}, \mathcal{M}, \mathcal{W}) \leftarrow \mathsf{Setup}(1^\lambda)$ *where* $\mathcal{M} \subseteq \mathcal{W} \subseteq \mathbb{Z}^n$ *and* $\iota \in \mathcal{I}$ *the commitment function* $\mathsf{Commit}(\mathsf{pp}_\iota, \cdot) : \mathcal{M} \to \mathbb{G}$ *is the restriction* $h|_{\mathcal{M}}$ *of a group homomorphism* $h : \mathbb{Z}^n \to \mathbb{G}$. *We say that* Γ *is a* $\mathbb{Z}$*-linear deterministic commitment scheme.*

Definition 5 (Rational openings). *Let* $\Gamma = (\mathsf{Setup}, \mathcal{G}, \mathsf{Commit}, \mathsf{Open})$ *be* $\mathbb{Z}$*-linear deterministic commitment scheme where commitments are contained within a finite group* $\mathbb{G}$. *Let* $\mathcal{W}^* \subseteq \mathbb{Q}^n$ *and let* $\mathsf{Setup}^*(1^\lambda)$ *denote a new setup algorithm that runs* $\mathsf{Setup}(1^\lambda)$ *but replaces* $\mathcal{W}$ *with* $\mathcal{W}^*$. *Let* $\mathsf{Open}^*(\mathsf{pp}, C, \mathbf{x}/z, (z, \mathbf{x}, \sigma))$ *denote a new opening verification algorithm which on inputs* $z \in \mathbb{Z}$, $\mathbf{x} \in \mathbb{Z}^n$ *such that* $\mathbf{x}/z \in \mathcal{W}^*$ *and* $C \in \mathbb{G}$ *returns 1 if and only if* $z \neq 0 \bmod |\mathbb{G}|$, *and* $\mathsf{Open}(\mathsf{pp}, z \cdot C, \mathbf{x}, \sigma) = 1$.[5] *We call the opening hint*

---

[5] In a group of unknown order it may be difficult to check that $z \neq 0 \bmod |\mathbb{G}|$. If g is a generator (e.g., the generator of a subgroup of unknown order) then it suffices to check $z \cdot g = 0$. In any case, GUOs are typically used for commitments under the hardness assumption that it is difficult to compute any multiple of the order of $\mathbb{G}$, in which case checking $z \neq 0 \bmod |\mathbb{G}|$ can be dropped from verification.

$(z, \mathbf{x}, \sigma)$ a rational opening of C to $\mathbf{x}/z \in \mathcal{W}^*$. We say Γ is binding over rational openings to $\mathcal{W}^* \subseteq \mathbb{Q}^n$ if $\Gamma^* = (\textit{Setup}^*, \mathcal{G}, \textit{Commit}, \textit{Open}^*)$ satisfies the usual definition of commitment binding (See Definition 2).

Lemma 3 (trivial). If $(\textit{Setup}, \mathcal{G}, \textit{Commit}, \textit{Open})$ is a $\mathbb{Z}$-linear deterministic commitment scheme binding over $\mathcal{W} \subseteq \mathbb{Q}^n$ where $\textit{Commit}(pp_\iota, \cdot) : \mathbb{Z}^n \rightarrow \mathbb{G}_{com}$ and $h : \mathbb{Z}^n \rightarrow \mathbb{G}$ is any homomorphism, then the modified scheme $(\textit{Setup}, \mathcal{G}, \textit{Commit}, \textit{Open}^*)$ where:

- $\textit{Setup}(1^\lambda) \rightarrow pp$ and $\mathcal{G}(\iota, pp) \rightarrow pp_\iota$
- $\textit{Commit}^*(pp_\iota, \mathbf{x} \in \mathbb{Z}^n) \rightarrow (\textit{Commit}(pp_\iota, \mathbf{x}), h(\mathbf{x})) \in \mathbb{G}_{com} \times \mathbb{G}$
- $\textit{Open}^*(pp_\iota, (C, y) \in \mathbb{G}_{com} \times \mathbb{G}, \mathbf{x} \in \mathbb{Z}^n, s) \rightarrow \textit{Open}(pp_\iota, \mathbf{x}, s, C)$

is also a $\mathbb{Z}$-linear deterministic commitment scheme binding over $\mathcal{W}$.

Proof. Any break of the modified scheme includes a break of the original scheme, i.e. tuples $(\mathbf{x}, \iota, s, (C, y))$ and $(\mathbf{x}', \iota, s', (C, y))$ such that $\mathbf{x} \neq \mathbf{x}' \in \mathcal{W}$ and $\textit{Open}(pp_\iota, C, \mathbf{x}, s) = 1$ and $\textit{Open}(pp_\iota, C, \mathbf{x}', s') = 1$.

Commitment Schemes Binding Over Bounded Rationals. Let $\beta = \beta_n \cdot \beta_d$ for some $\beta_n, \beta_d > 0$. Let $\mathcal{W}(\beta_n, \beta_d) := \{\mathbf{x}/z \in \mathbb{Q}^n : z \in \mathbb{Z}, \|\mathbf{x}\| \leq \beta_n, |z| \leq \beta_d\}$. The following lemmas establish several families of integer vector commitment schemes that are binding over $\mathcal{W}(\beta_n, \beta_d)$.

Lemma 4. Let $\Gamma = (\textit{Setup}, \mathcal{G}, \textit{Commit}, \textit{Open})$ denote any $\mathbb{Z}$-linear deterministic commitment scheme that maps $\mathbb{Z}^n \rightarrow \mathbb{G}^k$ where for any $\iota \in \mathcal{I}$ and $pp_\iota = \mathcal{G}(pp, \iota)$ the algorithm $\textit{Open}(pp_\iota, C, \mathbf{x})$ receives no hint and simply checks $C = \textit{Commit}(pp_\iota, \mathbf{x}) = \langle \mathbf{x}, \mathbf{g}_{pp_\iota} \rangle$ where $\mathbf{g}_{pp_\iota} \in \mathbb{G}^{n \times k}$ is a basis for the homomorphism. Let $\mathcal{A}(pp)$ denote a polynomial time algorithm that on input $pp \leftarrow \textit{Setup}(1^\lambda)$ returns $\iota \in \mathcal{I}$, $(z, \mathbf{x}), (z', \mathbf{x}') \in \mathbb{Z} \times \mathbb{Z}^n$ and $Y \in \mathbb{G}$ such that with probability non-negligible in λ:

(a) $z' \mathbf{x} \neq z \mathbf{x}'$
(b) $\frac{\mathbf{x}}{z}, \frac{\mathbf{x}'}{z'} \in \mathcal{W}(\beta_n, \beta_d)$
(c) $z \cdot Y = \textit{Commit}(pp_\iota, \mathbf{x})$ and $z' \cdot Y = \textit{Commit}(pp_\iota, \mathbf{x}')$
(d) $z, z' \neq 0 \mod |\mathbb{G}|$ and either $\frac{\mathbf{x}}{z} \neq 0 \mod |\mathbb{G}|$ or $\frac{\mathbf{x}'}{z'} \neq 0 \mod |\mathbb{G}|$

If $|\mathbb{G}|$ is prime then $\mathcal{A}$ breaks the binding of Γ over $\mathcal{W}_\beta = \{\mathbf{x} \in \mathbb{Z}^n : \|\mathbf{x}\| \leq \beta\}$. Otherwise, $\mathcal{A}$ either breaks the binding property over $\mathcal{W}_\beta$ or outputs an element u in the span of $\mathbf{g}_{pp_\iota}$ and an integer multiple of its order.

Corollary 3 (Homomorphic prime-order commitments). Let $\Gamma = (\textit{Setup}, \mathcal{G}, \textit{Commit}, \textit{Open})$ denote any $\mathbb{Z}$-linear deterministic commitment scheme where the commitments are contained within a k-dimensional $\mathbb{Z}$-module $\mathbb{G}^k$ and $\mathbb{G}$ is a group of prime-order q. Suppose that for non-zero C the algorithm $\textit{Open}(pp_\iota, C, \mathbf{x})$ checks $\textit{Commit}(pp_\iota, \mathbf{x}) = C$ and the element $\mathbf{0}_\mathbb{G} \in \mathbb{G}^k$ is the unique valid commitment to $0 \in \mathbb{Z}^n$. If Γ is binding over $\mathcal{W}_\beta = \{\mathbf{x} \in \mathbb{Z}^n : \|\mathbf{x}\| \leq \beta\}$ then Γ is also binding over rational openings to $\mathcal{W}(\beta_n, \beta_d)$.

Homomorphic Prime-Order Examples. Examples of commitments to integer vectors that satisfy the conditions in Corollary 3 trivially include Pedersen commitments but also Ajtai commitments based on Integer-SIS/Ring-SIS/Module-SIS. Let q be a prime, let $n, \kappa \in \mathbb{N}$ denote security parameters, Let $\Phi_m(x)$ be the m-th cyclotomic polynomial[6] (i.e., its roots are the primitive m-th roots of unity). Let $\mathcal{R} = \mathbb{Z}[x]/\Phi_m$ and $\mathcal{R}_q = \mathbb{Z}_q[x]/\Phi_m$, and let $n = n(m)$ and $B = B(m)$ be functions.

- **Integer-SIS.** The problem $\text{SIS}_{n,q,m,B}$ is: given $\mathbf{A} \xleftarrow{\$} \mathbb{Z}_q^{m \times n}$, find $\mathbf{z} \in \mathbb{Z}^n$ such that $\mathbf{A} \cdot \mathbf{z} = 0^m \bmod q$ and $0 < \|\mathbf{z}\| \leq B$.

- **Ring-SIS.** The problem $\text{R-SIS}_{n,q,m,B}$ is: given $\mathbf{a} \xleftarrow{\$} \mathcal{R}_q^n$, find $\mathbf{z} \in \mathcal{R}^n$ such that $\mathbf{a} \cdot \mathbf{z} = 0 \bmod q$ and $0 < \|\mathbf{z}\| \leq B$.

- **Module-SIS.** For some $\kappa > 0$, the problem $\text{M-SIS}_{\kappa,n,q,m,B}$ is: given $\mathbf{A} \xleftarrow{\$} \mathcal{R}_q^{\kappa \times n}$, find $\mathbf{z} \in \mathcal{R}^n$ such that $\mathbf{A} \cdot \mathbf{z} = 0^\kappa \bmod q$ and $0 < \|\mathbf{z}\| \leq B$.

Note that SIS and R-SIS are both special cases of M-SIS, with appropriate setting of the parameters. For example, Ring-SIS is the same as Module-SIS when $\kappa = 1$. All three problems are related to certain worst case lattice problems, and are believed to be hard for appropriate settings of the parameters n, q, m, B, and κ. In particular, these problems are believed to be post-quantum secure when the following conditions holds:

- **Integer-SIS** [25,31] m sufficiently large and $n, \log(q) \leq poly(m)$ and $q \geq B\sqrt{m} \cdot \omega(\sqrt{\log m})$.

- **Module-SIS** [29, Th. 3.6]: $m\kappa$ sufficiently large and $q > B \cdot (m\kappa)^{1/2}\omega(\sqrt{\log m\kappa})$, and both n and $\log q$ are less than $poly(m\kappa)$.

Corollary 4 (Homomorphic GUO commitments). *Let $\Gamma = (Setup, \mathcal{G}, Commit, Open)$ denote any $\mathbb{Z}$-linear deterministic commitment scheme where for any pp, ι, and $pp_\iota = \mathcal{G}(pp, \iota)$ the function $Commit(pp_\iota) : \mathbb{Z}^n \to \mathbb{G}$ is a homomorphism with basis $\mathbf{g}_{pp_\iota}$. Suppose that the subgroup hidden order assumption for $\mathbb{G}$ holds[7] with respect to the distribution over subgroups $\langle \mathbf{g}_{pp_\iota} \rangle \subseteq \mathbb{G}$ induced by sampling pp $\leftarrow Setup(1^\lambda)$ and any adversarially sampled $\iota \in \mathcal{I}$. If Γ is binding over $\mathcal{W}_\beta = \{\mathbf{x} \in \mathbb{Z}^n : \|\mathbf{x}\| \leq \beta\}$ then Γ is also binding over rational openings to $\mathcal{W}(\beta_n, \beta_d)$.*

---

[6] When m is a power of two we have that $\Phi_m(x) = x^{m/2} + 1$.

[7] If the generators $\mathbf{g}_{pp_\iota}$ are uniformly distributed for any ι and $\mathbb{G}$ is cyclic (or more generally a random element in the span of $\mathbf{g}_{pp_\iota}$ is statistically close to uniform over $\mathbb{G}$) then this is equivalent to the assumption that it is hard to compute a multiple of the order of a random element, which is implied by the difficulty of taking square roots of random elements (the RSA assumption) for $\mathbb{G}$. In certain groups where it is difficult to compute any integer that shares a common factor with $|\mathbb{G}|$ then the assumption holds regardless of how $\mathbf{g}_{pp_\iota}$ is sampled. One such group is the multiplicative subgroup $\mathbb{H} = \{x^4 : x \in \mathbb{Z}_N^\times\}$ for $N = p \cdot q$, where p and q are unknown safe primes and thus $|\mathbb{H}| = (p-1)(q-1)/4 = p' \cdot q'$ for unknown primes p', q'.

Corollary 5 (*DARK* commitments). *The integer vector commitment scheme known as DARK [19] uses a group of unknown order $\mathbb{G}$ and for $\mathbf{x} \in \mathbb{Z}^n$ computes the homomorphism $\mathbf{x} \mapsto g^{f_{\mathbf{x}}(q)}$, where $f_{\mathbf{x}}(q) = \sum_{i=1}^{n} \mathbf{x}_i q^{i-1}$, given setup parameters $q \in \mathbb{N}$ and $g \in \mathbb{G}$ sampled uniformly at random. Setting $q = \lceil 2\sqrt{n}\beta \rceil$, DARK is binding over rational openings to $\mathcal{W}(\beta_n, \beta_d)$ based on the hidden order assumption in $\mathbb{G}$.*

Proof. For $\mathbf{x} \in \mathbb{Z}^n$ let $f_{\mathbf{x}}$ denote the univariate polynomial with coefficient vector $\mathbf{x}$. By Fact 1, $f_{\mathbf{x}}(q) \neq f_{\mathbf{x}'}(q)$ for all $\mathbf{x} \neq \mathbf{x}'$ of L_∞ norm at most $q/2$ which is guaranteed if the L_2 norm is at most $q/(2\sqrt{n})$. By the hidden order assumption (Assumption 1) no polynomial-time adversary can compute integers $x \neq y$ such that $g^x = g^y$ for $g \xleftarrow{\$} \mathbb{G}$. DARK is therefore binding over $\mathcal{W}_\beta = \{\mathbf{x} \in \mathbb{Z}^n : ||\mathbf{x}|| \leq \beta\}$ for $q \geq 2\sqrt{n}\beta$ by the hidden order assumption, and as a corollary to Lemma 4 it is also binding over $\mathcal{W}(\beta_n, \beta_d)$ under the hidden order assumption.

Definition 6. *We define a integer matrix norm family $\mathcal{F}$ as an infinite collection $\mathcal{F} = \{\mathcal{N}_{m,n}\}$ of matrix norms $\mathcal{N}_{m,n} : \mathbb{Z}^{m \times n} \to \mathbb{R}$. We say that the $\mathcal{F}$ is $\alpha(m,n,k)$-submultiplicative if for all $m,n,k \in \mathbb{N}$, $M \in \mathbb{Z}^{m \times n}$, and $X \in \mathbb{Z}^{n \times k}$:*

$$\mathcal{N}_{m,k}(M \cdot X) \leq \alpha(m,n,k) \cdot \mathcal{N}_{m,n}(M) \cdot \mathcal{N}_{n,k}(X)$$

Lemma 5. *Let (Setup, $\mathcal{G}$, Commit, Open) be any $\mathbb{Z}$-linear deterministic commitment scheme that is binding over $\mathcal{W}_\beta = \{\mathbf{x} \in \mathbb{Z}^n : ||\mathbf{x}|| \leq \beta\}$, where the norm $||\cdot||$ belongs to an α-submultiplicative norm family. Let $U : \mathbb{Z}^m \to \mathbb{Z}^n$ denote any injective linear map, i.e. $U \in \mathbb{Z}^{m \times n}$ is a full row rank matrix. Then the modified scheme (Setup, $\mathcal{G}$, Commit*, Open*) over $\mathbb{Z}^m$ where:*

- *Commit*$(pp, \mathbf{x} \in \mathbb{Z}^m) \to$ Commit$(pp, \mathbf{x} \cdot U)$
- *Open*$(pp, C, \mathbf{x} \in \mathbb{Z}^m, s) \to$ Open$(pp, C, \mathbf{x} \cdot U, s)$

is binding over $\mathcal{W}^* = \{\mathbf{x} \in \mathbb{Z}^m : ||\mathbf{x}|| \leq \frac{\beta}{\alpha \cdot ||U||}\}$.

Proof. Suppose $(C, \mathbf{x} \in \mathbb{Z}^m, s)$ and $(C, \mathbf{x}' \in \mathbb{Z}^m, s')$ are both accepted by Open* for distinct $\mathbf{x}, \mathbf{x}' \in \mathcal{W}^*$, then both $(C, \mathbf{x} \cdot U, s)$ and $(\mathbf{x}' \cdot U, s', C)$ are accepted by Open. Since U is injective, $\mathbf{x} \cdot U \neq \mathbf{x}' \cdot U$. Furthermore, since the norm is α-submultiplicative, $||\mathbf{x} \cdot U|| \leq \alpha \cdot ||\mathbf{x}|| \cdot ||U|| \leq \beta$. Similarly, $||\mathbf{x}' \cdot U|| \leq \beta$. This contradicts the binding of (Setup, $\mathcal{G}$, Commit, Open).

Lemma 6. *Let (Setup, $\mathcal{G}$, Commit, Open) be any $\mathbb{Z}$-linear deterministic commitment scheme that is binding over rational openings to $\mathcal{W}(\beta_n, \beta_d)$, where the norm $||\cdot||$ belongs to an α-submultiplicative norm family. Let $U : \mathbb{Z}^m \to \mathbb{Z}^n$ denote any injective linear map, i.e. $U \in \mathbb{Z}^{m \times n}$ is a full row rank matrix. Then the modified scheme (Setup, $\mathcal{G}$, Commit*, Open*) over $\mathbb{Z}^m$ where:*

- *Commit*$(pp, \mathbf{x} \in \mathbb{Z}^m) \to$ Commit$(pp, \mathbf{x} \cdot U)$
- *Open*$(pp, C, \mathbf{x} \in \mathbb{Z}^m, s) \to$ Open$(pp, C, \mathbf{x} \cdot U, s)$

is binding over $\mathcal{W}(\frac{\beta_n}{\alpha ||U||}, \beta_d)$.

Proof. Let $\beta_n^* = \frac{\beta_n}{\alpha||U||}$. Suppose $(C, \mathbf{x} \in \mathbb{Z}^m, z \in \mathbb{Z}, s)$ and $(C, \mathbf{x}' \in \mathbb{Z}^m, z' \in \mathbb{Z}, s')$ are both accepted by Open* for distinct $\mathbf{x}/z, \mathbf{x}'/z \in \mathcal{W}(\beta_n^*, \beta_d)$, then both $(C, \mathbf{x} \cdot U, z, s)$ and $(\mathbf{x}' \cdot U, z', s', C)$ are accepted by Open. Let $\mathbf{x}/z = \mathbf{x}_1/z_1$ in reduced form so that $||\mathbf{x}_1|| \leq \beta_n^*$ and $|z_1| \leq \beta_d$. Similarly, let $\mathbf{x}'/z' = \mathbf{x}_1'/z_1'$ in reduced form so that $||\mathbf{x}_1'|| \leq \beta_n^*$ and $|z_1'| \leq \beta_d$. Since the norm is α-submultiplicative, $||\mathbf{x}_1 \cdot U|| \leq \alpha \cdot ||\mathbf{x}_1|| \cdot ||U|| \leq \beta_n$. Similarly, $||\mathbf{x}_1' \cdot U|| \leq \beta_n$. This shows that $\mathbf{x} \cdot U/z \in \mathcal{W}(\beta_n, \beta_d)$ and $\mathbf{x}' \cdot U/z' \in \mathcal{W}(\beta_n, \beta_d)$. Furthermore, since $z'\mathbf{x} \neq z\mathbf{x}'$ and U is injective, $z'\mathbf{x} \cdot U \neq z\mathbf{x}' \cdot U$. This contradicts the binding of $(\mathsf{Setup}, \mathcal{G}, \mathsf{Commit}, \mathsf{Open})$.

7.1 Interactive Protocol for Short Rational Openings

The public input of the protocol is a homomorphism $\mathsf{com} : \mathbb{Z}^n \to \mathbb{G}$, a target value $C \in \mathbb{G}$, and a bound $\beta \in \mathbb{R}$. The honest prover has a witness $\mathbf{x}$ of L2 norm at most β such that $\mathsf{com}(\mathbf{x}) = C$. The prover's claim is that it knows some witness $(z, \mathbf{x})$ such that $\mathsf{com}(\mathbf{x}) = z \cdot C$ and $||\mathbf{x}|| \leq 2^{\lambda \log n}\sqrt{\xi} \cdot \beta$ and $|z| \leq \sqrt{\xi}/2^{\lambda \log n}$ for a *soundness slack* parameter ξ. In other words, setting $\beta_n = 2^{\lambda \log n}\sqrt{\xi} \cdot \beta$ and $\beta_d = \sqrt{\xi}/2^{\lambda \log n}$ so that $\beta_n \cdot \beta_d = \xi \cdot \beta$, the knowledge extractor for this protocol opens a valid rational opening for C as long as the commitment scheme is binding over $\mathcal{W}(\beta_n, \beta_d) := \{\mathbf{x}/z \in \mathbb{Q}^n : z \in \mathbb{Z}, ||\mathbf{x}||_2 \leq \beta_n, |z| \leq \beta_d\}$. We prove that it suffices to set $\xi = 2^{(16+2\mu)\lambda + 6\mathsf{CSZ}_{\mu, \lambda} + 2\mu + 6}$, where $\mathsf{CSZ}_{\log n, \lambda} \in O(\log^2 n + \lambda \log \log n)$ is derived from the Multilinear Composite Schwartz Zippel (Theorem 2). Hence $\xi \in 2^{O(\lambda \log n + \log^2 n)}$.

Let $\mathbf{g} = (\mathbf{g}_1, ..., \mathbf{g}_n)$ denote a basis of com such that $\mathsf{com}(\mathbf{x}) = \langle \mathbf{x}, \mathbf{g} \rangle$. The interactive protocol is essentially the succinct argument for homomorphism preimages from [2,10], but where the verifier additionally checks a bound on the prover's final message. This is also a special case of a sumcheck argument with a bound check, as described in [12]. The prover's final message is an integer $x^* \in \mathbb{Z}$ and the verifier immediately rejects the proof unless $|x|^* \leq \beta \cdot 2^{\lambda \log n}$. We include the full protocol in the figure below for completeness.

An important observation, as first noted in [16] and leveraged in Halo [14], is that the verifier does not use its input $\mathbf{g}$ unless $n = 1$. Thus, the verifier does not need to compute $\mathbf{g} \in \mathbb{G}^{2^i}$ at each round of recursion. Instead, it only needs to compute the final $g' \in \mathbb{G}$ at the final round, which can be computed as $g' = \sum_{i=1}^n u_i \mathbf{g}_i$ where u_i is the ith coefficient of the polynomial $u(X) = \prod_{j=1}^{\log n} (r_j + X^{2^{j-1}})$ where r_j is the verifier's challenge at the jth round.

Application: Polynomial Commitment Scheme. Given any prime p of size $|p| \geq \beta$ and any deterministic homomorphic commitment scheme $(\mathsf{Setup}, \mathsf{com}, \mathsf{Vf})$ that is binding over $D = \{\mathbf{x} \in \mathbb{Z}^n : ||\mathbf{x}|| \leq \xi \cdot \beta\}$, where $\mathsf{com} : \mathbb{Z}^n \to \mathbb{G}_{\mathsf{com}}$ is a homomorphism and ξ is the slack parameter of the homomorphism-preimage (HPI) protocol, we can commit to the coefficient vector $\mathbf{x} \in [0, p)^n$ of a degree-n polynomial $f_\mathbf{x}(Z) = \sum_i \mathbf{x}_i Z^i$ as $C = \mathsf{com}(\mathbf{x})$ and open evaluations of the committed polynomial at any point $z \in \mathbb{Z}_p$ to $t = f_\mathbf{x}(z)$

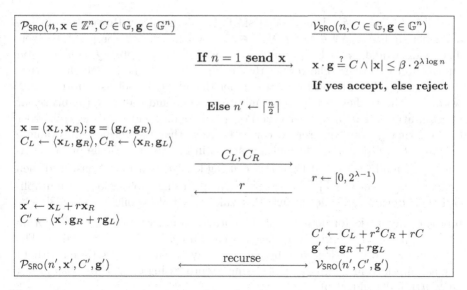

Fig. 1. *A succinct interactive protocol for short rational openings. The honest prover's input must have norm at most β. For simplicity n is a power of 2.*

by running the HPI protocol for the homomorphism $\mathbf{x} \mapsto (\mathrm{com}(\mathbf{x}), f_\mathbf{x}(z))$. Setting $\beta_1 = 2^{\lambda \log n} \sqrt{\xi} \cdot \beta$ and $\beta_2 = \sqrt{\xi}/2^{\lambda \log n}$, this protocol proves knowledge of a pair $(a, \mathbf{x}^*)$ such that $\mathrm{com}(\mathbf{x}^*) = a \cdot C$ and $f_{\mathbf{x}^*}(z) = a \cdot t \bmod p$ where $\|\mathbf{x}\| \leq \beta_1$ and $|a| \leq \beta_2$. This is a valid *rational opening* of C to $\mathbf{x}^*/a$, and by Corollary 3 the commitment is binding for rational openings in $\mathcal{W}(\beta_1, \beta_2)$. This proves for the polynomial $f(X) = \sum_i f_{\mathbf{x}^*,i}/aX^i \in \mathbb{Z}_p$, $f(z) = t$. The protocol has logarithmic communication complexity but requires a linear verifier to compute the final g' value.

Special Case: DARK Rational Openings with Log Verifier In the special case that $\mathbb{G}$ is a group of unknown order and $\mathrm{com}(\mathbf{x}) = g^{f_\mathbf{x}(q)}$ for $q \in \mathbb{N}$ and g a random element in $\mathbb{G}$, where $f_\mathbf{x}(q) = \sum_{i=1}^n \mathbf{x}_i q^{i-1}$, the verifier complexity can be made logarithmic by adding a *proof-of-exponentiation* (PoE) [37] step. By Corollary 5, for $q = \lceil \sqrt{n} 2\xi \beta \rceil$ this commitment scheme is binding over vectors in $\{\mathbf{x} \in \mathbb{Z}^n : \|\mathbf{x}\|_2 \leq \xi \beta\}$ and for any $\beta_n, \beta_d > 0$ such that $\beta_n \cdot \beta_d = \xi \beta$, is binding under rational openings to $\mathcal{W}(\beta_n, \beta_d) := \{\mathbf{x}/z \in \mathbb{Q}^n : z \in \mathbb{Z}, \|\mathbf{x}\|_2 \leq \beta_n, |z| \leq \beta_d\}$.

When using this as a linear-map vector commitment scheme over $\mathbb{F}_p$, where the honest prover may commit to any $\mathbf{x} \in [0, p)^n$ which has L2 norm at most $\beta = \sqrt{n} \cdot p$, we would set $q = \lceil n2\xi p \rceil$. The resulting interactive argument in this case is a slight variation of the DARK evaluation protocol.

The verifier complexity is made logarithmic using a PoE as follows. Recall that the verifier only needs to compute the final round $g' = \prod \mathbf{g}_i^{u_i}$ where u_i are the coefficients of $u(X) = \prod_{j=1}^{\log n}(r_j + X^{2^{j-1}})$. In this case, $\mathbf{g}_i = g^{(q^i)}$, and thus

$g' = g^{(\sum_i u_i q^i)} = g^{u(q)}$. The Wesolowski PoE [37] enables a Prover to convince a Verifier that $Y = X^a \in \mathbb{G}$ for $X, Y \in \mathbb{G}$ and $a \in \mathbb{Z}$. In the protocol, the verifier sends a random 2λ-bit prime ℓ, and the prover computes $Q \leftarrow g^{(\lfloor \frac{a}{\ell} \rfloor)}$ and sends it to the verifier. The verifier then computes $r \leftarrow a \bmod \ell$ and checks that $Y = X^r + Q^\ell$. The protocol is secure under the adaptive root assumption in $\mathbb{G}$. Note that the verifier just has to compute $a \bmod \ell$ and do two $O(\lambda)$-bit scalar multiplications. The prover runs the PoE protocol on input $(g, g', u(q))$ in order to show that g' was constructed correctly. Note that the verifier can evaluate $u(q) \bmod \ell$ in $O(\log(n))$ field multiplications in $\mathbb{F}_\ell$. To do this the prover computes $q^{(2^j)} \bmod \ell$ for $j \in [0, \log_2(n) - 1]$ using $\log_2(n)$ multiplications. And then evaluates $u(q) \bmod \ell = \prod_{j=1}^{\log n}(r_j + X^{2^{j-1}}) \bmod \ell$ using another $\log_2(n)$ multiplications. Alternatively, one can use Pietrzak's proof of exponentiation [33]. The protocol only works for powers of 2. The prover would send the $g_i \leftarrow g^{q^{2^i}}$ for all $i \in [0, \log_2(n))$. The verifier can efficiently compute $g^{u(q)}$ given the g_i values. The proof size would be $O(\log_2(n))$, but importantly, it can be instantiated without any assumptions in all groups [26]. Using preprocessing of q, it also has prover $O(\sqrt{(n)})$, independent of $|q|$.

7.2   Almost Special Soundness Analysis

Theorem 4 (Bulletproofs for short openings is AMSS). *Let $n = 2^\mu$ for $\mu \geq 1$. Let $\mathsf{CSZ}_{\mu,\lambda} = 8\mu^2 + \log_2(2\mu)\lambda$. Let $\Gamma = (\mathsf{Setup}, \mathcal{G}, \mathsf{Commit}, \mathsf{Open})$ denote any $\mathbb{Z}$-linear deterministic commitment scheme satisfying the following conditions:*

- *For $\beta_n = 2^{\lambda\mu}\sqrt{\xi} \cdot \beta$ and $\beta_d = \sqrt{\xi}/2^{\lambda\mu}$ where $\log \xi = (14 + 2\mu)\lambda + 6\mathsf{CSZ}_{\mu,\lambda} + 2(\mu + 4)$ it is binding to $\mathcal{W}(\beta_n, \beta_d) := \{\mathbf{x}/z \in \mathbb{Q}^n : z \in \mathbb{Z}, ||\mathbf{x}||_2 \leq \beta_n, |z| \leq \beta_d\}$ under rational openings.*
- *$\mathsf{Open}(pp_\iota, C, \mathbf{x})$ receives no hint, i.e. checks $\mathsf{Commit}(pp_\iota, \mathbf{x}) = C$.*
- *The group $\mathbb{G}$ defined for any $pp \leftarrow \mathsf{Setup}(1^\lambda)$ is a GUO (i.e., the hidden order assumption holds in $\mathbb{G}$) or a $\mathbb{Z}_q$-module for prime q (i.e., $\mathbb{G} = \mathbb{G}_1^k$ and $|\mathbb{G}_1| = q$).*

Let Π denote the interactive protocol which runs the protocol in Fig. 1 for parameters β and $\mathbf{g} \in \mathbb{G}^n$ defined by $pp \leftarrow \mathsf{Setup}(1^\lambda)$, an index $\iota \in \mathcal{I}$, $pp_\iota = \mathcal{G}(pp, \iota)$, and $\mathsf{Commit}(pp_\iota, \mathbf{x}) = \langle \mathbf{x}, \mathbf{g} \rangle$ for $\mathbf{x} \in \mathbb{Z}^n$. There exists a predicate pair $\phi = (\phi_a, \phi_b)$ and commitment scheme Γ^* such that Π is an $(4^{(\mu)}, \frac{3\mu}{2^\lambda}, \Gamma^*, \phi)$-almost-special-sound interactive argument for the relation:

$$\mathsf{SRO}_{\beta, pp_\iota} = \{(C, \mathsf{w} = (z, \mathbf{x})) : \langle \mathbf{x}, \mathbf{g} \rangle = z \cdot C \text{ and } \mathbf{x}/z \in \mathcal{W}(\beta_n, \beta_d)\}$$

Remark 8. Note that $\xi \in 2^{O(\lambda \log n + \log^2 n)}$. $\mathsf{CSZ}_{\mu,\lambda}$ is derived from the Multilinear Composite Schwartz Zippel Theorem (Theorem 2).

The proof of Theorem 4 is in the full version.

References

1. Albrecht, M.R., Lai, R.W.F.: Subtractive sets over cyclotomic rings. In: Malkin, T., Peikert, C. (eds.) CRYPTO 2021. LNCS, vol. 12826, pp. 519–548. Springer, Cham (2021). https://doi.org/10.1007/978-3-030-84245-1_18

2. Attema, T., Cramer, R.: Compressed Σ-protocol theory and practical application to plug & play secure algorithmics. In: Micciancio, D., Ristenpart, T. (eds.) CRYPTO 2020. LNCS, vol. 12172, pp. 513–543. Springer, Cham (2020). https://doi.org/10.1007/978-3-030-56877-1_18

3. Attema, T., Cramer, R., Kohl, L.: A compressed Σ-protocol theory for lattices. Cryptology ePrint Archive, Report 2021/307 (2021). https://eprint.iacr.org/2021/307

4. Attema, T., Cramer, R., Kohl, L.: A compressed Σ-protocol theory for lattices. In: Malkin, T., Peikert, C. (eds.) CRYPTO 2021. LNCS, vol. 12826, pp. 549–579. Springer, Cham (2021). https://doi.org/10.1007/978-3-030-84245-1_19

5. Attema, T., Fehr, S., Kloos, M.: Fiat-Shamir transformation of multi-round interactive proofs. Cryptology ePrint Archive, Report 2021/1377 (2021). https://eprint.iacr.org/2021/1377

6. Attema, T., Lyubashevsky, V., Seiler, G.: Practical product proofs for lattice commitments. In: Micciancio, D., Ristenpart, T. (eds.) CRYPTO 2020. LNCS, vol. 12171, pp. 470–499. Springer, Cham (2020). https://doi.org/10.1007/978-3-030-56880-1_17

7. Beullens, W., Seiler, G.: LaBRADOR: compact proofs for R1CS from module-SIS. Cryptology ePrint Archive, Report 2022/1341 (2022). https://eprint.iacr.org/2022/1341

8. Bishnoi, A., Clark, P.L., Potukuchi, A., Schmitt, J.R.: On zeros of a polynomial in a finite grid (2015). https://doi.org/10.48550/ARXIV.1508.06020. https://arxiv.org/abs/1508.06020

9. Block, A.R., Holmgren, J., Rosen, A., Rothblum, R.D., Soni, P.: Time- and space-efficient arguments from groups of unknown order. In: Malkin, T., Peikert, C. (eds.) CRYPTO 2021. LNCS, vol. 12828, pp. 123–152. Springer, Cham (2021). https://doi.org/10.1007/978-3-030-84259-8_5

10. Boneh, D., Drake, J., Fisch, B., Gabizon, A.: Halo Infinite: proof-carrying data from additive polynomial commitments. In: Malkin, T., Peikert, C. (eds.) CRYPTO 2021. LNCS, vol. 12825, pp. 649–680. Springer, Cham (2021). https://doi.org/10.1007/978-3-030-84242-0_23

11. Bootle, J., Cerulli, A., Chaidos, P., Groth, J., Petit, C.: Efficient zero-knowledge arguments for arithmetic circuits in the discrete log setting. In: Fischlin, M., Coron, J.-S. (eds.) EUROCRYPT 2016. LNCS, vol. 9666, pp. 327–357. Springer, Heidelberg (2016). https://doi.org/10.1007/978-3-662-49896-5_12

12. Bootle, J., Chiesa, A., Sotiraki, K.: Sumcheck arguments and their applications. In: Malkin, T., Peikert, C. (eds.) CRYPTO 2021. LNCS, vol. 12825, pp. 742–773. Springer, Cham (2021). https://doi.org/10.1007/978-3-030-84242-0_26

13. Bootle, J., Lyubashevsky, V., Nguyen, N.K., Seiler, G.: A non-PCP approach to succinct quantum-safe zero-knowledge. In: Micciancio, D., Ristenpart, T. (eds.) CRYPTO 2020. LNCS, vol. 12171, pp. 441–469. Springer, Cham (2020). https://doi.org/10.1007/978-3-030-56880-1_16

14. Bowe, S., Grigg, J., Hopwood, D.: Halo: recursive proof composition without a trusted setup. Cryptology ePrint Archive, Report 2019/1021 (2019). https://eprint.iacr.org/2019/1021

15. Buchmann, J., Hamdy, S.: A survey on IQ cryptography. In: Public-Key Cryptography and Computational Number Theory, pp. 1–15 (2001)
16. Bünz, B., Bootle, J., Boneh, D., Poelstra, A., Wuille, P., Maxwell, G.: Bulletproofs: short proofs for confidential transactions and more. In: 2018 IEEE Symposium on Security and Privacy, pp. 315–334. IEEE Computer Society Press (2018). https://doi.org/10.1109/SP.2018.00020
17. Bünz, B., Fisch, B.: Schwartz-Zippel for multilinear polynomials mod N. Cryptology ePrint Archive, Report 2022/458 (2022). https://eprint.iacr.org/2022/458
18. Bünz, B., Fisch, B., Szepieniec, A.: Transparent SNARKs from DARK Compilers. Cryptology ePrint Archive, Report 2019/1229 (2019). https://eprint.iacr.org/2019/1229
19. Bünz, B., Fisch, B., Szepieniec, A.: Transparent SNARKs from DARK compilers. In: Canteaut, A., Ishai, Y. (eds.) EUROCRYPT 2020. LNCS, vol. 12105, pp. 677–706. Springer, Cham (2020). https://doi.org/10.1007/978-3-030-45721-1_24
20. Campanelli, M., Nitulescu, A., Ràfols, C., Zacharakis, A., Zapico, A.: Linear-map vector commitments and their practical applications. Cryptology ePrint Archive, Report 2022/705 (2022). https://eprint.iacr.org/2022/705
21. Couteau, G., Peters, T., Pointcheval, D.: Removing the strong RSA assumption from arguments over the integers. In: Coron, J.-S., Nielsen, J.B. (eds.) EUROCRYPT 2017. LNCS, vol. 10211, pp. 321–350. Springer, Cham (2017). https://doi.org/10.1007/978-3-319-56614-6_11
22. DeMillo, R.A., Lipton, R.J.: A Probabilistic Remark on Algebraic Program Testing. Technical report, Georgia Inst of Tech Atlanta School of Information and Computer Science (1977)
23. Esgin, M.F., Nguyen, N.K., Seiler, G.: Practical exact proofs from lattices: new techniques to exploit fully-splitting rings. In: Moriai, S., Wang, H. (eds.) ASIACRYPT 2020. LNCS, vol. 12492, pp. 259–288. Springer, Cham (2020). https://doi.org/10.1007/978-3-030-64834-3_9
24. Gentry, C., Halevi, S., Lyubashevsky, V.: Practical non-interactive publicly verifiable secret sharing with thousands of parties. In: Dunkelman, O., Dziembowski, S. (eds.) EUROCRYPT 2022, Part I. LNCS, pp. 458–487. Springer, Heidelberg (2022). https://doi.org/10.1007/978-3-031-06944-4_16
25. Gentry, C., Peikert, C., Vaikuntanathan, V.: Trapdoors for hard lattices and new cryptographic constructions. In: Ladner, R.E., Dwork, C. (eds.) 40th ACM STOC, pp. 197–206. ACM Press (2008). https://doi.org/10.1145/1374376.1374407
26. Hoffmann, C., Hubácek, P., Kamath, C., Klein, K., Pietrzak, K.: Practical statistically- sound proofs of exponentiation in any group. In: Dodis, Y., Shrimpton, T. (eds.) CRYPTO 2022, Part II. LNCS, pp. 370–399. Springer, Heidelberg (2022). https://doi.org/10.1007/978-3-031-15979-4_13
27. Kabanets, V., Impagliazzo, R.: Derandomizing polynomial identity tests means proving circuit lower bounds. Comput. Complex. 13(1–2), 1–46 (2004). https://doi.org/10.1007/s00037-004-0182-6
28. Lai, R.W.F., Malavolta, G.: Subvector commitments with application to succinct arguments. In: Boldyreva, A., Micciancio, D. (eds.) CRYPTO 2019. LNCS, vol. 11692, pp. 530–560. Springer, Cham (2019). https://doi.org/10.1007/978-3-030-26948-7_19
29. Langlois, A., Stehlé, D.: Worst-case to average-case reductions for module lattices. Des. Codes Cryptogr. 75(3), 565–599 (2015)
30. Lyubashevsky, V., Nguyen, N.K., Seiler, G.: Shorter lattice-based zero-knowledge proofs via one-time commitments. In: Garay, J.A. (ed.) PKC 2021. LNCS, vol.

12710, pp. 215–241. Springer, Cham (2021). https://doi.org/10.1007/978-3-030-75245-3_9

31. Micciancio, D., Peikert, C.: Hardness of SIS and LWE with small parameters. In: Canetti, R., Garay, J.A. (eds.) CRYPTO 2013. LNCS, vol. 8042, pp. 21–39. Springer, Heidelberg (2013). https://doi.org/10.1007/978-3-642-40041-4_2

32. Nguyen, N.K., Seiler, G.: Practical sublinear proofs for R1CS from lattices. In: Dodis, Y., Shrimpton, T. (eds.) CRYPTO 2022, Part II. LNCS, pp. 133–162. Springer, Heidelberg (2022). https://doi.org/10.1007/978-3-031-15979-4_5

33. Pietrzak, K.: Proofs of catalytic space. In: Blum, A. (ed.) ITCS 2019, pp. 59:1–59:25. LIPIcs (2019). https://doi.org/10.4230/LIPIcs.ITCS.2019.59

34. Rivest, R.L., Shamir, A., Adleman, L.M.: A method for obtaining digital signatures and public-key cryptosystems. Commun. Assoc. Comput. Mach. **21**(2), 120–126 (1978)

35. Schwartz, J.T.: Fast probabilistic algorithms for verification of polynomial identities. J. ACM (JACM) **27**(4), 701–717 (1980)

36. Wahby, R.S., Tzialla, I., shelat, a., Thaler, J., Walfish, M.: Doubly-efficient zk-SNARKs without trusted setup. In: 2018 IEEE Symposium on Security and Privacy, pp. 926–943. IEEE Computer Society Press (2018). https://doi.org/10.1109/SP.2018.00060

37. Wesolowski, B.: Efficient verifiable delay functions. In: Ishai, Y., Rijmen, V. (eds.) EUROCRYPT 2019. LNCS, vol. 11478, pp. 379–407. Springer, Cham (2019). https://doi.org/10.1007/978-3-030-17659-4_13

38. Wikström, D.: Special soundness in the random oracle model. Cryptology ePrint Archive, Report 2021/1265 (2021). https://eprint.iacr.org/2021/1265

39. Zippel, R.: Probabilistic algorithms for sparse polynomials. In: International Symposium on Symbolic and Algebraic Manipulation, pp. 216–226 (1979)

Generalized Special-Sound Interactive Proofs and Their Knowledge Soundness

Thomas Attema[1,3](✉) [iD], Serge Fehr[1,2], and Nicolas Resch[4] [iD]

[1] CWI, Cryptology Group, Amsterdam, The Netherlands
serge.fehr@cwi.nl
[2] Leiden University, Mathematical Institute, Leiden, The Netherlands
[3] TNO, Cyber Security and Robustness, The Hague, The Netherlands
thomas.attema@tno.nl
[4] University of Amsterdam, Informatics Institute, Amsterdam, The Netherlands
n.a.resch@uva.nl

Abstract. A classic result in the theory of interactive proofs shows that a *special-sound* Σ-protocol is automatically a *proof of knowledge*. This result is very useful to have, since the latter property is typically tricky to prove from scratch, while the former is often easy to argue — *if* it is satisfied. While classic Σ-protocols often are special-sound, this is unfortunately not the case for many recently proposed, highly efficient interactive proofs, at least not in this strict sense. Motivated by this, the original result was recently generalized to k-special-sound Σ-protocols (for arbitrary, polynomially bounded k), and to multi-round versions thereof. This generalization is sufficient to analyze (e.g.) Bulletproofs-like protocols, but is still insufficient for many other examples.

In this work, we push the relaxation of the special soundness property to the extreme, by allowing an *arbitrary* access structure Γ to specify for which subsets of challenges it is possible to compute a witness, when given correct answers to these challenges (for a fixed first message). Concretely, for any access structure Γ, we identify parameters t_Γ and κ_Γ, and we show that any Γ-special-sound Σ-protocol is a proof of knowledge with knowledge error κ_Γ if t_Γ is polynomially bounded. Similarly for multi-round protocols.

We apply our general result to a couple of simple but important example protocols, where we obtain a tight knowledge error as an immediate corollary. Beyond these simple examples, we analyze the FRI protocol. Here, showing the general special soundness notion is non-trivial, but can be done (for a certain range of parameters) by recycling some of the techniques used to argue ordinary soundness of the protocol (as an IOP). Again as a corollary, we then derive that the FRI protocol, as an interactive proof by using a Merkle-tree commitment, has a knowledge extractor with almost optimal knowledge error, with the caveat that the extractor requires (expected) quasi-polynomial time.

Finally, building up on the technique for the parallel repetition of k-special-sound Σ-protocols, we show the same strong parallel repetition result for Γ-special-sound Σ-protocol and its multi-round variant.

© International Association for Cryptologic Research 2023
G. Rothblum and H. Wee (Eds.): TCC 2023, LNCS 14371, pp. 424–454, 2023.
https://doi.org/10.1007/978-3-031-48621-0_15

1   Introduction

Background. A key feature of an interactive proof is *soundness*, which requires that the verifier will not accept a false statement, i.e., an instance x that is not in the considered language, except with bounded probability. In many situations however, a stronger notion of soundness is needed: *knowledge soundness*. Informally, knowledge soundness requires the prover to *know* a witness w that certifies that x is a true statement, in order for the verifier to accept (except with bounded probability). More formally, this is captured by the existence of an efficient *extractor*, which has (rewindable) oracle access to any, possibly dishonest, prover, and which outputs a witness w for the considered statement x with a probability that is tightly related to the probability of the prover making the verifier accept.

Since their introduction, interactive proofs that satisfy knowledge soundness, typically referred to *proofs of knowledge* then, have found a myriad of applications. However, showing that an interactive proof satisfies knowledge soundness is typically non-trivial — often significantly more involved than showing ordinary soundness. By default, it involves *designing* the extractor, and *proving* that it "does the job." We got spoiled in the past, where most of the considered interactive proofs were Σ-protocols, i.e., public-coin 3-round interactive proofs, and had the additional property of being *special-sound*. Indeed, this made life rather easy since special-soundness is a property that is usually quite easy to prove, and that implies ordinary and knowledge soundness via a general classical result. Thus, knowledge soundness was often obtained (almost) for free. However, this has changed in recent years, where the focus has shifted towards finding *highly efficient* interactive proofs (where efficiency is typically measured via the communication complexity, verification time, etc.); many of these highly efficient solutions are *not* special-sound, and thus require a knowledge-soundness proof from scratch.

Given this situation, it would be desirable to have stronger versions of the generic "*special-soundness $\Rightarrow$ knowledge soundness*" result that applies to a *weaker* notion of special-soundness, which then hopefully is satisfied by these new cutting-edge interactive proofs. One step in this direction was recently made in [2,3], where the above implication was extended to k-special-sound interactive proofs, and, even more generally, to $(k_1, \ldots, k_\mu)$-special-sound *multi-round* public-coin interactive proofs, for arbitrary positive integer parameters, subject to being suitably bounded from above (e.g., $k \leq \text{poly}(|x|)$). Rather naturally, k-special-soundness means that from accepting responses to k pairwise distinct challenges for one fixed message, a witness can be efficiently computed (so that 2-special-soundness coincides with the classical special-soundness property); for the multi-round version, a suitable tree of transcripts is needed for computing a witness. This weaker notion of special-soundness is in particular sufficient to analyze Bulletproofs-like protocols, and so we directly obtain knowledge soundness for these protocols.

However, this weaker notion still falls short of capturing many of the recent highly-efficient interactive proofs. For instance, a commonly used amortization technique, where the prover proves a *random linear combination* of n statements (instead of proving all the statements individually), requires correct responses for n *linearly independent* challenge vectors in order to compute a witness. Another example comes from the design principle to first construct a highly efficient probabilistically checkable proof (PCP) or interactive *oracle* proof (IOP), and then to compile it into a standard (public-coin) interactive proof in the natural way by means of a Merkle-tree commitment [11–13]. Also here, one does not obtain a special-sound protocol in the above generalized sense (or then only for a too large parameter); instead, one requires challenges that correspond to sets whose union covers all (or sufficiently many of) the leaves of the Merkle tree, in order to obtain a witness.

Our Technical Results. In this paper, we push the weakening of the special-soundness property to the extreme. For Σ-protocols, in the spirit of ordinary or k-special-soundness, the notion of special-soundness that we consider in this work requires that a witness can be efficiently computed from accepting responses to *sufficiently many* pairwise distinct challenges, but now "sufficiently many" is captured by an arbitrary monotone (access) structure Γ, i.e., an arbitrary monotone set of subsets of the challenge set. This gives rise to the notion of Γ-special-soundness, which coincides with k-special-soundness in the special case where Γ is the threshold access structure with threshold k. This naturally extends to multi-round public-coin interactive proofs, leading to the notion of $(\Gamma_1, \ldots, \Gamma_\mu)$-special-soundness. Similar notions were considered in [9,10] in the setting of *commit-and-open* Σ-protocols, and in some more constrained form, where the monotone structures are replaced by matroids, in [14,15].

We cannot expect for every Γ that a Γ-special-sound protocol is a proof of knowledge. Instead, we identify parameters t_Γ and κ_Γ, determined by the structure Γ, and for any Γ-special-sound Σ-protocol we prove existence of an extractor that has an knowledge error κ_Γ and an expected running time that scales with t_Γ. Thus, as long as $t_\Gamma \leq \text{poly}(|x|)$, Γ-special-soundness implies knowledge soundness. Similarly for $(\Gamma_1, \ldots, \Gamma_\mu)$-special-sound multi-round protocols.

The construction of our extractor for Γ-special-sound protocols (and its multi-round generalization) is inspired by the extractor construction from [3]. As a nice consequence, we can recycle the line of reasoning from [3] to prove strong parallel repetition and extend it to our general notion of special-soundness, showing that also here the knowledge error of a parallel repetition decreases exponentially with the number of repetitions. For this result, we refer to the full version [1].

Applications. Our general technique gives immediate, tight results for simple but important example protocols. For example, applied to the above mentioned amortization technique of proving a random linear combination, we directly obtain knowledge extraction with a knowledge error that matches the trivial cheating probability. Similarly, applied to the natural interactive proof for a Merkle commitment, where the prover is challenged to open a random subset (of a certain size), we obtain a knowledge error that matches the probability of one faulty node not being opened.

In order to demonstrate the usefulness of our result beyond the above simple examples, we analyze the (interactive) FRI protocol [5].[1] We prove that for a certain range of parameters, when instantiated with a Merkle tree commitment using a collision resistant hash function (or with any non-interactive, computationally binding vector commitment scheme with local openings), the protocol admits a knowledge extractor with knowledge error essentially matching the trivial cheating probability with the following caveat: the knowledge extractor runs only in (expected) quasi-polynomial time. (At least, this is true if the protocol is run for logarithmically many rounds, as is typically done. For a natural constant-round variant, which requires more total communication, we can obtain nearly optimal knowledge soundness, i.e., here the knowledge extractor runs in expected polynomial time.) In more detail, for any proximity parameter δ up to $\delta < \frac{1-\rho}{4}$, where ρ is the relative rate of the considered code, we establish the existence a knowledge extractor running in expected time $N^{O(\log N)}$ which, when given oracle access to a (potentially dishonest) prover $\mathcal{P}^*$, succeeds with probability at least $\epsilon(\mathcal{P}^*) - ((1-\delta)^t + O(N/|\mathbb{F}|))$, where N is the length of the code, t is the number of repetitions of a certain verification step, and $\epsilon(\mathcal{P}^*)$ is the probability $\mathcal{P}^*$ convinces the verifier to accept.[2] For context, the trivial cheating probability for the protocol is $\max\{(1-\delta)^t, 1/|\mathbb{F}|\}$. In contrast to the above simple examples, arguing that the FRI protocol is $(\Gamma_1, \ldots, \Gamma_\mu)$-special-soundness is not trivial; however, technical results from [5] can be recycled in order to show this, and then the existence of the knowledge extractor follows immediately from our generic result. While proving the existence of a quasi-polynomial time extractor does not suffice for establishing the standard notion of knowledge soundness, we believe that it still offers a nontrivial guarantee with the potential for practical relevance.

A final example, which we would like to briefly discuss, is parallel repetition. This example shows that our generic technique does not always work. For simplicity, consider a k-special-sound Σ-protocol with $k > 2$ (but the discussion also applies to multi-round protocols, and to our generalized notion of special soundness). Then, its t-fold parallel repetition is *not* k-special-sound anymore (unless $k = 2$). One can argue that it is $((k-1)^t + 1)$-special-sound — but this parameter is exponential in t, and thus one cannot directly conclude knowledge soundness. On the other hand, equipped with our generalized notion, one can observe that the parallel repetition is Γ-special-sound for Γ being the structure that accepts a list of challenge vectors, each vector of length t, if there is one position where the challenge vectors feature at least k different values. Unfortunately, also here,

---

[1] We point out that, when considering the FRI protocol for an actual hash function (rather than the random oracle), ordinary soundness is meaningless: the *existence* of an opening of a Merkle commitment with a certain (not too obscure) property holds trivially. Thus, it is crucial to argue knowledge soundness in this case.

[2] For the constant-round variant, we obtain genuine knowledge-soundness $(1-\delta)^t + O(N/|\mathbb{F}|)$, that is here the knowledge extractor's expected running time is $N^{O(1)}$. We also point out that a simple argument can be used to show knowledge soundness $(1-2^\mu\delta)^t + O(N/|\mathbb{F}|)$, where μ is the number of rounds; however, this result is only meaningful for fairly extreme parameters.

the crucial parameter t_Γ turns out to be exponential for this structure Γ, and so our generic result does not imply knowledge soundness. Fortunately, for this particular and important example, the parallel repetition result from [3] applies in case of k-special-sound protocols (and its multi-round generalization), and our extension (see the full version [1]) of the parallel repetition applies in case of arbitrary $(\Gamma_1, \ldots, \Gamma_\mu)$-special-sound protocols. Thus, after all, we can still argue (optimal) knowledge soundness in this case.

In conclusion, we expect that with our generic result for $(\Gamma_1, \ldots, \Gamma_\mu)$-special-sound protocols (which requires control over certain parameters to be applicable), and with our general parallel repetition result, our work offers powerful tools for proving knowledge soundness of many sophisticated proofs of knowledge.

2   Preliminaries

We write $\mathbb{N}_0 = \mathbb{N} \cup \{0\}$ for the set of nonnegative integers. Further, for any $q \in \mathbb{Z}$, $\mathbb{Z}_q = \mathbb{Z}/q\mathbb{Z}$ denotes the ring of integers modulo q.

2.1   Interactive Proofs

Let us now introduce some standard terminology and definitions with respect to interactive proofs. We follow standard conventions as presented in [4].

Let $R \subseteq \{0,1\}^* \times \{0,1\}^*$ be a binary relation, containing statement-witness pairs $(x; w)$. We assume all relations to be NP-relations, i.e., verifying that $(x; w) \in R$ takes time polynomial in $|x|$. An interactive proof for a relation R aims to allow a prover $\mathcal{P}$ to convince a verifier $\mathcal{V}$ that a public statement x admits a (secret) witness w, i.e., $(x; w) \in R$, or even that the knows a witness w for x.

An interactive proof with three communication rounds, where we may assume the prover to send the first and final message, is called a Σ-protocol. Further, an interactive proof is said to be *public-coin* if the verifier publishes all its random coins. In this case, we may assume all the verifier's messages to be sampled uniformly at random from finite (challenge) sets.

An interactive proof is said to be *complete* if for any statement witness pair $(x; w)$ an honest execution results in an accepting transcript (with high probability). It is *sound* if a dishonest prover cannot convince an honest verifier on public inputs x that do not admit a witness w, i.e., on false statements x. More precisely, $(\mathcal{P}, \mathcal{V})$ is sound if $\mathcal{V}$ rejects false statements x with high probability. The stronger notion of *knowledge soundness* requires that (potentially dishonest) provers that succeed in convincing the verifier with large enough probability must actually "know" a witness w. We will mainly be interested in analyzing the knowledge soundness of interactive proofs. For this reason, we formally define this property below.

Definition 1 (Knowledge Soundness). *An interactive proof* $(\mathcal{P}, \mathcal{V})$ *for relation* R *is* knowledge sound *with knowledge error* $\kappa \colon \mathbb{N} \to [0,1]$ *if there exists a* *positive polynomial q and an algorithm $\mathcal{E}$, called a* knowledge extractor, *with the following properties. Given input x and black-box oracle access to a (potentially dishonest) prover $\mathcal{P}^*$, the extractor $\mathcal{E}$ runs in an expected number of steps that is polynomial in $|x|$ (counting queries to $\mathcal{P}^*$ as a single step) and outputs a witness $w \in R(x)$ with probability*

$$\Pr\big((x; \mathcal{E}^{\mathcal{P}^*}(x)) \in R\big) \geq \frac{\epsilon(\mathcal{P}^*, x) - \kappa(|x|)}{q(|x|)},$$

where $\epsilon(\mathcal{P}^*, x) := \Pr\big((\mathcal{P}^*, \mathcal{V})(x) = \text{accept}\big)$ is the success probability of $\mathcal{P}^*$ on public input x.

Remark 1 (Interactive Arguments). In some cases, soundness and knowledge soundness only hold with respect to computationally bounded provers, i.e., unbounded provers can falsely convince a verifier. Computationally (knowledge) sound protocols are referred to as interactive *arguments*. Proving soundness of interactive arguments can be significantly more complicated than proving soundness of interactive proofs. However, in the context of knowledge soundness, an interactive argument for relation R can oftentimes be cast as an interactive proof for a modified relation

$$R' = \{(x; w) : (x; w) \in R \text{ or } w \text{ solves some computational problem}\}.$$

Hence, in this case the knowledge extractor will either output a witness w with respect to the original relation w, or it will output the solution to some computational problem, e.g., a discrete logarithm relation. In fact, our analysis of the FRI protocol in Sect. 7 exemplifies this general principle. For this reason, knowledge soundness of interactive arguments can typically be analyzed via knowledge extractors that are originally defined for interactive proofs. Therefore, we will focus on the analyzes of interactive proofs.

Proving knowledge soundness of Σ-protocols directly is a nontrivial task, as it requires the construction of an efficient knowledge extractor. It is typically much easier to prove a related *threshold* special-soundness property, which states that a witness can be extracted from a sufficiently large set of colliding and accepting transcripts.

Definition 2 (k-out-of-N Special-Soundness). *Let $k, N \in \mathbb{N}$. A 3-round public-coin interactive proof $\Pi = (\mathcal{P}, \mathcal{V})$ for relation R, with challenge set of cardinality $N \geq k$, is k-out-of-N special-sound if there exists an algorithm that, on input a statement x and k accepting transcripts $(a, c_1, z_1), \ldots (a, c_k, z_k)$ with common first message a and pairwise distinct challenges $c_1, \ldots, c_k$, runs in polynomial time and outputs a witness w such that $(x; w) \in R$. We also say Π is k-special-sound and, if $k = 2$, it is simply said to be special-sound.*

It is known that k-out-of-N special-soundness implies knowledge soundness with knowledge error $(k - 1)/N$. Recently, the multi-round generalization $(k_1, \ldots, k_\mu)$-out-of-$(N_1, \ldots, N_\mu)$ special-soundness has become relevant. It is now known that also this generalization tightly implies knowledge soundness [2]. For a formal definition, we refer either to [2] or to Sect. 6 where we generalize this (multi-round) notion beyond the threshold setting.

2.2 Geometric Distribution

This work adapts the extractor of [3]. For this reason, we also need the following preliminaries on the geometric distribution from their work.

A random variable B with two possible outcomes, denoted 0 (failure) and 1 (success), is said to follow a Bernoulli distribution with parameter p if $p = \Pr(B = 1)$. Sampling from a Bernoulli distribution is also referred to as running a Bernoulli trial. The probability distribution of the number X of independent and identical Bernoulli trials needed to obtain a success is called the geometric distribution with parameter $p = \Pr(X = 1)$. In this case $\Pr(X = k) = (1 - p)^{k-1}p$ for all $k \in \mathbb{N}$ and we write $X \sim \mathrm{Geo}(p)$. For two independent geometric distributions we have the following lemma.

Lemma 1. *Let $X \sim \mathrm{Geo}(p)$ and $Y \sim \mathrm{Geo}(q)$ be independently distributed. Then,*

$$\Pr(X \leq Y) = \frac{p}{p + q - pq} \geq \frac{p}{p + q}.$$

3   A Generalized Notion of Special-Soundness for Σ-Protocols

In this section, we define a generalized notion of special-soundness. To this end, we first recall the definition of *monotone structures*.

Definition 3 (Monotone Structure). *Let $\mathcal{C}$ be a nonempty finite set and let $\Gamma \subseteq 2^{\mathcal{C}}$ be a family of subsets of $\mathcal{C}$. Then, Γ or $(\Gamma, \mathcal{C})$ is said to be a monotone structure if it is closed under taking supersets, i.e., $S \in \Gamma$ and $S \subseteq T \subseteq \mathcal{C}$ implies $T \in \Gamma$.*

In some textbooks monotone structures Γ do not contain the empty set $\emptyset$ by definition, which is equivalent to $\Gamma \neq 2^{\mathcal{C}}$, and they are required to be nonempty, which is equivalent to $\mathcal{C} \in \Gamma$. For convenience, we also consider $\Gamma = \emptyset$ and $\Gamma = 2^{\mathcal{C}}$ to be monotone structures. Then, for any $\mathcal{D} \subseteq \mathcal{C}$, the restriction

$$\Gamma|_{\mathcal{D}} = \{S \subseteq \mathcal{D} : S \in \Gamma\} \subseteq 2^{\mathcal{D}}$$

defines a monotone structure $(\Gamma|_{\mathcal{D}}, \mathcal{D})$.

Definition 4 (Minimal Set). *Let $(\Gamma, \mathcal{C})$ be a monotone structure. A set $S \in \Gamma$ is minimal if none of its proper subsets are in Γ, i.e., for all $T \subsetneq S$ it holds that $T \notin \Gamma$. Further, $M(\Gamma) \subseteq \Gamma$ denotes the set of minimal elements of Γ.*

Definition 5 (Distance to a Monotone Structure). *For a nonempty monotone structure* $(\Gamma, \mathcal{C})$, *we define the following distance function:*

$$d_\Gamma \colon 2^{\mathcal{C}} \to \mathbb{N}_0, \quad S \mapsto \min_{T \in \Gamma} |T \setminus S|.$$

Equivalently,

$$d_\Gamma \colon 2^{\mathcal{C}} \to \mathbb{N}_0, \quad S \mapsto \min_{T \subseteq \mathcal{C}} \{|T| : S \cup T \in \Gamma\}.$$

If $\Gamma = \emptyset$, *we define* d_Γ *to be identically equal to* ∞.

The value $d_\Gamma(S) \in \mathbb{N}_0$ equals the minimum number of elements that have to be added to the set S to obtain an element of Γ. In particular, $d_\Gamma(S) = 0$ if and only if $S \in \Gamma$. Hence, it shows how close S is to the monotone structure Γ.

The key observation is now that typical knowledge extractors for interactive proofs proceed by extracting some set of accepting transcripts from a dishonest prover attacking the interactive proof. Subsequently, the knowledge extractor computes a witness from this set of accepting transcripts. Clearly, the set of sets of accepting transcripts from which a witness can be computed is closed under taking supersets, i.e., it is a monotone structure. Therefore, the following special-soundness notion for 3-round Σ-protocols follows naturally.

Definition 6 (Γ-out-of-$\mathcal{C}$ Special-Soundness). *Let* $(\Gamma, \mathcal{C})$ *be a monotone structure. A 3-round public-coin interactive proof* $(\mathcal{P}, \mathcal{V})$ *for relation R, with challenge set $\mathcal{C}$, is Γ-out-of-$\mathcal{C}$ special-sound if there exists an algorithm that, on input a statement x and a set of accepting transcripts* $(a, c_1, z_1), \ldots, (a, c_k, z_k)$ *with common first message a and such that* $\{c_1, \ldots, c_k\} \in \Gamma$, *runs in polynomial time and outputs a witness* $w \in R(x)$. *We also say* $(\mathcal{P}, \mathcal{V})$ *is Γ-special-sound.*

The above definition is a generalization of k-out-of-N special-soundness, where the extractability is guaranteed when given k colliding accepting transcripts with common first message a and pairwise distinct challenges c_i that are elements of a challenge set with cardinality N. Hence, when Γ contains all sets of cardinality at least k, i.e., it is a *threshold* monotone structure, Γ-out-of-$\mathcal{C}$ special-soundness reduces to k-out-of-N special-soundness, where $N = |\mathcal{C}|$.

Remark 2. Formally, the monotone structure $(\Gamma, \mathcal{C})$ of Definition 6 may depend on the size $|x|$ of the public input x, i.e., it should actually be replaced by an ensemble $(\Gamma_\lambda, \mathcal{C}_\lambda)$ of monotone structures indexed by the size $\lambda \in \mathbb{N}$ of the public input of $(\mathcal{P}, \mathcal{V})$. For simplicity, we will abuse notation by ignoring this dependency and simply writing $(\Gamma, \mathcal{C})$.

4   Knowledge Extraction for Γ-out-of-$\mathcal{C}$ Special-Sound Σ-Protocols

Our goal is to prove that, for certain monotone structures $(\Gamma, \mathcal{C})$, Γ-out-of-$\mathcal{C}$ special-soundness (tightly) implies knowledge soundness, and to determine the corresponding knowledge error. In order to prove this, we construct a knowledge extractor that, by querying a prover $\mathcal{P}^*$ attacking the interactive proof, obtains a set of accepting transcripts with common first message and for which the challenges form a set in Γ. Without loss of generality we may assume $\mathcal{P}^*$ to be deterministic,[3] i.e., $\mathcal{P}^*$ always outputs the same first message a. Hence, $\mathcal{P}^*$ can be viewed as a (deterministic) function

$$\mathcal{P}^*: \mathcal{C} \to \{0,1\}^* \quad c \mapsto y = (a,c,z),$$

that on input a challenge $c \in \mathcal{C}$ outputs a protocol transcript $y = (a,c,z)$.

Let $A \subseteq \mathcal{C}$ be the set of challenges for which $\mathcal{P}^*$ succeeds, i.e., $A = \{c \in \mathcal{C} : V(\mathcal{P}^*(c)) = 1\}$. Then the goal of the extractor is to find a set $B \in \Gamma|_A$. The difficulty is that the extractor is only given oracle access to $\mathcal{P}^*$ and therefore does not know the set A. For this reason, extractors typically proceed recursively as follows: if at some point the extractor has found some $S \subseteq A$ with $S \notin \Gamma$, it will try new challenges $c \in \mathcal{C}$ until $\mathcal{P}^*$ succeeds. The hope is then that $S \cup \{c\} \subseteq A$ is "closer" to $\Gamma|_A$ than S. More precisely, the extractor tries to find a $c \in A \subseteq \mathcal{C}$ such that $d_{\Gamma|_A}(S \cup \{c\}) < d_{\Gamma|_A}(S)$. Note that not all challenges c shorten the distance to $\Gamma|_A$, e.g., $d_{\Gamma|_A}(S \cup \{c\}) = d_{\Gamma|_A}(S)$ for all $c \in S$. Since the extractor does not know the set A, it cannot evaluate this distance function.

However, for any S, the challenge set $\mathcal{C}$ can be partitioned into a partition of "useless" challenges and a partition of "potentially useful" challenges. The useless challenges are the $c \in \mathcal{C}$ such that $d_{\Gamma|_A}(S \cup \{c\}) = d_{\Gamma|_A}(S)$ for all $A \subseteq \mathcal{C}$ containing S, i.e., for all A useless challenges will not shorten the distance to $\Gamma|_A$. For instance, all $c \in S$ are useless challenges for any S and any Γ. However, in some settings the set of useless challenges is larger than S, and in general this observation is crucial for the extractor to be efficient. In fact, this is the case for all interactive proofs that warrant a generalization of the existing threshold special-soundness notion. All challenges $c \in \mathcal{C}$ that are not useless are potentially useful, i.e., for these challenges there exist an $A \subseteq \mathcal{C}$ containing S such that $d_{\Gamma|_A}(S \cup \{c\}) < d_{\Gamma|_A}(S)$. The set of useful challenges is denoted $U_\Gamma(S)$, where the function U_Γ is formally defined below.

Definition 7 (Useful Elements). *For a monotone structure $(\Gamma, \mathcal{C})$, we define the following function:*

$$U_\Gamma: 2^\mathcal{C} \to 2^\mathcal{C}, \quad S \mapsto \{c \in \mathcal{C} \setminus S : \exists A \in \Gamma \text{ s.t. } S \subset A \wedge A \setminus \{c\} \notin \Gamma\}.$$

Note that $\Gamma = \emptyset$ implies $U_\Gamma(S) = \emptyset$ for all $S \subseteq \mathcal{C}$. Moreover, if Γ is nonempty, $U_\Gamma(S) = \emptyset$ if and only if $S \in \Gamma$.

The following lemma shows that for any $c \in U_\Gamma(S)$, there exists an $A \in \Gamma$ containing $S \cup \{c\}$ such that

$$d_{\Gamma|_A}(S \cup \{c\}) < d_{\Gamma|_A}(S),$$

i.e., the challenges $c \in U_\Gamma(S)$ are indeed potentially useful to the extractor. Even more so, it is essential that the extractor considers *all* challenges $c \in U_\Gamma(S)$. For

---

[3] See [3] for a proof of this claim.

every $c \in U_\Gamma(S)$, it might namely be the case that the $A \in \Gamma$ that "certifies" c, i.e., the A such that $S \subset A$ and $A \setminus \{c\} \notin \Gamma$, corresponds to the challenges for which the prover $\mathcal{P}^*$ succeeds. Since $A \setminus \{c\} \notin \Gamma$, the extractor can only succeed if it considers the challenge $c \in U_\Gamma(S)$ at some point.

The same lemma shows that challenges $c \notin U_\Gamma(S)$ will never decrease the distance, i.e., they are indeed useless to the extractor. More precisely, if $c \notin U_\Gamma(S)$, for every $A \in \Gamma$ containing $S \cup \{c\}$ it holds that

$$d_{\Gamma|_A}(S \cup \{c\}) = d_{\Gamma|_A}(S).$$

Lemma 2. *Let $(\Gamma, \mathcal{C})$ be a monotone structure and $S \subset \mathcal{C}$. Then $c \in U_\Gamma(S)$ if and only if there exists an $A \in \Gamma$ containing $S \cup \{c\}$ such that*

$$d_{\Gamma|_A}(S \cup \{c\}) < d_{\Gamma|_A}(S).$$

For the proof of Lemma 2, we refer the to the full version [1].

We also derive the following lemma, which shows that even if all useless challenges $c \in \mathcal{C} \setminus U_\Gamma(S)$ are added to the set $S \in 2^{\mathcal{C}} \setminus \Gamma$, the resulting subset is still not in Γ.

Lemma 3. *Let $(\Gamma, \mathcal{C})$ be a monotone structure and $S \in 2^{\mathcal{C}} \setminus \Gamma$. Then, $(\mathcal{C} \setminus U_\Gamma(S)) \cup S \notin \Gamma$.*

For the proof of Lemma 3, we refer the to the full version [1].

The knowledge extractor will be restricted to sampling challenges that are potentially useful. The value t_Γ defines the maximum number of accepting transcripts that the extractor has to find, before it succeeds and obtains the accepting transcripts for a set $S \in \Gamma$. The efficiency of our knowledge extractor will depend on t_Γ. A formal definition is given below. Further, in Sect. 5, we describe the monotone structure and corresponding k-values for three (classes of) interactive proofs and explain their relevance.

Definition 8 (t-value). *Let $(\Gamma, \mathcal{C})$ be a monotone structure and $S \subseteq \mathcal{C}$. Then*

$$t_\Gamma(S) := \max\left\{ t \in \mathbb{N}_0 : \begin{array}{c} \exists c_1, \ldots, c_t \in \mathcal{C} \text{ s.t.} \\ c_i \in U_\Gamma(S \cup \{c_1, \ldots, c_{i-1}\}) \; \forall i \end{array} \right\}.$$

Further,

$$t_\Gamma := t_\Gamma(\emptyset).$$

It is easily seen that $t_\Gamma(S) = 0$ if and only if $S \in \Gamma$ or $\Gamma = \emptyset$. Further, the following lemma shows that adding an element $c \in U_\Gamma(S)$ to S decreases the corresponding k-value. This lemma plays a pivotal role in our recursive extraction algorithm.

Lemma 4. *Let $(\Gamma, \mathcal{C})$ be a nonempty monotone structure and let $S \subseteq \mathcal{C}$ such that $S \notin \Gamma$. Then, for all $c \in U_\Gamma(S)$,*

$$t_\Gamma(S \cup \{c\}) < t_\Gamma(S).$$

For the proof of Lemma 4, we refer the to the full version [1].

As in [3], we describe our technical results in a more abstract language. This will later allow us to easily derive composition results and handle more complicated scenarios, such as multi-round interactive proofs and parallel compositions. To this end, let us consider a finite set $\mathcal{C}$, a probabilistic algorithm $\mathcal{A}\colon \mathcal{C} \to \{0,1\}^*$ and a verification function $V\colon \mathcal{C} \times \{0,1\}^* \to \{0,1\}$. An output $y \leftarrow \mathcal{A}(c)$ of the algorithm $\mathcal{A}$ on input $c \in \mathcal{C}$ is said to be *accepting* or *correct* if $V(c, y) = 1$. The success probability of $\mathcal{A}$ is denoted as

$$\epsilon(\mathcal{A}) := \Pr\big(V\big(C, \mathcal{A}(C)\big) = 1\big),$$

where C is uniformly random in $\mathcal{C}$. The obvious instantiation of $\mathcal{A}$ is given by a deterministic dishonest prover $\mathcal{P}^*$ attacking an interactive proof Π on input x. Note that even though it is sufficient to consider deterministic provers $\mathcal{P}^*$, we allow the algorithm $\mathcal{A}$ to be probabilistic. This generalization is essential when considering multiround interactive proofs and parallel repetitions [3].

Now let $\Gamma \subseteq 2^{\mathcal{C}}$ be a nonempty monotone structure. Then, for any $S \subset \mathcal{C}$ with $U_\Gamma(S) \neq \emptyset$, we define

$$\epsilon_\Gamma(\mathcal{A}, S) := \Pr\big(V\big(C, \mathcal{A}(C)\big) = 1 \mid C \in U_\Gamma(S)\big).$$

Typically, $U_\Gamma(\emptyset) = \mathcal{C}$ and thus $\epsilon(\mathcal{A}) = \epsilon_\Gamma(\mathcal{A}, \emptyset)$, i.e., all challenges $c \in \mathcal{C}$ are potentially useful. However, this is not necessarily the case.

Given oracle access to $\mathcal{A}$, the goal of the extractor is to find *correct* outputs $y_1, \ldots, y_k$ for challenges $c_1, \ldots, c_k \in \mathcal{C}$ such that $\{c_1, \ldots, c_k\} \in \Gamma$, i.e., such that $V(c_i, y_i) = 1$ for all i. If $\mathcal{A}$ corresponds to a dishonest prover attacking a Γ-out-of-$\mathcal{C}$ special-sound interactive proof on some input x, a witness w for statement x can be efficiently computed from the outputs $y_1, \ldots, y_k$.

Let us further define the following quality measure for the algorithm $\mathcal{A}$:

$$\delta_\Gamma(\mathcal{A}) := \min_{S \notin \Gamma} \Pr\big(V\big(C, \mathcal{A}(C)\big) = 1 \mid C \notin S\big). \tag{1}$$

The value $\delta_\Gamma(\mathcal{A})$ defines a "punctured" success probability of $\mathcal{A}$, i.e., it equals the success probability of $\mathcal{A}$ when the challenge c is sampled uniformly at random from some set $\mathcal{C} \setminus S \supseteq U_\Gamma(S)$ such that S is not in the monotone structure. We will show that the value $\delta_\Gamma(\mathcal{A})$ measures how well we can extract from the algorithm $\mathcal{A}$. The value $\delta_\Gamma(\mathcal{A})$ is a generalization of the measure

$$\delta_k(\mathcal{A}) := \min_{S \subseteq \mathcal{C}:|S|=k-1} \Pr\big(V\big(C, \mathcal{A}(C)\big) = 1 \mid C \notin S\big),$$

defined in [3].[4] However, when restricting to threshold monotone structures, there is a syntactic difference between the definitions of $\delta_k(\mathcal{A})$ and $\delta_\Gamma(\mathcal{A})$. To see this, let $\mathcal{T}_k$ denote the monotone structure containing all subsets of $\mathcal{C}$ with cardinality at least k. Then, in the definition of $\delta_k(\mathcal{A})$ the minimum is over all

---

[4] In the original version of [3], the restriction was $|S| < k$. Here, when considering 3-round protocols, this makes no difference, but it does for the multi-round case.

sets of cardinality *exactly* $k-1$, whereas the corresponding $\delta_{T_k}(\mathcal{A})$ is a minimum over all sets of size *at most* $k-1$. In the threshold case this makes no difference: it is easily seen that there always exists a (maximal) set of size $k-1$ that minimizes $\delta_{T_k}(\mathcal{A})$ and so indeed $\delta_{T_k}(\mathcal{A}) = \delta_k(\mathcal{A})$. A similar result does not hold for arbitrary access structures, i.e., in general the minimum may not be attained by a maximal set $S \notin \Gamma$. This issue will reoccur in a more substantial way when addressing multi-round protocols.

For any set $T \in 2^{\mathcal{C}} \setminus \Gamma$, we also define

$$\delta_\Gamma(\mathcal{A}, T) := \min_{S : S \cup T \notin \Gamma} \Pr\big(V(C, \mathcal{A}(C)) = 1 \mid C \notin S\big).$$

Since $S \cup T \notin \Gamma$ implies $S \cup T' \notin \Gamma$ for all $T' \subseteq T$, it follows that

$$\delta_\Gamma(\mathcal{A}, T') \leq \delta_\Gamma(\mathcal{A}, T), \quad \forall T' \subseteq T. \tag{2}$$

Further, by Lemma 3, it follows that $(\mathcal{C} \setminus U_\Gamma(T)) \cup T \notin \Gamma$ for all $T \notin \Gamma$. Hence,

$$\begin{aligned}
\delta_\Gamma(\mathcal{A}, T) &= \min_{S : S \cup T \notin \Gamma} \Pr\big(V(C, \mathcal{A}(C)) = 1 \mid C \notin S\big) \\
&\leq \Pr\big(V(C, \mathcal{A}(C)) = 1 \mid C \notin \mathcal{C} \setminus U_\Gamma(T)\big) \\
&= \Pr\big(V(C, \mathcal{A}(C)) = 1 \mid C \in U_\Gamma(T)\big) \\
&= \epsilon_\Gamma(\mathcal{A}, T).
\end{aligned} \tag{3}$$

We are now ready to define and analyze our extraction algorithm for Γ-out-of-$\mathcal{C}$ special-sound interactive Σ-protocols. The extractor is defined in Fig. 1 and its properties are summarized in the following lemma.

Lemma 5 (Extraction Algorithm - Σ-protocols). *Let $(\Gamma, \mathcal{C})$ be a nonempty monotone structure and let $V : \mathcal{C} \times \{0, 1\}^* \to \{0, 1\}$. Then there exists an oracle algorithm $\mathcal{E}_\Gamma$ with the following properties: The algorithm $\mathcal{E}_\Gamma^{\mathcal{A}}$, given oracle access to a (probabilistic) algorithm $\mathcal{A} : \mathcal{C} \to \{0, 1\}^*$, requires an expected number of at most $2t_\Gamma - 1$ queries to $\mathcal{A}$ and, with probability at least $\delta_\Gamma(\mathcal{A})/t_\Gamma$, it outputs pairs $(c_1, y_1), (c_2, y_2), \ldots, (c_k, y_k) \in \mathcal{C} \times \{0, 1\}^*$ with $V(c_i, y_i) = 1$ for all i and $\{c_1, \ldots, c_k\} \in \Gamma$.*

Proof. The extractor $\mathcal{E}_\Gamma^{\mathcal{A}}(S)$ is formally defined in Fig. 1. It takes as input a subset $S \in 2^{\mathcal{C}} \setminus \Gamma$. The input S represents the set of accepting challenges that the extractor has already found, i.e., the goal of $\mathcal{E}_\Gamma^{\mathcal{A}}(S)$ is to find pairs (c_i, y_i) such that $V(c_i, y_i) = 1$ and $\{c_1, \ldots, c_k\} \cup S \in \Gamma$. Further, we define

$$\mathcal{E}_\Gamma^{\mathcal{A}} := \mathcal{E}_\Gamma^{\mathcal{A}}(\emptyset).$$

First note that, since $\Gamma \neq \emptyset$ and thus $U_\Gamma(S) \neq \emptyset$ for all $S \notin \Gamma$, the extractor is well-defined. Let us now analyze the success probability and the expected number of $\mathcal{A}$-queries of the extractor.

Parameters: a nonempty monotone structure $(\Gamma, \mathcal{C})$ and an $S \in 2^{\mathcal{C}} \setminus \Gamma$.

Oracle access to: Algorithm $\mathcal{A}\colon \mathcal{C} \to \{0,1\}^*$ and verification function $V\colon \mathcal{C} \times \{0,1\}^* \to \{0,1\}$.

- Sample $c_1 \in U_\Gamma(S)$ uniformly at random and evaluate $y_1 \leftarrow \mathcal{A}(c_1)$.
- If $V(c_1, y_1) = 0$, abort and output $\perp$.
- If $V(c_1, y_1) = 1$ and $\{c_1\} \cup S \in \Gamma$, output $(c_1, y_1) \in \mathcal{C} \times \{0,1\}^*$.
- Else, set $\text{COIN} = 0$ and repeat
  - run $\mathcal{E}_\Gamma^{\mathcal{A}}(S \cup \{c_1\})$;
  - set $\text{COIN} \leftarrow V\big(d, \mathcal{A}(d)\big)$ for $d \in U_\Gamma(S)$ sampled uniformly at random;
  until either $\mathcal{E}_\Gamma^{\mathcal{A}}(S \cup \{c_1\})$ outputs pairs $(c_2, y_2), \ldots, (c_k, y_k)$ (for some k) with $V(c_i, y_i) = 1$ for all i and $S \cup \{c_1, c_2, \ldots, c_k\} \in \Gamma$ or until $\text{COIN} = 1$.

Output: In the former case, output pairs $(c_1, y_1), \ldots, (c_k, y_k) \in \mathcal{C} \times \{0,1\}^*$ with $V(c_i, y_i) = 1$ for all i and $\{c_1, \ldots, c_k\} \cup S \in \Gamma$. In the latter case, output $\perp$.

Fig. 1. Recursive Expected Polynomial Time Extractor $\mathcal{E}_\Gamma^{\mathcal{A}}(S)$.

Success Probability. By induction over $t_\Gamma(S)$, we will prove that $\mathcal{E}_\Gamma^{\mathcal{A}}(S)$ succeeds with probability at least

$$\frac{\delta_\Gamma(\mathcal{A}, S)}{t_\Gamma(S)}.$$

We first consider the base case. To this end, let $S \subseteq \mathcal{C}$ with $t_\Gamma(S) = 1$. Then, by Lemma 4, for all $c_1 \in U_\Gamma(S)$, it holds that $t_\Gamma(S \cup \{c_1\}) = 0$ and thus $S \cup \{c_1\} \in \Gamma$. Therefore, the extractor succeeds if and only if $V\big(c_1, \mathcal{A}(c_1)\big) = 1$ for the c_1 sampled from $U_\Gamma(S)$. Hence, the success probability of the extractor equals

$$\epsilon_\Gamma(\mathcal{A}, S) \geq \delta_\Gamma(\mathcal{A}, S),$$

where the inequality follows from Eq. 3. This proves the bound on the success probability for the base case $t_\Gamma(S) = 1$.

Let us now consider an arbitrary subset $S \subseteq \mathcal{C}$ with $t_\Gamma(S) > 1$ and assume that the claimed bound holds for all subsets $T \subseteq \mathcal{C}$ with $t_\Gamma(T) < t_\Gamma(S)$.

In the first step, the extractor succeeds with probability $\epsilon_\Gamma(\mathcal{A}, S)$ in finding a $c_1 \in U_\Gamma(S)$ and $y_1 \leftarrow \mathcal{A}(c_1)$ with $V(c_1, y_1) = 1$. If $\{c_1\} \cup S \in \Gamma$, the extractor has successfully completed its task. If not, the extractor starts running two geometric experiments until one of them finishes. In the first geometric experiment the extractor repeatedly runs $\mathcal{E}_\Gamma^{\mathcal{A}}(S \cup \{c_1\})$. By Lemma 4, it holds that $t_\Gamma(S \cup \{c_1\}) < t_\Gamma(S)$. Hence, by the induction hypothesis, $\mathcal{E}_\Gamma^{\mathcal{A}}(S \cup \{c_1\})$ succeeds with probability

$$p \geq \frac{\delta_\Gamma(\mathcal{A}, S \cup \{c_1\})}{t_\Gamma(S \cup \{c_1\})} \geq \frac{\delta_\Gamma(\mathcal{A}, S)}{t_\Gamma(S) - 1},$$

where the second inequality follows from Eq. 2 and Lemma 4. In the second geometric experiment, the extractor tosses a coin that returns heads with probability

$$q := \epsilon_\Gamma(\mathcal{A}, S).$$

The second step of the extractor succeeds if the second geometric experiment does not finish before the first, and so by Lemma 1 this probability is lower bounded as follows

$$\Pr\big(\mathrm{Geo}(p) \le \mathrm{Geo}(q)\big) \ge \frac{p}{p+q} \ge \frac{\frac{\delta_\Gamma(\mathcal{A},S)}{t_\Gamma(S)-1}}{\frac{\delta_\Gamma(\mathcal{A},S)}{t_\Gamma(S)-1} + \epsilon_\Gamma(\mathcal{A}, S)}$$

$$\ge \frac{\frac{\delta_\Gamma(\mathcal{A},S)}{t_\Gamma(S)-1}}{\frac{\epsilon_\Gamma(\mathcal{A},S)}{t_\Gamma(S)-1} + \epsilon_\Gamma(\mathcal{A}, S)} = \frac{\delta_\Gamma(\mathcal{A}, S)}{t_\Gamma(S) \cdot \epsilon_\Gamma(\mathcal{A}, S)},$$

where the second inequality follows from the monotonicity of the function $x \mapsto \frac{x}{x+q}$ and the third inequality follows from the fact that $\delta_\Gamma(\mathcal{A}, S) \le \epsilon_\Gamma(\mathcal{A}, S)$ (Eq. 3).

Since the first step of the extractor succeeds with probability $\epsilon_\Gamma(\mathcal{A}, S)$, it follows that $\mathcal{E}_\Gamma^{\mathcal{A}}(S)$ succeeds with probability at least $\delta_\Gamma(\mathcal{A}, S)/t_\Gamma(S)$ for all $S \in 2^{\mathcal{C}} \setminus \Gamma$, which proves the claimed bound. In particular, $\mathcal{E}_\Gamma^{\mathcal{A}}$ succeeds with probability at least $\delta_\Gamma(\mathcal{A})/t_\Gamma$.

Expected Number of $\mathcal{A}$-Queries. By induction over $t_\Gamma(S)$, we will prove that the expected number of $\mathcal{A}$-queries $Q_\Gamma(S)$ made by $\mathcal{E}_\Gamma^{\mathcal{A}}(S)$ is upper bounded as follows:

$$Q_\Gamma(S) \le 2t_\Gamma(S) - 1.$$

We first consider the base case. To this end, let $S \subseteq \mathcal{C}$ with $t_\Gamma(S) = 1$. In this case, $\{c_1\} \cup S \in \Gamma$ for all $c_1 \in U_\Gamma(S)$. Hence, $\mathcal{E}_\Gamma^{\mathcal{A}}(S)$ either succeeds or fails after making exactly one $\mathcal{A}$-query, i.e., $Q_\Gamma(S) = 1 = 2t_\Gamma(S) - 1$, which proves the base case.

Let us now consider an arbitrary subset $S \subseteq \mathcal{C}$ with $t_\Gamma(S) > 1$ and assume that $Q_\Gamma(T) \le 2t_\Gamma(T) - 1$ for all subsets $T \subseteq \mathcal{C}$ with $t_\Gamma(T) < t_\Gamma(S)$.

The extractor $\mathcal{E}_\Gamma^{\mathcal{A}}(S)$ first samples $c_1 \leftarrow_R U_\Gamma(S)$ uniformly at random and evaluates $y_1 \leftarrow \mathcal{A}(c_1)$. This requires exactly one $\mathcal{A}$-query. After this step the extractor aborts with probability $1 - \epsilon_\Gamma(\mathcal{A}, S)$. Otherwise, and if $\{c_1\} \cup S \notin \Gamma$, it continues running the two geometric experiments until either one of them finishes. The second geometric experiment finishes in an expected number of $1/\epsilon_\Gamma(\mathcal{A}, S)$ trials and requires exactly one $\mathcal{A}$-query per trial. Hence, the total expected number of trials for both experiments is at most $1/\epsilon_\Gamma(\mathcal{A}, S)$. Further, since $t_\Gamma(S \cup \{c_1\}) < t_\Gamma(S)$ (Lemma 4) and by the induction hypotheses, the expected number of $\mathcal{A}$-queries of the first geometric experiment is at most

$$Q_\Gamma(S \cup \{c_1\}) \le 2t_\Gamma(S \cup \{c_1\}) - 1 \le 2t_\Gamma(S) - 3,$$

per iteration, where the second inequality follows again from Lemma 4. Hence, every iteration of the repeat loop requires an expected number of at most $2t_\Gamma(S) - 2$ $\mathcal{A}$-queries.

From this it follows that

$$Q_\Gamma(S) \le 1 + \epsilon_\Gamma(\mathcal{A}, S)\frac{2t_\Gamma(S) - 2}{\epsilon_\Gamma(\mathcal{A}, S)} = 2t_\Gamma(S) - 1,$$

for all $S \in 2^\mathcal{C} \setminus \Gamma$. In particular, $\mathcal{E}_\Gamma^\mathcal{A}$ requires an expected number of at most $2t_\Gamma - 1$ $\mathcal{A}$-queries, which completes the proof of the lemma.

□

By basic probability theory, for any $S \notin \Gamma$,

$$
\begin{aligned}
\Pr\big(V(C, \mathcal{A}(C)) = 1 \mid C \notin S\big) &= \frac{\Pr\big(V(C, \mathcal{A}(C)) = 1 \wedge C \notin S\big)}{\Pr\big(C \notin S\big)} \\
&\ge \frac{\Pr\big(V(C, \mathcal{A}(C)) = 1\big) - \Pr\big(C \in S\big)}{\Pr\big(C \notin S\big)} \\
&= \frac{\epsilon(\mathcal{A}) - \Pr\big(C \in S\big)}{1 - \Pr\big(C \in S\big)} \\
&= \frac{\epsilon(\mathcal{A}) - |S| / |\mathcal{C}|}{1 - |S| / |\mathcal{C}|}.
\end{aligned}
$$

Hence, taking the minimum over all $S \notin \Gamma$ shows that

$$\delta_\Gamma(\mathcal{A}) \ge \frac{\epsilon(\mathcal{A}) - \kappa_\Gamma}{1 - \kappa_\Gamma}, \tag{4}$$

where $\kappa_\Gamma = \max_{S \notin \Gamma} |S| / |\mathcal{C}|$. In Γ-out-of-$\mathcal{C}$ special-sound interactive proofs, a dishonest prover can potentially take any $S \notin \Gamma$ and choose the first message so that it will succeed if the verifier chooses a challenge $c \in S$. Hence, κ_Γ equals the trivial cheating strategy for Γ-out-of-$\mathcal{C}$ special-sound interactive proofs.

Since the extractor succeeds with probability at least $\delta_\Gamma(\mathcal{A})/t_\Gamma$, the following theorem follows.

Theorem 1. *Let $(\mathcal{P}, \mathcal{V})$ be a Γ-out-of-$\mathcal{C}$ special-sound Σ-protocol such that t_Γ is polynomial in the size $|x|$ of the public input statement x of $(\mathcal{P}, \mathcal{V})$ and sampling from $U_\Gamma(S)$ takes polynomial time (in $|x|$) for all S with $|S| < t_\Gamma$. Then $(\mathcal{P}, \mathcal{V})$ is knowledge sound with knowledge error $\kappa_\Gamma = \max_{S \notin \Gamma} |S| / |\mathcal{C}|$.*

5   Examples

In this section, we describe three very simple interactive proofs and their special-soundness properties. The first example shows that for the special case of k-out-of-N special-soundness notion, we recover the known results. The second and third example present techniques that have found numerous applications, but cannot be analyzed via their threshold special-soundness properties, i.e., these interactive proofs require an alternative analysis. Our knowledge extractor offers the means to easily handle these interactive proof as well. Finally, the fourth example shows that our generic techniques do not always suffice. In Sect. 7, we will consider a more complicated protocol and demonstrate how our techniques enable a knowledge soundness analysis of the multi-round protocol FRI [5].

Example 1 (Threshold Access Structures). Let $\mathcal{C}$ be a finite set with cardinality N, and let Γ be the monotone structure that contains all subsets of $\mathcal{C}$ of cardinality at least $k \leq N$. Then a Γ-out-of-$\mathcal{C}$ special-sound interactive proof is also k-out-of-N special-sound. Moreover, $U_\Gamma(A) = \mathcal{C} \setminus A$ for all $A \notin \Gamma$, $t_\Gamma = k$, and $\kappa_\Gamma = (k-1)/N$. Hence, in the case of k-out-of-N special-soundness, we recover the results from [3].

Example 2 (Standard Amortization Technique). Let $\mathbb{F}$ be a finite field and let Ψ be an $\mathbb{F}$-linear map. The following amortization technique, known from Σ-protocol theory, allows a prover to prove knowledge of n Ψ-preimages $x_1, \ldots, x_n$ of $P_1, \ldots, P_n$ for essentially the cost of one. The amortization technique is a 2-round protocol that proceeds as follows. First, the verifier samples a challenge vector $\mathbf{c} = (c_1, \ldots, c_n) \in \mathbb{F}^n$ uniformly at random. Second, upon receiving the challenge vector $\mathbf{c}$, the prover responds with the element $z = \sum_{i=1}^n c_i x_i$. Finally, the verifier checks that $\Psi(z) = \sum_{i=1}^n c_i P_i$. Hence, instead of sending n preimages the prover only has to send one preimage.

The n preimages $x_1, \ldots, x_n$ of $P_1, \ldots, P_n$ can be extracted from accepting transcripts $(\mathbf{c}_1, z_1), \ldots, (\mathbf{c}_k, z_k)$ if the challenge vectors $\mathbf{c}_1, \ldots, \mathbf{c}_k$ span the vector space $\mathbb{F}^n$. Hence, the amortization protocol is Γ-out-of-$\mathbb{F}^n$ special-sound, where Γ is the monotone structure that contains all subsets spanning $\mathbb{F}^n$. Further, $t_\Gamma = n$, $U_\Gamma(A) = \mathbb{F}^n \setminus \mathrm{span}(A)$ for all $A \notin \Gamma$; and $\kappa_\Gamma = 1/|\mathbb{F}|$; thus, we obtain optimal knowledge soundness.

At the same time, the amortization protocol is $(|\mathbb{F}|^{n-1}+1)$-out-of-$|\mathbb{F}|^n$ special-sound, i.e., the threshold special-soundness parameter of this protocol is $|\mathbb{F}|^{n-1}+1$, which is much larger than $t_\Gamma = n$. In fact, the parameter $|\mathbb{F}|^{n-1}+1$ is typically not polynomially bounded, in which case knowledge soundness can not be derived from this threshold special-soundness property.

Example 3 (Merkle Tree Commitments). Let us now consider an interactive proof for proving knowledge of the opening of a Merkle tree commitment P, i.e., P is the root of a Merkle tree and the prover claims to know all n leafs. To verify this claim, the verifier selects a subset S of k (distinct) indices between 1 and n uniformly at random. The prover sends the corresponding leafs together with their validation paths, which are checked by the verifier.

An opening of the commitment P can be extracted from accepting transcripts $(S_1, z_1), \ldots, (S_\ell, z_\ell)$ if the subsets S_i cover $\{1, \ldots, n\}$. Hence, this interactive proof is Γ-out-of-$\mathcal{C}$, where

$$\mathcal{C} = \{S \subseteq \{1, \ldots, n\} : |S| = k\} \quad \text{and} \quad \Gamma = \Big\{\mathcal{D} \subseteq \mathcal{C} : \bigcup_{S \in \mathcal{D}} S = \{1, \ldots, n\}\Big\}.$$

Further, $t_\Gamma = n - k + 1$, $U_\Gamma(\mathcal{D}) = \{A \in \mathcal{C} : A \nsubseteq \bigcup_{S \in \mathcal{D}} S\}$ for all $\mathcal{D} \notin \Gamma$, and $\kappa_\Gamma = (n-k)/n$; thus, we obtain optimal knowledge soundness.

The threshold special-soundness parameter of this protocol is $\binom{n-1}{k} + 1$ which is typically much larger than $t_\Gamma = n - k + 1$. Hence, also in this case our generalization provides a much more efficient knowledge extractor.

This simple interactive proof is an essential component in many more complicated protocols based on probabilistically checkable proofs (PCPs), interactive oracle proofs (IOPs) or MPC-in-the-head.

Example 4 (Parallel Repetition). Finally, we consider an example where our generic technique does not work. To this end, let Π^t be the t-fold parallel composition of a k-out-of-N special-sound interactive proof Π with challenge set $\mathcal{C}$, i.e., Π^t has challenge set $\mathcal{C}^t$. Then, as discussed in the introduction, Π^t is $((k - 1)^t + 1)$-out-of-N^t special-sound, i.e., its threshold special-soundness parameter $(k - 1)^t + 1$ grows exponentially in t (if $k > 2$).

The parallel repetition Π^t is also Γ-out-of-$\mathcal{C}^t$ special-sound, where Γ contains all subsets of challenge vectors $\mathbf{c} \in \mathcal{C}^t$ such that there is one position $1 \leq i \leq t$ where the challenge vectors feature at least k different values. Then, $\kappa_\Gamma = (k - 1)^t/N^t$. However, $t_\Gamma = (k-1)^t+1$, i.e., t_Γ equals the threshold special-soundness parameter and grows exponentially in t. Hence, in this particular example, the correct access structure does not yield an efficient extractor. Fortunately, here we can apply the parallel repetition result of [3].

6   Knowledge Extraction for Multi-round Interactive Proofs

Let us now move to the analysis of multi-round interactive proofs $(\mathcal{P}, \mathcal{V})$. To this end, we first generalize the notion of Γ-out-of-$\mathcal{C}$ special-soundness to multi-round interactive proofs. A $2\mu+1$-round interactive proof is said to be $(\Gamma_1, \ldots, \Gamma_\mu)$-out-of-$(\mathcal{C}_1, \ldots, \mathcal{C}_\mu)$ if there exists an efficient algorithm that can extract a witness from appropriate trees of transcripts. Before we formally define trees of transcripts, we first define the related trees of challenges.

Definition 9 (Tree of Challenges). *Let $(\Gamma_i, \mathcal{C}_i)$ be monotone structures for $1 \leq i \leq \mu$. A set containing a single challenge vector $(c_1, \ldots, c_\mu) \in \mathcal{C}_1 \times \cdots \times \mathcal{C}_\mu$ is also referred to as a $(1, \ldots, 1)$-tree of challenges. Further, for $1 \leq t \leq \mu$, a $(1, \ldots, 1, \Gamma_t, \ldots, \Gamma_\mu)$-tree T_t of challenges is the union of several $(1, \ldots, 1, \Gamma_{t+1}, \ldots, \Gamma_\mu)$-trees, such that*

- *The first $t - 1$ coordinates of all $\mathbf{c} \in T_t \subseteq \mathcal{C}_1 \times \cdots \times \mathcal{C}_\mu$ are equal;*
- *The t-th coordinates of the tree elements form an element in Γ_t, i.e.,*

$$\{c \in \mathcal{C}_t : \exists (c_1, \ldots, c_{t-1}, c, c_{t+1}, \ldots, c_\mu) \in T_t\} \in \Gamma_t.$$

Trivially, the verifier's messages in a transcript of a $2\mu + 1$-round interactive proof with challenge sets $\mathcal{C}_1, \ldots, \mathcal{C}_\mu$ form a $(1, \ldots, 1)$-tree of challenges. Hence, by adding the prover's messages we obtain a $(1, \ldots, 1)$-tree of transcripts, and thus, in the obvious way, we obtain the notion of a tree of transcripts. The only additional requirement is that the prover's messages *collide*, i.e., they are uniquely determined by the challenges received before sending the message. In particular, the first message of every transcript is the same. Note that if the transcripts are generated by a deterministic prover, this property is guaranteed to hold.

Definition 10 (Tree of Transcripts). *Let* $(\Gamma_i, \mathcal{C}_i)$ *be monotone structures for* $1 \leq i \leq \mu$. *Let* $(\mathcal{P}, \mathcal{V})$ *be a* $2\mu + 1$-*round public-coin interactive proof with challenge sets* $\mathcal{C}_1, \ldots, \mathcal{C}_\mu$. *A* $(\Gamma_1, \ldots, \Gamma_\mu)$-*tree of transcripts is a set of protocol transcripts, such that*

- *The corresponding set of challenge vectors, obtained by ignoring the prover's messages, is a* $(\Gamma_1, \ldots, \Gamma_\mu)$-*tree of challenges;*
- *The prover's messages* collide, *i.e., if two transcripts* $(a_0, c_1, a_1, \ldots, c_\mu, a_\mu)$ *and* $(a'_0, c'_1, a'_1, \ldots, c'_\mu, a'_\mu)$ *are both in the tree, and* $c_i = c'_i$ *for all* $i \leq j$, *then also* $a_i = a'_i$ *for all* $i \leq j$.

Prior works (e.g., [2,7,8]) considered $(k_1, \ldots, k_\mu)$-trees, where $k_i \in \mathbb{N}$ for all i. These are special cases of the above defined trees. More precisely, if $\Gamma_i = \{S \subseteq \mathcal{C}_i : |S| \geq k_i\}$, a $(k_1, \ldots, k_\mu)$-tree is the same as a $(\Gamma_1, \ldots, \Gamma_t)$-tree.

We are now ready to define a generalized multi-round special-soundness notion.

Definition 11 ($((\Gamma_1, \ldots, \Gamma_\mu)$-out-of-$(\mathcal{C}_1, \ldots, \mathcal{C}_\mu)$ Special-Soundness). *Let* $(\Gamma_i, \mathcal{C}_i)$ *be monotone structures for* $1 \leq i \leq \mu$. *A* $2\mu + 1$-*round public-coin interactive proof* $(\mathcal{P}, \mathcal{V})$ *for relation* R, *with challenge sets* $\mathcal{C}_1, \ldots, \mathcal{C}_\mu$, *is* $(\Gamma_1, \ldots, \Gamma_\mu)$-*out-of-$(\mathcal{C}_1, \ldots, \mathcal{C}_\mu)$ special-sound if there exists a polynomial time algorithm that, on input a statement* x *and a* $(\Gamma_1, \ldots, \Gamma_\mu)$-*tree of accepting transcripts, outputs a witness* $w \in R(x)$. *We also say that* $(\mathcal{P}, \mathcal{V})$ *is* $(\Gamma_1, \ldots, \Gamma_\mu)$-*special-sound.*

Remark 3. The monotone access structure $(\Gamma_{\text{TREE}}(\boldsymbol{\Gamma}), \mathcal{C}_1 \times \cdots \times \mathcal{C}_\mu)$, where $\boldsymbol{\Gamma} = (\Gamma_1, \ldots, \Gamma_\mu)$ and

$$\Gamma_{\text{TREE}}(\Gamma_1, \ldots, \Gamma_\mu) := \{S \subseteq \mathcal{C}_1 \times \cdots \times \mathcal{C}_\mu : S \text{ contains a } (\Gamma_1, \ldots, \Gamma_\mu)\text{-tree}\},$$

allows one to cast a multi-round $(\Gamma_1, \ldots, \Gamma_\mu)$-out-of-$(\mathcal{C}_1, \ldots, \mathcal{C}_\mu)$ special-sound interactive proof as a Γ-out-of-$\mathcal{C}$ special-sound interactive proof. Therefore, in principle, one could immediately apply the results from Sect. 4. However, typically, this results in an inefficient knowledge extractor. More precisely, the value $t_{\Gamma_{\text{TREE}}(\boldsymbol{\Gamma})}$, and thus the expected running time of the extractor, grows linearly in the product of the sizes of the challenge sets $\mathcal{C}_1, \ldots, \mathcal{C}_{\mu-1}$. For this reason, our multi-round knowledge extractor will proceed recursively over the different rounds.

Our goal is now to prove that, for appropriate monotone structures, $(\Gamma_1, \ldots, \Gamma_\mu)$-out-of-$(\mathcal{C}_1, \ldots, \mathcal{C}_\mu)$ special-soundness (tightly) implies knowledge soundness. As before, again borrowing the notation from [3], we present our results in a more abstract language. To this end, let $\mathcal{A}\colon \mathcal{C}_1 \times \cdots \times \mathcal{C}_\mu \to \{0,1\}^*$ be a probabilistic algorithm and

$$V\colon \mathcal{C}_1 \times \cdots \times \mathcal{C}_\mu \times \{0,1\}^* \to \{0,1\}$$

a verification function. The success probability of $\mathcal{A}$ is denoted as

$$\epsilon(\mathcal{A}) := \Pr\big(V\big(C,\mathcal{A}(C)\big) = 1\big)\,,$$

where C is distributed uniformly at random over $\mathcal{C}_1 \times \cdots \times \mathcal{C}_\mu$. The obvious instantiation of $\mathcal{A}$ is again a deterministic prover $\mathcal{P}^*$ attacking a $(\Gamma_1,\ldots,\Gamma_\mu)$-out-of-$(\mathcal{C}_1,\ldots,\mathcal{C}_\mu)$ special-sound interactive proof.

It turns out that defining the multi-round version of δ_Γ is somewhat subtle. In the case of a **k**-special sound protocol, it is defined in [3] as

$$\delta_{\mathbf{k}}^V(\mathcal{A}) :=$$
$$\min_{S_1\cdots S_\mu} \Pr\big(V(C,\mathcal{A}(C)) = 1 \,\big|\, C_1 \notin S_1, C_2 \notin S_2(C_1), C_3 \notin S_2(C_1,C2),\ldots\big)$$

where the minimum is over all sets $S_1 \subset 2^{\mathcal{C}_1}$ with $|S_1| = k_1 - 1$, all functions $S_2 : \mathcal{C}_1 \to 2^{\mathcal{C}_2}$ with $|S_2(c_1)| = k_2 - 1$ for all $c_1 \in \mathcal{C}_1$, etc.[5] Thus, the natural extension to $(\Gamma_1,\ldots,\Gamma_\mu)$-special-sound protocols would be to use the very same expression but minimize over all (maximal) sets $S_1 \subset 2^{\mathcal{C}_1}$ with $S_1 \notin \Gamma_1$, all functions $S_2 : \mathcal{C}_1 \to 2^{\mathcal{C}_2}$ with $S_2(c_1)$ (maximal and) not in Γ_2 for all $c_1 \in \mathcal{C}_1$, etc.

However, writing $\mathbf{\Gamma} = (\Gamma_1,\Gamma_2,\ldots,\Gamma_\mu)$, it turns out that defining $\delta_{\mathbf{\Gamma}}^V$ in this way will not lead to the desired results. In essence, the problem lies in the fact that the condition $C_2 \notin S_2(C_1)$ may bias the distribution of C_1, namely when $S_2(c_1)$ has different cardinality for different choices of c_1. This issue is avoided in the threshold case by requiring the S_i's to be maximal sets; here in the general case, this does not work, since different maximal sets may have different cardinality.

Because of this reason, we define $\delta_{\mathbf{\Gamma}}^V$ by the following, harder to comprehend, expression:

$$\delta_{\mathbf{\Gamma}}^V(\mathcal{A}) := \min_{S_1\cdots S_\mu} \sum_{\mathbf{c}} \Pr\big(V\big(C,\mathcal{A}(C)\big) = 1 \wedge C = \mathbf{c} \,\big|\, C_1 \notin S_1,$$
$$C_2 \notin S_2(c_1),\ldots,C_\mu \notin S_\mu(c_1,\ldots,c_\mu)\big)\,, \tag{5}$$

where, as in the above approach, the minimum is over all sets $S_1 \subset 2^{\mathcal{C}_1}$ with $S_1 \notin \Gamma_1$, all functions $S_2 : \mathcal{C}_1 \to 2^{\mathcal{C}_2}$ with $S_2(c_1) \notin \Gamma_2$ for all $c_1 \in \mathcal{C}_1$, etc.

---

[5] In the original version of [3], the restriction was $|S_i| < k_i$, i.e., the sets were not required to be maximal (this makes no difference for $\mu = 1$, but it does for the multi-round case, where the min is not necessarily attained by maximal sets). However, in an updated version, this was changed to the above (in essence because of a similar issue as discussed below).

Remark 4. Note that, in the special case of 3-round interactive proofs, i.e., if $\mu = 1$, it holds that

$$\delta_\Gamma^V(\mathcal{A}) = \min_{S \notin \Gamma} \sum_c \Pr\big(V(C, \mathcal{A}(C)) = 1 \wedge C = c \mid C \notin S\big)$$

$$= \min_{S \notin \Gamma} \Pr\big(V(C, \mathcal{A}(C)) = 1 \mid C \notin S\big).$$

Hence, the multi-round version of δ defined in Eq. 5, is indeed a generalization of the 3-round version defined in Eq. 1.

Remark 5. Let us consider the multi-round threshold case, i.e., let $\mathcal{T}_{\mathbf{k}} = (\mathcal{T}_{k_1}, \ldots, \mathcal{T}_{k_\mu})$ with $\mathcal{T}_{k_i}$ the monotone structure containing all subsets of $\mathcal{C}_i$ with cardinality at least k_i for all i. Then, although not immediately obvious, it turns out that $\delta_{\mathcal{T}_{\mathbf{k}}}(\mathcal{A}) = \delta_{\mathbf{k}}(\mathcal{A})$ for all $\mathcal{A}$.

By observing that for the non-vanishing terms in the sum, exploiting the independence of $V(\mathbf{c}, \mathcal{A}(\mathbf{c}))$ and C for a fixed $\mathbf{c}$,

$$\Pr\big(V(C, \mathcal{A}(C)) = 1 \mid C = \mathbf{c}, C_1 \notin S_1, C_2 \notin S_2(c_1), \cdots\big)$$
$$= \Pr\big(V(\mathbf{c}, \mathcal{A}(\mathbf{c})) = 1 \mid C = \mathbf{c}, C_1 \notin S_1, C_2 \notin S_2(c_1), \cdots\big)$$
$$= \Pr\big(V(\mathbf{c}, \mathcal{A}(\mathbf{c})) = 1\big),$$

we can re-write the definition as

$$\delta_\Gamma^V(\mathcal{A}) = \min_{S_1 \cdots S_\mu} \sum_{\mathbf{c}} \Pr\big(V(\mathbf{c}, \mathcal{A}(\mathbf{c})) = 1\big) \Pr\big(C = \mathbf{c} \mid C_1 \notin S_1, C_2 \notin S_2(c_1), \cdots\big)$$

$$= \min_{S_1 \cdots S_\mu} \sum_{\mathbf{c}} \Pr\big(V(\mathbf{c}, \mathcal{A}(\mathbf{c})) = 1\big) \Pr\big(C_1 = c_1 \mid C_1 \notin S_1\big) \cdots$$

$$\cdots \Pr\big(C_\mu = c_\mu \mid C_\mu \notin S_\mu(c_1, \ldots, c_{\mu-1})\big).$$

This shows that the definition captures the success probability of $\mathcal{A}$ when the challenges are samples as follows (for given sets/functions $S_1, S_2, \ldots$, over which the minimum is then taken): c_1 is sampled uniformly at random subject to being outside of S_1. Then, c_2 is sampled uniformly at random subject to being outside of $S_2(c_1)$. And so forth. We repeat, in general this is *not* the same as sampling $c_1, \ldots, c_\mu$ uniformly at random subject to $c_1 \notin S_2$, $c_2 \notin S_2(c_1)$, etc., which biases the choice of c_1 towards those for which $S_2(c_1)$ is small(er), while with the above sampling there is no bias on c_1 (beyond the exclusion from S_1). Defining δ_Γ^V in this way is crucial to our work. Oftentimes, the verification function V is clear from context, in which case we simply write $\delta_\Gamma(\mathcal{A})$ instead of $\delta_\Gamma^V(\mathcal{A})$.

Any choice of sets/functions $S_1, \ldots, S_\mu$ considered in the minimization in Eq. 5 defines a subset

$$X = \{(c_1, \ldots, c_\mu) \in \mathcal{C}_1 \times \cdots \times \mathcal{C}_\mu \mid c_1 \in S_1 \vee \cdots \vee c_\mu \in S_\mu(c_1, \ldots, c_{\mu-1})\}$$

that does not contain a Γ-tree. Hence, again the success probability is punctured by removing some set X from which we cannot extract and thus, for which a dishonest prover may (potentially) be successful. Moreover, every subset of $\mathcal{C}_1 \times \cdots \times \mathcal{C}_\mu$ that does not contain a Γ-tree is contained in a set X of this form. Hence, if a prover has positive success probability outside all such subsets X, i.e., if $\delta_\Gamma^V(\mathcal{A}) > 0$, then extraction of a Γ-tree of accepting transcripts is in principle possible. However, it is far less obvious that extraction can also be done efficiently. The following lemma shows that, for appropriate monotone structures $(\Gamma_i, \mathcal{C}_i)$, an efficient extraction algorithm indeed exists. This is a generalization of [3, Lemma 4]. Using the notation we introduced here, their proof almost immediately carries over to this more generic setting. For completeness, we present the proof below.

Lemma 6 (Multi-round Extraction Algorithm). *Let* $\Gamma = (\Gamma_1, \ldots, \Gamma_\mu)$ *and* $\mathcal{C} = \mathcal{C}_1 \times \cdots \times \mathcal{C}_\mu$ *be such that* $(\Gamma_i, \mathcal{C}_i)$ *are nonempty monotone structures for all* i. *Further, let* $T := \prod_{i=1}^{\mu} t_{\Gamma_i}$ *and* $V \colon \mathcal{C} \times \{0,1\}^* \to \{0,1\}$. *Then, there exists an algorithm* $\mathcal{E}^{\mathcal{A}}$ *so that, given oracle access to any (probabilistic) algorithm* $\mathcal{A} \colon \mathcal{C} \to \{0,1\}^*$, $\mathcal{E}^{\mathcal{A}}$ *requires an expected number of at most* $2^\mu \cdot T$ *queries to* $\mathcal{A}$ *and, with probability at least* $\delta_\Gamma(\mathcal{A})/T$, *outputs pairs* $(\mathbf{c}_i, y_i) \in \mathcal{C} \times \{0,1\}^*$ *such that* $\{\mathbf{c}_i\}_i$ *is a* Γ-*tree with* $V(\mathbf{c}_i, y_i) = 1$ *for all* i.

For the proof of Lemma 6, we refer to the full version [1].

Let us now derive a lower bound on the value $\delta_\Gamma^V(\mathcal{A})$. To this end, for $\mathbf{c} = (c_1, \ldots, c_\mu) \in \mathcal{C}_1 \times \cdots \times \mathcal{C}_\mu$, we write $V(\mathbf{c})$ as a shorthand for $V(\mathbf{c}, \mathcal{A}(\mathbf{c}))$. Furthermore, for any fixed choices of $S_1, S_2, \ldots, S_\mu$, as in the definition of $\delta_\Gamma(\mathcal{A})$ (Eq. 5), we introduce the event

$$\Omega(\mathbf{c}) := \left[C_1 \notin S_1 \wedge C_2 \notin S_2(c_1) \wedge \cdots \wedge C_\mu \notin S_\mu(c_1, \ldots, c_{\mu-1}) \right].$$

Then,

$$\sum_{\mathbf{c}} \Pr\big(V(\mathbf{c}) = 1 \wedge C = \mathbf{c} \mid \Omega(\mathbf{c})\big) \geq \sum_{\mathbf{c}} \Pr\big(V(\mathbf{c}) = 1 \wedge \Omega(\mathbf{c}) \wedge C = \mathbf{c}\big)$$

$$= \sum_{\mathbf{c}} \Pr\big(V(C) = 1 \wedge \Omega(C) \wedge C = \mathbf{c}\big)$$

$$= \Pr\big(V(C) = 1 \wedge \Omega(C)\big)$$

$$\geq \Pr\big(V(C) = 1\big) - \Pr\big(\neg\Omega(C)\big).$$

Now note that

$$\Pr\big(\neg\Omega(C)\big) = 1 - \Pr\big(\Omega(C)\big)$$

$$= 1 - \Pr\big(C_1 \notin S_1\big) \Pr\big(C_2 \notin S_2(C_1) \mid C_1 \notin S_1\big) \cdots$$

$$\leq 1 - \left(1 - \max_{S_1 \notin \Gamma_1} \frac{|S_1|}{|\mathcal{C}_1|}\right) \left(1 - \max_{S_2 \notin \Gamma_1} \frac{|S_2|}{|\mathcal{C}_2|}\right) \cdots \qquad (6)$$

$$= \kappa_\Gamma,$$

where

$$\kappa_\Gamma := \max_{S \notin \Gamma_{\text{TREE}}(\Gamma)} \frac{|S|}{|\mathcal{C}|} = 1 - \prod_{i=1}^{\mu} \left(1 - \max_{S_i \notin \Gamma_i} \frac{|S_i|}{|\mathcal{C}_i|}\right) = 1 - \prod_{i=1}^{\mu} (1 - \kappa_{\Gamma_i}).$$

We thus obtain that

$$\delta_\Gamma(\mathcal{A}) \geq \epsilon(\mathcal{A}) - \kappa_\Gamma . \tag{7}$$

These observations complete the proof of the following theorem.

Theorem 2. *Let* $(\mathcal{P}, \mathcal{V})$ *be a* $(\Gamma_1, \ldots, \Gamma_\mu)$-*out-of-*$(\mathcal{C}_1, \ldots, \mathcal{C}_\mu)$ *special-sound interactive proof such that* $T_\Gamma = \prod_{i=1}^\mu t_{\Gamma_i}$ *is polynomial in the size* $|x|$ *of the public input statement* x *of* $(\mathcal{P}, \mathcal{V})$ *and sampling from* $U_{\Gamma_i}(S_i)$ *takes polynomial time (in* $|x|$*) for all* $1 \leq i \leq \mu$ *and* $S_i \subset \mathcal{C}_i$ *with* $|S_i| < t_{\Gamma_i}$. *Then* $(\mathcal{P}, \mathcal{V})$ *is knowledge sound with knowledge error*

$$\kappa_\Gamma = 1 - \prod_{i=1}^\mu \left(1 - \max_{S_i \notin \Gamma_i} \frac{|S_i|}{|\mathcal{C}_i|} \right) .$$

7   Analysis of the FRI-Protocol

In this section we show how to use our generalized notion of special-soundness to demonstrate the existence of a quasi-polynomial time knowledge extractor with essentially optimal success probability for the Fast Reed-Solomon Interactive Oracle Proof of Proximity due to Ben-Sasson et al. [5], assuming it has been compiled into an interactive proof the natural way (i.e., the oracles are replaced by compact commitments to the vectors with a local opening functionality). We first provide the necessary background on the protocol before providing our analysis. We remark that we use ideas that were implicit in prior works; our main aim in this section is to demonstrate the utility of our generalized special-soundness notion and the accompanying knowledge extractor.

7.1   Preliminaries on Reed-Solomon Codes

Let $\mathbb{F}$ be a finite field of cardinality q and $S \subseteq \mathbb{F}$. Given a polynomial $f(X) \in \mathbb{F}[X]$ we let $f(S) = (f(s))_{s \in S}$ denote the vector of evaluations of f over the domain S (given in some arbitrary, but fixed, order). For an integer ℓ we write $S^{\cdot \ell}$ for the set of ℓ-powers of elements in S, i.e. $\{s^\ell : s \in S\}$.[6]

For any $0 \leq \rho \leq 1$, the Reed-Solomon code $\mathrm{RS}[\mathbb{F}, S, \rho] \subseteq \mathbb{F}^{|S|}$ consists of all evaluations over the domain S of polynomials $F(X) \in \mathbb{F}[X]$ of degree less than $\rho|S|$. In notation,

$$\mathrm{RS}[\mathbb{F}, S, \rho] := \{F(S) : F(X) \in \mathbb{F}[X] \wedge \deg(F) < \rho|S|\} .$$

In the sequel we will assume S is a multiplicative subgroup of $\mathbb{F}^*$ of order a power of 2, with the understanding that our analysis should generalize readily to other "smooth" evaluation domains for FRI protocols. We further set $\rho = 2^{-r}$

---

[6] We use this somewhat cumbersome notation as we will later need to denote j-fold Cartesian products of sets, and for this operation we will use the standard notation S^j.

for an integer $r < \log_2(|S|)$, which implies $\rho|S| \in \mathbb{N}$ and that the dimension of $\mathrm{RS}[\mathbb{F}, S, \rho]$ is precisely $\rho|S|$.

Letting $N = |S|$, we therefore have $S = \langle \omega \rangle = \{1, \omega, \omega^2, \ldots, \omega^{N-1}\}$, where ω is a primitive N-th root of unity. Note then that $S^{\cdot 2} = \langle \omega^2 \rangle = \{1, \omega^2, \omega^4, \ldots, \omega^{N-2}\}$ is a multiplicative subgroup of $\mathbb{F}^*$ of order $N/2$. More generally, for any $j = 1, 2, \ldots, \log_2(N)$, $S^{\cdot 2^j} = \langle \omega^{2^j} \rangle$ is multiplicative subgroup of $\mathbb{F}^*$ of order $N/2^j$.

Given two polynomials $f(X), g(X) \in \mathbb{F}[X]$ we let $d_S(f, g) := |\{s \in S : f(s) \neq g(s)\}|$ denote the number of points $s \in S$ on which f and g differ. Equivalently, it denotes the (unnormalized) Hamming distance between the vectors $f(S)$ and $g(S)$.

Given a polynomial $f \in \mathbb{F}[X]$, we let

$$\delta_S(f) := \frac{\min_F \{d_S(f, F) : F \in \mathbb{F}[X], \deg(F) < \rho|S|\}}{|S|} .$$

In other words, $\delta_S(f)$ denotes the relative Hamming distance of $f(S)$ to a closest codeword in $\mathrm{RS}[\mathbb{F}, S, \rho]$.

7.2 FRI-Protocol

Let $\mathcal{O}^f$ be an oracle implementing some function $f \colon S \to \mathbb{F}$, which of course uniquely corresponds to a polynomial of degree less than $N = |S|$. We are interested in the situation where a prover claims that $f(X)$ is in fact a polynomial of degree $< \rho N$, i.e., that $f(S) \in \mathrm{RS}[\mathbb{F}, S, \rho]$. In order to verify this, the verifier may make queries to $\mathcal{O}^f$, but it is easy to see that in order to catch a lying prover the verifier must query each $s \in S$ (or at least $\Omega(|S|)$ such points in order to catch the prover with good probability).

Thus, for soundness, we will be satisfied with rejecting oracles implementing functions that are *far* from low degree, i.e., such that $\delta_S(f) \geq \delta$. However, here as well we cannot hope to catch cheating verifiers without making at least $\rho N + 1$ queries (as ρN evaluations are always consistent with some polynomial of degree $< \rho N$). It turns out to be possible to make significantly less (i.e., just logarithmically many) oracle queries if we allow the verifier to *interact with* the prover.

The resulting protocols are referred to as *interactive oracle proofs of proximity* (IOPPs). In order to demonstrate the utility of our general special soundness notion, we will show how to analyze the Fast Reed-Solomon Interactive Oracle Proof of Proximity (FRI-protocol) [5].

In order to implement the oracle $\mathcal{O}^f$ cryptographically, one makes use of a compact commitment scheme, typically via a Merkle tree [6]. In the following we denote the commitment to the vector $F(S) = (F(s))_{s \in S}$ with public parameters pp by $P \leftarrow \mathrm{COM}_{\mathsf{pp}}(F(S))$ and the local opening information for $s \in S$ as γ_s. For example, in the case of a Merkle tree the public parameters pp would be a description of the hash function used, while γ_s would give hash values for the co-path of the leaf corresponding to s. We also assume access to a procedure $\mathrm{LOC}_{\mathsf{pp}}$

which takes as input a commitment P, a domain element s, a value $y_s \in \mathbb{F}$ and the opening information γ_s and outputs 1 if and only if γ_s indeed certifies that P opens to y_s on the element s.

We can therefore view the (cryptographically compiled version of the) FRI-protocol as an interactive proof for the pair of relations $(\mathfrak{R}_0, \mathfrak{R}_\delta \cup \mathfrak{R}_{\mathsf{coll}})$, where for a parameter $\beta \in [0,1)$ we define

$$\mathfrak{R}_\beta := \big\{ (P, \mathsf{pp}; F, B, (\gamma_s)_{s \in B}) : \deg(F) < \rho N \ \wedge \ |B| \geq (1-\beta)N$$
$$\wedge \ \forall s \in B, \ \mathrm{Loc}_{\mathsf{pp}}(P, s, F(s), \gamma_s) = 1 \big\},$$

while

$$\mathfrak{R}_{\mathsf{coll}} := \big\{ (\mathsf{pp}; s, y, y', \gamma, \gamma') : y \neq y' \ \wedge \ \mathrm{Loc}_{\mathsf{pp}}(P, s, y, \gamma) = 1$$
$$\wedge \ \mathrm{Loc}_{\mathsf{pp}}(P, s, y', \gamma') = 1 \big\}.$$

This means that completeness holds with respect to relation $\mathfrak{R}_0$ and soundness holds with respect to $\mathfrak{R}_\delta \cup \mathfrak{R}_{\mathsf{coll}}$, where the latter refers to the "or-relation" which accepts a witness for one or the other instance. On the one hand, this says that a prover that committed to a low-degree polynomial will indeed convince the verifier of this fact. On the other hand, if a prover has a good probability of convincing the verifier then we can either extract a commitment to many coordinates that agree with a low-degree polynomial, or we can extract two distinct local openings from the same commitment (invalidating the binding property of the commitment).[7]

Folding. An important ingredient in the FRI-protocol is a folding operation. For our specific choice of S, it is defined as follows: for $f(X) \in \mathbb{F}[X]$ and $c \in \mathbb{F}$, we define
$$\mathrm{Fold}\big(f(X), c\big) = g(X) \in \mathbb{F}[X]$$
such that
$$g(X^2) = \frac{f(X) + f(-X)}{2} + c \frac{f(X) - f(-X)}{2X}.$$

Intuitively, this folding operation considers the even-power monomials of $f(X)$ and the odd-power monomials separately, obtains from these terms two polynomials of degree $\deg(f)/2$, and takes a random linear combination of these polynomials. Importantly, the polynomial $g(X)$ can then naturally be viewed as having degree roughly $\deg(f)/2$ (i.e., the degree is halved) and its domain is naturally viewed as $S^{\cdot 2} = \langle \omega^2 \rangle$, which has order $N/2$. That is, the folded polynomial has its degree and domain halved.

A one round version of the FRI-protocol thus proceeds as follows. First, the prover commits to $F(S)$, where it promises that $F(S) \in \mathrm{RS}[\mathbb{F}, S, \rho]$. The verifier

---

[7] Observe that this is a concrete instantiation of the idea alluded to in Remark 1: we can either extract a witness to the desired relation, or a solution to a computationally hard problem.

picks a random challenge $c \in \mathbb{F}$, sends it to the prover, and the prover responds with the folding G of F around c. The verifier first checks that $\deg(G) < \rho N/2$. If yes, the verifier then chooses t points $s_1, \ldots, s_t \in S$ (each uniformly at random and thus possibly colliding), and asks for the evaluations of F on all points $\pm s_i$. It then checks that these evaluations are consistent with G, i.e., that $G(s_i^2) = \frac{f(s_i)+f(-s_i)}{2} + c\frac{f(s_i)-f(-s_i)}{2s_i}$ for all $1 \leq i \leq t$, and of course that these are indeed the values the prover committed to initially.

7.3 Analyzing the FRI-Protocol

In order to analyze the FRI-protocol, we must create an extractor that takes as input folding challenges and then openings for various points $s \in S$ that are consistent with the folded polynomials (which are assumed to be low-degree). From two distinct folding challenges $c, c' \in \mathbb{F}$, if $G(X)$ and $G'(X)$ are the foldings around c and c' respectively of the function the prover committed to, then we can create the following polynomial:

$$F(X) = X\frac{G(X^2) - G'(X^2)}{c - c'} + \frac{cG'(X^2) - c'G(X^2)}{c - c'}.$$

Note that if G and G' have degree less than $\rho N/2$, then indeed F would have degree less than ρN.

The extractor may also rewind the second phase of the protocol to obtain sets A and A' covering at least $(1 - \delta)$ fraction of S. We can then conclude that we have consistent openings on their intersection $A \cap A'$ (assuming that we do not violate the binding property of the commitment, i.e., that we do not extract a witness for the relation $\mathfrak{R}_{\mathsf{coll}}$). The intersection $A \cap A'$ covers a $(1 - 2\delta)$ fraction of S, so we have found a low-degree polynomial agreeing with the commitment on a $(1 - 2\delta)$ fraction of the points of S.

At this point, we could iterate this argument. However, iterating this argument over μ folding rounds would cause us to only prove that the prover committed to a function that agrees with a low-degree polynomial on a $(1-2^\mu\delta)$-fraction of the coordinates (assuming that we did not extract a collision in the commitment). This is quite unsatisfactory, as we would like to have μ logarithmic in N and $\delta \in (0,1)$ a constant. Fortunately, by relying on ideas from prior works (specifically, [5]) we can show that we can indeed extract a low-degree polynomial agreeing with the commitment on a $(1 - \delta)$ fraction of coordinates (or, of course, a violation to the binding property of the commitment).

In order to analyze the soundness of the FRI-protocol more effectively, we will need the following *coset-distance* from f to $\mathrm{RS}[\mathbb{F}, S, \rho]$:

$$\Delta_S(f) := \min_{F \in \mathbb{F}[X],\ \deg(F) < \rho N} \frac{|\{s \in S : f(s) \neq F(s) \vee f(-s) \neq F(-s)\}|}{N}.$$

This distance notion has been used in prior works [5]. Observe that $\Delta_S(f) \geq \delta_S(f)$. Intuitively, this measure is useful because it allows for a more careful accounting of how the Hamming metric behaves under the folding operation than the above naïve analysis. For this reason, our extractor will succeed assuming a bound on $\Delta_S(f)$ rather than just $\delta_S(f)$.

The following lemma quantifies this intuition, by characterizing the set of challenges c that could cause the Hamming metric to decrease when a function f is folded around c. These ideas are implicit in [5, Lemma 4.4]; we restate them in a language that is convenient for us. The full version of this work [1] includes a proof of the following lemma.

Lemma 7. *Let $f(X) \in \mathbb{F}[X]$ be such that $\Delta_S(f) < (1-\rho)/2$. The number of choices for $c \in \mathbb{F}$ such that $\delta_{S\cdot 2}\big(\mathrm{Fold}(f,c)\big) < \Delta_S(f)$ is at most N.*

In particular, if there exist pairwise distinct $c_0, \ldots, c_N \in \mathbb{F}$ such that $\delta_{S\cdot 2}\big(\mathrm{Fold}(f,c)\big) \leq \delta$ for all $i \in \{0, 1, \ldots, N\}$, then $\Delta_S(f) \leq \delta$.

We now precisely define the notion of special-soundness that we will prove the FRI-protocol with one folding iteration satisfies. Informally, for the folding round the previous lemma tells us we need $N+1$ challenges to extract, while for the second round we need enough local openings of the commitment to reveal a $(1-\delta)$-fraction of the values that the prover committed to. We now make this formal.

Let

$$\mathcal{C} := S^t = \big\{ (s_1, s_2, \ldots, s_t) : s_i \in S \ \forall i \big\} \ .$$

For a challenge $c = (s_1, \ldots, s_t) \in \mathcal{C}$ we denote by

$$B(c) = \{s_1, -s_1, s_2, -s_2, \ldots, s_t, -s_t\}$$

the set[8] of elements of S that appear in the challenge tuple c, along with their negations. That is, it is the set of points that will be queried by the verifier if it samples $(s_1, s_2, \ldots, s_t)$ in the final verification step. Let $(\Gamma_{N+1}, \mathbb{F})$ be the monotone structure that contains all subsets of $\mathbb{F}$ of cardinality at least $N+1$, and let $(\Gamma, \mathcal{C})$ be the monotone structure that contains all subsets of $\mathcal{C}$ that cover at least a $(1-\delta)$-fraction of S, i.e.,

$$A \in \Gamma \subset 2^{\mathcal{C}} \quad \Longleftrightarrow \quad \left| \bigcup_{c \in A} B(c) \right| \geq (1-\delta)N \ .$$

Theorem 3 (FRI-protocol (one folding iteration)). *Let $\rho = 2^{-r}$ for some $r \in \{0, 1, \ldots, m\}$ and let $\delta \in (0, 1)$ be such that $\delta < \frac{1-\rho}{4}$. The FRI-Protocol is perfectly complete with respect to relation $\mathfrak{R}_0$ and (Γ_{N+1}, Γ)-out-of-$(\mathbb{F}, \mathcal{C})$ special-sound with respect to relation $\mathfrak{R}_\delta \cup \mathfrak{R}_{coll}$.*

Proof. **Completeness:** This is immediate from prior work (e.g., [5]). To make our proof self-contained, we note that this follows immediately from the following facts concerning a polynomial $F(X) \in \mathbb{F}[X]$:

– if F has degree $< \rho N$ then $\mathrm{Fold}(F, c)$ has degree $< \rho N/2$ for any $c \in \mathbb{F}$; and

---

[8] That is, we explicitly remove repetitions, so $B(c)$ is *not* interpreted as a multi-set.

- for any $s \in S$ and $c \in \mathbb{F}$, $\mathrm{Fold}(F, c)(s^2) = \frac{F(s)+F(-s)}{2} + c\frac{F(s)-F(-s)}{2s}$.

Soundness: We must extract a witness for either the relation $\mathfrak{R}_\delta$ or the relation $\mathfrak{R}_{\mathrm{coll}}$ given a (Γ_{N+1}, Γ)-tree of accepting transcripts. Such a tree of transcripts consists of the following:

- folding challenges $c_0, \ldots, c_N \in \mathbb{F}$,
- polynomials $G_0, \ldots, G_N \in \mathbb{F}[X]$ of degree less than $\rho\frac{N}{2}$,
- subsets $A_0, \ldots, A_N \subseteq C$, each satisfying $\left|\bigcup_{c \in A_j} B(c)\right| \geq (1 - \delta)N$, and
- for each $0 \leq j \leq N$, for each $s \in \bigcup_{c \in A_j} B(c)$, opening information γ_{sj} for the element s. Let $y_{sj} \in \mathbb{F}$ be the element for which $\mathrm{Loc}_{\mathrm{pp}}(P, s, y_{sj}, \gamma_{sj}) = 1$.

Let $B_j := \bigcup_{c \in A_j} B(c)$ for $0 \leq j \leq N$, and observe that these sets are closed under negation (i.e., $s \in B_j \iff -s \in B_j$).

Suppose there exists $j \neq j'$ such that, for some $s \in B_j \cap B_{j'}$, $y_{sj} \neq y_{sj'}$. Then, we may output the following witness for the relation $\mathfrak{R}_{\mathrm{coll}}$: $(s, y_{sj}, y_{sj'}, \gamma_{sj}, \gamma'_{sj})$.

We may now assume that the above does not occur. In other words, for each $s \in \bar{B} := B_0 \cup \ldots \cup B_N$ the set $\{y_{sj} : s \in B_j\}$ is in fact a singleton set; denote its unique element by y_s. We also let $\gamma_s := \gamma_{sj}$ where j is the smallest element in $\{0, 1, \ldots, N\}$ such that $s \in B_j$ (this is just an arbitrary tie-breaking rule).

For each $j \in \{0, 1, \ldots, N\}$, the polynomial G_j and the elements y_s for $s \in B_j$ satisfy the following relation:

$$G_j(s^2) = \frac{y_s + y_{-s}}{2} + c_j \frac{y_s - y_{-s}}{2s} \ .$$

Let $f(X) \in \mathbb{F}[X]$ be a polynomial consistent with the y_s's, i.e., for all $s \in \bar{B}$ we have $f(s) = y_s$. Furthermore, for reasons to be clear later, we let f be different to the polynomial F_0 defined below outside of $\bar{B}$, i.e., $f(s) \neq F_0(s)$ for all $s \notin \bar{B}$. Then, for each $j \in \{0, 1, \ldots, N\}$ and all s^2 such that $\{\pm s\} \subseteq B_j$, we have

$$G_j(s^2) = \mathrm{Fold}\left(f, c_j\right)(s^2) \ .$$

We conclude that $\mathrm{Fold}\left(f, c_j\right)$ and G_j agree on at least $(1-\delta)\frac{N}{2}$ elements of $S^{\cdot 2}$. As $\deg(G_j) < \rho\frac{N}{2}$ it follows that

$$\delta_{S^{\cdot 2}}\left(\mathrm{Fold}\left(f, c_j\right)\right) \leq \delta \ .$$

By Lemma 7, if we establish that $\Delta_S(f) < \frac{1-\rho}{2}$, it in fact then follows that $\Delta_S(f) \leq \delta$, which in turn implies $\delta_S(f) \leq \delta$. As $2\delta < \frac{1-\rho}{2}$ by assumption, it suffices for us to show $\Delta_S(f) \leq 2\delta$. We focus on proving this now.

Consider the polynomial

$$F_0(X) := X\frac{G_0(X^2) - G_1(X^2)}{c_0 - c_1} + \frac{c_0 G_1(X^2) - c_1 G_0(X^2)}{c_0 - c_1} \ .$$

Since the degrees of G_0 and G_1 are smaller than $\rho\frac{N}{2}$, it follows that $\deg(F_0) < \rho N$. Furthermore, we note that for all $s \in B_0 \cap B_1$ we have $f(s) = F_0(s)$. Indeed,

$$
\begin{aligned}
F_0(s) &= s \cdot \frac{G_0(s^2) - G_1(s^2)}{c_0 - c_1} + \frac{c_0 G_1(s^2) - c_1 G_0(s^2)}{c_0 - c_1} \\
&= \frac{s}{c_0 - c_1} \left[\frac{f(s) + f(-s)}{2} + c_0 \frac{f(s) - f(-s)}{2s} \right. \\
&\quad \left. - \left(\frac{f(s) + f(-s)}{2} + c_1 \frac{f(s) - f(-s)}{2s} \right) \right] \\
&\quad + \frac{1}{c_0 - c_1} \left[c_0 \cdot \left(\frac{f(s) - f(-s)}{2} + c_1 \frac{f(s) - f(-s)}{2s} \right) \right. \\
&\quad \left. - c_1 \cdot \left(\frac{f(s) + f(-s)}{2} + c_0 \frac{f(s) - f(-s)}{2s} \right) \right] \\
&= \frac{s}{c_0 - c_1} \cdot (c_0 - c_1) \frac{f(s) - f(-s)}{2s} + \frac{1}{c_0 - c_1} \cdot (c_0 - c_1) \frac{f(s) + f(-s)}{2} \\
&= \frac{f(s) - f(-s)}{2} + \frac{f(s) + f(-s)}{2} = f(s) \ .
\end{aligned}
$$

From this, we can conclude that f and F_0 agree on at least $(1 - 2\delta)N/2$ pairs $\{\pm s\}$: here, we use the fact that as B_0 and B_1 are closed under negation, so is $B_0 \cap B_1$. Thus, the number of $s \in S$ for which $f(s) \neq F_0(s)$ or $f(-s) \neq F_0(-s)$ is at most $2\delta N$. Recalling $\deg(F_0) < \rho N$, we conclude $\Delta_S(f) \leq 2\delta$, as desired.

Thus, we have found that $\Delta_S(f) \leq \delta$, which in particular means $\delta_S(f) \leq \delta$, as desired. Let $F(X)$ denote the (necessarily unique) polynomial of degree $< \rho N$ such that $d_S(F(S), f(S)) \leq \delta N$. As $d_S(F_0(S), f(S)) \leq 2\delta N$ it also follows that $d_S(F_0(S), F(S)) \leq 3\delta N < 1 - \rho$. As $F_0(S), F(S) \in \mathrm{RS}[\mathbb{F}, S, \rho]$ and this code has minimum distance $1 - \rho$, it must be that $F_0(S) = F(S)$, which further implies $F_0(X) = F(X)$ (as polynomials).

We can therefore extract a polynomial of degree $< \rho N$ that agrees with the function $f(X)$ on a $(1 - \delta)$ fraction of coordinates: namely, the polynomial $F_0(X)$. Furthermore, since f differs from F_0 outside of $\bar{B} = B_0 \cup \ldots \cup B_N$ (by the choice of f), we can find a subset $B \subseteq \bar{B}$ of size at least $(1 - \delta)N$ for which $f(s) = F_0(s)$ for all $s \in B$. We may therefore output the following witness for $\mathfrak{R}_\delta$: $(F_0(X), B, (\gamma_s)_{s \in B})$. $\square$

We are now in position to apply the machinery developed in Sect. 6 to conclude the following bound on the knowledge error.

Corollary 1 (Knowledge Error of FRI-protocol (one folding iteration)). *Let $\rho = 2^{-r}$ for some $r \in \{0, 1, \ldots, m\}$ and let $\delta \in (0, 1)$ be such that $\delta < \frac{1-\rho}{4}$. The FRI-Protocol is knowledge sound with respect to relation $\mathfrak{R}_\delta \cup \mathfrak{R}_{coll}$ with knowledge error*

$$
\kappa := 1 - \left(1 - \frac{N}{|\mathbb{F}|} \right) \left(1 - \frac{(\lceil (1 - \delta)N \rceil - 1)^t}{N^t} \right) \leq \frac{N}{|\mathbb{F}|} + (1 - \delta)^t \ .
$$

Proof. Theorem 3 shows that the FRI-Protocol is (Γ_{N+1}, Γ)-out-of-$(\mathbb{F}, \mathcal{C})$ special-sound. To apply Theorem 2, we must first establish that $t_\Gamma \cdot t_{\Gamma_{N+1}} \leq N^{O(1)}$. And this is indeed the case, as

$$t_\Gamma \leq \lceil (1 - \delta)N \rceil \text{ and } t_{\Gamma_{N+1}} \leq N + 1 \, .$$

We now establish the knowledge error. For this, it suffices to note that $\max_{S \notin \Gamma_{N+1}} \frac{|S|}{|\mathbb{F}|} = \frac{N}{|\mathbb{F}|}$ while

$$\max_{A \notin \Gamma} \frac{|A|}{|\mathcal{C}|} = \frac{(\lceil (1 - \delta)N \rceil - 1)^t}{N^t} \leq (1 - \delta)^t \, .$$

To see the first equality, first note that if $A \notin \Gamma$ then $\bigcup_{c \in A} B(c)$ has cardinality less than $(1 - \delta)N$, so A the number of $s \in S$ which can appear in a challenge $c \in A$ is at most $(1 - \delta)N$; as this is an integer, it is at most $\lceil (1 - \delta)N \rceil - 1$. That is, for some subset $T \subseteq S$ with $|T| \leq \lceil (1 - \delta)N \rceil - 1$, $A \subseteq T^t$, and $|T^t| \leq ((1 - \delta)N/2)^t$. The equality holds as we can certainly choose $A = T^t$ for some $T \subseteq S$ of size $\lceil (1 - \delta)N \rceil - 1$. For the denominator, as $\mathcal{C} = S^t$ it has cardinality $|S|^t = N^t$. □

7.4   Additional Folding Iterations

The above analysis can naturally be extended to handle more folding iterations. Let $F_0 := F$ be the low degree polynomial the prover commits to in the first round. We have folding rounds $i = 1, \ldots, \mu$, and in round i the verifier sends a challenge $c_{i-1} \in \mathbb{F}$ and the prover provides a commitment to $F_i(S^{2^i})$ where $F_i(X) = \text{Fold}(F_{i-1}, c_{i-1})(X)$. After these folding iterations, the verifier picks t points $s_1, \ldots, s_t \in S$ independently and uniformly at random and then checks that for all $i = 1, \ldots, \mu$ and $j = 1, \ldots, t$, we have

$$F_i\left(s_j^{2^i}\right) = \frac{F_{i-1}\left(s_j^{2^{i-1}}\right) + F_{i-1}\left(-s_j^{2^{i-1}}\right)}{2} + c_{i-1} \frac{F_{i-1}\left(s_j^{2^{i-1}}\right) - F_{i-1}\left(-s_j^{2^{i-1}}\right)}{2s_j} \, .$$

The recursive structure of the extractor implies that after μ folding iterations we obtain a protocol with the following generalized special-soundness guarantee.

Theorem 4 (FRI-protocol (μ folding iterations).). *Let $\rho = 2^{-r}$ for some $r \in \{0, 1, \ldots, m\}$ and let $\delta \in (0, 1)$ be such that $\delta < \frac{1-\rho}{4}$. Let $\mu \in \mathbb{N}$ be such that $\mu \leq \log_2 N$, and for $i = 1, 2, \ldots, \mu$ let $N_i := N/2^{i-1}$. The FRI-protocol with μ folding iterations is perfectly complete with respect to relation $\mathfrak{R}_0$ and $(\Gamma_{N_1+1}, \Gamma_{N_2+1}, \ldots, \Gamma_{N_\mu+1}, \Gamma)$-out-of-$(\mathbb{F}, \mathbb{F}, \ldots, \mathbb{F}, \mathcal{C})$ special-sound with respect to relation $\mathfrak{R}_\delta \cup \mathfrak{R}_{coll}$.*

This yields the following corollary regarding the knowledge error. However, we note that for $\mu = \Omega(\log N)$ the knowledge extractor only runs in expected *quasi-polynomial* time, preventing us from being able to claim the standard notion of knowledge soundness. Nonetheless we believe that the guarantee is meaningful. For the proof, we refer to the full version [1].

Corollary 2 (Knowledge Error of FRI-protocol (μ folding iterations)).
Let $N = 2^n$ for some $n \in \mathbb{N}$, let $\rho = 2^{-r}$ for some $r \in \{0, 1, \ldots, m\}$ and let $\delta \in (0, 1)$ be such that $\delta < \frac{1-\rho}{4}$. Let $\mu \in \mathbb{N}$ be such that $\mu \leq \log_2 N$, and for $i = 1, 2, \ldots, \mu$ let $N_i := N/2^{i-1}$. There exists a function $q(N, \mu) = N^{O(\mu)}$ such that the following holds.

There exists an extraction algorithm that, when given oracle access to a (potentially dishonest prover) $\mathcal{P}^*$ and input x of size N for the FRI-protocol, runs in time $\leq q(N, \mu)$ and outputs a witness in the relation $\mathfrak{R}_\delta \cup \mathfrak{R}_{coll}$ with probability at least

$$\frac{\epsilon(\mathcal{P}^*, x) - \kappa(N, \mu)}{q(N, \mu)}$$

where

$$\kappa(N, \mu) := 1 - \left(\prod_{i=1}^{\mu} \left(1 - \frac{N_i}{|\mathbb{F}|} \right) \right) \cdot \left(1 - \frac{(\lceil (1 - \delta)N \rceil - 1)^t}{N^t} \right)$$

$$\leq \sum_{i=1}^{\mu} \frac{N_i}{|\mathbb{F}|} + (1 - \delta)^t \leq \frac{2N}{|\mathbb{F}|} + (1 - \delta)^t .$$

Acknowledgments. The first author has been supported by TNO's Early Research Program - Next Generation Cryptography. We would additionally like to thank Michael Klooß for pointing out to us that the extractor for the FRI-protocol only runs in quasi-polynomial time.

References

1. Full version of this paper. IACR ePrint 2023/818 (2023)
2. Attema, T., Cramer, R., Kohl, L.: A compressed Σ-protocol theory for lattices. In: CRYPTO, vol. 12826, pp. 549–579 (2021)
3. Attema, T., Fehr, S.: Parallel repetition of $(k_1, \ldots, k_\mu)$-special-sound multi-round interactive proofs. In: CRYPTO, vol. 13507, pp. 415–443 (2022)
4. Attema, T., Fehr, S., Klooß, M.: Fiat-shamir transformation of multi-round interactive proofs. In: TCC, vol. 13747, pp. 113–142 (2022)
5. Ben-Sasson, E., Bentov, I., Horesh, Y., Riabzev, M.: Fast reed-solomon interactive oracle proofs of proximity. In: ICALP, vol. 107, pp. 14:1–14:17 (2018)
6. Ben-Sasson, E., Chiesa, A., Spooner, N.: Interactive oracle proofs. In: TCC, vol. 9986, pp. 31–60 (2016)
7. Bootle, J., Cerulli, A., Chaidos, P., Groth, J., Petit, C.: Efficient zero-knowledge arguments for arithmetic circuits in the discrete log setting. In: EUROCRYPT, vol. 9666, pp. 327–357 (2016)
8. Bünz, B., Bootle, J., Boneh, D., Poelstra, A., Wuille, P., Maxwell, G.: Bulletproofs: short proofs for confidential transactions and more. In: IEEE (S&P), pp. 315–334 (2018)
9. Don, J., Fehr, S., Majenz, C., Schaffner, C.: Efficient NIZKs and signatures from commit-and-open protocols in the QROM. In: CRYPTO, vol. 13508, pp. 729–757 (2022)

10. Don, J., Fehr, S., Majenz, C., Schaffner, C.: Online-extractability in the quantum random-oracle model. In: Dunkelman, O., Dziembowski, S. (eds.) EUROCRYPT, vol. 13277, pp. 677–706 (2022)
11. Kilian, J.: A note on efficient zero-knowledge proofs and arguments (extended abstract). In: Kosaraju, S.R., Fellows, M., Wigderson, A., Ellis, J.A. (eds.) STOC, pp. 723–732 (1992)
12. Micali, S.: CS proofs (extended abstracts). In: FOCS, pp. 436–453 (1994)
13. Micali, S.: Computationally sound proofs. SIAM J. Comput. **30**(4), 1253–1298 (2000)
14. Wikström, D.: Special soundness revisited. IACR ePrint 2018/1157 (2018)
15. Wikström, D.: Special soundness in the random oracle model. IACR ePrint 2021/1265 (2021)

From Polynomial IOP and Commitments to Non-malleable zkSNARKs

Antonio Faonio[1]([✉]) [iD], Dario Fiore[2] [iD], Markulf Kohlweiss[3] [iD], Luigi Russo[1] [iD], and Michal Zajac[4]

[1] EURECOM, Sophia Antipolis, Biot, France
{faonio,russol}@eurecom.fr
[2] IMDEA Software Institute, Madrid, Spain
dario.fiore@imdea.org
[3] University of Edinburgh and Input Output, Edinburgh, Scotland
markulf.kohlweiss@ed.ac.uk
[4] Nethermind, London, England
michal@nethermind.io

Abstract. We study sufficient conditions to compile simulation-extractable zkSNARKs from information-theoretic interactive oracle proofs (IOP) using a simulation-extractable commit-and-prove system for its oracles. Specifically, we define simulation extractability for opening and evaluation proofs of polynomial commitment schemes, which we then employ to prove the security of zkSNARKS obtained from polynomial IOP proof systems. To instantiate our methodology, we additionally prove that KZG commitments satisfy our simulation extractability requirement, despite being naturally malleable. To this end, we design a relaxed notion of simulation extractability that matches how KZG commitments are used and optimized in real-world proof systems. The proof that KZG satisfies this relaxed simulation extractability property relies on the algebraic group model and random oracle model.

1   Introduction

Non-interactive succinct zero-knowledge arguments of knowledge (zkSNARKs) [45] are the new Swiss army knife of blockchain scalability and privacy. They effectively deliver the twin dream of probabilistically checkable proofs (PCP) [3] and zero-knowledge proofs (ZKP) [34] while also being non-interactive, short, and efficiently verifiable. These features make zkSNARKs of high practical and theoretical relevance. They are an active area of research that has seen rapid progress in multiple aspects, such as efficiency [7,33,35,36], security and versatility of their setups [6,37], and proof composition [13,15].

Simulation-extractable zkSNARKs. *Knowledge-soundness* is the basic security notion of zkSNARKs: informally speaking, it guarantees that, in isolation, a prover producing a valid proof must know the corresponding witness. In contrast, there exist real-world deployments and cryptographic applications

© International Association for Cryptologic Research 2023
G. Rothblum and H. Wee (Eds.): TCC 2023, LNCS 14371, pp. 455–485, 2023.
https://doi.org/10.1007/978-3-031-48621-0_16

of zkSNARKs that require a stronger property called *simulation extractability* (SE, for brevity) [38,47]. Intuitively, this notion considers attackers that can see proofs for some statements and may use this information in order to produce a proof for some other statement without knowing the witness. Interestingly, simulation extractability implies that proofs are *non-malleable* [23], a relevant property in practical applications. Most zkSNARKs in the literature are only proven to be knowledge-sound. In some cases, this is due to the fact that their proofs may indeed be malleable, e.g., as in [36] (see also [4]). In other cases, the lack of SE security proof is because it is challenging and may require more investigation.

From Polynomial Commitments to SNARKs. The design of modern zkSNARKs follows the common cryptographic approach of starting with protocols that achieve information-theoretic security in idealized models and then compiling them into efficient protocols by employing a smaller computationally secure primitive. In the world of SNARKs, the corresponding concepts are (polynomial) interactive oracle proofs F-IOP [16,17,20,28,48] and (polynomial) functional commitments F-COM [12,40,41]. An F-IOP employs two (idealized) oracles that share their state: the prover calls the first oracle *to commit* to functions $f \in F$ and the verifier calls the second *to query* the committed functions. Concretely, the F-IOP to SNARK compiler uses F-COM to replace oracles with commitments, opening proofs, and query proofs. As this only removes reliance on idealized function oracles but not interaction, the compiler additionally employs the usual Fiat-Shamir transformation for public-coin protocols to obtain the final zkSNARK. The benefits of this compilation paradigm are modularity and separation of concerns: once the compiler is proven, a line of research can address the problem of improving F-IOPs while another research line can tackle the problem of realizing F-COM schemes (e.g., with better efficiency, from different assumptions, etc.): this approach has been successfully adopted to construct several recent zkSNARKs. All this recent work, though, only shows that schemes obtained via this paradigm are knowledge-sound.

1.1 Our Work

We study the simulation extractability of a broad class of zkSNARKs built through this "natural" compilation approach. In particular, our primary goal includes showing that not only *existing* zkSNARKs but also any future zkSNARKs following this, by now standard, construction framework, provide simulation extractability. This goal has a twofold motivation. On the theoretical side, we are interested in understanding sufficient conditions on F-COM to compile an F-IOP into a simulation-extractable zkSNARK. On the practical side, by capturing existing compilers we can show that existing schemes that are under deployment, e.g., Plonk [28], have already this strong security property.[1]

---

[1] In fact as Mahak Pancholi and Akira Takahashi recently informed us of a flaw in the trapdoor-less zero-knowledge simulation of [29] this is arguably the first proof of simulation extractability of Plonk with deterministic KZG commitments.

For this reason, in our work, we focus on the popular case of the compiler where the F-IOP is a polynomial IOP (i.e., the oracle functions F are low-degree polynomials), and F-COM is a polynomial commitment. Furthermore, in terms of instantiations we are interested in covering the celebrated KZG polynomial commitment scheme [40] and on a polynomial IOP framework that is flexible enough to include recent constructions, e.g., [17,20,28,43,46]. The main contributions of our work are: (i) to introduce a relaxed notion of simulation extractability for polynomial commitments; (ii) to prove that the KZG scheme satisfies our relaxed SE notion in the algebraic group model (AGM) and random oracle model (ROM); and (iii) to prove that our notion is sufficient to compile a polynomial IOP into a simulation-extractable zkSNARK, using the usual compilation approach. By combining these results we obtain a simulation extractability proof for Plonk [28], Basilisk [46], and a slight variation of Marlin [20] and Lunar [17].

1.2   Our Techniques

Background. For our work, we chose the class of Polynomial (Holographic) IOPs (PIOP) as defined by [17] as a generalization of [16].[2] The oracle of the prover commits to low-degree polynomials over a finite field while the queries of the verifier check polynomial equations over these polynomials. These polynomial equations can depend on additional field elements sent by the prover and/or the verifier during the execution of the protocol. Slightly more in detail, the verifier can query an oracle polynomial $p(X)$ (or multiple polynomials simultaneously) by specifying polynomials G and v to test equations of the form $G(X, p(v(X))) \equiv 0$. Therefore, to be compiled, PIOPs need a commit-and-prove SNARK (CP-SNARK) for proving the validity of such equations concerning the committed polynomials. Notably, one can easily build this CP-SNARK from a CP-SNARK for polynomial evaluations (e.g., KZG) by testing the equations on a random point chosen by the random oracle.

Simulation Extractability Challenges. Intuitively, the use of a simulation-extractable CP-SNARK in the above compiler should result in a simulation-extractable zkSNARK: the zero-knowledge simulator samples random commitments (relying either on hiding property of commitments, or the randomness in the committed functions p). It then simulates evaluations of p that satisfy the verification equation of the PIOP. The reduction to PIOP soundness extracts all committed polynomials from their opening proofs and the final polynomial evaluations from the evaluation proofs. However, this approach presents two major challenges:

– The PIOP could be arbitrary. For example, consider a PIOP obtained by the sequential composition of two PIOP protocols for two independent statements. Very likely, the set of queries to the polynomials made by the two sub-protocols

---

[2] PIOPs can flexibly capture under the same hat all the most recent protocols based on the notions of [16], AHP [20], and ILDP [28].

are independent and (unless the PIOP specifies it explicitly) the evaluation queries of the first sub-protocol may be chosen based on the verifier's random challenges sent *before* the second sub-protocol even starts. The simulation extractability of the zkSNARK compiled from this protocol might be affected because one could strip off the second set of evaluation proofs and replace them with those for another statement[3].
- One needs to prove that existing, efficient, and practically deployable instantiations of polynomial commitment schemes are simulation-extractable.

Our Solutions. To solve the first challenge, motivated by our goal to show that existing zkSNARKs are simulation-extractable and that future zkSNARKs can seamlessly achieve simulation extractability, we define a (rather minimal) constraint on the PIOP. Namely, we require that at least one of the polynomial equations involves all the oracle polynomials and that the polynomial v chosen by the verifier (see above) is not constant.[4] Fortunately, this constraint is natural and easy to meet in practice: Plonk naturally meets our constraint meanwhile all the other proof systems based on Aurora's univariate sumcheck [8] can be easily (and at negligible cost) adapted by instantiating the proof of polynomial degree through an evaluation query on all the polynomials.

For the second challenge, unfortunately, the issue is that the most obvious candidate, the efficient and widely deployed KZG polynomial commitment scheme [40], is not simulation-extractable. Using bracket notation, KZG commitments are of the form $[p(s)]_1$ for a trapdoor secret s encoded in the parameters $([s^i]_1)_{i \in [0..d]}, [1, s]_2$, while evaluation proofs for an input x and output y are of the form $[\frac{p(s)-y}{s-x}]_1$. KZG is malleable: for example, given a commitment to p, anyone can compute $[p(s) + \Delta]_1$ and open it using the same proof to $(x, y + \Delta)$.

Our starting point is the observation that KZG retains a form of simulation extractability for evaluations at points that are randomly chosen *after* the commitment. Fortunately, this is the situation we encounter in the Fiat-Shamir part of the PIOP-to-SNARK compiler. The commitment forms part of the first commit-and-prove part of the statement which is hashed to determine the x of the second part of the statement. Thus, the evaluation point depends on the commitment and can be considered random in the RO model.

To formalize this important relaxation, we introduce the notion of policy-based simulation extractability (Φ-SE, w.r.t. a policy parameter Φ). In the standard simulation extractability experiment, the adversary can ask the simulator to generate proofs for statements of its choice and, eventually, must produce a *new* valid proof without knowing the witness. In Φ-SE, we consider a relaxation of the SE game in which all the simulation queries of the adversary must

---

[3] In particular, the adversary could have a simulated proof $\tilde{\pi} = (\pi, \pi')$ for (x, x') and then could choose x'' for which it knows a valid witness, and finally forge for (x, x'') using (π, π''), where π'' is honestly generated. As the simulated proof π is reused, extraction fails. Notice that this attack works even when the Fiat-Shamir challenges for π'' are derived by hashing a transcript that contains π.

[4] This can be for example implemented via a common random point chosen at the end of the protocol, on which all oracles are evaluated.

satisfy a predicate specified in Φ; similarly, Φ can constrain the winning condition of the adversary. For this reason, we refer to Φ as the *policy*. One can see that Φ-SE is a generalization of existing SE notions such as true-simulation extractability (where the adversary can only see simulated proofs on true statements) [22], or weak simulation extractability (where the adversary only wins if it provides a proof for a new statement and, contrary to (strong) SE, loses if it provides a new proof for a statement previously asked to the simulation oracle). Once having defined this framework, we analyze which policies Φ are strong enough to achieve simulation extractability in the compiled zkSNARK, while at the same time being weak enough for instantiation by KZG under plausible assumptions (in the AGM [27] and RO). Specifically, we isolate the (simulation) extractability properties needed for the compiler and verify it for KZG in the AGM. This is the only part of our results where we need the AGM. Given the broad applications of KZG in the field of practical zkSNARKs and beyond, the characterization of its (non-)malleability is interesting in its own right. In fact, our policy highlights some malleability attacks that we discovered and that we needed to handle. Finally, for our Φ we prove that KZG is Φ-SE in the AGM and ROM. This proof turned out to be highly non-trivial and is one of our main technical contributions.

1.3   Related Work

It is hard to be exhaustive, or even representative, in discussing related work on SNARKs. For the sake of our paper, we focus on related work on simulation extractability notions. Groth and Maller [38] give a simulation-extractable zkSNARK that consists of only 3 group elements. Their construction is neither universal nor updatable. The recent work of Ganesh, Orlandi, Pancholi, Takahashi and Tschudi [31] shows that Bulletproofs [14] are non-malleable in AGM. More recently, Dao and Grubbs show that Spartan and Bulletproofs are non-malleable even without AGM [21]. Both Ganesh et al. and Dao et al. work extend the framework introduced by Faust, Kohlweiss, Marson and Venturi in [25] to Fiat-Shamir applied to multi-round interactive arguments. On a similar path, the work of Ganesh, Khoshakhlagh, Kohlweiss, Nitulescu and Zajac [29] shows non-malleability for Plonk, Sonic and Marlin. Both [29,31] show that interactive *arguments* can be simulation-extractable after applying the Fiat-Shamir transform. In particular, their approach consists of defining new properties, like trapdoor-less zero-knowledge[5] and unique response[6] that *need to be proven on a case-by-case basis*. Namely, for each candidate SNARK (even if resulting from a generic compiler) one needs additional effort to show that it is simulation extractable. This is arguably more challenging and less generic than our approach. Thanks to our result, once having a Φ-SE polynomial commitment, one only needs to check a very simple property on the polynomial IOP.

---

[5] That is zero-knowledge where the simulator does not rely on the SRS's trapdoor but on the programmability of the random oracle.

[6] That is, at some point of the protocol, the prover becomes a deterministic algorithm.

The work of Abdolmaleki, Ramacher and Slamanig [2] shows a generic compiler to simulation-extractable SNARKs which requires key-homomorphic signatures. Their compiler produces universally-composable SNARKs (UC-SNARKs), which they prove through a black-box straight-line extractor. To obtain a black-box straight-line extractor, they append to the SNARK proof an encryption of the witness, thus achieving a relaxed succinctness w.r.t. the size of the circuit describing the relation. The recent work of Ganesh, Kondi, Orlandi, Pancholi and Takahashi [30] shows how to regain full succinctness in UC-SNARKs in the ROM through Fischlin's transform [26].

1.4 Open Problems

Our framework is general enough to handle compilation from polynomial commitment schemes different than KZG. Our contribution identifies a set of properties that a polynomial commitment scheme needs to have so that the resulting SNARK is simulation-extractable. We believe that thanks to the non-malleability of random oracles the FRI scheme [10] readily possesses the necessary properties, which would imply the simulation extractability of STARKs [6].

Another advantage of our formalization of PIOP over previous proposals such as [16] is that it naturally supports optimization tricks in the literature [17]. As an intermediate step of our compiler, we define a CP-SNARK for polynomial evaluations based on KZG. While we capture the important use case of batched evaluations on a common point, for the sake of simplicity, we leave further extensions and optimizations for future work. In particular, we do not capture the case of proving evaluations on *arbitrary* linear combinations of committed polynomials. We believe this extension could be handled at the PIOP level by extending the notion to *virtual* oracle polynomials obtained through linear combinations of other oracles (and thus using the homomorphic property of KZG). We leave open the problem to extend our result to other polynomial IOP models.

Recent works extend the polynomial evaluation proofs of KZG to multiple evaluation points [49,50]. Our simulation extractability strategy for KZG can be applied partially to these schemes; however, our technique uses a clever argument to separate the realm of commitments from the realm of proofs (in KZG proofs and commitments are both of the form $[p(s)]_1$ for some polynomial p) based on their degree as polynomials. Unfortunately, the same technique does not work when the degree of the polynomial in the proof depends on the number of evaluation points in the proved statement.

2   Preliminaries

A function f is negligible in λ (we write $f \in \mathsf{negl}(\lambda)$) if it approaches zero faster than the reciprocal of any polynomial: i.e., for every $c \in \mathbb{N}$ there is an integer λ_c such that $f(\lambda) \leq \lambda^{-c}$ for all $\lambda \geq \lambda_c$. For an integer $n \geq 1$, we use $[n]$ to denote the set $\{1, 2, \ldots, n\}$. Calligraphic letters denote sets, while set sizes are written as $|\mathcal{X}|$. Lists are represented as ordered tuples, e.g. $L :=$

$(L_i)_{i \in [n]}$ is a shortcut for the list of n elements $(L_1, \ldots, L_n)$. To get a specific value from a list, we also use the "dot" notation; e.g., we use $L.b$ to access the second element of the list $L := (a, b, c)$. An asymmetric bilinear group $\mathbb{G}$ is a tuple $(q, \mathbb{G}_1, \mathbb{G}_2, \mathbb{G}_T, e, P_1, P_2)$, where $\mathbb{G}_1, \mathbb{G}_2$ and $\mathbb{G}_T$ are groups of prime order q, the elements P_1, P_2 are generators of $\mathbb{G}_1, \mathbb{G}_2$ respectively, $e \colon \mathbb{G}_1 \times \mathbb{G}_2 \to \mathbb{G}_T$ is an efficiently-computable non-degenerate bilinear map, and there is no efficiently computable isomorphism between $\mathbb{G}_1$ and $\mathbb{G}_2$. Let GroupGen be some probabilistic polynomial-time (PPT) algorithm which on input 1^λ, where λ is the security parameter, returns a description of a bilinear group $\mathcal{G}$. Elements in $\mathbb{G}_i, i \in \{1, 2, T\}$ are denoted in implicit notation as $[a]_i := aP_i$, where $P_T := e(P_1, P_2)$. Every element in $\mathbb{G}_i$ can be written as $[a]_i$ for some $a \in \mathbb{Z}_q$, but note that, given $[a]_i$, it is in general hard to compute a (discrete logarithm problem). Given $a, b \in \mathbb{Z}_q$ we distinguish between $[ab]_i$, namely the group element whose discrete logarithm base $\mathcal{P}_i$ is ab, and $[a]_i \cdot b$, namely the execution of the multiplication of $[a]_i$ and b, and $[a]_1 \cdot [b]_2 = [a \cdot b]_T$, namely the execution of a pairing between $[a]_1$ and $[b]_2$. We do not use the implicit notation for variables, e.g. $\mathsf{c} = [a]_1$ indicates that c is a variable name for the group element whose logarithm is a.

Definition 1 (Algebraic algorithm, [27]). *An algorithm $\mathcal{A}$ is algebraic if for all group elements z that $\mathcal{A}$ outputs (either as returned by $\mathcal{A}$ or by invoking an oracle), it additionally provides the representation of z relative to all previously received group elements. That is, if elems is the list of group elements that $\mathcal{A}$ has received so far, then $\mathcal{A}$ must also provide a vector $\mathbf{r}$ such that $\mathsf{z} = \langle \mathbf{r}, \mathsf{elems} \rangle$.*

Definition 2 (Polynomial Commitment). *A polynomial commitment is a tuple of algorithms $\mathsf{PC} := (\mathsf{KGen}, \mathsf{Com}, \mathsf{VerCom})$ that works as follows:*

$\mathsf{KGen}(\mathsf{pp}_\mathbb{G}, d) \to \mathsf{ck}$ *takes as input group parameters $\mathsf{pp}_\mathbb{G} \leftarrow\!\!\$ \; \mathsf{GroupGen}(1^\lambda)$, and a degree bound d, and outputs a commitment key ck.*

$\mathsf{Com}(\mathsf{ck}, f) \to (c, o)$ *takes as input the commitment key ck, and a low degree polynomial $f \in \mathbb{F}_{\leq d}[X]$, and outputs a commitment c and an opening o.*

$\mathsf{VerCom}(\mathsf{ck}, c, f, o) \to b$ *takes as input ck, a commitment c, a polynomial f and an opening o, and accepts ($b = 1$) or rejects ($b = 0$).*

Definition 3 (Witness Sampleability, [39]). *A distribution $\mathcal{D}$ is witness samplable if there is a PPT algorithm $\tilde{\mathcal{D}}$ s.t. for any $\mathsf{pp}_\mathbb{G}$, the random variables $\mathbf{A} \leftarrow\!\!\$ \; \mathcal{D}(\mathsf{pp}_\mathbb{G})$ and $\left[\tilde{\mathbf{A}}\right]_1$, where $\tilde{\mathbf{A}} \leftarrow\!\!\$ \; \tilde{\mathcal{D}}(\mathsf{pp}_\mathbb{G})$, are equivalently distributed.*

Definition 4 ($\mathcal{D}_{\ell,k}$-Aff-MDH assumption). *Given a matrix distribution $\mathcal{D}_{\ell,k}$, the Affine Diffie-Hellman Problem is: given $\mathbf{A} \in \mathbb{G}_1^{\ell \times k}$, with $\mathbf{A} \leftarrow\!\!\$ \; \mathcal{D}_{\ell,k}$, find a nonzero vector $\mathbf{x} \in \mathbb{Z}_q^\ell$ and a vector $\mathbf{y} \in \mathbb{Z}_q^k$ such that $\left[\mathbf{x}^\top \mathbf{A}\right]_1 = [\mathbf{y}]_1$.*

Definition 5 ((d, d')-Power Polynomial in the Exponent). *The (d, d')-PEA Assumption holds for a bilinear group generator GroupGen if for every PPT adversary $\mathcal{A}$ that receives as input $\left(\left[1, \ldots, s^d\right]_1, \left[1, \ldots, s^{d'}\right]_2\right)$ and outputs a polynomial $p(X)$ of degree at most $\max\{d, d'\}$, and a value y, the probability that $p(s) = y$ is negligible. When $d = d'$ we use the shortcut d-PEA.*

Definition 6 (d-Power Discrete Logarithm [42]). *Given a degree bound $d \in \mathbb{N}$, the d-Power Discrete Logarithm (d-DL) assumption holds for a bilinear group generator GroupGen if for every PPT adversary $\mathcal{A}$ that receives as input $([1, \ldots, s^d]_1, [1, \ldots, s^d]_2)$, and outputs the value s', the probability that $s = s'$ is negligible. We also use DL as a shortcut for 1-DL.*

Lemma 1 (d-DL $\Rightarrow$ d-PEA). *We can make a reduction to the assumption that computes s. The reduction invokes the adversary, gets $p(X) - y$ of degree d, and computes s by factoring the polynomial $p(s) - y$. As $p(s) - y = 0$ we are guaranteed that s is a root.*

Lemma 2 (DL $\Rightarrow$ $\mathcal{U}_{\ell,k}$-Aff-MDH). *When considering the uniform random distribution $\mathcal{U}_{\ell,k}$, we can make a reduction to the assumption that computes s. The reduction samples at the exponent a uniformly random matrix $A = (a_{i,j})_{i,j} \in \mathbb{Z}_q^{\ell \times k}$ and invokes the adversary on input $[(a_{i,j})_{i,j}]_1$. Finally, let $p_i(s)$ be the i-the row of $x^\top A$. The reduction computes s by factoring one of the k polynomials $p_i(s) - y_i$.*

3   Policy-Based Simulation-Extractable NIZKs

We start by defining the basic syntax and properties for a Non-Interactive Zero-Knowledge Argument of Knowledge. Following Groth et al. [37], we define a PT relation $\mathcal{R}$ verifying triple (pp, x, w). We say that w is a witness to the instance x being in the relation defined by the parameters pp when (pp, x, w) $\in$ $\mathcal{R}$ (equivalently, we sometimes write $\mathcal{R}$(pp, x, w) = 1). For example, pp could be the description of a bilinear group or additionally contain a commitment key or a common reference string. A NIZK for a relation $\mathcal{R}$ (and group generator GroupGen) is a tuple of algorithms Π = (KGen, Prove, Verify) where:

- KGen(pp$_\mathbb{G}$) $\to$ srs is a probabilistic algorithm that takes as input the parameters pp$_\mathbb{G}$ $\leftarrow$\$ GroupGen(1^λ) and outputs srs := (ek, vk, pp), where ek is the evaluation key, vk is the verification key, and pp are the parameters for $\mathcal{R}$.
- Prove(ek, x, w) $\to$ π takes an evaluation key ek, a statement x, and a witness w such that $\mathcal{R}$(pp, x, w) holds, and returns a proof π.
- Verify(vk, x, π) $\to$ b takes a verification key, a statement x, and either accepts ($b = 1$) or rejects ($b = 0$) the proof π.

Definition 7 (Succinctness). *A NIZK Π is said succinct if the running time of Verify is poly($\lambda + |x| + \log |w|$) and the proof size is poly($\lambda + \log |w|$).*

CP-SNARKs. Commit-and-Prove succinct arguments of knowledge, or simply CP-SNARKs, are knowledge-sound and succinct NIZKs whose relations verify predicates over commitments (see Campanelli, Fiore and Querol [18]). We consider the following syntax. Briefly speaking, we refer to a CP-SNARK for a relation $\mathcal{R}$ and a commitment scheme CS as a tuple of algorithms CP = (KGen, Prove, Verify) where KGen(ck) $\to$ srs is an algorithm that takes as input a commitment key ck for CS and outputs srs := (ek, vk, pp); ek is the evaluation key, vk is the verification key, and pp are the parameters for the relation $\mathcal{R}$ (which include the commitment key ck). Moreover, if we consider the key generation algorithm KGen′ that upon group parameters pp_G first runs ck ←$ CS.KGen(pp_G), runs srs ←$ CP.KGen(ck) and outputs srs; then the tuple (KGen′, Prove, Verify) defines a SNARK.

Zero-Knowledge in the SRS (and RO) Model. The zero-knowledge simulator $\mathcal{S}$ of a NIZK is a stateful PPT algorithm that can operate in three modes:

- (srs, st_S) ← $\mathcal{S}(0, pp_G)$ takes care of generating the parameters and the simulation trapdoor (if necessary)
- (π, st_S) ← $\mathcal{S}(1, st_S, x)$ simulates the proof for a statement x
- (a, st_S) ← $\mathcal{S}(2, st_S, s)$ takes care of answering random oracle queries

The state st_S is updated after each operation. Similarly to [25, 31], we define the following wrappers.

Definition 8 (Wrappers for NIZK Simulator). *The following algorithms are stateful and share their state* st = (st_S, coms, $\mathcal{Q}_{sim}$, $\mathcal{Q}_{RO}$, $\mathcal{Q}_{aux}$) *where* st_S *is initially set to be the empty string, and* $\mathcal{Q}_{sim}$, $\mathcal{Q}_{RO}$ *and* $\mathcal{Q}_{aux}$ *are initially set to be the empty sets.*

- $\mathcal{S}_1(x, aux)$ *is an oracle that returns the first output of* $\mathcal{S}(1, st_S, x, aux)$.[7]
- $\mathcal{S}_1'(x, w)$ *is an oracle that first checks* (pp, x, w) $\in \mathcal{R}$ *where* pp *is part of* srs *and then runs (and returns the output of)* $\mathcal{S}_1(x)$.
- $\mathcal{S}_1^F(x, w)$ *is an oracle parameterized by a function F; first, it checks if* (pp, x, w) $\in \mathcal{R}$, *and then runs (and returns the output of)* $\mathcal{S}_1(x, F(x, w))$. *As explained below, this is useful to model leaky-zero-knowledge.*
- $\mathcal{S}_2(s, aux)$ *is an oracle that first checks if the query s is already present in* $\mathcal{Q}_{RO}$ *and in case answers accordingly, otherwise it returns the first output a of* $\mathcal{S}(2, st_S, s)$. *Additionally, the oracle updates the set* $\mathcal{Q}_{RO}$ *by adding the tuple* (s, aux, a) *to the set.*

Almost all the oracles in our definitions can take auxiliary information as additional input. We use this auxiliary information in a rather liberal form. For example, in the definition above, the auxiliary information for $\mathcal{S}_1$ refers to the (optional) leakage required by the simulator to work in some cases (see more in Definition 10), while the auxiliary information for $\mathcal{S}_2$ can contain, for example, the algebraic representations of the group elements in s (when we restrict to algebraic adversaries) or other information the security experiments might need.

Definition 9 (Zero-Knowledge). *A NIZK* NIZK *is (perfect) zero-knowledge if there exists a PPT simulator S such that for all adversaries* $\mathcal{A}$:

$$\Pr \begin{bmatrix} pp_G \leftarrow GroupGen(1^\lambda) \\ srs \leftarrow KGen(pp_G) \\ \mathcal{A}^{Prove(ek,\cdot,\cdot)}(srs) = 1 \end{bmatrix} \approx \Pr \begin{bmatrix} pp_G \leftarrow GroupGen(1^\lambda) \\ (srs, st_S) \leftarrow \mathcal{S}(0, pp_G) \\ \mathcal{A}^{\mathcal{S}_1'(\cdot,\cdot)}(srs) = 1 \end{bmatrix}$$

---

[7] More often, simulators need only the first three inputs, see Definition 9; abusing notation, we assume that such simulators simply ignore the auxiliary input aux.

Zero-knowledge is a security property that is only guaranteed for valid statements in the language, hence the above definition uses $\mathcal{S}'_1$ as a proof simulation oracle.

We also introduce a weaker notion of zero-knowledge. A NIZK is F-leaky zero-knowledge if its proofs may leak some information, namely a proof leaks $F(\mathbb{x}, \mathbb{w})$, where $(\mathbb{x}, \mathbb{w}) \in \mathcal{R}$. We formalize this by giving the zero-knowledge simulator the value $F(\mathbb{x}, \mathbb{w})$, which should be interpreted as a hint for the simulation of proofs. This notion could be seen as an extension of the bounded leaky zero-knowledge property defined in [17] and tailored for CP-SNARKs. Our notion is a special case of the leakage-resilient zero-knowledge framework of Garg, Jain and Sahai [32] where the leakage of the simulator is known ahead of time.

Definition 10 (Leaky Zero-Knowledge). *A NIZK* NIZK *is F-leaky zero-knowledge if there exists a PPT simulator $\mathcal{S}$ such that for all adversaries $\mathcal{A}$:*

$$\Pr\left[\begin{array}{l} \mathsf{pp}_\mathbb{G} \leftarrow \mathsf{GroupGen}(1^\lambda) \\ \mathsf{srs} \leftarrow \mathsf{KGen}(\mathsf{pp}_\mathbb{G}) \\ \mathcal{A}^{\mathsf{Prove}(\mathsf{ek},\cdot,\cdot)}(\mathsf{srs}) = 1 \end{array}\right] \approx \Pr\left[\begin{array}{l} \mathsf{pp}_\mathbb{G} \leftarrow \mathsf{GroupGen}(1^\lambda) \\ (\mathsf{srs}, \mathsf{st}_\mathcal{S}) \leftarrow \mathcal{S}(0, \mathsf{pp}_\mathbb{G}) \\ \mathcal{A}^{\mathcal{S}_1^F(\cdot,\cdot)}(\mathsf{srs}) = 1 \end{array}\right]$$

3.1   Policy-Based Simulation Extractability

An extraction policy defines the constraints under which the extractor must extract the witness. For example, we could consider the policy that checks that the forged instance and proof were not queried/output by the zero-knowledge simulator (thus modeling the classical simulation extractability notion), or we could consider a policy that only checks that the forged instance was not queried to the simulator, thus obtaining a weaker flavor of classical simulation extractability. Clearly, the more permissive the policy the stronger the security provided.

In our work, we also consider policies that constrain the behavior of the zero-knowledge simulator. For example, we could consider the policy that checks that the queried instances belong to the relation, thus obtaining a notion similar to true-simulation extractability (see Dodis et al. [22]). Looking ahead, contrary to the true-simulation extractability notion in [22], our policy-based version of the true-simulation extractability rather than disallowing certain queries, punishes the adversary at extraction time. It is not hard to see that the two definitional flavors, namely disallowing illegal queries versus punishing an adversary that made an illegal query are equivalent in the context of simulation extractability, because the adversary's goal is computational[8].

Extraction Policies. We define an extraction policy as a tuple $\Phi = (\Phi_0, \Phi_1)$ of PPT algorithms. This is used to define Φ-simulation extractability as follows. The security experiment starts by running the extraction policy algorithm Φ_0, which generates public information pp_Φ. The public information may contain,

---

[8] Observe that for decisional tasks disallowing and punishing flavors can result in different security notions, see Bellare, Hofheinz and Kiltz [5].

for example, random values that define the constraints later checked by Φ_1. Therefore, we feed pp_Φ to the adversary. In the case of commit-and-prove proof systems, the public information may contain commitments for which the adversary does not know openings (but on which it can still query simulated proofs). After receiving a forgery from the adversary, the security experiment runs the extraction policy Φ_1. The policy Φ_1 is a predicate that takes as input: (i) The public parameter pp_Φ; (ii) The forged instance and proof (x, π); (iii) The view of the experiment, denoted view. Such a view contains the public parameters, the set of simulated instances and proofs $\mathcal{Q}_{sim}$, and the set $\mathcal{Q}_{RO}$ of queries and answers to the random oracle[9]; (iv) Auxiliary information aux_Φ which might come along with the forged instance. We use aux_Φ to provide the adversary an interface with the policy.

Definition 11 (Simulation extractability). *A NIZK Π for a relation $\mathcal{R}$ and simulator $\mathcal{S}$ is Φ-simulation-extractable if for every PPT adversary $\mathcal{A}$ there is an efficient extractor $\mathcal{E}$ such that the following advantage is negligible in λ:*

$$\mathbf{Adv}^{\Phi\text{-}se}_{\Pi,\mathcal{A},\mathcal{S},\mathcal{E}}(\lambda) := \Pr\left[\mathbf{Exp}^{\Phi\text{-}se}_{\Pi,\mathcal{A},\mathcal{S},\mathcal{E}}(\lambda) = 1\right]$$

Below, we give a definition that explicitly considers the sub-class of PPT algebraic adversaries. To fit algebraic adversaries into our definitional framework we let the algebraic adversaries return the representation vectors (1) for any query to the simulator $\mathcal{S}$ into the auxiliary information aux and (2) for the forgery into the auxiliary information $aux_\mathcal{E}$.

Definition 12 (Simulation extractability in the AGM). *Let Π be a NIZK for a relation $\mathcal{R}$ with a simulator $\mathcal{S}$. Π is Φ-simulation-extractable (or simply Φ-SE) if there exists an efficient extractor $\mathcal{E}$ such that for every PPT algebraic adversary $\mathcal{A}$, the advantage $\mathbf{Adv}^{\Phi\text{-}se}_{\Pi,\mathcal{A},\mathcal{S},\mathcal{E}}(\lambda)$ (cf. Definition 11) is negligible in λ.*

4   Simulation Extractability of KZG in AGM

KZG [40] is a Polynomial Commitment scheme (see Definition 2) defined over bilinear groups $\mathbb{G} = (\mathbb{G}_1, \mathbb{G}_2, \mathbb{G}_T, e)$, that consists of the following algorithms:

$KGen(1^\lambda, d)$ on input the security parameter 1^λ, and a degree bound $d \in \mathbb{N}$, outputs $ck := (([s^j]_1)_{j \in [0,d]}, [1, s]_2)$, for secret $s \leftarrow\!\!\$\ \mathbb{F}_q$.
$Com(ck, f(X))$ on input ck, a polynomial $f(X)$, outputs $c := [f(s)]_1$.
$VerCom(ck, c, f(X))$ outputs 1 if $c = [f(s)]_1$.

The above scheme is (standard) binding under the d-DL assumption (see [35]), in fact, given two polynomials f and f' that evaluate to the same value on the secret point s, we can find s among the roots of the (non-zero) polynomial $f - f'$.

---

[9] Even if the given NIZK is not in the random oracle (namely neither the prover nor the verifier algorithms make random oracle queries) it still makes sense to assume the existence of the set $\mathcal{Q}_{RO}$. This is useful to model security for NIZK protocols that eventually are used as sub-protocols in ROM-based protocols.

$$\begin{array}{ll}
\underline{\mathsf{Exp}^{\varPhi\text{-}se}_{\mathcal{A},\mathcal{S},\mathcal{E}}(\lambda)} & \underline{\mathcal{S}_1(\mathbb{x},\mathsf{aux}):} \\[2pt]
\mathsf{pp}_{\mathbb{G}} \leftarrow\!\!\$\ \mathsf{GroupGen}(1^\lambda) & \pi,\mathsf{st}_{\mathcal{S}} \leftarrow \mathcal{S}(1,\mathsf{st}_{\mathcal{S}},\mathbb{x},\mathsf{aux}) \\
(\mathsf{srs},\mathsf{st}_{\mathcal{S}}) \leftarrow \mathcal{S}(0,\mathsf{pp}_{\mathbb{G}}) & \mathcal{Q}_{\mathsf{sim}} \leftarrow \mathcal{Q}_{\mathsf{sim}} \cup \{(\mathbb{x},\mathsf{aux},\pi)\} \\
\mathsf{pp}_{\varPhi} \leftarrow\!\!\$\ \varPhi_0(\mathsf{pp}_{\mathbb{G}}) & \mathbf{return}\ \pi \\
(\mathbb{x},\pi,\mathsf{aux}_{\mathcal{E}},\mathsf{aux}_{\varPhi}) \leftarrow \mathcal{A}^{\mathcal{S}_1,\mathcal{S}_2}(\mathsf{srs},\mathsf{pp}_{\varPhi}) & \\
\mathbb{w} \leftarrow \mathcal{E}(\mathsf{srs},\mathbb{x},\pi,\mathsf{aux}_{\mathcal{E}}) & \underline{\mathcal{S}_2(s,\mathsf{aux}):} \\
\mathsf{view} \leftarrow (\mathsf{srs},\mathsf{pp}_{\varPhi},\mathcal{Q}_{\mathsf{sim}},\mathcal{Q}_{\mathsf{RO}},\mathcal{Q}_{\mathsf{aux}}) & \mathbf{if}\ \nexists\ \mathsf{aux},a:(s,\mathsf{aux},a)\in\mathcal{Q}_{\mathsf{RO}}: \\
\mathbf{if}\ \varPhi_1((\mathbb{x},\pi),\mathsf{view},\mathsf{aux}_{\varPhi}) \wedge \mathsf{Verify}^{\mathcal{S}_2}(\mathsf{srs},\mathbb{x},\pi) & \quad a,\mathsf{st}_{\mathcal{S}} \leftarrow \mathcal{S}(2,\mathsf{st}_{\mathcal{S}},s,\mathsf{aux}) \\
\quad \wedge\ (\mathsf{pp},\mathbb{x},\mathbb{w}) \notin \mathcal{R}\ \mathbf{then\ return}\ 1 & \quad \mathcal{Q}_{\mathsf{RO}} \leftarrow \mathcal{Q}_{\mathsf{RO}} \cup \{(s,\mathsf{aux},a)\} \\
\mathbf{else\ return}\ 0 & \mathbf{return}\ a
\end{array}$$

Fig. 1. The $\varPhi$-simulation extractability experiments in ROM. The extraction policy $\varPhi$ takes as input the public view of the adversary view (namely, all the inputs received and all the queries and answers to its oracles). The set $\mathcal{Q}_{\mathsf{sim}}$ is the set of queries and answers to the simulation oracle. The set $\mathcal{Q}_{\mathsf{RO}}$ is the set of queries and answers to the random oracle. The set $\mathcal{Q}_{\mathsf{aux}}$ is the set of all the auxiliary information sent by the adversary (depending on the policy, this set might be empty or not). The wrappers $\mathcal{S}_1$ and $\mathcal{S}_2$ deal respectively with the simulation queries and the random oracle queries of $\mathcal{A}$ in the experiment.

We consider a CP-SNARK $\mathsf{CP}_{\mathsf{evl}}$ for the relation $\mathcal{R}_{\mathsf{evl}}((x,y),f) := f(x) = y$, where f is committed as $[f(s)]_1$. The scheme constructed in this section requires one $\mathbb{G}_1$ element to commit to $f(X)$, one $\mathbb{G}_1$ element for the evaluation proof, and checking this proof of evaluation requires two pairings, and is knowledge extractable in the AGM [20]. This is taken from [17] but adapted to AGM only.

$\mathsf{KGen}_{\mathsf{evl}}$: parse ck as $(([s^j]_1)_{j\in[0,d]},[1,s]_2)$ and define $\mathsf{ek} := \mathsf{ck}$ and $\mathsf{vk} := [1,s]_2$, and return $\mathsf{srs} := (\mathsf{ek},\mathsf{vk})$.

$\mathsf{Prove}_{\mathsf{evl}}(\mathsf{ek},\mathbb{x} = (\mathsf{c},x,y),\mathbb{w} = f)$: output $\pi := [\pi(s)]_1$, where $\pi(X)$ is the polynomial such that $\pi(X)(X - x) \equiv f(X) - y$.

$\mathsf{Verify}_{\mathsf{evl}}(\mathsf{vk},\mathbb{x} = (\mathsf{c},x,y),\pi)$: output 1 iff $e(\mathsf{c} - [y]_1,[1]_2) = e(\pi,[s - x]_2)$.

The Extraction Policy for $\mathsf{CP}_{\mathsf{evl}}$. We define $\boldsymbol{\varPhi}^{\mathsf{s\text{-}adpt}}_{\mathsf{evl}} = \{\varPhi_{\mathcal{D}}\}_{\mathcal{D}}$ as the family (indexed by a sampler $\mathcal{D}$) of *semi-adaptive* extraction policies for the KZG-based $\mathsf{CP}_{\mathsf{evl}}$ CP-SNARK. Indeed, as we show below, the evaluation points x_j for the instances for which the adversary can see simulated proofs are selectively chosen independently of the commitment key, while the evaluation values y can be adaptively chosen by the adversary. Each policy $\varPhi_{\mathcal{D}}$ is a tuple of the form $(\varPhi^{\mathcal{D}}_0,\varPhi_1)$, as defined in Sect. 3.1, where $\varPhi^{\mathcal{D}}_0$ outputs the parameters $\mathsf{pp}_{\varPhi}$ while $\varPhi_1$ outputs a bit. In particular, $\varPhi^{\mathcal{D}}_0$ on input group parameters $\mathsf{pp}_{\mathbb{G}}$ outputs $\mathsf{pp}_{\varPhi} := (\mathsf{coms},\mathcal{Q}_x)$, where coms is a vector of commitments sampled from $\mathcal{D}$, and $\mathcal{Q}_x$ is a set of evaluation points.

For sake of clarity, we define the policy $\varPhi_1$ as the logical conjunction of a "simulator" policy $\varPhi_{\mathsf{sim}}$ and an "extractor" policy $\varPhi_{\mathsf{ext}}$, i.e. $\varPhi_1 = \varPhi_{\mathsf{sim}} \wedge \varPhi_{\mathsf{ext}}$. The first policy defines rules under which we can classify a simulation query *legal*, while the second one defines rules under which the extractor must be able to extract a meaningful witness.

Definition 13. *Let Φ_{sim} be the policy that returns 1 if and only if:*

1. **Points check:** *let $(x_i, \text{aux}_i, \pi_i)_i$ be all the entries of $\mathcal{Q}_{\text{sim}}$. Recall that an instance x can be parsed as (c, x, y). Check that $\forall i : x_i.x \in \mathcal{Q}_x$.*
2. **Commitment Check:** *For all $i \in [Q_{\text{sim}}]$, parse aux_i as the representation vectors for $x_i.c$ and π_i such that $r_i = f_i \| c_i$ is the algebraic representation of the commitment $x_i.c$. For any i check that $\langle f_i, \text{ek} \rangle + \langle c_i, \text{coms} \rangle = x_i.c$.*
3. **Algebraic Consistency:** *Let $\mathcal{I}_j := \{i : x_i.x = x_j\}$ and let $R_j := (c_i)_{i \in \mathcal{I}_j}$. Check that $\forall j$: (i) the system of linear equations $R_j \cdot z = y_j$ has at least a solution, where z are the variables and $y_j = (x_i.y - \langle f_i, (1, x_j, \ldots, x_j^d) \rangle)_{i \in \mathcal{I}_j}$.*

In more intuitive terms, for every simulation query (c, x, y) made by the adversary: (1) ensures that x is in the set $\mathcal{Q}_x$ chosen at the beginning of the experiment (this is the semi-adaptive restriction); (2) ensures that c is computed as a linear combination of the simulated commitments and the $\mathbb{G}_1$ elements of the SRS, but *not of simulated proofs*; (3) ensures that overall the queried statements are plausibly true (e.g., the adversary does not ask to open the same (c, x) at two different $y \neq y'$). We notice that the "Algebraic Consistency" check is necessary since, if violated it would enable a class of generic attacks. We briefly mention one attack in the proof intuition and we refer the reader to [24] for the details.

Next, we define the policy Φ_{ext} as the logical disjunction of two policies, Φ_{ext}^{rnd} and Φ_{ext}^{der}. To this end, we first define some notation: let $g_c : \mathbb{G}_1 \times \{0,1\}^* \to \{0,1\}$ be a function that on inputs a group element c and a string s, that can be parsed as a list of group elements c_i followed by a second string $\tilde{s}$, outputs 1 iff $\exists i : c = c_i$.

Definition 14. *Let $\Phi_{\text{ext}}, \Phi_{\text{ext}}^{rnd}$ and Φ_{ext}^{der} be predicates that, parsing the forgery instance $x^* = (c^*, x^*, y^*)$, are defined as follows:*

- *Φ_{ext}^{rnd} returns 1 if and only if there exist a query (s, aux, a) to the random oracle and aux contains a non-constant polynomial $h(X)$ such that the following conditions are satisfied:*
  1. **Hashing check:** *$(s, \text{aux}, a) \in \mathcal{Q}_{\text{RO}}$, note that $\mathcal{Q}_{\text{RO}}$ is contained in view,*
  2. **Decoding check:** *$g_c(c^*, s) = 1$.*
  3. **Polynomial check:** *$g_h(h, \text{aux}) = 1$, where $g_h : \mathbb{F}[X] \times \{0,1\}^* \to \{0,1\}$ is a function that on input a polynomial $h(X)$ and a string aux outputs 1 iff $h(X)$ is encoded in aux.*
  4. **Computation check:** *$h(a) = x^*$.*
- *Φ_{ext}^{der} returns 1 iff $\exists (x, \cdot, \pi) \in \mathcal{Q}_{\text{sim}}$ s.t. $x := (c^*, x^*, y')$ and $(y', \pi) \neq (y^*, \pi^*)$.*
- *Φ_{ext} returns logical disjunction of Φ_{ext}^{rnd} and Φ_{ext}^{der}.*

More intuitively, Φ_{ext}^{rnd} checks that the point x^* is obtained from the random oracle *after* querying it on the commitment c^*, whereas Φ_{ext}^{der} checks if x^* is a strong forgery, namely it is a new evaluation proof for a statement (c^*, x^*) already queried to the simulation oracle.

Theorem 1. *For any witness samplable distribution $\mathcal{D}$ that is $\mathcal{D}$-Aff-MDH-secure (see Definition 4), any bilinear-group generator* GroupGen *that samples the generator of the group $\mathbb{G}_1$ uniformly at random, $\forall \Phi_{\mathcal{D}} \in \mathbf{\Phi}_{\text{evl}}^{\text{s-adpt}}$, KZG is $\Phi_{\mathcal{D}}$-simulation-extractable in the AGM. In particular, there exists $\mathcal{E}$ such that for any algebraic adversary $\mathcal{A}$:*

$$\mathbf{Adv}_{\mathsf{CP}_{\text{evl}},\mathcal{A},\mathcal{S},\mathcal{E}}^{\Phi_{\mathcal{D}}\text{-se}}(\lambda) \leq O(\epsilon_{(Q_x+d+1)\text{-DL}}(\lambda)) + O(\epsilon_{\text{Aff-MDH}}(\lambda)) + \mathsf{poly}(\lambda)\epsilon_h$$

where $Q_x := |\mathcal{Q}_x|$, d is the maximum degree supported by CP_{evl}, $\epsilon_{(Q_x+d+1)\text{-DL}}(\lambda)$ is the maximum advantage for any algebraic PT adversary against the $(Q_x + d + 1)$-strong Discrete-Log Assumption, $\epsilon_{\text{Aff-MDH}}(\lambda)$ is the maximum advantage for any algebraic PT adversary against the $\mathcal{D}$-Aff-MDH Assumption, h is the polynomial that satisfies the Polynomial check of $\Phi_{\mathcal{D}}$, and $\epsilon_h = \frac{\deg(h)}{q}$.

We show in the full version [24] how to generalize the scheme to support hiding commitments, and we extend our result to the hiding setting. Also, we consider a scheme $\mathsf{CP}_{\text{m-evl}}$ for batch evaluations which follows from [28,44].

Proof intuition of Theorem. 1 We consider an adversary whose forgery satisfies the predicate $\Phi_{\text{ext}}^{\text{rnd}}$. We first show an alternative way to simulate KZG proofs. This step allows one to move from a simulator whose trapdoor is a "secret exponent" s to a simulator whose trapdoor is a 'tower' of $\mathbb{G}_1$-elements $[s^i]_1$. The simulated SRS seen by the adversary includes only high-degree polynomials of the form $[p(s)s^i]_1$, while the simulator keeps the low-degree monomials $[s^i]_1$ for simulation. Here, p is a polynomial that vanishes in all the points to be asked in the simulation queries (this is reminiscent of the reduction technique for Boneh-Boyen signatures [11]). Since we program the SRS based on the queries our simulator is only *semi-adaptive*, namely it can simulate proofs for a (exponentially large) subset of all the statements. This first change essentially simplifies the objects involved in our analysis, from rational polynomials (with the formal variable being the trapdoor) to standard polynomials.

Next, we need to show that the adversary cannot mix the simulated commitments and the forgery material. In particular, we need to show that the forged proof is not derived as a linear combination involving simulated commitments. To show this, we use the fact that the degree of the proof must be smaller than the degrees of simulated commitments, otherwise we could break the d-DL assumption in the AGM. This intuitively comes from the fact that the verification equation *lifts* the degree of the polynomial in the forged proof (as it is multiplied by $(X - x^*)$). Similarly, we need to show that the forged instance cannot use a linear combination that involves the simulated commitments. For this, we use the Aff-MDH assumption to handle multiple evaluation proofs on different simulated commitments on the same evaluation point. In particular, we reduce the view of many simulated proofs over many commitments and many evaluation points to a view that only contains $[p(s)s^i]_1$ and (non-rational) polynomials $[p(s)/(s - x_j)]_1$. At this point, the attacker could still perform an attack if it could decide the evaluation point x^* arbitrarily. The attack works as follows:

(i) the adversary asks a simulation proof π for $\mathbf{x} = (\mathsf{c}, x, y)$, and (ii) produces the forgery $\mathbf{x}^* = (\mathsf{c} + \alpha\pi, x - \alpha, y), \pi$, for any $\alpha \in \mathbb{Z}_q$. It is easy to check that the forgery satisfies the verification equation. However, for this attack to work the attacker needs to set the commitment in the forged instance as a function of $x^* = x - \alpha$. The last part of our analysis shows that, indeed, the algebraic representation of the commitment in the forgery cannot depend on x^* and that this attack cannot be mounted when x^* is chosen after the commitment with sufficient randomness. For the second case, we can reduce a $\Phi_{\mathsf{ext}}^{\mathsf{der}}$ forgery to a $\Phi_{\mathsf{ext}}^{\mathsf{rnd}}$ forgery. In fact, such a forgery together with the simulated proofs set an algebraic inconsistency, a sub-case of the condition avoided by Item 3 of Definition 13, thus enabling an attack. In more detail, given a $\Phi_{\mathsf{ext}}^{\mathsf{der}}$-forgery $(\mathsf{c}, x, y), \pi$ and let $((\mathsf{c}, x, y'), \pi') \in \mathcal{Q}_{\mathsf{sim}}$ we can define a new $\Phi_{\mathsf{ext}}^{\mathsf{rnd}}$-forgery $(\mathsf{c}^*, x^*, y^*), \pi^*$ where $\mathsf{c}^* = (\pi' - \pi)$, $x^* = \mathsf{RO}(\mathsf{c}^*)$ and $\pi^* = \frac{\pi - \pi'}{x^* - x}$ and $y^* = \frac{y - y'}{x^* - x}$. We can prove that the verification equation holds noticing that $(\pi - \pi')(s - x) = [y - y']_1$ and by simple algebraic manipulations.

Proof (of Theorem 1). We stress that $\mathcal{A}$ is algebraic (cf. Definition 1), therefore for each group element output it additionally attaches a representation $\boldsymbol{r}$ of such a group element with respect to all the elements seen during the experiment (included elements in coms). In particular, we assume that for each query $(\mathbf{x}, \mathsf{aux})$ to the oracle $\mathcal{S}_1$ we can parse the value aux as $(\boldsymbol{r}, \mathsf{aux}')$ and $\boldsymbol{r}$ is a valid representation for $\mathbf{x}.\mathsf{c}$. Similarly, for the queries (s, aux) to $\mathcal{S}_2$, aux includes a valid representation for all the group elements $\mathbf{g}_i$ encoded in s, i.e. such that $g_c(\mathbf{g}_i, s) = 1$. Together with its forgery, the algebraic adversary encodes a polynomial $h(X)$ in aux_ϕ, and stores in $\mathsf{aux}_{\mathcal{E}}$ two representation vectors $\boldsymbol{r}_{\mathsf{c}^*}$ and $\boldsymbol{r}_{\pi^*}$ for the two group elements c^* and π^*. We can parse the vectors $\boldsymbol{r}_\tau := \boldsymbol{f}_\tau \| \boldsymbol{c}_\tau \| \boldsymbol{o}_\tau$ for $\tau \in \{\mathsf{c}^*, \pi^*\}$ where $\boldsymbol{f}_\tau$ is the vector of coefficients associated to group elements ek, $\boldsymbol{c}_\tau$ is the vector of coefficients associated to group elements $\mathsf{coms} = ([c_i]_1)_{i \in [Q_c]}$, and $\boldsymbol{o}_\tau$ is the vector of coefficients associated to the group elements of the simulated proofs proofs. Namely, for $\tau \in \{\mathsf{c}^*, \pi^*\}$ we have:

$$\tau = \langle \boldsymbol{f}_\tau, \mathsf{ek} \rangle + \langle \boldsymbol{c}_\tau, \mathsf{coms} \rangle + \langle \boldsymbol{o}_\tau, \mathsf{proofs} \rangle.$$

We can assume w.l.g. that all the simulation queries and the forgery of the adversary $\mathcal{A}$ agree with the policy $\Phi_{\mathcal{D}}$, as otherwise the adversary would automatically lose the experiment. We assume that $\boldsymbol{f}_{i,j} = \boldsymbol{0}, \forall i, j$, i.e., the adversary asks simulation queries on commitments that are a linear combination of coms only: this is also w.l.g. as we briefly show below. Given a commitement $\mathsf{c}_{i,j} = \mathbf{x}_{i,j}.\mathsf{c}$, whose representation is $\boldsymbol{r}_{i,j} = \boldsymbol{f}_{i,j} \| \boldsymbol{c}_{i,j}$, the adversary could compute a proof $\pi_{i,j}$ for the point x_j and the evaluation value y as follows:

1. let $y' = f_{i,j}(x_j)$, $\mathcal{A}$ computes the commitment $\mathsf{c}' \leftarrow \mathsf{Com}(\mathsf{ck}, f_{i,j}(X))$, and the "honest" proof π' for (c', x_j, y')
2. asks the simulation oracle to provide a proof $\tilde{\pi}$ for the instance $(\mathsf{c} - \mathsf{c}', x_j, y - y')$ with representation $\boldsymbol{0} \| \boldsymbol{c}_{i,j}$
3. recombines the proof $\pi_{i,j} = \pi' + \tilde{\pi}$

We define our extractor to be the *canonical* extractor that returns the polynomial $f(X) \leftarrow \langle f_{c^*}, (1, X, \ldots, X^d) \rangle$. We start by proving that for any algebraic adversary $\mathcal{A}$ whose forgery satisfies the predicate $\Phi_{\text{ext}}^{\text{der}}$, there exists an algebraic adversary $\mathcal{B}$ whose forgery satisfies the predicate $\Phi_{\text{ext}}^{\text{rnd}}$. Let $\{\Phi'_{\mathcal{D}}\}_{\mathcal{D}}$ be the family of policies defined exactly as $\Phi_{\text{evl}}^{\text{s-adpt}}$ with the difference that the extracion policy Φ_{ext} is equal to $\Phi_{\text{ext}}^{\text{rnd}}$ (i.e., there is no logical disjunction with $\Phi_{\text{ext}}^{\text{der}}$).

Lemma 3. *For any algebraic adversary $\mathcal{A}$ there is an algebraic adversary $\mathcal{B}$:*

$$\mathbf{Adv}_{\text{CP}_{\text{evl}}, \mathcal{A}, \mathcal{S}, \mathcal{E}}^{\Phi_{\mathcal{D}}\text{-se}}(\lambda) = \mathbf{Adv}_{\text{CP}_{\text{evl}}, \mathcal{B}, \mathcal{S}, \mathcal{E}}^{\Phi'_{\mathcal{D}}\text{-se}}(\lambda)$$

Proof. First, we notice that once we fix a commitment c, a point x, and a value y, there is a unique proof π that can satisfy the KZG verification equation. Thus, the predicate $\Phi_{\text{ext}}^{\text{der}}$ can be simplified as requiring that an adversary outputs a valid proof π^* and a value y^* such that $\exists((c^*, x^*, y'), \cdot, \pi) \in \mathcal{Q}_{\text{sim}}$ and $y^* \neq y'$.

The reduction $\mathcal{B}$ internally runs $\mathcal{A}$ forwarding all the simulation queries, up to the forgery (x^*, π^*), where $x^* = (c^*, x^*, y^*)$. If the simulation queries and/or the forgery of the adversary $\mathcal{A}$ do not agree with the policy $\Phi_{\mathcal{D}}$, i.e. $\mathcal{A}$ automatically loses its game, $\mathcal{B}$ aborts. Otherwise, it must be true that the forgery of $\mathcal{A}$ either (i) satisfies the extraction predicate $\Phi_{\text{ext}}^{\text{rnd}}$ or (ii) satisfies the extraction predicate $\Phi_{\text{ext}}^{\text{der}}$. Both cases can be efficiently checked by $\mathcal{B}$. In case (i) $\mathcal{B}$ would simply forward the forgery of $\mathcal{A}$ retaining the same advantage of $\mathcal{A}$. Otherwise, before submitting the forgery, $\mathcal{B}$ retrieves from $\mathcal{Q}_{\text{sim}}$ the statement $x := (c^*, x^*, y')$, where $y' \neq y^*$, and the corresponding proof π output by $\mathcal{S}_1$. Then $\mathcal{B}$ produces the forgery:

$$\hat{c} \leftarrow \pi^* - \pi, \qquad \hat{x} \leftarrow h(a), \qquad \hat{\pi} \leftarrow \frac{\pi - \pi^*}{\hat{x} - x^*}, \qquad \hat{y} \leftarrow \frac{y' - y^*}{\hat{x} - x^*}$$

which satisfies the verification equation (cf [24]), and the extraction predicate $\Phi_{\text{ext}}^{\text{rnd}}$ when $(\hat{c}, h, a) \in \mathcal{Q}_{\text{RO}}$. $\qquad \square$

Thanks to Lemma 3 we can assume that the forgery of $\mathcal{A}$ satisfies the extraction predicate $\Phi_{\text{ext}}^{\text{rnd}}$. We let $\mathbf{H}_0$ be the $\mathbf{Exp}_{\mathcal{A}, \mathcal{S}, \mathcal{E}}^{\Phi_{\mathcal{D}}\text{-se}}(\lambda)$ experiment, and we denote by ϵ_i the advantage of $\mathcal{A}$ to win $\mathbf{H}_i$, i.e. $\epsilon_i := \Pr[\mathbf{H}_i = 1]$.

Hybrid $\mathbf{H}_1$. Recall that $\mathcal{D}$ is witness samplable, thus according to Definition 3 there exists a PPT algorithm $\tilde{\mathcal{D}}$ associated with the sampler $\mathcal{D}$. The hybrid experiment $\mathbf{H}_1$ is identical to the previous one, but the group elements in coms are "sampled at exponent", i.e. we use $\tilde{\mathcal{D}}$ to generate the field elements γ, and we let coms $\leftarrow [\gamma]_1$; we also add γ to $\text{st}_{\mathcal{S}}$. By the witness sampleability of $\mathcal{D}$, $\mathbf{H}_0$ and $\mathbf{H}_1$ are perfectly indistinguishable, thus $\epsilon_1 = \epsilon_0$.

Hybrid $\mathbf{H}_2$. In this hybrid, we change the way we generate the SRS srs and the way in which $\mathcal{S}_1$ simulates the proofs. Let $((\mathbb{G}_1, \mathbb{G}_2, \mathbb{G}_T, e), [1]_1, [1]_2) \leftarrow\!\!\$ \text{GroupGen}(1^\lambda)$, sample $s \leftarrow\!\!\$ \mathbb{F}$ and compute $[s, \ldots, s^{D+d}]_1, [1, s]_2$, where $D \leftarrow Q_x + 1$. Let $x_r \leftarrow\!\!\$ \mathbb{F}$, and let $p(X)$ be the vanishing polynomial in $\mathcal{Q}_x \cup \{x_r\}$, namely $p(X) := (X - x_r) \prod_{x \in \mathcal{Q}_x} (X - x)$. Let also $p_j(X) := p(X)(X - x_j)^{-1}$, for $j \in [Q_x]$. In $\mathbf{H}_2$ we have that:

- $pp_\mathbb{G} := ((\mathbb{G}_1, \mathbb{G}_2, \mathbb{G}_T, e), [p(s)]_1, [1]_2)$,
- $srs := (ek, vk)$, where $ek \leftarrow [p(s), p(s)s, \ldots, p(s)s^d]_1$ and $vk \leftarrow [1, s]_2$,
- $st_\mathcal{S} := [1, s, \ldots, s^{D+d}]_1, [1, s]_2, \boldsymbol{\gamma}$.

Upon a query of the form $(\mathbb{x} = (c, x_j, y_k), aux = (\boldsymbol{r}_c, aux'))$ to $\mathcal{S}_1$, the latter outputs the proof $\pi \leftarrow [(\langle \boldsymbol{r}_c, \boldsymbol{\gamma} \rangle - y_k) \cdot p_j(s)]_1$, and updates $\mathcal{Q}_{sim}$ accordingly.

We now show that $\mathbf{H}_1 \equiv \mathbf{H}_2$, i.e., the view offered to the adversary $\mathcal{A}$ is identically distributed in the two experiments.

Lemma 4. $\epsilon_2 = \epsilon_1$.

Proof. Notice that in $\mathbf{H}_2$ we sample from GroupGen the description of the group, and then we set the generator of $\mathbb{G}_1$ to $[p(s)]_1$ which, thanks to the random root x_r, is distributed uniformly at random even given the value s. It is not hard to verify that the simulated proofs generated by the hybrid $\mathbf{H}_2$ pass the verification equations, in fact, we are assuming that queried commitment c are of the form $\langle \boldsymbol{r}_c, coms \rangle$. Additionally, since the proofs are uniquely determined given the SRS and the statements, the simulated proofs created in $\mathbf{H}_2$ are distributed as the simulated proofs generated by the simulator $\mathcal{S}_1$ in $\mathbf{H}_1$. Thus the advantage of $\mathcal{A}$ is the same in the two experiments. $\qquad \square$

Given an algebraic adversary $\mathcal{A}$ we can define a new adversary, $\mathcal{A}_c$, that we call the *core* adversary. Whenever the adversary $\mathcal{A}$ outputs a group element $\mathbf{g}$ it provides a representation vector $\boldsymbol{r}_\mathbf{g} := \boldsymbol{f}_\mathbf{g} \| \boldsymbol{c}_\mathbf{g} \| \boldsymbol{o}_\mathbf{g}$ for $\mathbf{g}$ such that:

$$\mathbf{g} = \langle \boldsymbol{f}_\mathbf{g}, ek \rangle + \langle \boldsymbol{c}_\mathbf{g}, coms \rangle + \langle \boldsymbol{o}_\mathbf{g}, proofs \rangle.$$

$\mathcal{A}_c$ runs internally $\mathcal{A}$ and forwards all the queries and answers from $\mathcal{A}$ to its simulation oracle. However, the way of simulating RO queries must ensure to not alter the result of the extractor policy, i.e. the "hash-check" for x^*. This is why we cannot simply forward the queries of $\mathcal{A}$ to the random oracle. Therefore, we keep track of the queries made by $\mathcal{A}$ in the list $\mathcal{Q}_{RO,\mathcal{A}}$ and the list of queries made by the core adversary in $\mathcal{Q}_{RO}$. More in detail, when $\mathcal{A}$ queries the RO with (s, aux), the adversary $\mathcal{A}_c$ makes a "core" RO query (s_c, aux_c) such that:

1. Let s be parsed as $(\mathbf{g}_i)_{i \in [k]}$ (the group elements in s whose representations $\boldsymbol{r}_{\mathbf{g}_i} := \boldsymbol{f}_{\mathbf{g}_i} \| \boldsymbol{c}_{\mathbf{g}_i} \| \boldsymbol{o}_{\mathbf{g}_i}$ are in aux) and a string $\tilde{s}$. Notice, since the adversary is algebraic we can un-ambiguously parse s as such.
2. For each i, $\mathcal{A}_c$ computes the group elements $\mathbf{g}'_i = \mathbf{g}_i - \langle \boldsymbol{f}_{\mathbf{g}_i}, ek \rangle$. $\mathcal{A}_c$ encodes into the string s' the group elements $(\mathbf{g}_i, \mathbf{g}'_i)_{i \in [k]}$.
3. $\mathcal{A}_c$ queries the RO with (s_c, aux_c), where $s_c := s' \| \tilde{s}$, and aux_c contains the representations of all the group elements in s' and the same function h encoded in aux. Finally, it forwards the output to $\mathcal{A}$, i.e. it adds (s, aux, a) to $\mathcal{Q}_{RO,\mathcal{A}}$, and adds (s, s_c) to (the initially empty) $\mathcal{Q}_s$.

Eventually, $\mathcal{A}$ outputs as forgery a string s and the tuple (c', x', y', π'), together with representation vectors $\boldsymbol{r}_{c'}$ and $\boldsymbol{r}_{\pi'}$. Let $f(X) := \langle \boldsymbol{f}_{c'}, (1, X, \ldots, X^d) \rangle$, $y := f(x')$, and $q(X)$ be such that $q(X)(X - x') = f(X) - y$. Let $\boldsymbol{f}_q$ be the vector of the coefficients of $q(X)$, namely $q(X) := \langle \boldsymbol{f}_q, (1, X, \ldots, X^d) \rangle$. The core adversary $\mathcal{A}_c$ returns for its forgery the string s_c such that $(s, s_c) \in \mathcal{Q}_s$, and the tuple (c^*, x', y^*, π^*), where $y^* \leftarrow y' - f(x')$ and:

$$c^* \leftarrow c' - \underbrace{[f(s)p(s)]_1}_{\mathsf{Com}(\mathsf{ck}, f(X))}, \qquad \pi^* \leftarrow \pi' - \underbrace{[q(s)p(s)]_1}_{\mathsf{Com}(\mathsf{ck}, q(X))}$$

inserting into aux_Φ the (correct) algebraic representations $(\boldsymbol{0}\|\boldsymbol{c}_{c'}\|\boldsymbol{o}_{c'})$ for c^* and $((\boldsymbol{f}_{\pi'} - \boldsymbol{f}_q)\|\boldsymbol{c}_{\pi'}\|\boldsymbol{o}_{\pi'})$ for π^*.

Hybrid $\mathbf{H}_3$. This hybrid is exactly the same of $\mathbf{H}_2$ but instead of running the experiment with the adversary $\mathcal{A}$ we run it with the core adversary $\mathcal{A}_c$.

Lemma 5. $\epsilon_3 = \epsilon_2$.

Proof. First, by construction, it is easy to verify that $\mathcal{A}_c$ is algebraic. Thus we need to show that the forgery of $\mathcal{A}$ is valid if and only if the forgery of $\mathcal{A}_c$ is valid. By the verification equation of the forgery of $\mathcal{A}_c$, we have:

$$e(c^* - [y^*]_1, [1]_2) - e(\pi^*, [s - x^*]_2) =$$
$$e(c' - [f(s)p(s)]_1 - [y' - f(x')]_1, [1]_2) - e(\pi' - [q(s)p(s)]_1, [s - x^*]_2) =$$
$$e(c' - [y']_1, [1]_2) - e(\pi', [s - x']_2) - [f(s)p(s) - f(x') - q(s)p(s)(s - x^*)]_T =$$
$$e(c' - [y']_1, [1]_2) - e(\pi', [s - x']_2),$$

where the last equation holds since $q(X)(X - x') = (f(X) - f(x'))$ and $x^* = x'$. Finally, notice that a forgery is valid for $\mathcal{A}$ if it provides a string s that satisfies the "hash check" of Φ_{ext}. We have that there exist s, aux, a, and $h(X)$ such that: (i) $g_c(c^*, s) = 1$, (ii) $g_h(h, \mathsf{aux}) = 1$, (iii) $(s, \mathsf{aux}, a) \in \mathcal{Q}_{\mathsf{RO}, \mathcal{A}}$, and (iv) $x^* = h(a)$ for the forgery of $\mathcal{A}$. The way $\mathcal{A}_c$ simulates the RO queries ensures that for the query s of $\mathcal{A}$ to the RO, the core adversary sent the "core" RO query s_c that encodes both c' and c^*, thus we have that (i) $g_c(c^*, s_c) = 1$, (ii) $g_h(h, \mathsf{aux}_c) = 1$, (iii) $(s_c, \mathsf{aux}_c, a) \in \mathcal{Q}_{\mathsf{RO}}$, and (iv) $x^* = h(a)$ for the forgery of $\mathcal{A}_c$. □

Notice that if we run the canonical extractor on the outputs of the core adversary $\mathcal{A}_c$, the extractor sets the extracted witness to be the zero polynomial.

Hybrid $\mathbf{H}_4$. The hybrid $\mathbf{H}_4$ additionally checks that $\boldsymbol{f}_{\pi^*} \neq \boldsymbol{0} \vee \boldsymbol{c}_{\pi^*} \neq \boldsymbol{0}$, and if the condition holds the adversary $\mathcal{A}_c$ loses the game.

Lemma 6. $\epsilon_3 \leq \epsilon_4 + \epsilon_{(Q_x + d + 1)\text{-DL}}$

Proof. Recall that from the definition of the experiment, upon a query $(\mathbf{x}, \mathsf{aux})$ from $\mathcal{A}_c$ to the simulation oracle of the form $\mathbf{x} = (c, x_j, y_k)$ and $\mathsf{aux} = \boldsymbol{r}$ where $c = \langle \boldsymbol{r}, \mathsf{coms} \rangle$, the adversary receives the proof $[\pi_{\boldsymbol{r}, j, k}(s)]_1$ where:

$$\pi_{\boldsymbol{r}, j, k}(X) := (\langle \boldsymbol{r}, (\gamma_i)_i \rangle - y_k) p_j(X).$$

Consider the following polynomials:

$$c^*(X) := \sum_{i \in [Q_c]} c_{c^*,i} \cdot \gamma_i p(X) + \sum_{r,j,k} o_{c^*,r,j,k} \cdot \pi_{r,j,k}(X)$$

$$\pi^*(X) := \sum_{i \in [Q_c]} c_{\pi^*,i} \cdot \gamma_i p(X) + \sum_{r,j,k} o_{\pi^*,r,j,k} \cdot \pi_{r,j,k}(X) + \sum_{i \in [d+1]} f_{\pi^*,i} X^{i-1} p(X)$$

$$v(X) := c^*(X) - y^* p(X) - (X - x^*) \pi^*(X)$$

By the guarantees of the AGM, we have $c^* = [c^*(s)]_1$ and $\pi^* = [\pi^*(s)]_1$, moreover, if the verification equation is satisfied by the forgery of $\mathcal{A}_c$, then $v(s) = 0$.

Next, we show that when the forgery of the adversary is valid the probability of $f_{\pi^*} \neq 0$ or $c_{\pi^*} \neq 0$ is bounded by $\epsilon_{(Q_x+d+1)\text{-DL}}$. First, notice that if the verification equation for $\mathcal{A}_c$ holds then the polynomial $v(X)$ must be equivalent to the zero polynomial with overwhelming probability. In fact, $v(s) = 0$ when the verification equation holds; if $v(X)$ is not the zero polynomial then, by Lemma 1, we can reduce $\mathcal{A}_c$ to an adversary to the $(Q_x + d + 1)$-DL assumption. Thus:

$$c^*(X) - y^* p(X) - (X - x^*) \pi^*(X) = v(X) = 0. \tag{1}$$

By the guarantees of the AGM, the polynomial $\pi^*(X)$ is a linear combination of elements that depend on $X^{i-1} p(X)$ for $i \in [d+1]$ and $p_j(X)$ for $j \in [Q_x]$. However, when the verification equation holds, the degree of $\pi^*(X)$ must be strictly less than the degree of $p(X)$, because, by Eq. 1, $v(X)$ would contain a non-zero coefficient of degree $Q_x + d + 1$ which in particular implies that $v(X) \not\equiv 0$. Then it must be the case that the forged proof $\pi^*(s)$ is a linear combination of the simulated proofs only, thus both f_{π^*} and c_{π^*} are null. □

The representation of c^* and π^* computed by the adversary (possibly) depends on the elements $\pi_{r,j,k}$ (i.e. the proof for the linear combination r of the elements of coms with evaluation point x_j and evaluation value y_k) of proofs. However, it is much more convenient to give a representation that depends on the polynomials $p_j(X)$. This motivates the definition of our next hybrid.

Hybrid H_5. The hybrid H_5 finds coefficients o''_τ, for $\tau \in \{c^*, \pi^*\}$ such that:

$$\langle o_\tau, \text{proofs} \rangle = \langle o''_\tau, ([p_j(s)]_1)_j \rangle. \tag{2}$$

Moreover, if $o_{c^*} \neq 0$ but $o''_{c^*} = 0$ the adversary loses the game.

Lemma 7. $\epsilon_4 \leq \epsilon_5 + \epsilon_{A\!f\!f\text{-}MDH}$

Proof. We begin by showing that the hybrid can compute such alternative representations efficiently. We proceed in steps. Let us parse the simulated proofs proofs $:= (\pi_{j,\ell})_{j,\ell}$ such that $\pi_{j,\ell}$ is the ℓ-th simulated proof obtained by $\mathcal{S}_1$ on a query involving the j-th point x_j, i.e., $((x_j, \hat{c}_{j,\ell}, y_{j,\ell}), \text{aux}_{j,\ell})$. Also, let $c_{j,\ell}$ be the algebraic representation for the group element $\hat{c}_{j,\ell}$ in $\text{aux}_{j,\ell}$. For every $j \in [Q_x]$, we define R_j as the $Q_c \times Q_c$ matrix whose ℓ-th column is $c_{j,\ell}$. By construction of $\mathcal{S}_1$ in this hybrid we have that for every $j \in [Q_x]$ it holds

$$\pi_{j,\ell} := \left[(c_{j,\ell}^\top \cdot \gamma - y_{j,\ell}) \, p_j(s) \right]_1$$

and thus $\boldsymbol{\pi}_j := \left[(\boldsymbol{R}_j^\top \boldsymbol{\gamma} - \boldsymbol{y}_j) p_j(s)\right]_1$ with $\boldsymbol{y}_j := (y_{j,\ell})_\ell$. Without loss of generality, we assume that for each x_j the adversary makes the maximum number of simulation queries (i.e., $\ell \in [Q_c]$); therefore $\boldsymbol{R}_j$ is a full rank matrix (this follows from the fact that the simulation queries of the adversary satisfy the policy Φ_{sim}, and in particular the algebraic consistency of the policy, see Item 3). Given any vector $\boldsymbol{o}_\tau$ with $\tau \in \{c^*, \pi^*\}$, its m-th entry $o_{\tau,m}$ corresponds to the m-th simulated proof in proofs. Therefore, similarly to above, we denote by $o_{\tau,j,\ell}$ the entry corresponding to proof $\pi_{j,\ell}$ and we define $\boldsymbol{o}_{\tau,j} := (o_{\tau,j,\ell})_\ell$. Then, for every $j \in [Q_x]$ we define $\boldsymbol{o}'_{\tau,j} \leftarrow \boldsymbol{R}_j \cdot \boldsymbol{o}_{\tau,j}$ and $\boldsymbol{\pi}'_j \leftarrow (\boldsymbol{R}_j^\top)^{-1} \cdot \boldsymbol{\pi}_j$, from which we derive:

$$\forall \tau \quad \sum_j \langle \boldsymbol{o}'_{\tau,j}, \boldsymbol{\pi}'_j \rangle = \sum_j \langle \boldsymbol{R}_j \cdot \boldsymbol{o}_{\tau,j}, (\boldsymbol{R}_j^\top)^{-1} \cdot \boldsymbol{\pi}_j \rangle = \sum_j \langle \boldsymbol{o}_{\tau,j}, \boldsymbol{\pi}_j \rangle$$

which is equal to $\langle \boldsymbol{o}_\tau, \text{proofs} \rangle$, up to a permutation of the indices j.

For all $j \in [Q_x]$ let $\boldsymbol{z}_j := (\boldsymbol{R}_j^\top)^{-1} \cdot \boldsymbol{y}_j$, and note that $\boldsymbol{\pi}'_j = [(\boldsymbol{\gamma} - \boldsymbol{z}_j) p_j(s)]_1$ namely $\pi'_{j,i}$ is a valid proof for the instance $(c_i, x_j, z_{j,i})$ w.r.t. the simulated SRS.

$\mathbf{H}_5$ computes $o''_{\tau,j} \leftarrow \langle \boldsymbol{o}'_{\tau,j}, (\boldsymbol{\gamma} - \boldsymbol{z}_j) \rangle$, and $\boldsymbol{o}''_\tau \leftarrow (o''_{\tau,j})_{j \in [Q_x]}$. By construction:

$$\sum_{j \in [Q_x]} \langle \boldsymbol{o}'_{\tau,j}, \boldsymbol{\pi}'_j \rangle = \sum_{j \in [Q_x]} o''_{\tau,j} \cdot [p_j(s)]_1.$$

which proves the first part of the lemma, i.e., computing $o''_{\tau,j}$ satisfying Eq. 2.

In what follows, we prove that if the event that $\mathbf{H}_5$ outputs 0 but $\mathbf{H}_4$ would output 1, namely that all the conditions of $\mathbf{H}_4$ hold but $\boldsymbol{o}_{c^*} \neq \boldsymbol{0} \wedge o''_{c^*} = 0$, then we can break the Aff-MDH assumption. First, notice that for any j $o_{c^*,j} \neq \boldsymbol{0}$ implies that $\boldsymbol{o}'_{c^*,j} \neq \boldsymbol{0}$, because the linear transformation applied to compute $\boldsymbol{o}'_{c^*,j}$ is full rank. Second, take an index j^* such that $o_{c^*,j^*} \neq \boldsymbol{0}$ and set $\boldsymbol{A} \leftarrow \boldsymbol{o}'_{c^*,j^*}$ and $\zeta \leftarrow \langle \boldsymbol{z}_{j^*}, \boldsymbol{o}'_{c^*,j^*} \rangle$. By the above definition of the values o''_{c^*,j^*} and our assumption that the "bad event" of this hybrid is $o''_{c^*} = 0$, we have that:

$$\langle \boldsymbol{A}, [\boldsymbol{\gamma}]_1 \rangle = \underbrace{[\langle \boldsymbol{o}'_{c^*,j^*}, (\boldsymbol{\gamma} - \boldsymbol{z}_{j^*}) \rangle]_1}_{o''_{c^*,j^*}=0} + \underbrace{[\langle \boldsymbol{o}'_{c^*,j^*}, \boldsymbol{z}_{j^*} \rangle]_1}_{\zeta} = [\zeta]_1.$$

The reduction $\mathcal{B}$ to the $\mathcal{D}$-Aff-MDH Assumption takes as input a distribution $[\boldsymbol{\gamma}]_1$ and runs the experiment as in $\mathbf{H}_4$ (it perfectly emulates $\mathbf{H}_4$, and in particular the simulation oracle, because it knows the trapdoor s "at the exponent"). Then $\mathcal{B}$ computes the coefficients $(A_i)_{i \in [Q_c]}$ and the value ζ as described above, which is a valid $\mathcal{D}$-Aff-MDH solution.   □

Hybrid $\mathbf{H}_6$. The hybrid $\mathbf{H}_6$ additionally checks that $r_{c^*} \neq \boldsymbol{0}$, and if the condition holds the adversary $\mathcal{A}_c$ loses the game.

Lemma 8. $\epsilon_5 \leq \epsilon_6 + \epsilon_{\text{Aff-MDH}} + 2\epsilon_{(Q_x+1+d)\text{-DL}} + \text{poly}(\lambda)\frac{\deg(h)}{q}$

Proof. We bound the probability that the adversary loses in $\mathbf{H}_6$ but not in $\mathbf{H}_5$, namely, the probability that $r_c^* \neq 0$ but the conditions of $\mathbf{H}_5$ hold. We show a reduction $\mathcal{B}$ to the Aff-MDH when this event happens. First of all, we can assume that the core adversary outputs coefficients $f_{c^*} = f_{\pi^*} = c_{\pi^*} = 0$, i.e. the adversary only makes use of previous commitments $c_i \in \text{coms}$ and simulated proofs $\pi_{r,j,k} \in \text{proofs}$ to represent c^*, and only uses the simulated proofs to represent the proof π^*. The reduction $\mathcal{B}$ takes as input a distribution $[\gamma]_1$ and runs the experiment as in $\mathbf{H}_5$. $\mathcal{B}$ aborts if the forgery (c^*, x^*, y^*, π^*) returned by the adversary is not valid (i.e. either the extraction predicate or the verification equation is not satisfied) or $r_{c^*} = 0$. Otherwise, we have that:

$$e(c^* - [p(s)y^*]_1, [1]_2) = e(\pi^*, [s - x^*]_2) \text{ and } r_{c^*} \neq 0$$

where $r_{c^*} \neq 0$ if $o_{c^*} \neq 0 \vee c_{c^*} \neq 0$. We can then rewrite the commitment and the proof of forgery of the core adversary as a function of the coefficients o''_{c^*} and o''_{π^*} (as computed in the $\mathbf{H}_5$):

$$c^* := \sum_{i \in [Q_c]} c_{c^*,i} [\gamma_i p(s)]_1 + \sum_{j \in [Q_x]} o''_{c^*,j} [p_j(s)]_1, \qquad \pi^* := \sum_{j \in [Q_x]} o''_{w^*,j} [p_j(s)]_1$$

Since the verification equation is satisfied, and plugging in the AGM representations we have:

$$\sum_{i \in [Q_c]} c_{c^*,i} \gamma_i p(s) + \sum_{j \in [Q_x]} o''_{c^*,j} p_j(s) - p(s)y^* = \sum_{j \in [Q_x]} o''_{\pi^*,j} p_j(s)(s - x^*) \qquad (3)$$

For all $j \in [Q_x]$, we define $\delta_j := x_j - x^*$. We can rewrite the r.h.s. of Eq. 3 as:

$$\sum_{j \in [Q_x]} o''_{\pi^*,j} p_j(s)(s - x^*) = \sum_{j \in [Q_x]} o''_{\pi^*,j} (p(s) + p_j(s)\delta_j).$$

In Eq. 3, we group all the terms that depend on $p(s)$ on the left side, and we move all the terms that depend on $p_j(s)$ to the right side, thus obtaining:

$$\underbrace{\left(\sum_{i \in [Q_c]} c_{c^*,i} \gamma_i - \sum_{j \in [Q_x]} o''_{w^*,j} - y^* \right)}_{A} p(s) = \sum_{j \in [Q_x]} \underbrace{\left(o''_{w^*,j} \delta_j - o''_{c^*,j} \right)}_{B_j} p_j(s) \qquad (4)$$

Let $f(X) := Ap(X) - \sum_{j \in [Q_x]} B_j p_j(X)$. Notice that because of Eq. 4 we have $f(s) = 0$, thus we can assume $f(X) \equiv 0$, as otherwise we can reduce, by Lemma 1, to the $(Q_x + d + 1)$-DL assumption. It must be the case that both $\sum_{j \in [Q_x]} B_j p_j(s) = 0$ and $A = 0$ because the degree of $p(X)$ and of $p_j(X)$ for any j are different. Moreover, the polynomials $p_j(X)$ are linearly independent, namely the only linear combination $\sum_j a_j p_j(X) = 0$ is the trivial one where the coefficients $a_j = 0^{10}$, thus $B_j = 0$ for all j. We have that $o''_{w^*,j}\delta_j - o''_{c^*,j} = 0, \forall j$.

---

[10] To see this, $\forall x_j \in \mathcal{Q}_x$ we have that $\sum_{j'} a_{j'} p_{j'}(x_j) = a_j p_j(x_j)$ since $p_j(x_j) \neq 0$ and $p_{j'}(x_j) = 0$ for $j \neq j'$, and $a_j p_j(x_j) = 0$ iff $a_j = 0$.

Thus we can rewrite the coefficients $o''_{\pi^*,j} = \frac{o''_{c^*,j}}{\delta_j}$, $\forall j$. Since A must be 0:

$$\sum_{i\in[Q_c]} c_{c^*,i}\gamma_i - \sum_{j\in[Q_x]} \frac{o''_{c^*,j}}{\delta_j} - y^* = 0. \tag{5}$$

$\mathcal{B}$ can plug the definition of the coefficients $o''_{c^*,j}$ in Eq. 5 and derive:

$$0 = \sum_{i\in[Q_c]} c_{c^*,i}\gamma_i - \sum_{i,j} \frac{o'_{c^*,i,j}(\gamma_i - z_{j_i})}{\delta_j} - y^*$$

$$= \sum_{i\in[Q_c]} (c_{c^*,i} - \sum_j \frac{o'_{c^*,i,j}}{\delta_j})\gamma_i + \sum_{i,j} \frac{o'_{c^*,i,j}z_{j_i}}{\delta_j} - y^*.$$

Above, in the last step we have grouped the terms depending on γ_i. In particular, the last equation shows that $\mathcal{B}$ can make a forgery in the Aff-MDH game since it knows $z := y^* - \sum_{i,j} \frac{o'_{c^*,i,j}z_{j_i}}{\delta_j}$ and coefficients $A_i := c_{c^*,i} - \sum_j \frac{o'_{c^*,i,j}}{\delta_j}$ such that: $\sum_{i\in[Q_c]} A_i [\gamma_i]_1 = [z]_1$. For this to be a valid solution in the Aff-MDH game, we need the existence of at least an index i such that $A_i \neq 0$. We show that this occurs with all but negligible probability, i.e., $\Pr[\exists i \in [Q_c] : A_i \neq 0] \geq 1-\mathsf{negl}(\lambda)$.

To this end, consider an arbitrary $\mu \in [Q_c]$, then we have $\Pr[\forall i \in [Q_c] : A_i = 0] \leq \Pr[A_\mu = 0]$. Thus, for any μ, we have:

$$\Pr[\exists i \in [Q_c] : A_i \neq 0] = 1 - \Pr[\forall i \in [Q_c] : A_i = 0] \geq 1 - \Pr[A_\mu = 0].$$

Below, we argue that $\Pr[A_\mu = 0]$ is negligible based on the randomness of x^* which is chosen by the random oracle after defining A_μ, and we make use of the assumption that $r_{c^*} \neq 0$. We claim that the value $A_\mu = c_{c^*\mu} - \sum_j \frac{o'_{c^*j,\mu}}{(x^*-x_j)}$ can be fixed before the random oracle query x^* is made. To this end, we start by showing that $o'_{c^*,j}$ does not depend on x^*. Let $B(j) \subseteq [Q_c]$ be the subset of indices of the simulation queries that involve x_j and that occurred before the random oracle query that returned x^*. We observe that for every $\eta \in B(j)$ it must be $o_{c^*,j,\eta} = 0$ since the simulated proof $\pi_{j,\eta}$ is not in the view of the adversary. Therefore:

$$o'_{c^*,j,i} = \sum_{\eta\in[Q_c]} R_{j,\eta,i} \cdot o_{c^*,j,\eta} = \sum_{\eta\in B(j)} R_{j,\eta,i} \cdot o_{c^*,j,\eta}$$

and observe that all the rows of R_j belonging to $B(j)$ can all be defined before x^* is sampled. Hence, we have that A_μ depends on the values $c_{c^*}, x^*, \{x_j\}_j$, and $o_{c^*,j}$ which can all be defined before the random oracle query x^* is made.

Now, we bound $\Pr[A_\mu = 0]$. Recall that, since the extractor policy Φ_{ext} holds true, we have that $x^* = h(a)$ and $(s, \mathsf{aux}, a) \in \mathcal{Q}_{\mathsf{RO}}$ where $g_c(c^*, s) = 1$ and the function h is the polynomial encoded in aux_ϕ: the adversary may want to encode up to $n \in \mathsf{poly}(\lambda)$ different polynomials h_i into aux_ϕ to maximize its advantage, and the extractor policy does not impose any restriction on this. Moreover, by the AGM, since $\mathcal{A}_c$ sends a query s (where c^* is encoded in s) to the random oracle it also defines coefficients for c^* before the value a, and therefore $x^* = h(a)$, is defined. Also, it is not hard to see that the representation vector of c^* defined by $\mathcal{A}_c$ when querying the random oracle must be the same representation vector used for the forgery. As otherwise we would break the $(Q_x + d + 1)$-DL assumption. Thus the coefficients c_{c^*} and $o'_{c^*,j}$ are defined by the adversary before seeing the random value x^*. Notice that, once the coefficients c_{c^*} and $o'_{c^*,j}$ are fixed, the coefficient A_μ can be seen as function of $x^* \in \mathbb{Z}_q$, i.e. $A_\mu = A_\mu(x^*)$, where:

$$A_\mu(X) = c_{c^*,\mu} + \sum_j \frac{o'_{c^*,j,\mu}}{X - x_j} = \frac{c_{c^*,\mu} \prod_j (X - x_j) + \sum_j (o'_{c^*,j,\mu} \prod_{j' \neq j} (x_{j'} - X))}{\prod_j X - x_j}.$$

Notice that $A_\mu(X)(\prod_j (X - x_j))$ vanishes in at most Q_x points in $\mathbb{F} \setminus \mathcal{Q}_x$ and vanishes in the set of points $\mathcal{Q}_x$. Let $\mathcal{R}$ be the set of the roots of such a polynomial, since $\forall i \in [n]$, h_i is defined before x^* is computed, and by union bound:

$$\Pr[\exists i : h_i(\mathsf{RO}(s)) \in \mathcal{R}] \leq \sum_{r \in \mathcal{R}} \Pr[\exists i : h_i(\mathsf{RO}(s)) = r] \leq n Q_x \frac{\max_i \deg(h_i)}{q}$$

for each string s that encodes c^*, To conclude, we notice that $\mathcal{A}$ can submit at most Q_{RO} queries to the RO with strings encoding c^*, say $s_1, \ldots s_{Q_{\mathsf{RO}}}$. Thus the probability that there exist $i \in [n], j \in [Q_{\mathsf{RO}}]$ such that $h_i(\mathsf{RO}(s_j)) \in \mathcal{R}$ is bounded by $n Q_{\mathsf{RO}} Q_x \frac{\max_i \deg(h_i)}{q}$. □

Hybrid $\mathbf{H_7}$. The hybrid $\mathbf{H_7}$ additionally checks that $y^* \neq 0$, and if the condition holds the adversary $\mathcal{A}_c$ loses the game. For space reasons, we give in [24] the proof of the following lemma.

Lemma 9. $\epsilon_6 \leq \epsilon_7 + \epsilon_{(Q_x + 1 + d)\text{-DL}} + \mathsf{poly}(\lambda) \frac{\deg(h)}{q}$

Finally, we have that the probability that the adversary wins in $\mathbf{H_7}$ is null, namely $\epsilon_7 = 0$. Indeed, the canonical extractor $\mathcal{E}$ outputs the 0 polynomial, moreover because of the condition introduced in $\mathbf{H_6}$, we have $c^* = [0]_1$, and because of the condition introduced in $\mathbf{H_7}$ we have $y^* = 0$, thus the witness extracted is valid for the instance $x^* = (c^* = [0]_1, x^*, y^* = 0)$. □

5   Simulation-Extractable Universal zkSNARKs

We provide a technical overview of our compiler for universal SNARKs based on polynomial IOPs. Rather than delving into extensive formal definitions and analysis, we aim to present this section in a more informal (and also more compact) manner and refer the reader to [24] for all the details.

We define an indexed relation $\mathcal{R}$ verifying tuple $(\mathsf{pp}, \mathsf{i}, \mathsf{x}, \mathsf{w})$. We say that w is a witness to the instance x being in the relation defined by the pp and index i when $(\mathsf{pp}, \mathsf{i}, \mathsf{x}, \mathsf{w}) \in \mathcal{R}$. Briefly, we say that a NIZK NIZK is *universal* if there exists a deterministic algorithm Derive that takes as input a (universal) srs and an index i, and outputs a specialized verification key for such an index. We say NIZK is a SNARK if the verification keys and the proofs are succinct. We say that a SNARK is *universal* if there exists a deterministic algorithm Derive that takes as input a (universal) srs and an index i, and outputs a specialized and succinct verification key for such an index.

Polynomial Interactive Oracle Proofs. A Polynomial (Holographic) IOP [17] consists of an r-rounds interaction between a prover P, sending oracle polynomials p_i (and additional messages π_i), and a verifier V, who sends uniformly random messages ρ_i; finally, V outputs a set of polynomial identities to be checked on the prover's polynomials of the form $(G^{(k)}, v_1^{(k)}, \ldots, v_n^{(k)})$, that is satisfied if and only if $F^{(k)}(X) \equiv 0$ where:

$$F^{(k)}(X) := G^{(k)}(X, \{p_i(v_i^{(k)}(X))\}_i, \{\pi_i\}_i). \tag{6}$$

In our work, we use PIOPs with two slight refinements.[11] The first one, called *(non-adaptive) algebraic verifiers*, says that the above polynomials $v_j^{(k)}$ do not depend on the instance and can be expressed as polynomial functions of $\mathcal{V}$'s random coins, i.e., $v_j^{(k)}(X) = \tilde{v}_j^{(k)}(X, \rho)$ for some instance-independent $\tilde{v}_j^{(k)}$. The second one is a more restrictive[12] concept of soundness called *state-restoration straight-line knowledge soundness*. This notion combines the notion of state-restoration soundness from [9] with the concept of straight-line extractability from [17]. For further clarification, the malicious prover engages in a game with the honest verifier and has the additional ability to *roll back* the interaction with the verifier to a previous state. At some point, the interaction may reach a final state. The prover is considered successful if it produces an accepting transcript, while the extractor, given such a transcript that includes all the oracle polynomials, fails to produce a valid witness. Similarly to previous work, we use the notion of bounded zero-knowledge of [17,20].

Compilation-safe PIOP. We must incorporate an additional element into the classical recipe. As stated in the introduction, mix-and-match attacks on compiled protocols, involving two or more independent sub-protocols, are unavoidable. Therefore, we identify a structural restriction on the PIOP that prevents such problematic scenarios. The restriction is easy to state and easy to meet:

Definition 15 (Compiler-safe PIOP). *A PIOP PIOP is compiler-safe if for any* i, x *and* $\rho := \rho_1, \ldots, \rho_{r-1}$ *and any tuple* $(G^{(k)}, v_1^{(k)}, \ldots, v_n^{(k)})_{j \in [n_e]} \leftarrow \mathcal{V}(\mathbb{F}, \mathsf{i}, \mathsf{x}, \rho)$ *there exists an index k such that for all j the polynomials $v_j^{(k)}$ are of degree at least one.*

---

[11] All the PIOPs that we are aware of satisfy both these properties.

[12] The (classical) notion of knowledge extractability implies state-restoration soundness through complexity leveraging [9].

The Compilation-Ready CP-SNARK. Instead of compiling directly a PIOP through a polynomial commitment in its simplest form (i.e., an evaluation proof for each polynomial queried in the PIOP), we take an alternative road similar to [17]. Namely, we assume the existence of a CP-SNARK that, w.r.t. a tuple of commitments $(c_j)_{j \in [n]}$, is capable of proving either knowledge of polynomials $(p_j)_{j \in [n]}$ opening these commitments or that the committed polynomials satisfy a statement like the one in Eq. 6 (i.e., that the oracles committed in $(c_j)_{j \in [n]}$ would make the PIOP verifier accept)[13]. We call this building block a *compilation-ready* CP-SNARK (CP, shortly), and informally we refer to the former type of statements as "proof of knowledge" and to the latter as "PIOP verifier". While our compilation strategy follows previous work, our novel contribution is to properly define the properties that this CP-SNARK must satisfy in order to argue that the result of the compiler is simulation-extractable, and not only knowledge-sound. These properties are mainly three. The first one is that the CP prover can "append" arbitrary messages to the proven instances. Looking ahead to our compiler, this feature is used so that the prover and the verifier can append the (hash of the) protocol's transcript to the proven instance, in such a way that a CP proof acts as a *signature of knowledge for the transcript* [19]. Note that this hashing of the transcript already happens in the standard PIOP compiler due to the application of the Fiat-Shamir transform; here, we highlight it explicitly as it plays an important role in the proof of simulation extractability. The second property, referred to as the *commitment simulator for PIOP*, intuitively requires the existence of a strategy to simulate commitments such that: adding them to the view preserves zero-knowledge, and the simulation respects the "commitment check" constraint in Item 2 of Definition 13. This is a very mild property that is trivially satisfied when employing hiding commitments, and is met by existing simulation strategies based on deterministic commitments to randomized polynomials [17,28]. The third property of CP is that it must be *simulation-extractable* w.r.t. a policy $\hat{\Phi}$ such that:

- The adversary can ask simulated proofs for "PIOP verifier" statements where all the $v_j^{(k)}$ of Eq. 6 are fixed at the beginning of the experiment.
- If the forgery of the adversary is a "proof of knowledge" for commitments $\mathbf{c}^*$, then the adversary must return as auxiliary output yet another forgery for a "PIOP verifier" statement such that: (1) All the commitments $\mathbf{c}^*$ appear in the second forgery, (2) the second forgery is valid according to the extractor policy described next.
- If the forgery of the adversary is for the "PIOP verifier" statement, then the statement-proof pair returned by the adversary must not be in the list of simulated statements-proofs, and (similarly to Definition 15) there exists a k such that for all j the polynomial $v_j^{(k)}$ has degree at least 1.

Theorem 2 (Informal). *Let* PIOP *be a PIOP for an indexed relation $\mathcal{R}$ that is state-restoration straight-line extractable, bounded zero-knowledge, and*

---

[13] The reason to assume a single CP-SNARK for both kinds of statements has to do with the security guarantees when we compose protocols in the AGM [1].

compiler-safe (cf. Definition 15). Let CP *be a compilation-ready CP-SNARK for* PIOP. *There exists a compiler that produces a simulation-extractable Universal zkSNARK for* $\mathcal{R}$.

We follow the classical compilation strategy where: for each of the r rounds, the zkSNARK prover sends commitments of the PIOP oracle polynomials (along with a proof of knowledge) and then computes the PIOP verifier's challenges using Fiat-Shamir; in the last round, the prover sends a CP proof that the PIOP verifier accepts, i.e., Eq. (6) holds w.r.t. all the commitments sent earlier. Notably, this CP proof is produced using the statement and the hash of the transcript as "message" for the signature of knowledge.

We briefly discuss how the properties of PIOP and CP play a role in the security of the compiled zkSNARK Π. We recall that in the simulation-extractability experiment, we have an adversary $\mathcal{A}$ who makes simulation queries for statements of its choice and eventually comes up with a forgery, which is a statement-proof that is new and valid. The goal is to show that for such an adversary there is an extractor that outputs a valid witness with overwhelming probability. Roughly speaking, we build this extractor by first extracting the committed oracle polynomials from the CP "proof of knowledge" in the random oracle query of $\mathcal{A}$ in each round,[14] and then by running the PIOP extractor to obtain the witness.

For this extraction strategy to work, we need two conditions: (A) The "proof of knowledge" extraction must be valid. (B) The zkSNARK extractor feeds the PIOP extractor with polynomials that pass the PIOP verification equations. A technicality about relying on CP extraction for (A) and (B) is that we actually have to make a reduction to its *policy-based simulation-extractability*. In particular, this means that we have to turn $\mathcal{A}$ into CP adversaries that comply with the policy $\hat{\Phi}$. To obtain (A), we use the second property of $\hat{\Phi}$ mentioned above, which ensures a valid extraction if the adversary later provides a valid proof of polynomial evaluation. This is however the case for us since a successful adversary must provide such proof. For (B), we rely on the following observations. If $\mathcal{A}$ produces a forgery for a new statement of Π then the CP proof (aka signature of knowledge) must use a new message, and thus we can build a CP adversary returning a new statement-proof pair. If $\mathcal{A}$ produces a forgery for a statement queried to the simulation oracle, then by strong simulation extractability the proof must be new, which means that: either the commitments in the transcript are different, or the commitments are all the same but the "PIOP verifier" proof is different. In the former case, we get a different transcript, which yields a CP forgery with a new message, as in the previous case. In the latter case, the transcript is the same and we get a CP forgery with the same message but fresh proof. Notably, in all the cases, the CP forgeries respect the degree-1 condition thanks to the compiler-safe property of the PIOP. Finally, the reduction CP adversaries that we build satisfy the first property of $\hat{\Phi}$ thanks to the algebraic verifier property of PIOP, which allows us to precompute the instance-independent polynomials

---

[14] Note, this avoids rewinding, since extraction is performed in the same moment when the adversary sends the proof of knowledge through a RO call.

$\tilde{v}_j^{(k)}$, and to the programmability of the random oracle that allows us to presample the verifier's challenges ρ, define $v_j^{(k)}(X) = \tilde{v}_j^{(k)}(X, \rho)$, and later program the random oracle to use these coins ρ.

Compilation-ready CP-SNARK from KZG. To connect together Sect. 4 and the results of this section, we show a simple compilation-ready CP-SNARK in the ROM based on batched KZG evaluation proofs. For a "PIOP verifier" statement, the prover RO-hashes the instance and obtains a random point ξ, evaluates the polynomials $v_j^{(k)}(\xi)$ for any j and outputs the evaluations $p_j(v_j^{(k)}(\xi))$ together with a batch evaluation proof for all of them. For a "proof of knowledge" statement, the prover does not output an explicit proof element (we call this a *vacuous proof*), and we rely on the AGM to argue its extractability. The idea is that, for an algebraic adversary that produces an alleged commitment c and its algebraic representation, we can find a way to *open* c, under some circumstances. For example, consider the adversary that, during the simulation-extractability experiment, hashes (i.e., makes a random oracle query) the commitment c, and later includes c in a "PIOP verifier" instance. Then the algebraic representation of c returned at hashing time must coincide with the same polynomial extracted at forgery time, otherwise one can break the standard binding of the commitment. Crucially, this scenario fits exactly the second part of the policy $\hat{\Phi}$. As for the third part of the policy, we notice that an attack similar to the mix-and-match malleability attack mentioned in the introduction applies to our compilation-ready CP-SNARK. For example, the adversary could ask a simulation for an instance that tests two (fake) commitments on constant values defined by the $v_j^{(k)}$, and then it can produce a forgery that includes one of the commitments by copying part of the simulated proof. Intuitively, this is why we require that the $v_j^{(k)}$ have a degree at least 1: when evaluated on a fresh random point ξ, a valid proof for $p_j(v_j^{(k)}(\xi))$ ensures that the prover knows p_j.

Acknowledgements. This work received funding from MESRI-BMBF French-German joint project named PROPOLIS (ANR-20-CYAL-0004-01), the European Research Council (ERC) under the European Union's Horizon 2020 research and innovation program under project PICOCRYPT (grant agreement No. 101001283), and from the Spanish Government under projects PRODIGY (TED2021-132464B-I00) and ESPADA (PID2022-142290OB-I00). The last two projects are co-funded by European Union EIE, and NextGenerationEU/PRTR funds.

References

1. Abdalla, M., Barbosa, M., Katz, J., Loss, J., Xu, J.: Algebraic adversaries in the universal composability framework. In: Tibouchi, M., Wang, H. (eds.) ASIACRYPT 2021, Part III. LNCS, vol. 13092, pp. 311–341. Springer, Cham (2021). https://doi.org/10.1007/978-3-030-92078-4_11
2. Abdolmaleki, B., Ramacher, S., Slamanig, D.: Lift-and-shift: obtaining simulation extractable subversion and updatable SNARKs generically. In: Ligatti, J., Ou, X., Katz, J., Vigna, G. (eds.) ACM CCS 2020, pp. 1987–2005. ACM Press, November 2020

3. Arora, S., Safra, S.: Probabilistic checking of proofs; a new characterization of NP. In: 33rd FOCS, pp. 2–13. IEEE Computer Society Press, October 1992
4. Baghery, K., Kohlweiss, M., Siim, J., Volkhov, M.: another look at extraction and randomization of Groth's zk-SNARK. In: Borisov, N., Diaz, C. (eds.) Financial Cryptography and Data Security. FC 2021. LNCS, vol. 12674, pp. 457–475. Springer, Berlin (2021). https://doi.org/10.1007/978-3-662-64322-8_22
5. Bellare, M., Hofheinz, D., Kiltz, E.: Subtleties in the definition of IND-CCA: when and how should challenge decryption be disallowed? J. Cryptol. **28**(1), 29–48 (2015)
6. Ben-Sasson, E., Bentov, I., Horesh, Y., Riabzev, M.: Scalable zero knowledge with no trusted setup. In: Boldyreva, A., Micciancio, D. (eds.) CRYPTO 2019, Part III. LNCS, vol. 11694, pp. 701–732. Springer, Cham (2019). https://doi.org/10.1007/978-3-030-26954-8_23
7. Ben-Sasson, E., Chiesa, A., Genkin, D., Tromer, E., Virza, M.: SNARKs for C: verifying program executions succinctly and in zero knowledge. In: Canetti, R., Garay, J.A. (eds.) CRYPTO 2013, Part II. LNCS, vol. 8043, pp. 90–108. Springer, Heidelberg (2013). https://doi.org/10.1007/978-3-642-40084-1_6
8. Ben-Sasson, E., Chiesa, A., Riabzev, M., Spooner, N., Virza, M., Ward, N.P.: Aurora: transparent succinct arguments for R1CS. In: Ishai, Y., Rijmen, V. (eds.) EUROCRYPT 2019, Part I. LNCS, vol. 11476, pp. 103–128. Springer, Cham (2019). https://doi.org/10.1007/978-3-030-17653-2_4
9. Ben-Sasson, E., Chiesa, A., Spooner, N.: Interactive oracle proofs. In: Hirt, M., Smith, A. (eds.) TCC 2016, Part II. LNCS, vol. 9986, pp. 31–60. Springer, Heidelberg (2016). https://doi.org/10.1007/978-3-662-53644-5_2
10. Ben-Sasson, E., Goldberg, L., Kopparty, S., Saraf, S.: DEEP-FRI: sampling outside the box improves soundness. In: Vidick, T. (ed.), ITCS 2020, vol. 151, pp. 5:1–5:32. LIPIcs, January 2020
11. Boneh, D., Boyen, X.: Short signatures without random oracles. In: Cachin, C., Camenisch, J.L. (eds.) EUROCRYPT 2004. LNCS, vol. 3027, pp. 56–73. Springer, Heidelberg (2004). https://doi.org/10.1007/978-3-540-24676-3_4
12. Boneh, D., Drake, J., Fisch, B., Gabizon, A.: Efficient polynomial commitment schemes for multiple points and polynomials. Cryptology ePrint Archive, Report 2020/081 (2020). https://eprint.iacr.org/2020/081
13. Boneh, D., Drake, J., Fisch, B., Gabizon, A.: Halo infinite: proof-carrying data from additive polynomial commitments. In: Malkin, T., Peikert, C. (eds.) CRYPTO 2021, Part I. LNCS, vol. 12825, pp. 649–680. Springer, Halo infinite: Proof-carrying data from additive polynomial commitments (2021). https://doi.org/10.1007/978-3-030-84242-0_23
14. Bünz, B., Bootle, J., Boneh, D., Poelstra, A., Wuille, P., Maxwell, G.: Bulletproofs: short proofs for confidential transactions and more. In: 2018 IEEE Symposium on Security and Privacy, pp. 315–334. IEEE Computer Society Press, May 2018
15. Bünz, B., Chiesa, A., Mishra, P., Spooner, N.: Recursive proof composition from accumulation schemes. In: Pass, R., Pietrzak, K. (eds.) TCC 2020. LNCS, vol. 12551, pp. 1–18. Springer, Cham (2020). https://doi.org/10.1007/978-3-030-64378-2_1
16. Bünz, B., Fisch, B., Szepieniec, A.: Transparent SNARKs from DARK compilers. In: Canteaut, A., Ishai, Y. (eds.) EUROCRYPT 2020, Part I. LNCS, vol. 12105, pp. 677–706. Springer, Cham (2020). https://doi.org/10.1007/978-3-030-45721-1_24

17. Campanelli, M., Faonio, A., Fiore, D., Querol, A., Rodríguez, H.: Lunar: a tool-box for more efficient universal and updatable zkSNARKs and commit-and-prove extensions. In: Tibouchi, M., Wang, H. (eds.) ASIACRYPT 2021, Part III. LNCS, vol. 13092, pp. 3–33. Springer, Cham (2021). https://doi.org/10.1007/978-3-030-92078-4_1

18. Campanelli, M., Fiore, D., Querol, A.: LegoSNARK: modular design and composition of succinct zero-knowledge proofs. In: Cavallaro, L., Kinder, J., Wang, X., Katz, J. (eds.) ACM CCS 2019, pp. 2075–2092. ACM Press, November 2019

19. Chase, M., Lysyanskaya, A.: On signatures of knowledge. In: Dwork, C. (ed.) CRYPTO 2006. LNCS, vol. 4117, pp. 78–96. Springer, Heidelberg (2006). https://doi.org/10.1007/11818175_5

20. Chiesa, A., Hu, Y., Maller, M., Mishra, P., Vesely, N., Ward, N.: Marlin: preprocessing zkSNARKs with universal and updatable SRS. In: Canteaut, A., Ishai, Y. (eds.) EUROCRYPT 2020, Part I. LNCS, vol. 12105, pp. 738–768. Springer, Cham (2020). https://doi.org/10.1007/978-3-030-45721-1_26

21. Dao, Q., Grubbs, P.: Spartan and bulletproofs are simulation-extractable (for Free!). In: Hazay, C., Stam, M. (eds.) Advances in Cryptology - EUROCRYPT 2023. EUROCRYPT 2023. LNCS, Part II, vol. 14005, pp. 531–562 Springer, Cham (2023). https://doi.org/10.1007/978-3-031-30617-4_18

22. Dodis, Y., Haralambiev, K., López-Alt, A., Wichs, D.: Efficient public-key cryptography in the presence of key leakage. In: Abe, M. (ed.) ASIACRYPT 2010. LNCS, vol. 6477, pp. 613–631. Springer, Heidelberg (2010)

23. Dolev, D., Dwork, C., Naor, M.: Non-malleable cryptography (extended abstract). In: 23rd ACM STOC, pp. 542–552. ACM Press, May 1991

24. Faonio, A., Fiore, D., Kohlweiss, M., Russo, L., Zajac, M.: From polynomial IOP and commitments to non-malleable zksnarks. Cryptology ePrint Archive, Paper 2023/569 (2023). https://eprint.iacr.org/2023/569

25. Faust, S., Kohlweiss, M., Marson, G.A., Venturi, D.: On the non-malleability of the fiat-shamir transform. In: Galbraith, S., Nandi, M. (eds.) INDOCRYPT 2012. LNCS, vol. 7668, pp. 60–79. Springer, Heidelberg (2012). https://doi.org/10.1007/978-3-642-34931-7_5

26. Fischlin, M.: Communication-efficient non-interactive proofs of knowledge with online extractors. In: Shoup, V. (ed.) CRYPTO 2005. LNCS, vol. 3621, pp. 152–168. Springer, Heidelberg (2005). https://doi.org/10.1007/11535218_10

27. Fuchsbauer, G., Kiltz, E., Loss, J.: The algebraic group model and its applications. In: Shacham, H., Boldyreva, A. (eds.) CRYPTO 2018, Part II. LNCS, vol. 10992, pp. 33–62. Springer, Cham (2018). https://doi.org/10.1007/978-3-319-96881-0_2

28. Gabizon, A., Williamson, Z.J., Ciobotaru, O.: PLONK: permutations over lagrange-bases for oecumenical noninteractive arguments of knowledge. Cryptology ePrint Archive, Report 2019/953 (2019). https://eprint.iacr.org/2019/953

29. Ganesh, C., Khoshakhlagh, H., Kohlweiss, M., Nitulescu, A., Zajac, M.: What makes fiat-shamir zksnarks (updatable SRS) simulation extractable? In: Galdi, C., Jarecki, S., (eds.), Security and Cryptography for Networks, SCN 2022, vol. 13409, LNCS, pp. 735–760, pp. 735–760. Springer, Cham (2022). https://doi.org/10.1007/978-3-031-14791-3_32

30. Ganesh, C., Kondi, Y., Orlandi, C., Pancholi, M., Takahashi, A., Tschudi, D.: Witness-succinct universally-composable snarks. Cryptology ePrint Archive, Paper 2022/1618 (2022). https://eprint.iacr.org/2022/1618

31. Ganesh, C., Orlandi, C., Pancholi, M., Takahashi, A., Tschudi, D.: Fiat-shamir bulletproofs are non-malleable (in the algebraic group model). In: Dunkelman, O., Dziembowski, S. (eds.) Advances in Cryptology - EUROCRYPT 2022. EUROCRYPT 2022. LNCS, Part II, vol. 13276, pp. 397–426. Springer, Cham (2022). https://doi.org/10.1007/978-3-031-07085-3_14

32. Garg, S., Jain, A., Sahai, A.: Leakage-resilient zero knowledge. In: Rogaway, P. (ed.) CRYPTO 2011. LNCS, vol. 6841, pp. 297–315. Springer, Heidelberg (2011). https://doi.org/10.1007/978-3-642-22792-9_17

33. Gennaro, R., Gentry, C., Parno, B., Raykova, M.: Quadratic span programs and succinct NIZKs without PCPs. In: Johansson, T., Nguyen, P.Q. (eds.) EUROCRYPT 2013. LNCS, vol. 7881, pp. 626–645. Springer, Heidelberg (2013). https://doi.org/10.1007/978-3-642-38348-9_37

34. Goldwasser, S., Micali, S., Rackoff, C.: The knowledge complexity of interactive proof-systems (extended abstract). In: 17th ACM STOC, pp. 291–304. ACM Press, May 1985

35. Groth, J.: Short pairing-based non-interactive zero-knowledge arguments. In: Abe, M. (ed.) ASIACRYPT 2010. LNCS, vol. 6477, pp. 321–340. Springer, Heidelberg (2010). https://doi.org/10.1007/978-3-642-17373-8_19

36. Groth, J.: On the Size of pairing-based non-interactive arguments. In: Fischlin, M., Coron, J.-S. (eds.) EUROCRYPT 2016, Part II. LNCS, vol. 9666, pp. 305–326. Springer, Heidelberg (2016). https://doi.org/10.1007/978-3-662-49896-5_11

37. Groth, J., Kohlweiss, M., Maller, M., Meiklejohn, S., Miers, I.: Updatable and universal common reference strings with applications to zk-SNARKs. In: Shacham, H., Boldyreva, A. (eds.) CRYPTO 2018, Part III. LNCS, vol. 10993, pp. 698–728. Springer, Cham (2018). https://doi.org/10.1007/978-3-319-96878-0_24

38. Groth, J., Maller, M.: Snarky signatures: minimal signatures of knowledge from simulation-extractable SNARKs. In: Katz, J., Shacham, H. (eds.) CRYPTO 2017, Part II. LNCS, vol. 10402, pp. 581–612. Springer, Cham (2017). https://doi.org/10.1007/978-3-319-63715-0_20

39. Jutla, C.S., Roy, A.: Shorter quasi-adaptive NIZK proofs for linear subspaces. J. Cryptology 30(4), 1116–1156 (2016). https://doi.org/10.1007/s00145-016-9243-7

40. Kate, A., Zaverucha, G.M., Goldberg, I.: Constant-size commitments to polynomials and their applications. In: Abe, M. (ed.) ASIACRYPT 2010. LNCS, vol. 6477, pp. 177–194. Springer, Heidelberg (2010). https://doi.org/10.1007/978-3-642-17373-8_11

41. Lee, J.: Dory: efficient, transparent arguments for generalised inner products and polynomial commitments. In: Nissim, K., Waters, B. (eds.) TCC 2021, Part II. LNCS, vol. 13043, pp. 1–34. Springer, Cham (2021). https://doi.org/10.1007/978-3-030-90453-1_1

42. Lipmaa, H.: Progression-free sets and sublinear pairing-based non-interactive zero-knowledge arguments. In: Cramer, R. (ed.) TCC 2012. LNCS, vol. 7194, pp. 169–189. Springer, Heidelberg (2012). https://doi.org/10.1007/978-3-642-28914-9_10

43. Maller, M., Bowe, S., Kohlweiss, M., Meiklejohn, S.: Sonic: zero-knowledge SNARKs from linear-size universal and updatable structured reference strings. In: Cavallaro, L., Kinder, J., Wang, X., Katz, J. (eds.) ACM CCS 2019, pp. 2111–2128. ACM Press, November 2019

44. Maller, M., Bowe, S., Kohlweiss, M., Meiklejohn, S.: Sonic: zero-knowledge SNARKs from linear-size universal and updateable structured reference strings. Cryptology ePrint Archive, Report 2019/099 (2019). https://eprint.iacr.org/2019/099

45. Micali, S.: CS proofs (extended abstracts). In: 35th FOCS, pp. 436–453. IEEE Computer Society Press, November 1994
46. Ràfols, C., Zapico, A.: An Algebraic framework for universal and updatable SNARKs. In: Malkin, T., Peikert, C. (eds.) CRYPTO 2021, Part I. LNCS, vol. 12825, pp. 774–804. Springer, Cham (2021). https://doi.org/10.1007/978-3-030-84242-0_27
47. Sahai, A.: Non-malleable non-interactive zero knowledge and adaptive chosen-ciphertext security. In: 40th FOCS, pp. 543–553. IEEE Computer Society Press, October 1999
48. Szepieniec, A.: Polynomial IOPs for linear algebra relations. Cryptology ePrint Archive, Report 2020/1022 (2020). https://eprint.iacr.org/2020/1022
49. Tomescu, A., Abraham, I., Buterin, V., Drake, J., Feist, D., Khovratovich, D.: Aggregatable subvector commitments for stateless cryptocurrencies. In: Galdi, C., Kolesnikov, V. (eds.) SCN 2020. LNCS, vol. 12238, pp. 45–64. Springer, Cham (2020). https://doi.org/10.1007/978-3-030-57990-6_3
50. Zapico, A., Buterin, V., Khovratovich, D., Maller, M., Nitulescu, A., Simkin, M.: Caulk: lookup arguments in sublinear time. In: Yin, H., Stavrou, A., Cremers, C., Shi, E. (eds.) ACM CCS 2022, pp. 3121–3134. ACM Press, November 2022

How to Compile Polynomial IOP into Simulation-Extractable SNARKs: A Modular Approach

Markulf Kohlweiss[1,2]([✉])[ID], Mahak Pancholi[3][ID], and Akira Takahashi[4]([✉])[ID]

[1] The University of Edinburgh, Edinburgh, UK
markulf.kohlweiss@ed.ac.uk
[2] Input Output Global, Singapore, Singapore
[3] Aarhus University, Aarhus, Denmark
mahakp@cs.au.dk
[4] J.P. Morgan AI Research & AlgoCRYPT CoE, New York, USA
takahashi.akira.58s@gmail.com

Abstract. Most succinct arguments (SNARKs) are initially only proven knowledge sound (KS). We show that the commonly employed compilation strategy from polynomial interactive oracle proofs (PIOP) via polynomial commitments to knowledge sound SNARKS actually also achieves other desirable properties: weak unique response (WUR) and trapdoorless zero-knowledge (TLZK); and that together they imply simulation extractability (SIM-EXT).

The factoring of SIM-EXT into KS + WUR + TLZK is becoming a cornerstone of the analysis of non-malleable SNARK systems. We show how to prove WUR and TLZK for PIOP compiled SNARKs under mild falsifiable assumptions on the polynomial commitment scheme. This means that the analysis of knowledge soundness from PIOP properties that inherently relies on non-falsifiable or idealized assumption such as the algebraic group model (AGM) or generic group model (GGM) need not be repeated.

While the proof of WUR requires only mild assumptions on the PIOP, TLZK is a different matter. As perfectly hiding polynomial commitments sometimes come at a substantial performance premium, SNARK designers prefer to employ deterministic commitments with some leakage. This results in the need for a stronger zero-knowledge property for the PIOP.

The modularity of our approach implies that any analysis improvements, e.g. in terms of tightness, credibility of the knowledge assumption and model of the KS analysis, or the precision of capturing real-world optimizations for TLZK also benefits the SIM-EXT guarantees.

The full version of this work is available at [34].

A. Takahashi—Work done while the author was affiliated with the University of Edinburgh.

G. Rothblum and H. Wee (Eds.): TCC 2023, LNCS 14371, pp. 486–512, 2023.
https://doi.org/10.1007/978-3-031-48621-0_17

1   Introduction

Succinct arguments and zero-knowledge proofs are being implemented and deployed. This is both due to their improved practicality and the popularity of use-cases that require efficient and private verification of statements. As it becomes harder to discern real information from automatically generated fakes, we have to increasingly rely on cryptographic chains of evidence [23,40]. Efficient zero-knowledge proofs help institutions become more transparent [10], help scale blockchains [7,11,43], and make applications more private [8,12,30,36].

As SNARKs become more prevalent, we must demand them to have optimal security and not just optimal speed. Recently, a number of new SNARK constructions have been proposed in the literature. They are typically proved to satisfy stand-alone security properties in isolation, namely zero-knowledge and (knowledge) soundness. These basic properties are often unsatisfactory both in theory and practice, due to the fact that NIZK proofs are inherently *transferable*, i.e., whoever observed an existing valid proof can prove a statement by reusing/modifying the proof, even without the knowledge of the corresponding witness. To prevent such *malleability attacks*, the seminal work of Sahai [42] introduced a stronger notion called *simulation-soundness*, which was later extended to *simulation-extractability* (SIM-EXT) [19]. Essentially, these notions state that no cheating prover can break (knowledge) soundness even after asking a ZK simulator to produce proofs on adaptively chosen statements. There is a long line of research that strengthens NIZK in a generic manner such that the proof system achieves simulation-soundness/extractability [2,3,6,16,19,21,29,32,35,37,38,41]. These generic lifting techniques often apply additional cryptographic primitives, such as (one-time) signature [19,29] and pseudo-random function [35], and then produce an extended proof for OR-statement derived from the target statement to be proven, without looking into inner workings of the base NIZK construction. In contrast, several recent works analyze particular exiting SNARK constructions *without modification* and successfully prove that some of the already deployed schemes satisfy simulation-extractability [5,18,25,27,28,31]. The downside of this approach is that analysis must be carried out in an ad-hoc way and tailored to each specific scheme.

Given this state of affairs, our question is whether it's possible to prove simulation-extractability for a large class of exiting SNARKs in an abstract manner. To this end, we turn to the popular paradigms of constructing highly efficient SNARKs from Polynomial Interactive Oracle Proofs (PIOP) [9,13,14, 17]. This paradigm allows for a modular design of zkSNARK, starting from an information theoretic object, compiling it into an interactive argument system via cryptographic *polynomial commitments*. It is then made non-interactive in the random oracle model via Fiat-Shamir transform [22].

1.1 Our Contribution

Framework for Proving SIM-EXT for PIOP-Based SNARKs. In this work, we provide a modular framework to prove SIM-EXT for a class of NIZK arguments constructed from PIOP in the random oracle model. We isolate sufficient and minimal properties required from the PIOP and the polynomial commitment schemes (PCOM) to conclude simulation-extractability (SIM-EXT) for the compiled zkSNARK, while relying on the existing knowledge soundness analysis in a black-box manner. An additional goal here is to minimize modifications to the exiting knowledge sound SNARK constructed via the compiler of [13,17].

Along the way, we generalize a theorem by [28] for proving SIM-EXT of Fiat-Shamir arguments in a modular fashion by adapting the notion of canonical simulator. Our canonical simulators supports access to a SRS and an internal PIOP simulator. Finally, we generalize the theorem of [28] to hold for both straight-line and rewinding-based extractors (assuming knowledge soundness, trapdoor-less zero knowledge (TLZK), and weak unique response (WUR) hold). Our analysis can now focus on proving TLZK and WUR and these properties do not even involve any extractor in the definition; our result holds for any extractor.

Generic Strategy for Proving Weak Unique Response. Since the SNARKs we study are obtained by applying Fiat-Shamir to multi-round interactive arguments, it is often required to show the so-called *(weak) unique response (WUR)* property to conclude SIM-EXT [28]. As indicated in the very recent works [18,28], proofs of unique response can be quite involved especially if the underlying interactive protocols have many rounds. We show that only a few mild properties of PCOM are sufficient to show that the PIOP-compiler generically outputs a NIZK argument satisfying WUR. Interestingly, this implies that exiting polynomial commitments already have a built-in mechanism to retain SIM-EXT .

Generic Strategy for Trapdoor-Less Zero-Knowledge Simulation. Another technical hurdle in proving SIM-EXT in a modular way is that, the zero knowledge simulation must be done in a trapdoor-less manner, i.e., the only additional power available to the zero-knowledge simulation is programming the random oracle. While this was trivial in previous work [18,27,28] that focus only on NIZK in the random oracle model, PIOP-based zkSNARKs often involve both a RO and structured reference string (SRS) generated by trusted setup. Consequently, the majority of existing ZK simulators for such systems take advantage of the SRS's trapdoor. In this work, we provide generic strategies for achieving trapdoorless simulation for all PIOP schemes satisfying the standard property of honest verifier zero-knowledge (HVZK). Additionally, we introduce a stronger version of HVZK and refine our simulation strategy for PIOP schemes that satisfy this stronger notion.

Case Studies for Concrete Schemes. To show applicability of our framework, we study a few concrete schemes. For PCOM schemes, we study KZG commitments, which is one of the most common commitment scheme used for compiling PIOPs. We also briefly sketch a simple PCOM scheme built using compressed sigma protocols of [4]. For PIOP schemes, we study trapdoorless zero-knowledge for Marlin, Lunar, and Plonk. As a consequence of our framework, we conclude that a slight modification of Marlin and Lunar when compiled with the deterministic KZG commitment scheme are SIM-EXT. On the other hand, we show that Plonk needs a hiding version of KZG to be SIM-EXT.

1.2 Technical Overview

We provide a high-level overview of our modular approach towards simulation-extractability.

PIOP and zkSNARK Compiler. Let us recap one of the popular paradigms of constructing efficient zkSNARKs [13,14,17]. The compiler we study in this paper mostly follows the formalization of Marlin [17]. Our starting point is a *polynomial interactive oracle proof* (PIOP) system. This is a public-coin interactive protocol between prover $\mathbf{P}(x, w)$ and verifier $\mathbf{V}(x)$, where x is a statement and w is a witness, respectively. For each round $i = 1, \ldots, r$, $\mathbf{P}$ sends a *polynomial oracle* $p_i \in \mathbb{F}[X]$ and the verifier $\mathbf{V}$ responds with uniformly sampled challenge ρ_i.[1] The challenge strings $\rho_1, \ldots, \rho_r$ are then used by $\mathbf{V}$ to derive *evaluation points* $z_1, \ldots, z_r$, which are queried to the polynomial oracles. Upon receiving $y_i = p_i(z_i)$ for $i = 1, \ldots, r$ from the oracles, $\mathbf{V}$ outputs a decision bit to accept or reject.

It is well known that the above information-theoretic object can be compiled into a non-interactive argument in the random oracle model, using a cryptographic primitive called *polynomial commitment* (PCOM). The compilation is two fold. First, one constructs an interactive argument, where for each round i, prover $\mathcal{P}$ internally runs a PIOP prover $\mathbf{P}$ to obtain a polynomial p_i, generates a commitment c_i to p_i, and sends c_i to $\mathcal{V}$, and $\mathcal{V}$ responds with ρ_i generated by the PIOP verifier $\mathbf{V}$. At the end of interaction, $\mathcal{P}$ outputs y_i with *evaluation proofs* π_i guaranteeing that $p_i(z_i) = y_i$ w.r.t. committed polynomials p_i. $\mathcal{V}$ accepts if and only if $\mathbf{V}$ accepts *and* all evaluation proofs are valid. Notice that this protocol follows the typical format of public-coin interactive argument. Therefore, assuming access to random oracle H, one can construct a corresponding non-interactive argument Π by applying a Fiat-Shamir transform.

From Knowledge Soundness to Simulation-Extractability in the PIOP Paradigm. Plain knowledge soundness of compiled protocol Π is already analyzed in the literature under various assumptions on PCOM and PIOP [13,14,17,24,39]. To benefit from existing knowledge soundness analyses in

---

[1] To sketch the core ideas, we provide a simplified version of PIOP where each round involves a single polynomial. Here, we also ignore the role of preprocessing for now. In the detailed proof, we deal with a more general case with multiple polynomials in every round, and the preprocessing phase, and multiple evaluation points for each polynomial.

a black-box manner, our goal is to lift knowledge soundness to simulation-extractability (SIM-EXT) while being agnostic of concrete behaviors of knowledge extractor. Fortunately, Ganesh et al. [28] recently proved that a property called *weak unique response (WUR)* is sufficient for Fiat-Shamir non-interactive arguments to have SIM-EXT in the ROM. Essentially, the WUR property of [28] requires the following: given a transcript $\pi = (a_1, \rho_1, \ldots, a_r, \rho_r, a_{r+1})$ output by simulator S for Fiat-Shamir non-interactive argument (constructed from $(2r+1)$-move multi-round public-coin interactive argument), for any $i \geq 2$, it is computationally hard to come up with another transcript π' with *shared prefix*, i.e., $\pi' = (a_1, \rho_1, \ldots, a_i', \rho_i', \ldots, a_r', \rho_r', a_{r+1}')$ such that $a_i' \neq a_i$.

However, their general theorem only covers a *transparent* case, while many recent PIOP-based zk-SNARKs require trusted generation of SRS in addition to the random oracle (e.g., if PCOM is instantiated with the well-known KZG scheme). It turns out that dependency on both SRS and RO introduces additional challenges in proving SIM-EXT in a modular fashion. In more detail, to invoke the general theorem similar to [28], one must show the existence of *trapdoor-less* ZK (TLZK) simulator, which only makes use of programmability of RO but without the knowledge of simulation trapdoor for SRS. We formalize this observation in Lemma 2.13. As the existing compiler theorems (such as Marlin and Lunar) do show zero-knowledge with trapdoor, we need an alternative way to prove zero-knowledge. In this work, we show two strategies of TLZK simulation, depending on the power of underlying PIOP simulator. The first path is straightforward: it requires honest verifier zero-knowledge (HVZK) of PIOP and hiding of PCOM similar to the Marlin compiler. As an alternative approach, if PIOP tolerates Ψ additional evaluations on polynomials which are *not* asked by honest PIOP verifier (Ψ-HVZK), then we show only a weak variant of hiding from PCOM is sufficient for Π to be TLZK. This is an observation implicit in several practical constructions, but to the best of our knowledge, no previous compiler theorem explicitly formalized it.

Proving Weak Unique Response for the Compiled Protocol. Given a TLZK simulator, our goal is to identify a set of properties allowing us to prove WUR. Recall that a transcript of Π is comprised of

$$(c_1, \rho_1, \ldots, c_r, \rho_r, (y_1, \ldots, y_r), (\pi_1, \ldots, \pi_r))$$

where $\rho_i = \mathsf{H}(\mathsf{srs}, \mathsf{i}, \mathsf{x}, c_1, \rho_1, \ldots, c_i)$. Focusing on the last round response, one can immediately see the need for unique proofs (i.e., for a fixed (c_i, z_i, y_i), there exists a unique proof π_i that verifies) and evaluation binding (i.e., for a fixed (c_i, z_i), there exists unique evaluation outcome y_i that verifies); otherwise, a cheating prover can maul either π_i or y_i of an existing transcript to create a valid transcript without knowing witness for x. We show that these mild properties are already satisfied by KZG which is the most common commitment scheme used for compilation. The hardest part is to prove that an adversary cannot maul a response in the middle of the transcript. Our crucial observation is that the compiler has a built-in mechanism similar to one-time signature, making it difficult for the prover to forge any part of the transcript. In more detail, if any prefix of the transcript is modified, then it inevitably triggers re-sampling of the final Fiat-Shamir challenge, leading to $\rho_r' \neq \rho_r$ with overwhelming probability. Since ρ_r' is used as a random coin to derive evaluation points $z_1', \ldots, z_r'$, without loss of generality, a cheating prover is forced to create a valid evaluation proof for c_1 w.r.t. an evaluation point $z_1' \neq z_1$.[2] However, if p_1 is randomized enough and the commitment c_1 together with an evaluation proof π_i leaks no more information than $p_1(z_1)$, then it must be hard for an adversary to extrapolate valid evaluation proof for $p_1(z_1')$ w.r.t. c_1. We formalize this intuition assuming the same evaluation binding and weak hiding assumptions.

1.3 Related Work

Broadly, there are currently three approaches to obtain simulation extractable SNARK:

Generic Lifting Techniques for SIM-EXT NIZK. Classically, it is well-known that any sound NIZK proof can be lifted to SIM-EXT NIZK in a general manner. For example, De Santis et al. [19] combine NIZK for a language L with one-time signature and PRF to realize SIM-EXT by having prover generate a proof for an extended OR-language L' related to the original language L. More recent lifting compilers [2,3,35] optimize the approach along these lines and further add *black-box and straight-line knowledge extraction* in order to achieve universally composable [15] zkSNARKs, but still introduce performance overhead in the size of SRS, proof size, and proving/verification time. Somewhat related, [26] introduced a straight-line extraction compiler to lift zkSNARKs which already satisfies SIM-EXT to UC-secure zkSNARKs in the random oracle model, while preserving the asymptotic succinctness of the output proof size.

Scheme Specific Techniques. The second is to prove directly that an existing SNARK scheme is simulation extractable [5,18,25,28,31]. This approach is taken by [25] for Plonk, Marlin, and Sonic, by [27,28] for Bulletproofs, and by [18] for Bulletproofs and Spartan, respectively. As these two works share close resemblance with ours, we investigate their strategy for proving specific schemes in some more detail.

All of [18,25,28] provide very similar frameworks for showing SIM-EXT for zkSNARKs obtained as Fiat-Shamir compiled multi-round protocols (in the updatable SRS setting for [25] and in the transparent setting for [18,28]). They observe that it suffices to prove that the schemes in question satisfy additional properties that together with existing properties, typically knowledge soundness, imply SIM-EXT. These properties are TLZK, and their specific variants

---

[2] As we elaborate in the full version, some PIOP protocols do not use the last round challenge ρ_r to derive z_1. However, one can cheaply patch them by introducing a random dummy polynomial p' in the first round and having the verifier query p' with a fresh evaluation point derived from ρ_r. Note that this can also be seen as a generic method to add weak unique response to *any* Fiat-Shamir NIZKAoK in the ROM.

of unique responses (UR). However, each of these properties is directly tied to the compiled zkSNARKs, and as such they have to be analyzed for each scheme separately, e.g., they provide three TLZK simulator and prove that they achieve zero-knowledge for Plonk, Marlin, and Sonic (in [25]), and prove the unique response property for each scheme (in all works). Moreover, [25] only considers zkSNARKs whose knowledge soundness proof is based on rewinding in the random oracle.

Our framework simplifies and generalizes the SIM-EXT analysis. We show that the PIOP to zkSNARK compiler [17] already achieves the additional TLZK and WUR under milder assumptions on the polynomial commitment. TLZK and WUR together with knowledge soundness then imply simulation-extractability.

Another difference from the work of [25] is in the simulation strategies for TLZK . We observe that the simulation for Plonk as presented in [25] is flawed as it only works for perfectly hiding commitments, and we explain more in the full version [34].

SE-SNARKS from PIOP and Polynomial Commitments. Our result thus falls into a third category which proves SIM-EXT for a PIOP to zkSNARK compiler rather than for individual schemes. As does the following concurrent work.

Concurrent Work. Faonio et al. [20] study simulation-extractability (SE) of zkSNARKs constructed from polynomial IOP and polynomial commitment. Their main goal is to identify properties of polynomial commitment such that a compiled zkSNARK satisfies simulation-extractability. Along the way, they define SE tailored to a polynomial commitment parameterized by a *policy predicate* Φ. The policy specifies additional conditions, on top of requiring a valid non-extractable proof, to determine the success of the adversary and is based on the following properties and variables in the SE game: (1) public parameters and honestly sampled commitments, (2) an adversarially created forgery (x, π), (3) the adversary's view, including the set of statement-proof pairs recorded by the simulation oracle, and the set of query-response pairs recorded by the random oracle, (4) auxiliary information which comes along with the forged instance. As a concrete example, they prove the KZG commitment is SE in the AGM w.r.t. a specific class of Φ and this implies SE of several existing zkSNARKs including Plonk and Marlin. In contrast, our approach to SE analysis of zkSNARKs only requires simpler, easy-to-state properties of polynomial commitment, namely, evaluation binding, unique proof and hiding. We expect that such properties are satisfied by other polynomial commitment than KZG such as inner-product based (IPA) polynomial commitments. Our analysis is also agnostic of the type of extractor for polynomial commitment thanks to the modularity of the generic result proved in [28].

Intuition from Proofs. We note that these two works take different routes to the same destination.[3] It is natural, that complex theorems can have multiple,

---

[3] As fellow travelers we have open lines of communications which even resulted in an author overlap.

conceptually very different proofs that yield different insights. Our intuition for where the proofs depart—early on, is that their work strengthens the extraction property of the polynomial commitment scheme to also work in the presence of a simulator using the secret trapdoor. In contrast, our work strengthens the zero-knowledge property and requires a simulator that does not have access to the trapdoor. Note that both works resort to random oracle programming for simulation.

More superficially, their polynomial IOP model stems from Lunar's PHP model [14] from where they also take the inspiration of treating polynomial commitments as commit-and-prove SNARKs, while our PIOP are inspired by Marlin's AHP model [17].

2 Preliminaries

We assume $[\ell]$ to denote integers $\{1, \ldots, \ell\}$ and $[k, \ell]$ to denote $\{k, \ldots, \ell\}$ for $k < \ell$. The security parameter is denoted by λ. A function $f(\lambda)$ is negligible in λ if for any polynomial $\mathsf{poly}(\lambda)$, $f(\lambda) \leq 1/\mathsf{poly}(\lambda)$ for sufficiently large λ. We denote $f(\lambda) \leq \mathsf{negl}(\lambda)$ to indicate f is negligible. By $y \xleftarrow{\rho} \mathcal{A}(x)$, we mean that a randomized algorithm $\mathcal{A}$ outputs y on input x using a random coin ρ sampled uniformly from a randomness space. For a finite field $\mathbb{F}$, $\mathbb{F}^d[X]$ denotes a set of polynomials over $\mathbb{F}$ of degree at most d.

2.1 Relations

An *indexed relation* $\hat{\mathcal{R}}$ is a set of triples $(\mathsf{i}, \mathsf{x}, \mathsf{w})$ where i is the index, x is the instance, and w is the witness. We assume $\hat{\mathcal{R}}$ can be partitioned using the security parameter $\lambda \in \mathbb{N}$ (e.g., by including the description of field $\mathbb{F}$ such that $|\mathbb{F}|$ is determined by a function of λ). Given a security parameter $\lambda \in \mathbb{N}$, we denote by $\hat{\mathcal{R}}_\lambda$ the restriction of $\hat{\mathcal{R}}$ to triples $(\mathsf{i}, \mathsf{x}, \mathsf{w}) \in \hat{\mathcal{R}}$ with appropriate length in λ. Given a fixed index i, we denote by $\hat{\mathcal{R}}_\mathsf{i}$ the restriction of $\hat{\mathcal{R}}$ to $\{(\mathsf{x}, \mathsf{w}) : (\mathsf{i}, \mathsf{x}, \mathsf{w}) \in \hat{\mathcal{R}}\}$. Given an indexed relation $\hat{\mathcal{R}}$, the corresponding *binary relation* can be defined as $\mathcal{R} = \{((\mathsf{i}, \mathsf{x}), \mathsf{w}) : (\mathsf{i}, \mathsf{x}, \mathsf{w}) \in \hat{\mathcal{R}}\}$.

Typically, i describes an arithmetic circuit over a finite field, x denotes public inputs, and w denotes private inputs, respectively. In the rest of this paper, we assume i and x to include the description of finite field $\mathbb{F}$ for the sake of simplicity, but our result holds even if the circuit is over a ring or module.

2.2 Polynomial Interactive Oracle Proofs

We define polynomial interactive oracle proofs (PIOP) with preprocessing. The formulation below is highly inspired by algebraic holographic proofs (AHP) [17]. We apply the following minor modifications: (1) Interaction starts with prover's message, instead of verifier's public coin. (2) We introduce an additional parameter t to allow multiple queries to a single polynomial. (3) We assume a single maximum degree bound d rather than a distinct bound for each polynomial oracle (following the PIOP formulation of [13]), since the degree bound check can be incorporated into PIOP by having prover output an oracle with shifted polynomial.

Definition 2.1 (Polynomial IOP). *A polynomial interactive oracle proof (PIOP) for an indexed relation $\hat{\mathcal{R}}$ is specified by a tuple* $\mathsf{PIOP} = (\mathsf{r}, \mathsf{s}, \mathsf{t}, \mathsf{d}, \mathbf{I}, \mathbf{P}, \mathbf{V})$, *where* $\mathsf{r}, \mathsf{s}, \mathsf{t}, \mathsf{d} : \{0,1\}^* \to \mathbb{N}$ *are polynomial-time computable functions and* $\mathbf{I}, \mathbf{P}, \mathbf{V}$ *are three algorithms known as the* indexer, prover, *and* verifier. *The parameter* r *specifies the number of interaction rounds,* s *specifies the number of polynomials in each round,* t *specifies the number of queries made to each polynomial, and* d *specifies a maximum degree bound on these polynomials. An execution of* $\mathsf{PIOP}\,(\mathsf{i}, \mathsf{x}, \mathsf{w}) \in \hat{\mathcal{R}}$ *involves interaction between* $\mathbf{P}$ *and* $\mathbf{V}$, *where* $b \leftarrow \langle \mathbf{P}(\mathsf{i}, \mathsf{x}, \mathsf{w}), \mathbf{V}^{\mathbf{I}(\mathsf{i})}(\mathsf{x}) \rangle$ *denotes the output decision bit, and* $(\text{view}; \mathsf{p}) \leftarrow [\![\mathbf{P}(\mathsf{i}, \mathsf{x}, \mathsf{w}), \mathbf{V}^{\mathbf{I}(\mathsf{i})}(\mathsf{x})]\!]$ *denotes the view (*view*) of* $\mathbf{V}$ *generated during the interaction and the responses of* $\mathbf{I}(\mathsf{i})$, *and the polynomial oracles (*p*) output by* $\mathbf{P}$. *The* view *consists of challenges* $\rho_1, \ldots, \rho_{\mathsf{r}}$ *that* $\mathbf{V}$ *sends to* $\mathbf{P}$ *and vector* y *of oracle responses defined below. The vector* p *consists of the polynomial oracles generated by* $\mathbf{P}$ *during the interaction. An execution of* PIOP *proceeds as follows:*

- *Offline phase. The indexer* $\mathbf{I}$ *receives as input index* i *for* $\hat{\mathcal{R}}$, *and outputs* $\mathsf{s}(0)$ *polynomials* $p_{0,1}, \ldots, p_{0,\mathsf{s}(0)} \in \mathbb{F}[X]$ *of degrees at most* $\mathsf{d}(|\mathsf{i}|)$. *Note that the offline phase does not depend on any particular instance or witness, and merely considers the task of encoding the given index* i.
- *Online phase. Given an instance* x *and witness* w *such that* $(\mathsf{i}, \mathsf{x}, \mathsf{w}) \in \hat{\mathcal{R}}$, *the prover* $\mathbf{P}$ *receives* $(\mathsf{i}, \mathsf{x}, \mathsf{w})$ *and the verifier* $\mathbf{V}$ *receives* x *and oracle access to the polynomials output by* $\mathbf{I}(\mathsf{i})$. *The prover* $\mathbf{P}$ *and the verifier* $\mathbf{V}$ *interact over* $(2\mathsf{r} + 1)$ *rounds where* $\mathsf{r} = \mathsf{r}(|\mathsf{i}|)$. *For* $i \in [\mathsf{r}]$, *in the i-th round of interaction, first the prover* $\mathbf{P}$ *sends* $\mathsf{s}(i)$ *oracle polynomials* $p_{i,1}, \ldots, p_{i,\mathsf{s}(i)} \in \mathbb{F}[X]$ *to the verifier* $\mathbf{V}$; *and* $\mathbf{V}$ *replies with a challenge* $\rho_i \in \mathsf{Ch}$, *where* Ch *is the challenge space determined by* i. *The last round challenge* $\rho_{\mathsf{r}} \in \mathsf{Ch}$ *serves as auxiliary input to* $\mathbf{V}$ *in subsequent phases. We assume the protocol to be public-coin, meaning that* ρ_i*'s are public and uniformly sampled from* Ch. *Moreover, observe that* $\mathbf{P}$ *can be interpreted as a series of next message functions such that polynomial oracles for round i are obtained by running* $(\mathsf{st}_P, p_{i,1}, \ldots, p_{i,\mathsf{s}(i)}) \leftarrow \mathbf{P}(\mathsf{st}'_P, \rho_{i-1})$, *where* st'_P *is the internal state of* $\mathbf{P}$ *after sending polynomials for round $i - 1$ and before receiving challenge* ρ_{i-1}, *and* st_P *is the updated state. Here,* ρ_0 *is assumed to be* $\bot$.
- *Query phase. Let* $\mathsf{p} = (p_{i,j})_{i \in [0,\mathsf{r}], j \in [\mathsf{s}(i)]}$ *be a vector consisting of all polynomials sent by the prover* $\mathbf{P}$. *The verifier may query any of the polynomials it has received any number of times. Concretely,* $\mathbf{V}$ *executes a subroutine* $\mathbf{Q}_{\mathbf{V}}$ *that receives* $(\mathsf{x}; \rho_1, \ldots, \rho_{\mathsf{r}})$ *and outputs a query vector* $\mathbf{z} = (\mathbf{z}_{i,j})_{i \in [0,\mathsf{r}], j \in [\mathsf{s}(i)]}$, *where each* $\mathbf{z}_{i,j}$ *is to be interpreted as a vector* $(z_{i,j,k})_{k \in [\mathsf{t}(i,j)]} \in \mathbb{D}^{\mathsf{t}(i,j)}$ *and* $\mathbb{D} \subseteq \mathbb{F}$ *is an evaluation domain determined by* i. *We write "*$\mathbf{y}_{i,j} = p_{i,j}(\mathbf{z}_{i,j})$*" to define an evaluation vector* $\mathbf{y}_{i,j} = (y_{i,j,k})_{k \in [\mathsf{t}(i,j)]}$ *where* $y_{i,j,k} = p_{i,j}(z_{i,j,k})$. *Likewise, we write "*$\mathbf{y} = \mathsf{p}(\mathbf{z})$*" to define* $\mathbf{y} = (\mathbf{y}_{i,j})_{i \in [0,\mathsf{r}], j \in [\mathsf{s}(i)]}$ *where* $\mathbf{y}_{i,j} = p_{i,j}(\mathbf{z}_{i,j})$.

– **Decision phase.** *The verifier outputs "accept" or "reject" based on the answers to the queries (and the verifier's randomness). Concretely,* **V** *executes a subroutine* $\mathbf{D_V}$ *that receives* $(\mathsf{x}, \mathbf{p}(\mathbf{z}); \rho_1, \ldots, \rho_r)$ *as input, and outputs the decision bit b.*
The function d *determines which provers to consider for the completeness and soundness properties of the proof system. In more detail, we say that a (possibly malicious) prover* $\tilde{\mathbf{P}}$ *is admissible for* PIOP *if, on every interaction with the verifier* **V***, it holds that for every round $i \in [r]$ and oracle index $j \in [\mathsf{s}(i)]$ we have* $\deg(p_{i,j}) \le \mathsf{d}(|\mathsf{i}|)$. *The honest prover* **P** *is required to be admissible under this definition.*

Typically PIOP should satisfy completeness, (knowledge) soundness and zero-knowledge as defined below.

Definition 2.2 (Completeness). *A* PIOP *is complete if for any* $(\mathsf{i}, \mathsf{x}, \mathsf{w}) \in \hat{\mathcal{R}}$,

$$\Pr\left[b \leftarrow \langle \mathbf{P}(\mathsf{i}, \mathsf{x}, \mathsf{w}), \mathbf{V}^{\mathbf{I}(\mathsf{i})}(\mathsf{x}) \rangle \ : \ b = 1 \right] = 1$$

Now we define a stronger notion of honest verifier zero knowledge (HVZK) for PIOP . First, a straightforward HVZK asks for simulatability of the view of honest verifier **V** which comprises of all public coins $\rho_1, \ldots, \rho_r$ and the outcome of evaluations **y**. It turns out that, if compiled with a non-hiding commitment scheme, the committing function leaks additional evaluations of polynomials which are not queried by an honest PIOP verifier **V** (modeled as $\mathbf{p}(\chi)$ below). In order to tolerate such additional leakages, we consider the existence of a more powerful simulator that, along with the proof string, is also able to output some polynomials, such that even after providing additional evaluations w.r.t. these polynomials, the view remains indistinguishable from the real execution.

Note that Lunar [14] also models a similar notion where zero-knowledge should hold even when the proof might leak some additional evaluation points. However, since their simulation strategy crucially uses the trapdoor information in order to satisfy this notion, our definition is stronger and harder to achieve. One interesting motivation that suggests that we need our stronger formulation is that Plonk [24] (as presented in [25]) happens to satisfy Lunar's definition but not ours. However, the trapdoorless simulation based on deterministic commitments, as suggested in [25], is flawed (as we expand more in the full version). This suggests that Lunar's formulation of leakage is not enough in the context of trapdoorless zero-knowledge; we require something stronger.

We also require the PIOP to satisfy a second condition called *non-extrapolatable first polynomial*. Roughly, it says that there is enough randomness in the first online polynomial p so that, given a certain number of evaluations, the next evaluation remains unpredictable. In this intuition, we implicitly assume that the first online polynomial of the PIOP encodes the witness somehow. Note that this requirement is very easily satisfied by most PIOPs already, since they do encode the witness in the first round polynomials with enough randomness used in the encoding to achieve zero-knowledge.

Game 1: HVZK for Polynomial IOP

$\underline{\text{HVZK-0}_{\mathbf{A}}(1^\lambda, \chi)}$
1: $b \leftarrow \mathbf{A}^{O_0}(1^\lambda)$
2: **return** b

$\underline{\text{NEXP-1}_{\mathbf{A}}(1^\lambda, \chi)}$
1: $(\mathsf{i}, \mathsf{x}) \leftarrow \mathbf{A}_1(1^\lambda)$
2: $(\text{view}, \mathrm{p}(\chi), \mathrm{p}(\mathrm{z})) \leftarrow \mathbf{O}_1'(\mathsf{i}, \mathsf{x})$
3: $(z^*, y^*) \leftarrow \mathbf{A}_2(\text{view}, \mathrm{p}(\chi), \mathrm{p}(\mathrm{z}))$
4: $b := (z^* \notin (\mathbf{z}, \chi)) \wedge (y^* = p(z^*))$
5: **return** b

$\underline{\mathbf{O}_0(\mathsf{i}, \mathsf{x}, \mathsf{w})}$
1: **if** $(\mathsf{i}, \mathsf{x}, \mathsf{w}) \notin \hat{\mathcal{R}}$ **then return** $\bot$
2: $(\text{view}; \mathrm{p}) \leftarrow [\![\mathbf{P}(\mathsf{i}, \mathsf{x}, \mathsf{w}), \mathbf{V}^{\mathbf{I}(\mathsf{i})}(\mathsf{x})]\!]$
3: $(\rho_1, \ldots, \rho_r, \mathbf{y}) := \text{view}$
4: $\mathbf{z} \leftarrow \mathbf{Q_V}(\mathsf{x}; \rho_1, \ldots, \rho_r)$
5: **return** $(\text{view}, \mathrm{p}(\chi), \mathrm{p}(\mathrm{z}))$

$\underline{\text{HVZK-1}_{\mathbf{A}}(1^\lambda, \chi)}$
1: $b \leftarrow \mathbf{A}^{O_1}(1^\lambda)$
2: **return** b

$\underline{\mathbf{O}_1(\mathsf{i}, \mathsf{x}, \mathsf{w})}$
1: **if** $(\mathsf{i}, \mathsf{x}, \mathsf{w}) \notin \hat{\mathcal{R}}$ **then return** $\bot$
2: $(\text{view}; \mathrm{p}) \leftarrow \mathbf{S}(\mathsf{i}, \mathsf{x})$
3: $(\rho_1, \ldots, \rho_r, \mathbf{y}) := \text{view}$
4: $\mathbf{z} \leftarrow \mathbf{Q_V}(\mathsf{x}; \rho_1, \ldots, \rho_r)$
5: **if** $\exists p_{i,j} \in \mathrm{p}, \deg(p_{i,j}) > \mathsf{d}(|\mathsf{i}|)$
   then return $\bot$
6: **return** $(\text{view}, \mathrm{p}(\chi), \mathrm{p}(\mathrm{z}))$

$\underline{\mathbf{O}_1'(\mathsf{i}, \mathsf{x})}$
1: $(\text{view}; \mathrm{p}) \leftarrow \mathbf{S}(\mathsf{i}, \mathsf{x})$
2: $(\rho_1, \ldots, \rho_r, \mathbf{y}) := \text{view}$
3: $\mathbf{z} \leftarrow \mathbf{Q_V}(\mathsf{x}; \rho_1, \ldots, \rho_r)$
4: **if** $\exists p_{i,j} \in \mathrm{p}, \deg(p_{i,j}) > \mathsf{d}(|\mathsf{i}|)$
   then return $\bot$
5: **return** $(\text{view}, \mathrm{p}(\chi), \mathrm{p}(\mathrm{z}))$

Definition 2.3 (Ψ-Honest Verifier Zero Knowledge (HVZK)). *Let* PIOP *be a polynomial IOP for relation* $\hat{\mathcal{R}}$. *Let* $\mathbb{D}$ *denote the domain of honest polynomial oracle queries. Let* $\chi = (\chi_{i,j})_{i \in [\mathsf{r}], j \in [\mathsf{s}(i)]}$ *denote an auxiliary query vector which is said to be valid if for each* $i \in [\mathsf{r}], j \in [\mathsf{s}(i)]$, $|\chi_{i,j}| \leq \Psi$ *and each query in* $\chi_{i,j}$ *comes from* $\mathbb{D}$. PIOP *is statistical* Ψ-*honest verifier zero knowledge, if there exists a* PPT *simulator* $\mathbf{S}$ *such that for any distinguisher* $\mathbf{A}$, *and for all valid auxiliary query vectors* χ, *it holds that*

$$\mathbf{Adv}_{\mathbf{A}}^{\Psi\text{-}HVZK}(\lambda, \chi) := \left| \Pr\left[HVZK\text{-}0_{\mathbf{A}}(1^\lambda, \chi) = 0 \right] - \Pr\left[HVZK\text{-}1_{\mathbf{A}}(1^\lambda, \chi) = 0 \right] \right| \leq \mathsf{negl}(\lambda)$$

where HVZK-0 and HVZK-1 are defined in Game 1 . If the operations highlighted in orange are not executed, then we simply say PIOP *satisfies HVZK.*

Definition 2.4 (Ψ-Non-Extrapolation for the First Polynomial). *Let* PIOP, $\mathbb{D}$, *and* χ *be as defined in Definition 2.3. Let* $\mathbf{S}$ *be the statistical* Ψ-*honest verifier zero knowledge simulator for the* PIOP , *and* t *be the number of distinct evaluations revealed for each polynomial in a* PIOP *proof. Let* $\mathbf{p}$ *be the vector of polynomials output by* $\mathbf{S}$, *and* p *denotes the first polynomial for the online phase in* $\mathbf{p}$. p *is said to be* Ψ-*Non-Extrapolatable if for any adversary* $\mathbf{A} := (\mathbf{A}_1, \mathbf{A}_2)$ *(where* $\mathbf{A}_1, \mathbf{A}_2$ *share internal state), and for all valid auxiliary query vectors* χ *(as defined in Definition 2.3), it holds that,*

$$\mathbf{Adv}_{\mathbf{A}}^{\Psi\text{-}NEXP}(\lambda, \chi) := \Pr\left[NEXP\text{-}1_{\mathbf{A}}(1^\lambda, \chi) = 1 \right] \leq \mathsf{negl}(\lambda)$$

where NEXP-1 is define in Game 1.

Min-entropy of $\mathbf{Q_V}$. Recall, the sub-routine $\mathbf{Q_V}$ takes input $(x; \rho_1, \ldots, \rho_r)$ and outputs a query vector $\mathbf{z} = (\mathbf{z}_{i,j})_{i \in [0,r], j \in [s(i)]}$ where each $\mathbf{z}_{i,j}$ can be parsed as a vector $(z_{i,j,k})_{k \in [t(i,j)]}$. We isolate one evaluation point $z_{1,1,1}$ for $p_{1,1}$ and require that $z_{1,1,1}$ is equal to some fixed value only with negligible probability. This is captured by assessing min-entropy of the $\mathbf{Q_V}$ algorithm.

Definition 2.5 (Min-entropy of $\mathbf{Q_V}$). *Let* PIOP $= (\mathsf{r}, \mathsf{s}, \mathsf{t}, \mathsf{d}, \mathbf{I}, \mathbf{P}, \mathbf{V})$ *be a PIOP for indexed relation $\hat{\mathcal{R}}$. $(\mathbf{Q_V}, \mathbf{D_V})$ denote the subroutines run by $\mathbf{V}$. Let* Ch *be the challenge space from which $\mathbf{V}$ samples ρ_i. For any fixed $\lambda \in \mathbb{N}$ and for any $(i, x, w) \in \hat{\mathcal{R}}_\lambda$, consider the maximum probability that $z_{1,1,1}$ is equal to a particular value:*

$$\mu(\lambda, x) = \max_{\rho_1, \ldots, \rho_{r-1} \in \mathsf{Ch}, a \in \mathbb{F}} \Pr\left[\rho_r \xleftarrow{\$} \mathsf{Ch}; \mathbf{z} \leftarrow \mathbf{Q_V}(x; \rho_1, \ldots, \rho_r) : z_{1,1,1} = a\right].$$

The min-entropy α *of sub-routine $\mathbf{Q_V}$ is*

$$\alpha(\lambda) = \min_{(i, x, w) \in \hat{\mathcal{R}}_\lambda} (-\log_2(\mu(\lambda, x))).$$

We say the min-entropy of $\mathbf{Q_V}$ is high if $\alpha \in \omega(\log(\lambda))$.

Remark 2.6. If the PIOP of interest does not have high min-entropy of $\mathbf{Q_V}$ and/or Ψ-non-extrapolatable first polynomial, one can easily patch in the following manner: a modified prover $\mathbf{P}$ additionally sends a dummy random polynomial $p^* \in \mathbb{F}^{\Psi+1}[X]$ in the first round and the verifier $\mathbf{V}$ queries p^* with a fresh evaluation point $z^* \in \mathbb{D}$ derived from ρ_r.

2.3   Non-interactive Argument and Simulation-Extractability in ROM

Below we write $\mathcal{A}^H$ to denote that an algorithm $\mathcal{A}$ has black-box access to the random oracle $H : \{0, 1\}^* \to \{0, 1\}^l$. To explicitly model preprocessed SRS in later sections, we also introduce indexed NARG (henceforth iNARG) $\hat{\Pi}$ for indexed relation $\hat{\mathcal{R}}$.

Definition 2.7 (Indexed Non-Interactive Argument (iNARG)). *An Indexed Non-Interactive Argument with Universal SRS in the random oracle model for indexed relation $\hat{\mathcal{R}}$ is a tuple $\hat{\Pi}_H = (\mathcal{G}, \mathcal{I}, \hat{\mathcal{P}}, \hat{\mathcal{V}})$ of three algorithms:*

- srs $\leftarrow \mathcal{G}(1^\lambda)$ *works as* $\mathcal{G}$ *of NARG.*
- $(\text{ipk}, \text{ivk}) \leftarrow \mathcal{I}(\text{i}, \text{srs})$ *is a deterministic* indexer[4] *that takes index* i *and* srs *as input, and produces a proving index key (*ipk*) and a verifier index key (*ivk*), used respectively by* $\hat{\mathcal{P}}$ *and* $\hat{\mathcal{V}}$.
- $\pi \leftarrow \hat{\mathcal{P}}^H(\text{ipk}, \text{x}, \text{w})$ *is a prover that outputs a proof* π *asserting* $(\text{i}, \text{x}, \text{w}) \in \hat{\mathcal{R}}$.
- $b \leftarrow \hat{\mathcal{V}}^H(\text{ivk}, \text{x}, \pi)$ *is a verifier that outputs a decision bit* b.

It is easy to convert $\hat{\Pi}$ for $\hat{\mathcal{R}}$ into the corresponding Π for binary relation $\mathcal{R} = \{((\text{i}, \text{x}), \text{w}) : (\text{i}, \text{x}, \text{w}) \in \hat{\mathcal{R}}\}$ by defining $\mathcal{P}^H(\text{srs}, (\text{i}, \text{x}), \text{w})$ to be an algorithm outputting π after running $(\text{ipk}, \text{ivk}) \leftarrow \mathcal{I}(\text{srs}, \text{i})$ and $\pi \leftarrow \hat{\mathcal{P}}^H(\text{ipk}, \text{x}, \text{w})$, and $\mathcal{V}^H(\text{srs}, (\text{i}, \text{x}), \pi)$ to be an algorithm outputting b after running $(\text{ipk}, \text{ivk}) \leftarrow \mathcal{I}(\text{srs}, \text{i})$ and $b \leftarrow \hat{\mathcal{V}}^H(\text{ivk}, \text{x}, \pi)$, respectively. Therefore, we only state security properties for NARG without loss of generality.

Definition 2.8 (Completeness). *A NARG* $\Pi_H = (\mathcal{G}, \mathcal{P}, \mathcal{V})$ *for relation* $\mathcal{R}$ *satisfies* perfect completeness *if for all* λ, *all* $N \in \mathbb{N}$, *and for all PPT adversaries* $\mathcal{A}$ *it holds that*

$$\Pr\left[\begin{array}{l} \text{srs} \leftarrow \mathcal{G}(1^\lambda); (\text{x}, \text{w}) \leftarrow \mathcal{A}^H(\text{srs}); \\ \pi \leftarrow \mathcal{P}^H(\text{srs}, \text{x}, \text{w}) \end{array} : \mathcal{V}^H(\text{srs}, \text{x}, \pi) = 1 \wedge (\text{x}, \text{w}) \in \mathcal{R}\right] = 1.$$

We define zero-knowledge for NARGs relying on both SRS and programmable RO. Note that in the general definition below, a simulator may take advantage of both the trapdoor of srs and programmability of the random oracle. Concretely, a simulated SRS generator $\mathcal{S}_0$ may potentially output a simulation trapdoor td. The zero-knowledge simulator $\mathcal{S}$ is defined as a stateful algorithm that operates in two modes. In the first mode, $(h, \text{st}') \leftarrow \mathcal{S}(1, \text{st}, t)$ responds to a random oracle query on input t. In the second mode, $(\pi, \text{st}') \leftarrow \mathcal{S}(2, \text{st}, (\text{srs}, \text{x}))$ simulates a proof string generated by an honest prover $\mathcal{P}$.

Definition 2.9 (Non-Interactive Zero Knowledge in the SRS and Programmable Random Oracle Model). *Let* $\Pi_H = (\mathcal{G}, \mathcal{P}, \mathcal{V})$ *be a NARG for relation* $\mathcal{R}$. Π_H *is* unbounded *non-interactive zero knowledge (NIZK) in the programmable random oracle model, if there exist a tuple of* PPT *algorithms* $(\mathcal{S}_0, \mathcal{S})$ *such that for all PPT distinguisher* $\mathcal{A}$, *it holds that*

$$\mathbf{Adv}_{\mathcal{A}}^{NIZK}(\lambda) := \left| \Pr\left[NIZK\text{-}0_{\mathcal{A}}(1^\lambda) = 0 \right] - \Pr\left[NIZK\text{-}1_{\mathcal{A}}(1^\lambda) = 0 \right] \right| \leq \mathsf{negl}(\lambda)$$

where NIZK-0 *and* NIZK-1 *are defined in Game 2. As a special case, if* Π_H *is* NIZK *w.r.t.* $\mathcal{S}_0 = \mathcal{G}$ *(and therefore it outputs* td $= \bot$*), then it is said to be* trapdoor-less *NIZK (TLZK).*

---

[4] In the literature, indexer is also referred to as Derive algorithm.

Game 2: NIZK

$\underline{\text{NIZK-0}_{\mathcal{A}}(1^\lambda)}$

  1: $\text{srs} \leftarrow \mathcal{G}(1^\lambda)$
  2: $b \leftarrow \mathcal{A}^{\text{H},\mathcal{P}^{\text{H}}(\text{srs},\cdot,\cdot)}(\text{srs})$
  3: **return** b

$\underline{\text{H}(t)}$

  1: **if** $\mathcal{Q}_{\text{H}}(t) = \bot$ **then**
  2:      $\mathcal{Q}_{\text{H}}(t) \xleftarrow{\$} \{0,1\}^l$
  3: **return** $\mathcal{Q}_{\text{H}}(t)$

$\underline{\text{NIZK-1}_{\mathcal{A}}(1^\lambda)}$

  1: $(\text{srs}, \text{td}) \leftarrow \mathcal{S}_0(1^\lambda)$
  2: $\text{st} := \text{td}$
  3: $b \leftarrow \mathcal{A}^{\mathcal{S}_1, \mathcal{S}_2}(\text{srs})$
  4: **return** b

$\underline{\mathcal{S}_1(t)}$

  1: $(h, \text{st}) \leftarrow \mathcal{S}(1, \text{st}, t)$
  2: **return** h

$\underline{\mathcal{S}_2(\text{x}, \text{w})}$

  1: **if** $(\text{x}, \text{w}) \notin \mathcal{R}$ **then**
  2:      **return** $\bot$
  3: $(\pi, \text{st}) \leftarrow \mathcal{S}(2, \text{st}, (\text{srs}, \text{x}))$
  4: **return** π

Now we define our final goal: an adaptive version of simulation-extractability for NARG in the ROM. On a high-level, the simulation-extractability (SIM-EXT) property ensures that extractability holds even if the cheating adversary is able to observe simulated proofs. Without the texts highlighted in orange (i.e., without access to the simulation oracle $\mathcal{S}_2'$), the property degrades to the standard extraction property (EXT). This is also known as knowledge soundness.

Definition 2.10 (Simulation-Extractability (SIM-EXT)). *Consider a NARG* $\Pi_{\text{H}} = (\mathcal{G}, \mathcal{P}, \mathcal{V})$ *for relation* $\mathcal{R}$ *with a NIZK simulator* $(\mathcal{S}_0, \mathcal{S})$. Π_{H} *is simulation-extractable (SIM-EXT) with respect to* $(\mathcal{S}_0, \mathcal{S})$, *if for any* PPT *adversary* $\mathcal{A}$, *there exists a* PPT *extractor* $\mathcal{E}_{\mathcal{A}}$ *such that, it holds that*

$$\text{Adv}_{\mathcal{A}}^{\text{SIM-EXT}}(\lambda) := \Pr\left[\, \text{SIM-EXT}_{\mathcal{A}}(1^\lambda) = 1 \right] \leq \text{negl}(\lambda)$$

where SIM-EXT is defined in Game 3.

Depending on whether $\mathcal{E}_{\mathcal{A}}(\text{srs}, \rho, \mathcal{Q}_1, \mathcal{Q}_2)$ depends on $\mathcal{A}$ and uses ρ, or there exists an $\mathcal{E}$ that is independent of $\mathcal{A}$ and uses only $\mathcal{Q}_1$ we get either white-box extraction, or "Fischlin's" straightline extraction, respectively.[5]

---

[5] Dependence or independence from $\mathcal{A}$ can be formalized by requiring that there exists a function f such that for any PPT adversary $\mathcal{A}$, there exists a PPT extractor $\mathcal{E}_{\mathcal{A}} = f(\mathcal{A})$. If f is a constant function we have independence otherwise dependence.

Game 3: SIM-EXT and WUR

$\text{WUR}_{\mathcal{A}}(1^\lambda)$

1: $\mathcal{Q}_1 := \varnothing; \mathcal{Q}_2 := \varnothing; \mathcal{Q}_{\mathsf{H}} := \varnothing$
2: $(\mathsf{srs}, \mathsf{td}) \leftarrow \mathcal{S}_0(1^\lambda)$
3: $\mathsf{st} := (\mathcal{Q}_{\mathsf{H}}, \mathsf{td})$
4: $(\mathsf{x}, \mathsf{st}_{\mathcal{A}}) \leftarrow \mathcal{A}_1^{\mathcal{S}_1}(\mathsf{srs})$
5: $\tilde{\pi} \leftarrow \mathcal{S}_2'(\mathsf{x})$
6: $\pi \leftarrow \mathcal{A}_2^{\mathcal{S}_1}(\mathsf{st}_{\mathcal{A}}, \tilde{\pi})$
7: $b \leftarrow \mathcal{V}^{\mathcal{S}_1}(\mathsf{srs}, \mathsf{x}, \pi)$
8: $b' \qquad\qquad :=$
$\quad (\exists i \in [1, \mathsf{r}] : \pi|_i = \tilde{\pi}|_i \ \wedge \ a_{i+1} \neq \tilde{a}_{i+1})$
9: **return** $b \wedge b'$

$\mathcal{S}_1(t)$

1: $(h, \mathsf{st}) \leftarrow \mathcal{S}(1, \mathsf{st}, t)$
2: $\mathcal{Q}_1(t) := h$
3: **return** h

$\mathcal{S}(1, \mathsf{st}, t)$

1: Retrieve $\mathcal{Q}_{\mathsf{H}}$ from st
2: **if** $\mathcal{Q}_{\mathsf{H}}(t) = \bot$ **then**
3: $\quad \mathcal{Q}_{\mathsf{H}}(t) \xleftarrow{\$} \{0,1\}^l$
4: $\mathsf{st} := \mathcal{Q}_{\mathsf{H}}$
5: **return** $(\mathcal{Q}_{\mathsf{H}}(t), \mathsf{st})$

$\text{SIM-EXT}_{\mathcal{A}}(1^\lambda)$

1: $\mathcal{Q}_1 := \varnothing; \mathcal{Q}_2 := \varnothing; \mathcal{Q}_{\mathsf{H}} := \varnothing$
2: $(\mathsf{srs}, \mathsf{td}) \leftarrow \mathcal{S}_0(1^\lambda)$
3: $\mathsf{st} := (\mathcal{Q}_{\mathsf{H}}, \mathsf{td})$
4: $(\mathsf{x}^*, \pi^*) \xleftarrow{\rho} \mathcal{A}^{\mathcal{S}_1, \mathcal{S}_2'}(\mathsf{srs})$
5: $b \leftarrow \mathcal{V}^{\mathcal{S}_1}(\mathsf{srs}, \mathsf{x}^*, \pi^*)$
6: $w^* \leftarrow \mathcal{E}_{\mathcal{A}}(\mathsf{srs}, \rho, \mathcal{Q}_1, \mathcal{Q}_2)$
7: **return** $b = 1 \wedge (\mathsf{x}^*, w^*) \notin$
$\quad \mathcal{R} \wedge (\mathsf{x}^*, \pi^*) \notin \mathcal{Q}_2$

$\mathcal{S}_2'(\mathsf{x})$

1: $(\pi, \mathsf{st}) \leftarrow \mathcal{S}(2, \mathsf{st}, (\mathsf{srs}, \mathsf{x}))$
2: $\mathcal{Q}_2 := \mathcal{Q}_2 \cup \{(\mathsf{x}, \pi)\}$
3: **return** π

$\mathcal{S}(2, \mathsf{st}, (\mathsf{srs}, \mathsf{x}))$

1: Retrieve $\mathcal{Q}_{\mathsf{H}}$ from st
2: $\pi = (a_1, \rho_1, \ldots, a_{\mathsf{r}+1}) \leftarrow \bar{\mathcal{S}}(\mathsf{srs}, \mathsf{x})$
3: **for** $i \in [1, \mathsf{r}]$ **do**
4: $\quad$ **if** $\mathcal{Q}_{\mathsf{H}}(\mathsf{srs}, \mathsf{x}, \pi|_i) \neq \bot$ **then**
5: $\quad\quad$ **return** abort
6: $\quad$ **else**
7: $\quad\quad \mathcal{Q}_{\mathsf{H}}(\mathsf{srs}, \mathsf{x}, \pi|_i) := \rho_i$
8: **return** $(\pi, \mathcal{Q}_{\mathsf{H}})$

2.4 Simulation-Extractability of Fiat-Shamir Non-interactive Arguments

In this paper, we consider a special class of NARG characterized as *Fiat-Shamir NARG (FS-NARG)*. $\Pi_{\mathsf{H}} = (\mathcal{G}, \mathcal{P}, \mathcal{V})$ is said to be FS-NARG, if $\mathcal{P}$ and $\mathcal{V}$ satisfy the following conditions:

- $\mathcal{P}^{\mathsf{H}}(\mathsf{srs}, \mathsf{x}, \mathsf{w})$ outputs a proof string that can be parsed as $\pi = (a_1, \rho_1, \ldots, a_{\mathsf{r}}, \rho_{\mathsf{r}}, a_{\mathsf{r}+1})$. We denote by $\pi|_i$ the i-th prefix $(a_1, \rho_1, \ldots, a_i)$ of π for $i \in [\mathsf{r}]$.
- There exists a PPT verdict algorithm Ver such that $\mathcal{V}^{\mathsf{H}}(\mathsf{srs}, \mathsf{x}, \pi)$ outputs 1 if and only if (1) $\mathsf{Ver}(\mathsf{srs}, \mathsf{x}, \pi) = 1$, and (2) $\rho_i = \mathsf{H}(\mathsf{srs}, \mathsf{x}, \pi|_i)$ for $i \in [\mathsf{r}]$.

In [27,28], the authors define the *weak unique response* property tailored to FS-NARGs but without SRS. In particular, this notion is useful for showing SIM-EXT of FS-NARGs constructed from multi-round public-coin protocols.

Definition 2.11 (WUR). *Consider a FS-NARG $\Pi_{\mathsf{H}} = (\mathcal{G}, \mathcal{P}, \mathcal{V})$ for $\mathcal{R}$ with a NIZK simulator $(\mathcal{S}_0, \mathcal{S})$. Π_{H} is said to have weak unique responses (WUR) with respect to $(\mathcal{S}_0, \mathcal{S})$, if given a proof string $\tilde{\pi} = (\tilde{a}_1, \tilde{\rho}_1, \ldots, \tilde{a}_{\mathsf{r}}, \tilde{\rho}_{\mathsf{r}}, \tilde{a}_{\mathsf{r}+1})$ simulated* *by $\mathcal{S}$, it is hard to find another accepting transcript $\pi = (a_1, \rho_1, \ldots, a_r, \rho_r, a_{r+1})$ that both have a common prefix up to the ith challenge for an instance* x. *That is, for all PPT adversaries $\mathcal{A} = (\mathcal{A}_1, \mathcal{A}_2)$ (where $\mathcal{A}_1$ and $\mathcal{A}_2$ share the internal states), it holds that*

$$\mathbf{Adv}_{\mathcal{A}}^{WUR}(\lambda) = \Pr\left[\, WUR_{\mathcal{A}}(1^\lambda) = 1 \right] \leq \mathsf{negl}(\lambda)$$

where WUR is defined in Game 3.

To capture typical behaviors of TLZK simulator in an abstract manner, we define the notion of canonical simulation.

Definition 2.12 (Canonical Simulator). *Let Π_H be a FS-NARG with TLZK simulator $\mathcal{S}$. $\mathcal{S}$ is said to be canonical, if $\mathcal{S}$ in mode 1 answers random oracle queries as defined in Game 3 , and $\mathcal{S}$ in mode 2 follows the procedures defined in Game 3 by invoking some stateless algorithm $\bar{\mathcal{S}}$.*

To enhance modularity of our security proof, we provide the following lemma updating extractability to simulation-extractability assuming weak unique response and a trapdoor-less canonical simulator. We note it can be seen as adaptation of [28, Lemma 3.2] which only covers NARGs without srs. In [18, Theorem 3.4], the authors prove a similar result in the transparent setting, although it relies on different assumptions, i.e., k-unique response (k-UR) and k-zero knowledge. In [25, Theorem 1], the authors deal with FS-NARG with (updatable) srs also assuming k-UR, but their analysis only covers the case where knowledge soundness is rewinding-based.

Lemma 2.13. *Consider FS-NARG $\Pi_H = (\mathcal{G}, \mathcal{P}, \mathcal{V})$ for relation $\mathcal{R}$ in the ROM. If Π_H satisfies EXT and additionally satisfies WUR w.r.t. a canonical TLZK simulator $\mathcal{S}$, then Π_H satisfies SIM-EXT w.r.t. $\mathcal{S}$.*

Proof. The proof is almost identical to that of [28, Lemma 3.2], thereby we often refer to their proof to avoid redundancy. Let $\hat{\mathcal{A}}$ be a SIM-EXT adversary. Consider the following hybrids:

- $\mathsf{Hyb}_0(1^\lambda)$: Identical to SIM-EXT except that there is no extractor in the experiment and it outputs 1 as long as $b = 1 \wedge (x^*, \pi^*) \notin \mathcal{Q}_2$.
- $\mathsf{Hyb}_1(1^\lambda)$: Identical to the previous, except that it aborts if there exists $(x^*, \pi) \in \mathcal{Q}_2$ such that $\exists i \in [1, r] : \pi^*|_i = \pi|_i \wedge \pi^* \neq \pi$. Assuming that $\hat{\mathcal{A}}$ makes at most $q_2(\lambda) \in \mathsf{poly}(\lambda)$ queries to $\mathcal{S}_2'$, the probability that Hyb_1 aborts can be bounded by $q_2 \cdot \mathbf{Adv}_{\mathcal{B}}^{WUR}(\lambda)$ for some reduction $\mathcal{B}$ [28, Lemma 3.2]. Therefore, the experiment only aborts with negligible probability.

Given $\hat{\mathcal{A}}$ causing Hyb_1 to output 1, we construct a EXT adversary $\mathcal{A}$ that only has access to the random oracle H. $\mathcal{A}$ proceeds as in [28, Alg.4]: (1) Upon receiving srs (corresponding to pp in [28]), $\mathcal{A}$ internally runs $\hat{\mathcal{A}}$. (2) Upon receiving a simulation query from $\hat{\mathcal{A}}$, $\mathcal{A}$ runs the algorithm of $\mathcal{S}$ in mode 2. (3) Upon receiving a random oracle query from $\hat{\mathcal{A}}$, $\mathcal{A}$ relays a query to H unless the input is already programmed by $\mathcal{S}$. (4) Upon receiving (x^*, π^*) from $\hat{\mathcal{A}}$, $\mathcal{A}$ outputs it unless the aforementioned abort conditions are met. Thanks to the hash prefix $(\mathsf{srs}, \mathsf{x})$, if $\mathsf{x}^* \neq \mathsf{x}$ for every previously queried x, then the random oracle entry prefixed by $(\mathsf{srs}, \mathsf{x}^*)$ has never been programmed by the canonical simulator $\mathcal{S}$. Moreover, if $\mathsf{x}^* = \mathsf{x}$ for some previously queried $(\mathsf{x}, \pi) \in \mathcal{Q}_2$, then the random oracle entry prefixed by $(\mathsf{srs}, \mathsf{x}, \pi^*|_i)$ has never been programmed by the canonical simulator $\mathcal{S}$ due to the abort condition of Hyb_1. Therefore, (x^*, π^*) output by $\mathcal{A}$ always gets accepted by $\mathcal{V}^{\mathsf{H}}$.

Overall, if $\hat{\mathcal{A}}$ outputs a valid proof in Hyb_0, then $\mathcal{A}$ also succeeds in outputting a valid proof w.r.t. H except with negligible probability. Since Π_{H} satisfies EXT, there exists a PPT extractor $\mathcal{E}_{\mathcal{A}}$ such that it can extract a valid witness from successful $\mathcal{A}$ except with negligible probability. Therefore, one can construct a $\mathsf{SIM}\text{-}\mathsf{EXT}$ extractor $\hat{\mathcal{E}}_{\hat{\mathcal{A}}}$ that internally runs the procedures of $\mathcal{A}$ and extracts a witness by invoking $\mathcal{E}_{\mathcal{A}}$. Overall such $\hat{\mathcal{E}}$ succeeds in extracting a valid witness from successful $\hat{\mathcal{A}}$ except with negligible probability. □

Remark 2.14. Note that trapdoor-less simulation is crucial for replicating the modular argument of [28]. In the above proof, an outer prover $\mathcal{A}$ only receives srs from an honest setup algorithm $\mathcal{G}$ while having to simulate the view of $\mathsf{SIM}\text{-}\mathsf{EXT}$ adversary $\hat{\mathcal{A}}$. Therefore, $\mathcal{A}$ cannot use the trapdoor and must perform simulation by programming the random oracle responses only.

2.5 Polynomial Commitment Scheme

We define a polynomial commitment scheme [33].

Definition 2.15 (Polynomial Commitment Scheme). *A polynomial commitment scheme denoted by* PCOM *is a tuple of algorithms* (KGen, Com, Eval, Check):

1. $\mathsf{ck} \leftarrow \mathsf{KGen}(1^\lambda, D)$: *Takes as input the security parameter λ and the maximum degree bound D and generates commitment key* ck *as output. We assume* ck *to include description of the finite field* $\mathbb{F}$.
2. $c \xleftarrow{\rho} \mathsf{Com}(\mathsf{ck}, f)$: *Takes as input* ck, *the polynomial $f \in \mathbb{F}^D[X]$, and outputs a commitment c. In case the commitment scheme is deterministic, $\rho = \bot$. We also denote $c := \mathsf{Com}(\mathsf{ck}, f; \rho)$ if the committing function deterministically generates c from fixed randomness ρ. If the input is a vector of polynomials* $\mathbf{f}$ *with dimension n, we assume* Com *to output a vector of commitments* $\mathbf{c}$ *with dimension n by invoking* Com *n times.*
3. $\pi \leftarrow \mathsf{Eval}(\mathsf{ck}, c, z, f, \rho)$: *Takes as input* ck, *the commitment c, evaluation point $z \in \mathbb{F}$, the polynomial f, and outputs a non-interactive proof of evaluation π. The randomness ρ must equal the one previously used in* Com. *If the input is vectors* $(\mathbf{c}, \mathbf{z}, \mathbf{f}, \boldsymbol{\rho})$ *with dimension n, we assume* Eval *to output a vector of proofs* $\boldsymbol{\pi}$ *with dimension n by invoking* Eval *n times.*
4. $b \leftarrow \mathsf{Check}(\mathsf{ck}, c, z, y, \pi)$: *Takes as input statement* (ck, c, z, y), *where $y \in \mathbb{F}$ is a claimed polynomial evaluation, and the proof of evaluation π and outputs a bit b. If the input is vectors* $(\mathbf{c}, \mathbf{z}, \mathbf{y}, \boldsymbol{\pi})$ *with dimension n, we assume* Check *to invoke* Check *n times and output 1 if and only if all of them output 1.*

We define security properties for PCOM. All of the experiments are described in Game 4.

Definition 2.16 (Completeness). *A* PCOM *is said to be* complete, *if for any* $\lambda \in \mathbb{N}$, $D \in \mathbb{N}$, *polynomial* $f \in \mathbb{F}^D[X]$, *evaluation point* $z \in \mathbb{F}$

$$\Pr \left[\begin{matrix} \mathsf{ck} \leftarrow \mathsf{KGen}(1^\lambda, D); c \leftarrow \mathsf{Com}(\mathsf{ck}, f); \\ \pi \leftarrow \mathsf{Eval}(\mathsf{ck}, c, z, f, \rho) \end{matrix} : \mathsf{Check}(\mathsf{ck}, c, z, f(z), \pi) = 1 \right] = 1.$$

The evaluation binding property essentially guarantees that, it is infeasible to open the same commitment c to two distinct outcomes of evaluation y and y' for the fixed evaluation point z.

Definition 2.17 ((Weak) Evaluation Binding). PCOM *is said to be evaluation binding if, for any* $\lambda \in \mathbb{N}$, $D \in \mathbb{N}$, *for all* PPT *adversaries* $\mathcal{A}$,

$$\mathbf{Adv}_{\mathcal{A}}^{PC\text{-}EBIND}(\lambda) := \Pr \left[\textit{PC-EBIND}_{\mathcal{A}}(1^\lambda) = 1 \right] \le \mathsf{negl}(\lambda).$$

If instead

$$\mathbf{Adv}_{\mathcal{A}}^{PC\text{-}wEBIND}(\lambda) := \Pr \left[\textit{PC-wEBIND}_{\mathcal{A}}(1^\lambda) = 1 \right] \le \mathsf{negl}(\lambda)$$

then PCOM *is* weak *evaluating binding.*

The unique proof states that, it is infeasible to create two distinct valid proofs π and π' for fixed c, z, y.

Definition 2.18 ((Weak) Unique Proof). PCOM *is said to be unique proof if, for any* $\lambda \in \mathbb{N}$, $D \in \mathbb{N}$, *for all* PPT *adversaries* $\mathcal{A}$,

$$\mathbf{Adv}_{\mathcal{A}}^{PC\text{-}UNIQ}(\lambda) := \Pr \left[\textit{PC-UNIQ}_{\mathcal{A}}(1^\lambda) = 1 \right] \le \mathsf{negl}(\lambda).$$

If instead

$$\mathbf{Adv}_{\mathcal{A}}^{PC\text{-}wUNIQ}(\lambda) := \Pr \left[\textit{PC-wUNIQ}_{\mathcal{A}}(1^\lambda) = 1 \right] \le \mathsf{negl}(\lambda)$$

then PCOM *is* weak *unique proof.*

Unlike the usual hiding definition for a commitment scheme, Com inevitably leaks evaluations of the committed polynomials. As we shall see later, some schemes such as KZG further leak evaluation at an additional point $\chi \in \mathbb{F}$. To capture this, we consider a weak variant of hiding.

Definition 2.19 ((Weak) Hiding). PCOM *is said to be weak hiding if, for any* $\lambda \in \mathbb{N}$, $D \in \mathbb{N}$, *there exists a* PPT *simulator* (SKGen, SCom) *such that for all* PPT *adversaries* $\mathcal{A}$,

$$\mathbf{Adv}_{\mathcal{A}}^{PC\text{-}wHIDE}(\lambda) := \left| \Pr \left[\textit{PC-wHIDE}_{\mathcal{A}}(1^\lambda) = 1 \right] - 1/2 \right| \le \mathsf{negl}(\lambda).$$

As a special case, if SKGen *outputs* $\chi = \bot$ *(and thus* $f(\chi) = \bot$*), then* PCOM *is said to be* hiding.

For our results, we require the probability that a commitment is equal to a fixed value is low. This requirement is captured by assessing min-entropy of the PCOM commitment scheme.

Definition 2.20 (Min-entropy of commitments). *Let PCOM be a polynomial commitment scheme over* $\mathbb{F}$. *For any fixed* $\lambda \in \mathbb{N}$, $D \in \mathbb{N}$, $\mathsf{ck} \in \mathsf{KGen}(1^\lambda, D)$, *and* $f \in \mathbb{F}^D[X]$, *consider the maximum probability that a commitment to* f *is equal to a particular value:*

$$\mu(\lambda, \mathsf{ck}, f) = \max_c \Pr\left[\,\mathsf{Com}(\mathsf{ck}, f) = c\,\right].$$

The min-entropy α *of scheme PCOM is*

$$\alpha(\lambda) = \min_{\mathsf{ck} \in \mathsf{KGen}(1^\lambda, D) \,\wedge\, f \in \mathbb{F}^D[X]} (-\log_2(\mu(\lambda, \mathsf{ck}, f))).$$

We say that PCOM has high min-entropy if $\alpha \in \omega(\log(\lambda))$.

3   Analysis of PIOP Compiled into Non-interactive Argument

In this section, we analyze a standard compiler that outputs iNARG (Definition 2.7) in the random oracle model. The formal description of the compiler is provided in the full version [34]. The compiler takes following building blocks as input:

- Polynomial IOP PIOP = $(\mathsf{r}, \mathsf{s}, \mathsf{t}, \mathsf{d}, \mathbf{I}, \mathbf{P}, \mathbf{V})$ (Definition 2.1) for an indexed relation $\hat{\mathcal{R}}$.
- Polynomial commitment PCOM = $(\mathsf{KGen}, \mathsf{Com}, \mathsf{Eval}, \mathsf{Check})$ (Definition 2.15)

It then outputs iNARG $\hat{\Pi}_{\mathsf{H}} = (\mathcal{G}, \mathcal{I}, \hat{\mathcal{P}}, \hat{\mathcal{V}})$. On a high-level, the outer prover $\hat{\mathcal{P}}$ internally runs a PIOP prover $\mathbf{P}$ in order to obtain polynomials and then commit to them using the polynomial commitment scheme. Then by hashing the transcript obtained until i-th round, $\hat{\mathcal{P}}$ obtains PIOP challenge ρ_i, which is fed to $\mathbf{P}$ to advance to the next round. When the PIOP prover terminates, $\hat{\mathcal{P}}$ runs a PIOP query algorithm to sample query points $\mathbf{z}$ and evaluates polynomial oracles on $\mathbf{z}$. Finally, $\hat{\mathcal{P}}$ produces evaluation proofs to guarantee that polynomial evaluations are done correctly with respect to commitments produced in earlier rounds.

Remark 3.1. The iNARG $\hat{\Pi}_{\mathsf{H}}$ is almost identical to the compiled protocol in [17], except that we are explicit about strings hashed to derive Fiat-Shamir challenge (the Marlin compiler does not specify what needs to be hashed when applying Fiat-Shamir). We stress it is crucial to hash index i (i.e., the circuit description) on top of statement x and transcript; otherwise, the proof system is susceptible to the following malleability attack. Suppose the adversary receives an honestly generated proof π for (i, x). Then the adversary constructs a modified i* such that for any w, it holds that $(i^*, x, w) \in \hat{\mathcal{R}}$ iff $(i, x, w) \in \hat{\mathcal{R}}$, e.g. by introducing redundancy in the circuit. In this way, π is a valid proof for (i^*, x) which allows the adversary to trivially win the SIM-EXT game. Although syntactically ivk now contains (srs, i), this does not penalize verification performance in practice because hashing of the prefix srs, i can be preprocessed.

As mentioned in Sect. 2.3, iNARG can be converted into NARG $\Pi_H = (\mathcal{G}, \mathcal{P}, \mathcal{V})$ (Definition 2.7) for the corresponding binary relation $\mathcal{R}$, which is amenable to analysis of simulation-extractability. In the rest of the section we will state the main results satisfying the following security properties under certain assumptions on PIOP and PCOM . The detailed analysis is deferred to the full version.

- Sect. 3.1 Trapdoor-less zero knowledge (TLZK) with canonical simulation (Definition 2.12),
- Sect. 3.2 Weak unique response (WUR) with respect to simulators provided in Sect. 3.1.

Knowledge soundness of Π_H is already proved in the literature from knowledge soundness of PIOP and extractability of PCOM under various assumptions [13,14, 17,24,39]. Put together with Lemma 2.13 we conclude SIM-EXT for the compiled Π_H.

Corollary 3.2. *Let Π_H be the FS-NARG protocol derived from $\hat{\Pi}_H$.*

1. *Suppose the PIOP satisfies Ψ-HVZK and Ψ-NEXP with $\Psi = 1$, and $\mathbf{Q_V}$ has high min-entropy. PCOM satisfies PC-wHIDE , PC-wEBIND PC-wEBIND , PC-wUNIQ. If Π_H is non-trivial and knowledge sound, then it is SIM-EXT.*
2. *Suppose the PIOP satisfies HVZK, high min-entropy of $\mathbf{Q_V}$, and $t(1,1) \leq d(|i|)$. PCOM has high min-entropy (Definition 2.20), and satisfies PC-HIDE, PC-wEBIND, PC-wUNIQ. If Π_H is knowledge sound, then it is SIM-EXT.*

3.1 Trapdoor-Less Non-interactive Zero Knowledge of Compiled NARG

Our analysis for showing TLZK will be split in two directions, which will exploit the type of properties satisfied by the two core building blocks, PIOP and PCOM schemes. First, we consider a class of PIOPs satisfying the *stronger* property of Ψ-HVZK , which in turn, requires only a *weaker* hiding property from the PCOM scheme. Namely, it suffices to use a deterministic PCOM scheme for the compilation. This characterization allows us to reuse randomness already introduced by the PIOP while committing to the polynomials. Note that the previous generic PIOP -to-iNARG compilers do not give us a clear picture of scenarios when using a deterministic commitment suffices for trapdoorless NIZK : Marlin [17, Thorem 8.4] and Dark [13, Theorem 4] require a hiding commitment scheme as well as trapdoor to perform simulation; and Lunar [14, Theorem 5] requires a weaker "somewhat hiding" commitment scheme, which however, crucially relies on the knowledge of commitment trapdoor.

In the second direction, we consider all other PIOP s that satisfy the *weaker* property of HVZK , and require the PCOM scheme to be hiding. This is similar to Marlin, however, unlike Marlin, we cannot use the trapdoor information in order to simulate. Hence, we present a more direct trapdoorless simulation strategy similar to Dark.[6]

Compilation with Weak Hiding Polynomial Commitments. We first handle the case where PCOM only satisfies a weak variant of hiding, which means that commitment and evaluation are potentially deterministic. In this case, the committing function itself does not have high min-entropy as in Definition 2.20. Combined with a "sufficiently randomized first polynomial" of PIOP , we can still retain high min-entropy of the compiled protocol, which we formalize below. Non-triviality is often required for Fiat-Shamir to retain zero knowledge (cf. [1]), and existing PIOP-based zkSNARKs are already non-trivial.

Definition 3.3. (Min-entropy of the first commitment). *Let* $\mathsf{Coin}_P(\lambda)$ *be the set of random coins used by the PIOP prover* $\mathbf{P}$ *on any input* $(\mathsf{i}, \mathsf{x}, \mathsf{w}) \in \hat{\mathcal{R}}_\lambda$. *For any fixed* $\lambda \in \mathbb{N}$, $\mathsf{ck} \in \mathsf{KGen}(1^\lambda)$, *and* $(\mathsf{i}, \mathsf{x}, \mathsf{w}) \in \hat{\mathcal{R}}_\lambda$, *consider the maximum probability that a commitment to the first polynomial hits a particular value:*

$$\mu(\mathsf{ck}, \mathsf{i}, \mathsf{x}, \mathsf{w}) = \max_c \Pr \left[r \xleftarrow{\$} \mathsf{Coin}_P(\lambda); (p_{1,1}, \dots) \leftarrow \mathbf{P}((\mathsf{i}, \mathsf{x}, \mathsf{w}); r) \; : \; \mathsf{Com}(\mathsf{ck}, p_{1,1}) = c \right]$$

The min-entropy $\alpha_{\hat{\Pi}}$ *of protocol* $\hat{\Pi}$ *is*

$$\alpha_{\hat{\Pi}}(\lambda) := \min_{\mathsf{ck} \in \mathsf{KGen}(1^\lambda) \wedge (\mathsf{i}, \mathsf{x}, \mathsf{w}) \in \hat{\mathcal{R}}_\lambda} (-\log_2 \mu(\mathsf{ck}, \mathsf{i}, \mathsf{x}, \mathsf{w}))$$

We say that $\hat{\Pi}$ *is non-trivial if* $\alpha_{\hat{\Pi}} \in \omega(\log(\lambda))$.

Lemma 3.4. *If* PIOP *is* Ψ-*HVZK with* $\psi = 1$, PCOM *is weak hiding (* PC-wHIDE *), and the corresponding iNARG* $\hat{\Pi}_H$ *is non-trivial. Then FS-NARG protocol* Π_H *derived from* $\hat{\Pi}_H$ *is TLZK with canonical simulator.*

Compilation with Hiding Polynomial Commitments. For completeness, we provide an alternative simulation strategy in the full version for when the compilation takes place using hiding polynomial commitments.

Lemma 3.5. *If* PIOP *is HVZK and PCOM is hiding (* PC-HIDE *) and has high min-entropy (Definition 2.20), then the FS-NARG protocol* Π_H *derived from* $\hat{\Pi}_H$ *is TLZK with canonical simulator.*

---

[6] They assume PIOP is HVZK, a committing function Com is hiding, and Eval satisfies HVZK. The latter two roughly correspond to our combined notion of hiding for PCOM .

3.2   Weak Unique Response of Compiled NARG

For a PIOP satisfying stronger Ψ-HVZK along with Ψ-NEXP and high min-entropy for the $\mathbf{Q_V}$ algorithm, we only need weaker hiding property for PCOM . For a PIOP satisfying just HVZK along with high min-entropy for the $\mathbf{Q_V}$ algorithm, and the constraint that $t(1,1) \leq d(|i|)$, we require PCOM to be hiding in a stronger sense. In both cases, we require the assumption that $\mathbf{Q_V}$ has high min-entropy. This condition is met by PIOP s such as Plonk, but is not met by other PIOP s such as Marlin and Lunar. The latter can be modified slightly to meet the condition: add a dummy polynomial in the first round and evaluate it on a random point chosen in the last round. In the first case, we require the PIOP to also satisfy Ψ-NEXP , which as remarked in Sect. 2.2, just captures the intuition that many PIOP s encode the witness in the first polynomial and thus generate it with enough randomness in order to achieve zero-knowledge. Finally, in the second case, we require that the PIOP does not reveal the entire first polynomial as a part of the proof. When the first polynomial encodes the witness, this constraint again is easily satisfied by most PIOP s in order to achieve zero-knowledge.

We state our main theorem now.

Theorem 3.6. *Let $\mathcal{S}$ and $\mathcal{S}'$ be canonical TLZK simulators for FS-NARG Π_H derived from $\hat{\Pi}_H$.*

1. *If PIOP satisfies Ψ-NEXP , high min-entropy of $\mathbf{Q_V}$, and if PCOM is weak evaluation binding (PC-wEBIND), weak unique proof (PC-wUNIQ), and weak hiding (PC-wHIDE), then Π_H satisfies weak unique responses (WUR) with respect to $\mathcal{S}$. Concretely, for every PPT adversary $\mathcal{A}$ against WUR of Π_H that makes q queries to $\mathcal{S}_1$, there exist adversaries $\mathcal{B}, \mathcal{C}, \mathcal{D}$ such that,*

$$\mathbf{Adv}_{\mathcal{A},\mathcal{S}}^{WUR}(\lambda) \leq \mathbf{Adv}_{\mathcal{B}}^{PC\text{-}wUNIQ}(\lambda) + 2 \cdot \mathbf{Adv}_{\mathcal{C}}^{PC\text{-}wEBIND}(\lambda)$$
$$+ 2 \cdot \mathbf{Adv}_{\mathcal{D}}^{PC\text{-}wHIDE}(\lambda) + \frac{q\ell}{2^\alpha} + \mathsf{negl}(\lambda)$$

   where $\ell := \sum_{i=0}^{i=r} \left(\sum_{j=1}^{s(i)} t(i,j) \right)$, and α is the min-entropy of $\mathbf{Q_V}$ (Definition 2.5).

2. *If PIOP satisfies high min-entropy of $\mathbf{Q_V}$, $t(1,1) \leq d(|i|)$, and if PCOM is hiding (PC-HIDE) and satisfies all the other properties above, then Π_H satisfies weak unique responses (WUR) with respect to $\mathcal{S}'$. Concretely,*

$$\mathbf{Adv}_{\mathcal{A},\mathcal{S}'}^{WUR}(\lambda) \leq \mathbf{Adv}_{\mathcal{B}}^{PC\text{-}wUNIQ}(\lambda) + 2 \cdot \mathbf{Adv}_{\mathcal{C}}^{PC\text{-}wEBIND}(\lambda)$$
$$+ 5 \cdot \mathbf{Adv}_{\mathcal{D}}^{PC\text{-}HIDE}(\lambda) + \frac{q\ell}{2^\alpha} + \mathsf{negl}(\lambda)$$

Game 4: PCOM Security Games Version 1

$\underline{\text{PC-EBIND}_{\mathcal{A}}(1^{\lambda}), \text{PC-wEBIND}_{\mathcal{A}}(1^{\lambda})}$

1: $ctr \quad := \quad 0; \mathcal{Q}_{\text{Com-0}} \quad = \quad \varepsilon; \mathcal{Q}_{\text{Eval-0}} := \varepsilon$

2: $\mathcal{Q}_{\text{Com-1}} = \varepsilon; \mathcal{Q}_{\text{Eval-1}} := \varepsilon; \mathcal{Q}_{\mathbf{z}} = \varepsilon$

3: $\text{ck} \leftarrow \text{KGen}(1^{\lambda}, D)$

4: $(i, b, c, z, y, y', \pi, \pi') \quad \leftarrow \mathcal{A}^{\mathcal{O}_{\text{Com}}, \mathcal{O}_{\text{Eval}}}(\text{ck})$

5: **if** $\mathcal{Q}_{\text{Eval-b}}(i) \neq (*, *, c, z, y, \pi)$ **then**

6:      return 0

7: $b \leftarrow \text{Check}(\text{ck}, c, z, y, \pi)$

8: $b' \leftarrow \text{Check}(\text{ck}, c, z, y', \pi')$

9: **return** $(y \neq y') \wedge b \wedge b'$

$\underline{\text{PC-UNIQ}_{\mathcal{A}}(1^{\lambda}), \text{PC-wUNIQ}_{\mathcal{A}}(1^{\lambda})}$

1: $ctr := 0; \mathcal{Q}_{\text{Eval}} := \varepsilon$

2: $\text{ck} \leftarrow \text{KGen}(1^{\lambda}, D)$

3: $(i, c, z, y, \pi, \pi') \quad \leftarrow \mathcal{A}^{\mathcal{O}_{\text{ComEval-0}}}(\text{ck})$

4: **if** $\mathcal{Q}_{\text{Eval}}(i) \neq (*, *, c, z, y, \pi)$ **then**

5:      return 0

6: $b \leftarrow \text{Check}(\text{ck}, c, z, y, \pi)$

7: $b' \leftarrow \text{Check}(\text{ck}, c, z, y, \pi')$

8: **return** $(\pi \neq \pi') \wedge b \wedge b'$

$\underline{\text{PC-wHIDE}_{\mathcal{A}}(1^{\lambda})}$

1: $b \xleftarrow{\$} \{0, 1\}$

2: **if** $b = 0$ **then**

3:      $\text{ck} \leftarrow \text{KGen}(1^{\lambda}, D)$

4: **else**

5:      $(\text{ck}, \chi) \leftarrow \text{SKGen}(1^{\lambda}, D)$

6: $b' \leftarrow \mathcal{A}^{\mathcal{O}_{\text{ComEval-b}}(1, *, *)}(\text{ck})$

7: **return** $(b = b')$

$\underline{\mathcal{O}_{\text{Com}}(f, b)}$

1: **if** $\deg(f) > D$ **then return** $\perp$

2: **if** $b=0$ **then** $\rho := \perp$

3: $c \xleftarrow{\rho} \text{Com}(\text{ck}, f)$

4: $ctr := ctr + 1$

5: $\mathcal{Q}_{\text{Com-b}}(ctr) := \{(f, \rho, c)\}$

6: **return** c

$\underline{\mathcal{O}_{\text{Eval}}(i, b, z)}$

1: **if** $\mathcal{Q}_{\text{Com-b}}(i) = \varepsilon$ **then return** $\perp$

2: **if** $z \in \mathcal{Q}_{\mathbf{z}}$ **then return** $\perp$

3: $(f, \rho, c) := \mathcal{Q}_{\text{Com-b}}(i)$

4: $\pi \leftarrow \text{Eval}(\text{ck}, c, z, f, \rho)$

5: $\mathcal{Q}_{\text{Eval-b}}(i) := (f, \rho, c, z, f(z), \pi)$

6: $\mathcal{Q}_{\mathbf{z}} := \mathcal{Q}_{\mathbf{z}} \cup \{z\}$.

7: **return** (y, π)

$\underline{\mathcal{O}_{\text{ComEval-0}}(b, f, (z_1, \ldots, z_n))}$

1: **if** $\deg(f) > D$ **then return** $\perp$

2: **if** $\exists i, j : i \neq j \wedge z_i = z_j$ **then return** $\perp$

3: **if** $b=0$ **then** $\rho := \perp$

4: $c \xleftarrow{\rho} \text{Com}(\text{ck}, f)$

5: **for** $i = 1, \ldots, n$ **do**

6:      $ctr := ctr + 1$

7:      $\pi_i \leftarrow \text{Eval}(\text{ck}, c, z_i, f, \rho)$

8:      $\mathcal{Q}_{\text{Eval}}(ctr) \quad := \{(f, \rho, c, z_i, f(z_i), \pi_i)\}$

9: **return** $(c, (\pi_1, \ldots, \pi_n))$

$\underline{\mathcal{O}_{\text{ComEval-1}}(b, f, (z_1, \ldots, z_n))}$

1: **if** $\deg(f) > D$ **then return** $\perp$

2: **if** $\exists i, j : i \neq j \wedge z_i = z_j$ **then return** $\perp$

3: $(c, \boldsymbol{\pi}) \quad \leftarrow \text{SCom}(\text{ck}, \chi, f(\chi), \mathbf{z}, f(z_1), \ldots, f(z_n))$

4: **return** $(c, \boldsymbol{\pi})$

Acknowledgment. We thank Matteo Campanelli, Antonio Faonio, Dario Fiore, Luigi Russo and Michal Zajac for helpful comments and discussions. Mahak Pancholi was supported by the European Research Council (ERC) under the European Unions's Horizon 2020 research and innovation programme under grant agreement No 803096 (SPEC).k Akira Takahashi was supported by the Protocol Labs Research Grant Program PL-RGP1-2021-064 while at the University of Edinburgh. This paper was prepared in part for information purposes by the Artificial Intelligence Research group of JPMorgan Chase & Co and its affiliates ("JP Morgan"), and is not a product of the Research Department of JP Morgan. JP Morgan makes no representation and warranty whatsoever and disclaims all liability, for the completeness, accuracy or reliability of the information contained herein. This document is not intended as investment research or investment advice, or a recommendation, offer or solicitation for the purchase or sale of any security, financial instrument, financial product or service, or to be used in any way for evaluating the merits of participating in any transaction, and shall not constitute a solicitation under any jurisdiction or to any person, if such solicitation under such jurisdiction or to such person would be unlawful. 2023 JP Morgan Chase & Co. All rights reserved.

References

1. Abdalla, M., An, J.H., Bellare, M., Namprempre, C.: From identification to signatures via the Fiat-Shamir transform: minimizing assumptions for security and forward-security. In: Knudsen, L.R. (ed.) EUROCRYPT 2002. LNCS, vol. 2332, pp. 418–433. Springer, Heidelberg (2002). https://doi.org/10.1007/3-540-46035-7_28

2. Abdolmaleki, B., Glaeser, N., Ramacher, S., Slamanig, D.: Universally composable NIZKs: circuit-succinct, non-malleable and CRS-updatable. Cryptology ePrint Archive, Paper 2023/097 (2023). https://eprint.iacr.org/2023/097

3. Abdolmaleki, B., Ramacher, S., Slamanig, D.: Lift-and-shift: obtaining simulation extractable subversion and updatable SNARKs generically. In: ACM CCS 2020, November 2020

4. Attema, T., Cramer, R.: Compressed Σ-protocol theory and practical application to plug & play secure algorithmics. In: Micciancio, D., Ristenpart, T. (eds.) CRYPTO 2020. LNCS, vol. 12172, pp. 513–543. Springer, Cham (2020). https://doi.org/10.1007/978-3-030-56877-1_18

5. Baghery, K., Kohlweiss, M., Siim, J., Volkhov, M.: Another look at extraction and randomization of Groth's zk-SNARK. In: Borisov, N., Diaz, C. (eds.) FC 2021. LNCS, vol. 12674, pp. 457–475. Springer, Heidelberg (2021). https://doi.org/10.1007/978-3-662-64322-8_22

6. Baghery, K., Sedaghat, M.: TIRAMISU: black-box simulation extractable NIZKs in the updatable CRS model. In: Conti, M., Stevens, M., Krenn, S. (eds.) CANS 2021. LNCS, vol. 13099, pp. 531–551. Springer, Cham (2021). https://doi.org/10.1007/978-3-030-92548-2_28

7. Ben-Sasson, E., Bentov, I., Horesh, Y., Riabzev, M.: Scalable zero knowledge with no trusted setup. In: Boldyreva, A., Micciancio, D. (eds.) CRYPTO 2019. LNCS, vol. 11694, pp. 701–732. Springer, Cham (2019). https://doi.org/10.1007/978-3-030-26954-8_23

8. Ben-Sasson, E., et al.: Zerocash: decentralized anonymous payments from bitcoin. In: 2014 IEEE Symposium on Security and Privacy, May 2014

9. Ben-Sasson, E., Chiesa, A., Spooner, N.: Interactive oracle proofs. In: Hirt, M., Smith, A. (eds.) TCC 2016. LNCS, vol. 9986, pp. 31–60. Springer, Heidelberg (2016). https://doi.org/10.1007/978-3-662-53644-5_2

10. Bitan, D., Canetti, R., Goldwasser, S., Wexler, R.: Using zero-knowledge to reconcile law enforcement secrecy and fair trial rights in criminal cases. In: Weitzner, D.J., Feigenbaum, J., Yoo, C.S. (eds.) Proceedings of the 2022 Symposium on Computer Science and Law, CSLAW 2022, Washington DC, USA, 1–2 November 2022, pp. 9–22. ACM (2022). https://doi.org/10.1145/3511265.3550452

11. Bonneau, J., Meckler, I., Rao, V., Shapiro, E.: Coda: decentralized cryptocurrency at scale. Cryptology ePrint Archive, Report 2020/352 (2020). https://eprint.iacr.org/2020/352

12. Bünz, B., Agrawal, S., Zamani, M., Boneh, D.: Zether: towards privacy in a smart contract world. In: Bonneau, J., Heninger, N. (eds.) FC 2020. LNCS, vol. 12059, pp. 423–443. Springer, Cham (2020). https://doi.org/10.1007/978-3-030-51280-4_23

13. Bünz, B., Fisch, B., Szepieniec, A.: Transparent SNARKs from DARK compilers. In: Canteaut, A., Ishai, Y. (eds.) EUROCRYPT 2020. LNCS, vol. 12105, pp. 677–706. Springer, Cham (2020). https://doi.org/10.1007/978-3-030-45721-1_24

14. Campanelli, M., Faonio, A., Fiore, D., Querol, A., Rodríguez, H.: Lunar: a toolbox for more efficient universal and updatable zkSNARKs and commit-and-prove extensions. In: Tibouchi, M., Wang, H. (eds.) ASIACRYPT 2021. LNCS, vol. 13092, pp. 3–33. Springer, Cham (2021). https://doi.org/10.1007/978-3-030-92078-4_1

15. Canetti, R.: Universally composable security: a new paradigm for cryptographic protocols. In: 42nd FOCS, October 2001

16. Chase, M., Lysyanskaya, A.: On signatures of knowledge. In: Dwork, C. (ed.) CRYPTO 2006. LNCS, vol. 4117, pp. 78–96. Springer, Heidelberg (2006). https://doi.org/10.1007/11818175_5

17. Chiesa, A., Hu, Y., Maller, M., Mishra, P., Vesely, N., Ward, N.: Marlin: preprocessing zkSNARKs with universal and updatable SRS. In: Canteaut, A., Ishai, Y. (eds.) EUROCRYPT 2020. LNCS, vol. 12105, pp. 738–768. Springer, Cham (2020). https://doi.org/10.1007/978-3-030-45721-1_26

18. Dao, Q., Grubbs, P.: Spartan and bulletproofs are simulation-extractable (for free!). In: Hazay, C., Stam, M. (eds.) Advances in Cryptology - EUROCRYPT 2023 - 42nd Annual International Conference on the Theory and Applications of Cryptographic Techniques, Lyon, France, 23–27 April 2023, Proceedings, Part II. LNCS, vol. 14005, pp. 531–562. Springer, Cham (2023). https://doi.org/10.1007/978-3-031-30617-4_18

19. De Santis, A., Di Crescenzo, G., Ostrovsky, R., Persiano, G., Sahai, A.: Robust noninteractive zero knowledge. In: Kilian, J. (ed.) CRYPTO 2001. LNCS, vol. 2139, pp. 566–598. Springer, Heidelberg (2001). https://doi.org/10.1007/3-540-44647-8_33

20. Faonio, A., Fiore, D., Kohlweiss, M., Russo, L., Zajac, M.: From polynomial IOP and commitments to non-malleable zksnarks. Cryptology ePrint Archive, Paper 2023/569 (2023). https://eprint.iacr.org/2023/569

21. Faust, S., Kohlweiss, M., Marson, G.A., Venturi, D.: On the non-malleability of the Fiat-Shamir transform. In: Galbraith, S., Nandi, M. (eds.) INDOCRYPT 2012. LNCS, vol. 7668, pp. 60–79. Springer, Heidelberg (2012). https://doi.org/10.1007/978-3-642-34931-7_5

22. Fiat, A., Shamir, A.: How to prove yourself: practical solutions to identification and signature problems. In: Odlyzko, A.M. (ed.) CRYPTO 1986. LNCS, vol. 263, pp. 186–194. Springer, Heidelberg (1987). https://doi.org/10.1007/3-540-47721-7_12

23. Fiore, D., Fournet, C., Ghosh, E., Kohlweiss, M., Ohrimenko, O., Parno, B.: Hash first, argue later: adaptive verifiable computations on outsourced data. In: ACM CCS 2016, October 2016

24. Gabizon, A., Williamson, Z.J., Ciobotaru, O.: PLONK: permutations over lagrange-bases for oecumenical noninteractive arguments of knowledge. Cryptology ePrint Archive, Report 2019/953 (2019). https://eprint.iacr.org/2019/953

25. Ganesh, C., Khoshakhlagh, H., Kohlweiss, M., Nitulescu, A., Zajac, M.: What makes Fiat-Shamir zksnarks (updatable SRS) simulation extractable? In: Galdi, C., Jarecki, S. (eds.) SCN 2022. LNCS, vol. 13409, pp. 735–760. Springer, Cham (2022). https://doi.org/10.1007/978-3-031-14791-3_32

26. Ganesh, C., Kondi, Y., Orlandi, C., Pancholi, M., Takahashi, A., Tschudi, D.: Witness-succinct universally-composable snarks. In: Hazay, C., Stam, M. (eds.) Advances in Cryptology - EUROCRYPT 2023 - 42nd Annual International Conference on the Theory and Applications of Cryptographic Techniques, Lyon, France, 23–27 April 2023, Proceedings, Part II. LNCS, vol. 14005, pp. 315–346. Springer, Cham (2023). https://doi.org/10.1007/978-3-031-30617-4_11

27. Ganesh, C., Orlandi, C., Pancholi, M., Takahashi, A., Tschudi, D.: Fiat-Shamir bulletproofs are non-malleable (in the algebraic group model). In: Dunkelman, O., Dziembowski, S. (eds.) EUROCRYPT 2022, Part II. LNCS, vol. 13276. Springer, Cham, pp. 397–426 (2022). https://doi.org/10.1007/978-3-031-07085-3_14

28. Ganesh, C., Orlandi, C., Pancholi, M., Takahashi, A., Tschudi, D.: Fiat-Shamir bulletproofs are non-malleable (in the random oracle model). Cryptology ePrint Archive, Paper 2023/147 (2023). https://eprint.iacr.org/2023/147

29. Garay, J.A., MacKenzie, P.D., Yang, K.: Strengthening zero-knowledge protocols using signatures. J. Cryptol. 19(2), 169–209 (2006)

30. Garman, C., Green, M., Miers, I.: Decentralized anonymous credentials. In: NDSS 2014, February 2014

31. Groth, J., Maller, M.: Snarky signatures: minimal signatures of knowledge from simulation-extractable SNARKs. In: Katz, J., Shacham, H. (eds.) CRYPTO 2017. LNCS, vol. 10402, pp. 581–612. Springer, Cham (2017). https://doi.org/10.1007/978-3-319-63715-0_20

32. Jain, A., Pandey, O.: Non-malleable zero knowledge: black-box constructions and definitional relationships. In: Abdalla, M., De Prisco, R. (eds.) SCN 2014. LNCS, vol. 8642, pp. 435–454. Springer, Cham (2014). https://doi.org/10.1007/978-3-319-10879-7_25

33. Kate, A., Zaverucha, G.M., Goldberg, I.: Constant-size commitments to polynomials and their applications. In: Abe, M. (ed.) ASIACRYPT 2010. LNCS, vol. 6477, pp. 177–194. Springer, Heidelberg (2010). https://doi.org/10.1007/978-3-642-17373-8_11

34. Kohlweiss, M., Pancholi, M., Takahashi, A.: How to compile polynomial IOP into simulation-extractable snarks: a modular approach. Cryptology ePrint Archive, Paper 2023/1067 (2023). https://eprint.iacr.org/2023/1067

35. Kosba, A., et al.: C∅c∅: a framework for building composable zero-knowledge proofs. Cryptology ePrint Archive, Report 2015/1093 (2015). https://eprint.iacr.org/2015/1093

36. Kosba, A.E., Miller, A., Shi, E., Wen, Z., Papamanthou, C.: Hawk: the blockchain model of cryptography and privacy-preserving smart contracts. In: 2016 IEEE Symposium on Security and Privacy, May 2016

37. Lysyanskaya, A., Rosenbloom, L.N.: Efficient and universally composable noninteractive zero-knowledge proofs of knowledge with security against adaptive cor-

ruptions. Cryptology ePrint Archive, Paper 2022/1484 (2022). https://eprint.iacr.org/2022/1484

38. Lysyanskaya, A., Rosenbloom, L.N.: Universally composable sigma-protocols in the global random-oracle model. Cryptology ePrint Archive, Report 2022/290 (2022). https://eprint.iacr.org/2022/290

39. Maller, M., Bowe, S., Kohlweiss, M., Meiklejohn, S.: Sonic: zero-knowledge SNARKs from linear-size universal and updatable structured reference strings. In: ACM CCS 2019, November 2019

40. Naveh, A., Tromer, E.: PhotoProof: cryptographic image authentication for any set of permissible transformations. In: 2016 IEEE Symposium on Security and Privacy, May 2016

41. Pass, R., Rosen, A.: New and improved constructions of non-malleable cryptographic protocols. In: 37th ACM STOC, May 2005

42. Sahai, A.: Non-malleable non-interactive zero knowledge and adaptive chosen-ciphertext security. In: 40th FOCS, October 1999

43. StarkWare: ethSTARK documentation. Cryptology ePrint Archive, Report 2021/582 (2021). https://eprint.iacr.org/2021/582

Author Index

© International Association for Cryptologic Research 2023
G. Rothblum and H. Wee (Eds.): TCC 2023, LNCS 14371, pp. 513–514, 2023.
https://doi.org/10.1007/978-3-031-48621-0

Printed in the United States
by Baker & Taylor Publisher Services